Everyone and Everything in George Eliot

George Eliot at age 30
by François D'Albert Durade

EVERYONE AND EVERYTHING IN GEORGE ELIOT

Volume I

The Complete Fiction: Prose and Poetry

Compiled and Edited by

GEORGE NEWLIN

Routledge
Taylor & Francis Group
LONDON AND NEW YORK

First published 2006 by M.E. Sharpe

Published 2015 by Routledge
2 Park Square, Milton Park, Abingdon, Oxon OX14 4RN
711 Third Avenue, New York, NY 10017, USA

Routledge is an imprint of the Taylor & Francis Group, an informa business

Library of Congress Cataloging-in-Publication Data

Everyone and everything in George Eliot / edited by George Newlin.
p. cm.
Includes bibliographical references and indexes.
Contents: v. 1. The complete fiction : prose and poetry—v. 2. The complete nonfiction, the taxonomy, and the topicon.
ISBN 0-7656-1589-4 (alk. paper)
1. Eliot, George, 1819–1880—Handbooks, manuals, etc. 2. Eliot, George, 1819–1880—Stories, plots, etc. 3. Eliot, George, 1819–1880—Characters. 4. Eliot, George, 1819–1880—Settings. I. Newlin, George. II. Eliot, George, 1819–1880.

PR4688.E94 2006
823'.8—dc22 2005057489

ISBN 13: 9780765615893 (Set)
ISBN 13: 9781032316321 (Volume 1)

IN MEMORY OF PHILIP WELLINGTON CLARK (1930-1999),
OUR DEAR FRIEND FROM EARLY GRAMMAR SCHOOL,
AND IN GRATITUDE TO LOUISE KINSEY CLARK,
HIS WIDOW, FORTUNATELY STILL WITH US

Contents

Illustrations

George Eliot's Works, published by Thomas Y. Crowell & Co., New York (1894), is the source of most of the illustrations reproduced in this work. Those from *Romola,* however, were commissioned for the first edition by Smith and Elder.

Volume I

Volume II

Preface

One of the pleasures I find in being a direct descendant of George Henry Lewes, famous to all the literary world as the consort of George Eliot and a distinguished figure in letters and science in his own right, is the opportunity to keep up to date on the evolution of George Eliot scholarship. When my grandmother Elinor Southwood Ouvry (*née* Lewes) died in 1974, she left me by her Will the copyright in all unpublished writings of George Eliot, since when I have filled several bulging files with correspondence from all over the world (but principally from the United States).

The continuing prominence of this great woman has given rise to much diligent work by highly respected scholars and enthusiastic readers—a process which seems to grow and accelerate with each passing year. As the President of the George Eliot Fellowship, I have the pleasure of meeting many such scholars and readers. The ability to use email in recent years has greatly facilitated contact with correspondents.

It is a particular pleasure to me to be in on the rediscovery of forgotten Eliot material, such as the two essays George Newlin recently came upon at Princeton University. They had been first noticed and published in 1980 and then immediately disappeared, but these volumes should ensure that this cannot happen again.

Newlin's work, which, in addition to its other achievements, canvasses all Eliot's nonfiction with unprecedented thoroughness, adds another cubit to the structure of appreciation and knowledge which has been rising ever since Eliot died on the 22nd December 1880, just 125 years ago as I write. These volumes, which cover everything Eliot wrote—fiction and nonfiction, prose and poetry—are a fine new commemorative and will be consulted for many years to come.

—Jonathan Ouvry
Blackheath, London
United Kingdom
December 22, 2005

Introduction

by Janice Carlisle

To see George Eliot's work through the lens offered by George Newlin's compendium is to be struck by the magnitude of her achievement as a novelist, as an essayist, and even as a poet. Although the editor in his introduction describes the value of these volumes to "the general reader" and "the young scholar," this compilation provides a salutary lesson for any Victorianist, amateur or professional, by setting George Eliot's fiction in the context of her nonfiction prose and her efforts in poetry, many of both of which are reproduced here in full. Comprehensiveness characterizes each section of *Everyone and Everything in George Eliot* from its accounts of her early fictional sketches in the Coventry *Herald and Observer* and its Taxonomy, which lists, among other things, Eliot's characters and place names, to the extensive Topicon, which extracts passages from her works on a wide array of themes. The main goal of this work is to offer its readers information, and generous transcriptions of Eliot's words are carefully selected and placed in contexts that reveal their connections to other passages and other works. At times, however, the interpretive aims of this collection come to the fore, and the editor shares his views on the achievements of this "great lady," as he calls Eliot in his characteristically courtly fashion. Readers of all kinds will profit from the rich resources of both information and interpretation with which this collection provides them.

Anyone looking for an account of one of George Eliot's novels, tales, essays, or poems will find it here, along with either the text of the piece if it is relatively brief or numerous quotations from it if transcription in full is impractical. In the treatments of her fiction, lengthy extracts describe the characters and their reactions to plot developments. Then categories are created for the materials relevant to a specific text according to what the editor finds remarkable about it: "foreshadowings" merit an entry for *The Mill on the*

Floss, "significant bachelors" appear among the headings for *Middlemarch*, and twelve "other clerical figures" are listed for "The Sad Fortunes of Amos Barton." One of the most revealing categories recurs in each account of a fictional work: after "minor figures" come those "also mentioned." These genuinely insignificant characters often never appear directly in a narrative, but they are important because references to their existence create a sense of the densely populated towns and villages of Eliot's imagination. Moreover, the "also mentioned" reveal the ways in which her characters live within complicated networks of people, about some of whom they may have only heard, but whose experiences necessarily impinge on their own. There are thirty such figures in "The Sad Fortunes," and the numbers increase as George Eliot's novels become more elaborate, with more than eighty in *Felix Holt* and over one hundred in *Middlemarch*.

The first volume of this collection, which treats both Eliot's fiction and her poetry, contains in its summaries and excerpts some genuine revelations: by offering the narrative portions of Eliot's earliest essays from the Coventry *Herald and Observer* and of her last work, *Impressions of Theophrastus Such*, George Newlin makes a case for the continuities of her career: her earliest works may seem awkwardly jejune, even though she was in her twenties when she wrote them, but they also address concerns that will be central to "The Lifted Veil" and *Middlemarch*, just as the political conservatism of *Theophrastus Such* looks back to the Tory sympathies of *Adam Bede*. Noteworthy as well are two items in the section on Eliot's poetry: a fragment that posits a revealing equation—sense plus image equals thought—and a short poem on London, a powerful evocation of the city as a fog-bound prison that recalls both Blake and Dickens (I: 726-27). A compilation of the poetic epigraphs that Eliot wrote for her fiction starting with *Felix Holt* makes it clear why one of her nineteenth-century fans, a young man named Alexander Main, was moved to publish his *Wise, Witty, and Tender Sayings in Prose and Verse: Selected from the Works of George Eliot* (1872): in her epigraphs as well as in her narrative commentary, she seems self-consciously to have promoted herself as a writer of wisdom literature.

Most remarkable of the items offered in the sections dealing with each of George Eliot's works, however, are the two once-published and then forgotten essays that George Newlin came upon in the rare-books collection at Princeton University. The second, here titled "A Note on Truth in Art," recalls the famous argument of the seventeenth chapter of *Adam Bede*, though it casts its call for "severely veracious likenesses," not in terms of genre painting, as the narrator of *Adam Bede* does, but in terms of portraiture, praising Rembrandt, Bellini, Holbein, and Titian as artists who eschew the creation of "ideal portraits" (II: 228). The first of these essays, called "Thoughts on Anthropology," invites speculation about its relation to *Middlemarch*. It recalls the descriptions of social processes in that novel—"constantly increasing complexity or interaction of various conditions"—but more important is its concern with theories of cultural origins. Eliot argues that the natural "limits" on the forms of human life—the range of sounds that the voice can make, the structure of the body "as our four limbs & trunk" (II: 227, 226)—ensure that the qualities of different cultures, no matter how distant in time or space from each other, will be similar in certain basic ways. After applying this idea to practices that are often used to distinguish one culture from another— language, costume—Eliot uses these examples to denounce "that irrational exclusiveness of theory which insists on interpreting the resemblances between the mythologies & legends of different people as a result of tradition or identity of descent" (II: 227). Here we enter the realm of Casaubon and his unfinished "Key to All Mythologies": without naming him here, Eliot has gone through a careful process of thought to prove him wrong, as Will Ladislaw does in *Middlemarch* by pointing out his fatal lack of German. Remarkably in this instance, however, Eliot mounts a case against Casaubon's bad scholarship, not by citing the early nineteenth-century thinkers who discounted the theory that many mythologies could be traced to one origin, but by referring to the new conceptions of culture that were developing in the 1860s and 1870s. This essay sheds light, I think, on George Eliot's greatest novel by revealing how careful she was to provide in it explanations consonant with its earlier historical setting even when—especially when—the impetus for a particular depiction may have come from much later sources contemporaneous with her writing of the novel.

In more general ways, the section on George Eliot's nonfiction prose encourages a new sense of the extent and importance of her work as a journalist. Serving as a reviewer for the *Leader*, *Fraser's Magazine*, the *Saturday Review*, and the *Pall Mall Gazette*, as well as the *Westminster Review*, she was a thorough professional who frequently dealt with a staggering range of topics and literatures. Simply looking at the table of contents for the second volume of this compilation makes that point. It is supported even more effectively by the material summarized in George Newlin's account of just one essay on *"Belles Lettres"* for the *Westminster Review*: in the article for January 1856, George Eliot commented on Browning's *Men and Women*; poetry by Augustine Daganne, Longfellow, Mrs. D. Ogilvy, and N. L. Frothingham; translations of *Agamemnon* and Greek romances, as well as an edition of Cicero; a tale from the Italian; an autobiographical sketch by Beatrice Reynolds; novels by Holme Lee, Currer Bell, Edmund About, G. F. Pardon, Friedrich Gerstäcker, Ludwig Bechstein, Theodor König; an instructive narrative for "young servant girls" by Margaret Maria Brewster; Brougham's essays; a study of da Vinci; an account of a French art exhibition; and Thoreau's *Walden*.

Such a list, amplified by Newlin's copious extracts from the text of the review, is a testament to George Eliot's enormous erudition and the difficulties she must have faced in dealing with this mass of diverse works—I had almost said "mess." This account also reveals how out of touch with the variety and prodigality of Victorian literary culture we have become. Most impressive about George Eliot's journalism was her ability to pick out of the torrent of texts that she encountered those that would stand the test of time: Thoreau's *Walden* she finds notable for both its "sturdy sense" and "unworldliness" (II: 171); Arnold's poetry appears "prosaic" (II: 150), but Tennyson's will last "as long as the English language is spoken" (II: 160); and Charlotte Brontë's *Villette* is more worth reading "for the third time than most new novels for the first" (II: 170). These views, like Tennyson's poetry, have tended to last.

Those who fancy lists will find much pleasure in the various entries in the Taxonomy in the second volume here. Characters are presented by given name and surname; occupations are catalogued; relationships are enumerated; and characteristics defined and tallied, as are localities, pets, and historical figures. Much of this information reflects the values and practices of the Victorian world in which George Eliot wrote her fiction—the occupation most frequently held by women in her fiction is, as it was in her society, that of domestic servant—but it also attests to the relative gentility of the fictional world that she created. The three traditional professions of medicine, church, and law dominate the occupations pursued by her male figures. Even the names she chose for characters reflect their social status: there is only one Dorothea, but there are three Selina's. Index XI, which treats the literary, biblical, musical and mythological allusions in George Eliot's works, offers an impressive insight into her mental world: although references to her contemporaries occur with some frequency, and Wordsworth appears fairly often, writers of the eighteenth century are cited more than one would have expected. Goldsmith, Gray, and Johnson are all important reference points for Eliot, but Milton is even more so; and citations of Shakespeare predictably outnumber them all—except, of course, for references to the Bible, which George Newlin traces in the second part of this section of the Taxonomy, helpfully offering the actual words cited as well as the relevant chapter and verse. The section on "Words and Thoughts" provides an anthology of sayings of both the narrators and the characters in Eliot's works, so that if one wants to find out, for instance, where one of her narrators says that "the happiest women, like the happiest nations, have no history," one can do so easily (II: 411). (The answer is the third chapter of the sixth book of *The Mill on the Floss.*)

Although there are points in the first volume of *Everyone and Everything in George Eliot* when George Newlin offers an opinion on a particular work—he makes a good case for taking *The Spanish Gypsy* more seriously than most Eliot scholars do—he allows his interpretive skills freer range in the second volume. Included there are three "essays," one on Eliot's re-use of character types and plot devices, another treating her "ineptitude" in dealing with legal matters (II: 297), and a third on the possibility that Gwendolen Harleth of *Daniel Deronda* suffers the after effects of having been sexually abused by her step-father. George Newlin has good evidence for his claims in all three—his account of the numerous instances of failed fathers and foster fathers and missing mothers makes his point about the extent to which Eliot "revisited" her earlier fictions throughout her career (II: 278-79)—but the last of these essays is the most controversial. Citing the narrator's oddly extreme choice of words to describe Gwendolen's childhood before her step-father's death and childhood in general—"evils" and "foulness," respectively—and her thoughts of her step-father when she sees her husband die (II: 318, 320, 322), Newlin offers an incitement for more discussion on this topic.

That effect is also the outcome of reading other, more apparently neutral presentations of information in the second volume. Like the Taxonomy, the Topicon is a selection; and since any selection is an act of interpretation, the choices that have been made here often provide implicit critical assessments. The section on "social classes," for instance, offers a passage from *Felix Holt*: "the sense of ranks and degrees has its repulsions corresponding to the repulsions dependent on difference of race and colour" (II: 545)—a reminder to American readers in particular not to underestimate the power of class in Victorian culture to make damaging and sometimes even violent discriminations. The passage also emphasizes the economic issues, the bases for "ranks and degrees," that form so crucial a part of the love story in *Felix Holt* and in virtually every other piece of fiction that George Eliot wrote. At points in the Topicon, as in his three essays, George Newlin boldly presents his views. Under the entry for "duty" appears transcribed the entire fortieth chapter of *Romola*, the scene in which the heroine listens as Savonarola encourages her to embrace renunciation. According to Newlin's note, "George Eliot chose to write *Romola* so she could write this scene . . . . [resulting in] the greatest achievement of her life" (II: 485). That judgment has two bracing effects, asking readers to reconsider, first, whether *Romola* is a much better novel than it is usually taken to be and, second, whether one ought to take more seriously, as Eliot clearly did, the emotional appeal of the religion that she otherwise so bravely rejected. Such moments in *Everyone and Everything in George Eliot* simply epitomize what will be its effect on anyone who reads its entries with care or even browses through the wealth offered in its pages: its enormously comprehensive as well as judiciously selected compilations will send its readers back to George Eliot's texts with a fresh appreciation of the scope of her achievements in matters both small and great.

—JC
Yale University
New Haven CT
January 30, 2006

Editor's Introduction

This work is the editor's third "CIA"—Concordance, Index, Anthology—of great mid-Victorian authors. Charles Dickens appeared this way in 1995 (three volumes from Greenwood Press) and 1996, and Anthony Trollope (four volumes—M.E. Sharpe) arrived in 2004. The gestation of each was about seven years. George Eliot, with a much smaller *oeuvre,* has come quicker—not much more than two years—and, if anything, with even more joy.

Our essential goal with each of these works is (1) to identify and assemble the *complete* work of the author in question and (2) make it accessible to the general reader and particularly to the young scholar, by an organizational scheme which in effect spares the student a great deal of "scut work" and encourages the development of new ideas and explorations with the data ready at hand to build upon.

The satisfaction accruing to me is enormous, arising from the nature of the assignment I gave myself: to read or reread *everything* by the author within a close time-frame and organize it while the works are fresh in my mind. Instead of picking a single novel, or a couple, from the production of a great author, I must read them all—and by so doing I see immediately relationships between the various books which could otherwise easily escape notice.

One of the results, in the case of George Eliot, is an overview which exposes the degree to which she re-used plot ideas and character configurations—not necessarily in a manner to heighten our admiration. (See "Parallels and Echoes: Eliot Revisits Eliot" at II: 275.) But often this kind of insight adds to our pleasure, perhaps by showing how an idea gained maturity on re-use, or sparkles freshly in a different context, and thus enhances our appreciation of the author's ability to achieve variety even while renewing her acquaintance with old devices.

Another aspect of my gratification is the ability I have now, and expect to expand on in the future, to take an overview of each author and make comparisons between them. I can say, if anyone were to ask, defensively on Eliot's behalf, whether *all* authors didn't do that, "Well, no: at least not Dickens, who waited to start a new novel until a totally fresh idea or 'gimmick' had occurred to him"; or Trollope, who somehow miraculously over 47 novels never really repeats himself even while writing about people of almost exclusively the same social class. But Eliot, despite working in only eight different major works of fiction, seems to turn to the same idea (the missing mother, the defective or unsuccessful father, the lost and foundling heiress, the exotic maiden's rescue) with almost perfunctory frequency.

But make no mistake about it, I agree with John Blackwood's famous and frequent dictum, "What a *wonderful* woman!"

To live for years inside the mind of George Eliot is a privilege I am proud to have been able to create for myself. I will never forget the many moments of wonder and delight, admiration, and spiritual inspiration she has given me. To leaf through and browse in the *Topicon,* for example (II: 418ff), is to enjoy an unimaginably provocative richness. There is wit in abundance; humour, tolerance, humanity, spirituality, scientific knowledge, beautiful writing, variety, vividness— every virtue we can hope for from a great writer. Reading her usually lapidary essays on an immense variety of subjects with her fictional achievements bubbling in the back of my mind induces a sense of prayerful awe, almost of incredulity.

And then, to look at the Taxonomy and to see, for example, the proofs of her enormous erudition (the historical figures of Index X, the literary and biblical references of Index XI), is to get a sense of why many today consider George Eliot not only the most brilliant woman of her time, but the brightest, most thoroughly educated (except in the law) and insightful *person* of her age.

There is another aspect of my mode of working which I feel bound to share with the reader. The discipline of reading *everything* in the case of Eliot produced a thorough understanding and appreciation of her knottiest challenge: *Impressions of Theophrastus Such.* The number of citations to and quotations from this work in the *Topicon* is out of all proportion to its length.

Even beyond this unexpected treasure-house, there were the immense rewards I obtained from slogging through all those columns of *Belles Lettres* in the *Westminster Review.* When I saw that Eliot had been the first British reviewer to look at and quote something called *Leaves of Grass* (no author mentioned), I tingled from face to feet. I was looking at an epochal instance of literary history not made—a great opportunity missed. That feeling was worth all my thirty months of labour by itself. Her unseeing glance at Whitman seems to have gone unremarked by Eliot scholars, though not, I gather, by Whitman specialists (II: 190).

And, finally, there was the thrill of excitement, disbelief, and elation when a staffer at Princeton's Firestone Library handed me the bound manuscript with "Three Essays" on the spine, and I suspected that I had found something which not only had been lost but that no scholar, biographer, or even husband had ever *known* had been lost: two essays by George Eliot as erudite, as polished, as thought-provoking as anything in the *oeuvre.* (They begin at II: 225.) This must have been the feeling Thomas Pinney had when he found and gave back to us "Notes on Form in Art" (II: 232). My later discovery that these essays had indeed been found and published (in 1980) was a dasher, but I take heart from the fact that, as now rediscovered, they can never be lost again (that is, unless *my* work is also lost).

To think I'm getting paid for this!

Acknowledgments

My long-time friend David Parker, Curator Emeritus of the Dickens House Museum in London, Fellow of Kingston College, London, and distinguished author, offered aid of a kind no editor has a right to expect of another. He went physically to the Colindale repository of the British Library, hunted out the Coventry *Herald and Observer* for the requisite dates, transcribed into his laptop computer, and transmitted to me by the modern electronic miracle of the internet, two articles I needed and had not known I needed when I last visited David and his wife Elinor for a blissful weekend of rambles in Devon. His effort allows me a reasonable hope that I have provided the reader with every published piece of Eliot's nonfiction. Words cannot express my gratitude to David, a colleague and friend beyond price.

I am very grateful to Jonathan Ouvry, the present generation's lineal descendant of George Henry Lewes, for permission to publish four essays by George Eliot, including the two I rediscovered at Princeton described below, and for writing the Preface to this work. Jonathan retired seven years ago from a family law practice in the third generation of serving private clients. His great-great uncle Frederic Ouvry was, of all things, solicitor to Charles Dickens.

Janice Carlisle, Professor of English at Yale University, was my colleague in younger days at the Dickens Universe in Santa Cruz, California, and I re-encountered her when my brother Carl audited her course at Yale in the Victorians last year. I am especially gratified that she was able to budget the time to write the Introduction to this work, and grateful to her for her extraordinary investment of effort and insight, and for her kind words.

I lived in Princeton, New Jersey, for two years while I completed my work on Anthony Trollope (*Everyone and Everything in Trollope,* M.E. Sharpe, Inc., 2004), in the course of which I came to know well many of the staff at the Department of Rare Books and Manuscript Collections at Firestone Library. When I went on to George Eliot, still in place there, I asked if they had anything, and they made available a bound volume of manuscripts, from which I transcribed, with amazement and delight, eight pages of holograph containing the two essays given the reader at pages 225-8 of Volume II. I am grateful to Princeton's library staff for their support and the photocopies they provided at nominal cost, and especially grateful to the unknown library representative who had the wit to bid for and obtain these theretofore unknown works at Parke-Bernet in 1955.

The later discovery that the essays had been noticed and published in 1980 (thereafter apparently quite forgotten) only mildly mitigated my satisfaction, and I salute Professor K. K. Collins for her scholarship in resurrecting these pieces in a special issue of *Nineteenth Century Fiction* (Vol. 35, No. 3; Dec. 1980) and for her fine commentary upon them. The issue's title is "Special Issue: George Eliot, 1880-1980," and to it I enthusiastically refer the reader (and, with an admonitory nod, the editors of the *Oxford Reader's Companion to George Eliot*, published in 2000, which makes no mention of it).

From Princeton to Yale (I took degrees from both sometime last century): the staff at the Beinecke Library, in particular Jill Haines, were cordial and efficient in promptly connecting me with the manuscript of Eliot's "Versification" (Volume II, page 229), which I happily transcribed on the premises (having no intimation that Antonie van den Broek had recently done the same thing), and for furnishing me with Yale's examples of the Blackwood Stereotyped edition of some of the Eliot novels.

My dear friend and fellow Quaker at Princeton Monthly Meeting, Michael Dawson, generously and trustingly let me borrow and burrow into a valuable and now very rare edition of Eliot's complete works: the twelve-volume set published in 1894 by Thomas Crowell under the supervision of Eliot's widower, John Cross. Without the aid of this edition I could not have provided most of the more or less contemporaneous illustrations which appear in these volumes, nor could I have organized the poetry as I did, the van den Broek edition of the shorter poetry (see *Bibliography*, page xxiiff) being still on the wrong side of the horizon at the time.

Beryl Gray, editor of the *George Eliot Review,* put me in touch with Eliot's literary executor, Jonathan Ouvry, an indispensable assistance.

I am blessed to continue to have to help me the staunch and resourceful editors at M.E. Sharpe, particularly Lynn Taylor, and my indefatigable production editors, Jane Lerner and Ana Erlic, all of whom have always been ready with counsel and corrective.

Abbreviations and Dates

3M	"Three Months in Weimar"	*Fraser's Magazine*	June 1855
3N	Reviews of three novels	*Westminster Review*	Oct 1856
AA	"The Art of the Ancients" (review)	*Leader*	March 17 1855
AAG	"The Art and Artists of Greece"	*Saturday Review*	May 31, 1856
AB	**Adam Bede**	Blackwood (3 vols)	Feb 1 1859
AG	*Agatha*	*Atlantic Monthly*	August 1869
AM	"The Antigone and Its Moral"	*Leader*	March 29 1856
AN	*Arion*		1874
AR	*Armgart*	*Macmillan's, Atlantic Mo*	*wr* July 1871
ATS	"A Tragic Story"	*Leader*	July 19, 1856
BJ	*Brother Jacob* (written summer 1860)	*Cornhill Magazine*	July 1864
BL	*Belles Lettres*	*Westminster Review*	sundry dates
BL 1	*Belles Lettres* (reviews Kingsley's *Westward Ho!*; a novel by Jewsbury)		July 1955
BL 2	*Belles Lettres* (reviews Tennysons *Maud*; a study of Milton)		Oct 1855
BL 3	*Belles Lettres* (reviews Browning's *Men and Women*; and *Hiawatha*)		Jan 1856
BL 4	*Art and Belles Lettres* (reviews Ruskin's *Modern Painters*, vol. 3)		April 1856
BL 5	*Belles Lettres and Art* (reviews several books of poetry, others on art)		July 1856
BL 6	*Belles Lettres* (reviews Stowe's *Dred*, poetical works, a Charles Reade novel)		Oct 1856
BL 7	*Belles Lettres* (reviews E. B. Browning's *Aurora Leigh*, miscellaneous works)		Jan 1857
BS	*Brother and Sister* (sonnet sequence)		*wr* July 1869 pub 1874
CA	"Memoirs of the Court of Austria" (review)	*Westminster Review*	April 1855
CA2	"The Court of Austria"	*Leader*	April 12, 1856
CB	*A College Breakfast-Party* (extended poem)	*Macmillan's*	July 1878
CC	"The Creed of Christendom" (Greg; review)	*Leader*	Sept 20 1851
CH	*Constance Herbert* (Jewsbury; review)	*Westminster Review*	July 1855
CH19	"Church History of the Nineteenth Century"	*Leader*	April 5 1856
CHE	*The Comic History of England* (review)	Cov'try *Herald, Observer*	Nov. 13 1846
DD	**Daniel Deronda**	*Blackwood's Magazine*	Feb- Sept 1876
DM	*The Death of Moses*	Blackwood	1878
E	*Erinna*		1874-5?
EH	Essays in Holograph (two unpublished works)	*Nineteenth Century Fiction*	Dec 1980
EOL	*Ex Oriente Lux*		1865
ET	Evangelical Teaching: Dr Cumming	*Westminster Review*	Oct 1855
F	Farewell (Knowing that shortly I must . . .)	*Christian Observer*	Jan 1840
FC	"Ferny Combes" (review)	*Leader*	Aug 16 1856
FF	"Futile Falsehoods"	*Pall Mall Gazette*	April 3 1865
FGP	"The Future of German Philosophy" (review)	*Leader*	July 28 1855
FH	**Felix Holt, the Radical**	Blackwood (3 vols)	June 14, 1866
FO	"Felice Orsini"	*Leader*	Aug 30 1856
GL	**Mr Gilfil's Love-Story** (SCL 2)	*Blackwood's Magazine*	Apr-July 1857
GML	"German Mythology and Legend" (review)	*Leader*	Sept 22 1855
GO	"The Grammar of Ornament"	*Fortnightly Review*	May 15 1865
HB	"History, Biography, Voyages and Travels"	*Westminster Review*	Jan 1857
HBS	"Heine's Book of Songs"	*Saturday Review*	April 26 1856
HGP	"History of German Protestantism" (review)	*Leader*	Feb 9 1856
HH	"German Wit: Heinrich Heine"	*Westminster Review*	Jan 1856
HL	*How Lisa Loved the King*	*Blackwood's Magazine*	May 1869
HP	"Heine's Poems" (review)	*Leader*	Sept 1 1855

IG	"Introduction to Genesis"	*Leader*	Jan 12 1856
IR	"The Influence of Rationalism"	*Fortnightly Review*	May 15 1865
JR	**Janet's Repentance** (SCL 3)	*Blackwood's Magazine*	Aug-Nov 1857
JS	*The Life of John Sterling* (Carlyle; review)	*Westminster Review*	Jan 1852
LB	"Lord Brougham's Litereature" (review)	*Leader*	July 7 1855
LD	"Love in the Drama" (review)	*Leader*	August 25 1855
LFN	"Pictures of Life in French Novels"	*Saturday Review*	May 17, 1856
LJ	*The Legend of Jubal*	*Macmillan's, Atlantic Mo.*	May 1870
LL1	*Letters on the Laws of Man's Nature* (review)	*Leader* (first of two)	March 1, 1851
LL2	*Letters on the Laws of Man's Nature* (review)	*Leader* (second of two)	March 8, 1851
LNB	"Leaves from a Note-book"	not published	1884
LOM	"Life and Opinions of Milton"	*Leader*	August 4 1955
LS	"The Lover's Seat" (review)	*Leader*	August 2 1856
LV	*The Lifted Veil*	*Blackwood's Magazine*	July 1859
LW	"Liszt, Wagner and Weimar"	*Fraser's Magazine*	July 1855
LWG	*Life and Works of Goethe* (Lewes; review)	*Leader*	Nov 3 1855
MF	**The Mill on the Floss**	Blackwood (3 vols)	April 4 1860
MFI	"Margaret Fuller's Letters from Italy"	*Leader*	May 17, 1856
MFW	"Margaret Fuller and Mary Wollstonecraft"	*Leader*	Oct 13 1855
MGC	"Menander and the Greek Comedy"	*Leader*	June 16, 1855
MH	"Modern Housekeeping"	*Pall Mall Gazette*	May 13 1865
MM	**Middlemarch**	*Blackwood's* (8 pts)	Dec 1871-Dec '72
MP	*A Minor Prophet*	Blackwood	1874
MR	"Michelet on the Reformation" (review)	*Leader*	Sept 15 1865
MW	"The Morality of *Wilhelm Meister*"	*Leader*	July 21 1855
NE	"From the Notebook of an Eccentric"	Coventry *Herald and Observer*	Dec 4 1846-Feb 19, 1847
NF	"Froude's *The Nemesis of Faith*" (review)	Coventry *Herald and*	March 16 1849
NFA	"Notes on Form in Art (1868)	Thomas Pinney	1963
NH	"The Natural History of German Life: Riehl"	*Westminster Review*	July 1856
OM	*"O May I Join the Choir Invisible"*		1867
PI	*The Progress of the Intellect* (review)	*Westminster Review*	Jan 1851
PPA	"The Poets and Poetry of America" (review)	*Leader*	March 1 1856
PY	"Worldliness and Other-Worldliness: the Poet Young"	*Westminster Rev.*	Jan 1857
QM	"Quinet and Michelet" (review)	Cov'try *Herald, Observer*	Oct 30 1846
R	**Romola**	*Cornhill Magazine*	July 1862-Aug '63
RG	"Rachel Gray" (review)	*Leader*	Jan 5 1856
RH	"Recollections of Heine"	*Leader*	August 23 1856
RMP	*Modern Painters* (Ruskin vol 3; review)	*Westminster Review*	April 1856
RSM	"The Romantic School of Music"	*Leader*	Oct 28 1854
S	*Stradivarius*	Blackwood	1874
SAL	*Self and Life*	Blackwood	1878
SBB	"Story of a Blue-Bottle"	*Leader*	April 26, 1856
SCL	**Scenes of Clerical Life**	*Blackwood's Magazine*	Jan-Nov 1857
SE	*"Sweet Evenings Come and Go, Love"*	Blackwood	1878
SF	**The Sad Fortunes of the Rev. Amos Barton** (SCL 1)	*Blackwood's*	Jan-Feb 1857
SG	*The Spanish Gypsy*	Blackwood	1859
SGT	"Sight-seeing in Germany and the Tyrol"	*Saturday Review*	Sept 6 1856
SL	"Servants' Logic"	*Pall Mall Gazette*	March 17 1865
SM	**Silas Marner**	Wm Blackwood & Sons	April 2 1861
SN	"Silly Novels by Lady Novelists"	*Westminster Review*	Oct 1856
SS	"The Shaving of Shagpat" (review)	*Leader*	Jan. 5 1856
TC	"Thomas Carlyle" (review)	*Leader*	Oct 27 1855
TL	*Two Lovers*		1866
TS	**Impressions of Theophrastus Such**	Wm Blackwood & Sons	May 19 1879
TT	"Translations and Translators"	*Leader*	Oct 20 1855
V	"Versification"	unpublished	1867
WF	"Woman in France: Madame de Sablé" (rev)	*Westminster Review*	Oct 1854
WG	"A Word for the Germans"	*Pall Mall Gazette*	March 7 1865
WH	"Westward Ho!" (Kingsley; review)	*Leader*	May 19 1855
WM	"Address to Working Men, by Felix Holt"	*Blackwood's Magazine*	Jan 1868
WN?	"Who Wrote the Waverley Novels?"	*Leader*	April 19 1856

Alphabetic Locators

Prose Fiction

Poetry

Chronology
Life and Works

The brief summary below is provided as a convenience. The Oxford *Reader's Companion to George Eliot* has an excellent time chart (page 495), and some of the biographies include carefully crafted versions, not extending to the outside world as completely as does Oxford. I have expanded the data usually supplied to include more of the nonfiction.

	Events	Works
1819	Birth at South Farm, Arbury Nov. 22 Christened Mary Anne Evans	
1820	The family moves to Griff House	
1824	First schooling commences	
1828	Begins boarding school at Nuneaton	
1832	School in Coventry with the Misses Franklin	
1836	Her mother dies	
1837	Her sister Chrissey marries She takes over the household at Griff	
1839	Begins to study Italian	Farewell (poem) Sonnet
1840	Begins to study German	Question and Answer (poem)
1841	Leaves Griff for Coventry with her father	
1842	First break with her father over church attendance	"Mind the rich store of nature's gifts"
1844	Begins work on the translation of *Das Leben Jesu*	
1846		*Das Leben Jesu* (anonymous) "Quinet and Michelet" *Poetry and Prose from the Notebook of an Eccentric*
1849	Spinoza translation started Her father dies; she goes abroad Lodgings in Geneva	
1850	Returns to England Begins with the *Westminster Review*	
1851	Editing at the *Review*	Mackay's *The Progress of the Intellect*

		"The Creed of Christendom"
1853	Relationship with Lewes begins	
1854	Leaves for Germany with Lewes	Feuerbach's "The Essence of Christianity" translation published under her name
1855	Back in England, living with Lewes	essays and reviews proliferate Eliot's first *Belles Lettres* for the *Westminster Review* (July) "Memoirs of the Court of Austria" "Three Months in Weimar" "Menander and the Greek Comedy" "The Morality of Wilhelm Meister" "The Future of German Philosophy" "Heine's Poems" "Evangelical Teaching: Dr Cumming"
1856	Spinoza's *Ethics* completed (not published)	"The Natural History of German Life" "German Wit: Heinrich Heine" "The Antigone and its Moral" "The Art and Artists of Greece" —many other essays and reviews *The Sad Fortunes of Amos Barton* submitted as by George Eliot
1857	Brother Isaac breaks with her over her liaison with Lewes	*The Sad Fortunes* published *Mr Gilfil's Love-Story* *Janet's Repentance* "Worldliness and Other-worldliness: The Poet Young"
1858	Meets John Blackwood and reveals her identity to him Second visit to Germany	***Scenes of Clerical Life***
1859	Chrissey dies	***Adam Bede*** *The Lifted Veil*
1860	Holiday in Italy	***The Mill on the Floss***
1861	Second trip to Italy (research)	***Silas Marner***
1862	Receives £7,000 advance for *Romola*	***Romola*** serialization begins
1863	Buys her first house, the Priory	***Romola*** in volume form
1864	Work on *The Spanish Gypsy*	*Brother Jacob* "The Influence of Rationalism: Lecky's History"
1865	Depression forces suspension of her work on *The Spanish Gypsy*	Other articles for the *Pall Mall Gazette*, the *Fortnightly Review* A Minor Prophet (poem) Two Lovers (poem) In a London Drawing-Room (poem)
1866	Accepts £5,000 for *Felix Holt*	***Felix Holt, the Radical*** Arms! To Arms! (poem) Ex Oriente Lux (poem)
1867	Tours of France and Spain	"O May I Join the Choir Invisible" In the South (poem)
1868	Holiday in Switzerland, the Schwarzwald Darwin visits	"Address to Working Men" ***The Spanish Gypsy***
1869	Lewes's son Thornton dies Henry James visits	The Legend of Jubal (poem) Agatha (poem) How Lisa Loved the King (poem) Brother and Sister (sonnet cycle)
1870	Lionized in Berlin and Vienna Work on *Middlemarch*	

1871	Turgenev visits; meets Tennyson	Armgart (poem)
1872	Travels in Germany	***Middlemarch*** (Dec. 1871-Dec. 1872)
1873	Studying Judaism	Stradivarius (poem) Arion (poem)
1874	First kidney attack	A College Breakfast-Party (poem) "I Grant You Ample Leave" (poem) *The Legend of Jubal and Other Poems*
1875	Lewes's son Bertie dies	
1876	Health problems mount	***Daniel Deronda***
1877	Cabinet edition of works agreed on	
1878	George Henry Lewes dies in November	Self and Life (poem) "Sweet Evenings Come and Go" (poem) The Death of Moses (poem) *The Legend of Jubal and Other Poems, Old and New*
1879	John Blackwood dies	***Impressions of Theophrastus Such***
1880	Marriage to John Cross (four proposals) Health deteriorates; death December 22	

Bibliography

As Jonathan Ouvry's remarks in his Preface to this work suggest, scholarship and discovery in the field of George Eliot is a burgeoning and dynamic field. It is at times fraught with peril and surprise to a laborer in that vineyard with a project lasting years, who is continually at risk of superseding developments. The following lists cannot be definitive, only illustrative, and of perhaps modest value as a convenience to other laborers. As to perils and surprises, see the Supplementary Comment below.

Certain of the works listed have been mentioned frequently enough in this work to warrant abbreviation in reference, as indicated in **bold**.

Volumes

Allen, Walter. *George Eliot.* Macmillan, 1964 (Masters of World Literature Series, Louis Kronenberger, ed.)

Ashton, Rosemary. *George Eliot: A Life.* Hamish Hamilton, 1996; Penguin Books, 1997 ("**Ashton**")

—*George Eliot: Selected Critical Writings.* Oxford, 1992

—*The Mill on the Floss: A Natural History.* Twayne Publishers, 1990

Baker, Wm., and John C. Ross, eds. *George Eliot: A Bibliographical History.* Oak Knoll Press/British Library, 2002

Bennett, Joan. *George Eliot: Her Mind and Her Art.* Cambridge University Press, 1948

Blind, Mathilde. *George Eliot.* University Press of the Pacific, 2003; reprint of 1883

Bodenheimer, Rosemarie. *The Real Life of Mary Ann Evans: George Eliot; Her Letters and Fiction.* Cornell University Press, 1996

Bullett, Gerald William. *George Eliot: Her Life and Books.* Greenwood Press, 1971

Byatt, A. S., and Nicholas Warren, eds. *George Eliot: Selected Essays, Poems and Other Writings.* Penguin Books, 1990

Correa, Delia da Sousa. *George Eliot, Music and Victorian Culture.* Palgrave, 2003

Dodd, Valerie A. *George Eliot: An Intellectual Life.* St. Martin's Press, 1990

Ermarth, Elizabeth Deeds. *George Eliot.* Twayne Publishers, 1985

Feuerbach, Ludwig. *The Essence of Christianity.* George Eliot, transl. Harper, 1957

Gardner, Charles. *The Inner Life of George Eliot.* Sir Isaac Pitman & Sons, 1912

Gray, Beryl. *George Eliot and Music.* Macmillan, 1989

Haight, Gordon S. *George Eliot, a Biography.* Oxford University Press, 1968; reprint Viking Penguin, 1993 ("**Haight**")

—ed. *The George Eliot Letters.* Yale University Press and Oxford University Press, 1954-78; 9 vols.

Hands, Timothy. *George Eliot Chronology.* Macmillan, 1988

Hartnoll, Phyllis. *Who's Who in George Eliot.* Taplinger Publishing, 1977

Hornback, Bert G. *Middlemarch: A Novel of Reform.* Twayne Publishers, 1988

Hughes, Kathryn. *George Eliot: The Last Victorian.* Farrar Straus & Giroux, 1989

Jankins, Lucien, ed. *George Eliot: Collected Poems.* Skoob Books, 1989

Karl, Frederick. *George Eliot: Voice of a Century.* Macmillan, 1995

Kaufmann, David. *George Eliot and Judaism: An Attempt to Appreciate 'Daniel Deronda.'* Transl. J. W. Ferrier; first published 1888; facsimile Haskell House, 1970

Kenyon, F. W. *The Consuming Flame: The Story of George Eliot.* Dodd Mead, 1970

Laski, Margherita. *George Eliot.* Thames and Husdon, 1987

MacKenzie, K. A. *Edith Simcox and George Eliot.* Greenwood Press, 1978

McSweeney, Kerry. *George Eliot (Mary Ann Evans): A Literary Life.* St. Martin's Press, 1991

Main, Alexander, ed. *Wise, Witty, and Tender Sayings in Prose and Verse, Selected from the Works of George Eliot.* William Blackwood and Sons, 1871-1896

Mudge, Isadore Gilbert. *George Eliot: Dictionary.* MSO House, 1972

Paris, Bernard J. *Experiments in Life: George Eliot's Quest for Value.* Wayne State University Press, 1965

Pinion, F. B., ed. *A George Eliot Miscellany: A Supplement to her Novels.* Barnes & Noble, 1982

Pinney, Thomas, ed. *Essays of George Eliot.* Routledge and Kegan Paul, 1963 ("**Pinney**")

Rignall, John, ed. *Oxford Reader's Companion to George Eliot.* Oxford University Press, 2000 ("**ORC**")

Sheppard, Nathan. *The Essays of George Eliot.* Funk and Wagnalls, 1883

Smith, Anne, ed. George Eliot: *Centenary Essays and an Unpubished Fragment.* Vision Press, London 1980

Taylor, Ina. *George Eliot; Woman of Contradictions,* 1989

Uglow, Jenny. *George Eliot.* Knopf, 1987

van den Broek, Antonie, ed., and William Baker, consult. ed. *The Complete Shorter Poetry of George Eliot.* Pickering Chatto, 2005; 2 vols. ("**CSP**")

Viont, Elfrida. *Towards a High Attic: The Early Life of George Eliot.* Holt, Rinehart & Winston, 1970

Wiesenfarth, Joseph, ed. *George Eliot, A Writer's Notebook 1854-1879, and Uncollected Writings.* University Press of Virginia, 1981

Articles

Collins, K. K. "Questions of Method: Some Unpublished Late Essays," *Nineteenth Century Fiction,* Vol. 35, No. 3, Special Issue: George Eliot, 1880-1980 (Dec., 1980), 385-405

Higdon, David L. "George Eliot and the Art of the Epigraph," *Nineteenth Century Fiction,* 25 (1970), 127-51

Hudd, Louise. "The Politics of a Feminist Poetics: 'Armgart' and George Eliot's Critical Response to *Aurora Leigh,*" in Kate Flint, ed. *Poetry and Politics,* D. S. Brewer, 1996, 62-83

La Porte, Charles. "George Eliot, the Poetics as Prophet," *Victorian Literature and Culture* (2003), 159-79

Paris, Bernard J. "George Eliot's Unpublished Poetry," *Studies in Philology* 56 (July 1959), 539-58

Works of George Eliot

Folio Society of London, 1999 (general editor not identified):

Scenes of Clerical Life, introduction by Jill Payton Walsh; following the cheap edition published in one volume by William Blackwood and Sons, 1863

Adam Bede, introduction by Jane Gardam; following the cheap edition published in one volume by Blackwood, 1862

The Mill on the Floss, introduction by Bel Mooney; following the cheap edition published in one volume by Blackwood, 1862

Silas Marner, the Weaver of Raveloe, introduction by Jill Paton Walsh, following the Cabinet edition published by Blackwood, 1878

Romola, introduction by Gillian Beer; following the cabinet edition published in two volumes by Blackwood, 1877 and 1878

Felix Holt, the Radical, introduction by Kathryn Hughes; following the first edition published by Blackwood, 1866

Middlemarch, a Study of Provincial Life, introduction by Penelope Fitzgerald; following the single-volume edition published by Blackwood, 1874

Daniel Deronda, introduction by A. S. Byatt; following the Cabinet edition published by Blackwood, 1878

Henry, Nancy, ed. *Impressions of Theophrastus Such.* University of Iowa Press, 1994

Lewes, Charles Lee, ed. *The Complete Works of George Eliot.* Thomas W. Crowell, 1884; 12 vols.

Shuttleworth, Sally, ed. *The Lifted Veil* and *Brother Jacob.* Penguin Classics, 2001

Supplementary Comment

Cynthia Ann Secor's unpublished doctoral dissertation on George Eliot's poetry (Cornell University, 1969) may be one of the most seminally influential works of scholarship never to have found its way to the public under a publisher's rubric. It is generously acknowledged in Antonie Gerard van den Broek's *The Complete Shorter Poetry of George Eliot,* which appeared just after we had submitted this work to the publisher for processing. We saw CSP advertised in the *George Eliot Review,* gulped at the price and paid it. We are glad we did, as it buttressed and confirmed our work (based primarily on the 1884 edition of Eliot's complete works edited by Charles Lewes) and added valuable insights, historical background and careful textual analysis in its introductory comments to each of the poetical works covered and in its elaborate notes on variants in Eliot's holographs.

We salute Mr van den Broek for an achievement of high importance to all who are fascinated by the full range of George Eliot's *oeuvre.* We differ only in that we do not include the poem "On Being Called a Saint," which may have been schoolgirl Mary Ann Evans's work or, on the other hand, may have been written by one of her school friends, as Mr van den Broek carefully notes. Mentioned and partially quoted in Haight (but attributed only tentatively), it contains seven complete quatrains but ends in a fragment and can be found at pages 5-6 of the first volume of CSP.

Mr van den Broek's admirable Introduction to his work contains in its notes much bibliographical citation which will be of use to scholars wishing to explore the subject of the Poetry. And the book is more nearly complete than this one in that it quotes *all* of the shorter poems in their entirety, though without the *précis* we provide.

So, that was a surprise. The peril narrowly averted arose from the undeserved obscurity of K. K. Collins's discovery and astute analysis of two unpublished essays of Eliot—essays we had long thought we were the first to unearth. But we learned in time that she had been ahead of us—a quarter of a century ahead of us—and we are thankful we avoided a modest embarrassment. (*See* II: 225)

Guide to the Use of These Volumes

Each principal segment of this work begins with a summary table showing what is to follow. You are encouraged to take a little time at first to look around and get acquainted with the organization scheme.

The table of Abbreviations and Dates covering all the works of George Eliot is an essential reference point. The abbreviations which are omnipresent in the Taxonomy and the *Topicon* are here explained. Each volume has an alphabetic locator covering the works in that volume, with page references. There follows a Chronology of Eliot's life events, with her works presented in parallel.

As will have been apparent from a persual of the Table of Contents, Volume I is organized primarily on a chronological philosophy, with first the Prose Fiction and then the Poetry presented. The two short stories follow the novelistic works, and in their placement chronology is disregarded.

The works of nonfiction in Volume II are divided into the two principal segments of Essays and Reports, and then Reviews and Notes, each again presented in chronological sequence. Then there follow the elements of the Taxonomy, with three editor's essays interspersed, succeeded by the *Topicon*, or topical concordance. There is a Glossary and a summary of Words and Phrases which will be of interest.

If you know a character's name but do not remember the work, refer to the Indexes at the back of Volume I. There are Indexes as well at the back of Volume II, covering all figures mentioned in the nonfiction, as well as the Notable Individuals highlighted in the *Topicon*.

Citations to the prose fiction are by chapter. Quotations of poetry are usually by line.

Where the symbol ¶ appears, it indicates that we have broken Eliot's paragraphing, which is often far less frequent than modern usage would favor, to improve readability and page appearance.

THE PROSE FICTION

Poetry and Prose,
From the Notebook of an Eccentric
(fictional elements)

Despite the title, there is no proper verse in these pieces, but there is deep and extraordinary poetry in passages on Purpose in Life and other philosophical matters (II: 8ff). Though most editors, if they notice these pieces at all, consider this material under the heading of Essays, there is noteworthy fiction here—Eliot's first published fiction—and accordingly these two small pieces begin this Volume.

Introductory (December 4, 1846)

Macarthy wanders and spends his inheritance, then comes home to see his friend, the narrator, and to die, leaving behind some manuscripts from which the narrator evidently makes extracts.

"The churchyard in which Macarthy lies looks not like a Gottes-acker, but a vicar's acre, the profits of which (including the grazing of half-a-dozen sheep) go to eke out the curate's yearly hundred, upon which he supports, or rather diets, the gentility of his wife and ten children."

Macarthy. "My friend was one of whom the world proved itself not worthy, for it never made a true estimate of him. His soul was a lyre of exquisite structure, but men knew not how to play on it: it was a bird endowed with rich and varied notes, which it was ready to bestow on human hearers; but their coarse fondling or brutal harshness scared it away, and the poor bird ceased to sing, save in the depths of the forest or the silence of night. To those who saw only the splendour of his genius, and the nobility of his sentiments, his childhood and youth seemed to promise a brilliant career; but any who were capable of a more discriminating estimate and refined analysis of his character, must have had a foreboding that it contained elements which would too probably operate as non-conductors, interposed between his highly charged mind and the negatively electrified souls around him. The quality on which a good prophet would have pronounced my friend's fate to hang, was one which will be held to have placed him not above, but simply out of, the sphere of his fellow men. It was a morbid sensitiveness in his feeling of the beautiful, which I can compare to nothing but those alleged states of mesmeric lucidity, in which the patient obtains an unenviable cognizance of irregularities, happily imperceptible to us in the ordinary state of our consciousness.

"His ideal was not, as with most men, an enshrined object of worship, but a beautiful shadow which was ever floating before him, importunately presenting itself as a twin object with all realities, whether external or mental, and turning all their charms into mockery. He moved among the things of this earth like a lapidarian among false gems, which fetch high prices and admiration from others, but to him are mere counterfeits. He seemed to have a preternaturally sharpened vision, which saw knots and blemishes, where all was smoothness to others. The unsightly condition of the masses—their dreary ignorance, the conventional distortion of human nature in upper classes—the absence of artistic harmony and beauty in the details of outward existence, were with him not merely themes for cold philosophy, indignant philippics, or pointed satire; but positively painful elements in his experience, sharp iron entering into his soul. Had his nature been less noble, his benevolence less God-like, he would have been a misanthropist, all compact of bitter sarcasm, and therefore no poet. As it was, he was a humourist—one who sported with all the forms of human life, as if they were so many May-day mummings, uncouth, monstrous disguises of poor human nature, which has not discovered its dignity. While he laughed at the follies of men, he wept over their sorrows; and while his wit lashed them as with a whip of scorpions, there was a stream of feeling in the deep caverns of his soul, which was all the time murmuring, 'Would that I could die for thee, thou poor humanity!' "

A Little Fable with a Great Moral (February 12, 1847)
A tale of two hamadryads.

"Now, the hamadryads are a race of nymphs that inhabit the forests. Whenever a little acorn, or a beech nut, or any other seed of a forest tree begins to sprout, a little hamadryad is born, and grows up and lives and dies with the tree. So you see the hamadryads, the daughters of trees, live far longer than the daughters of men—some of them even a thousand years; still they do at last get old, and faded, and shrivelled."

One, self-admiring, gets angry as she grows old and at last leaves the lake and its mirroring surface and dies lonely and sad; the other, self-indifferent, dies without ever knowing she has grown old.

Idione "loved to look into the lake because she saw herself there; she would sit on the bank, weaving leaves and flowers in her silken hair, and smiling at her own image all the day long, and if the pretty water-lilies or any other plants began to spread themselves on the surface below her, and spoil her mirror, she would tear them up in anger."

Hieria "cared not to look at herself in the lake; she only cared about watching the heavens as they were reflected in its bosom—the foamy clouds on the clear blue by day, and the moon and the stars by night. She did not mind that the water-lilies grew below her, for she was always looking farther off, into the deep part of the lake; she only thought the lilies pretty, and loved them."

"Until one morning, after she had been watching the stars in the lake, she went home to her tree, and lying down, she fell into a gentle sleep, and dreamed that she had left her mouldering tree, and had been carried up to live in a star, from which she could still look down on her lake that she had loved so long. And while she was dreaming this, men came and cut down her tree, and Hieria died without knowing that she had become old."

Scenes of Clerical Life

The Sad Fortunes of the Reverend Amos Barton

The Narrator [who then disappears] depicts Shepperton Church today and in his childhood. **Amos Barton** is the impecunious curate. The **Hackits** and **Mr Pilgrim** are having tea with **Mrs Patten** and discussing their parson. 1 Barton has had tea with the **Farquhars**, leaving the girls unimpressed. He comes home to his lovely wife **Milly**. The butcher needs a payment; **Caroline Czerlaski** has invited them for dinner. Amos must borrow. The children need shoes. Amos goes to the workhouse to preach and comes home irritable. 2

The Bartons dine with the Countess and her half-brother, **Mr Bridmain**. **John**, the footman, spills soup on Milly's dress, to her anguish. Cleanup follows. The Countess hints at preferment for Amos through her influence. Amos and Bridmain play chess. At a neighbouring parsonage, **Mr Ely**'s, **Mr Farquhar** gossips ignorantly about the Countess, believing Bridmain to be no brother. Ely is temperate. 3 The truth about Countess Czerlaski and Bridmain is much less exciting than the public thinks. He is honest, successful, and under her thumb. She is self-absorbed and looking for a husband. 4

Admittedly, Amos is ordinary. A borrowed £20 staves off the butcher and gets him a greatcoat. Milly has a new dress, thanks to Bridmain. She is ill. **Mrs Hackit** visits and then sends port-wine. The Countess calls, distraught. Her brother is going to marry the maid. She asks for shelter. It is granted. She stays and stays. Barton's reputation suffers. 5 Mr Pilgrim gossips with Mmes. Patten and Hackit. A clerical dinner at Mr Ely's leads to some gossip about Amos. A fine clerical specimen, **Martin Cleves**, is described. 6

The Countess stays and stays. Money gets very short. Milly is unwell. The maid-of-all-work, **Nanny**, speaks out. The Countess sees it is time to leave. Milly has another baby. 7 Dying, she sends for the children. The baby dies. Mrs Hackit comes. Milly dies. 8 Mr Cleves handles the obsequies. Amos is generally pitied, scandal forgotten. Friends rally with help, with money and aid for the children. But the Vicar writes that he will take over the church. 9 The Bartons pack and move. 10 Twenty years later, Amos and Patty revisit the grave. **Dickey Barton** has turned out well. *Conclusion*

The Title Role: Rev. Amos Barton

—disliked by his bassoonist: "a confounded, methodistical, meddlesome chap, who must be putting his finger in every pie." 1

—music preference: " 'But Mr Barton is all for the hymns, and a sort of music as I can't join in at all.'

" 'And so', said **Mr Pilgrim** . . . 'he called out Silence! Did he? When he got into the pulpit; and gave a hymn out himself to some meeting-house tune?'

" 'Yes', said **Mrs Hackit** . . . and turned as red as a turkeycock. I often say, when he preaches about meekness, he gives himself a slap in the face. He's like me—he's got a temper of his own.' " 1

—appraised as a preacher: " 'But our parson's no gift at all that way [for extempore speaking]; he can preach as good a sermon as need be heard when he writes it down. But when he tries to preach wi'out book, he rambles about, and doesn't stick to his text; and every now and then he flounders about like a sheep as has cast itself, and can't get on its legs again.' " 1

—ecclesiastical campaigner: "He, excellent man! was meditating fresh pastoral exertions on the morrow; he would set on foot his Lending Library; in which he had introduced some books that would be a pretty sharp blow to the Dissenters—one especially, purporting to be written by a working-man who, out of pure zeal for the welfare of his class, took the trouble to warn them in this way against those hypocritical thieves, the Dissenting preachers. The Rev. Amos Barton profoundly believed in the existence of that working-man, and had thoughts of writing to him. Dissent, he considered, would have its head bruised in Shepperton, for did he not attack it in two ways? He preached Low-Church doctrine—as evangelical as anything to be heard in the Independent Chapel; and he made a High-Church assertion of ecclesiastical powers and functions. Clearly, the Dissenters would feel that 'the parson' was too many for them. Nothing like a man who combines shrewdness with energy. The wisdom of the serpent, Mr Barton considered, was one of his strong points." 2

—characteristics: " . . . as Mr Barton hangs up his hat in the passage, you see that a narrow face of no particular complexion—even the smallpox that has attacked it seems to have been of a mongrel, indefinite kind—with features of no particular shape, and an eye of no particular expression, is surmounted by a slope of baldness gently rising from brow to crown. You judge him, rightly, to be about forty." 2

—amused: "Here Mr Barton laughed—he had a way of laughing at criticisms that other people thought damaging—and thereby showed the remainder of a set of teeth which, like the remnants of the Old Guard, were few in number, and very much the worse for wear." 2

—*a gap:* "Mr Barton had not the gift of perfect accuracy in English orthography and syntax, which was unfortunate, as he was known not to be a Hebrew scholar, and not in the least suspected of being an accomplished Grecian. These lapses, in a man who had gone through the Eleusinian mysteries of a university education, surprised the young ladies of his parish extremely; especially the **Misses Farquhar** . . . . The persons least surprised at the Rev. Amos's deficiencies were his clerical brethren, who had gone through the mysteries themselves." 2

—*oratory:* "We read, indeed, that the walls of Jericho fell down before the sound of trumpets; but we nowhere hear that those trumpets were hoarse and feeble. Doubtless they were trumpets that gave forth clear ringing tones, and sent a mighty vibration through brick and mortar. But the oratory of the Rev. Amos resembled rather a Belgian railway-horn, which shows praiseworthy intentions inadequately fulfilled. He often missed the right note both in public and private exhortation, and got a little angry in consequence." 2

—*wrong profession:* "For though Amos thought himself strong, he did not *feel* himself strong. Nature had given him the opinion, but not the sensation. Without that opinion he would probably never have worn cambric bands, but would have been an excellent cabinetmaker and deacon of an Independent church, as his father was before him . . . . He might then have sniffed long and loud in the corner of his pew in Gun Street Chapel; he might have indulged in halting rhetoric at prayer-meetings, and have spoken faulty English in private life; and these little infirmities would not have prevented him, honest, faithful man that he was, from being a shining light in the Dissenting circle of Bridgeport." 2

—*susceptible:* "Now, the Rev. Amos Barton was one of those men who have a decided will and opinion of their own; he held himself bolt upright, and had no self-distrust. He would march very determinedly along the road he thought best; but then it was wonderfully easy to convince him which *was* the best road. And so a very little unwonted reading and unwonted discussion made him see that an Episcopalian Establishment was much more than unobjectionable, and on many other points he began to feel that he held opinions a little too far-sighted and profound to be crudely and suddenly communicated to ordinary minds.

"He was like an onion that has been rubbed with spices; the strong original odour was blended with something new and foreign. The Low-Church onion still offended refined High-Church nostrils, and the new spice was unwelcome to the palate of the genuine onion-eater." ¶2

—*mediocre:* "[He] never came near the borders of a vice. His very faults were middling—he was not *very* ungrammatical. It was not in his nature to be superlative in anything; unless, indeed, he was superlatively middling, the quintessential extract of mediocrity." 5

—*incompetent:* If there was any one point on which he showed an inclination to be excessive, it was confidence in his own shrewdness and ability in practical matters, so that he was very full of plans which were something like his moves in chess—admirably well calculated, supposing the state of the case were otherwise." 5

—*reacting to gossip:* "But, in the first place, he still believed in the **Countess** as a charming and influential woman, disposed to befriend him, and, in any case, he could hardly hint departure to a lady guest who had been kind to him and his, and who might any day spontaneously announce the termination of her visit; in the second place, he was conscious of his own innocence, and felt some contemptuous indignation towards people who were ready to imagine evil of him; and, lastly, he had, as I have already intimated, a strong will of his own, so that a certain obstinacy and defiance mingled itself with his other feelings on the subject." 7

—bereaved: "Amos Barton had been an affectionate husband, and while Milly was with him, he was never visited by the thought that perhaps his sympathy with her was not quick and watchful enough; but now he relived all their life together, with that terrible keenness of memory and imagination which bereavement gives, and he felt as if his very love needed a pardon for its poverty and selfishness." 9

—in later years: "Amos himself was much changed. His thin circlet of hair was nearly white, and his walk was no longer firm and upright. But his glance was calm, and even cheerful, and his neat linen told of a woman's care. **Milly** did not take all her love from the earth when she died. She had left some of it in **Patty**'s heart." *Conclusion*

Other Clerical Figures

Mr Baird "has since gained considerable celebrity as an original writer and metropolitan lecturer, but at that time he used to preach in a little church something like a barn, to a congregation consisting of three rich farmers and their servants, about fifteen labourers, and the due proportion of women and children. The rich farmers understood him to be 'very high learned', but if you had interrogated them for a more precise description, they would have said that he was 'a thinnish-faced man, with a sort o' cast in his eye, like'. " 6

Rev. Carpe (6). "Those were days when a man could hold three small livings, starve a curate apiece on two of them, and live badly himself on the third. It was so with the Vicar of Shepperton, a vicar given to bricks and mortar, and thereby running into debt far away in a northern county—who executed his vicarial functions towards Shepperton by pocketing the sum of thirty-five pounds ten per annum, the net surplus remaining to him from the proceeds of that living, after the disbursement of eighty pounds as the annual stipend of his curate." 1

Rev. Martin Cleves, "a man about forty—middle-sized, broad-shouldered, with a negligently tied cravat, large irregular features, and a large head, thickly covered with lanky brown hair. To a superficial glance, Mr Cleves is the plainest and least clerical-looking of the party; yet, strange to say, *there* is the true parish priest, the pastor beloved, consulted, relied on by his flock; a clergyman who is not associated with the undertaker, but thought of as the surest helper under a difficulty, as a monitor who is encouraging rather than severe. Mr Cleves has the wonderful art of preaching sermons which the wheelwright and the blacksmith can understand; not because he talks condescending twaddle, but because he can call a spade a spade, and knows how to disencumber ideas of their wordy frippery.

"Look at him more attentively, and you will see that his face is a very interesting one—that there is a great deal of humour and feeling playing in his grey eyes, and about the corners of his roughly cut mouth: a man, you observe, who has most likely sprung from the harder-working section of the middle class, and has hereditary sympathies with the chequered life of the people. He gets together the working men in his parish on a Monday evening, and gives them a sort of conversational lecture on useful practical matters, telling them stories, or reading some select passages from an agreeable book, and commenting on them; and if you were to ask the first labourer or artisan in Tripplegate what sort of man the parson was, he would say—'a uncommon knowin', sensable, free-spoken gentleman; very kind an' good-natur'd too'. Yet for all this, he is perhaps the best Grecian of the party . . . . " ¶6

—aid after death: "Mr Cleves succeeded in collecting thirty pounds among his richer clerical brethren, and, adding ten pounds himself sent the sum to **Amos**, with the kindest and most delicate words of Christian fellowship and manly friendship." 9

Rev. Archibald Duke. "At **Mr Ely**'s right hand you see a very small man with a sallow and somewhat puffy face, whose hair is brushed straight up, evidently with the intention of giving him a height somewhat less disproportionate to his sense of his own importance than the measure of five feet three accorded him by an oversight of nature. This is the Rev. Archibald Duke, a very dyspeptic and evangelical man, who takes the gloomiest view of mankind and their prospects, and thinks the immense sale of the 'Pickwick Papers', recently completed, one of the strongest proofs of original sin. Unfortunately, though Mr Duke was not burdened with a family, his yearly expenditure was [*sic.*] apt considerably to exceed his income; and the unpleasant circumstances resulting from this, together with heavy meat-breakfasts, may probably have contributed to his desponding views of the world generally." 6

Mr Ely " 'was there to dinner, but went away rather early. **Miss Arabella** is setting her cap at him with a vengeance. But I don't think he's much smitten. I've a notion Ely's engaged to someone at a distance, and will astonish all the ladies who are languishing for him here, by bringing home his bride one of these days. Ely's a sly dog; he'll like that.' " 2

—characteristics: "Mr Ely was a tall, dark-haired, distinguished-looking man of three-and-thirty. By the laity of Milby and its neighbourhood he was regarded as a man of quite remarkable powers and learning, who must make a considerable sensation in London pulpits and drawing-rooms on his occasional visits to the metropolis, and by his brother clergy he was regarded as a discreet and agreeable fellow. Mr Ely never got into a warm discussion; he suggested what might be thought, but rarely said what he thought himself; he never let either men or women see that he was laughing at them, and he never gave anyone an opportunity of laughing at *him*. In one thing only he was injudicious. He parted his dark wavy hair down the middle; and as his head was rather flat than otherwise, that style of coiffure was not advantageous to him." 3

—dinner host: "Mr Ely was particularly worthy of [his guests'] confidence, and his virtues as an *Amphitryon* had probably contributed quite as much as the central situation of Milby to the selection of his house as a clerical rendezvous. He looks particularly graceful at the head of his table, and, indeed, on all occasions where he acts as president or moderator: he is a man who seems to listen well, and is an excellent amalgam of dissimilar ingredients." 6

Mr Fellowes. "At the other end of [**Mr Ely**'s] table, as 'Vice', sits Mr Fellowes, rector and magistrate, a man of imposing appearance, with a mellifluous voice and the readiest of tongues. Mr Fellowes once obtained a living by the persuasive charm of his conversation, and the fluency with which he interpreted the opinions of an obese and stammering baronet, so as to give that elderly gentleman a very pleasing perception of his own wisdom. Mr

Fellowes is a very successful man, and has the highest character everywhere except in his own parish, where, doubtless because his parishioners happen to be quarrelsome people, he is always at fierce feud with a farmer or two, a colliery proprietor, a grocer who was once churchwarden, and a tailor who formerly officiated as clerk." 6

" . . . the florid and highly peptic Mr Fellowes" 7

Mr Furness, "a tall young man, with blond hair and whiskers, who was plucked at Cambridge entirely owing to his genius; at least I know that he soon afterwards published a volume of poems, which were considered remarkably beautiful by many young ladies of his acquaintance. Mr Furness preached his own sermons, as anyone of tolerable critical acumen might have certified by comparing them with his poems: in both, there was an exuberance of metaphor and simile entirely original, and not in the least borrowed from any resemblance in the things compared." 6

Mr Gilfil, "the clergyman . . . an excellent old gentleman, who smoked very long pipes and preached very short sermons . . . his life . . . had its little romance, as most lives have between the ages of teetotum and tobacco." 1

Mr Parry. "A certain amount of religious excitement created by the popular preaching of Mr Parry, **Amos**'s predecessor, had nearly died out, and the religious life of Shepperton was falling back towards low-water mark." 2

Prior. " 'that canting Prior, who died a little while ago—a fellow who soaked himself with spirits, and talked of the Gospel through an inflamed nose.' " 6

Mr Pugh. "On **Mr Furness**'s left you see Mr Pugh, another young curate, of much less marked characteristics. He had not published any poems; he had not even been plucked; he had neat black whiskers and a pale complexion; read prayers and a sermon twice every Sunday, and might be seen any day sallying forth on his parochial duties in a white tie, a well-brushed hat, a perfect suit of black, and well-polished boots—an equipment which he probably supposed hieroglyphically to represent the spirit of Christianity to the parishioners of Whittlecombe." 6

Mr Sargent. " 'By the by,' said **Mr Ely**, 'do you know who is the man to whom **Lord Watling** has given the Bramhill living?'

" 'A man named Sargent [said **Mr Fellowes**]. I knew him at Oxford. His brother is a lawyer, and was very useful to Lord Watling in that ugly Brounsell affair. That's why Sargent got the living.'

" 'Sargent,' said Mr Ely. 'I know him. Isn't he a showy, talkative fellow; has written travels in Mesopotamia, or something of that sort?'

" 'That's the man.'

" 'He was at Witherington once, as Bagshawe's curate. He got into rather bad odour there, through some scandal about a flirtation, I think.' " 6

The Other Principal

Mrs Amelia (10; **Milly**) **Barton**. "She was a lovely woman—Mrs Amos Barton; a large, fair, gentle Madonna, with thick, close, chestnut curls beside her well-rounded cheeks, and with large, tender, short-sighted eyes. The flowing lines of her tall figure made the limpest dress look graceful, and her old friend black silk seemed to repose on her bust and limbs with a placid elegance and sense of distinction, in strong contrast with the uneasy sense of being no fit, that seemed to express itself in the rustling of **Mrs Farquhar**'s *gros de Naples.* The caps she wore would have been pronounced, when off her head, utterly heavy and hideous—for in those days even fashionable caps were large and floppy; but surmounting her long arched neck, and mingling their borders of cheap lace and ribbon with her chestnut curls, they seemed miracles of successful millinery. Among strangers she was shy and tremulous as a girl of fifteen; she blushed crimson if anyone appealed to her opinion; yet that tall, graceful, substantial presence was so imposing in its mildness, that men spoke to her with an agreeable sensation of timidity.

"Soothing, unspeakable charm of gentle womanhood! which supersedes all acquisitions, all accomplishments. You would never have asked, at any period of Mr Amos Barton's life, if she sketched or played the piano. You would even perhaps have been rather scandalised if she had descended from the serene dignity of *being* to the assiduous unrest of *doing*. Happy the man, you would have thought, whose eye will rest on her in the pauses of his fireside reading—whose hot aching forehead will be soothed by the contact of her cool, soft hand—who will recover himself from dejection at his mistakes and failures in the loving light of her unreproaching eyes!.

"You would not, perhaps, have anticipated that this bliss would fall to the share of precisely such a man as **Amos Barton**, whom you have already surmised not to have the refined sensibilities for which you might have imagined Mrs Barton's qualities to be destined by pre-established harmony. But I, for one, do not grudge Amos Barton his sweet wife. I have all my life had a sympathy for mongrel ungainly dogs, who are nobody's pets; and I would rather surprise one of them by a pat and a pleasant morsel, than meet the condescending advances of the loveliest Skye terrier who has his cushion by my lady's chair.

"That, to be sure, is not the way of the world: if it happens to see a fellow of fine proportions and aristocratic mien, who makes no *faux pas*, and wins golden opinions from all sorts of men, it straightway picks out for him the loveliest of unmarried women, and says, There would be a proper match!! Not at all, say I: let that successful, well-shapen, discreet and able gentleman put up with something less than the best in the matrimonial department; and let the sweet woman go to make sunshine and a soft pillow for the poor devil whose legs are not models, whose efforts are often blunders, and who in general gets more kicks than halfpence. She—the sweet woman—will like it as well, for her sublime capacity of loving will have all the more scope; and I venture to say, Mrs Barton's nature would never have grown half so angelic if she had married the man you would perhaps have had in your eye for her—a man with sufficient income and abundant personal éclat. Besides, Amos was an affectionate husband, and, in his way, valued his wife as his best treasure." ¶2

—*ingenious at repair:* "She had at that moment on her feet a pair of slippers which had long ago lived through the prunella phase of their existence, and were now running a respectable career as black silk slippers, having been neatly covered with that material by Mrs Barton's own neat fingers. Wonderful fingers those! they were never empty; for if she went to spend a few hours with a friendly parishioner, out came her thimble and a piece of calico or muslin, which, before she left, had become a mysterious little garment with all sorts of hemmed ins and outs. She was even trying to persuade her husband to leave off tight pantaloons, because if he would wear the ordinary guncases, she knew she could make them so well that no one would suspect the sex of the tailor." 2

—in bed: "Her body was very weary, but her heart was not heavy, in spite of **Mr Woods** the butcher, and the transitory nature of shoe-leather; for her heart so overflowed with love, she felt sure she was near a fountain of love that would care for husband and babes better than she could foresee; so she was soon asleep." 2

—going: "It seemed as if Milly had heard the little footsteps on the stairs, for when **Amos** entered her eyes were wide open, eagerly looking towards the door . . . .

" '**Patty**, I'm going away from you. Love your papa. Comfort him, and take care of your little brothers and sisters. God will help you' . . . .

"The mother motioned with her pallid lips for the dear child to lean towards her and kiss her . . . . " 8

—last words: " 'My dear—dear—husband—you have been—very—good to me. You—have—made me—very—happy' . . . .

"Music—music—didn't you hear it?' " 8

Supporting Roles

Edmund (5) **Bridmain**, "a stiff and rather thickset man, gave his welcome with a laboured cordiality. It was astonishing how very little he resembled his beautiful sister." 3

—conversationalist: "Mr Bridmain studied conversation as an art. To ladies he spoke of the weather, and was accustomed to consider it under three points of view: as a question of climate in general, comparing England with other countries in this respect; as a personal question, enquiring how it affected his lady interlocutor in particular; and as a question of probabilities, discussing whether there would be a change or a continuance of the present atmospheric conditions. To gentlemen he talked politics, and he read two daily papers expressly to qualify himself for this function." 3

—truth told: " . . . Mr Bridmain was neither more nor less than her half-brother, who, by unimpeached integrity and industry, had won a partnership in a silk-manufactory, and thereby a moderate fortune, that enabled him to retire, as you see, to study politics, the weather, and the art of conversation at his leisure. Mr Bridmain, in fact, quadragenarian bachelor as he was, felt extremely well pleased to receive his sister in her widowhood, and to shine in the reflected light of her beauty and title . . . . Mr Bridmain had put his neck under the yoke of his handsome sister, and though his soul was a very little one—of the smallest description indeed—he would not have ventured to call it his own . . . he submitted to all his sister's caprices, never grumbled because her dress and her maid formed a considerable item beyond her own little income of sixty pounds per annum, and consented to lead with her a migratory life, as personages on the debatable ground between aristocracy and commonality, instead of settling in some spot where his five hundred a year might have won him the definite dignity of a parochial magnate." 4

Countess Caroline Czerlaski "was undeniably beautiful . . . the tasteful dress, the rich silk of a pinkish lilac hue (the Countess always wore delicate colours in an evening), the black lace pelerine, and the black lace veil falling at the back of the small closely-braided head . . . small hands and feet, a tall lithe figure, large dark eyes, and dark silken braided hair. All these the Countess possessed, and she had, moreover, a delicately formed nose, the least bit curved, and a clear brunette complexion. Her mouth, it must be admitted, receded too much from her nose and chin, and to a prophetic eye threatened 'nutcrackers' in advanced age. But by the light of fire and wax-candles that age seemed very far off indeed, and you would have said that the Countess was not more than thirty." 3

—*widowed state:* "After three years of widowhood, she had brought her feelings to contemplate giving a successor to her lamented **Czerlaski**, whose fine whiskers, fine air, and romantic fortunes had won her heart ten years ago, when, as pretty **Caroline Bridmain**, in the full bloom of five-and-twenty, she was governess to **Lady Porter**'s daughters . . . . She had had seven years of sufficiently happy matrimony with Czerlaski, who had taken her to Paris and Germany, and introduced her there to many of his old friends with large titles and small fortunes." 4

—*current views:* "[She] had had considerable experience of life, and had gathered therefrom, not, indeed, any very ripe and comprehensive wisdom, but much external polish, and certain practical conclusions of a very decided kind. One of these conclusions was, that there were things more solid in life than fine whiskers and a title, and that, in accepting a second husband, she would regard these items as quite subordinate to a carriage and a settlement." 4

—*socially eligible:* "There was nothing here so very detestable. It is true, the Countess was a little vain, a little ambitious, a little selfish, a little shallow and frivolous, a little given to white lies. But who considers such slight blemishes, such moral pimples as these, disqualifications for entering into the most respectable society!" 4

—*religion:* "And she was especially eager for clerical notice and friendship, not merely because that is quite the most respectable countenance to be obtained in society, but because she really cared about religious matters, and had an uneasy sense that she was not altogether safe in that quarter. She had serious intentions of becoming *quite* pious—without any reserves—when she had once got her carriage and settlement." 4

—*predilections:* "And as she had by no means such fine taste and insight in theological teaching as in costume, the **Rev. Amos Barton** seemed to her a man not only of learning—*that* is always understood with a clergyman—but of much power as a spiritual director. As for **Milly**, the Countess really loved her as well as the preoccupied state of her affections would allow. For you have already perceived that there was one being to whom the Countess was absorbingly devoted, and to whose desires she made everything else subservient—namely, Caroline Czerlaski, née Bridmain." 4

—*spoken to plainly:* "The Countess was stunned for a few minutes, but when she began to recall **Nanny**'s words, there was no possibility of avoiding very unpleasant conclusions from them, or of failing to see her position in the Vicarage in an entirely new light. The interpretation too of Nanny's allusion to a 'bad name' did not lie out of the reach of the Countess's imagination, and she saw the necessity of quitting Shepperton without delay." 7

Others

Alice, "the buxom lady's-maid, wearing a much better dress than **Mrs Barton**'s, now appeared to take **Mr Bridmain**'s place in retrieving the mischief . . . . " 3

—*surprise:* " 'I am a most wretched woman [said the **Countess**]. To be deceived by a brother to whom I have been so devoted—to see him degrading himself—giving himself utterly to the dogs! . . .

" 'He is going to be married—to marry my own maid, that deceitful Alice, to whom I have been the most indulgent mistress. Did you ever hear of anything so disgraceful? so mortifying? so disreputable? . . .

" 'I went into the dining room suddenly and found him kissing her—disgusting at his time of life, is it not?—and when I reproved her for allowing such liberties, she turned round saucily, and said she was engaged to be married to my brother, and she saw no shame in allowing him to kiss her.' " 5

Dickey Barton, "the second boy, had insisted on superseding **Chubby** in the guidance of a headless horse, of the red-wafered species, which she was drawing round the room, so that when Papa opened the door Chubby was giving tongue energetically." 2

—with his mother: "Little Dickey, a boisterous boy of five, with large pink cheeks and sturdy legs, was having his turn to sit with mamma, and was squatting quiet as a mouse at her knee, holding her soft white hand between his little red black-nailed fists. He was a boy whom **Mrs Hackit**, in a severe mood, had pronounced 'stocky' (a word that etymologically, in all probability, conveys some allusion to an instrument of punishment for the refractory); but seeing him thus subdued into goodness, she smiled at him with her kindest smile, and, stooping down, suggested a kiss—a favour which Dickey resolutely declined." 5

—at graveside: "Dickey had rebelled against his black clothes, until he was told that it would be naughty to mamma not to put them on, when he at once submitted; and now, though he had heard **Nanny** say that mamma was in heaven, he had a vague notion that she would come home again tomorrow, and say he had been a good boy and let him empty her work-box. He stood close to his father, with great rosy cheeks, and wide-open blue eyes, looking first up at **Mr Cleves** and then down at the coffin, and thinking he and **Chubby** would play at that when they got home." 9

—in later years: "Dickey, you will be glad to hear, had shown remarkable talents as an engineer. His cheeks are still ruddy, in spite of mixed mathematics, and his eyes are still large and blue; but in other respects his person would present no marks of identification for his friend **Mrs Hackit**, if she were to see him; especially now that her eyes must be grown very dim, with the wear of more than twenty additional years. He is nearly six feet high, and has a proportionately broad chest; he wears spectacles, and rubs his large white hands through a mass of shaggy brown hair. But I am sure you have no doubt that Mr Richard Barton is a thoroughly good fellow, as well as a man of talent, and you will be glad any day to shake hands with him, for his own sake as well as his mother's." *Conclusion And see* **Mrs Hackit**—*motherly*

Patty Barton. "Nearest her mother sits the nine-year-old Patty, the eldest child, whose sweet fair face is already rather grave sometimes, and who always wants to run upstairs to save mamma's legs, which get so tired of an evening." 2

—death approaches: "Patty understood the great sorrow that was come upon them, and tried to check her sobs as she heard her papa's footsteps." 8

—a promise: " 'Love your papa. Comfort him; and take care of your little brothers and sisters. God will help you.'

"Patty stood perfectly quiet, and said, 'Yes, mamma.'

" . . . then Patty's great anguish overcame her, and she burst into sobs . . .

"Patty at first begged to stay at home and not go to **Mrs Bond**'s again; but when **Nanny** reminded her that she had better go to take care of the younger ones, she submitted at once . . . . " 8

—*at the grave:* "Patty alone of all the children felt that mamma was in that coffin, and that a new and sadder life had begun for papa and herself. She was pale and trembling, but she clasped his hand more firmly as the coffin went down, and gave no sob." 9

—*there again:* [**Amos**] held on his arm a young woman, with a sweet, grave face, which strongly recalled the expression of **Mrs Barton**'s, but was less lovely in form and colour. She was about thirty, but there were some premature lines round her mouth and eyes, which told of early anxiety . . . .

"Patty alone remains by her father's side, and makes the evening sunshine of his life." *Conclusion*

Miss Janet Gibbs, "a single lady of fifty, who has refused the most ineligible offers out of devotion to her aged aunt [**Mrs Patten**], is pouring the rich cream into the fragrant tea with a discreet liberality." 1

—*suppressed:* " . . . the snubbed Janet, whose ankles were only tight in the sense of looking extremely squeezed by her boots. But Janet seemed always to identify herself with her aunt's personality, holding her own under protest." 1

Hackit, "expressing his views more literally, reminded his wife that 'money breeds money.' "

"Mr Hackit is a shrewd substantial man, whose advice about crops is always worth listening to, and who is too well off to want to borrow money." 1

Mrs Hackit, "her epigrammatic neighbour . . . sarcastically accounted for [**Mrs Patten**'s wealth] by supposing that 'sixpences grew on the bents of Cross Farm' . . . . " 1

—*at tea:* "Mrs Hackit declines cream; she has so long abstained from it with an eye to the weekly butter-money, that abstinence, wedded to habit, has begotten aversion. She is a thin woman with a chronic liver complaint, which would have secured her **Mr Pilgrim**'s entire regard and unreserved good word, even if he had not been in awe of her tongue, which was as sharp as his own lancet." 1

—*the weather:* "[She] regulated her costume by the calendar, and brought out her furs on the first of November, whatever might be the temperature. She was not a woman weakly to accommodate herself to shilly-shally proceedings. If the season didn't know what it ought to do, Mrs Hackit did. In her best days, it was always sharp weather at 'Gunpowder Plot', and she didn't like new fashions." 5

—*motherly:* "When the spring came, Mrs Hackit begged that she might have **Dickey** to stay with her, and great was the enlargement of Dickey's experience from that visit. Every morning he was allowed—being well wrapped up as to his chest by Mrs Hackit's own hands, but very bare and red as to his legs—to run loose in the cow- and poultry-yard, to persecute the turkeycock by satirical imitations of his gobble-gobble, and to put difficult questions to the **groom** as to the reasons why horses had four legs, and other transcendental matters. Then **Mr Hackit** would take Dickey up on horseback when he rode round his farm, and Mrs Hackit had a large plum cake in cut, ready to meet incidental attacks of hunger. So that Dickey had considerably modified his views as to the desirability of Mrs Hackit's kisses." 9

Mrs Patten, "a childless old lady, who had got rich chiefly by the negative process of spending nothing. Mrs Patten's passive accumulation of wealth, through all sorts of 'bad times', on the farm of which she had been sole tenant since her husband's death . . . . " 1

—*at tea:* "Quiescence in an easy-chair, under a sense of compound interest perpetually accumulating, has long seemed an ample function to her, and she does her malevolence gently. She is a pretty little old woman of eighty, with a close cap and tiny flat white curls round her face, as natty and unsoiled and invariable as the waxen image of a little old lady under a glass case; once a lady's-maid, and married for her beauty. She used to adore her husband, and now she adores her money, cherishing a quiet blood relation's hatred for her niece, **Janet Gibbs**, who, she knows, expects a large legacy, and whom she is determined to disappoint." 1

Mr Pilgrim, "the doctor from the nearest market town, who, though occasionally affecting aristocratic airs, and giving late dinners with enigmatic side-dishes and poisonous port, is never so comfortable as when he is relaxing his professional legs in one of those excellent farmhouses where the mice are sleek and the mistress sickly." 1

—*elocution:* "Mr Pilgrim generally spoke with an intermittent kind of splutter . . . . But when he came to what he conceived the pith of his argument or the point of his joke, he mouthed out his words with slow emphasis; as a hen, when advertising her accouchement, passes at irregular intervals from pianissimo semiquavers to fortissimo crotchets." 1

" . . . Mr Pilgrim had emitted a succession of little snorts, something like the treble grunts of a guinea-pig, which were always with him the sign of suppressed disapproval." 1

Minor Figures

Chubby Barton: *see* **Dickey Barton** O

Fred Barton. " 'Poor Fred must have some new shoes; I couldn't let him go to Mrs Bond's yesterday because his toes were peeping out, dear child! and I can't let him walk anywhere except in the garden.' " 2

Walter Barton, "the year-old baby, who looks over her shoulder with large wide-open eyes, while the patient mother pats his back with her soft hand . . . .

"**Nanny** is that moment putting him in the little cot by his mother's bedside; the head, with its thin wavelets of brown hair, indents the little pillow; and a tiny, waxen, dimpled fist hides the rosy lips, for baby is given to the infantine peccadillo of thumb-sucking." 2

Betty. "**Miss Gibbs** . . . suspected Betty, the dairymaid, of frying the best bacon for the **shepherd**, when he sat up with her to 'help brew'; whereupon Mrs Hackit replied that she had always thought Betty false . . . . " 1

Bond. " 'I never saw the like to parsons,' **Mr Hackit** said one day in conversation with his brother churchwarden, Mr Bond; 'they're al'ys for meddling with business, an they know no more about it than my black filly.'

" 'Ah, said Mr Bond, 'they're too high learned to have much common sense.' " 5

Mr Brand, "the Shepperton doctor so obnoxious to **Mr Pilgrim**, ordered [**Milly**] to drink port-wine . . . . " 5

Mrs Brick. "Perfectly wide-awake . . . was Mrs Brick, one of those hard undying old women, to whom age seems to have given a network of wrinkles, as a coat of magic armour against the attacks of winters, warm or cold. The point on which Mrs Brick was still sensitive—the theme on which you might possibly excite her hope and fear—was snuff. It seemed to be an embalming powder, helping her soul to do the office of salt." 2

Cook. " 'You'd a deal sooner not ha' throwed it down at all, I should think,' responded the unsympathetic cook, to whom **John** did not make love. 'Who d'you think's to make gravy anuff, if you're to baste people's gownds wi' it?' " 3

Mrs Cramp, "the charwoman, on her way home from the Vicarage, where she had been helping **Nanny** to pack up the day before the departure. . . . " 10

Count Czerlaski. " . . . her husband had been the veritable Count Czerlaski, who had had wonderful escapes, as she said, and who, as she did *not* say, but as was said in certain circulars once folded by her fair hands, had subsequently given dancing lessons in the metropolis . . . . " 4

Miss Arabella Farquhar "wondered why [**Mr Barton**] always said he was going *for* to do a thing." 2

Miss Julia Farquhar "had observed that she never heard anyone sniff so frightfully as Mr Barton did—she had a great mind to offer him her pocket-handkerchief . . . . " 2

Mr Farquhar, "the secondary squire of the parish . . . . " 2

"Mr Farquhar, though not a parishioner of **Mr Ely**'s, was one of his warmest admirers, and thought he would make an unexceptionable son-in-law, in spite of his being of no particular 'family'. Mr Farquhar was susceptible on the point of 'blood'—his own circulating fluid, which animated a short and somewhat flabby person, being, he considered, of very superior quality.

" 'By the by,' he said, with a certain pomposity counteracted by a lisp, 'what an ath **Barton** makth of himthelf, about that **Bridmain** and the **Counteth**, ath she callth herthelf.' " 3

Mrs Farquhar. " 'Mithith Farquhar ith very fond of Mithith **Barton**, and ith quite dithtrethed that she should athothiate with thuch a woman, tho she attacked him on the thubject purpothly.' " 3

Fitchett, "who had once been a footman in the **Oldinport** family, and in that giddy elevation had enunciated a contemptuous opinion of boiled beef, which had been traditionally handed down in Shepperton as the direct cause of his ultimate reduction to pauper commons. His calves were now shrunken, and his hair was grey without the aid of powder; but he still carried his chin as if he were conscious of a stiff cravat; he set his dilapidated hat on with a knowing inclination towards the left ear; and when he was on field-work, he carted and uncarted the manure with a sort of flunkey grace, the ghost of that jaunty demeanour with which he used to usher in my lady's morning visitors. The flunkey nature was nowhere completely subdued but in his stomach, and he still divided society into gentry, gentry's flunkeys, and the people who provided for them . . . . Mr Fitchett had an irrepressible tendency to drowsiness under spiritual instruction, and in the recurrent regularity with which he dozed off until he nodded and awaked himself, he looked not unlike a piece of mechanism, ingeniously contrived for measuring the length of **Mr Barton**'s discourse." 2

Poll Fodge. "Next to [**Old Maxum**] sat Poll Fodge—known to the magistracy of her county as **Mary Higgins**—a one-eyed woman, with a scarred and seamy face, the most notorious rebel in the workhouse, said to have once thrown her broth over the master's coat-tails, and who, in spite of Nature's apparent safeguards against that contingency, had contributed to the perpetuation of the Fodge characteristics in the person of a small boy, who was behaving naughtily on one of the back benches. Miss Fodge fixed her one sore eye on **Mr Barton** with a sort of hardy defiance." 2

Fodge boy. "The inveterate culprit was a boy of seven, vainly contending against a cold in his nose by feeble sniffing." 2

Mrs Jackson. " . . . **Milly**'s aunt, who had lived with her ever since her marriage, had withdrawn herself, her furniture, and her yearly income, to the household of another niece, prompted to that step, very probably, by a slight 'tiff' with the **Rev. Amos**, which occurred while Milly was upstairs, and proved one too many for the elderly lady's patience and magnanimity." 5

Jet. "Whether Jet the spaniel, being a much more knowing dog than was suspected, wished to express his disapproval of the **Countess**'s last speech, as not accordant with his ideas of wisdom and veracity, I cannot say; but at this moment he jumped off her lap, and, turning his back upon her, placed one paw on the fender, and held the other up to warm, as if affecting to abstract himself from the current of conversation." 3

John, "the manservant, approached **Mrs Barton** with a gravy-tureen, and also with a slight odour of the stable, which usually adhered to him throughout his indoor functions. John was rather nervous, and the Countess happening to speak to him at this inopportune moment, the tureen slipped and emptied itself on Mrs Barton's newly turned black silk." 3

Mrs Landor: *see* **Mrs Phipps**

Dr Madeley, "the physician from Rotherby . . . .

" 'They sent for Dr Madeley i' the middle o' the day yisterday, an' he's here again now.' " 8

Nanny. "[The door] is opened without delay by the nurse, cook, and housemaid, all at once—that is to say, by the robust maid-of-all-work . . . . " 2

—speaking out: " 'What do you mean by behaving this way?'

" 'Mean? Why I mean as the missis is a-slavin' her life out an' a-sittin' up o' nights, for folks as are better able to wait of her, i'stid o'lyin' a-bed an' doin' nothin' all the blessed day, but mek work.'

" 'Leave the room and don't be insolent.'

" 'Insolent! I'd better be insolent than like what some folks is—a-livin' on other folks, an' bringin' a bad name on 'em into the bargain.'

"Here Nanny flung out of the room, leaving the lady to digest this unexpected breakfast at her leisure." 7

—pleased: "As for Nanny, she was perfectly aware of the relation between cause and effect in the affair, and secretly chuckled over her outburst of 'sauce' as the best morning's work she had ever done." 7

Old Maxum. "Right in front of [**Amos**]—probably because he was stone-deaf, and it was deemed more edifying to hear nothing at a short distance than at a long one—sat 'Old Maxum', as he was familiarly called, his real patronymic remaining a mystery to most persons. A fine philological sense discerns in this cognomen an indication that the pauper patriarch had once been considered pithy and sententious in his speech; but now the weight of ninety-five years lay heavy on his tongue as well as in his ears, and he sat before the clergyman with protruded chin, and munching mouth, and eyes that seemed to look at emptiness." 2

Oldinport. " 'If he agrees to attend service there [in the workhouse] once or twice, the other people will come. Net the large fish, and you're sure to have the small fry.' " 2

—sympathetic: "Mr Oldinport wrote to express his sympathy, and enclosed another twenty-pound note, begging that he might be permitted to contribute in this way to the relief of **Mr Barton**'s mind from pecuniary anxieties, under the pressure of a grief which all his parishioners must share; and offering his interest towards placing the two eldest girls in a school expressly founded for clergymen's daughters." 9

Mrs Phipps, "the banker's wife, and **Mrs Landor**, the attorney's wife, had invested part of their reputation for acuteness in the supposition that **Mr Bridmain** was not the **Countess**'s brother.

Miss Phipps. "Moreover, Miss Phipps was conscious that if the **Countess** was not a disreputable person, she, Miss Phipps, had no compensating superiority in virtue to set against the other lady's manifest superiority in personal charms. Miss Phipps's stumpy figure and unsuccessful attire, instead of looking down from a mount of virtue with an aureole round its head, would then be seen on the same level and in the same light as the Countess Czerlaski's Diana-like form and well-chosen drapery. Miss Phipps, for her part, didn't like dressing for effect—she had always avoided that style of appearance which was calculated to create a sensation." 4

Rachel, "the housemaid, came in and said—

" 'If you please 'm, the shepherd says, have you heard as **Mrs Barton**'s wuss, and not expected to live?' " 8

Silly Jim. "Beyond this member of the softer sex [**Poll Fodge**], at the end of the bench, sat 'Silly Jim', a young man afflicted with hydrocephalus, who rolled his head from side to side, and gazed at the point of his nose." 2

Spratt. " . . . a certain number of refractory children, over whom Mr Spratt, the master of the workhouse, exercised an irate surveillance . . . .

"Mr Spratt was a small-featured, small-statured man, with a remarkable power of language, mitigated by hesitation, who piqued himself on expressing unexceptionable sentiments in unexceptionable language on all occasions." 2

Jacob Tomms, "a young gentleman in the tailoring line, who occasionally—simply out of a taste for dialogue—looked into the Vicarage kitchen of an evening." 7

Tozer. "Old stiff-jointed Mr Tozer, who was still able to earn a little by gardening 'jobs', stopped **Mrs Cramp** . . . and enquired very particularly into Mr Barton's prospects.

" 'Ah, poor mon,' he was heard to say, 'I'm sorry for un. He hadn't much here, but he'll be wuss off theer. Half a loaf's better nor ne'er un.' " 10

Woodcock " 'was immensely taken with [the **Countess**], and insisted on his wife's calling on her and asking her to dinner; but I think **Mrs Woodcock** turned restive after the first visit, and wouldn't invite her again.' " 3

Woods. " 'And, dear, Woods the butcher called, to say he must have some money next week. He has a payment to make up.' " 2

Also mentioned

Amphitryon, a figure in Greek mythology, cuckolded by Zeus; known for hospitality	6
Sophy Barton, one of the children asked to carry books steadily	2
Betty, a milkmaid for Mrs Patten	1
blacksmith, a Catholic with plans once the Emancipation Bill is passed	1
Lord Blarney, allegedly known to the Countess	3
Dolby, architect for the Shepperton Church	6
footman to Mr Farquhar, who heard some news from Nanny	7
Granby, the host of a dinner-party	6
groom at the Hackits' farm	9
Jim Hood, the bassoon-man.	1
Bishop Jebb, whose Memoirs Mr Ely is reading	3
Mr Johns, mentor to Amos Barton at Gun Street Chapel	2
landlord at the Jolly Colliers	7
Landor, the attorney	4
Nisbett, retailing gossip to Mr Fellowes	6
Oldinport family, with escutcheons in Shepperton Church	1
Patten, the late husband of Mrs Patten	1
Phipps, the banker	4
Lady Porter, a friend of the Countess	3
Sir William Porter, whose name is dropped by the Countess	3
Dean of Radborough, allegedly known to the Countess	3
schoolmaster, who heard of the Countess's departure	7
schoolmistress, observing the Countess's departure	7
shepherd, in Mrs Patten's employ	1
Mrs Short, owner of Camp Villa; landlady to the Countess	3
Mr Simeon, mentor to Amos Barton at Cambridge	2
St Lawrence	1
Lord Watling, a gentleman farmer favouring black angus on his farm at Tetterley	6
Princess Wengstein, with whom the Countess is acquainted	3
Mrs Woodcock, who did not care for the Countess	3

Scenes of Clerical Life

Mr Gilfil's Love-Story

Mr Gilfil, dead thirty years, was mourned in black bombasine. We learn the story of his sending **Dame Fripp** a great piece of bacon, and other anecdotes of his relations with his parishioners and their children, and of his quarrel with **Squire Oldinport**. Mr Gilfil adapts himself to the lowly and the high. There is a room in his house, furnished in feminine style, which no one enters. **Mrs Patten** remembers **Mrs Gilfil** and describes her: an Italian girl soon ill and then dead to Mr Gilfil's great grief. 1 Back to June 21, 1788: **Caterina** (**Tina**) and **Lady Cheverel** are observed on the lawn at Cheverel Manor by **Sir Christopher**, his nephew the exquisite **Captain Anthony Wybrow**, and young **Rev. Maynard Gilfil**. The widow **Hartopp** comes to plead to be left on her farm. The baronet is firm, but will have a cottage for her. Tina is miserable and distraught because Anthony is leaving to take a wife. Gilfil, who loves her, tries to provide comfort. She sings gorgeously for them all. Later Wybrow pursues her in the gloaming and makes excuses. 2

Flashback 15 years: in Milan, Lady Cheverel's singing teacher suggests a copyist, **Sarti**, who works for her, but shortly sends a desperate note. By the time she reaches him, he is dead, a baby girl seated on his bed. His wife and other children had died. The Cheverels take Caterina back to England to raise as their protégée (not as a daughter). 3 The servants enjoy her; she has a happy childhood but is badly spoiled. Sir Christopher's project to Gothicize his house gets underway. Tina grows, and reveals her musical talent. It elevates her to real family status. And the baronet's young ward, **Maynard** Gilfil, comes each summer and devotes himself to her. But her love is Anthony, now summoned by his uncle to seek **Beatrice Assher** in marriage. He goes. 4

Tina waits in agony. Anthony reports success. Lady Assher and Beatrice arrive to meet his family. Beatrice is statuesque and gracious, her mother a stupid bore. Tina has a singing triumph but then flees to her room in jealous pain. 5 She copes, but then Anthony finds a moment and kisses her. She rushes away. Beatrice has seen them together. 6 Tina visits her friend gardener **Bates**, but his admiration of Beatrice and pleased talk of the forthcoming marriage drives her away. 7 Beatrice is watchful. She sees Tina brusque with Anthony, who feigns nonchalance. Beatrice taxes him. He asks for trust and reassures her. She believes. They go out to ride. 8

Gilfil comes to Tina and urges restraint. Beatrice is watching. Tina's heart is breaking. 9 Anthony, whose health is delicate, meditates on his troubles. He asks Beatrice to be kind to Tina, and she is, to Tina's torment. Night after night of suffering wears her down. 10 Tina looks unwell, causing alarm. But she is rude to Beatrice, then makes a scene with Anthony. Beatrice walks in on it. 11 Beatrice taxes Anthony severely, accusing him of prior flirtation. He speaks to Sir Christopher, asking him to further Gilfil's suit with Tina. The baronet puts it to Maynard, who strongly demurs. But Sir Christopher insists: he will speak to Tina. Maynard writes Tina to warn her, saying that Anthony has fomented the proposal. She is at first enraged, then bitterly sad, regretting that she must disappoint the baronet. She destroys Anthony's keepsake. 12

Sir Christopher puts it to Tina. He has set his heart on her marrying Gilfil. Anthony tells Beatrice he will speak with Tina. She approves. But when Tina comes to her to hold her silks, she mentions the meeting, and words follow. Tina rushes out and seizes a dagger, then runs to her meeting with Anthony. She finds him lying dead in the path. 13 Sir Christopher and Gilfil are talking when Tina rushes in with the news. She faints. Gilfil finds and takes the dagger. 14 Tina begins to wake. She eludes Gilfil and goes out but meets a cortège bringing back the body. She has forgotten the dagger. 15 Alone, she contemplates what has happened and what she has done and tried to do. She thinks she should go away and be forgotten. She packs and makes ready. 16

Mrs Sharp, Lady Cheverel's maid, finds Tina's bed unslept-in. She goes to Gilfil, who fears suicide. He asks Bates's aid: they will drag the ponds if Tina cannot be found. He is in deepest anguish, and fears also for the baronet. 17 He goes to the grieving Sir Christopher and says Tina is missing. The baronet asks if she had loved Anthony: Gilfil says yes, and that Anthony had behaved badly to her. Sir Christopher takes the news in quietly: he will talk to his wife. 18 The inquest proceeds normally Tina cannot be found. Gilfil sees a man he recognizes on horseback. It is coachman Daniel Knott, who married Tina's friend Dorcas. Tina is at his home in bed speaking to no one. Gilfil rides at once and Tina recognizes him and speaks, to ask about the dagger. He tells her it is put away: no one saw it. She weeps long, at last. They talk and talk, and sit and sit; she seems much calmer. He will take her to his sister's to get well. 19

At Foxholm Parsonage, the **Herons** care for Tina; little **Ozzy** at five is a huge health benefit. When he bangs his whip on the harpsichord, Tina vibrates at last and begins to play, then to sing, and to love Maynard. 20 The wedding occurs in May 1790, with the Cheverels present. The new heir-designee, a son of Sir Christopher's no-longer-estranged elder daughter, participates. Tina lives on, but only a little while. She dies loving her husband, who never loved again. 21 An epilogue comments on the present Vicar, forever wounded, forever strong; respected and beloved.

The Title Role: Rev. Maynard Gilfil

"You already suspect that the Vicar did not shine in the more spiritual functions of his office; and indeed, the utmost I can say for him in this respect is, that he performed those functions with undeviating attention to brevity and despatch. He had a large heap of short sermons, rather yellow and worn at the edges, from which he took two every Sunday, securing perfect impartiality in the selection by taking them as they came, without reference to topics; and having preached one of these sermons at Shepperton in the morning, he mounted his horse and rode hastily with the other in his pocket to Knebley, where he officiated in a wonderful little church . . . . Here, in an absence of mind to which he was prone, Mr Gilfil would sometimes forget to take off his spurs before putting on his surplice, and only become aware of the omission by feeling something mysteriously tugging at the skirts of that garment as he stepped into the reading-desk. But the Knebley farmers would as soon have thought of criticising the moon as their pastor. He belonged to the course of nature, like markets and toll-gates and dirty banknotes; and being a vicar, his claim on their veneration had never been counteracted by an exasperating claim on their pockets." 1

—encountering a pig: "Mr Gilfil laughed, and I am obliged to admit that he said goodby to **Dame Fripp** without asking her why she had not been to church, or making the slightest effort for her spiritual edification. But the next day he ordered his man David to take her a great piece of bacon, with a message, saying, the parson wanted to make sure that Mrs Fripp would know the taste of bacon fat again. So, when Mr Gilfil died, Dame Fripp manifested her gratitude and reverence . . . . " 1

—quarrelsome: "[He] was of an extremely caustic turn, his satire having a flavour of originality which was quite wanting in his sermons; and as **Mr Oldinport**'s armour of conscious virtue presented some considerable and conspicuous gaps, the Vicar's keen-edged retorts probably made a few incisions too deep to be forgiven." 1

—mode of speech: " . . . a superficial observer might have seen little difference, beyond his superior shrewdness, between the Vicar and his bucolic parishioners, for it was his habit to approximate his accent and mode of speech to theirs, doubtless because he thought it a mere frustration of the purposes of language to talk of 'shear-hogs' and 'ewes' to men who habitually said 'sharrags' and 'yowes'. Nevertheless the farmers themselves were perfectly aware of the distinction between them and the parson, and had not at all the less belief in him as a gentleman and a clergyman for his easy speech and familiar manners." 1

—dining out: " . . . you would have inferred that the earlier period of his life had been passed in more stately society than could be found in Shepperton, and that his slipshod chat and homely manners were but like weather-stains on a fine old block of marble, allowing you still to see here and there the fineness of the grain, and the delicacy of the original tint." 1

—at home: "But in his later years . . . he was rarely to be found anywhere of an evening beyond the bounds of his own parish—most frequently, indeed, by the side of his own sitting-room fire, smoking his pipe, and maintaining the leasing antithesis of dryness and moisture by an occasional sip of gin-and-water." 1

—close: "His nose was not rubicund; on the contrary, his white hair hung around a pale and venerable face. He drank [gin-and-water] chiefly, I believe,

because it was cheap; and here I find myself alighting on another of the Vicar's weaknesses . . . . It is undeniable that, as the years advanced, Mr Gilfil became . . . more and more 'close-fisted', though the growing propensity showed itself rather in the parsimony of his personal habits, than in withholding help from the needy. He was saving—so he represented the matter to himself—for a nephew, the only son of a sister who had been the dearest object, all but one, in his life." 1

—*his wife:* " 'As for him, I niver see'd a man so wrapped up in a woman. He looked at her as if he was worshippin' her, an' as if he wanted to lift her off the ground ivery minute, to save her the trouble o' walkin'. Poor man, poor man! It had like to ha' killed him when she died, though he niver gev way, but went on ridin' about and preachin'. But he was wore to a shadow, an' his eyes used to look as dead—you wouldn't ha' knowed 'em.' " 1

Rev. Maynard Gilfil. "It is the evening of the 21st of June 1788 . . . [his] legs and profile were not at all of a kind to make him peculiarly alive to the impertinence and frivolity of personal advantages. His healthy open face and robust limbs were after an excellent pattern for everyday wear . . . . " 2

—*flashback:* "When [**Caterina**] was no more than seven, a ward of **Sir Christopher's** —a lad of fifteen, Maynard Gilfil by name—began to spend his vacations at Cheverel Manor, and found there no playfellow so much to his mind as Caterina. Maynard was an affectionate lad, who retained a propensity to white rabbits, pet squirrels, and guinea-pigs, perhaps a little beyond the age at which young gentlemen usually look down on such pleasures as puerile. He was also much given to fishing, and to carpentry, considered as a fine art, without any base view to utility. And in all these pleasures it was his delight to have Caterina as his companion, to call her little pet names, answer her wondering questions, and have her toddling after him as you may have seen a Blenheim spaniel trotting after a large setter." 4

—*first love:* "With Maynard the boyish affection had insensibly grown into ardent love . . . of a kind to make him prefer being tormented by **Caterina** to any pleasure, apart from her, which the most benevolent magician could have devised for him. It was the way with those tall large-limbed men, from **Samson** downwards." 4

—*modest:* " . . . he would have been content with very little, being one of those men who pass through life without making the least clamour about themselves; thinking neither the cut of his coat, nor the flavour of his soup, nor the precise depth of a servant's bow, at all momentous." 4

—*a heavy report:* " 'I must tell you now, for her sake, what nothing but this should ever have caused to pass my lips. **Captain Wybow** won her affections by attentions which, in his position, he was bound not to show her. Before his marriage was talked of, he had behaved to her like a lover.' " 18 *This is the only direct intimation in the work that Tina had given herself to Anthony, but the absence of detail in GE's description of the relationship is consistent with Victorian discretion in this delicate area.*

—*distraught:* "Anyone looking at that face, usually so full of calm goodwill, would have seen that the last week's suffering had left deep traces. By day he had been riding or wandering incessantly, either searching for **Caterina** himself, or directing enquiries to be made by others. By night he had not known sleep—only intermittent dozing, in which he seemed to be finding Caterina dead, and woke up with a start from this unreal agony to the real anguish of believing that he should see her no more.

"The clear grey eyes looked sunken and restless, the full careless lips had a strange tension about them, and the brow, formerly so smooth and open, was contracted as if with pain. He had not lost the object of a few months' passion; he had lost the being who was bound up with his power of loving, as the brook we played by or the flowers we gathered in childhood are bound up with our sense of beauty.

"Love meant nothing for him but to love Caterina. For years, the thought of her had been present in everything, like the air and the light; and now she was gone, it seemed as if all pleasure had lost its vehicle: the sky, the earth, the daily ride, the daily talk might be there, but the loveliness and the joy that were in them had gone for ever." ¶19

—farewell: "And so the dear old Vicar, though he had something of the knotted whimsical character of the poor lopped oak, had yet been sketched out by nature as a noble tree. The heart of him was sound, the grain was of the finest; and in the grey-haired man who filled his pocket with sugar-plums for the little children, whose most biting words were directed against the evildoing of the rich man, and who, with all his social pipes and slipshod talk, never sank below the highest level of his parishioners' respect, here was the main trunk of the same brave, faithful, tender nature that had poured out the finest, freshest forces of its life-current in a first and only love . . . . " *Epilogue*

The Feminine Principal

Mrs Gilfil. "There were not many people in the parish, besides Martha, who had any very distinct remembrance of Mr Gilfil's wife, or indeed who knew anything of her, beyond the fact that there was a marble tablet, with a Latin inscription in memory of her, over the Vicarage pew . . . the utmost you could gather from [the parishioners] was that Mrs Gilfil looked like a 'furriner, wi' such eyes, you can't think, an' a voice as went through you when she sung at church.' " 1

—remembered: " '**Mr Tarbett** preached that day, and **Mr Gilfil** sat i' the pew with his wife. I think I see him now, a'leading her up the aisle, an' her head not reachin' much above his elber: a little pale woman, with eyes as black as sloes, an' yet lookin' blank-like as if she see'd nothing with 'em.' " 1

—singing: " 'An' so she did; an' her voice seemed sometimes to fill the room; an' then it went low an' soft, as if it was whisperin' close to your heart like' . . . .

" 'She was sickly then, and she died in a few months after. She wasn't in the parish much more nor half a year altogether.' " 1

Caterina (Tina) Sarti. "It is the evening of the 21st of June 1788 . . . . The soft turf gives way even under the faëry tread of the younger lady, whose small stature and slim figure rest on the tiniest of full-grown feet . . . . You are at once arrested by her large dark eyes, which, in their inexpressive unconscious beauty, resemble the eyes of a fawn, and it is only by an effort of attention that you notice the absence of bloom on her young cheek, and the southern yellowish tint of her small neck and face, rising above the little black lace kerchief which presents the too immediate comparison of her skin with her white muslin gown. Her large eyes seem all the more striking because the dark hair is gathered away from her face, under a little cap set at the top of her head, with a cherry-coloured bow on one side." 2

—in performance: "It happened this evening that the sentiment of these airs . . . in both of which the singer pours out his yearning after his lost love,

came very close to Caterina's own feeling. But her emotion, instead of being a hindrance to her singing, gave her additional power. Her singing was what she could do best; it was her one point of superiority, in which it was probable she would excel the high-born beauty whom **Anthony** was to woo; and her love, her jealousy, her pride, her rebellion against her destiny, made one stream of passion which welled forth in the deep rich tones of her voice. She had a rare contralto . . . . " 2

—*in babyhood:* "On the foot of the bed was seated a tiny child, apparently not three years old, her head covered by a linen cap, her feet clothed with leather boots, above which her little yellow legs showed thin and naked. A frock, made of what had once been a gay flowered silk, was her only other garment. Her large dark eyes shone from out her queer little face, like two precious stones in a grotesque image carved in old ivory." 3

—*status in England:* "**Sir Christopher** . . . loved children, and took at once to the little black-eyed monkey—his name for Caterina all through her short life. But neither he nor **Lady Cheverel** had any idea of adopting her as their daughter, and giving her their own rank in life. They were much too English and aristocratic to think of anything so romantic. No! the child would be brought up at Cheverel Manor as a protégée, to be ultimately useful, perhaps, in sorting worsteds, keeping accounts, reading aloud, and otherwise supplying the place of spectacles when her ladyship's eyes should wax dim." 3

—*discomfort:* " . . . cleanliness is sometimes a painful good, as anyone can vouch who has had his face washed the wrong way, by a pitiless hand with a gold ring on the third finger. If you, reader, have not known that initiatory anguish it is idle to expect that you will form any approximate conception of what Caterina endured under **Mrs Sharp**'s new dispensation of soap-and-water." 3

—*comfort:* "Happily, this purgatory came presently to be associated in her tiny brain with a passage straightway to a seat of bliss—the sofa in **Lady Cheverel**'s sitting-room, where there were toys to be broken, a ride was to be had on **Sir Christopher**'s knee, and a spaniel of resigned temper was prepared to undergo small tortures without flinching." 3

—*spoiled:* "Indeed, in the long monotonous leisure of that great country house, you may be sure there was always someone who had nothing better to do than to play with Tina. So that the little southern bird had its northern nest lined with tenderness, and caresses, and pretty things. A loving sensitive nature was too likely, under such nurture, to have its susceptibility heightened into unfitness for an encounter with any harder experience; all the more, because there were gleams of fierce resistance to any discipline that had a harsh or unloving aspect. For the only thing in which Caterina showed any precocity was a certain ingenuity in vindictiveness." 4

—*growing up:* "While Cheverel Manor was growing from ugliness into beauty, Caterina too was growing from a little yellow bantling into a whiter maiden, with no positive beauty indeed, but with a certain light airy grace, which, with her large appealing dark eyes, and a voice that, in its low-toned tenderness, recalled the love-notes of the stock-dove, gave her a more than usual charm. Unlike the building, however, Caterina's development was the result of no systematic or careful appliances. She grew up very much like the primroses, which the gardener is not sorry to see within his enclosure, but takes no pans to cultivate . . . . It is very likely that to her dying day Caterina thought the earth stood still, and that the sun and stars moved round it . . . ." 4

—*a talent:* "The truth is, that, with one exception, her only talent lay in loving; and there, it is probable, the most astronomical of women could not have surpassed her. Orphan and protégée though she was, this supreme talent of hers found plenty of exercise at Cheverel Manor, and Caterina had more people to love than many a small lady and gentleman affluent in silver mugs and blood relations. I think the first place in her childish heart was given to **Sir Christopher**, for little girls are apt to attach themselves to the finest-looking gentleman at hand, especially as he seldom has anything to do with discipline. Next to the Baronet, came **Dorcas** . . . . " 4

—*a great talent:* "The one other exceptional talent, you already guess, was music. When the fact that Caterina had a remarkable ear for music, and a still more remarkable voice, attracted **Lady Cheverel**'s notice, the discovery was very welcome both to her and **Sir Christopher**. Her musical education became at once an object of interest. Lady Cheverel devoted much time to it; and the rapidity of Tina's progress surpassing all hopes, an Italian singing-master was engaged, for several years, to spend some months together at Cheverel Manor. This unexpected gift made a great alteration in Caterina's position . . . . Insensibly she came to be regarded as one of the family, and the servants began to understand that Miss Sarti was to be a lady after all.

" 'And the raight on't too,' said **Mr Bates**, 'for she hasn't the cut of a gell as must work for her bread; she's as nesh an' dilicate as a paich blossom—welly laike a linnet, wi' on'y joost body anoof to hold her voice.' " 4

—*first lover:* "As for Tina, the little minx was perfectly well aware that **Maynard** was her slave; he was the one person in the world whom she did as she pleased with; and I need not tell you that this was a symptom of her being perfectly heartwhole as far as he was concerned . . . . " 4

—*jealous:* "Alas! you see what jealousy was doing in this poor young soul. Caterina, who had passed her life as a little unobtrusive singing-bird, nestling so fondly under the wings that were outstretched for her, her heart beating only to the peaceful rhythm of love, or fluttering with some easily stifled fear, had begun to know the fierce palpitations of triumph and hatred." 5

—*kissed by surprise:* "Caterina tore herself from **Anthony** with the desperate effort of one who has just self-recollection enough left to be conscious that the fumes of charcoal will master his senses unless he bursts a way for himself to the fresh air; but when she reached her own room, she was still too intoxicated with that momentary revival of old emotions, too much agitated by the sudden return of tenderness in her lover, to know whether pain or pleasure predominated. It was as if a miracle had happened in her little world of feeling, and made the future all vague—a dim morning haze of possibilities, instead of the sombre wintry daylight and clear rigid outline of painful certainty." 7

—*appraised:* " 'She gets moor nesh and dillicat than iver,' he said, half to himself and half to **Hester**. 'I shouldn't woonder if she fades away laike them cyclamens as I transplanted. She puts me i' maind on 'em somehow, hangin' on their little thin stalks, so whaite an' tinder.' " 7

—*tormented:* "And yet—oh, he *was* cruel to her. She could never have behaved so to him. To make her love him so—to speak such tender words—to give her such caresses, and then to behave as if such things had never been.

He had given her the poison that seemed so sweet while she was drinking it, and now it was in her blood, and she was helpless.

"With this tempest pent up in her bosom, the poor child went up to her room every night, and there it all burst forth. There, with loud whispers and sobs, restlessly pacing up and down, lying on the hard floor, courting cold and weariness, she told to the pitiful listening night the anguish which she could pour into no mortal ear. But always sleep came at last, and always in the morning the reactive calm that enabled her to live through the day." 10

—health affected: "The very delicacy of Caterina's usual appearance, her natural paleness and habitually quiet mouse-like ways, made any symptoms of fatigue and suffering less noticeable . . . it was only **Mr Gilfil** who discerned with anxiety the feverish spot that sometimes rose on her cheek, the deepening violet tint under her eyes, and the strange absent glance, the unhealthy glitter of the beautiful eyes themselves." 10

—sarcasm: " 'Say? . . . say that I am a poor silly girl, and have fallen in love with you, and am jealous of her; but that you have never had any feeling but pity for me . . . . '

"Tina uttered this as the bitterest sarcasm her ideas would furnish her with, not having the faintest suspicion that the sarcasm derived any of its bitterness from truth. Underneath all her sense of wrong, which was rather instinctive than reflective—underneath all the madness of her jealousy, and her ungovernable impulses of resentment and vindictiveness—underneath all this scorching passion there were still left some hidden crystal dews of trust, of self-reproof, of belief that **Anthony** was trying to do the right. Love had not all gone to feed the fires of hatred. Tina still trusted that Anthony felt more for her than he seemed to feel; she was still far from suspecting him of a wrong which a woman resents even more than inconstancy." 11

—infuriated: "See how she rushes noiselessly, like a pale meteor, along the passages and up the gallery stairs! Those gleaming eyes, those bloodless lips, that swift silent tread, make her look like the incarnation of a fierce purpose, rather than a woman." 13

—intent on murder: "Poor child! poor child! she who used to cry to have the fish put back into the water—who never willingly killed the smallest living thing—dreams now, in the madness of her passion, that she can kill the man whose very voice unnerves her.

"But what is that lying among the dank leaves on the path three yards before her?

"Good God! it is he—lying motionless . . . . His eyes are fixed; he does not see her. She sinks down on her knees, takes the dear head in her arms, and kisses the cold forehead.

" '**Anthony**, Anthony! speak to me—it is Tina—speak to me! O God, he is dead!' " 13

—what now: "The poor child never thought of suicide. No sooner was the storm of anger passed than the tenderness and timidity of her nature returned, and she could do nothing but love and mourn. Her inexperience prevented her from imagining the consequences of her disappearance from the Manor; she foresaw none of the terrible details of alarm and distress and search that must ensue." 16

—*music after long illness:* "**Ozzy**, roaming about the room in quest of a forbidden pleasure, came to the harpsichord, and struck the handle of his whip on a deep bass note.

"The vibration rushed through Caterina like an electric shock: it seemed as if at that instant a new soul were entering into her, and filling her with a deeper, more significant life. She looked round, rose from the sofa, and walked to the harpsichord. In a moment her fingers were wandering with their old sweet method among the keys, and her soul was floating in its true familiar element of delicious sound, as the water-plant that lies withered and shrunken on the ground expands into freedom and beauty when once more bathed in its native flood . . . .

"She paused, and burst into tears—the first tears she had shed since she had been at Foxholm. Maynard could not help hurrying towards her, putting his arm round her, and leaning down to kiss her hair. She nestled to him, and put up her little mouth to be kissed.

"The delicate-tendrilled plant must have something to cling to. The soul that was born anew to music was born anew to love." 20

—*envoi:* "She had come to lean entirely on his love, and to find life sweet for his sake. Her continual languor and want of active interest was a natural consequence of bodily feebleness, and the prospect of her becoming a mother was a new ground for hoping the best.

"But the delicate plant had been too deeply bruised, and in the struggle to put forth a blossom it died." 21

Supporting Roles

Beatrice Assher. " 'I shall not succeed. Miss Assher very likely prefers someone else; and you know I have the best will in the world to fail [said **Captain Wybrow**].' " 2

—*first appearance:* "Miss Assher was tall, and gracefully though substantially formed, carrying herself with an air of mingled graciousness and self-confidence; her dark-brown hair, untouched by powder, hanging in bushy curls round her face, and falling behind in long thick ringlets nearly to her waist. The brilliant carmine tint of her well-rounded cheeks, and the finely cut outline of her straight nose, produced an impression of splendid beauty, in spite of commonplace brown eyes, a narrow forehead, and thin lips. She was in mourning, and the dead black of her crape dress, relieved here and there by jet ornaments, gave the fullest effect to her complexion, and to the rounded whiteness of her arms, bare from the elbow. The first *coup d'oeil* was dazzling, and as she stood looking down with a gracious smile on **Caterina**, whom **Lady Cheverel** was presenting to her, the poor little thing seemed to herself to feel, for the first time, all the folly of her former dream." 5

—*gracious:* "Miss Assher turned to **Mr Gilfil** with her most beaming smile, and expressed her thanks with the elaborate graciousness of a person who means to be thought charming, and is sure of success." 5

—*unmusical:* " . . . that air of ostentatious admiration which belongs to the absence of real enjoyment . . . . " 5

—*reassured:* " 'One has a brotherly affection for such a woman as **Tina**; but it is another sort of woman that one loves.'

"These last words were made doubly significant by a look of tenderness, and a kiss imprinted on the hand **Captain Wybrow** held in his. Miss Assher was conquered. It was so far from probable that Anthony should love that pale insignificant little thing—so highly probable that he should adore the beautiful Miss Assher. On the whole, it was rather gratifying that other women should be languishing for her handsome lover; he really was an exquisite creature. Poor Miss Sarti! Well, she would get over it." 8

—an entrance: "As she entered, her face wore the smile appropriate to the exits and entrances of a young lady who feels that her presence is an interesting fact . . . . " 11

Sir Christopher Cheverel, Bart., "was as fine a specimen of the old English gentleman as could well have been found in those venerable days of cocked-hats and pigtails. His dark eyes sparkled under projecting brows, made more prominent by bushy grizzled eyebrows, but any apprehension of severity excited by these penetrating eyes, and by a somewhat aquiline nose, was allayed by the good-natured lines about the mouth, which retained all its teeth and its vigour of expression in spite of sixty winters. The forehead sloped a little from the projecting brows, and its peaked outline was made conspicuous by the arrangement of the profusely powdered hair, drawn backward and gathered into a pigtail. He sat in a small hard chair, which did not admit the slightest approach to a lounge, and which showed to advantage the flatness of his back and the breadth of his chest. In fact, Sir Christopher Cheverel was a splendid old gentleman . . . . " 2

—enthusiasm: "As for Sir Christopher, he was perfectly indifferent to criticism. 'An obstinate, crotchety man,' said his neighbours. But I, who have seen Cheverel Manor, as he bequeathed it to his heirs, rather attribute that unswerving architectural purpose of his, conceived and carried out through long years of systematic personal exertion, to something of the fervour of genius, as well as inflexibility of will; and in walking through these rooms, with their splendid ceilings and their meagre furniture, which tell how all the spare money had been absorbed before personal comfort was thought of, I have felt that there dwelt in this old English baronet some of that sublime spirit which distinguishes art from luxury, and worships beauty apart from self-indulgence." 4

—wishful thinking: " 'With **Caterina** for a wife, too,' Sir Christopher soon began to think; for though the good Baronet was not at all quick to suspect what was unpleasant and opposed to his views of fitness, he was quick to see what would dovetail with his own plans; and he had first guessed, and then ascertained, by direct enquiry, the state of **Maynard**'s feelings. He at once leaped to the conclusion that Caterina was of the same mind, or at least would be, when she was old enough." 4

—unforgiving: " . . . [there had been] an implacable quarrel with his elder sister; for a power of forgiveness was not among Sir Christopher's virtues." 4

—complacent: " 'Yes, **Maynard**,' said Sir Christopher, chatting with Mr Gilfil in the library, 'it really is a remarkable thing that I never in my life laid a plan, and failed to carry it out. I lay my plans well, and I never swerve from them—that's it. A strong will is the only magic. And next to striking out one's plans, the pleasantest thing in the world is to see them well accomplished.' " 14

—contretemps: "**Anthony** was no longer in the Rookery: they were carrying him stretched on a door, and there behind him was Sir Christopher, with the firmly set mouth, the deathly paleness, and the concentrated expression

of suffering in the eye, which mark the suppressed grief of the strong man." 15

—stunned by grief: "[**Gilfil**] was struck to see how a single day and night of grief had aged the fine old man. The lines in his brow and about his mouth were deepened; his complexion looked dull and withered; there was a swollen ridge under his eyes; and the eyes themselves, which used to cast so keen a glance on the present, had the vacant expression which tells that vision is no longer a sense, but a memory." 18

Henrietta Lady Cheverel. "She is tall, and looks the taller because her powdered hair is turned backward over a toupee, and surmounted by lace and ribbons. She is nearly fifty, but her complexion is still fresh and beautiful, with the beauty of an auburn blonde; her proud pouting lips, and her head thrown a little backward as she walks, give an expression of hauteur which is not contradicted by the cold grey eye. The tucked-in kerchief, rising full over the low tight bodice of her blue dress, sets off the majestic form of her bust, and she treads the lawn as if she were one of **Sir Joshua Reynolds**'s stately ladies, who had suddenly stepped from her frame to enjoy the evening cool." 2

—underneath: "Lady Cheverel, though not very tender-hearted, still less sentimental, was essentially kind, and liked to dispense benefits like a goddess, who looks down benignly on the halt, the maimed, and the blind that approach her shrine. She was smitten with compassion at the sight of poor **Sarti**, who struck her as the mere battered wreck of a vessel that might have once floated gaily enough on its outward voyage, to the sound of pipes and tabors. She spoke gently as she pointed out to him the operatic selections she wished him to copy, and he seemed to sun himself in her auburn, radiant presence . . . . " 3

—awful: " . . . once, when Lady Cheverel took her doll from [**Caterina**], because she was affectionately licking the paint off its face, the little minx straightway climbed on a chair and threw down a flower-vase that stood on a bracket. This was almost the only instance in which her anger overcame her awe of Lady Cheverel, who had the ascendancy always belonging to kindness that never melts into caresses, and is severely but uniformly beneficent." 4

—deferring: "[Her neighbours'] pity was quite gratuitous, as the most plentiful pity always is; for though Lady Cheverel did not share her husband's architectural enthusiasm, she had too rigorous a view of a wife's duties, and too profound a deference for **Sir Christopher**, to regard submission as a grievance." 4

—observant: "Lady Cheverel's enthusiasm never rose above the temperate mark of calm satisfaction, and, having quite her share of the critical acumen which characterises the mutual estimates of the fair sex, she had a more moderate opinion of **Miss Assher**'s qualities. She suspected that the fair Beatrice had a sharp and imperious temper; and being herself, on principle and by habitual self-command, the most deferential of wives, she noticed with disapproval Miss Assher's occasional air of authority towards **Captain Wybrow** . . . . Lady Cheverel, however, confined her criticisms to the privacy of her own thoughts, and, with a reticence which I fear may seem incredible, did not use them as a means of disturbing her husband's complacency." 10

Captain Anthony Wybrow, "in whom a certain resemblance to the Baronet, in the contour of the nose and brow, seemed to indicate a family relationship. If this young man had been less elegant in his person, he would have been remarked for the elegance of his dress. But the perfections of his slim well-proportioned figure were so striking that no one but a tailor could notice the perfection of his velvet coat; and his small white hands, with their blue veins and taper-fingers, quite eclipsed the beauty of his lace ruffles. The face, however—it was difficult to say why—was certainly not pleasing. Nothing could be more delicate than the blond complexion—its bloom set off by the powdered hair—than the veined overhanging eyelids, which gave an indolent expression to the hazel eyes; nothing more finely cut than the transparent nostril and the short upper-lip. Perhaps the chin and lower jaw were too small for an irreproachable profile, but the defect was on the side of that delicacy and *finesse* which was the distinctive characteristic of the whole person, and which was carried out in the clear brown arch of the eyebrows, and the marble smoothness of the sloping forehead. Impossible to say that this face was not eminently handsome, yet, for the majority both of men and women, it was destitute of charm. Women disliked eyes that seemed to be indolently accepting admiration instead of rendering it; and men, especially if they had a tendency to clumsiness in the nose and ankles, were inclined to think this *Antinous* in a pigtail a 'confounded puppy.' " 3

—in boyhood: " . . . a beautiful boy with brown curls and splendid clothes, on whom **Caterina** had looked with shy admiration. This was Anthony Wybrow, the son of **Sir Christopher**'s younger sister, and chosen heir of Cheverel Manor. The Baronet had sacrificed a large sum, and even straitened the resources by which he was to carry out his architectural schemes, for the sake of removing the entail from his estate, and making this boy his heir . . . . At length, on the death of Anthony's mother, when he was no longer a curly-headed boy, but a tall young man, with a captain's commission, Cheverel Manor became *his* home too, whenever he was absent from his regiment. Caterina was then a little woman, between sixteen and seventeen, and I need not spend many words in explaining what you perceive to be the most natural thing in the world." 4

—dalliance: "What man can withstand the temptation of a woman to fascinate, and another man to eclipse?—especially when it is quite clear to himself that he means no mischief, and shall leave everything to come right again by-and-by. At the end of eighteen months, however . . . he found that matters had reached a point which he had not at all contemplated. Gentle tones had led to tender words, and tender words had called forth a response of looks which made it impossible not to carry on the *crescendo* of love-making. To find oneself adored by a little, graceful, dark-eyed, sweet-singing woman, whom no one need despise, is an agreeable sensation, comparable to smoking the finest Latakia, and also imposes some return of tenderness as a duty." 4

—cool: "He was a young man of calm passions, who was rarely led into any conduct of which he could not give a plausible account to himself; and the tiny fragile **Caterina** was a woman who touched the imagination and the affections rather than the senses. He really felt very kindly towards her, and would very likely have loved her—if he had been able to love anyone. But nature had not endowed him with that capability. She had given him an admirable figure, the whitest of hands, the most delicate of nostrils, and a large amount of serene self-satisfaction; but, as if to save such a delicate piece of work from any risk of being shattered, she had guarded him from the liability to a strong emotion." 4

—compliant: "Captain Wybrow always did the thing easiest and most agreeable to him from a sense of duty: he dressed expensively, because it was a duty he owed to his position; from a sense of duty he adapted himself to **Sir**

Christopher's inflexible will, which it would have been troublesome as well as useless to resist; and, being of a delicate constitution, he took care of his health from a sense of duty. His health was the only point on which he gave anxiety to his friends . . . . " 4

—snubbed: "Captain Wybrow was silent. He wished very much to avoid allusions to the past or comments on the present. And yet he wished to be well with **Caterina**. He would have liked to caress her, make her presents, and have her think him very kind to her. But these women are plaguy perverse! There's no bringing them to looking rationally at anything." 6

—health issue: "[He] seated himself with an air of considerable lassitude before his mirror. The reflection there presented of his exquisite self was certainly paler and more worn than usual, and might excuse the anxiety with which he first felt his pulse, and then laid his hand on his heart." 10

—soliloquy: "Here am I, doing nothing to please myself, trying to do the best thing for everybody else, and all the comfort I get is to have fire shot at me from women's eyes, and venom spirted at me from women's tongues . . . any hitch in this marriage . . . might be a fatal business for the old gentleman. I wouldn't have such a blow fall upon him for a great deal. Besides a man must be married some time in his life, and I could hardly do better than marry **Beatrice**. She's an uncommonly fine woman, and I'm really very fond of her; and as I shall let her have her own way, her temper won't signify much. I wish the wedding was over and done with, for this fuss doesn't suit me at all. I haven't been half so well lately . . . . Heigho! Those are lucky fellows that have no women falling in love with them. It's a confounded responsibility." 10

—death: "The young and supple limbs, the rounded cheeks, the delicate ripe lips, the smooth white hands, were lying cold and rigid; and the aged face was bending over them in silent anguish; the aged deep-veined hands were seeking with tremulous enquiring touches for some symptom that life was not irrevocably gone." 13

Others

Lady Assher, "who had been **Sir Christopher**'s earliest love, but who, as things will happen in this world, had married another baronet instead of him . . . . **Anthony** had already been kindly received by Lady Assher as the nephew of her early friend . . . . " 4

—a relief: "Lady Cheverel, too, serenely radiant in the assurance a single glance had given her of Lady Assher's inferiority . . . .

" . . . a round-shouldered, middle-sized woman, who had once had the transient pink-and-white beauty of a blonde, with ill-defined features and early embonpoint." 5

—in speech: " 'We are enchanted with your place, **Sir Christopher**,' said Lady Assher, with a feeble kind of pompousness, which she seemed to be copying from someone else . . . . " 5

—a bore: "Lady Assher was sure cammomile tea would make all the difference in the world—**Caterina** must see if it wouldn't—and then went dribbling on like a leaky shower-bath, until the early entrance of the gentlemen created a diversion, and she fastened on **Sir Christopher**, who probably began to think that, for poetical purposes, it would be better not to meet one's first love again, after a lapse of forty years." 5

Bates, the gardener. “Mr Bates was by no means an average person, to be passed without special notice. He was a sturdy Yorkshireman, approaching forty, whose face nature seemed to have coloured when she was in a hurry, and had no time to attend to nuances, for every inch of him visible above his neckcloth was of one impartial redness; so that when he was at some distance your imagination was at liberty to place his lips anywhere between his nose and chin. Seen closer, his lips were discerned to be of a peculiar cut, and I fancy this had something to do with the peculiarity of his dialect, which, as we shall see, was individual rather than provincial. Mr Bates was further distinguished from the common herd by a perpetual blinking of the eyes; and this, together with the red-rose tint of his complexion, and a way he had of hanging his head forward, and rolling it from side to side as he walked, gave him the air of a **Bacchus** in a blue apron, who, in the present reduced circumstances of Olympus, had taken to the management of his own vines. Yet, as gluttons are often thin, so sober men are often rubicund; and Mr Bates was sober, with that manly, British, churchman-like sobriety which can carry a few glasses of grog without any perceptible clarification of ideas.” 4

—*a song:* “Mr Bates, urged thus flatteringly, stuck his thumbs into the armholes of his waistcoat, threw himself back in his chair with his head in that position in which he could look directly towards the zenith, and struck up a remarkably staccato rendering of ‘Roy’s Wife of Aldivalloch.’ ” 4

—*his home:* “The mossy turf, studded with the broad blades of marsh-loving plants, told that Mr Bates’s nest was rather damp in the best of weather; but he was of opinion that a little external moisture would hurt no man who was not perversely neglectful of that obvious and providential antidote, rum-and-water.” 7

—*visited:* “Mr Bates’s hair was now grey, but his frame was none the less stalwart, and his face looked all the redder, making an artistic contrast with the deep blue of his cotton neckerchief, and of his linen apron twisted into a girdle round his waist.” 7

Dame Fripp. “Even dirty Dame Fripp, who was a very rare churchgoer, had been to **Mrs Hackit** to beg a bit of old crape, and with this sign of grief pinned on her little coal-scuttle bonnet, was seen dropping her curtsy opposite the reading-desk. This manifestation of respect towards **Mr Gilfil**’s memory on the part of Dame Fripp had no theological bearing whatever. It was due to an event which had occurred some years back, and which, I am sorry to say, had left that grimy old lady as indifferent to the means of grace as ever.

—*occupations:* “Dame Fripp kept leeches, and was understood to have such remarkable influence over those wilful animals in inducing them to bite under the most unpromising circumstances, that though her own leeches were usually rejected, from a suspicion that they had lost their appetite, she herself was constantly called in to apply the more lively individuals furnished from **Mr Pilgrim**’s surgery. . . . Moreover, she drove a brisk trade in lollipop with epicurean urchins, who recklessly purchased that luxury at the rate of two hundred per cent.” 1

—*boon companion:* “ . . . by her side a large pig, who, with that ease and confidence belonging to perfect friendship, was lying with his head in her lap, and making no effort to play the agreeable beyond an occasional grunt . . . .

" 'My son gev him me two 'ear ago, an' he's been company to me iver sin'. I couldn't find i' my heart to part wi'm, if I niver knowed the taste o' bacon-fat again' . . . .

" 'Oh, he picks a bit up hisself wi' rootin', and I dooant mind doing wi'out to gi' him summat. A bit o' coompany's meat an' drink too, an' he follers me about, and grunts when I spake to'm, just like a Christian.' " 1

Mrs Hackit, "who, though she always said **Mrs Fripp** was 'as false as two folks', and no better than a miser and a heathen, had yet a leaning towards her as an old neighbour.

" 'There's that case-hardened old Judy a-coming after the tea-leaves again,' Mrs Hackit would say; 'an' I'm fool enough to give 'em her, though **Sally** wants 'em all the while to sweep the floors with!' " 1

—sermons: "Mrs Hackit expressed herself greatly edified by the sermon on honesty, the allusion to the unjust weight and deceitful balance having a peculiar lucidity for her, owing to a recent dispute with her grocer; but I am not aware that she ever appeared to be much struck by the sermon on anger." 1

Mrs Lucy Heron, "whose soft blue eyes and mild manners were very soothing to the poor bruised child—the more so as they had an air of sisterly equality which was quite new to her . . . there was a sweetness before unknown in having a young and gentle woman, like an elder sister, bending over her caressingly, and speaking in low loving tones." 20

Oswald (Ozzy) Heron, "the broad-chested boy, was perhaps her most beneficial companion. With something of his uncle's person, he had inherited also his uncle's early taste for a domestic menagerie, and was very imperative in demanding **Tina**'s sympathy in the welfare of his guinea-pigs, squirrels, and dormice. With him she seemed now and then to have gleams of her childhood coming athwart the leaden clouds, and many hours of winter went by the more easily for being spent in Ozzy's nursery." 20

—music: "Little Ozzy stood in the middle of the room, with his mouth open and his legs very wide apart, struck with something like awe at this new power in 'Tin-Tin', as he called her, whom he had been accustomed to think of as a playfellow not at all clever, and very much in need of his instruction on many subjects. A genie soaring with broad wings out of his milk-jug would not have been more astonishing." 20

Mr Oldinport, "the cousin and predecessor of the **Mr Oldinport** who flourished in the **Rev. Amos Barton**'s time. That quarrel [with **Mr Gilfil**] was a sad pity, for the two had had many a good day's hunting together when they were younger, and in those friendly times not a few members of the hunt envied Mr Oldinport the excellent terms he was on with his vicar . . . . " 1

—landlord: " . . . the Shepperton tenantry, with whom Mr Oldinport was in the worst odour as a landlord, having kept up his rents in spite of falling prices, and not being in the least stung to emulation by paragraphs in the provincial newspapers . . . . The fact was, Mr Oldinport had not the slightest intention of standing for Parliament, whereas he had the strongest intention of adding to his unentailed estate. Hence, to the Shepperton farmers it was as good as lemon with their grog to know that the Vicar had thrown out sarcasms against the Squire's charities, as little better than those of the man who stole a goose, and gave away the giblets in alms." 1

Sarti, "a small meagre man, sallow and dingy, with a restless wandering look in his dull eyes, and an excessive timidity about his deep reverences, which gave him the air of a man who had been long a solitary prisoner. Yet through all this squalor and wretchedness there were some traces discernible of comparative youth and former good looks." 3

—his story: "It was ten years at least since Sarti had seen anything so bright and stately and beautiful as **Lady Cheverel**. For the time was far off in which he had trod the stage in satin and feathers, the *primo tenore* of one short season. He had completely lost his voice in the following winter, and had ever since been little better than a cracked fiddle, which is good for nothing but firewood. For, like many Italian singers, he was too ignorant to teach, and if it had not been for his one talent of penmanship, he and his young helpless wife might have starved. Then, just after their third child was born, fever came, swept away the sickly mother and the two eldest children, and attacked Sarti himself, who rose from his sickbed with enfeebled brain and muscles, and a tiny baby on his hands, scarcely four months old." 3

Mrs Sharp, "my lady's maid, of somewhat vinegar aspect and flaunting attire . . . . " 2

—touched: "Even Mrs Sharp had been so smitten with pity by the scene she had witnessed when she was summoned upstairs to fetch **Caterina**, as to shed a small tear, though she was not at all subject to that weakness; indeed, she abstained from it on principle, because, as she often said, it was known to be the worst thing in the world for the eyes." 3

—no plans: "So Mrs Sharp, who had been heard to say that she had no thoughts at all of marrying **Mr Bates**, though he was 'a sensable, fresh-coloured man as many a woman 'ud snap at for a husband', enforced **Mr Bellamy**'s appeal [for a song]." 4

Minor Figures

Sir John Assher, Bart. " 'You never saw Sir John, **Lady Cheverel**. He was a large tall man, with a nose just like Beatrice, and so very particular about his shirts.' " 5

Bellamy, the butler, "in threadbare but well-brushed black, who, as he was placing [the coffee] on the table, said—

" 'If you please, **Sir Christopher**, there's the widow **Hartopp** a-crying i' the still-room, and begs leave to see your honour.' " 2

Mrs Bellamy. " . . . the women headed by Mrs Bellamy, the natty little old housekeeper, in snowy cap and apron . . . . " 2

—appalled: " 'Dear heart alive!' said Mrs Bellamy, 'we shall be pisoned wi' lime an' plaster, an' hev the house full o' workmen colloguing wi' the maids, an' makin' no end o' mischief.' " 4

—bringing comfort: " 'You look sadly, my dear,' said the old housekeeper, 'an' you're all of a quake wi' cold. Get you to bed, now do. **Martha** shall come an' warm it, an' light your fire. See now, here's some nice arrowroot, wi' a drop o' wine in it. Take that, an' it'll warm you. I must go down again, for I can't awhile to stay. There's so many things to see to; an' **Miss Assher**'s in hysterics constant, an' her maid's ill i' bed—a poor creachy thing—an' **Mrs Sharp**'s wanted every minute.' " 16

Blackbird. "[**Knott** said,] 'I've rode twenty mile upon Blackbird, as thinks all the while he's a–ploughin', an' turns sharp roun', every thirty yards, as if he was at the end of a furrow. I've hed a sore time wi' him, I can tell you, sir.' " 19

Mr Bond "often said, no man knew more than the Vicar about the breed of cows and horses." 1

Tommy Bond, "who had recently quitted frocks and trousers for the severe simplicity of a tight suit of corduroys, relieved by numerous brass buttons. Tommy was a saucy boy, impervious to all impressions of reverence, and excessively addicted to humming-tops and marbles, with which recreative resources he was in the habit of immoderately distending the pockets of his corduroys." 1

Sir Anthony Cheverel, "who in the reign of **Charles II** was the renovator of the family splendour, which had suffered some declension from the early brilliancy of that **Chevreuil** who came over with the Conqueror. A very imposing personage was this Sir Anthony, standing with one arm akimbo, and one fine leg and foot advanced, evidently with a view to the gratification of his contemporaries and posterity. You might have taken off his splendid peruke, and his scarlet cloak, which was thrown backward from his shoulders, without annihilating the dignity of his appearance." 2

Lady Cheverel. " . . . his lady, hanging opposite to him, with her sunny brown hair drawn away in bands from her mild grave face, and falling in two large rich curls on her snowy gently sloping neck, which shamed the harsher hue and outline of her white satin robe, was a fit mother of 'large-acred' heirs." 2

Dorcas, "the merry rosey-cheeked damsel who was **Mrs Sharp**'s lieutenant in the nursery, and thus played the part of the raisins in a dose of senna. It was a black day for **Caterina** when Dorcas married the coachman [**Daniel Knott**], and went, with a great sense of elevation in the world, to preside over a 'public' in the noisy town of Sloppeter. A little china box, bearing the motto 'Though lost to sight, to memory dear', which Dorcas sent her as a remembrance, was among Caterina's treasures ten years after." 4

" ' "Dear Dorkis," says she, "tek me in"; an' then went off into a faint, an' not a word has she spoken since.' " 19

Ford. " 'Well, that theer's whut I call a pictur,' said old 'Mester' Ford, a true Staffordshire patriarch, who leaned on a stick and held his head very much on one side, with the air of a man who had little hope of the present generation, but would at all events give it the benefit of his criticism." 21

Hackit, " . . . the very week after the quarrel, when presiding at the annual dinner of the Association for the Prosecution of Felons, held at the Oldinport Arms, he contributed an additional zest to the conviviality on this occasion by informing the company that 'the parson had given the squire a lick with the rough side of his tongue.' " 1

Dr Hart, "acquainted with **Captain Wybrow**'s previous state of health, had given his opinion that death had been imminent from long-established disease of the heart, though it had probably been accelerated by some unusual emotion." 19

Mrs Bessie Hartopp. " 'Your honour,' pleaded the **butler** . . . 'the poor woman's dreadful overcome, and says she can't sleep a wink this blessed night without seeing your honour, and she begs you to pardon the great freedom she's took to come at this time. She cries fit to break her heart.' " 2

"She was a buxom woman approaching forty, her eyes red with the tears which had evidently been absorbed by the handkerchief gathered into a damp ball in her right hand." 2

Rev. Arthur Heron "presented himself on the doorstep, eager to greet his returning **Lucy**, and holding by the hand a broad-chested tawny-haired boy of five, who was smacking a miniature hunting-whip with great vigour." 20

Mrs Higgins. " . . . as [she] observed in an undertone to Mrs Parrot when they were coming out of church, 'Her husband, who'd been born i' the parish, ought ha' told her better.' An unreadiness to put on black on all available occasions, or too great an alacrity in putting it off, argued, to Mrs Higgins's opinion, a dangerous levity of character, and an unnatural insensibility to the essential fitness of things . . . .

"Mrs Higgins, who was an elderly widow, 'well left' . . . . " 1

Mrs Jennings, "at the Wharf, by appearing the first Sunday after **Mr Gilfil**'s death in her salmon-coloured ribbons and green shawl, excited the severest remark. To be sure, Mrs Jennings was a newcomer, and town-bred, so that she could hardly be expected to have very clear notions of what was proper . . . . " 1

Daniel Knott, "the coachman who had married the rosey-cheeked **Dorcas** ten years before." 19

"[**Gilfil**] hung upon Daniel's moon-face, and listened to his small piping voice, with the same solemn yearning expectation with which he would have given ear to the most awful messenger from the land of shades." 19

Baby **Knott**, "**Becky**, a red-armed damsel, emerged from the adjoining back-kitchen, and possessed herself of baby, whose feelings or fat made him conveniently apathetic under the transference." 19

Bessie Knott, "a curly-headed little girl of three, who was twisting a corner of her mother's apron, and opening round eyes at the gentleman . . . . " 19

Young **Daniel Knott**, "a flaxen-haired lad of nine, prematurely invested with the *toga virilis,* or smock-frock, who ran forward to let in the unusual visitor." 19

Lady Felicia Oldinport "[and her husband], to whom Knebley Church was a sort of family temple, made their way among the bows and curtsies of their dependants to a carved and canopied pew in the chancel, diffusing as they went a delicate odour of Indian roses on the unsusceptible nostrils of the congregation." 1

Bessie Parrot, "a flaxen-headed 'two-shoes', very white and fat as to her neck, always had the admirable directness and sincerity to salute [**Mr Gilfil**] with the question—'What zoo dot in zoo pottet?' " 1

Mrs Parrot. " 'Ah,' said Mrs Parrot, who was conscious of inferiority in this respect, 'there isn't many families as have had so many deaths as yours, **Mrs Higgins**.' " 1

"Mrs Parrot smoothed her apron and set her cap right with the utmost solicitude when she saw the Vicar coming, made him her deepest curtsy, and every Christmas had a fat turkey ready to send him with her 'duty.' " 1

Miss Selina Parrot "put off her marriage a whole month when **Mr Gilfil** had an attack of rheumatism, rather than be married in a makeshift manner by the Milby curate." 1

La Pazzini, "a stout virago, loud of tongue and irate in temper, but who had had children born to her, and so had taken care of the tiny yellow, black-eyed *bambinetta,* and tended **Sarti** himself through his sickness." 3

Mrs Patten "understood that if she turned out ill-crushed cheeses, a just retribution awaited her; though, I fear, she made no particular application of the sermon on backbiting." 1

"[Her] strong memory and taste for personal narrative made her a great source of oral tradition in Shepperton." 1

Rev. Mr Pickard, "of the Independent Meeting, had stated, in a sermon preached at Rotherby, for the reduction of a debt on New Zion, built, with an exuberance of faith and a deficiency of funds, by seceders from the original Zion, that he lived n a parish where the Vicar was very 'dark' . . . . " 1

Rupert, "pet blood-hound, who, in his habitual place at the **Baronet**'s right hand, behaved with great urbanity during dinner; but when the cloth was drawn, invariably disappeared under the table; apparently regarding the claret-jug as a mere human weakness, which he winked at, but refused to sanction." 2

—at a death: "Rupert was there too, waiting and watching; licking first the dead and then the living hands; then running off on **Mr Bates**'s track as if he would follow and hasten his return, but in a moment turning back again, unable to quit the scene of his master's sorrow." 14

Sir Jasper Sitwell "observed, 'next to a man's wife, there's nobody can be such an infernal plague to you as a parson, always under your nose on your own estate.' " 1

"Old Sir Jasper Sitwell would have been glad to see [**Mr Gilfil**] every week . . . . " 1

Lady Sitwell. " . . . if you had seen [**Mr Gilfil**] conducting Lady Sitwell in to dinner, or had heard him talking to her with quaint yet graceful gallantry, you would have inferred that the earlier period of his life had been passed in more stately society than could be found in Shepperton . . . . " 1

Tom Stokes, "a flippant town youth, greatly scandalised his excellent relatives by declaring that he could write as good a sermon as **Mr Gilfil**'s; whereupon [his uncle] **Mr Hackit** sought to reduce the presumptuous youth to utter confusion, by offering him a sovereign if he would fulfil his vaunt. The sermon was written, however, and though it was not admitted to be anywhere within reach of Mr Gilfil's, it was yet so astonishingly like a sermon, having a text, three divisions, and a concluding exhortation beginning 'And now, my brethren', that the sovereign, though denied formally, was bestowed informally, and the sermon was pronounced, when Master Stokes's back was turned, to be 'an uncommon cliver thing.' " 1

Mr Warren, "Sir Christopher's venerable valet." 2

Also mentioned

Albani, Maestro; singing teacher to Lady Cheverel	3
Viscount Blethers, a landlord	1
Brooks, old man to whom Bates will give his comforter	7
Chevreuil, who came over with the Conqueror	2
coachman at Cheverel Manor, who married Dorcas and went off to run a 'public'	4
Crichley, the rector whose living is Mr Gilfil's expectation	12
David, groom and gardener at the Vicarage	1
Francesco, artisan working on Cheverel Manor ceilings	2
Griffin, Lady Assher's maid; obstinate about bitters	5
Hester, Mr Bates's old, hump-backed housekeeper	7
Miss Hibbert, who sang at the Asshers' home	5
Lady Sara Linter, who had been riding the mare Mr Gilfil has found for Beatrice	5
Markham, steward at Cheverel Manor	2
Martha, Mr Gilfil's housekeeper	1
Martha, housemaid at Cheverel Manor	5
nephew of Sir Christopher, son of his elder sister and now heir to the estate	21
Parrot, whose heifer was driven off	1
Ponto, Mr Gilfil's old brown setter	1
Hon. Augustus Purwell, a landlord	1
Patty Richards, who died, looking happy in her decline	11
Sally, maid at Mrs Hackit's	1
Signora Sarti, who had three children and died of fever	3
Sarti children (two), who died of fever	3
Mr Tarbett, who preached at Shepperton Church	1
Uncle of Daniel Knott, bailiff to Squire Ramble; left Knott a legacy	19
under-gardener at Cheverel Manor, scolded by Bates	5
valet to Captain Wybrow	2
Mrs Wybrow, Sir Christopher's younger sister	4

Scenes of Clerical Life

Janet's Repentance

In the bar at the Red Lion twenty-five years or so ago, Lawyer **Dempster** vociferously objects to Evangelical inroads in Milby. **Byles** is unfairly put down for contradicting Dempster's erroneous history of Presbyterianism. Who are the anti-**Tryan**ites who will sign a petition, and who are those favouring the Evangelical preacher? **Mr Pilgrim**, the doctor, appears. A note summons Dempster. 1 The town of Milby is described in unflattering terms. Curate **Crewe** is depicted as no preacher but avaricious, yet respected. The recent history of Dissent in the town is reviewed. Doctors Pilgrim and **Pratt** are contrasted. Tryan will seek authority from nonresident rector **Prendergast** to establish a Sunday evening lecture at the parish church. Dempster, churchwarden **Budd** and rich miller **Tomlinson** lead the opposition. 2

Ladies of the town meet to prepare books for Mr Tryan's library. They discuss **Janet Dempster**'s marriage and difficult life. Her husband drinks, and now so does she. But she goes out much on charitable errands. Tryan reports defeat on his evening lecture proposal. He vows to fight on. He has glimpsed Janet and been impressed. 3 The opposition celebrate boisterously. Dempster addresses them, then goes home drunk. Janet does not hear his banging. At last she appears, seemingly drunk herself. He is furious and beats her. 4 It is two weeks later. The **Narrator** reveals himself as a genteel youth, now in coat-tails, home for summer holidays and confirmation. **Miss Townley**'s pupils ready themselves to meet the Bishop. Janet visits her mother, **Mrs Raynor**. 5 The service passes without incident or tears, and we learn in the bar of the Red Lion that the Bishop has approved the evening lecture series. 6

A happy morning at the Dempsters', and a profile of Mrs Dempster. Her son takes her for a walk in the garden. He has made a plan to discommode Mr Tryan in his lecture. 7 **Mrs Jerome** is irked, waiting for Mr Tryan to come to tea. He arrives at last and **Mr Jerome**, a good man and appreciative of good preaching, greets him. He is dropping Dempster as his lawyer. Tryan plans a show of support. Jerome will join. He is much touched by Jerome's goodness. 8 A procession to the lecture, harassed and jeered at; a satirical broadside which the Dempsters had prepared; and a sad premonition of Tryan's later death. 9

The lectures are gaining adherents; Dempster is losing some. Evangelicalism is making its way in Milby. Mr Jerome is sad not to see Mrs Dempster any more: he speaks to her in the street, observed by the husband. A discourse on religion and its progress. 10 Tryan overworks. A worried Jerome offers him a horse. He fobs it off. Many worry about him. 11 Janet avoids him and will not hear him; but she encounters him when she is on a charitable errand. They exchange a long look, and her prejudice vanishes. 12 Dempster's law-business has more setbacks. The marriage sinks. Nemesis approaches. 13

Dempster announces four males for dinner. Janet goes to her mother, distraught at her life. The two women prepare for the evening. When Dempster returns, Janet has laid out his clothes. He spurns the attention and throws the clothes at her. Defiantly she does not pick them up. They are still on the floor when guests come. After the dinner, Dempster thrusts her in her nightdress outside in the cold and locks the door on her. 14 In the cold, Janet thinks over her life. At last she rouses herself to find shelter with kind neighbour **Mrs Pettifer**, who makes tea and puts her to bed. 15

Despairing and hopeless, she thinks of Tryan and asks for him. 16 Dempster remembers everything. He expects Janet to return by nightfall. His gig is late. In a fury, he lashes at **Dawes**, his man, cutting his face with his whip. Dawes walks out, letting him drive himself. 17 Tryan comes to Janet. She confesses her addiction. He tells her of his past: the ruination of a young girl who later killed herself. He speaks tellingly of the mercy of Christ. Janet hears. 18

She will remain where she is, hiding from her husband. Her mother comes to her; they connect in peace and joyful tears. 19 The new day begins with courage and calm. Mrs Raynor suggests **Benjamin Landor** as an advisor. 20 Kitty the maid and Betty the cook are concerned about Janet. Kitty goes to Mrs Raynor's, who on learning that Dempster is away, fetches Janet's clothes for church. She goes and hears Tryan and is kindly welcomed. She is undone. At home with Mrs Pettifer she weeps, dreading her husband. He returns, carried on a door, but she is unaware of this. 21

Dempster is not dead but near it, with a badly broken leg and other injuries, having been thrown from his gig by a frantic horse. Pilgrim describes his condition to Tryan as grave. Tryan advises Janet to be patient but keeps her in ignorance of the accident. 22 Janet impulsively runs off on a charitable errand, over Mrs Pettifer's objections. Janet sees Pilgrim going into her house. She runs over to find out why. She finds Dempster under restraint, raving in delirium tremens. She insists on remaining. 23 She nurses and prays. He dies without speaking again. 24

Dempster has left Janet most of his fortune. Old friends come to call. Mrs Raymor is called away. Janet is suddenly alone. Looking through papers, she comes upon brandy and is almost overwhelmed. She throws it down and rushes out. After sitting in the churchyard, she walks to Tryan's abode, fearing a relapse without his aid. He prays with her, wants to walk her home; she refuses his offer, urging him to take care of himself. She walks back alone, infused now with serenity and trust. She makes a plan: Mrs Pettifer will be her tenant and will take Tryan into a pleasant house Janet has inherited. 25 Janet makes steady progress, shedding her addiction. Tryan is sickening, probably of consumption. Janet and he meet in the road and go together to see the house, now ready. Tryan sinks rapidly. 27 He is buried. The tranquil Janet is his best memorial. 28

Title Role: Janet Dempster, *née* Raynor

—her marriage: " 'Well . . . Janet had nothing to look to but being a governess; and it was hard for **Mrs Raynor** to have to work at millinering—a woman well brought up, and her husband a man who held his head as high as any man in Thurston. And it isn't everybody that sees everything fifteen years beforehand. **Robert Dempster** was the cleverest man in Milby; and there weren't many young men fit to talk to Janet.' " 3

" 'It is a thousand pities,' said **Miss Pratt** . . . 'for I certainly did consider Janet Raynor the most promising young woman of my acquaintance—a little too much lifted up, perhaps, by her superior education, and too much given to satire, but able to express herself very well indeed about any book I recommended to her perusal. There is no young woman in Milby now who can be compared with what Janet was when she was married, either in mind or person.' " 3

" 'I never see her but she has something pretty to say to me—living in the same street, you know [said **Mrs Pettifer**]. I can't help seeing her often, though I've never been to the house since Dempster broke out on me in one of his drunken fits. She comes to me sometimes, poor thing, looking so strange, anybody passing her in the street may see plain enough what's the matter; but she's always got some little good-natured plan in her head for all that.' " 3

—her pride: " ' . . . you know she stands up for everything her husband says and does. She never will admit to anybody that he's not a good husband.'

" 'That is her pride,' said **Miss Pratt**. 'She married him in opposition to the advice of her best friends, and now she is not willing to admit that she was wrong . . . she has always pretended to have the highest respect for her husbands qualities.' " 3

" 'Pride or no pride,' said **Mrs Pettifer**, 'I shall always stand up for Janet Dempster . . . . There's great excuses for her. When a woman can't think of her husband coming home without trembling, it's enough to make her drink something to blunt her feelings—and no children either, to keep her from it.' " 3

—glimpsed: " 'I found Mrs Dempster there [said **Mr Tryan**]. I had often met her in the street, but did not know it was Mrs Dempster. It seems she goes among the poor a good deal. She is really an interesting-looking woman. I was quite surprised, for I have heard the worst account of her habits—that she is almost as bad as her husband. She went out hastily as soon as I entered.' " 3

—roused in the night: "She had on a light dress which sat loosely about her figure, but did not disguise its liberal, graceful outline. A heavy mass of straight jet-black hair had escaped from its fastening, and hung over her shoulders. Her grandly cut features, pale with the natural paleness of a

brunette, had premature lines about them, telling that the years had been lengthened by sorrow, and the delicately curved nostril, which seemed made to quiver with the proud consciousness of power and beauty, must have quivered to the heart-piercing griefs which had given that worn look to the corners of the mouth. Her wide-open black eyes had a strangely fixed, sightless gaze, as she paused at the turning, and stood silent before her husband.

" . . . Janet, not trembling, no! it would be better if she trembled—standing stupidly unmoved in her great beauty, while the heavy arm is lifted to strike her. The blow falls—another—and another." 4

—*two weeks later:* "Yes; no other woman in Milby has those searching black eyes, that tall graceful unconstrained figure, set off by her simple muslin dress and black lace shawl, that massy black hair now so neatly braided in glossy contrast with the white satin ribbons of her modest cap and bonnet. No other woman has that sweet, speaking smile . . . there are those sad lines about the mouth and eyes on which that sweet smile lays like sunbeams on the storm-beaten beauty of the full and ripened corn." 5

—*partisan:* " 'I would give my crooked guinea, and all the luck it will ever bring me, to have [**Tryan**] beaten, for I can't endure the sight of the man coming to harass dear old **Mr** and **Mrs Crewe** in their last days. Preaching the Gospel indeed! That is the best Gospel that makes everybody happy and comfortable . . . . ' " 5

—*misery abated:* "Janet looked glad and tender now—but what scene of misery was coming next? She was too like the cistus flowers in the little garden before the window, that, with the shades of evening, might lie with the delicate white and glossy dark of their petals trampled in the roadside dust. When the sun had sunk, and the twilight was deepening, Janet might be sitting there, heated, maddened, sobbing out her griefs with selfish passion, and wildly wishing herself dead." 5

—*bright moment:* " 'I've a capital idea, Gypsy!' (that was his name for his dark-eyed wife when he was in an extraordinarily good humour), 'and you shall help me. It's just what you're up to.'

" 'What is it?' said Janet, her face beaming at the sound of the pet name, now heard so seldom." 7

—*overhearing:* "Janet was surprised, and forgot her wish not to encounter **Mr Tryan**; the tone and the words were so unlike what she had expected to hear. There was none of the self-satisfied unction of the teacher, quoting, or exhorting, or expounding . . . but a simple appeal for help, a confession of weakness . . . .

"The most brilliant deed of virtue could not have inclined Janet's goodwill towards Mr Tryan so much as this fellowship in suffering, and the softening thought was in her eyes when he appeared in the doorway, pale, weary, and depressed. The sight of Janet standing there with the entire absence of self-consciousness which belongs to a new and vivid impression, made him start and pause a little. Their eyes met, and they looked at each other gravely for a few moments. Then they bowed, and Mr Tryan passed out." 12 *See Topicon* FM:Charity—*glance*

—*degeneration:* "Poor Janet! how heavily the months rolled on for her, laden with fresh sorrows as the summer passed into autumn, the autumn into winter, and the winter into spring again. Every feverish morning, with its blank listlessness and despair, seemed more hateful than the last; every coming night more impossible to brave without arming herself in leaden stupor." 13

—childless: "If she had babes to rock to sleep—little ones to kneel in their nightdress and say their prayers at her knees—sweet boys and girls to put their young arms round her neck and kiss away her tears, her poor hungry heart would have been fed with strong love, and might never have needed that fiery poison to still its cravings . . . . Yes! if Janet had been a mother, she might have been saved from much sin, and therefore from much of her sorrow." 13

—defiance: "Janet's bitterness would overflow in ready words; she was not to be made meek by cruelty; she would repent of nothing in the face of injustice, though she was subdued in a moment by a word or a look that recalled the old days of fondness . . . poor Janet's soul was kept like a vexed sea, tossed by a new storm before the old waves have fallen. Proud, angry resistance and sullen endurance were now almost the only alternations she knew . . . she would not admit her wretchedness; she had married him blindly, and she would bear it out to the terrible end, whatever that might be. Better this misery than the blank that lay for her outside her married home." 13

—making a call: " . . . there in the passage . . . stood Janet, her eyes worn as if by night-long watching, her dress careless, her step languid. No cheerful morning greeting to her mother—no kiss." 14

—breaking out: " 'You don't ask me what it is I have had to bear. You are tired of hearing me. You are cruel, like the rest; everyone is cruel in this world. Nothing but blame—blame—blame; never any pity. God is cruel to have sent me into the world to bear all this misery.

" ' . . . Why didn't you tell me, mother?—why did you let me marry? You knew what brutes men could be; and there's no help for me—no hope. I can't kill myself; I've tried; but I can't leave this world and go to another. There may be no pity for me there, as there is none here.' " 14

—beauty nevertheless: "[**Mrs Raynor**] could not help pausing a moment in sorrowful admiration at the tall rich figure, looking all the grander for the plainness of the deep mourning-dress, and the noble face with its massy folds of black hair, made matronly by a simple white cap. Janet had an enduring beauty which belongs to pure majestic outline and depth of tint. Sorrow and neglect leave their traces on such beauty, but it thrills us to the last, like a glorious Greek temple, which, for all the loss it has suffered from time and barbarous hands, has gained a solemn history, and fills our imagination the more because it is incomplete to the sense." 14

—abandonment: "Janet felt she was alone: no human soul had measured her anguish, had understood her self-despair, had entered into her sorrows and her sins with that deep-sighted sympathy which is wiser than all blame, more potent than all reproof—such sympathy as had swelled her own heart for many a sufferer. And if there was any Divine Pity, she could not feel it; it kept aloof from her, it poured no balm into her wounds, it stretched out no hand to bear up her weak resolve, to fortify her fainting courage." 15

—weakness: "She had a vague notion of some protection the law might give her, if she could prove her life in danger from him; but she shrank utterly, as she had always done, from any active, public resistance or vengeance: she felt too crushed, too faulty, too liable to reproach, to have the courage, even if she had had the wish, to put herself openly in the position of

a wronged woman seeking redress. She had no strength to sustain her in a course of self-defence and independence: there was darker shadow over her life than the dread of her husband—it was the shadow of self-despair." 16

—relief of spirit: "A door had opened in Janet's cold dark prison of self-despair, and the golden light of morning was pouring in its slanting beams through the blessed opening. There was sunlight in the world; there was a divine love caring for her; it had given her an earnest of good things; it had been preparing comfort for her in the very moment when she had thought herself most forsaken." 21

—all-forgiving: "Janet's was a nature in which hatred and revenge could find no place; the long bitter years drew half their bitterness from her ever-living remembrance of the too short years of love that went before; and the thought that her husband would ever put her hand to his lips again, and recall the days when they sat on the grass together, and he laid scarlet poppies on her black hair, and called her his gypsy queen, seemed to send a tide of loving oblivion over all the harsh and stony space they had traversed since. The Divine love that had already shone upon her would be with her; she would lift up her soul continually for help . . . . " 24

—watching: "She was almost as pale as her dying husband, and there were dark lines under her eyes, for this was the third night since she had taken off her clothes; but the eager straining gaze of her dark eyes, and the acute sensibility that lay in every line about her mouth, made a strange contrast with the blank unconsciousness and emaciated animalism of the face she was watching." 24

—her affection: "The chief strength of her nature lay in her affection, which coloured all the rest of her mind: it gave a personal sisterly tenderness to her acts of benevolence; it made her cling with tenacity to every object that had once stirred her kindly emotions. Alas! it was unsatisfied, wounded affection that had made her trouble greater than she could bear. And now there was no check to the full flow of that plenteous current in her nature—no gnawing secret anguish—no overhanging terror—no inward shame. Friendly faces beamed on her; she felt that friendly hearts were approving her, and wishing her well, and that mild sunshine of goodwill fell beneficently on her new hopes and efforts, as the clear shining after rain falls on the tender leaf-buds of spring, and wins them from promise to fulfilment." 25

—sudden assault: "An impetuous desire shook Janet through all her members; it seemed to master her with the inevitable force of strong fumes that flood our senses before we are aware. Her hand was on the decanter; pale and excited, she was lifting it out of its niche, when, with a start and a shudder, she dashed it to the ground, and the room was filled with the odour of the spirit." 25

—serenity returned: "The Divine Presence did not now seem far off, where she had not wings to reach it; prayer itself seemed superfluous in those moments of calm trust. The temptation which had so lately made her shudder before the possibilities of the future, was now a source of confidence; for had she not been delivered from it? Had not rescue come in the extremity of danger? Yes; Infinite Love was caring for her. She felt like a little child whose hand is firmly grasped by its father, as its frail limbs make their way over the rough ground; if it should stumble, the father will not let it go.

"That walk in the dewy starlight remained for ever in Janet's memory as one of those baptismal epochs, when the soul, dipped in the sacred waters of joy and peace, rises from them with new energies, with more unalterable longings." 25

—prospect of loss: "She felt no rebellion under this prospect of bereavement, but rather a quiet submissive sorrow. Gratitude that his influence and guidance had been given her, even if only for a little while—gratitude that she was permitted to be with him, to take a deeper and deeper impress from daily communion with him, to be something to him in these last months of his life, was so strong in her that it almost silenced regret. Janet had lived through the great tragedy of woman's life. Her keenest personal emotions had been poured forth in her early love—her wounded affection with its years of anguish—the agony of unavailing pity over that deathbed seven months ago." 27

—another aspect: "The thought of **Mr Tryan** was associated for her with repose from that conflict of emotion, with trust in the unchangeable, with the influx of a power to subdue self. To have been assured of his sympathy, his teaching, his help, all through her life, would have been to her like a heaven already begun—a deliverance from fear and danger; but the time was not yet come for her to be conscious that the hold he had on her heart was any other than that of the heaven-sent friend who had come to her like the angel in the prison, and loosed her bonds, and led her by the hand till she could look back on the dreadful doors that had once closed her in." 27

—after the burial: "Janet felt a deep stillness within. She thirsted for no pleasure; she craved no worldly good. She saw the years to come stretch before her like an autumn afternoon, filled with resigned memory. Life to her could never more have any eagerness; it was a solemn service of gratitude and patient effort. She walked in the presence of unseen witnesses—of the Divine love that had rescued her, of the human love that waited for its eternal repose until it had seen her endure to the end." 28

Other Principals

Robert Dempster. " 'No!' said lawyer Dempster, in a loud, rasping, oratorical tone, struggling against chronic huskiness, 'as long as my Maker grants me power of voice and power of intellect, I will take every legal means to resist the introduction of demoralising, methodistical doctrine into this parish; I will not supinely suffer an insult to be inflicted on our venerable pastor, who has given us sound instruction for half a century.' "1

—characteristics: "He was a tall and rather massive man, and the front half of his large surface was so well dredged with snuff, that the cat, having inadvertently come near him, had been seized with a severe fit of sneezing—an accident which, being cruelly misunderstood, had caused her to be driven contumeliously from the bar. Mr Dempster habitually held his chin tucked in, and his head hanging forward, weighed down, perhaps, by a preponderant occiput and a bulging forehead, between which his closely clipped coronal surface lay like a flat and new-mown tableland. The only other observable features were puffy cheeks and a protruding yet lipless mouth. Of his nose I can only say that it was snuffy; and as Mr Dempster was never caught in the act of looking at anything in particular, it would have been difficult to swear to the colour of his eyes." 1

—pontificator: " 'The Presbyterians,' said Mr Dempster, in rather a louder tone than before, holding that every appeal for information must naturally be addressed to him, 'are a sect founded in the reign of **Charles the First**, by a man named **John Presbyter**, who hatched all the brood of Dissenting vermin that crawl about in dirty alleys, and circumvent the lord of the manor in order to get a few yards of ground for their pigeon-house conventicles.' " 1

—debater: " 'Will you tell me, sir, that I don't know the origin of Presbyterianism? I, sir, a man known through the county, entrusted with the affairs of half a score parishes; while you, sir, are ignored by the very fleas that infest the miserable alley in which you were bred.'

"A loud and general laugh, with 'You'd better let him alone, **Byles**'; 'You'll not get the better of Dempster in a hurry,' drowned the retort of the too well-informed Mr Byles, who, white with rage, rose and walked out of the bar." 1

—successful practice: "Hardly a landholder, hardly a farmer, hardly a parish within ten miles of Milby, whose affairs were not under the legal guardianship of **Pittman** and Dempster; and I think the clients were proud of their lawyers' unscrupulousness . . . . Dempster's talent in 'bringing through' a client was a very common topic of conversation . . . . 'He's a long-headed feller, Dempster; why, it shows yer what a headpiece Dempster has, as he can drink a bottle of brandy at a sittin', an' yit see further through a stone wall when he's done, than other folks 'll see through a glass winder.' " 2

—joyous word: " 'The pulpit from which our venerable pastor has fed us with sound doctrine for half a century is not to be invaded by a fanatical, sectarian, double-faced, Jesuitical interloper! We are not to have a preacher obtruding himself upon us, who decries good works, and sneaks into our homes perverting the faith of our wives and daughters! We are not to be poisoned with doctrines which damp every innocent enjoyment, and pick a poor man's pocket of the sixpence with which he might buy himself a cheerful glass after a hard day's work, under pretence of paying for Bibles to send to the Chocktaws!' " 4

—as a son: "The hard, astute, domineering attorney was still that little old woman's pet, as he had been when she watched with triumphant pride his first tumbling effort to march alone across the nursery floor. 'See what a good son he is to me!' she often thought. 'Never gave me a harsh word. And so he might have been a good husband.' " 7

—with his mother: "It was rather sad, and yet pretty, to see that little groups passing out of the shadow into the sunshine, and out of the sunshine into the shadow again: sad, because this tenderness of the son for the mother was hardly more than a nucleus of healthy life in an organ hardening by disease, because the man who was linked in this way with an innocent past, had become callous in worldliness, fevered by sensuality, enslaved by chance impulses; pretty, because it showed how hard it is to kill the deep-down fibrous roots of human love and goodness—how the man from whom we make it our pride to shrink, has yet a close brotherhood with us through some of our most sacred feelings." 7

—reminiscence: " 'I niver lighted on a cliverer, promisiner young man nor he was then. They talked of his bein' fond of a extry glass now an' then, but niver nothing' like what he's come to since.' " 8

—harassed: "Persecution and revenge, like courtship and toadyism, will not prosper without a considerable expenditure of time and ingenuity, and

these are not to spare with a man whose law-business and liver are both beginning to show unpleasant symptoms. Such was the disagreeable turn affairs were taking with Mr Dempster, and, like the general distracted by home intrigues, he was too much harassed himself to lay ingenious plans for harassing the enemy." 10

—deterioration: "[**Mrs Raynor**] noticed many indications not only that he was drinking to greater excess, but that he was beginning to lose that physical power of supporting excess which had long been the admiration of such fine spirits as **Mr Tomlinson**. It seemed as if Dempster had some consciousness of this—some new distrust of himself; for, before winter was over, it was observed that he had renounced his habit of driving out alone, and was never seen in his gig without a servant by his side." 13

—temper controlled: "An outbreak of temper towards his man was not common with him; for Dempster, like most tyrannous people, had that dastardly kind of self-restraint which enabled him to control his temper where it suited his own convenience to do so . . . . " 17

—dying: "How changed he was since that terrible Monday, nearly a fortnight ago! He lay motionless, but for the irregular breathing that stirred his broad chest and thick muscular neck. His features were no longer purple and swollen; they were pale, sunken, and haggard. A cold perspiration stood in beads on the protuberant forehead, and on the wasted hands stretched motionless on the bedclothes. It was better to see the hands so, than convulsively picking the air, as they had been a week ago." 24

—the end: "Suddenly a slight movement, like the passing away of a shadow, was visible in his face, and he opened his eyes full on **Janet**.

"It was almost like meeting him again on the resurrection morning, after the night of the grave . . . .

"But the moment of speech was for ever gone—the moment for asking pardon of her, if he wanted to ask it. Could he read the full forgiveness that was written in her eyes? She never knew; for, as she was bending to kiss him, the thick veil of death fell between them, and her lips touched a corpse." 24

Rev. Edgar Tryan. " . . . innovation made its appearance in the person of the Rev. Mr Tryan, the new curate, at the chapel-of-ease on Paddiford Common. It was soon notorious in Milby that Mr Tryan held peculiar opinions; that he preached extempore; that he was founding a religious lending library in his remote corner of the parish; that he expounded the Scriptures in cottages; and that his preaching was attracting the Dissenters, and filling the very aisles of his church." 2

" ' . . . he preaches without book, they say, just like a Dissenter. It must be a rambling sort of a concern.' " 2

—barroom attack: " 'That's not the worst,' said **Mr Dempster**; 'he preaches against good works; says good works are not necessary to salvation —a sectarian, antinomian, Anabaptist doctrine. Tell a man he is not to be saved by his works, and you open the flood gates of all immorality. You see it in all these canting innovators; they're all bad ones by the sly; smooth-faced, drawling, hypocritical fellows, who pretend ginger isn't hot in their mouths, and cry down all innocent pleasures; their hearts are all the blacker for their sanctimonious outsides. Haven't we been warned against those who make clean the outside of the cup and the platter? There's this Tryan, now, he goes about praying with old women, and singing with charity children; but what

has he really got his eye on all the while? A domineering ambitious Jesuit, gentlemen; all he wants is to get his foot far enough into the parish to step into **Crewe**'s shoes when the old gentleman dies. Depend upon it, whenever you see a man pretending to be better than his neighbours, that man has either some cunning end to serve, or his heart is rotten with spiritual pride.' " 1

—first appearance: "But Mr Tryan had entered the room, and the strange light from the golden sky falling on his light-brown hair, which is brushed high up round his head, makes it look almost like an aureole. His grey eyes, too, shine with unwonted brilliancy this evening. They were not remarkable eyes, but they accorded completely in their changing light with the changing expression of his person, which indicated the paradoxical character often observable in a large-limbed sanguine blond; at once mild and irritable, gentle and overbearing, indolent and resolute, self-conscious and dreamy. Except that the well-filled lips had something of the artificially compressed look which is often the sign of a struggle to keep the dragon undermost, and that the complexion was rather pallid, giving the idea of imperfect health, Mr Tryan's face in repose was that of an ordinary whiskerless blond, and it seemed difficult to refer a certain air of distinction about him to anything in particular, unless it were his delicate hands and well-shapen feet." 3

—reporting bad news: " 'It seems,' he began, in a low and silvery tone, 'I need a lesson of patience; there has been something wrong in my thought or action about this evening lecture. I have been too much bent on doing good to Milby after my own plan—too reliant on my own wisdom' . . . .

"Mr Tryan's utterance had been getting rather louder and more rapid in the course of this speech, and he now added, in the energetic chest-voice, which, both in and out of the pulpit, alternated continually with his more silvery notes—

" 'But [**Dempster**'s] triumph will be a short one. If he thinks he can intimidate me by obloquy or threats, he has mistaken the man he has to deal with.' " 3

—susceptible: " . . . Mr Tryan turned to **Miss Eliza Pratt**, and the pre-occupied expression of his face melted into that beaming timidity with which a man almost always addresses a pretty woman." 3

—his home: " 'On Paddiford Common, where I live, you know, the bushes are all sprinkled with soot, and there's never any quiet except in the dead of night . . . .

" 'I've no face to go and preach resignation to those poor things in their smoky air and comfortless homes, when I come straight from every luxury myself. There are many things quite lawful for other men, which a clergyman must forgo if he would do any good in a manufacturing population like this.' " 8

—sensibility: "[He] was not cast in the mould of the gratuitous martyr. With a power of persistence which had been often blamed as obstinacy, he had an acute sensibility to the very hatred or ridicule he did not flinch from provoking. Every form of disapproval jarred him painfully; and, though he fronted his opponents manfully, and often with considerable warmth of temper, he had no pugnacious pleasure in the contest. It was one of the weaknesses of his nature to be too keenly alive to every harsh wind of opinion; to wince under the frowns of the foolish; to be irritated by the

injustice of those who could not possibly have the elements indispensable for judging him rightly; and with all this acute sensibility to blame, this dependence on sympathy, he had for years been constrained into a position of antagonism. No wonder, then, that good old **Mr Jerome**'s cordial words were balm to him. He had often been thankful to an old woman for saying 'God bless you'; to a little child for smiling at him; to a dog for submitting to be patted by him." 8

—limitations: " . . . anyone looking at him with the bird's-eye glance of a critic might perhaps say that he made the mistake of identifying Christianity with a too narrow doctrinal system; that he saw God's work too exclusively in antagonism to the world, the flesh, and the devil; that his intellectual culture was too limited . . . .

"But I am not poised at that lofty height. I am on the level and in the press with him, as he struggles his way along the stony road, through the crowd of unloving fellow men. He is stumbling, perhaps; his heart now beats fast with dread, now heavily with anguish; his eyes are sometimes dim with tears, which he makes haste to dash away; he pushes manfully on, with fluctuating faith and courage, with a sensitive failing body; at last he falls, the struggle is ended, and the crowd closes over the space he has left." 10 *GE fails technically here: she has introduced an occasional Narrator of sorts: a boy home from school who gets confirmed; but this omniscient observer is not he. The young Narrator plays no further role.*

—obsessive: "Mr Tryan's most unfriendly observers were obliged to admit that he gave himself no rest. Three sermons on Sunday, a night-school for young men on Tuesday, a cottage lecture on Thursday, addresses to schoolteachers, and catechising of school children, with pastoral visits, multiplying as his influence extended beyond his own district . . . would have been enough to tax severely the powers of a much stronger man. **Mr Pratt** remonstrated with him on his imprudence, but could not prevail on him so far to economise time and strength as to keep a horse. On some ground or other, which his friends found difficult to explain to themselves, Mr Tryan seemed bent on wearing himself out." 11

—discussed: " 'What is so wonderful to me in Mr Tryan is the way he puts himself on a level with one, and talks to one like a brother [said **Mrs Pettifer**]. I'm never afraid of telling him anything. He never seems to look down on anybody. He knows how to lift up those that are cast down, if ever man did.'

" 'Yes,' said **Mary**. 'And when I see all the faces turned up to him in Paddiford Church, I often think how hard it would be for any clergyman who had to come after him; he has made the people love him so.' " 11

—a confession: " 'But a dear friend to whom I opened my mind showed me it was just such as I—the helpless who feel themselves helpless—that God specially invites to come to Him, and offers all the riches of his salvation: not forgiveness only; forgiveness would be worth little if it left us under the powers of our evil passions; but strength—that strength which enables us to conquer sin.' " 18

—nearing the end: "He looked at her then, and smiled. There is an unspeakable blending of sadness and sweetness in the smile of a face sharpened and paled by slow consumption. That smile of Mr Tryan's pierced poor **Janet**'s heart: she felt in it at once the assurance of grateful affection

and the prophecy of coming death. Her tears rose; they turned round without speaking, and went back again along the lane." 26

—resistance: "He was conscious that he did not wish for prolonged life solely that he might reclaim the wanderers and sustain the feeble: he was conscious of a new yearning for those pure human joys which he had voluntarily and determinedly banished from his life—for a draught of that deep affection from which he had been cut off by a dark chasm of remorse. For now, that affection was within his reach; he saw it there, like a palm-shadowed well in the desert; he *could* not desire to die in sight of it." 27

—a last perspective: " . . . the pale wasted form in the easy-chair (for he sat up to the last), of the grey eyes so full even yet of enquiring kindness, as the thin, almost transparent hand was held out to give the pressure of welcome; and of the sweet woman, too, whose dark watchful eyes detected every want, and who supplied the want with a ready hand." 27

—envoi: " 'Let us kiss each other before we part.'

"She lifted up her face to his, and the full life-breathing lips met the wasted dying ones in a sacred kiss of promise." 27

—memorials: "There is a simple gravestone in Milby churchyard, telling that in this spot lie the remains of Edgar Tryan, for two years officiating curate at the Paddiford chapel-of-ease, in this parish . . . .

"But there is another memorial of Edgar Tryan, which bears a fuller record: it is **Janet Dempster**, rescued from self-despair, strengthened with divine hopes, and now looking back on years of purity and helpful labour. The man who has left such a memorial behind him, must have been one whose heart beat with true compassion, and whose lips were moved by fervent faith." 28

Supporting Roles

Mr Crewe, the curate, "in a brown Brutus wig, delivered inaudible sermons on a Sunday, and on a weekday imparted the education of a gentleman—that is to say, an arduous inacquaintance with Latin through the medium of the Eton Grammar—to three pupils in the upper grammar school." 2

" . . . there was almost always something funny about old Mr Crewe. His brown wig was hardly ever put on quite right, and he had a way of raising his voice for three or four words, and lowering it again to a mumble, so that we could scarcely make out a word he said; though, as **my mother** observed, that was of no consequence in the prayers, since everyone had a prayer-book; and as for the sermon, she continued with some causticity, we all of us heard more of it than we could remember when we got home." 2

—comfortable: "Old Mr Crewe, the curate, for example, was allowed to enjoy his avarice in comfort, without fear of sarcastic parish demagogues; and his flock liked him all the better for having scraped together a large fortune out of his school and curacy, and the proceeds of the three thousand pounds he had with his little deaf wife. It was clear he must be a learned man, for he had once had a large private school in connection with the grammar school, and had even numbered a young nobleman or two among his pupils. The fact that he read nothing at all now, and that his mind seemed absorbed in the commonest matters, was doubtless due to his having exhausted the resources of erudition earlier in life. It is true he was not spoken of in terms of high respect, and old Crewe's stingy housekeeping was a frequent subject of

jesting; but this was a good old-fashioned characteristic in a parson who had been part of Milby life for half a century: it was like the dents and disfigurements in an old family tankard, which no one would like to part with for a smart new piece of plate fresh from Birmingham. The parishioners saw no reason at all why it should be desirable to venerate the parson or anyone else: they were much more comfortable to look down a little on their fellow creatures." 2

Mamsey Dempster. "**Mr Dempster**, whom you have hitherto seen only as the orator of the Red Lion, and the drunken tyrant of a dreary midnight home, was the first-born darling son of a fair little mother. The mother was living still, and her own large black easy-chair, where she sat knitting through the livelong day, was now set ready for her at the breakfast-table, by her son's side, a sleek tortoiseshell cat acting as provisional incumbent . . . .

"A very little old lady she was, with a pale, scarcely wrinkled face, hair of that peculiar white which tells that the locks have once been blonde, a natty pure-white cap on her head, and a white shawl pinned over her shoulders. You saw at a glance that she had been a *mignonne* blonde, strangely unlike her tall, ugly, dingy-complexioned son . . . . " 7

—and daughter-in-law: "In spite of **Janet**'s tenderness and attention to her, she had had little love for her daughter-in-law from the first, and had witnessed the sad growth of home-misery through long years, always with a disposition to lay the blame on the wife rather than on the husband . . . . " 7

—silent: "But old Mrs Dempster had that rare gift of silence and passivity which often supplies the absence of mental strength; and, whatever were her thoughts, she said no word to aggravate the domestic discord. Patient and mute she sat at her knitting through many a scene of quarrel and anguish; resolutely she appeared unconscious of the sounds that reached her ears, and the facts she divined after she had retired to her bed; mutely she witnessed poor **Janet**'s faults, only registering them as a balance of excuse on the side of her son." 7

—death: "The housemaid found her seated motionless in her armchair, her knitting fallen down, and the tortoiseshell cat reposing on it unreproved. The little white old woman had ended her wintry age of patient sorrow, believing to the last that '**Robert** might have been a good husband as he had been a good son.' " 13

Thomas Jerome. "Even Mr Jerome, chief member of the congregation at Salem Chapel, an elderly man of very strict life, was one of **Dempster**'s clients, and had quite an exceptional indulgence for his attorney's foibles, perhaps attributing them to the inevitable incompatibility of law and gospel." 2

"Mr Jerome, a retired corn-factor, and the most eminent member of the [Independent] congregation, was one of the richest men in the parish." 2

—despised: "But of all **Pratt**'s patients, Mr Jerome was the one on whom **Mr Pilgrim** heaped the most unmitigated contempt. In spite of the surgeon's wise tolerance, Dissent became odious to him in the person of Mr Jerome. Perhaps it was because that old gentleman, being rich, and having very large yearly bills for medical attendance on himself and his wife, nevertheless employed Pratt—neglected all the advantages of 'active treatment', and paid away his money without getting his system lowered. On any other ground it is hard to explain a feeling of hostility to Mr Jerome, who was an excellent old gentleman, expressing a great deal of goodwill towards his neighbours, not

only in imperfect English, but in loans of money to the ostensibly rich, and in sacks of potatoes to the obviously poor." 2

—in his garden: "[He] followed leisurely with his full broad shoulders in rather a stooping posture, and his large good-natured features and white locks shaded by a broad-brimmed hat." 8

—greeting a guest: "If you had heard the tone of mingled goodwill, veneration, and condolence in which this greeting was uttered, even without seeing the face that completely harmonised with it, you would have no difficulty in inferring the ground-notes of Mr Jerome's character. To a fine ear that tone said as plainly as possible—'Whatever recommends itself to me, Thomas Jerome, as piety and goodness, shall have my love and honour. Ah, friends, this pleasant world is a sad one, too, isn't it? Let us help one another, let us help one another." 8

—religion: "And it was entirely owing to this basis of character, not at all from any clear and precise doctrinal discrimination, that Mr Jerome had very early in life become a Dissenter. In his boyish days he had been thrown where Dissent seemed to have the balance of piety, purity, and good works on its side, and to become a Dissenter seemed to him identical with choosing God instead of mammon . . . he had not gone further than to question whether a Christian man was bound in conscience to distinguish Christmas and Easter by any peculiar observance beyond the eating of mince-pies and cheesecakes. It seemed to him that all seasons were alike good for thanking God, departing from evil and doing well, whereas it might be desirable to restrict the period for indulging in unwholesome forms of pastry." 8

—combative: "The evening lecture was a subject of warm interest with him, and the opposition **Mr Tryan** met with gave that interest a strong tinge of partisanship; for there was a store of irascibility in Mr Jerome's nature which must find a vent somewhere, and in so kindly and upright a man could only find it in indignation against those whom he held to be enemies of truth and goodness." 8

"That old gentleman had in him the vigorous remnant of an energy and perseverance which had created his own fortune; and being . . . given to chewing the cud of a righteous indignation with considerable relish, he was determined to carry on his retributive war against the persecuting attorney." 13

Mr Pilgrim, "the doctor, who had presented his large top-booted person within the bar while **Mr Dempster** was speaking. Mr Pilgrim had just returned from one of his long day's rounds among the farmhouses, in the course of which he had sat down to two hearty meals . . . he was in that condition which his **groom** indicated with poetic ambiguity by saying that 'master had been in the sunshine.' " 1

—enunciation: "Mr Pilgrim was not a man to sit quiet under a sarcasm, nature having endowed him with a considerable share of self-defensive wit. In his most sober moments he had an impediment in his speech, and as copious gin-and-water stimulated not the speech but the impediment, he had time to make his retort sufficiently bitter." 1

—ecumenical: "Mr Pilgrim, too, was always [at the chapel's annual charity sermon] with his half-sovereign; for as there was no Dissenting doctor in Milby, Mr Pilgrim looked with great tolerance on all shades of religious opinion that did not include a belief in cures by miracle." 2

—colleague: see **Richard Pratt**

—*comparisons:* "But by their respective patients these two distinguished men were pitted against each other with great virulence. **Mrs Lowme** could not conceal her amazement that **Mrs Phipps** should trust her life in the hands of **Pratt**, who let her feed herself up to that degree, it was really shocking to hear how short her breath was; and Mrs Phipps had no patience with Mrs Lowme, living, as she did, on tea and broth, and looking as yellow as any crow-flower, and yet letting Pilgrim bleed and blister her and give her lowering medicine till her clothes hung on her like a scarecrow's. On the whole, perhaps, Mr Pilgrim's reputation was at the higher pitch, and when any lady under Mr Pratt's care was doing ill, she was half disposed to think that a little more 'active treatment' might suit her better." 2

—*patient prejudice:* "The doctor's estimate, even of a confiding patient, was apt to rise and fall with the entries in the day-book; and I have known Mr Pilgrim discover the most unexpected virtues in a patient seized with a promising illness. At such times you might have been glad to perceive that there were some of Mr Pilgrim's fellow creatures of whom he entertained a high opinion, and that he was liable to the amiable weakness of a too admiring estimate. A good inflammation fired his enthusiasm, and a lingering dropsy dissolved him into charity. Doubtless this crescendo of benevolence was partly due to feelings not at all represented by the entries in the day-book; for in Mr Pilgrim's heart, too, there was a latent store of tenderness and pity which flowed forth at the sight of suffering. Gradually, however, as his patients became convalescent, his view of their characters became more dispassionate; when they could relish mutton chops, he began to admit that they had foibles, and by the time they had swallowed their last dose of tonic, he was alive to their most inexcusable faults. After this, the thermometer of his regard rested at the moderate point of friendly backbiting, which sufficed to make him agreeable in his morning visits to the amiable and worthy persons who were yet far from convalescent." 2

—*sensitive:* " . . . [he spoke] in that low tone of sympathetic feeling which sometimes gave a sudden air of gentleness to this rough man . . . . " 24

Mrs Raynor, mother-in-law to **Dempster**. " 'Poor Mrs Raynor! She's glad to do anything for the sake of peace and quietness,' said **Mrs Pettifer**; 'but it's no trifle at her time of life to part with a doctor who knows her constitution.' " 3

—*her portrait:* "There was a portrait of Janet's mother, a grey-haired, dark-eyed old woman, in a neatly fluted cap, hanging over the mantelpiece. Surely the aged eyes take on a look of anguish as they see Janet . . . .

"Poor grey-haired woman! Was it for this you suffered a mother's pangs in your lone widowhood five-and-thirty years ago? Was it for this you kept the little worn morocco shoes Janet had first run in, and kissed them day by day when she was away from you, a tall girl at school Was it for this you looked proudly at her when she came back to you in her rich pale beauty, like a tall white arum that has just unfolded its grand pure curves to the sun?

"The mother lies sleepless and praying in her lonely house, weeping the difficult tears of age, because she dreads this may be a cruel night for her child." 4

—*visited:* "Mrs Raynor looked over her spectacles, and met her daughter's glance with eyes as dark and loving as her own. She was a much smaller woman than **Janet**, both in figure and feature, the chief resemblance lying in the eyes and the clear brunette complexion. The mother's hair had long been grey, and was gathered under the neatest of caps, made by her own clever fingers . . . . Always the same clean, neat old lady, dressed in black silk, was Mrs Raynor: a patient, brave woman, who bowed with resignation under the burden of remembered sorrow, and bore with meek fortitude the new load that the new days brought with them." 5

—her religion: "Mrs Raynor had her faith and her spiritual comforts, though she was not in the least evangelical and knew nothing of doctrinal zeal. I fear most of Mr Tryan's hearers would have considered her destitute of saving knowledge, and I am quite sure she had no well-defined views on justification. Nevertheless, she read her Bible a great deal, and thought she found divine lessons there—how to bear the cross meekly, and be merciful. Let us hope that there is a saving ignorance, and that Mrs Raynor was justified without knowing exactly how." 5

—her great sorrow: "The poor patient woman could do little more than mourn with her daughter: she had humble resignation enough to sustain her own soul, but she could no more give comfort and fortitude to **Janet**, than the withered ivy-covered trunk can bear up its strong, full-boughed offspring crashing down under an Alpine storm." 15

Others

Budd. "Mr Budd was a small, sleek-headed bachelor of five-and-forty, whose scandalous life had long furnished his more moral neighbours with an after-dinner joke. He had no other striking characteristic, except that he was a currier of choleric temperament, so that you might wonder why he had been chosen as clergyman's churchwarden, if I did not tell you that he had recently been elected through **Mr Dempster**'s exertions, in order that his zeal against the threatened evening lecture might be backed by the dignity of office." 1

—on duty: "Standing in the aisle close to [**Mr Tryan**], and repeating the responses with edifying loudness, was Mr Budd, churchwarden and delegate, with a white staff in his hand and a backward bend of his small head and person, such as, I suppose, he considered suitable to a friend of sound religion." 6

—in retreat: "Even Mr Budd and **Mr Tomlinson**, when they saw **Mr Tryan** passing pale and worn along the street, had a secret sense that this man was somehow not that very natural and comprehensible thing, a humbug—that, in fact, it was impossible to explain him from the stomach-and-pocket point of view. Twist and stretch their theory as they might, it would not fit Mr Tryan; and so, with that remarkable resemblance as to mental processes which may frequently be observed to exist between plain men and philosophers, they concluded that the less they said about him the better." 26

Luke Byles, "who piqued himself on his reading, and was in the habit of asking casual acquaintances if they knew anything of **Hobbes**; 'it is right enough that the lower orders should be instructed. But this sectarianism within the Church ought to be put down. In point of fact, these evangelicals are not Churchmen at all; they're no better than Presbyterians.' " 1

Mrs Crewe. "Little deaf Mrs Crewe would often carry half her own spare dinner to the sick and hungry . . . . " 2

—hostess: " 'You should have seen her lift up her hands yesterday, and pray heaven to take her before ever she should have another collation to get ready for the Bishop. She said, " . . . I wouldn't mind, **Janet**, if it was to feed

all the old hungry cripples in Milby; but so much trouble and expense for people who eat too much every day of their lives!" ' " 5

Lizzie Jerome. "[**Mr Jerome**] had set down the basket of strawberries on the gravel, and had lifted up little Lizzie in his arms to look at a bird's nest. Lizzie peeped, and then looked at her grandpa with round blue eyes, and then peeped again.

" D'ye see it, Lizzie?' he whispered.

" 'Yes,' she whispered in return, putting her lips very near grandpa's face. At this moment **Sally** appeared . . . .

"[She] trotted submissively along, her little head in eclipse under a large nankin bonnet . . . . " 8

—reappearing: "It is a pretty surprise, when one visits an elderly couple, to see a little figure enter in a white frock with a blonde head as smooth as satin, round blue eyes, and a cheek like an apple blossom." 8

Mrs Susan Jerome. "Mrs Jerome was like her china, handsome and old-fashioned. She was a buxom lady of sixty, in an elaborate lace cap fastened by a frill under her chin, a dark, well-curled front concealing her forehead, a snowy neckerchief exhibiting its ample folds as far as her waist, and a stiff grey silk gown. She had a clean damask napkin pinned before her to guard her dress during the process of tea-making . . . . " 8

—religion: "Mrs Jerome . . . had not a keen susceptibility to shades of doctrine, and it is probable that, after listening to Dissenting eloquence for thirty years, she might safely have re-entered the Establishment without performing any spiritual quarantine. Her mind, apparently, was of the non-porous flinty character which is not in the least danger from surrounding damp." 8

Miss Mary Linnet, "whose manuscript was the neatest type of zigzag, was seated at a small table apart, writing on green paper tickets . . . . Miss Linnet had other accomplishments besides that of a neat manuscript, and an index to some of them might be found in the ornaments of the room. She had always combined a love of serious and poetical reading with her skill in fancy-work . . . Miss Linnet had dark ringlets, a sallow complexion, and an amiable disposition. As to her features, there was not much to criticise in them, for she had little nose, less lip, and no eyebrow; and as to her intellect, her friend **Mrs Pettifer** often said: 'She didn't know a more sensible person to talk to than Mary Linnet . . . she said there were many things to bear in every condition of life, and nothing should induce her to marry without a prospect of happiness . . . . She always spoke very prettily, did Mary Linnet; very different, indeed, from **Rebecca**.' " 3

" . . . even her female friends said nothing more ill-natured of her, than that her face was like a piece of putty with two Scotch pebbles stuck in it. . . . " 3

And see Topicon A:Old Maid—*contrasts*

Miss Rebecca Linnet, "indeed, was not a general favourite . . . [she] was always spoken of sarcastically, and it was a customary kind of banter with young ladies to recommend her as a wife to any gentleman they happened to be flirting with—her fat, her finery, and her thick ankles sufficing to give piquancy to the joke . . . . Miss Rebecca, however, possessed the accomplishment of music, and her singing of 'Oh no, we never mention her', and 'The Soldier's Tear', was so desirable an accession to the pleasures of a tea-party that no one cared to offend her, especially as Rebecca had a high spirit of her own, and in spite of her expansively rounded contour, had a particularly sharp tongue." 3

—and her sister: "Thus there was a good deal of family unlikeness between Rebecca and her sister, and I am afraid there was also a little family dislike; but **Mary**'s disapproval had usually been kept imprisoned behind her thin lips, for Rebecca was not only of a headstrong disposition, but was her mother's pet; the old lady being herself stout, and preferring a more showy style of cap than she could prevail on her daughter Mary to make up for her." 3

—transformed: " . . . her appearance this evening, as she sits pasting on the green tickets, is in striking contrast with what it was three or four months ago. Her plain grey gingham dress and plain white collar could never have belonged to her wardrobe before that date; and though she is not reduced in size, and her brown hair will do nothing but hang in crisp ringlets down her large cheeks, there is a change in her air and expression which seems to shed a softened light over her person, and make her look like a peony in the shade, instead of the same flower flaunting in a parterre in the hot sunlight.

"No one could deny that Evangelicalism had wrought a change for the better in Rebecca Linnet's person . . . . " 3

And see Topicon A:Old Maid*—contrasts*

Mrs Linnet. " . . . it was much pleasanter in Mrs Linnet's parlour than in the bar of the Red Lion . . . Mrs Linnet's house was situated quite on the outskirts of Puddiford Common . . . . " 3

—a reader: "Mrs Linnet had become a reader of religious books since **Mr Tryan**'s advent, and as she was in the habit of confining her perusal to the purely secular portions, which bore a very small proportion to the whole, she could make rapid progress through a large number of volumes. On taking up the biography of a celebrated preacher, she immediately turned to the end to see what disease he died of; and if his legs swelled, as her own occasionally did, she felt a stronger interest in ascertaining any earlier facts in the history of the dropsical divine—whether he had ever fallen off a stagecoach, whether he had married more than one wife, and, in general, any adventures or repartees recorded of him previous to the epoch of his conversion. She then glanced over the letters and diary, and wherever there was a predominance of Zion, the River of Life, and notes of exclamation, she turned over to the next page; but any passage in which she saw such promising nouns as 'smallpox', 'pony', or 'boots and shoes', at once arrested her." 3

Lowme. "You might still less have suspected that the figure in light fustian and large grey whiskers, leaning against the grocer's doorpost in High Street, was no less a person than Mr Lowme, one of the most aristocratic men in Milby, said to have been 'brought up a gentleman', and to have had the gay habits accordant with that station, keeping his harriers and other expensive animals. He was now quite an elderly **Lothario**, reduced to the most economical sins; the prominent form of his gaiety being this of lounging at **Mr Gruby**'s door, embarrassing the servant-maids who came for grocery, and talking scandal with the rare passers-by. Still it was generally understood that Mr Lowme belonged to the highest circle of Milby society; his sons and daughters held up their heads very high indeed; and in spite of his condescending way of chatting and drinking with inferior people, he would himself have scorned any closer identification with them." 2

—*important moment:* "The most capacious punch-bowl was put in requisition; and that born gentleman, Mr Lowme, seated opposite **Mr Dempster** as 'Vice', undertook to brew the punch, defying the criticisms of the envious men out of office, who, with the readiness of irresponsibility, ignorantly suggested more lemons." 4

Lucy. " 'At college [said **Tryan**] I had an attachment to a lovely girl of seventeen; she was very much below my own station in life, and I never contemplated marrying her, but I induced her to leave her father's house. I did not mean to forsake her when I left college, and I quieted all scruples of conscience by promising myself that I would always take care of poor Lucy. But on my return from a vacation spent in travelling, I found that Lucy was gone—gone away with a gentleman, her neighbours said . . . three years since I had lost sight of Lucy . . . as I was walking along Gower Street, I saw a knot of people on the causeway before me. . . . The body of a woman, dressed in fine clothes, was lying against a doorstep. Her head was bent on one side, and the long curls had fallen over her cheek. A tremor seized me when I saw the hair: it was light chestnut—the colour of Lucy's. I knelt down and turned aside the hair; it was Lucy—dead—with paint on her cheeks. I found out afterwards that she had taken poison—that she was in the power of a wicked woman—that the very clothes on her back were not her own.' " 18

Mrs Phipps, "for her part, declared she would never accept an invitation to **Dempster**'s again; it was getting so very disagreeable to go there, **Mrs Dempster** was often 'so strange.' " 13

" 'Lors! why, **Liza** told me herself as Mrs Phipps was as skinny as skinny i' the kitchen, for all they keep so much company; and as for follyers, she's as cross as a turkeycock if she finds 'em out.' " 21

Pittman. "Old lawyer Pittman had once been a very important person indeed, having in his earlier days managed the affairs of several gentlemen in those parts, who had subsequently been obliged to sell everything and leave the country, in which crisis Mr Pittman accommodatingly stepped in as a purchaser of their estates, taking on himself the risk and trouble of a more leisurely sale; which, however, happened to turn out very much to his advantage. Such opportunities occur quite unexpectedly in the way of business. But I think Mr Pittman must have been unlucky in his later speculations, for now, in his old age, he had not the reputation of being very rich; and though he rode slowly to his office in Milby every morning on an old white hackney, he had to resign the chief profits, as well as the active business of the firm, to his younger partner, **Dempster**. No one in Milby considered old Pittman a virtuous man, and the elder townspeople were not at all backward in narrating the least advantageous portions of his biography in a very round unvarnished manner. Yet I could never observe that they trusted him any the less, or liked him any the worse. Indeed, Pittman and Dempster were the popular lawyers of Milby and its neighbourhood . . . . " 2

" 'I have a task to impose upon you, **Mrs Dempster**,' he said, with a certain toothless pomposity habitual to him . . . . " 25

Miss Eliza Pratt. "**Miss Pratt** having kept her brother's house during his long widowhood, his daughter, Miss Eliza, had had the advantage of being educated by her aunt, and thus of imbibing a very strong antipathy to all that remarkable woman's tastes and opinions. The silent handsome girl of two-and-twenty . . . is Miss Eliza Pratt . . . . " 3

" . . . whose fine grey eyes allowed few things to escape her silent observation . . . Miss Eliza, as she bent her handsome head and large cannon curls with apparent calmness over her work, felt a considerable internal flutter when she heard [**Mr Tryan**'s] knock on the door." 3

—concerned: "Miss Eliza Pratt had at one time passed through much sleepless cogitation on the possibility of **Mr Tryan**'s being attached to some lady at a distance . . . and her fine eyes kept close watch lest any symptom of engaged affections on his part should escape her." 11

Richard Pratt. " 'Oh, I thought, as Pratt had declared himself a Tryanite, we should be sure to get **Pilgrim** on our side.' " 1

—contrasted with a colleague: " . . . it was remarkable how strongly these two clever men were contrasted. Pratt was middle-sized, insinuating, and silvery-voiced; **Pilgrim** was tall, heavy, rough-mannered, and stuttering. Both were considered to have great powers of conversation, but Pratt's anecdotes were of the fine old crusted quality to be procured only of **Joe Miller**; Pilgrim's had the full fruity flavour of the most recent scandal. Pratt elegantly referred all diseases to debility, and, with a proper contempt for symptomatic treatment, went to the root of the matter with port-wine and bark; Pilgrim was persuaded that the evil principle in the human system was plethora, and he made war against it with cupping, blistering, and cathartics.

"They had both been long established in Milby, and as each had a sufficient practice, there was no very malignant rivalry between them; on the contrary, they had that sort of friendly contempt for each other which is always conducive to a good understanding between professional men; and when any new surgeon attempted, in an ill-advised hour, to settle himself in the town, it was strikingly demonstrated how slight and trivial are theoretic differences compared with the broad basis of common human feeling. There was the most perfect unanimity between Pratt and Pilgrim in the determination to drive away the obnoxious and too probably unqualified intruder as soon as possible." ¶2

Miss Pratt, "the thin stiff lady in spectacles . . . who always had a peculiar repulsion for 'females with a gross habit of body.' Miss Pratt was an old maid, but that is a no more definite description than if I had said she was in the autumn of life." 3 *See Topicon* A:Old Maid*—contrasts*

—blue-stocking: "Miss Pratt was the one bluestocking of Milby, possessing, she said, no less than five hundred volumes, competent, as her brother the doctor often observed, to conduct a conversation on any topic whatever, and occasionally dabbling a little in authorship, though it was understood that she had never put forth the full powers of her mind in print. Her 'Letters to a Young Man on His Entrance into Life', and 'De Courcy, or the Rash Promise, a Tale for Youth', were mere trifles which she had been induced to publish because they were calculated for popular utility, but they were nothing to what she had for years had by her in manuscript. Her latest production had been 'Six Stanzas', addressed to the **Rev. Edgar Tryan**, printed on glazed paper with a neat border, and beginning, 'Forward, young wrestler for the truth!' " 3

—commenting: "Miss Pratt has enough to do in commenting on the heap of volumes before her, feeling it a responsibility entailed on her by her great powers of mind to leave nothing without the advantage of her opinion.

Whatever was good must be sprinkled with the chrism of her approval; whatever was evil must be blighted by her condemnation." 3

—her favourite cleric: " ' . . . I assure you I have tested **Mr Tryan**'s [acquirements] by questions which are a pretty severe touchstone. It is true, I sometimes carry him a little beyond the depth of the other listeners. Profound learning . . . has not many to estimate it in Milby.' " 3

" ' . . . **Eliza** tells me what very fine cambric handkerchiefs he uses. My eyes are not good enough to see such things, but I know what breeding is as well as most people, and it is easy to see that Mr Tryan is quite *comme il faw,* to use a French expression.' " 3

Prendergast " 'might not take the protest well if **Deb Traunter** went with you.' " 1

"The alarm reached its climax when it was reported that **Mr Tryan** was endeavouring to obtain authority from Mr Prendergast, the non-resident rector, to establish a Sunday-evening lecture in the parish church, on the ground that old **Mr Crewe** did not preach the Gospel." 2

—result: " 'Mr Prendergast has been false to his own conscience in this business [said **Tryan**]. He knows as well as I do that he is throwing away the souls of the people by leaving things as they are in the parish. But I shall appeal to the **Bishop**—I am confident of his sympathy.' " 3

—impressive: " . . . Mr Prendergast looked much more dignified [than the **Bishop**] with his plain white surplice and black hair. He was a tall commanding man, and read the Liturgy in a strikingly sonorous and uniform voice, which I tried to imitate the next Sunday at home, until my little **sister** began to cry, and said I was 'yoaring at her.' " 6

Tomlinson. " 'Well! I'll not stick at giving myself trouble to put down such hypocritical cant,' said Mr Tomlinson, the rich miller. 'I know well enough what your Sunday-evening lectures are good for—for wenches to meet their sweethearts, and brew mischief. There's work enough with the servant-maids as it is—such as I never heard the like of in my mother's time, and it's all along o' your schooling and newfangled plans.' " 1

—in retreat: see **Budd**

Minor Figures

Armstrong, "a wealthy client . . . the prospect of a lucrative and exciting bit of business in Mr Armstrong's probable lawsuit . . . . " 7

" . . . Mr Armstrong's lawsuit, which was threatening to take a turn rather depreciatory of **Dempster**'s professional prevision . . . . " 13

Molly Beale, "a brawny old virago, descrying wiry **Dame Ricketts** peeping out from her entry, seized the opportunity of renewing the morning's skirmish." 4

Betty. " 'It's very odd,' said **Kitty**, the housemaid, as she trimmed her next week's cap, while Betty, the middle-aged cook, looked on . . . .

" . . . 'She's p'raps gone away, an's made up her mind not to come back again.'

" 'And i' the right on't, too,' said Betty. 'I'd ha' overrun him long afore now, if it had been me. I wouldn't stan' bein' mauled as she is by no husband, not if he was the biggest lord i' the land. It's poor work bein' a wife at that price: I'd sooner be a cook wi'out perkises, an' hev roast, an' boil, an' fry, an' bake, all to mind at once. She may well do as she does. I know I'm glad enough of a drop o' summat myself when I'm plagued. I feel very low, like, tonight; I think I shall put my beer i' the saucepan an' warm it.' " 21

Bishop. " . . . the Bishop was an old man, and probably venerable (for though he was not an eminent Grecian, he was the brother of a Whig lord). . . he had small delicate womanish hands adorned with ruffles, and, instead of laying them on the girls' heads, just let them hover over each in quick succession, as if it were not etiquette to touch them, and as if the laying on of hands were like the theatrical embrace—part of the play, and not to be really believed in. To be sure there were a great many heads, and the Bishop's time was limited." 6

Boots, "though aware that the lawyer could 'carry his liquor like Old Nick', with whose social demeanour Boots seemed to be particularly well acquainted, nevertheless thought it might be as well to see so good a customer in safety to his own door, and walked quietly behind his elbow out of the inn-yard . . . . " 4

Sally Butts, " 'as had to sell her mangle, though she was as decent a woman as need to be' . . . . " 26

Phib Cook "left her evening washtub and appeared at her door in soap-suds, a bonnet-poke, and general dampness . . . . " 4

Dawes. " . . . feeling the value of Dawes, a steady punctual fellow, [**Dempster**] not only gave him high wages, but usually treated him with exceptional civility." 17

—*insulted:* "Dawe's blood was now fairly up. 'I'll look out for a master as has got a better chariсter nor a lyin', bletherin' drunkard, an' I shouldn't hev to go fur.' " 17

Dunn, a draper. "In this persuasive power of convenience lay Mr Dunn's ultimate security from martyrdom. His drapery was the best in Milby; the comfortable use and wont of procuring satisfactory articles at a moment's notice proved too strong for anti-Tryanite zeal; and the draper could soon look forward to his next stock-taking without the support of a Scriptural parallel." 10

Mary Dunn, "a draper's daughter in Milby and a distant relation of the **Miss Linnets**. Her pale lanky hair could never be coaxed into permanent curl, and this morning the heat had brought it down to its natural condition of lankiness earlier than usual. But that was not what made her sit melancholy and apart at the lower end of the form. Her parents were admirers of **Mr Tryan**, and had been persuaded, by the Miss Linnets' influence, to insist that their daughter should be prepared for confirmation by him, over and above the preparation given to **Miss Townley**'s pupils by **Mr Crewe**. Poor Mary Dunn!" 5

Maria Gardner, "who was much taller [than **Ellen Marriott**], and had a lovely 'crop' of dark-brown ringlets, and who, being also about to take upon herself the vows made in her name at her baptism, had oiled and twisted her ringlets with especial care." 4

Jim Hardy, "the coal-carrier, 'as lost his hoss' . . . . " 26

Rev. Mr Horner, "elected with brilliant hopes, was discovered to be given to tippling and quarrelling with his wife . . . . " 2

Kitty. " '**Liza Thomson**, as is at **Phipps**'s, said to me last Sunday, "I wonder you'll stay at **Dempster**'s," she says, "such going-on as there is." But

I says, "There's thing to put up wi' in ivery place, an' you may change, an' change, an' not better yourself when all's said an' done." ' " 21

—*a display:* " . . . Kitty, with the elaborate manifestation of alarm which servants delight in, rushed in without knocking, and, holding her hands on her heart as if the consequences to that organ were like to be very serious, said—

" 'If you please 'm, is the missis here?' " 21

Jonathan Lamb, "the old parish clerk." 5

Benjamin Landor, "whom no one had anything particular to say against, had a very meagre business in comparison [with **Pittman** and **Dempster**]." 2

Ben Landor " 'has a way of keeping himself neutral in everything, and he doesn't like to oppose his father.' " 1

Eustace Landor, "being nearly of age, had recently acquired a diamond ring, together with the habit of rubbing his hand through his hair. He was tall and dark, and thus had an advantage . . . . " 2

Miss Landor, "the belle of Milby, clad regally in purple and ermine, with a plume of feathers neither dropping nor erect, but maintaining a discreet medium . . . . [She was] considered remarkably clever, and a terrible quiz. . . . " 2

Landor " 'is a regular Tryanite.' " 1 " . . . there was only one close carriage in the place, and that was old Mr Landor's, the banker, who, I think, never drove more than one horse." 2

Low-Church clergymen, "one was a Welshman of globose figure and unctuous complexion, and the other a man of atrabiliar aspect, with lank black hair, and a redundance of limp cravat—in fact, the sort of thing you might expect in men who distributed the publications of the Religious Tract Society, and introduced Dissenting hymns into the Church." 3

Bob Lowme, "who had such beautiful whiskers meeting under his chin." 2

Mrs Lowme. "I promised Mrs Lowme to go and sit with her. She's confined to her room, and both the **Miss Lowmes** are out; so I'm going to read the newspaper to her and amuse her.' " 7

Ellen Marriott "assured [**Clara Robins**] with great confidence that it was only the clever men who were made rectors. Ellen Marriott was going to be confirmed. She was a short, fair, plump girl, with blue eyes and sandy hair, which was this morning arranged in taller cannon curls than usual, for the reception of the Episcopal benediction, and some of the young ladies thought her the prettiest girl in the school . . . . " 4

Sally Martin, " 'the deformed girl that's in a consumption.' " 3

Joseph Mercer. " 'The old man tells me how precious he finds your reading to him, now he is no longer able to go to church.'

"**Miss Eliza** only answered by a blush, which made her look all the handsomer . . . . " 3

Mat Paine. " . . . it had been settled that Mat Paine, **Dempster**'s clerk, should ride out on Thursday morning to meet [the delegates to **Prendergast**] at Whitlow . . . that he might gallop back and prepare an ovation for the triumvirate in case of their success." 4

Mr Parry. " 'I saw him the other day at **Mrs Bond**'s [said **Mrs Pettifer**]. He may be a very good man, and a fine preacher; they say he is; but I thought to myself, What a difference between him and **Mr Tryan**! He's a sharp-sort-of-looking man, and hasn't that feeling way with him that Mr Tryan has.' " 11

Mrs Pettifer, "a superior-minded widow, much valued in Milby, being such a very respectable person to have in the house in case of illness, and of quite too good a family to receive any money payment—you could always send her garden stuff that would make her ample amends." 3

Mr Phipps, "amiable and laconic, wondered how it was women were so fond of running each other down." 13

Alfred Phipps, "who, like his sister, was blond and stumpy, [and] found it difficult to overtake [the taller **Eustace Landor**], even by the severest attention to shirt-studs, and the particular shade of brown that was best relieved by gilt buttons." 2

Miss Phipps, "with a crimson bonnet, very much tilted up behind, and a cockade of stiff feathers on the summit . . . with her cockade of red feathers, had a filial heart, and lighted her father's pipe with a pleasant smile . . . . " 2

Ned Phipps, "who knelt against me, and I am sure made me behave much worse than I should have done without him, whispered that he thought the **Bishop** was a 'guy' . . . . " 6

Misses Pittman. "There were the four tall Miss Pittmans, old lawyer Pittman's daughters, with cannon curls surmounted by large hats, and long, drooping ostrich feathers of parrot green." 2

Bill Powers. "It was time for Bill Powers, a plethoric **Goliath**, who presided over the knot of beer-drinkers at the Bear and Ragged Staff, to issue forth with his companions, and, like the enunciator of the ancient myth, make the assemblage distinctly conscious of the common sentiment that had drawn them together . . . . Bill Powers, whose blood-shot eyes, bent hat, and protuberant altitude, marked him out as the natural leader of the assemblage, undertook to interpret the common sentiment by stopping the chaise, advancing to the door with raised hat, and begging to know of **Mr Dempster**, whether the Rector had forbidden the 'canting lecture.' " 4

Pryme, "who was one of the most substantial ratepayers in the neighbouring parish of Dingley, and who had himself a complex and long-standing private account with **Dempster**. **Mr Jerome** stirred up this gentleman to an investigation of some suspicious points in the attorney's conduct of the parish affairs. The natural consequence was a personal quarrel between Dempster and Mr Pryme; the client demanded his account, and then followed the old story of an exorbitant lawyer's bill, with the unpleasant anticlimax of taxing." 13

Anna Raymor. " ' . . . she's been taken worse . . . . That dropsy is carrying her off at last, I dare say. Poor thing! it will be a happy release. I must go, my dear—she's your father's last sister' . . . . " 25

Dame Ricketts "peeping out from her entry . . . . " 4

Clara Robins "wondered why some clergymen were rectors and others not." 5

Rev. Mr Rose. "[His] doctrine was a little too 'high,' verging on antinomianism . . . . " 2

Sally. " 'Dear heart, **Miss Lizzie**, you've stained your pinafore, an' I shouldn't wonder if it's gone through to your frock. There's be fine work! Come along wi' me, do' . . . .

"Sally, regarding the washtub from a different point of view, looked sourly serious, and hurried away with Lizzie . . . . " 8

Squire Sandeman. " 'When I was a boy [said **Mr Jerome**] I lived at Tilston . . . the best part o' the land there belonged to Squire Sandeman; he'd a club-foot, had Squire Sandeman—lost a deal o'money by canal shares.' " 8

Silly Caleb, "an idiot well known in Dog Lane, but more of a stranger in the Bridge Way, was seen slouching along with a string of boys hooting at his heels . . . . " 4

Rev. Mr Smith, "a distinguished minister much sought after in the iron districts, with a talent for poetry, became objectionable from an inclination to exchange verses with the young ladies of his congregation. It was reasonably argued that such verses as Mr Smith's must take a long time for their composition, and the habit alluded to might entrench seriously on his pastoral duties." 2

Rev. Mr Stickney. "[His] gift as a preacher was found to be less striking on a more extended acquaintance . . . . " 2

"It was a great anomaly to the Milby mind that a canting evangelical parson [like **Mr Tryan**]. . . should have so much the air of a gentleman, and be so little like the splay-footed Mr Stickney of Salem, to whom he approximated so closely in doctrine." 3

—observing a colleague: "Mr Stickney, of Salem, who considered all voluntary discomfort as a remnant of the legal spirit, pronounced a severe condemnation on this self-neglect, and expressed his fear that **Mr Tryan** was still far from having attained true Christian liberty." 11

Thrupp, " 'the clerk at the bank, who had been waiting at the Red Lion to hear the result, came to let us know. He said **Dempster** had been making a speech to the mob out the window.' " 3

Misses Tomlinson. "There were the three Miss Tomlinsons, who imitated **Miss Landor**, and also wore ermine and feathers; but their beauty was considered of a coarse order, and their square forms were quite unsuited to the round tippet which fell with such remarkable grace on Miss Landor's sloping shoulders." 2

Miss Townley. " . . . the pupils at Miss Townley's, who were absolved from all lessons, and were going to church to see the Bishop . . . . " 4

"The anti-**Tryan**ite spirit, you perceive, was very strong at Miss Townley's, imported probably by day scholars, as well as encouraged by the fact that that clever woman was herself strongly opposed to innovation . . . . " 5

Deb Traunter. " '. . . there's a report all over the town that Deb Traunter swears you [**Mr Budd**] shall take her with you as one of the delegates, and they say there's to be a fine crowd at your door the morning you start, to see the row.' " 1

—social: "Deb Traunter, in a pink flounced gown and floating ribbons, was observed talking with great affability to two men in sealskin caps and fustian, who formed her cortège." 4

Mrs Wagstaff. " 'It is a great privilege for us, **Mr Tryan** living at Mrs Wagstaff's, for he is often able to take us on his way backwards and forwards into the town.' " 3

" . . . she's a very pious woman. And I'm sure she thinks it too great a privilege to have Mr Tryan with her, not to do the best she can to make him comfortable. She can't help her rooms being shabby.' " 11

Jacob Wright. " ' . . . I went to a night-school as was kept by a Dissenter [said **Mr Jerome**], one Jacob Wright; an' it was from that man, sir, as I got my little schoolin' an' my knowledge o' religion.' " 8

Also mentioned

Ann, Mrs Raynor's servant	21
Bishop of the diocese where Milby is located	3
Brady, dealer in horse tack; repairs	17
Mrs Brinley, the carpenter's wife	13
daughter of Janet; adopted	28
De Courcy, the hero of a work by Miss Pratt	3
Father Clement, protagonist in a book for the new library	3
Felix Neff, memoirist whose book is being covered for the new library	3
grandson of Janet, by adoption of his mother	28
groom for Mr Pilgrim	1
Gruby, a shopkeeper	1
Jesson, a shopkeeper near Mrs Pettifer's home	17
Job, who comes calling on Kitty at the Dempsters'	21
Lakin family, in deep distress	23
Legh Richmond, whose biography is part of the new library	3
The **Misses Lowme**, who will be out today	7
Dr Madely of Rotherby, called in to consult on Mr Tryan's health	27
Henry Martyn [H], a missionary whose biography inspires Janet to go out and work	23
two men in sealskin caps and fustian, chatting with Deb Traunter	4
Phoebe, house servant to Mrs Pettifer	16
John Presbyter, a figment of the Dempster imagination	1
Proctor, the local printer	7
Radcliffe, a waiter in the bar at the Red Lion	6
Radley, with a livery-stable	11
Raynor, the late father of Janet	3
Rector at Tilston, a terrible-drinking, fox-hunting man	8
Ribbon-weavers, three; narrow-chested in rusty black	4
sister of the Narrator	6
Liza Thomson, a housemaid at the Phippses	21
Mrs Tooke, to whom Janet carried parcels	13
Lord Trufford, where the Bishop was to dine after the Confirmation	6
Trower, a client of Dempster's	1
Mr Walsh, the new curate for Paddiford church	27

Adam Bede

Book First: Carpenters are working in **Jonathan Burge**'s workshop in the village of Hayslope, Loamshire, in the northern midlands. We meet **Adam** and **Seth Bede**, brothers; **Jim Salt** (Sandy Jim); **Ben Cranage** (Wiry Ben); and **Mum Taft**. As the clock strikes six, work ceases. Seth is off to Methodist meeting. Adam heads for home, noticed and admired for his stalwart figure and carriage by a **traveller** on horseback. 1 The traveller arrives at the inn, **Mr Casson** landlord, who orients him on the **Donnithorne** and Bede families. Blacksmith **Chad Cranage** and shoemaker **Joshua Rann**, the parish clerk, await an open-air preaching by a Methodist woman, **Dinah Morris**.. The Salt family and **Bessy Cranage** appear. Dinah arrives and speaks eloquently for an hour. Her hearers are transfixed. The traveller tears himself away. 2

Seth and Dinah walk together. He pleads his suit: she tells him her calling prevents marriage. He walks home, heartbroken. 3 Adam's mother **Lisbeth**, querulous and idolatrous of him, tells him his drunken father has not done promised work and is out. Adam stays up all night to complete the needed coffin. He hears a rap on the door, as of a willow wand: an omen of death. He and Seth deliver the coffin and, returning, find **Thias Bede**'s drowned body. 4

We visit the Rectory of the aristocratic **Rev. Adolphus Irwine** and meet him in detail, as well as his handsome mother and sisters: **Kate** and invalid **Anne**. The reverend's bachelor status results from a too-modest income. His sterling qualities of tolerance and bonhomie shine forth. Joshua Rann's report on Dinah's preaching disturbs him not a whit. He rides out with his visitor, **Captain Arthur Donnithorne**. 5 He wants to look at Dinah, and Arthur wants to look at **Hetty Sorrel**, the dairy-maid at the Hall Farm, which is described. **Mrs Rachel Poyser** is an indefatigable manager and talker. 6

Arthur admires the dairy and the cloyingly bewitching Hetty. Mrs Poyser talks cheese-making and, on request, fetches little **Totty Poyser**, to whom Arthur presents a present of six-pences. 7 Irwine and Dinah converse with instant mutual liking and respect. Dinah has heard of Adam's father's death, and sets off to sit with Lisbeth. Hetty is unmoved by the drowning. 8

Luxury-seeking Hetty Sorrel will never marry Adam: she is set dreaming by Arthur's glances. 9 Lisbeth is distraught and distrait, and her plaints try Adam, but Dinah's visit soothes and calms her. 10 Adam is awake, and Dinah sees him for the first time—and blushes. Adam is struck and impressed. 11 A picture of Arthur Donnithorne: good-natured, well-meaning, self-esteeming, so far unchallenged. He wants to avoid his suggested meeting with Hetty at a grove but finds himself unable not to ride back to be there. They find each other and are lost to all else. He suddenly tears himself away. He scolds himself for meeting her, then decides he must see her again to end it. 12

In the evening they meet again at the Hermitage, a summer-house in the wood, and kiss. He tears himself away again and vows to himself to tell Mr Irwine all. 13 Hetty gets home late, having met Dinah on the way, and Mrs Poyser questions her but baby Totty distracts, and Hetty goes to bed. 14 Dinah and Hetty have adjoining rooms. Hetty pulls out earrings and a lace shawl and dreams of marriage to Arthur. Dinah hears her and visits, to offer her help in trouble. Hetty is startled and fearful. She rejects the idea of trouble. Dinah returns to bed and prays for Hetty's welfare. 15 With Irwine, Arthur talks of love and temptation, then denies any personal reference, perhaps to avoid burning his bridges. He goes, unconfessed. 16

Book Second: The "story pauses a little" for a discourse on Mr Irwine's approach to religion, Adam's opinions on the subject, and an insight into the author's views. 17 A set-piece on a country funeral. Hetty is bitterly disappointed not to see Arthur in the church. Parish clerk **Joshua Rann** stars, singing and reading. Lisbeth is comforted. 18 Walking to work, Adam thinks of Hetty. His is the picture not of an average man, but one of excellent value. 19

Adam calls at the Hall Farm, where he is very welcome. He finds Hetty in the garden and startles her. Her blush misleads him. She is softened in concern about Arthur. **Molly**, discomfited by Mrs Poyser's stern eye, drops a pitcher of beer. Mrs Poyser drops her own pitcher, startled by Hetty's appearance in quakerly garb. She has responded to Adam's admiration of Dinah's dress. 20 Adam visits his old schoolmaster, **Bartle Massey**, who is conducting lessons with three adults learning to read, and groups of boys. He tells Adam of talk that he will be made master of the Donnithorne woods. 21

Book Third: Arthur has given Hetty expensive earrings, which she can only admire in her room. And she has a locket. Arthur is about to come of age, and a big party is in prospect. He and Irwine talk about the squire and Adam's prospects. Adam will dine upstairs with the important tenants. 22 He does so. Martin Poyser is President, Casson 'Vice,' and Adam is where he can watch Hetty, who smiles at him. 23 There are toasts, and Adam is made much of. Hetty is miserable because Arthur can pay no attention to her. 24 There are games. Bessy Cranage wins a disappointing prize. Wiry Ben dances. 25 Then all dance in the big hall. Arthur leads out Mrs Poyser. Adam has a dance with Hetty but later, taking Totty from her, sees her locket and is puzzled. 26

Book Fourth: Adam comes upon Arthur and Hetty kissing in the grove. He is transfixed. Hetty runs off, Arthur tries to make light of it. Adam reveals his love for Hetty and challenges Arthur to fight. At last they do: Arthur falls. 27 At first Adam fears he is dead, but he revives. Adam brings him water, then goes for brandy after taking him to his summer-house. Arthur finds a pink neckerchief and hides it. Adam apologizes for his hastiness. But he demands that Arthur write to Hetty, undeceiving her, before he goes away. He hedges; Adam insists; he promises. Adam helps him home. Until tomorrow. 28

Arthur agonizes: to write Hetty or to go to her and do something mad? He dreads one possibility but thrusts it out his mind. He goes riding and makes up his mind to write the letter Adam has demanded. He does so and gives it to Adam for delivery. 29 Adam finds the chance to speak to Hetty, who denies any knowledge that Arthur will not marry her. Adam gives her the letter. He talks to Seth about Dinah and reads her long letter to him. 30 Hetty reads Arthur's letter and is devastated. She cries herself to sleep. She asks her uncle to let her go for a lady's maid, but the Poysers adamantly oppose this. 31

The Squire calls on the Poysers with a proposition for a swap of land to suit a new tenant's wishes. Mrs Poyser sends him away with a flea in his ear. 32 Adam thinks Hetty is recovering and is more in love than ever. 33 Adam asks Hetty to marry him, and she silently assents, thinking of Arthur. They will be married at Easter. 34 The next chapter's title "The Hidden Dread" tells it all. Hetty thinks of drowning but decides to run away: not to write Arthur, since he cannot give her what she wants. But she will go to him at Windsor. She tells the Poysers she is going to visit Dinah, and ask her to come to her wedding. 35

Book Fifth: Miserably, Hetty starts on her journey. She gains help from kind coachmen. At Windsor at last, she learns Arthur's unit has gone to Ireland. She faints in the arms of the **landlady**. 36 Hetty gets money from the landlord for her jewelry and starts back toward Stoniton and Dinah; but her despair deepens. Thoughts of suicide surge. 37 Adam is puzzled by Hetty's long absence and walks to Stoniton. Dinah is not there; Hetty has never been there. He returns, stricken, and tells Seth he will go after Arthur in Ireland. He sees shocked, sad Martin Poyser. Adam decides to confide in Irwine. 38

Irwine has had terrible news: Hetty is arrested for infanticide. Adam is at first incredulous, then deeply stricken. He speaks of going to Ireland, but Irwine tells him Arthur is on his way home, having had a letter from the Squire. 39 The Squire is dead. The Poysers feel deeply disgraced and will leave the parish. They want Dinah, as does Lisbeth. Massey and Irwine commiserate. 40 A weary Adam watches and waits. Irwine adjures him to avoid vengeful thoughts. 41 Bartle Massey reports to Adam: Hetty continues to deny having a child. Adam decides to go to court. 42 A witness, **Sarah Stone**, tells of taking Hetty in and of the birth of the baby. Hetty disappeared with the baby; this gives Adam a moment's hope. Labourer **John Olding**, however, connects Hetty and the baby he found dead in a hole: Guilty, and to be hanged. 43

A joyful Arthur is home. He had heard of Adam's betrothal. He will enter upon his inheritance. In his first opened letter Irwine tells him of Hetty's trial. He rushes off to Stoniton. 44 The traveller, never yet identified, stands at the prison gate. Dinah appears. He is **Colonel Townley**, a magistrate, and can get her in. She prays with Hetty, who breaks at last and tells her story. 45 Dinah comes to Adam and says Hetty wants to see him. He goes. She asks forgiveness: he says he forgave her long ago. They kiss in final parting. 46

Dinah prays fervently in the gallows-cart. The crowd's shout announces Arthur's frantic arrival, waving Hetty's reprieve. 47 The Poysers are leaving. The Bedes will go with them. Adam makes a last visit to the grove where he fought Arthur. They meet there again and go to the Hermitage to talk. Arthur tells him he is leaving for the army and pleads for Adam to stay and persuade the Poysers to do so. At first resistant, Adam is moved. He agrees to stay and will urge the Poysers also. They shake hands and say farewell. 48

Book Sixth: Eighteen months later, Dinah is preparing to leave the happy Poysers and return to duty. She is inclined to blush when Adam is about. The two leave for his home. 49 Dinah helps in the house. Adam loves having her there. Intimations of courtship happening unaware. 50 Lisbeth wants to talk to Adam about Dinah. Seth discourages her, but she gets the nerve and does it. Adam is thunderstruck and immediately enthusiastic: he will speak to Dinah. But first he sounds Seth. Would he be hurt? No. 51 Adam goes to the Hall Farm and states his case. Dinah admits her love but says she must do God's will. She asks for time, will go home meanwhile. 52

Harvest Supper at the Hall Farm: Bartle Massey and Mrs Poyser have it out on the merits of their respective sexes. Dinah has departed. 53 Adam has waited and now impatiently goes to meet Dinah. On the brow of a hill he speaks, she turns, she comes to him. They walk on together. 54 The wedding takes place a month later. Dinah is in Quaker grey. **Mary Burge** is bridesmaid. For once, Lisbeth Bede has nothing to complain about. 55

Epilogue: Nine years later, Dinah with her children Lisbeth and Addy, and their uncle Seth, go to meet Adam, who has met with the returned Arthur, recovering from fever. Hetty has died on her trip home from Australia. Dinah Bede no longer preaches: Methodist Conference orders.

Mrs Poyser's famous put-down of the stingy Squire is set forth complete in the *Topicon* at LC:Communication—*speaking truth to power*

Dinah Morris's stunning prayer for Hetty Sorrel is set forth in the *Topicon* at S:Prayer—*with another*

The Harvest Supper duel between Mrs Poyser and Bartle Massey is in the *Topicon* at LM:The Sexes—*verbal combat*

Contents

Title Role

—Adam singing: "Such a voice could only come from a broad chest, and the broad chest belonged to a large-boned muscular man nearly six feet high, with a back so flat and a head so well poised that when he drew himself up to take a more distant survey of his work, he had the air of a soldier standing at ease. The sleeve rolled up above the elbow showed an arm that was likely to win the prize for feats of strength, yet the long supple hand, with its broad finger-tips, looked ready for works of skill. In his tall stalwartness Adam Bede was a Saxon, and justified his name, but the jet-black hair, made the more noticeable by its contrast with the light paper cap, and the keen glance of the dark eyes that shone from under strongly marked, prominent, and mobile eyebrows, indicated a mixture of Celtic blood. The face was large and roughly hewn, and when in repose had no other beauty than such as belongs to an expression of good-humoured honest intelligence." 1

—working garb: " . . . the stalwart workman in paper cap, leather breeches, and dark-blue worsted stockings." 1

—brother's view: " 'Think how he's stood by us all when it's been none so easy—paying his savings to free me from going for a soldier, an' turnin' his earnin's into wood for father, when he's got plenty o' uses for his money, and many a young man like him 'ud ha' been married and settled before now. He'll never turn round and knock down his own work, and forsake them as it's been the labour of his life to stand by.' " 4

—a shudder: "Adam was not a man to be gratuitously superstitious; but he had the blood of the peasant in him as well as of the artisan . . . . Besides, he had that mental combination which is at once humble in the region of mystery and keen in the region of knowledge: it was the depth of his reverence quite as much as his hard common-sense, which gave him his disinclination to doctrinal religion . . . . If a new building had fallen down and he had been told that this was a divine judgment, he would have said, 'May be; but the bearing o' the roof and walls wasn't right, else it wouldn't ha' come down;' yet he believed in dreams and prognostics, and you see he shuddered at the idea of the stroke with the willow wand." 4

—another world? " 'Maybe there's a world about us as we can't see, but th' ear's quicker than the eye, and catches a sound from't now and then. Some people think they get a sight on't too, but they're mostly folks whose eyes are not much use to 'em at anything else. For my part, I think it's better to see when your perpendicular's true, than to see a ghost.' " 4

—appraised: " '[He] is like the patriarch **Joseph**, for his great skill and knowledge, and the kindness he shows to his brother and his parents.' " 8

—susceptible: "[**Hetty Sorrel**] knew that this Adam, who was often rather stern to other people, and not much given to run after the lasses, could be made to turn pale or red any day by a word or a look from her." 9

—repute: "[**Hetty**] couldn't help perceiving that Adam was 'something like' a man; always knew what to say about things, could tell her uncle how to prop the hovel, and had mended the churn in no time; knew, with only looking at it, the value of the chestnut tree that was blown down, and why the damp came in the walls, and what they must do to stop the rats; and wrote a beautiful hand that you could read off, and could do figures in his head—a degree of accomplishment totally unknown among the richest farmers of that country-side." 9

Adam Bede

—weary in bereavement: "His face, unwashed since yesterday, looked pallid and clammy; his hair was tossed shaggily about his forehead, and his closed eyes had the sunken look which follows upon watching and sorrow. His brow was knit, and his whole face had an expression of weariness and pain." 10

—another girl: "It was like dreaming of the sunshine, and awaking in the moonlight . . . her slim figure, her plain black gown, and her pale serene face, impressed him with all the force that belongs to a reality contrasted with a preoccupying fancy . . . .

" 'I don't wonder at thee for loving her, **Seth**. She's got a face like a lily. . . .

" 'She's made out of stuff with a finer grain than most o' the women, I can see that clear enough. But if she's better than they are in other things, I canna think she'll fall short of 'em in loving.' " 11

—a friend: "Next to his own brother **Seth**, Adam would have done more for **Arthur Donnithorne** than for any other young man in the world. There was hardly anything he would not rather have lost than the two-feet ruler which he always carried in his pocket; it was Arthur's present, bought with his pocket-money when he was a fair-haired lad of eleven . . . . " 16

" ' . . . it 'ud be a poor look-out if folks didn't remember what they did and said when they were lads. We should think no more about old friends than we do about new uns, then.' " 16

—respecting rank: "Adam, I confess, was very susceptible to the influence of rank, and quite ready to give an extra amount of respect to every one who had more advantages than himself, not being a philosopher, or a proletaire with democratic ideas, but simply a stout-limbed clever carpenter with a large fund of reverence in his nature, which inclined him to admit all established claims unless he saw very clear grounds for questioning them." 16

—integrity in carpentry: "He had no theories about setting the world to rights, but he saw there was a great deal of damage done by building with ill-seasoned timber—by ignorant men in fine clothes making plans for outhouses and workshops and the like, without knowing the bearings of things—by slovenly joiners' work, and by hasty contracts that could never be fulfilled without ruining somebody; and he resolved, for his part, to set his face against such doings." 16

" 'I wouldn't give a penny for a man as 'ud drive a nail in slack because he didn't get extra pay for it.' " 16

—on fighting: " 'I used to fight for fun; but I've never done that since I was the cause o' poor **Gil Tranter** being laid up for a fortnight. I'll never fight any man again, only when he behaves like a scoundrel. If you get hold of a chap that's got no shame nor conscience to stop him, you must try what you can do by bunging his eyes up.' " 16

—on religion: " 'But I've seen pretty clear ever since I was a young un, as religion's something else besides doctrines and notions. I look at it as if the doctrines was like finding names for your feelings, so as you can talk of 'em when you've never known 'em, just as a man may talk o' tools when he knows their names, though he's never so much as seen 'em, still less handled 'em. I've heard a deal o' doctrine i' my time, for I used to go after the dissenting preachers . . . but I thought I could pick a hole or two in their notions, and I got disputing wi' one o' the class-leaders . . . and harassed him so, first o' this side and then o' that, till at last he said, 'Young man, it's the devil making

use o' your pride and conceit as a weapon to war against the simplicity o' the truth.' I couldn't help laughing then, but . . . I began to see as all this weighing and sifting what this text means and that text means, and whether folks are saved all by God's grace, or whether there goes an ounce o' their own will to't, was no part o' real religion at all. You may talk o' these things for hours on end, and you'll only be all the more coxy and conceited for't.

" 'So I took to going nowhere but to church, and hearing nobody but **Mr Irwine**, for he said nothing but what was good, and what you'd be the wiser for remembering. And I found it better for my soul to be humble before the mysteries o' God's dealings, and not be making a clatter about what I could never understand. And they're poor foolish questions after all; for what have we got either inside or outside of us but what comes from God? If we've got a resolution to do right, He gave it us, I reckon, first or last; but I see plain enough we shall never do it without a resolution, and that's enough for me.' " ¶17

—*in church:* "And to Adam the church service was the best channel he could have found for his mingled regret, yearning, and resignation; its interchange of beseeching cries for help, with outbursts of faith and praise—its recurrent responses and the familiar rhythm of its collects, seemed to speak for him as no other form of worship could have done: as, to those early Christians who had worshipped from their childhood upward in catacombs, the torchlight and shadows must have seemed nearer the Divine presence than the heathenish daylight of the streets." 18

—*regret:* " 'It seems to me now, if I was to find father at home to-night, I should behave different; but there's no knowing—perhaps nothing 'ud be a lesson to us if it didn't come too late. It's well we should feel as life's a reckoning we can't make twice over; there's no real making amends in this world, any more nor you can mend a wrong subtraction by doing your addition right." 18

—*looking ahead:* "Like all strong natures, Adam had confidence in his ability to achieve something in the future; he felt sure he should some day, if he lived, be able to maintain a family, and make a good broad path for himself; but he had too cool a head not to estimate to the full the obstacles that were to be overcome." 19

—*his puzzling choice:* " . . . it was impossible to come to any but fluctuating conclusions about **Hetty**'s feelings. She was like a kitten, and had the same distractingly pretty looks, that meant nothing, for everybody that came near her." 19

—*conviction to a fault:* "Whenever Adam was strongly convinced of any proposition, it took the form of a principle in his mind: it was knowledge to be acted on, as much as the knowledge that damp will cause rust. Perhaps here lay the secret of the hardness he had accused himself of: he had too little fellow-feeling with the weakness that errs in spite of foreseen consequences. Without this fellow-feeling, how are we to get enough patience and charity towards our stumbling, falling companions in the long and changeful journey? And there is but one way in which a strong determined soul can learn it—by getting his heart-strings bound round the weak and erring, so that he must share not only the outward consequences of their error, but their inward suffering." 19

—*a snap-shot:* "Look at this broad-shouldered man with the bare muscular arms, and the thick firm black hair tossed about like trodden meadow-grass whenever he takes off his paper cap, and with the strong barytone voice bursting every now and then into loud and solemn psalm-tunes, as if seeking some outlet for superfluous strength, yet presently checking himself, apparently crossed by some thought which jars with the singing. Perhaps, if you had not been already in the secret, you might not have guessed what sad memories, what warm affection, what tender fluttering hopes, had their home in this athletic body with the broken finger-nails—in this rough man, who knew no better lyrics than he could find in the Old and New Version and an occasional hymn; who knew the smallest possible amount of profane history; and for whom the motion and shape of the earth, the course of the sun, and the changes of the seasons, lay in the region of mystery just made visible by fragmentary knowledge." 19

—self-education: "It had cost Adam a great deal of trouble, and work in over-hours, to know what he knew over and above the secrets of his handicraft, and that acquaintance with mechanics and figures, and the nature of the materials he worked with, which was made easy to him by inborn inherited faculty—to get the mastery of his pen, and write a plain hand, to spell without any other mistakes than must in fairness be attributed to the unreasonable character of orthography rather than to any deficiency in the speller, and, moreover, to learn his musical notes and part-singing, Besides all this, he had read his Bible, including the apocryphal books; 'Poor Richard's Almanac,' **Taylor**'s 'Holy Living and Dying,' 'The Pilgrim's Progress,' with **Bunyan**'s Life and 'Holy War,' a great deal of **Bailey**'s Dictionary, 'Valentine and Orson,' and part of a 'History of Babylon' which **Bartle Massey** had lent him." 19

—an unusual man: "Adam, you perceive, was by no means a marvellous man, nor, properly speaking, a genius, yet I will not pretend that his was an ordinary character among workmen; and it would not be at all a safe conclusion that the next best man you may happen to see with a basket of tools over his shoulder and a paper cap on his head has the strong conscience and the strong sense, the blended susceptibility and self-command of our friend Adam. He was not an average man." 19

—misunderstanding: "Like many another man, he thought the signs of love for another were signs of love towards himself." 20

—a flaw: "**Hetty**'s love of finery was just the thing that would most provoke his mother, and he himself disliked it as much as it was possible for him to dislike anything that belonged to her." 20

—plain talk: " 'Well, well, my boy [said **Bartle Massey**], if good-luck knocks at your door, don't you put your head out at window and tell it to be gone about its business, that's all. You must learn to deal with odd and even in life, as well as in figures . . . you're overhasty and proud, and apt to set your teeth against folks that don't square to your notions.' " 21

—in love: " 'God bless her!' he said inwardly; 'I'd make her life a happy un, if a strong arm to work for her, and a heart to love her, could do it.'

"And then there stole over him delicious thoughts of coming home from work, and drawing **Hetty** to his side, and feeling her cheek softly pressed against his, till he forgot where he was, and the music and the tread of feet might have been the falling of rain and the roaring of the wind, for what he knew." 26

—his need: "A nature like Adam's, with a great need of love and reverence in it, depends for so much of its happiness on what it can believe

and feel about others! And he had no ideal world of dead heroes; he knew little of the life of men in the past; he must find the beings to whom he could cling with loving admiration among those who came within speech of him." 27

—his delight: "Adam delighted in a fine tree of all things: as the fisherman's sight is keenest on the sea, so Adam's perceptions were more at home with trees than with other objects." 27

—revelation: "If he had moved a muscle, he must inevitably have sprung upon **Arthur** like a tiger; and in the conflicting emotions that filled those long moments, he had told himself that he would not give loose [*sic*] to passion, he would only speak the right thing. He stood as if petrified by an unseen force, but the force was his own strong will." 27

"And I say it again, you're acting the part of a selfish, light-minded scoundrel, though it cuts me to th' heart to say so, and I'd rather ha' lost my right hand.' " 27

—blinded by pain: "Adam at this moment could only feel that he had been robbed of **Hetty**—robbed treacherously by the man in whom he had trusted; and he stood close in front of **Arthur**, with fierce eyes glaring at him, with pale lips and clenched hands, the hard tones in which he had hitherto been constraining himself to express no more than a just indignation, giving way to a deep agitated voice that seemed to shake him as he spoke.

" 'No, it'll not be soon forgot, as you've come in between her and me, when she might ha' loved me—it'll not soon be forgot, as you've robbed me o' my happiness, while I thought you was my best friend, and a noble-minded man, as I was proud to work for. And you've been kissing her, and meaning nothing, have you? And I never kissed her i' my life, but I'd ha' worked hard for years for the right to kiss her. And you make light of it. You think little o' doing what may damage other folks so as you get your bit o' trifling, as means nothing. I throw back your favours, for you're not the man I took you for. I'll never count you my friend any more. I'd rather you'd act as my enemy, and fight me where I stand—it's all th' amends you can make me.' " 27

—speaking hard truth: " 'Nay, sir, things don't lie level between **Hetty** and you. You're acting with your eyes open, whatever you may do; but how do you know what's been in her mind? She's all but a child—as any man with a conscience in him ought to feel bound to take care on. And whatever you may think, I know you've disturbed her mind. I know she's been fixing her heart on you; for there's a many things clear to me now as I didn't understand before. But you seem to make light o' what *she* may feel—you don't think o' that.' " 28

—rationalizing: "How busy his thoughts were . . . in devising pitying excuses for her folly; in referring all her weakness to the sweet lovingness of her nature; in blaming **Arthur**, with less and less inclination to admit that his conduct might be extenuated too! . . . Adam was a clear-sighted, fair-minded man—a fine fellow, indeed, morally as well as physically. But if **Aristides the Just** was ever in love and jealous, he was at that moment not perfectly mag-nanimous." 30

—resigned: " 'I'm not th' only man that's got to do without much happiness i' this life. There's many a good bit o' work done with a sad heart. It's God's will, and that's enough for us.' " 30

—his brother: " . . . he was inclined to interchange a word or two of brotherly affection and confidence with **Seth**. That was a rare impulse in him, much as the brothers loved each other. They hardly ever spoke of

personal matters, or uttered more than an allusion to their family troubles. Adam was by nature reserved in all matters of feeling, and Seth felt a certain timidity towards his more practical brother." 30

—yearning after his love: "Possibly you think that Adam was not at all sagacious in his interpretations, and that it was altogether extremely unbecoming in a sensible man to behave as he did—falling in love with a girl who really had nothing more than her beauty to recommend her, attributing imaginary virtues to her, and even condescending to cleave to her after she had fallen in love with another man, waiting for her kind looks as a patient trembling dog waits for his master's eye to be turned upon him . . . For my part, however, I respect him none the less: nay, I think the deep love he had for that sweet, rounded, blossom-like, dark-eyed Hetty, of whose inward self he was really very ignorant, came out of the very strength of his nature, and not out of any inconsistent weakness." 33

—imagining: "He only knew that the sight and memory of her moved him deeply, touching the spring of all love and tenderness, all faith and courage within him. How could he imagine narrowness, selfishness, hardness in her? He created the mind he believed in out of his own, which was large, unselfish, tender." 33

—thankful: ""Every now and then there was a rush of more intense feeling . . . a wondering thankfulness that all this happiness was given to him—that this life of ours had such sweetness in it. For our friend Adam had a devout mind, though he was perhaps rather impatient of devout words; and his tenderness lay very close to his reverence, so that the one could hardly be stirred without the other. But after feeling had welled up and poured itself out in this way, busy thought would come back with the greater vigour; and this morning it was intent on schemes by which the roads might be improved that were so imperfect all through the country . . . . " 38

—bereft: "[**Seth**] stood still in the doorway, smitten with a sudden shock at the sight of Adam seated listlessly on the bench, pale, unwashed, with sunken blank eyes, almost like a drunkard in the morning . . . .

"Adam was unable to speak: the strong man, accustomed to suppress the signs of sorrow, had felt his heart swell like a child's at this first approach of sympathy. He fell on Seth's neck and sobbed.

"Seth was prepared for the worst now, for, even in his recollections of their boyhood, Adam had never sobbed before." 38

—stricken: ". . . the sight of Adam . . . with that look of sudden age which sometimes comes over a young face in moments of terrible emotion—the hard bloodless look of the skin, the deep lines about the quivering mouth, the furrows in the brow—the sight of this strong firm man shattered by the invisible stroke of sorrow, moved [**Mr Irwine**] so deeply that speech was not easy. Adam stood motionless, with his eyes vacantly fixed in this way for a minute or two: in that short space he was living through all his love again." 39

—on watch: "You would hardly have known it was Adam without being told. His face has got thinner this last week: he has the sunken eyes, the neglected beard of a man just risen from a sick-bed. His heavy black hair hangs over his forehead, and there is no active impulse in him which inclines him to push it off, that he may be more awake to what is around him." 41

—*powerless:* "This brave active man, who would have hastened towards any danger or toil to rescue **Hetty** from an apprehended wrong or misfortune, felt himself powerless to contemplate irremediable evil and suffering." 42

—*breakthrough:* " 'Adam . . . I'm very sorry . . . I behaved very wrong to you . . . will you forgive me . . . before I die?'

"Adam answered with a half-sob: 'Yes, I forgive thee, **Hetty**: I forgave thee long ago.'

"It had seemed to Adam as if his brain would burst with the anguish of meeting Hetty's eyes in the first moments; but the sound of her voice uttering these penitent words, touched a chord which had been less strained: there was a sense of relief from what was becoming unbearable, and the rare tears came—they had never come before, since he had hung on **Seth**'s neck in the beginning of his sorrow." 46

—*reminiscent visit:* " . . . if he had had the basket of tools over his shoulder, he might have been taken, with his paled wasted face, for the spectre of the Adam Bede who entered the Grove on that August evening eight months ago. But he had no basket of tools, and he was not walking with the old erectness, looking keenly round him; his hands were thrust in his side pockets, and his eyes rested chiefly on the ground." 48

—*brothers together:* "Adam, with knit brows, shaggy hair, and dark vigorous colour, absorbed in his 'figureing;' **Seth**, with large rugged features, the close copy of his brother's, but with thin wavy brown hair and blue dreamy eyes, as often as not looking vaguely out of the window instead of at his book . . . . " 50

—*still in pain:* "For Adam, though you see him quite master of himself, working hard and delighting in his work after his inborn inalienable nature, had not outlived his sorrow—had not felt it slip from him as a temporary burthen, and leave him the same man again . . . there was still a great remnant of pain, which he felt would subsist as long as *her* pain was not a memory, but an existing thing, which he must think of as renewed with the light of every new morning." 50

—*regeneration unaware:* "He conceived no picture of the future but one made up of hard-working days such as he lived through, with growing contentment and intensity of interest, every fresh week: love, he thought, could never be anything to him but a living memory—a limb lopped off, but not gone from consciousness. He did not know that the power of loving was all the while gaining new force within him; that the new sensibilities bought by a deep experience were so many new fibres by which it was possible, nay, necessary to him, that his nature should intertwine with another." 50

—*a new possibility:* " . . . he had only said the simplest truth in telling **Dinah** that he put her above all other friends in the world. Could anything be more natural? For in the darkest moments of memory the thought of her always came as the first ray of returning comfort: the early days of gloom at the Hall Farm had been gradually turned into soft moonlight by her presence; and in the cottage, too—for she had come at every spare moment to soothe and cheer poor **Lisbeth** . . . . He had become used to watching her light quiet movements, her pretty loving ways to the children . . . to listen for her voice as for a recurrent music; to think everything she said and did was just right, and could not have been better." 50

—*revelation:* " ' . . . she's as fond o' thee as e'er I war o' **Thias**, poor fellow.'

"The blood rushed to Adam's face, and for a few moments he was not quite conscious where he was: his mother and the kitchen had vanished for him, and he saw nothing but **Dinah**'s face turned up towards him. It seemed as if there were a resurrection of his dead joy." 51

"Adam had thrust his hands in his pockets, and was looking down at the book on the table, without seeing any of the letters. He was trembling like a gold-seeker, who sees the strong promise of gold, but sees in the same moment a sickening vision of disappointment . . . now the suggestion had been made to him, he remembered so many things, very slight things, like the stirring of the water by an imperceptible breeze, which seemed to him some confirmation of his mother's words." 51

—seeing the light: " . . . he was amazed at the way in which this new thought of **Dinah**'s love had taken possession of him, with an overmastering power that made all other feelings give way before the impetuous desire to know that the thought was true. Strange, that till that moment the possibility of their ever being lovers had never crossed his mind, and yet now, all his longing suddenly went out towards that possibility; he had no more doubt or hesitation as to his own wishes than the bird that flies towards the opening through which the daylight gleams and the breath of heaven enters." 51

"Her love was so like that calm sunshine that they seemed to make one presence to him, and he believed in them both alike. And Dinah was so bound up with the sad memories of his first passion, that he was not forsaking them, but rather giving them a new sacredness by loving her. Nay, his love for her had grown out of that past: it was the noon of that morning." 51

—avowal: see Topicon LM:Love*—avowal and response*

—making his argument: " 'I don't believe your loving me could shut up your heart; it's only adding to what you've been before, not taking away from it; for it seems to me it's the same with love and happiness as with sorrow—the more we know of it the better we can feel what other people's lives are or might be, and so we shall only be more tender to 'em, and wishful to help 'em. The more knowledge a man has the better he'll do's work; and feeling's a sort o' knowledge.' " 52

—insight: " 'I should never ha' come to know that her love 'ud be the greatest o' blessings to me, if what I counted a blessing hadn't been wrenched and torn away from me, and left me with a greater need, so as I could crave and hunger for a greater and a better comfort.' " 53

—soliloquy: "Tender and deep as his love for **Hetty** had been—so deep that the roots of it would never be torn away—his love for **Dinah** was better and more precious to him; for it was the outgrowth of that fuller life which had come to him from his acquaintance with deep sorrow. 'It's like as if it was a new strength to me,' he said to himself, 'to love her, and know as she loves me. I shall look t' her to help me to see things right. For she's better than I am— there's less o' self in her, and pride. And it's a feeling as gives you a sort o' liberty, as if you could walk more fearless, when you've more trust in another than y' have in yourself. I've always been thinking I knew better than them as belonged to me, and that's a poor sort o' life, when you can't look to them nearest to you t' help you with a bit better thought than what you've got inside you a'ready.' " 54

—*married:* "Adam, as he pressed her arm to his side, walked with his old erectness and his head thrown rather backward as if to face all the world better; but it was not because he was particularly proud this morning, as is the wont of bridegrooms, for his happiness was of a kind that had little reference to men's opinion of it. There was a tinge of sadness in his deep joy: **Dinah** knew it, and did not feel aggrieved." 55

Other Principals

Captain Arthur Donnithorne, "known in Hayslope, variously, as 'the young squire,' 'the heir,' and 'the captain.' He was only a captain in the Loamshire Militia; but to the Hayslope tenants he was more intensely a captain than all the young gentlemen of the same rank in His Majesty's regulars—he outshone them as the planet Jupiter outshines the Milky Way." 5

—*characteristics:* "If you want to know more particularly how he looked, call to your remembrance some tawny-whiskered, brown-locked, clear-complexioned young Englishman whom you have met with in a foreign town, and been proud of as a fellow-countryman—well-washed, high-bred, white-handed, yet looking as if he could deliver well from the left shoulder, and floor his man: I will not be so much of a tailor as to trouble your imagination with the difference of costume, and insist on the striped waistcoat, long-tailed coat, and low-top boots." 5

—*self-esteem:* "His own approbation was necessary to him, and it was not an approbation to be enjoyed quite gratuitously; it must be won by a fair amount of merit. He had never yet forfeited that approbation, and he had considerable reliance on his own virtues. No young man could confess his faults more candidly; candour was one of his favourite virtues, and how can a man's candour be seen in all its lustre unless he has a few failings to talk of? But he had an agreeable confidence that his faults were all of a generous kind— impetuous, warm-blooded, leonine, never crawling, crafty, reptilian. It was not possible for Arthur Donnithorne to do anything mean, dastardly, or cruel. 'No! I'm a devil of a fellow for getting myself into a hobble, but I always take care the load shall fall on my own shoulders.' Unhappily there is no inherent poetical justice in hobbles, and they will sometimes obstinately refuse to inflict their worst consequences on the prime offender, in spite of his loudly-expressed wish. It was entirely owing to this deficiency in the scheme of things that Arthur had ever brought any one into trouble besides himself." 12

—*good-natured:* "He was nothing, if not good-natured; and all his pictures of the future, when he should come into the estate, were made up of a prosperous, contented tenantry, adoring their landlord, who would be the model of an English gentleman—mansion in first-rate order, all elegance and high taste—jolly housekeeping—finest stud in Loamshire—purse open to all public objects—in short, everything as different as possible from what was now associated with the name of Donnithorne." 12

—*so far, so good:* "Whether he would have self-mastery enough to be always as harmless and purely beneficent as his good-nature led him to desire, was a question that no one had yet decided against him: he was but twenty-one, you remember; and we don't inquire too closely into character in the case of a handsome generous young fellow, who will have property enough to support numerous peccadilloes—who, if he should unfortunately break a man's legs in his rash driving, will be able to pension him handsomely; or if he should happen to spoil a woman's existence for her, will make it up to her with expensive *bon-bons,* packed up and directed by his own hand." 12

"One thing is clear: Nature has taken care that he shall never go far astray with perfect comfort and satisfaction in himself; he will never get beyond that borderland of sin, where he will be perpetually harassed by assaults from the other side of the boundary. He will never be a courtier of Vice, and wear her orders in his buttonhole." 12

—infatuated: "The desire to see **Hetty** had rushed back like an ill-stemmed current; he was amazed himself at the force with which this trivial fancy seemed to grasp him: he was even rather tremulous as he brushed his hair . . . . " 12

—first moments with his love: "It may seem a contradiction, but Arthur gathered a certain carelessness and confidence from his timidity; it was an entirely different state of mind from what he had expected in such a meeting with **Hetty**; and full as he was of vague feeling, there was room, in those moments of silence, for the thought that his previous debates and scruples were needless." 12

"Arthur had laid his hand on the soft arm that was nearest to him, and was stooping towards Hetty with a look of coaxing entreaty. Hetty lifted her long dewy lashes, and met the eyes that were bent towards her with a sweet, timid, beseeching look. What a space of time those three moments were, while their eyes met and his arms touched her! . . . While Arthur gazed into Hetty's dark beseeching eyes, it made no difference to him what sort of English she spoke; and even if hoops and powder had been in fashion, he would very likely not have been sensible just then that Hetty wanted those signs of high breeding." 12

—reflecting: "He was getting in love with **Hetty**—that was quite plain. He was ready to pitch everything else—no matter where—for the sake of surrendering himself to this delicious feeling which had just disclosed itself. It was no use blinking the fact now—they would get too fond of each other, if he went on taking notice of her—and what would come of it? He should have to go away in a few weeks, and the poor little thing would be miserable. He *must not* see her alone again; he must keep out of her way." 12

—a rationale: "He wondered if the dear little thing were thinking of him too—twenty to one she was. How beautiful her eyes were with the tear on their lashes! He would like to satisfy his soul for a day with looking at them, and he *must* see her again—he must see her simply to remove any false impression from her mind about his manner to her just now. He would behave in a quiet, kind way to her—just to prevent her from going home with her head full of wrong fancies. Yes, that would be the best thing to do, after all." 12

—first kiss: "Hetty turned her head towards him, whispered, 'I thought you wouldn't come,' and slowly got courage to lift her eyes to him. The look was too much: he must have had eyes of Egyptian granite not to look too lovingly in return . . . .

"His arm is stealing round the waist again, it is tightening its clasp; he is bending his face nearer and nearer to the round cheek, his lips are meeting those pouting child-lips, and for a long moment time has vanished. He may be a shepherd in Arcadia for aught he knows, he may be the first youth kissing the first maiden, he may be *Eros* himself, sipping the lips of *Psyche*—it is all one." 13

—cold feet: "He was of an impressionable nature, and lived a great deal in other people's opinions and feelings concerning himself; and the mere fact that he was in the presence of an intimate friend, who had not the slightest notion that he had had any such serious internal struggle as he came to confide, rather shook his own belief in the seriousness of the struggle. It was not, after all, a thing to make a fuss about; and what could **Irwine** do for him that he could not do for himself?" 16

—hearing his love praised: " . . . other men's opinion, you know, was like a native climate to Arthur's feelings: it was the air on which they thrived the best, and grew strong. Yes! she *was* enough to turn any man's head: any man in his place would have done and felt the same. And to give her up after all, as he was determined to do, would be an act that he should always look back upon with pride." 25

—in uniform: "Arthur had put on his uniform to please the tenants, he said, who thought as much of his militia dignity as if it had been an elevation to the premiership. He had not the least objection to gratify them in that way: his uniform was very advantageous to his figure." 26

—her look: "That pale look came upon Arthur like the beginning of a dull pain, which clung to him, though he must dance and smile and joke all the same . . . . That look of **Hetty**'s oppressed Arthur with a dread which yet had something of a terrible unconfessed delight in it, that she loved him too well. There was hard task before him, for at that moment he felt he would have given up three years of his youth for the happiness of abandoning himself without remorse to his passion for Hetty." 26

—ordered to stop: "Confound the fellow! Arthur felt his temper rising. A patronising disposition always has its meaner side, and in the confusion of his irritation and alarm there entered the feeling that a man to whom he had shown so much favour as to **Adam**, was not in a position to criticise his conduct. And yet he was dominated, as one who feels himself in the wrong always is, by the man whose good opinion he cares for. In spite of pride and temper, there was as much depreciation as anger in his voice when he [spoke]." 27

—a revelation: "Arthur's lips were now as pale as **Adam**'s; his heart was beating violently. The discovery that Adam loved **Hetty**, was a shock which made him for the moment see himself in the light of Adam's indignation, and regard Adam's suffering as not merely a consequence, but an element of his error. The words of hatred and contempt—the first he had ever heard in his life—seemed like scorching missiles that were making ineffaceable scars on him. All screening self-excuse, which rarely falls quite away while others respect us, forsook him for an instant, and he stood face to face with the first great irrevocable evil he had ever committed. He was only twenty-one—and three months ago—nay, much later—he had thought proudly that no man should ever be able to reproach him justly." 27

—fighting: "The delicate-handed gentleman was a match for the workman in everything but strength, and Arthur's skill in parrying enabled him to protract the struggle for some long moments. But between unarmed men, the battle is to the strong, where the strong is no blunderer . . . Arthur fell . . . . " 27

—embarrassing secret: "Arthur was in the wretched position of an open, generous man, who has committed an error which makes deception seem a necessity. The native impulse to give truth in return for truth, to meet trust

with frank confession, must be suppressed, and duty was become a question of tactics. His deed was reacting upon him—was already governing him tyrannously, and forcing him into a course that jarred with his habitual feelings . . . he had to be judicious, and not truthful." 28

—*naturally loving:* "Arthur's as you know, was a loving nature. Deeds of kindness were as easy to him as a bad habit: they were the common issue of his weaknesses and good qualities, of his egoism and his sympathy. He didn't like to witness pain, and he liked to have grateful eyes beaming on him as the giver of pleasure." 29

—*telling incident:* "When he was a lad of seven, he one day kicked down an old gardener's pitcher of broth, from no motive but a kicking impulse, not reflecting that it was the old man's dinner; but on learning that sad fact, he took his favourite pencil-case and a silver-hafted knife out of his pocket and offered them as compensation. He had been the same Arthur ever since, trying to make all offences forgotten in benefits." 29

—*awkward fact:* "[**Adam**] stood like an immovable obstacle against which no pressure could avail; an embodiment of what Arthur most shrank from believing in—the irrevocableness of his own wrong-doing." 29

—*twice-awkward history:* " . . . when he had first talked to [**Hetty**] about his going away, she had asked him tremblingly to let her go with him and be married . . . . He had said no word with the purpose of deceiving her, her vision was all spun by her own childish fancy; but he was obliged to confess to himself that it was spun half out of his own actions . . . . The temporary sadness for Hetty was the worst consequence: he resolutely turned away his eyes from any bad consequence that was not demonstrably inevitable." 29

—*guilt:* "Self-accusation was too painful to him—he could not face it. He must persuade himself that he had not been very much to blame; he began even to pity himself for the necessity he was under of deceiving Adam: it was a course so opposed to the honesty of his own nature. But then, it was the only right thing to do." 29

—*fatuous:* "Arthur told himself, he did not deserve that things should turn out badly—he had never meant beforehand to do anything his conscience disapproved—he had been led on by circumstances. There was a sort of implicit confidence in him that he was really such a good fellow at bottom, Providence would not treat him harshly." 29

—*disaster to come:* " ' . . . he will suffer, long and bitterly [said **Mr Irwine**]. He has a heart and a conscience: I can't be entirely deceived in his character. I am convinced—I am sure he didn't fall under temptation without a struggle. He may be weak, but he is not callous, not coldly selfish. I am persuaded that this will be a shock of which he will feel the effects all his life.' " 41

—*home again, still susceptible:* "Sweet—sweet little **Hetty**! The little puss hadn't cared for him half as much as he cared for her; for he was a great fool about her still—was almost afraid of seeing her—indeed, had not cared much to look at any other woman since he parted from her. That little figure coming towards him in the grove, those dark-fringed childish eyes, the lovely lips put up to kiss him—that picture had got no fainter with the lapse of months. And she would look just the same. It was impossible to think how he could meet her: he should certainly tremble." 44

—*last carefree moment:* "The level rays of the low afternoon sun entered directly at the window, and as Arthur seated himself in his velvet chair with their pleasant warmth upon him, he was conscious of that quiet wellbeing which perhaps you and I have felt on a sunny afternoon, when, in our brightest youth and health, life has opened on a new vista for us, and long to-morrows of activity have stretched before us like a lovely plain, which there was no need for hurrying to look at, because it was all our own." 44

—a new beginning: " '**Hetty Sorrel** is in prison, and will be tried on Friday for the crime of child-murder' . . .

"Arthur read no more. He started up from his chair, and stood for a single minute with a sense of violent convulsion in his whole frame, as if the life were going out of him with horrible throbs." 44

—at the last minute: "The horse is hot and distressed, but answers to the desperate spurring; the rider looks as if his eyes were glazed by madness, and he saw nothing but what was unseen by others. See, he has something in his hand—he is holding it up as if it were a signal." 47

—explanation: " '**Adam**,' Arthur said, impelled to full confession now, 'it would never have happened, if I'd known you loved her. That would have helped to save me from it. And I *did* struggle: I never meant to injure her. I deceived you afterwards—and that led on to worse; but I thought it was forced upon me. I thought it was the best thing I could do. And in that letter, I told her to let me know if she were in any trouble: don't think I would not have done everything I could. But I was all wrong from the very first, and horrible wrong has come of it . . . I'd give my life if I could undo it.' " 48

Dinah Morris. "While she was near **Seth**'s tall figure she looked short, but when she had mounted the cart, and was away from all comparison, she seemed above the middle height of woman, though in reality she did not exceed it—an effect which was due to the slimness of her figure, and the simple line of her black stuff dress . . . . [She] walked as simply as if she were going to market, and seemed as unconscious of her outward appearance as a little boy: there was no blush, no tremulousness, which said, 'I know you think me a pretty woman, too young to preach'; no casting up or down of the eyelids, no compression of the lips, no attitude of the arms, that said, 'But you must think of me as a saint.'

"She held no book in her ungloved hands, but let them hang down lightly crossed before her, as she stood and turned her grey eyes on the people. There was no keenness in the eyes; they seemed rather to be shedding love than making observations; they had the liquid look which tells that the mind is full of what it has to give out, rather than impressed by external objects. She stood with her left hand towards the descending sun; and leafy boughs screened her from its rays; but in this sober light the delicate colouring of her face seemed to gather a calm vividness, like flowers at evening.

"It was a small oval face, of a uniform transparent whiteness, with an egg-like line of cheek and chin, a full but firm mouth, a delicate nostril, and a low perpendicular brow, surmounted by a rising arch of parting, between smooth locks of pale reddish hair. The hair was drawn straight back behind the ears, and covered, except for an inch or two above the brow, by a net quaker cap. The eyebrows, of the same colour as the hair, were perfectly horizontal and firmly pencilled; the eyelashes, though no darker, were long and abundant, nothing was left blurred or unfinished. It was one of those faces that make one think of white flowers with light touches of colour on their pure petals. The eyes had no peculiar beauty; beyond that of expression; they looked so simple, so candid, so gravely loving, that no accusing scowl, no light sneer, could help melting away before their glance." ¶2

—*transfixing:* "Hitherto the **traveller** had been chained to the spot against his will by the charm of Dinah's mellow treble tones, which had a variety of modulation like that of a fine instrument touched with the unconscious skill of musical instinct. The simple things she said seemed like novelties, as a melody strikes us with a new feeling when we hear it sung by the pure voice of a boyish chorister; the quiet depth of conviction with which she spoke seemed in itself an evidence for the truth of her message. He saw that she had thoroughly arrested her hearers." 2

—*her power:* " . . . she came to the words, 'Lost!—Sinners!' when there was a great change in her voice and manner. She had made a long pause before the exclamation, and the pause seemed to be filled by agitating thoughts that showed themselves in her features. Her pale face became paler; the circles under her eyes deepened, as they do when tears half gather without falling; and the mild loving eyes took an expression of appalled pity, as if she had suddenly discerned a destroying angel hovering over the heads of the people. Her voice became deep and muffled, but there was still no gesture. Nothing could be less like the ordinary type of the Ranter than Dinah. She was not preaching as she heard others preach, but speaking directly from her own emotions, and under the inspiration of her own simple faith.

"But now she had entered into a new current of feeling. Her manner became less calm, her utterance more rapid and agitated, as she tried to bring home to the people their guilt, their wilful darkness, their state of disobedience to God—as she dwelt on the hatefulness of sin, the Divine holiness, and the sufferings of the Saviour by which a way had been opened for their salvation. At last it seemed as if, in her yearning desire to reclaim the lost sheep, she could not be satisfied by addressing her hearers as a body. She appealed first to one and then to another, beseeching them with tears to turn to God while there was yet time; painting to them the desolation of their souls, lost in sin, feeding on the husks of this miserable world, far away from God their Father; and then the love of the Saviour, who was waiting and watching for their return." 2

—*demeanour:* "It was an expression of unconscious placid gravity—of absorption in thoughts that had no connection with the present moment or with her own personality: an expression that is most of all discouraging to a lover. Her very walk was discouraging: it had that quiet elasticity that asks for no support." 3

—*in the moment:* " 'It is good to live only a moment at a time, as I've read in one of **Mr Wesley**'s books. It isn't for you and me to lay plans; we've nothing to do but to obey and to trust.' " 3

—*encountered:* " 'She looked like **St Catherine** in a quaker dress. It's a type of face one rarely sees among our common people.' " 5

—*admonished:* " 'But what's the use o' talking, if you wonna be persuaded, and settle down like any other woman in her senses, istead o' wearing yourself out, with walking and preaching, and giving away every penny you get, so as you've nothing saved against sickness; and all the things you've got i' the world, I verily believe, 'ud go into a bundle no bigger nor a double cheese. And all because you've got notions i' your head about religion more nor what's i' the Catechism and the Prayer-book.' " 6

—her story: " 'I'd been used from the time I was sixteen to talk to the little children and teach them, and sometimes I had had my heart enlarged to speak in class, and was much drawn out in prayer with the sick. But I had felt no call to preach; for when I'm not greatly wrought upon, I'm too much given to sit still and keep by myself: it seems as if I could sit silent all day long with the thought of God overflowing my soul—as the pebbles lie bathed in the Willow Brook. For thoughts are so great—aren't they, sir? They seem to lie upon us like a deep flood; and it's my besetment to forget where I am and everything about me, and lose myself in thoughts that I could give no account of, for I could neither make a beginning nor ending of them in words. That was my way as long as I can remember; but sometimes it seemed as if speech came to me without any will of my own, and words were given to me that came out as the tears come, because our hearts are full and we can't help it. And those were always times of great blessing, though I had never thought it could be so with me before a congregation of people. But, sir, we are led on, like the little children, by a way that we know not. I was called to preach quite suddenly, and since then I have never been left in doubt about the work that was laid upon me.' " 8

—called: " ' . . . as I passed along by the cottages and saw the aged trembling women at the doors, and the hard looks of the men, who seemed to have their eyes no more filled with the sight of the Sabbath morning than if they had been dumb oxen that never looked up to the sky, I felt a great movement in my soul, and I trembled as if I was shaken by a strong spirit entering into my weak body. And I went to where the little flock of people was gathered together, and stepped on the low wall that was built against the green hill-side, and I spoke the words that were given to me abundantly. And they all came round me out of all the cottages, and many wept over their sins and have since been joined to the Lord. That was the beginning of my preaching, sir, and I've preached ever since.'

"Dinah had let her work fall during this narrative, which she uttered in her usual simple way, but with that sincere, articulate, thrilling treble, by which she always mastered her audience." 8

—and her beauty? "I've no room for such feelings, and I don't believe the people ever take notice about that. I think, sir, when God makes his presence felt through us, we are like the burning bush: **Moses** never took any heed what sort of bush it was—he only saw the brightness of the Lord.' " 8

—the comfortable; the afflicted: " . . . in these villages where the people lead a quiet life among the green pastures and the still waters, tilling the ground and tending the cattle, there's a strange deadness to the Word, as different as can be from the great towns, like Leeds, where I once went to visit a holy woman who preaches there. It's wonderful how rich is the harvest of souls up those high-walled streets, where you seem to walk as in a prison-yard, and the ear is deafened with the sounds of worldly toil. I think maybe it is because the promise is sweeter when this life is so dark and weary, and the soul gets more hungry when the body is ill at ease.' " 8

—earliest years: " 'No, I never knew a father or mother; my aunt brought me up from a baby. She had no children, for she was never married, and she brought me up as tenderly as if I'd been her own child.' " 10

Dinah Morris

—*calming influence:* "This was what Dinah had been trying to bring about, through all her still sympathy and absence from exhortation. From her girlhood upwards she had had experience among the sick and the mourning, among minds hardened and shrivelled through poverty and ignorance, and had gained the subtlest perception of the mode in which they could best be touched, and softened into willingness to receive words of spiritual consolation or warning. As Dinah expressed it, 'She was never left to herself, but it was always given her when to keep silence and when to speak.' " 10

—*another man:* "Dinah, for the first time in her life, felt a painful self-consciousness; there was something in the dark penetrating glance of this strong man so different from the mildness and timidity of his brother **Seth**. A faint blush came, which deepened as she wondered at it." 11

—*adversity congenial:* 'O, I love the Stonyshire side,' said Dinah; 'I shouldn't like to set my face towards the countries where they're rich in corn and cattle, and the ground so level and easy to tread; and to turn my back on the hills where the poor people have to live such a hard life, and the men spend their days in the mines away from the sunlight. It's very blessed on a bleak cold day, when the sky is hanging dark over the hill, to feel the love of God in one's soul, and carry it to the lonely, bare, stone houses, where there's nothing else to give comfort.' " 11

—*open glance:* "which told that her heart lived in no cherished secrets of its own, but in feelings which it longed to share with all the world." 14

—*centering:* "She closed her eyes, that she might feel more intensely the presence of a Love and Sympathy deeper and more tender than was breathed from the earth and sky. That was often Dinah's mode of praying in solitude. Simply to close her eyes, and to feel herself enclosed by the Divine Presence: then gradually her fears, her yearning anxieties for others, melted away like ice-crystals in a warm ocean. She had sat in this way perfectly still, with her hands crossed on her lap, and the pale light resting on her calm face, for at least ten minutes . . . . " 15

—*her neighbour:* "She saw too clearly the absence of any warm, self-devoting love in **Hetty**'s nature, to regard the coldness of her behaviour towards **Adam** as any indication that he was not the man she would like to have for a husband. And this blank in Hetty's nature, instead of exciting Dinah's dislike, only touched her with a deeper pity: the lovely face and form affected her as beauty always affects a pure and tender mind, free from selfish jealousies: it was an excellent divine gift, that gave a deeper pathos to the need, the sin, the sorrow with which it was mingled, as the canker in a lily-white bud is more grievous to behold than in a common pot-herb." 15

—*sympathetic imagination:* " . . . she saw the poor thing [**Hetty**] struggling torn and bleeding, looking with tears for rescue and finding none. It was in this way that Dinah's imagination and sympathy acted and reacted habitually, each heightening the other." 15

—*aunt's report:* " 'But eh, poor thing, as soon as she'd said us 'good-by,' an' got into the cart, an' looked back at me with her pale face, as is welly like her aunt **Judith** come back from heaven, I begun to be frightened to think o' the set-downs I'd given her; for it comes over you sometimes as if she'd a way o' knowing the rights o' things more nor other folks have. But I'll niver give in as that's 'cause she's a Methodist, no more nor a white calf's white 'cause it eats out o' the same bucket wi' a black un.' " 18

—appreciated: " 'For she's one o' them things as looks the brightest on a rainy day, and loves you the best when you're most i' need on't.' " 20

—centering: "Then [at twilight] the inward light shines the brighter, and we have a deeper sense of resting on the Divine strength. I sit on my chair in the dark room and close my eyes, and it is as if I was out of the body and could feel no want for evermore." 30

—come to prison: "There was no agitation visible in her, but a deep concentrated calmness, as if, even when she was speaking, her soul was in prayer reposing on an unseen support." 45

—in the gallows-cart: "And in a low voice, as the cart went slowly along through the midst of the gazing crowd, she poured forth her soul with the wrestling intensity of a last pleading, for the trembling creature that clung to her and clutched her as the only visible sign of love and pity." 47

—a blush: " . . . there was certainly a change come over Dinah, for she never used to change colour; but, as it was, he merely observed that her face was flushed at that moment. **Mr Poyser** thought she looked the prettier for it: it was a flush no deeper than the petal of a monthly rose. Perhaps it came because her uncle was looking at her so fixedly; but there is no knowing; for just then **Adam** was saying . . . . " 49

—caught off guard: "As it often happens, the words intended to relieve her were just too much for Dinah's susceptible feelings at this moment. The tears came into the grey eyes too fast to be hidden . . . . " 49

—more blushes: " . . . she could not prevent him from seeing her face. It struck him with surprise, for the grey eyes, usually so mild and grave, had the bright uneasy glance which accompanies suppressed agitation, and the slight flush in her cheeks, with which she had come down stairs, was heightened to a deep rose-colour. She looked as if she were only sister to Dinah. **Adam** was silent with surprise and conjecture . . . . " 50

—hearing a beloved voice: "It was as if Dinah had put her hands unawares on a vibrating chord; she was shaken with an intense thrill, and for the instant felt nothing else; then she knew her cheeks were glowing, and dared not look round, but stood still, distressed because she could not say good-morning in a friendly way." 50

—first response: " . . . from my childhood upward I have been led towards another path; all my peace and my joy have come from having no life of my own, no wants, no wishes for myself, and living only in God and those of his creatures whose sorrows and joys he has given me to know. Those have been very blessed years to me, and I feel that if I was to listen to any voice that would draw me aside from that path, I should be turning my back on the light that has shone upon me, and darkness and doubt would take hold of me. We could not bless each other, **Adam**, if there were doubts in my soul, and if I yearned, when it was too late, after that better part which had once been given me and I had put away from me.' " 52

—decision: " ' . . . since my affections have been set above measure on you, I have had less peace and joy in God; I have felt as it were a division in my heart. And think how it is with me, Adam:—that life I have led is like a land I have trodden in blessedness since my childhood; and if I long for a moment to follow the voice which calls me to another land that I know not, I cannot but fear that my soul might hereafter yearn for that early blessedness which I had forsaken; and where doubt enters, there is not perfect love. I must wait for clearer guidance: I must go from you, and we must submit

ourselves entirely to the Divine Will. We are sometimes required to lay our natural, lawful affections on the altar.' " 52

—her answer: "What a look of yearning love it was that the mild grey eyes turned on the strong dark-eyed man! She did not start again at the sight of him; she said nothing, but moved towards him so that his arm could clasp her round.

"And they walked on so in silence, while the warm tears fell . . . .

" '**Adam**,' she said, 'it is the Divine Will. My soul is so knit to yours that it is but a divided life I live without you. And this moment, now you are with me, and I feel that our hearts are filled with the same love, I have a fulness of strength to bear and do our heavenly Father's will, that I had lost before . . . .

" 'Then we'll never part any more, Dinah, till death parts us.'

"And they kissed each other with a deep joy." 54

—her wedding dress: "She was not in black this morning, for her aunt **Poyser** would by no means allow such a risk of incurring bad luck, and had herself made a present of the wedding dress, made all of grey, though in the usual Quaker form, for on this point Dinah could not give way. So the lily face looked out with sweet gravity from under a grey Quaker bonnet, neither smiling nor blushing, but with lips trembling a little under the weight of solemn feelings." 55

Sayings

" 'I'm not free to leave Snowfield, where I was first planted, and have grown deep into it, like the small grass on the hill-top.' " 8

" 'It makes no difference—whether we live or die, we are in the presence of God.' " 45

" 'God's love and mercy can overcome all things—our ignorance, and weakness, and all the burthen of our past wickedness—all things but our wilful sin; sin that we cling to, and will not give up.' " 45

" 'He can't bless you while you have one falsehood in your soul; his pardoning mercy can't reach you until you open your heart to him . . . . ' " 45

" 'I must resist, lest the love of the creature should become like a mist in my soul shutting out the heavenly light.' " 49

Hetty Sorrel "often took the opportunity, when her aunt's back was turned, of looking at the pleasing reflection of herself . . . . " 6

—visited: "But one gets only a confused notion of these details [of the dairy] when they surround a distractingly pretty girl of seventeen, standing on little pattens and rounding her dimpled arm to lift a pound of butter out of the scale.

"Hetty blushed a deep rose-colour when **Captain Donnithorne** entered the dairy and spoke to her; but it was not all a distressed blush, for it was inwreathed with smiles and dimples, and with sparkles from under long curled dark eye-lashes; and while her aunt was discoursing to him . . . Hetty tossed and patted her pound of butter with quite a self-possessed, coquettish air, slyly conscious that no turn of her head was lost." 7

—exquisite: "It is of little use for me to tell you that Hetty's cheek was like a rose-petal, that dimples played about her pouting lips, that her large dark eyes hid a soft roguishness under their long lashes, and that her curly hair, though all pushed back under her round cap while she was at work, stole back in dark delicate rings on her forehead, and about her white shell-

like ears; it is of little use for me to say how lovely was the contour of her pink and white neckerchief, tucked into her low plum-coloured stuff bodice, or how the linen butter-making apron, with its bib, seemed a thing to be imitated in silk by duchesses, since it fell in such charming lines, or how her brown stockings and thick-soled buckled shoes [*but she is in pattens*] lost all that clumsiness which they must certainly have had when empty of her foot and ankle;—of little use, unless you have seen a woman who affected you as Hetty affected her beholders, for otherwise, though you might conjure up the image of a lovely woman, she would not in the least resemble that distracting kitten-like maiden." 7

—of nature: "I might mention all the divine charms of a bright spring day, but if you had never in your life utterly forgotten yourself in straining your eyes after the mounting lark, or in wandering through the still lanes when the fresh-opened blossoms fill them with a sacred, silent beauty like that of fretted aisles, where would be the use of my descriptive catalogue? I could never make you know what I meant by a bright spring day. Hetty's was a springtide beauty; it was the beauty of young frisking things, round-limbed, gambolling, circumventing you by a false air of innocence—the innocence of a young star-browed calf, for example, that, being inclined for a promenade out of bounds, leads you a severe steeple-chase over hedge and ditch, and only comes to a stand in the middle of a bog." 7

—at work: "And they are the prettiest attitudes and movements into which a pretty girl is thrown in making up butter—tossing movements that give a charming curve to the arm, and a sideward inclination of the round white neck; little patting and rolling movements with the palm of the hand, and nice adaptations and finishings which cannot at all be effected without a great play of the pouting mouth and the dark eyes. And then the butter itself seems to communicate a fresh charm—it is so pure, so sweet-scented; it is turned off the mould with such a beautiful firm surface, like marble in a pale yellow light! Moreover, Hetty was particularly clever at making up the butter; it was the one performance of hers that her aunt allowed to pass without severe criticism; so she handled it with all the grace that belongs to mastery." 7

—admired: "Bright, admiring glances from a handsome young gentleman, with white hands, a gold chain, occasional regimentals, and wealth and grandeur immeasurable—these were the warm rays that set poor Hetty's heart vibrating, and playing its little foolish tunes over and over again." 9

—not in love: "But as to marrying **Adam**, that was a very different affair! There was nothing in the world to tempt her to do that. Her cheeks never grew a shade deeper when his name was mentioned; she felt no thrill when she saw him passing along the causeway by the window, or advancing towards her unexpectedly in the footpath across the meadow; she felt nothing when his eyes rested on her, but the cold triumph of knowing that he loved her, and would not care to look at **Mary Burge**: he could no more stir in her the emotions that make the sweet intoxication of young love, than the mere picture of a sun can stir the spring sap in the subtle fibres of the plant." 9

—her dreams: "And Hetty's dreams were all of luxuries to sit in a carpeted parlour and always wear white stockings; to have some large beautiful earrings, such as were all the fashion; to have Nottingham lace round the top of her gown, and something to make her handkerchief smell nice . . . and not to be obliged to get up early or be scolded by anybody." 9

Hetty Sorrel

—*intoxicant:* " . . . a new influence had come over Hetty—vague, atmospheric, shaping itself into no self-confessed hopes or prospects, but producing a pleasant narcotic effect, making her tread the ground and go about her work in a sort of dream, unconscious of weight or effort, and showing her all things through a soft-liquid veil, as if she were living not in this solid world of brick and stone, but in a beautified world, such as the sun lights up for us in the waters. Hetty had become aware that Mr **Arthur Donnithorne** would take a good deal of trouble for the chance of seeing her. . . .

" . . . Hetty was quite uneducated—a simple farmer's girl, to whom a gentleman with a white hand was dazzling as an Olympian God." 9

—*danger:* "Ah, there she comes: first, a bright patch of colour, like a tropic bird among the boughs, then a tripping figure, with a round hat on, and a small basket under her arm; then a deep-blushing, almost frightened, but bright-smiling girl, making her curtsy with a fluttered yet happy glance, as **Arthur** came up to her. If Arthur had had time to think at all, he would have thought it strange that he should feel fluttered too, be conscious of blushing too—in fact, look and feel as foolish as if he had been taken by surprise instead of meeting just what he expected.

"Poor things! It was a pity they were not in that golden age of childhood when they would have stood face to face, eyeing each other with timid liking, then given each other a little butterfly kiss, and toddled off to play together. Arthur would have gone home to his silk-curtained cot, and Hetty to her home-spun pillow, and both would have slept without dreams, and to-morrow would have been a life hardly conscious of a yesterday." ¶12

—*ecstasy:* "As for Hetty, her feet rested on a cloud, and she was borne along by warm zephyrs; she had forgotten her rose-coloured ribbons, she was no more conscious of her limbs than if her childish soul had passed into a water-lily, resting on a liquid bed, and warmed by the midsummer sunbeams." 12

—*question:* "Would he come? Her little butterfly soul fluttered incessantly between memory and dubious expectation." 13

—*daydream:* "It was as if she had been wooed by a river-god, who might any time take her to his wondrous halls below a watery heaven. There was no knowing what would come since this strange entrancing delight had come. If a chest full of lace and satin and jewels had been sent her from some unknown source, how could she but have thought that her whole lot was going to change, and that to-morrow some still more bewildering joy would befall her? Hetty had never read a novel: if she had ever seen one, I think the words would have been too hard for her: how then could she find a shape for her expectations? They were as formless as the sweet languid odours of the garden at the Chase, which had floated past her as she walked by the gate." 13

—*looking at **Dinah**:* "Hetty looked at her much in the same way as one might imagine a little perching bird that could only flutter from bough to bough, to look at the swoop of the swallow or the mounting of the lark . . . . " 14

—*hair down:* " . . . the dark hyacinthine curves fell on her neck. It was not heavy, massive, merely rippling hair, but soft and silken, running at every opportunity into delicate rings." 15

—*strutting alone:* "[She] began to pace with a pigeon-like stateliness backwards and forwards along her room, in her coloured stays and coloured skirt, and the old black lace scarf round her shoulders, and the great glass earrings in her ears.

"How pretty the little puss looks in that odd dress! It would be the easiest folly in the world to fall in love with her: there is such a sweet baby-like roundness about her face and figure; the delicate dark rings of hair lie so charmingly about her ears and neck; her great dark eyes with their long eyelashes touch one so strangely, as if an imprisoned frisky sprite looked out of them." 15

—*adorable:* "The dear young, round, soft, flexible thing! Her heart must be just as soft, her temper just as free from angles, her character just as pliant. If anything ever goes wrong, it must be the husband's fault there: he can make her what he likes, that is plain. And the lover himself thinks so too: the little darling is so fond of him, her little vanities are so bewitching, he wouldn't consent to her being a bit wiser; those kitten-like glances and movements are just what one wants to make one's hearth a paradise." 15

—*shallow:* "Does any sweet or sad memory mingle with this dream of the future—any loving thought of her second parents—of the children she had helped to tend—of any youthful companion, any pet animal, any relic of her own childhood even? Not one. There are some plants that have hardly any roots: you may tear them from their native nook of rock or wall, and just lay them over your ornamental flower-pot, and they blossom none the worse." 15

—*selfish:* "It was wonderful how little she seemed to care about waiting on her uncle, who had been a good father to her: she hardly ever remembered to reach him his pipe at the right time without being told, unless a visitor happened to be there, who would have a better opportunity of seeing her as she walked across the hearth. Hetty did not understand how anybody could be very fond of middle-aged people." 15

—*hard:* "The round downy chicks peeping out from under their mother's wing never touched Hetty with any pleasure; that was not the sort of prettiness she cared about; but she did care about the prettiness of the new things she would buy for herself at Treddleston fair with the money they fetched. And yet she looked so dimpled, so charming, as she stooped down to put the soaked bread under the hen-coop, that you must have been a very acute personage indeed to suspect her of that hardness." 15

—*character understood:* " 'She's no better than a peacock, as 'ud strut about on the wall and spread its tail when the sun shone if all the folks i' the parish was dying: there's nothing seems to give her a turn i' th' inside, not even when we thought **Totty** had tumbled into the pit . . . Hetty niver minded it, I could see, though she's been at the nussin' o' the child iver since it was a babby. It's my belief her heart's as hard as a pibble.' " 15

—*a neighbour:* "What a strange contrast the two figures made! Visible enough in that mingled twilight and moonlight, Hetty, her cheeks flushed and her eyes glistening from her imaginary drama, her beautiful neck and arms bare, her hair hanging in a curly tangle down her back, and the baubles in her ears. **Dinah**, covered with her long white dress, her pale face full of subdued emotion, almost like a lovely corpse into which the soul has returned charged with sublimer secrets and a sublimer love. They were nearly of the same height, Dinah evidently a little the taller, as she put her arm round Hetty's waist, and kissed her forehead." 15

—timorous: " . . . she had the timidity of a luxurious pleasure-seeking nature, which shrinks from the hint of pain." 15

—dressed for a funeral: "If ever a girl looked as if she had been made of roses, that girl was Hetty in her Sunday hat and frock. For her hat was trimmed with pink, and her frock had pink spots sprinkled on a white ground. There was nothing but pink and white about her, except in her dark hair and eyes and her little buckled shoes." 18

—proud: "Hetty had a certain strength in her vain little nature: she would have borne anything rather than be laughed at, or pointed at with any other feeling than admiration; she would have pressed her own nails into her tender flesh rather than people should know a secret she did not want them to know." 18

—a softening: " . . . the anxieties and fears of a first passion, with which she was trembling, had become stronger than vanity, had given her for the first time that sense of helpless dependence on another's feeling which awakens the clinging deprecating womanhood even in the shallowest girl that can ever experience it, and creates in her a sensibility to kindness which found her quite hard before . . . .

"Hetty, we know, was not the first woman that had behaved more gently to the man who loved her in vain, because she had herself begun to love another. It was a very old story; but Adam knew nothing about it, so he drank in the sweet delusion." 20

—irritated: " . . . if Hetty had been plain she would have looked very ugly and unamiable at that moment, and no one's moral judgment upon her would have been in the least beguiled. But really there was something quite charming in her pettishness: it looked so much more like innocent distress than ill-humour; and the severe **Adam** felt no movement of disapprobation; he only felt a sort of amused pity, as if he had seen a kitten setting up its back, or a little bird with its feathers ruffled." 23

—foreshadowing: "Hetty thought this was going to be the most miserable day she had had for a long while: a moment of chill daylight and reality came across her dream: **Arthur**, who had seemed so near to her only a few hours before, was separated from her, as the hero of a great procession is separated from a small outsider in the crowd." 24

—apprehensive: "But the uncertainty of the future, the possibilities to which she could give no shape, began to press upon her like the invisible weight of air; she was alone on her little island of dreams, and all round her was the dark unknown water where **Arthur** was gone." 30

—devastated: "Slowly Hetty had read [**Arthur**'s] letter; and when she looked up from it there was the reflection of a blanched face in the old dim glass—a white marble face with rounded childish forms, but with something sadder than a child's pain in it. Hetty did not see the face—she saw nothing—she only felt that she was cold and sick and trembling . . . . Presently she took up the letter with a firmer hand, and began to read it through again. The tears came this time—great rushing tears, that blinded her and blotched the paper. She felt nothing but that Arthur was cruel—cruel to write so, cruel not to marry her. Reasons why he could not marry her had no existence for her mind; how could she believe in an misery that could come to her from the fulfillment of all she had been longing for and dreaming of? She had not the ideas that could make up the notion of that misery.

"As she threw down the letter again, she caught sight of her face in the glass; it was reddened now, and wet with tears; it was almost like a companion that she might complain to—that would pity her. She leaned forward on her elbows, and looked into those dark overflooding eyes, and at that quivering mouth, and saw how the tears came thicker and thicker, and how the mouth became convulsed with sobs.

"The shattering of all her little dream-world, the crushing blow on her new-born passion, afflicted her pleasure-craving nature with an overpowering pain that annihilated all impulse to resistance, and suspended her anger. She sat sobbing till the candle went out, and then wearied, aching, stupified with crying, threw herself on the bed without undressing, and went to sleep." 31

—spoiled: "For her short poisonous delights had spoiled for ever all the little joys that had once made the sweetness of her life—the new frock ready for Treddleston fair, the party at **Mr Britton**'s at Broxston wake, the beaux that she would say 'No' to for a long while, and the prospect of the wedding that was to come at last when she would have a silk gown and a great many clothes all at once." 31

—self-indulgent: "But Hetty's was not a nature to face difficulties—to dare to loose her hold on the familiar and rush blindly on some unknown condition. Hers was a luxurious and vain nature, not a passionate one; and if she were ever to take any violent measure, she must be urged to it by the desperation of terror." 31

—her great fear: "For Hetty looked out from her secret misery towards the possibility of [the **Poysers**'] ever knowing what had happened, as the sick and weary prisoner might think of the possible pillary. They would think her conduct shameful; and shame was torture. That was poor little Hetty's conscience." 31

—judged by her aunt: " 'It's what rag she can get to stick on her as she's thinking on from morning till night; as I often ask her if she wouldn't like to be the mawkin i' the field, for then she'd be made o' rags inside an' out. I'll never gi' my consent to her going for a lady's-maid, while she's got good friends to take care on her till she's married to somebody better nor one o' them valets, as is neither a common man nor a gentleman, an' must live on the fat o' the land, an's like enough to stick his hands under his coat tails and expect his wife to work for him.' " 31

" 'Eh, there's no knowing what she's got a liking to, for things take no more hold on her than if she was a dried pea . . . . I'm fonder on her nor she deserves— a little hard-hearted hussy; wanting to leave us i' that way . . . like a fool as I am for thinking aught about her, as is no better nor a cherry wi' a hard stone inside it.' " 31

—impulsive: "Yes, the actions of a little trivial soul like Hetty's, struggling amidst the serious, sad destinies of a human being, are strange. So are the motions of a little vessel without ballast tossed about on a stormy sea. How pretty it looked with its particoloured sail in the sunlight, moored in the quiet bay!

" 'Let that man bear the loss who loosed it from its moorings.'

"But that will not save the vessel—the pretty thing that might have been a life-long joy." 31

—changed: " . . . the cheeks were as pink as ever, and she smiled as much as she had ever done of late, but there was something different in her

eyes, in the expression of her face, in all her movements, **Adam** thought —something harder, older, less child-like." 33

—betrothed: " 'Do you really love me, Hetty? Will you be my own wife, to love and take care of as long as I live?'

"Hetty did not speak, but Adam's face was very close to hers, and she put up her round cheek against his, like a kitten. She waned to be caressed—she wanted to feel as if **Arthur** were with her again . . . .

"Adam's attachment to her, Adam's caress, stirred no passion in her, were no longer enough to satisfy her vanity; but they were the best her life offered her now—they promised her some change." 34

—that great fear compounded: "[A stranger] would not know that hidden behind the apple-blossoms, or among the golden corn, or under the shrouding boughs of the wood, there might be a human heart beating heavily with anguish: perhaps a young blooming girl, not knowing where to turn for refuge from swift-advancing shame; understanding no more of this life of ours than a foolish lost lamb wandering farther and farther in the nightfall on the lonely heath; yet tasting the bitterest of life's bitterness.

" . . . the sound of the gurgling brook, if you came close to one spot behind a small bush, would be mingled for your ear with a despairing human sob. No wonder man's religion has much sorrow in it: no wonder he needs a Suffering God." 35

"Her great dark eyes wander blankly over the fields like the eyes of one who is desolate, homeless, unloved, not the promised bride of a brave, tender man. But there are no tears in them: her tears were all wept away in the weary night before she went to sleep . . . . She sits down on the grassy bank, against the stooping stem of the great oak that hangs over the dark pool. She has thought of this pool often in the nights of the month that has just gone by, and now at last she is come to see it. She clasps her hands round her knees and leans forward, and looks earnestly at it, as if trying to guess what sort of bed it would make for her young round limbs.

"No, she has not courage to jump into that cold watery bed, and if she had, they might find her—they might find out why she had drowned herself. There is but one thing left to her: she must go away, go where they can't find her." 35

—a refuge? "She must run away; she must hide herself where no familiar eyes could detect her; and then the terror of wandering out into the world, of which she knew nothing made the possibility of going to **Arthur** a thought which brought some comfort with it. She felt so helpless now, so unable to fashion the future for herself, that the prospect of throwing herself on him had a relief in it which was stronger than her pride . . . the hope that he would receive her tenderly—that he would care for her and think for her—was like a sense of lulling warmth, that made her for the moment indifferent to everything else; and she began now to think of nothing but the scheme by which she should get away." 35

—on the road: "Now for the first time, as she lay down to-night in the strange hard bed, she felt that her home had been a happy one, that her uncle had been very good to her, that her quiet lot at Hayslope among the things and people she knew, with her little pride in her one best gown and bonnet, and nothing to hide from any one, was what she would like to wake up to as a reality, and find that all the feverish life she had known besides was a short nightmare. She thought of all she had left behind with yearning regret for

her own sake: her own misery filled her heart: there was no room in it for other people's sorrow." 36

—at a loss: "She was too ignorant of everything beyond the simple notions and habits in which she had been brought up, to have any more definite idea of her probable future than that **Arthur** would take care of her somehow, and shelter her from anger and scorn. He would not marry her and make her a lady; and apart from that she could think of nothing he could give towards which she looked with longing and ambition." 36

—dreads: "And the dread of bodily hardship mingled with the dread of shame; for Hetty had the luxurious nature of a round, soft-coated pet animal." 37

—her religion: "Religious doctrines had taken no hold on Hetty's mind: she was one of those numerous people who have had godfathers and godmothers, learned their catechism, been confirmed, and gone to church every Sunday, and yet, for any practical result of strength in life, or trust in death, have never appropriated a single Christian idea or Christian feeling. You would misunderstand her thoughts during these wretched days, if you imagined that they were influenced either by religious fears or religious hopes." 37

—new expression: "And yet, even in her most self-conscious moments, the face was sadly different from that which had smiled at itself in the old speckled glass, or smiled at others when they glanced at it admiringly. A hard and even fierce look had come in the eyes, though their lashes were as long as ever, and they had all their dark brightness. And the cheek was never dimpled with smiles now. It was the same rounded, pouting, childish prettiness, but with all love and belief in love departed from it—the sadder for its beauty, like that wondrous **Medusa**-face, with the passionate, passionless lips." 37

—suicide? "The horror of this cold, and darkness, and solitude—out of all human reach—became greater every long minute: it was almost as if she were dead already, and knew that she was dead, and longed to get back to life again. But no: she was alive still; she had not taken the dreadful leap. She felt a strange contradictory wretchedness and exultation: wretchedness, that she did not dare to face death; exultation, that she was still in life—that she might yet know light and warmth again . . . . Tears came—she had never shed tears before since she left Windsor—tears and sobs of hysterical joy that she had still hold of life, that she was still on the familiar earth, with the sheep near her. The very consciousness of her own limbs was a delight to her: she turned up her sleeves, and kissed her arms with the passionate love of life. . . . at last deep dreamless sleep came . . . the poor soul, driven to and fro between two equal terrors, found the one relief that was possible to it—the relief of unconsciousness." 37

—reaction: "Life now, by the morning light, with the impression of that [**old**] **man**'s hard wondering look at her, was as full of dread as death:—it was worse; it was a dread to which she felt chained, from which she shrank and shrank as she did from the black pool, and yet could find no refuge from it." 37

—moving on: "Poor wandering Hetty, with the rounded childish face, and the hard unloving despairing soul looking out of it—with the narrow heart and narrow thoughts, no room in them for any sorrows but her own, and tasting that sorrow with the more intense bitterness. My heart bleeds for her

as I see her toiling along on her weary feet, or seated in a cart, with her eyes fixed vacantly on the road before her, never thinking or caring whither it tends, till hunger comes and makes her desire that a village may be near.

"What will be the end?—the end of her objectless wandering, apart from all love, caring for human beings only through her pride, clinging to life only as the hunted wounded brute clings to it?" 37

—bad report: " 'I'm afraid it will go hard with her [said **Mr Irwine**]: the evidence is very strong. And one bad symptom is that she denies everything— denies that she has had a child, in the face of the most positive evidence. I saw her myself, and she was obstinately silent to me: she shrank up like a frightened animal when she saw me. I was never so shocked in my life as at the change in her.' " 40

—imprisoned: " 'You know she shrinks from seeing any one, **Adam**. It is not only you—some fatal influence seems to have shut up her heart against her fellow-creatures. She has scarcely said anything more than "No," either to me or the chaplain. Three or four days ago, before you were mentioned to her, when I asked her if there was any one of her family whom she would like to see—to whom she could open her mind, she said, with a violent shudder, "Tell them not to come near me—I won't see any of them." ' " 41

—in the dock: "There they were—the sweet face and neck, with the dark tendrils of hair, the long dark lashes, the rounded cheek and the pouting lips: pale and thin—yes—but like Hetty, and only Hetty. Others thought she looked as if some demon had cast a blighting glance upon her, withered up the woman's soul in her, and left only a hard despairing obstinacy . . . to Adam, this pale hard-looking culprit was the Hetty who had smiled at him in the garden under the apple-tree boughs—she was that Hetty's corpse, which he had trembled to look at the first time, and then was unwilling to turn away his eyes from." 43

—visited: "Slowly, while **Dinah** was speaking, Hetty rose, took a step forward, and was clasped in Dinah's arms.

"They stood so a long while, for neither of them felt the impulse to move apart again. Hetty, without any distinct thought of it, hung on this something that was come to clasp her now, while she was sinking helpless in a dark gulf; and Dinah felt a deep joy in the first sign that her love was welcomed by the wretched lost one." 45

—new report: " 'Although her poor soul is very dark, and discerns little beyond the things of the flesh, she is no longer hard: she is contrite—she has confessed all to me. The pride of her heart has given way, and she leans on me for help, and desires to be taught.' " 46

—a last visit: "But he began to see through the dimness—to see the dark eyes lifted up to him once more, but with no smile in them. O God, how sad they looked! The last time they had met his was when he parted from her with his heart full of joyous, hopeful love, and they looked out with a tearful smile from a pink, dimpled, childish face. The face was marble now; the sweet lips were pallid and half-open, and quivering; the dimples were all gone—all but one, that never went; and the eyes—O! the worst of all was the likeness they had to Hetty's. They were Hetty's eyes looking at him with that mournful gaze, as if she had come back to him from the dead to tell him of her misery." 46

Hetty has a Visitor

Supporting Roles

Lisbeth Bede. "Lisbeth Bede loves her son with the love of a woman to whom her first-born has come late in life. She is an anxious, spare, yet vigorous old woman, clean as a snowdrop. Her grey hair is turned neatly back under a pure linen cap with a black band round it; her broad chest is covered with a buff neckerchief, and below this you see a sort of short bed-gown made of blue-checkered linen, tied round the waist and descending to the hips, from whence there is a considerable length of linsey-wolsey petticoat. For Lisbeth is tall, and in other points too there is a strong likeness between her and her son **Adam**. Her dark eyes are somewhat dim now—perhaps from too much crying —but her broadly-marked eyebrows are still black, her teeth are sound, and as she stands knitting rapidly and unconsciously with her work-hardened hands, she has as firmly-upright an attitude as when she is carrying a pail of water on her head from the spring. There is the same type of frame and the same keen activity of temperament in mother and son, but it is not from her that Adam got his well-filled brow and his expression of large-hearted intelligence." 4

—*querulous:* " . . . at once patient and complaining, self-renouncing and exacting, brooding the livelong day over what happened yesterday, and what is likely to happen tomorrow, and crying very readily both at the good and the evil. But a certain awe mingled itself with her idolatrous love of **Adam**, and when he said, 'leave me alone,' she was always silenced." 4

—*vicarious piety:* "Lisbeth, though disposed always to take the negative side in her conversations with **Seth**, had a vague sense that there was some comfort and safety in the fact of his piety, and that it somehow relieved her from the trouble of any spiritual transactions on her own behalf." 4

—*plaint:* " 'There's no comfort for me no more,' she went on, the tears coming when she began to speak, 'now thy poor feyther's gone, as I'n washed for and mended, an' got's victual for 'm for thirty 'ear, an' him allays so pleased wi' iverything I done for 'em, an' used to be so handy an' do the jobs for me when I war ill an' cumbered wi' th' babby . . . .' " 10

—*grief soothed:* "Yet she cried less to-day than she had done any day since her husband's death: along with all her grief there was mixed an unusual sense of her own importance in having a 'burial,' and in **Mr Irwine**'s reading a special service for her husband; and besides, she knew the funeral psalm was going to be sung for him. She felt this counter-excitement to her sorrow still more strongly as she walked with her sons towards the church door, and saw the friendly sympathetic nods of their fellow-parishioners." 18

—*jealous:* "Her joy and pride in the honour paid to her darling son **Adam** was beginning to be worsted in the conflict with the jealousy and fretfulness which had revived when Adam came to tell her that **Captain Donnithorne** desired him to join the dancers in the hall. Adam was getting more and more out of her reach; she wished all the old troubles back again, for then it mattered more to Adam what his mother said and did." 26

—*a favourite:* "**Dinah** was moving away, but Lisbeth held her fast, while she was taking off her bonnet, and looked at her face, as one looks into a newly-gathered snowdrop, to renew the old impressions of purity and gentleness." 50

—*a scene:* " . . . there was the broad-shouldered, large-featured, hardy old woman, in her blue jacket and buff kerchief, with her dim-eyes anxious looks turned continually on the lily face and the slight form in the black dress that were either moving lightly about in helpful activity, or seated close by the old woman's arm-chair, holding her withered hand, with eyes lifted up towards her to speak a language which Lisbeth understood far better than the Bible or the hymn-book." 50

—bliss: "Sunday morning was the happiest time in all the week to Lisbeth; for as there was no service at Hayslope church till the afternoon, **Adam** was always at home, doing nothing but reading, an occupation in which she could venture to interrupt him. Moreover, she had always a better dinner than usual to prepare for her sons—very frequently for Adam and herself alone, **Seth** being often away the entire day; and the small of the roast-meat before the clear fire in the clean kitchen, the clock ticking in a peaceful Sunday manner, her darling Adam seated near her in his best clothes, doing nothing very important, so that she could go and stroke her hand across his hair if she liked, and see him look up at her and smile, while **Gyp**, rather jealous, poked his muzzle up between them—all these things made poor Lisbeth's earthly paradise." 51

—observant: " 'But I can see as she doesna behave tow'rt thee as she does tow'rt **Seth**. She makes no more o' Seth's comin' a-nigh her nor if he war **Gyp**, but she's all of a tremble when thee't a-sittin' down by her at breakfast, an' a-lookin' at her. Thee think'st thy mother knows nought, but she war alive afore thee wast born.' " 51

Sayings

" 'Thee't allays stay till the last child's born.' " 4

" 'Thee allays makes a peck o' thy own words out o' a pint o' the Bible's.' " 4

" 'When one end o' th' bridge tumbles down, where's th' use o' th' other stannin'? I might as well foller my old man.' " 10

" ' . . . the minutes to look at the corpse is like the meltin' snow.' " 10

" 'One old coat 'ull do to patch another, but it's good for noght else.' " 10

" 'He could no more ha' done wi'out me nor one side o' the scithers can do wi'out the tother.' " 10

" 'I'm no better nor an old haft when the blade's gone.' " 10

" 'If the Methodies are fond o' trouble, they're like to thrive: it's a pity they canna ha' all, an' take it away from them as donna like it.' " 10

" 'It's a choice o' mislikins is all I'n got i' this world. One mossel's as good as another when your mouth's out o' taste.' " 11

" 'How's she to get a likin' for 'm, I'd like to know? No more nor the cake 'ull come wi'out th' leaven.' " 14

" 'Folks mun allays choose by contrairies, as if they must be sorted like the pork—a bit o' good meat wi' a bit of offal.' " 14

" 'It's poor luck for the platter to wear well when it's broke i' two.' " 18

" 'It 'ud be better if folks 'ud make much on us before hand, istid o' beginnin' when we're gone. It's but little good you'll do a-watering the last year's crop.' " 18

" 'That's what comes o' marr'in' young wenches. She'll be a poor dratchell by then she's thirty, a-marr'in' a-that'n, afore her teeth's all come.' " 20

" 'But happen, thee'dst like a husband better as isna just the cut o' thysen: th' runnin' brook isna athirst for th' rain.' " 51

" 'Said? nay, she'll say nothin'. It's oon'y the men as have to wait till folks say things afore they find 'em out.' " 51

" 'It's no matter what's put it into my head: my head's none so hollow as it must get in, an' nought to put it there.' " 51

" 'I know she's fond on him, as I know th' wind's comin' in at th' door, an' that's anoof.' " 51

" 'Happen he knowsna as he wants t' see her; he knowsna as I put salt in's broth, but he'd miss it pretty quick if it warna there.' " 51

" 'An' what's it sinnify her bein' a Methody? It's on'y th' marigold i' th' parridge.' " 51

Seth Bede. "He is nearly as tall, he has the same type of features, the same hue of hair and complexion, but the strength of the family likeness seems only to render more conspicuous the remarkable difference of expression both in form and face. Seth's broad shoulders have a slight stoop; his eyes are grey; his eyebrows have less prominence and more repose than his brother's, and his glance, instead of being keen, is confiding and benignant. He has thrown off his paper cap, and you see that his hair is not thick and straight, like Adam's, but thin and wavy, allowing you to discern the exact contour of a coronal arch that predominates very decidedly over the brow." 1

—*in love:* "When Seth had once begun to urge his suit, he went on earnestly, and almost hurriedly, lest **Dinah** should speak some decisive word before he had poured forth all the arguments he had prepared. His cheeks became flushed as he went on, his mild grey eyes filled with tears, and his voice trembled as he spoke the last sentence." 3

—*unsuccessful in love:* "Poor Seth! . . . instead of bursting out into wild accusing apostrophes to God and destiny, he is resolving, as he now walks homeward under the solemn starlight, to repress his sadness, to be less bent on having his own will, and to live more for others, as **Dinah** does." 3

—*thinking of her:* "**Dinah** had never been more constantly present with him than in this scene [of dancing], where everything was so unlike her. He saw her all the more vividly after looking at the thoughtless faces and gay-coloured dresses of the young women—just as one feels the beauty and the greatness of a pictured Madonna the more, when it has been for a moment screened from us by a vulgar head in a bonnet." 26

Rev. Adolphus Irwine, "Rector of Broxton, Vicar of Hayslope, and Vicar of Blythe, a pluralist at whom the severest Church-reformer would have found it difficult to look sour." 5

—*characteristics:* "You suspect at once that the inhabitants of this room have inherited more blood than wealth, and would not be surprised to find that Mr Irwine had a finely-cut nostril and upper lip; but at present we can only see that he has a broad flat back and an abundance of powdered hair, all thrown backward and tied behind with a black ribbon—a bit of conservatism in costume which tells you that he is not a young man." 5

"It is very pleasant to see some men turn round; pleasant as a sudden rush of warm air in winter, or the flash of fire-light in the chill dusk. Mr Irwine was one of those men. He bore the same sort of resemblance to his mother that our loving memory of a friend's face often bears to the face itself: the lines were all more generous, the smile brighter, the expression heartier. If the outline had been less finely cut, his face might have been called jolly;

but that was not the right word for its mixture of bonhomie and distinction." 5

—tolerant: " 'Let evil words die as soon as they're spoken. If you can bring me any proof that [**Will Maskery**] interferes with his neighbours, and creates any disturbance, I shall think it my duty as a clergyman and a magistrate to interfere. But it wouldn't become wise people, like you and me, to be making a fuss about trifles, as if we thought the Church was in danger because Will Maskery lets his tongue wag rather foolishly, or a young woman talks in a serious way to a handful of people on the Green. We must "live and let live," **Joshua**, in religion as well as in other things. You go on doing your duty, as parish clerk and sexton, as well as you've always done it, and making those capital thick boots for your neighbours, and things won't go far wrong in Hayslope, depend upon it .' " 5

—bachelorhood: "And if that handsome, generous-blooded clergyman, the Rev. Adolphus Irwine, had not had these two hopelessly-maiden sisters, his lot would have been shaped quite differently: he would very likely have taken a comely wife in his youth, and now, when his hair was getting grey under the powder, would have had tall sons and blooming daughters—such possessions, in short, as men commonly think will repay them for all the labour they take under the sun. As it was—having with all his three livings no more than seven hundred a-year, and seeing no way of keeping his splendid mother and his sickly sister, not to reckon a second sister, who was usually spoken of without any adjective, in such lady-like ease as became their birth and habits, and at the same time providing for a family of his own—he remained, you see, at the age of eight-and-forty, a bachelor, not making any merit of that renunciation, but saying, laughingly, if any one alluded to it, that he made it an excuse for many indulgences which a wife would never have allowed him." 5

—generosity: "And perhaps he was the only person in the world who did not think his sisters uninteresting and superfluous; for his was one of those large-hearted, sweet-blooded natures that never know a narrow or a grudging thought; epicurean, if you will, with no enthusiasm, no self-scourging sense of duty; but yet, as you have seen, of a sufficiently subtle moral fibre to have an unwearying tenderness for obscure and monotonous suffering. It was his large-hearted indulgence that made him ignore his mother's hardness towards her daughters, which was the more striking from its contrast with her doting fondness towards himself: he held it no virtue to frown at irremediable faults." 5

—relaxed in religion: "He really had no very lofty aims, no theological enthusiasm . . . he felt no serious alarms about the souls of his parishioners, and would have thought it a mere loss of time to talk in a doctrinal and awakening manner to old '**Feyther Taft**,' or even to **Chad Cranage** the blacksmith. If he had been in the habit of speaking theoretically, he would perhaps have said that the only healthy form religion could take in such minds was that of certain dim but strong emotions, suffusing themselves as a hallowing influence over the family affections and neighbourly duties. He thought the custom of baptism more important than its doctrine, and that the religious benefits the peasant drew from the church where his fathers worshipped and the sacred piece of turf where they lay buried, were but slightly dependent on a clear understanding of the Liturgy or the sermon.

"Clearly, the Rector was not what is called in these days an 'earnest' man: he was fonder of church history than of divinity, and had much more insight into men's characters than interest in their opinions; he was neither laborious, nor obviously self-denying, nor very copious in alms-giving, and his theology, you perceive, was lax. His mental palate, indeed, was rather pagan, and found a savouriness in a quotation from **Sophocles** or **Theocritus** that was quite absent from any text in **Isaiah** or **Amos**. But if you feed your young setter on raw flesh, how can you wonder at its retaining a relish for uncooked partridge in after life? And Mr Irwine's recollections of young enthusiasm and ambition were all associated with poetry and ethics that lay aloof from the Bible." ¶5

—his best side: " . . . I must plead . . . that he was not vindictive—and some philanthropists have been so; that he was not intolerant—and there is a rumour that some zealous theologians have not been altogether free from that blemish; that although he would probably have declined to give his body to be burned in any public cause, and was far from bestowing all his goods to feed the poor, he had that charity which has sometimes been lacking to very illustrious virtue—he was tender to other men's failings, and unwilling to impute evil. He was one of those men, and they are not the commonest, of whom we can know the best only by following them away from the market-place, the platform, and the pulpit, entering with them into their own homes, hearing the voice with which they speak to the young and aged about their own hearthstone, and witnessing their thoughtful care for the everyday wants of everyday companions, who take all their kindness as a matter of course, and not as a subject for panegyric." 5

—fitting in: " . . . if you had met him that June afternoon riding on his grey cob, with his dogs running beside him—portly, upright, manly, with a good-natured smile on his finely-turned lips as he talked to his dashing young companion on the bay mare, you must have felt that, however ill he harmonised with sound theories of the clerical office, he somehow harmonised extremely well with that peaceful landscape." 5

—moved by a woman preacher: " 'He must be a miserable prig who would act the pedagogue here: one might as well go and lecture the trees for growing in their own shape.' " 8

—on farming: " ' . . . a man who has no feeling for the classics couldn't make a better apology for coming into the world than by increasing the quantity of food to maintain scholars—and rectors who appreciate scholars.' " 16

—on love: ". . . there's this difference between love and small-pox, or bewitchment either—that if you detect the disease at an early stage and try change of air, there is every chance of complete escape, without any further development of symptoms. And there are certain alternative doses which a man may administer to himself by keeping unpleasant consequences before his mind: that gives you a sort of smoked glass through which you may look at the resplendent fair one and discern her true outline; though I'm afraid, by the by, the smoked glass is apt to be missing just at the moment it is most wanted.' " 16

—on man's actions: " 'A man can never do anything at variance with his own nature. He carries within him the germ of his most exceptional action; and if we wise people make eminent fools of ourselves on any particular occasion, we must endure the legitimate conclusion that we carry a few grains of folly to our ounce of wisdom.' " 16

—*on the struggle against temptation:* " 'I pity him, in proportion to his struggles, for they foreshadow the inward suffering which is the worst form of Nemesis. Consequences are unpitying. Our deeds carry their terrible consequences, quite apart from any fluctuations that went before—consequences that are hardly ever confined to ourselves. And it is best to fix our minds on that certainty, instead of considering what may be the elements of excuse for us.' " 16

—*later report:* " 'Now Mester Irwine was as different as could be [from **Mr Ryde**]: as quick!—he understood what you meant in a minute; and he knew all about building, and could see when you'd made a good job. And he behaved as much like a gentleman to the farmers, and th' old women, and the labourers, as he did to the gentry. You never saw *him* interfering and scolding, and trying to play th' emperor. Ah! he was a fine man as ever you set eyes on; and so kind to 's mother and sisters. That poor sickly **Miss Anne**—he seemed to think more of her than of anybody else in the world. There wasn't a soul in the parish had a word to say against him; and his servants stayed with him till they were so old and pottering, he had to hire other folks to do their work.' " 17

—*on duty:* " . . . imagine Mr Irwine looking round on this scene, in his ample white surplice that became him so well, with his powdered hair thrown back, his rich brown complexion, and his finely-cut nostril and upper lip; for there was a certain virtue in that benignant yet keen countenance, as there is in all human faces from which a generous soul beams out." 18

—*aristocratic:* "The superior refinement of his face was much more striking than that of **Arthur**'s when seen in comparison with the people round them. Arthur's was a much commoner British face, and the splendour of his new-fashioned clothes was more akin to the young farmer's taste in costume than Mr Irwine's powder, and the well-brushed but well-worn black which seemed to be his chosen suit for great occasions, for he had the mysterious secret of never wearing a new-looking coat." 24

—*with heavy news:* "But when [**Adam**] entered the study and looked in Mr Irwine's face, he felt in an instant that there was a new expression in it, strangely different from the warm friendliness it had always worn for him before . . . .

" 'You know who's the man I've reckoned my greatest friend, . . . and used to be proud to think as I should pass my life i' working for him, and had felt so ever since we were lads' . . .

"Mr Irwine, as if all self-control had forsaken him, grasped Adam's arm, which lay on the table, and, clutching it tightly like a man in pain, said, with pale lips and a low hurried voice,

" 'No, Adam, no—don't say it, for God's sake!' . . . Mr Irwine threw himself back in his chair, saying, 'Go on—I must know it' . . . .

"During Adam's narrative, Mr Irwine had had time to recover his self-mastery . . . it was cruel to think how thin a film had shut out rescue from all this guilt and misery . . . . His own agitation was quelled by a certain awe that comes over us in the presence of a great anguish; for the anguish he must inflict on Adam was already present to him." 39

—*a report:* " 'Ay, ay, he's good metal; he gives the right ring when you try him, our parson does. A man o' sense—says no more than's needful. He's not one of those that think they can comfort you with chattering, as if folks who stand by and look on knew a deal better what the trouble was than those who have to bear it.' " 42

Bartle Massey " 'come from nobody knows where, wi' his counter-singin' and fine anthems, as puts everybody out but himself . . . . ' " 5

" 'But he's got a tongue like a sharp blade, Bartle has: it never touches anything but it cuts.' " 16

—teaching adults: "The face wore its mildest expression: the grizzled bushy eyebrows had taken their more acute angle of compassionate kindness, and the mouth, habitually compressed with a pout of the lower lip, was relaxed so as to be ready to speak a helpful word or syllable in a moment. This gentle expression was the more interesting because the schoolmaster's nose, an irregular aquiline twisted a little on one side, had rather a formidable character, and his brow, moreover, had that peculiar tension which always impresses one as a sign of a keen impatient temperament: the blue veins stood out like cords under the transparent yellow skin, and this intimidating brow was softened by no tendency to baldness, for the grey bristly hair, cut down to about an inch in length, stood round it in as close ranks as ever." 21

—softened: "[Teaching adults to read] touched the tenderest fibre in Bartle Massey's nature, for such full-grown children as these were the only pupils for whom he had no severe epithets, and no impatient tones. He was not gifted with an imperturbable temper, and on music-nights it was apparent that patience could never be an easy virtue to him; but this evening, as he glances over his spectacles at **Bill Downes**, the sawyer, who is turning his head on one side with a desperate sense of blankness before the letters d, r, y, his eyes shed their mildest and most encouraging light." 21

—teaching boys: " 'You go whistling about, and take no more care what you're thinking than if your heads were gutters for any rubbish to swill through that happened to be in the way; and if you get a good notion in 'em, it's pretty soon washed out again . . . . I'll send no man away because he's stupid: if **Billy Taft**, the idiot, wanted to learn anything, I'd not refuse to teach him. But I'll not throw away good knowledge on people who think they can get it by the sixpenn'orth, and carry it away with 'em as they would an ounce of snuff. So never come to me again, if you can't show that you've been working with your own heads, instead of thinking you can pay for mine to work for you. That's the last word I've got to say to you.' " 21

—lame: "He was no sooner on the ground than it became obvious why the stick was necessary—the left leg was much shorter than the right. But the schoolmaster was so active with his lameness, that it was hardly thought of as a misfortune; and if you had seen him make his way along the schoolroom floor, and up the step into his kitchen, you would perhaps have understood why the naughty boys sometimes felt that his pace might be indefinitely quickened, and that he and his stick might overtake them even in their swiftest run." 21

—misogynist: " 'I hate the sound of women's voices; they're always either a-buzz or a-squeak, always either a-buzz or a-squeak. **Mrs Poyser** keeps at the top o' the talk, like a fife; and as for the young lasses, I'd as soon look at water-grubs—I know what they'll turn to—stinging gnats, stinging gnats.' " 21

" 'Nonsense! It's the silliest lie a sensible man like you ever believed, to say a woman makes a house comfortable. It's a story got up, because the women are there, and something must be found for 'em to do. I tell you there isn't a thing under the sun that needs to be done at all, but what a man can do better than a woman, unless it's bearing children, and they do that in a poor make-shift way; it had better ha' been left to the men—it had better ha' been left to the men . . . . Don't tell me about God having made such creatures to be companions for us! I don't say but he might make **Eve** to be a companion to **Adam** in Paradise—there was no cooking to be spoilt there, and no other woman to cackle with and make mischief; though you see what mischief she did as soon as she'd an opportunity. But it's an impious, unscriptural opinion to say a woman's a blessing to a man now; you might as well say adders and wasps, and hogs and wild beasts, are a blessing, when they're only the evils that belong to this state o' probation, which it's lawful for a man to keep as clear of as he can in this life, hoping to get quit of 'em for ever in another —hoping to get quit of 'em for ever in another.' " 21

—experience: "**Adam** was used to hear him talk in this way, but had never learned so much of Bartle's past life as to know whether his view of married comfort was founded on experience. On that point Bartle was mute; and it was even a secret where he had lived previous to the twenty years in which, happily for the peasants and artisans of this neighbourhood, he had been settled among them as their only schoolmaster." 21

—speech critic: " 'The right language!' said Bartle Massey contemptuously. 'You're about as near the right language as a pig's squeaking is like a tune played on a key-bugle.'

" 'Well, I don't know,' answered **Mr Casson**, with an angry smile. 'I should think a man as has lived among the gentry from a by, is likely to know what's the right language pretty nigh a well as a schoolmaster.'

" 'Ay, ay, man,' said Bartle, with a tone of sarcastic consolation, 'you talk the right language for you. When **Mike Holdsworth**'s goat says ba-a-a, it's all right—it 'ud be unnatural for it to make any other noise.' " 32

—agitated: " 'For as for that bit o' pink-and-white they've taken the trouble to put in jail, I don't value her a rotten nut—not a rotten nut—only for the harm or good that may come out of her to an honest man . . . . '

"Bartle was heated by the exertion of walking fast in an agitated frame of mind, and was not able to check himself on this first occasion of venting his feelings. But he paused now to rub his moist forehead, and probably his moist eyes also." 40

—judging: " '. . . it's stuff and nonsense for the innocent to care about her being hanged. For my own part, I think the sooner such women are put out o' the world the better; and the men that help 'em to do mischief had better go along with 'em, for that matter. What good will you do by keeping such vermin alive? eating the victual that 'ud feed rational beings." 40

—exception to misogyny: " 'Well . . . if there must be women to make trouble in the world it's but fair there should be women to be comforters under it; and she's one—she's one. It's a pity she's a Methodist; but there's no getting a woman without some foolishness or other.' " 46

—uncharacteristic concession: "Bartle Massey had consented to attend the wedding at **Adam's** earnest request, under protest against marriage in general, and the marriage of a sensible man in particular. Nevertheless, **Mr Poyser** had a joke against him after the wedding dinner, to the effect that in the vestry he had given the bride one more kiss than was necessary." 55

Martin Poyser "was not a frequenter of public-houses, but he liked a friendly chat over his own home-brewed; and though it was pleasant to lay down the law to a stupid neighbour who had no notion how to make the best of his farm, it was also an agreeable variety to learn something from a clever fellow like **Adam Bede**." 9

—physiognomy: " 'That common round red face one sees sometimes in the men—all cheek and no features, like Martin Poyser's . . . . ' " 9

—visited: " . . . the doorway was filled by a portly figure, with a ruddy black-eyed face, which bore in it the possibility of looking extremely acute, and occasionally contemptuous, on market-days, but had now a predominant after-supper expression of hearty good nature." 14

—martinet: " . . . he was of so excellent a disposition that he had been kinder and more respectful than ever to his old father since he had made a deed of gift of all his property; and no man judged his neighbours more charitably on all personal matters; but for a farmer, like **Luke Britton**, for example . . . Martin Poyser was as hard and implacable as the north-east wind. Luke Britton could not make a remark, even on the weather, but Martin Poyser detected in it a taint of that unsoundness and general ignorance which was palpable in all his farming operations." 14

—dancing: "There was but one thing to mar Martin Poyser's pleasure in this dance: it was, that he was always in close contact with **Luke Britton**, that slovenly farmer. He thought of throwing a little glazed coldness into his eye in the crossing of hands; but then, as **Miss Irwine** was opposite to him instead of the offensive Luke, he might freeze the wrong person. So he gave his face up to hilarity, unchilled by moral judgments." 26

—his landlord's visit: "As he stood, red, rotund, and radiant before the small, wiry, cool, old gentleman, he looked like a prize apple by the side of a withered crab." 32

—dressed for a funeral: "Mr Poyser was in his Sunday suit of drab, with a red and green waistcoat, and a green watch-ribbon having a large cornelian seal attached, pendent like a plumb-line from that promontory where his watch-pocket was situated; a silk handkerchief of a yellow tone round his neck, and excellent grey ribbed stockings, knitted by **Mrs Poyser**'s own hand, setting off the proportions of his leg. Mr Poyser had no reason to be ashamed of his leg, and suspected that the growing abuse of top-boots and other fashions tending to disguise the nether limbs, had their origin in a pitiable degeneracy of the human calf. Still less had he reason to be ashamed of his round jolly face, which was good-humour itself . . . . " 18

—animus: " 'Nay,' said Mr Poyser, with as near an approach to a snarl as his good-nature would allow; 'I'n no opinion o' the Methodists. It's on'y tradesfolks as turn Methodists; you niver knew a farmer bitten wi' them maggots.' " 18

—commiserating: " 'Shake hands wi' me, lad: I wish I could make thee amends.'

"There was something in Martin Poyser's throat at that moment which caused him to bring out those scanty words in rather a broken fashion. Yet **Adam** knew what they meant all the better; and the two honest men grasped each other's hard hands in mutual understanding." 38

—feeling disgrace: "He and his father were simple-minded farmers, proud of their untarnished character, proud that they came of a family which had held up its head and paid its way as far back as its name was in the

parish register; and **Hetty** had brought disgrace on them all—disgrace that could never be wiped out. That was the all-conquering feeling in the mind both of father and son—the scorching sense of disgrace, which neutralised all other sensibility; and **Mr Irwine** was struck with surprise to observe that **Mrs Poyser** was less severe than her husband." 39

—*bitterness:* " 'We thought it 'ud be bad luck if th' old **Squire** gave us notice this Lady Day, but I must gi' notice myself now, an' see if there can anybody be got to come an' take to the crops as I'n put i' the ground; for I wonna stay upo' that man's land a day longer nor I'm forced to't. An' me, as thought him such a good upright young man, as I should be glad when he come to be our landlord. I'll ne'er lift my hat to 'm again, nor sit i' the same church wi'm . . . a man as has brought shame on respectable folks . . . an' pretended to be such a friend t' everybody . . . . Poor Adam there . . . a fine friend he's been t' Adam, making speeches an' talking so fine, an' all the while poisoning the lad's life, as it's much if he can stay i' this country any more nor we can.' " 40

—*in court:* " 'But when she heard her uncle's name, there seemed to go a shiver right through her; and when they told him to look at her, she hung her head down, and cowered, and hid her face in her hands. He'd much ado to speak, poor man, his voice trembled so. And the counsellors—who look as hard as nails mostly—I saw, spared him as much as they could. **Mr Irwine** put himself near him, and went with him out o' court.' " 42

Sayings

" '**Adam**'s sure enough . . . . There's no fear but he'll yield well i' the threshing. He's not one o' them as is all straw and no grain.' " 14

" 'Them young gells are like th' unripe grain; they'll make good meal by-and-by; but they're squashy as yit.' " 15

Mrs Rachel Poyser. "Do not suppose . . . that Mrs Poyser was elderly or shrewish in her appearance; she was a good-looking woman, not more than eight-and-thirty, of fair complexion, and sandy hair, well-shapen, light-footed: the most conspicuous article in her attire was an ample checkered linen apron, which almost covered her skirt; and nothing could be plainer or less noticeable than her cap and gown, for there was no weakness of which she was less tolerant than feminine vanity, and the preference of ornament to utility.

"The family likeness between her and her niece, **Dinah Morris**, with the contrast between her keenness and Dinah's seraphic gentleness of expression, might have served a painter as an excellent suggestion for a **Martha** and **Mary**. Their eyes were just of the same colour, but a striking test of the difference in their operation was seen in the demeanour of **Trip**, the black and tan terrier, whenever that much-suspected dog unwarily exposed himself to the freezing arctic ray of Mrs Poyser's glance. Her tongue was not less keen than her eye, and, whenever a damsel came within ear-shot, seemed to take up an unfinished lecture, as a barrel-organ takes up a tune, precisely at the point where it had left off." ¶6

—*interrupted:* " 'Cold, is it, my darling? Bless your sweet face!' said Mrs Poyser, who was remarkable for the facility with which she could relapse from her official objurgatory tone to one of fondness or of friendly converse." 6

—*conversationalist:* "Mrs Poyser, once launched into conversation, always sailed along without any check from her preliminary awe of the gentry. The confidence she felt in her own powers of exposition was a motive force that overcame all resistance." 6

—musical solecism: " 'Dear heart, dear heart! But you must have a cup o' tea first, child,' said Mrs Poyser, falling at once from the key of B with five sharps to the frank and genial C." 8 *One has to rise, not fall, from B to C.*

—deference due: "The woman who manages a dairy has a large share in making the rent, so she may well be allowed to have her opinion on stock and their 'keep'—an exercise which strengthens her understanding so much that she finds herself able to give her husband advice on most other subjects." 18

—hospitality: " . . . she would have held it a deep disgrace not to make her neighbours welcome to her house: personal likes and dislikes must not interfere with that sacred custom." 18

—flattery: "Mrs Poyser was not to be caught in the weakness of smiling at a compliment, but a quiet complacency overspread her face like a stealing sunbeam, and gave a milder glance than usual to her blue-grey eyes . . . . " 20

—proprieties: " . . . Mrs Poyser was strict in adherence to her own rules of propriety, and she considered that a young girl was not to be treated sharply in the presence of a respectable man who was courting her. That would not be fair play: every woman was young in her turn, and had her chances of matrimony, which it was a point of honour for other women not to spoil—just as one market-woman who has sold her own eggs must not try to balk another of a customer." 20

—inveterate activity: "[She] now came back into the house-place, knitting with fierce rapidity, as if that movement were a necessary function, like the twittering of a crab's antennae." 31

—restraining herself: " . . . she was not the woman to misbehave towards her betters, and fly in the face of the catechism, without severe provocation." 32

—her exploit discussed: "[**Mrs Irwine**] declared that if she were rich she should like to allow Mrs Poyser a pension for life, and wanted to invite her to the Parsonage, that she might hear an account of the scene from Mrs Poyser's own lips . . . .

" 'Well, I like that woman even better than her cream-cheese,' said Mrs Irwine. 'She has the spirit of three men, with that pale face of hers, and she says such sharp things too.'

" ' Sharp! Yes, her tongue is like a new-set razor. She's quite original in her talk, too; one of those untaught wits that help to stock a country with proverbs. I told you that capital thing I heard her say about **Craig**—that he was like a cock who thought the sun had risen to hear him crow. Now that's an Æsop's fable in a sentence.' " 33

Nature's word-smith

" 'What are you stanning there for, like a jack as is run down?' " 6

" 'I might as well talk to the running brook, and tell it to stan' still.' " 6

" 'When there's a bigger maggot than usial in your head you call it "direction"; and then nothing can stir you—you look like the statty o' the outside o' Treddles'on church, a-starin' and a-smilin' whether it's fair weather or foul. I hanna common patience with you.' " 6

" 'As for farming, it's putting money into your pocket wi' your right hand and fetching it out wi' your left. As far as I can see, it's raising victual for other folks, and just getting a mouthful for yourself and your children as you go along.' " 6

" 'It's poor fun, losing money, I should think, though I understan' it's what the great folks i' London lay at more than anything.' " 6

" 'It's more than flesh and blood 'ull bear sometimes, to be toiling and striving, and up early and down late, and hardly sleeping a wink when you lie down for thinking as the cheese may swell, or the cows may slip their calf, or the wheat may grow green again i' the sheaf—and after all, at th' end o' the year, it's like as if you'd been cooking a feast and had got the smell of it for your pains.' " 6

" 'It' summat-like to see such a man as [**Irwine**] i' the desk of a Sunday! . . . it's like looking at a full crop o' wheat, or a pasture with a fine dairy o' cows in it; it makes you think the world's comfortable-like.' " 8

" 'As for such creaturs as you Methodisses run after, I'd so as soon go to look at a lot o' bare-ribbed runts on a common.' " 8

" 'Fine folks they are to tell you what's right, as look as if they'd never tasted nothing better than bacon-sword and sourcake i' their lives.' " 8

" 'It's the flesh and blood folks are made on as makes the difference. Some cheeses are made o' skimmed milk and some o' new milk and it's no matter what you call 'em, you may tell which is which by the look and the smell.' " 8

" 'It's all very fine having a ready-made rich man, but may-happen he'll be a ready-made fool; and it's no use filling your pocket full o' money if you've got a hole in the corner.' " 9

" 'It'll do you no good to sit in a spring-cart o' your own, if you've got a soft to drive you: he'll soon turn you over into the ditch.' " 9

" 'I allays said I'd never marry a man as had got no brains; for where's the use of a woman having brains of her own if she's tackled to a geck as everybody's a-laughing at? She might as well dress herself fine to sit back'ards on a donkey.' " 9

" 'What, you'd be wanting the clock set by gentlefolks's time, would you? An' sit up burnin' candle, an' lie a-bed wi' the sun a-bakin' you, like a cowcumber i' the frame?' " 14

" 'Wi' them three gells in the house I'd need have twice the strength, to keep 'em up to their work. It's like having roast meat at three fires; as soon as you've basted one, another's burnin.' " 15

" 'Mrs Poyser used to say—you know she would have her word about everything—she said, **Mr Irwine** was like a good meal o' victual, you were the better for him without thinking on it, and **Mr Ryde** was like a dose o' physic, he griped you and worreted you, and after all he left you much the same.' " 17

" 'Ah, I often think it's wi' th' old folks as it is wi' the babbies . . . they're satisfied wi' looking, no matter what they're looking at. It's God A'mighty's way o' quietening 'em, I reckon, afore they go to sleep.' " 18

" 'Ay, them as choose a soft for a wife may's well buy up the short-horns, for if you get your head stuck in a bog your legs may's well go after it.' " 18

" 'What care I what the men 'ud run after? It's well seen what choice the most of 'em know how to make, by the poor draggle-tails o' wives you see, like bits o' gauze ribbin, good for nothing when the colour's gone.' " 18

" 'There's **Chowne**'s wife ugly enough to turn the milk an' save the rennet, but she'll niver save nothing any other way.' " 18

" 'You make but a poor trap to catch luck if you go and bait it wi' wickedness.' " 18

" 'And as for the weather, there's One above makes it, and we must put up wi't: it's nothing of a plague to what the wenches are.' " 18

" 'Husbands and wives must be content when they've lived to rear their children and see one another's hair grey.' " 18

" 'I think [**Mr Craig**'s] welly like a cock as thinks the sun's rose o' purpose to hear him crow.' " 18

" 'Nothing to say again him; on'y it was a pity he couldna be hatched o'er again, an' hatched different.' " 18

" 'An' there's no trustin' the children to gether it, for they put more into their own mouths nor into the basket; you might as well set the wasps to gether the fruit.' " 20

" 'I know you're fond o' whey, as most folks is when they hanna got to crush it out.' " 20

" 'The smell o' bread's sweet t'everybody but the baker.' " 20

" 'It's poor eating where the flavour o' the meat lies i' the cruets. There's folks as make bad butter, and trusten to the salt t' hide it.' " 20

" 'Wooden folks had need ha' wooden things t' handle.' " 20

" 'Looks 'ull mend no jugs, nor laughing neither.' " 20

" 'When your broth's ready made for you, you mun swallow the thickenin', or else let the broth alone.' " 26

" 'I'd sooner ha' brewin' day and washin' day together than one o' these pleasurin' days. There's no work so tirin' as danglin' about an' starin' an' not rightly knowin' what you're goin' to do next; an' keepin' your face i' smilin' order like a grocer o' market-day, for fear people shouldna think you civil enough. An you've nothing to show for't when it's done, if it isn't a yellow face wi' eatin' things as disagree.' " 26

" 'I was never over-fond o' gentlefolks's servants—they're mostly like the fine ladies' fat dogs, nayther good for barking nor butcher's meat, but on'y for show.' " 27

" ' . . . that set at **Casson**'s, a-sittin' soakin'-in drink, and looking as wise as a lot o' cod-fish wi' red faces.' " 32

" 'Good-day, Mrs Poyser,' said the old **Squire**, peering at her with his short-sighted eyes—a mode of looking at her which, as Mrs Poyser observed, 'allays aggravated her: it was as if you was a insect, and he was going to dab his finger-nail on you.' " 32

" ' . . . it's seldom I see other folks's butter, though there's some on it as one's no need to see—the smell's enough.' " 32

" 'If you could make a pudding wi' thinking o' the batter, it 'ud be easy getting dinner.' " 32

" 'But there's folks 'ud hold a sieve under the pump and expect to carry away the water.' " 32

" 'There's no pleasure i' living, if you're to be corked up for iver, and only dribble your mind out by the sly, like a leaky barrel.' " 32

" 'Christian folks can't be married like cuckoos, I reckon.' " 34

" 'You must go back to that bare heap o' stones [Stoniton] as the very crows fly over an' won't stop at.' " 49

" '[**Bessy Cranage**]'ll no more go on in her new ways without you, than a dog 'ull stand on its hind-legs when there's nobody looking.' " 49

" 'I suppose you must be a Methodist to know what a Methodist 'ull do. It's ill guessing what the bats are flying after.' " 49

" 'Them as ha' never had a cushion don't miss it.' " 49

" 'It's allays the way wi' them meek-faced people; you may's well pelt a bag o' feathers as talk to 'em.' " 49

" 'It's a small joke sets men laughing when they sit a-staring at one another with a pipe i' their mouths . . . . If the chaff-cutter had the making of us, we should all be straw, I reckon.' " 49

" 'Why, what dost think has just jumped into my head?'

" 'Summat as hadna far to jump, for it's just under our nose.' " 52

" 'I'm not one o' those as can see the cat i' the dairy, an' wonder what she's come after.' " 52

" 'Well, I aren't like a bird-clapper, forced to make a rattle when the wind blows on me. I can keep my own counsel when there's no good i' speaking.' " 52

" 'She's like the driven snow: anybody might sin for two as had her at their elbow.' " 52

" 'Scarceness o' victual 'ull keep: there's no need to be hasty wi' the cooking. An' scarceness is what there's the biggest stock of i' that country.' " 52

" 'It's hard work to tell which is Old Harry when everybody's got boots on.' " 53

Others

Jonathan Burge, "a carpenter and builder in the village of Hayslope. . . ." 1

" . . . who held his hands behind him, and leaned forward coughing asthmatically; with an inward scorn of all knowingness that could not be turned into cash." 18

" . . . at the beginning of November, Jonathan Burge, finding it impossible to replace **Adam**, had at last made up his mind to offer him a share in the business, without further condition than that he should continue to give his energies to it, and renounce all thought of having a separate business of his own. Son-in-law or no son-in-law, Adam had made himself too necessary to be parted with . . . . " 33

Mary Burge, " 'that nice modest girl . . . . ' " 9

"Mary was a good girl, not given to indulge in evil feelings, but she said to herself, that, since **Hetty** had a bad temper, it was better **Adam** should know it." 23

Casson, landlord. "Mr Casson's person was by no means of that common type which can be allowed to pass without description. On a front view it appeared to consist principally of two spheres, bearing about the same relation to each other as the earth and the moon: that is to say, the lower sphere might be said, at a rough guess, to be thirteen times larger than the upper, which naturally performed the function of a mere satellite and tributary. But here the resemblance ceased, for Mr Casson's head was not at all a melancholy-looking satellite, nor was it a 'spotty globe,' as **Milton** has irreverently called the moon; on the contrary, no head and face could look more sleek and healthy, and its expression, which was chiefly confined to a pair of round and ruddy cheeks, the slight knot and interruptions forming the nose and eyes being scarcely worth mention, was one of jolly contentment, only tempered by that sense of personal dignity which usually made itself felt in his attitude and bearing. This sense of dignity could hardly be considered excessive in a man who had been butler to 'the family' for fifteen years, and who, in his present high position, was necessarily very much in contact with his inferiors." 2

—voice: " . . . a treble and wheezy voice, with a slightly mincing accent." 2

—at church: " . . . in his most striking attitude—that is to say, with the forefinger of his right hand thrust between the buttons of his waistcoat, his left hand in his breeches pocket, and his head very much on one side; looking, on the whole, like an actor who has only a monosyllable part intrusted to him, but feels sure that the audience discern his fitness for the leading business. . . ." 18

—pride in his speech: " 'I daresay he'd think me a hodd talker, as you Loamshire folks allays does hany wonn as talks the right language.' " 32

Craig, "the gardener at the Chase, was over head and ears in love with [**Hetty**], and had lately made unmistakable avowals in luscious strawberries and hyperbolical peas." 9

—as a suitor: "And as for Mr Craig, the gardener, he was a sensible man enough, to be sure, but he was knock-kneed, and had a queer sort of sing-song in his talk; moreover, on the most charitable supposition, he must be far on the way to forty." 9

—informative: "Mr Craig, like a superior man, was very fond of giving information." 18

—cautious: "Mr Craig was a man of sober passions, and was already in his tenth year of hesitation as to the relative advantages of matrimony and bachelorhood. It is true that, now and then, when he had been a little heated by an extra glass of grog, he had been heard to say of **Hetty** that the 'lass was well enough,' and that 'a man might do worse'; but on convivial occasions men are apt to express themselves strongly." 18

—characteristics: "Mr Craig was an estimable gardener, and was not without reasons for having a high opinion of himself. He had also high shoulders and high cheek-bones, and hung his head forward a little, as he walked along with his hands in his breeches pockets. I think it was his pedigree only that had the advantage of being Scotch, and not his 'bringing up'; for except that he had a stronger burr in his accent, his speech differed little from that of the Loamshire people about him." 18

—observant: "Him [**Arthur Donnithorne**] and th' old Squire fit one another like frost and flowers.' " 18

—not a singer: " 'A man that's got the names and the natur o' plants in's head isna likely to keep a hollow place t'hold tunes in.' " 23

—authority: "Mr Craig was not above talking politics occasionally, though he piqued himself rather on a wise insight than on specific information. He saw so far beyond the mere facts of a case, that really it was superfluous to know them." 53

Ben Cranage (**'Wiry Ben'**). " 'Hoorray!' shouted a small lithe fellow, called Wiry Ben, running forward and seizing the door." 1

—*at the preaching:* "Wiry Ben was feeling very uncomfortable, and almost wishing he had not come to hear **Dinah**; he thought what she said would haunt him somehow. Yet he couldn't help liking to look at her and listen to her, though he dreaded every moment that she would fix her eyes on him, and address him in particular." 2

—*agile:* " . . . a long list of challenges to such ambitious attempts as that of walking as many yards as possible on one leg—feats in which it was generally remarked that Wiry Ben, being 'the lissom'st, springiest fellow i' the country,' was sure to be pre-eminent." 25

—*dancing:* "Have you ever seen a real English rustic perform a solo dance? Perhaps you have only seen a ballet rustic, smiling like a merry countryman in crockery, with graceful turns of the haunch and insinuating movements of the head. That is as much like the real thing as the 'Bird Waltz' is like the song of birds. Wiry Ben never smiled: he looked as serious as a dancing monkey—as serious as if he had been an experimental philosopher ascertaining in his own person the amount of shaking and the varieties of angularity that could be given to the human limbs . . . .

" 'What dost think o' that?' [**Martin Poyser**] said to his wife. 'He goes as pat to the music as if he was made o' clockwork . . . . '

" 'It's little matter what his limbs are, to my thinking,' returned **Mrs Poyser**. 'He's empty enough i' the upper story, or he'd niver come jigging an' stamping i' that way, like a mad grasshopper, for the gentry to look at him.' " 25

—*speaking out:* "[**Bessy**'s] cousin Wiry Ben, who stood near her, judiciously suggested, **Dinah** was not going away, and if Bessy was in low spirits, the best thing for her to do was to follow Dinah's example, and marry an honest fellow who was ready to have her." 55

Bessy Cranage, "the blacksmith's buxom daughter, known to her neighbours as **Chad's Bess**, who wondered 'why the folks war a-mekin' faces a that'ns.' Chad's Bess was the object of peculiar compassion, because her hair, being turned back under a cap which was set at the top of her head, exposed to view an ornament of which she was much prouder than of her red cheeks, namely a pair of large round earrings with false garnets in them, ornaments contemned not only by the Methodists, but by her own cousin and namesake **Timothy's Bess**, who, with much cousinly feeling, often wished 'them earrings' might come to good." 2

—*puzzled:* "[She] had shown an unwonted quietude and fixity of attention ever since **Dinah** had begun to speak. Not that the matter of the discourse had arrested her at once, for she was lost in a puzzling speculation as to what pleasure and satisfaction there could be in life to a young woman who wore a cap like Dinah's. Giving up this inquiry in despair, she took to studying Dinah's nose, eyes, mouth, and hair, and wondering whether it was better to have such a sort of pale face as that, or fat red cheeks and round black eyes like her own." 2

—*frightened:* "But gradually the influence of the general gravity told upon her, and she became conscious of what **Dinah** was saying. The gentle tones, the loving persuasion, did not touch her, but when the more severe appeals came she began to be frightened. Poor Bessy had always been considered a naughty girl; she was conscious of it; if it was necessary to be very good, it was clear she must be in a bad way. She couldn't find her places at church as **Sally Rann** could, she had often been tittering when she 'curcheyed' to **Mr Irwine**, and these religious deficiencies were accompanied by a corresponding slackness in the minor morals, for Bessy belonged unquestionably to that unsoaped, lazy class of feminine characters with whom you may venture to eat 'an egg, an apple, or a nut.' All this she was generally conscious of, and hitherto had not been greatly ashamed of it. But now she began to feel very much as if the constable had come to take her up and carry her before the justice for some undefined offence. She had a terrified sense that God, whom she had always thought of as very far off, was very near to her, and that **Jesus** was close by looking at her, though she could not see him." 2

—triumphant: " 'Here's a delicate bit of womanhood, or girlhood, coming to receive a prize, I suppose,' said **Mr Gawaine**. 'She must be one of the racers in the sacks . . . . '

"The 'bit of womanhood' was our old acquaintance Bessy Cranage, otherwise Chad's Bess, whose large red cheeks and blowsy person had undergone an exaggeration of colour, which, if she had happened to be a heavenly body, would have made her sublime. Bessy, I am sorry to say, had taken to her earrings again since **Dinah**'s departure, and was otherwise decked out in such small finery as she could muster. Any one who could have looked into poor Bessy's heart would have seen a striking resemblance between her little hopes and anxieties and **Hetty**'s. The advantage, perhaps, would have been on Bessy's side in the matter of feeling. But then, you see, they were so very different outside! You would have been inclined to box Bessy's ears, and you would have longed to kiss Hetty." 25

Chad Cranage, "the blacksmith himself, who stood with his black brawny arms folded, leaning against the door-post, and occasionally sending forth a bellowing laugh at his own jokes, giving them a marked preference over the sarcasms of **Wiry Ben** . . . . " 2

—on Sunday: "Chad Cranage looks like quite a new acquaintance to-day; for he has got his clean Sunday face, which always makes his little granddaughter cry at him as a stranger. But an experienced eye would have fixed on him at once as the village blacksmith, after seeing the humble deference with which the big saucy fellow took off his hat and stroked his hair to the farmer; for Chad was accustomed to say . . . that men who had horses to be shod must be treated with respect." 18

—frightened: "**Bessy** could bear it no longer: a great terror was upon her, and wrenching her earrings from her ears, she threw them down before her, sobbing aloud. Her father Chad, frightened lest he should be 'laid hold on' too, this impression on the rebellious Bess striking him as nothing less than a miracle, walked hastily away, and began to work at his anvil by way of reassuring himself 'Folks mun ha' hoss-shoes, praichin' or no praichin': the divil canna lay hould o' me for that,' he muttered to himself." 2

Lydia Donnithorne. "[**Hetty**] knew Miss Lydia was passing, and though Hetty liked so much to look at her fashionable little coal-scuttle bonnet, with the wreath of small roses round it, she didn't mind it to-day." 18

—to dance: "**Mr Gawaine** brought Miss Lydia, looking neutral and stiff in an elegant peach-blossom silk . . . . " 25

—bereaved: "Aunt Lydia was the only person in the house who knew nothing about **Hetty**: her sorrow as a maiden daughter was unmixed with

any other thoughts than those of anxiety about funeral arrangements and her own future lot; and, after the manner of women, she mourned for the father who had made her life important, all the more because she had a secret sense that there was little mourning for him in other hearts." 44

Squire Donnithorne. " . . . that gentleman had the meanness to receive his own rents and make bargains about his own timber." 18

" . . . he always came first, the wrinkled small old man, peering round with short-sighted glances at the bowing and curtsying congregation . . . . " 18

—*his grandson's view:* " 'There's the most curious contradiction in my grandfather: I know he means to leave me all the money he has saved, and he is likely enough to have cut off poor aunt **Lydia**, who has been a slave to him all her life, with only five hundred a-year, for the sake of giving me all the more; and yet I sometimes think he positively hates me because I'm his heir. I believe if I were to break my neck, he would feel it the greatest misfortune that could befall him, and yet it seems a pleasure to him to make my life a series of petty annoyances.' " 22

—*to dance:* "Old Mr Donnithorne, the delicately-clean, finely-scented, withered old man, led out **Miss Irwine**, with his air of punctilious, acid politeness." 25

—*understood:* "The old Squire, before sitting down, walked round the hall to greet the tenants and make polite speeches to the wives: he was always polite; but the farmers had found out, after long puzzling, that this polish was one of the signs of hardness." 26

—*mode of speech:* "He always spoke in the same deliberate, well-chiselled, polite way, whether his words were sugary or venomous." 32

—*discomfited: see Topicon* LC:Communication—*speaking truth to power*

—*age:* " 'It struck me [said **Mrs Irwine**] on **Arthur**'s birthday that the old man was a little shaken: he's eighty-three, you know. It's really an unconscionable age. It's only women who have a right to live as long as that.' " 33

Mrs Irwine. " . . . we can look at that stately old lady, [the rector's] mother, a beautiful aged brunette, whose rich-toned complexion is well set off by the complex wrappings of pure white cambric and lace about her head and neck. She is as erect in her comely embonpoint as a statue of *Ceres*, and her dark face, with its delicate aquiline nose, firm proud mouth, and small intense black eye, is so keen and sarcastic in its expression that you instinctively substitute a pack of cards for the chess-men, and imagine her telling your fortune. The small brown hand with which she is lifting her queen is laden with pearls, diamonds, and turquoises, and a large black veil is very carefully adjusted over the crown of her cap, and falls in sharp contrast on the white folds about her neck. It must take a long time to dress that old lady in the morning! But it seems a law of nature that she should be drest so: she is clearly one of those children of royalty who have never doubted their right divine, and never met with any one so absurd as to question it." 5

"That fine old lady herself was worth driving ten miles to see, any day; her beauty, her well-preserved faculties, and her old-fashioned dignity, made her quite a graceful subject for conversation . . . . " 5

old **Martin Poyser**, "a hale but shrunken and bleached image of his portly black-haired son—his head hanging forward a little, and his elbows pushed backward so as to allow the whole of his fore-arm to rest on the arm of the chair. His blue handkerchief was spread over his knees, as was usual indoors, when it was not hanging over his head, and he sat watching what went forward with the quiet *outward* glance of healthy old age . . . ." 15

—useful: "Old Martin opened the gate as he saw the family procession approaching, and held it wide open, leaning on his stick—pleased to do this bit of work; for, like all old men whose life has been spent in labour, he liked to feel that he was still useful—that there was a better crop of onions in the garden because he was by at the sowing—and that the cows would be milked the better if he staid at home on a Sunday afternoon to look on. He always went to church on Sacrament Sundays, but not very regularly at other times: on wet Sundays, or whenever he had a touch of rheumatism, he used to read the first chapters of Genesis instead." 18

Marty and **Tommy Poyser**, "boys of nine and seven, in little fustian tailed coats and knee-breeches, relieved by rosy cheeks and black eyes; looking as much like their father as a very small elephant is like a very large one . . . conscious of a marble or two in their pockets, which they looked forward to handling a little, secretly, during the sermon." 18

—distracted: "The fact was that this Sunday walk through the fields was fraught with great excitement to Marty and Tommy, who saw a perpetual drama going on in the hedgerows, and could no more refrain from stopping and peeping than if they had been a couple of spaniels or terriers. Marty was quite sure he saw a yellowhammer on the boughs of the great ash, and while he was peeping, he missed the sight of a white-throated stoat, which had run across the path and was described with much fervour by the junior Tommy. Then there was a little greenfinch, just fledged, fluttering along the ground, and it seemed quite possible to catch it, till it managed to flutter under the blackberry bush . . . .

" . . . Mary ran on first, shouting, 'We've found the speckled turkey's nest, mother!' with the instinctive confidence that people who bring good news are never in fault." 18

Totty (Charlotte) Poyser. "The small chirruping voice . . . came from a little sunny-haired girl between three and four, who, seated on a high chair at the end of the ironing-table, was arduously clutching the handle of a miniature iron with her tiny fat fist, and ironing rags with an assiduity that required her to put her little red tongue out as far as anatomy would allow." 6

—in mischief: "Totty, however, had descended from her chair with great swiftness, and was already in retreat towards the dairy, with a sort of waddling run, and an amount of fat on the nape of her neck, which made her look like the metamorphosis of a white sucking pig." 6

—now older: "Totty, looking as serenely unconscious of remark as a fat white puppy, was set down at the door-place, and the mother enforced her reproof with a shower of kisses." 49

—upset: " . . . **Tommy**, no longer expectant of cake, was lifting up his eyelids with his forefingers, and turning his eyeballs towards Totty, in a way that she felt to be disagreeably personal." 49

—discipline: " 'Mother,' said Totty, with her treble pipe, '**Dinah** was saying her prayers and crying ever so.'

" 'Hush, hush,' said the mother: 'little gells mustn't chatter.'

"Whereupon the father, shaking with silent laughter, set Totty on the white deal table, and desired her to kiss him. **Mr** and **Mrs Poyser**, you perceive, had no correct principles of education." 49

Joshua Rann. "Mr Rann's leathern apron and subdued griminess can leave no one in any doubt that he is the village shoemaker; the thrusting out of his chin and stomach, and the twirling of his thumbs, are more subtle indications, intended to prepare unwary strangers for the discovery that they are in the presence of the parish clerk. 'Old Joshway,' as he is irreverently called by his neighbours, is in a state of simmering indignation; but he has not yet opened his lips except to say in a resounding bass undertone, like the tuning of a violoncello . . . a quotation which may seem to have slight bearing on the present occasion, but, as with every other anomaly, adequate knowledge will show it to be a natural sequence. Mr Rann was inwardly maintaining the dignity of the Church in the face of this scandalous irruption of Methodism, and as that dignity was bound up with his own sonorous utterance of the responses, his argument naturally suggested a quotation from the psalm he had read the last Sunday afternoon." 2

—surprised: "[Seeing **Dinah Morris** for the first time,] Joshua Rann gave a long cough, as if he were clearing his throat in order to come to a new understanding with himself . . . . " 2

—reading in church: "But there was one reason why even a chance comer would have found the service in Hayslope Church more impressive than in most other village nooks in the kingdom—a reason, of which I am sure you have not the slightest suspicion. It was the reading of our friend Joshua Rann. Where that good shoemaker got his notion of reading from, remained a mystery even to his most intimate acquaintances. I believe, after all, he got it chiefly from Nature, who had poured some of her music into this honest conceited soul, as she had been known to do into other narrow souls before his. She had given him, at least, a fine bass voice and a musical ear; but I cannot positively say whether these alone had sufficed to inspire him with the rich chant in which he delivered the responses. The way he rolled from a rich deep forte into a melancholy cadence, subsiding, at the end of the last word, into a sort of faint resonance, like the lingering vibrations of a fine violoncello, I can compare to nothing for its strong calm melancholy but the rush and cadence of the wind among the autumn boughs. This may seems a strange mode of speaking about the reading of a parish clerk—a man in rusty spectacles, with stubbly hair, a large occiput, and a prominent crown." 18

Mr Ryde, "who came there twenty years afterwards, when **Mr Irwine** had been gathered to his fathers. It is true Mr Ryde insisted strongly on the doctrines of the Reformation, visited his flock a great deal in their own homes, and was severe in rebuking the aberrations of the flesh—put a stop, indeed, to the Christmas rounds of the church singers, as promoting drunkenness and too light a handling of sacred things. But I gathered from **Adam Bede**, to whom I talked of these matters in his old age, that few clergymen could be less successful in winning the hearts of their parishioners than Mr Ryde." 17

—a report: " 'Somehow, the congregation began to fall off [said **Adam**], and people began to speak light o' Mr Ryde. I believe he meant right at bottom; but, you see, he was sourish-tempered, and was for beating down prices with the people as worked for him; and his preaching wouldn't go down well with that sauce. And he wanted to be like my lord judge i' the parish, punishing folks for doing wrong; and he scolded 'em from the pulpit as if he'd

been a Ranter, and yet he couldn't abide the Dissenters, and was a deal more set against 'em than **Mr Irwine** was. And then he didn't keep within his income, for he seemed to think at first go-off that six hundred a-year was to make him as big a man as **Mr Donnithorne** . . . . Mr Ryde was a deal thought on at a distance, I believe, and he wrote books; but as for math'-matics and the natur o' things, he was as ignorant as a woman. He was very knowing about doctrines, and used to call 'em the bulwarks of the Reformation; but I've always mistrusted that sort of learning as leaves folks foolish and unreasonable about business.' " 27

John Wesley [H]. " 'I remember his face well [said **Dinah**]: he was a very old man, and had very long white hair; his voice was very soft and beautiful, not like any voice I had ever heard before. I was a little girl, and scarcely knew anything, and this old man seemed to me such a different sort of a man from anybody I had ever seen before, that I thought he had perhaps come down from the sky to preach to us, and I said, "Aunt, will he go back to the sky to-night, like the picture in the Bible?"

" 'That man of God was Mr Wesley, who spent his life in doing what our blessed Lord did—preaching the Gospel to the poor—and he entered into his rest eight years ago [1791].' " 2

Minor Figures

Alick, "the shepherd, in his new smock-frock, [was] taking an uneasy siesta, half-sitting half-standing on the granary steps. Alick was of opinion that church, like other luxuries, was not to be indulged in often by a foreman who had the weather and the ewes on his mind. 'Church! nay—I'n gotten summat else to think on,' was an answer which he often uttered in a tone of bitter significance that silenced further question. I feel sure Alick meant no irreverence; indeed, I know that his mind was not of a speculative, negative cast, and he would on no account have missed going to church on Christmas Day, Easter Sunday, and 'Whissuntide.' But he had a general impression that public worship and religious ceremonies, like other non-productive employments, were intended for people who had leisure." 18

—at the harvest supper: "Then, at the end of the table, opposite his master, there was Alick, the shepherd and head man, with the ruddy face and broad shoulders . . . not by any means a honeyed man: his speech had usually something of a snarl in it, and his broad-shouldered aspect something of the bulldog expression . . . but he was honest even to the splitting of an oat-grain rather than take beyond his acknowledged share, and as 'close-fisted' with his master's property as if it had been his own—throwing very small handfuls of damaged barley to the chickens, because a large handful affected his imagination painfully with a sense of profusion." 53

Kester Bale (**Beale**), "the old man with the close leather cap, and the network of wrinkles on his sun-browned face. Was there any man in Loamshire who knew better the 'natur' of all farming work? One of those invaluable labourers who can not only turn their hand to everything, but excel in everything they turn their hand to. It is true, Kester's knees were much bent outward by this time, and he walked with a perpetual curtsy, as if he were among the most reverent of men . . . . He always thatched the ricks; for if anything were his forte more than another, it was thatching; and when the last touch had been put to the last beehive rick, Kester . . . would take a walk to the rickyard in his best clothes on a Sunday morning, and stand in the lane, at a due distance, to contemplate his own thatching . . . . Kester was an old bachelor, and reputed to have stockings full of coin, concerning which his master cracked a joke with him every pay-night . . . . I am not ashamed of commemorating old Kester: you and I are indebted to the hard hands of such men—hands that have long ago mingled with the soil they tilled so faithfully, thriftily making the best they could of the earth's fruits, and receiving the smallest share as their own wages." 53

Addy Bede. "**Seth** . . . being taller than usual by the black head of a sturdy two-year-old nephew, who had caused some delay by demanding to be carried on uncle's shoulder." *E*

Lisbeth Bede, "a small fair creature with pale auburn hair and grey eyes, little more than four years old, who ran out silently and put her hand into her mother's." *E*

Thias Bede. " 'If I wasn't sharp with him [said **Adam**], he'd sell every bit of stuff i' th' yard, and spend it on drink. I know there's a duty to be done by my father, but it isn't my duty to encourage him in running headlong to ruin.' " 4

—disgrace: "**Adam** remembered well the night of shame and anguish when he first saw his father quite wild and foolish, shouting a song out fitfully among his drunken companions at the 'Waggon Overthrown.' " 4

Brimstone "was a Methodist brickmaker, who, after spending thirty years of his life in perfect satisfaction with his ignorance, had lately 'got religion,' and along with it the desire to read the Bible . . . . [He] had been a notorious poacher, and was suspected, though there was no good evidence against him, of being the man who had shot a neighbouring gamekeeper in the leg . . . though he was still known in the neighbourhood by his old sobriquet of 'Brimstone,' there was nothing he held in so much horror as any farther transactions with that evil-smelling element. He was a broad-chested fellow with a fervid temperament, which helped him better in imbibing religious ideas than in the dry process of acquiring the mere human knowledge of the alphabet." 21

Luke Britton sr., "whose fallows were not well cleaned, who didn't know the rudiments of hedging and ditching, and showed but a small share of judgment in the purchase of winter stock . . . . " 14

Luke Britton "of Broxton came to Hayslope Church on a Sunday afternoon on purpose that he might see [**Hetty**]; and . . . would have made much more decided advances if her uncle **Poyser**, thinking but lightly of a young man whose father's land was so foul as **old Luke Britton**'s, had not forbidden her aunt to encourage him in any civilities." 9

—tongue-tied: " . . . that slouching Luke Britton, who, when [**Hetty**] once walked with him all the way from Broxton to Hayslope, had only broken silence to remark that the grey goose had begun to lay." 9

Carrol. " '[**Arthur**'s] said in plenty of people's hearing [said **Bartle**] that he'd make you [**Adam**] manager of the woods to-morrow, if he'd the power. Why, Carrol, **Mr Irwine**'s butler, heard him say so to the parson not many days ago. Carrol looked in when we were smoking our pipes o' Saturday night at **Casson**'s, and he told us about it . . . . ' " 21

—spreading news: " . . . Carrol, who kept his ears open to all that passed at the Rectory, had framed an inferential version of the story, and found early opportunities of communicating it." 40

Chaplain. " 'The jail chaplain is rather harsh in his manner.' " 41

" ' . . . he's a sharp ferrety-faced man—another sort o' flesh and blood to **Mr Irwine**. They say the jail chaplains are mostly the fag-end o' the clergy.' " 42

Child, auditor. " ' . . . there was one stout curly-headed fellow about three or four year-old, that I never saw there before. He was as naughty as could be at the beginning while I was praying, and while we was singing, but when we all sat down and **Dinah** began to speak, th' young 'un stood stock-still all at once, and began to look at her with's mouth open, and presently he run away from's mother and went up to Dinah, and pulled at her, like a little dog, for her to take notice of him. So Dinah lifted him up and held th' lad on her lap, while she went on speaking; and he was as good as could be till he went t' sleep—and the mother cried to see him.' " 51

Chowne. "Well, Chowne's been wantin' to buy **Sally**, so we can get rid of her, if thee lik'st,' said Mr Poyser . . . . " 18

Mrs Chowne. " 'What's it sinnify what Chowne's wife likes?—a poor soft thing, wi' no more head-piece nor a sparrow. She'd take a big cullender to strain her lard wi', and then wonder as the scratchins run through. I've seen enough of her to know as I'll niver take a servant from her house again. . . .' " 18

Coachman. "The burly old coachman from Oakbourne, seeing such a pretty young woman among the outside passengers, had invited her to come and sit beside him . . . . After many cuts with his whip and glances at **Hetty** out of the corner of his eye, he lifted his lips above the edge of his wrapper, and said,

" 'He's pretty nigh six foot, I'll be bound, isna he, now?' " 36

Coachman, "[who] came up, and begged [**Hetty**] to 'remember him.' She put her hand in her pocket and took out the shilling, but the tears came with the sense of exhaustion and the thought that she was giving away her last means of getting food . . . 'Can you give me back sixpence?'

" 'No, no,' he said, gruffly, 'never mind—put the shilling up again.' " 36

Counsel. " ' . . . there's the counsel they've got for [**Hetty**] puts a spoke in the wheel whenever he can, and makes a deal to do with cross-examining the witnesses, and quarrelling with the other lawyers. That's all he can do for the money they give him; and it's a big sum—it's a big sum. But he's a 'cute fellow, with an eye that 'ud pick the needles out of the hay in no time.' " 42

Dalton, "the coachman, whose person stood out in high relief as he smoked his pipe against the stable wall, when **John** brought up **Rattler** . . . .

" 'Ay; he'd hev a deal habler groom nor what he hes now,' observed Dalton, and the joke appeared to him so good, that being left alone upon the scene, he continued at intervals to take his pipe from his mouth in order to wink at an imaginary audience, and shake luxuriously with a silent, ventral laughter; mentally rehearsing the dialogue from the beginning, that he might recite it with effect in the servants' hall." 12

David. "The amatory David was a young man of an unconscious abstracted expression, which was due probably to a squint of superior intensity rather than to any mental characteristic; for he was not indifferent to **Ben**'s invitation [to sing], but blushed and laughed and rubbed his sleeve over his mouth in a way that was regarded as a symptom of yielding. And for some time the company appeared to be much in earnest about the desire to hear David's song. But in vain." 53

Dolly, "a clean old woman, in a dark-striped linen gown, a red kerchief, and a linen cap, talking to some speckled fowls which appeared to have been drawn towards her by an illusory expectation of cold potatoes or barley. The old woman's sight seemed to be dim . . . . " 1

"[**Lisbeth**'s] favourite Dolly, the old housekeeper at **Mr Burge**'s, who had come to condole with her in the morning as soon as she heard of **Thias**'s death, was too dim-sighted to be of much use." 10

Bill Downes "was a sturdy fellow, aged four-and-twenty, an excellent stone-sawyer, who could get as good wages as any man in the trade of his years, but he found a reading lesson in words of one syllable a harder matter to deal with than the hardest stone he had ever had to saw. The letters, he complained, were so 'uncommon alike, there was no tellin' 'em one from another,' the sawyer 's business not being concerned with minute differences such as exist between a letter with its tail turned up and a letter with its tail turned down . . . . So here he was, pointing his big finger towards three words at once, and turning his head on one side that he might keep better hold with his eye of the one word which was to be discriminated out of the group. The amount of knowledge **Bartle Massey** must possess was something so dim and vast that Bill's imagination recoiled before it: he would hardly have ventured to deny that the schoolmaster might have something to do in bringing about the regular return of daylight and the changes in the weather." 21

Job Dummilow. "If any one had asked old Job Dummilow who gave him his flannel jacket, he would have answered, 'the gentlefolks, last winter'. . . . " 5

Dyer, "a much more promising pupil. He was a tall but thin and wiry man, nearly as old as **Brimstone**, with a very pale face, and hands stained a deep blue. He was a dyer, who, in the course of dipping home-spun wool and old women's petticoats, had got fired with the ambition to learn a great deal more about the strange secrets of colour. He had already a high reputation in the district for his dyes, and he was bent on discovering some method by which he could reduce the expense of crimsons and scarlets. The **druggist** at Treddleston had given him a notion that he might save himself a great deal of labour and expense if he could learn to read, and so he had begun to give his spare-hours to the night-school . . . . " 21

Gedge. "I have often heard Mr Gedge, the landlord of the Royal Oak, who used to turn a bloodshot eye on his neighbours in the village of Shepperton, sum up his opinion of the people in his own parish—and they were all the people he knew—in these emphatic words: 'Ay, sir, I've said it often, and I'll say it again, they're a poor lot i' this parish— a poor lot, sir, big and little.' " 17

Gyp, "a rough grey shepherd-dog . . . was lying with his nose between his fore-paws, occasionally wrinkling his brows to cast a glance at the tallest of the five workmen . . . . " 1

—helpful: "The basket was the one which on workdays held **Adam**'s and **Seth**'s dinner, and no official, walking in procession, could look more resolutely unconscious of all acquaintances than Gyp with his basket, trotting at his master's heels." 1

Michael Holdsworth. " . . . for had not Michael Holdsworth had a pair of oxen 'sweltered' while he was ploughing on Good Friday? That was a demonstration that work on sacred days was a wicked thing . . . . " 18

Innkeeper, "seeing that **Adam** was in great anxiety, and entering into this new incident with the eagerness of a man who passes a great deal of time with his hands in his pockets looking into an obstinately monotonous street, offered to take him back to Oakbourne in his own 'taxed cart' this very evening." 38

Anne Irwine. " 'It's no use, child; she can't speak to you. **Kate** says she has one of her worst headaches this morning.'

" 'O she likes me to go and see her just the same; she's never too ill to care about that.' " 5

—invalid: "It was a small face, that of the poor sufferer; perhaps it had once been pretty, but now it was worn and sallow . . . . Anne's eyes were closed, and her brow contracted as if from intense pain. **Mr Irwine** went to the bedside, and took up one of the delicate hands and kissed it; a slight pressure from the small fingers told him that it was worth while to have come up-stairs for the sake of doing that." 5

Miss Kate Irwine, "the thin middle-aged lady standing by the bedside, would not have had light enough for any other sort of work than the knitting which lay on the little table near her. But at present she was doing what required only the dimmest light—sponging the aching head that lay on the pillow with fresh vinegar." 5

—indictment: "And **Mr Irwine**'s sisters, as any person of family within ten miles of Broxton could have testified, were such stupid uninteresting women! It was quite a pity handsome, clever **Mrs Irwine** should have had such commonplace daughters . . . no one ever thought of mentioning the Miss Irwines, except the poor people of Broxton village, who regarded them as deep in the science of medicine, and spoke of them vaguely as 'the gentlefolks.' " 5

" . . . the general impression was quite in accordance with the fact that both the sisters were old maids for the prosaic reason, that they had never received an eligible offer." 5

John. "[The squire] persisted in retaining as head groom an old dolt whom no sort of lever could move out of his old habits, and who was allowed to hire a succession of raw Loamshire lads as his subordinates . . . . "

"Old John's wooden, deep-wrinkled face was the first object that met **Arthur**'s eyes as he entered the stable-yard, and it quite poisoned for him the bark of the two bloodhounds that kept watch there. He could never speak quite patiently to the old blockhead." 12

"John considered a young master as the natural enemy of an old servant, and young people in general as a poor contrivance for carrying on the world." 12

Judith. " 'You look th' image o' your aunt Judith, **Dinah** . . . only her hair was a deal darker than yours, and she was stouter and broader i' the shoulders . . . . I allays said that o' Judith, as she'd bear a pound weight any day, to save anybody else carrying a ounce. And she was just the same from the first o' my remembering her; it made no difference in her, as I could see, when she took to the Methodists, only she talked a bit different, and wore a different sort o' cap; but she'd never in her life spent a penny on herself more than keeping herself decent.'

" 'She was a blessed woman,' said Dinah; 'God had given her a loving, self-forgetting nature, and he perfected it by grace. And she was very fond of you too, Aunt **Rachel**. I've often heard her talk of you in the same sort of way.' " 6

Kitty. " 'There's a piece o' sheeting I could give you as that squinting Kitty spun—she was a rare girl to spin, for all she squinted, and the children couldn't abide her . . . .' " 6

Landlady. " 'Ah, it's plain enough what sort of business it is,' said the wife. 'She's not a common flaunting dratchell, I can see that. She looks like a respectable country girl, and she comes from a good way off, to judge by her tongue . . . .

" 'It 'ud have been a good deal better for her if she'd been uglier and had more conduct,' said the landlady, who on any charitable construction must have been supposed to have more 'conduct' than beauty." 36

—an offer: "I will not say that in this accommodating proposition the landlady had no regard whatever to the possible reward of her good-nature in the ultimate possession of the locket and earrings: indeed, the effect they would have in that case on the mind of the grocer's wife had presented itself with remarkable vividness to her rapid imagination." 37

Landlord "of the Green Man . . . was a man whose abundant feeding served to keep his good-nature, as well as his person, in high condition. And that lovely tearful face of **Hetty**'s would have found out the sensitive fibre in most men." 36

—touched: " 'I never saw a prettier young woman in my life,' said the husband. 'She's like a pictur in a shop-winder. It goes to one's 'eart to look at her.' " 36

Mrs Maskery, " 'as they say's a big Methody, isna pleasant to look at, at all. I'd as lief look at a tooad [said **Lisbeth**].' " 10

Will Maskery, wheelwright. " ' . . . an' there's Will hisself, lookin' as meek as if he couldna knock a nail o' th' head for fear o' hurtin't.' " 2

—as a speaker: " 'Will Maskery is no preacher himself, I think.'

" 'Nay, sir [said **Joshua Rann**], he's no gift at stringin' the words together wi'out book; he'd be stuck fast like a cow i' wet clay. But he's got tongue enough to speak disrespectful about's neebors, for he said as I was a blind Pharisee; —a-usin' the Bible i' that way to find nicknames for folks as are his elders an' betters . . . . ' "

—reformed: " 'Will Maskery might be a great deal worse fellow than he is. He used to be a wild drunken rascal, neglecting his work and beating his wife, they told me; now he's thrifty and decent, and he and his wife look comfortable together.' " 5

—critic: " 'An' he said as our Christmas singin' was no better nor the cracklin' o' thorns under a pot.' " 5

Meg. "The pretty creature arched her bay neck in the sunshine, and pawed the gravel, and trembled with pleasure when her master stroked her nose, and patted her, and talked to her even in a more caressing tone than usual. He loved her the better because she knew nothing of his secrets. But Meg was quite as well acquainted with her master's mental state as many others of her sex with the mental condition of the nice young gentlemen towards whom their hearts are in a state of fluttering expectation." 29

Molly. "To all appearance Molly had got through her after-dinner work in an exemplary manner, had 'cleaned herself' with great despatch, and now came to ask, submissively, if she should sit down to her spinning till milking-time." 6

—*kind:* "Molly, the housemaid, with a turn-up nose and a protuberant jaw, was really a tenderhearted girl, and, as **Mrs Poyser** said, a jewel to look after the poultry; but her stolid face showed nothing of this maternal delight, any more than a brown earthenware pitcher will show the light of the lamp within it." 15

—*cooperative:* "[She] was called on for her ready sympathy, and peeped with open mouth wherever she was told, and said 'Lawks!' whenever she was expected to wonder." 18

Nancy, kitchen-maid " . . . the fuller the cart the better, because then the jolting would not hurt so much, and Nancy's broad person and thick arms were an excellent cushion to be pitched on." 22

Old man. "And there was a face looking down on [**Hetty**]; but it was an unknown face, belonging to an elderly man in a smock-frock.

" 'Why, what do you do here, young woman?' the man said roughly." 37

—*offered money:* "He looked slowly at the sixpence, and then said, 'I want none o' your money. You'd better take care on't, else you'll get it stool from yer, if you go trapesin' about the fields like a mad woman a-that'n.' " 37

Old woman, "with a slow palsied shake of the head . . . slow of speech and apprehension . . . .

" 'Nay, I'n seen no young woman.' " 38

John Olding, labourer. " 'I saw the prisoner, in a red cloak, sitting under a bit of a haystack not far off the stile. She got up when she saw me . . . she looked white and scared . . . I heard a strange cry. I thought it didn't come from any animal I knew, but I wasn't for stopping to look about just then. But it went on and seemed so strange to me in that place . . . . But when I came back the same way pretty nigh an hour after, I couldn't help laying down my stakes to have another look . . . I saw something odd and round and whitish lying on the ground under a nut-bush by the side of me. And I stooped down on hands and knees to pick it up. And I saw it was a little baby's hand.' " 43

Mrs Pomfret. " 'It isn't **Mrs Best**, it's Mrs Pomfret, the lady's-maid, as I go to see [said **Hetty**]. She's teaching me tent-stitch and the lacemending. I'm going to tea with her to-morrow afternoon.' " 7

—*noticing:* "Even Mrs Pomfret's preoccupied mind did not prevent her from noticing what looked like a new flush of beauty in the little thing as she tied on her hat before the looking-glass.

" 'That child gets prettier and prettier every day, I do believe,' was her inward comment. 'The more's the pity. She'll get neither a place nor a husband any the sooner for it. Sober well-to-do men don't like such pretty wives. When I was a girl I was more admired than if I'd been so very pretty. However, she's reason to be grateful to me for teaching her something to get her bread with, better than farmhouse work. They always told me I was good-natured' and that's the truth . . . . ' " 13

Pug, "who is dozing, with his black muzzle aloft, like a sleepy president." 5

Pym, valet. "Even the presence of Pym, waiting on him with the usual deference, was a reassurance to [**Arthur**] after the scenes of yesterday." 29

Mr Roe, "the 'travelling preacher' stationed at Treddleston, had included **Mr Irwine** in a general statement concerning the church clergy in the surrounding district, whom he described as men given up to the lusts of the flesh and the pride of life; hunting and shooting, and adorning their own houses; asking what shall we eat, and what shall we drink, and wherewithal shall we be clothed?—careless of dispensing the bread of life to their flocks, preaching at best but a carnal and soul-benumbing morality, and trafficking in the souls of men by receiving money for discharging the pastoral office in parishes where they did not so much as look on the faces of the people more than once a-year." 5

Ben Salt, "a sturdy fellow of five in knee-breeches and red legs, who had a rusty milk-can round his neck by way of drum, and was very carefully avoided by **Chad**'s small terrier. This young olive-branch, notorious under the name of **Timothy's Bess's Ben**, being of an inquiring disposition, unchecked by any false modesty, had advanced beyond the group of women and children, and was walking round the Methodists, looking up in their faces with his mouth wide open, and beating his stick against the milk-can by way of musical accompaniment. But one of the elderly women bending down to take him by the shoulder, with an air of grave remonstrance, Timothy's Bess's Ben first kicked out vigorously, then took to his heels and sought refuge behind his father's legs." 2

Bess Salt. "**Timothy's Bess**, though retaining her maiden appellation among her familiars, had long been the wife of **Sandy Jim**, and possessed of a handsome set of matronly jewels, of which it is enough to mention the heavy **baby** she was rocking in her arms, and [**Ben**] the sturdy fellow of five. . . ." 2

Jim Salt, "a burly red-haired man, known as **Sandy Jim**, paused from his planing . . . . " 1

—paternal: " 'Ye gallows young dog,' said Sandy Jim, with some paternal pride, 'if ye dunna keep that stick quiet, I'll tek it from ye. What d'ye mane by kickin' foulks?' " 2

—at the preaching: "She had already addressed Sandy Jim . . . and the big soft-hearted man had rubbed away some tears with his fist, with a confused intention of being a better fellow, going less to the Holly Bush down by the Stone Pits, and cleaning himself more regularly of a Sunday." 2

Satchell. " ' . . . I know [**Adam**] would make twice the money of them that my grandfather does, with that miserable old Satchell to manage, who understands no more about timber than an old carp' [said the Captain]." 5

—appraised: " 'He's been a selfish, tale-bearing, mischievous fellow [said **Adam**]; but, after all, there's nobody he's done so much harm to as to th' old Squire. Though it's the Squire himself as is to blame—making a stupid fellow like that a sort o' man-of-all-work, just to save th' expense of having a proper steward to look after th' estate.' " 21

Servants at the Chase. "They had the partisanship of household servants who like their places, and were not inclined to go the full length of the severe indignation felt against him by the farming tenants, but rather to make excuses for him; nevertheless, the upper servants, who had been on terms of neighbourly intercourse with the **Poysers** for many years, could not help feeling that the longed-for event of the young Squire's coming into the estate had been robbed of all its pleasantness." 44

Mrs Sorrel. " 'I'd hard work t'hould her in [said **old Martin**], an' she married i' spite o' me—a feller wi' on'y two head o' stock when there should ha' been ten on's farm—she might well die o' th' inflammation afore she war thirty.'

"It was seldom the old man made so long a speech; but his son's question had fallen like a bit of dry fuel on the embers of a long unextinguished resentment, which had always made the grandfather more indifferent to **Hetty** than to his son's children. Her mother's fortune had been spent by that good-for-nought **Sorrel**, and Hetty had Sorrel's blood in her veins." 31

Mrs Steene. " . . . widow Steene dwelt much on the virtues of the 'stuff' the gentlefolks gave her for her cough." 5

Sarah Stone. " 'I am a widow, and keep a small shop licensed to sell tobacco, snuff, and tea . . . . The prisoner at the bar is the same young woman who came, looking ill and tired, with a basket on her arm . . . her prettiness, and her condition, and something respectable about her clothes and looks, and the trouble she seemed to be in, made me as I couldn't find in my heart to send her away at once." 43

Jacob Storey. "[**Bartle Massey**] was a little more severe than usual on Jacob Storey's Z's, of which poor Jacob had written a pageful, all with their tops turned the wrong way, with a puzzled sense that they were not right 'somehow.' " 21

Mum Taft, "who, true to his name, had kept silence throughout the previous conversation, had flung down his hammer as he was in the act of lifting it . . . .

" 'Ay, ay, **Adam** lad, ye talk like a young un. When y' are six an' forty like me, istid o' six an' twenty, ye wonna be so flush o' workin for nought.' " 1

Old Taft. "Every generation in the village was there, from 'old Feyther Taft' in his brown worsted night-cap, who was bent nearly double, but seemed tough enough to keep on his legs a long while, leaning on his short stick . . . . " 2

" 'Well, Mester Taft,' shouted **old Martin**, at the utmost stretch of his voice—for though he knew the old man was stone deaf, he could not omit the propriety of a greeting—'you're hearty yit. You can enjoy yoursen to-day, for all you're ninety an' better.'

" 'Your sarvant, mesters, your sarvant,' said Feyther Taft in a treble tone, perceiving that he was in company." 22

Tom Tholer. "**Martin Poyser** . . . watched half-witted Tom Tholer, otherwise known as 'Tom Saft,' receiving his second plateful of beef. A grin of delight broke over Tom's face as the plate was set down before him, between his knife and fork, which he held erect, as if they had been sacred tapers; but the delight was too strong to continue smouldering in a grin—it burst out the next instant in a long-drawn 'haw, haw!' followed by a sudden collapse into utter gravity, as the knife and fork darted down on the prey." 53

Ben Tholoway, "a very powerful thresher, but detected more than once in carrying away his master's corn in his pockets: an action which, as Ben was not a philosopher, could hardly be ascribed to absence of mind. However, his master had forgiven him, and continued to employ him; for the Tholoways had lived on the Common, time out of mind, and had always worked for the

Poysers. And on the whole, I daresay, society was not much the worse because Ben had not six months of it at the treadmill; for his views of depredation were narrow, and the House of Correction might have enlarged them. As it was, Ben ate his roast-beef to-night with a serene sense of having stolen nothing more than a few peas and beans, as seed for his garden, since the last harvest-supper, and felt warranted in thinking that **Alick**'s suspicious eye, for ever upon him, was an injury to his innocence." 53

Tim. " . . . many 'whups' from Tim the ploughman, as if the heavy animals who held down their meek, intelligent heads, and lifted their shaggy feet so deliberately, were likely to rush wildly in every direction but the right." 20

—at the harvest supper: "Good-tempered Tim, the waggoner, who loved his horses, had his grudge against **Alick** in the matter of corn: they rarely spoke to each other, and never looked at each other, even over their dish of cold potatoes . . . . " 53

Traveller [Colonel Townley]. " . . . an elderly horseman, with his portmanteau strapped behind him, stopped his horse when **Adam** had passed him, and turned round to have another long look at the stalwart workman. . . . " 1

—seeing the preacher: " 'A sweet woman,' the stranger said to himself, 'but surely nature never meant her for a preacher.' " 2 *See* **Dinah Morris** OP *—transfixing*

—reappearance: " . . . no less than a second appearance of the smart man in top-boots, said by some to be a mere farmer in treaty for the Chase Farm, by others to be the future steward; but by **Mr Casson** himself, the personal witness to the stranger's visit, pronounced contemptuously to be nothing better than a bailiff . . . . " 32 *The "smart man" seems a GE mistake. She may have had a plan for the mysterious figure, but she truncated it at best.*

—another reappearance: " . . . an elderly gentleman was standing with his back against the smaller entrance-door of Stoniton jail, saying a few last words to the departing **chaplain**. The chaplain walked away, but the elderly gentleman stood still, looking down on the pavement, and stroking his chin, with a ruminating air when he was roused by a sweet clear woman's voice, saying,

" 'Can I get into the prison, if you please?' . . .

" 'I have seen you before,' he said, at last. 'Do you remember preaching on the village green at Hayslope in Loamshire?'

" 'Yes, sir, surely. Are you the gentleman that staid to listen on horse-back?' " 45

"After speaking to the jailer, the magistrate turned to her and said, 'The **turnkey** will take you to the prisoner's cell, and leave you there for the night, if you desire it; but you can't have a light during the night—it is contrary to rules. My name is **Colonel Townley**: if I can help you in anything, ask the jailer for my address, and come to me.' " 45

Vixen "could not even see her master look at [her puppies] without painful excitement: she got into the hamper and got out again the next moment, and behaved with true feminine folly, though looking all the while as wise as a dwarf with a large old-fashioned head and body on the most abbreviated legs." 21

—personal remark: " ' . . . I'm pretty sure the father was that hulking, bull-terrier of **Will Baker**'s—wasn't he now, eh, you sly hussey?' (Here Vixen tucked her tail between her legs, and ran forward into the house. Subjects are sometimes broached which a well-bred female will ignore.)" 21

Waggoner, "a large ruddy man, with a sack over his shoulders by way of scarf or mantle . . . .

" 'Aw,' said the big fellow, with that slowly-dawning smile which belongs to heavy faces, 'I can take y' up fawst enough wi'out bein' paid for't, if you dooant mind lyin' a bit closish a-top o' the wool-packs.' " 36

Jim Wakefield, " 'as they used to call "Gentleman Wakefield," used to do the same of a Sunday as o' week-days, and took no heed to right or wrong, as if there was nayther God nor devil. An' what's he come to? Why, I saw him myself last market-day a-carrying a basket wi' oranges in't.' " 18

Women in court. " 'And there's a lot o' foolish women in fine clothes, with gewgaws all up their arms and feathers on their heads, sitting near the judge: they've dressed themselves out in that way, one 'ud think, to be scarecrows and warnings against any man ever meddling with a woman again; they put up their glasses, and stared and whispered.' " 42

Youths, "between sixteen and nineteen, came up with imaginary bills of parcels, which they had been writing out on their slates, and were now required to calculate 'off-hand'—a test which they stood with such imperfect success, that **Bartle Massey**, whose eyes had been glaring at them ominously through his spectacles for some minutes, at length burst out in a bitter, high-pitched tone, pausing between every sentence to rap the floor with a knobbed stick which rested between his legs." 21

Also mentioned

Sister **Allen**, in a decline and needing Dinah Morris	3
Richard Arkwright [H], inventor and owner of water-powered cotton mills at Cromford	1
aunt of Dinah Morris, who took her to hear John Wesley, having brought her up	2
Miss Bacon, the miller's daughter, who was called the beauty of Treddleston	14
Will Baker, whose bull-terrier may have impregnated Bartle Massey's Vixen	21
Mrs Best, housekeeper for the Donnithornes	55
Bethell, a driver employed by the Squire	32
Betty, dairy-maid at the Hall Farm	6
Blick, Rev. Irwine's predecessor	5
Bradwell, a farmer needing Adam's help with his barn	16
Bridget, housemaid for the Irwines	5
Bygate, the lawyer, who greeted Arthur on his return	44
Chester, a boy at the Donnithorne estate who does chores for Mr Craig	18
Choyce, a tenant on the Donnithorne estate	6
constable who arrested Hetty and brought Irwine dreadful tidings	39
Crabtree, a farmer in Hayslope	32
Lord and **Lady Dacey** (of some thickness); his law-suit was fretting her to death	5, 15
—eldest son who lost thousands to the Prince of Wales	6
Dent, a game-keeper	16
Dingall, the grocer who gives a bad price for butter	18, 32
Mrs Dingall, a sensible woman who had very good kin	18
D'Oyley, a cleric formerly at Treddleston	16
druggist at Treddleston, who had advised the dyer to learn to read	21
Mrs Fletcher (who was **Miss Bosanquet**) [H], an early Wesleyan preacher	8, 51
Gawaine, a friend of Arthur Donnithorne's, living at Norburne	12
Godwin, doctor attending Captain Donnithorne's arm	5
Growler, a watch-dog at the Hall Farm	22

Justice Hardy, who heard an information on a dead baby	43
James, the Doctor's assistant, who married his niece secretly	15
Knowles, a wagon-driver	32
landlord at Snowfield: too chatty for Adam's taste	54
Mills, the butler at the Chase	23, 44
Old Brown, a sober horse pulling Mr Poyser's cart and pricking his ears to the music	22
ostler, a lad in a smock frock at the Donnithorne Arms	2
ostler, at the Royal Oak, Oakbourne; he remembered Hetty	38
Ottley, Molly's former employer	6
Prince of Wales, who won money from Lord Dacey's son	6
Sally Rann, who sat with Bessy Cranage in church	2
Rattler, a horse in the Donnithorne stables intended for Arthur's valet Pym	12
Salkeld, a friend of Arthur's who took solace in daily port	12
Sally, a meek short-horned cow which lay chewing its cud	18
baby **Salt**, a heavy baby carried first by mother, then by Sandy Jim, the father	2
Mrs Satchell, with whose dairy management the Squire was not happy	32
Sheriff at Stoniton, who sees Arthur arrive with Hetty's reprieve	47
Sorrel, Hetty's father, who married her mother despite Martin Poyser's opposition	31
Billy Taft, the village idiot	21
Bob Tholer, for whom a coffin had been ordered	4
Josh Tod, innkeeper at the Holly Bush	1
Tommy, farm boy at the Hall Farm	6
Tradgett, the maiden name of Arthur Donnithorne's mother	5
Tradgett cousin, who would inherit if Arthur does not return	48
Gil Tranter, who was laid up for a fortnight after fighting Adam	16
Trent, Betty's former employer	6
Trip, a black and tan terrier at the Hall Farm	6
Trot, a tiny spaniel and Meg's inseparable companion in the stable	12
turnkey, at the Stoniton jail	45
West, a wool factor based in Rosseter	6
Sarah Williamson, Methodist preacher at Leeds	40

The Mill on the Floss

Book First: Boy and Girl

A scene of the river Floss, the stream Ripple, and the mill. A little girl watches the mill wheel. 1 The **Tullivers** are talking: **Tom** is to go to school, but where? **Maggie** enters, all dishevelled, and Mrs Tulliver directs her to clean up and come do her patchwork. She crossly declines and leaves. 2 Auctioneer and appraiser **Riley** visits, after a successful negotiation over water rights on Tulliver's behalf. Riley recommends the **Rev. Walter Stelling**, to school Tom, for personal political reasons and not knowing Stelling's qualifications. 3 Maggie is furious at not being allowed to go and meet Tom, back from school. She dunks her head in water to frustrate her mother's curling and runs off to the attic. As the weather and her temper improve, she heads for the yard and dog **Yap**, then visits miller **Luke Moggs** and his wife. She is reminded she promised Tom to feed his rabbits. She forgot: they are all dead. 4

Tom arrives. Maggie is thrilled. He has brought her a new fishing-line, which he had paid for after some fighting at school. She tells him about the rabbits, and he turns on her. No fishing for her. He loves her no more. Heartbroken, she flees to the attic. Her parents wonder where she is and send Tom for her. Reconciliation. Fishing the next day: a halcyon morning. The narrator's reflections on childhood and the good earth. 5 **Bob Jakin**, a child of nature and the lesser orders, walks with Tom. They get into a scrap over Bob's cheating on a call of a coin. Tom wins and walks off. Bob throws after him a knife Tom had given him. Tom ignores it. Bob picks it up again. 6

The aunts and uncles come for dinner. We meet aunts **Glegg** (acidic), **Pullet** (weepy) and **Deane** (sallow) and their husbands—also adorable **Lucy Deane**. They discuss Maggie's hair, so she runs out and cuts it off, which produces an uproar. Her father comforts her. The children are sent out; Mr Tulliver explains his plan to send Tom to a parson, and discussion leads to a row with aunt Glegg, who walks out. 7 Mrs Tulliver fears sister Glegg will call a loan to her husband. Mr Tulliver decides to call a loan he has made to his brother-in-law **Moss** and rides to see him. His sister's comments on brothers' loyalty to sisters hit home with him. He leaves the loan alone. 8 Mrs Tulliver and children, with Lucy, visit the Pullets. Maggie is irritable and accidentally knocks down Tom's pagoda of cards. He is furious and turns his attention all to Lucy. They hear the Pullet music-box, and in her pleasure Maggie knocks over Tom's cowslip wine. The children go off; Mrs Tulliver and aunt Pullet commiserate on them and Mr Tulliver. Shock interrupts them. 9

Lucy is shown in covered with mud. Tom has taken her to the pond to show her delicious sights and jealous Maggie has pushed her down. The house is stirred up. Maggie has disappeared. 10 She runs off to the gypsies, finds them not what she expected, gets frightened, and is taken toward the mill on a donkey. Her father meets her in the road. She tells of Tom's anger and her misery. He says a word at home. 11 The Gleggs at home: she is vexed, as usual, and takes it out on her husband, here described as good-natured and stingy. He hints at excellent will provision for her, and after half a day upstairs she is mollified. 12 Mrs Pullet finds her intervention for Tulliver unnecessary, but Mrs Tulliver has put her foot in it and aroused her husband's pride. He has written Mrs Glegg of his intent to repay the loan. He borrows £500 on bond from a client of his arch-enemy, the successful, unethical lawyer **Wakem**. 13

Book Second: School-Time

Tom reads and tries to learn **Euclid** and Latin with dogmatic, ambitious, and good-hearted Mr Stelling, and is at sea and miserable. His respite is airing baby **Laura**. Maggie visits and cheers him. She tries to understand his work and help him, and he is grateful for her company. He fears her quickness, but Stelling puts her down: girls are quick but shallow. Maggie is crushed. She goes home, and Tom regrets. The first half-year ends. 1 Tom is home for Christmas and hears much of his father's ire and legal woes. A neighbour upstream, **Pivart**, is doing some damming and irrigating. Wakem is his counsel. Tulliver fulminates. Tom learns that **Philip Wakem** will be at school with him. 2 On arrival he meets the slight, deformed Philip and is impressed by his drawing skill. Philip promises to help Tom with his Latin and tell him classic tales. 3

Tom is ambivalent about Philip, and Philip is sensitive to slight. But Tom is beguiled by Philip's drawing skill.. The narrator discourses on education "in those days": Tom was luckier than many. **Mr Poulter** comes to drill Tom and tells him tales of the Peninsular War. He brings his sword and shows manoeuvres with it. Tom is frightened but excited. He interrupts Philip at the piano urging him to come watch. Philip is furious. The two exchange wounding words. Poulter leaves his sword with Tom for secret practice. 4 Maggie comes again, and Tom shows off to her. The sword falls on his foot: he faints. 5 Will Tom be lame? Philip asks and reports: no. Their bond renews but fades as Tom recovers. 6 Maggie comes with terrible news: their father is ruined, having lost his lawsuit, and he has fallen from his horse and is in bed knowing no one. The children leave the school together, to enter a wilderness of sorrow and care. 7

Book Third: The Downfall

Flashback: Tulliver at first seems to be resilient and begins to plan. But his money troubles are great: he owes £250 as surety for the deceased Riley; there is a bill of sale for his household furniture and effects on the £500 he borrowed to repay Mrs Glegg. He gets a letter from his lawyer: his enemy Wakem is his creditor. He has a stroke. Maggie is sent for; then she goes for Tom. 1 Mrs Tulliver is beside herself: her china and other precious effects will be sold. Bailiffs are in the house. Maggie is furious: her father is being disregarded. 2 The sisters and husbands arrive for a conclave. Maggie flares out at them. Aunt Moss arrives, distraught. Tom says the Moss note must be destroyed: his father would wish it. 3 When they seek the note in a strongbox, the lid falls and Tulliver is startled awake. He says £50 must be paid to his foreman **Luke**, and the Moss note destroyed. Excited, he then relapses. 4

Tom goes to his uncle **Deane** to ask for advice and a job. Deane probes and equivocates. Tom's education is no help. Tom is hurt and irked. He takes it out on Maggie, who is miserable. 5 The sale of Tulliver effects takes place. Bob Jakin turns up. He has been rewarded for dousing a fire. He offers the nine sovereigns remaining to Tom, who is touched but declines. Bob will be a packman. Maggie offers friendship. 6 Tulliver makes progress. Mr Deane considers whether his firm might acquire the mill but is wary of Wakem, holder of the mortgage. Dim-witted Bessy Tulliver puts her foot in it and gives Wakem the idea of outbidding Guest & Co. for the mill. Tom has a warehouse job. 7 The mill goes to Wakem, Tulliver to be manager. Bessy tells him, and he submits for her sake. 8 He broods, but the pull of Home holds him to his word. He summons the family and has Tom write his perpetual unforgiveness of Wakem in the Bible. "You'll make him and his feel it." Maggie is horrified. 9

Book Fourth: The Valley of Humiliation

A meditation contrasting ruins on the Rhône and the Rhine, and a discourse on the Dodsons—conventional, prosaic, judging, image-conscious, loyal to kin. 1 The two senior Tullivers cope with financial disgrace and privation in different ways. Maggie endures, but with pain. 2 Tulliver is subject to rages, terrifying Maggie, who is desperately lonely. Bob Jakin pays a cheering call and leaves some books: she picks up and reads **Thomas à Kempis**. Her inner life benefits greatly: courage and self-abnegation meet. Tulliver broods. 3

Book Fifth: Wheat and Tares

Maggie sees Philip and is reminded of his kindness. He waylays her at her favourite haunt, an abandoned quarry called the Red Deeps. She thanks him for the past and tells him they cannot see each other. He argues. She is tempted by this new interest. She refuses to take a novel he offers. She will think. 1 Tom progresses. Bob offers to help him trade for his own account. Tom speaks to his father, who fears a loss. Tom and Bob go to the Gleggs, and Mrs Glegg is maneuvered into a purchase from the pack. The Gleggs give Tom a stake. He succeeds and foresees paying off the family debts in one year. 2

Maggie meets Philip to tell him it must end. He fights eloquently against this. Philip's need. There is a hint that Maggie will weaken. 3 Nearly a year has passed: Maggie is in the Red Deeps. So is Philip. They discuss books he has given her. Philip speaks of love. Maggie is astounded. She will do nothing to wound her father. She kisses him in parting. 4 Mrs Pullet mentions seeing Philip near the Red Deeps. Tom hears; Maggie blushes. He confronts her: she acknowledges all, saying she loves Philip. On the bible, she promises not to communicate with Philip again without Tom's knowledge. He insists on going with her to meet Philip, and he vents his indignation at him bitterly. Maggie scorns him as a Pharisee but will obey for her father's sake. He is hard, sure. 5

Tom comes home in triumph. He announces the debt will be paid. Tulliver is nearly undone. A sweet moment for Tom; Bob Jakin's role is admired. But Tulliver is vengeful. 6 The creditors' lunch brings loud applause for Tulliver and for Tom. Exhilarated, Tulliver rides home but encounters Wakem, who scolds him for a farming error. Enraged, Tulliver rides on him. Wakem falls from his horse. Tulliver belabours him with his crop until Maggie pulls him off. Entering the house, he is fainting. He is put to bed; early next morning he calls his children: he dies. 7

Book Sixth: The Great Temptation

Two years later, Lucy and her swain **Stephen Guest** are in the Deanes' drawing-room. Mrs Deane has died. Mrs Tulliver is housekeeper. Maggie is home from the schoolroom where she has been teaching. Stephen and Lucy sing and lovingly part. 1 Lucy and Maggie divert each other. Stephen arrives, and Maggie stuns him with her beauty and uniqueness. He suggests they go boating. Maggie tries to learn to row, has a little slip: he rescues her. 2 Maggie is very stirred by intimations of beauty, romance, poetry—which she had tried to bypass in resignation. Lucy comes to her: they talk of Philip, and Maggie tells the whole story. There is relief in the confidence—perhaps illusory. 3

Maggie calls at Bob Jakin's to see Tom. She tells him Philip will be coming to Lucy's. Tom is firm but tells her it is her choice. 4 Tom meets with uncle **Deane**, who tells him the firm is pleased and ready to offer him a partnership. He says he'd like to recover the mill and hopes the firm would buy it and let him acquire it over time. Deane is surprised but says they will think of it. 5 Lucy's popularity spills over: Maggie is invited into Society. Silent tense awareness builds between her and Stephen, who calls one evening when Lucy is out. They sit, speechless, then briefly walk. He is infatuated; she wishes for Philip. 6

Philip visits at Lucy's. Maggie greets him tenderly. Stephen arrives; Philip suspects. Lucy gets him to the piano. He observes Stephen placing a stool for Maggie and grows disturbed. Lunch interrupts. Deane queries Philip about his father's farming (the mill has a farm). Lucy asks her father about this, and learning that the mill might be acquired for Tom, wants to enlist Philip to help. Deane consents. 7 Lucy talks with Philip, who gets his father to his studio. As he had foreseen, Wakem sees his portraits of Maggie. Philip tells him of his love; Wakem at first is furious. He leaves—but returns, softened. He will help. And he will sell the mill. 8 Maggie is a great hit at the bazaar, but she is deeply troubled about Stephen. Kind **Mr Kenn**, the new rector, sees her distress and offers his help when she wants it. Philip watches Stephen. He is angrily suspicious. Lucy tells of her triumph about the mill, but Maggie says she has a new situation and will leave to take it up. She cannot marry Philip now: She will not divide herself from her brother. There will be one last party. 9

A ball at the Guests'. Lucy is the queen. Maggie dances. Stephen suspects a bond between Philip and Maggie. He goes to Maggie, and she walks with him as though in a dream. But overmastered, he seizes her arm and kisses it. She is stunned and furious. Shock gives her back self-command. She goes home with Lucy. Philip calls the following day. She tells him that only Tom stands between them. There must be time. 10 She visits aunt Moss, and Stephen appears. He avows his love and asks forgiveness. He begs her to marry him. She says they are caught: pity and faithfulness would punish her forever. He begs and gets one kiss. He goes; she weeps on her aunt's shoulder. 11

A family party at the Pullets: Guest & Co. has purchased the mill. Lucy tells Tom how Philip helped, thinking he will be easier now. She fails completely: he is unsoftened and will sanction no connection with the Wakems. 12 Philip, observing Stephen and Maggie again, is now certain there is something between them. He broods himself into illness and sends word he cannot boat with the ladies: Stephen was to go in his place. Lucy, thinking Philip will be with Maggie, goes shopping. Stephen arrives. Maggie goes to the boat with him in a trance. He rows, she floats in a dream. When she wakes they have gone well beyond their destination. She is horrified. He is penitent and desperate. She feels his pain. The drift continues. A vessel picks them up. She sleeps. 13 She wakes, appalled. They land. At a hotel she tells him it is over. He argues with her passionately and eloquently. She holds her own and leaves. It is over. 14

Book Seventh: The Final Rescue

Maggie comes home to Tom, who rejects her out of hand. She and her mother go together to Bob Jakin's, who shows her the new baby, named after her. She asks him to bring Mr Kenn to her. He reports that Mrs Kenn has just died. She must wait a few days. Bob asks only whether anyone has injured her. She says no. He leaves his dog **Mumps** to guard her. 1 The world's wife condemns Maggie. It disregards Stephen's exculpatory letter to his father. He is in Holland, Philip is invisible. Lucy is prostrate, unspeaking. Maggie endures snubs but goes to Mr Kenn. He tells her of Stephen's letter. He warns her of imputations despite it. He advises her to take a situation elsewhere; he foresees nothing but trouble if she stays. She will remain, at least for now. 2

Aunt Glegg turns up trumps: she castigates Tom for judging Maggie prematurely. She sends word to her to come and live in her house. Maggie won't go: she wants to be independent. Lucy has been able to hear Stephen's letter and is getting better. At last a long, loving, reassuring, and supportive letter from Philip. 3 Dr Kenn cannot overcome public sentiment, so he takes Maggie in himself as governess. Scandal has a new subject. Sitting in near-terminal despair, Maggie has a visitor: cousin Lucy, sweet, understanding, forgiving. She is going to the coast but will return and will seek Maggie out. They part in deep friendship and love. 4 Maggie has been to Dr Kenn's. He tells her scandal is damaging him as rector: will she consent to leave town for a while and take a situation he can find for her? She broods. A letter comes from Stephen: a passionate reproach. He begs her to call him to her. She is sorely tempted. As she kneels in prayer, water rushes in: it is the flood. She awakes the Jakins, and Bob and family take to one of the two boats. She takes the other and rows to the Mill to rescue Tom should he be trapped. He is: he boards, and at last he seems to see Maggie clearly. He is humiliated, grateful; but the boat is crushed by heavy objects borne downstream by the flood. Brother and sister die, drowned clinging to each other. 5 The Conclusion foretells reconciliation between Stephen and Lucy. The boy and the girl are below a tomb inscribed:

In their death they were not divided

Contents

Tom Tulliver's purgatory of Latin and Euclid under the Rev. Mr Stelling is depicted in the *Topicon* at M:Education—*rote formula*

Maggie's exploit in the flood on the Floss is in the *Topicon* at N:River—*flood and rescue*

Foreshadowings

Though anything but a novice even in this, her second novel, George Eliot seems rather to belabor the common fictional device of leaving clues to warn the alert reader of what is coming.

" 'Maggie . . . where's the use o' my telling you to keep away from the water? You'll tumble in and be drownded some day, an' then you'll be sorry you didn't do as mother told you.' " I 2

" . . . the great Floss along which they wandered with a sense of travel, to see the rushing spring tide—the awful Eagre—come up like a hungry monster. . . . " I 5

" ' . . . there was a big flood once when the Round Pool was made. I know there was, 'cause father says so. And the sheep and cows were all drowned, and the boats went all over the fields ever such a way.' " I 6

" 'They're such children for the water, mine are,' she said aloud, without reflecting that there was no one to hear her. 'They'll be brought in dead and drownded some day. I wish that river was far enough.' " I 10 *Along about now, the reader might be thinking that GE is overdoing it.*

"Journeying down the Rhône on a summer's day, you have perhaps felt the sunshine made dreary by those ruined villages which stud the banks in certain parts of its course, telling how the swift river once rose, like an angry, destroying god sweeping down the feeble generations whose breath is in their nostrils and making their dwellings a desolation." IV 1

"Maggie's destiny, then, is at present hidden, and we must wait for it to reveal itself like the course of an unmapped river: we only know that the river is full and rapid, and that for all rivers there is the same final home." VI 6

"[Philip] fell into a doze in which he fancied Maggie was slipping down a glistening, green, slimy channel of a waterfall, and he was looking on helpless." VI 8

Boy and Girl

Maggie Tulliver

—*parental views:* " 'The little un takes after my side, now: she's twice as 'cute as **Tom**. Too 'cute for a woman, I'm afraid, continued **Mr Tulliver**. . . ." I 2

" ' . . . I'm sure [said her mother] the child's half a idiot i' some things, for if I send her up-stairs to fetch anything she forgets what she's gone for, an' perhaps 'ull sit down on the floor i' the sunshine an' plait her hair an' sing to herself like a Bedlam creatur', all the while I'm waiting for her down-stairs.' " I 2

—*loyal:* "There were few sounds that roused Maggie when she was dreaming over her book, but **Tom**'s name served as well as the shrillest whistle: in an instant she was on the watch, with gleaming eyes, like a Skye terrier suspecting mischief, or at all events determined to fly at any one who threatened it towards Tom." I 3

—*proud father:* " 'She understands what one's talking about so as never was. And you should hear her read—straight off, as if she knowed it all beforehand. An' allays at her book! . . . she'll read the books and understand 'em, better nor half the folks as are growed up.' " I 3

—*hideaway:* "This attic was Maggie's favourite retreat on a wet day, when the weather was not too cold: here she fretted out all her ill-humours, and talked aloud to the worm-eaten floors and the worm-eaten shelves and the dark rafters festooned with cobwebs, and here she kept a Fetish which she punished for all her misfortunes." 3 *See Topicon* A:Childhood—*doll —punished*

—*stricken:* " 'O dear **Luke**, **Tom** told me to be sure and remember the rabbits every day—but how could I, when they did not come into my head, you know?' " I 4

—*misery:* " 'And you're a naughty girl, and you shan't go fishing with me to-morrow.'

"With this terrible conclusion, **Tom** ran away from Maggie . . . .

"Maggie stood motionless, except from her sobs, for a minute or two; then she turned round and ran into the house and up to her attic, where she sat on the floor and laid her head against the worm-eaten shelf, with a crushing sense of misery. Tom was come home and she had thought how happy she should be—and now he was cruel to her. What use was anything if Tom didn't love her? O, he was very cruel! Hadn't she wanted to give him the money and said how very sorry she was? She knew she was naughty to her mother, but she had never been naughty to Tom—had never *meant* to be naughty to him.

" 'O he is cruel!' Maggie sobbed aloud, finding a wretched pleasure in the hollow resonance that came through the long empty space of the attic. She never thought of beating or grinding her Fetish; she was too miserable to be angry." I 5

—*pride overcome:* "No, she would never go down if **Tom** didn't come to fetch her. This resolution lasted in great intensity for five dark minutes behind the tub; but then the need of being loved, the strongest need in poor Maggie's nature, began to wrestle with her pride and soon threw it. She crept from behind her tub into the twilight of the long attic . . . . " I 5

—*reconciliation:* "But she rushed to him and clung round his neck, sobbing, 'O **Tom**, please forgive me—I can't bear it—I will always be good—always remember things—do love me—please, dear Tom.'

" . . . Maggie and Tom were still very much like young animals, and so she could rub her cheek against his, and kiss his ear in a random, sobbing way, and there were tender fibres in the lad that had been used to answer to Maggie's fondling: so that he behaved with a weakness quite inconsistent with his resolution to punish her as much as she deserved: he actually began to kiss her in return and say,

" 'Don't cry then, Maggie—here, eat a bit o' cake.'

"Maggie's sobs began to subside, and she put out her mouth for the cake and bit a piece; and then Tom bit a piece, just for company, and they ate together and rubbed each other's cheeks and brows and noses together while they ate, with a humiliating resemblance to two friendly ponies." I 5

—*catching a fish:* "O Magsie! you little duck! Empty the basket.'

"Maggie was not conscious of unusual merit, but it was enough that **Tom** called her Magsie, and was pleased with her. There was nothing to mar her delight in the whispers and the dreamy silences, when she listened to the light dipping sounds of the rising fish and the gentle rustling, as if the willows and the reeds and the water had their happy whisperings also. Maggie thought it would make a very nice heaven to sit by the pool in that way, and never be scolded. She never knew she had a bite till Tom told her, but she liked fishing very much." I 5

—*a grief:* " . . . every holiday-time Maggie was sure to have days of grief because [**Tom**] had gone off with **Bob**.

"Well! There was no hope for it: he was gone now, and Maggie could think of no comfort but to sit down by the holly or wander by the hedgerow, and fancy it was all different, refashioning her little world into just what she should like it to be.

"Maggie's was a troublous life, and this was the form in which she took her opium." I 6

—*a radical step:* " 'Here, **Tom**, cut it behind for me,' said Maggie, excited by her own daring and anxious to finish the deed.

" 'You'll catch it, you know,' said Tom, nodding his head in an admonitory manner, and hesitating a little as he took the scissors.

" 'Never mind—make haste!' said Maggie, giving a little stamp with her foot. Her cheeks were quite flushed.

"The black locks were so thick—nothing could be more tempting to a lad who had already tasted the forbidden pleasure of cutting the pony's mane. I speak to those who know the satisfaction of making a pair of shears meet through a duly resisting mass of hair. One delicious grinding snip, and then another and another, and the hinder locks fell heavily on the floor, and Maggie stood cropped in a jagged uneven manner, but with a sense of clearness and freedom, as if she had emerged from a wood into the open plain." I 7

—*afterthoughts:* "[**Tom**] hurried down-stairs and left poor Maggie to that bitter sense of the irrevocable which was almost an everyday experience of her small soul. She could see clearly enough now the thing was done that it was very foolish, and that she should have to hear and think more about her hair than ever; for Maggie rushed to her deeds with passionate impulse, and then saw not only their consequences, but what would have happened if they had not been done, with all the detail and exaggerated circumstances of an active imagination." I 7

—*regret:* "But Maggie, as she stood crying before the glass, felt it impossible that she should go down to dinner and endure the severe eyes and severe words of her aunts, while **Tom**, and **Lucy**, and **Kezia** who waited at table, and perhaps her father and her uncles, would laugh at her—for if Tom had laughed at her of course every one else would: and if she had only let her hair alone, she could have sat with Tom and Lucy and had the apricot pudding and the custard! What could she do but sob? She sat as helpless and despairing among her black locks as **Ajax** among the slaughtered sheep." I 7

—*comfort:* " 'Come, come, my wench,' said her father soothingly putting his arms round her, 'never mind. You was i' the right to cut it off if it plagued you. Give over crying: father'll take your part.'

"Delicious words of tenderness! Maggie never forgot any of these moments when her father 'took her part': she kept them in her heart and thought of them long years after, when every one else said that her father had done very ill by his children." I 7

—*a scheme:* " . . . she had been so often told she was like a gypsy and 'half wild' that when she was miserable it seemed to her the only way of escaping opprobrium and being entirely in harmony with circumstances, would be to live in a little brown tent on the commons: the gypsies, she considered, would gladly receive her and pay her much respect on account of her superior knowledge." I 11

—*running away:* "She crept through the bars of the gate and walked on with new spirit, though not without haunting images of **Apollyon**, and a highwayman with a pistol, and a blinking dwarf in yellow with a mouth from ear to ear, and other miscellaneous dangers. For poor little Maggie had at once the timidity of an active imagination, and the daring that comes from overmastering impulse." I 11

—*unsophisticated:* "Maggie Tulliver, you perceive, was by no means that well-trained, well-informed young person that a small female of eight or nine necessarily is in these days: she had only been to school a year at St Ogg's, and had so few books that she sometimes read the dictionary; so that in travelling over her small mind you would have found the most unexpected ignorance as well as unexpected knowledge. She could have informed you that there was such a word as 'polygamy' and being also acquainted with 'polysyllable,' she had deduced the conclusion that 'poly' meant 'many'; but she had had no idea that gypsies were not well supplied with groceries, and her thoughts generally were the oddest mixture of clear-eyed acumen and blind dreams." I 11

—*crushed:* " '**Mr Stelling**,' she said . . . 'couldn't I do **Euclid**, and all **Tom**'s lessons, if you were to teach me instead of him?' . . .

" '[Girls] can pick up a little of everything, I daresay,' said Mr Stelling. They've a great deal of superficial cleverness: but they couldn't go far into anything. They're quick and shallow.'

"Tom, delighted with this verdict, telegraphed his triumph by wagging his head at Maggie behind Mr Stelling's chair. As for Maggie, she had hardly ever been so mortified: she had been so proud to be called 'quick' all her little life, and now it appeared that this quickness was the brand of inferiority. It would have been better to be slow, like Tom." II 1

—predilection: "Maggie moreover had rather a tenderness for deformed things; she preferred the wry-necked lambs, because it seemed to her that the lambs which were quite strong and well made wouldn't mind so much about being petted, and she was especially fond of petting objects that would think it very delightful to be petted by her. She loved **Tom** very dearly, but she often wished that he *cared* more about her loving him." II 5

—noticed: " What was it, [**Philip**] wondered, that made Maggie's dark eyes remind him of the stories about princesses being turned into animals? . . . I think it was, that her eyes were full of unsatisfied intelligence and unsatisfied, beseeching affection." II 5

—sensitive: "Maggie, young as she was, felt her mistake. Hitherto she had instinctively behaved as if she were quite unconscious of **Philip**'s deformity; her own keen sensitiveness and experience under family criticism sufficed to teach her this, as well as if she had been directed by the most finished breeding." II 6

—defending her father: "Maggie, almost choked with mingled grief and anger, left the room, and took her old place on her father's bed. Her heart went out to him with a stronger movement than ever at the thought that people would blame him. Maggie hated blame: she had been blamed all her life, and nothing had come of it but evil tempers. Her father had always defended and excused her, and her loving remembrance of his tenderness was a force within her that would enable her to do or bear anything for his sake." III 2

—weary: "As for Maggie, she was peculiarly depressed this morning: she had been called up, after brief rest, at three o'clock, and had that strange dreamy weariness which comes from watching in a sick-room through the chill hours of early twilight and breaking day—in which the outside daylight life seems to have no importance and to be a mere margin to the hours in the darkened chamber." III 3

—scolded and miserable: "They were very bitter tears: everybody in the world seemed so hard and unkind to Maggie: there was no indulgence, no fondness, such as she imagined when she fashioned the world afresh in her own thoughts. In books there were people who were always agreeable or tender, and delighted to do things that made one happy, and who did not show their kindness by finding fault. The world outside the books was not a happy one, Maggie felt: it seemed to be a world where people behaved the best to those they did not pretend to love and that did not belong to them. And if life had no love in it, what else was there for Maggie?" III 5

—longings: "Maggie in her brown frock with her eyes reddened and her heavy hair pushed back, looking from the bed where her father lay, to the dull walls of this sad chamber which was the centre of her world, was a creature full of eager, passionate longings for all that was beautiful and glad: thirsty for all knowledge: with an ear straining after dreamy music that died away and would not come near to her: with a blind, unconscious yearning for something that would link together the wonderful impressions of this mysterious life and give her soul a sense of home in it. *As clearly autobiographical a passage as any in the work: GE spent more than two years as her father's housekeeper and nurse.*

"No wonder, when there is this contrast between the outward and the inward, that painful collisions come of it. A girl of no startling appearance, and who will never be a **Sappho** or a **Madame Roland** or anything else that the world takes wide note of, may still hold forces within her as the living plant-seed does, which will make a way for themselves, often in a shattering, violent manner." III 5

—at thirteen: "To the usual precocity of the girl, she added that early experience of struggle, of conflict between the inward impulse and outward fact which is the lot of every imaginative and passionate nature: and the years since she hammered the nails into her wooden fetish among the worm-eaten shelves of the attic, had been filled with so eager a life in the triple world of reality, books and waking dreams, that Maggie was strangely old for her years in everything except in her entire want of that prudence and self-command which were the qualities that made **Tom** manly in the midst of his intellectual boyishness." IV 2

—devotion: "But now she got no answer to her little caresses, either from her father or from **Tom**—the two idols of her life." IV 2

—yearning: " . . . she wanted some key that would enable her to understand and, in understanding, endure, the heavy weight that had fallen on her young heart. If she had been taught real learning and wisdom, such as great men knew, she thought she should have held the secrets of life; if she had only books that she might learn for herself what wise men knew! Saints and martyrs had never interested Maggie so much as sages and poets. She knew little of saints and martyrs, and had gathered, as a general result of her teaching, that they were a temporary provision against the spread of Catholicism and had all died at Smithfield." IV 3

—rebellion: "She rebelled against her lot, she fainted under its loneliness, and fits even of anger and hatred towards her father and mother who were so unlike what she would have them to be—towards **Tom**, who checked her and met her thought or feeling always by some thwarting difference—would flow out over her affections and conscience like a lava stream and frighten her with the sense that it was not difficult for her to become a demon." IV 3

—fantasy: "Then her brain would be busy with wild romances of a flight from home in search of something less sordid and dreary:—she would go to some great man—**Walter Scott**, perhaps, and tell him how wretched and how clever she was, and he would surely do something for her." IV 3

—lonely: "Poor child! . . . She was as lonely in her trouble as if she had been the only girl in the civilised world of that day, who had come out of her school-life with a soul untrained for inevitable struggles—with no other part of her inherited share in the hard-won treasures of thought, which generations of painful toil have laid up for the race of men than shreds and patches of feeble literature and false history . . . but unhappily quite without that knowledge of the irreversible laws within and without her which, governing the habits, becomes morality, and, developing the feelings of submission and dependence, becomes religion:—as lonely in her trouble as if every other girl besides herself had been cherished and watched over by elder minds, not forgetful of their own early time when need was keen and impulse strong." IV 3

—new inspiration: "A strange thrill of awe passed through Maggie while she read, as if she had been wakened in the night by a strain of solemn music, telling of beings whose souls had been astir while hers was in stupor. She went on from one brown mark to another, where the quiet hand seemed to point, hardly conscious that she was reading—seeming rather to listen while a low voice said,

Why dost thou here gaze about, since this is not the place of thy rest? In heaven ought to be thy dwelling, and all earthly things are to be looked on as they forward thy journey thither. All things pass away, and thou together with them. Beware thou cleave not unto them, lest thou be entangled and perish . . . . If a man should give all his substance, yet it is as nothing. And if he should do great penances, yet are they but little. And if he should attain to all knowledge, he is yet far off. And if he should be of great virtue, and very fervent devotion, yet is there much wanting; to wit, one thing, which is most necessary for him. What is that? That having left all, he leave himself, and go wholly out of himself, and retain nothing of self-love . . . . I have often said unto thee, and now again I say the same: Forsake thyself, resign thyself, and thou shalt enjoy much inward peace . . . . Then shall all vain imaginations, evil perturbations, and superfluous cares fly away; then shall immoderate fear leave thee and inordinate love shall die. *GE's ellipses*

"Maggie drew a long breath and pushed her heavy hair back, as if to see a sudden vision more clearly. Here, then, was a secret of life that would enable her to renounce all other secrets—here was a sublime height to be reached without the help of outward things—here was insight, and strength, and conquest, to be won by means entirely within her own soul, where a supreme teacher was waiting to be heard." IV 3 *See Topicon* SR:Spiritual insight—*reading Thomas à Kempis*

—enthusiasm: "Now and then that sort of enthusiasm [*see Topicon* S:Religious Observance—*labouring class*] finds a far-echoing voice that comes from an experience springing out of the deepest need. And it was by being brought within the long lingering vibrations of such a voice that Maggie, with her girl's face and unnoted sorrows, found an effort and a hope that helped her through two years of loneliness, making out a faith for herself without the aid of established authorities and appointed guides—for they were not at hand, and her need was pressing. From what you know of her, you will not be surprised that she threw some exaggeration and wilfulness, some pride and impetuosity even into her self-renunciation: her own life was still a drama for her, in which she demanded of herself that her part should be played with intensity. And so it came to pass that she often lost the spirit of humility by being excessive in the outward act: she often strove after too high a flight and came down with her pour little half-fledged wings dabbled in the mud." IV 3

—changed look: "Hanging diligently over her sewing, Maggie was a sight any one might have been pleased to look at. That new inward life of hers, notwithstanding some volcanic upheavings of imprisoned passions, yet shone out in her face with a tender soft light that mingled itself as added loveliness with the gradually enriched colour and outline of her blossoming youth." IV 3

—at seventeen: " . . . her tall figure and old lavender gown visible through an hereditary black silk shawl of some wide-meshed net-like material . . . . One would certainly suppose her to be farther on in life than her seventeenth year—perhaps because of the slow resigned sadness of the glance, from which all search and unrest seem to have departed, perhaps because her broad-chested figure has the mould of early womanhood. Youth and health have withstood well the involuntary and voluntary hardships of her lot, and the nights in which she has lain on the hard floor for a penance have left no obvious trace: the eyes are liquid, the brown cheek is firm and rounded, the full lips are red. With her dark colouring and jet crown surmounting her tall fig-

ure, she seems to have a sort of kinship with the grand Scotch firs, at which she is looking up as if she loved them well." V 1

—a delight: " . . . her innate delight in admiration and love . . . . Comparing herself with elegant, wealthy young ladies, it had not occurred to her that she could produce any effect with her person." V 1

—accepting: " 'I've been a great deal happier . . . since I have given up thinking about what is easy and pleasant, and being discontented because I couldn't have my own will. Our life is determined for us—and it makes the mind very free when we give up wishing and only think of bearing what is laid upon us and doing what is given us to do.' " V 1

—tempted: "Yet the music would swell out again, like chimes borne onward by a recurrent breeze, persuading her that the wrong lay all in the faults and weaknesses of others, and that there was such a thing as futile sacrifice for one, to the injury of another." V 1

—offered a book: " 'No thank you,' said Maggie, putting it aside with her hand and walking on. 'It would make me in love with this world again, as I used to be; it would make me long to see and know many things—it would make me long for a full life.' " V 1

—first memory: " '. . . the first thing I ever remember in my life is standing with **Tom** by the side of the Floss while he held my hand—everything before that is dark to me.' " V 1

—overmastered: "Maggie had an awe of him, against which she struggled, as something unfair to her consciousness of wider thoughts and deeper motives; but it was of no use to struggle." V 2

—a confession: " 'I was never satisfied with a *little* of anything. That is why it is better for me to do without earthly happiness altogether . . . . I never felt that I had enough music—I wanted voices to be fuller and deeper.' " V 3

—new concept: "Maggie smiled, with glistening tears, and then stooped her tall head to kiss the low pale face that was full of pleading, timid love—like a woman's.

"She had a moment of real happiness then—a moment of belief that if there were sacrifice in this love—it was all the richer and more satisfying.

"She turned away and hurried home, feeling that in the hour since she had trodden this road before, a new era had begun for her. The tissue of vague dreams must now get narrower and narrower, and all the threads of thought and emotion be gradually absorbed in the woof of her actual daily life." V 4

—discovered, and incensed: " 'You have no pity—you have no sense of your own imperfection and your own sins. It is a sin to be hard—it is not fitting for a mortal—for a Christian. You are nothing but a Pharisee. You thank God for nothing but your own virtues—you think they are great enough to win you everything else. You have not even a vision of feelings by the side of which your shining virtues are mere darkness!' " V 5

—and yet: " . . how was it that she was now and then conscious of a certain dim background of relief in the forced separation from **Philip**? Surely it was only because the sense of a deliverance from concealment was welcome at any cost?" V 5

—the family triumph: " . . . Maggie couldn't help forgetting her own grievances. Tom *was* good; and in the sweet humility that springs in us all in

moments of true admiration and gratitude, she felt that the faults he had to pardon in her had never been redeemed, as his faults were. She felt no jealousy this evening that for the first time, she seemed to be thrown into the background in her father's mind." V 6

—trapped in a schoolroom: " 'It is with me as I used to think it would be with the poor uneasy white bear I saw at the show. I thought he must have got so stupid with the habit of turning backwards and forwards in that narrow space that he would keep doing it if they set him free. One gets a bad habit of being unhappy.' " VI 2

—confession: " 'I don't enjoy their happiness as you do—else I should be more contented. I do feel for them when they are in trouble—I don't think I could ever bear to make any one *un*happy—and yet, I often hate myself, because I get angry sometimes at the sight of happy people. I think I get worse as I get older—more selfish.' " VI 2

—discontented:: "The sight of the old scenes had made the rush of memories so painful that even yesterday she had only been able to rejoice in her mother's restored comfort and **Tom**'s brotherly friendliness as we rejoice in good news of friends at a distance rather than in the presence of a happiness which we share. Memory and imagination urged upon her a sense of privation too keen to let her taste what was offered in the transient present: her future, she thought, was likely to be worse than her past, for after her years of contented renunciation, she had slipped back into desire and longing: she found joyless days of distasteful occupation harder and harder—she found the image of the intense and varied life she yearned for and despaired of, becoming more and more importunate." VI 2

—a Man: "For one instant **Stephen** could not conceal his astonishment at the sight of this tall dark-eyed nymph with her jet-black coronet of hair, the next Maggie felt herself, for the first time in her life, receiving the tribute of a very deep blush and a very deep bow from a person towards whom she herself was conscious of timidity. This new experience was very agreeable to her—so agreeable that it almost effaced her previous emotion about **Philip**. There was a new brightness in her eyes, and a very becoming flush on her cheek as she seated herself." VI 2

—literal: "Poor Maggie! She was so unused to society that she could take nothing as a matter of course, and had never in her life spoken from the lips merely, so that she must necessarily appear absurd to more experienced ladies, from the excessive feeling she was apt to throw into very trivial incidents. . . . It did not occur to her that her irritation was due to the pleasanter emotion which had preceded it, just as when we are satisfied with a sense of glowing warmth an innocent drop of cold water may fall upon us as a sudden smart." VI 2

—a slip and a rescue: " 'You have not hurt yourself at all, I hope?' he said, bending to look in her face with anxiety. It was very charming to be taken care of in that kind graceful manner by some one taller and stronger than oneself. Maggie had never felt just in the same way before." VI 2

—stirred up: "She had been hearing some fine music sung by a fine bass voice—but then it was sung in a provincial amateur fashion, such as would have left your critical ear much to desire. And she was conscious of having been looked at a great deal in rather a furtive manner from beneath a pair of well-marked horizontal eyebrows, with a glance that seemed somehow to have caught the vibratory influence of the voice. Such things could have had

no perceptible effect on a thoroughly well-educated young lady with a perfectly balanced mind, who had had all the advantages of fortune, training and refined society. But if Maggie had been that young lady, you would probably have known nothing about her; her life would have had so few vicissitudes that it could hardly have been written . . . . " VI 3

—*unresigned:* " . . . she felt the half-remote presence of a world of love and beauty and delight, made up of vague, mingled images from all the poetry and romance she had ever read, or had ever woven in her dreamy reveries. Her mind glanced back once or twice to the time when she had courted privation, when she had thought all longing, all impatience was subdued, but that condition seemed irrecoverably gone, and she recoiled from the remembrance of it. No prayer, no striving now would bring back that negative peace: the battle of her life, it seemed, was not to be decided in that short and easy way—by perfect renunciation at the very threshold of her youth." VI 3

—*need for music: see Topicon* H:Music and Music-making—*craved*

—*need for love:* "When Maggie was not angry, she was as dependent on kind or cold words as a daisy on the sunshine or the cloud: the need of being loved would always subdue her as in old days it subdued her in the worm-eaten attic." VI 4

—*sibling struggle:* " 'But your ideas and mine never accord, and you will not give way. Yet you might have sense enough to see that a brother, who goes out into the world and mixes with men, necessarily knows better what is right and respectable for his sister than she can know herself . . . I never feel certain about anything with you. At one time you take pleasure in a sort of perverse self-denial, and at another, you have not resolution to resist a thing that you know to be wrong.'

"There was a terrible cutting truth in **Tom**'s words—that hard rind of truth which is discerned by unimaginative, unsympathetic minds. Maggie always writhed under this judgment of Tom's: she rebelled and was humiliated in the same moment: it seemed as if he held a glass before her to show her her own folly and weakness—as if he were a prophetic voice predicting her future failings—and yet, all the while, she judged him in return: she said inwardly, that he was narrow and unjust, that he was below feeling those mental needs which were often the source of the wrong-doing or absurdity that made her life a planless riddle to him." VI 4

—*warming:* " 'I can only warn you. I wish to be as good a brother to you as you will let me.'

"There was a little tremor in **Tom**'s voice as he uttered the last words, and Maggie's ready affection came back with as sudden a glow as when they were children and bit their cake together as a sacrament of conciliation." VI 4

—*condescended to:* "And Maggie was so entirely without those pretty airs of coquetry which have the traditional reputation of driving gentlemen to despair, that she won some feminine pity for being so ineffective in spite of her beauty. She had not had many advantages, poor thing! And it must be admitted there was no pretension about her: her abruptness and unevenness of manner were plainly the result of her secluded and lowly circumstances." VI 6 *See* The Miss **Guests** O

—*music revived:* "It was pleasant too . . . to sit down at the piano alone, and find that the old fitness between her fingers and the keys remained and revived, like a sympathetic kinship not to be worn out by separation—to get the tunes she had heard the evening before and repeat them again and again until she had found out a way of producing them so as to make them a more pregnant, passionate language to her. The mere concord of octaves was a delight to Maggie, and she would often take up a book of Studies rather than any melody, that she might taste more keenly by abstraction the more primitive sensation of intervals.

"Not that her enjoyment of music was of the kind that indicates a great specific talent: it was rather that her sensibility to the supreme excitement of music was only one form of that passionate sensibility which belonged to her whole nature and made her faults and virtues all merge in each other—made her affection sometimes an angry demand, but also prevented her vanity from taking the form of mere feminine coquetry and device, and gave it the poetry of ambition." ¶VI 6

—a gentleman caller: "As for Maggie she had no distinct thought—only the sense of a presence like that of a closely-hovering broad-winged bird in the darkness, for she was unable to look up and saw nothing but **Minny**'s black wavy coat." VI 6

—her eyes: "Was it possible to quarrel with a creature who had such eyes —defying and deprecating, contradicting and clinging, imperious and beseeching—full of delicious opposites." VI 6

—transparent: "[She] had little more power of concealing the impressions made upon her than if she had been constructed of musical strings . . . . " VI 7

—a refuge: "For **Philip** . . . had now, in this short space, become a sort of outward conscience to her, that she might fly to for rescue and strength. Her tranquil, tender affection for Philip, with its root deep down in her childhood, and its memories of long quiet talk confirming by distinct successive impressions the first instinctive bias—the fact that in him the appeal was more strongly to her pity and womanly devotedness than to her vanity or other egoistic excitability of her nature—seemed now to make a sort of sacred place, a sanctuary where she could find refuge from an alluring influence which the best part of herself must resist, which must bring horrible tumult within, wretchedness without." VI 7

—insight: " 'But I begin to think there can never come much happiness to me from loving: I have always had so much pain mingled with it. I wish I could make myself a world outside it, as men do.' " VI 7

—transfixed: " . . . all her intentions were lost in the vague state of emotion produced by the inspiring duet—emotion that seemed to make her at once strong and weak, strong for all enjoyment, weak for all resistance. When the strain passed into the minor she half started from her seat with the sudden thrill of that change. Poor Maggie! She looked very beautiful when her soul was being played on in this way by the inexorable power of sound. You might have seen the slightest perceptible quivering through her whole frame, as she leaned a little forward, clasping her hands as if to steady herself, while her eyes dilated and brightened into that wide-open, childish expression of wondering delight which always came back in her happiest moments." VI 7

—coming out: "The culmination of Maggie's career as an admired member of society in St Ogg's was certainly the day of the Bazaar, when her simple noble beauty, clad in a white muslin of some soft-floating kind, which I suspect must have come from the stores of aunt **Pullet**'s wardrobe, appeared with marked distinction among the more adorned and conventional women around her." VI 9

—*snide comment:* "There was something rather bold in Miss Tulliver's direct gaze, and something undefinably coarse in the style of her beauty, which placed her, in the opinion of all feminine judges, far below her cousin **Miss Deane** . . . . " VI 9

—*vanity, and more:* "It may be surprising that Maggie, among whose many imperfections an excessive delight in admiration and acknowledged supremacy were not absent now, any more than when she was instructing the gypsies . . . was not more elated on a day when she had had the tribute of so many looks and smiles, together with that satisfactory consciousness which had necessarily come from being taken before **Lucy**'s cheval glass and made to look at the full length of her tall beauty, crowned by the night of her massy hair.

"Maggie had smiled at herself then, and for the moment had forgotten everything in the sense of her own beauty. If that state of mind could have lasted, her choice would have been to have **Stephen Guest** at her feet, offering her a life filled with all luxuries, with daily incense of adoration near and distant, with all possibilities of culture at her command.

"But there were things in her stronger than vanity—passion, and affection, and long deep memories of early discipline and effort, of early claims on her love and pity; and the stream of vanity was soon swept along and mingled imperceptibly with that wider current which was at its highest force today, under the double urgency of the events and inward impulses brought by the last week." ¶VI 9

—*the answer to a question:* " 'Yes, **Lucy**—I would choose to marry [**Philip**]. I think it would be the best and highest lot for me—to make his life happy. He loved me first. No one else could be quite what he is to me. But I can't divide myself from my brother for life. I must go away, and wait.' " VI 9

—*an illicit kiss:* "A mad impulse seized on **Stephen**; he darted towards the arm, and showered kisses on it, clasping the wrist.

"But the next moment Maggie snatched it from him and glared at him like a wounded war-goddess, quivering with rage and humiliation.

" 'How dare you?'—she spoke in a deeply shaken, half-smothered voice, 'What right have I given you to insult me?' . . .

"A horrible punishment was come upon her, for the sin of allowing a moment's happiness that was treachery to **Lucy**, to **Philip**—to her own better soul. That momentary happiness had been smitten with a blight—a leprosy: Stephen thought more lightly of *her* than he did of Lucy." VI 10

—*a cold shock:* "All the pride of her nature was stung into activity: the hateful weakness which had dragged her within reach of this wound to her self-respect, had at least wrought its own cure. The thoughts and temptations of the last month should all be flung away into an unvisited chamber of memory: there was nothing to allure her now; duty would be easy, and all the old calm purposes would reign peacefully once more." VI 10

—*declaration:* " 'That book [of their past together] will never will be closed, **Philip**,' she said, with grave sadness. 'I desire no future that will break the ties of the past. But the tie to my brother is one of the strongest. I can do nothing willingly that will divide me always from him.' " VI 10

—*watershed decision:* " 'We should break all these mistaken ties that were made in blindness—and determine to marry each other.'

" 'I would rather die than fall into that temptation,' said Maggie, with deep, slow distinctness—all the gathered spiritual force of painful years coming to her aid in this extremity . . . .

" 'You feel, as I do, that the real tie lies in the feelings and expectations we have raised in other minds. Else all pledges might be broken, when there was no outward penalty. There would be no such thing as faithfulness.' " VI 11

—the crux: " 'O it is difficult—life is very difficult. It seems right to me sometimes that we should follow our strongest feeling;—but then, such feelings continually come across the ties that all our former life has made for us—the ties that have made others dependent on us—and would cut them in two. If life were quite easy and simple, as it might have been in paradise, and we could always see that one being first towards whom . . . . I mean, if life did not make duties for us before love comes—love would be a sign that two people ought to belong to each other.

" 'But I see—I feel that it is not so now: there are things we must renounce in life—some of us must resign love. Many things are difficult and dark to me—but I see one thing quite clearly—that I must not, cannot seek my own happiness by sacrificing others. Love is natural—but surely pity and faithfulness and memory are natural too. And they would live in me still, and punish me if I didn't obey them. I should be haunted by the suffering I had caused. Our love would be poisoned. Don't urge me; help me—help me, *because* I love you.' " ¶VI 11

—fondest wish: "To have no cloud between herself and **Tom** was still a perpetual yearning in her, that had its root deeper than all change." VI 12

—tormented: "But under this torpor there was a fierce battle of emotions, such as Maggie in all her life of struggle had never known or foreboded: it seemed to her as if all the worst evil in her had lain in ambush till now and had suddenly started up full-armed with hideous, overpowering strength. There were moments in which a cruel selfishness seemed to be getting possession of her: why should not **Lucy**—why should not **Philip** suffer? *She* had had to suffer through many years of her life, and who had renounced anything for her?

"And when something like that fulness of existence—love, wealth, ease, refinement—all that her nature craved was brought within her reach, why was she to forego it, that another might have it—another, who perhaps needed it less? But amidst all this new passionate tumult there were the old voices making themselves heard with rising power till, from time to time, the tumult seemed quelled. *Was* that existence which tempted her, the full existence she dreamed? Where, then, would be all the memories of early striving, all the deep pity for another's pain which had been nurtured in her through years of affection and hardship, all the divine presentiment of something higher than mere personal enjoyment which had made the sacredness of life?

"She might as well hope to enjoy walking by maiming her feet, as hope to enjoy an existence in which she set out by maiming the faith and sympathy that were the best organs of her soul. And then, if pain were so hard to *her*—what was it to others?—Ah, God! Preserve me from inflicting—give me strength to bear it.

"How had she sunk into this struggle with a temptation that she would once have thought herself as secure from, as from deliberate crime? When was that first hateful moment in which she had been conscious of a feeling that clashed with her truth, affection, and gratitude, and had not shaken it from her with horror, as if it had been loathsome thing?—and yet, since this strange, sweet, subduing influence did not, should not conquer her—since it was to remain simply her own suffering . . . her mind was meeting **Stephen**'s in that thought of his, that they might still snatch moments of mute confession before the parting came.

"For was not he suffering too? She saw it daily—saw it in the sickened look of fatigue with which as soon as he was not compelled to exert himself he relapsed into indifference towards everything but the possibility of watching her. Could she refuse sometimes to answer that beseeching look which she felt to be following her like a low murmur of love and pain? She refused it less and less, till at last the evening for them both was sometimes made of a moment's mutual gaze—they thought of it till it came, and when it had come, they thought of nothing else." ¶VI 13

—a prop: "She had always additional strength of resistance when **Philip** was present, just as we can restrain our speech better in a spot that we feel to be hallowed." VI 13

—a trance: "Maggie felt that she was being led down the garden among the roses, being helped with firm tender care into the boat, having the cushion and cloak arranged for her feet, and her parasol opened for her (which she had forgotten)—all by this stronger presence that seemed to bear her along without any act of her own will, like the added self which comes with the sudden exalting influence of a strong tonic—and she felt nothing else. Memory was excluded." VI 13

—awake: "Maggie listened—passing from her startled wonderment to the yearning after that belief that the tide was doing it all—that she might glide along with the swift, silent stream and not struggle any more. But across that stealing influence came the terrible shadow of past thoughts; and the sudden horror lest now at last the moment of fatal intoxication was close upon her, called up a feeling of angry resistance towards **Stephen**.

" 'Let me go!' she said, in an agitated tone, flashing an indignant look at him, and trying to get her hands free. You have wanted to deprive me of any choice. You knew we were come too far—you have dared to take advantage of my thoughtlessness. It is unmanly to bring me into such a position.' " VI 13

—disarmed: "Maggie was paralysed: it was easier to resist **Stephen**'s pleading, than this picture he had called up of himself suffering, while she was vindicated—easier even to turn away from his look of tenderness than from this look of angry misery, that seemed to place her in selfish isolation from him. He had called up a state of feeling in which the reasons which had acted on her conscience seemed to be transmuted into mere self-regard. The indignant fire in her eyes was quenched—and she began to look at him with timid distress. She had reproached him for being hurried into irrevocable trespass—*she,* who had been so weak herself.

" 'As if I shouldn't feel what happened to you—just the same'—she said, with reproach of another kind—the reproach of love, asking for more trust. This yielding to the idea of Stephen's suffering was more fatal than the other yielding, because it was less distinguishable from that sense of others' claims which was the moral basis of her resistance." VI 13

—weakened: "Every influence tended to lull her into acquiescence: that dreamy gliding in the boat, which had lasted for four hours and had brought some weariness and exhaustion—the recoil of her fatigued sensations from

the impracticable difficulty of getting out of the boat at this unknown distance from home, and walking for long miles—all helped to bring her into more complete subjection to that strong mysterious charm which made a last parting from **Stephen** seem the death of all joy—which made the thought of wounding him like the first touch of the torturing iron before which resolution shrank. And then, there was the present happiness of being with him, which was enough to absorb all her languid energy." VI 13

—falling asleep: "Behind all the delicious visions of these last hours which had flowed over her like a soft stream and made her entirely passive, there was the dim consciousness that the condition was a transient one, and that the morrow must bring back the old life of struggle—that there were thoughts which would presently avenge themselves for this oblivion. But now nothing was distinct to her: she was being lulled to sleep with that soft stream still flowing over her, with those delicious visions melting and fading like the wondrous aërial land of the west." VI 13

—catastrophe: "The irrevocable wrong that must blot her life had been committed—she had brought sorrow into the lives of others—into the lives that were knit up with hers by trust and love. The feeling of a few short weeks had hurried her into the sins her nature had most recoiled from—breach of faith and cruel selfishness; she had rent the ties that had given meaning to duty, and had made herself an outlawed soul with no guide but the wayward choice of her own passion.

"And where would that lead her?—where had it led her now? She had said she would rather die than fall into that temptation. She felt it now—now that the consequences of such a fall had come before the outward act was completed. There was at least this fruit from all her years of striving after the highest and best—that her soul, though betrayed, beguiled, ensnared, could never deliberately consent to a choice of the lower.

"And a choice of what? O God—not a choice of joy—but of conscious cruelty and hardness; for could she ever cease to see before her **Lucy** and **Philip** with their murdered trust and hopes? Her life with **Stephen** could have no sacredness: she must for ever sink and wander vaguely, driven by uncertain impulse; for she had let go the clue of life—that clue which once in the far off years her young need had clutched so strongly. She had renounced all delights then, before she knew them, before they had come within her reach: Philip had been right when he told her that she knew nothing of renunciation: she had thought it was quiet ecstasy; she saw it face to face now—that sad patient living strength which holds the clue of life, and saw that the thorns were for ever pressing on its brow. That yesterday which could never be revoked—if she could exchange it now for any length of inward silent endurance she would have bowed beneath that cross with a sense of rest." VI 14

—parting dread: "The worst bitterness of parting—the thought that urged the sharpest inward cry for help was the pain it must give to *him.* But surmounting everything was the horror at her own possible failure, the dread lest her conscience should be benumbed again and not rise to energy till it was too late.—Too late! It was too late now, not to have caused misery—too late for everything, perhaps, but to rush away from the last act of baseness—the tasting of joys that were wrung from crushed hearts." VI 14

—the unanswerable: " 'If the past is not to bind us, where can duty lie? We should have no law but the inclination of the moment . . . .

"Faithfulness and constancy mean something else besides doing what is easiest and pleasantest to ourselves. They mean renouncing whatever is opposed to the reliance others have in us—whatever would cause misery to those whom the course of our lives has made dependent on us. If we—if I had been better, nobler—those claims would have been so strongly present with me, I should have felt them pressing on my heart so continually, just as they do now in the moments when my conscience is awake—that the opposite feeling would never have grown in me, as it has done—it would have been quenched at once —I should have prayed for help so earnestly—I should have rushed away, as we rush from hideous danger. I feel no excuse for myself—none—I should never have failed towards **Lucy** and **Philip** as I have done, if I had not been weak and selfish and hard—able to think of their pain without a pain to myself that would have destroyed all temptation.' " VI 14

—her integrity: " 'I couldn't live in peace if I put the shadow of a wilful sin between myself and God. I have caused sorrow already—I know—I feel it—but I have never deliberately consented to it—I have never said, "They shall suffer, that I may have joy." It has never been my will to marry you—if you were to win consent from the momentary triumph of my feeling for you, you would not have my whole soul. If I could wake back again into the time before yesterday, I would choose to be true to my calmer affections and live without the joy of love.' " VI 14

—divinity: " 'We can't choose happiness either for ourselves or for another —we can't tell where that will lie. We can only choose whether we will indulge ourselves in the present moment or whether we will renounce that for the sake of obeying the divine voice within us—for the sake of being true to all the motives that sanctify our lives. I know that belief is hard—it has slipped away from me again and again; but I have felt that if I let it go for ever, I should have no light through the darkness of this life.' " VI 14

—the last dream: "In the darkness of that night she saw **Stephen**'s face turned towards her in passionate, reproachful misery—She lived through again all the tremulous delights of his presence with her that made existence an easy floating in a stream of joy instead of a quiet resolved endurance and effort:—the love she had renounced came back upon her with a cruel charm—she felt herself opening her arms to receive it once more and then it seemed to slip away and fade and vanish, leaving only the dying sound of a deep, thrilling voice that said, 'Gone—for ever gone.' " VI 14

—essential fear: "Her brother was the human being of whom she had been most afraid, from her childhood upwards—afraid with that fear which springs in us when we love one who is inexorable, unbending, unmodifiable—with a mind that we can never mould ourselves upon, and yet that we cannot endure to alienate from us." MF VII 1

—condemnation: "Maggie had returned without a *trousseau,* without a husband—in that degraded and outcast condition to which error is well known to lead; and the world's wife, with that fine instinct which is given her for the preservation of society, saw at once that Miss Tulliver's conduct had been of the most aggravated kind. Could anything be more detestable?" VII 1

—grim prognosis: "The idea of ever recovering happiness never glimmered in her mind for a moment; it seemed as if every sensitive fibre in her were too entirely preoccupied by pain ever to vibrate again to another influence. Life stretched before her as one act of penitence, and all she craved as she dwelt on her future lot, was something to guarantee her from more fal-

ling: her own weakness haunted her like a vision of hideous possibilities that made no peace conceivable except such as lay in the sense of a sure refuse." VII 2

—sacrifice: " '**Lucy**,' Maggie began again, '*he* struggled too. He wanted to be true to you. He will come back to you. Forgive him—he will be happy then . . . . '

"These words were wrung forth from Maggie's deepest soul with an effort like the convulsed clutch of a drowning man." VII 4

—to leave for a time: "She must be a lonely wanderer; she must go out among fresh faces, that would look at her wonderingly, because the days did not seem joyful to her; she must begin a new life, in which she would have to rouse herself to receive new impressions—and she was so unspeakably, sickeningly weary! . . . But ought she to complain? Ought she to shrink in this way from the long penance of life, which was all the possibility she had of lightening the load to some other sufferers, and so changing that passionate error into a new force of unselfish human love?" VII 5

—tempted again: "And here—close within her reach—urging itself upon her even as a claim—was another future, in which hard endurance and effort were to be exchanged for easy delicious leaning on another's loving strength! And yet that promise of joy in the place of sadness did not make the dire force of the temptation to Maggie. It was Stephen's tone of misery—it was the doubt in the justice of her own resolve, that made the balance tremble, and made her once start from her seat to reach the pen and paper, and write, 'Come!' " VII 5

—the answer: "No—she must wait—she must pray—the light that had forsaken her would come again: she should feel again what she had felt, when she had fled away, under an inspiration strong enough to conquer agony—to conquer love . . . .

"She sat quite still, far on into the night: with no impulse to change her attitude, without active force enough even for the mental act of prayer: only waiting for the light that would surely come again.

"It came with the memories that no passion could long quench: the long past came back to her and with it the fountains of self-renouncing pity and affection, of faithfulness and resolve. The words that were marked by the quiet hand in the little old book that she had long ago learned by heart [*The Imitation of Christ*], rushed even to her lips, and found a vent for themselves in a low murmur that was quite lost in the loud driving of the rain against the window and the load moan and roar of the wind: 'I have received the Cross, I have received it from thy hand; I will bear it, and bear it till death, as thou hast laid it upon me.' " VII 5

—the last prayer: "Her soul went out to the Unseen Pity that would be with her to the end. Surely there was something being taught her by this experience of great need; and she must be learning a secret of human tenderness and long-suffering, that the less erring could hardly know? 'O God, if my life is to be long, let me live to bless and comfort—' " VII 5

—the flood: "In the first moments Maggie felt nothing, thought of nothing, but that she had suddenly passed away from that life which she had been dreading: it was the transition of death, without its agony—and she was alone in the darkness with God." VII 5 *And see Topicon* N:River—*flood and rescue*

—reconcilement? "Along with the sense of danger and possible rescue for those long-remembered beings at the old home, there was an undefined sense of reconcilement with her brother: what quarrel, what harshness, what unbelief in each other can subsist in the presence of a great calamity when all the artificial vesture of our life is gone, and we are all one with each other in primitive mortal needs? Vaguely, Maggie felt this;—in the strong resurgent love towards her brother that swept away all the later impressions of hard, cruel offence and misunderstanding; and left only the deep, underlying, unshakable memories of early union." VII 5

—staking all: "More and more strongly the energies seemed to come and put themselves forth, as if her life were a stored-up force that was being spent in this hour, unneeded for any future." VII 5 *And see* Tom Tulliver—*revelation,* and *—death; also the Topicon* N:River—*flood and rescue*

Tom Tulliver

—appraised: " ' . . . he's got a notion o' things out o' door, an' a sort o' commonsense, as he'd lay hold of things by the right handle. But he's slow with his tongue, you see, and he reads but poorly, and can't abide the books, and spells all wrong, they tell me, an' as shy as can be wi' strangers, an' you never hear him say 'cute things like the little wench.' " I 3

—characteristics: "He was one of those lads that grow everywhere in England, and, at twelve or thirteen years of age, look as much alike as goslings:—a lad with light brown hair, cheeks of cream and roses, full lips, indeterminate nose and eyebrows—a physiognomy in which it seems impossible to discern anything but the generic character of boyhood; as different as possible from poor **Maggie**'s phiz, which Nature seemed to have moulded and coloured with the most decided intention. But that same Nature has the deep cunning which hides itself under the appearance of openness, so that simple people think they can see through her quite well, and all the while she is secretly preparing a refutation of their confident prophecies. Under these average boyish physiognomies that she seems to turn off by the gross, she conceals some of her most rigid inflexible purposes, some of her most unmodifiable characters, and the dark-eyed, demonstrative, rebellious girl may after all turn out to be a passive being compared with this pink and white bit of masculinity with the indeterminate features." I 5

—hard in anger: " 'More rabbits? I don't want any more.'

" 'O, but Tom, they're all dead.'

"Tom stopped immediately in his walk and turned round towards **Maggie**. 'You forgot to feed 'em then, and **Harry** forgot,' he said, his colour heightening for a moment, but soon subsiding. 'I'll pitch into Harry—I'll have him turned away. And I don't love you, Maggie. You shan't go fishing with me to-morrow. I told you to go and see the rabbits every day.' He walked on again.

" 'Yes, but I forgot—and I couldn't help it, indeed, Tom. I'm so very sorry,' said Maggie, while the tears rushed fast.

" 'You're a naughty girl,' said Tom, severely, 'and I'm sorry I bought you the fish-line. I don't love you.' " I 5

—sense of justice: "Tom never disobeyed his father, for **Mr Tulliver** was a peremptory man . . . but he went out rather sullenly, carrying his piece of plum-cake, and not intending to reprieve **Maggie**'s punishment, which was

no more than she deserved. Tom was only thirteen, and had no decided views in grammar and arithmetic, regarding them for the most part as open questions, but he was particularly clear and positive on one point, namely that he would punish everybody who deserved it: why, he wouldn't have minded being punished himself if he deserved it, but then, he never *did* deserve it." I 5

—and his sister: "Tom, indeed, was of opinion that Maggie was a silly little thing: all girls were silly—they couldn't throw a stone so as to hit anything, couldn't do anything with a pocket-knife, and were frightened at frogs. Still, he was very fond of his sister, and meant always to take care of her, make her his housekeeper, and punish her when she did wrong." I 5

—stern uprightness: "But Tom, you perceive, was rather a **Rhadamanthine** personage, having more than the usual share of boys' justice in him—that justice that desires to hurt culprits as much as they deserve to be hurt, and is troubled with no doubts concerning the exact amount of their deserts . . . . It is not pleasant to give up a rat-catching when you have set your mind on it. But if Tom had told his strongest feeling at that moment, he would have said, 'I'd do just the same again.' That was his usual mode of viewing his past actions; whereas **Maggie** was always wishing she had done something different." I 6

—in company: "He stood looking at nothing in particular, with the blushing awkward air and semi-smile which are common to shy boys when in company—very much as if they had come into the world by mistake and found it in a degree of undress that was quite embarrassing." I 7

—confidence: "Tom never did the same sort of foolish things as **Maggie**, having a wonderful, instinctive discernment of what would turn to his advantage or disadvantage, and so it happened that though he was much more wilful and inflexible than Maggie, his mother hardly ever called him naughty. But if Tom did make a mistake of that sort he espoused it and stood by it: he 'didn't mind':—if he broke the lash of his father's gig-whip by lashing the gate, he couldn't help it—the whip shouldn't have got caught in the hinge. If Tom Tulliver whipped a gate he was convinced, not that the whipping of gates by all boys was a justifiable act, but that he Tom Tulliver was justifiable in whipping that particular gate, and he wasn't going to be sorry." I 7

—ordering his existence: "In very tender years, when he still wore a lace border under his out-door cap, he was often observed peeping through the bars of a gate and making minatory gestures with his small forefinger while he scolded the sheep with an inarticulate burr, intended to strike terror into their astonished minds: indicating, thus early, that desire for mastery over the inferior animals wild and domestic, including cockchafers, neighbours' dogs, and small sisters, which in all ages has been an attribute of so much promise for the fortunes of our race." MF I 9

—out of his depth: " . . . poor Tom . . . had never been used to jokes at all like **Mr Stelling**'s, and for the first time in his life he had a painful sense that he was all wrong somehow. When Mr Stelling said, as the roast beef was being uncovered, 'Now, Tulliver! which would you rather decline, roast beef or the Latin for it?'—Tom, to whom in his coolest moments a pun would have been a hard nut, was thrown into a state of embarrassed alarm that made everything dim to him except the feeling that he would rather not have anything to do with Latin: of course he answered, 'Roast beef' . . . . " II 1

—good intention: "He was of a very firm, not to say obstinate, disposition, but there was no brute-like rebellion and recklessness in his nature: the

human sensibilities predominated, and if it had occurred to him that he could enable himself to show some quickness at his lessons and so acquire **Mr Stelling**'s approbation, by standing on one leg for an inconvenient length of time or rapping his head moderately against the wall, or any voluntary action of that sort, he would certainly have tried it." II 1

—*his best side:* "If Tom had had a worse disposition, he would certainly have hated the little cherub **Laura**, but he was too kind-hearted a lad for that—there was too much in him of the fibre that turns to true manliness, and to protecting pity for the weak." II 1 *See* **Laura Stelling** O

—*weak spot:* "**Laura** was a sort of playfellow—and O how Tom longed for playfellows! In his secret heart, he yearned to have **Maggie** with him, and was almost ready to doat on her exasperating acts of forgetfulness; though when he was at home, he always represented it as a great favour on his part to let Maggie trot by his side on his pleasure excursions." II 1

—*schoolfellow:* "Tom never quite lost the feeling that **Philip**, being the son of a 'rascal,' was his natural enemy, never thoroughly overcame his repulsion to Philip's deformity: he was a boy who adhered tenaciously to impressions once received: as with all minds in which mere perception predominates over thought and emotion, the external remained to him rigidly what it was in the first instance." II 4

—*getting on better:* "Tom was gradually allowed to shuffle through his lessons with less rigour, and having **Philip** to help him, he was able to make some show of having applied his mind in a confused and blundering way, without being cross-examined into a betrayal that his mind had been entirely neutral in the matter. He thought school much more bearable under this modification of circumstances; and he went on contentedly enough, picking up a promiscuous education chiefly from things that were not intended as education at all. What was understood to be his education, was simply the practice of reading, writing and spelling, carried on by an elaborate appliance of unintelligible ideas and by much failure in the effort to learn by rote." II 4

—*in costume:* "Dissatisfied with the pacific aspect of a face which had no more than the faintest hint of flaxen eyebrow, together with a pair of amiable blue-grey eyes and round pink cheeks that refused to look formidable let him frown as he would before the looking-glass . . . he had had recourse to that unfailing source of the terrible, burnt cork, and had made himself a pair of black eyebrows that met in a satisfactory manner over his nose and were matched by a less carefully adjusted blackness about the chin. He had wound a red handkerchief round his cloth cap to give it the air of a turban, and his red comforter across his breast as a scarf—an amount of red which, with the tremendous frown on his brow, and the decision with which he grasped the sword as he held it with its point resting on the ground, would suffice to convey an approximate idea of his fierce and bloodthirsty disposition." II 5

—*nearing graduation:* "He was a tall youth now, carrying himself without the least awkwardness, and speaking without more shyness than was a becoming symptom of blended diffidence and pride: he wore his tailed coat and his stand-up collars, and watched the down on his lip with eager impatience looking every day at his virgin razor, with which he had provided himself in the last holidays." II 7

—*terrible news:* "Tom felt that pressure of the heart which forbids tears: he had no distinct vision of their troubles as **Maggie** had, who had been at home: he only felt the crushing weight of what seemed unmitigated misfortune . . . his face looked rigid and tearless—his eyes blank—as if a black curtain of cloud had suddenly fallen on his path." II 7

—distress of mind: "And Tom was very unhappy: he felt the humiliation as well as the prospective hardships of his lot with all the keenness of a proud nature; and with all his resolute dutifulness towards his father there mingled an irrepressible indignation against him which gave misfortune the less endurable aspect of a wrong . . . it was a significant indication of Tom's character, that though he thought his aunts ought to do something more for his mother, he felt nothing like **Maggie**'s violent resentment against them for showing no eager tenderness and generosity. There were no impulses in Tom that led him to expect what did not present itself to him as a right to be demanded." III 5

—independent spirit: "It was very hard upon him that he should be put at this disadvantage in life by his father's want of prudence, but he was not going to complain and to find fault with people because they did not make everything easy for him. He would ask no one to help him, more than to give him work and pay him for it." III 5

—hurt: " 'I hope I should never do you any discredit, uncle,' said Tom, hurt, as all boys are at the statement of the unpleasant truth that people feel no ground for trusting them. 'I care about my own credit too much for that'. . . .

"Apparently he, Tom Tulliver, was likely to be held of small account in the world, and for the first time he felt a sinking of heart under the sense that he really was very ignorant and could do very little." III 5

—future prospect: "Two hours ago, as Tom was walking to St Ogg's, he saw the distant future before him, as he might have seen a tempting stretch of smooth sandy beach beyond a belt of flinty shingles: he was on the grassy bank then, and thought the shingles might soon be passed. But now his feet were on the sharp stones: the belt of shingles had widened, and the stretch of sand had dwindled into narrowness." III 5

—sibling interchange: "Poor Tom! He had just come from being lectured and made to feel his inferiority: the reaction of his strong, self-asserting nature must take place somehow, and here was a case in which he could justly show himself dominant. **Maggie**'s cheek flushed and her lip quivered with conflicting resentment and affection and a certain awe as well as admiration of Tom's firmer and more effective character." III 5

—practical: "Tom had very clear prosaic eyes not apt to be dimmed by mists of feeling or imagination." IV 2

—hard at it: "But now Tom's strong will bound together his integrity, his pride, his family regrets and his personal ambition, and made them one force, concentrating his efforts and surmounting discouragements. His uncle **Deane**, who watched him closely, soon began to conceive hopes of him, and to be rather proud that he had brought into the employment of the firm a nephew who appeared to be made of such good commercial stuff." V 2

" . . . there were certain milestones to be passed and one of the first was the payment of his father's debts. Having made up his mind on that point, he strode along without swerving, contracting some rather saturnine sternness, as a young man is likely to do who has a premature call upon him for self-reliance. Tom felt intensely that common cause with his father which springs from family pride, and was bent on being irreproachable as a son; but his growing experience caused him to pass much silent criticism on the rashness and imprudence of his father's past conduct: their dispositions were not in sympathy, and Tom's face showed little radiance during his few home hours." V 2

—*trading secretly:* "In not telling his father, he was influenced by that strange mixture of opposite feelings which often gives equal truth to those who blame an action and those who admire it: partly, it was that disinclination to confidence which is seen between near kindred—that family repulsion which spoils the most sacred relations of our lives; partly, it was the desire to surprise his father with a great joy. He did not see that it would have been better to soothe the interval with a new hope, and prevent the delirium of a too sudden elation." V 2

—*repelled:* "Tom's was a nature which had a sort of superstitious repugnance to everything exceptional. A love for a deformed man would be odious in any woman—in a sister intolerable." V 5

—*prejudice:* "He did not know how much of an old boyish repulsion and of mere personal pride and animosity was concerned in the bitter severity of the words by which he meant to do the duty of a son and a brother. Tom was not given to inquire subtly into his own motives, any more than into other matters of an intangible kind; he was quite sure that his own motives as well as actions were good, else he would have had nothing to do with them." V 5

—*impending triumph:* "There is a very pleasant light in Tom's blue-grey eyes as he glances at the house-windows: that fold in his brow never disappears but it is not unbecoming—it seems to imply a strength of will that may possibly be without harshness, when the eyes and mouth have their gentlest expression. His firm step becomes quicker, and the corners of his mouth rebel against the compression which is meant to forbid a smile." V 6

—*a great moment:* " 'Shake hands wi' me, my lad,' [**Mr Tulliver**] said, suddenly putting out his hand. 'It's a great thing when a man can be proud as he's got a good son. I've had *that* luck.'

"Tom never lived to taste another moment so delicious as that . . . . " V 6

—*exploit:* " 'They think of doing something for young Tulliver—he saved them from a considerable loss by riding home in some marvellous way, like **Turpin**, to bring them news about the stoppage of a bank or something of that sort.' " VI 1

—*in love?* " 'An' it worrets me as Mr Tom 'ull sit by himself so glumpish, a-knittin' his brow an' a-lookin' at the fire of a night. He should be a bit livelier now—a fine young fellow like him. My wife says, when she goes in sometimes an' he takes no notice of her, he sits lookin' into the fire and frownin' as if he was watchin' folks at work in it . . . .

" 'He's close, Mr Tom is, but I'm a 'cute chap, I am, an' I thought tow'rt last Christmas, as I'd found out a soft place in him. It was about a little black spaniel—a rare bit o' breed—as he made a fuss to get. But since then summat's come over him as he's set his teeth again' things more nor iver . . . .

" 'I'm afraid I have very little power over him, **Bob**,' said **Maggie**, a good deal moved by Bob's suggestion. It was a totally new idea to her mind, that Tom could have his love troubles. Poor fellow!—and in love with **Lucy** too! But it was perhaps a mere fancy of Bob's too officious brain. The present of the dog meant nothing more than cousinship and gratitude." VI 4

—*adamant:* "Our good upright Tom Tulliver's . . . inward criticism of his father's faults did not prevent him from adopting his father's prejudice; it was a prejudice against a man of lax principle and lax life, and it was a meeting-point for all the disappointed feelings of family and personal pride. Other feelings added their force to produce Tom's bitter repugnance to **Philip** and to **Maggie**'s union with him; and notwithstanding **Lucy**'s power over her strong-willed cousin, she got nothing but a cold refusal ever to sanction such a marriage . . . . " VI 12

—rejection out of hand: " 'You will find no home with me,' he answered with tremulous rage. 'You have disgraced us all—you have disgraced my father's name. You have been a curse to your best friends. You have been base—deceitful—no motives are strong enough to restrain you. I wash my hands of you for ever. You don't belong to me.' " VII 1

—tunnel vision: "Poor Tom! he judged by what he had been able to see: and the judgment was painful enough to himself. He thought he had the demonstration of facts observed through years by his own eyes which gave no warning of their imperfection, that **Maggie**'s nature was utterly untrustworthy and too strongly marked with evil tendencies to be safely treated with leniency: he would act on that demonstration at any cost—but the thought of it made his days bitter to him. Tom, like every one of us, was imprisoned within the limits of his own nature, and his education had simply glided over him, and left a slight deposit of polish." VII 3

—disillusion: "There had arisen in Tom a repulsion towards Maggie that derived its very intensity from their early childish love in the time when they had clasped tiny fingers together, and their later sense of nearness in a common duty and a common sorrow: the sight of her, as he had told her, was hateful to him." VII 3

—revelation: "It was not till Tom had pushed off and they were on the wide water—he face to face with **Maggie**—that the full meaning of what had happened rushed upon his mind. It came with so overpowering a force—such an entirely new revelation to his spirit, of the depths in life, that had lain beyond his vision which he had fancied so keen and clear, that he was unable to ask a question. They sat mutely gazing at each other: Maggie with eyes of intense life looking out from a weary, beaten face—Tom pale with a certain awe and humiliation. Thought was busy though the lips were silent: and though he could ask no question, he guessed a story of almost miraculous divinely-protected effort. But at last a mist gathered over the blue-grey eyes, and the lips found a word they could utter: the old childish—'Magsie!'

"Maggie could make no answer but a long deep sob of that mysterious wondrous happiness that is one with pain." VII 5

—death: " 'It is coming, **Maggie**,' Tom said, in a deep hoarse voice, loosing the oars, and clasping her.

"The next instant the boat was no longer seen upon the water—and the huge mass was hurrying on in hideous triumph.

"But soon the keel of the boat reappeared, a black speck on the golden water.

"The boat reappeared—but brother and sister had gone down in an embrace never to be parted—living through again in one supreme moment, the days when they had clasped their little hands in love, and roamed the daisied fields together." VII 5

Their Parents

Mr Tulliver. "If Mr Tulliver had been a susceptible man in his conjugal relations, he might have supposed that she drew out the key to aid her imagination in anticipating the moment when he would be in a state to justify the production of the best Holland sheets. Happily he was not so: he was only susceptible in respect of his right to water-power; moreover, he had the marital habit of not listening very closely . . . . " I 2

—fatherly ambition: " 'I want **Tom** to be such a sort o' man as **Riley**, you know—as can talk pretty nigh as well as if it was all wrote out for him, and knows a good lot o' words as don't mean much, so as you can't lay hold of 'em i' law; and a good solid knowledge o' business too.' " I 2

" 'I want him to know figures, and write like print, and see into things quick, and know what folks mean, and how to wrap things up in words as aren't actionable.' " I 3

—flaw: "Mr Tulliver was on the whole a man of safe traditional opinions; but on one or two points he had trusted to his unassisted intellect and had arrived at several questionable conclusions, among the rest, that rats, weevils, and lawyers were created by Old Harry." I 3

—fatherly apprehension: " ' . . . why, if I made him a miller an' farmer, he'd be expectin' to take to the mill an' the land, an' a-hinting at me as it was time for me to lay by an' think o' my latter end. Nay, nay, I've seen enough o' that wi' sons. I'll niver pull my coat off before I go to bed. I shall give **Tom** an eddication an' put him to a business, as he may make a nest for himself an' not want to push me out o' mine. Pretty well if he gets it when I'm dead an' gone. I shan't be put off wi' spoon-meat afore I've lost my teeth.' " I 3

—matrimonial: " 'I picked the mother because she wasn't o'er 'cute—bein' a good-looking woman too, an' come of a rare family for managing—but I picked her from her sisters o' purpose 'cause she was a bit weak, like; for I wasn't a-goin' to be told the rights o' things by my own fireside. ' " I 3

—on genetics: " 'But, you see, when a man's got brains himself, there's no knowing where they'll run to; an' a pleasant sort o' soft woman may go on breeding you stupid lads and 'cute wenches, till it's like as if the world was turned topsy-turvy. It's an uncommon puzzlin' thing.' " I 3

—fatherly insight: " 'You go and fetch her down, **Tom**,' said Mr Tulliver, rather sharply, his perspicacity or his fatherly fondness for **Maggie** making him suspect that the lad had been hard upon 'the little un,' else she would never have left his side." I 5

—impulsive: "Mr Tulliver, when under the influence of a strong feeling, had a promptitude in action that may seem inconsistent with that painful sense of the complicated puzzling nature of human affairs under which his more dispassionate deliberations were conducted; but it is really not improbable that there was a direct relation between these apparently contradictory phenomena, since I have observed that for getting a strong impression that a skein is tangled, there is nothing like snatching hastily at a single thread." I 8

—financial standing: "For Mr Tulliver was in a position neither new nor striking but, like other everyday things, sure to have a cumulative effect that will be felt in the long run: he was held to be a much more substantial man than he really was. And as we are all apt to believe what the world believes about us, it was his habit to think of failure and ruin with the same sort of

remote pity with which a spare long-necked man hears that his plethoric short-necked neighbour is stricken with apoplexy." I 8

—good-nature: "Our friend Mr Tulliver had a good-natured fibre in him, and did not like to give harsh refusals even to a sister . . . . " I 8

—softened: "Evidently, after his fit of promptitude, Mr Tulliver was relapsing into the sense that this is a puzzling world . . . .

"And so the respectable miller returned along the Basset lanes rather more puzzled than before as to ways and means, but still with the sense of a danger escaped. It had come across his mind that if he were hard upon his sister, it might somehow tend to make **Tom** hard upon **Maggie**, at some distant day, when her father was no longer there to take her part; for simple people, like our friend Mr Tulliver, are apt to clothe unimpeachable feelings in erroneous ideas, and this was his confused way of explaining to himself that his love and anxiety for 'the little wench' had given him a new sensibility towards his sister." I 8

—correspondent: "Mr Tulliver did not willingly write a letter, and found the relation between spoken and written language, briefly known as spelling, one of the most puzzling things in this puzzling world . . . if the spelling differed from **Mrs Glegg**'s—why, she belonged, like himself, to a generation with whom spelling was a matter of private judgment." I 13

—legal dogma: " 'It's plain enough what's the rights and the wrongs of water, if you look at it straight forrard; for a river's a river, and if you've got a mill, you must have water to turn it; and it's no use telling me, **Pivart**'s erigation and nonsense won't stop my wheel: I know what belongs to water better than that. Talk to me o' what th' engineers say! I saw it's common sense, as Pivart's dykes must do me an injury.' " II 2

—perverse: "Not that **Mrs Tulliver**'s feeble beseeching could have had this feather's weight in virtue of her single personality; but whenever she departed from entire assent to her husband, he saw in her the representative of the **Dodson** family; and it was a guiding principle with Mr Tulliver, to let the Dodsons know that they were not to domineer over *him,* or—more specifically—that a male Tulliver was far more than equal to four female Dodsons, even though one of them was **Mrs Glegg**." II 2

—huge setback: "All the obstinacy and defiance of his nature, driven out of their old channel, found a vent for themselves in the immediate formation of plans by which he would meet his difficulties and remain Mr Tulliver of Dorlcote Mill in spite of them." III 1

—the future: "But with poor Tulliver, death was not to be a leap: it was to be a long descent under thickening shadows." III 4

—consenting to servitude: " 'You may do as you like wi' me, **Bessy**,' he said in a low voice, 'I'n been the bringing of you to poverty . . . this world's too many for me . . . I'm nought but a bankrupt—it's no use standing up for anything now.' " III 8

—the pull of Home: "But the strongest influence of all was the love of the old premises where he had run about when he was a boy, just as Tom had done after him. The Tullivers had lived on this spot for generations, and he had sat listening on a low stool on winter evenings while his father talked of the old half-timbered mill that had been there before the last great floods, which damaged it so that his grandfather pulled it down and built the new one. It was when he got able to walk about and look at all the old objects, that he felt the strain of this clinging affection for the old home as part of his

life, part of himself. He couldn't bear to think of himself living on any other spot than this, where he knew the sound of every gate and door, and felt that the shape and colour of every roof and weather stain and broken hillock was good, because his growing senses had been fed on them.

"Our instructed vagrancy which has hardly time to linger by the hedgerows, but runs away early to the tropics and is at home with palms and banyans—which is nourished on books of travel and stretches the theatre of its imagination to the Zambesi can hardly get a dim notion of what an old-fashioned man like Tulliver felt for this spot where all his memories centred and where life seemed like a familiar smooth-handled tool that the fingers clutch with loving ease. And just now he was living in that freshened memory of the far-off time which comes to us in the passive hours of recovery from sickness." ¶III 9

—*as a churchman:* "Mr Tulliver regarded [the **vicar**] with dutiful respect, as he did everything else belonging to the church-service; but he considered that church was one thing and common sense another, and he wanted nobody to tell *him* what common sense was. Certain seeds which are required to find a nidus for themselves under unfavourable circumstances have been supplied by nature with an apparatus of hooks, so that they will get a hold on very unreceptive surfaces. The spiritual seed which had been scattered over Mr Tulliver had apparently been destitute of any corresponding provision, and had slipped off to the winds again from a total absence of hooks." IV 1

—*sullen:* " . . . now, instead of childlike dependence there had come a taciturn hard concentration of purpose in strange contrast with his old vehement communicativeness and high spirit, and this listed from day to day and from week to week, the dull eye never brightening with any eagerness or any joy." IV 2

—*concentration:* "To save something towards the repayment of those creditors was the object towards which he was now bending all his thoughts and efforts; and under the influence of this all-compelling demand of his nature, the somewhat profuse man who hated to be stinted or to stint any one else in his own house, was gradually metamorphosed into the keen-eyed grudger of morsels." IV 2

—*valuing his daughter:* " 'I knew well enough what she'd be, before now— it's nothing new to me. But it's a pity she isn't made o' commoner stuff—she'll be thrown away, I doubt: there'll be nobody to marry her as is fit for her.' " IV 3

—*unconsoled:* "In a mind charged with an eager purpose and an unsatisfied vindictiveness, there is no room for new feelings: Mr Tulliver did not want spiritual consolation—he wanted to shake off the degradation of debt and to have his revenge." IV 3

—*wonderful news:* "[He] was silent: the flood of emotion hemmed in all power of speech. Both **Tom** and **Maggie** were struck with fear lest the shock of joy might even be fatal. But the blessed relief of tears came. The broad chest heaved, the muscles of the face gave way, and the grey-haired man burst into loud sobs. The fit of weeping gradually subsided and he sat quiet, recovering the regularity of his breathing. At last he looked up at his wife and said, in a gentle tone,

" '**Bessy**, you must come and kiss me now—the lad has made y' amends. You'll see a bit o' comfort again belike.' " V 6

—*temperate:* "Mr Tulliver was an essentially sober man—able to take his glass and not averse to it, but never exceeding the bounds of moderation. He had naturally an active **Hotspur** temperament, which did not crave liquid fire to set it aglow; his impetuosity was usually equal to an exciting occasion, without any such reinforcements . . . . " V 7

—*credit restored:* " . . . when he was seated at table with his creditors, his eye kindling and his cheek flushed with the consciousness that he was about to make an honourable figure once more, he looked more like the proud, confident, warm-hearted and warm-tempered Tulliver of old times, than might have seemed possible to any one who had met him a week before, riding along as had been his wont for the last four years since the sense of failure and debt had been upon him—with his head hanging down, casting brief, unwilling looks on those who forced themselves on his notice . . . the streak of irritation and hostile triumph seemed to melt for a little while into purer fatherly pride and pleasure . . . . " V 7

—*epitaph:* " 'Does God forgive raskills? . . . but if He does, He won't be hard wi' me.' " V 7

Mrs Elizabeth (Bessy) Tulliver, "a blond comely woman in a fan-shaped cap . . . nearly forty . . . . " I 2

—*motherly:* " 'However, if **Tom**'s to go to a new school, I should like him to go where I can wash him and mend him; else he might as well have calico as linen, for they'd be one as yallow as th' other before they'd been washed half-a-dozen times. And then, when the box is goin' backards and forrards, I could send the lad a cake, or a pork-pie, or an apple; for he can do with an extry bit, bless him, whether they stint him at the meals or no. My children can eat as much victuals as most, thank God.' " I 2

—*housekeeper:* " ' . . . as for them best Holland sheets, I should repent buying 'em, only they'll do to lay us out in. An' if you was to die to-morrow, **Mr Tulliver**, they're mangled beautiful, an' all ready, an' smell o' lavender as it 'ud be a pleasure to lay 'em out. An' they lie at the left-hand corner o' the big oak linen-chest, at the back: not as I should trust anybody to look 'em out but myself.' " I 2

—*amiable:* "Mrs Tulliver was what is called a good-tempered person—never cried when she was a baby on any slighter ground than hunger and pins, and from the cradle upwards had been healthy, fair, plump, and dull-witted, in short, the flower of her family for beauty and amiability. But milk and mildness are not the best things for keeping, and when they turn only a little sour they may disagree with young stomachs seriously." I 2

—*aroused:* "Mrs Tulliver was a mild woman, but even a sheep will face about a little when she has lambs." I 6

—*her hair:* "So if **Mrs Glegg**'s front to-day was more fuzzy and lax than usual, she had a design under it: she intended the most pointed and cutting allusion to Mrs Tulliver's bunches of blond curls separated from each other by a due wave of smoothness on each side of the parting. Mrs Tulliver had shed tears several times at sister Glegg's unkindness on the subject of these unmatronly curls, but the consciousness of looking the handsomer for them naturally administered support." I 7

—*propitiating:* "Mrs Tulliver never went the length of quarrelling with her [sister Glegg], any more than a waterfowl that puts out its leg in a deprecating manner can be said to quarrel with a boy who throws stones." I 7

—*slow learner:* "Mrs Tulliver had lived thirteen years with her husband, yet she retained in all the freshness of her early married life a facility of saying things which drove him in the opposite direction to the one she desired. Some minds are wonderful for keeping their bloom in this way, as a patriarchal goldfish apparently retains to the last its youthful illusion that it can swim in a straight line beyond the encircling glass. Mrs Tulliver was an amiable fish of this kind, and after running her head against the same resisting medium for thirteen years would go at it again to-day with undulled alacrity." I 8

—*response to resistance:* "Mrs Tulliver cried a little in a trickling quiet way as she put on her nightcap; but presently sank into a comfortable sleep, lulled by the thought that she would talk everything over with her **sister Pullet** tomorrow when she was to take the children to Garum Firs to tea. Not that she looked forward to any distinct issue from that talk, but it seemed impossible that past events should be so obstinate as to remain unmodified when they were complained against." I 8

—*dressed to visit:* "Mrs Tulliver had on her visiting costume with a protective apparatus of brown holland, as if she had been a piece of satin furniture in danger of flies . . . . " I 9

—*imagination:* "Her imagination was not easily acted on, but she could not help thinking that her case was a hard one—since it appeared that other people thought it hard." I 9

—*spirit:* "Amiable Mrs Tulliver, who was never angry in her life, had yet her mild share of that spirit without which she could hardly have been at once a **Dodson** and a woman. Being always on the defensive towards her own sisters, it was natural that she should be keenly conscious of her superiority, even as the weakest Dodson, over [**Mrs Moss**]." II 2

—*paradoxical influence:* "Mrs Tulliver, as we have seen, was not without influence over her husband. No woman is: she can always incline him to do either what she wishes, or the reverse; and on the composite impulses that were threatening to hurry Mr Tulliver into 'law,' Mrs Tulliver's monotonous pleading had doubtless its share of force; it might even be comparable to that proverbial feather which has the credit or discredit of breaking the camel's back . . . . " II 2

—*phlegmatic:* "[She] came down . . . with her comely face a little distorted nearly as it would have been if she had been crying: she was not a woman who could shed abundant tears, except in moments when the prospect of losing her furniture became unusually vivid, but she felt how unfitting it was to be quite calm under present circumstances." III 3

—*worn out:* "Mrs Tulliver's blond face seemed aged ten years by the last thirty hours: the poor woman's mind had been busy divining when her favourite things were being knocked down by the terrible hammer, her heart had been fluttering at the thought that first one thing and then another had gone to be identified as hers in the hateful publicity of the Golden Lion; and all the while she had to sit and make no sign of this inward agitation. Such things bring lines in well-rounded faces, and broaden the streaks of white among the hairs that once looked as if they had been dipped in pure sunshine." III 6

—*intervening:* "Imagine a truly respectable and amiable hen, by some portentous anomaly, taking to reflection and inventing combinations by which she might prevail on **Hodge** not to wring her neck or send her and her chicks to market: the result could hardly be other than much cackling and fluttering." III 7

—bereft: "It was piteous to see the comely blond stout woman getting thinner and more worn under a bodily as well as mental restlessness which made her often wander about the empty house after her work was done, until **Maggie**, becoming alarmed about her, would seek her and bring her down by telling her how it vexed **Tom** that she was injuring her health by never sitting down and resting herself." IV 2

—maternal: "Yet amidst this helpless imbecility, there was a touching trait of humble self-devoting maternity . . . . She would let **Maggie** do none of the work that was heaviest and most soiling to the hands, and was quite peevish when Maggie attempted to relieve her from her grate-brushing and scouring . . . . And she would still brush and carefully tend Maggie's hair, which she had become reconciled to, in spite of its refusal to curl, now it was so long and massy . . . the womanly heart, so bruised in its small personal desires, found a future to rest on in the life of this young thing, and the mother pleased herself with wearing out her own hands to save the hands that had so much more life in them." IV 2

—her own integrity: "Mrs Tulliver carried the proud integrity of the **Dodsons** in her blood, and had been brought up to think that to wrong people of their money, which was another phrase for debt, was a sort of moral pillory: it would have been wickedness, to her mind, to have run counter to her husband's desire to 'do the right thing' and retrieve his name. She had a confused dreamy notion that if the creditors were all paid, her plate and linen ought to come back to her, but she had an inbred perception that while people owed money they were unable to pay, they couldn't rightly call anything their own." IV 2

—taking a stand: "Slowly **Maggie** was turning away, with despair in her heart. But the poor frightened mother's love leaped out now, stronger than all dread.

" 'My child! I'll go with you. You've got a mother.'

"O the sweet rest of that embrace to the heart-stricken Maggie! More helpful than all wisdom is one draught of simple human pity that will not forsake us." VII 1

Their Relations

Lucy Deane. " '[She's] such a good child—you may set her on a stool, and there she'll sit for an hour together and never offer to get off—I can't help loving the child as if she was my own, and I'm sure she's more like my child than **sister Deane**'s, for she'd allays a very poor colour for one of our family, sister Deane had.' " I 6

"And **Maggie** always looked twice as dark as usual when she was by the side of Lucy." I 7

—a contrast: "Certainly the contrast between the cousins was conspicuous and to superficial eyes was very much to the disadvantage of **Maggie**, though a connoisseur might have seen 'points' in her which had a higher promise for maturity than Lucy's natty completeness: it was like the contrast between a rough, dark, overgrown puppy and a white kitten. Lucy put up the neatest little rosebud mouth to be kissed: everything about her was neat—her little round neck with the row of coral beads, her little straight nose, not at all snubby, her little clear eyebrows, rather darker than her curls, to match

her hazel eyes which looked up with shy pleasure at Maggie, taller by the head, though scarcely a year older." I 7

—*neat:* "As for Lucy, she was just as pretty and neat as she had been yesterday: no accidents ever happened to her clothes, and she was never uncomfortable in them . . . . " I 9

—*and then:* "The startling object . . . was no other than little Lucy, with one side of her person, from her small foot to her bonnet-crown, wet and discoloured with mud, holding out two tiny blackened hands and making a very piteous face." I 10

—*pitying the trouble:* "One day [her father] brought Lucy, who was come home for the Christmas holidays, and the little blond angel-head had pressed itself against **Maggie**'s darker cheek with many kisses and some tears. These fair slim daughters keep [*sic*] up a tender spot in the heart of many a respectable partner in a respectable firm, and perhaps Lucy's anxious pitying questions about her poor cousins helped to make **uncle Deane** more prompt in finding **Tom** a temporary place in the warehouse, and in putting him in the way of getting evening lessons in book-keeping and calculation." III 7

—*a good-bye:* "And there was that slight pressure of the hands and momentary meeting of the eyes, which will often leave a little lady with a slight flush and smile on her face that do not subside immediately when the door is closed, and with an inclination to walk up and down the room rather than to seat herself quietly at her embroidery, or other rational and improving occupation." VI 1

—*wishing all things well:* "Even now, that she is walking up and down with a little triumphant flutter of her girlish heart at the sense that she is loved by the person of chief consequence in her small world, you may see in her hazel eyes an ever present sunny benignity in which the momentary harmless flashes of personal vanity are quite lost, and if she is happy in thinking of her lover it is because the thought of him mingles readily with all the gentle affections and good-natured offices with which she fills her peaceful days." VI 1

—*rare quality:* " . . . a woman who was loving and thoughtful for other women, not giving them Judas-kisses with eyes askance on their welcome defects, but with real care and vision for their half-hidden pains and mortifications, with long ruminating enjoyment of little pleasures prepared for them." VI 1

—*little:* " . . . her slight, aërial cousin, whose figure was quite subordinate to her faultless drapery of silk and crape." VI 2

—*lack of jealousy:* "Is it an inexplicable thing that a girl should enjoy her lover's society the more for the presence of a third person, and be without the slightest spasm of jealousy that the third person had the conversation habitually directed to her? Not when that girl is as tranquil-hearted as Lucy, thoroughly possessed with a belief that she knows the state of her companions' affections, and not prone to the feelings which shake such a belief in the absence of positive evidence against it." VI 6

—*voice:* " 'This was very good and virtuous of you,' she said, in her pretty treble, like the low conversational notes of little birds." VI 7

—*envisioned:* " . . . **Maggie** was haunted by a face cruel in its very gentleness: a face that had been turned on hers with glad sweet looks of trust and love from the twilight time of memory: changed now to a sad and weary face by a first heart-stroke . . . the picture grew and grew into more speaking definiteness under the avenging hand of remorse; the soft hazel eyes in their look of pain, were bent for ever on Maggie and pierced her the more because she could see no anger in them." VII 4

Mr Deane, "a large but alert-looking man with a type of physique to be seen in all ranks of English society—bald crown, red whiskers, full forehead, and general solidity without heaviness. You may see noblemen like Mr Deane, and you may see grocers or day-labourers like him; but the keenness of his brown eyes was less common than his contour." I 7

—respected: "Mr Deane, he considered, was the 'knowingest' man of his acquaintance and he had besides a ready causticity of tongue which made an agreeable supplement to **Mr Tulliver**'s own tendency that way, which had remained in rather an embryonic or inarticulate condition." I 7

—an interview: " 'Ah, young gentleman,' said Mr Deane, with that tendency to repress youthful hopes which stout and successful men of fifty find one of their easiest duties, 'that's sooner said than done. . . .

" 'Ay, ay, sir,' said Mr Deane, spreading himself in his chair a little, and entering with great readiness into a retrospect of his own career. 'But I'll tell you how I got on: it wasn't by getting astride a stick and thinking it would turn into a horse if I sat on it long enough. I kept my eyes and ears open, sir, and I wasn't too fond of my own back, and I made my master's interest my own.' " III 5

—hearing of success: "Mr Deane was rather puzzled, and suspected that there had been something 'going on' among the young people to which he wanted a clue. But to men of Mr Deane's stamp, what goes on among the young people is as extraneous to the real business of life as what goes on among the birds and butterflies—until it can be shown to have a malign bearing on monetary affairs. And in this case the bearing appeared to be entirely propitious." VI 8

Mrs Susan Deane. " 'I'd as lief not invite sister Deane this time,' said **Mrs Tulliver**, 'for she's as jealous and having as can be, and's allays trying to make the worst o' my poor children to their aunts and uncles.' " I 6

"It was quite unaccountable that Mrs Deane, the thinnest and sallowest of all the **Miss Dodsons**, should have had this child who might have been taken for Mrs Tulliver's any day." I 7

"Mrs Deane was not a woman to take part in a scene where missiles were flying." I 7

—cautious: "Mrs Deane was a thin-lipped woman who made small well-considered speeches on peculiar occasions, repeating them afterwards to her husband and asking him if she had not spoken very properly." III 3

The Dodsons "were a very respectable family indeed—as much looked up to as any in their own parish or the next to it. The Miss Dodsons had always been thought to hold up their heads very high, and no one was surprised the two eldest had married so well:—not at an early age, for that was not the practice of the Dodson family.

"There were particular ways of doing everything in that family: particular ways of bleaching the linen, of making the cowslip wine, curing the hams and keeping the bottled gooseberries, so that no daughter of that house could be indifferent to the privilege of having been born a Dodson, rather than a **Gibson** or a **Watson**. Funerals were always conducted with peculiar propriety in the Dodson family: the hatbands were never of a blue shade, the gloves never split at the thumb, everybody was a mourner who ought to be, and there were always scarfs for the bearers. When one of the family was in trouble or sickness, all the rest went to visit the unfortunate member, usually at the same time, and did not shrink from offering the most disagreeable truths that correct family feeling dictated: if the illness or trouble was the sufferer's own fault, it was not in the practice of the Dodson family to shrink from saying so.

"In short, there was in this family a peculiar tradition as to what was the right thing in household management and social demeanour, and the only bitter circumstance attending this superiority was a painful inability to approve the condiments or the conduct of families ungoverned by the Dodson tradition. A female Dodson, when in 'strange houses,' always ate dry bread with her tea and declined any sort of preserves, having no confidence in the butter and thinking that the preserves had probably begun to ferment from want of due sugar and boiling.

"There were some Dodsons less like the family than others—that was admitted—but in so far as they were 'kin,' they were of necessity better than those who were 'no kin.' And it is remarkable that while no individual Dodson was satisfied with any other individual Dodson, each was satisfied, not only with him or herself, but with the Dodsons collectively.

"The feeblest member of a family—the one who has the least character—is often the merest epitome of the family habits and traditions, and **Mrs Tulliver** was a thorough Dodson, though a mild one, as small beer, so long as it is anything, is only describable as very weak ale. And though she had groaned a little in her youth under the yoke of her elder sisters, and still shed occasional tears at their sisterly reproaches, it was not in Mrs Tulliver to be an innovator on the family ideas: she was thankful to have been a Dodson, and to have one child who took after her own family, at least in his features and complexion, in liking salt, and in eating beans, which a Tulliver never did." ¶ I 6

—the ruin: " . . . there was a general family sense that a judgment had fallen on **Mr Tulliver**, which it would be an impiety to counteract by too much kindness." III 1

—their religion: "The religion of the Dodsons consisted in revering whatever was customary and respectable: it was necessary to be baptised, else one could not be buried in the churchyard, and to take the sacrament before death as a security against more dimly understood perils; but it was of equal necessity to have the proper pall-bearers and well-cured hams at one's funeral, and to leave an unimpeachable will." IV 1 *See Topicon* S:Religious Observance—*Protestantism*

—their propriety: "A Dodson would not be taxed with the omission of anything that was becoming, or that belonged to that eternal fitness of things which was plainly indicated in the practice of the most substantial parishioners, and in the family traditions—such as obedience to parents, faithfulness to kindred, industry, rigid honesty, thrift, the thorough scouring of wooden and copper utensils, the hoarding of coins likely to disappear from the currency, the production of first-rate commodities for the market, and the general preference for whatever was home-made." IV 1

—their pride: "The Dodsons were a very proud race, and their pride lay in the utter frustration of all desire to tax them with a breach of traditional duty or propriety. A wholesome pride in many respects; since it identified

honour with perfect integrity, thoroughness of work, and faithfulness to admitted rules; and society owes some worthy qualities in many of her members to mothers of the Dodson class, who made their butter and their fromenty well and would have felt disgraced to make it otherwise." IV 1

—their image: "To be honest and poor was never a Dodson motto, still less, to seem rich though being poor; rather, the family badge was to be honest and rich, and not only rich, but richer than was supposed." IV 1

—clinging to kin: "To live respected and have the proper bearers at your funeral was an achievement of the ends of existence that would be entirely nullified if on the reading of your Will, you sank in the opinion of your fellowmen either by turning out to be poorer than they expected or by leaving your money in a capricious manner without strict regard to degrees of kin. The right thing must always be done towards kindred: the right thing was to correct them severely, if they were other than a credit to the family, but still not to alienate from them the smallest rightful share in the family shoe-buckles and other property. A conspicuous quality in the Dodson character was its genuineness: its vices and virtues alike were phases of a proud, honest egoism which had a hearty dislike to whatever made against its own credit and interest, and would be frankly hard of speech to inconvenient 'kin' but would never forsake or ignore them—would not let them want bread, but only require them to eat it with bitter herbs." IV 1

—stable: "On the other hand, nobody had ever heard of a Dodson who had ruined himself: it was not the way of that family." IV 1

Mr Glegg, "a kind-looking, white-haired old gentleman, said—

" 'Heyday! what little gell's this—why, I don't know her. Is it some little gell you've picked up in the road, **Kezia**?' " I 7

—humour: " 'What, do you think the parson'll teach him to know a good sample o' wheat when he sees it, neighbour **Tulliver**?' said Mr Glegg, who was fond of his jest, and, having retired from business, felt that it was not only allowable but becoming in him to take a playful view of things." I 7

—occupation: " . . . spending his time among 'them flowers and vegetables.' For Mr Glegg having retired from active business as a wool-stapler for the purpose of enjoying himself through the rest of his life, had found this last occupation so much more severe than his business, that he had been driven into amateur hard labour as a dissipation, and habitually relaxed by doing the work of two ordinary gardeners." I 12

—stingy: "Now good Mr Glegg himself was stingy in the most amiable manner: his neighbours called him 'near,' which always means that the person in question is a lovable skinflint. If you expressed a preference for cheese-parings, Mr Glegg would remember to save them for you with a good-natured delight in gratifying your palate, and he was given to pet all animals which required no appreciable keep. There was no humbug or hypocrisy about Mr Glegg: his eyes would have watered with true feeling over the sale of a widow's furniture, which a five-pound note from his side-pocket would have prevented: but a donation of five pounds to a person 'in a small way of life' would have seemed to him a mad kind of lavishness rather than 'charity' which had always presented itself to him as a contribution of small aids, not a neutralising of misfortune." I 12

—compatibility: "The true **Harpagon**s were always marked and exceptional characters: not so the worthy taxpayers who having once pinched from real necessity retained even in the midst of their comfortable retirement, with

their wall-fruit and wine-bins, the habit of regarding life as an ingenious process of nibbling out one's livelihood without leaving any perceptible deficit, and who would have been as immediately prompted to give up a newly-taxed luxury when they had their clear five hundred a year as when they had only five hundred pounds of capital. Mr Glegg was one of these men, found so impracticable by chancellors of the exchequer; and knowing this, you will be the better able to understand why he had not swerved from the conviction that he had made an eligible marriage, in spite of the too pungent seasoning that nature had given to the eldest **Miss Dodson**'s virtues. A man with an affectionate disposition, who finds a wife to concur with his fundamental idea of life, easily comes to persuade himself that no other woman would have suited him so well, and does a little daily snapping and quarrelling without any sense of alienation." I 12

—kind-hearted: "Mr Glegg's unmistakable kind-heartedness was shown in this, that it pained him more to see his wife at variance with others—even with **Dolly**, the servant—than to be in a state of cavil with her himself . . . . " I 12

—judging: "[**Mrs Glegg**] quarrelled with Mr Glegg, whose kindness, flowing entirely into compassion for **Lucy** made him as hard in his judgment of **Maggie** as **Mr Deane** himself was . . . . " VII 3

Mrs Jane Glegg. "The **Dodsons** were certainly a handsome family, and Mrs Glegg was not the least handsome of the sisters . . . for a woman of fifty she had a very comely face and figure . . . . It is true she despised the advantages of costume, for though, as she often observed, no woman had better clothes, it was not her way to wear her new things out before her old ones. Other women, if they liked, might have their best thread lace in every wash, but when Mrs Glegg died, it would be found that she had better lace laid by in the right-hand drawer of her wardrobe, in the Spotted Chamber, than ever **Mrs Wooll** of St Ogg's had bought in her life . . . . So of her curled fronts. Mrs Glegg had doubtless the glossiest and crispest brown curls in her drawers, as well as curls in various degrees of fuzzy laxness; but to look out on the week-day world from under a crisp and glossy front would be to introduce a most dreamlike and unpleasant confusion between the sacred and the secular. Occasionally, indeed, Mrs Glegg wore one of her third-best fronts on a week-day visit, but not at a sister's house; especially not at **Mrs Tulliver**'s, who since her marriage had hurt her sisters' feelings greatly by wearing her own hair, though, as Mrs Glegg observed to **Mrs Deane**, a mother of a family, like **Bessy**, with a husband always going to law, might have been expected to know better. But Bessy was always weak!" I 7

—attire: "Mrs Glegg chose to wear her bonnet in the house today—untied and tilted slightly, of course—a frequent practice of hers when she was on a visit and happened to be in a severe humour: she didn't know what draughts there might be in strange houses. For the same reason she wore a small sable tippet which reached just to her shoulders and was very far from meeting across her well-formed chest, while her long neck was protected by a *chevaux-de-frise* of miscellaneous frilling. One would need to be learned in the fashions of those times to know how far in the rear of them Mrs Glegg's slate-coloured silk gown must have been, but from certain constellations of small yellow spots upon it, and a mouldy odour about it suggestive of a damp clothes-chest, it was probable that it belonged to a stratum of garments just old enough to have come recently into wear." I 7

—*hectoring:* "Aunt Glegg always spoke to them in this loud emphatic way, as if she considered them deaf or perhaps rather idiotic: it was a means, she thought, of making them feel that they were accountable creatures, and might be a salutary check on naughty tendencies. **Bessy**'s children were so spoiled— they'd need have somebody to make them feel their duty." I 7

—*a mystery:* "That a creature made—in a genealogical sense—out of a man's rib, and in this particular case maintained in the highest respectability without any trouble of her own, should be normally in a state of contradiction to the blandest propositions and even to the most accommodating concessions, was a mystery in the scheme of things to which he had often in vain sought a clue in the early chapters of Genesis. **Mr Glegg** had chosen the eldest **Miss Dodson** as a handsome embodiment of female prudence and thrift, and being himself of a money-getting, money-keeping turn, had calculated on much conjugal harmony. But in that curious compound the feminine character, it may easily happen that the flavour is unpleasant in spite of excellent ingredients; and a fine systematic stinginess may be accompanied with a seasoning that quite spoils its relish." I 12

—*suited to her mate:* "**Mr Glegg**, being of a reflective turn, and no longer occupied with wool, had much wondering meditation on the peculiar constitution of the female mind as unfolded to him in his domestic life: and yet he thought Mrs Glegg's household ways a model for her sex: it struck him as a pitiable irregularity in other women if they did not roll up their table-napkins with the same tightness and emphasis as Mrs Glegg did, if their pastry had a less leathery consistence, and their damson cheese a less venerable hardness than hers: nay, even the peculiar combination of grocery and drug-like odours in Mrs Glegg's private cupboard impressed him as the only right thing in the way of cupboard-smells. I am not sure that he would not have longed for the quarrelling again, if it had ceased for an entire week; and it is certain that an acquiescent mild wife would have left his meditations comparatively jejune and barren of mystery." I 12

—*anticipation:* "To survive **Mr Glegg** and talk eulogistically of him, as a man who might have his weaknesses, but who had done the right thing by her notwithstanding his numerous poor relations—to have sums of interest coming in more frequently and secrete it in various corners baffling to the most ingenious of thieves (for, to Mrs Glegg's mind, banks and strong boxes would have nullified the pleasure of property—she might as well have taken her food in capsules)—finally, to be looked up to by her own family and the neighbourhood, so as no woman can ever hope to be who has not the praeterite and present dignity comprised in being a 'widow well left,'—all this made a flattering and conciliatory view of the future." I 12

—*calling in lugubrious circumstances:* "Mrs Glegg had on her fuzziest front, and garments which appeared to have had a recent resurrection from rather a creasy form of burial: a costume selected with the high moral purpose of instilling perfect humility into **Bessy** and her children." III 3

—*typical complaint:* " 'Though it's other people must see the joke in a niece's putting a slight on her mother's eldest sister, as is the head o' the family; and only coming in and out on short visits all the time she's been in the town, and then settling to go away without my knowledge—as I'd laid caps out on purpose for her to make 'em up for me—and me as have divided my money so equal—' " VI 12

—*unexpected reaction:* "As long as **Maggie** had not been heard of, Mrs Glegg had half closed her shutters and drawn down her blinds: she felt assured that Maggie was drowned: that was far more probable than that her niece and legatee should have done anything to wound the family honour in the tenderest point. When, at last, she learned from **Tom** that Maggie had come home, and gathered from him what was her explanation of her absence, she burst forth in severe reproof of Tom for admitting the worst of his sister until [*sic;* before] he was compelled. If you were not to stand by your 'kin' as long as there was a shred of honour attributable to them, pray what were you to stand by? Lightly to admit conduct in one of your own family that would force you to alter your will, had never been the way of the **Dodsons**; and though Mrs Glegg had always augured ill of Maggie's future at a time when other people were perhaps less clear-sighted, yet fair play was a jewel, and it was not for her own friend to help to rob the girl of her fair fame, and to cast her out from family shelter to the scorn of the outer world, until she had become unequivocally a family disgrace." VII 3

—*armed:* " . . . **Mr Glegg** brought from **Mr Deane** the news of **Stephen**'s letter. Then Mrs Glegg felt that she had adequate fighting-ground. . . .

"Again she had a scene of remonstrance with **Tom**, all the more severe, in proportion to the greater strength of her present position. But Tom, like other immovable things, seemed only the more rigidly fixed under that attempt to shake him." VII 3

Mr Moss, "who when he married **Miss Tulliver** had been regarded as the buck of Basset, now wore a beard nearly a week old and had the depressed, unexpectant air of a machine horse." I 8

—*captive audience:* "[**Mr Tulliver**] had no male audience today except Mr Moss, who knew nothing, as he said, of the 'natur' o' mills,' and could only assent to Mr Tulliver's arguments on the *a priori* ground of family relationship and monetary obligation . . . good Mr Moss made strong efforts to keep his eyes wide open, in spite of the sleepiness which an unusually good dinner produced in his hard-worked frame." II 2

Mrs Gertrude Moss. 'As for **Maggie**, she was the picture of her aunt Moss, **Mr Tulliver**'s sister, a large-boned woman who had married as poorly as could be, had no china, and had a husband who had much ado to pay his rent." I 7

" . . . who had not only come into the world in that superfluous way characteristic of sisters, creating a necessity for mortgages, but had quite thrown herself away in marriage and had crowned her mistakes by having an eighth baby. . . . poor Gritty had been a good-looking wench before she married **Moss** . . . ." I 8

—*at home:* "Mrs Moss heard the sound of the horse's feet and when her brother rode up, was already outside the kitchen door with a half-weary smile on her face, and a black-eyed **baby** in her arms. Mrs Moss's face bore a faded resemblance to her brother's: baby's little fat hand pressed against her cheek seemed to show more strikingly that the cheek was faded." I 8

—*long-suffering:* "But she thought it was in the order of nature that people who were poorly off should be snubbed. Mrs Moss did not take her stand on the equality of the human race: she was a patient, loosely-hung, child-producing woman." I 8

—*low in pecking order:* " . . . besides being poorly off, and inclined to 'hang on' her brother, [she] had the good natured submissiveness of a large, easy-tempered, untidy, prolific woman, with affection enough in her not only for her own husband and abundant children, but for any number of collateral relations." II 2

—family meeting: "The tall, worn, dark-haired woman was a strong contrast to the **Dodson** sisters as she entered in her shabby dress, with her shawl and bonnet looking as if they had been hastily huddled on, and with that entire absence of self-consciousness which belongs to keenly felt trouble." III 3

Mr Pullet, gentleman farmer, "was a small man with a high nose, small twinkling eyes and thin lips, in a fresh-looking suit of black and a white cravat that seemed to have been tied very tight on some higher principle than that of mere personal ease. He bore about the same relation to his tall, good-looking wife, with her balloon sleeves, abundant mantle and large be-feathered and be-ribboned bonnet, as a small fishing-smack bears to a brig with all its sails spread." I 7

—obfuscated: " . . . uncle Pullet belonged to that extinct class of British yeomen who dressed in good broadcloth, paid high rates and taxes, went to church, and ate a particularly good dinner on Sunday, without dreaming that the British constitution in Church and State had a traceable origin any more than the solar system and the fixed stars. It is melancholy, but true, that Mr Pullet had the most confused idea of a bishop as a sort of a baronet, who might or might not be a clergyman; and as the rector of his own parish was a man of high family and fortune, the idea that a clergyman could be a schoolmaster was too remote from Mr Pullet's experience to be readily conceivable. I know it is difficult for people in these instructed times to believe in uncle Pullet's ignorance; but let them reflect on the remarkable results of a great natural faculty under favouring circumstances. And uncle Pullet had a great natural faculty for ignorance." I 7

—talent: "**Lucy** thought it was by reason of some exceptional talent in uncle Pullet that the snuff-box played such beautiful tunes, and indeed the thing was viewed in that light by the majority of his neighbours in Garum. Mr Pullet had bought the box, to begin with, and he understood winding it up, and knew which tune it was going to play beforehand . . . . " I 9

—social stratagem: "But uncle Pullet when entreated to exhibit his accomplishment, never depreciated it by a too ready consent. 'We'll see about it,' was the answer he always gave, carefully abstaining from any sign of compliance till a suitable number of minutes had passed. Uncle Pullet had a programme for all great social occasions, and in this way fenced himself in from much painful confusion and perplexing freedom of will." I 9

—interested: " . . . beginning to nurse his knee and shelter it with his pocket handkerchief, as was his way when the conversation took an interesting turn." I 9

—investor: "Mr Pullet was nervous about his investments, and did not see how a man could have any security for his money unless he turned it into land." I 9

—puzzled: " 'Miss **Lucy**'s called the bell o' St Ogg's, they say—that's a cur'ous word,' observed Mr Pullet, on whom the mysteries of etymology sometimes fell with an oppressive weight." V 5

Mrs Sophy Pullet. "Sister Pullet was in tears when the one-horse chaise stopped before **Mrs Tulliver**'s door, and it was apparently requisite that she should shed a few more before getting out, for though her husband

and Mrs Tulliver stood ready to support her, she sat still and shook her head sadly as she looked through her tears at the vague distance . . . .

"Mrs Pullet brushed each doorpost with great nicety, about the latitude of her shoulders (at that period a woman was truly ridiculous to an instructed eye if she did not measure a yard and a half across the shoulders), and having done that sent the muscles of her face in quest of fresh tears as she advanced into the parlous where **Mrs Glegg** was seated." I 7

—calmer: "Mrs Pullet was silent, having to finish her crying, and rather flattered than indignant at being upbraided for crying too much. It was not everybody who could afford to cry so much about their neighbours who had left them nothing; but Mrs Pullet had married a gentleman farmer, and had leisure and money to carry her crying and everything else to the highest pitch of respectability." I 7

—medicated: " 'Ah!' sighed Mrs Pullet, shaking her head at the idea that there were few who could enter fully into her experiences in pink mixture and white mixture, strong stuff in small bottles, and weak stuff in large bottles, damp boluses at a shilling, and draughts at eighteenpence." I 7

—housekeeper: "Mrs Pullet's front-door mats were by no means intended to wipe shoes on: the very scraper had a deputy to do its dirty work. **Tom** rebelled particularly against this shoe-wiping, which he always considered in the light of an indignity to his sex . . . he had once been compelled to sit with towels wrapped round his boots . . . .

"The next disagreeable was . . . the mounting of the polished oak stairs, which had very handsome carpets rolled up and laid by in a spare bedroom, so that the ascent of these glossy steps might have served in barbarous times as a trial by ordeal from which none but the most spotless virtue could have come off with unbroken limbs." I 9

—hypochondria: " 'Pullet keeps all my physic-bottles . . . . He won't have one sold. He says it's nothing but right, folks should see 'em when I'm gone. They fill two o' the long store-room shelves a'ready—but,' she added beginning to cry, 'it's well if they ever fill three. I may go before I've made up the dozen o' these last sizes. The pill-boxes are in the closet in my room—you'll remember that, sister—but there's nothing to show for the boluses, if it isn't the bolls.' " I 9

—lachrymose: "Mrs Pullet entered crying, as a compendious mode, at all times, of expressing what were her views of life in general, and what, in brief, were the opinions she held concerning the particular case before her." III 3

—lares and penates: " ' . . . you'll be blundering with the keys, and never remember as that on the third shelf o' the left hand wardrobe, behind the night-caps with the broad ties—not the narrow-frilled ones—is the key o' the drawer in the Blue Rom, where the key o' the Blue Closet is. You'll make a mistake and I shall niver be worthy to know it. You've a memory for my pills and draughts, wonderful—I'll allays say that of you—but you're lost among the keys.' This gloomy prospect of the confusion that would ensue on her decease was very affecting to Mrs Pullet." VI 12

Supporting Roles

Stephen Guest, " 'who'll have nothing to do but sign cheques all his life, and may as well have Latin inside his head as any other sort of stuffing.' " III 5

—*in dalliance:* " . . . whose diamond ring, attar of roses, and air of nonchalant leisure at twelve o'clock in the day are the graceful and odoriferous result of the largest oil-mill and the most extensive wharf in St Ogg's. . . . a large-headed, long-limbed young man . . . . " VI 1

"He might have been sitting for his portrait, which would have represented a rather striking young man of five and twenty, with a square forehead, short dark-brown hair standing erect with a slight wave at the end like a thick crop of corn, and a half-ardent, half-sarcastic glance from under his well-marked horizontal eyebrows." VI 1

—*a guess:* " ' . . . a fat round girl, with round blue eyes, who will stare at us silently.'

" 'O yes!' exclaimed Lucy, laughing wickedly and clapping her hands, 'that is just my cousin Maggie. You must have seen her!' " VI 1

—*his choice:* " . . . perhaps he approved his own choice of her chiefly because she did not strike him as a remarkable rarity. A man likes his wife to be pretty: well, **Lucy** was pretty, but not to a maddening extent. A man likes his wife to be accomplished, gentle, affectionate and not stupid; and Lucy had all these qualifications. Stephen was not surprised to find himself in love with her, and was conscious of excellent judgment in preferring her to **Miss Leyburn**, the daughter of the county member . . . besides, he had had to defy and overcome a slight unwillingness and disappointment in his **father** and **sisters**—a circumstance which gives a young man an agreeable consciousness of his own dignity. Stephen was aware that he had sense and independence enough to choose the wife who was likely to make him happy, unbiassed by any indirect considerations. He meant to choose Lucy: she was a little darling, and exactly the sort of woman he had always most admired." VI 1

—*opinion solicited:* " 'Too tall . . . and a little too fiery. She is not my type of woman, you know.'

" . . . you, who have a higher logic than the verbal to guide you, have already foreseen, as the direct sequence to that unfavourable opinion of Stephen's, that he walked down to the boathouse calculating, by the aid of a vivid imagination, that **Maggie** must give him her hand at least twice in consequence of this pleasant boating plan, and that a gentleman who wishes ladies to look at him is advantageously situated when he is rowing them in a boat. What then? Had he fallen in love with this surprising daughter of **Mrs Tulliver** at first sight? Certainly not—such passions are never head of in real life. Besides, he was in love already, and half engaged to the dearest little creature in the world, and he was not a man to make a fool of himself in any way." VI 2

—*susceptible:* "But when one is five and twenty, one has not chalk-stones at one's finger ends that the touch of a handsome girl should be entirely indifferent. It was perfectly natural and safe to admire beauty and enjoy looking at it—at least under such circumstances as the present. And there was really something very interesting about this girl, with her poverty and troubles: it was gratifying to see the friendship between the two cousins. Generally, Stephen admitted, he was not fond of women who had any peculiarity of character—but here the peculiarity seemed really of a superior kind: and provided one is not obliged to marry such women—why, they certainly make a variety in social intercourse." VI 2

—a silent creep: "His personal attentions to **Maggie** were comparatively slight . . . . If Stephen came in when **Lucy** was out of the room—if Lucy left them together, they never spoke to each other: Stephen, perhaps, seemed to be examining books or music, and Maggie bent her head assiduously over her work. Each was oppressively conscious of the other's presence, even to the finger-ends. Yet each looked and longed for the same thing to happen the next day. Neither of them had begun to reflect on the matter, or silently to ask, 'To what does all this tend?' . . . Stephen wilfully abstained from self-questioning, and would not admit to himself that he felt an influence which was to have any determining effect on his conduct." VI 6

—alone with her: "He thought it was becoming a sort of monomania with him, to want that long look from Maggie, and he was racking his invention continually to find out some means by which he could have it without its appearing singular and entailing subsequent embarrassment." VI 6

—recrimination: "He wished he had never seen this **Maggie Tulliver**, to be thrown into a fever by her in this way: she would make a sweet, strange, troublesome, adorable wife to some man or other—but he would never have chosen her himself. Did she feel as he did? He hoped she did—not. He ought not to have gone. He would master himself in future. He would make himself disagreeable to her—quarrel with her perhaps." VI 6 *See* Maggie Tulliver*—her eyes*

—greeting a friend: " . . . I wish you'd conduct yourself a little less like a sparrow with a residence on the house-top and not go in and out constantly without letting the servants know. This is about the twentieth time I've had to scamper up those countless stairs to that painting room of yours, all to no purpose, because your people thought you were at home. Such incidents embitter friendship.' " VI 7

—a struggle: " . . . there was some attachment between [**Maggie**] and **Philip**; at least there was an attachment on his side, which made her feel in some bondage. Here then, Stephen told himself, was another claim of honour which called on him to resist the attraction that was continually threatening to overpower him. He told himself so: and yet he had once or twice felt a certain savage resistance, and at another moment a shuddering repugnance, to this intrusion of Philip's image which almost made it a new incitement to rush towards Maggie and claim her for himself." VI 10

—exquisite moment: " . . . does not a supreme poet blend light and sound into one, calling darkness mute, and light eloquent? Something strangely powerful there was in the light of Stephen's long gaze, for it made **Maggie**'s face turn towards it and look upward at it—slowly, like a flower at the ascending brightness. And they walked unsteadily on, without feeling that they were walking—without feeling anything but that long grave mutual gaze which has the solemnity belonging to all deep human passion. The hovering thought that they must and would renounce each other made this moment of mute confession more intense in its rapture." VI 10

—apology and avowal: " 'As if it were not enough that I'm entangled in this way—that I'm mad with love for you—that I resist the strongest passion a man can feel, because I try to be true to other claims—but you must treat me as if I were a coarse brute who would willingly offend you. And when, if I

had my own choice, I should ask you to take my hand, and my fortune and my whole life, and do what you liked with them. I know I forgot myself—I took an unwarrantable liberty—I hate myself for having done it. But I repented immediately—I've been repenting ever since. You ought not to think it unpardonable—a man who loves with his whole soul, as I do you, is liable to be mastered by his feelings for a moment; but you know—you must believe—that the worst pain I could have is to have pained you—that I would give the world to recall the error.' " VI 11

—responding to a plea: "Stephen had the fibre of nobleness in him that vibrated to her appeal; but in the same moment—how could it be otherwise?—that pleading beauty gained new power over him." *See* **Maggie Tulliver**—*the crux*

—rationalization: "There was nothing to conceal between them: they knew—they had confessed their love, and they had renounced each other—they were going to part. Honour and conscience were going to divide them—Maggie, with that appeal from her inmost soul had decided it: but surely they might cast a lingering look at each other across the gulf, before they turned away never to look again till that strange light had forever faded out of their eyes." VI 13

—subterfuge: "One other thing Stephen seemed now and then to care for, and that was, to sing: it was a way of speaking to **Maggie**—perhaps he was not distinctly conscious that he was impelled to it by a secret longing, running counter to all his self-confessed resolves, to deepen the hold he had on her." VI 13

—advocate: " 'See, **Maggie**, how everything has come without our seeking—in spite of all our efforts. We never thought of being alone together again—it has all been done by others. See how the tide is carrying us out—away from all those unnatural bonds that we have been trying to make faster round us—and trying us in vain. It will carry us on . . . and never pause a moment till we are bound to each other so that only death can part us. It is the only right thing—dearest—it is the only way of escaping from this wretched entanglement. Everything has concurred to point it out to us. We have contrived nothing, we have thought of nothing ourselves.' " VI 13

—conscience pricked: "He had the uneasy consciousness that he had robbed her of perfect freedom yesterday: there was too much native honour in him, for him not to feel that if her will should recoil, his conduct would have been odious, and she would have a right to reproach him." VI 14

—passionate message "**Maggie**! whose pain can have been like mine? Whose injury is like mine? Who besides me has met that long look of love that has burnt itself into my soul, so that no other image can come there? Maggie, call me back to you!—call me back to life and goodness! I am banished from both now. I have no motives: I am indifferent to everything. Two months have only deepened the certainty that I can never care for life without you. Write me one word—say "Come!" In two days I should be with you." VII 5

Bob Jakin. "**Tom** . . . had another companion besides **Yap**—naughty Bob Jakin, whose official, if not natural function, of frightening the birds, was just now at a standstill. **Maggie** felt sure that Bob was wicked, without very distinctly knowing why . . . . " I 6

—a character: "**Maggie** thought it very likely that the round house had snakes on the floor, and bats in the bedroom; for she had seen Bob take off

his cap to show Tom a little snake that was inside it, and another time he had a handful of young bats: altogether, he was an irregular character, perhaps even slightly diabolical, judging from his intimacy with snakes and bats . . . . " I 6

—*attributes:* "Bob knew, directly he saw a bird's egg, whether it was a swallow's or a tomtit's or a yellowhammer's; he found out all the wasps' nests and could set all sorts of traps; he could climb the trees like a squirrel, and had quite a magical power of detecting hedgehogs and stoats; and he had courage to do things that were rather naughty, such as making gaps in the hedgerows, throwing stones after sheep, and killing a cat that was wandering *incognito*. Such qualities in an inferior who could always be treated with authority in spite of his superior knowingness, had necessarily a fatal fascination for **Tom** . . . . " I 6

—*characteristics:* "For a person suspected of preternatural wickedness, Bob was really not so very villainous-looking; there was even something agreeable in his snub-nosed face with its close-curled border of red hair. But then his trousers were always rolled up at the knee for the convenience of wading on the slightest notice, and his virtue, supposing it to exist, was undeniably 'virtue in rags' which, on the authority even of bilious philosophers, who think all well-dressed merit overpaid, is notoriously likely to remain unrecognised (perhaps because it is seen so seldom)." I 6

—*changing his mind:* "What is life without a pocket-knife to him who has once tasted a higher existence? . . . Poor Bob! he was not sensitive on the point of honour—not a chivalrous character. That fine moral aroma would not have been thought much of by the public opinion of Kennel Yard, which was the very focus or heart of Bob's world, even if it could have made itself perceptible there. Yet, for all that, he was not utterly a sneak and a thief, as our friend **Tom** had hastily decided." I 6

—*reappeared:* " . . . **Tom** had not even an indefinite sense of any acquaintance with the rather broad-set but active figure, perhaps two years older than himself, that looked at him with a pair of blue eyes set in a disc of freckles, and pulled some curly red locks with a strong intention of respect. A low-crowned oilskin-covered hat and a certain shiny deposit of dirt on the rest of the costume, as of tablets prepared for writing upon, suggested a calling that had to do with boats, but this did not help Tom's memory." III 6

—*options considered:* " . . . there war a many trades I'd thought on, for as for the barge I'm clean tired out wi't, for it pulls the days out till they're as long as pig's chitterlings. An' I thought first I'd ha' ferrets an' dogs an' be a rot-ketcher an' then I thought as I should like a bigger way o' life, as I didn't know so well; for I'n seen to the bottom o' rotketching; an' I thought an' thought till at last I settled I'd be a packman, for they're knowin' fellers, the packmen are—an' I'd carry the lightest things I could i' my pack—an' there'd be a use for a feller's tongue, as is no use, neither wi' rots nor barges. An' I should go about the country far an' wide, an' come round the women wi' my tongue, an' get my dinner hot at the public—lors, it 'ud be a lovely life!' " III 6

—*turning up:* "It was not **Tom** who was entering, but a man in a sealskin cap and a blue plush waistcoat, carrying a pack on his back, and followed closely by a bull-terrier . . . ." IV 3

—*worshipper:* "The days of chivalry are not gone, notwithstanding **Burke**'s grand dirge over them [*see* Index XI Part I] they live still in that far-off worship paid by many a youth and man to the woman of whom he never dreams that he shall touch so much as her little finger or the hem of her robe. Bob, with the pack on his back, had as respectful an adoration for this dark-eyed maiden as if he had been a knight in armour calling aloud on her name as he pricked on to the fight." IV 3

Dr Kenn. " 'I think Kenn one of the finest fellows in the world. I don't care much about the tall candle-sticks he has put on the communion table, and I shouldn't like to spoil my temper by getting up to early prayers every morning. But he's the only man I ever knew personally who seems to me to have anything of the real apostle in him—a man who has eight hundred a year and is contented with deal furniture and boiled beef because he gives away two thirds of his income . . . .

" 'And one admires that sort of action in Kenn all the more,' said **Stephen**, 'because his manners in general are rather cold and severe. There's nothing sugary and maudlin about him.' " VI 2

—offering comfort: " . . . it was Dr Kenn's face that was looking at her:—that plain, middle-aged face, with a grave, penetrating kindness in it, seeming to tell of a human being who had reached a firm, safe strand, but was looking with helpful pity towards the strugglers still tossed by the waves, had an effect on **Maggie** at that moment which was afterwards remembered by her as if it had been a promise." VI 9

—counselling: "There was an entire absence of effusive benevolence in his manner; there was something almost cold in the gravity of his look and voice. If **Maggie** had not known that his benevolence was persevering in proportion to its reserve, she might have been chilled and frightened." VII 2

—the problem: "The tone of **Stephen**'s letter, which he had read, and the actual relations of all the persons concerned, forced upon him powerfully the idea of an ultimate marriage between Stephen and **Maggie** as the least evil; and the impossibility of their proximity in St Ogg's on any other supposition, until after years of separation, threw an insurmountable prospective difficulty over Maggie's stay here." VII 2

—powerless: "Even with his twenty years' experience as a parish priest, he was aghast at the obstinate continuance of imputations against [**Maggie**] in the face of evidence . . . in attempting to open the ears of women to reason and their consciences to justice on behalf of Maggie Tulliver, he suddenly found himself as powerless as he was aware he would have been if he had attempted to influence the shape of bonnets." VII 4

—pertinacious: "Dr Kenn, having great natural firmness, began, in the presence of this opposition, as every firm man would have done, to contract a certain strength of determination over and above what would have been called forth by the end in view. He himself wanted a daily governess for his younger children; and though he had hesitated in the first instance to offer this position to **Maggie**, the resolution to protest with the utmost force of his personal and priestly character against her being crushed and driven away by slander, was now decisive." VII 4 *See* **Miss Kirke** and **Mrs James Torry** MF

—a warning: "Dr Kenn, at first enlightened only by a few hints as to the new turn which gossip and slander had taken in relation to **Maggie**, had recently been made more fully aware of it by an earnest remonstrance from one of his male parishioners against the indiscretion of persisting in the attempt to overcome the prevalent feeling in the parish by a course of resistance." VII 5

—cornered: "Dr Kenn, having a conscience void of offence in the matter, was still inclined to persevere—was still averse to give way before a public sentiment that was odious and contemptible; but he was finally wrought upon by the consideration of the peculiar responsibility attached to his office, of avoiding the appearance of evil—and that 'appearance' is always dependent on the average quality of surrounding minds. Where these minds are low and gross, the area of that 'appearance' is proportionately widened. Perhaps he was in danger of acting from obstinacy; perhaps it was his duty to succumb: conscientious people are apt to see their duty in that which is the most painful course; and to recede was always painful to Dr Kenn. He made up his mind that he must advise **Maggie** to go away from St Ogg's for a time . . . . " VII 5

Rev. Walter Stelling. "If there were anything that was not thoroughly genuine about Mr Stelling, it lay quite beyond **Tom**'s power to detect it: it is only by a wide comparison of facts that the wisest full-grown man can distinguish well-rolled barrels from more supernal thunder." II 1

—characteristics: "Mr Stelling was a well-sized, broad-chested man, not yet thirty, with flaxen hair standing erect, and large lightish-grey eyes, which were always very wide open; he had a sonorous bass voice, and an air of defiant self-confidence inclining to brazenness. He had entered on his career with great vigour, and intended to make a considerable impression on his fellow-men." II 1

—goals: "The Rev. Walter Stelling was not a man who would remain among the 'inferior clergy' all his life. He had a true British determination to push his way in the world. As a schoolmaster, in the first place: for there were capital masterships of grammar-schools to be had, and Mr Stelling meant to have one of them. But as a preacher also, for he meant always to preach in a striking manner, so as to have his congregation swelled by admirers from neighbouring parishes, and to produce a great sensation whenever he took occasional duty for a brother clergyman of minor gifts." II 1

—life-style: "A clergyman who has such vigorous intentions naturally gets a little into debt at starting: it is not to be expected that he will live in the meagre style of a man who means to be a poor curate all his life, and if the few hundreds **Mr Timpson** advanced towards his daughter's fortune did not suffice for the purchase of handsome furniture together with a stock of wine, a grand piano, and the laying-out of a superior flower-garden, it followed in the most rigorous manner, either that these things must be procured by some other means, or else, that the Rev. Mr Stelling must go without them—which last alternative would be an absurd procrastination of the fruits of success, where success was certain." II 1

—amenable: "Not that Mr Stelling was a harsh-tempered or unkind man —quite the contrary: he was jocose with **Tom** at table, and corrected his provincialisms and his deportment in the most playful manner . . . . " II 1

—underneath: "**Mr Tulliver** was not be any means an exception in mistaking brazenness for shrewdness: most laymen thought Stelling shrewd, and a man of remarkable powers generally; it was chiefly by his clerical brethren that he was considered rather a dull fellow." II 1

—judgment: "And Mr Stelling was convinced that a boy so stupid at signs and abstractions must be stupid at everything else, even if that reverend gentleman could have taught him everything else." II 4

—*limitations:* "Gentlemen with broad chests and ambitious intentions do sometimes disappoint their friends by failing to carry the world before them. Perhaps it is, that high achievements demand some other unusual qualification besides an unusual desire for high prizes; perhaps it is that these stalwart gentlemen are rather indolent, their *divinae particulam aurae* being obstructed from soaring by a too hearty appetite. Some reason or other there was why Mr Stelling deferred the execution of many spirited projects—why he did not begin the editing of his Greek play, or any other work of scholarship in his leisure hours, but, after turning the key of his private study with much resolution, sat down to one of **Theodore Hook**'s novels." II 4

—*best side:* "Mr Stelling felt like a kind-hearted man: he foresaw a probable money loss for himself, but this had no appreciable share in his feeling while he looked with grave pity at the brother and sister for whom youth and sorrow had begun together." II 7

John Wakem, "to [**Mr Tulliver**'s] certain knowledge, was (metaphorically speaking) at the bottom of **Pivart**'s irrigation: Wakem had tried to make **Dix** stand out, and go to law about the dam: it was unquestionably Wakem who had caused Mr Tulliver to lose the suit about the right of road and the bridge that made a thoroughfare of his land for every vagabond . . . all lawyers were more or less rascals, but Wakem's rascality was of that peculiarly aggravated kind which placed itself in opposition to that form or fight embodied in Mr Tulliver's interests and opinions. . . . . A hook-nosed glib fellow! as cool as a cucumber—always looking so sure of his game!" II 2

—*first appearance:* " . . . a tallish man, with an aquiline nose and abundant iron-grey hair. You have not seen Mr Wakem before, and are possibly wondering whether he was really as eminent a rascal and as crafty, bitter an enemy of honest humanity in general and of **Mr Tulliver** in particular, as he is represented to be in that eidolon or portrait of him which we have seen to exist in the miller's mind. . . . .

"It is still possible to believe that the attorney was not more guilty towards him, than an ingenious machine which performs its work with much regularity is guilty towards the rash man who, venturing too near it, is caught up by some fly-wheel or other, and suddenly converted into unexpected sausages." III 7

—*outburst:* " '[**Tulliver**]'s a pig-headed, foul-mouthed fool!' burst out Mr Wakem, forgetting himself." III 7

—*a new idea:* "Although when Mr Wakem entered his office that morning, he had had no intention of purchasing Dorlcote Mill, his mind was already made up: **Mrs Tulliver** had suggested to him several determining motives, and his mental glance was very rapid: he was one of those men who can be prompt without being rash, because their motives run in fixed tracks, and they have no need to reconcile conflicting aims." III 7

—*above animus:* "To suppose that Wakem had the same sort of inveterate hatred towards **Tulliver**, that Tulliver had towards him, would be like supposing that a pike and a roach can look at each other from a similar point of view. The roach necessarily abhors the mode in which the pike gets his living, and the pike is likely to think nothing further even of the most indignant roach than that he is excellent good eating . . . . If Mr Tulliver had ever seriously injured or thwarted the attorney, Wakem would not have refused him the distinction of being a special object of vindictiveness . But when Mr Tulliver called Wakem a rascal at the market dinner-table, the attorney's clients were not a whit inclined to withdraw their business from him . . . he maintained perfect *sang-froid,* and knew quite well that the majority of substantial men then present were perfectly contented with the fact that 'Wakem was Wakem,' that is to say, a man who always knew the stepping-stones that would carry him through very muddy bits of practice. A man who had made a large fortune, had a handsome house among the trees at Tofton, and decidedly the finest stock of port wine in the neighbourhood of St Ogg's, was likely to feel himself on a level with public opinion." III 7

—but vindictive: "Wakem was not without this parenthetic vindictiveness towards the uncomplimentary miller, and now **Mrs Tulliver** had put the notion into his head it presented itself to him as a pleasure to do the very thing that would cause **Mr Tulliver** the most deadly mortification, and a pleasure of a complex kind, not made up of crude malice but mingling with it the relish of self-approbation . . . . He had once had the pleasure of putting an old enemy of his into one of the St Ogg's almshouses, to the rebuilding of which he had given a large subscription; and here was an opportunity of providing for another by making him his own servant." III 7

—not honest: "**Tulliver** was known to be a man of proud honesty, and Wakem was too acute not to believe in the existence of honesty. He was given to observing individuals, not to judging of them according to maxims, and no one knew better than he, that all men were not like himself." III 7

—the good side: "For Wakem was not a mere man of business: he was considered a pleasant fellow in the upper circles at St Ogg's, chatted amusingly over his port wine, did a little amateur farming, and had certainly been an excellent husband and father: at church, when he went there, he sat under the handsomest of mural monuments erected to the memory of his wife. Most men would have married again under his circumstances but he was said to be more tender to his deformed son than most men were to their best shapen offspring." III 7

—aroused father: " 'Find a single person in St Ogg's who will not tell you that a beautiful creature like her would be throwing herself away on a pitiable object like me.'

" 'Not she!' said Wakem, rising again, and forgetting everything else in a burst of resentful pride, half fatherly, half personal. 'It would be a deuced fine match for her. It's all stuff about an accidental deformity, when a girl's really attached to a man.' " VI 8

—giving in: " 'I don't care about the Mill,' he said at last with a sort of angry compliance. 'I've had an infernal deal of bother lately about the Mill. Let them pay me for my improvements, that's all. But there's one thing you needn't ask me. I shall have no direct transactions with young **Tulliver**. If you like to swallow him for his sister's sake you may; but I've no sauce that will make him go down.' " VI 8

Philip Wakem. "**Tom** felt in an uncomfortable flutter . . . . He had seen Philip Wakem at St Ogg's, but had always turned his eyes away from him as quickly as possible. He would have disliked having a deformed boy for his companion even if Philip had not been the son of a bad man. And Tom did not see how a bad man's son could be very good." II 3

—first impressions: "An anatomist . . . would have seen that the deformity of Philip's spine was not a congenital hump, but the result of an accident in infancy . . . [a] melancholy boy's face: the brown hair round it waved and curled at the ends like a girl's—**Tom** thought that truly pitiable. This Wakem

was a pale, puny fellow, and it was quite clear he would not be able to play at anything worth speaking of; but he handled his pencil in an enviable manner, and was apparently making one thing after another without any trouble." II 3

—amused: "Philip felt some bitter complacency in the promising stupidity of this well-made active-looking boy; but made polite by his own extreme sensitiveness as well as by his desire to conciliate, he checked his inclination to laugh . . . . " II 3

—irritable: "The slight spurt of peevish susceptibility which had escaped him in their first interview, was a symptom of a perpetually recurring mental ailment—half of it nervous irritability, half of it the heart-bitterness produced by the sense of his deformity. In these fits of susceptibility every glance seemed to him to be charged either with offensive pity or with ill-repressed disgust—at the very least it was an indifferent glance, and Philip felt indifference as a child of the south feels the chill air of a northern spring. Poor **Tom**'s blundering patronage when they were out of doors together would sometimes make him turn upon the well-meaning lad quite savagely, and his eyes, usually sad and quiet, would flash with anything but playful lightning." II 4

—happy: "Tom ran in to Philip, who was enjoying his afternoon's holiday at the piano in the drawing-room, picking out tunes for himself and singing them. He was supremely happy perched like an amorphous bundle on the high stool, with his head thrown back, his eyes fixed on the opposite cornice, and his lips wide open, sending forth, with all his might, impromptu syllables to a tune of **Arne**'s, which had hit his fancy." II 4

—interrupted and furious: "Philip shuddered visibly as he paused from his music. Then turning red, he said, with violent passion,

" 'Get away, you lumbering idiot! Don't come bellowing at me—you're not fit to speak to anything but a cart horse!' " II 4

—the unkindest cut: " 'I'm fit to speak to something better than you—you poor-spirited imp!' said **Tom**, lighting up immediately at Philip's fire. 'You know I won't hit you—because you're no better than a girl. But I'm an honest man's son, and your father's a rogue—everybody says so!' " II 4

—blandished: "[**Mrs Stelling**] meant him to feel that she behaved exceedingly well to him. Philip, however, met her advances towards a good understanding very much as a caressed mollusc meets an invitation to show himself out of his shell." II 4

—wounded: " . . . there was no malignity in his disposition, but there was a susceptibility that made him peculiarly liable to a strong sense of repulsion. The ox . . . is not given to use his teeth as an instrument of attack; and Tom was an excellent bovine lad, who ran at questionable objects in a truly ingenuous bovine manner; but he had blundered on Philips tenderest point, and had caused him as much acute pain as if he had studied the means with the nicest precision and the most envenomed spite." II 5

—grown: " . . . his face was wonderfully little altered—it was only a larger, more manly copy of the pale small-featured boy's face, with the grey eyes and the boyish waving brown hair; there was the old deformity to awaken the old pity . . . . " V 1

—blameable: "You can hardly help blaming him severely He was four or five years older than **Maggie**, and had a full consciousness of his feeling towards her to aid him in foreseeing the character his contemplated interviews with her would bear in the opinion of a third person." V 1

—on the other hand: "But you must not suppose that he was capable of a gross selfishness, or that he could have been satisfied without persuading himself that he was seeking to infuse some happiness into Maggie's life—seeking this even more than any direct ends for himself. He could give her sympathy—he could give her help. There was not the slightest promise of love towards him in her manner . . . [but] he clutched passionately the possibility, that she *might* love him: perhaps the feeling would grow, if she could come to associate him with that watchful tenderness, which her nature would be so keenly alive to. If any woman could love him—surely Maggie was that woman: there was such wealth of love in her, and there was no one to claim it all. Then —the pity of it that a mind like hers should be withering in its very youth, like a young forest tree, for want of the light and space it was formed to flourish in! Could he not hinder that, by persuading her out of her system of privation? He would be her guardian angel; he would do anything, bear anything for her sake—except not seeing her." V 1

—many talents: " 'I'm cursed with susceptibility in every direction, and effective faculty in none. I care for painting and music—I care for classic literature, and mediaeval literature and modern literature—I flutter all ways, and fly in none.' " V 3

—compensation: "His longing to see **Maggie** and make an element in her life, had in it some of that savage impulse to snatch an offered joy which springs from a life in which the mental and bodily constitution have made pain predominate. He had not his full share in the common good of men: he could not even pass muster with the insignificant, but must be singled out for pity, and excepted from what was a matter of course with others. Even to Maggie he was an exception: it was clear that the thought of his being her lover had never entered her mind." V 3

—lack of a mother: "Philip had never been soothed by that mother's love which flows out to us in the greater abundance because our need is greater, which clings to us the more tenderly because we are the less likely to be winners in the game of life; and the sense of his father's affection and indulgence towards him was marred by the keener perception of his father's faults. Kept aloof from all practical life as Philip had been, and by nature half feminine in sensitiveness, he had some of the woman's intolerant repulsion towards worldliness and the deliberate pursuit of sensual enjoyment, and this one strong natural tie in his life—his relation as a son—was like an aching limb to him. Perhaps there is inevitably something morbid in a human being who is in any way unfavourably excepted from ordinary conditions until the good force has had time to triumph, and it has rarely had time for that at two-and-twenty. That force was present in Philip in much strength, but the sun himself looks feeble through the morning mists." V 3

—stoical: " . . . like all persons who have passed through life with little expectation of sympathy, he seldom lost his self-control, and shrank with the most sensitive pride from any noticeable betrayal of emotion. A little extra paleness, a little tension of the nostril when he spoke, and the voice pitched in rather a higher key, that to strangers would seem expressive of cold indifference, were all the signs Philip usually gave of an inward drama that was not without its fierceness." VI 7

—eager to play: " . . . there is no feeling . . . that does not make a man sing or play the better; and Philip had an abundance of pent-up feeling at this moment, as complex as any trio or quartet that was ever meant to ex-

press love and jealousy and resignation and fierce suspicion all at the same time." VI 7

—tortured: "Philip went home soon after in a state of hideous doubt mingled with wretched certainty. It was impossible for him now to resist the conviction that there was some mutual consciousness between **Stephen** and **Maggie**; and for half the night his irritable, susceptible nerves were pressed upon almost to frenzy by that one wretched fact: he could attempt no explanation that would reconcile it with her words and actions. When, at last, the need for belief in Maggie rose to its habitual predominance, he was not long in imagining the truth—she was struggling, she was banishing herself—this was the clue to all he had seen since his return." VI 13

Others

Blessed Virgin. " 'And it came to pass when she stepped ashore, that her rags were turned into robes of flowing white, and her face became bright with exceeding beauty and there was a glory around it so that she shed a light on the water like the moon in its brightness. And she said, "**Ogg**, the son of **Beorl**, thou art blessed, in that thou didst not question and wrangle with the heart's need but wast smitten with pity and didst straightway relieve the same. And from henceforth whoso steps into thy boat shall be in no peril from the storm, and whenever it puts forth to the rescue it shall save the lives both of men and beasts." And when the floods came, many were saved by reason of that blessing on the boat.' " I 12 *See Foreshadowings*

Dix, "who had a mill on the stream, was a feeble auxiliary of Old Harry compared with **Pivart**: Dix had been brought to his senses by arbitration . . . in the intensity of his indignation against Pivart, [**Mr Tulliver**'s] contempt for a baffled adversary like Dix began to wear the air of a friendly attachment." II 2

Mr Gore, "a bald, round-featured man, with bland manners and fat hands: a game-cock that you would be rash to bet upon against **Wakem**. Gore was a sly fellow: his weakness did not lie on the side of scrupulosity: but the largest amount of winking, however significant, is not equivalent to seeing through a stone wall . . . . " II 2

The **Miss Guests**, "who associated chiefly on terms of condescension with the families of St Ogg's, and were the glass of fashion there, took some exception to **Maggie**'s manners. She had a way of not assenting at once to the observations current in good society and of saying that she didn't know whether those observations were true or not which gave her an air of *gaucherie* and impeded the even flow of conversation; but it is a fact capable of an amiable interpretation that ladies are not the worse disposed towards a new acquaintance of their own sex because she has points of inferiority . . . . It was only a wonder that there was no tinge of vulgarity about her, considering what the rest of poor **Lucy**'s relations were: an allusion which always made the Miss Guests shudder a little." VI 6

—at the Bazaar: "The Miss Guests were much too well-bred to have any of the grimaces and affected tones that belong to pretentious vulgarity; but their stall being next to the one where **Maggie** sat, it seemed newly obvious today that **Miss Guest** held her chin too high, and that **Miss Laura** spoke and moved continually with a view to effect.' " VI 9

—after the fall: "The Miss Guests saw an alleviation to the sorrow of witnessing a folly in their rector: at least, their brother would be safe; and their

knowledge of **Stephen**'s tenacity was a constant ground of alarm to them, lest he should come back and marry **Maggie**. They were not among those who disbelieved their brother's letter; but they had no confidence in Maggie's adherence to her renunciation of him . . . . They had always thought her disagreeable: they now thought her artful and proud; having quite as good grounds for that judgment as you and I probably have for many strong opinions of the same kind." VII 4

Gypsy men. "The elder of the two carried a bag, which he flung down, addressing the women in a loud and scolding tone, which they answered by a shower of treble sauciness; while a black cur ran barking up to Maggie and threw her into a tremor that only found a new cause in the curses with which the younger man called the dog off, and gave him a rap with a great stick he held in his hand." I 11

Mr Jacobs, "himself, familiarly known as Old Goggles, from his habit of wearing spectacles, imposed no painful awe; and if it was the property of snuffy old hypocrites like him to write like copperplate and surround their signatures with arabesques, to spell without forethought, and to spout 'My name is **Norval**' without bungling, **Tom** for his part was rather glad he was not in danger of those mean accomplishments. He was not going to be a snuffy schoolmaster . . . . " II 1

Kezia. " . . . 'a puff o' wind 'ud make 'em blow about like feathers,' Kezia, the housemaid said, feeling proud to live under a mistress [**Mrs Tulliver**] who could make such pastry . . . . " I 6

—embattled: "Already at three o'clock, Kezia, the good-hearted, bad-tempered housemaid, who regarded all people that came to the sale as her personal enemies, the dirt on whose feet was of a peculiarly vile quality, had begun to scrub and swill with an energy much assisted by a continual low muttering against 'folks as came to buy up other folks's things' . . . she was bent on bringing the parlour, where that 'pipe-smoking pig' the **bailiff** had sat, to such an appearance of scant comfort as could be given to it by cleanliness and the few articles of furniture bought in for the family. Her mistress and the young folks should have their tea in it that night, Kezia was determined." III 6

—high fettle: "Having declared her intention of staying till the master could get about again, 'wage or no wage,' she had found a certain recompense in keeping a strong hand over her mistress, scolding her for 'moithering' herself and going about all day without changing her cap and looking as if she was 'mushed.' Altogether this time of trouble was rather a Saturnalian time to Kezia; she could scold her betters with unreproved freedom." III 8

Ladies of St Ogg's. "[They] were not beguiled by any wide speculative conceptions; but they had their favourite abstraction, called society, which served to make their consciences perfectly easy in doing what satisfied their own egoism—thinking and speaking the worst of **Maggie Tulliver** and turning their backs upon her." VII 4

Luke Moggs, "the head miller, a tall broad-shouldered man of forty, black-eyed and black-haired, subdued by a general mealiness, like an auricula." I 4

—on Dutchmen: " ' . . . my old master, as war a knowin' man, used to say, says he, "If e'er I sow my wheat wi'out brinin', I'm a Dutchman," says he; an' that war as much as to say as a Dutchman war a fool, or next door. Nay, nay,

I aren't goin' to bother mysen about Dutchmen. There's fools enoo—an' rogues enoo—wi'out lookin' i' books for 'em.' " I 4

—on reading: " 'Nay, Miss, I'n got to keep 'count o' the flour an' corn—I can't do wi' knowin' so many things besides my work. That's what brings folk to the gallows—knowin' everything but what they'n got to get their bread by. An' they're mostly lies, I think, what's printed i' the books: them printed sheets are, anyhow, as the men cry i' the streets.' " I 4

—loyal: "Good Luke felt, after the manner of contented hard-working men whose lives have been spent in servitude, that sense of natural fitness in rank which made his master's downfall a tragedy to him. He was urged, in his slow way, to say something that would express his share in the family sorrow, and these words which he had used over and over again to **Tom**, when he wanted to decline the full payment of his fifty pounds out of the children's money, were the most ready to his tongue." III 8

—conservative: " 'I can't abide new plazen mysen: things is allays awk'ard —narrow-wheeled waggins, belike, and the stiles all another sort, an' oat-cake i' some plazen, tow'rt th' head o' the Floss, there. It's poor work, changing your country side.' " III 9

Ogg, the son of **Beorl**, "says my private hagiographer, 'was a boatman who gained a scanty living by ferrying passengers across the river Floss. And it came to pass one evening when the winds were high, that there sat moaning by the brink of the river a woman with a child in her arms; and she was clad in rags, and had a worn and withered look. And she craved to be rowed across the river . . . . But Ogg the son of Beorl came up, and said, "I will ferry thee across: it is enough that thy heart needs it." And he ferried her across . . . [and] it was witnessed in the floods of after-time, that at the coming on of even, Ogg the son of Beorl was always seen with his boat upon the wide-spreading waters, and the **Blessed Virgin** sat in the prow shedding a light around as of the moon in its brightness, so that the rowers in the gathering darkness took heart and pulled anew.' " I 12

Mr Pivart, "who, having lands higher up the Ripple, was taking measures for their irrigation which either were or would be or were bound to be (on the principle that water was water) an infringement on **Mr Tulliver**'s legitimate share of water-power." II 2

—recent arrival: " 'New name? Yes—I should think it *is* a new name,' said **Mr Tulliver**, with angry emphasis. 'Dorlcote Mill's been in our family a hundred year and better, and nobody ever heard of a Pivart meddling with the river, till this fellow came and bought **Bincome**'s farm out of hand, before anybody else could so much as say "snap." But I'll *Pivart* him!' added Mr Tulliver lifting his glass with a sense that he had defined his resolution in an unmistakable manner." II 2

Mr Poulter, "the village schoolmaster, who, being an old Peninsular soldier, was employed to drill Tom—a source of high mutual pleasure. Mr Poulter, who was understood by the company at the Black Swan to have once struck terror into the hearts of the French, was no longer personally formidable. He had rather a shrunken appearance, and was tremulous in the mornings, not from age, but from the extreme perversity of the King's Lorton boys which nothing but gin could enable him to sustain with any firmness. Still, he carried himself with martial erectness, had his clothes scrupulously brushed, and his trousers tightly strapped, and on the Wednesday and Saturday afternoons when he came to Tom, he was always inspired with gin and old memories, which gave him an exceptionally spirited air, as of a superannuated charger who hears the drum." II 4

—*private exercise:* "But Mr Poulter was a host in himself; that is to say, he admired himself more than a whole army of spectators could have admired him." II 4

Mr Rappit, "the hair-dresser from St Ogg's who had spoken in the severest terms of the condition in which he had found her hair, holding up one jagged lock after another and saying, 'See here! tut—tut—tut!' in a tone of mingled disgust and pity, which to Maggie's imagination was equivalent to the strongest expression of public opinion. Mr Rappit . . . with his well-anointed coronal locks tending wavily upward, like the simulated pyramid of flame on a monumental urn, seemed to her at that moment the most formidable of her contemporaries, into whose street at St Ogg's she would carefully refrain from entering through the rest of her life." I 9

Riley. " ' . . . a sort o' engineer, or a surveyor, or an auctioneer and vallyer, like Riley . . . for Riley looks Lawyer **Wakem** i' the face as hard as one cat looks another. *He's* none frighted at him.' " I 2

—*visiting:* "The gentleman in the ample white cravat and shirt-frill, taking his brandy and water so pleasantly with his good friend **Tulliver**, is Mr Riley: a gentleman with a waxen complexion and fat hands, rather highly educated for an auctioneer and appraiser, but large-hearted enough to show a great deal of *bonhommie* [*sic*] towards simple country acquaintances of hospitable habits. Mr Riley spoke of such acquaintances kindly as 'people of the old school.' " I 3

—*education:* " . . . though Mr Riley had received a tincture of the classics at the great Mudport Free School and had a sense of understanding Latin generally, his comprehension of any particular Latin was not ready. Doubtless there remained a subtle aroma from his juvenile contact with the *De Senectute* and the Fourth Book of the *Aeneid*, but it had ceased to be distinctly recognisable as classical, and was only perceived in the higher finish and force of his auctioneering style." I 3

—*millstone:* "There was that suretyship for poor Riley, who had died suddenly last April, and left his friend saddled with a debt of two hundred and fifty pounds: a fact which had helped to make **Mr Tulliver**'s banking book less pleasant reading than a man might desire towards Christmas." III 1

Sally "looked at them in speechless amaze, with a piece of bread-and-butter in her mouth and a toasting-fork in her hand, 'Sally, tell mother it was **Maggie** pushed **Lucy** into the mud.'

" 'But Lors ha' massy, how did you get near such mud as that?' said Sally, making a wry face, as she stooped down and examined the *corpus delicti.*" I 10

"Sally . . . lost no time in presenting Lucy at the parlour door, for to have so dirty an object introduced into the house at Garum Firs was too great a weight to be sustained by a single mind." I 10

Laura Stelling. "The little cherub Laura, not being an accomplished walker at present, had a ribbon fastened round her waist, by which **Tom** held her as if she had been a little dog, during the minutes in which she chose to walk, but as these were rare, he was for the most part carrying this fine child round and round the garden, within sight of Mrs Stelling's window—according to orders." II 1

Mrs Louisa Stelling, *née* **Timpson**. " 'There isn't a kinder little soul in the world; I know her family well. She has very much your complexion—light curly hair. She comes of a good Mudport family . . . . ' " I 3

—compatible: "As for **Mrs Tulliver**, finding that Mrs Stelling's views as to the airing of linen and the frequent recurrence of hunger in a growing boy, entirely coincided with her own, moreover, that Mrs Stelling, though so young a woman, and only anticipating her second confinement, had gone through very nearly the same experience as herself with regard to the behaviour and fundamental character of the monthly nurse—she expressed great contentment to her husband when they drove away, at leaving **Tom** with a woman who, in spite of her youth, seemed quite sensible and motherly, and asked advice as prettily as could be." II 1

—contriving: "When the wife of a poor curate contrives under all her disadvantages to dress extremely well, and to have a style of coiffure which requires that her nurse shall occasionally officiate as lady's maid—when, moreover, her dinner parties and her drawing-room show that effort at elegance and completeness of appointment to which ordinary women might imagine a large income necessary, it would be unreasonable to expect of her that she should employ a second nurse or even act as a nurse herself. **Mr Stelling** knew better: he saw that his wife did wonders already, and was proud of her . . . Among the many means whereby Mr Stelling intended to be more fortunate than the bulk of his fellowmen, he had entirely given up that of having his own way in his own house." II 1

—hated: "I'm afraid [**Tom**] hated Mrs Stelling, and contracted a lasting dislike to pale blond ringlets and broad plaits as directly associated with haughtiness of manner and a frequent reference to other people's 'duty.' " II 1

—unloving: "Mrs Stelling was not a loving, tender-hearted woman: she was a woman whose skirt sat well, who adjusted her waist, and patted her curls with a preoccupied air when she inquired after your welfare. These things, doubtless, represent a great social power, but it is not the power of love . . . . " II 4

Minor Figures

Bailiff. "There was a coarse, dingy man . . . sitting in his father's chair, smoking, with a jug and glass beside him . . . .

" 'How do you do, sir?' said the man, taking the pipe out of his mouth with rough, embarrassed civility. The two young startled faces made him a little uncomfortable." III 2

Boy. "It was not without a leaping of the heart that [**Maggie**] caught sight of a small pair of bare legs sticking up, feet uppermost, by the side of a hillock; they seemed something hideously preternatural—a diabolical kind of fungus; for she was too much agitated at the first glance to see the ragged clothes and the dark shaggy head attached to them. It was a boy asleep . . . . " I 11

Mr Carr. " 'It's much if he ever gets up again [said **Mrs Pullet**], and if he does he'll most like be childish, as Mr Carr was, poor man! They fed him with a spoon as if he'd been a babby for three year. He'd quite lost the use of his limbs; but then, he'd got a Bath chair, and somebody to draw him . . . .

" ' . . . if you've got anything disrespectful to say o' Mr Carr, I do beg of you, as you won't say it to me. *I* know what he was,' she added, with a sigh.

'His breath was short to that degree as you could hear him two rooms off.' " III 3

Dickison, landlord at the Marquis of Granby, "leaning against the door-post with a melancholy pimpled face looking as irrelevant to the daylight as a last night's guttered candle . . . . " I 8

Dolly, servant to the Gleggs (who immediately becomes **Sally**). I 12

Furley. "There was Furley, who held the mortgage on the land—a reasonable fellow who would see his own interest, **Mr Tulliver** was convinced, and who would glad not only to purchase the whole estate including the mill and homestead, but would accept Mr Tulliver as tenant, and be willing to advance money to be repaid with high interest out of the profits of the business which would be made over to him . . . . " III 1

Gypsy-mother, "a young woman with a baby in her arm . . . this face with the bright dark eyes and the long hair was really something like what [**Maggie**] used to see in the glass before she cut her hair off." I 11

Gypsy men. "The elder of the two carried a bag, which he flung down, addressing the women in a loud and scolding tone, which they answered by a shower of treble sauciness; while a black cur ran barking up to **Maggie** and threw her into a tremor that only found a new cause in the curses with which the younger man called the dog off, and gave him a rap with a great stick he held in his hand." I 11

Harry. " 'I reckon Master **Tom** told Harry to feed [his rabbits], but there's no countin' on Harry—*he's* a offal creatur as iver come about the primises, he is. He remembers nothin' but his own inside—an' I wish it 'ud gripe him.' " I 4

Mrs Jakin senior "was a dreadfully large fat woman, who lived at a queer round house down the river, and once, when **Maggie** and **Tom** had wandered thither there rushed out a brindled dog that wouldn't stop barking, and when **Bob**'s, mother came out after it, and screamed above the barking to tell them not to be frightened, Maggie thought she was scolding them fiercely and her heart beat with terror." I 6

Mrs Prissy Jakin. "It was Bob's wife who opened the door to **Maggie**. She was a tiny woman, with the general physiognomy of a Dutch doll, looking, in comparison with Bob's mother who filled up the passage in the rear, very much like one of those human figures which the artist finds conveniently standing near a colossal statue to show the proportions." VI 4

Maggie Jakin, "a two months' old baby—quite the liveliest of its age that had ever been born to prince or packman." VII 1

Jetsome. " ' He's a loose fish—that young Jetsome,' said **Tom**. 'He's taking to drinking, and they say he's letting the business go down . . . . I was thinking, if things went on in that way, **Wakem** might be more willing to part with the Mill.' " VI 5

"To think that . . . that unfortunate young Jetsome, whom Mr Wakem had placed at the Mill, had been pitched off his horse in a drunken fit, and was lying at St Ogg's in a dangerous state . . . . " VI 12

Mrs Kenn, "whose delicate state of health, threatening to become confirmed illness through an attack of bronchitis, obliged her to resign her functions at the coming bazaar . . . . " VI 6

Miss Kirke "who had a spinal complaint and wanted a reader and companion, felt quite sure that **Maggie**'s mind must be of a quality with which she, for her part, could not risk *any* contact." VII 4

Minny, "who had intrenched himself, trembling, in his basket as soon as the music began, found this thunder so little to his taste that he leaped out and scampered under the remotest *chiffonnière*, as the most eligible place in which a small dog could await the crack of doom." VI 1

Mrs Moggs, Luke's wife, was a decidedly agreeable acquaintance: she exhibited her hospitality in bread and treacle and possessed various works of art . . . a remarkable series of pictures representing the **Prodigal Son** in the costume of **Sir Charles Grandison** . . . . " I 4

Baby Moss. "**Tom** . . . unthinkingly withdrew a small rattle he was amusing Baby Moss with, whereupon she, being a baby that knew her own mind with remarkable clearness, instantaneously expressed her sentiments in a piercing yell, and was not to be appeased even by the restoration of the rattle . . . . " II 2

Lizzy Moss, "a black-eyed child of seven, looked very shy when her mother drew her forward, for the small Mosses were much in awe of their uncle from Dorlcote Mill. She was inferior enough to **Maggie** in fire and strength of expression to make the resemblance between the two entirely flattering to **Mr Tulliver**'s fatherly love." I 8

Moss children. "Maggie . . . making an epoch for her cousins great and small, who were learning her words and actions by heart, as if she had been a transient avatar of perfect wisdom and beauty.." VI 11

Mumps, "a bull-terrier of brindled coat and defiant aspect." IV 3

—indifferent: " 'Why, the gentry stops to look at him, but you won't catch Mumps a-looking at the gentry much—he minds his own business—he does.'

"The expression of Mumps's face, which seemed to be tolerating the superfluous existence of objects in general, was strongly confirmatory of this high praise." IV 3

—visiting: " . . . a huge brindled bull-terrier, who walked with a slow swaying movement from side to side, and glanced from under his eyelids with a surly indifference which might after all be a cover to the most offensive designs." V 2

Nephew. " 'It's a nice sort o' man as **Mrs Sutton** has left her money to, for he's troubled with the asthmy and goes to bed every night at eight o'clock. He told me about it himself, as free as could be, one Sunday when he came to our church. He wears a hare-skin on his chest, and has a trembling in his talk—quite a gentleman sort o' man.' " I 7

Sally. " 'Sally,' [**Mrs Glegg**] said, rising from her chair, and speaking in rather a choked voice, light a fire upstairs, and put the blinds down.' " I 12
Mrs Pullet's maid is also Sally: does GE make a mistake? She first calls the Pullet servant "Dolly."

Salt, "that eminently 'briny chap'—having been discovered in a cloud of tobacco smoke at the Anchor Tavern, **Mr Glegg** commenced inquiries which turned out satisfactorily enough to warrant the advance of the 'nest-egg'. . . ." V 2

Mr Spray "the independent minister had begun to preach political sermons in which he distinguished with much subtlety between his fervent belief in the right of the Catholics to the franchise and his fervent belief in their eternal perdition." I 12

Mrs Sutton. " 'Died the day before yesterday,' continued **Mrs Pullet**. 'An' her legs was as thick as my body,' she added, with deep sadness, after a pause. 'They'd tapped her no end o' times, they say you might ha' swum in the water as came from her . . . .

"She's so much acquaintance as I've seen her legs when they was like bladders . . . . And an old lady as had doubled her money over and over again, and kept it all in her own management to the last, and had her pocket with her keys in under her pillow constant. There isn't many old *par*ish'ners like her, I doubt.' " I 7

Tilt. " 'There's poor Mr Tilt got his mouth drawn all o' one side, and couldn't laugh if he was to try.' " VI 12

Timpson "was one of the most useful and influential men in the parish, and had a good deal of business which he knew how to put into the right hands." I 3

Mrs James Torry "could not think of taking **Maggie** as a nursery governess, even temporarily—a young woman about whom 'such things had been said,' and about whom 'gentlemen joked' . . . . " VII 4

Young **Torry**. " 'He might look at me through an eyeglass stuck in his eye, making a hideous face, as young Torry does . . . I never felt any pity for young Torry. I've never any pity for conceited people because I think they carry their comfort about with them.' " V 4

—struck: " . . . young Torry fatigued his facial muscles more than usual in order that 'the dark-eyed girl there, in the corner,' might see him in all the additional style conferred by his eyeglass . . . . " VI 6

—envious " '**Guest** is a great coxcomb,' young Torry observed, 'but then he is a privileged person in St Ogg's—he carries all before him: if another fellow did such things [as wear a scarlet Fez], everybody would say he made a fool of himself.' (Young Torry had red hair.)" VI 9

Ralph Tulliver. "**Mr Tulliver**'s **grandfather** had been heard to say that he was descended from one Ralph Tulliver, a wonderfully clever fellow who had ruined himself.—It is likely enough that the clever Ralph was a high liver, rode spirited horses, and was very decidedly of his own opinion." IV 1

Mr Turnbull. "But Mr Turnbull came now to meet her: a medical man is the good angel of the troubled house, and **Maggie** ran towards the kind old friend whom she remembered as long as she could remember anything . . . . " III 1

Miss Unit "declares she will never visit **Mr** and **Mrs Stephen Guest** —such nonsense! pretending to be better than other people." MF VII 2

Vicar. "The vicar of [the **Dodsons**'] pleasant rural parish was not a controversialist, but a good hand at whist, and one who had a joke always ready for a blooming female parishioner." IV 1

—benign: "It was not that any harm could be said concerning the vicar of that charming rural parish to which Dorlcote Mill belonged: he was a man of excellent family, an irreproachable bachelor, of elegant pursuits, had taken honours, and held a fellowship . . . . " IV 1

Emily Wakem. " 'But your mother looked gentler—she had that brown wavy hair, and grey eyes, like yours. You can't remember her very well. It was a thousand pities I'd no likeness of her.' " VI 8

Counsellor Wylde. "But then, if they went to law, there was a chance for **Mr Tulliver** to employ Counsellor Wylde on his side, instead of having that admirable bully against him, and the prospect of seeing a witness of **Wakem**'s made to perspire and become confounded, as Mr Tulliver's witness had once been, was alluring to the love of retributive justice." II 2

Yap, "the queer white and brown terrier with one ear turned back, trotting about and sniffing vaguely as if he were in search of a companion . . . Yap pranced and barked round [**Maggie**], as much as to say, if there was any noise wanted, he was the dog for it." I 4

—and jam puffs: "[He] had also been looking on while the eatables vanished with an agitation of his ears and feelings which could hardly have been without bitterness. Yet the excellent dog accepted **Tom**'s attention with as much alacrity as if he had been treated quite generously." I 6

Also mentioned

Abbott, a cousin of the Dodson sisters	I 7, VII 3
Alice, lady's maid to Lucy Deane	VII 4
Mr Askern, surgeon who attends Tom when the sword falls on his foot	II 5
Margaret Beaton, Mr Tulliver's mother, who died at forty-seven	III 8
Bincome, whose farm on the Ripple was sold to Pivart	II 2
boy serving in the mill; beaten by Tulliver	IV 3
Dick Brumby, childhood friend whom Bob Jakin "leathered" frequently	III 6
Brumley, a litigant represented by Mr Wakem: he lost his suit	II 2
Mrs Bucks, with a cork leg; a customer of Bob Jakin's pack	V 2
choir members, who sing carols after midnight in the countryside	II 2
clerk, one-armed and elderly, who gave Tom lessons in book-keeping and calculation	III 7
Miss Clint, who married Mr Wakem; the mother of Philip	III 7
cook at Garum Firs, who brought in the tea	I 10
cowboy at the Moss farm	I 8
Sir James Crake, Master of the Harriers, whom Tom would hope to emulate	II 3
Squire Darleigh, who had the Dodson sisters to dances in their youth	III 7
Dodson, a brother with a mole who died	I 2
Dodson senior, the late	I 7
Bill Fawks, who gave Bob Jakin a terrier pup instead of drowning it	III 6
Miss Firniss, schoolmistress at Laceham on the Floss	II 7
Frances, an aunt of the Dodson daughters	I 7
Garnett, and his son; an example for Mr Tulliver in his plans for Tom	I 7
Gell, a new partner in Guest & Co.	VI 5
George IV, in portrait: depressed cranium, voluminous neck-cloth	IV 3
John Gibbs, waggoner hired by Mr Tulliver, who died	I 2
Gibson, a schoolmate who fought Tom to make him share	I 2
Goodrich, drawing-master	II 4
Grattan lad, who shot his mother by accident; rescued by Dr Kenn	VI 2
Mrs Gray, milliner to aunt Pullet	I 9
Guest, senior; wealthy businessman, not very enthusiastic about Lucy Deane	VI 1
gypsy children, shock-headed, lying prone, resting on their elbows like small sphinxes	I 11
Job Haxey, who wove the Tulliver table cloths	III 2
Mr Hyndmarsh, grocer of St Ogg's, who knew the Dodsons and recognized Tom	III 5, 7
Jacobs, headmaster at the Academy, whom Mr Tulliver does not regard highly	I 7
Kenn baby, age three	VII 2
lawyer friend of the Rev. Stelling, not yet a lord chancellor	II 1
Miss Leyburn, the daughter of the county member; a prospect for Stephen Guest	VI 1
Morton, a businessman who has died	I 12
Georgy Moss, who ran for his father	I 8
Willy Moss, asked to hold a horse	VI 11

old gypsy-man, fierce-eyed and frightening to Maggie	I 11
old gypsy-woman seated on the ground poking a skewer into a round kettle	I 11
Partridge, whose effects were sold at auction	I 3
Patch, the old parish clerk who goes out to sing Christmas carols	II 2
Pelley, a banker of whose failure Tom was able to warn Guest & Co. in time	VI 5
Mrs Pepper, a customer of Bob Jakin's pack	V 2
publican of St Ogg's, a client of Tulliver's	III 5
Riley daughter, now an under-teacher at Miss Firniss's	III 8
Salt, supercargo on the ship which will take Tom's goods	V 2
servant to Mr Kenn	VII 2
servant at the Tullivers' unnamed; in Mr Tulliver's illness	III 2
Spence, managing clerk at Mr Deane's bank	III 5
Spouncer, a schoolmate who fought Tom to make him share	I 5
Stowe, in Tom's place at the wharf while he is out	V 2
Torry, a miller with a business connection of Guest & Co.	III 5, 6
Miss Torry, who brought Lucy a request from Mrs Kenn	VI 6
Grandfather **Tulliver**, who spoke of his ancestor Ralph	IV 1
Mrs Tulliver, senior; a fine dark-eyed woman whom Maggie resembles	III 9
Mrs and **Miss Turnbull**, who snub Maggie in the street	VII 2
waggoner, managing his horses	I 1
Wakem sons, including a favourite lad he had meant to bring along in the world	III 7
Winship, the auctioneer for the sale of Dorlcote Mill	III 7
Mrs Wooll, well-dressed denizen of St Ogg's; negative gossip about Maggie	I 7, VII 3

Silas Marner

The Weaver of Raveloe

Silas Marner, linen-weaver, lives in a cottage next to a deserted quarry near Raveloe, in central England. Subject to catalepsy, he knows herbs and has done cures, so he is a little feared and generally avoided except by customers. He is reputed to have amassed a fortune. At his former home he was an active speaker and participant in a religious sect in Lantern Yard. The senior deacon became ill; Silas and his friend **William Dane** divided the watch; and on Silas's watch the deacon died. He was summoned to explain why his pocket knife was found in a drawer where the meeting's funds, now missing, were kept. The money bag was found at his lodgings. He realized William had framed him. The sect drew lots, which went against Silas; his fiancée **Sarah** broke their engagement. William and Sarah married. Disillusioned, Silas left town. 1

Established at Raveloe, he weaves and earns gold. He remembers his mother's dropsy and gives a foxglove preparation to the cobbler's wife to help her; but his refusal to trade on this isolates him the more from the suspicious rustics. He concentrates on weaving and loves the money he makes more and more. He lives like that, his life narrowing into a fixation on his gold, for 15 years. 2 **Squire Cass**'s sons **Godfrey** and **Dunstan** quarrel: Dunstan knows of Godfrey's impulsive marriage to drunken **Molly Farren**. He has extorted £100 Godfrey had collected from their father's tenant. It is agreed that he will take Godfrey's hunter to ride and sell, to permit Godfrey to pay his father. Godfrey yearns for **Nancy Lammeter**, who would keep him straight. 3

Dunstan takes Wildfire on a hunt but overrides and causes the horse's death soon after contracting to sell him for £120. He has to walk back in a deepening mist. He has seen Silas's cottage going out and thought of his gold as a resource for Godfrey. Now he reaches the cottage and knocks. No one is there. Dunstan walks in and sits by the fire. He quickly divines the location of two bags of gold under the bricks of the floor and gets them out. Hurriedly he goes out, closes the door behind him and steps out into pitch darkness. 4

Silas returns from his errand and continues his meal preparation. But he decides to have his gold for company with his supper. It is not there. He is amazed, incredulous, then frantic. He suspects a poacher, Jem Rodney.

He heads for the Rainbow, the local tavern, to report his loss. 5 Tavern denizens are in conversation. **Dowlas**, the farrier, taxes butcher **Lundy** over a cow. The new deputy parish clerk, **Tookey**, is derided by wheelwright **Winthrop** as a poor choir singer. Parish clerk **Macey** tells of the original **Lammeter** arrival and wedding, and of the deranged **Cliff**, former owner of the Lammeter house, who went mad after his son died and is now believed to haunt the place. 6

Silas manifests in the middle of the floor like a pale apparition. The group is disconcerted, but then he speaks: 'Robbed!' and adjures Jem to return his gold if he has taken it. Jem is insulted, then absolved by the landlord, who agrees to go with Silas to constable **Kench**, accompanied by Dowlas. 7 There is an inquiry afoot, with a mysterious **pedlar** an object of suspicion. Dunstan is missing, and Godfrey worries about him and Wildfire. He encounters **Bryce**, who would have bought Wildfire and now tells him he is dead. Godfrey is stuck. 8

After a bad night, Godfrey goes to his father and tells him of Wildfire and the £100. Furious, his father threatens vaguely. He offers to speak to Lammeter about Godfrey's marrying Nancy. Godfrey tries to dissuade him. He hopes for some chance rescue. 9 Silas moans over his loss. His neighbours no longer fear him: there is human feeling. A tinder-box found near the cottage leads to a search for a gypsy pedlar. Silas's life is a blank of grief, little assuaged by small kindnesses of others. Macey pays a call. **Dolly Winthrop** brings her son **Aaron** and lard-cakes for Silas. Aaron sings a carol. Christmas is come, and New Year's. There is a great party at the Casses'. 10

Nancy Lammeter is a focus of attention at the New Year's ball, and the country gentry lead the dancing as usual. Nancy's dress is damaged, and she must sit. Godfrey escorts her and takes the moment to avow regret for the past and intent to do better. Nancy is startled but keeps her poise. 11 **Molly Farren Cass**, bar-maid, walks through snow and cold to confront Godfrey and his father. She carries her infant daughter. An opium-addict, she takes her last bit to stave off the cold and lies down to sleep. The baby is attracted by the light of Silas's fire and toddles in past Silas, caught in catalepsy. She falls asleep on the hearth. Silas recovers, sits, and sees gold on his hearth. It is the baby's curls. He is dumbfounded. He realizes her boots are soaked and divines that she has walked in out of the night. He finds Molly dead in the snow. 12

Silas walks into the Cass house, carrying the baby and looking for the doctor to attend the woman he found. **Kimble** gets up from his cards. At the suggestion that Silas give up the baby he realizes he wants it. Godfrey is compelled to go to learn the best, or worst: Molly is dead. Godfrey is silent. 13 Silas enlists Dolly to help him learn to bring up baby. She insists on proper churching, beginning with christening. He picks his dead little sister's name: **Hephzibah** and will call the baby **Eppie**. With Dolly's guidance and advice, Silas raises Eppie. She makes him a companion to his neighbours and the world. 14 Godfrey is free, he thinks, and happily headed for matrimony. 15

Sixteen years have passed. Eppie is eighteen. We see Godfrey and Nancy, now long married, coming from church. Silas and Eppie, blooming and auburn-haired now, follow, and Aaron Winthrop, Eppie's admirer, comes behind. He offers to help with a garden Eppie plans. Godfrey has been a benefactor of the Marner household. Silas has acclimated himself on Eppie's behalf and has begun to tell Dolly of his sad past. Eppie and Silas discuss their garden: it will need a fence. They notice the water level at the old quarry has dropped: draining is going forward. Eppie broaches her and Aaron's plan to marry and have Silas to live with them. 16 **Nancy Cass** reflects on her childlessness and her adamant refusal to adopt despite Godfrey's pleas. She will not flout the intent of Providence. There is agitation in the street. She awaits Godfrey. 17

Godfrey comes: they have found Dunstan's skeleton in the Stone-pits. The money he stole is with him. Godfrey confesses that Eppie is his child, and Nancy's reaction is deep regret: she would have reared Eppie as her own, and the loss of her own baby would have been assuaged. They will go to Silas. 18 Silas is transfixed by the excitement; Eppie is with him. The Casses appear. They offer to take Eppie and bring her up a lady. They will provide for Silas. Eppie declines. In heat, Godfrey tells her he is her father. He presses his right and his duty. Silas bows to it and leaves it to Eppie. She is firmer than ever. She says she has her man. The Casses leave. 19 At home, Godfrey expresses himself clearheadedly. He and Nancy resign themselves to what they have. 20

Silas tells Eppie he wants to travel to Lantern Yard and find his minister. She is delighted. They go: Lantern Yard is gone, replaced by a factory. Silas is stunned. On return to Raveloe, he is resigned and settled in his mind. 21 There is a simple wedding in Raveloe. Nancy has provided the dress. Godfrey absents himself. The Winthrops follow the bride and groom, and Silas Marner is beside them. They will live together in an expanded stone cottage by the Stone-pits. The garden is a success. *Conclusion*

Contents

Silas's great discovery is in the *Topicon* at A:Baby—*transcending alchemy.*

Title Role

Silas Marner "worked at his vocation in a stone cottage that stood among the nutty hedgerows near the village of Raveloe, and not far from the edge of a deserted stone-pit." 1

—*eyes:* "For how was it possible to believe that those large brown protuberant eyes in Silas Marner's pale face really saw nothing very distinctly that was not close to them, and not rather that their dreadful stare could dart cramp, or rickets, or a wry mouth at any boy who happened to be in the rear?" 1

—*catalepsy:* " . . . on coming up to him, [**Jem Rodney**] saw that Marner's eyes were set like a dead man', and he spoke to him, and shook him, and his limbs were stiff, and his hands clutched the bag as if they'd been made of iron; but just as he had made up his mind that the weaver was dead, he came all right again, like, as you might say, in the winking of an eye, and said 'Good night,' and walked off." 1

—honest after a fit: "A less truthful man than he might have been tempted into the subsequent creation of a vision in the form of resurgent memory: a less sane man might have believed in such a creation; but Silas was both sane and honest, though as with many honest and fervent men, culture had not defined any channels for his sense of mystery, and so it spread itself over the proper pathway of inquiry and knowledge." 1

—medicinal knowledge: "He had inherited from his mother some acquaintance with medicinal herbs and their preparation—a little store of wisdom which she had imparted to him as a solemn bequest—but of late years he had had doubts about the lawfulness of applying this knowledge, believing that herbs could have no efficacy without prayer, and that prayer might suffice without herbs, so that his inherited delight to wander through the fields in search of foxglove and dandelion and coltsfoot, began to wear to him the character of a temptation." 1

—naïve in friendship: "But whatever blemishes others might discern in **William**, to his friend's mind he was faultless; for Marner had one of those impressible self-doubting natures which, at an inexperienced age, admire imperativeness and lean on contradiction. The expression of trusting simplicity in Marner's face, heightened by that absence of special observation, that defenceless, deer-like gaze which belongs to large prominent eyes, was strongly contrasted by the self-complacent suppression of inward triumph that lurked in the narrow slanting eyes and compressed lips of William **Dane**." 1

—occupation: "His first movement after the shock had been to work in his loom; and he went on with this unremittingly, never asking himself why, now he was come to Raveloe, he worked far on into the night to finish the tale of **Mrs Osgood**'s table-linen sooner than she expected—without contemplating beforehand the money she would put into his hand for the work. He seemed to weave, like the spider, from pure impulse, without reflection . . . Silas's hand satisfied itself with throwing the shuttle, and his eye with seeing the little squares in the cloth complete themselves under his effort." 2

—numb: "He hated the thought of the past; there was nothing that called out his love and fellowship toward the strangers he had come amongst; and the future was all dark, for there was no Unseen Love that cared for him. Thought was arrested by utter bewilderment, now its old narrow pathway was closed, and affection seemed to have died under the bruise that had fallen on its keenest nerves." 2

—bright spot: "Now, for the first time in his life, he had five bright guineas put into his hand; no man expected a share of them, and he loved no man that he should offer him a share. But what were the guineas to him who saw no vista beyond countless days of weaving? It was needless for him to ask that, for it was pleasant to him to feel them in his palm, and look at their bright faces, which were all his own . . . that habit of looking towards the money and grasping it with a sense of fulfilled effort made a loam that was deep enough for the seeds of desire, and as Silas walked homeward across the fields in the twilight, he drew out the money and thought it was brighter in the gathering gloom." 2

—life narrowing "So, year after year, Silas Marner had lived in this solitude, his guineas rising in the iron pot, and his life narrowing and hardening itself more and more into a mere pulsation of desire and satisfaction that had no relation to any other being. His life had reduced itself to the functions of weaving and hoarding, without any contemplation of an end towards which the functions tended . . . . The prominent eyes that used to look trusting and

dreamy, now looked as if they had been made to see only one kind of thing that was very small, like tiny grain, for which they hunted everywhere: and he was so withered and yellow, that, though he was not yet forty, the children always called him 'Old Master Marner.' " 2

—his guineas: "He spread them out in heaps and bathed his hands in them; then he counted them and set them up in regular piles, and felt their rounded outline between his thumb and fingers, and thought fondly of the guineas that were only half earned by the work in his loom, as if they had been unborn children . . . his life had shrunk away, like a rivulet that has sunk far down from the grassy fringe of its old breadth into a little shivering thread, that cuts a groove for itself in the barren sand." 2

—alone and unobserved: "Any one who had looked at him as the red light shone upon his pale face, strange straining eyes, and meagre form, would perhaps have understood the mixture of contemptuous pity, dread, and suspicion with which he was regarded by his neighbours in Raveloe. Yet few men could be more harmless than poor Marner. In his truthful simple soul, not even the growing greed and worship of gold could beget any vice directly injurious to others. The light of his faith quite put out, and his affections made desolate, he had clung with all the force of his nature to his work and his money, and like all objects to which a man devotes himself, they had fashioned him into correspondence with themselves. His loom, as he wrought in it without ceasing, had in its turn wrought on him, and confirmed more and more the monotonous craving for its monotonous response. His gold, as he hung over it and saw it grow, gathered his power of loving together into a hard isolation like its own." 5

—robbed and desperate: "The sight of the empty hole made his heart leap violently, but the belief that his gold was gone could not come at once—only terror, and the eager effort to put an end to the terror. He passed his trembling hand all about the hole, trying to think it possible that his eyes had deceived him; then he held the candle in the hole and examined it curiously, trembling more and more. At last he shook so violently that he let fall the candle, and lifted his hands to his head, trying to steady himself, that he might think . . . .

"Silas got up from his knees trembling, and looked round at the table: didn't the gold lie there after all? The table was bare. Then he turned and looked behind him—looked all round his dwelling, seeming to strain his brown eyes after some possible appearance of the bags where he had already sought them in vain. He could see every object in his cottage—and his gold was not there.

"Again he put his trembling hands to his head, and gave a wild ringing scream, the cry of desolation . . . the cry had relieved him from the first maddening pressure of the truth." 5

—deprivation: "But in reality it had been an eager life, filled with immediate purpose which fenced him in from the wide, cheerless unknown. It had been a clinging life; and though the object round which its fibres had clung was a dead disrupted thing, it satisfied the need for clinging. But now the fence was broken down—the support was snatched away . . . .

The Old Gold

"He filled up the blank with grief. As he sat weaving, he every now and then moaned low, like one in pain: it was the sign that his thoughts had come round again to the sudden chasm—to the empty evening time. And all the evening, as he sat in his loneliness by his dull fire, he leaned his elbows on his knees, and clasped his head with his hands, and moaned very low—not as one who seeks to be heard." 10

—neighbours: "Formerly, his heart had been as a locked casket with its treasures inside, but now the casket was empty, and the lock was broken. Left groping in darkness, with his prop utterly gone, Silas had inevitably a sense, though a dull and half-despairing one, that if any help came to him it must come from without; and there was a slight stirring expectation at the sight of his fellow-men, a faint consciousness of dependence on their good-will." 10

—loveless still: "[**Dolly**'s] simple view of life and its comforts, by which she had tried to cheer him, was only like a report of unknown objects, which his imagination could not fashion. The fountains of human love and of faith in a divine love had not yet been unlocked, and his soul was still the shrunken rivulet, with only this difference, that its little groove of sand was blocked up, and it wandered confusedly against dark obstruction." 10

—looking and longing: "During the last few weeks, since he had lost his money, he had contracted the habit of opening his door and looking out from time to time, as if he thought that his money might be somehow coming back to him, or that some trace, some news of it, might be mysteriously on the road, and be caught by the listening ear or the straining eye. It was chiefly at night . . . that he fell into this repetition of an act for which he could have assigned no definite purpose, and which can hardly be understood except by those who have undergone a bewildering separation from a supremely loved object. In the evening twilight, and later whenever the night was not dark, Silas looked out on that narrow prospect round the Stone-pits, listening and gazing, not with hope, but with mere yearning and unrest." 12

—seizure: "He went in again, and put his right hand on the latch of the door to close it—but he did not close it: he was arrested, as he had been already since his loss, by the invisible wand of catalepsy, and stood like a graven image, with wide but sightless eyes, holding open his door, powerless to resist either the good or evil that might enter there." 12 *See Topicon* A:Baby—*transcendent alchemy*

—revelation: " 'No—no—I can't part with it, I can't let it go,' said Silas, abruptly: 'It's come to me—I've a right to keep it.'

"The proposition to take the child from him had come to Silas quite unexpectedly, and his speech, uttered under a strong sudden impulse, was almost like a revelation to himself: a minute before, he had no distinct intention about the child." 13

—taking possession: " 'But,' he added, uneasily, leaning forward to look at Baby with some jealousy, as she was resting her head backward against **Dolly**'s arm, and eyeing him contentedly from a distance—'But I want to do things for it myself, else it may get fond o' somebody else, and not fond o' me. I've been used to fending for myself in the house—I can learn, I can learn.' " 14

The New Gold

—his new gold: "The gold had kept his thoughts in an ever-repeated circle, leading to nothing beyond itself; but **Eppie** was an object compacted of changes and hopes that forced his thoughts onward, and carried them far away from the old eager pacing towards the same blank limit—carried them away to the new things that would come with the coming years, when Eppie would have learned to understand how her father Silas cared for her; and made him look for images of that time in the ties and charities that bound together the families of his neighbours.

"The gold had asked that he should sit weaving longer and longer, deafened and blinded more and more to all things except the monotony of his loom and the repetition of his web; but Eppie called him away from his weaving, and made him think all its pauses a holiday, reawakening his sense with her fresh life, even to the old winter-flies that came crawling forth in the early spring sunshine, and warming him into joy because *she* had joy." ¶14

—waking: "As the child's mind was growing into knowledge, his mind was growing into memory: as her life unfolded, his soul, long stupefied in a cold narrow prison, was unfolding too, and trembling gradually into full consciousness." 14

—discipline: " ' . . . there's one of 'em you must choose—ayther smacking or the coal-hole—else she'll get so masterful, there'll be no holding her.'

"Silas was impressed with the melancholy truth of this last remark; but his force of mind failed before the only two penal methods open to him, not only because it was painful to him to hurt **Eppie**, but because he trembled at a moment's contention with her, lest she should love him the less for it . . . . It was clear that Eppie, with her short toddling steps, must lead father Silas a pretty dance on any fine morning when circumstances favoured mischief." 14

—the difference: "Hitherto he had been treated very much as if he had been a useful gnome or brownie—a queer and unaccountable creature, who must necessarily be looked at with wondering curiosity and repulsion, and with whom one would be glad to make all greetings and bargains as brief as possible, but who must be dealt with in a propitiatory way, and occasionally have a present of pork or garden stuff to carry home with him, seeing that without him there was no getting the yarn woven. But now Silas met with open smiling faces and cheerful questioning, as a person whose satisfactions and difficulties could be understood. Everywhere he must sit a little and talk about the child, and words of interest were always ready for him . . . .

"No child was afraid of approaching Silas when Eppie was near him: there was no repulsion around him now, either for young or old; for the little child had come to link him once more with the whole world. There was love between him and the child that blent them into one, and there was love between the child and the world—from men and women with parental looks and tones, to the red lady-birds and the round pebbles." 14

—money: "The disposition to hoard had been utterly crushed at the very first by the loss of his long-stored gold: the coins he earned afterwards seemed as irrelevant as stones brought to complete a house suddenly buried by an earthquake; the sense of bereavement was too heavy upon him for the old thrill of satisfaction to arise again at the touch of the newly-earned coin. And now something had come to replace his hoard which gave a growing purpose to the earnings, drawing his hope and joy continually onward beyond the money." 14

—*sixteen years on:* "But it is impossible to mistake Silas Marner. His large brown eyes seem to have gathered a longer vision, as is the way with eyes that have been short-sighted in early life, and they have a less vague, a more answering gaze; but in everything else one sees signs of a frame much enfeebled by the lapse of the sixteen years. The weaver's bent shoulders and white hair give him almost the look of advanced age, though he is not more than five-and-fifty . . . . " 16

—*acclimatised:* "By seeking what was needful for **Eppie**, by sharing the effect that everything produced on her, he had himself come to appropriate the forms of custom and belief which were the mould of Raveloe life; and as, with reawakening sensibilities, memory also reawakened, he had begun to ponder over the elements of his old faith, and blend them with his new impressions, till he recovered a consciousness of unity between his past and present." 16

—*painful reminiscence:* " 'Ah! that was what fell on me like as if it had been red-hot iron; because, you see, there was nobody as cared for me or clave to me above nor below. And him [**William Dane**] as I'd gone out and in wi' for ten year and more, since when we was lads and went halves—mine own familiar friend in whom I trusted, had lifted up his heel again' me, and worked to ruin me.' " 16

—*roused:* " 'Then sir,' he answered, with an accent of bitterness that had been silent in him since the memorable day when his youthful hope had perished—'then, sir, why didn't you say so sixteen year ago, and claim her before I'd come to love her, i'stead o' coming to take her from me now, when you might as well take the heart out o' my body? God gave her to me because you turned your back upon her, and He looks upon her as mine: you've no right to her! When a man turns a blessing from his door, it falls to them as take it in.' " 19

—*a final word:* " 'Since the time the child was sent to me and I've come to love her as myself, I've had light enough to trusten by; and now she says she'll never leave me, I think I shall trusten till I die.' " 21

Other Principals

Eppie [**Cass**]. "Suddenly as the child rolled downward on its mother's knees, all wet with snow, its eyes were caught by a bright glancing light on the white ground, and, with the ready transition of infancy, it was immediately absorbed in watching the bright living thing running towards it, yet never arriving. That bright living thing must be caught . . . [she] toddled on to the open door of **Silas Marner**'s cottage, and right up to the warm hearth, where there was a bright fire of logs and sticks, which had thoroughly warmed the old sack (Silas's greatcoat) spread out on the bricks to dry. The little one, accustomed to be left to itself for long hours without notice from its mother, squatted down on the sack, and spread its tiny hands towards the blaze, in perfect contentment, gurgling and making many inarticulate communications to the cheerful fire, like a new-hatched gosling beginning to find itself comfortable. But presently the warmth had a lulling effect, and the little golden head sank down on the old sack, and the blue eyes were veiled by their delicate half-transparent lids." 12

—*a handful:* " 'For she'll get busier and mischievouser every day—she will, bless her. It's lucky as you've got that high hearth i'stead of a grate, for that keeps the fire more out of her reach: but if you've got anything as can be split or broke, or as is fit to cut her fingers off, she'll be at it—and it is but right you should know.' " 14

—demanding: "Unlike the gold which needed nothing, and must be worshipped in close-locked solitude—which was hidden away from the daylight, was deaf to the song of birds, and started to no human tones—Eppie was a creature of endless claims and ever-growing desires, seeking and loving sunshine, and living sounds, and living moments; making trial of everything, with trust in new joy, and stirring the human kindness in all eyes that looked on her." 14

—mischief: "Also, by the time Eppie was three years old, she developed a fine capacity for mischief, and for devising ingenious ways of being troublesome, which found much exercise, not only for **Silas**'s patience, but for his watchfulness and penetration." 14

—the victor: "So Eppie was reared without punishment, the burden of her misdeeds being borne vicariously by father **Silas**. The stone hut was made a soft nest for her, lined with downy patience: and also in the world that lay beyond the stone hut she knew nothing of frowns and denials." 14

—growing world: "Servant maidens were fond of carrying her out to look at the hens and chickens, or to see if any cherries could be shaken down in the orchard; and the small boys and girls approached her slowly, with cautious movement and steady gaze, like little dogs face to face with one of their own kind, till attraction had reached the point at which the soft lips were put out for a kiss." 14

—sixteen years on: " . . . there is the freshest blossom of youth close by [**Silas**'s] side—a blond dimpled girl of eighteen, who has vainly tried to chastise her curly auburn hair into smoothness under her brown bonnet: the hair ripples as obstinately as a brooklet under the March breeze, and the little ringlets burst away from the restraining comb behind and show themselves below the bonnet-crown. Eppie cannot help being rather vexed about her hair, for there is no other girl in Raveloe who has hair at all like it, and she thinks hair ought to be smooth." 16

—lovely sight: "Yet it was a sight that might well arrest wandering thoughts: Eppie, with the rippling radiance of her hair and the whiteness of her rounded chin and throat set off by the dark-blue cotton gown, laughing merrily as the kitten held on with her four claws to one shoulder, like a design for a jug-handle, while **Snap** on the right hand and Puss on the other put up their paws towards a morsel which she held out of the reach of both—Snap occasionally desisting in order to remonstrate with the cat by a cogent worrying growl on the greediness and futility of her conduct; till Eppie relented, caressed them both, and divided the morsel between them." 16

—protected: "The tender and peculiar love with which **Silas** had reared her in almost inseparable companionship with himself, aided by the seclusion of their dwelling, had preserved her from the lowering influences of the village talk and habits, and had kept her mind in that freshness which is sometimes falsely supposed to be an invariable attribute of rusticity." 16

—an offer: "Eppie took her hand from her father's head; and came forward a step. Her cheeks were flushed, but not with shyness this time: the sense that her father was in doubt and suffering banished that sort of self-consciousness. She dropt a low curtsy, first to **Mrs Cass** and then **Mr Cass**, and said—

" 'Thank you, ma'am—thank you, sir. But I can't leave my father, nor own anybody nearer than him. And I don't want to be a lady—thank you all the same' (here Eppie dropped another curtsy). 'I couldn't give up the folks I've been used to.' " 19

—her father revealed: " 'Thank you, ma'am—thank you, sir, for your offers—they're very great, and far above my wish. For I should have no delight i' life any more if I was forced to go away from my father, and knew he was sitting at home, a-thinking of me and feeling lone. We've been used to be happy together every day, and I can't think o' no happiness without him. And he says he'd nobody i' the world till I was sent to him, and he'd have nothing when I was gone. And he's took care o' me and loved me from the first, and I'll cleave to him as long as he lives, and nobody shall ever come between him and me.' " 19

—the convincing straw: " 'And,' she ended passionately, while the tears fell, 'I'm promised to marry a working-man, as'll live with father; and help me to take care of him.' " 19

—a bride: "Seen at a little distance as she walked across the churchyard and down the village, she seemed to be attired in pure white, and her hair looked like the dash of gold on a lily. One hand was on her husband's arm, and with the other she clasped the hand of her father **Silas**." *Conclusion*

—a final word: " 'Oh father,' said Eppie, 'what a pretty home ours is! I think nobody could be happier than we are.' " *Conclusion*

Godfrey Cass. " . . . it would be a thousand pities if Mr Godfrey, the eldest, a fine open-faced good-natured young man who was to come into the land some day, should take to going along the same road with his brother, as he had seemed to do of late. If he went on in that way, he would lose **Miss Nancy Lammeter** . . . . There was something wrong, more than common—that was quite clear; for Mr Godfrey didn't look half so fresh-coloured and open as he used to do . . . if Mr Godfrey didn't turn over a new leaf, he might say 'Good-bye' to Miss Nancy Lammeter." 3

—characteristics: "That big muscular frame of his held plenty of animal courage, but helped to no decision when the dangers to be braved were such as could neither be knocked down nor throttled. His natural irresolution and moral cowardice were exaggerated by a position in which dreaded consequences seemed to press equally on all sides, and his irritation had no sooner provoked him to defy **Dunstan** and anticipate all possible betrayals, than the miseries he must bring on himself by such a step seemed more unendurable to him than the present evil . . . . From the near vision of that certainty he fell back on suspense and vacillation with a sense of repose." 3

—bleak prospect: "The disinherited son of a small squire, equally disinclined to dig and to beg, was almost as helpless as an uprooted tree, which, by the favour of earth and sky, has grown to a handsome bulk on the spot where it first shot upward . . . he could imagine no future for himself on the other side of confession but that of ' 'listing for a soldier'—the most desperate step, short of suicide, in the eyes of respectable families. No! he would rather trust to casualties than to his own resolve—rather go on sitting at the feast, and sipping the wine he loved, though with the sword hanging over him and terror in his heart, than rush away into the cold darkness where there was no pleasure left." 3

—ghastly mistake: "A movement of compunction, helped by those small indefinable influences which every personal relation exerts on a pliant na-

ture, had urged him into a secret marriage, which was a blight on his life. It was an ugly story of low passion, delusion, and waking from delusion, which needs not to be dragged from the privacy of Godfrey's bitter memory . . . he had something else to curse—his own vicious folly, which now seemed as mad and unaccountable to him as almost all our follies and vices do when their promptings have long passed away." 3

—dream of better: "For four years he had thought of **Nancy Lammeter**, and wooed her with tacit patient worship, as the woman who made him think of the future with joy: she would be his wife, and would make home lovely to him, as his father's home had never been; and it would be easy, when she was always near, to shake off those foolish habits that were no pleasures, but only a feverish way of annulling vacancy.

"Godfrey's was an essentially domestic nature, bred up in a home where the hearth had no smiles, and where the daily habits were not chastised by the presence of household order. His easy disposition made him fall in unresistingly with the family courses, but the need of some tender permanent affection, the longing for some influence that would make the good he preferred easy to pursue, caused the neatness, purity, and liberal orderliness of the Lammeter household, sunned by the smile of Nancy, to seem like those fresh bright hours of the morning when temptations go to sleep and leave the ear open to the voice of the good angel, inviting to industry, sobriety, and peace.

"And yet the hope of this paradise had not been enough to save him from a course which shut him out of it for ever. Instead of keeping fast hold of the strong silken rope by which Nancy would have drawn him safe to the green banks where it was easy to step firmly, he had let himself be dragged back into mud and slime, in which it was useless to struggle. He had made ties for himself which robbed him of all wholesome motive and were a constant exasperation." 3

—scruple: "He felt that in letting **Dunstan** have the money, he had already been guilty of a breach of trust hardly less culpable than that of spending the money directly for his own behoof; and yet there was a distinction between the two acts which made him feel that the one was so much more blackening than the other as to be intolerable to him.

" 'I don't pretend to be a good fellow,' he said to himself; 'but I'm not a scoundrel—at least, I'll stop short somewhere. I'll bear the consequences of what I *have* done sooner than make believe I've done what I never would have done. I'd never have spent the money for my own pleasure—I was tortured into it.' " 8

—lack of guidance: "He was not likely to be very penetrating in his judgments, but he had always had a sense that his father's indulgence had not been kindness, and had had a vague longing for some discipline that would have checked his own errant weakness and helped his better will." 9

—question of courage: "Deeper down, and half-smothered by passionate desire and dread, there was the sense that he ought . . . to accept the consequences of his deeds, own the miserable wife, and fulfil the claims of the helpless child. But he had not moral courage enough to contemplate that active renunciation of **Nancy** as possible for him: he had only conscience and heart enough to make him for ever uneasy under the weakness that forbade the renunciation. And at this moment his mind leaped away from all restraint towards the sudden prospect of deliverance from his long bondage." 13

—*a last look:* "He cast only one glance at the dead face on the pillow, which **Dolly** had smoothed with decent care; but he remembered that last look at his unhappy hated wife so well, that at the end of sixteen years every line in the worn face was present to him when he told the full story of this night." 13

—*his child:* "The wide-open blue eyes looked up at Godfrey's without any uneasiness or sign of recognition: the child could make no visible [or] audible claim on its father; and the father felt a strange mixture of feelings, a conflict of regret and joy, that the pulse of that little heart had no response for the half-jealous yearning in his own, when the blue eyes turned away from him slowly, and fixed themselves on the weaver's queer face . . . . " 13

—*rationale:* "Perhaps it would be just as happy in life without being owned by its father, seeing that nobody could tell how things would turn out, and that—is there any other reason wanted?—well, then, that the father would be much happier without owning the child." 13

—*free at last:* "He felt a reformed man, delivered from temptation; and the vision of his future life seemed to him as a promised land for which he had no cause to fight. He saw himself with all his happiness centred on his own hearth, while **Nancy** would smile on him as he played with the children.

"And that other child, not on the hearth—he would not forget it; he would see that it was well provided for. That was a father's duty." 15

—*sixteen years on:* "The tall blond man of forty is not much changed in feature from the Godfrey Cass of six-and-twenty: he is only fuller in flesh, and has only lost the indefinable look of youth—a loss which is marked even when the eye is undulled and the wrinkles are not yet come." 16

—*class myopia:* " . . . we must remember that many of the impressions which Godfrey was likely to gather concerning the labouring people around him would favour the idea that deep affections can hardly go along with callous palms and scant means; and he had not had the opportunity, even if he had had the power, of entering intimately into all that was exceptional in the weaver's experience." 17

—*better side:* "It was only the want of adequate knowledge that could have made it possible for Godfrey deliberately to entertain an unfeeling project: his natural kindness had outlived that blighting time of cruel wishes, and **Nancy**'s praise of him as a husband was not founded entirely on a wilful illusion." 17

—*shocking news:* "[He] turned towards [**Nancy**] with a pale face and a strange unanswering glance, as if he saw her indeed, but saw her as part of a scene invisible to herself . . . .

" 'It's **Dunstan**—my brother Dunstan, that we lost sight of sixteen years ago. We've found him—found his body—his skeleton' . . .

" 'The Stone-pit has gone dry suddenly—from the draining, I suppose; and there he lies . . . .

"Godfrey paused: it was not so easy to say what came next. 'Do you think he drowned himself?' said Nancy . . . .

" 'No, he fell in,' said Godfrey, in a low but distinct voice, as if he felt some deep meaning in the fact. Presently he added: 'Dunstan was the man that robbed **Silas Marner**.' " 18

—*rejected:* "Godfrey felt an irritation inevitable to almost all of us when we encounter an unexpected obstacle. He had been full of his own penitence and resolution to retrieve his error as far as the time was left to him; he was possessed with all-important feelings, that were to lead to a predetermined course of action which he had fixed on as the right, and he was not prepared to enter with lively appreciation into other people's feelings counteracting his virtuous resolves." 19

—angered: "It seemed to him that the weaver was very selfish (a judgment readily passed by those who have never tested their own power of sacrifice) to oppose what was undoubtedly for **Eppie**'s welfare; and he felt himself called upon, for her sake, to assert his authority.

" ' . . . You ought to remember your own life's uncertain, and she's at an age now when her lot may soon be fixed in a way very different from what it would be in her father's home: she may marry some low working-man, and then, whatever I might do for her, I couldn't make her well-off. You're putting yourself in the way of her welfare; and though I'm sorry to hurt you after what you've done, and what I've left undone, I feel now it's my duty to insist on taking care of my own daughter. I want to do my duty.' " 19

—convinced: "Godfrey looked up at **Nancy** with a flushed face and smarting dilated eyes. This frustration of a purpose towards which he had set out under the exalted consciousness that he was about to compensate in some degree for the great demerit of his life, made him feel the air of the room stifling.

" 'Let us go,' he said, in an undertone.' " 19

—clearheaded at last: " 'No,' said Godfrey, with a keen decisiveness of tone, in contrast with his usually careless and unemphatic speech—'there's debts we can't pay like money debts, by paying extra for the years that have slipped by. While I've been putting off and putting off, the trees have been growing—it's too late now. **Marner** was in the right in what he said about a man's turning away a blessing from his door: it falls to somebody else. I wanted to pass for childless once, **Nancy**—I shall pass for childless now against my wish.' " 20

Miss Nancy Lammeter. " . . . it was well known that she had looked very shyly on [**Godfrey Cass**] ever since last Whitsuntide twelvemonth, when there was so much talk about his being away from home days and days together . . . . What a handsome couple he and Miss Nancy Lammeter would make! and if she could come to be mistress at the Red House, there would be a fine change, for the Lammeters had been brought up in that way, that they never suffered a pinch of salt to be wasted, and yet everybody in their household had of the best, according to his place. Such a daughter-in-law would be a saving to the old **Squire**, if she never brought a penny to her fortune . . . . " 3

—looking good: "Some women, I grant, would not appear to advantage seated on a pillion, and attired in a drab joseph [long riding-coat] and a drab beaver-bonnet, with a crown resembling a small stew-pan; for a garment suggesting a coachman's greatcoat, cut out under an exiguity of cloth that would only allow of miniature capes, is not well adapted to conceal deficiencies of contour, nor is drab a colour that will throw sallow cheeks into lively contrast. It was all the greater triumph to Miss Nancy Lammeter's beauty that she looked thoroughly bewitching in that costume . . . . " 11

—surprising: "[The **Miss Gunns**] were so taken by surprise at finding such a lovely face and figure in an out-of-the-way country place, that they be-

gan to feel some curiosity about the dress she would put on when she took off her joseph." 11

—*reflecting:* "[Her] thoughts were always conducted with the propriety and moderation conspicuous in her manners . . . . " 11

—*her aunt:* " . . . Miss Nancy's mind resembled her aunt's to a degree that everybody said was surprising considering the kinship was on **Mr Osgood**'s side; and though you might not have supposed it from the formality of their greeting, there was a devoted attachment and mutual admiration between aunt and niece. Even Miss Nancy's refusal of her cousin **Gilbert Osgood** (on the ground solely that he was her cousin), though it had grieved her aunt greatly, had not in the least cooled the preference which had determined her to leave Nancy several of her hereditary ornaments, let Gilbert's future wife be whom [*sic*] she might." 11

—*meticulous:* "Everything belonging to Miss Nancy was of delicate purity and nattiness: not a crease was where it had no business to be, not a bit of her linen professed whiteness without fulfilling its profession; the very pins on her pincushion were stuck in after a pattern from which she was careful to allow no aberration; and as for her own person, it gave the same idea of perfect unvarying neatness as the body of a little bird.

"It was true that her light-brown hair was cropped behind like a boy's, and was dressed in front in a number of flat rings, that lay quite away from her face; but there was no sort of coiffure that could make Miss Nancy's cheek and neck look otherwise than pretty; and when at last she stood complete in her silvery twilled silk, her lace tucker, her coral necklace, and coral eardrops, the Miss Gunns could see nothing to criticise except her hands, which bore the traces of butter-making, cheese-crushing, and even still coarser work." ¶11

—*education:* "Miss Nancy, indeed, had never been to any school higher than **Dame Tedman**'s: her acquaintance with profane literature hardly went beyond the rhymes she had worked in her large sampler under the lamb and the shepherdess; and in order to balance an account, she was obliged to effect her subtraction by removing visible metallic shillings and sixpences from a visible metallic total." 11

—*lady:* "There is hardly a servant-maid in these days who is not better informed than Miss Nancy; yet she had the essential attributes of a lady—high veracity, delicate honour in her dealings, deference to others, and refined personal habits—and lest these should not suffice to convince grammatical fair ones that her feelings can at all resemble theirs, I will add that she was slightly proud and exacting, and as constant in her affection towards a baseless opinion as towards an erring lover." 11

—*lover:* "It certainly did make some difference to Nancy that the lover she had given up was the young man of quite the highest consequence in the parish . . . not the most dazzling rank should induce her to marry a man whose conduct showed him careless of his character, but . . . 'love once, love always,' was the motto of a true and pure woman, and no man should ever have any right over her which would be a call on her to destroy the dried flowers that she treasured, and always would treasure, for **Godfrey Cass**'s sake." 11

—*calm:* "And Nancy was capable of keeping her word to herself under very trying conditions. Nothing but a becoming blush betrayed the moving thoughts that urged themselves upon her as she accepted the seat next to **Mr**

Crackenthorp; for she was so instinctively neat and adroit in all her actions, and her pretty lips met each other with such quiet firmness, that it would have been difficult for her to appear agitated." 11

—*sudden declaration:* "It was a long, long while since **Godfrey** had said anything so direct as that, and Nancy was startled. But her instinctive dignity and repugnance to any show of emotion made her sit perfectly still, and only throw a little more decision into her voice . . . .

" . . . Nancy really felt much agitated by the possibility Godfrey's words suggested, but this very pressure of emotion that she was in danger of finding too strong for her roused all her power of self-command." 11

—now **Cass**

—*sixteen years on:* "Perhaps the pretty woman, not much younger than he, who is leaning on his arm, is more changed than her husband: the lovely bloom that used to be always on her cheek now comes but fitfully, with the fresh morning air or with some strong surprise; yet to all who love human faces best for what they tell of human experience, Nancy's beauty has a heightened interest.

"Often the soul is ripened into fuller goodness while age has spread an ugly film, so that mere glances can never divine the preciousness of the fruit. But the years have not been so cruel to Nancy. The firm yet placid mouth, the clear veracious glance of the brown eyes, speak now of a nature that has been tested and has kept its highest qualities; and even the costume, with its dainty neatness and purity, has more significance now the coquetries of youth can have nothing to do with it." 16

—*introspection:* "She was not theologically instructed enough to discern very clearly the relation between the sacred documents of the past which she opened without method, and her own obscure, simple life; but the spirit of rectitude, and the sense of responsibility for the effect of her conduct on others, which were strong elements in Nancy's character, had made it a habit with her to scrutinise her past feelings and actions with self-questioning solicitude.

"Her mind not being courted by a great variety of subjects, she filled the vacant moments by living inwardly, again and again, through all her remembered experience, especially through the fifteen years of her married time, in which her life and its significance had been doubled. She recalled the small details, the words, tones, and looks, in the critical scenes which had opened a new epoch for her by giving her a deeper insight into the relations and trials of life, or which had called on her for some little effort of forbearance, or of painful adherence to an imagined or real duty—asking herself continually whether she had been in any respect blamable." ¶17

—*wounded:* "And Nancy's deepest wounds had all come from the perception that the absence of children from their hearth was dwelt on in her husband's mind as a privation to which he could not reconcile himself . . . .

" . . . Had she really been right in the resistance which had cost her so much pain six years ago, and again four years ago—the resistance to her husband's wish that they should adopt a child?" 17

—*rigidly principled:* "It was as necessary to her mind to have an opinion on all topics, not exclusively masculine, that had come under her notice, as for her to have a precisely marked place for every article of her personal property: and her opinions were always principles to be unwaveringly acted on. They were firm, not because of their basis, but because she held them with a tenacity inseparable from her mental action.

"On all the duties and proprieties of life, from filial behavior to the arrangements of the evening toilet, pretty Nancy Lammeter, by the time she was three-and-twenty, had her unalterable little code, and had formed every one of her habits in strict accordance with that code. She carried these decided judgments within her in the most unobtrusive way: they rooted themselves in her mind, and grew there as quietly as grass." ¶17

—principle and superstition: "To adopt a child, because children of your own had been denied you, was to try and choose your lot in spite of Providence: the adopted child, she was convinced, would never turn out well, and would be a curse to those who had wilfully and rebelliously sought what it was clear that, for some high reason, they were better without. When you saw a thing was not meant to be, said Nancy, it was a bounden duty to leave off so much as wishing for it. And so far, perhaps, the wisest of men could scarcely make more than a verbal improvement in her principle.

"But the conditions under which she held it apparent that a thing was not meant to be, depended on a more peculiar mode of thinking. She would have given up making a purchase at a particular place if, on three successive times, rain, or some other cause of Heaven's sending, had formed an obstacle; and she would have anticipated a broken limb or other heavy misfortune to any one who persisted in spite of such indications." 17

—truly upright: "It was impossible to have lived with her fifteen years and not be aware that an unselfish clinging to the right, and a sincerity clear as the flower-born [*sic*] dew, were her main characteristics; indeed, **Godfrey** felt this so strongly, that his own more wavering nature, too averse to facing difficulty to be unvaryingly simple and truthful, was kept in a certain awe of this gentle wife who watched his looks with a yearning to obey them." 17

—truth told at last: " '**Godfrey**, if you had but told me this six years ago, we could have done some of our duty by the child. Do you think I'd have refused to take her in, if I'd known she was yours? . . .

" 'And—Oh, Godfrey—if we'd had her from the first, if you'd taken to her as you ought, she'd have loved me for her mother—and you'd have been happier with me: I could better have bore [*sic*] my little baby dying, and our life might have been more like what we used to think it 'ud be.'

"The tears fell, and Nancy ceased to speak." 18

—the what if: " 'I can't say what I should have done about that, **Godfrey**. I should never have married anybody else. But I wasn't worth doing wrong for—nothing is in this world. Nothing is so good as it seems beforehand—not even our marrying wasn't, you see.' There was a faint sad smile on Nancy's face as she said the last words." 18

Nancy and Godfrey Cass

Supporting Roles

Dunstan (**Dunsey**) **Cass**, "whose taste for swapping and betting might turn out to be a sowing of something worse than wild oats. To be sure, the neighbours said, it was no matter what became of Dunsey—a spiteful jeering fellow, who seemed to enjoy his drink the more when other people went dry—always provided that his doings did not bring trouble on a family like **Squire Cass**'s . . . . " 3

—*morning appearance:* "The door opened, and a thick-set, heavy-looking young man entered, with the flushed face and the gratuitously elated bearing which mark the first stage of intoxication." 3

—*mendacious:* " 'Oh, I've swopped with him,' said Dunstan, whose delight in lying, grandly independent of utility, was not to be diminished by the likelihood that his hearer would not believe him—'**Wildfire**'s mine now.' " 4

—*heedless:* "Dunstan, whose nature it was to care more for immediate annoyances than for remote consequences, no sooner recovered his legs, and saw that it was all over with **Wildfire**, than he felt a satisfaction at the absence of witnesses . . . to walk many miles without a gun in his hand and along an ordinary road, was as much out of the question to him as to other spirited young men of his kind." 4

Squire Cass. "The greatest man in Raveloe was Squire Cass, who lived in the large red house with the handsome flight of stone steps in front and the high stables behind it, nearly opposite the church. He was only one among several landed parishioners, but he alone was honoured with the title of Squire . . . Squire Cass had a tenant or two, who complained of the game to him quite as if he had been a lord." 3

—*money problems:* " . . . it was to be feared that, notwithstanding his incomings, there were more holes in his pocket than the one where he put his own hand in." 3

—*unyielding:* "The old Squire was an implacable man: he made resolutions in violent anger, and he was not to be moved from them after his anger had subsided—as fiery volcanic matters cool and harden into rock. Like many violent and implacable men, he allowed evils to grow under favour of his own heedlessness, till they pressed upon him with exasperating force, and then he turned round with fierce severity and became unrelentingly hard. This was his system with his tenants: he allowed them to get into arrears, neglect their fences, reduce their stock, sell their straw, and otherwise go the wrong way—and then, when he became short of money in consequence of this indulgence, he took the hardest measures and would listen to no appeal." 8

—*characteristics:* " . . . a tall, stout man of sixty, with a face in which the knit brow and rather hard glance seemed contradicted by the slack and feeble mouth. His person showed marks of habitual neglect, his dress was slovenly; and yet there was something in the presence of the old Squire distinguishable from that of the ordinary farmers in the parish, who were perhaps every whit as refined as he, but, having slouched their way through life with a consciousness of being in the vicinity of their 'betters,' wanted that self-possession and authoritativeness of voice and carriage which belonged to a man who thought of superiors as remote existences with whom he had personally little more to do than with America or the stars. The Squire had been used to parish homage all his life, used to the presupposition that his family, his tankards, and everything that was his, were the oldest and best; and as he never associated with any gentry higher than himself, his opinion was not disturbed by comparisons." 9

—*elevated:* "By this advanced hour of the day, the Squire was always in higher spirits than we have seen him in at the breakfast-table, and felt it quite pleasant to fulfil the hereditary duty of being noisily jovial and patronising: the large silver snuff-box was in active service and was offered without fail to all neighbours from time to time, however often they might have declined the favour . . . as the evening deepened, his hospitality rayed out more widely, till he had tapped the youngest guests on the back and shown a peculiar fondness for their presence, in the full belief that they must feel their lives made happy by their belonging to a parish where there was such a hearty man as Squire Cass to invite them and wish them well." 11

—*joking:* "[He] regarded physic and doctors as many loyal churchmen regard the church and the clergy—tasting a joke against them when he was in health, but impatiently eager for their aid when anything was the matter with him." 11

Priscilla Lammeter. "For the little bit of pork was a present from that excellent housewife [*sic*], Miss Priscilla Lammeter, to whom he had this day carried home a handsome piece of linen . . . . " 5

—*dress:* " 'What do you think o' *these* gowns, aunt **Osgood**? . . .

" 'I'm obliged to have the same as **Nancy**, you know, for all I'm five years older, and it makes me look yellow; for she never *will* have anything without I have mine just like it, because she wants us to look like sisters. And I tell her, folks 'ull think it's my weakness makes me fancy as I shall look pretty in what she looks pretty in. For I am ugly—there's no denying that: I feature my father's family. But, law! I don't mind, do you?" Priscilla here turned to the **Miss Gunns**, rattling on in too much preoccupation with the delight of talking, to notice that her candour was not appreciated." 11

" . . . any one who did not know the character of both might certainly have supposed that the reason why the square-shouldered, clumsy, high-featured Priscilla wore a dress the facsimile of her pretty sister's, was either the mistaken vanity of the one, or the malicious contrivance of the other in order to set off her own rare beauty. But the good-natured self-forgetful cheeriness and common-sense of Priscilla would soon have dissipated the one suspicion, and the modest calm of Nancy's speech and manners told clearly of a mind free from all disavowed devices." 11

Aaron Winthrop, "an apple-cheeked youngster of seven, with a clean starched frill which looked like a plate for the apples, needed all his adventurous curiosity to embolden him against the possibility that the big-eyed weaver might do him some bodily injury . . . . " 10

—*offered a cake:* " . . . **Silas**, seeming to notice him for the first time, tried to return Dolly's signs of good-will by offering the lad a bit of lard-cake. Aaron shrank back a little, and rubbed his head against his mother's shoulder, but still thought the piece of cake worth the risk of putting his hand out for it." 10

—*a carol:* "Aaron was not indisposed to display his talents, even to an ogre, under protecting circumstances; and after a few more signs of coyness, consisting chiefly in rubbing the backs of his hands over his eyes, and then peeping between them at Master **Marner**, to see if he looked anxious for the 'carril,' he at length allowed his head to be duly adjusted, and standing behind the table, which let him appear above it only as far as his broad frill, so that he looked like a cherubic head untroubled with a body, he began with a clear chirp, and in a melody that had the rhythm of an industrious hammer. . . . " 10

—sixteen years on: "That good-looking young fellow, in a new fustian suit, who walks behind her, is not quite sure upon the question of hair in the abstract, when **Eppie** puts it to him, and thinks that perhaps straight hair is the best in general, but he doesn't want Eppie's hair to be different. She surely divines that there is some one behind her who is thinking about her very particularly, and mustering courage to come to her side as soon as they are out in the lane . . . . " 16

Mrs Dolly Winthrop, "the wheelwright's wife . . . was in all respects a woman of scrupulous conscience, so eager for duties that life seemed to offer them too scantily unless she rose at half-past four, though this threw a scarcity of work over the more advanced hours of the morning, which it was a constant problem with her to remove. Yet she had not the vixenish temper which is sometimes supposed to be a necessary condition of such habits: she was a very mild, patient woman, whose nature it was to seek out all the sadder and more serious elements of life, and pasture her mind upon them.

"She was the person always first thought of in Raveloe when there was illness or death in a family, when leeches were to be applied, or there was a sudden disappointment in a monthly nurse. She was a 'comfortable woman'—good-looking, fresh-complexioned, having her lips always slightly screwed, as if she felt herself in a sick-room with the doctor or the clergyman present. But she was never whimpering; no one had seen her shed tears; she was simply grave and inclined to shake her head and sigh, almost imperceptibly, like a funeral mourner who is not a relation. It seemed surprising that Ben Winthrop, who loved his quart-pot and his joke, got along so well with Dolly; but she took her husband's jokes and joviality as patiently as everything else, considering that 'men would be so,' and viewing the stronger sex in the light of animals whom it had pleased Heaven to make naturally troublesome, like bulls and turkey-cocks." ¶10

—largesse: " 'I'd a baking yesterday, Master **Marner**, and the lard-cakes turned out better nor common, and I'd ha' asked you to accept some, if you'd thought well. I don't eat such things myself, for a bit o' bread's what I like from one year's end to the other; but men's stomichs are made so comical, they want a change—they do, know, God help 'em.' " 10

—encouraging a journey: " 'You'd be easier in your mind for the rest o' your life, Master **Marner**,' said Dolly—'that you would. And if there's any light to be got up the yard as you talk on, we've need of it i' this world, and I'd be glad on it myself, if you could bring it back.' " 21

Dolly Winthrop, Coach and Teacher

Others

Mr Crackenthorp. " . . . a higher consultation was being carried on within, under the presidency of Mr Crackenthorp, the rector, assisted by **Squire Cass** and other substantial parishioners." 8

—reaching out: "Mr Crackenthorp, too, while he admonished **Silas** that his money had probably been taken from him because he thought too much of it and never came to church, enforced the doctrine by a present of pigs' petti-toes, well calculated to dissipate unfounded prejudices against the clerical character." 10

—cravat: "He was not in the least lofty or aristocratic, but simply a merry-eyed, small-featured, grey-haired man, with his chin propped by an ample many-creased white neck-cloth which seemed to predominate over every other point in his person, and somehow to impress its peculiar character on his remarks; so that to have considered his amenities apart from his cravat would have been a severe, and perhaps a dangerous, effort of abstraction." 11

—dancer: see **Macey***—acute dance critic*

William Dane. "Among the members of [**Silas**'s] church there was one young man, a little older than himself, with whom he had long lived in such close friendship that it was the custom of their Lantern Yard brethren to call them **David** and **Jonathan**. The real name of the friend was William Dane, and he, too, was regarded as a shining instance of youthful piety, though somewhat given to over-severity towards weaker brethren, and to be so dazzled by his own light as to hold himself wiser than his teachers." 1

—accused: " 'The last time I remember using my knife [said **Silas**], was when I took it out to cut a strap for you. I don't remember putting it in my pocket again. *You* stole the money , and you have woven a plot to lay the sin at my door. But you may prosper, for all that there is no just God that governs the earth righteously, but a God of lies, that bears witness against the innocent.'

"There was a general shudder at this blasphemy.

"William said meekly, 'I leave our brethren to judge whether this is the voice of Satan or not. I can do nothing but pray for you, Silas.' " 1

See Title Role*—painful reminiscence*

Molly Farren. " 'I might tell the **Squire** [said **Dunsey**] how his handsome son was married to that nice young woman, Molly Farren, and was very unhappy because he couldn't live with his drunken wife . . . . " 3

—walk in the cold: "This journey on New Year's Eve was a premeditated act of vengeance . . . her husband would be smiling and smiled upon, hiding *her* existence in the darkest corner of his heart. But she would mar his pleasure: she would go in her dingy rags, with her faded face, once as handsome as the best, with her little child that had its father's hair and eyes, and disclose herself to the **Squire** as his eldest son's wife." 12

—addiction: "Molly knew that the cause of her dingy rags was not her husband's neglect, but the demon Opium to whom she was enslaved, body and soul, except in the lingering mother's tenderness that refused to give him her hungry child. She knew this well; and yet, in the moments of wretched unbenumbed consciousness, the sense of her want and degradation transformed it self continually into bitterness towards **Godfrey**. He was well off;

and if she had her rights she would be well off too. The belief that he repented his marriage, and suffered from it, only aggravated her vindictiveness. Just and self-reproving thoughts do not come to us too thickly, even in the purest air and with the best lessons of heaven and earth; how should those white-winged delicate messengers make their way to Molly's poisoned chamber, inhabited by no higher memories than those of a barmaid's paradise of pink ribbons and gentlemen's jokes?" 12

—*self-betrayal:* "In that moment the mother's love pleaded for painful consciousness rather than oblivion—pleaded to be left in aching weariness, rather than to have the encircling arms benumbed so that they could not feel the dear burden. In another moment Molly had flung something away, but it was not the black remnant—it was an empty phial. And she walked on again under the breaking cloud, from which there came now and then the light of a quickly veiled star, for a freezing wind had sprung up since the snowing had ceased. But she walked always more and more drowsily, and clutched more and more automatically the sleeping child at her bosom." 12

—*coming death:* "Slowly the demon was working his will, and cold and weariness were his helpers. Soon she felt nothing but a supreme immediate longing that curtained off all futurity—the longing to lie down and sleep." 12

—*doctor's report:* " 'There's nothing to be done. She's dead—has been dead for hours, I should say.'

" 'What sort of woman is she?' said **Godfrey**, feeling the blood rush to his face.

" 'A young woman, but emaciated, with long black hair. Some vagrant—quite in rags. She's got a wedding-ring on, however. They must fetch her away to the workhouse to-morrow.' " 13

The **Miss Gunns**, "the wine merchant's daughters from Lytherly, dressed in the height of fashion, with the tightest skirts and the shortest waists, and gazed at by **Miss Ladbrook** (of the Old Pastures) with a shyness not unsustained by inward criticism." 11

—*observed:* "**Miss Nancy** . . . remarked to herself that the Miss Gunns were rather hard-featured than otherwise, and that such very low dresses as they wore might have been attributed to vanity if their shoulders had been pretty, but that, being as they were, it was not reasonable to suppose that they showed their necks from a love of display, but rather from some obligation not inconsistent with sense and modesty." 11

Mr and **Mrs Kimble**. "The doctor and his wife, uncle and aunt Kimble, were there [at the **Casses**'], and the annual Christmas talk was carried through without any omissions, rising to the climax of Mr Kimble's experience when he walked the London hospitals thirty years back, together with striking professional anecdotes then gathered. Whereupon cards followed, with aunt Kimble's annual failure to follow suit, and uncle Kimble's irascibility concerning the odd trick which was rarely explicable to him, when it was not on his side, without a general visitation of tricks to see that they were formed on sound principles: the whole being accompanied by a strong steaming odour of spirits-and-water." 10

"**Mrs Kimble** was the **Squire**'s sister, as well as the doctor's wife—a double dignity, with which her diameter was in direct proportion . . . . " 11

"But **Doctor Kimble** (country apothecaries in old days enjoyed that title without authority of diploma), being a thin and agile man, was flitting about the room with his hands in his pockets, making him self agreeable to his feminine patients, with medical impartiality; and being welcomed everywhere as a doctor by hereditary right—not one of those miserable apothecaries who canvass for practice in strange neighbourhoods, and spend all their income in starving their one horse, but a man of substance, able to keep an extravagant table like the best of his patients." 11

—at cards: " . . . uncle Kimble, who, being always volatile in sober business hours, became intense and bitter over cards and brandy, shuffled before his adversary's deal with a glare of suspicion, and turned up a mean trump-card with an air of inexpressible disgust, as if in a world where such things could happen one might as well enter on a course of reckless profligacy." 13

—medical principle: "**Silas** had taken to smoking a pipe daily during the last two years, having been strongly urged to it by the sages of Raveloe, as a practice 'good for the fits'; and this advice was sanctioned by Dr Kimble, on the ground that it was as well to try what could do no harm—a principle which was made to answer for a great deal of work in that gentleman's medical practice." 16

Mr Lammeter, "who was the soberest and best man in that country-side, only a little hot and hasty now and then, if things were not done to the minute." 11

—his daughter complimented: " . . . her father gave a slight additional erectness to his back, as he looked across the table at her with complacent gravity. That grave and orderly senior was not going to bate a jot of his dignity by seeming elated at the notion of a match between his family and the **Squire**'s: he was gratified by any honour paid to his daughter; but he must see an alteration in several ways before his consent would be vouchsafed. His spare but healthy person, and high-featured firm face, that looked as if it had never been flushed by excess, was in strong contrast, not only with the Squire's, but with the appearance of the Raveloe farmers generally—in accordance with a favourite saying of his own, that 'breed was stronger than pasture.' " 11

Macey, "clerk of the parish, shook his head, and asked if anybody was ever known to go off in a fit and not fall down." 1

"Mr Macey, tailor and parish-clerk, the latter of which functions rheumatism had of late obliged him to share . . . held his white head on one side, and twirled his thumbs with an air of complacency, slightly seasoned with criticism." 6

—oracular: " 'Ay, ay,' said Mr Macey . . . 'you're right there, **Tookey**: there's allays two 'pinions; there's the 'pinion a man has of himsen, and there's the 'pinion other folks have on him. There'd be two 'pinions about a cracked bell, if the bell could hear itself.' " 6

—complimentary: "Mr Macey, for example, coming one evening expressly to let **Silas** know that recent events had given him the advantage of standing more favourably in the opinion of a man whose judgment was not formed lightly, opened the conversation by saying, as soon as he had seated himself and adjusted his thumbs—

" 'Come, Master Marner, why, you've no call to sit a-moaning. You're a deal better off to ha' lost your money, nor to ha' kep it by foul means. I used to think, when you first come into these parts, as you were no better nor you should be; you were younger a deal than what you are now; but you were allays a staring, white-faced creatur, partly like a bald-faced calf, as I may say. But there's no knowing: it isn't every queer-looksed thing as Old Harry's had the making of—I mean, speaking o' toads and such; for they're often harmless, and useful against varmin. And it's pretty much the same wi' you, as fur as I can see.' " 10

—acute dance critic: " 'The **Squire**'s pretty springe, considering his weight,' said Mr Macey, 'and he stamps uncommon well. But **Mr Lammeter** beats 'em all for shapes: you see he holds his head like a sodger, and he isn't so cushiony as most o' the oldish gentlefolks—they run fat in general, and he's got a fine leg. The parson's nimble enough, but hasn't got much of a leg: it's a bit too thick down'ard, and his knees might be a bit nearer wi'ut damage, but he might do worse, he might do worse. Though he hasn't that grand way o' waving his hand as the Squire has.' " 11

—sixteen years on: " . . . Mr Macey, now a very feeble old man of fourscore and six, never seen except in his chimney-corner or sitting in the sunshine at his door-sill, was of opinion that when a man had done what **Silas** had done by an orphan child, it was a sign that his money would come to light again . . . . " 16

Solomon Macey. " 'To be sure . . . we're fond of our clerk; it's nat'ral, and him used to be such a singer, and got a brother as is known for the first fiddler in this country-side. Eh, it's a pity but what Solomon lived in our village, and could give us a tune when we liked; eh, Mr Macey? I'd keep him in liver and lights for nothing—that I would [said the butcher].' " 6

—in action: "Solomon Macey, a small hale old man, with an abundant crop of long white hair reaching nearly to his shoulders, advanced to the indicated spot, bowing reverently while he fiddled, as much as to say that he respected the company though he respected the keynote more." 11

Justice Malam "was naturally regarded in Tarley and Raveloe as a man of capacious mind, seeing that he could draw much wider conclusions without evidence than could be expected of his neighbours who were not on the Commission of the Peace. Such a man was not likely to neglect the clue of the tinder-box . . . . " 10

Mrs Osgood. " . . . an elderly lady came forward, whose full white muslin kerchief, and mob-cap round her curls of smooth grey hair, were in daring contrast with the puffed yellow satins and top-knotted caps of her neighbours. She approached **Miss Nancy** with much primness, and said, with a slow, treble suavity—

" 'Niece, I hope I see you well in health.' " 11

—dancer: " 'Talk o' nimbleness, look at Mrs Osgood,' said **Ben Winthrop** . . . . 'She trips along with her little steps, so as nobody can see how she goes—it's like as if she had little wheels to her feet. She doesn't look a day older nor last year: she's the finest-made woman as is, let the next be where she will.' " 11

pedlar. " . . . **Mr Snell** gradually recovered a vivid impression of the effect produced on him by the pedlar's countenance and conversation. He had a 'look with his eye' which fell unpleasantly on Mr Snell's sensitive organism. . . . Moreover, he had a swarthy foreignness of complexion which boded little honesty.

" . . . on the spread of inquiry among the villagers it was stated with gathering emphasis, that the parson had wanted to know whether the pedlar wore ear-rings in his ears, and an impression was created that a great deal depended on the eliciting of this fact. Of course, every one who heard the question, not having any distinct image of the pedlar as *without* ear-rings, immediately had an image of him *with* ear-rings, larger or smaller, as the case might be; and the image was presently taken for a vivid recollection. . . . " 8

—another view: "**Godfrey Cass** . . . had treated it lightly, stating that he himself had bought a pen-knife of the pedlar, and thought him a merry grinning fellow enough; it was all nonsense, he said, about the man's evil looks." 8

—sought: " . . . an inquiry was set on foot concerning a pedlar, name unknown, with curly black hair and a foreign complexion, carrying a box of cutlery and jewellery, and wearing large rings in his ears." 10

Jem Rodney "the mole-catcher, averred that one evening as he was returning homeward he saw **Silas Marner** leaning against a stile with a heavy bag on his back, instead of resting the bag on the stile as a man in his senses would have done . . . . " 1

—suspected: "There was Jem Rodney, a known poacher, and otherwise disreputable: he had often met **Marner** in his journeys across the fields, and had said something jestingly about the weaver's money; nay, he had once irritated Marner, by lingering at the fire when he called to light his pipe, instead of going about his business. Jem Rodney was the man . . . . " 5

—absolved: " 'It isn't Jem Rodney as has done this work, Master **Marner**,' said the landlord. 'You mustn't be a-casting your eye at poor Jem. There may be a bit of a reckoning against Jem for the matter of a hare or so, if anybody was bound to keep their eyes staring open, and niver to wink, but Jem's been a-sitting here drinking his can, like the decentest man i' the parish, since before you left your house, Master Marner, by your own account.' " 7

Sarah, "a young servant-woman . . . [her] manner towards [**Silas**] began to exhibit a strange fluctuation between an effort at an increased manifestation of regard and involuntary signs of shrinking and dislike. He asked her if she wished to break off their engagement; but she denied this: their engagement was known to the church, and had been recognised in the prayer-meetings; it could not be broken off without strict investigation, and Sarah could render no reason that would be sanctioned by the feeling of the community." 1

John Snell, "the landlord, a man of a neutral disposition, accustomed to stand aloof from human differences as those of beings who were all alike in need of liquor, broke silence . . . . " 6

—pacifier: " 'Come, come,' said the landlord, who felt that paying people for their absence was a principle dangerous to society, 'a joke's a joke. We're all good friends here, I hope. We must give and take. You're both right and you're both wrong, as I say.' " 6

Mr Tookey, "a small-featured young man who sat opposite . . . . 'If you're pointing at me, **Mr Macey**,' said the deputy-clerk, with an air of anxious propriety, 'I'm nowise a man to speak out of my place.' " 6

—attacked for his singing: " 'Well, **Mr Macey**,' said poor Tookey, serious amidst the general laughter, 'I undertook to partially fill up the office of parish-clerk by **Mr Crackenthorp**'s desire, whenever your infirmities should make you unfitting; and it's one of the rights thereof to sing in the choir—else why have you done the same yourself?' " 6

" 'But as for you, Master Tookey, you'd better stick to your "Amens": your voice is well enough when you keep it up in your nose. It's your inside as isn't right made for music: it's no better nor a hollow stalk . . . .

" 'Nay, nay, Tookey,' said **Ben Winthrop**. 'We'll pay you your share to keep out of it—that's what we'll do. There's things folks 'ud pay to be rid on, besides varmin.' " 6

Ben Winthrop. " 'Well, then, I wish you'd keep hold o' the tune, when it's set for you, if you're for prac*tis*ing, I wish you'd prac*tise* that,' said a large jocose-looking man, an excellent wheelwright in his week-day capacity, but on Sundays leader of the choir. He winked, as he spoke, at two of the company, who were known officially as the 'bassoon,' and the 'key-bugle,' in the confidence that he was expressing the sense of the musical profession in Raveloe." 6

Minor Figures

Bryce. " 'Heyday!' said Bryce, who had long had his eye on **Wildfire**, 'you're on your brother's horse to-day: how's that?' " 4

Bob Cass. " 'Bob's my father's favourite—you know that very well. He'd only think himself well rid of you.' " 3

—dancing: "Bob Cass was figuring in a hornpipe, and his father, very proud of this lithe son, whom he repeatedly declared to be just like himself in his young days in a tone that implied this to be the very highest stamp of juvenile merit, was the centre of a group who had placed themselves opposite the performer . . . . " 13

Cliff " 'as came and built the big stables at the Warrens . . . he thought o' nothing but hunting, Cliff didn't—a Lunnon tailor, some folks said, as had gone mad wi' cheating. For he couldn't ride; lor bless you! they said he'd got no more grip o' the hoss than if his legs had been cross-sticks . . . . ' " 6

—deranged: " . . . the father didn't live long after [his son], for he got queerer nor ever, and they said he used to go out i' the dead o' the night, wi' a lantern in his hand, to the stables, and set a lot o' lights burning, for he got as he couldn't sleep; and there he'd stand, cracking his whip and looking at his hosses . . . . ' " 6

Cliff son, " 'A lad o' sixteen, and nothing would his father have him do, but he must ride and ride—though the lad was frighted, they said. And it was a common saying as the father wanted to ride the tailor out o' the lad, and make a gentleman on him . . . . Howsomever, the poor lad got sickly and died . . . . " 6

Mrs Crackenthorp. " . . . a small blinking woman, who fidgeted incessantly with her lace, ribbons, and gold chain, turning her head about and making subdued noises, very much like a guinea-pig that twitches its nose and soliloquises in all company indiscriminately—now blinked and fidgeted towards the Squire . . . . " 11

—in procession: " . . . Mrs Crackenthorp herself, the summit of whose perpendicular feather was on a level with the **Squire**'s shoulder . . . . " 11

Dowlas. " 'Was it a red Durham?' said the farrier, taking up the thread of discourse after the lapse of a few minutes . . . .

" 'Then you needn't tell *me* who you bought it of,' said the farrier, looking round with some triumph; 'I know who it is has got the red Durhams o' this country-side. And she'd a white star on her brow, I'll bet a penny?' The farrier leaned forward with his hands on his knees as he put this question, and his eyes twinkled knowingly." 6

—*local character:* "Mr Dowlas was the negative spirit in the company, and was proud of his position." 6

Mr Drumlow. " '—poor old gentleman, I was fond on him, though he'd got a bit confused in his head, what wi' age and wi' taking a drop o' summat warm when the service come of a cold morning.' " 6

Fowler. " 'And there's that damned Fowler, I won't put up with him any longer; I've told **Winthrop** to go to **Cox** this very day. The lying scoundrel told me he'd be sure to pay me a hundred last month. He takes advantage because he's on that outlying farm, and thinks I shall forget him.' " 9

Glazier's wife, "a well-intentioned woman, not given to lying, and whose house was among the cleanest in the village, was ready to declare, as sure as ever she meant to take the sacrament the very next Christmas that was ever coming, that she had seen big ear-rings, in the shape of the young moon, in the pedlar's two ears . . . . " 8

Jane. "It was, in fact, a little before the usual time for tea; but Jane had her reasons .. . .

" 'I don't know whether you've seen 'em,' continued Jane, after a pause, 'but there's folks making haste all one way, afore the front window. I doubt something's happened.' " 17

Betty Jay "scented the boiling of **Squire Cass**'s hams, but her longing was arrested by the unctuous liquor in which they were boiled . . . . " 3

Miss Ladbrook. "Partly, Miss Ladbrook felt that her own skirt must be regarded as unduly lax by the **Miss Gunns**, and partly, that it was a pity the Miss Gunns did not show that judgment which she herself would show if she were in their place, by stopping a little on this side of the fashion." 11

Mrs Ladbrook "was standing in skullcap and front, with her turban in her hand, curtsying and smiling blandly and saying, 'After you, ma'am,' to another lady in similar circumstances, who had politely offered the precedence at the looking-glass." 11

Lammeter senior. " ' . . . a fine old gentleman he was [said **Macey**]—as fine, and finer nor the **Mr Lammeter** as now is. He came from a bit north'ard . . . only it couldn't be far north'ard, nor much different from this country, for he brought a fine breed o' sheep with him, so there must be pastures there, and everything reasonable. We heared tell as he'd sold his own land to come and take the Warrens . . . along of his wife's dying . . . . ' " 6

Bob Lundy, "the butcher, a jolly, smiling, red-haired man, was not disposed to answer rashly . . . .

" 'Red it was,' said the butcher, in his good-humoured husky treble—'and a Durham it was.' " 6

—*questioned:* " 'Well; yes—she might [have a star],' said the butcher, slowly, considering that he was giving a decided affirmative. 'I don't say contrairy.' " 6

—*challenged:* " 'I tell no lies,' said the butcher, with the same mild huskiness as before, 'and I contradick none—not if a man was to swear himself black: he's no meat o' mine, nor none o' my bargains. All I say is, it's a lovely carkiss. And what I say I'll stick to; but I'll quarrel wi' no man.' " 6

Jinny Oates, "the cobbler's daughter, being a more imaginative person, stated not only that she had seen [the **pedlar**'s ear-rings] too, but that they had made her blood creep, as it did at that very moment while there she stood." 8

Sally Oates. ". . . **Marner** had cured Sally Oates, and made her sleep like a baby, when her heart had been beating enough to burst her body, for two months and more, while she had been under the doctor's care." 1

"One day, taking a pair of shoes to be mended, he saw the cobbler's wife seated by the fire, suffering from the terrible symptoms of heart-disease and dropsy, which he had witnessed as the precursors of his mother's death. He felt a rush of pity at the mingled sight and remembrance, and, recalling the relief his mother had found from a simple preparation of foxglove, he promised Sally Oates to bring her something that would ease her, since the doctor did her no good." 2

Miss Osgood, of old. " 'And the young man, that's the **Mr Lammeter** as now is, for he'd niver a sister—began to court Miss Osgood, that's the sister o' the **Mr Osgood** as now is, and a fine handsome lass she was . . . . ' " 6

Mr Osgood's "family was also understood to be of timeless origin—the Raveloe imagination having never ventured back to that fearful blank when there were no Osgoods—still, he merely owned the farm he occupied . . . ." 3

Snap. "The sharp bark was the sign of an excited welcome that was awaiting them from a knowing brown terrier . . . . " 16

Snuff, "the brown spaniel . . . now jumped up in impatience for the expected caress. But **Godfrey** thrust her away . . . and left the room, followed humbly by the unresenting Snuff—perhaps because she saw no other career open to her." 3

Wildfire. "**Dunstan** . . . took one fence too many, and got his horse pierced with a hedge-stake . . . poor Wildfire, unconscious of his price, turned on his flank and painfully panted his last." 4

Also mentioned

Dr Blick of Flitton, likely to succeed to the Kimble practice	11
brush-maker in Shoe Lane, where Lantern Yard used to be	21
Cass sons, younger	9
Ann Coulter, who had an idiot child	2
Cox, lawyer for Squire Cass	9
Lord Cromleck, in the market for a good horse	4
dairy-maid at the Lammeters' to be married and distracted accordingly	17
Bessie Fawkes, who died leaving her children behind	16
Jortin, who owns a mare	4
Keating, with Bryce a riding companion of Dunstan Cass's	4
Kench, the constable, sick in bed when Marner is robbed	7
Grandfather **Macey**, who made the livery for the grooms at the Warrens	6
baby **Marner**, Silas's little sister, who died in infancy	12
Mott, the village gardener now retiring: Aaron Winthrop will succeed to his work	16
Gilbert Osgood, Nancy Lammeter's first cousin; his proposal declined for that reason	11
Mr Paston, the old minister at Lantern Yard	21
senior deacon who became ill; was watched by Silas and died during that period	1
Mrs Snell, who has lost her sense of smell	6, 13
stable-keeper, who promised to do no more business with Dunstan Cass	4
Dame Tedman, at whose school Nancy Lammeter received her education	11
Winthrop, bailiff or managing-man for Squire Cass (related to the wheelwright?)	9

Romola

Serialized in the *Cornhill Magazine*
July 1862-August 1863
Smith Elder & Co (3 vols. 1863)

Romola

Book I

The preamble shows the Spirit of **Lorenzo de' Medici** returned to look at present Florence. There is a review of the character of the city of his day: its political life, something of its mind, art, and religion. *Proem* A hawker of old iron, **Bratti Ferravecchi**, finds a stranger sleeping in the street and scolds him for carelessness with a valuable ring. The two go to the old market, where there is great agitation at the death just announced of the great Lorenzo. The stranger disappears. 1 Penniless and hungry, he sees a pretty girl in the market and begs a drink of milk. **Tessa**'s mother tries to drive him off. Bratti and the barber **Nello** come upon them, and Nello takes him away. 2

Charmed by the stranger, the talkative, name-dropping Nello shaves him, gives him good advice, and, learning there are jewels to be sold, mentions **Bartolommeo Scala** [H], Secretary of the Republic, to whom a letter from **Bardo de' Bardi** [H], a blind scholar with a beautiful daughter, might be effective. 3 Customers arrive; Nello presents the stranger, who at last gives his name: **Tito Melema**. **Piero di Cosimo** [H] asks Tito to sit for his painting of a treachery. Tito is shocked but recovers. He shows his ring to goldsmith **Domenico Cennini**, who takes him away for a scholarship test. 4

The narrator gives us background on the Bardi family and a description of the house where Bardo lives with his daughter **Romola**. We follow their old servant **Maso** and meet the two. She is reading to her father. He bemoans the desertion of his son. She is hurt. He speaks of his library and collections as all he has to leave to carry on his name. He is bitter that he will be forgotten. She is sympathetic. Nello is announced. 5 He introduces Tito, whose beauty startles Romola. Bardo asks him about his background, and he tells of the loss of his adoptive father at sea. They talk of scholarly matters, and Bardo is delighted. As Tito is about to leave, Bardo asks for his hand to feel, and he strokes Tito's hair and touches his face. **Bernardo del Nero** [H], an old friend and Romola's god-father, walks in and appraises Tito keenly. After Tito leaves, he warns Bardo to be careful: Tito could ingratiate himself anywhere. 6

Tito visits Scala, immersed in a literary feud with **Politian** whose suit for his daughter Scala had spurned. Tito makes a hit. 7 There is a procession to observe the feast of San Giovanni, On a balcony, Tito gets a meaning look from a friar he does not recognise, and a glimpse of Tessa. 8 Tito charms, impresses, gains favour. He sells his last jewels, amassing 500 gold florins, enough to ransom **Baldassarre Calvo**, his foster-father, last seen a Turkish prisoner. Tito decides the risk to himself of going there and trying to find the old man is too great. He may already be dead (Tito hopes so). He decides to put the money out at interest and ignore any feeling of shame and guilt. 9

Walking along enjoying the holiday crowds, Tito hears Tessa calling. He intervenes and rescues her from a street-conjuror. Can he take her home? She clings to him, and his gentle nature weakens him. He naps, then gives her a token from his purse. He retrieves his ring and puts it on. Minutes later, the strange friar accosts him and gives me a package: there is a description mentioning the ring, and a message that Baldassarre is a slave and being taken to Antioch. "The gems alone will serve to ransom me." 10 Tito decides to go slow. He does not love his father, who was demanding and brusque. Gratitude is a chimera. He calls to see the friar but hears he is in Fiesole, very ill. 11

At Bardo's, Tito speaks his love to Romola, who responds in kind. **Monna Brigida**, cousin to Bardo's late wife and foster-mother to Romola, appears. She mentions "Dino," and Bardo flares up: "my son is dead to me." Tito deduces that the mysterious friar Fra Luca and Dino the same. Bardo speaks his gratitude at Tito's help, and Tito asks for Romola's hand. She says she wants Tito. Bardo will consult Bernardo. 12 Tito is amazed to meet Romola in the street. She is going to her brother. Certain that Fra Luca will inquire about her and her father, and that she will report her engagement, Tito faces disaster: he can devise no way to explain his betrayal of his father. 13

Tito wanders into a street fair in a reckless mood. The conjuror **Vaiano** is performing mock marriages. Tito remembers Tessa. He finds her in church. He takes her to eat. They wander, and find themselves by Vaiano's display. The conjuror offers to marry them. Tessa believes it. Needing someone to trust him, Tito does not disabuse her. He makes her promise to keep their marriage a secret and sends her home. 14 At the convent, Romola sees Dino, who describes a portentous vision he has had three times: a powerful warning against her marrying. He speaks of nothing else. His companion, **Savonarola**, exhorts Romola to kneel. She does so. Dino expires She accepts the crucifix he intended for her. She has not learned of Tito's betrayal of his father. 15

Comic relief: a "Florentine Joke." Nello has a grudge against a visiting doctor, who has treated patients in his square: he is competition. Shaving him, he tells him he is in danger, that boys have spied on him and seen him making medicines illicitly. A disguised countrywoman (actually Vaiano) appears, with a baby she says desperately needs attention. It is Vaiano's monkey, and once released from constraint it leaps on the doctor's recalcitrant horse. Off they tear, to the delight of all. Maso comes to Tito: Romola is waiting for him. 16 She rushes into his arms; he is in bliss. Amorous glances and a few words: he wants to marry soon, and so does she. 17 He goes to Piero di Cosimo and commissions a special work: a tryptich on a box for Romola. Piero has a commission for which he wants Bardo and Romola to sit. He will take Romola for Tito's Ariadne and will not charge him if he can get her and Bardo. He shows Tito a painting he has done of him looking terrified. Tito feigns indifference. 18

Bernardo is firm in demanding a full year in Florence for Tito before any marriage. Bardo agrees but is impressed by news of Tito's successes. His ties with Bardo and Romola engender sympathy. Bardo's property is so depleted that he has no means to preserve his library, but he will not admit this. 19 Tito has been summoned for a trip to Rome and has begged to be betrothed first. He walks toward the house; Tessa sees and follows him. He scolds her sharply but tenderly. He reaches Romola and gives her the box with tryptich to contain (and conceal) Dino's crucifix. He keeps the key. As they come out of the church after the ceremony, Romola is horrified to see part of Dino's vision: mummers as sheeted dead following a Winged Time with scythe. 20

Book II

Eighteen months have passed. Florence has expelled Lorenzo's heir, **Piero de' Medici** [H]. **Ludovico Sforza** [H] in Milan has invited **Charles VIII** [H] of France to enter Italy and take Naples, stopping at Florence en route. Savonarola points to this occupation as a needed cleansing. Florence waits. 21 The French king and his army enter Florence. A group of soldiers harry three Italian prisoners, one of whom, an older man, refuses to kowtow. A boy cuts him free, and he gains sanctuary in the duomo, but as he stumbles on the steps he clutches Tito for balance. It is **Baldassarre Calvo**, Tito's abandoned father. They recognize each other in a moment of terror for Tito, incredulity and hatred for Calvo. Queried, Tito says, "he is a madman," denying him. 22

Piero di Cosimo twits Tito for his fright. Tito wishes he had had better presence of mind, but it is too late: vengeance stalks him in the streets of the city. He does not think of murder, but of self-defence. 23 Calvo is surprised to find many people in the cathedral. They are listening to Savonarola, whose words of retribution and vengeance resonate in Calvo's soul. Romola observes him. He is consumed with ideas of vengeance. 24 Piero di Cosimo offers him aid and asks him to pose: he declines. Savonarola's eloquence and audience, with its varying politics, are described, as are the flaws of his egoism and need for power and ascendancy. 25 Charles VIII's army arrives in magnificent procession, and Tito is obliged to welcome the monarch in his good French. Tito ponders his danger. He buys a shirt of chainmail—a coat of fear. 26

Romola mourns her father's death and struggles with her resentment and disappointment in Tito, who neglected Bardo for several months before his end. His library is now her sacred trust. She waits for Tito, and wonders. He comes, awkward and frozen by his fear that she may discover his secret. Caressing him, she feels his chainmail shirt. He denies any specific fear. She tells him of seeing Baldassarre and of Piero's attention to him. Tito's fear intensifies. 27 Visiting Piero's studio, Romola sees his painting of a terrified Tito. Piero is too anxious to make nothing of it, and Romola's suspicions begin to grow. 28 There is gossip at the barber shop, interrupted by news, announced to the people by Tito, that negotiations with Charles VIII have been successful for the city. As Tito jumps down from his podium, he encounters a shaven, cleaned-up Calvo. 29

Calvo knows he is enfeebled, though far from mad. But he fears he has irreparably lost memory and knowledge. His only effective focus is revenge. He finds an amulet in a bag around his neck and acquires a poniard, pumping the seller, Bratti, for information about Tito. 30 Tito has concluded for safety he must leave Florence. Therefore, he must dispose of Bardo's library, despite Romola's likely indignation. So he is cold, and she gets colder. Bernardo visits and sees Piero's portrait of Bardo. He says the French are leaving. 31 The French do leave; Romola is delighted. Tito comes home early. She is happy until he tells her he has sold her father's collections. There is a stormy scene: she scorns him, he keeps his head. Bernardo will be reimbursed. Tito leaves. 32

Baldassarre does chores for a bed on a hillside. Tessa lives there. She is delighted to have a person to bring food to and talk with. She tells him of her babies and her husband. Her companion, **Monna Lisa**, agrees he shall stay, but the man who pays her must not know. Tessa asks him his name; he cannot remember. 33 Tito's history with his two women is sketched. His need for comfort and his innate kindness have combined; but now the storm with Romola disturbs him and he comes to Tessa to relax. She tells him of the old man; he realizes who it is and decides to propitiate him in hopes of neutralizing a threat. Before he can speak, Baldassarre strikes to kill. The chain mail breaks the poniard. A graceful apology, not heartfelt but seeking convenience, meets hatred: agony is to come. Baldassarre will leave at once. Tito goes. 34

The debate between the more democratic and more aristocratic tendencies in Florence intensifies. Savonarola shows his preference for the former. 35 Romola reflects. Tito stops by briefly: he is to Rome. Romola completes her preparations to leave him and Florence. She takes off her betrothal ring. She will seek guidance from a wise woman in Venice. 36 Romola writes to Tito and Bernardo. Maso goes ahead of her. She walks out of Florence, passing two monks, and stops to rest. 37 To his joy, Baldassarre has recovered his memory and knowledge. His thoughts instantly turn to vengeance. He has followed Tito and researched his life. Now he follows him to Rucellai's house. 38

A gathering of Mediceans at the Rucellai Gardens. Political discussion and new prospects for Tito are interrupted by Calvo's accusing appearance. But he loses his presence of mind and fails a test of memory. Tito's story of a deranged, homicidal manservant is believed; Calvo is taken away. 39 Romola's rest on her journey is interrupted: Savonarola recognizes her and exhorts her to return to duty in Florence. She accedes. 40 Her confessor, **Fra Salvestro Maruffi**, does not engender confidence, but her renunciation holds: she goes to her home, destroys her letters to Tito and her god-father, and settles in. 41

Book III

Florence is besieged and in famine. On an errand of mercy, Romola comes upon Baldassarre apparently dead in the street. He revives; she recognizes him. Hungry bystanders observe. One of them, **Cecco**, offers to watch Calvo until Romola returns. 42 Romola is offered rest in a house; her return is blocked by a procession of monks of many orders following the unseen madonna of L'Impruneta, revered as Florence's traditional saviour. Tito arrives on horseback with news that favourable winds have allowed foodstuffs to be landed: the city is saved. 43 Calvo is galvanized: he has seen Tito. Romola comes to him and takes him to her home. He realizes who she is. She gives him money, which he takes and immediately uses to buy a knife. Romola wonders about him. She goes to tell people she has cared for the good news. Her trust in and dependence upon Savonarola now are central to her. 44

Gossip and observation at the barber-shop. A hint of awareness between Tito and **Dolfo Spini**, head of a disaffected group. Tito is discussed, not entire-ly fondly. 45 Tito and Romola are walking home at night when Spini appears. He is indiscreet, not seeing Romola, giving away a plot to abduct Savonarola. Romola warns Tito she will denounce him if harm comes to the Frate. He is reassuring but very angry with her. 46 Romola, sleepless, decides to go to the Frate. On the way, she sees Tito at the barbershop and speaks to him openly. Her question betrays him to one hearer, the multiple spy-traitor **Ceccone**. 47 Tito confronts Romola, ordering more discretion, implying danger to Bernardo. Their breach is total. Tito decides to leave her behind on quitting Florence. 48

Savonarola's party is ascendant. Hot-tempered **Francesco Valori** is Gonfaloniere. There will be a Burning of the Vanities—indecent books and ribald objects—in a sacred parody of the old Carnival. Romola walks in the city and smiles on it all. 49 Tessa gets Tito's permission to go to see the Carnival, and she happily walks into the city. Bratti sells her a cross and gets her address, promising to visit. The boys seeking vanities waylay her and demand her necklace, but Romola intervenes. All the time, Baldassarre follows. 50 In the novel's only comic sequence, the boys frighten Monna Brigida into giving up her false hair and makeup. Trying not to smile, Romola comforts her. 51

The Frate's preaching is becoming, under mounting attacks, more shrill and exasperated. Romola gets an urgent invitation to visit **Camilla Rucellai**, prophetess, who fiercely attacks Bernardo del Nero. Romola is revolted, and her faith in Savonarola is shaken. She fears plotting from the right, fanaticism from the left: she prays. Calvo appears. 52 He tells her his and Tito's story. He tells of Tessa. Vengeance is his only thought. They will meet tomorrow. 53 Romola rushes to Bernardo. She warns him passionately of treachery but cannot give details. He sends her home. Guns awaken her: the exiled Piero de' Medici is at the gates with an army. He has lost surprise, and he retreats; but his supporters in the city are suspect. Calvo has disappeared. 54

Plague is come, and the Excommunication of Savonarola. Romola is invigorated in her work and her adherence; but Calvo does not appear. 55 In the street Romola finds a lost little boy. It is Tessa's **Lillo**. He finds his home. Tessa's prattle reveals to Romola who her "husband" is. Romola gives her a lock of her hair and goes home to think. She decides to tell Tito her wish to live apart, hoping for his consent. Tito returns, and before she can speak he tells her Bernardo is arrested for conspiracy, with other betrayed Mediceans. 56 Tito's treachery is detailed, and it is recognised as such. The spy Ceccone watches as he leaves the council chamber after giving his evidence. 57

The question of sentence for the Mediceans is referred to an assembly of dignitaries, but the Council of Eight has passed sentence, which is now to be appealed under a law Savonarola caused to be adopted. Tito comes to tell Romola this. She excoriates him for his treachery to Baldassarre but does not mention Tessa. 58 Romola goes to Savonarola to plead for her god-father and Appeal to the Signoria. She is eloquent almost to bitterness; the Frate is stung but at last unmoved. When he says the cause of his party is God's cause, she walks out. 59 Fierce debate: grant Appeal, or execute at once? Hot-head Valori threatens mob action against his opponents, who give in. The five condemned are paraded in fetters and led to the scaffold. Romola says farewell to Bernardo. Tito does not watch. He fears Romola and is glad Bernardo will not be there to support her against him. Romola endures and will now depart. 60

At the seashore, Romola acquires a small boat and sets sail. She lies in it and drifts out to sea, hoping for death. 61 An enormous crowd in the Piazza di San Marco hears Savonarola, excommunicated and banned from the Duomo, preach in the open air. He challenges God to destroy him if his words are unworthy. A wait. The sun suddenly illuminates him, and the crowd is enraptured. Tito, is struck but not moved. 62 A Franciscan offers to walk through fire with the Frate. The people are interested, and curious about a posted notice in Latin. Tito translates. Dolfo Spini appears. A signal is given. Tito goes to Dolfo's, and the discussion shows he is fomenting the fire challenge. Tito humours Dolfo, who asks if Ceccone can be useful. Tito cannot say no. But he fears him, and rightly so: Ceccone hates him as a successful rival. 63

Tito goes to Savonarola, who is perplexed by the Trial by Fire: how can he evade it? Tito tells him a courier will be going to France. The Frate has a letter ready, calling for the French king's assistance in deposing the Pope. Tito adroitly entices the Frate to consign the letter to him, and he sends it, alerting the Duke of Milan to intercept. 64 A huge crowd gathers to see a miracle. Tito watches, with satisfaction because his betrayal has worked: he will be in good odor in Milan and Rome, and he will leave Florence in a day. A theological dispute delays the Trial, and the rain blots it out. Spini's men try to seize the Frate but are driven back. The crowd is furious with disappointment and disillusion. Savonarola knows he has been defeated: his honour is forfeit. 65

Much fighting ensues. The monks defend San Marco. The government sends troops to arrest Savonarola. Led by Spini's forces, the mob loots houses of Savonarola supporters. There is a huge revulsion of feeling against Valori and his party. He is murdered by relatives of the executed. Dolfo Spini hears poisonous words against Tito from Ceccone and **Francesco Cei** [H], also Tito's enemy, and vows punishment. 66 Baldassarre scavenges at the Arno. Spini's men are going to sack Tito's house. They intercept Tito, who escapes by throwing purse and belt to them and diving from the bridge into the river. He swims on and on and, exhausted, at last is thrown by the river current onto the bank just where Baldassarre is watching and waiting. He climbs on Tito, who opens his eyes and wonders if he is already in Hell. Baldassarre throttles him. Both die. A cart brings them to the city. Savonarola is under torture. 67

Romola's little boat has landed. She hears a baby cry and finds a little one with a family of Jewish exiles all dead of pestilence. She recruits a priest and a youth to help, and she stays for months caring for the sick and the well. 68 All suicidal gloom is gone. The village healthy, **Benedetto** cared for, she leaves for Florence. 69 She learns of Tito's death, Savonarola's torture. She searches in vain for Tessa and the children. Then she sees Tessa's necklace in Bratti's cart and reclaims her and hers, bringing them home to Brigida. 70 Savonarola has confessed, and his words are analyzed and summed up as admirable. 71 But Papal torturers come and his agony is renewed. He retracts his confession and retracts his retraction. At last he is burned at the stake: no last words. 72

Nine years later, Romola, Tessa, Nillo, Ninna and Brigida are at peace. *E*

Contents

The *Topicon* contains Romola's brother Dino's vision at M:Consciousness—*vision of portent* and, at S:Duty—*the call*, the *full text* of Chapter 40, the fulcrum of the novel, which describes the confrontation between Savonarola and Romola on a path outside Florence.

Savonarola

Romola di Bardi

—introduced: "The only spot of bright colour in the room was made by the hair of a tall maiden of seventeen or eighteen, who was standing before a carved *leggio,* or reading-desk . . . . The hair was of a reddish gold colour, enriched by an unbroken small ripple, such as may be seen in the sunset clouds on grandest autumnal evenings. It was confined by a black fillet above her small ears, from which it rippled forward again, and made a natural veil for her neck above her square-cut gown of black *rascia,* or serge. Her eyes were bent on a large volume placed before her: one long white hand rested on the reading-desk, and the other clasped the back of her father's chair . . . .

" . . . [Her] cheeks were also without any tinge of the rose. There was the same refinement of brow and nostril in both, counterbalanced by a full though firm mouth and powerful chin, which gave an expression of proud tenacity and latent impetuousness: an expression carried out in the backward poise of the girl's head, and the grand line of her neck and shoulders. It was a type of face of which one could not venture to say whether it would inspire love or only that unwilling admiration which is mixed with dread: the question must be decided by the eyes, which often seem charged with a more direct message from the soul." 5

—revealed: " . . . a fine ear would have detected in her clear voice and distinct utterance, a faint suggestion of weariness struggling with habitual patience. But as she approached her father and saw his arms stretched out a little with nervous excitement to seize the volume, her hazel eyes filled with pity; she hastened to lay the book on his lap, and kneeled down by him, looking up at him as if she believed that the love in her face must surely make its way through the dark obstruction that shut out everything else. At that moment the doubtful attractiveness of Romola's face, in which pride and passion seemed to be quivering in the balance with native refinement and intelligence, was transfigured to the most lovable womanliness by mingled pity and affection: it was evident that the deepest fount of feeling within her had not yet wrought its way to the less changeful features, and only found its outlet through her eyes." 5

—filial sympathy: "Romola was moved with sympathetic indignation, for in her nature too there lay the same large claims, and the same spirit of struggle against their denial. She tried to calm her father by a still prouder word than his." 5

—deceptive: " . . . the most penetrating observer would hardly have divined that this proud pale face, at the slightest touch on the fibres of affection or pity, could become passionate with tenderness, or that this woman, who imposed a certain awe on those who approached her, was in a state of girlish simplicity and ignorance concerning the world outside her father's books." 5

—surprise: "Romola's astonishment could hardly have been greater if the stranger had worn a panther-skin and carried a thyrsus; for the cunning barber had said nothing of the Greek's age or appearance; and among her father's scholarly visitors, she had hardly ever seen any but middle-aged or grey-headed men . . . . But the habitual attitude of her mind towards strangers—a proud self-dependence and determination to ask for nothing even by a smile—confirmed in her by her father's complaints against the world's injustice, was like a snowy embankment hemming in the rush of admiring surprise." 6

The Blind Scholar and his Daughter

—impact: "**Tito**'s bright face showed its rich-tinted beauty without any rivalry of colour above his black *sajo* or tunic reaching to the knees. It seemed like a wreath of spring, dropped suddenly in Romola's young but wintry life, which had inherited nothing but memories—memories of a dead mother, of a lost brother, of a blind father's happier time—memories of far-off light, love, and beauty, that lay embedded in dark mines of books, and could hardly give out their brightness again until they were kindled for her by the torch of some known joy. Nevertheless, she returned Tito's bow, made to her on entering, with the same pale proud face as ever; but, as he approached, the snow melted, and when he ventured to look towards her again, while **Nello** was speaking, a pink flush overspread her face, to vanish again almost immediately, as if her imperious will had recalled it." 6

—paternal criticism: " 'I constantly marvel at the capriciousness of my daughter's memory, which grasps certain objects with tenacity, and lets fall all those minutiæ whereon depends accuracy, the very soul of scholarship.' " 6

—commiseration: " . . . at the accusation against her memory [**Tito**'s] face broke into its brightest smile, which was reflected as inevitably as sudden sunbeams in Romola's. Conceive the soothing delight of that smile to her! Romola had never dreamed that there was a scholar in the world who would smile at a deficiency for which she was constantly made to feel herself a culprit. It was like the dawn of a new sense to her—the sense of comradeship. They did not look away from each other immediately, as if the smile had been a stolen one; they looked and smiled with frank enjoyment." 6

—eager projection: "He looked so bright and gentle: he must feel as she did, that in this eagerness of blind age there was piteousness enough to call forth inexhaustible patience. How much more strongly he would feel this if he knew about her brother! A girl of eighteen imagines the feelings behind the face that has moved her with its sympathetic youth, as easily as primitive people imagined the humours of the gods in fair weather: what is she to believe in, if not in this vision woven from within?" 6

—self-deprecating: " 'I am by no means sufficient to my father. I have not the gifts that are necessary for scholarship.'

"Romola did not make this self-depreciatory statement in a tone of anxious humility, but with a proud gravity.

" 'Nay, my Romola,' said her father . . . 'thou art not destitute of gifts; rather, thou art endowed beyond the measure of women; but thou hast withal the woman's delicate frame, which ever craves repose and variety, and so begets a wandering imagination.' " 6

—the moment: " ' . . . if you will only let me say, I love you—if you will only think me worth loving a little.'

"His speech was the softest murmur, and the dark beautiful face, nearer to hers than it had ever been before, was looking at her with beseeching tenderness.

" 'I do love you,' murmured Romola; she looked at him with the same simple majesty as ever, but her voice had never in her life before sunk to that murmur. It seemed to them both that they were looking at each other a long while before her lips moved again; yet it was but a moment till she said, 'I know *now* what it is to be happy.'

"The faces just met, and the dark curls mingled for an instant with the rippling gold . . . . They were both contented to be silent and separate, for that first blissful experience of mutual consciousness was all the more exquisite for being unperturbed by immediate sensation." 12

"Each woman creates in her own likeness the love-tokens that are offered to her; and Romola's deep calm happiness encompassed **Tito** like the rich but quiet evening light which dissipates all unrest." 12

—avowal: " 'Nothing has ever come to me before that I have wished for strongly: I did not think it possible that I could care so much for anything that could happen to myself.'

"It was a brief and simple plea; but it was the condensed story of Romola's self-repressing colourless young life, which had thrown all its passion into sympathy with aged sorrows, aged ambition, aged pride and indignation. It had never occurred to Romola that she should not speak as directly and emphatically of her love for Tito as of any other subject." 12

—swain: "[He] now turned away, lifting his cap—a sign of reference rarely made at that time by native Florentines, and which excited **Bernardo del Nero**'s contempt for **Tito** as a fawning Greek, while to Romola, who loved homage, it gave him an exceptional grace." 13

—disgust: "There was an unconquerable repulsion for her in [**Dino**'s] monkish aspect; it seemed to her the brand of the dastardly undutifulness which had left her father desolate—of the grovelling superstition which could give such undutifulness the name of piety." 15

—negation of religion: "Her father, whose proud sincerity and simplicity of life had made him one of the few frank pagans of his time, had brought her up with a silent ignoring of any claims the Church could have to regulate the belief and action of beings with a cultivated reason." 15

—new feeling: "Slowly Romola fell on her knees, and in the very act a tremor came over her; in the renunciation of her proud erectness, her mental attitude seemed changed, and she found herself in a new state of passiveness." 15

—her brother's vision: " . . . a strange awe had come over her. Her mind was not apt to be assailed by sickly fancies; she had the vivid intellect and the healthy human passion, which are too keenly alive to the constant relations of things to have any morbid craving after the exceptional. Still the images of the vision she despised jarred and distressed her like painful and cruel cries." 15

—her brother's death: "And it was the first time she had witnessed the struggle with approaching death: her young life had been sombre, but she had known nothing of the utmost human needs, no acute suffering—no heart-cutting sorrow; and this brother, come back to her in his hour of supreme agony, was like a sudden awful apparition from an invisible world . . . .

" '**Dino**!' said Romola, with a low but piercing cry, as the certainty came upon her that the silence of misunderstanding could never be broken.

" 'Take the crucifix, my daughter,' said **Fra Girolamo**, after a few minutes. 'His eyes behold it no more.'

"Romola stretched out her hand to the crucifix, and this act appeared to relieve the tension of her mind. A great sob burst from her. She bowed her head by the side of her dead brother, and wept aloud.

"It seemed to her as if this first vision of death must alter the daylight for her for evermore." 15

—reaction: " . . . it was **Tito** who had first brought the warm stream of hope and gladness into her life, and who had first turned away the keen edge of pain in the remembrance of her brother. She would tell Tito everything; there was no one else to whom she could tell it . . . . Proud and self-controlled to all the world beside, Romola was as simple and unreserved as a child in her love for Tito. She had been quite contented with the days when they had only looked at each other; but now, when she felt the need of clinging to him, there was no thought that hindered her." 17

—a kiss: "A sweet pink blush spread itself with the quickness of light over **Romola**'s face and neck as she bent towards him. It seemed impossible that their kisses could ever become common things." 17

—blossoming: "For it was pleasant to look at Romola's beauty; to see her, like old **Firenzuola**'s type of womanly majesty, 'sitting with a certain grandeur, speaking with gravity, smiling with modesty, and casting around, as it were, an odour of queenliness'; and she seemed to unfold like a strong white lily under this genial breath of admiration and homage; it was all one to her with her new bright life in **Tito**'s love." 19

—betrothal garb: "Romola entered, all white and gold, more than ever like a tall lily. Her white silk garment was bound by a golden girdle, which fell with large tassels; and above that was the rippling gold of her hair, surmounted by the white mist of her long veil, which was fastened on her brow by a band of pearls . . . and was now parted off her face so that it all floated backward . . . .

" . . . she stood in calm delight, with that exquisite self-consciousness which rises under the gaze of admiring love." 20

—touched: "She had looked long and attentively at **Baldassarre**, for grey hairs made a peculiar appeal to her; and the stamp of some unwonted suffering in the face, confirmed by the cord round his neck, stirred in her those sensibilities towards the sorrows of age, which her whole life had tended to develop." 24

—creeping disillusion: "The breath of sadness that still cleaved to her lot while she saw her father month after month sink from elation into new disappointment as **Tito** gave him less and less of his time, and made bland excuses for not continuing his own share of the joint work—that sadness was no fault of Tito's, she said, but rather of their inevitable destiny . . . . But all the while inwardly her imagination was busy trying to see how Tito could be as good as she had thought he was, and yet find it impossible to sacrifice those pleasures of society which were necessarily more vivid to a bright creature like him than to the common run of men . . . she tried to persuade herself that the inferiority was on her side. Tito was really kinder than she was, better tempered, less proud and resentful; he had no angry retorts, he met all complaints with perfect sweetness; he only escaped as quietly as he could from things that were unpleasant." 27

—resisting it: "Disappointment? Yes, there was no other milder word that would tell the truth. Perhaps all women had to suffer the disappointment of ignorant hopes, if she only knew their experience. Still, there had been something peculiar in her lot: her relation to her father had claimed unusual sacrifices from her husband. **Tito** had once thought that his love would make those sacrifices easy; his love had not been great enough for that. She was not justified in resenting a self-delusion. No! resentment must not rise:

all endurance seemed easy to Romola rather than a state of mind in which she would admit to herself that Tito acted unworthily." 27

—a commitment: "The laborious simple life, pure from vulgar corrupting ambitions, embittered by the frustrations of the dearest hopes, imprisoned at last in total darkness—a long seed-time without a harvest—was at an end now, and all that remained of it besides the tablet in Sante [*sic*] Croce and the unfinished commentary on **Tito**'s text, was the collection of manuscripts and antiquities, the fruit of half a century's toil and frugality. The fulfilment of her father's lifelong ambition about this library was a sacramental obligation for Romola." 27

—unawakened: "All Romola's ardour had been concentrated in her affections. Her share in her father's learned pursuits had been for her little more than a toil which was borne for his sake; and **Tito**'s airy brilliant faculty had no attraction for her that was not merged in the deeper sympathies that belong to young love and trust. Romola had had contact with no mind that could stir the larger possibilities of her nature; they lay folded and crushed like embryonic wings, making no element in her consciousness beyond an occasional vague uneasiness." 27

—an interest: " . . . this fanatical preacher of tribulations was after all a man towards whom it might be possible for her to feel personal regard and reverence. The denunciations and exhortations simply arrested her attention. She felt no terror, no pangs of conscience: it was the roll of distant thunder, that seemed grand, but could not shake her." 27

—stronger: "But when she heard **Savonarola** invoke martyrdom, she sobbed with the rest: she felt herself penetrated with a new sensation—a strange sympathy with something apart from all the definable interests of her life. It was not altogether unlike the thrill which had accompanied certain rare heroic touches in history and poetry; but the resemblance was as that between the memory of music, and the sense of being possessed by actual vibrating harmonies." 27

—an undermining: "Romola was labouring, as a loving woman must, to subdue her nature to her husband's. The great need of her heart compelled her to strangle, with desperate resolution, every rising impulse of suspicion, pride, and resentment; she felt equal to any self-infliction that would save her from ceasing to love. That would have been like the hideous nightmare in which the world had seemed to break away all round her, and leave her feet overhanging the darkness. Romola had never distinctly imagined such a future for herself; she was only beginning to feel the presence of effort in that clinging trust which had once been mere repose." 27

—a shift: "The eighteen months had produced a more definable change in Romola's face than in **Tito**'s; the expression was more subdued, less cold, and more beseeching, and, as the pink flush overspread her face now, in her joy that the long waiting was at an end, she was much lovelier than on the day when Tito had first seen her. On that day, any on-looker would have said that Romola's nature was made to command, and Tito's to bend; yet now Romola's mouth was quivering a little, and there was some timidity in her glance." 27

—shut out: "Romola, keenly sensitive to the absence of the usual response, took away her hand and said, 'I am going, **Tito**' . . . .

"Still Tito did not look up, and Romola went out without saying any more. Very slight things make epochs in married life; and this morning for the first time she admitted to herself not only that Tito had changed, but that he had changed towards her." 31

—pride still: " 'You are contented then, Madonna Orgogliosa?' said **Bernardo**, smiling, as he moved to the door.

" 'Assuredly.'

"Poor Romola! There was one thing that would have made the pang of disappointment in her husband harder to bear; it was, that any one should know he gave her cause for disappointment. This might be a woman's weakness, but it is closely allied to a woman's nobleness." 31

—apprehensive: " . . . she was determined never to submit her mind to his judgment on this question of duty to her father; she was inwardly prepared to encounter any sort of pain in resistance." 32

—a stand: " 'Because it was a trust,' said Romola, in a low but distinct voice. 'He trusted me, he trusted you, **Tito**. I did not expect you to feel anything else about it—to feel as I do—but I did expect you to feel that.' " 32

" 'But I will not give up that duty. What have I to do with your arguments? It was a yearning of *his* heart, and therefore it is a yearning of mine.' " 32

—love is going: "As that fluent talk fell on her ears there was a rising contempt within her, which only made her more conscious of her bruised, despairing love, her love for the **Tito** she had married and believed in. Her nature, possessed with the energies of strong emotion, recoiled from this hopelessly shallow readiness which professed to appropriate the widest sympathies and had no pulse for the nearest." 32

—indictment: " 'You talk of substantial good, **Tito**! Are faithfulness, and love, and sweet grateful memories, no good? Is it no good that we should keep our silent promises on which others build because they believe in our love and truth? Is it no good that a just life should be justly honoured? Or, is it good that we should harden our hearts against all the wants and hopes of those who have depended on us? What good can belong to men who have such souls? To talk cleverly, perhaps, and find soft couches for themselves, and live and die with their base selves as their best companions.' " 32

—revelation: " 'You have *sold* them?' she asked, as if she distrusted her ears . . . .

" 'You are a treacherous man!' she said, with something grating in her voice, as she looked down at him . . . .

"Her eyes were flashing, and her whole frame seemed to be possessed by impetuous force that wanted to leap out in some deed. All the crushing pain of disappointment in her husband, which had made the strongest part of her consciousness a few minutes before, was annihilated by the vehemence of her indignation. She could not care in this moment that the man she was despising as he leaned there in his loathsome beauty—she could not care that he was her husband; she could only feel that she despised him. The pride and fierceness of the old **Bardo** blood had been thoroughly awaked in her for the first time." 32

—intimidating nobility: "She, too [like **Tessa**], knew little of the actual world; she, too, trusted him; but he had an uneasy consciousness that behind her frank eyes there was a nature that could judge him, and that any ill-founded trust of hers sprang not from pretty brute-like incapacity, but from a nobleness which might prove an alarming touchstone." 34

—aftermath: " . . . the night had been one long waking to her, and, in spite of her healthy frame, sensation had become a dull continuous pain, as if she had been stunned and bruised." 35

—dressed for exile: "To herself she looked strangely like her brother **Dino**: the full oval of the cheek had only to be wasted; the eyes, already sad, had only to become a little sunken. Was she getting more like him in anything else? Only in this, that she understood now how men could be prompted to rush away for ever from earthly delights, how they could be prompted to dwell on images of sorrow rather than of beauty and joy." 36

—her ring: "If that beloved **Tito** who had placed the betrothal ring on her finger was not in any valid sense the same Tito whom she had ceased to love, why should she return to him the sign of their union, and not rather retain it as a memorial? And this act, which came as a palpable demonstration of her own and his identity, had a power unexplained to herself, of shaking Romola . . . . But there was a passionate voice speaking within her that presently nullified all such muffled murmurs.

" 'It cannot be! I cannot be subject to him. He is false. I shrink from him. I despise him!'

"She snatched the ring from her finger and laid it on the table against the pen with which she meant to write." 36

—her law: "Again she felt that there could be no law for her but the law of her affections. That tenderness and keen fellow-feeling for the near and the loved which are the main outgrowth of the affections, had made the religion of her life: they had made her patient in spite of natural impetuosity; they would have sufficed to make her heroic . . . .

"She was not acting after any precedent, or obeying any adopted maxims. The grand severity of the stoical philosophy in which her father had taken care to instruct her, was familiar enough to her ears and lips, and its lofty spirit had raised certain echoes within her; but she had never used it, never needed it as a rule of life. She had endured and forborne because she loved: maxims which told her to feel less, and not to cling close lest the onward course of great Nature should jar her, had been as powerless on her tenderness as they had been on her father's yearning for just fame. She had appropriated no theories: she had simply felt strong in the strength of affection, and life without that energy came to her as an entirely new problem." 36

—a touchstone: "Her life could never be happy any more, but it must not, could not, be ignoble." 36

—rejecting a chimera: "True as the voice of foreboding had proved, Romola saw with unshaken conviction that to have renounced **Tito** in obedience to a warning like that, would have been meagre-hearted folly. Her trust had been delusive, but she would have chosen over again to have acted on it rather than be a creature led by phantoms and disjointed whispers in a world where there was the large music of reasonable speech, and the warm grasp of living hands." 36

—her brother's calling: "If there were much more of such experience as his in the world, she would like to understand it—would even like to learn the thoughts of men who sank in ecstasy before the pictured agonies of martyrdom. There seemed to be something more than madness in that supreme fellowship with suffering." 36

Escaped

'Father, I Will be Guided'

—*out:* "Out! Once past the houses of the Borgo . . . she would have entered on her new life—a life of loneliness and endurance, but of freedom. She had been strong enough to snap asunder the bonds she had accepted in blind faith: what ever befell her, she would no more feel the breath of soft hated lips warm upon her cheek, no longer feel the breath of an odious mind stifling her own." 37

—*arrested:* "While **Savonarola** spoke with growing intensity, his arms tightly folded before him still, as they had been from the first, but his face alight as from an inward flame, Romola felt herself surrounded and possessed by the glow of his passionate faith. The chill doubts all melted away; she was subdued by the sense of something unspeakably great to which she was being called by a strong being who roused a new strength within herself. In a voice that was like a low, prayerful cry, she said—

" 'Father, I will be guided. Teach me! I will go back.' " 40 *See Topicon* S:Duty—*the call*

—*her mentor's wish:* " 'I desire to behold you among the feebler and more ignorant sisters as the apple-tree among the trees of the forest, so that your fairness and all natural gifts may be but as a lamp through which the Divine light shines the more purely.' " 41

—*a disappointment:* "After her first angry resistance of **Savonarola** had passed away, she had lost all remembrance of the old dread lest any influence should drag her within the circle of fanaticism and sour monkish piety. But now again, the chill breath of that dread stole over her. It could have no decisive effect against the impetus her mind had just received; it was only like the closing of the grey clouds over the sunrise, which made her returning path monotonous and sombre." 41

—*privation:* "Her own pale face had the slightly pinched look and the deepening of the eye-socket which indicate unusual fasting in the habitually temperate, and the large direct gaze of her hazel eyes was all the more impressive." 42

—*service:* "Romola, whose heart had been swelling, half with foreboding, half with that enthusiasm of fellowship which the life of the last two years had made as habitual to her as the consciousness of costume to a vain and idle woman, gave a deep sigh, as at the end of some long mental tension, and re-mained on her knees for very languor . . . . " 43

—*mystified:* "Yet what could she have done if the truth had proved to be the burden of some painful secret about her husband, in addition to the anxieties that already weighed upon her? Surely a wife was permitted to desire ignorance of a husband's wrong-doing, since she alone must not protest and warn men against him. But that thought stirred too many intricate fibres of feeling to be pursued now in her weariness." 44

—*helping:* " 'Bless you, madonna! bless you!' said the faint chorus, in much the same tone as that in which they had a few minutes before praised and thanked the unseen Madonna.

"Romola cared a great deal for that music. She had no innate taste for tending the sick and clothing the ragged, like some women to whom the details of such work are welcome in themselves, simply as an occupation. Her early training had kept her aloof from such womanly labours; and if she had not brought to them the inspiration of her deepest feelings, they would have been irksome to her. But they had come to be the one unshaken resting-place of her mind, the one narrow pathway on which the light fell clear." 44

—vindication: "Whatever else made her doubt, the help she gave to her fellow-citizens made her sure that **Fra Girolamo** had been right to call her back. According to his unforgotten words, her place had not been empty: it had been filled with her love and her labour. Florence had had need of her, and the more her own sorrow pressed upon her, the more gladness she felt in the memories, stretching through the two long years, of hours and moments in which she had lightened the burden of life to others. All that ardour of her nature which could no longer spend itself in the woman's tenderness for father and husband, had transformed itself into an enthusiasm of sympathy with the general life. She had ceased to think that her own lot could be happy—had ceased to think of happiness at all: the one end of her life seemed to her to be the diminishing of sorrow." 44

—her mentor: "Her enthusiasm was continually stirred to fresh vigour by the influence of **Savonarola**. In spite of the wearisome visions and allegories from which she recoiled in disgust when they came as stale repetitions from other lips than his, her strong affinity for his passionate sympathy and the splendour of his aims had lost none of its power." 44

"[Savonarola] had created in her a new consciousness of the great drama of human existence in which her life was a part; and through her daily helpful contact with the less fortunate of her fellow-citizens this new consciousness became something stronger than a vague sentiment; it grew into a more and more definite motive of self-denying practice. She thought little about dogmas, and shrank from reflecting closely on the Frate's prophecies of the immediate scourge and closely-following regeneration.

"She had submitted her mind to his and had entered into communion with the Church, because in this way she had found an immediate satisfaction for moral needs which all the previous culture and experience of her life had left hungering. Fra Girolamo's voice had waked in her mind a reason for living, apart from personal enjoyment and personal affection; but it was a reason that seemed to need feeding with greater forces than she possessed within herself, and her submissive use of all offices of the Church was simply a watching and waiting if by any means fresh strength might come. The pressing problem for Romola just then was not to settle questions of controversy, but to keep alive that flame of unselfish emotion by which a life of sadness might still be a life of active love." ¶44

—accepting: "Romola was so deeply moved by the grand energies of **Savonarola**'s nature, that she found herself listening patiently to all dogmas and prophecies, when they came in the vehicle of his ardent faith and believing utterance." 44

—her trust: "Romola's trust in **Savonarola** was something like a rope suspended securely by her path, making her step elastic while she grasped it; if it were suddenly removed, no firmness of the ground she trod could save her from staggering, or perhaps from falling." 44

—alienation: "In the first ardour of her self-conquest . . . Romola had made many timid efforts towards the return of a frank relation between them. But to her such a relation could only come by open speech about their differences, and the attempt to arrive at a moral understanding; while **Tito** could only be saved from alienation from her by such a recovery of her effusive tenderness as would have presupposed oblivion of their differences. He cared for no explanation between them; he felt any thorough explanation impossible: he would have cared to have Romola fond again, and to her, fondness was impossible. She could be submissive and gentle, she could repress

any sign of repulsion; but tenderness was not to be feigned. She was helplessly conscious of the result: her husband was alienated from her." 46

—*ambivalence:* "The first rush of indignation and alarm in Romola had begun to give way to more complicated feelings, which rendered speech and action difficult. In that simpler state of vehemence, open opposition to the husband from whom she felt her soul revolting had had the aspect of temptation for her; it seemed the easiest of all courses. But now, habits of self-questioning, memories of impulse subdued, and that proud reserve which all discipline had left unmodified, began to emerge from the flood of passion." 46

—*estrangement:* " . . . they had never approached an avowal of that past which, both in its young love and in the shock that shattered the love, lay locked away from them like a banquet-room where death had once broken the feast." 48

—*contrite:* "Her sweet pale face, with all its anger gone and nothing but the timidity of self-doubt in it, seemed to give a marked predominance to her husband's dark strength." 48

—*killjoy:* "Romola's life had given her an affinity for sadness which inevitably made her unjust towards merriment. That subtle result of culture which we call Taste was subdued by the need for deeper motive; just as the nicer demands of the palate are annihilated by urgent hunger. Moving habitually amongst scenes of suffering, and carrying woman's heaviest disappointment in her heart, the severity which allied itself with self-renouncing beneficent strength had no dissonance for her." 49 *The rarest of the rare: Eliot gives us not one, but two dangling participles in the same sentence.*

—*strengthened:* "As Romola walked, often in weariness, among the sick, the hungry, and the murmuring, she felt it good to be inspired by something more than her pity—by the belief in a heroism [of **Savonarola**] struggling for sublime ends, towards which the daily action of her pity could only tend feebly, as the dews that freshen the weedy ground to-day tend to prepare an unseen harvest in the years to come." 52

—*enthusiasm at risk:* "Romola, kneeling with buried face on the altar-step, was enduring one of those sickening moments, when the enthusiasm which had come to her as the only energy strong enough to make life worthy, seemed to be inevitably bound up with vain dreams and wilful eye-shutting." 52

—*reacting against bigotry:* " . . . she felt that to keep the Government of Florence pure, and to keep out a vicious rule, was a sacred cause; the **Frate** was right there, and had carried her understanding irrevocably with him. But at this moment the assent of her understanding went alone; it was given unwillingly. Her heart was recoiling from a right allied to so much narrowness; a right apparently entailing that hard systematic judgment of men which measures them by assents and denials quite superficial to the manhood within them. Her affection and respect were clinging with new tenacity to her godfather, and with him to those memories of her father which were in the same opposition to the division of men into sheep and goats by the easy mark of some political or religious symbol." 52

—*illumination:* "If Romola's intellect had been less capable of discerning the complexities in human things, all the early loving associations of her life would have forbidden her to accept implicitly the denunciatory exclusiveness of **Savonarola**. She had simply felt that his mind had suggested deeper and more efficacious truth to her than any other, and the large breathing-room she found in his grand view of human duties had made her patient towards that part of his teaching which she could not absorb, so long as its practical effect came into collision with no strong force in her.

"But now a sudden insurrection of feeling had brought about that collision. Her indignation, once roused by **Camilla**'s visions, could not pause there, but ran like an illuminating fire over all the kindred facts in Savonarola's teaching, and for the moment she felt what was true in the scornful sarcasms she heard continually flung against him, more keenly than she felt what was false." ¶52

—the truth revealed: "A vision had risen of what **Tito** was to her in those first days when she thought no more of wrong in him than a child thinks of poison in flowers. The yearning regret that lay in that memory brought some relief from the tension of horror. With one great sob the tears rushed forth." 53

—another wife! "The first shock that passed through Romola was visibly one of anger. The woman's sense of indignity was inevitably foremost." 53

—verdict: "What else had **Tito**'s crime towards **Baldassarre** been but that abandonment working itself out to the most hideous extreme of falsity and ingratitude?" 56

—on the march: "And the inspiring consciousness breathed into her by **Savonarola**'s influence that her lot was vitally united with the general lot had exalted even the minor details of obligation into religion. She was marching with a great army; she was feeling the stress of a common life. If victims were needed, and I was uncertain on whom the lot might fall, she would stand ready to answer to her name." 56

—the Question: "It flashed upon her mind that the problem before here was essentially the same as that which had lain before **Savonarola**—the problem where the sacredness of obedience ended, and where the sacredness of rebellion began. To her, as to him, there had come one of those moments in life when the soul must dare to act on its own warrant, not only without external law to appeal to, but in the face of a law which is not unarmed with Divine lightnings—lightnings that may yet fall if the warrant has been false." 56

—supervening intelligence: "When Tito had named the men of whom she felt certain he was the confederate, she said, with a recoiling gesture and low-toned bitterness—

" 'And you—you are safe?'

" 'You are certainly an amiable wife, my Romola,' said Tito, with the coldest irony. Yes; I am safe.'

"They turned away from each other in silence." 56

—losing eloquently: " 'Then,' said Romola, her indignation rising again, 'you can be indifferent that Florentines should inflict death which you do not desire, when you might have protested against it—when you might have helped to hinder it, by urging the observance of a law which you held it good to get passed. Father, you used not to stand aloof: you used not to shrink from protesting. Do not say you cannot protest where the lives of men are concerned; say, rather, you desire their death. Say rather, you hold it good for Florence that there shall be more blood and more hatred. Will the death of five Mediceans put an end to parties in Florence? Will the death of a noble

old man like **Bernardo del Nero** save a city that holds such men as **Dolfo Spini**?' " 59

—the crux: " 'Take care, father, lest your enemies have some reason when they say, that in your visions of what will further God's kingdom you see only what will strengthen your own party.'

" 'And that is true!' said **Savonarola**, with flashing eyes. Romola's voice had seemed to him in that moment the voice of his enemies. 'The cause of my party *is* the cause of God's kingdom.'

" 'I do not believe it!' said Romola, her whole frame shaken with passionate repugnance. 'God's kingdom is something wider—else, let me stand outside it with the beings that I love.'

"The two faces were lit up, each with an opposite emotion, each with an opposite certitude. Further words were impossible. Romola hastily covered her head and went out in silence." 59

—transcending horror: "She needed no arm to support her; she shed no tears. She felt that intensity of life which seems to transcend both grief and joy . . . . Romola was feeling the full force of that sympathy with the individual lot that is continually opposing itself to the formulæ by which actions and parties are judged. She was treading the way with her second father to the scaffold, and nerving herself to defy ignominy by the consciousness that it was not deserved." 60

—marriage gone: "The vision of any great purpose, any end of existence which could ennoble endurance and exalt the common deeds of a dusty life with divine ardours, was utterly eclipsed for her now by the sense of a confusion in human things which made all effort a mere dragging at tangled threads; all fellowship, either for resistance or advocacy, mere unfairness and exclusiveness." 61

—bitter disillusion: "And now that her keen feeling for her god-father had thrown her into antagonism with the Frate, she saw all the repulsive and inconsistent details in his teaching with a painful lucidity which exaggerated their proportions. In the bitterness of her disappointment she said that his striving after the renovation of the Church and the world was a striving after a mere name which told no more than the title of a book: a name that had come to mean practically the measures that would strengthen his own position in Florence; nay, often questionable deeds and words, for the sake of saving his influence from suffering by his own errors." 61

—tired out: "Romola felt even the springs of her once active pity drying up, and leaving her to barren egoistic complaining. Had not *she* had her sorrows too? And few had cared for her, while she had cared for many. She had done enough; she had striven after the impossible, and was weary of this stifling crowded life. She longed for that repose in mere sensation which she had sometimes dreamed of in the sultry afternoons of her early girlhood, when she had fancied herself floating naïad-like in the waters." 61

—floating away: "Romola felt orphaned in those wide spaces of sea and sky. She read no message of love for her in that far-off symbolic writing of the heavens, and with a great sob she wished that she might be gliding into death.

Floating away

"She drew the cowl over her head again and covered her face, choosing darkness rather than the light of the stars, which seemed to her like the hard light of eyes that looked at her without seeing her. Presently she felt that she was in the grave, but not resting there: she was touching the hands of the beloved dead beside her, and trying to wake them." 61

—*a new life:* "Every day the Padre and **Jacopo** and the small flock of surviving villagers paid their visit to this cottage to see the blessed Lady, and to bring her of their best as an offering—honey, fresh cakes. eggs, and polenta. It was a sight they could none of them forget, a sight they all told of in their old age—how the sweet and sainted lady with her fair face, her golden hair, and her brown eyes that had a blessing in them, lay weary with her labours after she had been sent over the sea to help them in their extremity, and how the queer little black **Benedetto** used to crawl about the straw by her side and want everything that was brought to her, and she always gave him a bit of what she took, and told them if they loved her they must be good to Benedetto.

"Many legends were afterwards told in that valley about the blessed Lady who came over the sea, but they were legends by which all who heard might know that in times gone by a woman had done beautiful loving deeds there, rescuing those who were ready to perish." 68

—*rejuvenation:* " . . . from the moment after her waking when the cry had drawn her, she had not even reflected, as she used to do in Florence, that she was glad to live because she could lighten sorrow—she had simply lived, with so energetic an impulse to share the life around her, to answer the call of need and do the work which cried aloud to be done, that the reasons for living, enduring, labouring, never took the form of argument.

"The experience was like a new baptism to Romola. In Florence the simpler relations of the human being to his fellow-men had been complicated for her with all the specialties of marriage, the State, and religious discipleship, and when these had disappointed her trust, the shock seemed to have shaken her aloof from life and stunned her sympathy. But now she said, 'It was mere baseness in me to desire death. If everything else is doubtful, this suffering that I can help is certain; if the glory of the cross is an illusion, the sorrow is only the truer.' " 69

—*reassessment:* "That rare possibility of self-contemplation which comes in any complete severance from our wonted life made her judge herself as she had never done before: the compunction which is inseparable from a sympathetic nature keenly alive to the possible experience of others, began to stir in her with growing force. She questioned the justness of her own conclusions, of her own deeds: she had been rash, arrogant, always dissatisfied that others were not good enough, while she herself had not been true to what her soul had once recognised as the best. She began to condemn her flight: after all, it had been cowardly self-care; the grounds on which **Savonarola** had once taken her back were truer, deeper than the grounds she had had for her second flight. How could she feel the needs of others and not feel, above all, the needs of the nearest?" 69

—*mentor reconsidered:* "Her indignant grief for her godfather had no longer complete possession of her, and her sense of debt to **Savonarola** was recovering predominance. Nothing that had come, or was to come, could do away with the fact that there had been a great inspiration in him which had waked a new life in her." 69

The Visible Madonna

—*new mission:* " . . . she needed something that she was bound specially to care for; she yearned to clasp the children and to make them love her. This at least would be some sweet result, for others as well as herself, from all her past sorrow." 70

—*lesson for a son:* " 'And remember, if you were to choose something lower, and make it the rule of your life to seek your own pleasure and escape from what is disagreeable, calamity might come just the same; and it would be calamity falling on a base mind, which is the one form of sorrow that has no balm in it, and that may well make a man say—'It would have been better for me if I had never been born.' " *E*

Tito Melema

—*aroused:* " . . . lying on the pavement, [he] was looking upward with the startled gaze of a suddenly-awakened dreamer." 1

—*startled:* " 'Anybody might say the saints had sent you a dead body; but if you took the jewels, I hope you buried him—and you can afford a mass or two for him into the bargain.'

"Something like a painful thrill appeared to dart through the frame of the listener, and arrest the careless stretching of his arms and chest. For an instant he turned on **Bratti** with a sharp frown; but he immediately recovered an air of indifference, took off the red Levantine cap which hung like a great purse over his left ear, pushed back his long dark-brown curls . . . . " 1

—*penniless:* " 'Not an obolus, by Jupiter!' he murmured, in a language which was not Tuscan or even Italian. 'I thought I had one poor piece left. I must get my breakfast for love, then!' " 2

—*scolded:* "The young stranger drew back and looked at the speaker with a glance provokingly free from alarm and deprecation, and his slight expression of saucy amusement broke into a broad beaming smile as he surveyed the figure of his threatener . . . .

"There was something irresistibly propitiating in that bright young smile . . . . " 2

—*defended:* "Tito Melema started and looked round with a pale astonishment in his face as if at a sudden accusation; but **Nello** left him no time to feel at a loss for an answer: **'Piero**,' said the barber . . . . 'What trick wilt thou play with the fine visage of this young scholar to make it suit thy traitor? . . . make him a young **Bacchus**, or say rather a **Phoebus Apollo**, for his face is as warm and bright as a summer morning; it made me his friend in the space of a "credo." ' " 4

—*meeting a lady:* "Tito's glance . . . had that gentle, beseeching admiration in it which is the most propitiating of appeals to a proud shy woman, and is perhaps the only atonement a man can make for being too handsome. The finished fascination of his air came chiefly from the absence of demand and assumption. It was that of a fleet, soft-coated, dark-eyed animal that delights you by not bounding away in indifference from you, and unexpectedly pillows its chin on your palm, and looks up at you desiring to be stroked—as if it loved you." 6

—*acquiescent:* "He was pleased that **Bardo** should take an interest in him; and he did not dwell with enough seriousness on the prospect of the work in which he was to be aided, to feel moved by it to anything else than that easy, good-humoured acquiescence which was natural to him." 6

—*equable in success:* "His face wore that bland liveliness, as far removed from excitability as from heaviness or gloom, which marks the companion popular alike amongst men and women—the companion who is never obtrusive or noisy from uneasy vanity or excessive animal spirits, and whose brow is never contracted by resentment or indignation. He showed . . . that added radiance of good fortune, which is like the just perceptible perfecting of a flower after it has drunk a morning's sunbeams." 8

—*reticent:* "Tito had an innate love of reticence—let us say a talent for it—which acted as other impulses do, without any conscious motive, and, like all people to whom concealment is easy, he would now and then conceal something which had as little the nature of a secret as the fact that he had seen a flight of crows." 9

—*falling in love:* "[He remembered] the transient pink flush on **Romola**'s face and neck, which subtracted nothing from her majesty, but only gave it the exquisite charm of womanly sensitiveness, heightened still more by what seemed the paradoxical boy-like frankness of her look and smile . . . he felt himself strangely in subjection to Romola with that simplicity of hers: he felt for the first time, without defining it to himself, that loving awe in the presence of noble womanhood, which is perhaps something like the worship paid of old to a great nature-goddess, who was not all-knowing, but whose life and power were something deeper and more primordial than knowledge." 9

—*simplicity and awe:* "One day in Greece, as he was leaning over a wall in the sunshine, a little black-eyed **peasant girl**, who had rested her water-pot on the wall, crept gradually nearer and nearer to him, and at last shyly asked him to kiss her, putting up her round olive cheek very innocently. Tito was used to love that came in this unsought fashion. But **Romola**'s love would never come in that way: would it ever come at all?—and yet it was that topmost apple on which he had set his mind. He was in his fresh youth—not passionate, but impressible: it was as inevitable that he should feel lovingly towards Romola as that the white irises should be reflected in the clear sunlit stream; but he had no coxcombry, and he had an intimate sense that Romola was something very much above him. Many men have felt the same before a large-eyed, simple child." 9

—*well patronized:* "Tito was thus sailing under the fairest breeze, and besides convincing fair judges that his talents squared with his good fortune, he wore that fortune so easily and unpretentiously that no one had yet been offended by it." 9

—*social gift:* "For where could a handsome young scholar not be welcome when he could touch the lute and troll a gay song? That bright face, that easy smile, that liquid voice, seemed to give life a holiday aspect; just as a strain of gay music and the hoisting of colours make the work-worn and the sad rather ashamed of showing themselves. Here was a professor likely to render the Greek classics amiable to the sons of great houses." 9

—*moral crisis: see* **Baldassarre Calvo**—*present plight* "If he were saying to himself, 'Tito will find me: he had but to carry our manuscripts and gems to Venice; he will have raised money, and will never rest till he finds me out'? If that were certain, could he, Tito, see the price of the gems lying before him, and say, 'I will stay at Florence, where I am fanned by soft airs of promised love and prosperity; I will not risk myself for his sake'? No, surely not, *if it were certain.* But nothing could be farther from certainty . . . . What, probably enough, would be the result if he were to quit Florence and go to Venice; get authoritative letters—yes, he knew that might be done—and set out for the Archipelago? Why, that he should be himself seized, and spend all his florins on preliminaries, and be again a destitute wanderer—with no more gems to sell.

"Tito had a clearer vision of that result than of the possible moment when he might find his father again, and carry him deliverance. It would surely be an unfairness that he, in his full ripe youth . . . should turn his back on promised love and distinction, and perhaps never be visited by that promise again. 'And yet,' he said to himself, 'if I were certain that **Baldassarre Calvo** was alive, and that I could free him, by whatever exertions or perils, I would go now—now I have the money: it was useless to debate the matter before. I would go now to **Bardo** and **Bartolommeo Scala**, and tell them the whole truth.' Tito did not say to himself so distinctly that if those two men had known the whole truth . . . there would have been no alternative for him but to go in search of his benefactor, who, if alive, was the rightful owner of the gems, and whom he had always equivocally spoken of as 'lost'; he did not say to himself—what he was not ignorant of—that Greeks of distinction had made sacrifices, taken voyages again and again, and sought help from crowned and mitred heads for the sake of freeing relatives from slavery to the Turks. Public opinion did not regard this as exceptional virtue." 9

—*retrospect:* "The feelings that gather fervour from novelty will be of little help towards making the world a home for dimmed and faded human beings; and if there is any love of which they are not widowed, it must be the love that is rooted in memories and distils perpetually the sweet balms of fidelity and forbearing tenderness.

"But surely such memories were not absent from Tito's mind? Far in the backward vista of his remembered life, when he was only seven years old, **Baldassarre** had rescued him from blows, had taken him to a home that seemed like opened paradise, where there was sweet food and soothing caresses, all had on Baldassarre's knee; and from that time till the hour they had parted, Tito had been the one centre of Baldassarre's fatherly cares." 9

—*childhood:* "And he had been docile, pliable, quick of apprehension, ready to acquire: a very bright lovely boy, a youth of even splendid grace, who seemed quite without vices, as if that beautiful form represented a vitality so exquis-itely poised and balanced that it could know no uneasy desires, no unrest—a radiant presence for a lonely man to have won for himself. If he were silent when his father expected some response, still he did not look moody; if he declined some labour—why, he flung himself down with such a charming, half-smiling, half-pleading air, that the pleasure of looking at him made amends to one who had watched his growth with a sense of claim and possession: the curves of Tito's mouth had ineffable good-humour in them. And then, the quick talent to which everything came readily, from philosophical systems to the rhymes of a street ballad caught up at a hearing! Would any one have said that Tito had not made a rich return to his benefactor, or that his gratitude and affection would fail on any great demand?

"He did not admit that his gratitude had failed; but *it was not certain* that Baldassarre was in slavery; not certain that he was living." 9

Tito and the Escaped Prisoner

—*his choice:* "When, the next morning, Tito put this determination into act [putting his money out at interest] he had chosen his colour in the game, and had given an inevitable bent to his wishes. He had made it impossible that he should not from henceforth desire it to be the truth that his father was dead, impossible that he should not be tempted to baseness rather than that the precise facts of his conduct should not remain for ever concealed." 9

—*no turning back*: "Besides, in this first distinct colloquy with himself the ideas which had previously been scattered and interrupted had now concentrated themselves; the little rills of selfishness had united and made a channel, so that they could never again meet with the same resistance. Hitherto Tito had left in vague indecision the question whether, with the means in his power, he would not return, and ascertain his father's fate; he had now made a definite excuse to himself for not taking that course; he had avowed to himself a choice which he would have been ashamed to avow to others, and which would have made him ashamed in the resurgent presence of his father." 9

—*seemingly serene:* " . . . he showed all the outward signs of a mind at ease. How should it be otherwise? He never jarred with what was immediately around him, and his nature was too joyous, too unapprehensive, for the hidden and the distant to grasp him in the shape of a dread . . . there was no brand of duplicity on his brow; neither was there any stamp of candour: it was simply a finely-formed, square, smooth young brow.

"And the slow absent glance he cast around at the upper windows of the houses had neither more dissimulation in it, nor more ingenuousness, than belongs to a youthful well-opened eye-lid with its unwearied breadth of gaze; to perfectly pellucid lenses; to the undimmed dark of a rich brown iris, and to a pure cerulean-tinted angle of whiteness streaked with the delicate shadows of long eyelashes.

"Was it that Tito's face attracted or repelled according to the mental attitude of the observer? Was it a cypher with more than one key? The strong, unmistakable expression in his whole air and person was a negative one, and it was perfectly veracious; it declared the absence of any uneasy claim, any restless vanity, and it made the admiration that followed him as he passed among the troop of holiday-makers a thoroughly willing tribute." ¶10

—*his nature:* "Tito's nature was all gentleness." 10

"The softness of his nature required that all sorrow should be hidden away from him." 10

—*self-indulgent:* "Tito had an unconquerable aversion to anything unpleasant, even when an object very much loved and desired was on the other side of it." 10

—*mental coping:* "[He] set himself to throw extra animation into the evening, though all the while his consciousness was at work like a machine with complex action, leaving deposits quite distinct from the line of talk; and by the time he descended the stone stairs and issued from the grim door in the starlight, his mind had really reached a new stage in its formation of a purpose." 11

—*a lie needed:* "Tito had never had occasion to fabricate an ingenious lie before: the occasion was come now—the occasion which circumstance never fails to beget on tacit falsity; and his ingenuity was ready." 11

—*hedonist:* "But, after all, *why* was he bound to go? What, looked at closely, was the end of all life, but to extract the utmost sum of pleasure?

And was not his own blooming life a promise of incomparably more pleasure, not for himself only, but for others, than the withered wintry life of a man who was past the time of keen enjoyment, and whose ideas had stiffened into barren rigidity? Those ideas had all been sown in the fresh soil of Tito's mind, and were lively germs there: that was the proper order of things—the order of nature, which treats all maturity as a mere nidus for youth. **Baldassarre** had done his work, had had his draught of life. Tito said it was *his* turn now." 11

—theft rationalized: "Certainly the gems and therefore the florins were, in a sense, **Baldassarre**'s: in the narrow sense by which the right of possession is determined in ordinary affairs; but in that large and more radically natural view by which the world belongs to youth and strength, they were rather his who could extract the most pleasure out of them. That, he was conscious, was not the sentiment which the complicated play of human feelings had engendered in society. The men around him would expect that he should immediately apply those florins to his benefactor's rescue. But what was the sentiment of society?—a mere tangle of anomalous traditions and opinions, which no wise man would take as a guide except so far as his own comfort was concerned." 11

—gratitude inoperative: "Any maxims that required a man to fling away the good that was needed to make existence sweet, were only the lining of human selfishness turned outward: they were made by men who wanted others to sacrifice themselves for their sake. He would rather that **Baldassarre** should not suffer: he liked no one to suffer; but could any philosophy prove to him that he was bound to care for another's suffering more than for his own? To do so he must have loved Baldassarre devotedly, and he did *not* love him: was that his own fault? Gratitude! seen closely, it made no valid claim: his father's life would have been dreary without him: are we convicted of a debt to men for the pleasures they give themselves?" 11

—anomaly: "Yet **Romola**'s life seemed an image of that loving, pitying devotedness, that patient endurance of irksome tasks, from which he had shrunk and excused himself. But he was not out of love with goodness, or prepared to plunge into vice: he was in his fresh youth, with soft pulses for all charm and loveliness; he had still a healthy appetite for ordinary human joys, and the poison could only work by degrees. He had sold himself to evil, but at present life seemed so nearly the same to him that he was not conscious of the bond." 12

—in love: "And he cared supremely for **Romola**; he wished to have her for his beautiful and loving wife. There might be a wealthier alliance within the ultimate reach of successful accomplishments like his, but there was no woman in all Florence like Romola. When she was near him, and looked at him with her sincere hazel eyes, he was subdued by a delicious influence as strong and inevitable as those musical vibrations which take possession of us with a rhythmic empire that no sooner ceases than we desire it to begin again." 12

—a task: "Tito might have been excused for shrugging his shoulders at the prospect before him, but he was not naturally impatient; moreover, he had been bred up in that laborious erudition, at once minute and copious, which was the chief intellectual task of the age; and with **Ramola** near, he was floated along by waves of agreeable sensation that made everything seem easy." 12

A Kiss

—venal regret: "As Tito kissed **Romola** on their parting that evening, the very strength of the thrill that moved his whole being at the sense that this woman, whose beauty it was hardly possible to think of as anything but the necessary consequence of her noble nature, loved him with all the tenderness that spoke in her clear eyes, brought a strong reaction of regret that he had not kept himself free from that first deceit which had dragged him into the danger of being disgraced before her. There was a spring of bitterness mingling with that fountain of sweets. Would the death of **Fra Luca** arrest it? He hoped it would." 12

—burning words: " ' . . . though, if you had seen your father forsaken by one to whom he had given his chief love—by one in whom he had planted his labour and his hopes—forsaken when his need was becoming greatest—even you, Tito, would find it hard to forgive.'

"What could he say? He was not equal to the hypocrisy of telling **Romola** that such offences ought not to be pardoned, and he had not the courage to utter any words of dissuasion.

" 'You are right, my Romola; you are always right, except in thinking too well of me.'

"There was really some genuineness in those last words, and Tito looked very beautiful as he uttered them, with an unusual pallor in his face, and a slight quivering of his lip." 13

—catastrophe: "**Fra Luca** would tell all he knew and conjectured, and Tito saw no possible falsity by which he could now ward off the worst consequences of his former dissimulation. It was all over with his prospects in Florence . . . . For the first time in his life he felt too fevered and agitated to trust his power of self-command . . . .

"He was at one of those lawless moments which come to us all if we have no guide but desire, and if the pathway where desire leads us seems suddenly closed; he was ready to follow any beckoning that offered him an immediate purpose." 13

—needy: "The absence of presumptuous self-conceit in Tito made him feel all the more defenceless under prospective obloquy: he needed soft looks and caresses too much ever to be impudent . . . .

"Poor little **Tessa** had disappeared behind the curtain among the crowd of peasants; but the love which formed one web with all his worldly hopes, with the ambitions and pleasures that must make the solid part of his days—the love that was identified with his larger self—was not to be banished from his consciousness." 14

—too late a thought: "He cared so much for the pleasures that could only come to him through the good opinion of his fellow-men, that he wished now he had never risked ignominy by shrinking from what his fellowmen called obligations." 16

—modest: "He had never for a moment relied on **Romola**'s passion for him as likely to be too strong for the repulsion created by the discovery of his secret; he had not the presumptuous vanity which might have hindered him from feeling that her love had the same root with her belief in him." 17

—relief: "He was in paradise: disgrace, shame, parting—there was no fear of them any longer. This happiness was too strong to be marred by the sense that **Romola** was deceived in him; nay, he could only rejoice in her delusion; for, after all, concealment had been wisdom. The only thing he

could regret was his needless dread; if, indeed, the dread had not been worth suffering for the sake of this sudden rapture." 17

—reaction: " . . . Tito had at that moment a nauseating weariness of simulation. He was well out of the possible consequences that might have fallen on him from that initial deception, and it was no longer a load on his mind; kind fortune had brought him immunity, and he thought it was only fair that she should. Who was hurt by it? The results to **Baldassarre** were too problematical to be taken into account. But he wanted now to be free from any hidden shackles that would gall him, though ever so little, under his ties to **Romola**. He was not aware that that very delight in immunity which prompted resolutions not to entangle himself again, was deadening the sensibilities which alone could save him from entanglement." 18

—getting ahead: " . . . the bright young Greek who had a tongue that was always ready without ever being quarrelsome, was more and more wished for at gay suppers in the Via Larga, and at Florentine games, in which he had no pretension to excel, and could admire the incomparable skill of **Piero de' Medici** in the most graceful manner in the world." 19

—hint of corruption: "He wore nothing but black, for he was in mourning; but the black was presently to be covered by a red mantle, for he too was to walk in procession as Latin Secretary to the Ten. Tito Melema had become conspicuously serviceable in the intercourse with the French guests, from his familiarity with Southern Italy, and his readiness in the French tongue . . . . The lustre of good fortune was upon him; he was smiling, listening, and explaining, with his usual graceful unpretentious ease, and only a very keen eye bent on studying him could have marked a certain amount of change in him which was not to be accounted for by the lapse of eighteen months. It was that change which comes from the final departure of moral youthfulness—from the distinct self-conscious adoption of a part in life. The lines of the face were as soft as ever, the eyes as pellucid, but something was gone—something as indefinable as the changes in the morning twilight." 22

—hard to insult: ". . . Tito, besides his natural disposition to overcome ill-will by good-humour, had the unimpassioned feeling of the alien towards names and details that move the deepest passions of the native." 22

—a small triumph: "It was a delightful moment for Tito, for he was the only one of the party who could have made so amusing an interpreter, and without any disposition to triumphant self-gratulation he revelled in the sense that he was an object of liking—he basked in approving glances." 22

—confrontation: "The two men looked at each other, silent as death: **Baldassarre**, with dark fierceness and a tightening grip of the soiled worn hands on the velvet-clad arm; Tito, with cheeks and lips all bloodless, fascinated by terror. It seemed a long while to them—it was but a moment . . . .

"The first sound Tito heard was the short laugh of **Piero di Cosimo**, who stood close by him and was the only person that could see his face.

" 'Ha, ha! I know what a ghost should be now.' " 22

—denial: " 'This is another escaped prisoner,' said **Lorenzo Tornabuoni**. 'Who is he, I wonder?'

" *'Some madman, surely,'* said Tito.

"He hardly knew how the words had come to his lips . . . .

"The two men had not taken their eyes off each other, and it seemed to Tito, when he had spoken, that some magical poison had darted from **Baldassarre**'s eyes, and that he felt it rushing through his veins." 22

—physical coward: "Tito shrank with shuddering dread from disgrace; but he had also that physical dread which is inseparable from a soft pleasure-loving nature, and which prevents a man from meeting wounds and death as a welcome relief from disgrace." 23

—a piece missing: "He might have turned back; sought **Baldassarre** again, confessed everything to him—to **Romola**—to all the world. But he never thought of that. The repentance which cuts off all mooring to evil, demands something more than selfish fear. He had no sense that there was strength and safety in truth; the only strength he trusted lay in his ingenuity and his dissimulation." 23 *GE nowhere tells us what Tito experienced before his foster-father rescued him at age seven from the street. His origins are a blank.*

—nonviolent: "It was a characteristic fact in Tito's experience at this crisis, that no direct measures for ridding himself of Baldassarre ever occurred to him. All other possibilities passed through his mind, even to his own flight from Florence; but he never thought of any scheme for removing his enemy. His dread generated no active malignity, and he would still have been glad not to give pain to any mortal. He had simply chosen to make life easy to himself—to carry his human lot, if possible, in such a way that it should pinch him nowhere; and the choice had, at various times, landed him in unexpected positions. The question now was, not whether he should divide the common pressure of destiny with his suffering fellow-men; it was whether all the resources of lying would save him from being crushed by the consequences of that habitual choice." 23

—presence of mind: "His presence of mind . . . had been a ready instrument this time. It was an excellent livery servant that never forsook him when danger was not visible." 26

—frozen: "The terrible resurrection of secret fears, which, if **Romola** had known them, would have alienated her from him for ever, caused him to feel an alienation already begun between them—caused him to feel a certain repulsion towards a woman from whose mind he was in danger. The feeling had taken hold of him unawares, and he was vexed with himself for behaving in this new cold way to her. He could not suddenly command any affectionate looks or words; he could only exert himself to say what might serve as an excuse." 27

—new discovery: "It was very easy, very pleasant, this exercise of speaking to the general satisfaction: a man who knew how to persuade need never be in danger from any party; he could convince each that he was feigning with all the others. The gestures and faces of weavers and dyers were certainly amusing when looked at from above in this way." 29

—softly dishonest: " . . . he could not, on a sudden, master an involuntary shrinking from her, which, by a subtle relation, depended on those very characteristics in him that made him desire not to fail in his marks of affection. He was about to take a step which he knew would arouse her deep indignation; he would have to encounter much that was unpleasant before he could win her forgiveness. And Tito could never find it easy to face displeasure and anger; his nature was one of those most remote from defiance or impudence, and all his inclinations leaned towards preserving **Romola**'s tenderness." 31

—*prisoner of success:* "Success had given him a growing appetite for all the pleasures that depend on an advantageous social position, and at no moment could it look like a temptation to him, but only like a hideous alternative, to decamp under dishonour, even with a bag of diamonds, and incur the life of an adventurer." 31

—*trammelled:* "She was the wife of his first love—he loved her still; she belonged to that furniture of life which he shrank from parting with. He winced under her judgment, he felt uncertain how far the revulsion of her feeling towards him might go; and all that sense of power over a wife which makes a husband risk betrayals that a lover never ventures on, would not suffice to counteract Tito's uneasiness. This was the leaden weight which had been too strong for his will, and kept him from raising his head to meet her eyes. Their pure light brought too near him the prospect of a coming struggle.

"But it was not to be helped; if they had to leave Florence, they must have money; indeed, Tito could not arrange life at all to his mind without a considerable sum of money. And that problem of arranging life to his mind had been the source of all his misdoing. He would have been equal to any sacrifice that was not unpleasant." 31

—*egoistic:* "He was glad of her silence; for, much as he had feared the strength of her feeling, it was impossible for him, shut up in the narrowness that hedges in all merely clever, unimpassioned men, not to overestimate the persuasiveness of his own arguments. His conduct did not look ugly to himself, and his imagination did not suffice to show him exactly how it would look to **Romola**." 32

—*challenge direct*: " 'Have you robbed somebody else, who is *not* dead? Is that the reason you wear armour?'

"**Romola** had been driven to utter the words as men are driven to use the lash of the horsewhip. At first, Tito felt horribly cowed; it seemed to him that the disgrace he had been dreading would be worse than he had imagined it. But soon there was a reaction: such power of dislike and resistance as there was within him was beginning to rise against a wife whose voice seemed like the herald of a retributive fate." 32

—*looking back to love:* "It was true that the kindness was manifested towards a pretty trusting thing whom it was impossible to be near without feeling inclined to caress and pet her; but it was not less true that Tito had movements of kindness towards her apart from any contemplated gain to himself. Otherwise, charming as her prettiness and prattle were in a lazy moment, he might have preferred to be free from her; for he was not in love with **Tessa**—he was in love for the first time in his life with an entirely different woman, whom he was not simply inclined to shower caresses on, but whose presence possessed him so that the simple sweep of her long tresses across his cheek seemed to vibrate through the hours. All the young ideal passion he had in him had been stirred by **Romola**, and his fibre was too fine, his intellect too bright, for him to be tempted into the habit of a gross pleasure-seeker." 34

—*a mistress:* "The elements of kindness and self-indulgence are hard to distinguish in a soft nature like Tito's, and the annoyance he had felt under **Tessa**'s pursuit of him on the day of his betrothal, the thorough intention of revealing the truth to her with which he set out to fulfil his promise of seeing her again, were a sufficiently strong argument to him that in ultimately leaving Tessa under her illusion and providing a home for her, he had been overcome by his own kindness." 34

—needing a respite: " . . . it was **Romola**, and not **Tessa**, that belonged to the world where all the larger desires of a man who had ambition and effective faculties must necessarily lie. But he wanted a refuge from a standard disagreeably rigorous, of which he could not make himself independent simply by thinking it folly; and Tessa's little soul was that inviting refuge." 34

—amends? "Tito was quite . . . unconscious of his own attitude: he was in that wrapt [*sic*] state in which a man will grasp painful roughness, and press and press it closer, and never feel it. A new possibility had risen before him, which might dissolve at once the wretched conditions of fear and suppression that were marring his life. Destiny had brought within his reach an opportunity of retrieving that moment on the steps of the Duomo, when the Past had grasped him with living quivering hands, and he had disowned it A few steps, and he might be face to face with his father, with no witness by; he might seek forgiveness and reconciliation . . . . " 34

—an easy way: "It was not repentance with a white sheet round it and taper in hand, confessing its hated sin in the eyes of men, that Tito was preparing for: it was a repentance that would make all things pleasant again, and keep all past unpleasant things secret. And Tito's soft-heartedness, his indisposition to feel himself in harsh relations with any creature, was in strong activity towards his father, now his father was brought near to him. It would be a state of ease that his nature could not but desire, if the poisonous hatred in **Baldassarre**'s glance could be replaced by something of the old affection and complacency." 34

—comfortableness: "Tito longed to have his world once again completely cushioned with goodwill, and longed for it the more eagerly because of what he had just suffered from the collision with **Romola**. It was not difficult to him to smile pleadingly on those whom he had injured, and offer to do them much kindness: and no quickness of intellect could tell him exactly the taste of that honey on the lips of the injured." 34

—murder foiled: "Tito had felt one great heart-leap of terror as he had staggered under the weight of the thrust: he felt no the triumph of deliverance and safety. His armour had been proved, and vengeance lay helpless before him. But the triumph raised no devilish impulse; on the contrary, the sight of his father close to him and unable to injure him, made the effort at reconciliation easier." 34

—apology: " '*Padre mio!*' There was a pause after those words, but no movement or sound till he said—

" 'I come to ask your forgiveness! . . .

" 'I was taken by surprise that morning. I wish now to be a son to you again. I wish to make the rest of your life happy, that you may forget what you have suffered.' " 34

—coldness withal: "Tito put out his hand to help him, and so strangely quick are men's souls that in this moment, when he began to feel his atonement was accepted, he had a darting thought of the irksome efforts it entailed." 34

A Recognition

—spurned: "If it had been a deep yearning emotion which had brought him to ask his father's forgiveness, the denial of it might have caused him a pang which would have excluded the rushing train of thought that followed [his father's] decisive words. As it was, though the sentence of unchangeable hatred grated on him and jarred him terribly, his mind glanced round with a self-preserving instinct to see how far those words could have the force of a substantial threat." 34

—change of emphasis: "As the freshness of young passion faded, life was taking more and more decidedly for him the aspect of a game in which there was an agreeable mingling of skill and chance." 35

—new perspective: "Tito felt that **Romola** was a more unforgiving woman than he had imagined; her love was not that sweet clinging instinct, stronger than all judgments, which, he began to see now, made the great charm of a wife." R 36

—prospect of power: "Hitherto he had seen success only in the form of favour; it now flashed on him in the shape of power—of such power as is possible to talent without traditional ties, and without beliefs. Each party that thought of him as a tool might become dependent on him. His position as an alien, his indifference to the ideas or prejudices of the men amongst whom he moved, were suddenly transformed into advantages; he became newly conscious of his own adroitness in the presence of a game that he was called on to play. And all the motives which might have made Tito shrink from the triple deceit that came before him as a tempting game, had been slowly strangled in him by the successive falsities of his life." 39

—mortal threat: "He had never yet done an act of murderous cruelty even to the smallest animal that could utter a cry; but at that moment he would have been capable of treading the breath from a smiling child for the sake of his own safety." 39

—trapped: "Nay, so distinct sometimes is the working of a double consciousness within us, that Tito himself, while he triumphed in the apparent verification of his lie, wished that he had never made the lie necessary to himself—wished he had recognised his father on the steps—wished he had gone to seek him—wished everything had been different. But he had borrowed from the terrible usurer Falsehood, and the loan had mounted and mounted with the years, till he belonged to the usurer, body and soul." 39

—reaction in relief: "Tito's heart was palpitating, and the wine tasted no better to him than if it had been blood.

"To-night he had paid a heavier price than ever to make himself safe. He did not like the price, and yet it was inevitable that he should be glad of the purchase.

"And after all he led the chorus. He was in a state of excitement in which oppressive sensations, and the wretched consciousness of something hateful but irrevocable, were mingled with a feeling of triumph which seemed to assert itself as the feeling that would subsist and be master of the morrow." 39

—peripheral vision: " . . . he had the power of seeing everything without seeming to see it." 43

—good cover: " . . . the doubleness of feigning attachment to the popular government, while at heart a Medicean, was common to Tito with more than half the Medicean party. He only feigned with more skill than the rest . . . . " 45

—civility: "Tito and **Romola** never jarred, never remonstrated with each other. They were too hopelessly alienated in their inner life ever to have that contest which is an effort towards agreement." 46

—manipulator: "Tito himself did not much care for the result. He managed his affairs so cleverly, that all results, he considered, must turn to his advantage. Whichever party came uppermost, he was secure of favour and money. That is an indecorously naked statement; the fact, clothed as Tito habitually clothed it, was that his acute mind, discerning the equal hollowness of all parties, took the only rational course in making them subservient to his own interest." 46

—jeopardized: "Tito himself felt that a crisis was come in his married life. The husband's determination to mastery, which lay deep below all blandness and beseechingness, had risen permanently to the surface now, and seemed to alter his face, as a face is altered by a hidden muscular tension with which a man is secretly throttling or stamping out the life from something feeble, yet dangerous." 48

—hardened: "The good-humoured, tolerant Tito, incapable of hatred, incapable almost of impatience, disposed always to be gentle towards the rest of the world, felt himself becoming strangely hard towards this wife whose presence had once been the strongest influence he had known. With all his softness of disposition, he had a masculine effectiveness of intellect and purpose which, like sharpness of edge, is itself an energy, working its way without any strong momentum." 48

—lecture: " 'You are so constituted as to have certain strong impressions inaccessible to reason: I cannot share those impressions, and you have withdrawn all trust from me in consequence. You have changed towards me; it has followed that I have changed towards you. It is useless to take any retrospect. We have simply to adapt ourselves to altered conditions.' " 48

—cutting tongue: " 'Your impetuosity about trifles, **Romola**, has a freezing influence that would cool the baths of **Nero**.' " 48

—turning point: "With the project of leaving Florence as soon as his life there had become a high enough stepping-stone to a life elsewhere, perhaps at Rome or Milan, there was now for the first time associated a desire to be free from **Romola**, and to leave her behind him. She had ceased to belong to the desirable furniture of his life: there was no possibility of an easy relation between them without genuineness on his part. Genuineness implied confession of the past, and confession involved a change of purpose. But Tito had as little bent that way as a leopard has to lap milk when its teeth are grown. From all relations that were not easy and agreeable, we know that Tito shrank: why should he cling to them?" 48

—haven: "And certainly the charm of that bright, gentle-humoured Tito who woke up . . . on a Lenten morning five years before, not having yet given any hostages to deceit, never returned so nearly as in the person of **Naldo**, seated in that straight-backed, carved arm-chair which he had provided for his comfort when he came to see **Tessa** and the children. Tito himself was surprised at the growing sense of relief which he felt in these moments. No guile was needed towards Tessa: she was too ignorant and too innocent to suspect him of anything. And the little voices calling him 'Babbo' were very sweet in his ears for the short while that he heard them. When he thought of leaving Florence, he never thought of leaving Tessa and the little ones behind . . . . Poor **Romola**, with all her self-sacrificing effort, was really helping to

harden Tito's nature by chilling it with a positive dislike which had before had seemed impossible in him; but Tessa kept open the fountains of kindness." 50

—*secret of success:* "The principle of duplicity admitted by the Mediceans on their own behalf deprived them of any standard by which they could measure the trustworthiness of a colleague who had not, like themselves, hereditary interests, alliances, and prejudices, which were intensely Medicean . . . in using Tito's facile ability, they were not keenly awake to the fact that the absence of traditional attachments which made him a convenient agent was also the absence of what among themselves was the chief guarantee of mutual honour." 57

—*a heavy price:* " . . . if he could have chosen, he would have declined to see himself disapproved by men of the world. He had never meant to be disapproved; he had meant always to conduct himself so ably that if he acted in opposition to the standard of other men they should not be aware of it . . . . He shrank from condemnatory judgments as from a climate to which he could not adapt himself. But things were not so plastic in the hands of cleverness as could be wished, and events had turned out inconveniently." 57

—*rationale for treachery:* " . . . was he to relinquish all the agreeable fruits of life because [his friends'] party had failed? . . . Florentines whose passions were engaged in their petty and precarious political schemes might have no self-interest separable from family pride and tenacity in old hatreds and attachments; a modern simpleton who swallowed whole one of the old systems of philosophy, and took the indigestion it occasioned for the signs of a divine afflux or the voice of an inward monitor, might see his interest in a form of self-conceit which he called self-rewarding virtue; fanatics who believed in the coming Scourge and Renovation might see their own interest in a future palm-branch and white robe: but no man of clear intellect allowed his course to be determined by such puerile impulses or questionable inward fumes." 57

—*palpable step downward:* "It was a faint prognostic of that hissing . . . which gave his present conduct the character of an epoch to him, and made him dwell on it with argumentative vindication. It was not that he was taking a deeper step in wrong-doing, for it was not possible that he should feel any tie to the Mediceans to be stronger than the tie to his father; but his conduct to his father had been hidden by successful lying: his present act did not admit of total concealment—in its very nature it was a revelation. And Tito winced under his new liability to disesteem." 57

—*cynicism:* " '**Fra Girolamo** is a man to make one understand that there was a time when the monk's frock was a symbol of power over men's minds rather than over the keys of women's cupboards.' " 62

—*looking good:* "The exceptional reverence was really exacted by the splendour and grace of Tito's appearance, which made his black mantle, with its gold fibula, look like a regal robe, and his ordinary black velvet cap like an entirely exceptional head-dress. The hardening of his cheeks and mouth, which was the chief change in his face since he came to Florence, seemed to a superficial glance only to give his beauty a more masculine character." 63

—*coup of treachery:* "There was no malignity in Tito Melema's satisfaction: it was the mild self-gratulation of a man who has won a game that has employed hypothetic skill, not a game that has stirred the muscles and heated the blood . . . **Fra Girolamo**'s existence had been highly convenient to

Tito Melema, furnishing him with that round of the ladder from which he was about to leap on to a new and smooth footing very much to his heart's content." 65

—*on the run:* "Falsehood had prospered and waxed strong; but it had nourished the twin life, Fear. He no longer wore his armour, he was no longer afraid of **Baldassarre**; but from the corpse of that dead fear a spirit had risen—the undying *habit* of fear. He felt he should not be safe till he was out of this fierce, turbid Florence; and now he was ready to go." 67

—*the end:* "Rigid—rigid still. Those eyes with the half-fallen lids were locked against vengeance. Could it be that he was dead? . . .

"Surely at last the eyelids were quivering: the eyes were no longer rigid. There was a vibrating light in them: they opened wide.

" 'Ah, yes! You see me—you know me!'

"Tito knew him; but he did not know whether it was life or death that had brought him into the presence of his injured father. It might be death—and death might mean this chill gloom with the face of the hideous past hanging over him for ever." 67

—*his wife to his (unknowing) son:* " 'There was a man to whom I was very near, so that I could see a great deal of his life, who made almost every one fond of him, for he was young, and clever, and beautiful, and his manners to all were gentle and kind. I believe, when I first knew him, he never thought of anything cruel or base. But because he tried to slip away from everything that was unpleasant, and cared for nothing else so much as his own safety, he came at last to commit some of the basest deeds—such as make men infamous. He denied his father, and left him to misery; he betrayed every trust that was reposed in him, that he might keep himself safe and get rich and prosperous. Yet calamity overtook him.' " *E*

Will His Eyes Ever Open?

Other Principals

Bardo de' Bardi [H] " 'is so blind that he can see no more of his daughter than, as he says, a glimmering of something bright when she comes very near him: doubtless her golden hair . . . . ' " 3

—*situation:* "In one of these **Neri** houses there lived, however, a descendant of the Bardi . . . a descendant who had inherited the old family pride and energy, the old love of pre-eminence, the old desire to leave a lasting track of his footsteps on the fast-whirling earth. But the family passions lived on in him under altered conditions: the descendant of the Bardi was not a man swift in street warfare, or one who loved to play the signor, fortifying strongholds and asserting the right to hang vassals, or a merchant and usurer of keen daring, who delighted in the generalship of wide commercial schemes: he was a man with a deep-veined hand cramped by much copying of manuscripts, who ate sparing dinners, and wore threadbare clothes, at first from choice and at last from necessity; who sat among his books and his marble fragments of the past, and saw them only by the light of those far-off younger days which still shone in his memory: he was a moneyless, blind old scholar—the Bardo de' Bardi to whom **Nello**, the barber, had promised to introduce the young Greek, **Tito Melema**." 5

—*introduced:* "The blind father sat with head uplifted and turned a little aside towards his daughter, as if he were looking at her. His delicate paleness, set off by the black velvet cap which surmounted his drooping white hair, made all the more perceptible the likeness between his aged features and those of the young maiden . . . . " 5 *And see* **Romola di Bardi**—*introduced*

—*walking:* "While Bardo had been sitting, he had seemed hardly more than sixty: his face, though pale, had that refined texture in which wrinkles and lines are never deep; but now that he began to walk he looked as old as he really was—rather more than seventy; for his tall spare frame had the student's stoop of the shoulders, and he stepped with the undecided gait of the blind." 5

—*closest to his heart:* " 'There will be nothing else to preserve my memory and carry down my name as a member of the great republic of letters—nothing but my library and my collection of antiquities.' " 5

—*bemoaning his fate:* "The old man's voice had become at once loud and tremulous, and a pink flush overspread his proud, delicately-cut features, while the habitually raised attitude of his head gave the idea that behind the curtain of his blindness he saw some imaginary high tribunal to which he was appealing against the injustice of Fame." 5

" '*Inanis?* yes, if it is a lying fame; but not if it is the just meed of labour and a great purpose. I claim my right: it is not fair that the work of my brain and my hands should not be a monument to me—it is not just that my labour should bear the name of another man. It is but little to ask . . . that my name should be over the door—that men should own themselves debtors to the Bardi Library in Florence.' " 5

—*a change:* " 'For my mind, as I have often said, was shut up as by a dam; the plenteous waters lay dark and motionless; but you, my **Tito**, have opened a duct for them, and they rush forward with a force that surprises myself.' " 12

—*enraged:* " 'Silenzio!' said Bardo, in a loud agitated voice . . . .

" 'Donna!' said Bardo, again, 'hear once more my will. Bring no reports about that name to this house; and thou, **Romola**, I forbid thee to ask. My son is dead.'

"Bardo's whole frame seemed vibrating with passion, and no one dared to break silence again." 12

—neglected: "The blind old scholar—whose proud truthfulness would never enter into that commerce of feigned and preposterous admiration which, varied by a corresponding measurelessness in vituperation, made the woof of all learned intercourse—had fallen into neglect even among his fellow-citizens, and when he was alluded to at all, it had long been usual to say that, though his blindness and the loss of his son were pitiable misfortunes, he was tiresome in contending for the value of his own labours; and that his discontent was a little inconsistent in a man who had been openly regardless of religious rites, and who in days past had refused offers made to him from various quarters, on the slight condition that he would take orders, without which it was not easy for patrons to provide for every scholar." 19

—remembered: " 'Your father had a great deal of fire in his eyes when he was young [said **Bernardo**]. It was what I could never understand, that he, with his fiery spirit, which seemed much more impatient than mine, could hang over the books and live with shadows all his life. However, he had put his heart into that.' " 31

Baldassarre Calvo. " ' . . . he made enemies [said his son]—chiefly, I believe, by a certain impetuous candour; and they hindered his advancement, so that he lived in obscurity. And he would never stoop to conciliate: he could never forget an injury.' " 6

—present plight: "If now, under this mid-day sun, on some hot coast far away, a man somewhat stricken in years—a man who long years ago had rescued a little boy from a life of beggary, filth, and cruel wrong, had reared him tenderly, and been to him as a father—if that man were now under this summer sun toiling as a slave, hewing wood and drawing water, perhaps being smitten and buffeted because he was not deft and active?" 9

—irksome: "Baldassarre was exacting; and had got stranger as he got older: he was constantly scrutinising **Tito**'s mind to see whether it answered to his own exaggerated expectations; and age—the age of a thick-set, heavy-browed, bald man beyond sixty, whose intensity and eagerness in the grasp of ideas have long taken the character of monotony and repetition, may be looked at from many points of view without being found attractive." 9

—a call for help: " *'I am sold for a slave: I think they are going to take me to Antioch. The gems alone will serve to ransom me.'* " 10

—emerged: "But the third man remained obstinately silent under all the strokes from the knotted cord . . . he had passed the boundary of old age, and could hardly be less than four or five and sixty. His beard, which had grown long in neglect, and the hair which fell thick and straight round his baldness, were nearly white. His thickset figure was still firm and upright, though emaciated, and seemed to express energy in spite of age—an expression that was partly carried out in the dark eyes and strong dark eyebrows, which had a strangely isolated intensity of colour in the midst of his yellow, bloodless, deep-wrinkled face with its lank grey hairs. And yet there was something fitful in the eyes which contradicted the occasional flash of energy: after looking round with quick fierceness at windows and faces, they fell again with a lost

and wandering look. But his lips were motionless, and he held his hands resolutely down. He would not beg." 22

—*a stumble:* " [He] was only able to recover his balance as he clutched one of the [signori] by the arm.

"It was **Tito Melema** who felt that clutch. He turned his head, and saw the face of his adoptive father, Baldassarre Calvo, close to his own.

"The two men looked at each other, silent as death: Baldassarre, with dark fierceness and tightening grip of the soiled worn hands on the velvet-clad arm; Tito, with cheeks and lips all bloodless, fascinated by terror. It seemed a long while to them—it was but a moment." 22

—*vengeful:* "Baldassarre living, and in Florence, was a living revenge, which would no more rest than a winding serpent would rest until it had crushed its prey. It was not in the nature of that man to let an injury pass unavenged: his love and his hatred were of that passionate fervour which subjugates all the rest of the being, and makes a man sacrifice himself to his passion as if it were a deity to be worshipped with self-destruction." 23

—*mad-looking:* "The old man looked strange and wild; with his eager heart and brain, suffering was likely enough to have produced madness. If it were so, the vengeance that strove to inflict disgrace might be baffled." 23

—*violent:* "Baldassarre belonged to a race to whom the thrust of the dagger seems almost as natural an impulse as the outleap of the tiger's talons." 23

—*in sanctuary:* "The rope indicated plainly enough that he was an escaped prisoner, but in that case the church was a sanctuary which he had a right to claim; his advanced years and look of wild misery were fitted to excite pity rather than alarm; and as he stood motionless, with eyes that soon wandered absently from the wide scene before him to the pavement at his feet, those who had observed his entrance presently ceased to regard him . . . . " 24

—*bewildered:* "Images from the past kept urging themselves upon him like delirious visions strangely blended with thirst and anguish. No distinct thought for the future could shape itself in the midst of that fiery passion: the nearest approach to such thought was the bitter sense of enfeebled powers, and a vague determination to universal distrust and suspicion." 24

—*a cord in tune:* "Among all the human beings present, there was perhaps not one whose frame vibrated more strongly than his to the tones and words of [**Savonarola**]; but it had vibrated like a harp of which all the strings had been wrenched away except one. That threat of a fiery inexorable vengeance—of a future into which the hated sinner might be pursued and held by the avenger in an eternal grapple, had come to him like the promise of an unquenchable fountain to unquenchable thirst . . . . The thunder of denunciation fell on his passion-wrought nerves with all the force of self-evidence: his thought never went beyond it into questions—he was possessed by it as the war-horse is possessed by the clash of sounds. No word that was not a threat touched his consciousness; he had no fibre to be thrilled by it . . . .

" 'I rescued him—I cherished him—if I might clutch his heart-strings for ever! Come, O blessed promise! Let my blood flow; let the fire consume me!' "

"The one cord vibrated to its utmost." 24

—*described:* " 'There was even [said **Romola**] a wretched-looking man, with a rope round his neck—an escaped prisoner, I should think, who had run in for shelter—a very wild-eyed old man: I saw him with great tears rolling down his cheeks, as he looked and listened quite eagerly.' " 27

—a report: " 'I went to the hospital to inquire . . . they said he showed no signs of madness—only took no notice of questions, and seemed to be planting a vine twenty miles off. He was a mysterious old tiger. I should have liked to know something more about him' [said **Piero di Cosimo**]." 29

—cleaned up: "The face of this man was clean-shaven, his hair close-clipped, and he wore a decent felt hat. A single glance would hardly have sufficed to assure any one but **Tito** that this was the face of the escaped prisoner who had laid hold of him on the steps." 29

—his fear: " . . . when the words '*some madman, surely,*' had fallen from **Tito**'s lips, it was not their baseness and cruelty only that had made their viper sting—it was Baldassarre's instantaneous bitter consciousness that he might be unable to prove the words false . . . . He was not mad; for he carried within him that piteous stamp of sanity, the clear consciousness of shattered faculties; he measured his own feebleness." 30

—his caution: "With the first movement of vindictive rage awoke a vague caution, like that of a wild beast that is fierce but feeble—or like that of an insect whose little fragment of earth has given way, and made it pause in a palsy of distrust. It was this distrust, this determination to take no step which might betray anything concerning himself, that had made Baldassarre reject **Piero di Cosimo**'s friendly advances." 30

—appearance now: "No, he was not so changed as that [**Tito** might have failed to recognize him]. He himself had known the wrinkles as they had been three years ago; they were only deeper now: there was the same rough, clumsy skin, making little superficial bosses on the brow, like so many cipher-marks; the skin was only yellower, only looked more like a lifeless rind. That shaggy white beard—it was no disguise to eyes that had looked closely at him for sixteen years . . . . There was something different in his glance, but it was a difference that should only have made the recognition of him the more startling; for is not a known voice all the more thrilling when it is heard as a cry? But the doubt was folly: he had felt that Tito knew him . . . .

"Was there something wandering and imbecile in his face—something like what he felt in his mind?" 30

—lost memory and knowledge: see Topicon M:Mind*—damaged*

—his discovery: "A man at Genoa, on whose finger he had seen Tito's ring, had told him that he bought that ring at Florence, of a young Greek, well dressed, and with a handsome dark face . . . . Until then he had clung with all the tenacity of his fervent nature to his faith in **Tito**, and had not for a moment believed himself to be wilfully forsaken." 30

—despair and hope: " . . . the illness had come from which he had risen with body and mind so shattered that he was worse than worthless to his owners, except for the sake of the ransom that did not come . . . . Sitting in his new feebleness and despair, supporting his head between his hands, with blank eyes and lips that moved uncertainly, he looked so much like a hopelessly imbecile old man, that his owners were contented to be rid of him . . . there was still a hope for Baldassarre—faint, perhaps, and likely to be long deferred, but still a hope, that he might find his child, his cherished son again; might yet again clasp hands and meet face to face with the one being who remembered him as he had been before his mind was broken." 30

'But You will Help Me?'

—revenge: "And now again Baldassarre said, 'I am not alone in the world; I shall never be alone, for my revenge is with me.'

"It was as the instrument of that revenge, as something merely external and subservient to his true life, that he bent down again to examine himself with hard curiosity—not, he thought, because he had any care for a withered, forsaken old man, whom nobody loved, whose soul was like a deserted home, where the ashes were cold upon the hearth, and the walls were bare of all but the marks of what had been." 30

—a sort of love: " 'I was a loving fool—I worshipped a woman once, and believed she could care for me; and then I took a helpless child and fostered him; and I watched him as he grew, to see if he would care for me only a little —care for me over and above the good he got from me. I would have torn open my breast to warm him with my life-blood if I could only have seen him care a little for the pain of my wound.

" 'I have laboured, I have strained to crush out of this hard life one drop of unselfish love. Fool! men love their own delights; there is no delight to be had in me. And yet I watched till I believed I saw what I watched for. When he was a child he lifted soft eyes towards me, and held my hand willingly: I thought, this boy will surely love me a little: because I give my life to him and strive that he shall know no sorrow, he will care a little when I am thirsty—the drop he lays on my parched lips will be a joy to him . . .

" 'Curses on him! I wish I may see him lie with those red lips white and dry as ashes, and when he looks for pity I wish he may see my face rejoicing in his pain. It is all a lie—this world is a lie—there is no goodness but in hate. Fool! not one drop of love came with all your striving: life has not given you one drop. But there are deep draughts in this world for hatred and revenge. I have memory left for that, and there is strength in my arm—there is strength in my will—and if I can do nothing but kill him——' " ¶30

—drawn-out revenge: "His whole soul had been thrilled into immediate unreasoning belief in that eternity of vengeance where he, an undying hate, might clutch for ever an undying traitor, and hear that fair smiling hardness cry and moan with anguish." 30

—work? "He wondered whether the sight of written characters would so stimulate his faculties that he might venture to try and find work as a copyist: that might win him some credence for his past scholarship. But no! he dared trust neither hand nor brain. He must be content to do the work that was most like that of a beast of burden: in this mercantile city many porters must be wanted, and he could at least carry weights. Thanks to the justice that struggled in this confused world in behalf of vengeance, his limbs had got back some of their old sturdiness. He was stripped of all else that men would give coin for." 30

—description: " 'His face is yellow, and he has deep marks in it; and his hair is white, but there is none on the top of his head: and his eyebrows are black, and he looks from under them at me, and says, "Poor thing!" to me, as if he thought I was beaten as I used to be; and that seems as if he couldn't be in his right mind, doesn't it? And I asked him his name once, but he couldn't tell it me: yet everybody has a name . . . . ' " 34

—blankness: "He was in one of his most wretched moments of conscious helplessness: he had been poring, while it was light, over the book that lay open beside him; then he had been trying to recall the names of his jewels, and the symbols engraved on them; and though at certain other times he had

recovered some of those names and symbols, to-night they were all gone into darkness. And this effort at inward seeing had seemed to end in utter paralysis of memory." 34

—monomania: "He was reduced to a sort of mad consciousness that he was a solitary pulse of just rage in a world filled with defiant baseness. He had clutched and unsheathed his dagger, and for a long while had been feeling its edge, his mind narrowed to one image, and the dream of one sensation—the sensation of plunging that dagger into a base heart, which he was unable to pierce in any other way." 34

—one idea: " 'I saved you—I nurtured you—I loved you. You forsook me—you robbed me—you denied me. What can you give me? You have made the world bitterness to me; but there is one draught of sweetness left—*that you shall know agony.'* " 34

—lucid memory: " . . . Baldassarre was sitting in that state of after-tremor known to every one who is liable to great outbursts of passion: a state in which physical powerlessness is sometimes accompanied by an exceptional lucidity of thought, as if that disengagement of excited passion had carried away a fire-mist and left clearness behind it. He felt unable to rise and walk away just yet; his limbs seemed benumbed; he was cold, and his hands shook. But in that bodily helplessness he sat surrounded, not by the habitual dimness and vanishing shadows, but by the clear images of the past; he was living again in an unbroken course through that life which seemed a long preparation for the taste of bitterness." 38

—fixation: " . . . a dark deity in the inmost cell . . . his thoughts centred themselves on **Tito**. That fair slippery viper could not escape him now; thanks to struggling justice, the heart that never quivered with tenderness for another had its sensitive selfish fibres that could be reached by the sharp point of anguish. The soul that bowed to no right, bowed to the great lord of mortals, Pain." 38

—focus: "Baldassarre felt the indestructible independent force of a supreme emotion, which knows no terror, and asks for no motive, which is itself an ever-burning motive, consuming all other desire. And now in this morning light, when the assurance came again that the fine fibres of association were active still, and that his recovered self had not departed, all his gladness was but the hope of vengeance." 38

—preparation useless: "Baldassarre . . . had been making anew the digest of the evidence he would bring to prove his identity and **Tito**'s baseness, recalling the description and history of his gems, and assuring himself by rapid mental glances that he could attest his learning and his travels. It might be partly owing to this nervous strain that the new shock of rage he felt as Tito's lie fell on his ears brought a strange bodily effect with it: a cold stream seemed to rush over him, and the last words of the speech seemed to be drowned by ringing chimes. Thought gave way to a dizzy horror, as if the earth were slipping away from under him." 39

—appearance against him: "And the originally common type of Baldassarre's person, coarsened by years of hardship, told as a confirmation of **Tito**'s lie. If Baldassarre, to begin with, could have uttered precisely the words he had premeditated, there might have been something in the form of his accusation which would have given it the stamp not only of true experience but of mental refinement. But there had been no such testimony in his impulsive agitated words: and there seemed the very opposite testimony in

the rugged face and the coarse hands that trembled beside it, standing out in strong contrast in the midst of that velvet-clad, fair-handed company." 39

—stunned: "Baldassarre was still in that half-stunned state in which he was susceptible to any prompting, in the same way as an insect that forms no conception of what the prompting leads to." 39

—after prison: "Those wild dark eyes opening in the sallow deep-lined face, with the white beard, which was now long again, were like an unmistakable signature to a remembered handwriting." 42

—revived: "There was a striking change in him: the blank, dreamy glance of a half-returned consciousness had given place to a fierceness which, as [**Romola**] advanced and spoke to him, flashed upon her as if she had been its object. It was the glance of caged fury that sees its prey passing safe beyond the bars." 44

—lying in wait: "His long imprisonment had so intensified his timid suspicion and his belief in some diabolic fortune favouring **Tito**, that he had not dared to pursue him, except under cover of a crowd or of the darkness; he felt, with instinctive horror, that if Tito's eyes fell upon him, he should again be held up to obloquy, again be dragged away; his weapon would be taken from him, and he should be cast helpless into a prison-cell. His fierce purpose had become as stealthy as a serpent's, which depends for its prey on one dart of the fang." 50

—obsession: "Both these wives had been kind to Baldassarre, and their acts towards him, being bound up with the very image of them, had not vanished from his memory; yet the thought of their pain could not present itself to him as a check. To him it seemed that pain was the order of the world for all except the hard and base. If any were innocent, if any were noble, where could the utmost gladness lie for them? Where it lay for him—in unconquerable hatred and triumphant vengeance." 50

—destitute and hopeless: "His knife was gone, and he was too feeble in body to win another by work, too feeble in mind, even if he had had the knife, to contrive that it should serve its one purpose. He was a shattered, bewildered, lonely old man; yet he desired to live: he waited for something of which he had no distinct vision—something dim, formless—that startled him, and made strong pulsations within him, like that unknown thing which we look for when we start from sleep, though no voice or touch has waked us." 67

Girolamo Savonarola [H]. "That very Quaresima or Lent of 1492 in which he died, still in his erect old age, [**Lorenzo de' Medici**] had listened in San Lorenzo, not without a mixture of satisfaction, to the preaching of a Dominican Friar . . . who denounced with a rare boldness the worldliness and vicious habits of the clergy, and insisted on the duty of Christian men not to live for their own ease when wrong was triumphing in high places, and not to spend their wealth in outward pomp even in the churches, when their fellow-citizens were suffering from want and sickness. The Frate carried his doctrine rather too far for elderly ears, yet it was a memorable thing to see a preacher move his audience to such a pitch that the women even took off their ornaments, and delivered them to be sold for the benefit of the needy." *P*

—face: " 'Your Fra Girolamo has a high nose and a large under-lip. I saw him once—he is not handsome . . . . ' " 8 *See* page 235

—his voice: " 'Kneel, my daughter, for the Angel of Death is present, and waits while the message of heaven is delivered: bend thy pride before it is

bent for thee by a yoke of iron,' said a strong rich voice, startlingly in contrast with **Fra Luca**'s.

"The tone was not that of imperious command, but of quiet self-possession and assurance of the right, blended with benignity." 15

—his hands: " . . . her eyes fell at once on his hands, which were folded across his breast and lay in relief on the edge of his black mantle. They had a marked physiognomy which enforced the influence of the voice: they were very beautiful and almost of transparent delicacy." 15

—his face: " . . . the features of the monk had the full light of the tapers on them. They were very marked features, such as lend themselves to popular description. There was the high arched nose, the prominent under lip, the coronet of thick dark hair above the brow, all seeming to tell of energy and passion; there were the blue-grey eyes, shining mildly under auburn eyelashes, seeming, like the hands, to tell of acute sensitiveness." 15

—the voice again: " 'Kneel, my daughter,' the penetrating voice said again, 'the pride of the body is a barrier against the gifts that purify the soul.'

"He was looking at her with mild fixedness while he spoke, and again she felt that subtle mysterious influence of a personality by which it has been given to some rare men to move their fellows." 15

—power: "His audience, some of whom were held to be among the choicest spirits of the age—the most cultivated men in the most cultivated of Italian cities . . . listened with shuddering awe. For this man had a power rarely paralleled, of impressing his beliefs on others, and of swaying very various minds. And as long as four years ago he had proclaimed from the chief pulpit of Florence that a scourge was about to descend on Italy, and that by this scourge the Church was to be purified. Savonarola appeared to believe, and his hearers more or less waveringly believed, that he had a mission like that of the Hebrew prophets, and that the Florentines amongst whom his message was delivered were in some sense a second chosen people . . . .

"While in others the gift of prophecy was very much like a farthing candle illuminating small corners of human destiny with prophetic gossip, in Savonarola it was like a mighty beacon shining far out for the warning and guidance of men. And to some of the soberest minds the supernatural character of his insight into the future gathered a strong attestation from the peculiar conditions of the age." ¶21

—revelation: "In brilliant Ferrara, seventeen years before, the contradiction between men's lives and their professed beliefs had pressed upon him with a force that had been enough to destroy his appetite for the world, and at the age of twenty-three had driven him into the cloister. He believed that God had committed to the Church the sacred lamp of truth for the guidance and salvation of men, and he saw that the Church, in its corruption, had become a sepulchre to hide the lamp." 21

—personal view: "But the real force of demonstration for Girolamo Savonarola lay in his own burning indignation at the sight of wrong; in his fervent belief in an Unseen Justice that would put an end to the wrong, and in an Unseen Purity to which lying and uncleanness were an abomination. To his ardent, power-loving soul, believing in great ends, and longing to achieve those ends by the exertion of its own strong will, the faith in a supreme and righteous Rule became one with the faith in a speedy divine interposition that would punish and reclaim." 21

—*his message:* " 'And forasmuch as it is written that God will do nothing but he revealeth it to his servants the prophets, he has chosen me, his unworthy servant, and made his purpose present to my soul in the living word of the Scriptures, and in the deeds of his providence; and by the ministry of angels he has revealed it to me in visions. And his word possesses me so that I am but as the branch of the forest when the wind of heaven penetrates it, and it is not in me to keep silence, even though I may be a derision to the scorner. And for four years I have preached in obedience to the Divine will: in the face of scoffing I have preached three things, which the Lord has delivered to me: that *in these times God will regenerate his Church,* and that *before the regeneration must come the scourge over all Italy,* and that *these things will come quickly.'* " 24

—*sudden silence:* "His silence, instead of being the signal for small movements amongst his audience, seemed to be as strong a spell to them as his voice. Through the vast area of the cathedral men and women sat with faces upturned, like breathing statues, till the voice was heard again . . . . " 24

—*climax:* "Every changing tone, vibrating through the audience, shook them into answering emotion. There were plenty among them who had very moderate faith in the Frate's prophetic mission, and who in their cooler moments loved him little; nevertheless, they too were carried along by the great wave of feeling which gathered its force from sympathies that lay deeper than all theory. A loud responding sob rose at once from the wide multitude, while Savonarola had fallen on his knees and buried his face in his mantle. He felt in that moment the rapture and glory of martyrdom without its agony." 24

—*his preaching:* "Perhaps, while no preacher ever had a more massive influence than Savonarola, no preacher ever had more heterogeneous materials to work upon. And one secret of the massive influence lay in the highly mixed character of his preaching . . . there were strains that appealed to the very finest susceptibilities of men's natures, and there were elements that gratified low egoism, tickled gossiping curiosity, and fascinated timorous superstition." 25

—*his egoism:* "His need of personal predominance, his labyrinthine allegorical interpretations of the Scriptures, his enigmatic visions, and his false certitude about the Divine intentions, never ceased, in his own large soul, to be ennobled by that fervid piety, that passionate sense of the infinite, that active sympathy, that clear-sighted demand for the subjection of selfish interests to the general good, which he had in common with the greatest of mankind. But for the mass of his audience all the pregnancy of his preaching lay in his strong assertion of supernatural claims, in his denunciatory visions, in the false certitude which gave his sermons the interest of a political bulletin; and having once held that audience in his mastery, it was necessary to his nature—it was necessary for their welfare—that he should *keep* the mastery. The effect was inevitable. No man ever struggled to retain power over a mixed multitude without suffering vitiation; his standard must be their lower needs and not his own best insight." 25

—*his character:* "The mysteries of human character have seldom been presented in a way more fitted to check the judgments of facile knowingness than in Girolamo Savonarola; but we can give him a reverence that needs no shutting of the eyes to fact, if we regard his life as a drama in which there were great inward modifications accompanying the outward changes. And up to this period, when his more direct action on political affairs had only just begun, it is probable that his imperious need of ascendancy had burned undiscernibly in the strong flame of his zeal for God and man." 25

—flawed: "It was the fashion of old, when an ox was led out for sacrifice to **Jupiter**, to chalk the dark spots, and give the offering a false show of unblemished whiteness. Let us fling away the chalk, and boldly say—the victim is spotted, but it is not therefore in vain that his mighty heart is laid on the altar of men's highest hopes." 25

—political leader: "To Savonarola . . . . The Great Council was the only practicable plan for giving an expression to the public will large enough to counteract the vitiating influence of party interests: it was a plan that would make honest impartial public action at least possible. And the purer the government of Florence would become—the more secure from the designs of men who saw their own advantage in the moral debasement of their fellows— the nearer would the Florentine people approach the character of a pure community, worthy to lead the way in the renovation of the Church and the world. And Fra Girolamo's mind never stopped short of that sublimest end: the objects towards which he felt himself working had always the same moral magnificence. He had no private malice—he sought no party gratification. Even in the last terrible days, when ignominy, torture, and the fear of torture, had laid bare every hidden weakness of his soul, he could say to his importunate judges: 'Do not wonder if it seems to you that I have told but few things; for my purposes were few and great.' " 35

—spiritual power: *see Topicon* S:Duty*—the call*

—priorities: " . . . whose preaching never insisted on gifts to the invisible powers, but only on help to visible need . . . . " 43

"His burning indignation against the abuses and oppression that made the daily story of the Church and of States had kindled the ready fire in [**Romola**] too. His special care for liberty and purity of government in Florence, with his constant reference of this immediate object to the wider end of a universal regeneration, had created in her a new consciousness of the great drama of human existence in which her life was a part . . . . " 44

—enemies: " 'He is accumulating three sorts of hatred on his head [said **Macchiavelli**]—the hatred of average mankind against every one who wants to lay on them a strict yoke of virtue; the hatred of the stronger powers in Italy who want to farm Florence for their own purposes; and the hatred of the people, to whom he has ventured to promise good in this world, instead of confining his promises to the next.' " 45

—nearing his peak: " . . . he knew that excommunication was imminent, and he had reached the point of defying it. He held up the condition of the Church in the terrible mirror of his unflinching speech, which called things by their right names and dealt in no polite periphrases; he proclaimed with heightening confidence the advent of renovation—of a moment when there would be a general revolt against corruption. As to his own destiny, he seemed to have a double and alternating prevision: sometimes he saw himself taking a glorious part in that revolt, sending forth a voice that would be heard through all Christendom, and making the dead body of the Church tremble into new life, as the body of **Lazarus** trembled when the Divine voice pierced the sepulchre; sometimes he saw no prospect for himself but persecution and martyrdom:— this life for him was only a vigil, and only after death would come the dawn." 52

—driven to extremes: "It followed that the spirit of contention and self-vindication pierced more and more conspicuously in his sermons; that he was urged to meet the popular demands not only by increased insistence and detail concerning visions and private revelations, but by a tone of defiant confidence against objectors; and from having denounced the desire for the miraculous, and declared that miracles had no relation to true faith, he had come to assert that at the right moment the Divine power would attest the truth of his prophetic preaching by a miracle. And continually, in the rapid transitions of excited feeling, as the vision of triumphant good receded behind the actual predominance of evil, the threats of coming vengeance against vicious tyrants and corrupt priests gathered some impetus from personal exasperation, as well as from indignant zeal." 52

—adherent: "[**Romola**] could not witness the silencing and excommunication of a man whose distinction from the great mass of the clergy lay, not in any heretical belief, not in his superstitions, but in the energy with which he sought to make the Christian life a reality, without feeling herself drawn strongly to his side." 55

—hardened: "Owing to his seclusion since he had been excommunicated, it had been an unusually long while since she had seen him, and the last months had visibly deepened in his face the marks of over-taxed mental activity and bodily severities; and yet **Romola** was not so conscious of this change as of another, which was less definable. Was it that the expression of serene elevation and pure human fellowship which had once moved her was no longer present in the same force, or was it that the sense of his being divided from her in her feeling about her god-father roused the slumbering sources of alienation, and marred her own vision? Perhaps both causes were at work . . . .

"It was true that Savonarola's glance at Romola had some of the hardness which is caused by an egotistic prepossession." 59

—but noble: "Savonarola was too keen not to divine something of the conflict that was arresting her—too noble, deliberately to assume in calm speech that self-justifying evasiveness into which he was often hurried in public by the crowding impulses of the orator." 59

—fairly stung: "Savonarola had that readily-roused resentment towards opposition, hardly separable from a power-loving and powerful nature, accustomed to seek great ends that cast a reflected grandeur on the means by which they are sought. His sermons have much of that red flame in them. And if he had been a meaner man his susceptibility might have shown itself in irritation at **Romola**'s accusatory freedom, which was in strong contrast with the deference he habitually received from his disciples." 59

—the struggle of his life: "But at this moment such feelings were nullified by that hard struggle which made half the tragedy of his life—the struggle of a mind possessed by a never-silent hunger after purity and simplicity, yet caught in a tangle of egoistic demands, false ideas, and difficult outward conditions, that made simplicity impossible." 59

—at last unmoved: "Keenly alive to all the suggestions of **Romola**'s remonstrating words, he was rapidly surveying, as he had done before, the courses of action that were open to him, and their probable results. But it was a question on which arguments could seem decisive only in proportion as they were charged with feeling, and he had received no impulse that could alter his bias." 59

—*intimidating:* "But the stillness was not broken, for the Frate's audiences with Heaven were yet charged with electric awe for that mixed multitude, so that those who had already the will to stone him felt their arms unnerved." 62

—*again his hands:* "Then he stretched out his hands, which, in their exquisite delicacy, seemed transfigured from an animal organ for grasping into vehicles of sensibility too acute to need any gross contact: hands that came like an appealing speech from that part of his soul which was masked by his strong passionate face, written on now with deeper lines about the mouth and brow than are made by forty-four years of ordinary life." 62

—*his essential need:* "After the utterance of this blessing, Savonarola himself fell on his knees and hid his face in temporary exhaustion. Those great jets of emotion were a necessary part of his life; he himself had said to the people long ago, 'Without preaching I cannot live.' But it was a life that shattered him." 62

—*a timely ray of sun:* "It was his last moment of untroubled triumph, and in its rapturous confidence he felt carried to a grander scene yet to come, before an audience that would represent all Christendom, in whose presence he should again be sealed as the messenger of the supreme righteousness, and feel himself full charged with Divine strength." 62

—*political analysis:* " 'The Frate, wanting to be master, and to carry out his projects against the Pope, requires the lever of a foreign power, and requires Florence as a fulcrum. I used to think him a narrow-minded bigot, but now, I think him a shrewd ambitious man who knows what he is aiming at. . . .' " 63

—*his conscience:* "But under this particular white tunic there was a heart beating with a consciousness inconceivable to the average monk, and perhaps hard to be conceived by any man who has not arrived at self-knowledge through a tumultuous inner life: a consciousness in which irrevocable errors and lapses from veracity were so entwined with noble purposes and sincere beliefs, in which self-justifying expediency was so inwoven with the tissue of a great work which the whole being seemed as unable to abandon as the body was unable to abandon glowing and trembling before the objects of hope and fear, that it was perhaps impossible, whatever course might be adopted, for the conscience to find perfect repose." 64

—*the problem of a miracle:* "Not that Savonarola had uttered and written a falsity when he declared his belief in a future supernatural attestation of his work; but his mind was so constituted that while it was easy for him to believe in a miracle which, being distant and undefined, was screened behind the strong reasons he saw for its occurrence, and yet easier for him to have a belief in inward miracles such as his own prophetic inspiration and divinely-wrought intuitions; it was at the same time insurmountably difficult to him to believe in the probability of a miracle which, like this of being carried unhurt through the fire, pressed in all its details on his imagination and involved a demand not only for belief but for exceptional action." 64

—*his complex nature:* "[It] was one of those in which opposing tendencies coexist in almost equal strength: the passionate sensibility which, impatient of definite thought, floods every idea with emotion and tends towards contemplative ecstasy, alternated in him with a keen perception of outward facts and a vigorous practical judgment of men and things." 64

—expression: "The muscles of Fra Girolamo's face were eminently under command, as must be the case with all men whose personality is powerful, and in deliberate speech he was habitually cautious, confiding his intentions to none without necessity. But under any strong mental stimulus, his eyes were liable to a dilatation and added brilliancy that no strength of will could control." 64

—rain intervenes: "As that rain fell, and plashed on the edge of the Loggia, and sent spray over the altar and all garments and faces, the Frate knew that the demand for him to enter the fire was at an end. But he knew too, with a certainty as irresistible as the damp chill that had taken possession of his frame, that the design of his enemies was fulfilled, and that his honour was not saved." 65

—after torture: "It must be clear to all impartial men that if this examination represented the only evidence against the Frate, he would die, not for any crime, but because he had made himself inconvenient to the Pope, to the rapacious Italian States that wanted to dismember their Tuscan neighbour, and to those unworthy citizens who sought to gratify their private ambition in opposition to the common weal.

"Not a shadow of political crime had been proved against him. Not one stain had been detected on his private conduct: his fellow-monks, including one who had formerly been his secretary for several years, and who, with more than the average culture of his companions, had a disposition to criticise Fra Girolamo's rule as Prior, bore testimony, even after the shock of his retractation, to an unimpeachable purity and consistency in his life, which had commanded their unsuspecting veneration." 70

—conclusion: "Even in this confession, and without expurgation of the notary's [**Ceccone**'s] malign phrases, Fra Girolamo shone forth as a man who had sought his own glory indeed, but sought it by labouring for the very highest end—the moral welfare of men—not by vague exhortations, but by striving to turn beliefs into energies that would work in all the details of life." 71

—superiority manifest: "It was the habit of Savonarola's mind to conceive great things, and to feel that he was the man to do them. Iniquity should be brought low; the cause of justice, purity, and love should triumph; and it should triumph by his voice, by his work, by his blood. In moments of ecstatic contemplation, doubtless, the sense of self melted in the sense of the Unspeakable, and in that part of his experience lay the elements of genuine self-abasement; but in the presence of his fellow-men for whom he was to act, pre-eminence seemed a necessary condition of his life." 71

—sad consequence: "Every vulgar self-ignorant person in Florence was glibly pronouncing on this man's demerits, while *he* was knowing a depth of sorrow which can only be known to the soul that has loved and sought the most perfect thing, and beholds itself fallen." 71

—martyr: "There is no jot of worthy evidence that from the time of his imprisonment to the supreme moment, Savonarola thought or spoke of himself as a martyr. The idea of martyrdom had been to him a passion dividing the dream of the future with the triumph of beholding his work achieved. And now, in place of both, had come a resignation which he called by no glorifying name.

"*But therefore he may the more fitly be called a martyr by his fellow-men to all time.* For power rose against him not because of his sins, but because of his greatness—not because he sought to deceive the world, but because he sought to make it noble. And through that greatness of his he endured a double agony: not only the reviling, and the torture, and the death-throe, but the agony of sinking from the vision of glorious achievement into that deep shadow where he could only say, 'I count as nothing: darkness encompasses me: yet the light I saw was the true light.' " 71 *Emphasis is Eliot's*

The City of Florence

—arts in cultivation: "It was his pride besides, that he was duly tinctured with the learning of his age, and judged not altogether with the vulgar, but in harmony with the ancients: he, too, in his prime, had been eager for the most correct manuscripts, and had paid many florins for antique vases and for disinterred busts of the ancient immortals—some, perhaps, *truncis naribus,* wanting as to the nose, but not the less authentic; and in his old age had had made haste to look at the first sheets of that fine **Homer** which was among the early glories of the Florentine press." *P*

—mind: "Our resuscitated Spirit was not a pagan philosopher, nor a philosophising pagan poet, but a man of the fifteenth century, inheriting its strange web of belief and unbelief, of Epicurean levity and fetichistic dread; of pedantic impossible ethics uttered by rote, and crude passions acted out with childish impulsiveness; of inclination towards a self-indulgent paganism, and inevitable subjection to that human conscience which, in the unrest of a new growth, was filling the air with strange prophecies and presentiments." *P*

—prototype: "He loved his honours and his gains, the business of his counting-house, of his guild, of the public council-chamber; he loved his enmities too, and fingered the white bean which was to keep a hated name out of the *borsa* with more complacency than if it had been a golden florin. He loved to strengthen his family by a good alliance, and went home with a triumphant light in his eyes after concluding a satisfactory marriage for his son or daughter under his favourite loggia in the evening cool; he loved his game at chess under that same loggia, and his biting jest, and even his coarse joke, as not beneath the dignity of a man eligible for the highest magistracy.

"He had gained an insight into all sorts of affairs at home and abroad: he had been of the 'Ten' who managed the war department, of the 'Eight' who attended to home discipline, of the Priori or Signori who were the heads of the executive government; he had even risen to the supreme office of Gonfaloniere; he had made one in embassies to the Pope and to the Venetians; and he had been commissary to the hired army of the Republic, directing the inglorious bloodless battles in which no man died of brave breast wounds—*virtuosi colpi*—but only of casual falls and tramplings. And in this way he had learned to distrust men without bitterness; looking on life mainly as a game of skill, but not dead to traditions of heroism and clean-handed honour." ¶*P*

—religion: " . . . look, if you will, into the churches, and hear the same chants, see the same images as of old—the images of willing anguish for a great end, of beneficent love and ascending glory; see upturned living faces, and lips moving to the old prayers for help. These things have not changed. The sunlight and shadows bring their old beauty and waken the old heart-strains at morning, noon, and eventide; the little children are still the symbol of the eternal marriage between love and duty; and men still yearn for the reign of peace and righteousness—still own *that* life to be the highest which is a conscious voluntary sacrifice." *P*

Florence in the late Fifteenth Century

—growth: "The name of Florence had been growing prouder and prouder in all the courts of Europe, nay, in Africa itself, on the strength of purest gold coinage, finest dyes and textures, preeminent statesmanship and banking: it was a name so omnipresent that a Pope with a turn for epigram had called Florentines 'the fifth element.' " 8

—reservations: " 'There is something grim and grave to me always about Florence,' said **Tito** . . . 'and even in its merriment there is something shrill and hard—biting rather than gay.' " 17

—Carnival: "It was the last week of the Carnival, and the streets of Florence were at their fullest and noisiest: there were the masqued processions, chanting songs, indispensable now they had once been introduced by **Lorenzo** the Magnificent; there was the favourite rigoletto, or round dance, footed 'in piazza' under the blue frosty sky; there were practical jokes of all sorts, from throwing comfits to throwing stones—especially stones. For the boys and striplings, always a strong element in Florentine crowds, became at the height of Carnival-time as loud and unmanageable as tree-crickets, and it was their immemorial privilege to bar the way with poles to all passengers, until a tribute had been paid towards furnishing those lovers of strong sensations with suppers and bonfires: to conclude with the standing entertainment of stone-throwing, which was not entirely monotonous, since the consequent maiming was various, and it was not always a single person who was killed.

"So the pleasures of the Carnival were of a checkered kind, and if a painter were called upon to represent them truly, he would have to make a picture in which there would be so much grossness and barbarity that it must be turned with its face to the wall, except when it was taken down for the grave historical purpose of justifying a reforming zeal which, in ignorance of the facts, might be unfairly condemned for its narrowness. Still there was much of that more innocent picturesque merriment which is never wanting among a people with quick animal spirits and sensitive organs: there was not the heavy sottishness which belongs to the thicker northern blood, nor the stealthy fierceness which in the more southern regions of the peninsula makes the brawl lead to the dagger-thrust." ¶20

—politics: "Life had its zest for the old Florentine . . . . His politics had an area as wide as his trade, which stretched from Syria to Britain, but they had also the passionate intensity, and the detailed practical interest, which could belong only to a narrow scene of corporate action; only to the members of a community shut in close by the hills and by walls of six miles' circuit, where men knew each other as they passed in the street, set their eyes every day on the memorials of their commonwealth, and were conscious of having not simply the right to vote, but the chance of being voted for." *P*

—the parties:

Piagnoni: "There were men of high birth, accustomed to public charges at home and abroad, who had become newly conspicuous not only as enemies of the Medici and friends of popular government, but as thorough Piagnoni, espousing to the utmost the doctrines and practical teaching of the Frate, and frequenting San Marco as the seat of another Samuel: some of them men of authoritative and handsome presence, like **Francesco Valori**, and perhaps also of a hot and arrogant temper, very much gratified by an immediate divine authority for bringing about free dome in their own way; others, like **Soderini**, with less of the ardent Piagnone, and more of the wise politician." 25

" ' . . . the Frate has an acute mind . . . but it is not likely that **Pagolantonio** Soderini, who has had long experience of affairs, and has specially studied the Venetian Council, should be much indebted to a monk for ideas on that subject. No, no; Soderini loads the cannon; though, I grant you, Fra Girolamo brings the powder and lights the match.' " 39

Republicans: Others were since advocates of a free government, but regarded **Savonarola** simply as an ambitious monk—half sagacious, half fanatical—who had made himself a powerful instrument with the people, and must be accepted as an important social fact." 25 *See* **Piero Capponi** MF

Mediceans: "Some were Mediceans who had already, from motives of fear and policy, begun to show the presiding spirit of the popular party a feigned deference." 25

"[**Bernardo Rucellai**] welcomed **Tito** with more marked favour than usual and gave him a place between **Lorenzo Tornabuoni** and **Giannozzo Pucci**, both of them accomplished young members of the Medicean party." 39

—arrested: " 'The accused have too many family ties with all parties not to escape; and Messer **Bernardo del Nero** has other things in his favour besides his age . . . .

" ' . . . along with him are three, at least, whose names have a commanding interest even among the popular party—**Niccolò Ridolfi**, **Lorenzo Torna-buoni**, and **Giannozzo Pucci**.' " 56

Anti-Mediceans: "There were even some of [the Frate's] bitter enemies: members of the old aristocratic anti-Medicean party—determined to try and get the reins once more tight in the hands of certain chief families; or else licentious young men, who detested him as the killjoy of Florence." 25

Arrabbiati: "We are not strong enough to make head on our own behalf [said **Tornabuoni**]; and if the Frate and the popular party were upset, every one who hears me knows perfectly well what other party would be uppermost just now: **Nerli**, **Alberti**, **Pazzi**, and the rest—*Arrabbiati,* as somebody christened them the other day—who instead of giving us an amnesty, would be inclined to fly at our throats like mad dogs, and not be satisfied till they had banished half of us.' " 56

Compagnacci, or Evil Companions: " . . . **Dolfo Spini**, leader of the Compagnacci . . .that is to say, of all the dissolute young men belonging to the old aristocratic party, enemies of the Mediceans, enemies of the popular government, but still more bitter enemies of **Savonarola**." 45

Supporting Roles

Bernardo del Nero [H], "a tall elderly man in a handsome black silk lucco, who, unwinding his becchetto from his neck and taking off his cap, disclosed a head as white as **Bardo**'s . . . .

" 'Well, god-daughter,' said the stately man, as he touched **Romola**'s shoulder, '**Maso** said you had a visitor, but I came in nevertheless.' " 6

—*introduced:* " 'Ah, a Greek, as I augur,' said Bernardo, returning **Tito**'s reverence but slightly, and surveying him with that sort of glance which seems almost to cut like fine steel . . . .

" 'I had expected [your name] to be at least as long as the names of a city, a river, a province, and an empire all put together. We Florentines mostly use names as we do prawns, and strip them of all flourishes before we trust them to our throats.' " 6

—*a warning:* " 'Remember, **Bardo**, thou hast a rare gem of thy own; take care no one gets it who is not likely to pay a worthy price. That pretty Greek has a lithe sleekness about him, that seems marvellously fitted for slipping easily into any nest he fixes his mind on.' " 6

" 'Ah, said **Nello**, 'he is the dragon that guards the remnant of old **Bardo**'s gold, which, I fancy, is chiefly that virgin gold that falls about the fair **Romola**'s head and shoulders, eh, my Apollino?' he added, patting Tito's head." 8

—*defended:* " 'He has never agreed with my father about disowning **Dino**, and you know he has always said that we ought to wait until you have been at least a year in Florence. Do not think hardly of my godfather. I know he is prejudiced and narrow, but yet he is very noble. He has often said that it is folly in my father to want to keep his library apart, that it may bear his name; yet he would try to get my father's wish carried out. That seems to me very great and noble—that power of respecting a feeling which he does not share or understand.' " 17

—*teasing:* " 'Thy father has thought of shutting woman's folly out of thee by cramming thee with Greek and Latin; but thou hast been as ready to believe in the first pair of bright eyes and the first soft words that have come within reach of thee, as if thou couldst say nothing by heart but Paternosters, like other Christian men's daughters.' " 19

—*grudging admiration:* " . . . as [**Tito**] gave with fulness and precision the results of his inquiries and interviews, Bernardo del Nero, who was at that time one of the Ten, could not withhold his admiration. He would have withheld it if he could, for his original dislike of Tito had returned, and become stronger, since the sale of the library. **Romola** had never uttered a word to her godfather on the circumstances . . . but he felt sure that the breach of her father's wish had been a blighting grief to her, and the old man's observant eyes discerned other indications that her married life was not happy." 45

—*reflections:* " 'These women, if they are not happy, and have no children, must either take to folly or to some overstrained religion that makes them think they've got all heaven's work on their shoulders. And as for my poor child **Romola**, it is as I always said—the cramming with Latin and Greek has left her as much a woman as if she had done nothing all day but prick her fingers with the needle. And this husband of hers, who gets employed everywhere, because he's a tool with a smooth handle, I wish **Tornabuoni** and the rest may not find their fingers cut.' " 45

—admired: "[**Romola**'s] mind rushed back with a new attraction towards the strong worldly sense, the dignified prudence, the untheoretic virtues of her godfather, who was to be treated as a sort of **Agag** because he held that a more restricted form of government was better than the Great Council, and because he would not pretend to forget old ties to the banished [**Medici**] family." 52

—the end: "Suddenly there was a stillness, and the very tapers seemed to tremble into quiet. The executioner was ready on the scaffold, and Bernardo del Nero was seen ascending it with a slow firm step. **Romola** made no visible movement, uttered not even a suppressed sound: she stood more firmly, caring for *his* firmness. She saw him pause, saw the white head kept erect, while he said, in a voice distinctly audible—

" 'It is but a short space of life that my fellow-citizens have taken from me' . . . . " 60

Dino (Bernardino) de' Bardi. (**Fra Luca**) " ' . . . my son, whom I had brought up to replenish my ripe learning with young enterprise, left me and all liberal pursuits that he might lash himself and howl at midnight with besotted friars—that he might go wandering on pilgrimages befitting men who know of no past older than the missal and the crucifix—left me when the night was already beginning to fall on me.' " 5

—remembered: "There was only one masculine face, at once youthful and beautiful, the image of which remained deeply impressed on [**Romola's**] mind: it was that of her brother, who long years ago had taken her on his knee, kissed her, and never come back again: a fair face, with sunny hair, like her own." 6

—face in the crowd: "[**Tito**] saw a man's face upturned towards him, and fixing on him a gaze that seemed to have more meaning in it than the ordinary passing observation of a stranger. It was a face with tonsured head, that rose above the black mantle and white tunic of a Dominican friar . . . but the glance had something peculiar in it for Tito. There was a faint suggestion in it, certainly not of an unpleasant kind." 8

—in the street: "Seen closer, the face looked more evidently worn by sickness and not by age, and again it brought some strong but indefinite reminiscences to **Tito**." 10

—a father's anathema: " 'But he left me—he is dead to me. I have disowned him for ever. He was a ready scholar, as you [**Tito**] are, but more fervid and impatient, and yet sometimes rapt and self-absorbed, like a flame fed by some fitful source; showing a disposition from the very first to turn away his eyes from the clear lights of reason and philosophy; and to prostrate himself under the influences of a dim mysticism which eludes all rules of human duty as it eludes all argument. And so it ended. We will speak no more of him: he is dead to me. I wish his face could be blotted from that world of memory in which the distant seems to grow clearer and the near to fade.' " 12

—his death-bed: " . . . two tapers placed behind a truckle-bed, showed the emaciated face of Fra Luca, with the tonsured crown of golden hair above it, and with deep-sunken hazel eyes fixed on a small crucifix which he held before him. He was propped up into nearly a sitting posture . . . . " 15

The Dying Message

—*challenged:* " 'No; I have never repented fleeing from the stifling poison-breath of sin that was hot and thick around me, and threatened to steal over my sense like besotting wine . . . . My father has lived amidst human sin and misery without believing in them: he has been like one busy picking shining stones in a mine, while there was a word dying of plague above him.' " 15

—*his call:* "I felt that there was a life of perfect love and purity for the soul; in which there would be no uneasy hunger after pleasure, no tormenting questions, no fear of suffering. Before I knew the history of the saints, I had a foreshadowing of their ecstasy. For the same truth had penetrated even into pagan philosophy: that it is a bliss within the reach of man to die to mortal needs, and live in the life of God as the Unseen Perfectness.

" 'But to attain that I must forsake the world: I must have no affection, no hope, wedding me to that which passeth away; I must live with my fellow-beings only as human souls related to the eternal unseen life. The need was urging me continually: it came over me in visions when my mind fell away weary from the vain words which record the passions of dead men: it came over me after I had been tempted into sin and had turned away with loathing from the scent of the emptied cup . . . I saw the meaning of the Crucifix . . . .

" 'I fled—fled to lands where danger and scorn and want bore me continually, like angels, to repose on the bosom of God. I have lived the life of a hermit, I have ministered to pilgrims; but my task has been short: the veil has worn very thin that divides me from my everlasting rest . . . . " ¶15

—*his vision: see Topicon* M:Consciousness—*vision of portent*

—*missing ingredient:* "The prevision that Fra Luca's words had imparted to **Romola** had been such as comes from the shadowy region where human souls seek wisdom apart from the human sympathies which are the very life and substance of our wisdom; the revelation that might have come from the simple questions of filial and brotherly affection had been carried into irrevocable silence." 15

Monna Brigida " 'may well serve as a scarecrow and a warning.' " 5

—*first entrance:* "It was the figure of a short stout black-eyed woman, about fifty, wearing a black velvet berretta, or close cap, embroidered with pearls, under which surprisingly massive black braids surmounted the little bulging forehead, and fell in rich plaited curves over the ears, while an equally surprising carmine tint on the upper region of the fat cheeks contrasted with the surrounding sallowness. Three rows of pearls and a lower necklace of gold reposed on the horizontal cushion of her neck; the embroidered border of her trailing black-velvet gown and her embroidered long-drooping sleeves of rose-coloured damask, were slightly faded, but they conveyed to the initiated eye the satisfactory assurance that they were the splendid result of six months' labour by a skilled workman; and the rose-coloured petticoat, with its dimmed white fringe and seed-pearl arabesques, was duly exhibited in order to suggest a similar pleasing reflection. A handsome coral rosary hung from one side of an inferential belt, which emerged into certainty with a large clasp of silver wrought in niello, and, on the other side, where the belt again became inferential, hung a scarsella, or large purse, of crimson velvet, stitched with pearls. Her little fat right hand, which looked as if it had been made of paste and had risen out of shape under partial baking, held a small book of devotions, also splendid with velvet, pearls, and silver." 12

—status: " . . . Monna Brigida was a frequent visitor at **Bardo**'s, being excepted . . . on the ground of her cousinship to his dead wife and her early care for **Romola** . . . . " 12

—scolded: "Monna Brigida lifted her shoulders and her hands in mute dismay; then she rose as quietly as possible . . . and stole out of the room like a culpable fat spaniel who has barked unseasonably." 12

—enhancements: "And Monna Brigida had begun to have frequent struggles at her toilet. If her soul would prosper better without them, was it really worth while to put on the rouge and the braids? But when she lifted up the hand-mirror and saw a sallow face with baggy cheeks, and crows'-feet that were not to be dissimulated by any simpering of the lips—when she parted her grey hair, and let it lie in simple Piagnone fashion round her face, her courage failed." 51

—rationalization: "Every woman who was not a Piagnone would give a shrug at the sight of her, and the men would accost her as if she were their grandmother. Whereas, at fifty-five a woman was not so very old—she only required making up a little. So the rouge and the braids and the embroidered berretta went on again, and Monna Brigida was satisfied with the accustomed effect; as to her neck, if she covered it up, people might suppose it was too old to show, and, on the contrary, with the necklaces round it, it looked better than **Monna Berta**'s." 51

—dissolution: "The heavy black plait fell down over Monna Brigida's face, and dragged the rest of the head-gear forward. It was a new reason for not hesitating: she put up her hands hastily, undid the other fastenings, and flung down into the basket of doom her beloved crimson-velvet berretta, with all its unsurpassed embroidery of seed-pearls, and stood an unrouged woman, with grey hair pushed backward from a face where certain deep lines of age had triumphed over *embonpoint*." 51

—indulgent: "However, Monna Brigida wanted to give the children too many sweets for their supper, and confessed to **Romola**, the last thing before going to bed, that it would be a shame not to take care of such cherubs." 70

—later: "Monna Brigida was asleep at this moment . . . . Her hair, parting backward under her black hood, had that soft whiteness which is not like snow or anything else, but is simply the lovely whiteness of aged hair. Her chin had sunk on her bosom, and her hands rested on the elbow of her chair. She had not been weaving flowers or doing anything else: she had only been looking on as usual, and as usual had fallen asleep." *E*

Charles the Eighth of France [H]. "An unexampled visitor! For he had come through the passes of the Alps with such an army as Italy had not seen before: with thousands of terrible Swiss, well used to fight for love and hatred as well as for hire; with a host of gallant cavaliers proud of a name; with an unprecedented infantry; in which every man in a hundred carried an arquebus; nay, with cannon of bronze, shooting not stones but iron balls, drawn not by bullocks but by horses, and capable of firing a second time before a city could mend the breach made by the first ball." 21

—awesome augury: "And there was a very widely spread conviction that the advent of the French king and his army into Italy was one of those events at which marble statues might well be believed to perspire, phantasmal fiery warriors to fight in the air, and quadrupeds to bring forth monstrous births—that it did not belong to the usual order of Providence, but was in a peculiar sense the work of God. It was a conviction that rested less on the necessarily

momentous character of a powerful foreign invasion than on certain moral emotions to which the aspect of the times gave the form of presentiments: emotions which had found a very remarkable utterance in the voice of a single man [—**Savonarola**]." 21

—deformed: "Also, if the young monarch under the canopy, seated on his charger with his lance upon his thigh, had looked more like a **Charlemagne** and less like a hastily modelled grotesque, the imagination of his admirers would have been much assisted. It might have been wished that the scourge of Italian wickedness and 'Champion of the honour of women' had had a less miserable leg, and only the normal sum of toes; that his mouth had been of a less reptilian width of slit, his nose and head of a less exorbitant outline." 26

—losing heart: "For the French king, that new Charlemagne, who had entered Italy in anticipatory triumph, and had conquered Naples without the least trouble, had gone away again fifteen months ago [July 1495], and was even, it was feared, in his grief for the loss of a new-born son, losing the languid intention of coming back again to redress grievances and set the Church in order." 42

Bratti Ferravecchi. "He was a grey-haired, broad-shouldered man, of the type which, in Tuscan phrase, is moulded with the fist and polished with the pickaxe; but the self-important gravity which had written itself out in the deep lines about his brow and mouth seemed intended to correct any contemptuous inferences from the hasty workmanship which Nature had bestowed on his exterior." 1 *The name means "old iron."*

—at a fair: "[He] stood with his back against a pillar, and his mouth pursed up in disdainful silence, eyeing every one who approached him with a cold glance of superiority, and keeping his hand fast on a serge covering which concealed the contents of the basket slung before him." 14

—curious customer: " 'Before I answer that, Monna, I must know whether you mean to buy. I can't show such wares as mine in this fair for every fly to settle on and pay nothing. My goods are a little too choice for that. Besides, I've only two left, and I've no mind to sell them; for with the chances of the pestilence that wise men talk of, there is likelihood of their being worth their weight in gold. No, no; *andate con Dio.*' " 14

—egoism: "It never occurred to Bratti that the decent man (who was rather deaf, apparently, asking him to say many things twice over) had any curiosity about **Tito**; the curiosity was doubtless about himself, as a truly remarkable pedlar." 30

—sales pitch: " 'Young woman . . . you come from some castello a good way off, it seems to me, else you'd never think of walking about, this blessed Carnival, without a red cross in your hand. Santa Madonna! Four white quattrini is a small price to pay for your soul—prices rise in purgatory, let me tell you.' " 50

—making a sale: " 'You're in the right, madonna,' said Bratti, taking the coin quickly, and thrusting the cross into her hand; 'I'll not offer you change, for I might as well rob you of a mass. What! we must all be scorched a little, but you'll come off the easier; better fall from the window than the roof.' " 51

Nello, a barber, "a man of slim figure, whose eye twinkled rather roguishly. He wore a close jerkin, a skull-cap lodged carelessly over his left ear as if it had fallen there by chance, a delicate linen apron tucked up on one side, and a razor stuck in his belt." 1

—*talkative:* "[His] loquacity, like an over-full bottle, could never pour forth a small dose." 3

—*his specialty:* " 'And first of all, in the matter of your hair. That beard, my fine young man, must be parted with, were it as dear to you as the nymph of your dreams. Here at Florence, we love not to see a man with his nose projecting over a cascade of hair. But, remember, you will have passed the Rubicon, when once you have been shaven: if you repent, and let your beard grow after it has acquired stoutness by a struggle with the razor, your mouth will be and by show no longer what **Messer Angelo** calls the divine prerogative of lips, but will appear like a dark cavern fringed with horrent brambles.' " 3

—*his shop:* " 'For my shop is a no less fitting haunt of the Muses, as you will acknowledge when you feel the sudden illumination of understanding and the serene vigour of inspiration that will come to you with a clear chin.' " 3

—*tactless:* " 'But it is said of the Greeks that their honesty begins at what is the hanging point with us, and that since the old Furies went to sleep, your Christian Greek is of so easy a conscience that he would make a stepping-stone of his father's corpse.'

"The flush on the stranger's [**Tito**'s] face indicated what seemed so natural a movement of resentment, that the good-natured Nello hastened to atone for his want of reticence." 3

—*appraised:* " 'Nello is a good-hearted prodigal,' said **Bardo**; 'and though, with that ready ear and ready tongue of his, he is too much like the ill-famed Margites—knowing many things and knowing them all badly, as I hinted to him but now—he is nevertheless "abnormis sapiens," after the manner of our born Florentines.' " 6

—*curious:* "[His] Florentine curiosity was of that lively canine sort which thinks no trifle too despicable for investigation . . . . " 8

—*amorous:* " 'What is it, my **Orpheus**?' here Nello stretched out his arms to their full length, and then brought them round till his hands grasped **Tito**'s curls, and drew them out playfully. 'What is it you want of your well-tamed Nello? For I perceive a coaxing sound in that soft strain of yours. Let me see the very needle's eye of your desire, as the sublime poet says, that I may thread it.' " 13

—*adroit:* " 'Come, come, **Francesco** [**Cei**], you are out of humour with waiting,' said the conciliatory Nello. 'Let me stop your mouth with a little lather. I must not have my friend **Cronaca** made angry: I have a regard for his chin; and his chin is in no respect altered since he became a Piagnone.' " 16

—*defending his favourite:* " 'What is it against my *bel erudito* that he looked startled when he felt a pair of claws upon him and saw an unchained madman at his elbow? . . . We Florentines count some other qualities in a man besides that vulgar stuff called bravery, which is to be got by hiring dunderheads at so much per dozen. I tell you, as soon as men found out that they had more brains than oxen, they set the oxen to draw for them; and when we Florentines found out that we had more brains than other men we set them to fight for us.' " 29

—*comment:* " '*Va,* Nello,' growled **Piero**, 'thy tongue runs on as usual, like a mill when the Arno's full—whether there's grist or not.' " 29

Piero di Cosimo [H]. " ' . . . he says his pictures are an appendix which Messer Domeneddio [familiarity with God] has been pleased to make to the universe, and if any man is in doubt what they mean, he had better inquire of Holy Church. He has been asked to paint a picture after the sketch, but he puts his fingers to his ears and shakes his head at that: the fancy is past, he says—a strange animal, our Piero.' " 3

—*proposal:* "Meanwhile the man who had entered the shop . . . a tall figure, about fifty, with a short trimmed beard, wearing an old felt hat and a thread-bare mantle—had kept his eye fixed on the Greek, and now said abruptly—

" 'Young man, I am painting a picture of **Sinon** deceiving old **Priam**, and I should be glad of your face for my Sinon, if you'd give me a sitting.' " 4

—*at the festival:* "Piero di Cosimo was raising a laugh . . . by his grimaces and anathemas at the noise of the bells, against which no kind of ear-stuffing was a sufficient barricade, since the more he stuffed his ears the more he felt the vibration of his skull; and declaring that he would bury himself in the most solitary spot of the Valdarno on a *festa,* if he were not condemned, as a painter, to lie in wait for the secrets of colour that were sometimes to be caught from the floating of banners and the chance grouping of the multitude." 8

—*instinct:* "**Nello** . . . gave a challenging look at Piero di Cosimo, whom he had never forgiven for his refusal to see any prognostics of character in his favourite's handsome face. Piero, who was leaning against the other door-post, close to **Tito**, shrugged his shoulders: the frequent recurrence of such challenges from Nello had changed the painter's first declaration of neutrality into a positive inclination to believe ill of the much-praised Greek." 16

—*at home:* " . . . the door opened, and Piero presented himself in a red night-cap and a loose brown serge tunic, with sleeves rolled up to the shoulder . . . . " 18

—*mollified:* "The painter's manners were too notoriously odd to all the world for this reception to be held a special affront; but even if **Tito** had suspected any offensive intention, the impulse to resentment would have been less strong in him than the desire to conquer goodwill.

"Piero made a grimace which was habitual with him when he was spoken to with flattering suavity. He grinned, stretched out the corners of his mouth, and pressed down his brows, so as to defy any divination of his feelings under that kind of stroking." 18

—*disorganized:* "Piero was so uncertain in his work—sometimes, when the demand was not peremptory, laying aside a picture for months, sometimes thrusting it into a corner or coffer, where it was likely to be utterly forgotten—that [**Romola**] felt it necessary to watch over his progress. She was a favourite with the painter, and he was inclined to fulfil any wish of hers, but no general inclination could be trusted as a safeguard against his sudden whims." 28

—*snappish:* " 'You crusty Piero! I forgot how snappish you are. Here, put this nice sweetmeat in your mouth,' said **Romola**, smiling through her tears, and taking something very crisp and sweet from the little basket.

"Piero accepted it very much as that proverbial bear that dreams of pears might accept an exceedingly mellow 'swan-egg'—really liking the gift, but accustomed to have his pleasures and pains concealed under a shaggy coat." 28

Piero Shows Romola a Frightened Tito

—*bad deceiver:* "Piero was too sanguine, as open-hearted men are apt to be when they attempt a little clever simulation." 28

—*unflattering:* " 'Yes, you ought to have been there,' said Piero, in his biting way, 'just to see your favourite Greek look as frightened as if **Satanasso** had laid hold of him. I like to see your ready-smiling Messeri caught in a sudden wind and obliged to show their lining in spite of themselves. What colour do you think a man's liver is, who looks like a bleached deer as soon as a chance stranger lays hold of him suddenly?' " 29

—*Pyramid of Vanities:* " 'What think you of this folly, Madonna **Romola**?' said a brusque voice close to her ear. Your Piagnoni will make *l'inferno* a pleasant prospect to us, if they are to carry things their own way on earth . . . . '

" 'There are some things in [*The Decameron*] I do not want ever to forget,' said Romola, 'but you must confess, Piero, that a great many of those stories are only about low deceit for the lowest ends. Men do not want books to make them think lightly of vice, as if life were a vulgar joke. And I cannot blame **Fra Girolamo** for teaching that we owe our time to something better.'

" 'Yes, yes, it's very well to say so now you've read them,' said Piero, bitterly, turning on his heel and walking away from her.

"Romola, too, walked on, smiling at Piero's innuendo, with a sort of tenderness towards the old painter's anger, because she knew that her father would have felt something like it." 49

Bartolommeo Scala [H], secretary of the Republic. " 'He came to Florence [said **Nello**] as a poor adventurer himself—a miller's son—a "branny monster," as he has been nicknamed by our honey-lipped **Poliziano**, who agrees with him as well as my teeth agree with lemon-juice.' " 3

—*achievement:* " . . . the miller's son held his ascent to honours by his own efforts a fact to be proclaimed without wincing. The secretary was a vain and pompous man, but he was also an honest one: he was sincerely convinced of his own merit, and could see no reasons for feigning. The topmost round of his azure ladder had been reached by this time: he had held his secretaryship these twenty years—had long since made his orations on the *ringhiera* or platform of the Old Palace, as the custom was, in the presence of princely visitors, while Marzocco, the republican lion, wore his gold crown on the occasion, and all the people cried, 'Viva Messer Bartolommeo!'—had been on an embassy to Rome, and had there been made titular Senator, Apostolical Secretary, Knight of the Golden Spur, and had, eight years ago, been Gonfaloniere—last goal of the Florentine citizen's ambition. Meantime he had got richer and richer, and more and more gouty, after the manner of successful mortality; and the Knight of the Golden Spur had often to sit with helpless cushioned heel under the handsome loggia he had built for himself, overlooking the spacious gardens and lawn at the back of his palace." 7

—*weakness:* "Scala was a meritorious public servant, and, moreover, a lucky man—naturally exasperating to an offended scholar; but then—O beautiful balance of things!—he had an itch for authorship, and was a bad writer—one of those excellent people who, sitting in gouty slippers, 'penned poetical trifles' entirely for their own amusement, without any view to an audience, and, consequently sent them to their friends in letters, which were the literary periodicals of the fifteenth century. Now Scala had an abundance of friends who were ready to praise his writings: friends like **Ficino** and **Landino**—amiable browsers in the Medicean park along with himself—who found his Latin prose style elegant and masculine . . . . But when was the fatal coquetry inherent in superfluous authorship ever quite contented with the ready praise of friends? That critical supercilious **Politian**—a fellow-browser, who was far from amiable—must be made aware that the solid secretary showed, in his leisure hours, a pleasant fertility in verses, which indicated pretty clearly how much he might do in that way if he were not a man of affairs." 7

—feud: "The quarrel could not end there. The logic could hardly get worse, but the secretary got more pompously self-asserting, and the scholarly poet's temper more and more venomous . . . . The secretary was ashamed of the age in which he lived, and blushed for it. *Some,* indeed, there were who wanted to have their own works praised and exalted to a level with the divine monuments of antiquity; but he, Scala, could not oblige them. And as to the honours which were offensive to the envious, they had been well earned: witness his whole life since he came in penury to Florence." *See* **Poliziano**—*crescendo*

—good host: "[He,] excellent man, not seeking publicity through the book-sellers, was never unprovided with 'hasty uncorrected trifles,' as a sort of sherbet for a visitor on a hot day, or, if the weather were cold, why then as a cordial—had a few little matters in the shape of Sonnets, turning on well-known foibles of **Politian**'s, which he would not like to go any farther, but which would, perhaps, amuse the company." 7

Dolfo Spini [H]. " 'I will engage to make myself the special confidant of that thick-headed Dolfo Spini, and know his projects before he knows them himself [said **Tito**].' " 39

—costume: "Yet the tall, broad-shouldered personage greeted in that slight way looked like one who had considerable clams. He wore a richly-embroidered tunic, with a great show of linen, after the newest French mode, and at his belt there hung a sword and poniard of fine workmanship. His hat, with a red plume in it, seemed a scornful protest against the gravity of Florentine costume, which had been exaggerated to the utmost under the influence of the Piagnoni. Certain undefinable indications of youth made the breadth of his face and the large diameter of his waist appear the more emphatically a stamp of coarseness, and his eyes had that rude desecrating stare at all men and things which to a refined mind is as intolerable as a bad odour or a flaring light." 45

—political role: " . . . this broad-shouldered man with the red feather was Dolfo Spini, leader of the Compagnacci . . . [who] had organised these young men into an armed band, as sworn champions of extravagant suppers and all the pleasant sins of the flesh, against reforming pietists who threatened to make the world chaste and temperate to so intolerable a degree that there would soon be no reason for leaving . . . . " 45

—problematic: "But Spino was an inconvenient colleague. He had cunning enough to delight in plots, but not the ability or self-command necessary to so complex an effect as secrecy. He frequently got excited with drinking . . . and in spite of the agreement between him and **Tito**, that their public recognition of each other should invariably be of the coolest sort, there was always the possibility that on an evening encounter he would be suddenly blurting and affectionate. The delicate sign of casting the becchetto over the left shoulder was understood in the morning, but the strongest hint short of a threat might not suffice to keep off a fraternal grasp of the shoulder in the evening." 46

A Dangerous Colleague

Tessa, "a young girl, apparently not more than sixteen, with a red hood surrounding her face, which was all the more baby-like in its prettiness from the entire concealment of her hair." 2

—lost and worried: "The corners of the pouting mouth went down piteously, and the poor little bosom with the beads on it above the green serge gown heaved so, that there was no longer any help for it: a loud sob *would* come, and the big tears fell as if they were making up for lost time." 10

—calmed: "The apron fell, and Tessa's face began to look as contented as a cherub's budding from a cloud. The diabolical conjuror, the anger and the beating, seemed a long way off.

" 'I think I'll go home, if you'll take me,' she said, in a half whisper, looking up at **Tito** with wide blue eyes, and with something sweeter than a smile —with a childlike calm." 10

—oblivious " . . . she took no note of [**Tito**'s] dress; he was simply a voice and face to her, something come from Paradise into a world where most things seemed hard and angry; and she prattled with as little restraint as if he had been an imaginary companion born of her own lovingness and the sunshine." 10

—found at the fair: "Her head hung a little aside with a look of weariness, and her blue eyes were directed rather absently towards an altar-piece . . . her round cheek was paled, either by the light or by the weariness that was expressed in her attitude: her lips were pressed poutingly together, and every now and then her eyelids half fell: she was a large image of a sweet sleepy child." 14

—new situation: "She turned away from her shutter with rather an excited expression in her childish face, which was as pretty and pouting as ever. Her garb was still that of a simple contadina, but of a contadina prepared for a *festa:* her gown of dark-green serge, with its red girdle, was very clean and neat; she had the string of red glass beads round her neck; and her brown hair, rough from curliness, was duly knotted up, and fastened with the silver pin. She had but one new ornament, and she was very proud of it, for it was a fine gold ring." 33

—dressed for Carnival: "Tessa did not think at all of showing her figure, for no one had ever told her it was pretty; but she was quite sure that her necklace and clasp were the prettiest sort ever worn by the richest contadina, and she arranged her white hood over her head so that the front of her necklace might be well displayed. These ornaments, she considered, must inspire respect for her as the wife of some one who could afford to buy them." 50

—later: "Tessa's fingers had not become more adroit with the years—only very much fatter. She . . . never ceased to be astonished at the wisdom of her children. She still wore her contadina gown: it was only broader than the old one; and there was the silver pin in her rough curly brown hair, and round her neck the memorable necklace . . . . Her rounded face wore even a more perfect look of childish content than in her younger days: everybody was so good in the world, Tessa thought; even **Monna Brigida** never found fault with her now, and did little else than sleep, which was an amiable practice in everybody, and one that Tessa liked for herself." *E*

Tessa at Home

Others

Pope Alexander VI (**Rodrigo Borgia**) [H]. "A league had been formed against [**Charles VIII**]—a Holy League, with Pope Borgia at its head . . . but, looked at more closely, the Holy League seemed very much like an agreement among certain wolves to drive away all other wolves, and then to see which among themselves could snatch the largest share of the prey." 42

" . . . in [**Savonarola**'s] excommunication [**Romola**] only saw the menace of hostile vice: on one side she saw a man whose life was devoted to the ends of public virtue and spiritual purity, and on the other the assault of alarmed selfishness, headed by a lustful, greedy, lying, and murderous old man, once called Rodrigo Borgia, and now lifted to the pinnacle of infamy as Pope Alexander the Sixth." 55

—*dealing with a critic*: "Not to try and rid himself of a man who wanted to stir up the Powers of Europe to summon a General Council and depose him, would have been adding ineptitude to iniquity. There was no denying that towards Alexander the Sixth **Savonarola** was a rebel, and, what was much more, a dangerous rebel." 71

Niccolò Caparra, a blacksmith with "a bass voice, with a note that dropped like the sound of a great bell in the midst of much tinkling . . . .

"The speaker had joined the group only in time to hear the conclusion of Nello's speech, but he was one of those figures for whom all the world instinctively makes way, as it would for a battering-ram. He was not much above the middle height, but the impression of enormous force which was conveyed by his capacious chest and brawny arms bared to the shoulder, was deepened by the keen sense and quiet resolution expressed in his glance and in every furrow of his cheek and brow.

"He had often been an unconscious model to **Domenico Ghirlandajo**, when that great painter was making the walls of the churches reflect the life of Florence, and translating pale aerial traditions into the deep colour and strong lines of the faces he knew. The naturally dark tint of his skin was additionally bronzed by the same powdering deposit that gave a polished black surface to his leathern apron: a deposit which habit had probably made a necessary condition of perfect ease, for it was not washed off with punctilious regularity." ¶1

—*barbered:* "That famous worker in iron . . . was this morning dressed in holiday suit, and as he sat submissively while **Nello** skipped round him, lathered him, seized him by the nose, and scraped him with magical quickness, he looked much as a lion might if it had donned linen and tunic and was preparing to go into society." 16

—*at work:* "Against the red light framed in by the outline of the fluted tiles and columns stood in black relief the grand figure of Niccolò, with his huge arms in rhythmic rise and fall, first hiding and then disclosing the profile of his firm mouth and powerful brow. Two slighter ebony figures, one at the anvil, the other at the bellows, served to set off his superior massiveness." 26

—*scruple:* " 'I'm rather nice about what I sell, and whom I sell to. I like to know who's my customer.'

" 'I know your scruples, Niccolò. But that is only defensive armour: it can hurt nobody.'

Niccolò the blacksmith at Work

" 'True, but it may make the man who wears it feel himself all the safer if he should want to hurt somebody. No, no; it's not my own work; but it's fine work of **Maso** of Brescia; I should be loth for it to cover the heart of a scoundrel. I must know who is to wear it.' " 26

—selling: " 'Take the coat. It's made to cheat sword, or poniard, or arrow. But, for my part, I would never put such a thing on. It's like carrying fear about with one.' " 26

Piero Capponi [H]. "There were men, also of family, like Piero Capponi, simply brave undoctrinal lovers of a sober republican liberty, who preferred fighting to arguing, and had no particular reasons for thinking any ideas false that kept out the **Medici** and made room for public spirit." 25

—great deed: " 'The Most Christian King demanded a little too much—was obstinate—said at last, "I shall order my trumpets to sound." Then, Florentine citizens! your Piero Capponi, speaking with the voice of a free city, said, "If you sound your trumpets, we will ring our bells!" He snatched the copy of the dishonouring conditions from the hands of the secretary, tore it in pieces, and turned to leave the royal presence.' " 29

—cheered: "The moment belonged to another man of firm presence, as little inclined to humour the people as to humour any other unreasonable claimants—loving order, like one who by force of fortune had been made a merchant, and by force of nature had become a soldier. It was not till he was seen at the entrance of the piazza that the silence was broken, and then one loud shout of 'Capponi, Capponi! Well done, Capponi!' rang through the piazza.

"The simple, resolute man looked round him with grave joy. His fellow-citizens gave him a great funeral two years later, when he had died in fight; there were torches carried by all the magistracy, and torches again, and trains of banners. But it is not known that he felt any joy in the oration that was delivered in his praise, as the banners waved over his bier. Let us be glad that he got some thanks and praise while he lived." 29

Ser Ceccone [H]. "There were present not only genuine followers of the **Frate**, but Ser Ceccone, the notary, who at that time, like **Tito** himself, was secretly an agent of the Mediceans.

"Ser Francesco di Ser Barone, more briefly known to infamy as Ser Ceccone, was not learned, not handsome, not successful, and the reverse of generous. He was a traitor without charm. It followed that he was not fond of Tito Melema." 47

" . . . also [like **Tito**] willing to serve the State by giving information against unsuccessful employers." 57

—hatred for a rival: "He also had been privy to the unexecuted plot, and was willing to tell what he knew, but knew much less to tell [than **Tito**]. He also would have been willing to go on treacherous errands, but a more eligible agent had forestalled him. His propositions were received coldly; the council, he was told, was already in possession of the needed information, and since he had been thus busy in sedition, it would be well for him to retire out of the way of mischief, otherwise the government might be obliged to take note of him. Ser Ceccone wanted no evidence to make him attribute his failure to Tito, and his spite was the more bitter because the nature of the case compelled him to hold his peace about it." 63

—unplacated: "Now Ser Ceccone had no positive knowledge that Tito had an underhand connection with the Arrabbiati and the Court of Milan, but he

had a suspicion of which he chewed the cud with as strong a sense of flavour as if it had been a certainty.

"This fine-grown vigorous hatred could swallow the feeble opiate of Tito's favours, and be as lively as ever after it." 63

Francesco Cei [H]. " 'Besides, that loud-barking "hound of the Lord" [**Savonarola**] is not in Florence just now,' said Francesco Cei, the popular poet; 'he has taken **Piero de' Medici**'s hint, to carry his railing prophecies on a journey for a while.' " 8

—anti-semitic: " '. . . and then comes the famous Art of Money-changers.'

" 'Many of them matriculated also to the noble art of usury before you were born,' interrupted Francesco Cei, 'as you may discern by a certain fitful glare of the eye and sharp curve of the nose which manifest their descent from the ancient Harpies, whose portraits you see supporting the arms of the Zecca [Mint]. Shaking off old prejudices now, such a procession as that of some four hundred passably ugly men carrying their tapers in open daylight, **Diogenes**-fashion, as if they were looking for a lost quattrino, would make a merry spectacle for the Feast of Fools.' " 8 *See* **Pietro Cennini**—*offended*

—acute: " 'I'm of our old **Piero di Cosimo**'s mind,' said Francesco Cei. 'I don't half like **Melema**. That trick of smiling gets stronger than ever—no wonder he has lines about the mouth.' " 45

Pietro Cennini. " 'My brother Pietro, who is a better judge of scholarship than I, will perhaps be able to supply you with a task that may test your capabilities." 4

" . . . the erudite corrector of proof-sheets . . . . " 8

—offended: " 'Blaspheme not against the usages of our city,' said Pietro Cennini [to **Cei**], much offended. 'There are new wits who think they see things more truly because they stand on their heads to look at them, like tumblers and mountebanks, instead of keeping the attitude of rational men. . . .

" 'Keep your jest then till your end of the pole is uppermost,' said Cennini, still angry, 'and that is not when the great bond of our Republic is expressing itself in ancient symbols, without which the vulgar would be conscious of nothing beyond their own petty wants of back and stomach, and never rise to the sense of community in religion and law. There has been no great people without processions, and the man who thinks himself too wise to be moved by them to anything but contempt, is like the puddle that was proud of standing alone while the river rushed by.' " 8

Lillo. " 'Ah, it is not true! He is prettier than anything . . . only he's asleep, and you can't see his eyes or his tongue, and I can't show you his hair—and it grows—isn't it wonderful? Look at him! It's true his face is very much all alike when he's asleep, there is not so much to see as when he's awake.' " 34

"Lillo, whose great dark eyes looked all the darker because his curls were of a light brown like his mother's, jumped off Babbo's knee, and went forthwith to attest his intelligence by thumping **Monna Lisa** . . . . " 50

—lost: " . . . she saw, a few yards before her, a little child not more than three years old, with no other clothing than his white shirt, pause from a waddling run and look around him. In the first moment of coming nearer she could only see his back—a boy's back, square and sturdy, with a cloud of reddish-brown curls above it; but in the next he turned towards her, and she

could see his dark eyes wide with tears, and his lower lip pushed up and trembling, while his fat brown fists clutched his shirt helplessly.

" . . . presently the outburst ceased with that strange abruptness which belongs to childish joys and griefs: his face lost its distortion, and was fixed in an open-mouthed gaze at **Romola**." 55

—later: "Lillo sat on the ground with his back against the angle of the door-post, and his long legs stretched out, while he held a large book open on his knee, and occasionally made a dash with his hand at an inquisitive fly, with an air of interest stronger than that excited by the finely-printed copy of **Petrarch** . . . . " *E*

"Lillo was a handsome lad, but his features were turning out to be more massive and less regular than his father's. The blood of the Tuscan peasant was in his veins." *E*

" 'I should like to be something that would make me a great man, and very happy besides—something that would not hinder me from having a good deal of pleasure.' " *E*

Lorenzo de' Medici [H]. "The Spirit is clothed in his habit as he lived: the folds of his well-lined black silk garment or *lucco* hang in grave unbroken lines from neck to ankle, his plain cloth cap, with its *becchetto,* or long hanging strip of drapery, to serve as a scarf in case of need, surmounts a penetrating face, not, perhaps, very handsome, but with a firm, well-cut mouth, kept distinctly human by a close-shaven lip and chin." *P*

—mourned: " 'There is but one Lorenzo, I imagine, whose death could throw the Mercato into an uproar, set the lantern of the Duomo leaping in desperation, and cause the lions of the Republic to feel under an immediate necessity to devour one another. I mean Lorenzo de' Medici, the **Pericles** of our Athens . . . . ' " 3

—change: "Lorenzo the magnificent and subtle was dead, and an arrogant, incautious **Piero** was come in his room, an evil change for Florence, unless, indeed, the wise horse prefers the bad rider, as more easily thrown from the saddle . . . . " 8

Niccolò di Macchiavelli [*sic;* H], " 'himself keen enough [said **Nello**] . . . and a great lover of delicate shaving, though his beard is hardly of two years' date, that no sooner do the hairs begin to push themselves, than he perceives a certain grossness of apprehension creeping over him.' " 3 *Of all things, in a work so profoundly informed by GE's meticulous, indeed obsessive, research, she misspells the name of one of the great figures of the age she describes. The spelling with two "c's" is an Anglicization and a solecism here.*

—characteristics: "He was a young man about **Tito**'s own age, with keen features, small close-clipped head, and close-shaven lip and chin, giving the idea of a mind as little encumbered as possible with material that was not nervous. The keen eyes were bright with hope and friendliness, as so many other young eyes have been that have afterwards closed on the world in bitterness and disappointment, for at that time there were none but pleasant predictions about Niccolò Macchiavelli, as a young man of promise, who was expected to mend the broken fortunes of his ancient family." 16

—wrong politics: " '[He] might have done for us if he had been on our [the Medicean] side, but hardly so well [as you, **Tito**]. He is too much bitten with notions, and has not your power of fascination. All the worse for him. He has lost a great chance in life, and you have got it.' " 39

Niccolò Macchiavelli

—observant: "For leaning against the door-post in the centre of the group [of Compagnacci] was a close-shaven, keen-eyed personage . . . who, young as he was, had penetrated all the small secrets of egoism.

" 'Messer **Dolfo**'s head,' he was saying, 'is more of a pumpkin than I thought. I measure men's dulness by the devices they trust in for deceiving others. Your dullest animal of all is he who grins and says he doesn't mind just after he has had his shins kicked.' " 45

—jocular insult: " 'If I were a trifle duller, now,' he went on, smiling as the circle opened to admit **Tito**, 'I should pretend to be fond of this **Melema**, who has got a secretaryship that would exactly suit me—as if Latin ill-paid could love better Latin that's better paid! Melema, you are a pestiferously clever fellow, very much in my way, and I'm sorry to hear you've had another piece of good-luck to-day.' " 45

—a warning: " ' . . . where personal ties are strong, the hostilities they raise must be taken due account of. Many of these half-way severities are mere hot-headed blundering. The only safe blows to be inflicted on men and parties are the blows that are too heavy to be avenged.

" ' . . . Ask our Frate, our prophet, how his universal renovation is to be brought about: he will tell you, first, by getting a free and pure government; and since it appears that this cannot be done by making all Florentines love each other, it must be done by cutting off every head that happens to be obstinately in the way. Only if a man incurs odium by sanctioning a severity that is not thorough enough to be final, he commits a blunder.' " 60

Fra Salvestro Maruffi. "It was not that there was anything manifestly repulsive in Fra Salvestro's face and manner, any air of hypocrisy, any tinge of coarseness; his face was handsomer than **Fra Girolamo**'s, his person a little taller. He was the long-accepted confessor of many among the chief personages in Florence, and had therefore had large experience as a spiritual director. But his face had the vacillating expression of a mind unable to concentrate itself strongly in the channel of one great emotion or belief—an expression which is fatal to influence over an ardent nature like **Romola**'s. Such an expression is not the stamp of insincerity; it is the stamp simply of a shallow soul, which will often be found sincerely striving to fill a high vocation, sincerely composing its countenance to the utterance of sublime formulas, but finding the muscles twitch or relax in spite of belief, as prose insists on coming instead of poetry to the man who has not the divine frenzy.

"Fra Salvestro had a peculiar liability to visions, dependent apparently on a constitution given to somnambulism. Savonarola believed in the supernatural character of these visions, while Fra Salvestro himself had originally resisted such an interpretation of them, and had even rebuked Savonarola for his prophetic preaching: another proof, if one were wanted, that the relative greatness of men is not to be gauged by their tendency to disbelieve the superstitions of their age. For of these two there can be no question which was the great man and which the small." ¶41

Ninna. "The mummy looked very lively, having unusually large dark eyes, though no more than the usual indication of a future nose." 33

" 'Ninna is very good without me now,' began **Tessa** . . . 'I can leave her with **Monna Lisa** any time, and if she is in the cradle and cries, **Lillo** is as sensible as can be—he goes and thumps Monna Lisa' . . . .

"Ninna was a blue-eyed thing, at the tottering, tumbling age—a fair solid, which, like a loaded die, found its base with a constancy that warranted prediction." 50

—*later:* " . . . a delicate blue-eyed girl of thirteen, tossing her long light-brown hair out of her eyes, as she made selections for the wreaths she was weaving, or looked up at her mother's work in the same kind, and told her how to do it with a little air of instruction." *E*

Angelo Poliziano (**Politian**) [H]. "You are of the same mind as **Michele Marullo**, ay, and as Angelo Poliziano himself, in spite of his canonicate, when he relaxes himself a little in my shop after his lectures, and talks of the gods awaking from their long sleep and making the woods and streams vital once more. But he rails against the Roman scholars who want to make us all talk Latin again: "My ears," he says, "are sufficiently flayed by the barbarisms of the learned, and if the vulgar are to talk Latin I would as soon have been in Florence the day they took to beating all the kettles in the city because the bells were not enough to stay the wrath of the saints." ' " 3

—*feud:* "Politian, having been a rejected pretender to the love and the hand of **Scala**'s daughter, kept a very sharp and learned tooth in readiness against the too prosperous and presumptuous secretary, who had declined the greatest scholar of the age for a son-in-law . . . .

"Ineffable moment when the man you secretly hate sends you a Latin epigram with a false gender—hendecasyllables with a questionable elision, at least a toe too much—attempts at poetic figures which are manifest solecisms. That moment had come to Politian: the secretary had put forth his soft head from the official shell, and the terrible lurking crab was down upon him." 7

—*crescendo:* "The elegant scholar, in reply, was not surprised that **Scala** found the Age distasteful to him, since he himself was so distasteful to the Age; nay, it was with perfect accuracy that he, the elegant scholar, had called Scala a branny monster, inasmuch as he was formed from the offscourings of monsters, born amidst the refuse of a mill, and eminently worthy the long-eared office of turning the paternal millstones . . . . " 7

—*appraised:* " ' . . . that Messer Angelo has more genius and erudition than I can find in all the other Florentine scholars put together [said **Tito**]. It may answer very well for them to cry me up now, when Poliziano is beaten down with grief, or illness, or something else. I can try a flight with such a sparrow-hawk as **Pietro Crinito**, but for Poliziano, he is a large-beaked eagle who would swallow me, feathers and all, and not feel any difference.' " 13

—*requiescat:* " ' . . . the incomparable Poliziano, not two months since, gone to——well, well, let us hope he is not gone to the eminent scholars in the Malebolge [**Dante**'s eighth circle of Hell].' " 29

—*summarized:* " . . . Angelo Poliziano, chief literary genius of that age, a born poet, and a scholar without dulness, whose phrases had blood in them and are alive still . . . . " 39

Bernardo Rucellai [H]. " 'And our Bernardo, who stands out more prominently than the rest . . . had added all sorts of distinction to the family name: he had married the sister of **Lorenzo de' Medici**, and had had the most splendid wedding in the memory of Florentine upholstery; and for these and other virtues he had been sent on embassies to France and Venice, and had been chosen Gonfaloniere; he had not only built himself a fine palace, but had finished putting the black and white marble façade to the church of

Santa Maria Novella; had planted a garden with rare trees, and had made it classic ground by receiving within it the meetings of the Platonic Academy, orphaned by the death of Lorenzo; he had written an excellent, learned book, of a new topographical sort, about ancient Rome; he had collected antiquities; he had a pure Latinity. The simplest account of him, one sees, reads like a laudatory epitaph, at the end of which the Greek and Ausonian Muses might be confidently requested to tear their hair, and Nature to desist from any second attempt to combine so many virtues with one set of viscera." 38

"[He] was a man to hold a distinguished place in that [Platonic] Academy even before he became its host and patron. He was still in the prime of life, not more than four and forty, with a somewhat haughty, cautiously dignified presence; conscious of an amazingly pure Latinity, but, says **Erasmus**, not to be caught speaking Latin—no word of Latin to be sheared off him by the sharpest of Teutons." 39

Camilla Rucellai [H]. " 'She prophesied two years ago [said **Francesco Cei**] that Pico would die in the time of lilies. He has died in November. "Not at all the time of lilies," said the scorners. "Go to!" says Camilla; "it is the lilies of France I meant, and it seems to me they are close enough under your nostrils." I say, "Euge, Camilla!" If the Frate can prove that any one of his visions has been as well fulfilled, I'll declare myself a Piagnone to-morrow.' " 29

—antagonistic vision: "[**Romola**] found the nervous grey-haired woman in a chamber arranged as much as possible like a convent cell. The thin fingers clutching Romola as she sat, and the eager voice addressing her at first in a loud whisper, caused her a physical shrinking that made it difficult for her to keep her seat.

" . . . She had a constitutional disgust for the shallow excitability of women like Camilla, whose faculties seemed all wrought up into fantasies, leaving nothing for emotion and thought. The exhortation was not yet ended when she started up and attempted to wrench her arm from Camilla's tightening grasp. It was of no use. The prophetess kept her hold like a crab, and, only incited to more eager exhortation by Romola's resistance, was carried beyond her own intention into a shrill statement of other visions . . . .

" 'Let me go!' said Romola, in a deep voice of anger. 'God grant you are mad! else you are detestably wicked.' " 52

Pagolantonio Soderini [H] " 'Have you heard the news **Domenico Cennini**, here, has been telling us?—that Pagolantonio Soderini has given **Ser Piero da Bibbiena** a box on the ear for setting on **Piero de' Medici** to interfere with the marriage between young **Tommaso Soderini** and **Fiammetta Strozzi**, and is to be sent ambassador to Venice as a punishment?' " See **The City of Florence**—*politics*—*Piagnoni*

" 'I don't know which I envy him most,' said **Macchiavelli**, 'the offence or the punishment. The offence will make him the most popular man in all Florence, and the punishment will take him among the only people in Italy who have known how to manage their own affairs.' " 16

—on the Frate's confession: "And keen Florentines like Soderini and **Piero Guicciardini** may well have had an angry smile on their lips at a severity which dispensed with all law in order to hang and burn a man in whom the seductions of a public career had warped the strictness of his veracity; may well have remarked that if the Frate had mixed a much deeper fraud with a zeal and ability less inconvenient to high personages, the fraud would

have been regarded as an excellent oil for ecclesiastical and political wheels." 71

Vaiano. "The conjuror—a man with one of those faces in which the angles of the eyes and eyebrows, of the nostrils, mouth, and sharply-defined jaw, all tend upward—showed his small regular teeth in an impish but not ill-natured grin, as he let go **Tessa**'s hands, and stretched out his own backward, shrugging his shoulders, and bending them forward a little in a half-apologetic, half-protesting manner." 10

—at a fair: ". . . [in] a white mitre with yellow cabalistic figures upon it.

" 'Behold, my children!' **Tito** heard him saying, 'behold your opportunity! neglect not the holy sacrament of matrimony when it can be had for the small sum of a white quattrino—the cheapest matrimony ever offered, and dissolved by special bull beforehand at every man's own will and pleasure.' " 14

Francesco Valori [H], " 'that I've danced with in the Via Larga when he was a bachelor . . . how we ought to keep to the rules the Signory laid down heaven knows when, that we were not to wear this or that, and not to eat this and that—and how our manners were corrupted and we read bad books. . . .' " 12 *See* **The City of Florence**—*politics—Piagnone*

—in power: " . . . the relief which had come in extremity . . . was making that party so triumphant, that Francesco Valori, hot-tempered chieftain of the Piagnoni, had been elected Gonfaloniere at the beginning of the year, and was making haste to have as much of his own liberal way as possible during his two months of power. That seemed for the moment like a strengthening of the party most attached to freedom, and a reinforcement of protection to **Savonarola** . . . . " 49

—attributes: "Francesco Valori . . . was the head of the Piagnoni, a man with certain fine qualities that were not incompatible with violent partisanship, with an arrogant temper that alienated his friends, nor with bitter personal animosities—one of the bitterest being directed against **Bernardo del Nero**." 57

—needing evidence: " . . . additional and stronger facts were desirable, especially against **Bernardo del Nero**, who, so far as appeared hitherto, had simply refrained from betraying the late plot after having tried in vain to discourage it: for the welfare of Florence demanded that the guilt of Bernardo del Nero should be put in the strongest light. So Francesco Valori zealously believed; and perhaps he was not himself aware that the strength of his zeal was determined by his hatred." 57

Minor Figures

Leon Battista Alberti [H], "a reverend senior when those three (**Pico**, **Ficino**, and **Poliziano**) were young, and of a much grander type than they, a robust, universal mind, at once practical and theoretic, artist, man of science, inventor, poet . . . . " 39

Lamberto dell' Antella, " 'has been seized within the territory: a letter has been found on him of very dangerous import to the chief Mediceans, and the scoundrel, who was once a favourite hound of **Piero de' Medici**, is ready now to swear what any one pleases against him or his friends.' " 56

"[He] had been tortured in aid of his previous willingness to tell more than he knew . . . . " 57

Benedetto. " . . . and the Hebrew baby was a tottering tumbling Christian, Benedetto by name, having been baptised in the church on the mountain-side." 68

Girolamo Benevieni [H], "the mystic poet . . . hastening, perhaps, to carry tidings of the beloved Frate's speedy coming to his friend **Pico della Mirandola**, who was never to see the light of another morning." 25

Monna Berta "would certainly burst out laughing at [**Monna Brigida**], and call her an old hag, and as Monna Berta was really only fifty-two, she had a superiority which would make the observation cutting." 51

Boys, collecting Anathema.

" . . . a **small fellow** of ten, his olive wreath resting above cherubic cheeks and wide brown eyes, his imagination really possessed with a hovering awe at existence as something in which great consequences impended on being good or bad, his longings nevertheless running in the direction of mastery and mischief, was the first to reach **Monna Brigida** and place himself across her path . . . .

" 'In truth you are old, buona madres,' said the cherubic boy, in a sweet soprano. 'You look very ugly with the red on your cheeks and that black glistening hair, and those fine things. It is only **Satan** who can like to see you. Your Angel is sorry. He wants you to rub away the red.' " 51

"But it was not the cherubic-faced young one who first addressed her; it was a **youth** of fifteen, who held one handle of a wide basket.

" 'Venerable mother!' he began, 'the blessed Jesus commands you to give up the Anathema which you carry upon you. That cap embroidered with pearls, those jewels that fasten up your false hair—let them be given up and sold for the poor; and cast the hair itself away from you, as a lie that is only fit for burning. Doubtless, too, you have other jewels under your silk mantle.' " 51

" 'Yes, lady,' said the **youth** at the other handle, who had many of **Fra Girolamo**'s phrases by heart, 'they are too heavy for you: they are heavier than a millstone, and are weighting you for perdition. Will you adorn yourself with the hunger of the poor, and be proud to carry God's curse upon your head?' " 51

Burchiello. " 'Now a barber can be dispassionate [said **Nello**]; the only thing he necessarily stands by is the razor, always providing he is not an author. That was the flaw in my great predecessor Burchiello: he was a poet, and had consequently a prejudice about his own poetry.' " 3

Butcher. " ' . . . it's my belief **Piero** will be a good while before he wants to come back, for he looked as frightened as a hunted chicken, when we hustled and pelted him in the piazza. He's a coward, else he might have made a better stand when he'd got his horsemen. But we'll swallow no **Medici** any more, whatever else the French king wants to make us swallow.' " 22

Demetrio Calcondila [H], " 'who is loved by many, and not hated immoderately even by the most renowned scholars.' " 3

" . . . for a long time Demetrio Calcondila, one of the most eminent and respectable among the emigrant Greeks, had also held a Greek chair . . . . Calcondila was now gone to Milan, and there was no counterpoise or rival to **Politian** such as was desired for him by the friends who wished him to be taught a little propriety and humility." 9

Calderino (**Domizio Calderini**) [H], " 'who, as Poliziano has well shown, [has] recourse to impudent falsities of citation to serve the ends of their vanity and secure a triumph to their own mistakes.' " 12

Cecco "was a wild-looking figure: a very ragged tunic, made shaggy and variegated by cloth-dust and clinging fragments of wool, gave relief to a pair of bare bony arms and a long sinewy neck; his square jaw shaded by a bristly black beard, his bridgeless nose and low forehead, made his face look as if it had been crushed down for purposes of packing, and a narrow piece of red rag tied over his ears seemed to assist in the compression: **Romola** looked at him with some hesitation.

" 'Don't distrust me, madonna,' said Cecco, who understood her look perfectly; 'I am not so pretty as you, but I've got an old mother who eats my porridge for me. What! there's a heart inside me, and I've bought a candle for the most Holy Virgin before now.' " 42

Bernardo Cennini, "who, twenty years before, having heard of the new process of printing carried on by Germans, had cast his own types in Florence . . . . " 4

Domenico Cennini, goldsmith. "The grave elderly man . . . remained necessarily in lathered silence and passivity while **Nello** showered this talk in his ears, but turned a slow sideway gaze on the stranger." 4

—*expert:* " 'This is a curious and valuable ring, young man. This intaglio of the fish with the crested serpent above it, in the black stratum of the onyx, or rather nicolo, is well shown by the surrounding blue of the upper stratum. The ring has, doubtless, a history?' added Cennini, looking up keenly at the young stranger." 4

Ser Cioni [H], a notary. " . . . a thin-lipped, eager-looking personage in spectacles, wearing a pen-and-ink case at his belt . . . .

" ' 'Tis well said you Florentines are blind,' he began, in an incisive high voice. 'It appears to me, you need nothing but a diet of hay to make cattle of you. What! do you think the death of **Lorenzo** is the scourge God has prepared for Florence? Go! you are sparrows chattering praise over the dead hawk. What! a man who was trying to slip a noose over every neck in the Republic that he might tighten it at his pleasure!' " 1

—*changed times:* "His biting words could get only a contemptuous reception two years and a half before in the Mercato, but now he spoke with the more complacent humour of a man whose party is uppermost, and who is conscious of some influence with the people." 21

Contadina (false—it is **Vaiano**). " . . . a sturdy-looking, broad-shouldered contadina, with her head-drapery folded about her face so that little was to be seen but a bronzed nose and a pair of dark eyes and eyebrows. She carried her child packed up in the stiff mummy-shaped case in which Italian babies have been from time immemorial introduced into society, turning its face a little towards her bosom, and making those sorrowful grimaces which women are in the habit of using as a sort of pulleys to draw down reluctant tears." 16

Luca Corsini [H], "doctor of law, felt his heart palpitating a little with the sense that he had a Latin oration to read . . . . " 21

"Messer Luca Corsini himself, for example, who on a memorable occasion yet to come was to raise his learned arms in street stone-throwing for the cause of religion, freedom, and the Frate." 25

Pietro Crinito [H]. " ' . . . banquets and other follies . . . [have] been too much the fashion of scholars, especially when, like our Pietro Crinito, they think their scholarship needs to be scented and broidered, to squander with one hand till they have been fain to beg with the other.' " 9

Fra Cristoforo, confessor to **Monna Brigida**. 12 "[He] was not at hand to reinforce her distrust of Dominican teaching, and she was helplessly possessed and shaken by a vague sense that a supreme warning was come to her." 51

Cronaca. " 'The Frate neither rails nor prophesies against any man,' said a middle-aged personage seated at the other corner of the window; 'he only prophesies against vice. If you think that an attack on your poems, **Francesco**, it is not the Frate's fault.' " 8

" 'Cronaca, you are becoming sententious,' said the printer; '**Fra Girolamo**'s preaching will spoil you, and make you take life by the wrong handle. Trust me, your cornices will lose half their beauty if you begin to mingle bitterness with them . . . . The next palace you build we shall see you trying to put the Frate's doctrine into stone.' " 8

—partisan: " 'We have had the best testimony to his words since the last Quaresima; for even to the wicked wickedness has become a plague; and the ripeness of vice is turning to rottenness in the nostrils even of the vicious. There has not been a change since the Quaresima, either in Rome or at Florence, but has put a new seal on the Frate's words that the harvest of sin is ripe, and that God will reap it with a sword.' " 16

Bernardo Dovizi of Bibbiena [H], " 'whose wit is so rapid that I see no way of outrivalling it save by the scent of orange-blossoms' . . . .

" 'Never talk of rivalry, bel giovane mio: Bernardo Dovizi is a keen youngster, who will never carry a net out to catch the wind; but he has something of the same sharp-muzzled look as his brother . . . . ' " 13

Ser Piero Dovizi da Bibbiena [H], " 'the weasel that **Piero de' Medici** keeps at his beck to slip through small holes for him.' " 13 *See* **Pagolantonio Soderini**

Fra Domenico, "**Savonarola**'s fervent follower . . . no sooner heard of this new challenge, than he took up the gauntlet for his master, and declared himself ready to walk through the fire with **Fra Francesco**." 63

—dress for fire: " . . . the flame-coloured velvet cope in which Fra Domenico was arrayed as he headed the procession, cross in hand, his simple mind totally exalted with faith, and with the genuine intention to enter the flames for the glory of God and **Fra Girolamo**." 65

Marsilio Ficino [H]. " ' . . . why is Ficino [said **Bardo**], whose Latin is an offence to me, and who wanders purblind among the superstitious fancies that marked the decline at once of art, literature, and philosophy, to descend to posterity as the very high priest of Platonism, while I, who am more than their equal, have not effected anything but scattered work, which will be appropriated by other men?' " 5

" . . . innocent, laborious Marsilio Ficino, picked out young to be reared as a Platonic philosopher, and fed on Platonism in all its stages till his mind was perhaps a little pulpy from that too exclusive diet . . . . " 39

Fellow in a red cap. " 'Do you keep your bread for those that can't swallow, madonna?' said a rough-looking fellow, in a red night-cap . . . .

" 'Come, madonna . . . the old thief doesn't eat the bread, you see: you'd better try *us*. We fast so much, we're half saints already.' " 42

—faced down: "The man in the night-cap looked rather silly, and backed, thrusting his elbow into his neighbour's ribs with an air of moral rebuke." 42

Matteo Franco [H]. " ' "Here is this untainted sceptic, Matteo Franco, who wants hotter sauce than any of us." "Because he has a strong opinion of *himself,"* flashes out **Luigi** [**Pulci**], "which is the original egg of all other opinion. *He* a sceptic? He believes in the immortality of his own verses. He is such a logician as that preaching friar who described the pavement of the bottomless pit." ' " 39

Francesco Gaddi [H]. " 'Somebody step forward and say a few words in French,' said **Soderini**. But no one of high importance chose to risk a second failure. 'You, Francesco Gaddi—you can speak.' But Gaddi, distrusting his own promptness, hung back, and pushing **Tito**, said, 'You, **Melema**.' " 26

Monna Ghita. "She was a stout but brawny woman, with a man's jerkin slipped over her green serge gamurra or gown, and the peaked hood of some departed mantle fastened round her sun-burnt face, which, under all its coarseness and premature wrinkles, showed a half-sad, half-ludicrous maternal resemblance to the tender baby-face of the little maiden [**Tessa**]—the sort of resemblance which often seems a more croaking, shudder-creating prophecy than that of the death's head." 2

—gone: " '[She] had a fatal seizure before I was called in . . . .'

" 'Monna Ghita!' said **Nello** . . . 'Peace be with her angry soul! The Mercato will want a whip the more if her tongue is laid to rest.' " 16

Cardinal **Giovanni de' Medici** [H}, "youngest of red-hatted fathers, who has since presented his broad dark cheek very conspicuously to posterity as **Pope Leo the Tenth** . . . . " 13

Goro, a wool-beater. " 'I tell you I saw it myself,' said a fat man, with a bunch of newly-purchased leeks in his hand. 'I was in Santa Maria Novella, and saw it myself. The woman started up and threw out her arms, and cried out and said she saw a big bull with fiery horns . . . . ' " 1

" 'Goro is a fool . . . . Let him carry home his leeks and shake his flanks over his wool-beating. He'll mend matters more that way than by showing his tun-shaped body in the piazza, as if everybody might measure his grievances by the size of his paunch. The burdens that harm him most are his heavy carcass and his idleness' . . . .

"Goro turned his fat cheek and glassy eye on the frank speaker with a look of deprecation rather than of resentment." 1

Cristoforo Landino [H] " 'said that the excellent **Bardo** was one of those scholars who lie overthrown in their learning, like cavaliers in heavy armour,* and then get angry because they are over-ridden—which pithy remark, it seems to me, was not a herb out of his own garden; for of all men, for feeding one with an empty spoon and gagging one with vain expectation by long discourse, Messer Cristoforo is the pearl.' " 13 **The gravamen of the criticism widely made of this work by the likes of Henry James and Leslie Stephen.*

Camillo Leonardi [H]. " 'I . . . wear certain rings, which the discreet Camillo Leonardi prescribed to me by letter when two years ago I had a certain infirmity of sudden numbness [said **Bardo**].' " 6

Monna Lisa, "a shrivelled, hardy old woman [who] was untying a goat with two kids . . . she fetched a hatchet from the house, and, showing [**Baldassarre**] a clump that lay half covered with litter in a corner, asked him if he would chop that up for her: if he would, he might lie in the outhouse for one night. He agreed, and Monna Lisa stood with her arms akimbo to watch him, with a smile of gratified cunning . . . . " 33

—*meek:* " 'Holy Mother!' said Monna Lisa, in her meek, thick tone . . . .

"**Romola** went to look at the sleeping **Ninna**, and Monna Lisa, one of the exceptionally meek deaf, who never expect to be spoken to, returned to her salad." 55

Lollo, "the conjuror's impish lad . . . who was dancing and jeering in front of the ingenuous boys that made the majority of the crowd. Lollo had no great compassion for the **prisoners**, but being conscious of an excellent knife which was his unfailing companion, it had seemed to him from the first that to jump forward, cut a rope, and leap back again before the soldier who held it could use his weapon, would be an amusing and dexterous piece of mischief." 22

Mariotto. " . . . and now a well-looking, merry-eyed youth of seventeen, in a loose tunic and red cap, pushed forward, holding by the hand a plump **brunette**, whose scanty ragged dress displayed her round arms and legs very picturesquely.

" 'Fetter us without delay, Maestro!' said the youth, 'for I have got to take my bride home and paint her under the light of a lantern.' " 14

Marullo [H], " 'who may be said to have married the Italic Muse in more senses than one, since he has married our learned and lovely **Alessandra Scala** [H].' " 3

" . . . the Greek soldier-poet . . . . " 7

Maso, "the old serving-man, when he returned from the Mercato with the stock of cheap vegetables, had to make his slow way up to the second storey before he reached the door of his master, **Bardo**. . . . " 5

"Maso had been taken into her confidence only so far that he knew her intended journey was a secret; and to do just what she told him was the thing he cared most for in his withered wintry age." 36

Mischief. "**Dolfo Spini** sat playing with a fine stag-hound which alternately snuffed at a basket of pups and licked his hands with that affectionate disregard of her master's morals sometimes held to be one of the most agreeable attributes of her sex." 63

Nanni, a tailor. " 'Thou art pleased to scoff, **Nello**,' said the sallow, round-shouldered man . . . 'but it is not the less true that every revelation, whether by visions, dreams, portents, or the written word, has many meanings, which it is given to the illuminated only to unfold.' " 1

—*reformer:* " 'And that reform is not far off, **Niccolò**' . . . seizing his opportunity like a missionary among the too light-minded heathens; 'for a time of tribulation is coming, and the scourge is at hand. And when the Church is purged of cardinals and prelates who traffic in her inheritance that their hands may be full to pay the price of blood and to satisfy their own lusts, the State will be purged too—and Florence will be purged of men who love to see avarice and lechery under the red hat and the mitre because it gives them the screen of a more hellish vice than their own.' " 1

Jacopo Nardi [H]. " . . . also looking on in painful doubt concerning the man who had won his early reverence, was a young Florentine of two-and-twenty, named Jacopo Nardi, afterwards to deserve honour as one of the very few who, feeling **Fra Girolamo**'s eminence, have written about him with the simple desire to be veracious." 72

Nofri. "It was true [**Tessa**'s] obedience had been a little helped by her own dread lest the alarming stepfather Nofri should turn up even in this quarter, so far from the Por' del Prato, and beat her at least, if he did not drag her back to work for him." 33

" 'What! [said **Bratti**] you've done none the worse, then, for running away from father Nofri? You were in the right of it, for he goes on crutches now, and a crabbed fellow with crutches is dangerous; he can reach across the house and beat a woman as he sits.' " 50

Pico della Mirandola [H], "once a quixotic young genius with long curls, astonished at his own powers and astonishing Rome with heterodox theses; afterwards a more humble student with a consuming passion for inward perfection, having come to find the universe more astonishing than his own cleverness . . . . " 39

Piero de' Medici [H] " 'has abundant intelligence; his faults are only the faults of hot blood. I love the lad—lad he will always be to me, as I have always been "little father" to him' [said **Bernardo del Nero**]." 6

Pistoian women. "[**Tito**] found himself at one moment close to the trotting procession of barefooted, hard-heeled contadine, and could see their sun-dried, bronzed faces, and their strange, fragmentary garb, dim with hereditary dirt, and of obsolete stuffs and fashions, that made them look, in the eyes of the city people, like a way-worn ancestry returning from a pilgrimage on which they had set out a century ago. Just then it was the hardy-scant-feeding peasant-women from the mountains of Pistoia, who were entering with a year's labour in a moderate bundle of yarn on their backs, and in their hearts that meagre hope of good and that wide dim fear of harm, which were somehow to be cared for by the Blessed Virgin . . . . " 14

Pontanus or **Merula** [H], " 'whose names will be foremost on the lips of posterity, because they sought patronage and found it, because they had tongues that could flatter, and blood that was used to be nourished from the client's basket.' " 5

—two-faced: "Did not Pontanus, poet and philosopher of unrivalled Latinity, make the finest possible oration at Naples to welcome the French king, who had come to dethrone the learned orator's royal friend and patron? and still Pontanus held up his head and prospered." 57

Porter. " 'Are you a servant of Messer **Tito**?'

" 'No, friend [said **Baldassarre**], I am not a servant; I am a scholar.'

"There are men to whom you need only say, 'I am a buffalo' in a certain tone of quiet confidence, and they will let you pass. The porter gave way at once." 38

Priest, "with a broad, harmless face, his black frock much worn and soiled, stood, bucket in hand, looking at [**Romola**] timidly and still keeping aloof as he took the path towards the cow in silence." 68

Prisoners. "They were young and hardy, and, in the scant clothing which the avarice of their captors had left them, looked like vulgar, sturdy mendicants." 22

Giannozzo Pucci [H], Medicean "who was more fraternal and less patronising in his manner than **Tornabuoni** . . . . " 39

Fra Francesco di Puglia [H]. " . . . excitement was to be had in Santa Croce, where the Franciscan appointed to preach the Quaresimal sermons had offered to clench his arguments by walking through the fire with **Fra Girolamo** . . . if the fire consumed him, his falsity would be manifest; and that he might have no excuse for evading the test, the Franciscan declared himself willing to be a victim to this high logic, and to be burned for the sake of securing the necessary minor premiss." 53

Luigi Pulci [H]. " 'For what says Luigi Pulci? "**Dombruno**'s sharp-cutting scimitar had the fame of being enchanted; but," says Luigi, "I am rather of opinion that it cut sharp because it was of strongly-tempered steel." ' " 16

—quoted: " 'Our Luigi Pulci would have said this delicate boiled kid must be eaten with an impartial mind. I remember one day at Careggi, when Luigi was in his rattling vein, he was maintaining that nothing perverted the palate like opinion. "Opinion," said he, "corrupts the saliva—that's why men took to pepper. Scepticism is the only philosophy that doesn't bring a taste in the mouth" . . . . Poor Luigi! his mind was like the sharpest steel that can touch nothing without cutting.'

" 'And yet a very gentle-hearted creature,' said **Giannozzo Pucci**. 'It seemed to me his talk was a mere blowing of soap-bubbles. What dithyrambs he went into about eating and drinking! And yet he was as temperate as a butterfly.' " 39

Niccolò Ridolfi [H], "a middle-aged man, with that negligent ease of manner which, seeming to claim nothing, is really based on the life-long consciousness of commanding rank." 39

Sandro, "a solemn-looking dark-eyed youth, who made way for them on the threshold [of **Nello**'s shop]." 3

" '[He] does not deserve even to be called a *tonsor inequalis,* but rather to be pronounced simply a bungler in the vulgar tongue.' " 6

—a plot: "**Nello** whispered in the ear of Sandro, who rolled his solemn eyes, nodded, and, following up these signs of understanding with a slow smile, took to his heels with surprising rapidity." 16

Ludovico Sforza [H], "copious in gallantry, splendid patron of an incomparable **Leonardo da Vinci**—holding the ducal crown of Milan in his grasp, and wanting to put it on his own head rather than let it rest on that of a feeble **nephew** who would take very little to poison him . . . . " 21

Soldiers. "The men who held the ropes were French soldiers, and by broken Italian phrases and strokes from the knotted end of the rope, they from time to time stimulated their prisoners to beg . . . .

"The soldiers themselves began to dislike their position, for, with a strong inclination to use their weapons, they were checked by the necessity for keeping a secure hold on their prisoners, and they were now hurrying along in the hope of finding shelter in a hostelry." 22

Maestro Tacco, "a round-headed, round-bodied personage, seated on a raw young horse, which held its nose out with an air of threatening obstinacy, and by a constant effort to back and go off in an oblique line showed free views about authority very much in advance of the age." 16

—disliked: " 'And I have a few more adventures in pickle for him,' continued **Nello** . . . . 'He's a doctor from Padua . . . and now he's come to Flor-

ence to see what he can net. But his great trick is making rounds among the contadini . . . . It stirs my gall to see the toad-faced quack fingering the greasy quattrini, or bagging a pigeon in exchange for his pills and powders. But I'll put a few thorns in his saddle, else I'm no Florentine.' " 16

—hat off: " . . . taking off his bonnet, and giving to full view a bald low head and flat broad face, with high ears, wide lipless mouth, round eyes, and deep arched lines above the projecting eyebrows, which altogether made **Nello**'s epithet 'toad-faced' dubiously complimentary to the blameless batrachian." 16

Lorenzo Tornabuoni [H]. " 'He pretends to look well satisfied—that deep Tornabuoni—but he's a Medicean in his heart; mind that.' " 22

"[He] possessed that power of dissembling annoyance which is demanded in a man who courts popularity . . . . " 22

'Monna Trecca' "(equivalent to 'Dame Green-grocer') turned round . . . with a half-fierce, half-bewildered look, first at the speaker, then at her disarranged commodities, and then at the speaker again.

" 'A bad Easter and a bad year to you, and may you die by the sword!' she burst out, rushing towards her stall . . . . " 1

Lorenzo Valla [H]. " 'But inasmuch as Valla, though otherwise of dubious fame, is held in high honour for his severe scholarship, whence the epigrammatist has jocosely said of him that since he went among the shades, **Pluto** himself has not dared to speak in the ancient languages, it is the more needful that his name should not be as a stamp warranting false wares. . . .' " 12

Young man "in an excellent cloth tunic, whose face showed no signs of want. 'The Frate has been preaching to the birds, like **Saint Anthony**, and he's been telling the hawks they were made to feed the sparrows, as every good Florentine citizen was made to feed six starving beggarmen from Arezzo or Bologna. Madonna, there, is a pious Piagnone: she's not going to throw away her good bread on honest citizens who've got all the Frate's prophecies to swallow.' " 42

Also mentioned

Saints

Sant' Anna, mother of the Virgin	13, 51
St Anthony (San Antonio)	8, 42, 61
St Augustine	8
San Bartolommeo, said to have been killed by flaying	3
Saint Benedict	15
St Bernard, in a picture by Lippi	52
Saint Catherine of Egypt (Alexandria)	49
St Christopher, the patron saint of travellers	1, 14
San Cosma, who gave medical aid without fee	16
San Damiano, who gave medical aid without fee	16
San Domenico; Saint Dominick, Saint Dominic	1, 15, 65
San Francisco; Saint Francis	1, 12, 15, 36
San Giovanni Battista, patron saint of Florence: his feast day June 24	1, 8, 29
San Giuseppe	12
Saint Margaret, whose trials included ingestion by a large dragon and beheading	18
St Michael	1
San Niccolò	1
Saint Peter	62
St Philip	6
Saint Sebastian	4

San Stefano, who was stoned to death 16
San Zenobio, revered bishop of Florence a thousand years before 43

Others

Dianola Acciajoli [H], a new bride 12
Accursius [H], scholar of Roman law 25
Alberti [H], a leader of the *Arrabbiati* party 39
Albizzi [H], Dianola's groom 12
Albizzi, the; a sub-party of toughs associated with Valori and the Frate's party 63
Pope **Alexander the Sixth** [H], whose name Vaiano takes in vain at a street fair 14, 16
apprentice in Caparra's shop, who sold Calvo a knife 44
Archbishop in gorgeous cope, with a canopy held above him 43
Giovanni Argiropulo [H], Greek scholar brought to Florence; tutored Poliziano 3, 5
Cecco d'Ascoli, alleged to have been burned alive for excessive brains 16
Augustinian monk, who advised Tito to go to Florence, not to Rome 3
Augustinians of San Spirito, in black, with cultured human faces above it 43
Giovanni Aurispa [H], who brought manuscripts back from Greece 6
Baccio [H], Florentine painter who became Fra Bartolommeo 49
barber who shaved Baldassarre and gave him a mirror 30
Michelozzo di Bartolomeo [H], architect *P*
Seneschal de Beaucaire, " 'the great favourite of the Cristianissimo.' " 31
Fra Benedetto, a colleague and friend of Savonarola's 64
Benedictines, in white; reformed 43
Antonio Benevieni, " 'the greatest master of the chirurgic art.' " 16
Ser Benghi, a figure in a story of a recalcitrant steed 3
Monna Berta, evidently with a poor opinion of Monna Brigida's ostentatious finery 12
two blacksmith's labourers, slight ebony figures at anvil and bellows 26
Giovanni Boccaccio [H], who had a fine collection made by himself alone 5
Domenico Bonsi [H], Florentine delegate in treaty negotiation with France 29
boy in a white surplice trying to control Vaiano's monkey 14
Brunelleschi [H], designer of the cupola of the cathedral 3
brunette contadina in a ragged dress at the fair 14
Leonardo Bruno [H], scholar noted for his complaint at the cost of his wedding 20
Michelangelo Buonarotti [H], a "promising youth" 20
Christoforo Buondelmonte [H], who wrote the *Isolario* 6
The **Buondelmonti** [H], patrons of the Church of L'Impruneta 42
bystander, rough-looking and hungry, with a red cap; faced down by Romola 42
Denetrio Calcondila [H], Greek professor who comes to be shaved by Nello 2, 5
Andrea Cambini, with rumours about the convicted Mediceans 59
Carmelites, in procession; white over dark 43
Cecca [H], artist and engineer who designed displays for feast days 8
cheesemonger, in oratorical flight making notes on his piece of *marzolino* 1
Ciriaco of Ancona [H], author and traveller 6
Philippe de Comines [H], Frenchman owed a debt by Florence 64
Constantine the Great [H], Roman emperor who converted to Christianity 8
Piero di Cosimo [H], "a strange, freakish painter" 3
Joannes Crisolara [H], a tutor at the court of the King of Naples 5, 6
Diogenes, Greek philosopher who carried a lantern by day in search of an honest man 8
Fra Domenico, of the convent of San Marco; a lieutenant to Savonarola 12, 49
Dominican monk, formerly secretary to Fra Girolamo for several years 70
Donatello [H], sculptor: his statue of Plenty stood in the old market 1, 8
Piero Dovizi [H], a Medicean serving Piero de' Medici 13
envoy from France, commenting on feminine emotions in politics 60
Gian Fantoni, who gave his house to Romola to rest in 43
Ferdinand, king of Naples [H] 21
Cassandra Fidele [H], exceptional woman of great learning 5, 36
Francesco Filelfo [H], a "wonder of juvenile learning" 4, 5, 6, 16
Firenzuola [H], who wrote the quoted *Delle Bellezza delle Donne* 19
fisherman, who had a boat Romola coveted 61

Poggio (Bracchiolini) [H], admirable but not wholly exemplary in Bardo's opinion	5
Antonio Pollajuolo [H], painter and designer enticed to Rome from Florence	39
Pontanus (Giovano Pantano) [H], who had patronage and may leave a name	5
Raphael [H], who painted a portrait of the keen-eyed Cardinal da Bibbiena	20
The **Ridolfi** family [H], prominent in Florence	1
Gian Battista Ridolfi [H], brother of Niccolì and a Piagnone	58
Alemanno Rinuccini [H], humanist and author in Florence	3, 17
Cosimo Rosselli [H], employer of Piero di Cosimo	4
Franco Sacchetti [H], who wrote a book of tales	12, 29
Marco Salviati, adherent of Savonarola, commanding 300 at the Trial by Fire	65
Salviati, the; a sub-party of toughs allied with Valori	63
Count di San Severino, a purchaser of the Bardo collections	32
Andrea del Sarto [H], whose frescoes were not yet in place at the Nunziata	14
Meo di Sasso, who was bringing wonderful news when his horse broke down	43
Alessandra Scala [H] a daughter who delights in gems: her "winter flowers"	6
Joseph Scaliger [H], a 16th century humanist who thought little of Scala's Latin	7
sculptor who wore his white-streaked cap and tunic with a jaunty air	63
Servites, a famous Florentine order founded by seven merchants	43
The **Sforza** family [H], rulers in Milan	1
Gian Galeazzo Sforza, feeble nephew of Ludovico; ducal incumbent	21
shoemaker, with bunches of slippers hanging over his shoulders	63
sleek shopkeeper; correcting Goro on the challenge to walk through fire	63
Tommaso Soderini [H], son of Pagolantonio Soderini; engaged to Fiammetta Strozzi	16
Dolfo (Ridolpho) Spini [H], dissolute aristocrat and Troublemaker	25
Fiametta Strozzi [H], engaged to Tommaso Soderini	16
Pope **Sylvester** [H], in the days when San Giovanni deposed Mars in Florence	8
Taddeo, ruffian in the employ of Dolfo Spini	66
Theodolinda [H], Queen of Lombardy; chose San Giovanni as Florence's patron saint	8
Thomas of Sarzana [H] who became Pope	5
Ambrogio Traversari [H], vicar-general of the Camaldolite order	6
Farinata degli Uberti [H], whose definition of "party" survives	6
Frati Umiliati, from Ognissanti, early in the wool trade	43
Vallambrosan Benedictines, in procession	43
vendor of old clothes, who hung hose absent-mindedly around his own neck	1
Giovanni Vespucci [H], who wanted a painting	18
Guidantonio Vespucci [H], Florentine delegate in treaty negotiation with France	29
Giovanni Villani [H], historian of Lombardy and Florence	8
wife of Bratti Ferravecchi	1
stout woman at Fantoni's house, giving way to Romola; three children	43
tall woman upon whose head Vaiano's monkey jumped	14
young woman at Dolfo Spini's, who opens the door for Tito	63

Felix Holt

The Radical

"The poets have told us of a dolorous enchanted forest in the under world. The thorn-bushes there, and the thick-barked stems, have human histories hidden in them; the power of unuttered cries dwells in the passionless-seeming branches, and the red warm blood is darkly feeding the quivering nerves of a sleepless memory that watches through all dreams. These things are a parable." *Introduction*

Volume I

The Introduction depicts the rural midlands of England: the coaches, the hedgerows, the hamlets; and then the manufacturing areas toward the north: the miners, the Dissenting chapels, the weavers, the factories. **Sampson** the coachman is full of information concerning those who live on the lands he drives through, including the **Transome-Durfey** claims and law-suits, the present Transome (the name assumed) family and their lawyer, **Jermyn**. *I* It is September, 1832 **Harold Transome**, the younger son but now the heir, and rich in his own right, is coming home after fifteen years in the near East, with a little son. Harold is self-confident, independent; not inclined to consult his mother. **Mrs Transome** married money and had an imbecile son before Harold. She is disappointed and fearful. She has a past and a terrible secret eating at her soul. 1

Harold visits his uncle, the Rector **Lingon** and gets background. He will keep Jermyn to fight his election, then get rid of him. At breakfast, Harold tells him he will run as a Radical. His mother remonstrates and is put down. Jermyn observes and is apprehensive. Harold and he talk politics after breakfast. Harold avoids touchy subjects and later encounters his uncle, who is determined to be friends despite Radicalism. 2 A survey of Treby Magna, now a polling-place, its history and the rise of Dissent with the coming of mines. 3 The **Rev. Rufus Lyon** receives **Mrs Holt**, who complains that her son refuses to allow her income from quack medicines developed by the late **Mr Holt**. Mr Lyon asks her to send **Felix Holt** to him and eases her out. 4

Felix calls on Mr Lyon, and they talk. **Esther Lyon** appears, startling Felix with her obvious high breeding. He attacks her for reading **Byron**. Startled, she defends herself with wit and charm. She tells her father

Jermyn wants to meet. He is puzzled: his are the wrong politics. Felix tells of his talks with the workers. He goes. Esther is let down to hear he is a watchmaker. He thinks of her. 5 Esther is not popular with the Dissenters: she is too accomplished. Her father has never spoken of his wife. We learn the story: **Annette Ledru**, lost and outcast by circumstances, cried for help one evening, and the successful minister Lyon responded. He took her and the baby in and found he was obliged to leave his church as a result. After a year's struggle, he asks her to marry him. She trembles, miserably. He cuts off the discussion but becomes seriously ill. She tends him, pays attention, then offers to marry him. They are wed. She fades slowly away and dies after four years of life together. 6

Sir Maximus Debarry, staunch Tory, and his lady call on Mrs Transome. They see little **Harry Transome**, who bites his grandmother fiercely. As they drive home, factotum **Maurice Christian** intercepts them with dreadful news: Harold Transome will stand as a Radical. Sir Maximus is appalled and furious. At his home, the servants live a gay life. Gossip alludes to an old lawsuit over the Transome estate, in which one **Henry Scaddon** was discomfited. The butler **Scales** attacks Christian as of doubtful background. Christian is cool. 7 Harold sees signs of bad mismanagement but is cautious: Jermyn is his election agent. Harold's past life is reviewed, and his nature and present goals. His mother is bitterly unhappy and fearful despite his kindness. Jermyn calls. 8

The former lovers talk about Harold: his attitude toward affairs on the property. She demands a promise that Jermyn never quarrel with her son: he refuses to give it, showing his savage side. But he is determined to win the election, anticipating Harold's better mood thereafter. 9 Felix is routinely at the Lyons' now, mostly in friendly disputation with the minister. He calls one afternoon to see Esther. She is reading a book he thinks silly. He castigates her for the feminine frivolity which weakens men. She is mortified, yet heart-struck by the thought that he must care something for her to speak so. 10

In **Chubb**'s public-house at Sproxton, Felix plans a campaign to win the men from beer to supporting a school for their children. He is interrupted by an election agent, **Johnson**, who talks up Transome to the colliers. His remarks lead Chubb to ask him to leave. Johnson talks about gentle roughness to teach the wrong interests a lesson. 11 Scales has played a joke on Christian and inadvertently caused the loss of a packet of letters important to **Philip Debarry**. He confesses; a search is made: no packet is found. 12

Walking in the park, Felix steps on the packet and finds a notebook and a locket and chain. He takes them to Lyon, wishing no contact with the Debarrys. Lyon sees something upsetting but is silent. Esther, softened by Felix's confrontation and her ensuing tears, is tender to her father, to his surprised delight. 13 The Debarrys receive Lyon's note about the packet. Philip is greatly relieved and writes a letter of thanks, offering vague reciprocation. He sends Christian to collect the objects (the locket and chain are Christian's property). Lyon fears the locket will prove his visitor to be Annette's husband and Esther's father. He delivers locket and chain, tries to get more information. Christian faces him down: does Lyon know something of "**Bycliffe**"? 14

Volume II

Lyon decides to seek a debate with the Rector, as his reward from Philip. He writes Philip. Esther reminds him Jermyn is coming. He is abstracted. Esther thinks of Felix. 15 Jermyn and Harold visit, Harold seeing Esther for the first time. He is impressed; she is delighted. Lyon enters; canvassing begins. The topic of the ballot is interrupted by Felix, who reports roughness recruited by Harold's people. Harold goes with him to investigate. 16 At Jermyn's, they present their concerns. Felix then leaves. Jermyn's subagent, Johnson, is there and gives strong arguments for changing nothing. Harold gives in but is curt with Jermyn, who dislikes it and vows to even things. 17

Jermyn has visited Lyon at his request and now knows everything about the locket and the past. He has promised to track Christian. There are to be speeches: Jermyn invites Esther to join his party. Esther is tender with her father but is vexed that Felix has stopped visiting. 18 "Parson Jack" Lingon, speaks first and puts the crowd in good humour. Harold does well. Observed by Jermyn, Christian sees Esther with the Jermyn daughters and is struck by her resemblance to someone. He has known Harold's man **Dominic** abroad. 19

Conversation on politics at the market-dinner at "the Marquis" in Treby introduces a string of local characters. Christian makes a figure. A reference to **Tommy Trounsem**'s recent turning-up meets Jermyn's affected indifference. He invites Christian to stop by at his home. 20 He receives him in some state and tells him his name **is Henry Scaddon**, whose life was in earlier days disreputable. As a prisoner of the French he exchanged identities with another, **Maurice Christian Bycliffe**, who was desperate to get to England. Christian at first denies all, then assents. Jermyn asks what items of personal property of Bycliffe's Christian retains. Christian tells him, then leaves. Jermyn writes to Johnson asking what is known about any Bycliffe marriage and fatherhood. Narration reveals Jermyn's unsavoury machinations: falsely imprisoning the true Bycliffe to defend the Durfey-Transomes' interests and then embezzling and manipulating their estate. He will use his special knowledge to checkmate any move now by Harold to expose and banish him, because he has the Lyon evidence of Esther's status as a putative heir, and no one else knows of it. 21

Esther makes an occasion to visit Felix (her watch loses) and comes away impressed and perhaps in love. 22 The Rev. Lyon's note received, Philip Debarry laughs his way to the Rectory, but there he encounters stiff opposition from his uncle, the **Rev. Augustus Debarry**. The Rector dragoons his new curate, **Sherlock**, to debate Lyon. 23 All is ready, but Sherlock does not show up. Philip Debarry goes to find him. He has taken the coach and fled. During the wait, Christian learns that Esther is Lyon's daughter. Her resemblance, especially her carriage, to his past acquaintance Bycliffe is striking. 24

Christian decides to pump Lyon and asks for his time. Lyon at first refers him to Jermyn, which gives Christian a clue. Christian tells him their talk must not be known to Jermyn. He asks directly about Esther's parentage, and Lyon reveals it. Christian explains that she may have some legal right Jermyn would wish to stifle. Lyon realizes he must tell Esther the facts. 25 The next morning, he does so. Esther is deeply touched and remorseful at her lack of tenderness to him. He is overjoyed. He tells of Christian's visit and of some possibility of fortune for her. They will be cautious. 26 Esther is sitting, pale and sad, when Felix comes to call. He takes her for a walk, and they talk deeply and to good purpose. She says she could live a hard, if good, life. 27

Christian looks up Trounsem, who is bill-sticking for Transome. After a drink, they go off to paste over Debarry placards, Christian covertly substituting bills Quorlen has given him. Tommy tells him of a meeting with Jermyn and later one with Johnson: he knows his life matters but he doesn't. Christian discovers mention of Bycliffe on some of the bills and abstracts these. 28 The Narrator explains the intricate legal history of the "Durfey-Transomes." *See* **Thomas Transome**. 29 On the hustings in Duffield, Felix is inspired to speak, and he holds Johnson up to ridicule as a manipulator without conscience. In the crowd, Christian identifies Johnson as a man who has information he wants on the Transome estate. The two meet and guardedly exchange knowledge. 30

The election day at Treby develops heat, which ebbs and flows. The magistrates seem to be keeping order. 31 Felix, at his bench, hears alarming noise and rushes out at last to check on Esther. She is glad to see him. Their discussion is deep and revealing. They know they love, but he thinks he must renounce this happiness. He leaves; she weeps. 32 Felix walks into town. Constable **Crow**'s threats of soldiers enrage the mob and it becomes destructive. Felix tries to lead it into harmlessness, but criminal elements take advantage, and the Debarry mansion is invaded. Troops arrive; Felix is shot through the shoulder and arrested for riot and for manslaughter of Constable **Tucker**, who had misunderstood his actions and died in a scuffle. 33

Volume III

Harold is disgusted and uneasy at the mob behaviour on election day. He knows he is at fault and that Felix has been unfairly dealt with. He is reluctant to take action for fear of liability and loss of reputation. 34 At a meeting with Harold, Jermyn comes loaded for bear. He threatens the Transome estate: he knows there is a proper heir—a Bycliffe—alive. He will suppress the evidence if Harold drops malfeasance proceedings against him Harold says he will hold that in abeyance while he thinks it over. 35 He is torn: he hates to let Jermyn off; he hates the idea of cheating the unknown heir. Christian calls: he knows who the heir is, and for the promise of £1,000 he gives the details to Harold, who immediately asks his mother to join him in calling on Esther. 36

Hearing the news of Felix, Mr Lyon rushes out to get the facts, calling first on Mrs Holt. He prays for Felix by name, scandalizing his congregation. A letter to Esther: she is heir to the Transome estate, worth £5,000 to £6,000 a year. She and her father are stupefied. Johnson has instigated the letter. 37 Esther ponders her new situation; Harold and his mother visit and invite her to visit Transome Court. Esther goes to pack; her father and Harold discuss Felix. Esther rides off with the Transomes. 38 Mrs Transome is feeling miserable and frightened. Her faithful servant **Denner** dresses and comforts her. 39 Harry thoroughly enjoys Esther. So does Harold, surprised at how much. Conversation verges on intimacy; Esther wants to see her father. 40

Esther has a happy visit, except on hearing that Felix assumes she will marry Harold. 41 Jermyn hears that Esther is at Transome Court and fears his game is up. He calls on Mrs Transome. She tells him Esther's rights are known. He reminds her of his past illegitimate defense of Transome interests. He now regrets causing Bycliffe to end in prison. He suggests that she help, putting his foot in it. She calls him a dastard and says she never will, now. 42

Mrs Holt intercepts Esther and Harold walking and states that Felix and Esther had been walking out together. Her eloquence is effective on Felix's behalf, and Harold promises action with the king. Mrs Holt and Mr Transome have an exchange, and Esther manages her departure. 43 Esther visits her father, who fears for Felix. Esther wants to see him. It is clear she loves him. 44 At the prison, the lovers talk, but Felix does not believe. As Esther is on the point of going, he calls to her: she rushes to him and they kiss. 45

The trial: minor witnesses for the prosecution; Felix's statement which may not be understood; character witnesses: the Rev. Lyon, Harold Transome, and working man **Michael Brincey**. Esther decides to speak for Felix. Her words move all; the verdict is guilty nevertheless. 46 A meeting of gentry to discuss moves for a pardon: Sir Maximus takes the lead, influenced by his son Philip. Harold is deeply in it, sure that Esther only admires Felix. Jermyn barges in to accost Harold. He reaches him; they grapple. Jermyn says, "I am your father," and Harold's view of them both in the mirror confirms the fact. 47

Harold goes to his mother to test for slander. His face tells her all; her face confirms its truth. 48 Esther awaits word about Felix. Harold comes to her, full of his new situation, avows his love and tells her he will be going away. He gets around to telling her that a strong memorial for Felix's pardon has gone to the Home Secretary. Her relief is intense, but Harold does not understand. She stalls for time and goes to her room. In the night she hears, then sees, Mrs Transome pacing the hall. 49 Denner finds her mistress in deep distress. She sends her servant away and waits. Then she walks, and Esther finds and tends her to sleep. In the morning, Esther begs Harold to watch by his mother and be with her when she awakes. She loves another, she renounces the estate and will go home. 50 At home, she waits. Felix comes, free. Esther is free too, but she will have a small income to take care of his mother and her father—and buy books for him. 51 They marry the following May, to much admiring comment and acclaim. They and the Rev. Lyon move away to an undisclosed location. There is a young Felix. *E*

Contents

Title Role

Felix Holt. "There could hardly have been a lot less like **Harold Transome**'s than this of the quack doctor's son, except in the superficial facts that he called himself a Radical, that he was the only son of his mother, and that he had lately returned to his home with ideas and resolves not a little disturbing to that mother's mind." 3

—*startling:* "The minister, accustomed to the respectable air of provincial townsmen, and especially to the sleek well-clipped gravity of his own male congregation, felt a slight shock as his glasses made perfectly clear to him the shaggy-headed, large-eyed, strong-limbed person of this questionable young man, without waistcoat or cravat." 5

—*inheritance renounced:* " 'I know there's a stage of speculation in which a man may doubt whether a pickpocket is blameworthy—but I'm not one of your subtle fellows who keep looking at the world through their own legs. If I allowed the sale of those medicines to go on, and my mother to live out of the proceeds when I can keep her by the honest labour of my hands, I've not the least doubt that I should be a rascal.' " 5

—*conversion:* " 'I was converted by six weeks' debauchery . . . .

" 'If I had not seen that I was making a hog of myself very fast, and that pig-wash, even if I could have got plenty of it, was a poor sort of thing, I should never have looked life fairly in the face to see what was to be done with it . . . . Then I began to see what else it could be turned into. Not much, perhaps. This world is not a very fine place for a good many of the people in it. But I've made up my mind it shan't be the worse for me, if I can help it. They may tell me I can't alter the world—that there must be a certain number of sneaks and robbers in it, and if I don't lie and filch somebody else will. Well, then, somebody else shall, for I won't. That's the upshot of my conversion, **Mr Lyon**, if you want to know it.' " 5

—*view on employment*: " 'I'll take no employment that obliges me to prop up my chin with a high cravat, and wear straps, and pass the livelong day with a set of fellows who spend their spare money on shirt-pins. That sort of work is really lower than many handicrafts; it only happens to be paid out of proportion. That's why I set myself to learn the watchmaking trade.' " 5

—*advice to a preacher:* " 'Teach any truth you can, whether it's in the Testament or out of it. It's little enough anybody can get hold of, and still less what he can drive into the skulls of a pence-counting, parcel-tying generation, such as mostly fill your chapels.' " 5

—*head measured:* " . . . a phrenologist at Glasgow told me I had large veneration; another man there, who knew me, laughed out and said I was the most blasphemous iconoclast living. 'That,' says my phrenologist, 'is because of his large Ideality, which prevents him from finding anything perfect enough to be venerated.' " 5

—*observed:* "She had time to remark that he was a peculiar-looking person, but not insignificant, which was the quality that most hopelessly consigned a man to perdition. He was massively built. The striking points in his face were large clear grey eyes and full lips." 5

—*literary critic:* " 'A misanthropic debauchee [**Byron**] . . . whose notion of a hero was that he should disorder his stomach and despise mankind. His corsairs and renegades, his Alps and **Manfred**s, are the most paltry puppets that were ever pulled by the strings of lust and pride.' " 5

—love at first sight: " 'I could grind my teeth at such self-satisfied minxes, who think they can tell everybody what is the correct thing, and the utmost stretch of their ideas will not place them on a level with the intelligent fleas. I should like to see if she could be made ashamed of herself.' " 5

—dress: " 'Good afternoon, **Miss Lyon**,' said Felix, taking off his cloth cap: he resolutely declined the expensive ugliness of a hat, and in a poked cap and without a cravat, made a figure at which his mother cried every Sunday, and thought of with a slow shake of the head at several passages in the minister's prayer." 10

—compliment: " 'You have enough understanding to make it wicked that you should add one more to the women who hinder men's lives from having any nobleness in them.' " 10

—forthright: " 'I want you to change. Of course I am a brute to say so. I ought to say you are perfect. Another man would, perhaps. But I say, I want you to change . . . .

" 'You don't care to be better than a bird trimming its feathers, and pecking about after what pleases it. You are discontented with the world because you can't get just the small things that suit your pleasure, not because it's a world where myriads of men and women are ground by wrong and misery, and tainted with pollution.' " 10

—for education: "There was nothing better than a dame school in the hamlet; he thought that if he could move the fathers, whose blackened weekday persons and flannel caps, ornamented with tallow candles by way of plume, were a badge of hard labour for which he had a more sympathetic fibre than for any ribbon in the button-hole—if he could move these men to save something from their drink and pay a schoolmaster for their boys, a greater service would be done them than if **Mr Garstin** and his company were persuaded to establish a school." 11

—spurious rival: "Felix felt himself in danger of getting into a rage. There is hardly any mental misery worse than that of having our own serious phrases, our own rooted beliefs, caricatured by a charlatan or a hireling. He began to feel the sharp lower edge of his tin pint-measure, and to think it a tempting missile." 11

—self-knowledge: " 'There's some reason in me as long as I keep my temper, but my rash humour is drunkenness without wine.' " 13

—repulsion: "It was a constant source of irritation to him that the public men on his side were, on the whole, not conspicuously better than the public men on the other side; that the spirit of innovation, which with him was a part of religion, was in many of its mouthpieces no more of a religion than the faith in rotten boroughs; and he was thus predisposed to distrust **Harold Transome**." 16

—mistrusted: "The inconvenient chance [**Jermyn**] guessed at once to be represented by Felix Holt, whom he knew very well by Trebian report to be a young man with so little of the ordinary Christian motives as to making an appearance and getting on in the world, that he presented no handle to any judicious and respectable person who might be willing to make use of him." 17

Felix Holt and Job Tudge

—thought: "He had thought a great deal of **Esther** with a mixture of strong disapproval and strong liking, which both together made a feeling the reverse of indifference; but he was not going to let her have any influence on his life." 22

—comforting a lady: "He had been very kind ever since that morning when she had called at his home, more disposed to listen indulgently to what she had to say, and less blind to her looks and movements. If he had never railed at her or ignored her, she would have been less sensitive to the attention he gave her; but as it was, the prospect of seeing him seemed to light up her life, and to disperse the old dulness." 24

—confession: " 'The fact is, there are not many easy lots to be drawn in the world at present; and such as they are I am not envious of them. I don't say life is not worth having: it is worth having to a man who has some sparks of sense and feeling and bravery in him. And the finest fellow of all would be the one who could be glad to have lived because the world was chiefly miserable, and his life had come to help some one who needed it. He would be the man who had the most powers and the fewest selfish wants. But I'm not up to the level of what I see to be best. I'm often a hungry discontented fellow.' " 27

—his stand: " 'I would never choose to withdraw myself from the labour and common burthen of the world; but I do choose to withdraw myself from the push and the scramble for money and position. Any man is at liberty to call me a fool, and say that mankind are benefited by the push and the scramble in the long-run. But I care for the people who live now and will not be living when the long-run comes. As it is, I prefer going shares with the unlucky.' " 27

—credo: "It all depends on what a man gets into his consciousness—what life thrusts into his mind, so that it becomes present to him as remorse is present to the guilty, or a mechanical problem to an inventive genius. There are two things I've got present in that way: one of them is the picture of what I should hate to be. I'm determined never to go about making my face simpering or solemn, and telling professional lies for profit; or to get tangled in affairs where I must wink at dishonesty and pocket the proceeds, and justify that knavery as part of a system that I can't alter. If I once went into that sort of struggle for success, I should want to win—I should defend the wrong that I had once identified myself with. I should become everything that I see now beforehand to be detestable. And what's more, I should do this, as men are doing it every day, for a ridiculously small prize—perhaps for none at all— perhaps for the sake of two parlours, a rank eligible for the churchwardenship, a discontented wife and several unhopeful children.' " 27

" 'The other thing that's got into my mind like a splinter,' said Felix, after a pause, 'is the life of the miserable—the spawning life of vice and hunger. I'll never be one of the sleek dogs. The old Catholics are right, with their higher rule and their lower. Some are called to subject themselves to a harder discipline, and renounce things voluntarily which are lawful for others. It is the old word—"necessity is laid upon me." ' " 27

—avowal—sort of: " 'You are very beautiful.'

"She started and looked round at him, to see whether his face would give some help to the interpretation of this novel speech. He was looking up at her quite calmly, very much as a reverential Protestant might look at a picture of the Virgin, with a devoutness suggested by the type rather than by the image. **Esther**'s vanity was not in the least gratified: she felt that, somehow or other Felix was going to reproach her.

" 'I wonder,' he went on, still looking at her, 'whether the subtle measuring of forces will ever come to measuring the force there would be in one beautiful woman whose mind was as noble as her face was beautiful—who made a man's passion for her rush in one current with all the great aims of his life.' " 27 *See* **Esther Lyon** TL—*challenged*

—*his future:* " 'I want to be a demagogue of a new sort; an honest one, if possible, who will tell the people they are blind and foolish, and neither flatter them nor fatten on them. I have my heritage—an order I belong to. I have the blood of a line of handicraftsmen in my veins, and I want to stand up for the lot of the handicraftsman as a good lot, in which a man may be better trained to all the best functions of his nature than if he belonged to the grimacing set who have visiting-cards, and are proud to be thought richer than their neighbours.' " 27

—*his fault:* "The weak point to which Felix referred was his liability to be carried completely out of his own mastery by indignant anger. His strong health, his renunciation of selfish claims, his habitual preoccupation with large thoughts and with purposes independent of everyday casualties, secured him a fine and even temper, free from moodiness or irritability. He was full of long-suffering towards his unwise mother, who 'pressed him daily with her words and urged him, so that his soul was vexed'; he had chosen to fill his days in a way that required the utmost exertion of patience, that required those little rill-like out-flowings of goodness which in minds of great energy must be fed from deep sources of thought and passionate devotedness. In this way his energies served to make him gentle; and now, in this twenty-sixth year of his life, they had ceased to make him angry, except in the presence of something that roused his deep indignation. When once exasperated, the passionateness of his nature threw off the yoke of a long-trained consciousness in which thought and emotion had been more and more completely mingled, and concentrated itself in a rage as ungovernable as that of boyhood. . . . Felix had a terrible arm: he knew that he was dangerous; and he avoided the conditions that might cause him exasperation, as he would have avoided intoxicating drinks if he had been in danger of intemperance." 30

—*conspicuous:* "Everyone looked at him: the well-washed face and its educated expression along with a dress more careless than that of most well-to-do workmen on a holiday, made his appearance strangely arresting." 30

—*on the hustings:* "He was considerably taller [than the previous speaker], his head and neck were more massive, and the expression of his mouth and eyes was something very different from the mere acuteness and rather hard-lipped antagonism of the trades-union man. Felix Holt's face had the look of habitual meditative abstraction from objects of mere personal vanity or desire, which is the peculiar stamp of culture, and makes a very roughly-cut face worthy to be called 'the human face divine'. Even lions and dogs know a distinction between men's glances; and doubtless those Duffield men, in the expectation with which they looked up at Felix, were unconsciously influenced by the grandeur of his full yet firm mouth, and the calm clearness of his grey eyes, which were somehow unlike what they were accustomed to see along with an old brown velveteen coat, and an absence of chin-propping." 30

—*worried:* "But he was of a fibre that vibrated too strongly to the life around him to shut himself away in quiet, even from suffering and irremediable wrong. As the noises grew louder, and wrought more and more strongly on his imagination, he was obliged to lay down his delicate wheel-work." 32

—tongue untied: " 'I want you to tell me—once—that you know it would be easier to me to give myself up to loving and being loved, as other men do, when they can, than to—'

"This breaking-off in speech was something quite new in Felix. For the first time he had lost his self-possession, and turned his eyes away. He was at variance with himself. He had begun what he felt that he ought not to finish." 32

—renouncing: " 'We shall always be the better for thinking of each other,' he said, leaning his elbow on the back of the sofa, and supporting his head as he looked at her with calm sadness. 'This thing can never come to me twice over. It is my knighthood. That was always a business of great cost.' " 32

—renounced: "He could not help seeing that he was very important to her; and he was too simple and sincere a man to ape a sort of humility which would not have made him any the better if he had possessed it. Such pretences turn our lives into sorry dramas. And Felix wished **Esther** to know that her love was dear to him as the beloved dead are dear. He felt that they must not marry—that they would ruin each other's lives. But he had longed for her to know fully that his will to be always apart from her was renunciation, not an easy preference. In this he was thoroughly generous; and yet, now some subtle, mysterious conjuncture of impressions and circumstances had made him speak, he questioned the wisdom of what he had done. Express confessions give definiteness to memories that might more easily melt away without them; and Felix felt for Esther's pain as the strong soldier, who can march on hungering without fear that he shall faint, feels for the young brother—the maiden-cheeked conscript whose load is too heavy for him." 32

—sad diagnosis: " 'My poor young friend is being taught with mysterious severity the evil of a too confident self-reliance,' [**Lyon**] said to **Esther** . . . . " 37

—message from gaol: " 'Tell her . . . whatever they sentence me to, she knows they can't rob me of my vocation. With poverty for my bride, and preaching and pedagoguy [*sic*] for my business, I am sure of a handsome establishment.' " 37

—visited in prison: "He was just the same—no, something inexpressibly better, because of the distance and separation, and the half-weary novelties, which made him like the return of morning." 45

—on failure: " 'The only failure a man ought to fear is failure in cleaving to the purpose he sees to be best. As to just the amount of result he may see from his particular work—that's a tremendous uncertainty: the universe has not been arranged for the gratification of his feelings. As long as a man sees and believes in some great good, he'll prefer working towards that in the way he's best fit for, come what may. I put effects at their minimum, but I'd rather have the minimum of effect, if it's of the sort I care for, than the maximum of effect I don't care for—a lot of fine things that are not to my taste—and if they were, the conditions of holding them while the world is what it is, are such as would jar on me like grating metal.' " 45

—in the dock: "It was now for the first time that **Esther** had a feeling of pride in him on the ground simply of his appearance. At this moment, when he was the centre of a multitudinous gaze, which seemed to act on her own vision like a broad unmitigated daylight, she felt that there was something

pre-eminent in him, not withstanding the vicinity of numerous gentlemen. No apple-woman would have admired him; not only to feminine minds like **Mrs Tiliot**'s, but to many minds in coat and waistcoat, there was something dangerous and perhaps unprincipled in his bare throat and great Gothic head; and his somewhat massive person would doubtless have come out very oddly from the hands of a fashionable tailor of that time. But as Esther saw his large grey eyes looking round calmly and undefiantly, first at the audience generally, and then with a more observant expression at the lawyers and other persons immediately around him, she felt that he bore the outward stamp of a distinguished nature." 46

"Felix might have come from the hands of a sculptor in the later Roman period, when the plastic impulse was stirred by the grandeur of barbaric forms—when rolled collars were not yet conceived, and satin stocks were not." 46

The Lyons

Esther Lyon. "The daughter was probably some prim Miss, neat, sensible, pious, but all in a small feminine way . . . . " 5

—in actuality: "The minister's daughter was not the sort of person he expected. She was quite incongruous with his notion of ministers' daughters in general, and though he had expected something nowise delightful, the incongruity repelled him. A very delicate scent, the faint suggestion of a garden, was wafted as she went. He would not observe her, but he had a sense of an elastic walk, the tread of small feet, a long neck and a high crown of shining brown plaits with curls that floated backward—things, in short, that suggested a fine lady to him, and determined him to notice her as little as possible." 5

—voice: "Esther had that excellent thing in woman, a soft voice with a clear fluent utterance. Her sauciness was always charming, because it was without emphasis, and was accompanied with graceful little turns of the head." 5

—viewed askance: "She was not much liked by her father's church and congregation. The less serious observed that she had too many airs and graces, and held her head much too high; the stricter sort feared greatly that **Mr Lyon** had not been sufficiently careful in placing his daughter among God-fearing people, and that, being led astray by the melancholy vanity of giving her exceptional accomplishments, he had sent her to a French school, and allowed her to take situations where she had contracted notions not only above her own rank, but of too worldly a kind to be safe in any rank." 6

—impressive, but: " . . . she had secured an astonished admiration of her cleverness from the girls of various ages who were her pupils; indeed, her knowledge of French was generally held to give a distinction to Treby itself as compared with other market-towns . . . . As for the Church people who engaged Miss Lyon to give lessons in their families, their imaginations were altogether prostrated by the incongruity between accomplishments and Dissent, between weekly prayer-meetings and a conversance with so lively and altogether worldly a language as the French." 6

—susceptible: " . . . all her native tendencies towards luxury, fastidiousness, and scorn of mock gentility, were strengthened by witnessing the habits of a well-born and wealthy family." 6

Esther Lyon

—*fastidious:* "She had one of those exceptional organizations which are quick and sensitive without being in the least morbid; she was alive to the finest shades of manner, to the nicest-distinctions of tone and accent; she had a little code of her own about scents and colours, textures and behaviour, by which she secretly condemned or sanctioned all things and persons. And she was well satisfied with herself for her fastidious taste, never doubting that hers was the highest standard.

"She was proud that the best-born and handsomest girls at school had always said that she might be taken for a born lady. Her own pretty instep, clad in a silk stocking, her little heel, just rising from a kid slipper, her irreproachable nails and delicate wrist, were the objects of delighted consciousness to her; and she felt that it was her superiority which made her unable to use without disgust any but the finest cambric handkerchiefs and freshest gloves. Her money all went in the gratification of these nice tastes, and she saved nothing from her earnings." ¶6

—*generous:* " . . . she felt sure that she was generous: she hated all meanness, would empty her purse impulsively on some sudden appeal to her pity, and if she found out that her father had a want, she would supply it with some pretty device of a surprise." 6

—*embarrassed:* "Esther had affection for her father: she recognized the purity of his character, and a quickness of intellect in him which responded to her own liveliness, in spite of what seemed a dreary piety . . . . But his old clothes had a smoky odour, and she did not like to walk with him . . . . Esther had a horror of appearing ridiculous even in the eyes of vulgar Trebians. She fancied that she should have loved her mother better than she was able to love her father . . . . " 6

—*at school:* "It was understood that Esther would contract no Papistical superstitions, and this was perfectly true; but she contracted, as we see, a good deal of non-Papistical vanity." 6

—*piqued:* "But she had begun to find [**Felix**] amusing, and also rather irritating to her woman's love of conquest. He always opposed and criticized her; and besides that, he looked at her as if he never saw a single detail about her person—quite as if she were a middle-aged woman in a cap. She did not believe that he had ever admired her hands, or her long neck, or her graceful movements . . . . Felix ought properly to have been a little in love with her. . . . But it was quite clear that, instead of feeling any disadvantage on his own side, he held himself to be immeasurably her superior: and, what was worse, Esther had a secret consciousness that he was her superior.

"She was all the more vexed at the suspicion that he thought slightly of her; and wished in her vexation that she could have found more fault with him—that she had not been obliged to admire more and more the varying expressions of his open face and his deliciously good-humoured laugh, always loud at a joke against himself." ¶10

—*setting a scene:* "On this particular Sunday afternoon, when she heard the knock at the door, she was seated in the kitchen corner between the fire and the window reading 'Réné' [*sic*]. Certainly, in her well-fitting light-blue dress—she almost always wore some shade of blue—with her delicate sandalled slipper stretched towards the fire, her little gold watch, which had cost her nearly a quarter's earnings, visible at her side, her slender fingers playing with a shower of brown curls, and a coronet of shining plaits at the summit of her head, she was a remarkable **Cinderella**." 10

Esther receives Felix in her kitchen

—*scolded:* "He was outrageously ill-bred; but she felt that she would be lowering herself by telling him so, and manifesting her anger in that way: she would be confirming his accusation of a littleness that shrank from severe truth; and, besides, through all her mortification there pierced a sense that this exasperation of **Felix** against her was more complimentary than anything in his previous behaviour." 10

—*pride:* "The tumult of feeling in Esther's mind—mortification, anger, the sense of a terrible power over her that **Felix** seemed to have as his angry words vibrated through her—was getting almost too much for her self-control. She felt her lips quivering; but her pride, which feared nothing so much as the betrayal of her emotion, helped her to a desperate effort." 10

—*shaken into tears:* "Poor maiden! There was a strange contradiction of impulses in her mind in those first moments [alone]. She could not bear that **Felix** should not respect her, yet she could not bear that he should see her bend before his denunciation. She revolted against his assumption of superiority, yet she felt herself in a new kind of subjection to him . . . . For the first time in her life Esther felt herself seriously shaken in her self-contentment. She knew there was a mind to which she appeared trivial, narrow, selfish. Every word Felix had said to her seemed to have burnt itself into her memory. She felt as if she should for evermore be haunted by self-criticism, and never do anything to satisfy those fancies on which she had simply piqued herself before without being dogged by inward questions . . . . But now she had been stung—stung even into a new consciousness concerning her father. Was it true that his life was so much worthier than her own?" 10

—*softened:* "When Esther was lying down that night, she felt as if the little incidents between herself and her father on this Sunday had made it an epoch. Very slight words and deeds may have a sacramental efficacy, if we can cast our self-love behind us, in order to say or do them." 13

—*daydream:* "She was fond of netting, because it showed to advantage both her hand and her foot; and across this image of **Felix Holt**'s indifference and contempt there passed the vaguer image of a possible somebody who would admire her hands and feet, and delight in looking at their beauty, and long, yet not dare, to kiss them. Life would be much easier in the presence of such a love." 15

—*disturbed:* "Esther was beginning to lose her complacency at her own wit and criticism; to lose the sense of superiority in an awakening need for reliance on one whose vision was wider, whose nature was purer and stronger than her own. But then, she said to herself, that 'one' must be tender to her, not rude and predominating in his manners. A man with any chivalry in him could never adopt a scolding tone towards a woman—that is, towards a charming woman. But **Felix** had no chivalry in him. He loved lecturing and opinion too well ever to love any woman." 15

—*visitor:* "Esther was perfectly aware, as [**Harold Transome**] took a chair near her, that he was under some admiring surprise at her appearance and manner. How could it be otherwise? She believed that in the eyes of a high-bred man no young lady in Treby could equal her: she felt a glow of delight at the sense that she was being looked at." 16

—*exit:* " . . . bowing and floating out like a blue-robed Naïad, but not without a suffused blush as she passed through the doorway." 16

—*a new interest:* "It had been a pleasant variety in her monotonous days to see a man like **Harold Transome**, with a distinguished appearance and polished manners, and she would like to see him again: he suggested to her that brighter and more luxurious life on which her imagination dwelt without the painful effort it required to conceive the mental condition which would place her in complete sympathy with **Felix Holt**." 18

—*a new caring:* "[Her father] sat down obediently, while Esther took a towel, which she threw over his shoulders, and then brushed the thick long fringe of soft auburn hair. This very trifling act, which she had brought herself to for the first time yesterday, meant a great deal in Esther's little history. It had been her habit to leave the mending of her father's clothes to **Lyddy**; she had not liked even to touch his cloth garments; still less had it seemed a thing she would willingly undertake to correct his toilette, and use a brush for him. But having once done this, under her new sense of faulty omission, the affectionateness that was in her flowed so pleasantly, as she saw how much her father was moved by what he thought a great act of tenderness, that she quite longed to repeat it. This morning, as he sat under her hands, his face had such a calm delight in it that she could not help kissing the top of his bald head . . . . " 18

—*felt neglect:* "Esther felt vexed with herself that her heart was suddenly beating with unusual quickness, and that her last resolution not to trouble herself about what **Felix** thought, had transformed itself with magic swiftness into mortification that he evidently avoided coming to the house when she was there, though he used to come on the slightest occasion." 18

—*perceiving indifference:* "Poor Esther was quite helpless. The mortification which had come like a bruise to all the sensibilities that had been in keen activity, insisted on some relief. Her eyes filled instantly, and a great tear rolled down while she said in a loud sort of whisper, as involuntary as her tears,

" 'I wanted to tell you that I was not offended—that I am not ungenerous—I thought you might think—but you have not thought of it.' " 22

—*reflecting:* " 'There is something greater and better in him than I had imagined. His behaviour to-day—to his mother and me too—I should call it the highest gentlemanliness, only it seems in him to be something deeper. But he has chosen an intolerable life; though I suppose, if I had a mind equal to his, and if he loved me very dearly, I should choose the same life.' " 22

—*influenced:* "The favourite Byronic heroes were beginning to look something like last night's decorations seen in the sober dawn. So fast does a little leaven spread within us—so incalculable is the effect of one personality on another. Behind all Esther's thoughts, like an unacknowledged yet constraining presence, there was the sense, that if **Felix Holt** were to love her, her life would be exalted into something quite new—into a sort of difficult blessedness, such as one may imagine in beings who are conscious of painfully growing into the possession of higher powers." 22

—*at the debate:* "She looked unusually charming to-day, from the very fact that she was not vividly conscious of anything but of having a mind near her that asked her to be something better than she actually was. The consciousness of her own superiority amongst the people around her was superseded, and even a few brief weeks had given a softened expression to her eyes, a more feminine beseechingness and self-doubt to her manners. Perhaps, however, a little new defiance was rising in place of the old contempt—defiance of the Trebian views concerning **Felix Holt**." 24

—*knowledge has come:* "She wanted to speak, but the floodgates could not be opened for words alone. She threw her arms round the old man's neck and sobbed out with a passionate cry, 'Father, father! forgive me if I have not loved you enough. I will—I will!' " 26

—*hurt by an avowal:* "Esther's eyes got hot and smarting. It was no use trying to be dignified. She had turned away her head, and now said, rather bitterly, 'It is difficult for a woman ever to try to be anything good when she is not believed in—when it is always supposed that she must be contemptible.' " 27

—*challenged:* " 'I do believe in you [said **Felix**]; but I want you to have such a vision of the future that you may never lose your best self. Some charm or other may be flung about you—some of your atta-of-rose fascinations—and nothing but a good strong terrible vision will save you. And if it did save you, you might be that woman I was thinking of a little while ago when I looked at your face: the woman whose beauty makes a great task easier to men instead of turning them away from it.' " 27

—*in conflict:* "He was like no one else to her: he had seemed to bring at once a law, and the love that gave strength to obey the law. Yet the next moment, stung by his independence of her, she denied that she loved him; she had only longed for a moral support under the negations of her life. If she were not to have that support, all effort seemed useless." 27

—*religion:* "Esther had been so long used to hear the formulas of her father's belief without feeling or understanding them, that they had lost all power to touch her. The first religious experience of her life—the first self-questioning, the first voluntary subjection, the first longing to acquire the strength of greater motives and obey the more strenuous rule—had come to her through Felix Holt. No wonder that she felt as if the loss of him were inevitable backsliding." 27

—*visited on election day:* "It was in reality a little heaven to her that **Felix** was there, but she saw beyond it—saw that by-and-by he would be gone, and that they should be farther on their way, not towards meeting, but parting. His will was impregnable. He was a rock, and she was no more to him than the white clinging mist-cloud." 32

—*rising to the occasion:* "Esther, like a woman as she was—a woman waiting for love, never able to ask for it—had her joy in these signs of her power; but they made her generous, not chary, as they might have done if she had had a pettier disposition. She said, with deep yet timid earnestness,

" 'What you have chosen to do has only convinced me that your love would be the better worth having.'

"All the finest part of Esther's nature trembled in those words." 32

—*losing him:* "The charming sauciness was all gone from her face, but the memory of it made this childlike dependent sorrow all the more touching." 32

—*lost him:* "She cried bitterly. If she might have married **Felix Holt**, she could have been a good woman. She felt no trust that she could ever be good without him." 32

—*stature:* "Hers was not a childish beauty; and when the sparkle of mischief, wit, and vanity was out of her eyes, and the large look of abstracted sorrow was there, you would have been surprised by a certain grandeur which the smiles had hidden. That changing face was the perfect symbol of her mixed susceptible nature, in which battle was inevitable, and the side of victory uncertain." 37

—her hero: "She began to look on all that had passed between herself and **Felix** as something not buried, but embalmed and kept as a relic in a private sanctuary. The very entireness of her preoccupation about him, the perpetual repetition in her memory of all that had passed between them, tended to produce this effect. She lived with him in the past; in the future she seemed shut out from him. He was an influence above her life, rather than a part of it; some time or other, perhaps, he would be to her as if he belonged to the solemn admonishing skies, checking her self-satisfied pettiness with the suggestion of a wider life.

" . . . she could never think of him with pity, because he always seemed to her too great and strong to be pitied; he wanted nothing. He evaded calamity by choosing privation." 37

—her old daydream: "But her mind had fixed itself habitually on the signs and luxuries of ladyhood, for which she had the keenest perception. She had seen the very mat in her carriage, had scented the dried rose-leaves in her corridors, had felt the soft carpets under her pretty feet, and seen herself, as she rose from her sofa cushions, in the crystal panel that reflected a long drawing-room, where the conservatory flowers and the pictures of fair women left her still with the supremacy of charm. She had trodden the marble-firm gravel of her garden-walks and the soft deep turf of her lawn; she had had her servants about her filled with adoring respect, because of her kindness as well as her grace and beauty; and she had had several accomplished cavaliers all at once suing for her hand—one of whom, uniting very high birth with long dark eyelashes and the most distinguished talents, she secretly preferred, though his pride and hers hindered an avowal, and supplied the inestimable interest of retardation . . . no one who has not, like Esther, a strong natural prompting and susceptibility towards such things, and has at the same time suffered from the presence of opposite conditions, can understand how powerfully those minor accidents of rank which please the fastidious sense can preoccupy the imagination." 38

—daydream disturbing: " . . . she was compelled to gaze on the degrading hard experience of other human beings, and on a humiliating loss which was the obverse of her own proud gain. Even in her times of most untroubled egoism Esther shrank from anything ungenerous; and the fact that she had a very lively image of **Harold Transome** and his gipsy-eyed boy in her mind, gave additional distinctness to the thought that if she entered they must depart." 38

—awe: "It was only that she was conscious of being strangely awed by something that was called good fortune; and the awe shut out any scheme of rejection as much as any triumphant joy in acceptance." 38

—pleased: "Esther's pretty behaviour, it must be confessed, was not fed entirely from lofty moral sources: over and above her really generous feeling, she enjoyed **Mrs Transome**'s accent, the high-bred quietness of her speech, the delicate odour of her drapery. She had always thought that life must be particularly easy if one could pass it among refined people; and so it seemed at this moment. She wished, unmixedly, to go to Transome Court." 38

—in her element: "Her quick light movement was always ready to anticipate what **Mrs Transome** wanted; her bright apprehension and silvery speech were always ready to cap Mrs Transome's narratives or instructions

even about doses and liniments, with some lively commentary. She must have behaved charmingly; for one day when she had tripped across the room to put the screen just in the right place, Mrs Transome said, taking her hand, 'My dear, you make me wish I had a daughter.' " 40

—a new prospect: "Esther found it impossible to read in these days; her life was a book which she seemed herself to be constructing—trying to make character clear before her, and looking into the ways of destiny." 40

—a slip: " 'The person I liked best in the world was one who did nothing but scold me and tell me of my faults.'

"When Esther began to speak, she meant to do no more than make a remote unintelligible allusion, feeling, it must be owned, a naughty will to flirt and be saucy, and thwart **Harold**'s attempts to be felicitous in compliment. But she had no sooner uttered the words than they seemed to her like a confession. A deep flush spread itself over her face and neck, and the sense that she was blushing went on deepening her colour." 40

—comparing lovers: " . . . she found herself mentally protesting that, whatever **Harold** might think, there was a light in which he was vulgar compared with **Felix**. Felix had ideas and motives which she did not believe that Harold could understand. More than all, there was this test: she herself had no sense of inferiority and just subjection when she was with Harold Transome; there were even points in him for which she felt a touch, not of angry, but of playful scorn; whereas with Felix she had always a sense of dependence and possible illumination. In those large, grave, candid grey eyes of his, love seemed something that belonged to the high enthusiasm of life, such as might now be for ever shut out from her." 43

—devaluation: "And yet, this life at Transome Court was *not* the life of her day-dreams: there was dulness already in its ease, and in the absence of high demand; and there was the vague consciousness that the love of this not unfascinating man who hovered about her gave an air of moral mediocrity to all her prospects. She would not have been able perhaps to define this impression; but somehow or other by this elevation of fortune it seemed that the higher ambition which had begun to spring in her was for ever nullified. All life seemed cheapened; as it might seem to a young student who, having believed that to gain a certain degree he must write a thesis in which he would bring his powers to bear with memorable effect, suddenly ascertained that no thesis was expected, but the sum (in English money) of twenty-seven pounds ten shillings and sixpence." 43

—cause for concern: "Yet there was a lightning that shot out of her now and then, which seemed the sign of a dangerous judgment; as if she inwardly saw something more admirable than **Harold Transome**. Now, to be perfectly charming a woman should not see this." 43

—a challenge: "It is terrible—the keen bright eye of a woman when it has once been turned with admiration on what is severely true; but then, the severely true rarely comes within its range of vision. Esther had had an unusual illumination; **Harold** did not know how, but he discerned enough of the effect to make him more cautious than he had ever been in his life before." 43

—found out: "And Esther's renewed confusion, united with her silence about **Felix**, which now first seemed noteworthy, and with **Mrs Holt**'s graphic details as to her walking with him and letting him sit by her before all the town, were grounds not merely for a suspicion, but for a conclusion in **Harold**'s mind." 43

—*aroused and clarified:* " 'If it is eccentricity to be very much better than other men, he is certainly eccentric; and fanatical too, if it is fanatical to renounce all small selfish motives for the sake of a great and unselfish one. I never knew what nobleness of character really was before I knew **Felix Holt**.'

"It seemed to Esther as if, in the excitement of this moment, her own words were bringing her a clearer revelation . . . .

"Esther at that moment looked perfectly beautiful, with an expression which **Harold** had never hitherto seen. All the confusion which had depended on personal feeling had given way before the sense that she had to speak the truth about the man whom she felt to be admirable." 43

—*self-deceiving:* "She felt pleased with [**Harold**]; she was open to the fallacious delight of being assured that she had power over him to make him do what she liked, and quite forgot the many impressions which had convinced her that Harold had a padded yoke ready for the neck of every man, woman, and child that depended on him." 43

—*creeping languor:* " . . . she had begun to feel more profoundly that in accepting **Harold Transome** she left the high mountain air, the passionate serenity of perfect love for ever behind her, and must adjust her wishes to a life of middling delights, overhung with the languorous haziness of motiveless ease, where poetry was only literature, and the fine ideas had to be taken down from the shelves of the library when her husband's back was turned." 44

—*her first love:* "The first spontaneous offering of her woman's devotion, the first great inspiration of her life, was a sort of vanished ecstasy which had left its wounds. It seemed to her a cruel misfortune of her young life that her best feeling, her most precious dependence, had been called forth just where the conditions were hardest, and that all the easy invitations of circumstance were towards something which that previous consecration of her longing had made a moral descent for her." 44

—*barren prospect:* " . . . a solitary elevation to wealth, which out of Utopia she had no notion how she should manage, looked as chill and dreary as the offer of dignities in an unknown country." 44

—*intended to marry:* " . . . she was intensely of the feminine type, verging neither towards the saint nor the angel. She was 'a fair divided excellence, whose fulness of perfection' must be in marriage. And, like all youthful creatures, she felt as if the present conditions of choice were final. It belonged to the freshness of her heart that, having had her emotions strongly stirred by real objects, she never speculated on possible relations yet to come. It seemed to her that she stood at the first and last parting of the ways." 44

—*preoccupied:* " . . . she was full of an expectation that held her lips in trembling silence, and gave her eyes that sightless beauty which tells that the vision is all within." 45

—*misery transformed:* "Esther felt too miserable for tears to come. She looked helplessly at **Felix** for a moment, then took her hands from his, and, turning away mutely, walked dreamily towards her father, and said, 'Father, I am ready—there is no more to say.'

"She turned back again, towards the chair where her bonnet lay, with a face quite corpse-like above her dark garment.

" 'Esther!'

"She heard Felix say the word, with an entreating cry, and went towards him with the swift movement of a frightened child towards its protector. He clasped her, and they kissed each other.

"She never could recall anything else that happened, till she was in the carriage again with **Mrs Transome**." 45

—her moment approaches: "Some of that ardour which has flashed out and illuminated all poetry and history was burning to-day in the bosom of sweet Esther Lyon. In this, at least, her woman's lot was perfect: that the man she loved was her hero; that her woman's passion and her reverence for rarest goodness rushed together in an undivided current. And to-day they were making one danger, one terror, one irresistible impulse for her heart. Her feelings were growing into a necessity for action, rather than a resolve to act. She could not support the thought that the trial would come to an end, that sentence would be passed on **Felix**, and that all the while something had been omitted which might have been said for him. There had been no witness to tell what had been his behaviour and state of mind just before the riot. She must do it." 46

—in the moment: "There was no blush on her face: she stood, divested of all personal considerations whether of vanity or shyness. Her clear voice sounded as it might have done if she had been making a confession of faith. She began and went on without query or interruption. Every face looked grave and respectful . . . .

"There was something so naïve and beautiful in this action of Esther's, that it conquered every low or petty suggestion even in the commonest minds. The three men in that assembly who knew her best—even her father and **Felix Holt**—felt a thrill of surprise mingling with their admiration. This bright, delicate, beautiful-shaped [*sic*] thing that seemed most like a toy or ornament —some hand had touched the chords, and there came forth music that brought tears. Half a year before, Esther's dread of being ridiculous spread over the surface of her life; but the depth below was sleeping." 46

—wrought up: "And now, in these hours since her return from Loamford, her mind was in that state of highly-wrought activity, that large discourse, in which we seem to stand aloof from our own life—weighing impartially our own temptations and the weak desires that most habitually solicit us. 'I think I am getting that power **Felix** wished me to have: I shall soon see strong visions,' she said to herself . . . . " 49

—hearing renunciation: "Esther was keenly touched. With a paradoxical longing, such as often happens to us, she wished at that moment that she could have loved this man with her whole heart. The tears came into her eyes; she did not speak, but, with an angel's tenderness in her face, she laid her hand on his sleeve." 49

—wrong choice: "And on the other side there was a lot where everything seemed easy—but for the fatal absence of those feelings which, now she had once known them, it seemed nothing less than a fall and a degradation to do without. With terrible prescience which a multitude of impressions during her stay at Transome Court had contributed to form, she saw herself in a silken bondage that arrested all motive, and was nothing better than a well cushioned despair. To be restless amidst ease, to be languid among all appliances for leisure, was a possibility that seemed to haunt the rooms of this house, and wander with her under the oaks and elms of the park. And **Harold Transome**'s love, no longer a hovering fancy with which she played, but

become a serious fact, seemed to threaten her with a stifling oppression. The homage of a man may be delightful until he asks straight for love, by which a woman renders homage." 49

—*cautionary:* "The dimly-suggested tragedy of [**Mrs Transome**'s] life, the dreary waste of years empty of sweet trust and affection, afflicted her even to horror. It seemed to have come as a last vision to urge her towards the life where the draughts of joy sprang from the unchanging fountains of reverence and devout love." 50

Rev. Rufus Lyon, "minister of the Independent Chapel usually spoken of as 'Malthouse Yard'." 3

—*meditating:* "The book-shelves did not suffice for his store of old books, which lay about him in piles so arranged as to leave narrow lanes between them; for the minister was much given to walking about during his hours of meditation, and very narrow passages would serve for his small legs, unencumbered by any other drapery than his black silk stockings and the flexible, though prominent, bows of black ribbon that tied his knee-breeches.

"He was walking about now, with his hands clasped behind him, an attitude in which his body seemed to bear about the same proportion to his head as the lower part of a stone **Hermes** bears to the carven image that crowns it. His face looked old and worn, yet the curtain of hair that fell from his bald crown and hung about his neck retained much of its original auburn tint, and his large, brown, shortsighted eyes were still clear and bright. At the first glance, every one thought him a very odd-looking rusty old man . . . . But he was too shortsighted to notice those who tittered at him—too absent from the world of small facts and petty impulses in which titterers live.

"With Satan to argue against on matters of vital experience as well as of church government, with great texts to meditate on, which seemed to get deeper as he tried to fathom them, it had never occurred to him to reflect what sort of image his small person made on the retina of a light-minded beholder. The good Rufus had his ire and his egoism; but they existed only as the red heat which gave force to his belief and his teaching. He was susceptible concerning the true office of deacons in the primitive church, and his small nervous body was jarred from head to foot by the concussion of an argument to which he saw no answer. In fact, the only moments when he could be said to be really conscious of his body, were when he trembled under the pressure of some agitating thought." ¶4

—*parishioner's visit:* "Mr Lyon had placed himself in the chair against his desk, and waited with the resolute resignation of a patient who is about to undergo an operation. But his visitor did not speak.

" 'You have something on your mind, **Mistress Holt**?' he said, at last." 4

—*not credulous:* "His simplicity was strongly mixed with sagacity as well as sectarian prejudice, and he did not rely at once on a loud-spoken integrity— **Satan** might have flavoured it with ostentation." 5

—*speaking style:* "He spoke rapidly, as he always did, except when his words were specially weighted with emotion: he overflowed with matter, and in his mind matter was always completely organized into words . . . . 'I have to keep a special watch over myself in this matter, inasmuch as I have a need of utterance which makes the thought within me seem as a pent-up fire, until I have shot it forth, as it were, in arrowy words, each one hitting its mark. Therefore I pray for a listening spirit, which is a great mark of grace.' " 5

The Reverend Lyon receives a Christian of sorts

—status: "His gifts were admired, and tears were shed under best bonnets at his sermons; but the weaker tea was thought good enough for him; and even when he went to preach a charity sermon in a strange town. He was treated with home-made wine and the smaller bedroom." 6

—a wish: "But then the good man so seldom had a want—except the perpetual desire, which she could never gratify, of seeing her under convictions, and fit to become a member of the church." 6 *An autobiographical remark.*

—reticence: "He had not the courage to tell **Esther** that he was not really her father: he had not the courage to renounce that hold on her tenderness which the belief in his natural fatherhood must help to give him, or to incur any resentment that her quick spirit might feel at having been brought up under a false supposition." 6

—past standing: "Whenever noteworthy preachers were discussed, Rufus Lyon was almost sure to be mentioned as one who did honour to the Independent body; his sermons were said to be full of study yet full of fire; and while he had more of human knowledge than many of his brethren, he showed in an eminent degree the marks of a true ministerial vocation. But on a sudden this burning and shining light seemed to be quenched: Mr Lyon voluntarily resigned his charge and withdrew from the town." 6

—shattered: "He spent [the night] in misery, enduring a horrible assault of **Satan**. He thought a frenzy had seized him. Wild visions of an impossible future thrust themselves upon him. He dreaded lest the woman had a husband; he wished that he might call her his own, that he might worship her beauty, that she might love and caress him. And what to the mass of men would have been only one of many allowable follies—a transient fascination, to be dispelled by daylight and contact with those common facts of which common-sense is the reflex—was to him a spiritual convulsion. He was as one who raved, and knew that he raved.

"These mad wishes were irreconcilable with what he was, and must be, as a Christian minister; nay, penetrating his soul as tropic heat penetrates the frame, and changes for it all aspects and all flavours, they were irreconcilable with that conception of the world which made his faith. All the busy doubt which had before been mere impish shadows flitting around a belief that was strong with the strength of an unswerving moral bias, had now gathered blood and substance. The questioning spirit had become suddenly bold and blasphemous: it no longer insinuated scepticism—it prompted defiance; it no longer expressed cool inquisitive thought, but was the voice of a passionate mood. Yet he never ceased to regard it as the voice of the tempter: the conviction which had been the law of his better life remained within him as a conscience." ¶6

—vulnerable: "Those sensibilities which in most lives are diffused equally through the youthful years, were aroused suddenly in Mr Lyon, as some men have their special genius revealed to them by a tardy concurrence of conditions. His love was the first love of a fresh young heart full of wonder and worship." 6

—failure: " 'Can you love me, **Annette**? Will you be my wife?' Annette trembled and looked miserable.

" 'Do not speak—forget it,' said Mr Lyon, rising suddenly and speaking with loud energy. 'No, no—I do not want it—I do not wish it.' " 6

—transcended: "Those three years were to Mr Lyon a period of such self-suppression and life in another as few men know. Strange! that the passion

for this woman, which he felt to have drawn him aside from the right as much as if he had broken the most solemn vows . . . the passion for a being who had no glimpse of his thoughts induced a more thorough renunciation than he had ever known in the time of his complete devotion to his ministerial career. He had no flattery now, either from himself or the world; he knew that he had fallen, and *his* world had forgotten him, or shook their heads at his memory. The only satisfaction he had was the satisfaction of his tenderness—which meant untiring work, untiring patience, untiring wakefulness even to the dumb signs of feeling in a creature whom he alone cared for." 6

—*stimulated:* "To talk with this young man, who, though hopeful, had a singularity which some might at once have pronounced heresy, but which Mr Lyon persisted in regarding as orthodoxy 'in the making', was like a good bite to strong teeth after a too plentiful allowance of spoon meat. To cultivate his society with a view to checking his erratic tendencies was a laudable purpose; but perhaps if **Felix** had been rapidly subdued and reduced to conformity, little Mr Lyon would have found the conversation much flatter." 10

—*aroused:* "Tired, even exhausted, as the minister had been . . . the gathering excitement of speech gave more and more energy to his voice and manner; he walked away from the vestry table, he paused, and came back to it; he walked away again, then came back, and ended with his deepest-toned largo, keeping his hands clasped behind him, while his brown eyes were bright with the lasting youthfulness of enthusiastic thought and love." 13

—*ahem:* " . . . he vented from time to time a low guttural interjection, which was habitual with him when he was absorbed by an inward discussion." 15

—*visited:* "He placed himself at a right angle with his visitors, his worn look of intellectual eagerness, slight frame, and rusty attire, making an odd contrast with their flourishing persons, unblemished costume, and comfortable freedom from excitement. The group was fairly typical of the difference between the men who are animated by ideas and the men who are expected to apply them. Then he drew forth his spectacles, and began to rub them with the thin end of his coat-tail." 16

—*impulsive:* "Mr Lyon, like others who are habitually occupied with impersonal subjects, was liable to this impulsive sort of action. He snatched at the details of life as if they were darting past him—as if they were like the ribbons at his knees, which would never be tied all day if they were not tied on the instant. Through these spasmodic leaps out of his abstractions into real life, it constantly happened that he suddenly took a course which had been the subject of too much doubt with him ever to have been determined on by continuous thought." 16

—*his skill:* " . . . speech and exposition were so easy to him, that if he argued forcibly, he believed it to be simply because the truth was forcible. He was not proud of moving easily in his native medium. A panting man thinks of himself as a clever swimmer; but a fish swims much better, and takes his performances as a matter of course." 24

—*eager for debate:* "But the little man suffered from imprisoned ideas, and was as restless as a racer held in. He could not sit down again, but walked backwards and forwards, stroking his chin, emitting his low guttural interjection under the pressure of clauses and sentences which he longed to utter aloud, as he would have done in his own study." 24

—surprised by joy: "The old man's little delicate frame was shaken by a surprise and joy that were almost painful in their intensity. He had been going to ask forgiveness of her who asked it for herself. In that moment of supreme complex emotion one ray of the minister's joy was the thought, 'Surely the work of grace is begun in her—surely here is a heart that the Lord hath touched.' " 26

—heroic partisan: "Yet the minister, as we have seen, found in his Christian faith a reason for clinging the more to one who had not a large party to back him. That little man's heart was heroic: he was not one of those Liberals who make their anxiety for 'the cause' of Liberalism a plea for cowardly desertion." 37

The Transomes

Durfey Transome. "And the eldest son had been just such another as his father, only worse—A wild sort of half-natural, who got into bad company. They said his mother hated him and wished him dead . . . . " *I*

—mother's fond wish: "Somehow the hated Durfey, the imbecile eldest, who seemed to have become tenacious of a despicable squandering life, would be got rid of; vice might kill him." 1

—tenure: "[**Harold**] knew that affairs had been unpleasant in his youth— that there had been ugly lawsuits—and that his scapegrace brother Durfey had helped to lower still farther the depressed condition of the family." 2

—brother: "At home and at Eton [**Harold**] had been side by side with his stupid elder brother Durfey, whom he despised; and he very early began to reflect that since this **Caliban** in miniature was older than himself, he must carve out his own fortune." 8

Harold Transome. " . . . there hung a picture of a youthful face which bore a strong resemblance to her own: a beardless but masculine face, with rich brown hair hanging low on the forehead, and undulating beside each cheek down to the loose white cravat." 1

—first impression: "She heard herself called 'Mother!' and felt a light kiss on each cheek; but stronger than all that sensation was the consciousness which no previous thought could prepare her for, that this son who had come back to her was a stranger . . . though the likeness to herself was no longer striking, the years had overlaid it with another likeness which would have arrested her." 1

—not sensitive: "Harold . . . had no wish opposed to filial kindness, but his busy thoughts were imperiously determined by habits which had no reference to any woman's feeling; and even if he could have conceived what his mother's feeling was, his mind, after that momentary arrest, would have darted forward on its usual course." 1

—the younger son: " . . . with a precocious clearness of perception as to the conditions on which he could hope for any advantages in life. Like most energetic natures, he had a strong faith in his luck; he had been gay at their parting, and had promised to make his fortune . . . . " 1

—intimidating: "Harold's rapidity, decision, and indifference to any impressions in others which did not further or impede his own purposes, had made themselves felt by her as much as she would have felt the unmanageable strength of a great bird which had alighted near her, and allowed her to stroke its wing for a moment because food lay near her." 1

—*conversation:* "It was his habit to compress a great deal of effective conversation into a short space of time, asking rapidly all the questions he wanted to get answered, and diluting no subject with irrelevancies, paraphrase, or repetitions." 2

—*his father:* "Yet he remained good-humoured, saying something to his father now and then for the sake of being kind, and looking on with a pitying shrug as he saw him watch **Hickes** cutting his food." 2

—*practical and masterful:* "He was not to be turned aside from any course he had chosen; but he disliked all quarrelling as an unpleasant expenditure of energy that could have no good practical result. He was at once active and luxurious; fond of mastery, and good-natured enough to wish that every one about him should like his mastery; not caring greatly to know other people's thoughts, and ready to despise them as blockheads if their thoughts differed from his, and yet solicitous that they should have no colourable reason for slight thoughts about him.

"The blockheads must be forced to respect him. Hence, in proportion as he foresaw that his equals in the neighbourhood would be indignant with him for his political choice, he cared keenly about making a good figure before them in every other way. His conduct as a landholder was to be judicious, his establishment was to be kept up generously, his imbecile father treated with careful regard, his family relations entirely without scandal." ¶2

—*observed:* "**Jermyn** was closely observing Harold with an unpleasant sense that there was an expression of acuteness and determination about him which would make him formidable." 2

—*self-control:* "But in proportion as he found **Jermyn**'s manners annoying, he felt the necessity of controlling himself. He despised all persons who defeated their own projects by the indulgence of momentary impulses." 2

—*politics:* " 'I am a radical only in rooting out abuses . . . .

" 'I remove the rotten timbers . . . and substitute fresh oak, that's all.' " 2

"He himself was proceeding very cautiously, and preferred not even to know too much just at present, lest a certain personal antipathy he was conscious of towards **Jermyn**, and an occasional liability to exasperation, should get the better of a calm and clear-sighted resolve not to quarrel with the man while he could be of use. Harold would have been disgusted with himself if he had helped to frustrate his own purpose. And his strongest purpose now was to get returned for Parliament, to make a figure there as a Liberal member, and to become on all grounds a personage of weight in North Loamshire." 8

—*summary:* "Twenty years ago he had been a bright, active, good-tempered lad, with sharp eyes and a good aim; he delighted in success and in predominance; but he did not long for an impossible predominance, and become sour and sulky because it was impossible. He played at games he was clever in, and usually won; all other games he let alone, and thought them of little worth . . . . He turned his back on home very cheerfully, though he was rather fond of his mother, and very fond of Transome Court, and the river where he had been used to fish; but he said to himself as he passed the lodge-gates, 'I'll get rich somehow, and have an estate of my own, and do what I like with it.'

"This determined aiming at something not easy but clearly possible, marked the direction in which Harold's nature was strong; he had the energetic will and muscle, the self-confidence, the quick perception, and the narrow imagination which make what is admiringly called the practical mind." ¶8

—political goal: "He meant to stand up for every change that the economical condition of the country required, and he had an angry contempt for men with coronets on their coaches, but too small a share of brains to see when they had better make a virtue of necessity. His respect was rather for men who had no coronets, but who achieved a just influence by furthering all measures which the common sense of the country, and the increasing self-assertion of the majority, peremptorily demanded. He could be such a man himself." 8

—healthy egoist: "In fact Harold Transome was a clever, frank, good-natured egoist; not stringently consistent, but without any disposition to falsity; proud, but with a pride that was moulded in an individual rather than an hereditary form; unspeculative, unsentimental, unsympathetic, fond of sensual pleasures, but disinclined to all vice, and attached as a healthy, clear-sighted person, to all conventional morality, construed with a certain freedom, like doctrinal articles to which the public order may require subscription.

"A character is apt to look but indifferently, written out in this way. Reduced to a map, our premises seem insignificant, but they make, nevertheless, a very pretty freehold to live in and walk over; and so, if Harold Transome had been among your acquaintances, and you have observed his qualities through the medium of his agreeable person, bright smile, and a certain easy charm which accompanies sensuousness when unsullied by coarseness—through the medium also of the many opportunities in which he would have made himself useful or pleasant to you—you would have thought him a good fellow, highly acceptable as a guest, a colleague, or a brother-in-law. Whether all mothers would have liked him as a son, is another question." ¶8

—filial: "Yet Harold was a kind son: he kissed his mother's brow, offered her his arm, let her choose what she liked for the house and garden, asked her whether she would have bays or greys for her new carriage, and was bent on seeing her make as good a figure in the neighbourhood as any other woman of her rank." 8

—presented to a lady: "But we have some notions of beauty and fitness which withstand the centuries; and quite irrespective of dates, it would be pronounced that at the age of thirty-four Harold Transome was a striking and handsome man. He was one of those people, as **Denner** had remarked, to whose presence in the room you could not be indifferent: if you do not hate or dread them, you must find the touch of their hands, nay, their very shadows, agreeable.

"**Esther** felt a pleasure quite new to her as she saw his finely-embrowned face and full bright eyes turned towards her with an air of deference by which gallantry must commend itself to a refined woman who is not absolutely free from vanity. Harold Transome regarded women as slight things, but he was fond of slight things in the intervals of business; and he held it among the chief arts of life to keep these pleasant diversions within such bounds that they should never interfere with the course of his serious ambition." 16

—repulsion: "Harold, in his turn, disliked impracticable notions of loftiness and purity—disliked all enthusiasm; and he thought he saw a very troublesome, vigorous incorporation of that nonsense in **Felix**." 16

Harold Transome has a new interest

—*retrospect:* "At present, looking back on that day at Treby, it seems to me that the sadder illusion lay with Harold Transome, who was trusting in his own skill to shape the success of his own morrows, ignorant of what many yesterdays had determined for him beforehand." 16

—*practical ethics:* "It was not disgraceful to be neither a **Quixote** nor a theorist, aiming to correct the moral rules of the world; but whatever actually was, or might prove to be, disgraceful, Harold held in detestation." 17

—*a gift:* "Harold had smiles at command in the right place, but he was not going to smile when it was neither necessary nor agreeable. He was one of those good-humoured, yet energetic men, who have the gift of anger, hatred, and scorn upon occasion, though they are too healthy and self-contented for such feelings to get generated in them without external occasion." 17

—*on the hustings:* "Harold's speech 'did': it was not of the glib-nonsensical sort, not ponderous, not hesitating—which is much as to say, that it was remarkable among British speeches. Read in print the next day, perhaps it would be neither pregnant nor conclusive, which is saying no more than that its excellence was not of an abnormal kind, but such as is usually found in the best efforts of eloquent candidates. Accordingly the applause drowned the opposition, and content predominated." 19

—*setback:* "He had lost the election; but if that had been his only annoyance, he had good humour and good sense enough to have borne it as well as most men, and to have paid the eight or nine thousand, which had been the price of ascertaining that he was not to sit in the next Parliament, without useless grumbling." 34

—*anger:* "Harold himself did not look amiable just then, but his anger was of the sort that seeks a vent without waiting to give a fatal blow; it was that of a nature more subtly mixed than **Jermyn**'s—less animally forcible, less unwavering in selfishness, and with more of high-bred pride." 35

—*in conflict:* "His nature was not of a kind given to internal conflict, and he had never before been long undecided and puzzled. This unaccustomed state of mind was so painfully irksome to him—he rebelled so impatiently against the oppression of circumstances in which his quick temperament and habitual decision could not help him—that it added tenfold to his hatred of **Jermyn**, who was the cause of it. And thus, as the temptation to avoid all risk of losing the estate grew and grew till scruples looked minute by the side of it, the difficulty of bringing himself to make a compact with Jermyn seemed more and more insurmountable." 36

—*tempted:* "Harold listened as if he had been a legendary hero, selected for peculiar solicitation by the Evil One." 36

—*on a visit:* "[**Lyddy**] saw the tall lady sweep in arrayed in her rich black and fur, with that fine gentleman behind her whose thick topknot of wavy hair, sparkling ring, dark complexion, and general air of worldly exaltation unconnected with chapel, were painfully suggestive to Lyddy of **Herod**, **Pontius Pilate**, or the much-quoted **Gallio**." 38

—*his mother:* " . . . he spoke of his mother's lonely life and pinched circumstances, of her lack of comfort in her elder son, and of the habit she had consequently acquired of looking at the gloomy side of things. He hinted that she had been accustomed to dictate, and that, as he had left her when he was a boy, she had perhaps indulged the dream that he would come back a boy. She was still sore on the point of his politics. These things could not be helped, but, so far as he could, he wished to make the rest of her life as cheerful as possible." 40

—*the opposite sex:* "When [**Esther**] had been hardly a week in the house, he had made up his mind to marry her; and it had never entered into that mind that the decision did not rest entirely with his inclination . . . . To be deeply in love was a catastrophe not likely to happen to him; but he was readily amorous. No woman could make him miserable, but he was sensitive to the presence of women, and was kind to them; not with grimaces, like a man of mere gallantry, but beamingly, easily, like a man of genuine good-nature." 40

—*caution indicated:* "Along with **Esther**'s playful charm she conveyed an impression of personal pride and high spirit which warned Harold's acuteness that in the delicacy of their present position he might easily make a false move and offend her. A woman was likely to be credulous about adoration, and to find no difficulty in referring it to her intrinsic attractions; but Esther was too dangerously quick and critical not to discern the least awkwardness that looked like offering her marriage as a convenient compromise for himself. Beforehand, he might have said that such characteristics as hers were not lovable in a woman; but, as it was, he found that the hope of pleasing her had a piquancy quite new to him." 40

—*nonsense:* " 'A woman ought never to have any trouble. There should always be a man to guard her from it.' (Harold Transome was masculine and fallible; he had incautiously sat down this morning to pay his addresses by talk about nothing in particular; and, clever experienced man as he was, he fell into nonsense.)" 40

—*self-revealing:* "Harold was looking, as he felt, thoroughly enamoured of this bright woman, who was not at all to his preconceived taste. Perhaps a touch of hypothetic jealousy now helped to heighten the effect. But he mastered all indiscretion . . . . " 40

—*effective:* " . . . the attractive interest of noticing Harold's practical cleverness—the masculine ease with which he governed everybody and administered everything about him, without the least harshness, and with a facile good-nature which yet was not weak." 43

—*superficial:* "And his face did look very pleasant; she could not help liking him, although he was certainly too particular about sauces, gravies, and wines, and had a way of virtually measuring the value of everything by the contribution it made to his own pleasure. His very good-nature was unsympathetic: it never came from any thorough understanding or deep respect for what was in the mind of the person he obliged or indulged; it was like his kindness to his mother—an arrangement of his for the happiness of others, which, if they were sensible, ought to succeed." 43

—*rival discovered:* "It seemed to him that **Felix** was the least formidable person that he could have found out as an object of interest antecedent to himself. A young workman who had got himself thrown into prison, whatever recommendations he might have had for a girl at a romantic age in the dreariness of Dissenting society at Treby, could hardly be considered by Harold in the light of a rival . . . he was solicitous that his behaviour with regard to this young man should be such as to enhance his own merit in **Esther**'s eyes. At the same time he was not inclined to any euphemisms that would seem by any possibility to bring Felix into the lists with himself." 43

—*lack of experience:* "With all due regard to Harold Transome, he was one of those men who are liable to make the greater mistakes about a particular woman's feelings, because they pique themselves on a power of interpretation derived from much experience. Experience is enlightening, but with a difference. Experiments on live animals may go on for a long period, and yet the fauna on which they are made may be limited. There may be a passion in the mind of a woman which precipitates her, not along the path of any beguilement, but into a great leap away from it. Harold's experience had not taught him this; and **Esther**'s enthusiasm about **Felix Holt** did not seem to him to be dangerous." 43

—*witness:* "He had generosity and candour enough to bear **Felix Holt**'s proud rejection of his advances without any petty resentment; he had all the susceptibilities of a gentleman; and these moral qualities gave the right direction to his acumen, in judging of the behaviour that would best secure his dignity. Everything requiring self-command was easier to him because of **Esther**'s presence; for her admiration was just then the object which this well-tanned man of the world had it most at heart to secure.

" . . . He certainly looked like a handsome portrait by **Sir Thomas Lawrence**, in which that remarkable artist had happily omitted the usual excess of honeyed blandness mixed with alert intelligence, which is hardly compatible with the state of man out of paradise." 46

—*misled:* "Harold had a conviction that might have seemed like fatuity if it had not been that he saw the effect he produced on **Esther** by the light of his opinions about women in general. The conviction was, that **Felix Holt** could not be his rival in any formidable sense. Esther's admiration for this eccentric young man was, he thought, a moral enthusiasm, a romantic fervour, which was one among those many attractions quite novel in his own experience; her distress about the trouble of one who had been a familiar object in her former home, was no more than naturally followed from a tender woman's compassion . . . . Felix Holt was not the sort of man a woman would be likely to be in love with when she was wooed by Harold Transome." 47

—*at a peak:* "He looked brilliant that morning; his blood was flowing prosperously. He had come in after a ride, and was additionally brightened by rapid talk and the excitement of seeking to impress himself favourably, or at least powerfully, on the minds of neighbours nearer or more remote. He had just that amount of flush which indicates that life is more enjoyable than usual; and as he stood with his left hand caressing his whisker, and his right holding the paper and his riding-whip, his dark eyes running rapidly along the written lines, and his lips reposing in a curve of good-humour which had more happiness in it than a smile, all beholders might have seen that his mind was at ease." 47

—*the depths:* "The last five hours had made a change as great as illness makes. Harold looked as if he had been wrestling, and had some terrible blow. His eyes had that sunken look which, because it is unusual, seems to intensify expression." 48

—*decision taken:* "It was the most serious moment in Harold Transome's life: for the first time the iron had entered into his soul, and he felt the hard pressure of our common lot, the yoke of that mighty resistless destiny laid upon us by the acts of other men as well as our own." 49

—*avowal:* " 'I need not tell you that your regard has become very important to me—that if our mutual position had been different—that, in short, you must have seen—if it had not seemed to be a matter of worldly interest, I should have told you plainly already that I loved you, and that my happiness could be complete only if you would consent to marry me.' " 49

Harry Transome, "a black-maned little boy about three years old, who was urging [**Mr Transome**] on with loud encouraging noises and occasional thumps from a stick which he wielded with some difficulty . . . the little boy, finding something new to be looked at, let go the cord and came round in front of the company, dragging his stick, and standing at a safe war-dancing distance as he fixed his great black eyes on **Lady Debarry**." 7

—invitation and response: " 'But he's a charming little fellow: come to me, you round-cheeked cherub.'

"The black eyes continued fixed as if by a sort of fascination on **Lady Debarry**'s face, and her affable invitation was unheeded. At last, putting his head forward and pouting his lips, the cherub gave forth with marked intention the sounds, 'Nau-o-oom', many times repeated: apparently they summed up his opinion of Lady Debarry, and may perhaps have meant 'naughty old woman', but his speech was a broken lisping polyglot of hazardous interpretation . . . .

" 'Go, go, Harry; let poor **Puff** alone—he'll bite you,' said **Mrs Transome**, stooping to release her aged pet.

"Her words were too suggestive, for Harry immediately laid hold of her arm with his teeth, and bit with all his might. Happily the stuffs upon it were some protection, but the pain forced Mrs Transome to give a low cry; and **Sir Maximus** who had now turned to reseat himself, shook the little rascal off, whereupon he burst away and trotted into the library again." 7

—and a visitor: "This creature, with the soft broad brown cheeks, low forehead, great black eyes, tiny well-defined nose, fierce biting tricks towards every person and thing he disliked, and insistence on entirely occupying those he liked, was a human specimen such as **Esther** had never seen before . . . she had no sooner sat down on the sofa in the library than he climbed up to her, and began to treat her as an attractive subject in natural history, snatched up her curls with his brown fist, and, discovering that there was a little ear under them, pinched it and blew into it, pulled at her coronet of plaits, and seemed to discover with satisfaction that it did not grow at the summit of her head, but could be dragged down and altogether undone. Then finding that she laughed, tossed him back, kissed, and pretended to bite him—in fact, was an animal that understood fun—he rushed off and made **Dominic** bring a small menagerie of white-mice, squirrels, and birds, with **Moro**, the black spaniel, to make her acquaintance." 40

John Justus Transome. "[**Johnson**] had before him the whole history of the settlement of those estates made a hundred years ago by John Justus Transome, entailing them, whilst in his possession, on his son **Thomas** and his heirs-male, with remainder to the **Bycliffe**s in fee." 29

Mr Transome. " . . . he was as poor half-witted a fellow as you'd wish to see . . . . " *I*

—observed: "A man nearer seventy than sixty was in the act of ranging on a large library-table a series of shallow drawers, some of them containing dried insects, others mineralogical specimens. His pale mild eyes, receding lower jaw, and slight frame, could never have expressed much vigour, either bodily or mental; but he had now the unevenness of gait and feebleness of gesture which tell of a past paralytic seizure. His threadbare clothes were

thoroughly brushed; his soft white hair was carefully parted and arranged: he was not a neglected-looking old man . . . but when **Mrs Transome** appeared within the doorway, her husband paused in his work and shrank like a timid animal looked at in a cage where flight is impossible. He was conscious of a troublesome intention, for which he had been rebuked before: that of disturbing all his specimens with a view to a new arrangement." 1

—*appraised:* "Gad! what a wreck poor father is! Paralysis, eh? Terribly shrunk and shaken—crawls about among his books and beetles as usual, though. Well, it's a slow and easy death. But he's not much over sixty-five, is he?'

" 'Sixty-seven, counting by birthdays; but your father was born old . . . . ' " 1

—*released:* "The old man seemed so happy now in the new world created for him by **Dominic** and **Harry**, that he would perhaps have made a holocaust of his flies and beetles if it had been necessary in order to keep this living, lively kindness about him. He no longer confined himself to the library, but shuffled along from room to room, staying and looking on at what was going forward wherever he did not find **Mrs Transome** alone.

"To **Esther** the sight of this feeble-minded, timid, paralytic man, who had long abdicated all mastery over the things that were his, was something piteous." 40

—*after a nap:* "He had doffed his furred cap and cloak, but in lying down to sleep he had thrown over his shoulders a soft Oriental scarf which **Harold** had given him, and this still hung over his scanty white hair and down to his knees, held fast by his wooden-looking arms and laxly clasped hands, which fell in front of him." 43

Mrs Arabella Transome. " . . . but *she* was master, had come of a high family, and had a spirit—you could see it in her eye and the way she sat her horse. Forty years ago, when she came into this country, they said she was a pictur'; but her family was poor, and so she took up with a hatchet-faced fellow like this Transome." *I [Her given name is mentioned in 2, and never again.]*

—*in expectation:* " . . . there came forth from time to time a lady, who walked lightly over the polished stone floor, and stood on the door-steps and watched and listened. She walked lightly, for her figure was slim and finely formed, though she was between fifty and sixty. She was a tall, proud-looking woman, with abundant grey hair, dark eyes and eyebrows, and a somewhat eagle-like yet not unfeminine face. Her tight-fitting black dress was much worn; the fine lace of her cuffs and collar, and of the small veil which fell backwards over her high comb, was visibly mended; but rare jewels flashed on her hands, which lay on her folded black-clad arms like finely-cut onyx cameos." 1

—*anticipation:* "Could it be that now—when her hair was grey, when sight had become one of the day's fatigues, when her young accomplishments seemed almost ludicrous, like the tone of her first harpsichord and the words of the songs long browned with age—was she going to reap an assured joy?—to feel that the doubtful deeds of her life were justified by the result, since a kind Providence had sanctioned them?—to be no longer tacitly pitied by her neighbours for her lack of money, her imbecile husband, her graceless eldest-born, and the loneliness of her life; but to have at her side a rich, clever, possibly a tender, son?" 1

—*first words:* " 'Everything has changed, **Harold**. I am an old woman, you see.'

" 'But straighter and more upright than some of the young ones!' said Harold, inwardly, however, feeling that age had made his mother's face very anxious and eager." 1

—*a manager:* "Mrs Transome had not the feminine tendency to seek influence through pathos; she had been used to rule in virtue of acknowledged superiority. The consciousness that she had to make her son's acquaintance, and that her knowledge of the youth of nineteen might help her little in interpreting the man of thirty-four, had fallen like lead on her soul; but in this new acquaintance of theirs she cared especially that her son, who had seen a strange world, should feel that he was come home to a mother who was to be consulted on all things, and who could supply his lack of the local experience necessary to an English landholder." 1

—*past:* "Her part in life had been that of the clever sinner, and she was equipped with the views, the reasons, and the habits which belonged to that character: life would have little meaning for her if she were to be gently thrust aside as a harmless elderly woman. And besides, there were secrets which her son must never know." 1

—*shock:* " 'God forbid! I'm a radical.'

"Mrs Transome's limbs tottered; she sank into a chair. Here was a distinct confirmation of the vague but strong feeling that her son was a stranger to her. Here was a revelation to which it seemed almost as impossible to adjust her hopes and notions of a dignified life as if her son had said that he had been converted to Mahometanism at Smyrna, and had four wives, instead of one son . . . . There were rich Radicals, she was aware, as there were rich Jews and Dissenters, but she had never thought of them as county people." 1

—*lonely and unoccupied:* "She had begun to live merely in small immediate cares and occupations, and, like all eager-minded women who advance in life without any activity of tenderness or any large sympathy, she had contracted small rigid habits of thinking and acting, she had her 'ways' which must not be crossed, and learned to fill up the great void of life with giving small orders to tenants, insisting on medicines for infirm cottagers, winning small triumphs in bargains and personal economies, and parrying ill-natured remarks of **Lady Debarry**'s by lancet-edged epigrams." 1

—*high-born:* "She had that high-born imperious air which would have marked her as an object of hatred and reviling by a revolutionary mob. Her person was too typical of social distinctions to be passed by with indifference by any one: it would have fitted an empress in her own right, who had had to rule in spite of faction, to dare the violation of treaties and dread retributive invasions, to gasp after new territories, to be defiant in desperate circumstances, and to feel a woman's hunger of the heart for ever unsatisfied." 1

—*her tastes:* "She always thought that the dangerous French writers were wicked, and that her reading of them was a sin; but many sinful things were highly agreeable to her, and many things which she did not doubt to be good and true were dull and meaningless. She found ridicule of Biblical characters very amusing, and she was interested in stories of illicit passion: but she believed all the while that truth and safety lay in due attendance on prayers and sermons, in the admirable doctrines and ritual of the Church of England, equally remote from Puritanism and Popery; in fact, in such a view of this world and the next as would preserve the existing arrangements of

English society quite unshaken, keeping down the obtrusiveness of the vulgar and the discontent of the poor." 1

—early swath: "And it is astonishing how effective this education appeared in a handsome girl, who sat supremely well on horseback, sang and played a little, painted small figures in water-colours, had a naughty sparkle in her eyes when she made a daring quotation, and an air of serious dignity when she recited something from her store of correct opinions. But however such a stock of ideas may be made to tell in elegant society, and during a few seasons in town, no amount of bloom and beauty can make them a perennial source of interest in things not personal; and the notion that what is true and, in general, good for mankind, is stupid and drug-like, is not a safe theoretic basis in circumstances of temptation and difficulty.

"Mrs Transome had been in her bloom before this century began, and in the long painful years since then, what she had once regarded as her knowledge and accomplishments had become as valueless as old-fashioned stucco ornaments, of which the substance was never worth anything, while the form is no longer to the taste of any living mortal." 1

—latterly jaded: "Crosses, mortifications, money-cares, conscious blameworthiness, had changed the aspect of the world for her: there was anxiety in the morning sunlight; there was unkind triumph or disapproving pity in the glances of greeting neighbours; there was advancing age, and a contracting prospect in the changing seasons as they came and went. And what could then sweeten the days to a hungry much-exacting self like Mrs Transome's?" 1

—need for power: "Mrs Transome, whose imperious will had availed little to ward off the great evils of her life, found the opiate for her discontent in the exertion of her will about smaller things. She was not cruel, and could not enjoy thoroughly what she called the old woman's pleasure of tormenting; but she liked every little sign of power her lot had left her.

"She liked that a tenant should stand bareheaded below her as she sat on horseback. She liked to insist that work done without her orders should be undone from beginning to end. She liked to be curtsied and bowed to by all the congregation as she walked up the little barn of a church. She liked to change a labourer's medicine fetched from the doctor, and substitute a prescription of her own. If she had only been more haggard and less majestic, those who had glimpses of her outward life might have said she was a tyrannical griping harridan, with a tongue like a razor.

"No one said exactly that; but they never said anything like the full truth about her, or divined what was hidden under that outward life—a woman's keen sensibility and dread, which lay screened behind all her petty habits and narrow notions, as some quivering thing with eyes and throbbing heart may lie crouching behind withered rubbish." ¶1

—pathetic: "There were piteous sensibilities in this faded woman, who thirty-four years ago, in the splendour of her bloom, had been imperious to one of these men, and had rapturously pressed the other as an infant to her bosom, and now knew that she was of little consequence to either of them." 2

—observed: " 'She's a healthy woman enough, surely: see how upright she is, and she rides about like a girl of twenty.'

" 'She is so thin that she makes me shudder.'

" 'Pooh! she's slim and active; women are not bid for by the pound.' " 7

—hopes cast down: “After sharing the common dream that when a beautiful man-child was born to her, her cup of happiness would be full, she had travelled through long years apart from that child to find herself at last in the presence of a son of whom she was afraid, who was utterly unmanageable by her, and to whose sentiments in any given case she possessed no key.” 8

—trammelled: “The finest threads, such as no eye sees, if bound cunningly about the sensitive flesh, so that the movement to break them would bring torture, may make a worse bondage than any fetters. Mrs Transome felt the fatal threads about her, and the bitterness of this helpless bondage mingled itself with the new elegancies of the dining and drawing rooms, and all the household changes which **Harold** had ordered to be brought about with magical quickness. Nothing was as she had once expected it would be. If Harold had shown the least care to have her stay in the room with him—if he had really cared for her opinion—if he had been what she had dreamed he would be in the eyes of those people who had made her world—if all the past could be dissolved, and leave no solid trace of itself—mighty *ifs* that were all impossible —she would have tasted some joy; but now she began to look back with regret to the days when she sat in loneliness among the old drapery, and still longed for something that might happen.” 8

—former lover: “For years there had been a deep silence about the past between them: on her side, because she remembered; on his, because he more and more forgot.” 9

“It was a resolve which had become a habit, that she would never quarrel with this man—never tell him what she saw him to be. She had kept her woman’s pride and sensibility intact: through all her life there had vibrated the maiden need to have her hand kissed and be the object of chivalry.” 9

“But no sooner did the words ‘You have brought it on me’ rise within her than she heard within also the retort, ‘You brought it on yourself.’ Not for all the world beside could she bear to hear that retort uttered from without.” 9

“There was a possibility of fierce insolence in this man who was to pass with those nearest to her as her indebted servant, but whose brand she secretly bore. She was as powerless with him as she was with her son.” 9

—her foot in it: “ . . .she had not resisted the temptation to say something bitter about **Harold**’s failure to get returned as a Radical, helping, with feminine self-defeat, to exclude herself more completely from any consultation by him. In this way poor women, whose power lies solely in their influence, make themselves like music out of tune, and only move men to run away.” 34

—frightened: “She was still young and ardent in her terrors; the passions of the past were living in her dread . . . .

“. . . dull obscurity everywhere, except where the keen light fell on the narrow track of her own lot, wide only for a woman’s anguish . . . . Unable to walk about any longer, she sank into a large cushioned chair, helpless and prayerless. She was not thinking of God’s anger or mercy, but of her son’s. She was thinking of what might be brought, not by death, but by life.” 34

—caught aback: “Mrs Transome’s rising temper was turned into a horrible sensation, as painful as a sudden concussion from something hard and immovable when we have struck out with our fist, intending to hit something warm, soft, and breathing, like ourselves. Poor Mrs Transome’s strokes were sent jarring back on her by a hard unalterable past.” 36

—blindness: “Mrs Transome hardly noticed **Mr Lyon**, not from studied haughtiness, but from sheer mental inability to consider him—as a person

ignorant of natural history is unable to consider a fresh-water polyp otherwise than as a sort of animated weed, certainly not fit for table." 38

—charmed: "Since [**Harold**] had come home again, he had never seen her so much at her ease, or with so much benignancy in her face. The secret lay in the charm of **Esther**'s sweet young deference, a sort of charm that had not before entered into Mrs Transome's elderly life." 38

—abstracted: "Mrs Transome had herself unfastened her abundant grey hair, which rolled backward in a pale sunless stream over her dark dress. She was seated before the mirror apparently looking at herself, her brow knit in one deep furrow, and her jewelled hands laid one above the other on her knee. Probably she had ceased to see the reflection in the mirror, for her eyes had the fixed wide-open look that belongs not to examination, but to reverie. Motionless in that way, her clear-cut features keeping distinct record of past beauty, she looked like an image faded, dried, and bleached by uncounted suns, rather than a breathing woman who had numbered the years as they passed, and had a consciousness within her which was the slow deposit of those ceaseless rolling years." 39

—genealogy: "Poor Mrs Transome, with her secret bitterness and dread, still found a flavour in this sort of pride; none the less because certain deeds of her own life had been in fatal inconsistency with it. Besides, genealogies entered into her stock of ideas, and her talk on such subjects was as necessary as the notes of the linnet or the blackbird. She had no ultimate analysis of things that went beyond blood and family . . . . " 40

—an old lover: "This man, young, slim, and graceful, with a selfishness which then took the form of homage to her, had at one time kneeled to her and kissed those hands fervently; and she had thought there was a poetry in such passion beyond any to be found in everyday domesticity." 42

—excoriation: " 'You have said enough; I will speak now. I have made sacrifices too, but it was when I knew that they were not my happiness. It was after I saw that I *had* stooped—after I saw that you cared for yourself only, and not for me. I heard your explanations—of your duty in life—of our mutual reputation—of a virtuous young lady attached to you. I bore it; I let everything go; I shut my eyes; I might almost have let myself starve, rather than have scenes of quarrel with the man I had loved, in which I must accuse him of turning my love into a good bargain.' There was a slight tremor in Mrs Transome's voice in the last words, and for a moment she paused; but when she spoke again it seemed as if the tremor had frozen into a cutting icicle. 'I suppose if a lover picked one's pocket, there's no woman would like to own it. I don't say I was not afraid of you. I *was* afraid of you, and I know now I was right.'

" 'Mrs Transome,' said **Jermyn**, white to the lips, 'it is needless to say more. I withdraw any words that have offended you.'

" 'You can't withdraw them. Can a man apologize for being a dastard? . . . And I have caused you to strain your conscience, have I? —it is I who have sullied your purity? I should think the demons have more honour—they are not so impudent to one another. I would not lose the misery of being a woman, now I see what can be the baseness of a man. One must be a man—first to tell a woman that her love has made her your debtor, and then ask her to pay you by breaking the last poor threads between her and her son.' " 42

—*ironic ashes:* " 'I felt the horror of [**Harold**'s] not knowing the truth. I might have been dragged at last, by my own feeling—by my own memory—to tell him all, and make him as well as myself miserable, to save you . . . .

" 'But now you have asked me, I will never tell him! Be ruined—no—do something more dastardly to save yourself. If I sinned, my judgment went beforehand—that I should sin for a man like you.' " 42

—*sad consideration:* " 'My dear, I shall make this house dull for you. You sit with me like an embodied patience. I am unendurable; I am getting into a melancholy dotage. A fidgety old woman like me is as unpleasant to see as a rook with its wing broken. Don't mind me, my dear. Run away from me without ceremony. Everyone else does, you see. I am part of the old furniture with new drapery.' " 45

—*"who is my father?"* "She seemed as if age were striking her with a sudden wand—as if her trembling face were getting haggard before him. She was mute. But her eyes had not fallen; they looked up in helpless misery at her son." 48

—*a blight:* "The sense that Mrs Transome was unhappy, affected **Esther** more and more deeply as the growing familiarity which relaxed the efforts of the hostess revealed more and more the threadbare tissue of this majestic lady's life. Even the flowers and the pure sunshine and the sweet waters of Paradise would have been spoiled for a young heart, if the bowered walks had been haunted by an **Eve** grown grey with bitter memories of an **Adam** who had complained, 'The woman . . . she gave me of the tree, and I did eat.' " 49

—*comfort in the night:* "The disordered grey hair—the haggard face—the reddened eyelids under which the tears seemed to be coming again with pain, pierced **Esther** to the heart. A passionate desire to soothe this suffering woman came over her. She clung round her again, and kissed her poor quivering lips and eyelids, and laid her young cheek against the pale and haggard one. Words could not be quick or strong enough to utter her yearning. As Mrs Transome felt that soft clinging, she said,

" 'God has some pity on me.' " 50

Thomas Transome. "[**Johnson**] knew that Thomas, son of **John Justus**, proving a prodigal, had, without the knowledge of his father, the tenant in possession, sold his own and his descendants' rights to a lawyer-cousin named **Durfey**; that, therefore, the title of the Durfey-Transomes, in spite of that old Durfey's tricks to show the contrary, depended solely on the purchase of the 'base fee' thus created by Thomas Transome; and that the **Bycliffe**s were the 'remainder-men' who might fairly oust the Durfey-Transomes if ever the issue of the prodigal Thomas went clean out of existence, and ceased to represent a right which he had bargained away from them." 29

A later **Thomas Transome** "at Littleshaw, in Stonyshire, who was the representative of a pawned inheritance." 29 *See* **Tommy Trounsem** O

The Other Principal

Matthew Jermyn. "But heir or no heir, Lawyer Jermyn had had *his* picking out of the estate [said **Sampson**]. Not a door in his big house but what was the finest polished oak, all got off the Transome estate. If anybody liked to believe he paid for it, they were welcome. However, Lawyer Jermyn had sat on that box-seat many and many a time. He had made the wills of most people there-about. The coachman would not say that Lawyer Jermyn was not the man he would choose to make his own will some day. It was not so well for a lawyer to be over-honest, else he might not be up to other people's tricks." *I*

—*appraised:* " 'A fat-handed, glib-tongued fellow, with a scented cambric handkerchief; one of your educated low-bred fellows, a foundling who got his Latin for nothing at Christ's Hospital; one of your middle-class upstarts who want to rank with gentlemen, and think they'll do it with kid gloves and new furniture [said the **Rev. Lingon**].' " 2

—*past days:* "Jermyn used to smile at him, and speak to him affably, but **Harold**, half proud, half shy, got away from such patronage as soon as possible: he knew Jermyn was a man of business; his father, his uncle, and **Sir Maximus Debarry** did not regard him as a gentleman and their equal. He had known no evil of the man; but he saw now that if he were really a covetous upstart, there had been a temptation for him in the management of the **Transome** affairs; and it was clear that the estate was in a bad condition." 2

—*appearance:* "He was grey, but still remarkably handsome; fat, but tall enough to bear that trial to man's dignity. There was as strong a suggestion of toilette about him as if he had been five-and-twenty instead of nearly sixty. He chose always to dress in black, and was especially addicted to black satin waistcoats, which carried out the general sleekness of his appearance; and this, together with his white, fat, but beautifully-shaped hands, which he was in the habit of rubbing gently on his entrance into a room, gave him very much the air of a lady's physician." 2

—*manner of speaking:* "Mr Jermyn had a copious supply of words, which often led him into periphrase, but he cultivated a hesitating stammer, which, with a handsome impassiveness of face, except when he was smiling at a woman, or when the latent savageness of his nature was thoroughly roused, he had found useful in many relations, especially in business. No one could have found out that he was not at his ease." 2

—*concerned:* "Jermyn was not naturally flinty-hearted: at five-and-twenty he had written verses, and had got himself wet through in order not to disappoint a dark-eyed woman whom he was proud to believe in love with him; but a family man with grown-up sons and daughters, a man with a professional position and complicated affairs that make it hard to ascertain the exact relation between property and liabilities, necessarily thinks of himself and what may be impending." 9

"A man of sixty, with a wife whose Duffield connections were of the highest respectability, with a family of tall daughters, an expensive establishment, and a large professional business, owed a great deal more to himself as the mainstay of all those solidities, than to feelings and ideas which were quite unsubstantial." 9

—*insensitive:* "Jermyn felt annoyed—nothing more. There was nothing in his mind corresponding to the intricate meshes of sensitiveness in **Mrs Transome**'s. He was anything but stupid; yet he always blundered when he wanted to be delicate or magnanimous; he constantly sought to soothe others by praising himself. Moral vulgarity cleaved to him like an hereditary odour." 9

—useful quality: "But he was a man of resolution, who, having made out what was the best course to take under a difficulty, went straight to his work. The election must be won: that would put **Harold** in good-humour . . . . " 9

—irritating: " 'I don't approve it at all,' said **Harold**, who hated Jermyn's calculated slowness and conceit in his own impenetrability." 17

—annoyed but resilient: "When **Harold** was gone, Jermyn's handsome face gathered blackness. He hardly ever wore his worst expression in the presence of others, and but seldom when he was alone, for he was not given to believe that any game would ultimately go against him. His luck had been good. New conditions might always turn up to give him new chances; and if affairs threatened to come to an extremity between Harold and himself, he trusted to finding some sure resource." 17

—confident: "Jermyn was not afraid to show himself anywhere in Treby. He knew many people were not exactly fond of him, but a man can do without that, if he is prosperous. A provincial lawyer in those old-fashioned days was as independent of personal esteem as if he had been a Lord Chancellor." 20

—intimidating: " 'I'll tell you what Lawyer Jermyn was [said **Tommy Trounsem**]. He stands you there, and holds you away from him wi' a pole three yard long. He stares at you, and says nothing, till you feel like a Tom-fool; and then he threats you to set the justice on you; and then he's sorry for you, and hands you money, and preaches you a sarmint, and tells you you're a poor man, and he'll give you a bit of advice—and you'd better not be meddling wi' things belonging to the law, else you'll be catched up in a big wheel and fly to bits. And I went of a cold sweat, and I wished I might never come i' sight o' Lawyer Jermyn again. But he says, if you keep i' this neighbourhood, behave yourself well, and I'll pertect you.' " 28

—odious: "Jermyn was able and politic enough to have commanded a great deal of success in his life, but he could not help being handsome, arrogant, fond of being heard, indisposed to any kind of comradeship, amorous and bland towards women, cold and self-contained towards men." 29

—disliked: "Some one who . . . was disposed to revile Jermyn (perhaps it was **Sir Maximus**), had called him 'a cursed, sleek, handsome, long-winded, overbearing sycophant'; epithets which expressed, rather confusedly, the mingled character of the dislike he excited." 29

—black expression: "On the attorney's handsome face there was a black cloud of defiant determination, slightly startling to **Harold** . . . . Nobody was ever prepared beforehand for this expression of Jermyn's face, which seemed as strongly contrasted with the cold impenetrableness which he preserved under the ordinary annoyances of business as with the bland radiance of his lighter moments." 35

—obtuse: "And if Jermyn had been capable of feeling that he had thoroughly merited this infliction, he would not have uttered the words that drew it down on him . . . . He did not take into account (how should he?) the exasperation and loathing excited by his daring to urge the plea of right . . . . Some salt of generosity would have made Jermyn conscious that he had lost the citizenship which authorized him to plead the right; still more, that his self-vindication to **Mrs Transome** would be like the exhibition of a brand-mark, and only show that he was shame-proof." 42

—cornered: "It would be a vague intimation, carrying the effect of a threat, which should compel **Harold** to give him a private interview. To any counter-consideration that presented itself in his mind—to anything that an imagined voice might say—the imagined answer arose, 'That's all very fine, but I'm not going to be ruined if I can help it—least of all, ruined in that way.' Shall we call it degeneration or gradual development—this effect of thirty additional winters on the soft-glancing, versifying young Jermyn?" 47

—his last throw: " 'Let me go, you scoundrel!' said **Harold**, fiercely, 'or I'll be the death of you.'

" 'Do,' said Jermyn, in a grating voice; *'I am your father.'* " 47

Supporting Roles

Maurice Christian (actually **Henry Scaddon**), "a well-dressed man, who raised his hat to **Sir Maximus**, and called to the coachman to stop.

" 'Excuse me, Sir Maximus,' said this personage standing uncovered at the carriage-door, 'but I have just learned something of importance at Treby, which I thought you would like to know as soon as possible . . . . A new Radical candidate.' " 7

—appraised: " 'He's an uncommonly adroit, useful fellow, that factotum of **Philip**'s. I wish Phil would take my man and give me Christian. I'd make him house-steward; he might reduce the accounts a little.'

"Perhaps **Sir Maximus** would not have been so sanguine as to Mr Christian's economical virtues if he had seen that gentleman relaxing himself the same evening among the other distinguished dependants of the family and frequenters of the steward's room." 7

—cynosure: "The chief part in this scene was undoubtedly Mr Christian's, although he had hitherto been comparatively silent; but he occupied two chairs with so much grace, throwing his right leg over the seat of the second, and resting his right hand on the back; he held his cigar and displayed a splendid seal-ring with such becoming nonchalance, and had his grey hair arranged with so much taste, that experienced eyes would at once have seen even the great **Scales** himself to be but a secondary character." 7

—defending adroitly: " 'I don't intend to quarrel with you, **Scales**. Such talk as this is not profitable to either of us. It makes you purple in the face —you are apoplectic, you know—and it spoils good company. Better tell a few fibs about me behind my back—it will heat you less, and do me more harm. I'll leave you to it; I shall go and have a game at whist with the ladies.' " 7

—illness: "The fact was that Mr Christian, who had been remarkable through life for that power of adapting himself to circumstances which enables a man to fall safely on all-fours in the most hurried expulsions and escapes, was not exempt from bodily suffering . . . . Next to the pain itself he disliked that any one should know of it: defective health diminished a man's market value; he did not like to be the object of the sort of pity he himself gave to a poor devil who was forced to make a wry face or 'give in' altogether." 12

—loud visitor: "This rusty little man, in his dismal chamber, seemed to the **Ulysses** of the steward's room a pitiable sort of human curiosity, to whom a man of the world would speak rather loudly, in accommodation to an eccentricity which was likely to be accompanied with deafness. One cannot be eminent in everything, and if Mr Christian had dispersed his faculties in

study that would have enabled him to share unconventional points of view, he might have worn a mistaken kind of boot, and been less competent to win at *écarté,* or at betting, or in any other contest suitable to a person of figure." 14

—address: "Christian never allowed himself to be treated as a servant by any one but his master, and his master [**Philip Debarry**] treated a servant more deferentially than an equal." 20

—caught aback: " 'A—your name—a—is **Henry Scaddon**.'

"There was a start through Christian's frame which he was quick enough, almost simultaneously, to try and disguise as a change of position. He uncrossed his legs and unbuttoned his coat." 21

—unsavoury history: " '[Your father] died when you were barely of age, leaving an extensive business; before you were five-and-twenty you had run through the greater part of the property, and had compromised your safety by an attempt to defraud your creditors. Subsequently you forged a cheque on your father's elder brother, who had intended to make you his heir.' " 21

" . . . a somewhat shattered man of pleasure . . . having early exhausted the more impulsive delights of life, had become a sober calculator; and he had made up his mind that, for a man who had long ago run through his own money, servitude in a great family was the best kind of retirement after that of a pensioner; but if a better chance offered, a person of talent must not let it slip through his fingers." 25

—distrusted: " 'I have little confidence in this man's allegations,' **Mr Lyon** ended. 'I confess his presence and speech are to me as the jarring of metal. He bears the stamp of one who has never conceived aught of more sanctity than the lust of the eye and the pride of life.' " 26

—a legal question: "Christian in his time had gathered enough legal notions to be aware that possession by one man sometimes depended on the life of another; that a man might sell his own interest in property, and the interest of his descendants, while a claim on that property would still remain to some one else than the purchaser, supposing the descendants became extinct, and the interest they had sold were at an end. But under what conditions the claim might be valid or void in any particular case, was all darkness to him." 29

—decisive choice: "He was afraid of **Jermyn**; he utterly distrusted **Johnson**; but he thought he was secure in relying on **Harold Transome**'s care for his own interest; and he preferred above all issues the prospect of forthwith leaving the country with a sum that at least for a good while would put him at his ease." 36

—demeanour: "Christian wore this morning those perfect manners of a subordinate who is not servile, which he always adopted towards his unquestionable superiors. **Mr [Philip] Debarry**, who preferred having some one about him with as little resemblance as possible to a regular servant, had a singular liking for the adroit, quiet-mannered Christian, and would have been amazed to see the insolent assumption he was capable of in the presence of people like **Mr Lyon**, who were of no account in society. Christian had that sort of cleverness which is said to 'know the world'—that is to say, he knew the price-current of most things." 36

Rev. Augustus Debarry. "The Rector . . . really a fine specimen of the old-fashioned aristocratic clergyman, preaching short sermons, understanding business, and acting liberally about his tithe, had never before found himself in collision with Dissenters, but now he began to feel that these people were a nuisance in the parish, that his brother **Sir Maximus** must take care lest they should get land to build more chapels, and that it might not have been a bad thing if the law had furnished him as a magistrate with a power of putting a stop to the political sermons of the Independent preacher, which, in their way, were as pernicious sources of intoxication as the beerhouses." 3

"[He was] a refined and rather severe likeness of his brother, with a ring of fearlessness and decision in his voice which startled all flaccid men and unruly boys." 14

—*Conservative view:* " 'There's no end to the mischief done by these busy prating men. They make the ignorant multitude the judges of the largest questions, both political and religious, till we shall soon have no institution left that is not on a level with the comprehension of a huckster or a drayman. There can be nothing more retrograde—having all the results of civilization, all the lessons of Providence—letting the windlass run down after men have been turning at it painfully for generations. If the instructed are not to judge for the uninstructed, why let us set Dick Stubbs to make our almanacs, and have a President of the Royal Society elected by universal suffrage.' " 23

—*taste for authorship:* "He was a healthy-natured man, but that was not at all a reason why he should not have those sensibilities to the odour of authorship which belong to almost everybody who is not expected to be a writer—and especially to that form of authorship which is called suggestion, and consists in telling another man that he might do a great deal with a given subject, by bringing a sufficient amount of knowledge, reasoning, and wit to bear upon it." 23

—*on election day:* "**Mr Wace**, who was one of **Debarry**'s committee, had suggested to the Rector that it might be wise to send for the military from Duffield, with orders that they should station themselves at Hathercote, three miles off: there was so much property in the town that it would be better to make it secure against risks. But the Rector felt that this was not the part of a moderate and wise magistrate, unless the signs of riot recurred. He was a brave man, and fond of thinking that his own authority sufficed for the maintenance of the general good in Treby." 31

Sir Maximus Debarry, "a hale good-natured-looking man of sixty, whose hands rested on a knotted stick held between his knees . . . . " 7

"Sir Maximus laughed and showed his good teeth, which made his laughter very becoming." 7

—*staunch Tory:* " 'In the present state of the country it is our duty to look at a man's position and politics. **Philip** and my brother are both of that opinion, and I think they know what's right, if any man does. We are bound to regard every man of our party as a public instrument, and to pull all together. The **Transomes** have always been a good Tory family, but it has been a cipher of late years. This young fellow coming back with a fortune to give the family a head and a position is a clear gain to the county; and with Philip he'll get into the right hands . . . . All we have to ask is, whether a man's a Tory, and will make a stand for the country? . . . And I do beg of you, my dear, to set aside all these gossiping niceties, and exert yourself, like a woman of sense and spirit as you are, to bring the right people together.'

"Here Six Maximus gave a deep cough, took out his snuff-box, and tapped it: he had made a serious marital speech, an exertion to which he was rarely urged by anything smaller than a matter of conscience. And this outline of the whole duty of a Tory was matter of conscience with him . . . . " 7

—*indulgent:* "For Six Maximus, as every one said, was a gentleman of the right sort, condescended to no mean inquiries, greeted his head-servants with a 'good evening, gentlemen,' when he met them in the Park, and only snarled in a subdued way when he looked over the accounts, willing to endure some personal inconvenience in order to keep up the institutions of the country, to maintain his hereditary establishment, and do his duty in that station of life—the station of the long-tailed saurian—to which it had pleased Providence to call him." 7

—*vexed:* "He had great pride in his son's superiority even to himself; but he did not enjoy having his own opinion argued down as it always was . . . . " 14

Philip Debarry. "There is a portrait of Mr Philip Debarry still to be seen at Treby Manor, and a very fine bust of him at Rome, where he died fifteen years later, a convert to Catholicism. His face would have been plain but for the exquisite setting of his hazel eyes, which fascinated even the dogs of the household. The other features, though slight and irregular, were redeemed from triviality by the stamp of gravity and intellectual preoccupation in his face and bearing. As he read aloud, his voice was what his uncle's might have been if it had been modulated by delicate health and visitation of self-doubt." 14

—*handsome thanks:* "I shall consider myself doubly fortunate if at any time you can point out to me some method by which I may procure you as lively a satisfaction as I am now feeling, in that full and speedy relief from anxiety which I owe to your considerate conduct." 14

—*complimented:* " . . . the character you bear as a young man who aspires (albeit mistakenly) to engraft the finest fruits of public virtue on a creed and institutions, whereof the sap is composed rather of human self-seeking than of everlasting truth." 15

Mrs Mary Holt. " 'Mistress Holt is another who darkens counsel by words without knowledge, and angers the reason of the natural man. Lord, give me patience. My sins were heavier to bear than this woman's folly.' " 4

—*come to consult:* "She was a tall elderly woman, dressed in black, with a light-brown front and a black band over her forehead. She moved the chair a little and seated herself in it with some emphasis, looking fixedly at the opposite wall with a hurt and argumentative expression." 4

—*upset:* "Mrs Holt was not given to tears; she was much sustained by conscious unimpeachableness, and by an argumentative tendency which usually checks the too great activity of the lachrymal gland; nevertheless her eyes had become moist, her fingers played on her knee in an agitated manner, and she finally plucked a bit of her gown and held it with great nicety between her thumb and finger." 4

—*appraised:* " 'This woman has sat under the Gospel all her life, and she is as blind as a heathen, and as proud and stiff-necked as a Pharisee; yet she is one of the souls I watch for.' " 4

—*argumentative:* "[Her] strong powers of argument required the file of an imagined contradiction, if there were no real one at hand." 22

—*her son's troubles:* "She, regarding all her trouble about **Felix** in the light of a fulfilment of her own prophecies, treated the sad history with a preference for edification above accuracy, and for mystery above relevance, worthy of a commentator on the Apocalypse." 37

—sartorial reflection: "As Mrs Holt advanced into closer observation, it became more evident that she was attired with a view not to charm the eye, but rather to afflict it with all that expression of woe which belongs to very rusty bombazine and the limpest state of false hair." 43

—maternal: "Like many women who appear to others to have a masculine decisiveness of tone, and to themselves to have a masculine force of mind, and who come into severe collision with sons arrived at the masterful stage, she had the maternal cord vibrating strongly within her towards all tiny children." 43

John Johnson. "First came a smartly-dressed personage on horseback, with a conspicuous expansive shirt-front and figured satin stock. He was a stout man, and gave a strong sense of broadcloth." 11 (21)

" 'This gentleman is kind enough to treat the company,' [**Chubb**] added, looking round, 'and what's more he'll take a cup with 'em; and I think there's no man but what'll say that's a honour.' " 11

—spiel: " 'I've been into ale-houses where I've seen a fine fellow of a miner or a stone-cutter come in and have to lay down money for beer that I should be sorry to give to my pigs!' Here Mr Johnson leaned forward with squared elbows, hands placed on his knees, and a defiant shake of the head." 11

" 'We've got Reform, gentlemen, but now the thing is to make Reform work. It's a crisis—I pledge you my word it's a crisis.'

"Mr Johnson threw himself back as if from the concussion of that great noun. He did not suppose that one of his audience knew what a crisis meant; but he had large experience in the effect of uncomprehended words; and in this case the colliers were thrown into a state of conviction concerning they did not know what, which was a fine preparation for 'hitting out', or any other act carrying a due sequence to such a conviction." 11

—moderate disruption: " 'No pommelling—no striking first. There you have the law and the constable against you. A little rolling in the dust and knocking hats off, a little pelting with soft things that'll stick and not bruise—all that doesn't spoil the fun. If a man is to speak when you don't like to hear him, it is but fair you should give him something he doesn't like in return. And the same if he's got a vote and doesn't use it for the good of the country; I see no harm in splitting his coat in a quiet way. A man must be taught what's right if he doesn't know it. But no kicks, no knocking down, no pommelling.' " 11

—talkative: " ' . . . when **Mr Jermyn** first spoke to me about having the honour to assist in your canvass of North Loamshire'—here Johnson played with his watch-seals and balanced himself a moment on his toes—'the very first thing I said was, "And there's **Garstin** has got **Putty**! No Whig could stand against a Whig," I said, "who had Putty on his side: I hope **Mr Transome** goes in for something of a deeper colour" . . . . '

"It had been impossible to interrupt Johnson before, without the most impolitic rudeness. Jermyn was not sorry that he should talk, even if he made a fool of himself; for in that solid shape, exhibiting the average amount of human foibles, he seemed less of the *alias* which Harold had insinuated him to be, and had all the additional plausibility of a lie with a circumstance." 17

—subordinate: "Johnson was a most serviceable subordinate. Being a man who aimed at respectability, a family man, who had a good church-pew,

subscribed for engravings of banquet pictures where there were portraits of political celebrities, and wished his children to be more unquestionably genteel than their father, he presented all the more numerous handles of worldly motive by which a judicious superior might keep a hold on him." 29

—techy: "But this useful regard to respectability had its inconvenience in relation to such a superior: it was a mark of some vanity and some pride, which, if they were not touched just in the right handling-place, were liable to become raw and sensitive. **Jermyn** was aware of Johnson's weaknesses, and thought he had flattered them sufficiently . . . [But] Jermyn had often been unconsciously disagreeable to Johnson, over and above the constant offence of being an ostentatious patron. He would never let Johnson dine with his wife and daughters; he would not himself dine at Johnson's house when he was in town. He often did what was equivalent to pooh-poohing his conversation by not even appearing to listen, and by suddenly cutting it short with a query on a new subject." 29

—resentment building: "And serviceable John Johnson, himself sleek, and mindful about his broadcloth and his cambric fronts, had what he considered 'spirit' enough within him to feel that dislike of **Jermyn** gradually gathering force through years of obligation and subjection, till it had become an actuating motive disposed to use an opportunity, if not to watch for one." 29

—real at times: "If in an uncomplimentary spirit he might have been called **Jermyn**'s 'man of straw', it was a satisfaction to know that the unreality of the man John Johnson was confined to his appearance in annuity deeds, and that elsewhere he was solid, locomotive, and capable of remembering anything for his own pleasure and benefit." 29

—infuriating: "It was a little too exasperating to look at this pink-faced rotund specimen of prosperity, to witness the power for evil that lay in his vulgar cant, backed by another man's money, and to know that such stupid iniquity flourished the flags of Reform, and Liberalism, and justice to the needy." 30

—an attack: " 'What is poor Jack likely to do when he sees a smart stranger coming to him, who happens to be just one of those men that I say will be the masters till public opinion gets too hot for them? He's a middle-sized man, we'll say; stout, with coat upon coat of fine broadcloth, open enough to show a fine gold chain: none of your dark, scowling men, but one with an innocent pink-and-white skin and very smooth light hair—a most respectable man, who calls himself by a good, sound, well-known English name—as Green, or Baker, or Wilson, or, let us say, Johnson—'

"**Felix** was interrupted by an explosion of laughter from a majority of the bystanders. Some eyes had turned on Johnson . . . who had kept his ground till his name was mentioned, [and] now turned away, looking unusually white after being unusually red, and feeling by an attorney's instinct for his pocket-book, as if he felt it was a case for taking down the names of witnesses." 30

—treachery: "He was not going to be ruined, though **Jermyn** probably was: he was not a highflyer, but a mere climbing-bird, who could hold on and get his livelihood just as well if his wings were clipped a little." 37

Annette Ledru—*remembered:* " . . . a low voice spoke caressing French words to [**Esther**], and she in her turn repeated the words to her rag-doll; when a very small white hand, different from any that came after, used to pat her, and stroke her, and tie on her frock and pinafore . . . . She knew that her mother was a Frenchwoman, that she had been in want and distress, and that her maiden name was Annette Ledru." 6

—a husband: " . . . once, when she had asked him some question, he had said, 'My **Esther**, until you are a woman, we will only think of your mother: when you are about to be married and leave me, we will speak of her, and I will deliver to you her ring and all that was hers; but, without a great command laid upon me, I cannot pierce my heart by speaking of that which was and is not.' " 6

—rescued: "[**Lyon**] had nothing to do but to notice the loveliness of her face, which seemed to him as that of an angel, with a benignity in its repose that carried a more assured sweetness than any smile . . . .

"The grateful glance of those blue-grey eyes, with their long shadow-making eyelashes, was a new kind of good to Rufus Lyon; it seemed to him as if a woman had never really looked at him before. Yet this poor thing was apparently a blind French Catholic—of delicate nurture, surely, judging from her hands." 6

—a child: "Annette was one of those angelic-faced helpless women who take all things as manna from heaven: the good image of the well-beloved **Saint John** wished her to stay with him, and there was nothing else that she wished for except the unattainable . . . . She did not seem even to care about a priest, or about having her child baptized . . . . " 6

—changed: " . . . Annette was looking at him; he paused to look at her in return, and was struck with a new expression in her face, quite distinct from the merely passive sweetness which usually characterized it. She laid her little hand on his, which was now transparently thin, and said, 'I am getting very wise; I have sold some of the books to make money—the **doctor** told me where, and I have looked into the shops where they sell caps and bonnets and pretty things, and I can do all that, and get more money to keep us. And when you are well enough to get up, we will go out and be married—shall we not? See! and *la petite* . . . shall call you Papa—and then we shall never part.' " 6

—her religion: " 'There is nothing of my religion in this country. But the good God must be here, for you are good; I leave all to you.' " 6

—fading: "She was too indolent mentally, too little interested, to acquaint herself with any secrets of the isle. The transient energy, the more vivid consciousness and sympathy which had been stirred in her during **Mr Lyon**'s illness, had soon subsided into the old apathy to everything except her child. She withered like a plant in strange air, and the three years of life that remained were but a slow and gentle death." 6

Like every novelist, though some more than others, George Eliot paid more attention to character analysis and development than she did to plots. In Volume II of this work there is an essay, Parallelisms in Eliot's Fiction, *which addresses her repetitiveness, never burdensome or hackneyed but nevertheless not the sort of thing a plotster like Charles Dickens would ever have succumbed to. Mr Gilfil rescued and cherished the Italian orphan Tina; Daniel Deronda saved Mirah Lapidoth, a Jewess of exotic background, from drowning and married her; and here in* Felix Holt *we find the soft-hearted Rufus Lyon abandoning his pulpit to nurture and love a French lady fallen on tragically difficult times. There are many more such plot echoes, detailed in the essay. See* II: 275

Rufus Lyon encounters Annette Ledru in distress

Others

Michael Brincey, "otherwise **Michael Brindle** [*GE does not explain this 'otherwise'*] who gave evidence of the sayings and doings of the prisoner amongst the Sproxton men. Mike declared that **Felix** went 'uncommon again' drink, and pitch-and-toss, and quarrelling, and sich', and was 'all for schooling and bringing up the little chaps'; but on being cross-examined, he admitted that he 'couldn't give much account'; that Felix did talk again' idle folks, whether poor or rich, and that most like he meant the rich, who had 'a rights to be idle', which was what he, Mike, liked himself sometimes . . . . " 46

Maurice Christian Bycliffe, **Annette**'s first husband. " 'This old fellow [mused **Christian**] has got some secret in his head. It's not likely he can know anything about me; it must be about Bycliffe. But Bycliffe was a gentleman: how should he ever have had anything to do with such a seedy old ranter as [**Rufus Lyon**]?' " 14

—his daughter: "Her first father, she learned, had died disappointed and in wrongful imprisonment, and an undefined sense of Nemesis seemed half to sanctify her inheritance, and counteract its apparent arbitrariness." 38

William Chubb "was a remarkable publican; none of your stock Bonifaces, red, bloated, jolly, and joking. He was thin and sallow, and was never, as his constant guests observed, seen to be the worse (or the better) for liquor; indeed, as among soldiers an eminent general was held to have a charmed life, Chubb was held by the members of the Benefit Club to have a charmed sobriety, a vigilance over his own interest that resisted all narcotics." 11

—drink-inducer: "Mr Chubb was standing, as usual, with his hands nervously busy in his pockets, his eyes glancing round with a detective expression at the black landscape, and his lipless mouth compressed yet in constant movement. On a superficial view it might be supposed that so eager-seeming a personality was unsuited to the publican's business; but in fact it was a great provocative to drinking. Like the shrill biting talk of a vixenish wife, it would have compelled you to 'take a little something' by way of dulling your sensibility." 11

Mrs Hickes (**Denner**), "the small, neat exquisitely clean old woman who now presented herself . . . the butler's wife, who acted as housekeeper, lady's-maid, and superintendent of the kitchen . . . . Forty years ago she had entered Mrs Transome's service when that lady was beautiful **Miss Lingon**, and her mistress still called her Denner, as she had done in the old days." 1

—staunch retainer: "Denner had still strong eyes of that shortsighted kind which see through the narrowest chink between the eyelashes. The physical contrast between the tall, eagle-faced, dark-eyed lady, and the little peering waiting-woman who had been round-featured and of pale mealy complexion from her youth up, had doubtless had a strong influence in determining Denner's feeling towards her mistress, which was of that worshipful sort paid to a goddess in ages when it was not thought necessary or likely that a goddess should be very moral.

"There were different orders of beings—so ran Denner's creed—and she belonged to another order than that to which her mistress belonged. She had a mind as sharp as a needle, and would have seen through and through the ridiculous pretensions of a born servant who did not submissively accept the rigid fate which had given her born superiors. She would have called such pretensions the wrigglings of a worm that tried to walk on its tail.

"There was a tacit understanding that Denner knew all her mistress's secrets, and her speech was plain and unflattering; yet with wonderful subtlety of instinct she never said anything which Mrs Transome could feel humiliated by, as by a familiarity from a servant who knew too much. Denner identified her own dignity with that of her mistress. She was a hard-headed godless little woman, but with a character to be reckoned on as you reckon on the qualities of iron.

" . . . She spoke with a refined accent, in a low, quick, monotonous tone—

" 'Mr **Harold** is drest; he shook me by the hand in the corridor, and was very pleasant.'

" 'What an alteration, Denner! No likeness to me now.'

" 'Handsome, though, site of his being so browned and stout . . . . And as for likenesses, thirty-five and sixty are not much alike, only to people's memories.'

"**Mrs Transome** knew perfectly that Denner had divined her thoughts." ¶1

—comfort: " 'For my part, I've seen no young ones fit to hold up your train. Look at your likeness down below; and though you're older now, what signifies? . . . I would change with nobody, madam. And if troubles were put up to market, I'd sooner buy old than new. It's something to have seen the worst.' " 39

—forbearing: " . . . she suspected that the close **Dominic** knew the secret, and was more trusted than she was, in spite of her forty years' service; but any resentment on this ground would have been an entertained reproach against her mistress, inconsistent with Denner's creed and character." 39

—philosophy: " 'When I awake at cock-crow, I'd sooner have one real grief on my mind than twenty false. It's better to know one's robbed than to think one's going to be murdered.' " 39

—her lady's judgment: " 'There's no folly in you, and no heartache. You are made of iron. You have never had any trouble.' " 39

Dominic Lenoni. " 'O! one of those wonderful southern fellows that make one's life easy. He's of no country in particular. I don't know whether he's most of a Jew, a Greek, an Italian, or a Spaniard. He speaks five or six languages, one as well as another. He's cook, valet, major-domo, and secretary all in one; and what's more, he's an affectionate fellow—I can trust to his attachment. That's a sort of human specimen that doesn't grow here in England, I fancy. I should have been badly off if I could not have brought Dominic.' " 2

" . . . the olive-skinned Dominic, whose acute yet mild face was brightened by the occupation of amusing little **Harry** and rescuing from his tyrannies a King Charles puppy, with big eyes, much after the pattern of the boy's." 19

—in charge: "Skilful Dominic was always at hand to meet his master's demands, and his bland presence diffused itself like a smile over the household, infecting the gloomy English mind with the belief that life was easy, and making his real predominance seem as soft and light as a down quilt." 34

Rev. John Lingon "became very talkative over his second bottle of port, which was opened on his nephew's arrival. He was not curious about the manners of Smyrna, or about Harold's experience, but he unbosomed himself very freely as to what he himself liked and disliked, which of the farmers he suspected of killing the foxes, what game he had bagged that very morning, what spot he would recommend as a new cover, and the comparative flatness of all existing sport compared with cock-fighting, under which Old England had been prosperous and glorious, while, so far as he could see, it had gained little by the abolition of a practice which sharpened the faculties of men, gratified the instincts of the fowl, and carried out the designs of heaven in its admirable device of spurs.

"From these main topics, which made his points of departure and return, he rambled easily enough at any new suggestion or query; so that when Harold got home at a late hour, he was conscious of having gathered from amidst the pompous full-toned triviality of his uncle's chat some impressions which were of practical importance. Among the Rector's dislikes, it appeared, was Mr **Matthew Jermyn**." ¶2

—outdoorsman: " . . . shouldering a gun, and followed by one black and one liver-spotted pointer, his muscular person with its red eagle face set off by a velveteen jacket and leather leggings . . . . " 2

—on the hustings: "The Rector of Little Treby had been a favourite in the neighbourhood since the beginning of the century. A clergyman thoroughly unclerical in his habits had a piquancy about him which made him a sort of practical joke. He had always been called Jack Lingon, or Parson Jack—sometimes, in older and less serious days, even 'Cock-fighting Jack'. He swore a little when the point of a joke seemed to demand it, and was fond of wearing a coloured bandana [*sic*] tied loosely over his cravat, together with large brown leather leggings; he spoke in a pithy familiar way that people could understand, and had none of that frigid mincingness called dignity, which some have thought a peculiar clerical disease. In fact, he was 'a charicter'—something cheerful to think of, not entirely out of connection with Sunday and sermons. And it seemed in keeping that he should have turned sharp round in politics, his opinions being only part of the excellent joke called Parson Jack. When his red eagle face and white hair were seen on the platform, the Dissenters hardly cheered this questionable Radical; but to make amends, all the Tory farmers gave him a friendly 'hurray'. 'Let's hear what old Jack will say for himself,' was the predominant feeling among them; 'he'll have something funny to say, I'll bet a penny.' " 19

—impressions: "Honest Jack Lingon's first impressions quickly became traditions, which no subsequent evidence could disturb. He was fond of his sister, and seemed never to be conscious of any change for the worse in her since their early time. He considered that man a beast who said anything unpleasant about the persons to whom he was attached. It was not that he winked; his wide-open eyes saw nothing but what his easy disposition inclined him to see." 43

—a fan: "**Esther** was always glad when the old Rector came. With a contrariety to her former niceties she liked his rough attire and careless frank speech; they were something not point device that seemed to connect the life of Transome Court with that rougher, commoner world where her home had been." 43

Lyddy. "Here the door was opened, and old Lyddy, the minister's servant, put in her head to say, in a tone of despondency, finishing with a groan. . . . " 4

" 'There seemed no end of these great folks coming to Malthouse Yard since there was talk of the election; but they might be poor lost creatures the most of 'em.' Whereupon Lyddy shook her head and groaned, under an edifying despair as to the future lot of gentlemen callers." 15

"**Esther** always avoided asking questions of Lyddy, who found an answer as she found a key, by pouring out a pocketful of miscellanies." 15

—negligent: " 'That is Lyddy's fault, who sits crying over her want of Christian assurance instead of brushing your clothes and putting out your clean cravat. She is always saying her righteousness is filthy rags, and really I don't think that is a very strong expression for it. I'm sure it is dusty clothes and furniture.' " 41

Baruch Nolan, "the retired London hosier, a wiry old gentleman past seventy, whose square tight forehead, with its rigid hedge of grey hair, whose bushy eyebrows, sharp dark eyes, and remarkable hooked nose, gave a handsome distinction to his face in the midst of rural physiognomies. He had married a **Miss Pendrell** early in life, when he was a poor young Londoner, and the match had been thought as bad as ruin by her family; but fifteen years ago he had had the satisfaction of bringing his wife to settle amongst her own friends, and of being received with pride as a brother-in-law, retired from business, possessed of unknown thousands, and of a most agreeable talent for anecdote and conversation generally." 20

—visited: " 'Just so, my dear sir,' said the wiry-faced Nolan, pinching his under-lip between his thumb and finger, and giving one of those wonderful universal shrugs, by which he seemed to be recalling all his garments from a tendency to disperse themselves. 'Come in and see **Mrs Nolan**?' " 31

Mr Nuttwood, "the grocer, who was one of the deacons, was complaining to [**Rev. Lyon**] about the obstinate demeanour of the singers . . . .

" 'They are so headstrong,' said Mr Nuttwood, in a tone of sad perplexity, 'that if we dealt not warily with them, they might end in dividing the church, even now that we have had the chapel enlarged.' " 13

Sampson. "At this Mr Sampson (everybody in North Loamshire knew Sampson's coach) would screw his features into a grimace expressive of entire neutrality, and appear to aim his whip at a particular spot on the horse's flank. If the passenger was curious for further knowledge concerning the **Transome** affairs, Sampson would shake his head and say there had been fine stories in his time; but he never condescended to state what these stories were. Some attributed this reticence to a wise incredulity, others to a want of memory, others to simple ignorance." *I*

Scales, "house-steward and head-butler, a man most solicitous about his boots, wristbands, the roll of his whiskers, and other attributes of a gentleman, distributed cigars, cognac, and whisky, to various colleagues and guests who were discussing, with that freedom of conjecture which is one of our inalienable privileges as Britons, the probable amount of **Harold Transome**'s fortune, concerning which fame had already been busy long enough to have acquired vast magnifying power." 7

" 'A hundred thousand, my dear sir! fiddle-stick's end of a hundred thousand,' said Mr Scales, with a contempt very painful to be borne by a modest man." 7

—deliberate: "Here Mr Scales paused to puff, and pull down his waistcoat in a gentlemanly manner, and drink. He was wont in this way to give his hearers time for meditation." 7

—portentous: "When Mr Scales's strong need to make an impressive figure in conversation, together with his very slight need of any other premise than his own sense of his wide general knowledge and probable infallibility, led him to specify five hundred thousand as the lowest admissible amount of **Harold Transome**'s commercially-acquired fortune, it was not fair to put this down to poor old Miss Rumour, who had only told Scales that the fortune was considerable." 8

—a joke played: "Scales knew nothing of [**Christian**'s] errand to the Rectory; and as he noticed that there was something in the pocket, thought it was probably a large cigar-case. So much the better—he had not time to pause. He threw the coat-tail as far as he could . . . he hurried away. . . . not daring to explode in laughter until it was safe from the chance of waking the sleeper. And then the vision of the graceful well-appointed Mr Christian, who sneered at Scales about his 'get up', having to walk back to the house with only one tail to his coat, was a source of so much enjoyment to the butler, that . . . . Exit Scales, laughing, and presenting a fine example of dramatic irony to any one in the secret of Fate." 12

Rev. Theodore Sherlock,. "a young divine of good birth and figure, of sallow complexion and bashful address." 23

—tempted: "With all Mr Sherlock's timidity, there was fascination for him in this distinction. He reflected that he could take coffee and sit up late, and perhaps produce something rather fine. It might be a first step towards that eminence which it was no more than his duty to aspire to . . . . Mr Sherlock was not insensible to the pleasure of turning sentences successfully, and it was a pleasure not always unconnected with preferment. A diffident man likes the idea of doing something remarkable, which will create belief in him without any immediate display of brilliancy. Celebrity may blush and be silent, and win a grace the more. Thus Mr Sherlock was constrained, trembling all the while, and much wishing that his essay were already in print." 23

—repute: "[H] was known, apparently by an intuition concerning the nature of curates, to be a very clever young man; and he would show [the Church ladies] what learning had to say on the right side." 24

—fled: "That well-intentioned young divine was seen no more in Treby Magna. But the river was not dragged, for by the evening coach the Rector received an explanatory letter. The Rev. Theodore's agitation had increased so much during his walk, that the passing coach had been a means of deliverance not to be resisted; and, literally at the eleventh hour, he had hailed and mounted the cheerful Tally-ho! and carried away his portion of the debate in his pocket." 24

Tommy Trounsem. " 'These **Transome**'s are not the old blood.'

" 'Well, they're the oldest that's forthcoming, I suppose,' said **Mr Wace**, laughing. 'Unless you believe in mad old Tommy Trounsem. I wonder where that old poaching fellow is now.' " 20

—identified: " 'It's Tommy Trounsem—an old, crippling, half-mad fellow. Most people know Tommy . . . . '

" 'He was a stoutish fellow fifteen year ago, when he carried pots,' said **Mr Pink**.

" 'Ay, and has snared many a hare in his time,' said **Mr Sims**. 'But he was always a little cracked. Lord bless you! he used to swear he'd a right to the **Transome** estate' . . . .

" 'The lawing, sir—nothing but the lawing about the estate. There was a deal of it twenty year ago,' said Mr Pink. 'Tommy happened to turn up hereabout at that time; a big, lungeous fellow, who would speak disrespectfully of hanybody.'

" 'O, he meant no harm,' said Mr Sims. 'He was fond of a drop to drink, and not quite right in the upper storey, and he could hear no difference between Trounsem and Transome. It's an odd way of speaking they have in that part where he was born.' " 28

—offered a drink: "Tommy was not slower than a shaking hand obliged him to be in accepting this invitation. He was a tall broad-shouldered old fellow, who had once been good-looking; but his cheeks and chest were both hollow now, and his limbs were shrunken." 28

—a drinker: "He was one of the thoroughly inured, originally hale drunkards, and did not easily lose his head or legs or the ordinary amount of method in his talk. Strangers often supposed that Tommy was tipsy when he had only taken what he called 'one blessed pint', chiefly from that glorious contentment with himself and his adverse fortunes which is not usually characteristic of the sober Briton." 28

—dealing with a lawyer: " 'Thinks I, Tommy, you've done finely for yourself: you're a rat as has broke up your house to take a journey, and show yourself to a ferret. And then it jumps into my head: I'd once two ferrets as turned on one another, and the little un killed the big un. Says I to the landlady, "Missis, could you tell me of a lawyer," says I, "not very big or fine, but a second size—a pig-potato, like?" "That I can," says she; "there's one now in the bar parlour." "Be so kind as bring us together," says I. And she cries out—I think I hear her now—"**Mr Johnson**!" ' " 28

—a critical figure: " . . . **Johnson** could conceive: an heir or heiress of the **Bycliffe**s—if such a personage turned out to be in existence—might some time raise a new and valid claim when once informed that wretched old Tommy Trounsem the bill-sticker, tottering drunkenly on the edge of the grave, was the last issue remaining above ground from that dissolute **Thomas** who played his **Esau** part a century before. While the poor old bill-sticker breathed, the Durfey-Transomes could legally keep their possession in spite of a possible Bycliffe proved real; but not when the parish had buried the bill-sticker." 29

—on election day: "He had an immense light-blue cockade in his hat, and an amount of silver in a dirty little canvass bag which astonished himself. For some reason, at first inscrutable to him, he had been paid for his bill-sticking with great liberality at **Mr Jermyn**'s office . . . . " 31

Job Tudge "was a small fellow about five, with a germinal nose, large round blue eyes, and red hair that curled close to his head like the wool on the back of an infantine lamb. He had evidently been crying, and the corners of his mouth were still dolorous." 22

" . . . the droll little figure, set off by a ragged jacket with a tail about two inches deep sticking out above the funniest of corduroys." 22

" . . . a tiny red-haired boy, scantily attired as to his jacket, which merged into a small sparrow-tail a little higher than his waist, but muffled as to his throat with a blue woollen comforter." 43

—wedding suit: "Little Job Tudge had an entirely new suit, of which he fingered every separate brass button in a way that threatened an arithmetical mania . . . . " *E*

Wace, the brewer, "whose chief political tenet was, that it was all nonsense giving men votes when they had no stake in the country." 3

—hearing dire prediction: " 'I'm sorry to hear it from one of your experience, Mr Nolan,' said the brewer, a large happy-looking man. 'I'd make a good fight myself before I'd leave a worse world for my boys than I've found for myself . . . if we can't trust the Government just now, there's Providence and the good sense of the country; and there's a right in things—that's what I've always said—there's a right in things. The heavy end will get downmost.' " 20

—on Radicals: " 'I once heard two of 'em spouting away. They're a sort of fellow I'd never employ in my brewery, or anywhere else. I've seen it again and again. If a man takes to tongue-work it's all over with him. "Everything's wrong," says he. That's a big text. But does he want to make everything right? Not he. He'd lose his text. "We want every man's good," say they. Why, they never knew yet what a man's good is. How should they? It's working for his victual—not getting a slice of other people's.' " 20

—condescending: "Mr Wace turned his head to listen for **Christian**'s answer with that tolerance of inferiority which becomes men in places of public resort." 20

—a wedding: "But the majority of honest Trebians were affected somewhat in the same way as happy-looking Mr Wace was, who observed to his wife, as they walked from under the churchyard chestnuts, 'It's wonderful how things go through you—you don't know how. I feel somehow as if I believed more in everything that's good.' " *E*

Minor Figures

Bishop. " 'Nobody likes our Bishop: he's all Greek and greediness; too proud to dine with his own father.' " 2

Brent. " 'Come, that's a good one,' said the head-gardener, who was a ready admirer; 'I should like to hear the thing you don't understand, **Christian**.' " 7

Mike Brindle "was one of the head miners; he had a bright good-natured face, and had given especial attention to certain performances with a magnet which **Felix** carried in his pocket." 11

Sir James Clement. " '[He] is a poor baronet, hoping for an appointment and can't be expected to be liberal in that wider sense which commands majorities.' " 2

Clerk. "The oratorical clerk at the Factory, acting as the tribune of the Dissenting interest, and feeling bound to put questions, might have been troublesome; but his voice being unpleasantly sharp, while **Harold**'s was full and penetrating, the questioning was cried down." 19

Mr Crow, "the high constable of Treby, inwardly rehearsed a brief address to a riotous crowd in case it should be wanted . . . . " 31

"Presently Mr Crow, who held himself a tactician, took a well-intentioned step, which went far to fulfil his own prophecy . . . he showed himself at an upper window, and addressed the crowd, telling them that the soldiers had been sent for, and that if they did not disperse they would have cavalry upon them instead of constables.

"Mr Crow, like some other high constables more celebrated in history, 'enjoyed a bad reputation'; that is to say, he enjoyed many things which caused his reputation to be bad, and he was anything but popular in Treby. It is probable that a pleasant message would have lost something from his lips, and what he actually said was so unpleasant, that, instead of persuading the crowd, it appeared to enrage them." 33

Crowder, "an old respectable tenant, though much in arrear as to his rent, who condescended frequently to drink in the steward's room for the sake of the conversation . . . . " 7

"It was the voters for **Debarry** and **Garstin** who considered that they alone had the right to regard themselves as targets for evil-minded men; and Mr Crowder, if he could have got his ideas countenanced, would have recommended a muster of farm-servants with defensive pitchforks on the side of Church and King." 31

Jacob Cuff, "a Tory charity-man, who was a well-known ornament of the pothouse, and gave his mind much leisure for amusing devices . . . . " 31

Harriet Debarry. " 'Dear me, **Selina**,' said her elder sister, Harriet, whose forte was general knowledge, 'don't you remember "Woodstock"? They were in **Cromwell**'s time.' " 14

Lady Debarry, "a blue-eyed, well-featured lady, fat and middle-aged—a mountain of satin, lace, and exquisite muslin embroidery." 7

Selina Debarry. " 'How did Dissenters, and Methodists, and Quakers, and people of that sort first come up, uncle?' said Miss Selina, a radiant girl of twenty, who had given much time to the harp." 14

Dibbs. " 'I don't care two straws who I vote for,' said Dibbs, sturdily. 'I'm not going to make a wry face. It stands to reason a man should vote for his landlord.' " 20

" . . . Mr Dibbs, taking the more cheerful view of a prosperous man, reflected that if the Radicals were dangerous, it was safer to be on their side." 31

Dredge. " 'Ay, that's sin' the Reform,' said a big, red-whiskered man, called Dredge. 'That's brought the 'lections and the drink into these parts; for afore that, it was all kep up the Lord knows wheer.' " 11

The **Durfeys**, "very distant connections, who only called themselves Transomes because they had got the estate. But the Durfeys' claim had been disputed over and over again . . . . " *I See* **Thomas Transome**

Filmore, "the surgeon's assistant, a fast man, whose chief scene of dissipation was the Manor." 7

" 'All I know is, [**Christian**'s] a wonderful hand at cards,' said Mr Filmore, whose whiskers and shirt-pin were quite above the average." 7

Peter Garstin. " 'I couldn't help thinking that something would occur to prevent **Philip** from having such a man as Peter Garstin for his colleague.' " 7

"The head member of the company that worked the mines was Mr Peter Garstin, and the same company received the rent for the Sugar Loaf. Hence, as the person who had the most power of annoying **Mr Chubb**, and being of detriment to him, Mr Garstin was naturally the candidate for whom he had reserved his vote." 11

—competition: "Garstin was a harsh and wiry fellow; he seemed to suggest that sour whey, which some say was the original meaning of Whig in the

Scottish, and it might assist the theoretic advantages of Radicalism if it could be associated with a more generous presence." 16

Gentleman. " . . . another had something to say about the North Loamshire Hunt to a friend who was the reverse of good-looking, but who, nevertheless, while listening, showed his strength of mind by giving a severe attention also to his full-length reflection in the handsome tall mirror that filled the space between two windows." 47

George III [H]. " 'When our good old King George the Third heard his ministers talking about Catholic Emancipation, he boxed their ears all round. Ah, poor soul! he did indeed, gentlemen,' ended **Mr Nolan**, shaken by a deep laugh of admiration." 20

Gills, "a wide-mouthed wiry man . . . who wished for an exhaustive treatment of the subject [of making freestone], being a stone-cutter." 11

Mr Goffe, "of Rabbit's End, had never had it explained to him that, according to the true theory of rent, land must inevitably be given up when it would not yield a profit equal to the ordinary rate of interest; so that from want of knowing what was inevitable, and not from a Titanic spirit of opposition, he kept on his land. He often said of himself, with a melancholy wipe of his sleeve across his brow, that he 'didn't know what-a-way to turn'; and he would have been still more at a loss on the subject if he had quitted Rabbit's End with a waggonful of furniture and utensils, a file of receipts, a wife with five children, and a shepherd-dog in low spirits." 8

—the election: "[He] considered that 'one thing was as mauling as another', and that an election was no worse than the sheep-rot . . . . " 31

Gottlib. " ' "The Whigs for salt and mustard, the Tories for meat," Mr Gottlib the banker used to say to me [said **Nolan**]. Mr Gottlib was a worthy man. When there was a great run on Gottlib's bank in '16, I saw a gentleman come in with bags of gold, and say, "Tell Mr Gottlib there's plenty more where that came from." It stopped the run, gentlemen—it did indeed.' " 20

Hawkins. " . . . and Brother Hawkins, in his high tenor, observed that it was an occasion on which some stinging things might be said with all the extra effect of an *apropos*." 24

Hickes. " 'I'll have old Hickes. He was a neat little machine of a butler; his words used to come like the clicks of an engine. He must be an old machine now, though.' " 1

Holt. " ' . . . he had a wonderful gift in prayer . . . and he believed himself that the receipt for the Cancer Cure, which I've sent out in bottles till this very last April before September as now is, and have bottles standing by me—he believed it was sent him in answer to prayer; and nobody can deny it, for he prayed most regular, and read out of the green baize Bible.' " 4

" 'Moreover your father, who originally concocted these medicines and left them as a provision for your mother, was, as I understand, a man whose walk was not unfaithful.'

" 'My father was ignorant,' said **Felix**, bluntly. 'He knew neither the complication of the human system, nor the way in which drugs counteract each other. Ignorance is not so damnable as humbug, but when it prescribes pills it may happen to do more harm.' " 5

" 'My father was a weaver first of all. It would have been better for him if he had remained a weaver.' " 5

Louisa Jermyn. " 'Miss Jermyn said to me only the other day that she could not think how I came to be so well educated and ladylike. She always thought Dissenters were ignorant, vulgar people. I said, so they were, usually, and Church people also in small towns. She considers herself a judge of what is ladylike, and she is vulgarity personified—with large feet, and the most odious scent on her handkerchief, and a bonnet that looks like "The Fashion" printed in capital letters.' " 5

Job. "Even the patriarch Job, if he had been a gentleman of the modern West, would have avoided picturesque disorder and poetical laments; and the friends who called on him, though not less disposed than ***Bildad the Shuhite*** to hint that their unfortunate friend was in the wrong, would have sat on chairs and held their hats in their hands." 40

Joyce. " 'Take it! they'd be obliged to take it,' said the impetuous young Joyce, a farmer of superior information." 20

Kemp. " 'I cannot but think it a snare when a professing Christian has a bass voice like Brother Kemp's. It makes him desire to be heard of men; but the weaker song of the humble may have more power in the ear of God.' " 13

"Brother Kemp urged in his heavy bass that **Mr Lyon** should lose no time in sending an account of the affair to the 'Patriot' . . . . " 24

—on our hero: " 'a young Ishmaelite, whom we would fain see brought back from the lawless life of the desert, and seated in the same fold even with the sons of **Judah** and of **Benjamin**', a suitable periphrasis which Brother Kemp threw off without any effort, and with all the felicity of a suggestive critic." 37

Letty. " 'I wouldn't be Letty in the scullery because she's got red cheeks. She mayn't know she's a poor creature, but I know it, and that's enough for me: I know what sort of a dowdy draggletail she'll be in ten years' time.' " 39

Lady Fanny Lingon. " . . . how the brilliant Fanny, having married a country parson, became so niggardly that she had gone about almost begging for fresh eggs from the farmers' wives, though she had done very well with her six sons, as there was a bishop and no end of interest in the family, and two of them got appointments in India." 40

Lady Sara Lingon, "[whose] husband went off into jealous madness only a month after their marriage, and dragged that sweet blue-eyed thing by the hair . . . . " 40

Medical man. "The illness was a serious one, and the medical man one day hearing **Mr Lyon** in his delirium raving with an astonishing fluency in Biblical language, suddenly looked round with increased curiosity at **Annette**, and asked if she were the sick man's wife, or some other relative." 6

Lady Alicia Methurst, " '[who] got heart-disease from a sudden piece of luck—the death of her uncle, you know.' " 7

Muscat, cheese-maker. " 'He's turned tail, sure enough,' said Mr Muscat to the neighbour behind him, lifting his eyebrows and shoulders, and laughing in a way that showed that, deacon as he was, he looked at the affair in an entirely secular light." 24

Mrs Muscat and **Mrs Nuttwood**, Dissenting parishioners, "applied the principle of Christian equality by remarking that **Mr Lyon** had his oddities, and that he ought not to allow his daughter to indulge in such unbecoming expenditure on her gloves, shoes, and hosiery, even if she did pay for them out of her earnings." 6

—*on the preacher:* "('An odd man,' as Mrs Muscat observed, 'to have such a gift in the pulpit. But there's One knows better than we do—' which, in a lady who rarely felt her judgment at a loss, was a concession that showed much piety.)" 16

—*religion:* "Irreproachable Dissenting matrons, like Mrs Muscat, whose youth had been passed in a short-waisted boddice [*sic*] and tight skirt, had never been animated by the struggle for liberty, and had a timid suspicion that religion was desecrated by being applied to the things of this world." 18

—*eager for a meeting:* "Mrs Muscat, who had been a beauty, and was as nice in her millinery as any Trebian lady belonging to the Establishment, reflected that she should put on her best large embroidered collar, and that she should ask **Mrs Tiliot** where it was in Duffield that she once got her bed-hangings dyed so beautifully." 24

—*gossiping:* "Mrs Muscat lowered her blond eyelashes and swayed her neat head just perceptibly from side to side, with a sincere desire to be moderate in her expressions, notwithstanding any shock that facts might have given her." 24

Orator, "a grimy man in a flannel shirt, hatless and with turbid red hair, who was insisting on political points with much more ease than had seemed to belong to the gentlemen speakers on the hustings . . . . " 30

"[**Felix**] liked the look of the speaker, whose bare arms were powerfully muscular, though he had the pallid complexion of a man who lives chiefly amidst the heat of furnaces. He was leaning against the dark stone building behind him with folded arms, the grimy paleness of his shirt and skin standing out in high relief against the dark stone building behind him. He lifted up one forefinger, and marked his emphasis with it as he spoke. His voice was high and not strong, but Felix recognized the fluency and the method of a habitual preacher or lecturer." 30

Pack. "A man known among the 'butties' as Pack, who had already been mentioned by **Mr Chubb**, presently joined the party, and had a private audience of **Mr Johnson**, that he might be instituted as the 'shepherd' of this new flock." 11

—*on election day:* "It seemed natural . . . that Pack, the tall 'shepherd' of the Sproxton men, would be seen moving to and fro where there would be a frequent opportunity of cheering the voters for a gentleman who had the chief share in the Sproxton mines." 31

Ned Patch, " 'the pedlar, used to say to me, "You canna read, **Tommy**," says he. "No; thank you," says I; "I'm not going to crack my headpiece to make myself as big a fool as you." I was fond o' Ned. Many's the pot we've had together.' " 28

Pink, "the saddler . . . professed a deep-dyed Toryism; but he regarded all fault-finding as Radical and somewhat impious, as disturbing to trade, and likely to offend the gentry or the servants through whom their harness was ordered . . . . Mr Pink suggested impartially that lawyers must live . . . [and] felt that this speculation was complicated by the ordering of side-saddles for lawyers' daughters, and, returning to the firm ground of fact, stated that it was getting dusk." 28

—*on election day:* " . . . being stopped on his way and made to declare that he was going to vote for **Debarry**, got himself well chalked as to his coat, and pushed up an entry, where he remained the prisoner of terror combined with the want of any back outlet, and never gave his vote that day." 31

James Putty, " 'one of the first men in the country as an agent . . . . ' " 17

Quorlen, "the Tory printer, who was an intimate of [**Christian**'s]." 24

"Quorlen was a new man in Treby, who had so reduced the trade of **Dow**, the old hereditary printer, that Dow had lapsed to Whiggery and Radicalism and opinions in general, so far as they were contented to express themselves in a small stock of types. Quorlen had brought his Duffield wit with him, and insisted that religion and joking were the handmaids of politics; on which principle he and **Christian** undertook the joking, and left the religion to the Rector." 28

Timothy Rose, "a 'gentleman farmer' from Leek Malton, against whose independent position nature had provided the safeguard of a spontaneous servility. His large porcine cheeks, round twinkling eyes, and thumbs habitually twirling, expressed a concentrated effort not to get into trouble, and to speak everybody fair except when they were safely out of hearing." 20

—fearful: "He had left home with some foreboding, having swathed his more vital parts in layers of flannel, and put on two greatcoats as a soft kind of armour . . . he once more observed to **Mrs Rose** that these were hard times when a man of independent property was expected to vote 'willy-nilly'. . . ." 31

Salt, "the wool factor, a bilious man, who only spoke when there was a good opportunity of contradicting . . . . " 20

Sims, "the auctioneer, [said] everything was done for the sake of the lawyers . . . having a ready auctioneering wit, did not see that so many of them need live, or that babies were born lawyers." 28

Sircome. "[He] was an eminent miller who had considerable business transactions at the manor, and appreciated **Mr Scales**'s merits at a handsome percentage on the yearly account. He was a highly honourable tradesman, but in this and in other matters submitted to the institutions of his country; for great houses, as he observed, must have great butlers." 7

Sleck. " 'Well, but the Reform's niver come anigh Sprox'on,' said a grey-haired but stalwart man called Old Sleck. 'I don't believe nothing about'n, I don't.' " 11

Spilkins. " 'If I'd twenty votes, I'd give one for **Transome**, and I don't care who hears me.'

"The landlord peeped out from his fungous cluster of features with a beery confidence that the high figure of twenty had somehow raised the hypothetic value of his vote." 28

Spratt, "the hated manager of the Sproxton Colliery, in careless confidence that the colliers and other labourers under him would follow his orders, had provided carts to carry some loads of voteless enthusiasm to Duffield on behalf of **Garstin** . . . . " 30

—unpopular: "Also the Seven Stars sheltered Spratt; and to some Sproxton men in front of that inn it was exasperating that Spratt should be safe and sound on a day when blows were going, and justice might be rendered." 33

—at the trial: "Spratt had retained consciousness enough, in the midst of his terror, to swear that, when he was tied to the finger-post, **Felix** was presiding over the actions of the mob." 46

Mrs Tiliot. "When Mrs Tiliot was **Mary Salt**, the two ladies [**Mrs Muscat** the other] had been bosom friends; but **Mr Tiliot** had looked higher and higher since his gin had become so famous; and in the year '29 he had, in Mr Muscat's hearing, spoken of Dissenters as sneaks—a personality which could not be overlooked." 24

Lady Betty Transome, "who had lived a century and a half before . . . .

" 'That fair lady Betty looks as if she had been drilled into that posture, and had not will enough of her own ever to move again unless she had a little push given to her.' " 40

Dr Truncheon. " 'If **Mrs Transome** were wise she would go to town—she can afford it now—and consult Dr Truncheon. I should say myself he would order her digitalis.' " 7

Tucker. "One spirited fellow, named Tucker, who was a regular constable, feeling that no time was to be lost in meditation, called on his neighbour to follow him, and with the sabre that happened to be his weapon got a way for himself where he was not expected, by dint of quick resolution." 33

—*impetuous:* "**Felix** . . . sprang forward close to the cowering **Spratt**. As he did this, Tucker had cut his way to the spot, and imagining Felix to be the destined executioner of Spratt—for any discrimination of Tucker's lay in his muscles rather than his eyes—he rushed up to Felix, meaning to collar him and throw him down." 33

Vendor. " . . . others [listening] to a Scotch vendor of articles useful to sell, whose unfamiliar accent seemed to have a guarantee of truth in it wanting as an association with everyday English." 30

Wimple. " 'The character of the Establishment has suffered enough already through the Evangelicals, with their extempore incoherence and their pipe-smoking piety. Look at Wimple, the man who is vicar of Shuttleton—without his gown and bands, anybody would take him for a grocer in mourning.' " 23

Lady Wyvern "finally deciding not to send [**Mrs Transome**] invitations to dinner." 40

Young man. " 'Who is this **Johnson**?' said **Christian** to a young man who had been standing near him, and had been one of the first to laugh . . . .

" ' . . . he's a London man now—a very busy fellow—on his own legs in Bedford Row. Ha ha! It's capital, though, when these Liberals get a slap in the face from the working men they're so very fond of.' " 30

Also mentioned

apothecary, to whom Felix Holt had been apprenticed	5
Armenian banker, his life saved by Harold Transome, made his fortune	1
attorney for Felix Holt at his trial for manslaughter (oddly never identified or named)	46
Badgers, of Hillbury: a good family	40
bailiff for the Transomes	2
Banks, the bailiff at Transome Court, and his wife, who play whist with the Hickeses	1
Batt & Cowley, old lawyers for the Bycliffes (Medwin an associate)	21
Blenheim spaniel, fat and too old and sleepy to notice his mistress's restlessness	1
Bodkin, a bank clerk fired for being a Dissenter	5
Boys of Little Treby, on the lookout for the heir	1
Sir Francis Burdett [H], Radical MP "generally regarded as a madman"	1
butcher from Leek Malton; rich but modestly takes the lowest seat	20
Peggy Button, whose house in Sproxton serves for Dissenting preaching	11
Calibut, former colleague of Mr Nolan in a warehouse, now with a large rent-roll	20
Mrs Cherry, lady's-maid, with whom Scales was in a flirtation	12
clerk from Duffield, testifying at Felix's trial	46

clerk to Jermyn, who told the story of Harold Transome's radicalism	7
clerk to Mr Labron, who had heard about Harold Transome's radicalism	7
clerks to Mr Labron, and their hangers-on: heckling Parson Jack Lingon	19
counsel for the prosecution of Felix Holt for manslaughter (oddly not identified or named)	46
cousin of Mrs Transome, who was Harold's patron in the near East	1
Crowder, brother to the Treby Manor tenant; tenant at Transome Court	7
Lady Mary Debarry, wife of the Rector	23
two Dissenting swains of Esther, in the best style of Treby waistcoat	6
Dow, the hereditary printer in Treby	28
Dymock and Halliwell, lawyers for Harold Transome	35
Filmore, of Corpus Christi college	24
Lord Fortinbras, son-in-law of Calibut	20
governess to young Miss Lingon: superior, who held that a woman should be able to write	1
Greek wife of Harold Transome, no longer living but the mother of little Harry	1
Hawkins, a factory manager for Harold Transome	17
head-servant at Transome Court, who nodded and winked over Jermyn and Harold	39
Herons of Fenshore: a good family	40
inspector at the tape manufactory, eloquent on the extension of suffrage but tyrannical	3
Jabez, the footman at Transome Court: a "dolt"	1
Jermyn's eldest daughter, having a birthday	9
John, a footman at the Jermyns'	21
Kitty, kitchen-maid at Transome Court	1
Labron, political agent for the Debarrys and Salt's brother-in-law	2, 20
lady-visitor, deaf; kept up her ear-trumpet all evening to hear Jermyn's conversation	9
Lambert, a Dissenter with a house near the speaking	18
landlady at the Red Lion, Treby Magna: introduces Johnson to Tommy Trounsem	28
landlady of the Seven Stars, testifying at Felix's trial	46
Lingon, the family of Mrs Transome	40
Lodge-keeper, aged; he has opened his heavy gate for Harold Transome	1
—his lame wife left to do the honours while he rakes leaves	1
old **Miss Lukyn**, who drove out in a gig sometimes	22
Lukyns, a couple coming for dinner with the Jermyns	21
Magistrate colleague of the Rector	31
Makepiece, an election agent	17, 35
Maria, niece of the deaf lady-visitor	9
Matrons of Little Treby, waiting to stand and make a curtsy to the arriving heir	1
Medwin, a correspondent of Jermyn's	21
Mitchell, coachman to Sir Maximus	7
Moro, a King Charles spaniel at Transome Court	19
young **Muscat**, who sighs after Esther	22
Nimrod, a fine old black retriever, companion to Mr Transome	1
Mrs Nolan, helpmeet of Baruch Nolan	31
Pendrell, banker who will hire only adherents of the established Church	5
Mrs Pendrell, eager to hear Sherlock in debate	24
Mr Prowd, the watchmaker in Treby Magna to whom Felix Holt goes as journeyman	4, 22
revising barrister	20, 28
Mrs Rose, helpmeet of Timothy	31
Mary Salt, who became Mrs Tiliot	24
servant of Mr Lyon in the seaport town where he brought Annette and baby home	6
sexton waiting in the belfry ready to set the one bell going to welcome the heir	1
solicitor in Loamford, who would act for Felix without fee	37
Mrs Spilkins, landlady at the Cross-Keys; yellow and sickly	28
Mr Tiliot, a spirit merchant and established Church member; his gin became famous	3, 24
tradesmen from Treby, giving evidence in Felix's trial; influenced by John Johnson	46
Mrs Tucker, who will benefit from a pension	37
Tudge, a stone-breaker; grandfather of Job	22
Mary Wall, who became Mrs Holt	37
Willis, head game-keeper at Treby Manor	14
witnesses, respectable; swearing to Felix's encouragement of the rioters	46
Lord Wyvern, influential local Conservative with a large rent-roll	2, 20
Zachary, pew-opener at Malthouse Yard	15, 38
Little Zachary, presumably his son, mentioned in connection with a hard egg	26

Published in eight parts by John Blackwood
December 1871-December 1872

MM

Middlemarch

Book I: Miss Brooke

A Prelude invokes **Saint Theresa** of Avila, with commiseration for modern-day avatars given less scope for deeds which might shape the world.

We meet the **Brooke** orphan sisters: **Dorothea** and **Celia**, minors, each with £700 a year, living with their uncle **Arthur Brooke**. Dorothea, if she marries and has a son, would see him inherit Mr Brooke's estate, about £3,000 a year. Celia asks her sister to go over jewelry their mother has left. Dorothea at first looks down on the enterprise, then picks some emeralds, moved by their vividness. All the rest is for Celia. 1 Mr Brooke gives a dinner. A scholar, the frail, desiccated **Rev. Edward Casaubon**, 47 (with a handsome property independent of the church) is there. Dorothea is impressed. Her conversation interests him. **Sir James Chettam**, Bart., contemplates proposing to her. Imbued with idealism and a profound wish to lead an effective life, Dorothea's imagination is stirred by Mr Casaubon's researches in mythology. Chettam brings her a puppy. She rejects it. He tells her he has heard of her work planning tenants' cottages. She is enthusiastic. Chettam implements her cottage plans, but her mind is on Casaubon. 3

Her uncle tells her Casaubon wishes to marry her, while pointing out Chettam's interest. Good-hearted and stupid, he is puzzled by her preference for Casaubon but will not stand in the way, though she is not yet of age. 4 Dorothea reads Casaubon's stilted, self-centered proposal of marriage and falls on her knees in thankfulness. Her uncle is surprised at the speed of her assent. Celia suspects and digs in a needle. Dorothea reacts and tells her news. Celia had never turned so pale before. Casaubon comes for dinner; the happy lovers plan a marriage within six weeks. 5 **Mrs Cadwallader**, the Rector's wife, arrives at the Grange. Celia tells her the news. She is disgusted and goes to apprise Chettam. He is very upset at first. She starts him thinking about Celia. He goes to call. 6 Mr Casaubon is surprised at the moderation of his ardour, but he sees no defect in Dorothea to explain it. He begins teaching her Greek characters. Brooke observes this and is bemused. 7

Chettam, apprehensive for Dorothea, consults the tolerant Rector, **Mr Cadwallader**. We learn that Mr Casaubon's aunt was disowned for a bad marriage and that, much enriched as a result, he is educating her grandson, his cousin. Mrs Cadwallader joins the conference. Nothing will be done. 8 Mr Casaubon's behaviour on settlements is highly satisfactory to Mr Brooke. (*Life insurance on Mr Casaubon is not mentioned.*) Dorothea and Brooke drive over to see the manor house Mr Casaubon has owned since the death of his elder brother. She observes a portrait of **Julia**, elder sister of Mr Casaubon's mother. On their walk they encounter **Will Ladislaw**, sketching. He is Julia's grandson. Prepared to dislike Dorothea for loving his cousin, he is enraptured by her voice and amused by the scene. The picture as Mr Casaubon describes him to the others shows a dilettante. 9 Will leaves for Europe. Mr Casaubon is uncomfortable. Dorothea is eager. Mr Brooke gives a last dinner-party, inviting many town figures, including mayor **Vincy**; banker **Bulstrode**; and lawyer **Standish**. **Lydgate**, the new doctor in town, is present. He impresses **Lady Chettam**. He talks with Dorothea but finds her fatiguing. She marries Casaubon (offstage) and heads to Rome. 10

Scene at the Vincys': **Rosamond Vincy**, exquisite and ambitious, sees in the well-born Lydgate a suitable swain. Mrs Vincy is affable and indulgent of son **Fred**, self-absorbed and indolent. He has failed his degree at Cambridge. An uncle, **Peter Featherstone**, is old, rich from manganese found on his land, and fond of the Vincy children. 11 Peter's sister, **Jane Waule**, makes scandal to him about Fred's having gotten in debt and mentioning expectations. **Mary Garth**, serving Peter, refuses to discuss it. Peter taxes Fred with the report and demands he disprove it with a letter from Bulstrode. Rosamond sings, hoping Lydgate will come. He does at last. A love-glance: both are caught. Fred decides to tackle his father on Bulstrode. 12

Book II: Old and Young

Bulstrode is described. He talks with Lydgate about his hospital project and his ideas for its chaplain. Vincy comes to get his help for Fred. After hot words, he accedes. 13 Letter in hand, Fred goes to Featherstone, who gives him £100, not enough for his debts. Fred tries to advance his suit with Mary. She rebuffs him as idle and a gambler. They were childhood sweethearts. 14 A chapter devoted to Lydgate: background, medical vocation, the primitive medical milieu (emphasizing drugs), his ambitions to improve medicine generally—and a Paris adventure. He feels experienced now, and confident. 15

Bulstrode's standing in Middlemarch and his methods are detailed. Lydgate dines with the Vincys and puts his fellow doctors' backs up without meaning to. Rosamond impresses; when she plays Lydgate is entranced. The **Rev. Camden Farebrother** drops in. He plays excellent whist. Going home, Lydgate reflects on his exciting researches. Rosamond reflects on him. 16 Mr Farebrother at home, with his mother, aunt **Miss Noble**, and sister **Winifred**. Lydgate calls. After conversation, Farebrother shows his nature collections. Farebrother mentions the **Garth** family and particularly his esteem (in fact love) for Mary. He tells of Bulstrode's opposition to him for hospital chaplain and asks Lydgate not to let any negative vote impair their own relationship. 17 Lydgate ruminates on the hospital chaplaincy. Bulstrode wants him to vote for the canting **Tyke**, but he knows Farebrother needs the money. The hospital board meets and is split evenly before Lydgate arrives and casts his vote for Tyke. Farebrother remains friendly with him. 18

Ladislaw is in Rome, and so is Dorothea. At the Vatican with his painter friend **Adolf Naumann**, Will sees her, pensive. He is unreasonably irritated by Naumann's eagerness to paint her. A hint of love? 19 Dorothea is weeping bitterly: her husband is not what she had expected. His appreciation of art is entirely second-hand: he has no view of his own. There has been a scene: he is threatened by her enthusiasm and eagerness to see his work reach the public. They drive to the Vatican: she wonders abstractedly about the future. 20 Will calls. He sees she has been weeping. They talk about art. He is smitten. Casaubon comes home and has to invite him for dinner. 21 Will comes and charms. He urges a visit to a studio. At Naumann's, Dorothea is stimulated and pleased. He asks Casaubon to pose for St Thomas Aquinas. Casaubon is delighted. While he rests, a sketch of Dorothea. Both pictures are continued the following day. Casaubon will buy the Aquinas. Will is annoyed by Naumann's admiration of Dorothea. Will comes and talks at length with Dorothea. He is in love. He says he will give up Casaubon's stipend and go to work. She tells her husband: he is not interested, he says. 22

Book III: Waiting for Death

Fred Vincy owes horsedealer **Bambridge** £160. **Caleb Garth** signed the renewal note (not telling his wife). His late sister had married Featherstone, who subsequently married Fred's aunt. Fred and Mary were sweethearts as tots, and Fred still visits the Garths regularly though his mother doesn't like it. Fred is generally believed to be Featherstone's heir. He goes to the Houndsley horse fair with Bambridge and the 'vet' **Horrock** and is gulled into buying the 'hunter' **Diamond**. 23 Diamond is incorrigibly vicious. Fred has lost £80. He confesses to Garth and gives him the £50 he has left The redoubtable Mrs Garth is described. She is present as he breaks the news. The Garths are hit badly in their plans for **Alfred Garth**'s apprenticeship, but there is no bitterness; Fred has an intimation of what it is to injure others. 24

Fred's remorse is no comfort to Mary. But his misery touches her. Caleb comes to tell her all, and she gives him her savings. 25 Fred is ill. **Wrench** thinks it little. Fred gets worse. Rosamond sees Lydgate outside. Mrs Vincy calls him in. It is typhoid; the Vincys are outraged at Wrench's seeming indifference. Offended, he withdraws. 26 Fred recovers in Lydgate's care. The latter's frequent encounters with Rosamond engender a portentous consciousness in both. They come to flirting; but Lydgate thinks himself secure. 27 The Casaubons are home. Celia and Brooke visit. She is engaged to Chettam. 28

Casaubon has had a letter from Will. His insecurity and unease lead to a warning which Dorothea feels is insulting. She reveals wrath and stalks to her work. Half an hour later, Casaubon has an attack. She is frightened and contrite. Chettam calls and recommends Lydgate. He tells Celia the news. 29 Lydgate advises relaxation. Brooke suggests light reading. Lydgate speaks to Dorothea, urging watchful care. He leaves; she weeps. She reads Will's letters now. To Casaubon Will proposes to bring Naumann's picture to Lowick. Dorothea gives the letter to Brooke, asking him to reply staving off a visit. Brooke impulsively invites Will to his own home. He doesn't tell Dorothea. 30

Lydgate is being drawn in. **Mmes Bulstrode** and **Plymdale** discuss Rosamond's prospects. Mrs Bulstrode is surprised by the Lydgate possibility and goes to speak to her niece. Rosamond cannot say she is engaged and is silent. Mrs Bulstrode warns Lydgate about possible injury to Rosamond. He resolves to avoid the Vincys except on business. Rosamond is very unhappy. Lydgate has a message for her father but brings it to the house. Her sudden tears betray her and undo him. He leaves an engaged man. In a jovial mood, Vincy readily consents. 31 Peter Featherstone is dying. Relatives flock.

Mary as housekeeper feeds and deals with them. Peter will see none: not brothers **Solomon** (rich) and **Jonah** (poor), not sisters **Martha Cranch** (poor) and **Jane Waule** (rich). He somewhat favours pontificating auctioneer **Borthrop Trumbull**. 32 Mary is alone with her thoughts until Peter calls her at 3 a.m. He directs her to get out his will, saying he will burn it. She declines. He offers her his box of gold and notes. He asks her to get Fred. She adamantly insists on witnesses. He weeps frantically, quiets; dies. 33

Book IV: Three Love Problems

Peter Featherstone's ostentatious funeral is observed by the gentry, who note a frog-face in the churchyard not seen before and the presence of Will, who has come in response to Brooke's letter, bringing the painting. Casaubon infers that Dorothea instigated the invitation. 34 Lawyer Standish reports a surprise will, dated more recently than the one he had drawn, which he reads first. There are many small bequests, including £200 only to each sibling. There is a bequest of £10,000 to Fred. The land and residual estate go to frog-faced **Joshua Rigg**, sole executor. The second will revokes everything, but the land, with stock and furniture, goes to Rigg. The balance will build alms-houses. Shock and mortification. The solicitor is known; *no witnesses are mentioned.* The second will appears valid. 35 Fred is crushed, his father annoyed. He now opposes Rosamond's marriage, but she defeats him easily. It is generally known there is an engagement. Mrs Bulstrode expostulates to no avail. We have hints of Lydgate's impracticality, Rosamond's stubbornness. They decide to marry at once. Mr Vincy opposes, warning he cannot help. He demands that Lydgate insure his life, which he immediately does. 36

Brooke has secretly bought the Liberal "Pioneer" and invited Will to run it. Casaubon is jealous and uneasy. Will finds his way to Dorothea. He tells her of his grandfather and parents, both dead—his mother four years before—and of Brooke's offer. Dorothea suggests he consult Casaubon. She does so. Casaubon writes him, warning that if he takes the job, he is banned. Dorothea, knowing his will leaves the bulk of his property to her, asks Casaubon to provide for Will to compensate him for the wrongs forebears did his grandmother. Casaubon snubs her fiercely. Will writes, rejecting his views. Casaubon decides to remain silent, stewing in insecurity. 37 Chettam consults the Cadwalladers on Brooke's political activity. They are upset. Brooke's penny-pinching has left his tenants in hardship: Garth should be brought back to manage. Brooke calls. He is defensive but stubborn. 38

To gain leverage with him, Chettam drops Dorothea at his home. Will is electrified. He tells her he is forbidden her home. She is shocked and sorrowful. Brooke hears that a tenant's son has killed a leveret and goes to call. The farmer has 'dined' and insults him, threatening dire consequences from 'Rinform.' The flummoxed Brooke retreats. 39 The Garths at table: Mary expects a teaching job in York. There is a letter to Caleb with an offer to manage the Chettam and Brooke interests. Joy abounds: Mary will stay. Farebrother calls; he suspects that Mary loves Fred. Caleb has been asked by both Rigg and Bulstrode to appraise Stone Court. 40 Rigg is in residence, visited by **John Raffles**, his step-father, seeking a hand-out. Rigg refuses; as he goes for a parting brandy Raffles picks up a bit of paper to wedge his flask in its cover. He does not then see that it is a letter from Bulstrode. He raffishly departs. 41 Casaubon's jealous misery and fear of Will's influence on Dorothea's mind and views torment him. What if he died early and Will married her? He consults Lydgate. It is fatty degeneration of the heart, with complete uncertainty as to the end. He excludes Dorothea from his thoughts: she is angry but overcomes it, waits for him, and conducts him to his rest. 42

Book V: The Dead Hand

Dorothea calls on Lydgate to learn what he has told Casaubon. He is not at home. Rosamond and Will have been making music. Will offers to fetch Lydgate at the hospital, but she goes herself, unhappy at seeing him with another's wife. Will is mortified. Lydgate and Rosamond discuss him; she thinks he adores Dorothea. 43 Dorothea learns nothing new from Lydgate. She offers £200 a year for the hospital. Casaubon has no objection, but he mistrusts her love. 44 Medical opposition builds against the hospital and Lydgate, who does not dispense drugs. He is disparaged by Drs Wrench and **Toller**. Farebrother gives him wise advice: stay clear of Bulstrode; be careful of money. Lydgate tells Rosamond about **Vesalius**. She is not impressed. 45

Brooke and Will discuss Reform and Will's work on the "Pioneer." The eccentric, mercurial Will gains recognition, not always favourable. He is much at the Lydgates'. Tertius is irked by a dunning letter. 46 Will's devotion to his love is idealistic yet stubborn: he will not leave the place where she is. But he rarely sees her and knows his association with Brooke is not highly creditable. He goes to her church. Casaubon ignores him; she bows, on the verge of tears. He regrets coming. 47 Dorothea had hoped a reconciliation might occur: no such thing. She foresees a blank life with nothing to do. Celia has a baby. In the night, Casaubon asks her to promise to carry out his wishes if he dies, not saying what he has in mind. Thinking he wants her commitment to his work, she temporizes, having lost faith in it. She fears the treadmill. He goes out to walk; she sits, knowing she will give in for fear of injuring him. At last she goes to him—he is dead: his heart has failed. 48

Chettam and Brooke confer on how to keep from Dorothea: news of a codicil in Casaubon's will disinheriting her if she weds Ladislaw. Chettam is adamant for getting rid of Ladislaw. Brooke opposes that and wins the argument: it would look like mistrust of Dorothea. 49 Celia admires her baby. Dorothea sits by. She is concerned about the Lowick living. She wants to go over Casaubon's papers; Brooke fobs her off but she wants activity. Celia breaks the news. Dorothea is astounded, stunned; there is a revulsion from Casaubon, a sudden yearning toward Will. Lydgate sees her agitation and advises that she have freedom to follow her bent. She goes to Lowick and finds Casaubon's "Synoptical Tabulation." He had begun too late to prepare Dorothea to carry on his work; she is revolted now by his suspicion. She finds nothing in his papers: no explanation, no message whatsoever. Lydgate sees a chance to help Farebrother and recommends him for the living. Obliviously, he describes Will's squiring of Miss Noble on her charitable visits. 50

Will is busy with the election. He is ignorant of the codicil but fears imputations of fortune-hunting. It is hard to coach Brooke to commit for the Reform Bill. He speaks to the crowd in town but is confused, then harassed by an effigy and an echo. Eggs pelt the effigy and Brooke. Shouted down, he retreats inside. He withdraws from the election and will give up the "Pioneer." Ladislaw will not leave without a sign from Dorothea. 51 The Farebrother household is ecstatic at the news of the Lowick living. Fred, now a B.A., comes for advice: a clerical career is not for him. He asks Farebrother to sound Mary on her feelings. Like John Alden, he goes. She flatly will not accept Fred as a clergyman but cannot choose any one else. Farebrother hides his pain and goes to report. 52 Rigg sells Stone Court to Bulstrode and goes to the seashore to change money. Bulstrode is there when a drunken Raffles appears, looking for him. Bulstrode has him stay overnight and goes home, fearing future disgrace. After a payoff, Raffles spent ten years in America. Now he wants more: £200. Bulstrode goes to get it. Raffles remembers the married name of a girl he sought once: Ladislaw. In funds, he departs. 53

Book VI: The Widow and the Wife

Dorothea insists on returning to Lowick Manor. She longs to see Will. He calls, to say good-bye. Their conversation is allusive and elliptical; he cannot speak as he would wish. Chettam interrupts; Will says good-bye and leaves. 54 Mrs Cadwallader wants Dorothea to remarry, but not to Will. She says she will never marry again. 55 She works happily with Caleb Garth on Chettam's cottages. The railroad is coming, but countrymen are suspicious. They chase the railway surveyors with pitchforks. The mounted Fred sees **Tom**, Caleb's assistant, knocked down by them, and he charges the farmer group and scatters it. He puts the injured boy on his horse and takes his place with the measuring-chain for Caleb. On their way home, Fred asks Caleb to take him under him: he knows he should work in the out-of-doors. Caleb will. He tells his wife, and of Mary and Fred. Susan is vexed. She knows Farebrother has had hopes. Fred tells his father his decision. Vincy is amazed, then bitter at first. Mrs Vincy is devastated; her husband cheers her up. 56

On his way to Mary, Fred stops at the Garths' and talks to Susan, who gives him a piece of her mind, betraying her sentiments as to Farebrother. Fred is badly stung. He fears he must lose out to a better man. Mary laughs at him. She will not change, though the new idea impresses her. 57 Rosamond has lost her baby. Disobeying Tertius, she has ridden with his foppish cousin and had a fright which led to miscarriage. Her stubbornness amazes Tertius. He is worried about debt: he has spent too much and his income is not flourishing. He arrives home scowling; Ladislaw is there but soon leaves. Tertius thinks of selfish Laure and unselfish Dorothea. Gently he broaches his subject: there will be an inventory. She is shocked; tears come. She wants to speak to her father. He forbids that. She suggests leaving town. She brings him her jewels, offering any and all for return; she will go home on the morrow and miss the inventory. Lydgate persuades her to stay, and to keep all the jewels. There is a cool kiss in seeming reconciliation. 58

Fred mentions the codicil to Rosamond, who tells Ladislaw. He is stunned. He soon leaves. She has disobeyed Tertius again, going to her father for help. His negative was unequivocal. 59 All the town is at a festive auction at the **Larchers**'. Bulstrode has asked Ladislaw to advise his wife on a painting. Raffles turns up and recognises him. He accosts him, tells him his mother's name and the reason she ran from her family: their illicit business receiving stolen goods. Ladislaw walks and ponders: he believes it. 60

Raffles turns up at the Bulstrodes' and the dog shows him out. At the bank, he asks for £25 and says he may reside in Middlemarch. Bulstrode fears disgrace. He is haunted by unwanted memories: of happy early lay preaching years; years as a protégé of **Dunkirk**, wealthy pawn-broker; invitation to partnership; discovery of the shady side of the business; the death of Dunkirk following his son's death; the failure of a search for a run-away daughter; marriage to the widow. But the daughter had been found, and only Bulstrode and Raffles knew it. Mrs Bulstrode died; Bulstrode gradually withdrew his capital, but did not terminate the business. He came to Middlemarch with £100,000 and besides banking was a sleeping partner in new shadinesses. Desperate now to propitiate his God, he summons Ladislaw and offers him £500 a year and a proportional inheritance. Ladislaw probes harshly: did Bulstrode conceal his mother from her mother? was his business that of thieves and convicts? Will spurns the offer: Bulstrode is stricken. 61

Chettam has heard that Will frequents the Lydgates'. He gets Mrs Cadwallader to tell Dorothea, who reacts indignantly. She encounters Will at the Grange. They don't know what to say. When Will does speak, she misunderstands, thinking he refers to Rosamond. He speaks again, and now she knows it is not Rosamond but herself he loves: his honour carries him away from her, not from any other relationship. Her carriage passes him on the road. She cherishes her new knowledge; he is far less sure. He departs. 62

Book VII: Two Temptations

Mr Farebrother at a dinner-party hears comments on Lydgate's mode of living. He goes to see him and finds him agitated. Farebrother suspects opiates. There is a party at the Vincys'. Rosamond seems to ignore Tertius; her father barely speaks to him. Farebrother thanks Lydgate for his help over the Lowick living. Lydgate had wanted that to be a secret. He is very unhappy, and touchy at the suggestion that he needs help now himself. 63 He tries to talk economy to Rosamond. He has heard of a planned marriage of a wealthy couple who might like the Lydgate house. Rosamond is appalled and determines to frustrate him. She goes to **Mrs Plymdale** and encourages **Ned**'s taking a different house; she countermands Lydgate's plans to auction his leasehold. She asks how much is needed to keep things in place: £1,000. So she writes **Sir Godwin Lydgate**, Bart. She tells Lydgate she has instructed Trumbull to abandon advertising the house. Hs is dumbfounded but vulnerable to her accusation that he married her under false pretenses. She misses Ladislaw. Lydgate thinks of journeying north to talk to his uncle. 64

Rosamond waits for Sir Godwin's reply. It comes; Lydgate reads and turns white. His uncle scolds him for letting his wife do the dirty work. He speaks harshly: she is calm, despising him; he softens because he has no choice if there is to be any marriage. 65 By accident he stops in at a billiard room and plays, winning at first. Fred comes in, disposed to dissipation. Sobered by seeing Lydgate excited, now losing, he distracts him with news that Farebrother is below. Lydgate comes away. Farebrother warns Fred he could lose Mary's respect: that Mary could choose another. Fred is grateful. 66

Lydgate steels himself to appeal to Bulstrode, who asks for a consultation and tells him he will withdraw from Middlemarch and end his financial support of the Hospital. He has spoken to Mrs Casaubon about taking his place, and she is considering it. Lydgate broaches his own need; Bulstrode recommends bankruptcy. 67 Raffles has reappeared. Bulstrode had turned him out promising to cut him off if he ever returned. Bulstrode makes contingency plans to remove to the coast and agrees to Caleb's suggestion that Fred manage Stone Court as tenant. Mary and Fred could then marry. 68 But Garth resigns all: he has encountered Raffles, now ill at Stone Court, and he believes his story. The humiliated Bulstrode hopes Raffles has spoken to no one else. Lydgate prescribes complete rest, no alcohol. At home, the bailiffs are in the house. Rosamond suggests she go to her parents. Lydgate assents. 69

Bulstrode searches Raffles' baggage for clues as to past journeys. He regrets refusing Lydgate's request for aid: he might need a partisan. Raffles is worse. Lydgate comes with minute instructions as to moderate opiates and no alcohol whatsoever. Bulstrode tells him he will aid him, for the sake of his wife's niece, and gives him a cheque for £1,000. Lydgate rides home in joy. Bulstrode gives his housekeeper correct instructions and goes to bed. She comes to ask if she may not provide alcohol, and he gives her the needed key. Raffles sinks during the night. Bulstrode hides the brandy bottle. In the morning Lydgate sees that he is dying. He is uneasy and puzzled. Raffles dies. News of an execution on Lydgate has spread; Farebrother is anxious, but Lydgate reassures him: the debts are paid thanks to Bulstrode. 70

Bambridge is idling in the street when Hawley and others collect. They see Mr Bulstrode passing. Bambridge is reminded of meeting Raffles and hearing a story to Bulstrode's discredit. Hawley is eager to hear more, but the first news is of Raffles' death and funeral. A net is cast: Caleb's withdrawal is food for inference; Mr Farebrother fears for Lydgate and gratuitously imports the notion of "Jew pawnbroker." [*Is Dunkirk a Jewish name? Are all pawnbrokers Jews?*] Scandal connects Lydgate's new resources with Bulstrode's desire to see Raffles out of the way. Strong negative public feeling against Bulstrode is voiced by Hawley at a town meeting. Lydgate sees all in a flash. Bulstrode tries an *ad hominem* attack; Hawley fiercely replies. Rev. Mr **Thesiger** in the chair suggests that Bulstrode withdraw for the present. Trapped as the doctor in the house, Lydgate takes him out, feeling bitterly compromised. Brooke and Farebrother drive to Dorothea, who flatly refuses to believe ill of Lydgate: "Let's find out the truth and clear him." 71

Book VIII: Sunset and Sunrise

Farebrother is troubled over Lydgate. Dorothea prefers faith and action to caution. Chettam, Farebrother and Brooke all urge her to be cautious. Celia adds her voice. 72 Lydgate is furious at his fate and his marriage. But he will not flee: he will fight it out; and will not turn on Bulstrode. 73 **Mmes Hackbutt**, **Sprague** and **Plymdale** discuss Mrs Bulstrode's situation. She, knows nothing, but suspects. Lydgate is evasive. She visits Mrs Hackbutt, who piously hints. Mrs Plymdale hints also. Her brother tells her all. After a scorching wave of shame and isolation, her soul leaps to a decision for allegiance to her husband and her marriage. At home, she confronts her future and changes her dress for Methodist simplicity. She goes to her husband. They weep together. 74

Despite relief from bailiffs, Rosamond is resentful. She misses Ladislaw and constructs a fantasy of his love for her. A letter comes: he will return. She is joyful, and with new energy sends out dinner invitations. They are all declined. Puzzled, she goes to the Vincys and learns of the scandal. At home she is silent, and so is Lydgate. As he steels himself to gain her understanding, she asks him again to move to London. He walks out in despair. 75 Lydgate comes to Dorothea, as requested, to discuss the Hospital. She is eager to help him and assures him of her trust. He is greatly moved. She wants him to stay; he feels his obligation to Rosamond obliges him to leave. Dorothea asks leave to go to her. Lydgate leaves. Dorothea writes a cheque to him for £1,000 to replace Bulstrode's funds. She will take it with her when she visits Rosamond. 76

She arrives and is shown into a room by the servant who thought Rosamond upstairs. She sees Ladislaw holding Rosamond's hands and speaking fervently, Rosamond flushed and near tears (she has made a declaration and been rebuffed). Dorothea leaves her envelope and stalks out, filled with indignant energy and numb. 77 Beside himself with chagrin, Will is brutal to Rosamond. She is undone. He goes, she faints. She cannot move. Her maid helps her to bed. She seems grateful when Tertius comes and cherishes her.

78 Will calls on Lydgate and hears the whole Raffles story for the first time, including his role in the old history. Both men are foreseeing bleak futures. 79

Dorothea visits the Farebrothers. She is undone by a mention of Ladislaw. She goes home to a night of bitter sorrow, reflecting on the scene with Will and Rosamond. There comes a dawn of renunciation and peace. She will go again to Rosamond. 80 She hears that Lydgate accepts her aid and has sent his cheque to Bulstrode. Rosamond is amazed that she has come, is apprehensive and ready for hostility. She is disarmed by Dorothea's cordiality and earnest wish to reassure her about Tertius. They weep together. She tells Dorothea that the scene she had witnessed did not mean what she thought: "He has never had any love for me. No woman exists for him beside you." Dorothea knows the beginning of her joy. 81

Will had come to Middlemarch on a charitable project, but hopes to see Dorothea. Now he is in a quagmire over Rosamond. He calls, and Rosamond slips him a note: she has told Dorothea what their scene meant; he cannot reproach her now. He is glad but unsure how things will unfold. 82 Miss Noble appears at Lowick: Will is in the garden. Will Dorothea see him? She will. They speak haltingly. Thunder crashes outside. They take hands; a few more words, and they kiss. He says it is hopeless: he will never have enough money for them both. She bursts out: she has enough for both. 83

Brooke has bad news for the Chettams and Cadwalladers: Dorothea and Ladislaw will marry. Chettam is furious; Celia is alarmed; Mrs Cadwallader says I Told You So. Celia goes to Dorothea: she is adamant. 84 Bulstrode, in distress over his wife's misery, asks her if she wants anything. She says she would be glad to help her brother's family. Bulstrode proposes that the plan for Fred to take over Stone Court be revised. She must propose it; he cannot. 85 Garth and Mary walk and talk: he puts the proposal to her. It means she and Fred can marry. Fred is incredulous, then delighted. 86

Finale: Fred and Mary were a great success. Fred gained distinction as theoretic and practical farmer and published a book. Mary wrote a noted children's book. They had three boys. Lydgate died at fifty of diphtheria, having gained an excellent practice in London and at a continental spa. He wrote a book on gout. They had four children. Rosamond remarried an older man, wealthy and paternal. Will became an ardent public man and went into Parliament. His constituents paid his expenses. Dorothea had a son, and reconciliation with the Chettams ensued. Chettam advised Brooke not to change the entail. Brooke lived to a good old age, and a Ladislaw inherited. By percolation and diffusion, Dorothea's spirit still does good work in the world.

Contents

The *Topicon* contains Mr Casaubon's letter to Dorothea Brooke proposing marriage at LM:Courtship—*marriage proposal*; the story of Lydgate's aborted French passion at LM:Love—*infatuation;* the blue-eyed tears which undo him at LM:Love—*betrayed by tears;* and Dorothea's night of revelation and agony at LM:Love—*purgatory endured*

Couples who Will Marry

Dorothea (**Dodo** to her sister; 50*) **Brooke**. "Miss Brooke had that kind of beauty which seems to be thrown into relief by poor dress. Her hand and wrist were so finely formed that she could wear sleeves not less bare of style than those in which the Blessed Virgin appeared to Italian painters; and her profile as well as her stature and bearing seemed to gain the more dignity from her plain garments, which by the side of provincial fashion gave her the impressiveness of a fine quotation from the Bible—or from one of our elder poets—in a paragraph of to-day's newspaper." 1

*The chapter in which a naming detail—sometimes the actual given name—is first learned.

—*intelligence:* "She was usually spoken of as being remarkably clever, but with the addition that her sister **Celia** had more common-sense." 1

—*class standing:* " . . . the Brooke connections, though not exactly aristocratic, were unquestionably 'good': if you inquired backward for a generation or two, you would not find any yard-measuring or parcel-tying forefathers—anything lower than an admiral or a clergyman; and there was even an ancestor discernible as a Puritan gentleman who served under **Cromwell**, but afterwards conformed, and managed to come out of all political troubles as the proprietor of a respectable family estate." 1

—*dress:* "Dorothea knew many passages of **Pascal**'s *Pensées* and of **Jeremy Taylor** by heart; and to her the destinies of mankind, seen by the light of Christianity, made the solicitudes of feminine fashion appear an occupation for Bedlam. She could not reconcile the anxieties of a spiritual life involving eternal consequences, with a keen interest in guimp and artificial protrusions of drapery." 1

—*enthusiast:* "Her mind was theoretic, and yearned by its nature after some lofty conception of the world which might frankly include the parish of Tipton and her own rule of conduct there; she was enamoured of intensity and greatness, and rash in embracing whatever seemed to her to have those aspects; likely to seek martyrdom, to make retractions, and then to incur martyrdom after all in a quarter where she had not sought it." 1

—*marriageable?* "And how should Dorothea not marry?—a girl so handsome and with such prospects? Nothing could hinder it but her love of extremes, and her insistence on regulating life according to notions which might cause a wary man to hesitate before he made her an offer, or even might lead her at last to refuse all offers. A young lady of some birth and fortune, who knelt suddenly down on a brick floor by the side of a sick labourer and prayed fervidly as if she thought herself living in the time of the Apostles—who had strange whims of fasting like a Papist, and of sitting up at night to read old theological books! Such a wife might awaken you some fine morning with a new scheme for the application of her income which would interfere with political economy and the keeping of saddle-horses: a man would naturally think twice before he risked himself in such fellowship." 1

—*and her sister:* "The rural opinion about the new young ladies, even among the cottages, was generally in favour of **Celia**, as being so amiable and innocent-looking, while Miss Brooke's large eyes seemed, like her religion, too unusual and striking. Poor Dorothea! Compared with her, the innocent-looking Celia was knowing and worldly-wise; so much subtler is a human mind than the outside tissues which make a sort of blazonry or clock-face for it." 1

—*a favourite pastime:* "Most men thought her bewitching when she was on horseback. She loved the fresh air and the various aspects of the country, and when her eyes and cheeks glowed with mingled pleasure she looked very little like a devotee. Riding was an indulgence which she allowed herself in spite of conscientious qualms, she felt that she enjoyed it in a pagan sensuous way, and always looked forward to renouncing it." 1

—*dream of a husband:* "Dorothea, with all her eagerness to know the truths of life, retained very childlike ideas about marriage. She felt sure that she would have accepted the judicious **Hooker**, if she had been born in time to save him from that wretched mistake he made in matrimony; or **John Milton** when his blindness had come on; or any of the other great men whose odd habits it would have been glorious piety to endure; but an amiable handsome baronet, who said 'Exactly' to her remarks even when she expressed uncertainty—how would he affect her as a lover? The really delightful marriage must be that where your husband was a sort of father, and could teach you even Hebrew, if you wished it." 1

—*capable of sting:* "Across her imaginative adornment of those whom she loved, there darted now and then a keen discernment, which was not without a scorching quality. If Miss Brooke ever attained perfect meekness, it would not be for lack of inward fire." 1

—*falling in love:* "Dorothea by this time had looked deep into the unguaged reservoir of Mr **Casaubon**'s mind, seeing reflected there in vague labyrinthine extension every quality she herself brought; had opened much of her own experience to him, and had understood from him the scope of his great work, also of attractively labyrinthine extent." 3

—*impressible:* "Miss Brooke argued from words and dispositions not less unhesitatingly than other young ladies of her age. Signs are small measurable things, but interpretations are illimitable, and in girls of sweet, ardent nature, every sign is apt to conjure up wonder, hope, belief, vast as a sky, and coloured by a diffused thimbleful of matter in the shape of knowledge . . . . Because Miss Brooke was hasty in her trust, it is not therefore clear that **Mr Casaubon** was unworthy of it." 3

" . . . Dorothea heard and retained what he said with the eager interest of a fresh young nature to which every variety in experience is an epoch." 3

—*hairstyle:* " . . . she wore her brown hair flatly braided and coiled behind so as to expose the outline of her head in a daring manner at a time when public feeling required the meagreness of nature to be dissimulated by tall barricades of frizzed curls and bows, never surpassed by any great race except the Feejeean. This was a trait of Miss Brooke's asceticism." 3

—*uncertainty:* "For a long while she had been oppressed by the indefiniteness which hung in her mind, like a thick summer haze, over all her desire to make her life greatly effective. What could she do, what ought she to do?—she, hardly more than a budding woman, but yet with an active conscience and a great mental need, not to be satisfied by a girlish instruction comparable to the nibblings and judgments of a discursive mouse." 3

Dorothea and Mr Casaubon

—*soul-hunger:* "The intensity of her religious disposition, the coercion it exercised over her life, was but one aspect of a nature altogether ardent, theoretic, and intellectually consequent: and with such a nature, struggling in the hands of a narrow teaching, hemmed in by a social life which seemed nothing but a labyrinth of petty courses, a walled-in maze of small paths that led no whither, the outcome was sure to strike others as at once exaggeration and inconsistency. The thing which seemed to her best, she wanted to justify by the completest knowledge; and not to live in a pretended admission of rules which were never acted on. Into this soul-hunger as yet all her youthful passion was poured; the union which attracted her was one that would deliver her from her girlish subjection to her own ignorance, and give her the freedom of voluntary submission to a guide who would take her along the grandest path." 3

—*a conviction:* "He was all she had at first imagined him to be: almost everything he had said seemed like a specimen from a mine; or the inscription on the door of a museum which might open on the treasures of past ages. . . ." 3

—*sisterly comment:* " '. . . you went on as you always do, never looking just where you are, and treading in the wrong place. You always see what nobody else sees; it is impossible to satisfy you, yet you never see what is quite plain. That's your way, Dodo.' " 4

—*hands:* "They were not thin hands, or small hands; but powerful, feminine, maternal hands. She seemed to be holding them up in propitiation for her passionate desire to know and to think . . . . " 4

—*marriage:* " 'I know that I must expect trials, uncle. Marriage is a state of higher duties. I never thought of it as mere personal ease,' said poor Dorothea." 4

—*thankful:* Dorothea trembled while she read [**Mr Casaubon**'s proposal] letter, then she fell on her knees, buried her face, and sobbed. She could not pray; under the rush of solemn emotion in which thoughts became vague and images floated uncertainly, she could but cast herself, with a childlike sense of reclining, in the lap of a divine consciousness which sustained her own . . . .

"Now she would be able to devote herself to large yet definite duties; now she would be allowed to live continually in the light of a mind that she could reverence. This hope was not unmixed with the glow of proud delight—the joyous maiden surprise that she was chosen by the man whom her admiration had chosen. All Dorothea's passion was transfused through a mind struggling towards an ideal life; the radiance of her transfigured girlhood fell on the first object that came within its level." 5

—*a thrill:* "It seemed as if something like the reflection of a white sunlit wing had passed across her features, ending in one of her rare blushes." 5

—*naive*: "[**Mr Casaubon**] was being unconsciously wrought upon by the charms of a nature which was entirely without hidden calculations either for immediate effects or for remoter ends. It was this which made Dorothea so childlike, and, according to some judges, so stupid, with all her reputed cleverness; as, for example, in the present case of throwing herself, metaphorically speaking, at Mr Casaubon's feet, and kissing his unfashionable shoe-ties as if he were a Protestant Pope. She was not in the least teaching Mr Casaubon to ask if he were good enough for her, but merely asking herself anxiously how she could be good enough for Mr Casaubon." 5

Dorothea working for her man

"And she had not reached that point of renunciation at which she would have been satisfied with having a wise husband: she wished, poor child, to be wise herself. Miss Brooke was certainly very naïve with all her alleged cleverness." 7

—and painting: "To poor Dorothea these severe classical nudities and smirking Renaissance-**Correggio**sities were painfully inexplicable, staring into the midst of her Puritanic conceptions: she had never been taught how she could bring them into any sort of relevance with her life." 9

—already defending: " 'After all, people may really have in them some vocation which is not quite plain to themselves, may they not? They may seem idle and weak because they are growing. We should be very patient with each other, I think.' " 9

—her dream: " . . . eagerness for a binding theory which could bring her own life and doctrine into strict connection with that amazing [classical Greek] past and give the remotest sources of knowledge some bearing on her actions . . . something she yearned for by which her life might be filled with action at once rational and ardent, and . . . what lamp was there but knowledge? Surely learned men kept the only oil; and who more learned than **Mr Casaubon**?" 10

—dressed for dinner: "[She] was an agreeable image of serene dignity when she came into the drawing-room in her silver-grey dress—the simple lines of her dark-brown hair parted over her brow and coiled massively behind, in keeping with the entire absence from her manner and expression of all search after mere effect." 10

Dorothea Casaubon

—and then: "Not long after that dinner-party she had become **Mrs Casaubon**, and was on her way to Rome." 10

—at the Vatican: " . . . a breathing blooming girl, whose form, not shamed by the **Ariadne**, was clad in Quakerish grey drapery; her long cloak, fastened at the neck, was thrown backward from her arms, and one beautiful ungloved hand pillowed her cheek, pushing somewhat backward the white beaver bonnet which made a sort of halo to her face around the simply braided dark-brown hair. She was not looking at the sculpture, probably not thinking of it: her large eyes were fixed dreamily on a streak of sunlight which fell across the floor." 19

—pain: "I am sorry to add that she was sobbing bitterly, with such abandonment to this relief of an oppressed heart as a woman habitually controlled by pride on her own account and thoughtfulness for others will sometimes allow herself when she feels securely alone . . . .

"Yet Dorothea had no distinctly shapen grievance that she could state even to herself; and in the midst of her confused thought and passion, the mental act that was struggling forth into clearness was a self-accusing cry that her feeling of desolation was the fault of her own spiritual poverty . . . .

"But this stupendous fragmentariness [of Rome] heightened the dreamlike strangeness of her bridal life. Dorothea had now been five weeks in Rome, and in the kindly mornings when autumn and winter seemed to go hand in hand like a happy aged couple one of whom would presently survive in chiller loneliness, she had driven about at first with **Mr Casaubon**, but of late chiefly with **Tantripp** and their experienced courier." 20

Dorothea at the Vatican

—*honeymoon:* "She had been led through the best galleries, had been taken to the chief points of view, had been shown the grandest ruins and the most glorious churches, and she had ended by oftenest choosing to drive out to the Campagna where she could feel alone with the earth and sky, away from the oppressive masquerade of ages, in which her own life too seemed to become a masque with enigmatical costumes." 20

—*tumult:* "[Imagine] the gigantic broken revelations of that Imperial and Papal city thrust abruptly on the notions of a girl who had been brought up in English and Swiss Puritanism, fed on meagre Protestant histories and on art chiefly of the handscreen sort; a girl whose ardent nature turned all her small allowance of knowledge into principles, fusing her actions into their mould, and whose quick emotions gave the most abstract things the quality of a pleasure or a pain; a girl who had lately become a wife, and from the enthusiastic acceptance of untried duty found herself plunged in tumultuous preoccupation with her personal lot." 20

—*adjusting to wedlock:* " . . . that new future which was replacing the imaginary drew its material from the endless minutiae by which her view of Mr Casaubon and her wifely relation, now that she was married to him, was gradually changing with the secret motion of a watch-hand from what it had been in her maiden dream. It was too early yet for her fully to recognise or at least admit the change, still more for her to have readjusted that devotedness which was so necessary a part of her mental life that she was almost sure sooner or later to recover it." 20

—*deepening impatience:* "Permanent rebellion, the disorder of a life without some loving reverent resolve, was not possible to her . . . . [but] she had been becoming more and more aware, with a certain terror, that her mind was continually sliding into inward fits of anger and repulsion, or else into forlorn weariness." 20

—*affectionate:* "These characteristics, fixed and unchangeable as bone in Mr Casaubon, might have remained longer unfelt by Dorothea . . . if she could have fed her affection with those childlike caresses which are the bent of every sweet woman, who has begun by showering kisses on the hard pate of her bald doll, creating a happy soul within that woodenness from the wealth of her own love. That was Dorothea's bent. With all her yearning to know what was afar from her and to be widely benignant, she had ardour enough for what was near, to have kissed Mr Casaubon's coat-sleeve, or to have caressed his shoe-latchet . . . ." 20

—*frustrated:* "[Her] ideas and resolves seemed like melting ice floating and lost in the warm flood of which they had been but another form. She was humiliated to find herself a mere victim of feeling, as if she could know nothing except through that medium: all her strength was scattered in fits of agitation, of struggle, of despondency, and then again in visions of more complete renunciation, transforming all hard conditions into duty. Poor Dorothea! She was certainly troublesome—to herself chiefly . . . . " 20

"Dorothea . . . had a vivid memory of evenings in which she had supposed that Mr Casaubon's mind had gone too deep during the day to be able to get to the surface again." 20

—*blind spot:* "She was as blind to his inward troubles as he to hers: she had not yet learned those hidden conflicts in her husband which claim our pity. She had not yet listened patiently to his heart-beats, but only felt that her own was beating violently." 20

—regret: "However just her indignation might be, her ideal was not to claim justice, but to give tenderness." 20

—ideal: "But in Dorothea's mind there was a current into which all thought and feeling were apt sooner or later to flow—the reaching forward of the whole consciousness towards the fullest truth, the least partial good. There was clearly something better than anger and despondency." 20

—vulnerability: "She felt an immense need of some one to speak to, and she had never before seen any one who seemed so quick and pliable [as **Will**], so likely to understand everything." 21

—presentiment: "To-day she had begun to see that she had been under a wild illusion in expecting a response to her feeling from Mr Casaubon, and she had felt the waking of a presentiment that there might be a sad consciousness in his life which made as great a need on his side as on her own." 21

—trusting: "No nature could be less suspicious than hers: when she was a child she believed in the gratitude of wasps and the honourable susceptibility of sparrows, and was proportionately indignant when their baseness was made manifest." 22

—innocence: " 'I quite hoped that we should be friends when I first saw you—because of your relationship with Mr Casaubon.' There was a certain liquid brightness in her eyes, and **Will** was conscious that his own were obeying a law of nature and filling too. The allusion to Mr Casaubon would have spoiled all if anything at that moment could have spoiled the subduing power, the sweet dignity, of her noble unsuspicious inexperience." 22

—in her new home: "She was glowing from her morning toilette as only healthful youth can glow: there was gem-like brightness on her coiled hair and in her hazel eyes; there was warm red life in her lips; her throat had a breathing whiteness above the differing white of the fur which itself seemed to wind about her neck and cling down her blue-grey pelisse with a tenderness gathered from her own, a sentient commingled innocence which kept its loveliness against the crystalline purity of the out-door snow." 28

—the honeymoon over: "Marriage, which was to bring guidance into worthy and imperative occupation, had not yet freed her from the gentlewoman's oppressive liberty: it had not even filled her leisure with the ruminant joy of unchecked tenderness. Her blooming full-pulsed youth stood there in a moral imprisonment which made itself one with the chill, colourless, narrowed landscape, with the shrunken furniture, the never-read books, and the ghostly stag in a pale fantastic world that seemed to be vanishing from the daylight." 28

—her need: "Dorothea had little vanity, but she had the ardent woman's need to rule beneficently by making the joy of another soul. Hence the mere chance of seeing **Will** occasionally was like a lunette opened in the wall of her prison, giving her a glimpse of the sunny air; and this pleasure began to nullify her original alarm at what her husband might think about the introduction of Will as her uncle's guest." 37

—a fresh encounter: "She seated herself on a dark ottoman with the brown books behind her, looking in her plain dress of some thin woollen-white material, without a single ornament on her besides her wedding-ring, as if she were under a vow to be different from all other women; and **Will** sat down opposite her at two yards' distance, the light falling on his bright curls and delicate but rather petulant profile, with its defiant curves of lip and

chin. Each looked at the other as if they had been two flowers which had opened then and there. Dorothea for the moment forgot her husband's mysterious irritation against Will: it seemed fresh water at her thirsty lips to speak without fear to the one person whom she had found receptive; for in looking backward through sadness she exaggerated a past solace." 37

—*unconscious revelation:* " 'But it is very difficult to be learned; it seems as if people were worn out on the way to great thoughts, and can never enjoy them because they are too tired.' " 37

—*facing a central fact:* "She was no longer struggling against the perception of facts, but adjusting herself to their clearest perception; and now when she looked steadily at her husband's failure, still more at his possible consciousness of failure, she seemed to be looking along the one track where duty became tenderness." 37

—*oblivious purity:* "There was a peculiar fascination for Dorothea in this division [favouring **Ladislaw**] of property intended for herself, and always regarded by her as excessive. She was blind, you see, to many things obvious to others—likely to tread in the wrong places, as **Celia** had warned her; yet her blindness to whatever did not lie in her own pure purpose carried her safely by the side of precipices where vision would have been perilous with fear." 37

—*after a fierce snub:* "Hearing him breathe quickly after he had spoken, she sat listening, frightened, wretched—with a dumb inward cry for help to bear this nightmare of a life in which every energy was arrested by dread." 37

—*and paintings:* " 'that is one reason why I did not like the pictures here, dear uncle—which you think me stupid about. I used to come from the village with all that dirt and coarse ugliness like a pain within me, and the simpering pictures in the drawing-room seemed to me like a wicked attempt to find delight in what is false, while we don't mind how hard the truth is for the neighbours outside our walls.' " 39

—*principle:* " 'I think we have no right to come forward and urge wider changes for good, until we have tried to alter the evils which lie under our own hands.' " 39

—*and animals:* "She leaned her back against the window-frame, and laid her hand on the dog's head; for though, as we know, she was not fond of pets that must be held in the hands or trodden on, she was always attentive to the feelings of dogs, and very polite if she had to decline their advances." 39

—*creed:* " 'But I have a belief of my own, and it comforts me . . . .

" 'That by desiring what is perfectly good, even when we don't quite know what it is and cannot do what we would, we are part of the divine power against evil—widening the skirts of light and making the struggle with darkness narrower . . . .

" 'Please not to call it by any name . . . . You will say it is Persian, or something else geographical. It is my life. I have found it out, and cannot part with it. I have always been finding out my religion since I was a little girl. I used to pray so much—now I hardly ever pray. I try not to have desires merely for myself, because they may not be good for others, and I have too much already.' " 39

—*anger:* "She was in the reaction of a rebellious anger stronger than any she had felt since her marriage. Instead of tears there came words—

" 'What have I done—what am I—that he should treat me so? He never knows what is in my mind—he never cares. What is the use of anything I do? He wishes he had never married me.' " 42

"If he had drawn her towards him, she would never have surveyed him—never have said, 'Is he worth living for?' but would have felt him simply a part of her own life. Now she said bitterly, 'It is his fault, not mine.' In the jar of her whole being, Pity was overthrown. Was it her fault that she had believed in him—had believed in his worthiness? And what, exactly, was he?—She was able enough to estimate him—she who waited on his glances with trembling, and shut her best soul in prison, paying it only hidden visits, that she might be petty enough to please him. In such a crisis as this, some women begin to hate." 42

—contrition: "That energy that would animate a crime is not more than is wanted to inspire a resolved submission, when the noble habit of the soul reasserts itself. That thought with which Dorothea had gone out to meet her husband—her conviction that he had been asking about the possible arrest of all his work, and that the answer must have wrung his heart, could not be long without rising beside the image of him, like a shadowy monitor looking at her anger with sad remonstrance. It cost her a litany of pictured sorrows and of silent cries that she might be the mercy for those sorrows—but the resolved submission did come; and when the house was still, and she knew that it was near the time when Mr Casaubon habitually went to rest, she opened her door gently and stood outside in the darkness waiting for his coming upstairs with a light in his hand . . . .

" 'Dorothea!' he said, with a gentle surprise in his tone. 'Were you waiting for me?'

" 'Yes, I did not like to disturb you.'

" 'Come, my dear, come. You are young, and need not to extend your life by watching.'

"When the kind quiet melancholy of that speech fell on Dorothea's ears, she felt something like the thankfulness that might well up in us if we had narrowly escaped hurting a lamed creature. She put her hand into her husband's, and they went along the broad corridor together." 42

—calling: "Let those who know, tell us exactly what stuff it was that Dorothea wore in those days of mild autumn—that thin white woollen stuff soft to the touch and soft to the eye. It always seems to have been lately washed, and to smell of the sweet hedges—was always in the shape of a pelisse with sleeves hanging all out of the fashion . . . the grace and dignity were in her limbs and neck; and about her simply parted hair and candid eyes the large round poke which was then in the fate of women, seemed no more odd as a head-dress than the gold trencher we call a halo." 43

—dilemma: "She was always trying to be what her husband wished, and never able to repose on his delight in what she was. The thing that she liked, that she spontaneously cared to have, seemed to be always excluded from her life; for if it was only granted and not shared by her husband it might as well have been denied." 48

—ominous prospect: "She longed for work which would be directly beneficent like the sunshine and the rain, and now it appeared that she was to live more and more in a virtual tomb, where there was the apparatus of a ghastly labour producing what would never see the light." 48

—*integrity:* "It was a proof of the force with which certain characteristics in Dorothea impressed those around her, that her husband, with all his jealousy and suspicion, had gathered implicit trust in the integrity of her promises, and her power of devoting herself to her idea of the right and best. Of late he had begun to feel that these qualities were a peculiar possession for himself, and he wanted to engross them." 48

—*disillusioned:* "The poor child had become altogether disbelieving as to the trustworthiness of that Key which had made the ambition and the labour of her husband's life. It was not wonderful that, in spite of her small instruction, her judgment in this matter was truer than his: for she looked with unbiassed comparison and healthy sense at probabilities on which he had risked all his egoism." 48

—*asked to promise—what?* " . . . she simply felt that she was going to say 'Yes' to her own doom: she was too weak, too full of dread at the thought of inflicting a keen-edged blow on her husband, to do anything but submit completely . . . .

"She saw clearly enough the whole situation, yet she was fettered: she could not smite the stricken soul that entreated hers. If that were weakness, Dorothea was weak." 48

—*ready to promise:* "She went into the summer-house and said, 'I am come, **Edward**; I am ready.'

"He took no notice, and she thought that he must be fast asleep. She laid her hand on his shoulder, and repeated, 'I am ready!' Still he was motionless, and with a sudden confused fear, she leaned down to him, took off his velvet cap, and leaned her cheek close to his head, crying in a distressed tone,

" 'Wake, dear, wake! Listen to me. I am come to answer.'

"But Dorothea never gave her answer." 48

"Later in the day **Lydgate** was seated by her bedside, and she was talking deliriously, thinking aloud, and recalling what had gone through her mind the night before. She knew him, and called him by his name, but appeared to think it right that she should explain everything to him; and again, and again, begged him to explain everything to her husband.

" 'Tell him I shall go to him soon: I am ready to promise. Only, thinking about it was so dreadful—it has made me ill. Not very ill. I shall soon be better. Go and tell him.'

"But the silence in her husband's ear was never more to be broken." 48

Dorothea widowed

—*galvanized by shock:* "She might have compared her experience at that moment to the vague, alarmed consciousness that her life was taking on a new form, that she was undergoing a metamorphosis in which memory would not adjust itself to the stirring of new organs. Everything was changing its aspects: her husband's conduct, her own duteous feeling towards him, every struggle between them—and yet more, her whole relation to **Will Ladislaw**. Her world was in a state of convulsive change; the only thing she could say distinctly to herself was, that she must wait and think anew. One change terrified her as if it had been a sin; it was a violent shock of repulsion from her departed husband, who had had hidden thoughts, perhaps perverting everything she said and did. Then again she was conscious of another change which also made her tremulous; it was a sudden strange yearning of heart towards Will Ladislaw. It had never before entered her mind that he could, under any circumstances, be her lover; conceive the effect of the sudden revelation that another had thought of him in that light—that perhaps he himself had been conscious of such a possibility—and this with the hurrying crowding vision of unfitting conditions, and questions not soon to be solved." 50

—*a new point of view:* "... her judgment, instead of being controlled by duteous devotion, was made active by the embittering discovery that in her past union there had lurked the hidden alienation of secrecy and suspicion. The living, suffering man was no longer before her to awaken her pity: there remained only the retrospect of painful subjection to a husband whose thoughts had been lower than she had believed, whose exorbitant claims for himself had even blinded his scrupulous care for his own character, and made him defeat his own pride by shocking men of ordinary honour." 50

—*choices:* "Mr Casaubon had taken a cruelly effective means of hindering her: even with indignation against him in her heart, any act that seemed a triumphant eluding of his purpose revolted her." 50

GE neglects to provide a codicil mechanism to enforce its terms: a trust with named trustees to act if Dorothea marries Ladislaw. And there is no explanation of what will become of the estate if she does so. (Will appears to be the only living relative.) Nor does she anywhere address the issue of the original marriage settlements and the enforceability of this contravening provision. A single sentence disposes of the problem but explains nothing. See II:300

—*promulgation of religion:* " 'I have always been thinking of the different ways in which Christianity is taught, and whenever I find one way that makes it a wider blessing than any other, I cling to that as the truest—I mean that which takes in the most good of all kinds, and brings in the most people as sharers in it. It is surely better to pardon too much, than to condemn too much.' " 50

—*power:* " 'So far as self is concerned, I think it would be easier to give up power and money than to keep them. It seems very unfitting that I should have this patronage, yet I felt that I ought not to let it be used by some one else instead of me.' " 52

—*pity:* "The pity which had been the restraining compelling motive in her life with him still clung about [**Casaubon**'s] image, even while she remonstrated with him in indignant thought and told him that he was unjust. . . .

"The silent colloquy was perhaps only the more earnest because underneath and through it all there was always the deep longing which had really determined her to come to Lowick. The longing was to see **Will Ladislaw**." 54

—*the parting:* "In Dorothea, still in that time of youth when the eyes with their long full lashes look out after their rain of tears unsoiled and unwearied as a freshly-opened passion-flower, that morning's parting with **Will Ladislaw** seemed to be the close of their personal relations. He was going away into the distance of unknown years, and if ever he came back he would be another man. . . . Their young delight in speaking to each other, and saying what no one else would care to hear, was for ever ended, and become a treasure of the past. For this very reason she dwelt on it without inward check. That unique happiness too was dead, and in its shadowed silent chamber she might vent the passionate grief which she herself wondered at." 55

Will Ladislaw calls upon the Widow

—*ignorant resolve:* "She did not know then that it was Love who had come to her briefly, as in a dream before awaking, with the hues of morning on his wings—that it was Love to whom she was sobbing her farewell as his image was banished by the blameless rigour of irresistible day. She only felt that there was something irrevocably amiss and lost in her lot, and her thoughts about the future were the more readily shapen into resolve. Ardent souls, ready to construct their coming lives, are apt to commit themselves to the fulfilment of their own visions." 55

—*unexpectedly:* "As **Mrs Kell** closed the door behind her they met: each was looking at the other, and consciousness was overflowed by something that suppressed utterance. It was not confusion that kept them silent, for they both felt that parting was near, and there is no shamefacedness in a sad parting.

" . . . she had been used, when they were face to face, always to feel confidence and the happy freedom which comes with mutual understanding, and how could other people's words hinder that effect on a sudden? Let the music which can take possession of our frame and fill the air with joy for us, sound once more—what does it signify that we heard it found fault with in its absence?" 62

—*speech frozen:* "She was ready to say that it was as hard on her as on him, and that she was helpless; but those strange particulars of their relation which neither of them could explicitly mention kept her always in dread of saying too much . . . .

" . . . What could he say, since what had got obstinately uppermost in his mind was the passionate love for her which he forbade himself to utter? What could she say, since she might offer him no help—since she was forced to keep the money that ought to have been his?—since to-day he seemed not to respond as he used to do to her thorough trust and liking?" 62

—*Will's slip of the tongue:* "She sank into the chair, and for a few moments sat like a statue, while images and emotions were hurrying upon her. Joy came first, in spite of the threatening train behind it—joy in the impression that it was really herself whom **Will** loved and was renouncing, that there was really no other love less permissible, more blameworthy, which honour was hurrying him away from. They were parted all the same, but—Dorothea drew a deep breath and felt her strength return—she could think of him unrestrainedly. At that moment the parting was easy to bear: the first sense of loving and being loved excluded sorrow. It was as if some hard icy pressure had melted, and her consciousness had room to expand: her past was come back to her with larger interpretation. The joy was not the less—perhaps it was the more complete just then—because of the irrevocable parting; for there was no reproach, no contemptuous wonder to imagine in any eye or from any lips. He had acted so as to defy reproach, and make wonder respectful." 62

—*eager to vindicate:* "She disliked this cautious weighing of consequences, instead of an ardent faith in efforts of justice and mercy, which would conquer by their emotional force . . . .

" 'What do we live for, if it is not to make life less difficult to each other? I cannot be indifferent to the troubles of a man who advised me in *my* trouble, and attended me in my illness.' " 72

—her purity: "Nothing could have seemed more irrelevant to Dorothea than insistence on her youth and sex when she was moved to show her human fellowship." 76

—declaration to one under a cloud: " 'I know the unhappy mistakes about you. I knew them from the first moment to be mistakes. You have never done anything vile. You would not do anything dishonourable . . . .

" 'It is wicked to let people think evil of any one falsely, when it can be hindered.' " 76

—the dream: " 'So you see that what I should most rejoice at would be to have something good to do with my money: I should like it to make other people's lives better to them. It makes me very uneasy—coming all to me who don't want it.'

"A smile broke through the gloom of **Lydgate**'s face. The childlike grave-eyed earnestness with which Dorothea said all this was irresistible—blent into an adorable whole with her ready understanding of high experience. (Of lower experience such as plays a great part in the world, poor Mrs Casaubon had a very blurred shortsighted knowledge, little helped by her imagination.)" 76

—appraised: " 'This young creature has a heart large enough for the Virgin Mary. She evidently thinks nothing of her own future, and would pledge away half her income at once, as if she wanted nothing for herself but a chair to sit in from which she can look down with those clear eyes at the poor mortals who pray to her. She seems to have what I never saw in any woman before—a fountain of friendship towards men—a man can make a friend of her." 76

—no rival: "Dorothea, believing in **Will**'s love for her, believing with a proud delight in his delicate sense of honour and his determination that no one should impeach him justly, felt her heart quite at rest as to the regard he might have for **Mrs Lydgate**. She was sure that the regard was blameless." 77

—power in her trust: " . . . her own passionate faults lay along the easily-counted upon channels of her ardent character; and while she was full of pity for the visible mistakes of others, she had not yet any material within her experience for subtle constructions and suspicions of hidden wrong. But that simplicity of hers, holding up an ideal for others in her believing conception of them, was one of the great powers of her womanhood . . . . " 77

—a future with him? "She entertained no visions of their ever coming into nearer union, and yet she had taken no posture of renunciation. She had accepted her whole relation to **Will** very simply as part of her marriage sorrows, and would have thought it very sinful in her to keep up an inward wail because she was not completely happy . . . . " 77

—a future without him: " . . . any one looking at her might have thought that though she was paler than usual she was never animated by a more self-possessed energy. And that was really her experience. It was as if she had drunk a great draught of scorn that stimulated her beyond the susceptibility to other feelings. She had seen something so far below her belief, that her emotions rushed back from it and made an excited throng without an object. She needed something active to turn her excitement out upon. She felt power to walk and work for a day, without meat or drink . . . . She had never felt anything like this triumphant power of indignation in the struggle of her married life . . . . " 77

With the man she loves

—*purgatory endured: see Topicon* LM:Love—*purgatory endured*

—*hearing better news:* "The revulsion of feeling in Dorothea was too strong to be called joy. It was a tumult in which the terrible strain of the night and morning made a resistant pain—she could only perceive that this would be joy when she had recovered her power of feeling it." 81

—*superfluous energy:* "What was there to be done in the village? O dear! nothing. Everybody was well and had flannel, nobody's pig had died; and it was Saturday morning, when there was a general scrubbing of floors and door-stones, and when it was useless to go into the school." 83

—*a new step:* " 'Don't be sorry,' said Dorothea, in her clear tender tones. 'I would rather share all the trouble of our parting.'

"Her lips trembled and so did his. It was never known which lips were the first to move towards the other lips; but they kissed tremblingly, and then they moved apart." 83

—*he says good-bye:* " 'Oh, I cannot bear it—my heart will break,' said Dorothea, starting from her seat, the flood of her young passion bearing down all the obstructions which had kept her silent—the great tears rising and falling in an instant: 'I don't mind about poverty—I hate my wealth.'

"In an instant **Will** was close to her and had his arms round her, but she drew her head back and held his arms gently that she might go on speaking, her large tear-filled eyes looking at his very simply, while she said in a sobbing childlike way, 'We could live quite well on my own fortune—it is too much— seven hundred a year—I want so little—no new clothes—and I will learn what everything costs.' " 83

—*envoi:* "Her finely-touched spirit had still its fine issues, though they were not widely visible. Her full nature . . . spent itself in channels which had no great name on the earth. But the effect of her being on those around her was incalculably diffusive: for the growing good of the world is partly dependent on unhistoric acts; and that things are not so ill with you and me as they might have been, is half owing to the number who lived faithfully a hidden life, and rest in unvisited tombs." *Finale*

Rev. Edward Casaubon, "noted in the county as a man of profound learning, understood for many years to be engaged on a great work concerning religious history; also as a man of wealth enough to give lustre to his piety, and having views of his own which were to be more clearly ascertained on the publication of his book. His very name carried an impressiveness hardly to be measured without a precise chronology of scholarship." 1

—*manners:* "His manners, [**Dorothea**] thought, were very dignified; the set of his iron-grey hair and his deep eye-sockets made him resemble the portrait of **Locke**. He had the spare form and the pale complexion which became a student; as different as possible from the blooming Englishman of the red-whiskered type represented by **Sir James Chettam**." 2

—*conversation:* "He delivered himself with precision, as if he had been called upon to make a public statement; and the balanced sing-song neatness of his speech, occasionally corresponded to by a movement of his head, was the more conspicuous from its contrast with good **Mr Brooke**'s scrappy slovenliness. **Dorothea** said to herself that Mr Casaubon was the most interesting man she had ever seen . . . . " 2

—*elocution:* "And he delivered this statement with as much careful precision as if he had been a diplomatic envoy whose words would be attended with results. Indeed, Mr Casaubon was not used to expect that he should have to repeat or revise his communications of a practical or personal kind. The inclinations which he had deliberately stated on the 2d of October he would think it enough to refer to by the mention of that date; judging by the standard of his own memory, which was a volume where a *vide supra* could serve instead of repetitions, and not the ordinary long-used blotting-book which only tells of forgotten writing." 3

—discourse: "Mr Casaubon seemed even unconscious that trivialities existed, and never handed round that small-talk of heavy men which is as acceptable as stale bride-cake brought forth with an odour of cup-board. He talked of what he was interested in, or else he was silent and bowed with sad civility." *3*

—proposal of marriage: see Topicon LM:Courtship*—proposal of marriage*

—pleased: "Mr Casaubon was touched with an unknown delight (what man would not have been?) at [**Dorothea**'s] childlike unrestrained ardour: he was not surprised (what lover would have been?) that he should be the object of it." 5

" 'Hitherto I have known few pleasures save of the severer kind: my satisfactions have been those of the solitary student. I have been little disposed to gather flowers that would wither in my hand, but now I shall pluck them with eagerness, to place them in your bosom.'

"No speech could have been more thoroughly honest in its intention: the frigid rhetoric at the end was as sincere as the bark of a dog, or the cawing of an amorous rook." 5

—surprise: "[He had] made up his mind that it was now time for him to adorn his life with the graces of female companionship, to irradiate the gloom which fatigue was apt to hang over the intervals of studious labour with the play of female fancy, and to secure in this, his culminating age, the solace of female tendance for his declining years. Hence he determined to abandon himself to the stream of feeling, and perhaps was surprised to find what an exceedingly shallow rill it was. As in droughty regions baptism by immersion could only be performed symbolically, so Mr Casaubon found that sprinkling was the utmost approach to a plunge which his stream would afford him; and he concluded that the poets had much exaggerated the force of masculine passion. . . . there was clearly no reason to fall back upon but the exaggerations of human tradition." 7 *Is GE speaking in code? The metaphor is daringly apt.*

—appraised: " 'He is very good to his poor relations, pensions several of the women, and is educating a young fellow at a good deal of expense. [He] acts up to his sense of justice. His mother's sister made a bad match—a Pole, I think—lost herself—at any rate was disowned by her family. If it had not been for that, Casaubon would not have had so much money by half. I believe he went himself to find out his cousins, and see what he could do for them. Every man would not ring so well as that, if you tried his metal.' " 8

—not to be prejudged: "I protest against any absolute conclusion, any prejudice derived from **Mrs Cadwallader**'s contempt for a neighbouring clergyman's alleged greatness of soul, or **Sir James Chettam**'s poor opinion of his rival's legs—from **Mr Brooke**'s failure to elicit a companion's ideas, or from **Celia**'s criticism of a middle-aged scholar's personal appearance. I am not sure that the greatest man of his age, if ever that solitary superlative existed, could escape these unfavourable reflections of himself in various small

mirrors, and even **Milton**, looking for his portrait in a spoon, must submit to have the facial angle of a bumpkin. Moreover, if Mr Casaubon, speaking for himself, has rather a chilling rhetoric, it is not therefore certain that there is no good work or fine feeling in him." 10

—the inner man: "Suppose we turn from outside estimates of a man, to wonder, with keener interest, what is the report of his own consciousness about his doings or capacity: with what hindrances he is carrying on his daily labours; what fading of hopes, or what deeper fixity of self-delusion the years are marking off within him; and with what spirit he wrestles against universal pressure, which will one day be too heavy for him, and bring his heart to its final pause. Doubtless his lot is important in his own eyes; and the chief reason that we think he asks too large a place in our consideration must be our want of room for him, since we refer him to the Divine regard with perfect confidence; nay, it is even held sublime for our neighbour to expect the utmost there, however little he may have got from us. Mr Casaubon, too, was the center of his own world; if he was liable to think that others were providentially made for him, and especially to consider them in the light of their fitness for the author of a 'Key to all Mythologies,' this trait is not quite alien to us, and, like the other mendicant hopes of mortals, claims some of our pity." 10

—apprehension: "For in truth, as the day fixed for his marriage came nearer, Mr Casaubon did not find his spirits rising; nor did the contemplation of that matrimonial garden-scene, where, as all experience showed, the path was to be bordered with flowers, prove persistently more enchanting to him than the accustomed vaults where he walked taper in hand. He did not confess to himself, still less could he have breathed to another, his surprise that though he had won a lovely and noble-hearted girl he had not won delight—which he had also regarded as an object to be found by search. It is true that he knew all the classical passages implying the contrary; but knowing classical passages, we find, is a mode of motion, which explains why they leave so little extra force for their personal application." 10

—disillusion: "Poor Mr Casaubon had imagined that his long studious bachelorhood had stored up for him a compound interest of enjoyment, and that large drafts on his affections would not fail to be honoured . . . . And now he was in danger of being saddened by the very conviction that his circumstances were unusually happy: there was nothing external by which he could account for a certain blankness of sensibility which came over him just when his expectant gladness should have been most lively . . . . " 10

—lonely: "Here was a weary experience in which he was as utterly condemned to loneliness as in the despair which sometimes threatened him while toiling in the morass of authorship without seeming nearer to the goal. And his was that worst loneliness which would shrink from sympathy." 10

—no deceiver: " . . . no man was more incapable of flashy make-believe than Mr Casaubon: he was as genuine a character as any ruminant animal, and he had not actively assisted in creating any illusions about himself." 20

—his mind: "How was it that in the weeks since her marriage, Dorothea had not distinctly observed but felt with a stifling depression, that the large vistas and wide fresh air which she had dreamed of finding in her husband's mind were replaced by anterooms and winding passages which seemed to lead nowhither . . . . Having once embarked on your marital voyage, it is impossible not to be aware that you make no way and that the sea is not within sight—that, in fact, you are exploring an enclosed basin." 20

—*enthusiast—not:* " 'Should you like to go to the Farnesina, Dorothea? It contains celebrated frescoes designed or painted by **Raphael**, which most persons think it worth while to visit.'

"But do you care about them?' was always Dorothea's question.

" 'They are, I believe, highly esteemed . . . it you like these wall-paintings we can easily drive thither; and you will then, I think, have seen the chief works of Raphael, any of which it were a pity to omit in a visit to Rome. He is the painter who has been held to combine the most complete grace of form with sublimity of expression. Such at least I have gathered to be the opinion of cognoscenti.' " 20

—*enthusiasm—abortive:* "On other subjects indeed Mr Casaubon showed a tenacity of occupation and an eagerness which are usually regarded as the effect of enthusiasm . . . . Poor Mr Casaubon himself was lost among small closets and winding stairs, and in an agitated dimness about the Cabeiri [Samothracian fertility gods], or in an exposure of other mythologists' ill-considered parallels, easily lost sight of any purpose which had prompted him to these labours. With his taper stuck before him he forgot the absence of windows, and in bitter manuscript remarks on other men's notions about the solar deities, he had become indifferent to the sunlight." 20

—*reaction to feminine demonstrativeness:* " . . . pronouncing her, with his unfailing propriety, to be of a most affectionate and truly feminine nature, indicating at the same time by politely reaching a chair for her that he regarded these manifestations as rather crude and startling. Having made his clerical toilette with due care in the morning, he was prepared only for those amenities of life which were suited to the well-adjusted stiff cravat of the period, and to a mind weighted with unpublished matter." 20

—*achievement:* "He had not found marriage a rapturous state, but he had no idea of being anything else than an irreproachable husband, who would make a charming young woman as happy as she deserved to be." 20

—*threatened:* " 'All those rows of volumes—will you not now do what you used to speak of?—will you not make up your mind what part of them you will use, and begin to write the book which will make your vast knowledge useful to the world?' . . . Dorothea, in a most unaccountable, darkly-feminine manner, ended with a slight sob and eyes full of tears.

"The excessive feeling manifested would alone have been highly disturbing to Mr Casaubon, but there were other reasons why Dorothea's words were among the most cutting and irritating to him that she could have been impelled to use . . . . In Mr Casaubon's ear, Dorothea's voice gave loud emphatic iteration to those muffled suggestions of consciousness which it was possible to explain as mere fancy, the illusion of exaggerated sensitiveness: always when such suggestions are unmistakably repeated from without, they are resisted as cruel and unjust . . . . And this cruel outward accuser was there in the shape of a wife—nay, of a young bride, who instead of observing his abundant pen-scratches and amplitude of paper with the uncritical awe of an elegant-minded canary-bird, seemed to present herself as a spy watching everything with a malign power of interference. Here, towards this particular point of the compass, Mr Casaubon had a sensitiveness to match Dorothea's, and an equal quickness to imagine more than the fact." 20

—*riposte:* "For the first time since Dorothea had known him, Mr Casaubon's face had a quick angry flush upon it.

More wife than he had bargained for

" 'My love,' he said, with irritation reined in by propriety, 'you may rely upon me for knowing the times and the seasons, adapted to the different stages of a work which is not to be measured by the facile conjectures of ignorant onlookers. It had been easy for me to gain a temporary effect by a mirage of baseless opinion; but it is ever the trial of the scrupulous explorer to be saluted with the impatient scorn of chatterers who attempt only the smallest achievements, being indeed equipped for no other . . . .

"This speech was delivered with an energy and readiness quite unusual with Mr Casaubon. It was not indeed entirely an improvisation, but had taken shape in inward colloquy, and rushed out like the round grains from a fruit when sudden heat cracks it." 20

—*unpleasant surprise:* " . . . this charming young bride not only obliged him to much consideration on her behalf (which he had sedulously given), but turned out to be capable of agitating him cruelly just where he most needed soothing. Instead of getting a soft fence against the cold, shadowy, unapplausive audience of his life, had he only given it a more substantial presence?" 20

—*seeing his cousin:* "Mr Casaubon felt a surprise which was quite unmixed with pleasure . . . . " 21

—*jealousy:* " . . . he was too proud to betray that jealousy of disposition which was not so exhausted on his scholarly compeers that there was none to spare in other directions." 21

—*humanity:* "In spite of the blinking eyes and white moles objectionable to Celia, and the want of muscular curve which was morally painful to Sir James, Mr Casaubon had an intense consciousness within him, and was spiritually a-hungered like the rest of us." 29

—*marital choice:* "It had occurred to him that he must not any longer defer his intention of matrimony, and he had reflected that in taking a wife, a man of good position should expect and carefully choose a blooming young lady—the younger the better, because more educable and submissive—of a rank equal to his own, of religious principles, virtuous disposition, and good understanding. On such a young lady he would make handsome settlements, and he would neglect no arrangement for her happiness: in return, he should receive family pleasures and leave behind him that copy of himself which seemed so urgently required of a man—to the sonneteers of the sixteenth century." 29

—*goal to reach:* "Times had altered since then, and no sonneteer had insisted on Mr Casaubon's leaving a copy of himself: moreover, he had not yet succeeded in issuing copies of his mythological key; but he had always intended to acquit himself by marriage, and the sense that he was fast leaving the years behind him, that the world was getting dimmer and that he felt lonely, was a reason to him for losing no more time in overtaking domestic delights before they too were left behind by the years." 29

—*a burden:* "(Mr Casaubon was nervously conscious that he was expected to manifest a powerful mind.) . . . A wife, a modest young lady, with the purely appreciative, unambitious abilities of her sex, is sure to think her husband's mind powerful." 29

—*vitality missing:* "He had not had much foretaste of happiness in his previous life. To know intense joy without a strong bodily frame, one must have an enthusiastic soul. Mr Casaubon had never had a strong bodily frame, and his soul was sensitive without being enthusiastic: it was too languid to thrill out of self-consciousness into passionate delight; it went on fluttering in the swampy ground where it was hatched, thinking of its wings and never flying." 29

—scruples: "His experience was of that pitiable kind which shrinks from pity, and fears most of all that it should be known: it was that proud narrow sensitiveness which has not mass enough to spare for transformation into sympathy, and quivers thread-like in small currents of self-preoccupation or at best of an egoistic scrupulosity. And Mr Casaubon had many scruples: he was capable of a severe self-restraint; he was resolute in being a man of honour according to the code; he would be unimpeachable by any recognised opinion." 29

—hurt pride: "[He was] bitterly convinced that his old acquaintance **Carp** had been the writer of that depreciatory recension which was kept locked in a small drawer of Mr Casaubon's desk, and also in a dark closet of his verbal memory." 29

—pitiable: "For my part I am very sorry for him. It is an uneasy lot at best, to be what we call highly taught and yet not to enjoy: to be present at this great spectacle of life and never to be liberated from a small hungry shivering self—never to be fully possessed by the glory we behold, never to have our consciousness rapturously transformed into the vividness of a thought, the ardour of a passion, the energy of an action, but always to be scholarly and uninspired, ambitious and timid, scrupulous and dimsighted. Becoming a dean or even a bishop would make little difference, I fear, to Mr Casaubon's uneasiness." 29

—diversion: "[He] had slipped again into the library to chew a cud of erudite mistake about Cush and Mizraim." 34

—uneasy: "He had disliked **Will** while he helped him, but he had begun to dislike him still more now that Will had declined his help. That is the way with us when we have any uneasy jealousy in our disposition: if our talents are chiefly of the burrowing kind, our honey-sipping cousin (whom we have grave reasons for objecting to) is likely to have a secret contempt for us, and any one who admires him passes an oblique criticism on ourselves. Having the scruples of rectitude in our souls, we are above the meanness of injuring him—rather we meet all his claims on us by active benefits; and the drawing of cheques for him, being a superiority which he must recognise, gives our bitterness a milder infusion. Now Mr Casaubon had been deprived of that superiority (as anything more than a remembrance) in a sudden, capricious manner. His antipathy to Will did not spring from the common jealousy of a winter-worn husband: it was something deeper, bred by his lifelong claims and discontents; but **Dorothea**, now that she was present—Dorothea, as a young wife who herself had shown an offensive capability of criticism, necessarily gave concentration to the uneasiness which had before been vague." 37

—insecurity and mistrust: "Poor Mr Casaubon was distrustful of everybody's feeling towards him, especially as a husband. To let any one suppose that he was jealous would be to admit their (suspected) view of his disadvantages: to let them know that he did not find marriage particularly blissful would imply his conversion to their (probably) earlier disapproval. It would be as bad as letting **Carp**, and Brasenose generally, know how backward he was in organizing the matter for his 'Key to all Mythologies.' All through his life Mr Casaubon had been trying not to admit even to himself the inward sores of self-doubt and jealousy. *And on the most delicate of all personal subjects,* the habit of proud suspicious reticence told doubly." *Emphasis added.*

—an abhorrence: " . . . he shrank from pity; and if the suspicion of being pitied for anything in his lot surmised or known in spite of himself was embittering, the idea of calling forth a show of compassion by frankly admitting an alarm or a sorrow was necessarily intolerable to him." 42

—his failure: ". . . there are some kinds of authorship in which by far the largest result is the uneasy susceptibility accumulated in the consciousness of the author—one knows of the river by a few streaks amid a long-gathered deposit of uncomfortable mud. That was the way with Mr Casaubon's hard intellectual labours. Their most characteristic result was not the 'Key to all Mythologies,' but a morbid consciousness that others did not give him the place which he had not demonstrably merited—a perpetual suspicious conjecture that the views entertained of him were not to his advantage—a melancholy absence of passion in his efforts at achievement, and a passionate resistance to the confession that he had achieved nothing." 42

—his wife: "There was no denying that **Dorothea** was as virtuous and lovely a young lady as he could have obtained for a wife; but a young lady turned out to be something more troublesome than he had conceived. She nursed him, she read to him, she anticipated his wants, and was solicitous about his feelings; but there had entered into the husband's mind the certainty that she judged him, and that her wifely devotedness was like a penitential expiation of unbelieving thoughts—was accompanied with a power of comparison by which himself and his doings were seen too luminously as a part of things in general. His discontent passed vapour-like through all her gentle loving manifestations, and clung to that inappreciative world which she had only brought nearer to him.

" . . . To his suspicious interpretation Dorothea's silence now was a suppressed rebellion; a remark from her which he had not in any way anticipated was an assertion of conscious superiority; her gentle answers had an irritating cautiousness in them; and when she acquiesced it was a self-approved effort of forbearance. The tenacity with which he strove to hide this inward drama made it the more vivid for him; as we hear with the more keenness what we wish others not to hear.

"Instead of wondering at this result of misery in Mr Casaubon, I think it quite ordinary. Will not a tiny speck very close to our vision blot out the glory of the world, and leave only a margin by which we see the blot? I know no speck so troublesome as self." 42

—the final nail: " . . . there was a strong reason to be added, which he had not himself taken explicitly into account—namely, that he was not unmixedly adorable. He suspected this, however, as he suspected other things, without confessing it, and like the rest of us, felt how soothing it would have been to have a companion who would never find it out." 42

—dread-full thoughts: "This man has gained **Dorothea**'s ear: he has fascinated her attention . . . . If I die—and he is waiting here on the watch for that—he will persuade her to marry him. That would be calamity for her and success for him . . . . He thinks of an easy conquest and of entering into my nest. That I will hinder! . . . .

"The arrangements made by Mr Casaubon on her marriage left strong measures open to him . . . . " 42 *This is not explained and it is hard to credit unless Brooke was utterly careless and Chettam indifferent—both very unlikely.* See *our discussion at page 410.*

The haunted man is attended in the night

—*aged:* "Lydgate . . . felt some compassion when the figure . . . advancing towards him showed more markedly than ever the signs of premature age—the student's bent shoulders, the emaciated limbs, and the melancholy lines of the mouth." 42

—*portent:* "To a mind largely instructed in the human destiny hardly anything could be more interesting than the inward conflict implied in his formal measured address . . . are there many situations more sublimely tragic than the struggle of the soul with the demand to renounce a work which has been all the significance of its life—a significance which is to vanish as the waters which come and go where no man has need of them?" 42

—*having heard his fate:* "To Mr Casaubon now, it was as if he suddenly found himself on the dark river-brink and heard the plash of the oncoming oar, not discerning the forms, but expecting the summons. In such an hour the mind does not change its lifelong bias, but carries it onward in imagination to the other side of death, gazing backward—perhaps with the divine calm of beneficence, perhaps with the petty anxieties of self-assertion. What was Mr Casaubon's bias his acts will give us a clue to. He held himself to be, with some private scholarly reservations, a believing Christian, as to estimates of the present and hopes of the future. But what we strive to gratify, though we may call it a distant hope, is an immediate desire: the future estate for which men drudge up city alleys exists already in their imagination and love. And Mr Casaubon's immediate desire was not for divine communion and light divested of earthly conditions; his passionate longings, poor man, clung low and mist-like in very shady places." 42

—*his wife—again:* "Then she went towards him, and might have represented a heaven-sent angel coming with a promise that the short hours remaining should yet be filled with that faithful love which clings the closer to a comprehended grief. His glance in reply to hers was so chill that she felt her timidity increased; yet she turned and passed her hand through his arm.

"Mr Casaubon kept his hands behind him and allowed her pliant arm to cling with difficulty against his right arm." 42

"You may ask why, in the name of manliness, Mr Casaubon should have behaved in that way. Consider that his was a mind which shrank from pity. Have you ever watched in such a mind the effect of a suspicion that what is pressing it as a grief may be really a source of contentment, either actual or future, to the being who already offends by pitying?" 42

"But Mr Casaubon's theory of the elements which made the seed of all tradition was not likely to bruise itself unawares against discoveries: it floated among flexible conjectures no more solid than those etymologies which seemed strong because of likeness in sound until it was shown that likeness in sound made them impossible: it was a method of interpretation which was not tested by the necessity of forming anything which had sharper collisions than an elaborate notion of God and Magog: it was as free from interruption as a plan for threading the stars together." 48

—*pitiable:* "And here Dorothea's pity turned from her own future to her husband's past—nay, to his present hard struggle with a lot which had grown out of that past: the lonely labour, the ambition breathing hardly under the pressure of self-distrust; the goal receding, and the heavier limbs, and now at last the sword visibly trembling above him." 48

* *

Celia (**Kitty** to her sister; 50) **Brooke**. "Celia wore scarcely more trimmings; and it was only to close observers that her dress differed from her sister's, and had a shade of coquetry in its arrangements . . . . " 1

—in awe: "Celia's face had the shadow of a pouting expression in it, the full presence of the pout being kept back by an habitual awe of Dorothea and principle; two associated facts which might show a mysterious electricity if you touched them incautiously." 1

"Since they could remember, there had been a mixture of criticism and awe in the attitude of Celia's mind towards her elder sister. The younger had always worn a yoke; but is there any yoked creature without its private opinions?" 1

—not impressed: " 'He is remarkably like the portrait of **Locke**. He has the same deep eye-sockets' [said **Dorothea**].

" 'Had Locke those two white moles with hairs on them?' " 2

—reticent: " 'I cannot bear notions.'

"It was Celia's private luxury to indulge in this dislike. She dared not confess it to her sister in any direct statement, for that would be laying herself open to a demonstration that she was somehow or other at war with all goodness. But on safe opportunities, she had an indirect mode of making her negative wisdom tell upon **Dorothea** and calling her down from her rhapsodic mood by reminding her that people were staring, not listening. Celia was not impulsive: what she had to say could wait, and came from her always with the same quiet, staccato evenness. When people talked with energy and emphasis she watched their faces and features merely. She never could understand how well-bred persons consented to sing and open their mouths in the ridiculous manner required for that vocal exercise." 3

—equable: "It had been her nature when a child never to quarrel with any one—only to observe with wonder that they quarrelled with her, and looked like turkey-cocks; whereupon she was ready to play at cat's cradle with them whenever they recovered themselves." 5

—alert: "She was seldom taken by surprise . . . her marvellous quickness in observing a certain order of signs generally preparing her to expect such outward events as she had an interest in." 5

—stinging: ". . . . Celia's small and rather gutteral voice speaking in its usual tone . . . .

" 'I hope there is some one else. Then I shall not hear [**Mr Casaubon**] eat his soup so.'

" 'What is there remarkable about his soup-eating?'

" 'Really, Dodo, can't you hear how he scrapes his spoon? And he always blinks before he speaks. I don't know whether **Locke** blinked, but I'm sure I am sorry for those who sat opposite to him if he did.' " 5

—hearing news: " 'It is right to tell you, Celia, that I am engaged to marry Mr Casaubon.'

"Perhaps Celia had never turned so pale before. The paper man she was making would have had his leg injured, but for her habitual care of whatever she held in her hands. She laid the fragile figure down at once, and sat perfectly still for a few moments. When she spoke there was a tear gathering.

Celia

" 'O Dodo, I hope you will be happy.' Her sisterly tenderness could not but surmount other feelings at this moment, and her fears were the fears of affection." 5

—*an intimation:* " 'Only,' Celia added, with a slight blush (she sometimes seemed to blush as she breathed) I don't think he [**Chettam**] would have suited **Dorothea**.' " 6

—*dispassion:* "Celia, whose mind had never been thought too powerful, saw the emptiness of other people's pretensions much more readily [than **Dorothea**]. To have in general but little feeling, seems to be the only security against feeling too much on any particular occasion." 7

—*predilection:* " . . . **Sir James**, who talked so agreeably, always about things which had common-sense in them, and not about learning! Celia had those light young feminine tastes which grave and weather-worn gentlemen sometimes prefer in a wife; but happily **Mr Casaubon**'s bias had been different, for he would have had no chance with Celia." 9

—*touchy:* "[She] immediately dropped backward a little, because she could not bear Mr **Casaubon** to blink at her." 9

—*with news:* "Celia's colour changed again and again—seemed

'To come and go with tidings from the heart,
As it a running messenger had been.'

It must mean more than Celia's blushing usually did.

" 'It was because you went away, Dodo. Then there was nobody but me for Sir James to talk to,' said Celia, with a certain roguishness in her eyes." 28

—*concern:* " 'Shall you be glad to see him?'

" 'Of course I shall. How can you ask me?'

" 'Only I was afraid you would be getting so learned,' said Celia, regarding **Mr Casaubon**'s learning as a kind of damp which might in due time saturate a neighbouring body." 28

Celia Chettam

—*with a baby:* "Celia felt her advantage, and was determined to use it. None of them knew **Dodo** as well as she did, or knew how to manage her. Since Celia's baby was born, she had had a new sense of her mental solidity and calm wisdom. It seemed clear that where there was a baby, things were right enough, and that error, in general, was a mere lack of that central poising force." 50

—*her sister leaving:* " . . . in her quiet unemphatic way [she] shot off a needle-arrow of sarcasm." 54

—*sure of her influence:* "All through their girlhood she had felt that she could act on her sister by a word judiciously placed—by opening a little window for the daylight of her own understanding to enter among the strange coloured lamps by which Dodo habitually saw. And Celia the matron naturally felt more able to advise her childless sister. How could any one understand Dodo so well as Celia did, or love her so tenderly?" 84

There is nothing like a baby

Sir James Chettam. "He thought it probable that **Miss Brooke** liked him . . . . She was thoroughly charming to him, but of course he theorised a little about his attachment. He was made of excellent human dough, and had the rare merit of knowing that his talents, even if let loose, would not set the smallest stream in the country on fire: hence he liked the prospect of a wife to whom he could say, 'What shall we do?' about this or that, who could help her husband out with reasons, and would also have the property qualification for doing so . . . . In short, he felt himself to be in love in the right place, and was ready to endure a great deal of predominance, which, after all, a man could always put down when he liked." 2

—oblivious: "He was not in the least jealous of the interest with which **Dorothea** had looked up at **Mr Casaubon**: it never occurred to him that a girl to whom he was meditating an offer of marriage could care for a dried bookworm towards fifty, except, indeed, in a religious sort of way, as for a clergyman of some distinction." 2

—his choice: "[He] said to himself that the second **Miss Brooke** was certainly very agreeable as well as pretty, though not, as some people pretended, more clever and sensible than the elder sister. He felt that he had chosen the one who was in all respects the superior; and a man naturally likes to look forward to having the best." 2

—his readiness: "He came much oftener than **Mr Casaubon**, and **Dorothea** ceased to find him disagreeable since he showed himself so entirely in earnest; for he had already entered with much practical ability into **Lovegood**'s estimates, and was charmingly docile." 3

—disappointed: "Perhaps his face had never before gathered so much concentrated disgust as when he turned to **Mrs Cadwallader** and repeated, '**Casaubon**?' . . .

" 'Good God! It is horrible! He is no better than a mummy!' (The point of view to be allowed for, as that of a blooming and disappointed rival.)" 6

—the opposite sex: "Although Sir James was a sportsman, he had some other feelings towards women than towards grouse and foxes, and did not regard his future wife in the light of prey, valuable chiefly for the excitements of the chase. Neither was he so well acquainted with the habits of primitive races as to feel that an ideal combat for her, tomahawk in hand, so to speak, was necessary to the historical continuity of the marriage-tie." 6

—a certain relief: "He could not help rejoicing that he had never made the offer and been rejected . . . . He really did not like it: giving up Dorothea was very painful to him; but there was something in the resolve to make this visit forthwith and conquer all show of feeling, which was a sort of file-biting and counter-irritant And without his distinctly recognising the impulse, there certainly was present in him the sense that **Celia** would be there, and that he should pay her more attention than he had done before." 6

—mixed feelings: "Of course the forked lightning seemed to pass through him when he first approached [**Dorothea**], and he remained conscious throughout the interview of hiding uneasiness; but, good as he was, it must be owned that his uneasiness was less than it would have been if he thought his rival a brilliant and desirable match. He had no sense of being eclipsed by **Mr Casaubon**; he was only shocked that Dorothea was under a melancholy illusion, and his mortification lost some of its bitterness by being mingled with compassion." 8

—having to explain: "He did not usually find it easy to give his reasons: it seemed to him strange that people should not know them without being told, since he only felt what was reasonable." 8

—chivalrous: "Sir James had long ceased to have any regrets on his own account: his heart was satisfied with his engagement to **Celia**. But he had a chivalrous nature (was not the disinterested service of woman among the ideal glories of old chivalry?): his disregarded love had not turned to bitterness; its death had made sweet odours—floating memories that clung with a consecrating effect to **Dorothea**. He could remain her brotherly friend, interpreting her actions with generous trustfulness." 29

—interrupting: "Indeed, Sir James shrank with so much dislike from the association even in thought of **Dorothea** with **Ladislaw** as her possible lover, that he would himself have wished to avoid an outward show of displeasure which would have recognised the disagreeable possibility . . . . His aversion was all the stronger because he felt himself unable to interfere.

"But Sir James was a power in a way unguessed by himself. Entering at that moment, he was an incorporation of the strongest reasons through which Will's pride became a repellant force, keeping him asunder from Dorothea." 54

—matured: "[He] was no longer the diffident and acquiescent suitor: he was the anxious brother-in-law, with a devout admiration for his sister, but with a constant alarm lest she should fall under some new illusion almost as bad as marrying Casaubon. He smiled much less; when he said 'Exactly' it was more often an introduction to a dissentient opinion than in those submissive bachelor days; and Dorothea found to her surprise that she had to resolve not to be afraid of him—all the more because he was really her best friend." 72

—bad news: "[He] was almost white with anger, but he did not speak . . . .

" 'It would have been better if I had called him out and shot him a year ago,' said Sir James, not from bloody-mindedness, but because he needed something strong to say." 84

—propitiation: " 'But I can cut off the entail, you know. It will cost money and be troublesome; but I can do it, you know.'

" . . . He had touched a motive of which Sir James was ashamed. The mass of his feeling about **Dorothea**'s marriage to **Ladislaw** was due partly to excusable prejudice, or even justifiable opinion, partly to a jealous repugnance hardly less in Ladislaw's case than in **Casaubon**'s. He was convinced that the marriage was a fatal one for Dorothea. But amid that mass ran a vein of which he was too good and honourable a man to like the avowal even to himself: it was undeniable that the union of the two estates—Tipton and Freshitt—lying charmingly within a ring-fence, was a prospect that flattered him for his son and heir. Hence when **Mr Brooke** noddingly appealed to that motive, Sir James felt a sudden embarrassment; there was a stoppage in his throat; he even blushed. He had found more words than usual in the first jet of his anger, but Mr Brooke's propitiation was more clogging to his tongue than **Mr Cadwallader**'s caustic hint." 84

**

Tertius Lydgate "had the medical accomplishment of looking perfectly grave whatever nonsense was talked to him, and his dark steady eyes gave him impressiveness as a listener. He was as little as possible like the lamented **Hicks**, especially in a certain careless refinement about his toilette and utterance. Yet **Lady Chettam** gathered much confidence in him. He confirmed her view of her own constitution as being peculiar, by admitting that all constitutions might be called peculiar, and he did not deny that hers might be more peculiar than others. He did not approve of a too lowering system, including reckless cupping, nor, on the other hand, of incessant port-wine and bark. He said 'I think so' with an air of so much deference accompanying the insight of agreement, that she formed the most cordial opinion of his talents." 10

—smitten: " 'She is grace itself; she is perfectly lovely and accomplished. That is what a woman ought to be: she ought to produce the effect of exquisite music.' Plain women he regarded as he did the other severe facts of life, to be faced with philosophy and investigated by science. But **Rosamond Vincy** seemed to have the true melodic charm . . . . " 11

—fatiguing woman: " . . . Lydgate was disposed to give [adornment] the first place among wifely functions. To his taste . . . . here was the point on which **Miss Brooke** would be found wanting, notwithstanding her undeniable beauty. She did not look at things from the proper feminine angle. The society of such women was about as relaxing as going from your work to teach the second form, instead of reclining in a paradise with sweet laughs for bird-notes, and blue eyes for a heaven." 11

—offending: " 'My liking [said **Mary Garth**] always wants some little kindness to kindle it. I am not magnanimous enough to like people who speak to me without seeming to see me.' " 12

—described: " 'I can give you an inventory: heavy eyebrows, dark eyes, a straight nose, thick dark hair, large solid white hands—and—let me see—oh, an exquisite cambric pocket-handkerchief.' " 12

—voice: "One of the Lydgate's gifts was a voice habitually deep and sonorous, yet capable of becoming very low and gentle at the right moment." 13

—demeanour: "About his ordinary bearing, there was a certain fling, a fearless expectation of success, a confidence in his own powers and dignity much fortified by contempt for petty obstacles or seductions of which he had had no experience. But this proud openness was made lovable by an expression of unaffected good-will." 13

—conviction: " . . . he carried to his studies in London, Edinburgh, and Paris, the conviction that the medical profession as it might be was the finest in the world; presenting the most perfect interchange between science and art; offering the most direct alliance between intellectual conquest and the social good. Lydgate's nature demanded this combination: he was an emotional creature, with a flesh-and-blood sense of fellowship which withstood all the abstractions of special study. He cared not only for 'cases,' but for John and Elizabeth, especially Elizabeth." 15

—goal: "But he did not simply aim at a more genuine kind of practice than was common. He was ambitious of a wider effect: he was fired with the possibility that he might work out the proof of an anatomical conception and make a link in the chain of discovery . . . . Lydgate was ambitious above all to contribute towards enlarging the scientific, rational basis of his profession.

. . . Such was Lydgate's plan of his future: to do good small work for Middlemarch, and great work for the world." 15

—confident: "Lydgate was not blind to the dangers of such friction [cares, distractions, temptations], but he had plenty of confidence in his resolution to avoid it as far as possible: being seven-and-twenty, he felt himself experienced." 15

—reformist: "One of these reforms was to . . . simply prescribe, without dispensing drugs or taking percentage from druggists. This was an innovation for one who had chosen to adopt the style of general practitioner in a country town, and would be felt as offensive criticism by his professional brethren. But Lydgate meant to be innovative in his treatment also, and he was wise enough to see that the best security for his practising honestly according to his belief was to get rid of systematic temptations to the contrary." 15

—flawed humanity: "Among our valued friends is there not some one or other who is a little too self-confident and disdainful; whose distinguished mind is a little spotted with commonness; who is a little pinched here and protuberant there with native prejudices; or whose better energies are liable to lapse down the wrong channel under the influence of transient solicitations? All these things might be alleged against Lydgate, but then, they are the periphrases of a polite preacher, who talks of **Adam**, and would not like to mention anything painful to the pew-renters." 15

—conceit: "Lydgate's conceit was of the arrogant sort, never simpering, never impertinent, but massive in its claims and benevolently contemptuous. He would do a great deal for noodles, being sorry for them, and feeling quite sure that they could have no power over him . . . . All his faults were marked by kindred traits, and were those of a man who had a fine baritone, whose clothes hung well upon him, and who even in his ordinary gestures had an air of inbred distinction." 15

—commonness: "How could there be any commonness in a man so well-bred, so ambitious of social distinction, so generous and unusual in his views of social duty? As easily as there may be stupidity in a man of genius if you take him unawares on the wrong subject, or as many a man who has the best will to advance the social millennium might be ill-inspired in imagining its lighter pleasures; unable to go beyond **Offenbach**'s music, or the brilliant punning in the last burlesque. Lydgate's spots of commonness lay in the complexion of his prejudices, which, in spite of noble intention and sympathy, were half of them such as are found in ordinary men of the world: that distinction of mind which belonged to his intellectual ardour, did not penetrate his feeling and judgment about furniture, or women, or the desirability of its being known (without his telling) that he was better born than other country surgeons. He did not mean to think of furniture at present; but whenever he did so, it was to be feared that neither biology nor schemes of reform would lift him above the vulgarity of feeling that there would be an incompatibility in his furniture not being of the best." 15

—infatuation: "For those who want to be acquainted with Lydgate, it will be good to know what was that case of impetuous folly, for it may stand as an example of the fitful swerving of passion to which he was prone, together with the chivalrous kindness which helped to make him morally lovable." 15 *See* **Madame Laure** O, and the *Topicon* LM:Love—*infatuation*

—aftermath: "He was saved from hardening effects by the abundant kindness of his heart and his belief that human life might be made better. But he had more reason than ever for trusting his judgment, now that it was so experienced; and henceforth he would take a strictly scientific view of woman, entertaining no expectations but such as were justified before hand." 15

—susceptible: "Lydgate was almost forgetting that he must carry on the conversation, in thinking how lovely this creature was, her garment seeming to be made out of the faintest blue sky, herself so immaculately blond, as if the petals of some gigantic flower had just opened and disclosed her; and yet with this infantine blondness showing so much ready, self-possessed grace. Since he had had the memory of **Laure**, Lydgate had lost all taste for large-eyed silence: the divine cow no longer attracted him, and **Rosamond** was her very opposite." 16

"Lydgate felt sure that if ever he married, his wife would have that feminine radiance, that distinctive womanhood which must be classed with flowers and music, that sort of beauty which by its very nature was virtuous, being moulded only for pure and delicate joys." 16

—science and love: "He went home and read far into the smallest hour, bringing a much more testing vision of details and relations into this pathological study than he had ever thought it necessary to apply to the complexities of love and marriage, these being subjects on which he felt himself amply informed by literature, and that traditional wisdom which is handed down in the genial conversation of men." 16

—enthusiasm: "He was an ardent fellow, but at present his ardour was absorbed in love of his work and in the ambition of making his life recognised as a factor in the better life of mankind—like other heroes of science who had nothing but an obscure country practice to begin with." 16

—in a dilemma: "He could not help hearing within him the distinct declaration that **Bulstrode** was prime minister, and that the **Tyke** affair was a question of office or no office; and he could not help an equally pronounced dislike to giving up the prospect of office." 18

—dislike for play: "Lydgate was no Puritan, but he did not care for play, and winning money at it had always seemed a meanness to him; besides, he had an ideal of life which made this subservience of conduct to the gaining of small sums thoroughly hateful to him."

—money as a practical matter: "Hitherto in his own life his wants had been supplied without any trouble to himself, and his first impulse was always to be liberal with half-crowns as matters of no importance to a gentleman; it had never occurred to him to devise a plan for getting half-crowns. He had always known in a general way that he was not rich, but he had never felt poor, and he had no power of imagining the part which the want of money plays in determining the actions of men. Money had never been a motive to him." 18

—rationalization? "Lydgate did not like the consciousness that in voting for **Tyke** he should be voting on the side obviously convenient for himself. But would the end really be his own convenience? Other people would say so . . . . What he really cared for was a medium for his work, a vehicle for his ideas; and after all, was he not bound to prefer the object of getting a good hospital, where he could demonstrate the specific distinctions of fever and test therapeutic results, before anything else connected with this chaplaincy?

For the first time Lydgate was feeling the hampering threadlike pressure of small social conditions, and their frustrating complexity." 18

—*opposition building:* "It was clear that Lydgate, by not dispensing drugs, intended to cast imputations on his equals, and also to obscure the limit between his own rank as a general practitioner and that of the physicians, who, in the interest of the profession, felt bound to maintain its various grades. Especially against a man who had not been to either of the English universities and enjoyed the absence of anatomical and bedside study there, but came with a libellous pretension to experience in Edinburgh and Paris, where observation might be abundant indeed, but hardly sound." 18

—*overpraised:* "To be puffed by ignorance was not only humiliating, but perilous, and not more enviable than the reputation of the weather-prophet. He was impatient of the foolish expectations amidst which all work must be carried on, and likely enough to damage himself as much as **Mr Wrench** could wish, by an unprofessional openness." 26

—*portentous proximity:* "They were obliged to look at each other in speaking, and somehow the looking could not be carried through as the matter of course which it really was. Lydgate began to feel this sort of consciousness unpleasant, and one day looked down, or anywhere, like an ill-worked puppet. But that turned out badly: the next day, **Rosamond** looked down, and the consequence was that when their eyes met again, both were more conscious than before. There was no help for this in science, and as Lydgate did not want to flirt, there seemed to be no help for it in folly." 27

—*no danger:* "The preposterousness of the notion that he could at once set up a satisfactory establishment as a married man was a sufficient guarantee against danger. This play at being a little in love was agreeable, and did not interfere with graver pursuits." 27

—*appreciated:* "If Lydgate had been aware of all the pride he excited in that delicate bosom, he might have been just as well pleased as any other man, even the most densely ignorant of humoral pathology or fibrous tissue. He held it one of the prettiest attitudes of the feminine mind to adore a man's pre-eminence without too precise a knowledge of what it consisted in." 27

—*in danger:* "It is true, Lydgate had the counter-idea of remaining unengaged, but this was a mere negative, a shadow cast by other resolves which themselves were capable of shrinking. Circumstance was almost sure to be on the side of **Rosamond**'s idea, which had a shaping activity and looked through watchful blue eyes, whereas Lydgate's lay blind and unconcerned as a jelly-fish which gets melted without knowing it." 27

—*much moved:* " 'Oh, you are a wise man, are you not [said **Dorothea**]? You know all about life and death. Advise me. Think what I can do . . . . '

"For years after Lydgate remembered the impression produced in him by this involuntary appeal—this cry from soul to soul, without other consciousness than their moving with kindred natures in the same embroiled medium, the same troublous fitfully-illuminated life." 30

—*engaged and in love:* "And Lydgate fell to spinning that web from his inward self with wonderful rapidity, in spite of experience supposed to be finished off with the drama of **Laure**—in spite too of medicine and biology; for the inspection of macerated muscle . . . and other incidents of scientific inquiry, are observed to be less incompatible with poetic love than a native dulness or a lively addiction to the lowest prose." 36

—*heedless about money:* " . . . he would have despised any ostentation of expense; his profession had familiarised him with all grades of poverty; and he cared much for those who suffered hardships. He would have behaved perfectly at a table where the sauce was served in a jug with the handle off, and he would have remembered nothing about a grand dinner except that a man was there who talked well. But it had never occurred to him that he should live in any other than what he would have called an ordinary way, with green glasses for hock, and excellent waiting at table. In warming himself at French social theories he had brought away no smell of scorching. We may handle even extreme opinions with impunity while our furniture, our dinner-giving, and preference for armorial bearings in our own case, link us indissolubly with the established order." 36

—*the weak link:* "[His] tendency was not towards extreme opinions: he would have liked no barefooted doctrines, being particular about his boots: he was no radical in relation to anything but medical reform and the prosecution of discovery. In the rest of practical life he walked by hereditary habit; half from that personal pride and unreflecting egoism which I have already called commonness, and half from that naïveté which belong to preoccupation with favourite ideas." 36

—*urging early marriage:* "An unmistakable delight shone forth from the blue eyes that met his, and the radiance seemed to light up all his future with mild sunshine. Ideal happiness (of the kind known in the Arabian Nights, in which you are invited to step from the labour and discord of the street into a paradise where everything is given to you and nothing claimed) seemed to be an affair of a few weeks' waiting, more or less." 36

—*his imagining:* "[He] thought that after all his wild mistakes and absurd credulity, he had found perfect womanhood—felt as if already breathed upon by exquisite wedded affection such as would be bestowed by an accomplished creature who venerated his high musings and momentous labours and would never interfere with them; who would create order in the home and accounts with still magic, yet keep her fingers ready to touch the lute and transform life into romance at any moment; who was instructed to the true womanly limit and not a hair's-breadth beyond—docile, therefore, and ready to carry out behests which came from beyond that limit . . . .

"Lydgate, you perceive, had talked fervidly to **Rosamond** of his hopes as to the highest uses of his life, and had found it delightful to be listened to by a creature who would bring him the sweet furtherance of satisfying affection—beauty—repose—such help as our thoughts get from the summer sky and the flower-fringed meadows.

"Lydgate relied much on the psychological difference between what for the sake of variety I will call goose and gander: especially on the innate submissiveness of the goose as beautifully corresponding to the strength of the gander." 36

—*an expensive dinner service:* " 'I trust in heaven it won't be broken!'

" 'One must hire servants who will not break things,' said Lydgate. (Certainly, this was reasoning with an imperfect vision of sequences. But at that period there was no sort of reasoning which was not more or less sanctioned by men of science.)" 36

—*appraising a patient's prospects:* "Lydgate's instinct was fine enough to tell him that plain speech, quite free from ostentatious caution, would be felt by **Mr Casaubon** as a tribute of respect." 42

—ignorantly praised: "Various patients got well while Lydgate was attending them, some even of dangerous illnesses . . . . The trash talked on such occasions was the more vexatious to Lydgate, because it gave precisely the sort of prestige which an incompetent and unscrupulous man would desire. . . . But even his proud outspokenness was checked by the discernment that it was as useless to fight against the interpretations of ignorance as to whip the fog, and 'good fortune' insisted on using those interpretations." 45

—hated and opposed: "The medical aversion to Lydgate was hardly disguised now. Neither **Dr Sprague** nor **Dr Minchin** said that he disliked Lydgate's knowledge, or his disposition to improve treatment: what they disliked was his arrogance, which nobody felt to be altogether deniable. They implied that he was insolent, pretentious, and given to that reckless innovation for the sake of noise and show which was the essence of the charlatan." 45

—inspired: "A man conscious of enthusiasm for worthy aims is sustained under petty hostilities by the memory of great workers who had to fight their way not without wounds, and who hover in his mind as patron saints, invisibly helping . . . .

"There was something very fine in Lydgate's look just then, and any one might have been encouraged to bet on his achievement. In his dark eyes and on his mouth and brow there was that placidity which comes from the fulness of contemplative thought—the mind not searching, but beholding, and the glance seeming to be filled with what is behind it." 45

—not jealous: "For he was not at all a jealous husband, and preferred leaving a feather-headed young gentleman alone with his wife to bearing him company." 58

—illusions passing: " 'The fact is, you would wish me to be a little more like him [**Captain Lydgate**], Rosy,' said Lydgate, in a sort of resigned murmur, with a smile which was not exactly tender, and certainly not merry . . . .

"These words of Lydgate's were like a sad milestone marking how far he had travelled from his old dreamland, in which **Rosamond Vincy** appeared to be that perfect piece of womanhood who would reverence her husband's mind after the fashion of an accomplished mermaid, using her comb and looking glass and singing her song for the relaxation of his adored wisdom alone. He had begun to distinguish between that imagined adoration and the attraction towards a man's talent because it gives him prestige, and is like an order in his button-hole or an Honourable before his name." 58

—astounded: " . . . he secretly wondered over the terrible tenacity of this mild creature. There was gathering within him an amazed sense of his powerlessness over **Rosamond**. His superior knowledge and mental force, instead of being, as he had imagined, a shrine to consult on all occasions, was simply set aside on every practical question . . . . Lydgate was astounded to find in numberless trifling matters, as well as in this last serious case of the riding, that affection did not make her compliant. He had no doubt that the affection was there, and had no presentiment that he had done anything to repel it. For his own part he said to himself that he loved her as tenderly as ever, and could make up his mind to her negations; but—well!" 58

—a split: "Between him and her indeed there was that total missing of each other's mental track, which is too evidently possible even between persons who are continually thinking of each other. To Lydgate it seemed that he had been . . . bearing without betrayal of bitterness to look through less

and less of interfering illusion at the blank unreflecting surface her mind presented to his ardour for the more impersonal ends of his profession and his scientific study, an ardour which he had fancied that the ideal wife must somehow worship as sublime, though not in the least knowing why." 58

—debt: "And on Lydgate's enthusiasm there was constantly pressing not a simple weight of sorrow, but the biting presence of a petty degrading care, such as casts the blight of irony over all higher effort . . . .

" . . . He was now experiencing something worse than a simple deficit: he was assailed by the vulgar hateful trials of a man who has bought and used a great many things which might have been done without, and which he is unable to pay for, though the demand for payment has become pressing." 58

"He was intensely miserable, this strong young man of nine-and-twenty and of many gifts. He was not saying angrily within himself that he had made a profound mistake; but the mistake was at work in him like a recognised chronic disease, mingling its uneasy importunities with every prospect, and enfeebling every thought." 58

—warm-hearted and sad: "His native warm-heartedness took a great deal of quenching, and it is a part of manliness for a husband to feel keenly the fact that an inexperienced girl has got into trouble by marrying him." 58

—unhappy and proud: "So strangely determined are we mortals, that, after having been long gratified with the sense that he had privately done the Vicar a service, the suggestion that the Vicar discerned his need of a service in return made him shrink into unconquerable reticence. Besides, behind all making of such offers. What else must come?—that he should 'mention his case,' imply that he wanted specific things. At that moment, suicide seemed easier." 63

—frustration: "He was not an ill-tempered man; his intellectual activity, the ardent kindness of his heart, as well as his strong frame, would always, under tolerably easy conditions, have kept him above the petty uncontrolled susceptibilities which make bad temper. But he was now a prey to that worst irritation which arises not simply from annoyances, but from the second consciousness underlying those annoyances, of wasted energy and a degrading preoccupation, which was the reverse of all his former purposes." 64

—and women: " . . this rather abrupt man had much tenderness in his manners towards women, seeming to have always present in his imagination the weakness of their frames and the delicate poise of their health both in body and mind." 64

—undermined: " . . . he had a growing dread of **Rosamond**'s quiet elusive obstinacy, which would not allow any assertion of power to be final; and again, she had touched him in a spot of keenest feeling by implying that she had been deluded with a false vision of happiness in marrying him. As to saying that he was master, it was not the fact. The very resolution to which he had wrought himself by dint of logic and honourable pride was beginning to relax under her torpedo contact." 64

—an appeal to the baronet? "No sooner had Lydgate begun to represent this step to himself as the easiest than there was a reaction of anger that he—he who had long ago determined to live aloof from such abject calculations, such self-interested anxiety about the inclinations and the pockets of men with whom he had been proud to have no aims in common—should have fallen not simply to their level but to the level of soliciting them." 64

The Lydgates do not understand each other

—defeated: "He could not promise to shield her from the dreaded wretchedness, for he could see no sure means of doing so. When he left her to go out again, he told himself that it was ten times harder for her than for him: he had a life away from home, and constant appeals to his activity on behalf of others. He wished to excuse everything in her if he could—but it was inevitable that in that excusing mood he should think of her as if she were an animal of another and feebler species. Nevertheless she had mastered him." 65

—helped by his work: "He had no longer free energy enough for spontaneous research and speculative thinking, but by the bedside of patients the direct external calls on his judgment and sympathies brought the added impulse needed to draw him out of himself. It was not simply that beneficent harness of routine which enables silly men to live respectably and unhappy men to live calmly—it was a perpetual claim on the immediate fresh application of thought, and on the consideration of another's need and trial." 66

—addictions: " . . . he had once or twice tried a dose of opium. But he had no hereditary constitutional craving after such transient escapes from the hauntings of misery. He was strong, could drink a great deal of wine, but did not care about it; and when the men round him were drinking spirits, he took sugar and water, having a contemptuous pity even for the earliest stages of excitement from drink. It was the same with gambling. He had looked on at a great deal of gambling in Paris, watching it as if it had been a disease. He was no more tempted by such winning than he was by drink." 66

—dread: " . . . the coming destitution of everything which made his married life tolerable—everything which saved him and **Rosamond** from that bare isolation in which they would be forced to recognise how little of a comfort they could be to each other." 69

—a dream: " . . . he was beginning now to imagine how two creatures who loved each other, and had a stock of thoughts in common, might laugh over their shabby furniture, and their calculations how far they could afford butter and eggs. But . . . in poor **Rosamond**'s mind there was not room enough for luxuries to look small in." 69

—revelation and shock: "Lydgate, who himself was undergoing a shock as from the terrible practical interpretation of some faint augury, felt, nevertheless, that his own movement of resentful hatred was checked by that instinct of the Healer which thinks first of bringing rescue or relief to the sufferer, when he looked at the shrunken misery of **Bulstrode**'s livid face." 71

—frustrated and furious: "Lydgate thought of himself as the sufferer, and of others as the agents who had injured his lot. He had meant everything to turn out differently; and others had thrust themselves into his life and thwarted his purposes. His marriage seemed an unmitigated calamity; and he was afraid of going to **Rosamond** before he had vented himself in this solitary rage, lest the mere sight of her should exasperate him and make him behave unwarrantably." 73

—scowl of defiance: " . . . he was setting his mind on remaining in Middlemarch in spite of the worst that could be done against him. He would not retreat before calumny, as if he submitted to it. He would face it to the utmost, and no act of his should show that he was afraid. It belonged to the generosity as well as defiant force of his nature that he resolved not to shrink from showing to the full his sense of obligation to Bulstrode . . . he would not

turn away from this crushed fellow-mortal whose aid he had used, and make a pitiful effort to get acquittal for himself by howling against another." 73

—adaptation: "For he had almost learned the lesson that he must bend himself to her nature, and that because she came short in her sympathy, he must give the more." 75

—changed: "It was not the change of emaciation, but that effect which even young faces will very soon show from the persistent presence of resentment and despondency." 76

—in the presence of nobility and trust: "He sat down again, and felt that he was recovering his old self in the consciousness that he was the one who believed in it . . . .

" . . . Lydgate did not stay to think that she was Quixotic; he gave himself up for the first time in his life, to the exquisite sense of leaning entirely on a generous sympathy,. Without any check of proud reserve." 76

—nonmedical diagnosis: " 'It is one of those cases on which a man is condemned on the ground of his character—it is believed that he has committed a crime in some undefined way, because he had the motive for doing it; and **Bulstrode**'s character has enveloped me, because I took his money. I am simply blighted—like a damaged ear of corn—the business is done and can't be undone.' " 76

—decision and fate: " 'I must not at least sink into the degradation of being pensioned for work that I never achieved. It is very clear to me that I must not count on anything else than getting away from Middlemarch as soon as I can manage it . . . . I must do as other men do, and think what will please the world and bring in money; look for a little opening in the London crowd, and push myself, set up in a watering-place, or go to some southern town where there are plenty of the English, and get myself puffed—that is the sort of shell I must creep into and try to keep my soul alive in.' " 76

—after a crisis: "Poor **Rosamond**'s vagrant fancy had come back terribly scourged—meek enough to nestle under the old despised shelter. And the shelter was still there: Lydgate had accepted his narrowed lot with sad resignation. He had chosen this fragile creature, and had taken the burthen of her life upon his arms. He must walk as he could, carrying that burthen pitifully." 81

Rosamond Vincy "had excellent taste in costume, with that nymph-like figure and pure blondness which give the largest range of choice in the flow and colour of drapery. But these things made only part of her charm. She was admitted to be the flower of **Mrs Lemon**'s school, the chief school in the county, where the teaching included all that was demanded in the accomplished female—even to extras, such as the getting in and out of a carriage. Mrs Lemon herself had always held up Miss Vincy as an example: no pupil, she said, exceeded that young lady for mental acquisition and propriety of speech, while her musical execution was quite exceptional. We cannot help the way in which people speak of us, and probably if Mrs Lemon had undertaken to describe **Juliet** or **Imogen**, these heroines would not have seemed poetical. The first vision of Rosamond would have been enough with most judges to dispel any prejudice excited by Mrs Lemon's praise." 11

—bored: "Rosamond silently wished that her father would invite **Mr Lydgate**. She was tired of the faces and figures she had always been used to—the various irregular profiles and gaits and turns of phrase distinguishing those Middlemarch young men whom she had known as boys. She had

been at school with girls of higher position, whose brothers, she felt sure, it would have been possible for her to be more interested in, than in these inevitable Middlemarch companions." 11

—*smile:* " 'But'—here Rosamond's face broke into a smile which suddenly revealed two dimples. She herself thought unfavourably of these dimples and smiled little in general society. 'I shall not marry any Middlemarch young man.' " 11

—*fastidious:* " 'I would rather not have anything left to me if I must earn it by enduring much of my uncle's cough and his ugly relations.' " 11

—*beauty:* " . . . Rosamond took off her hat, adjusted her veil, and applied little touches of her finger-tips to her hair—hair of infantine fairness, neither flaxen nor yellow . . . with eyes of heavenly blue, deep enough to hold the most exquisite meanings an ingenious beholder could put into them, and deep enough to hide the meanings of the owner if these should happen to be less exquisite. Only a few children in Middlemarch looked blond by the side of Rosamond, and the slim figure displayed by her riding-habit had delicate undulations. In fact, most men in Middlemarch, except her brothers, held that Miss Vincy was the best girl in the world, and some called her an angel." 12

—*conscious:* " . . . rising to reach her hat, which she had laid aside before singing, so that her flower-like head on its white stem was seen in perfection above her riding-habit . . . .

"(Every nerve and muscle in Rosamond was adjusted to the consciousness that she was being looked at. She was by nature an actress of parts that entered into her *physique:* she even acted her own character, and so well, that she did not know it to be precisely her own.)" 12

—*the first glance:* "She bowed and looked at him: he of course was looking at her, and their eyes met with that peculiar meeting which is never arrived at by effort, but seems like a sudden divine clearance of haze. I think **Lydgate** turned a little paler than usual, but Rosamond blushed deeply and felt a certain astonishment." 12

—*a dream made real:* "And a stranger was absolutely necessary to Rosamond's social romance, which had always turned on a lover and bridegroom who was not a Middlemarcher, and who had no connections at all like her own: of late, indeed, the construction seemed to demand that he should somehow be related to a baronet. Now that she and the stranger had met, reality proved much more moving than anticipation, and Rosamond could not doubt that this was the great epoch of her life. She judged of her own symptoms as those of awakening love, and she held it still more natural that **Mr Lydgate** should have fallen in love at first sight of her.

"These things happened so often at balls, and why not by the morning light, when the complexion showed all the better for it? Rosamond . . . was rather used to being fallen in love with; but she, for her part, had remained indifferent and fastidiously critical towards both fresh sprig and faded bachelor. And here was Mr Lydgate suddenly corresponding to her ideal, being altogether foreign to Middlemarch, carrying a certain air of distinction congruous with good family, and possessing connections which offered vistas of that middle-class heaven, rank: a man of talent, also, whom it would be especially delightful to enslave: in fact, a man who had touched her nature quite newly, and brought a vivid interest into her life which was better than any fancied 'might-be' such as she was in the habit of opposing to the actual." ¶12

—money? "There was nothing financial, still less sordid, in her previsions: she cared about what were considered refinements, and not about the money that was to pay for them." 12

—adroit grace: "Certainly, small feet and perfectly turned shoulders aid the impression of refined manners, and the right thing said seems quite astonishingly right when it is accompanied with exquisite curves of lip and eyelid. And Rosamond could say the right thing; for she was clever with that sort of cleverness which catches every tone except the humorous. Happily she never attempted to joke, and this perhaps was the most decisive mark of her cleverness." 16

"But she remained simply serious, turned her long neck a little, and put up her hand to touch her wondrous hair-plaits—an habitual gesture with her as pretty as any movements of a kitten's paw. Not that Rosamond was in the least like a kitten: she was a sylph caught young and educated at **Mrs Lemon**'s." 16

—musical skill: "Rosamond played admirably . . . with an executant's instinct, [she] had seized [her master's] manner of playing, and gave forth his large rendering of noble music with the precision of an echo. It was almost startling, heard for the first time. A hidden soul seemed to be flowing forth from Rosamond's fingers . . . . Lydgate was taken possession of, and began to believe in her as something exceptional." 16

—impression made: "[She] had just the kind of intelligence one would desire in a woman—polished, refined, docile, lending itself to finish in all the delicacies of life, and enshrined in a body which expressed this with a force of demonstration that excluded the need for other evidence." 16

—inner life: "[She] had neither any reason for throwing her marriage into distant perspective, nor any pathological studies to divert her mind from that ruminating habit, that inward repetition of looks, words, and phrases, which makes a large part in the lives of most girls." 16

—the key: "In Rosamond's romance it was not necessary to imagine much about the inward life of the hero, or of his serious business in the world: of course, he had a profession and was clever, as well as sufficiently handsome; but the piquant fact about Lydgate was his good birth, which distinguished him from all Middlemarch admirers, and presented marriage as a prospect of rising in rank and getting a little nearer to that celestial condition on earth in which she would have nothing to do with vulgar people, and perhaps at last associate with relatives quite equal to the county people who looked down on the Middlemarchers. It was part of Rosamond's cleverness to discern very subtly the faintest aroma of rank . . . . " 16

—finished and polished: "For Rosamond never showed any unbecoming knowledge, and was always that combination of correct sentiments, music, dancing, drawing, elegant note-writing, private album for extracted verse, and perfect blond loveliness, which made the irresistible woman for the doomed man of that date. Think no unfair evil of her, pray: she had no wicked plots, nothing sordid or mercenary; in fact, she never thought of money except as something necessary which other people would always provide. She was not in the habit of devising falsehoods, and if her statements were no direct clue to fact, why, they were not intended in that light—they were among her elegant accomplishments intended to please. Nature had inspired many arts in finishing **Mrs Lemon**'s favourite pupil, who by general

consent (**Fred**'s excepted) was a rare compound of beauty, cleverness, and amiability." 27

—an attraction: " . . . sweet to look at as a half-opened blush-rose and adorned with accomplishments for the refined amusement of man." 27

—demure: "She was not a fiery young lady and had no sharp answers, but she meant to live as she pleased." 31

—avowal: " 'If I loved, I should love at once and without change,' said Rosamond, with a great sense of being a romantic heroine, and playing the part prettily." 31

—hearing of opposition: "Rosamond, examining some muslin-work, listened in silence, and at the end gave a certain turn of her graceful neck, of which only long experience could teach you that it meant perfect obstinacy." 36 *See* **Walter Vincy**—*not a chance* CHM

—engaged and in love: "As for Rosamond, she was in the water-lily's expanding wonderment at its own fuller life, and she too was spinning industriously at the mutual web." 36 *See* **Tertius Lydgate**—*engaged and in love* CWM

—irresistible: "She blushed and looked at him as the garden flowers look at us when we walk forth happily among them in the transcendent evening light: is there not a soul beyond utterance, half-nymph, half-child, in those delicate petals which glow and breathe about the centres of deep colour?" 36

Rosamond Lydgate

—making an impression: " . . . imagine Rosamond's infantine blondness and wondrous crown of hair-plaits, with her pale-blue dress of a fit and fashion so perfect that no dressmaker could look at it without emotion, a large embroidered collar which it was to be hoped all beholders would know the price of, her small hands duly set off with rings, and that controlled self-consciousness of manner which is the expensive substitute for simplicity." 43

—the crux of her character: "Rosamond had that victorious obstinacy which never wastes its energy in impetuous resistance. What she liked to do was to her the right thing, and all her cleverness was directed to getting the means of doing it." 58

—her skills: "No one quicker than Rosamond to see causes and effects which lay within the track of her own tastes and interests: she had seen clearly **Lydgate**'s pre-eminence in Middlemarch society, and could go on imaginatively tracing still more agreeable social effects when his talent should have advanced him; but for her, his professional and scientific ambition had no other relation to these desirable effects than if they had been the fortunate discovery of an ill-smelling oil. And that oil apart, with which she had nothing to do, of course she believed in her own opinion more than she did in his." 58

—hoping: "Rosamond was soon looking lovelier than ever at her work-table [*following the loss of her baby, to which she seems indifferent*], enjoying drives in her father's phaeton and thinking it likely that she might be invited to Quallingham. She knew that she was a much more exquisite ornament to the drawing-room there than any daughter of the family, and in reflecting that the gentlemen were aware of that, did not perhaps sufficiently consider whether the ladies would be eager to see themselves surpassed." 58

—*news of debt:* "Rosamond sat perfectly still. The thought in her mind was that if she had known how **Lydgate** would behave, she would never have married him." 58

—*alienated:* " . . . in her secret soul she was utterly aloof from him. The poor thing saw only that the world was not ordered to her liking, and Lydgate was part of that world." 64

" . . . it was not in Rosamond's nature to be repellent or sulky; indeed, she welcomed the signs that her husband loved her and was under control. But this was something quite distinct from loving *him.*" 64

—*tenacity in action:* "That she should be obliged to do what she intensely disliked, was an idea which turned her quiet tenacity into active invention. Here was a case in which it could not be enough simply to disobey and be serenely, placidly obstinate: she must act according to her judgment, and she said to herself that her judgment was right—'indeed, if had not been, she would not have wished to act on it.' " 64

—*another's anger:* "The effect of any one's anger on Rosamond had always been to make her shrink in cold dislike, and to become all the more calmly correct, in the conviction that she was not the person to misbehave, whatever others might do." 64

—*disillusion and dulness:* "Poor Rosamond for months had begun to associate her husband with feelings of disappointment, and the terribly inflexible relation of marriage had lost its charm of encouraging delightful dreams. It had freed her from the disagreeables of her father's home, but it had not given her everything that she had wished and hoped. The **Lydgate** with whom she had been in love had been a group of airy conditions for her, most of which had disappeared, while their place had been taken by everyday details which must be lived through slowly from hour to hour, not floated through with a rapid selection of favourable aspects. The habits of Lydgate's profession, his home preoccupation with scientific subjects, which seemed to her almost like a morbid vampire's taste, his peculiar views of things which had never entered into the dialogue of courtship—all these continually alienating influences, even without the fact of his having placed himself at a disadvantage in the town, and without that first check of revelation about **Dover**'s debt, would have made his presence dull to her." 64

—*her power:* "Rosamond had the double purchase over him of insensibility to the point of justice in his reproach, and of sensibility to the undeniable hardships now present in her married life . . . . Rosamond felt that she was aggrieved, and that this was what Lydgate had to recognise." 65

"She spoke and wept with that gentleness which makes such words and tears omnipotent over a loving-hearted man." 65

—*castle in the air:* "She had felt stung and disappointed by **Will**'s resolution to quit Middlemarch, for in spite of what she knew and guessed about his admiration for **Dorothea**, she secretly cherished the belief that he had, or would necessarily come to have, much more admiration for herself, Rosamond being one of these women who live much in the idea that each man they meet would have preferred them if the preference had not been hopeless . . . . He would have made, she thought, a much more suitable husband for her than she had found in **Lydgate**. No notion could have been falser than this, for Rosamond's discontent in her marriage was due to the conditions of marriage itself, to its demand for self-suppression and tolerance, and not to the nature of her husband; but the easy conception of an unreal Better had a sentimental charm which diverted her ennui." 75

—shame: "The shock to Rosamond was terrible. It seemed to her that no lot could be so cruelly had as hers—to have married a man who had become the centre of infamous suspicions. In many cases it is inevitable that the shame is felt to be the worst part of crime; and it would have required a great deal of disentangling reflection, such as had never entered into Rosamond's life, for her in these moments to feel that her trouble was less than if her husband had been certainly known to have done something criminal." 75

—disoriented: "Rosamond . . . was almost losing the sense of her identity, and seemed to be waking into some new terrible existence. She had no sense of chill resolute repulsion, of reticent self-justification such as she had known under **Lydgate**'s most stormy displeasure; all her sensibility was turned into a bewildering novelty of pain; she felt a new terrified recoil under a lash never experienced before. What another nature felt in opposition to her own was being burnt and bitten into her consciousness. When **Will** had ceased to speak she had become an image of sickened misery: her lips were pale, and her eyes had a tearless dismay in them." 78

—catastrophe: "The poor thing had no force to fling out any passion in return; the terrible collapse of the illusion towards which all her hope had been strained was a stroke which had too thoroughly shaken her: her little world was in ruins, and she felt herself tottering in the midst as a lonely bewildered consciousness." 78

—a new sensation: "It was a newer crisis in Rosamond's experience than even **Dorothea** could imagine: she was under the first great shock that had shattered her dream-world in which she had been easily confident of herself and critical of others; and this strange unexpected manifestation of feeling in a woman whom she had approached with a shrinking aversion and dread, as one who must necessarily have a jealous hatred towards her, made her soul totter all the more with a sense that she had been walking in an unknown world which had just broken in upon her." 81

**

Mary Garth "had the aspect of an ordinary sinner: she was brown; her curly dark hair was rough and stubborn; her stature was low; and it would not be true to declare, in satisfactory antithesis, that she had all the virtues. . . . At the age of two-and-twenty Mary had certainly not attained that perfect good sense and good principle which are usually recommended to the less fortunate girl, as if they were to be obtained in quantities ready mixed, with a flavour of resignation as required. Her shrewdness had a streak of satiric bitterness continually renewed and never carried utterly out of sight, except by a strong current of gratitude towards those who, instead of telling her that she ought to be contented, did something to make her so.

"Advancing womanhood had tempered her plainness, which was of a good human sort, such as the mothers of our race have very commonly worn in all latitudes under a more or less becoming head-gear. **Rembrandt** would have painted her with pleasure, and would have made her broad features look out of the canvas with intelligent honesty. For honesty, truth-telling fairness, was Mary's reigning virtue: she neither tried to create illusions, nor indulged in them for her own behoof, and when she was in a good mood she had humour enough in her to laugh at herself." ¶12

—*soft-hearted:* "There is often something maternal even in a girlish love, and Mary's hard experience had wrought her nature to an impressibility very different from that hard slight thing which we call girlishness. At Fred's last words she felt an instantaneous pang, something like what a mother feels at the imagined sobs or cries of her naughty truant child, which may lose itself and get harm. And when, looking up, her eyes met his dull despairing glance, her pity for him surmounted her anger and all her other anxieties." 25

—*meditating:* "There were intervals in which she could sit perfectly still, enjoying the outer stillness and the subdued light. The red fire with its gently audible movement seemed like a solemn existence calmly independent of the petty passions, the imbecile desires, the straining after worthless uncertainties, which were daily moving her contempt. Mary was fond of her own thoughts, and could amuse herself well sitting in twilight with her hands in her lap; for, having early had strong reason to believe that things were not likely to be arranged for her peculiar satisfaction, she wasted no time in astonishment and annoyance at that fact. And she had already come to take life very much as a comedy in which she had a proud, nay, a generous resolution not to act the mean or treacherous part." 33

—*grateful:* "Mary might have become cynical if she had not had parents whom she honoured, and a well of affectionate gratitude within her, which was all the fuller because she had learned to make no unreasonable claims." 33

—*amused:* " . . . people were so ridiculous with their illusions, carrying their fool's caps unawares, thinking their own lies opaque while everybody else's were transparent, making themselves exceptions to everything, as if when all the world looked yellow under a lamp they alone were rosy . . . .

"But she liked her thoughts: a vigorous young mind not overbalanced by passion, finds a good in making acquaintance with life, and watches its own powers with interest. May had plenty of merriment within." 33

—*her employer:* "Her thought was not veined by any solemnity or pathos about the old man on the bed: such sentiments are easier to affect than to feel about an aged creature whose life is not visibly anything but a remnant of vices. She had always seen the most disagreeable side of **Mr Featherstone**:

he was not proud of her, and she was only useful to him. To be anxious about a soul that is always snapping at you must be left to the saints of the earth; and Mary was not one of them. She had never returned him a harsh word, and had waited on him faithfully: that was her utmost. Old Featherstone himself was not in the least anxious about his soul, and had declined to see **Mr Tucker** on the subject." 33

—a skill: " 'Mary Garth might do some work for me now, I should think [said **Rosamond**]. Her sewing is exquisite; it is the nicest thing I know about Mary.' " 36

—her portrait: "They made a pretty picture in the western light which brought out the brightness of the apples on the old scant-leaved boughs—Mary in her lavender gingham and black ribbons holding a basket, while **Letty** in her well-worn nankin picked up the fallen apples. If you want to know more particularly how Mary looked, ten to one you will see a face like hers in the crowded street to-morrow, if you are there on the watch: she will not be among those daughters of Zion who are haughty, and walk with stretched-out necks and wanton eyes, mincing as they go: let all those pass, and fix your eyes on some small plump brownish person of firm but quiet carriage, who looks about her, but does not suppose that anybody is looking at her. If she has a broad face and square brow, well-marked eyebrows and curly dark hair, a certain expression of amusement in her glance which her mouth keeps the secret of, and for the rest features entirely insignificant—take that ordinary but not disagreeable person for a portrait of Mary Garth. If you made her smile, she would show you perfect little teeth; if you made her angry, she would not raise her voice, but would probably say one of the bitterest things you have ever tasted the flavour of; if you did her a kindness, she would never forget it." 40

—partiality: "At least, it was remarkable that the actual imperfections of the Vicar's clerical character never seemed to call forth the same scorn and dislike which she showed beforehand for the predicted imperfections of the clerical character sustained by **Fred Vincy** . . . . Will any one guess towards which of those widely different men Mary had the peculiar woman's tenderness?—the one she was most inclined to be severe on, or the contrary?" 40

—clerical vocation: "[**Fred**'s] being a clergyman would be only for gentility's sake, and I think there is nothing more contemptible than such imbecile gentility . . . he has plenty of sense, but I think he would not show it as a clergyman. He would be a piece of professional affectation.' " 52

—rooted love: "She had never thought that any man could love her except **Fred**, who had espoused her with the umbrella ring, when she wore socks and little strapped shoes.

" 'Since you think it my duty . . . I will tell you that I have too strong a feeling for Fred to give him up for any one else. I should never be quite happy if I thought he was unhappy for the loss of me. It has taken such deep root in me—my gratitude to him for always loving me best, and minding so much if I hurt myself, from the time when we were very little. I cannot imagine any new feeling coming to make that weaker. I should like better than anything to see him worthy of every one's respect. But please tell him I will not promise to marry him till then. I should shame and grieve my father and mother. He is free to choose some one else.' " 52

—*modest:* "Mary was accustomed to think rather rigorously of what was probable, and, if a belief flattered her vanity, she felt warned to dismiss it as ridiculous, having early had much exercise in such dismissals." 57

—*shaken:* "She was in a position in which she seemed to herself to be slighting **Mr Farebrother**, and this, in relation to a man who is much honoured, is always dangerous to the firmness of a grateful woman . . . Mary earnestly desired to be always clear that she loved **Fred** best . . . . It was impossible to help fleeting visions of another kind—new dignities and an acknowledged value of which she had often felt the absence. But these things with Fred outside them, Fred forsaken and looking sad for the want of her, could never tempt her deliberate thought." 57

—*her love:* " 'I don't love him because he is a fine match.'

" 'What for, then?'

" 'Oh, dear, because I have always loved him. I should never like scolding any one else so well; and that is a point to be thought of in a husband.' " 86

Fred Vincy, "the family laggard, who found any sort of inconvenience (to others) less disagreeable than getting up when he was called." 11

—*music:* "So Fred was gratified with nearly an hour's practice of 'Ar hyd y nos,' 'Ye banks and braes,' and other favourite airs from his 'Instructor on the Flute,' a wheezy performance, into which he threw much ambition and an irrepressible hopefulness." 11

—*kind:* "Fred, in spite of his irritation, had kindness enough in him to be a little sorry for the unloved, unvenerated old man [**Featherstone**], who with his dropsical legs looked more than usually pitiable in walking. While giving his arm, he thought that he should not himself like to be an old fellow with his constitution breaking up . . . . " 12

—*sanguine:* " . . . Fred had felt confident that he should meet the bill himself, having ample funds at disposal in his own hopefulness. You will hardly demand that his confidence should have a basis in external facts; such confidence, we know, is something less coarse and materialistic: it is a comfortable disposition leading us to expect that the wisdom of providence or the folly of our friends, the mysteries of luck or the still greater mystery of our high individual value in the universe, will bring about agreeable issues, such as are consistent with our good taste in costume, and our general preference for the best style of thing." 23

—*disliking a scene:* "He was too filial to be disrespectful to his father, and he bore the thunder with the certainty that it was transient; but in the mean time it was disagreeable to see his mother cry, and also to be obliged to look sulky instead of having fun; for Fred was so good-tempered that if he looked glum under scolding, it was chiefly for propriety's sake." 23

—*getting a name:* "Thus it came to pass that the friend whom he chose to apply to was at once the poorest and the kindest—namely, **Caleb Garth**." 23

—*hopeful:* " . . . he had kept twenty pounds in his own pocket as a sort of seed-corn, which, planted by judgment, and watered by luck, might yield more than threefold—a very poor rate of multiplication when the field as a young gentleman's infinite soul, with all the numerals at command." 23

—*a mind idea:* "Considering that Fred was not at all coarse, that he rather looked down on the manners and speech of young men who had not been to the university, and that he had written stanzas as pastoral and unvoluptuous as his flute-playing, his attraction towards **Bambridge** and **Hor-**

rock was an interesting fact which even the love of horse-flesh would not wholly account for without that mysterious influence of Naming which determinates so much of mortal choice. Under any other name than 'pleasure' the society of Messieurs Bambridge and Horrock must certainly have been regarded as monotonous . . . . " 23

—*self-centered:* "Curiously enough, his pain in the affair beforehand had consisted almost entirely in the sense that he must seem dishonourable, and sink in the opinion of the **Garths**: he had not occupied himself with the inconvenience and possible injury that his breach might occasion them . . . . " 24

—*having been very ill:* "**Mrs Vincy** told these messages to Fred when he could listen, and he turned towards her his delicate, pinched face, from which all the thick blond hair had been cut away, and in which the eyes seemed to have got larger, yearning for some word about **Mary** . . . . " 27

—*characteristics:* " . . . white complexion, long legs, and pinched delicacy of face . . . . " 32

—*no legacy:* "He had that withered sort of paleness which will sometimes come on young faces, and his hand was very cold when she shook it." 35

" . . . he was too utterly depressed. Twenty-four hours ago he had thought that instead of needing to know what he should do, he should by this time know that he needed to do nothing: that he should hunt in pink, have a first-rate hunter, ride to cover on a fine hack, and be generally respected for doing so; moreover, that he should be able at once to pay **Mr Garth**, and that **Mary** could no longer have any reason for not marrying him. And all this was to have come without study or other inconvenience, purely by the favour of providence in the shape of an old gentleman's caprice." 36

—*career choice:* " 'I don't like divinity, and preaching, and feeling obliged to look serious. I like riding across country, and doing as other men do. I don't mean that I want to be a bad fellow in any way; but I've no taste for the sort of thing people expect of a clergyman.' " 52

—*his love:* " ' . . . I have never been without loving **Mary**. If I had to give her up, it would be like beginning to live on wooden legs.' " 52

—*dilemma:* " . . . what secular avocation on earth was there for a young man whose friends could not get him an 'appointment' which was at once gentlemanly, lucrative, and to be followed without special knowledge?" 56

—*an accident helps:* "His spirits had risen, and he heartily enjoyed a good slip in the moist earth under the hedgerow, which soiled his perfect summer trousers. Was it his successful onset which had elated him, or the satisfaction of helping **Mary**'s father? Something more. The accidents of the morning had helped his frustrated imagination to shape an employment for himself which had several attractions. I am not sure that certain fibres in **Mr Garth**'s mind had not resumed their old vibration towards the very end which now revealed itself to Fred. For the effective accident is but the touch of fire where there is oil and tow; and it always appeared to Fred that the railway brought the needed touch." 56

—*a vision:* " 'I should like to have to do with outdoor things. I know a good deal about land and cattle already. I used to believe . . . that I should have land of my own. I am sure knowledge of that sort would come easily to me . . . . ' " 56

They will marry; yes, they will

—a rival: "Fred's light hopeful nature had perhaps never had so much of a bruise as from this suggestion that if he had been out of the way **Mary** might have made a thoroughly good match . . . . Notwithstanding his trust in **Mr Farebrother**'s generosity, notwithstanding what Mary had said to him, Fred could not help feeling that he had a rival: it was a new consciousness, and he objected to it extremely . . . . Certainly this experience was a discipline for Fred hardly less sharp than his disappointment about his uncle's will. The iron had not entered into his soul, but he had begun to imagine what the sharp edge would be." 57

—surprising contrast: "It was a strange reversal of attitudes: Fred's blond face and blue eyes, usually bright and careless, ready to give attention to anything that held out a promise of amusement, looking involuntarily grave and almost embarrassed as if by the sight of something unfitting; while **Lydgate**, who had habitually an air of self-possessed strength, and a certain meditativeness that seemed to lie behind his most observant attention, was acting, watching, speaking with that excited narrow consciousness which reminds one of an animal with fierce eyes and retractile claws." 66

—transfiguring moment: " 'I want you to make the happiness of her life and your own, and if there is any chance that a word of warning from me may turn aside any risk to the contrary—well, I have uttered it.'

"There was a drop in the Vicar's voice when he spoke the last words . . . . Fred was moved quite newly. Some one highly susceptible to the contemplation of a fine act has said, that it produces a sort of regenerating shudder through the frame, and makes one feel ready to begin a new life. A good degree of that effect as just then present in Fred Vincy." 66

Couples who Have Married

Nicholas (41) **Bulstrode**, "the philanthropic banker . . . who predominated so much in the town that some called him a Methodist, others a hypocrite, according to the resources of their vocabulary . . . . [He] seemed to be addressed, but that gentleman disliked coarseness and profanity, and merely bowed." 10

—characteristics: "The banker's speech was fluent, but it was also copious, and he used up an appreciable amount of time in brief meditative pauses. Do not imagine his sickly aspect to have been of the yellow, black-haired sort: he had a pale blond skin, thin grey-besprinkled brown hair, light grey eyes, and a large forehead. Loud men called his subdued tone an undertone, and sometimes implied that it was inconsistent with openness . . . . Mr Bulstrode had also a deferential bending attitude in listening, and an apparently fixed attentiveness in his eyes which made those persons who thought themselves worth hearing infer that he was seeking the utmost improvement from their discourse. Others, who expected to make no great figure, disliked this kind of moral lantern turned on them." 13

—favourably impressed: "Mr Bulstrode perhaps liked [**Lydgate**] better for the difference between them in pitch and manners; he certainly liked him the better, as **Rosamond** did, for being a stranger in Middlemarch. One can begin so many things with a new person!—even begin to be a better man." 13

—annoying: "To point out other people's errors was a duty that Mr Bulstrode rarely shrank from." 13

—power: "Mr Bulstrode's power was not due simply to his being a country banker, who knew the financial secrets of most traders in the town and

could touch the springs of their credit; it was fortified by a beneficence that was at once ready and severe—ready to confer obligations, and severe in watching the result. He had gathered, as an industrious man always at his post, a chief share in administering the town charities, and his private charities were both minute and abundant." 16

"It was a principle with Mr Bulstrode to gain as much power as possible, that he might use it for the glory of God. He went through a great deal of spiritual conflict and inward argument in order to adjust his motives, and make clear to himself what God's glory required." 16

—image: "There were many crass minds in Middlemarch whose reflective scales could only weigh things in the lump and they had a strong suspicion that since Mr Bulstrode could not enjoy life in their fashion, eating and drinking so little as he did, and worreting himself about everything, he must have a sort of vampire's feast in the sense of mastery." 16

" 'I am opposed to Bulstrode in many ways [said **Farebrother**]. I don't like the set he belongs to: they are a narrow ignorant set, and do more to make their neighbours uncomfortable than to make them better. Their system is a sort of worldly spiritual cliqueism: they really look on the rest of mankind as a doomed carcass which is to nourish them for heaven.' " 17

—large projects: " . . . when referring to the Hospital [**Caleb Garth**] often said that however Bulstrode might ring if you tried him, he liked good solid carpentry and masonry, and had a notion both of drains and chimneys. In fact, the Hospital had become an object of intense interest to Bulstrode, and he would willingly have continued to spare a large yearly sum that he might rule it dictatorially without any Board, but he had another favourite object which also required money for its accomplishment: he wished to buy some land in the neighbourhood of Middlemarch . . . . " 45

—serenity: "He was doctrinally convinced that there was a total absence of merit in himself; but that doctrinal conviction may be held without pain when the sense of demerit does not take a distinct shape in memory and revive the tingling of shame or the pang of remorse. Nay, it may be held with intense satisfaction when the depth of our sinning is but a measure for the depth of forgiveness, and a clenching proof that we are peculiar instruments of the divine intention." 53

—fear of disgrace: "In his closest meditations the life-long habit of Mr Bulstrode's mind clad his most egoistic terrors in doctrinal references to superhuman ends. But even while we are talking and meditating about the earth's orbit and the solar system, what we feel and adjust our movements to is the stable earth and the changing day. And now within all the automatic succession of theoretic phrases—distinct and inmost as the shiver and the ache of oncoming fever when we are discussing abstract pain, was the forecast of disgrace in the presence of his neighbours and of his own wife. For the pain, as well as the public estimate of disgrace, depends on the amount of previous profession. To men who only aim at escaping felony, nothing short of the prisoner's dock is disgrace. But Mr Bulstrode had aimed at being an eminent Christian." 53

—ethics: " . . . Mr Bulstrode shrank from the direct falsehood of denying true statements. It was one thing to look back on forgiven sins, nay, to explain questionable conformity to lax customs, and another to enter deliberately on the necessity of falsehood." 53

—former wife's business: "'... a little in what you may call the respectable thieving line—that high style of receiving-house—none of your holes and corners—first rate. Slap-up shop, high profits and no mistake.'" 60

—his present wife: "... he was rather afraid of this ingenuous wife, whose imitative piety and native worldliness were equally sincere, who had nothing to be ashamed of, and whom he had married out of a thorough inclination still subsisting. But his fears were such as belong to a man who cares to maintain his recognised supremacy: the loss of high consideration from his wife, as from every one else who did not clearly hate him out of enmity to the truth, would be as the beginning of death to him." 61

—fear: "It was not that he was in danger of legal punishment or of beggary: he was in danger only of seeing disclosed to the judgment of his neighbours and the mournful perception of his wife certain facts of his past life which would render him an object of scorn and an opprobrium of the religion with which he had diligently associated himself." 61

—rationalizing: "Metaphors and precedents were not wanting; peculiar spiritual experiences were not wanting which at last made the retention of his position seem a service demanded of him: the vista of a fortune had already opened itself, and Bulstrode's shrinking remained private ... Bulstrode found himself carrying on two distinct lives, his religious activity could not be incompatible with his business as soon as he had argued himself into not feeling it incompatible ....

"Mentally surrounded with that past again, Bulstrode had the same pleas —indeed, the years had been perpetually spinning them into intricate thickness, like masses of spider-web, padding the moral sensibility; nay, as age made egoism more eager but less enjoying, his soul had become more saturated with the belief that he did everything for God's sake, being indifferent to it for his own. And yet—if he could be back on that far-off spot with his youthful poverty—why, then he would choose to be a missionary." 61

—new shadinesses: "[He] was also a sleeping partner in trading concerns, in which his ability was directed to economy in the raw material, as in the case of the dyes which rotted **Mr Vincy**'s silk." 61

—hypocrite? "The spiritual kind of rescue was a genuine need with him. There may be coarse hypocrisies, who consciously affect beliefs and emotions for the sake of gulling the world, but Bulstrode was not one of them. He was simply a man whose desires had been stronger than his theoretic beliefs, and who had gradually explained the gratification of his desires into satisfactory agreement with those beliefs." 61 *See Topicon* S:Hypocrisy—*subtle*

—need for power: "But a man who believes in something else than his own greed, has necessarily a conscience or standard to which he more or less adapts himself. Bulstrode's standard had been his serviceableness to God's cause. 'I am sinful and nought—a vessel to be consecrated by use—but use me!—had been the mould into which he had constrained his immense need of being something important and predominating." 61

—seen by another: "... this pale-eyed sickly-looking piece of respectability, whose subdued tone and glib formality of speech were at this moment almost as repulsive to [**Ladislaw**] as their remembered contrast." 61

—self-deception: "For Bulstrode shrank from a direct lie with an intensity disproportionate to the number of his more indirect misdeeds. But many of these misdeeds were like the subtle muscular movements which are not taken account of in the consciousness, though they bring about the end that

we fix our mind on and desire. And it is only what we are vividly conscious of that we can vividly imagine to be seen by Omniscience." 68 [*GE begins three consecutive sentences with a conjunction. This is technically way below her usual mastery.*]

—*hearing the plain truth:* " 'If you led a harmful life for gain, and kept others out of their rights by deceit, to get the more for yourself, I daresay you repent—you would like to go back, and can't: that must be a bitter thing.' " 69

—*under challenge:* "Bulstrode's native imperiousness and strength of determination served him well. This delicate-looking man, himself nervously perturbed, found the needed stimulus in his strenuous circumstances, and through that difficult night and morning, while he had the air of an animated corpse returned to movement without warmth, holding the mastery by its chill impassibility, his mind was intensely at work thinking of what he had to guard against and what would win him security . . . . Should Providence in this case award death, there was no sin in contemplating death as the desirable issue—if he kept his hands from hastening it—if he scrupulously did what was prescribed." 70

—*pitiable:* "Strange, piteous conflict in the soul of this unhappy man, who had longed for years to be better than he was—who had taken his selfish passions into discipline and clad them in severe robes, so that he had walked with them as a devout quire, till now that a terror had risen among them, and they could chant no longer, but threw out their common cries for safety." 70

—*and Providence:* " . . . it was that haunting ghost of his earlier life which . . . he was trusting that Providence had delivered him from. Yes, Providence. He had not confessed to himself yet that he had done anything in the way of contrivance to this end; he had accepted what seemed to have been offered. It was impossible to prove that he had done anything which hastened the departure of that man's soul." 71

—*disaster:* "The quick vision that his life was after all a failure, that he was a dishonoured man, and must quail before the glance of those towards whom he had habitually assumed the attitude of a reprover—that God had disowned him before men and left him unscreened to the triumphant scorn of those who were glad to have their hatred justified—the sense of utter futility in that equivocation with his conscience in dealing with the life of his accomplice, an equivocation which now turned venomously upon him with the full-grown fang of a discovered lie:—all this rushed through him like the agony of terror which fails to kill, and leaves the ears still open to the returning wave of execration. The sudden sense of exposure after the re-established sense of safety came—not to the coarse organisation of a criminal—but to the susceptible nerve of a man whose intensest being lay in such mastery and predominance as the conditions of his life had shaped for him." 71

—*resilience:* "But in that intense being lay the strength of reaction. Through all his bodily infirmity there ran a tenacious nerve of ambitious self-preserving will, which had continually leaped out like a flame, scattering all doctrinal fears, and which, even while he sat an object of compassion for the merciful, was beginning to stir and glow under his ashy paleness." 71

—*breaking down:* *see* **Mrs Harriet Bulstrode**—*preparing for what is to come*

—*fearing condemnation:* "His equivocations with himself about the death of **Raffles** had sustained the conception of an Omniscience whom he prayed to, yet he had a terror upon him which would not let him expose them to judgment by a full confession to his wife: the acts which he had washed and diluted with inward argument and motive, and for which it seemed comparatively easy to win invisible pardon—what name would she call them? That she should ever silently call his acts Murder was what he could not bear. He felt shrouded by her doubt: he got strength to face her from the sense that she could not yet feel warranted in pronouncing that worst condemnation on him. Some time, perhaps—when he was dying—he would tell her all: in the deep shadow of that time, when she held his hand in the gathering darkness, she might listen without recoiling from his touch. Perhaps: but concealment had been the habit of his life, and the impulse to confession had no power against the dread of a deeper humiliation." 85

Mrs Harriet Bulstrode. "Mr **Vincy**'s sister had made a wealthy match in accepting Mr Bulstrode, who, however, as a man not born in the town, and altogether of dimly-known origin, was considered to have done well in uniting himself with a real Middlemarch family . . . . " 11

—uninspiring: "[Her] *naïve* way of conciliating piety and worldliness, the nothingness of this life and the desirability of cut glass, the consciousness at once of filthy rags and the best damask, was not a sufficient relief from the weight of her husband's invariable seriousness." 27

—familial: "[She] had a true sisterly feeling for her brother [**Vincy**]; always thinking that he might have married better, but wishing well to the children." 31

—confidante: "Now Mrs Bulstrode had a long-standing intimacy with **Mrs Plymdale**. They had nearly the same preferences in silks, patterns for under-clothing, china-ware, and clergymen: they confided their little troubles of health and household management to each other, and various little points of superiority on Mrs Bulstrode's side, namely, more decided seriousness, more admiration for mind, and a house outside the town, sometimes served to give colour to their conversation without dividing them: well-meaning women both; knowing very little of their own motives." 31

—characteristics: "Mrs Bulstrode was a feminine, smaller version of her brother, and had none of her husband's low-toned pallor. She had a good honest glance and used no circumlocution." 31

—trusting: "She believed that her husband was one of those men whose memoirs should be written when they died." 36

—a prejudice: "[She] felt that [**Ladislaw**'s] mode of talking about Catholic countries, as if there were any truce with Antichrist, illustrated the usual tendency to unsoundness in intellectual men." 46

— husband: "She believed in him as an excellent man whose piety carried a peculiar eminence in belonging to a layman, whose influence had raised her own mind towards seriousness, and whose share of perishable good had been the means of raising her own position. But she also liked to think that it was well in every sense for **Mr Bulstrode** to have won the hand of **Harriet Vincy**, whose family was undeniable in a Middlemarch light—a better light surely than any thrown in London thoroughfares or dissenting chapel-yards." 61

—standing: "Mrs Bulstrode was not an object of dislike, and had never consciously injured any human being. Men had always thought her a handsome comfortable woman, and had reckoned it among the signs of **Bulstrode**'s hypocrisy that he had chosen a red-blooded **Vincy**, instead of a

ghastly and melancholy person suited to his low esteem for earthly pleasure. When the scandal about her husband was disclosed they remarked of her—'Ah, poor woman! She's as honest as the day—she never suspected anything wrong in him, you may depend on it.' " 74

—with her brother: " . . . her knees trembled and her usually florid face was deathly pale. Something of the same effect was produced in him by the sight of her: he rose from his seat to meet her, took her by the hand, and said, with his impulsive rashness—

" 'God help you, Harriet! you know all.'

"That moment was perhaps worse than any which came after. It contained that concentrated experience which in great crises of emotion reveals the bias of a nature, and is prophetic of the ultimate act which will end an intermediate struggle." 74

—convulsion of soul: "Without that memory of **Raffles** she might still have thought only of monetary ruin, but now along with her brother's look and words there darted into her mind the idea of some guilt in her husband—then, under the working of terror came the image of her husband exposed to disgrace—and then, after an instant of scorching shame in which she felt only the eyes of the world, with one leap of her heart she was at his side in mournful but unreproaching fellowship with shame and isolation." 74

—preparing for what is to come: "She locked herself in her room. She needed time to get used to her maimed consciousness, her poor lopped life, before she could walk steadily to the place allotted her. A new searching light had fallen on her husband's character, and she could not judge him leniently: the twenty years in which she had believed in him and venerated him by virtue of his concealments came back with particulars that made them seem an odious deceit. He had married her with that bad past life hidden behind him and she had no faith left to protest his innocence of the worst that was imputed to him. Her honest ostentatious [?] nature made the sharing of a merited dishonour as bitter as it could be to any mortal.

"But this imperfectly-taught woman, whose phrases and habits were an odd patchwork, had a loyal spirit within her. The man whose prosperity she had shared through nearly half a life, and who had unvaryingly cherished her—now that punishment had befallen him it was not possible to her in any sense to forsake him. There is a forsaking which still sits at the same board and lies on the same couch with the forsaken soul, withering it the more by unloving proximity. She knew, when she locked her door, that she should unlock it ready to go down to her unhappy husband and espouse his sorrow, and say of his guilt, I will mourn and not reproach.

"But she needed time to gather up her strength; she needed to sob out her farewell to all the gladness and pride of her life. When she had resolved to go down, she prepared herself by some little acts which might seem mere folly to a hard onlooker; they were her way of expressing to all spectators visible or invisible that she had begun a new life in which she embraced humiliation. She took off all her ornaments and put on a plain black gown, and instead of wearing her much-adorned cap and large bows of hair, she brushed her hair down and put on a plain bonnet-cap, which made her look suddenly like an early Methodist." ¶74

The Bulstrodes

—*going to him:* "He dared not look up at her. He sat with his eyes bent down, and as she went towards him she thought he looked smaller—he seemed so withered and shrunken. A movement of new compassion and old tenderness went through her like a great wave, and putting one hand on his which rested on the arm of the chair, and the other on his shoulder, she said, solemnly but kindly—

" 'Look up, **Nicholas**.'

"He raised his eyes with a little start and looked at her half amazed for a moment: her pale face, her changed, mourning dress, the trembling about her mouth, all said, 'I know;' and her hands and eyes rested gently on him. He burst out crying and they cried together, she sitting at his side. They could not yet speak to each other of the shame which she was bearing with him, or of the acts which had brought it down on them. His confession was silent, and her promise of faithfulness was silent." 74

—*sadness:* "Set free by [her daughters'] absence from the intolerable necessity of accounting for her grief or of beholding their frightened wonder, she could live unconstrainedly with the sorrow that was every day streaking her hair with whiteness and making her eyelids languid . . . .

"**Bulstrode**, sitting opposite to her, ached at the sight of that grief-worn face, which two months before had been bright and blooming. It had aged to keep sad company with his own withered features." 85

**

Mrs Elinor Cadwallader, *née* **De Bracy**. "In spite of her shabby bonnet and very old Indian shawl, it was plain that the lodge-keeper regarded her as an important personage, from the low curtsy which was dropped on the entrance of the small phaeton." 6

" . . . a lady of immeasurably high birth, descended, as it were, from unknown earls, dim as the crowd of heroic shades—who pleaded poverty, pared down prices, and cut jokes in the most companionable manner, though with a turn of tongue that let you know who she was. Such a lady gave a neighbourliness to both rank and religion, and mitigated the bitterness of uncommuted tithe. A much more exemplary character with an infusion of sour dignity would not have furthered their comprehension of the Thirty-nine Articles, and would have been less socially uniting." 6

" . . . a thin but well-built figure." 6

—*poverty:* " 'I set a bad example—married a poor clergyman, and made myself a pitiable object among the **De Bracy**s—obliged to get my coals by stratagem, and pray to heaven for my salad oil.' " 6

—*mode of life:* "Her life was rurally simple, quite free from secrets either foul, dangerous, or otherwise important, and not consciously affected by the great affairs of the world. All the more did the affairs of the great world interest her, when communicated in the letters of high-born relations: the way in which fascinating younger sons had gone to the dogs by marrying their mistresses; the fine old-blooded idiocy of young **Lord Tapir**, and the furious gouty humours of old **Lord Megatherium**, the exact crossing of genealogies which had brought a coronet into a new branch and widened the relation of scandal— these were topics of which she retained details with the utmost accuracy, and reproduced them in an excellent pickle of epigrams, which she herself enjoyed the more because she believed as unquestioningly in birth and no-birth as she did in game and vermin." 6

—tart tongue: " 'A man always makes a fool of himself, speechifying: there's no excuse but being on the right side, so that you can ask a blessing on your humming and hawing. You will lose yourself, I forewarn you. You will make a Saturday pie of all parties' opinions, and be pelted by everybody.' " 6

" '**Casaubon** has money enough; I must do him that justice. As to his blood, I suppose the family quarterings are three cuttle-fish sable, and a commentator rampant . . . . A great bladder for dried peas to rattle in!' " 6

" ' . . . when a woman is not contradicted, she has no motive for obstinacy in her absurdities.' " 6

" 'Somebody put a drop [of **Mr Casaubon**'s blood] under a magnifying-glass, and it was all semi-colons and parentheses' . . . . " 8

" 'He dreams footnotes, and they run away with all his brains.' " 8

" 'Really, by the side of **Sir James** he looks like a death's head skinned over for the occasion.' " 10

"Priority is a poor recommendation in a husband if he has got no other. I would rather have a good second husband than an indifferent first.' " 55

—prejudice: "But her feeling towards the vulgar rich was a sort of religious hatred: they had probably made all their money out of high retail prices, and Mrs Cadwallader detested high prices for everything that was not paid in kind at the Rectory: such people were no part of God's design in making the world; and their accent was an affliction to the ears. A town where such monsters abounded was hardly more than a sort of low comedy, which could not be taken account of in a well-bred scheme of the universe." 6

—mind, "active as phosphorous, biting everything that came near into the form that suited it . . . . " 6

—on medicine: " 'It strengthens the disease,' said the Rector's wife, much too well-born not to be an amateur in medicine. 'Everything depends on the constitution: some people make fat, some blood, and some bile—that's my view of the matter; and whatever they take is a sort of grist to the mill.' " 10

—on sermons: " 'Oh, my dear, when you have a clergyman in your family you must accommodate your tastes: I did that very early. When I married **Humphrey** I made up my mind to like sermons, and I set out by liking the end very much. That soon spread to the middle and the beginning, because I couldn't have the end without them.' " 34

—pungent advice: " 'You will certainly go mad in that house alone, my dear. You will see visions. We have all got to exert ourselves a little to keep sane, and call things by the same names as other people call them by. To be sure, for younger sons and women who have no money, it is a sort of provision to go mad: they are taken care of then. But you must not run into that. I daresay you are little bored here with our good dowager; but think what a bore you might become yourself to your fellow-creatures if you were always playing tragedy queen and taking things sublimely. Sitting alone in that library at Lowick you may fancy yourself ruling the weather; you must get a few people round you who wouldn't believe you if you told them. That is a good lowering medicine.' " 54

Humphrey Cadwallader. " '[He] finds everybody charming. I never can get him to abuse **Casaubon**. He will even speak well of the bishop, though I tell him it is unnatural in a beneficed clergyman: what can one do with a husband who attends so little to the decencies?' " 6

—*characteristics:* "Mr Cadwallader was a large man, with full lips and a sweet smile; very plain and rough in his exterior, but with that solid imperturbable ease and good-humour which is infectious, and like great grassy hills in the sunshine, quiets even an irritated egoism, and makes it rather ashamed of itself." 8

—*indolent:* "He always saw the joke of any satire against himself. His conscience was large and easy, like the rest of him: it did only what it could do without any trouble." 8

—*on the mark:* " 'My dear fellow, we are rather apt to consider an act wrong because it is unpleasant to us' said the Rector, quietly. Like many men who take life easily, he had the knack of saying a home truth occasionally to those who felt themselves virtuously out of temper. **Sir James** took out his handkerchief and began to bite the corner." 84

**

Caleb Garth "had failed in the building business, which he had unfortunately added to his other avocations of surveyor, valuer, and agent, had conducted that business for a time entirely for the benefit of his assignees, and had been living narrowly, exerting himself to the utmost that he might after all pay twenty shillings in the pound. He had now achieved this . . . . " 23

—*unwary:* " . . a large amount of painful experience had not sufficed to make Caleb Garth cautious about his own affairs, or distrustful of his fellow-men when they had not proved themselves untrustworthy . . . . He was one of those rare men who are rigid to themselves and indulgent to others. He had a certain shame about his neighbours' errors, and never spoke of them willingly. . . . If he had to blame any one, it was necessary for him to move all the papers within his reach, or describe various diagrams with his stick or make calculations with the odd money in his pocket, before he could begin; and he would rather do other men's work than find fault with their doing. I fear he was a bad disciplinarian." 23

—*habits:* "[He] lowered his spectacles, measured the space at his command, reached his pen and examined it, dipped it in the ink and examined it again, then pushed the paper a little way from him, lifted up his spectacles again, showed a deepened depression in the outer angle of his bushy eyebrows, which gave his face a peculiar mildness (pardon these details for once—you would have learned to love them if you had known Caleb Garth). . . . " 23

—*his veneration:* "Caleb Garth often shook his head in meditation on the value, the indispensable might of that myriad-headed, myriad-handed labour by which the social body is fed, clothed, and housed. It had laid hold of his imagination in boyhood. The echoes of the great hammer where roof or keel were a-making, the signal-shouts of the workmen, the roar of the furnace, the thunder and plash of the engine, were a sublime music to him; the felling and lading of timber, and the huge trunk vibrating star-like in the distance along the highway; the crane at work on the wharf, the piled-up produce in warehouse, the precision and variety of muscular effort wherever exact work had to be turned out—all these sights of his youth had acted on him as poetry without the aid of the poets, had made a philosophy for him without the aid of philosophers, a religion without the aid of theology. His early ambition had been to have as effective a share as possible in this sublime labour, which was peculiarly dignified by him with the name of 'business,' and though he had only been a short time under a surveyor, and had been chiefly his own teacher, he knew more of land, building, and mining than most of the special men in the county." 24

"I think his virtual divinities were good practical schemes, accurate work, and the faithful completion of undertakings; his prince of darkness was a slack workman . . . he was ready to accept any number of systems, like any number of firmaments, if they did not obviously interfere with the best land-drainage, solid building, correct measuring, and judicious boring (for coal). In fact, he had a reverential soul with a strong practical intelligence." 24 *GE evokes her father.*

—weak spot: 'But he could not manage finance: he knew values well, but he had no keenness of imagination for monetary results in the shape of profit and loss: and having ascertained this to his cost, he determined to give up all forms of his beloved 'business' which required that talent. He gave himself up entirely to the many kinds of work which he could do without handling capital, and was one of those precious men within his own district whom everybody would choose to work for them, because he did his work well, charged very little, and often declined to charge at all. It is no wonder, then, that the Garths were poor, and 'lived in a small way.' However, they did not mind it." 24

—another weak spot: "[**Mary**] turned round to her father, and putting her arms round his neck kissed him with childish kisses which he delighted in—the expression of his large brows softening as the expression of a great beautiful dog softens when it is caressed. Mary was his favourite child, and whatever **Susan** might say, and right as she was on all other subjects, Caleb thought it natural that **Fred** or any one else should think Mary more lovable than other girls." 25

—paternal wisdom: " ' . . . what I am thinking of is—what it must be for a wife when she's never sure of her husband, when he hasn't got a principle in him to make him more afraid of doing the wrong thing by others than of getting his own toes pinched . . . . Young folks may get fond of each other before they know what life is, and they may think it all holiday if they can only get together; but it soon turns into working-day, my dear.' " 25

—his candour: " 'Garth is an independent fellow [said **Cadwallader**]: an original, simple-minded fellow. One day, when he was doing some valuation for me, he told me point-blank that clergymen seldom understood anything about business, and did mischief when they meddled; but he said it as quietly and respectfully as if he had been talking to me about sailors.' " 38

—good news: "His face had an expression of grave surprise, which alarmed [his wife] a little . . . till she saw him suddenly shaken by a little joyous laugh as he turned back to the beginning of the letter . . . . " 40

—linguistics: " . . . his talents did not lie in finding phrases, though he was very particular about his letter-writing, and regarded his wife as a treasury of correct language . . . .

" 'Things hang together,' he added, looking on the floor and moving his feet uneasily with a sense that words were scantier than thoughts." 40

" 'The soul of man . . . when it gets fairly rotten, will bear you all sorts of poisonous toad-stools, and no eye can see whence came the seed thereof.'

"It was one of Caleb's quaintnesses, that in his difficulty of finding speech for his thought, he caught, as it were, snatches of diction which he associated with various points of view or states of mind, and whenever he had a feeling of awe, he was haunted by a sense of Biblical phraseology, though he could hardly have given a direct quotation." 40

—his creed: " '. . . it's a fine thing to come to a man when he's seen into the nature of business to have the chance of getting a bit of the country into good fettle, as they say, and putting men into the right way with their farming, and getting a bit of good contriving and solid building done—that those who are living and those who come after will be the better for. I'd sooner have it than a fortune. I hold it the most honourable work that is.' " 40

—subtext: " 'There's no sort of work,' said Caleb, with fervour, putting out his hand and moving it up and down to mark his emphasis, 'that could ever be done well, if you minded what fools say. You must have it inside you that your plan is right, and that plan you must follow.' " 40

—strong language: " 'Duce knows,' said Caleb, who never referred the knowledge of discreditable doings to any higher power than the deuce." 40

—a rare quality: "But Caleb was peculiar: certain human tendencies which are commonly strong were almost absent from his mind, and one of these was curiosity about personal affairs. Especially if there was anything discreditable to be found out concerning another man, Caleb preferred not to know it; and if he had to tell anybody under him that his evil doings were discovered, he was more embarrassed than the culprit." 53

—and music: "Caleb was very fond of music, and when he could afford it went to hear an oratorio that came within his reach, returning from it with a profound reverence for this mighty structure of tones, which made him sit meditatively, looking on the floor and throwing much unutterable language into his outstretched hands." 56

—and labourers: "Caleb was a powerful man and knew little of any fear except the fear of hurting others and the fear of having to speechify. But he felt it his duty at this moment to try and give a little harangue. There was a striking mixture in him—which came from his having always been a hard-working man himself—of rigorous notions about workmen and practical indulgence towards them. To do a good day's work and to do it well, he held to be part of their welfare, as if was the chief part of his own happiness; but he had a strong sense of fellowship with them." 56

—speaking: " . . . taking as usual to brief phrases, which seemed pregnant to himself, because he had many thoughts lying under them, like the abundant roots of a plant that just manages to peep above the water." 56

—guidance to youth: " . . . lowering his voice, with the air of a man who felt himself to be saying something deeply religious. 'You must be sure of two things: you must love your work, and not be always looking over the edge of it, wanting your play to begin. And the other is, you must not be ashamed of your work, and think it would be more honourable to you to be doing something else. You must have a pride in your own work and in learning to do it well, and not be always saying, There's this and there's that—if I had this or that to do, I might make something of it. No matter what a man is—I wouldn't give twopence for him'—here Caleb's mouth looked bitter, and he snapped his fingers—'whether he was the prime minister or the rick-thatcher, if he didn't do well what he undertook to do.' " 56

—his mind made up: "With regard to a large number of matters about which other men are decided or obstinate, he was the most easily manageable man in the world. He never knew what meat he would choose, and if **Susan** had said that they ought to live in a four-roomed cottage, in order to save, he

would have said, 'Let us go,' without inquiring into details. But where Caleb's feeling and judgment strongly pronounced, he was a ruler; and in spite of his mildness and timidity in reproving, every one about him knew that on the exceptional occasions when he chose, he was absolute. He never, indeed, chose to be absolute except on some one else's behalf. On ninety-nine points Mrs Garth decided, but on the hundredth she was often aware that she would have to perform the singularly difficult task of carrying out her own principle, and to make herself subordinate." 56

—frank and true: " 'I am sorry. I don't judge you and say, he is wicked, and I am righteous. God forbid. I don't know everything. A man may do wrong, and his will may rise clear out of it, though he can't get his life clear. That's a bad punishment. If it is so with you—well, I'm very sorry for you. But I have that feeling inside me, that I can't go on working with you. That's all, **Mr Bulstrode**. Everything else is buried, so far as my will goes. And I wish you good-day.' " 69

—something to say: "**Mary** knew quite well that her father had something particular to say: his eyebrows made their pathetic angle, and there was a tender gravity in his voice: these things had been signs to her when she was **Letty**'s age." 86

Mrs Susan Garth. "Mrs Vincy had never been at her ease with Mrs Garth, and frequently spoke of her as a woman who had had to work for her bread— meaning that Mrs Garth had been a teacher before her marriage." 23

—disciplined: "Not that she was inclined to sarcasm and to impulsive sallies, as **Mary** was. In her present matronly age at least, Mrs Garth never committed herself by over-hasty speech; having, as she said, borne the yoke in her youth, and learned self-control. She had that rare sense which discerns what is unalterable, and submits to it without murmuring. Adoring her husband's virtues, she had very early made up her mind to his incapacity of minding his own interests, and had met the consequences cheerfully. She had been magnanimous enough to renounce all pride in teapots or children's frilling, and had never poured any pathetic confidences into the ears of her feminine neighbours concerning Mr Garth's want of prudence and the sums he might have had if he had been like other men. Hence these fair neighbours thought her either proud or eccentric, and sometimes spoke of her to their husbands as 'your fine Mrs Garth.' " 24

—and the sexes: "She was . . . apt to be a little severe towards her own sex, which in her opinion was framed to be entirely subordinate. On the other hand, she was disproportionately indulgent towards the failings of men, and was often heard to say that these were natural." 24

—pedagogic: "She thought it good for [her pupils] to see that she could make an excellent lather while she corrected their blunders 'without looking'—that a woman with her sleeves tucked up about her elbows might know all about the Subjunctive Mood or the Torrid Zone—that, in short, she might possess 'education' and other good things ending in 'tion,' and worthy to be pronounced emphatically, without being a useless doll. When she made remarks to this edifying effect, she had a firm little frown on her brow, which yet did not hinder her face from looking benevolent, and her words which came forth like a procession were uttered in a fervid agreeable contralto. Certainly the exemplary Mrs Garth had her droll aspects, but her character sustained her oddities, as a very fine wine sustains a flavour of skin." 24

—*characteristics:* "She was of the same curly-haired, square-faced type as Mary, but handsomer, with more delicacy of feature, a pale skin, a solid matronly figure, and remarkable firmness of glance." 24

—*bad news:* "Like the eccentric woman she was, she was at present absorbed in considering what was to be done, and did not fancy that the end could be better achieved by bitter remarks or explosions. But she had made **Fred** feel for the first time something like the tooth of remorse." 24

—*cogent:* " . . . boys cannot well be apprenticed ultimately: they should be apprenticed at fifteen.' " 24

—*torn:* " 'I say that young man's soul is in my hand; and I'll do the best I can for him, so help me God! It's my duty, Susan.'

"Mrs Garth was not given to tears, but there was a large one rolling down her face before her husband had finished. It came from the pressure of various feelings, in which there was much affection and some vexation. She wiped it away quickly, saying—

" 'Few men besides you would think it a duty to add to their anxieties in that way, **Caleb** . . . . '

"But she went out and had a hearty cry to make up for the suppression of her words. She felt sure that her husband's conduct would be misunderstood, and about **Fred** she was rational and unhopeful. Which would turn out to have the more foresight in it—her rationality or Caleb's ardent generosity?" 56

—*strategy:* "She was knitting, and could either look at **Fred** or not, as she chose—always an advantage when one is bent on loading speech with salutary meaning . . . . " 57

—*stirred:* "The power of admonition which had begun to stir in Mrs Garth had not yet discharged itself. It was a little too provoking even for her self-control that this blooming youngster should flourish on the disappointments of sadder and wiser people—making a meal of a nightingale and never knowing it—and that all the while his family should suppose that hers was in eager need of this sprig, and her vexation had fermented the more actively because of its total repression towards her husband. Exemplary wives will sometimes find scapegoats in this way." 57

**

Walter Vincy, "the newly-elected mayor of Middlemarch, who happened to be a manufacturer . . . .

" 'I should be glad of any treatment that would cure me without reducing me to a skeleton, like poor **Grainger**,' said [he], a florid man, who would have served for a study of flesh in striking contrast with the Franciscan tints of **Mr Bulstrode**." 10

—*circumspect:* "Mr Vincy was more inclined to general good-fellowship than to taking sides, but there was no need for him to be hasty in making any new man's acquaintance . . . . An alderman about to be mayor must by-and-by enlarge his dinner parties, but at present there were plenty of guests at his well-spread table." 11

—*impatient:* "When a man has the immediate prospect of being mayor, and is ready, in the interests of commerce, to take up a firm attitude on politics generally, he has naturally a sense of his importance to the framework of things which seems to throw questions of private conduct into the background." 13

—upset: " 'I tell you what, **Wrench**, this is beyond a joke,' said the Mayor, who of late had had to rebuke offenders with an official air, and now broadened himself by putting his thumbs in his armholes." 27

—reneging: "This was a not infrequent procedure with Mr Vincy—to be rash in jovial assent, and on becoming subsequently conscious that he had been rash, to employ others in making the offensive retraction." 36

—not a chance: "Apart from his dinners and his coursing, Mr Vincy, blustering as he was, had as little of his own way as if he had been a prime minister: The force of circumstances was easily too much for him, as it is for most pleasure-loving florid men; and the circumstance called **Rosamond** was particularly forcible by means of that mild persistence which, as we know, enables a white soft living substance to make its way in spite of opposing rock. Papa was not a rock: he had no other fixity than that fixity of alternating impulses sometimes called habit, and this was altogether unfavourable to his taking the only decisive line of conduct in relation to his daughter's engagement—namely to inquire thoroughly into **Lydgate**'s circumstances, declare his own inability to furnish money, and forbid alike either a speedy marriage or an engagement which must be too lengthy.

"That seems very simple and easy in the statement, but a disagreeable resolve formed in the chill hours of the morning had as many conditions against it as the early frost, and rarely persisted under the warming influences of the day. The indirect though emphatic expression of opinion to which Mr Vincy was prone suffered much restraint in this case: Lydgate was a proud man towards whom innuendoes were obviously unsafe, and throwing his hat on the floor was out of the question. Mr Vincy was a little in awe of him, a little vain that he wanted to marry Rosamond, a little indisposed to raise a question of money on which his own position was not advantageous, a little afraid of being worsted in dialogue with a man better educated and more highly bred than himself, and a little afraid of doing what his daughter would not like.

"The part Mr Vincy preferred playing was that of the generous host whom nobody criticised. In the earlier half of the day there was business to hinder any formal communication of an adverse resolve; in the later there was dinner, wine, whist, and general satisfaction. And in the meanwhile the hours were each leaving their little deposit and gradually forming the final reason for inaction, namely, that action was too late." ¶36

—disappointment: "Mr Vincy listened [to **Fred**'s new plans] in profound surprise without uttering even an exclamation, a silence which in his impatient temperament was a sign of unusual emotion. He had not been in good spirits about trade that morning, and the slight bitterness in his lips grew intense as he listened. When Fred had ended, there was a pause of nearly a minute, during which Mr Vincy replaced a book in his desk and turned the key emphatically. Then he looked at his son steadily, and said—

" 'So you've made up your mind at last, sir?'

" 'Yes, father.'

" 'Very well: stick to it. I've no more to say. You've thrown away your education, and gone down a step in life, when I had given you the means of rising, that's all . . . . I wash my hands of you. I only hope, when you have a son of your own he will make a better return for the pains you spend on him.'

"This was very cutting to Fred. His father was using that unfair advantage possessed by us all when we are in a pathetic situation and see our own past as if it were simply part of the pathos. In reality, Mr Vincy's wishes about his son had had a great deal of pride, inconsiderateness, and egoistic folly in them." 56

Mrs Lucy (26) **Vincy**. " . . . Mr Vincy had descended a little, having taken an innkeeper's daughter. But on this side too there was a cheering sense of money; for Mrs Vincy's sister had been second wife to rich old Mr **Featherstone** and had died childless years ago, so that her nephews and nieces might be supposed to touch the affections of the widower." 11

—*sunny:* "[Her instruction was given] without any change in the radiant good-humour of Mrs Vincy's face, in which forty-five years had delved neither angles nor parallels, and pushing back her pink cap-strings, she let her work rest on her lap, while she looked admiringly at her daughter." 11

" 'Look at my mother: you don't see her objecting to everything except what she does herself. She is my notion of a pleasant woman.' " 11

—*demeanour:* "She disliked anything which reminded her that her mother's father had been an innkeeper. Certainly any one remembering the fact might think that Mrs Vincy had the air of a very handsome good-humoured landlady, accustomed to the most capricious orders of gentlemen." 11

—*vulgar:* " . . . the matron's blooming good-natured face, with the too volatile pink strings floating from her fine throat, and her cheery manners to husband and children, was certainly among the great attractions of the Vincy house—attractions which made it all the easier to fall in love with the daughter. The tinge of unpretentious, inoffensive vulgarity in Mrs Vincy gave more effect to **Rosamond**'s refinement, which was beyond what **Lydgate** had expected." 16

—*a happy family:* "The Vincys had the readiness to enjoy, the rejection of all anxiety, and the belief in life as a merry lot, which made a house exceptional in most county towns at that time when Evangelicalism had cast a certain suspicion as of plague infection over the few amusements which survived in the provinces." 16

—*a mother distraught:* " . . . her brightness was all bedimmed; unconscious of her costume which had always been so fresh and gay, she was like a sick bird with languid eye and plumage ruffled, her senses dulled to the sights and sounds that used most to interest her. **Fred**'s delirium, in which he seemed to be wandering out of her reach, tore her heart. After her first outburst against **Mr Wrench** she went about very quietly: her one low cry was to **Lydgate**. She would follow him out of the room and put her hand on his arm moaning out, 'Save my boy.' Once she pleaded, 'He has always been good to me, Mr Lydgate: he never had a hard word for his mother,'—as if poor Fred's suffering were an accusation against him. All the deepest fibres of the mother's memory were stirred, and the young man whose voice took a gentler tone when he spoke to her, was one with the babe whom she had loved, with a love new to her, before he was born." 27

—*the worst over:* " . . . Mrs Vincy felt as if after all the illness had made a festival for her tenderness." 27

—*dressed for a funeral:* "[Her] expense in handsome crape seemed to imply the most presumptuous hopes, suggested by a bloom of complexion which told pretty plainly that she was not a blood-relation, but of the generally objectionable class called wife's kin." 34

—disappointment: " . . . she was inconsolable, having before her eyes what perhaps her husband had never thought of, the certainty that **Fred** would marry **Mary Garth**, that her life would henceforth be spoiled by a perpetual infusion of Garths and their ways, and that her darling boy, with his beautiful face and stylish air 'beyond anybody else's son in Middlemarch,' would be sure to get like that family in plainness of appearance and carelessness about his clothes . . . . Her temper was too sweet for her to show any anger, but she felt that her happiness had received a bruise, and for several days merely to look at Fred made her cry a little as if he were the subject of some baleful prophecy." 56

—comfort: " 'Come, Lucy my dear, don't be so down-hearted. You always have spoiled the boy, and you must go on spoiling him . . . . Don't make it worse by letting me see you out of spirits.'

" 'Well, I won't,' said Mrs Vincy, roused by this appeal and adjusting herself with a little shake as of a bird which lays down its ruffled plumage." 56

—prospective mother-in-law: "Mrs Vincy, in her fullest matronly bloom, looked at **Mary**'s little figure, rough wavy hair, and visage quite without lilies and roses, and wondered; trying unsuccessfully to fancy herself caring about Mary's appearance in wedding clothes, or feeling complacency in grandchildren who would 'feature' the **Garth**s." 63

Significant Bachelors

Arthur Brooke, "a man of nearly sixty, of acquiescent temper, miscellaneous opinions, and uncertain vote. He had travelled in his younger years, and was held in this part of the county to have contracted a too rambling habit of mind. Mr Brooke's conclusions were as difficult to predict as the weather: it was only safe to say that he would act with benevolent intentions, and that he would spend as little money as possible in carrying them out." 1

—weak point: "[He was] blamed in neighbouring families for not securing some middle-[aged lady as guide and companion to his nieces. But he himself dreaded so much the sort of superior woman likely to be available for such a position, that he allowed himself to be dissuaded by **Dorothea**'s objections. . . ." 1

—casual remark: " 'Young ladies are too flighty.'

" . . . the remark lay in his mind as lightly as the broken wing of an insect among all the other fragments there, and a chance current had sent it alighting on *her* [**Dorothea**]." 2

—conversational quirk: "[Speaking] from his usual tendency to say what he had said before. This fundamental principle of human speech was markedly exhibited in Mr Brooke." 4

—fundamental asset: "What feeling he, as a magistrate who had taken in so many ideas, could make room for, was unmixedly kind." 4

—puzzled: "Mr Brooke wondered, and felt that women were an inexhaustible subject of study, since even he at his age was not in a perfect state of scientific prediction about them. Here was a fellow like **Chettam** with no chance at all." 4

"In short, woman was a problem which, since Mr Brooke's mind felt blank before it, could be hardly less complicated than the revolutions of an irregular solid." 4

—*a bachelor:* " 'I never married myself . . . I never loved any one well enough to put myself into a noose for them. It is a noose, you know. Temper, now. There is temper. And a husband likes to be master.' " 4

—*a fear:* " . . . where is a country gentleman to go who quarrels with his oldest neighbours? Who could taste the fine flavour in the name of Brooke if it were delivered casually, like wine without a seal? Certainly a man can only be cosmopolitan up to a certain point." 6

—*appraised:* " 'Brooke is a very good fellow, but pulpy; he will run into any mould, but he won't keep shape.' " 8

—*coached, but with difficulty:* "Mr Brooke always ended by agreeing with **Ladislaw**, who still appeared to him a sort of **Burke** with a leaven of **Shelley**; but after an interval the wisdom of his own methods reasserted itself, and he was again drawn into using them with much hopefulness . . . his powers of convincing and persuading had not yet been tested by anything more difficult than a chairman's speech introducing other orators, or a dialogue with a Middlemarch voter, from which he came away with a sense that he was a tactician by nature, and that it was a pity he had not gone earlier into this kind of thing." 51

—*as speechmaker:* " . . . Mr Brooke's mind, if it had the burthen of remembering any train of thought, would let it drop, run away in search of it, and not easily come back again. To collect documents is one mode of serving your country, and to remember the contents of a document is another. No! the only way in which Mr Brooke could be coerced into thinking of the right arguments at the right time was to be well plied with them till they took up all the room in his brain.. But here there was the difficulty of finding room, so many things having been taken in beforehand. Mr Brooke himself observed that his ideas stood rather in his way when he was speaking." 51

"Pray pity him: so many English gentlemen make themselves miserable by speechifying on entirely private grounds! whereas Mr Brooke wished to serve his country . . . .

"The striking points in his appearance were his buff waistcoat, short-clipped blond hair, and neutral physiognomy." 51

—*sherry at the wrong moment:* "It was ill-chosen; for Mr Brooke was an abstemious man, and to drink a second glass of sherry quickly at no great interval from the first was a surprise to his system which tended to scatter his energies instead of collecting them." 51

Rev. Camden Farebrother. "**Mr Vincy** liked well enough the notion of the chaplain's having a salary, supposing it were given to Farebrother, who was as good a little fellow as ever breathed, and the best preacher anywhere, and companionable too." 16

—*arrival:* " . . . Mr Farebrother came in—a handsome, broad-chested but otherwise small man, about forty, whose black was very threadbare: the brilliancy was all in his quick grey eyes. He came like a pleasant change in the light, arresting little **Louisa** with fatherly nonsense as she was being led out of the room by **Miss Morgan**, greeting everybody with some special word, and seeming to condense more talk into ten minutes than had been held all through the evening." 16

—*at whist:* "[**Lydgate**] got interested in watching Mr Farebrother's play, which was masterly, and also his face, which was a striking mixture of the shrewd and the mild. . . . there was punch-drinking; but Mr Farebrother had only a glass of water. He was winning, but there seemed to be no reason why the renewal of rubbers should end . . . . " 16

—*conversation:* "The Vicar's frankness seemed not of the repulsive sort that comes from an uneasy consciousness seeking to forestall the judgment of others, but simply the relief of a desire to do with as little pretence as possible." 17

—*personal qualities:* "[That he] should have taken pains rather to warn off than to obtain his interest, showed an unusual delicacy and generosity, which **Lydgate**'s nature was keenly alive to. It went along with other points of conduct in Mr Farebrother which were exceptionally fine, and made his character resemble those southern landscapes which seem divided between natural grandeur and social slovenliness. Very few men could have been as filial and chivalrous as he was to the mother, aunt, and sister, whose dependence on him had in many ways shaped his life rather uneasily for himself; few men who feel the pressure of small needs are so nobly resolute not to dress up their inevitably self-interested desires in a pretext of better motives . . . . Besides, he was a likeable man: sweet-tempered, ready-witted, frank, without grins of suppressed bitterness or other conversational flavours which make half of us an affliction to our friends." 18

—*as a preacher:* "Then, his preaching was ingenious and pithy, like the preaching of the English Church in its robust age, and his sermons were delivered without book. People outside his parish went to hear him, and, since to fill the church was always the most difficult part of a clergyman's function, here was another ground for a careless sense of superiority." 18

—*the flaw:* " . . . it was a continually repeated shock, disturbing **Lydgate**'s esteem, that the Vicar should obviously play for the sake of money . . . . The Vicar was a first-rate billiard-player, and though he did not frequent the Green Dragon, there were reports that he had sometimes been there in the daytime and won money." 18

—*no Pharisee he:* "[He] had certainly escaped the slightest tincture of the Pharisee, and by dint of admitting to himself that he was too much as other men were, he had become remarkably unlike them in this—that he could excuse others for thinking slightly of him, and could judge impartially of their conduct even when it told against him." 18

—*admired:* "**Mary** admired the keen-faced handsome little Vicar in his well-brushed threadbare clothes more than any man she had had the opportunity of knowing. She had never heard him say a foolish thing, though she knew that he did unwise ones . . . . " 40

—*colloquy:* "The Vicar was holding an inward dialogue in which he told himself that there was probably something more between **Fred** and **Mary Garth** than the regard of old playfellows, and replied with a question whether that bit of womanhood were not a great deal too choice for that crude young gentleman. The rejoinder to this was the first shrug. Then he laughed at himself for being likely to have felt jealous, as if he had been a man able to marry, which, added he, it is as clear as any balance-sheet that I am not. Whereupon followed the second shrug." 40

—*wise advice:* " ' . . . try and keep clear of wanting small sums that you [**Lydgate**] haven't got. I am perhaps talking rather superfluously, but a man likes to assume superiority over himself, by holding up his bad example and sermonising on it.' " 45

—*summarized and recommended:* " 'I never heard such good preaching as his—such plain, easy eloquence [said **Lydgate**] . . . . His talk is just as good about all subjects: original, simple, clear. I think him a remarkable fellow; he ought to have done more than he has done . . . .

" 'He is very fond of Natural History and various scientific matters, and he is hampered in reconciling these tastes with his position. He has no money to spare—hardly enough to use; and that has led him into card-playing . . . . He does play for money, and he wins a good deal. Of course that takes him into company a little beneath him, and makes him slack about some things, and yet, with all that, looking at him as a whole, I think he is one of the most blameless men I ever knew. He has neither venom nor doubleness in him, and those often go with a more correct outside.' " 50

—*policy:* " 'I don't feel bound to give up St Botolph's. It is protest enough against the pluralism they want to reform if I give somebody else most of the money. The stronger thing is not to give up power, but to use it well.' " 52

—*conscience*: "He was one of the natures in which conscience gets the more active when the yoke of life ceases to gall them. He made no display of humility on the subject, but in his heart he felt rather ashamed that his conduct had shown laches which others who did not get benefices were free from." 52

—*hard duty done:* " . . . something indefinable, something like the resolute suppression of a pain in Mr Farebrother's manner, made [**Mary**] feel suddenly miserable . . . .

"In three minutes the Vicar was on horseback again, having gone magnanimously through a duty much harder than the renunciation of whist, or even than the writing of penitential meditations." 52

—*rumination:* " 'To think of the part one little woman can play in the life of a man, so that to renounce her may be a very good imitation of heroism, and to win her may be a discipline!' " 66

Peter Featherstone, widower, "holding his stick between his knees and settling his wig, while he gave [**Mrs Waule**] a momentary sharp glance, which seemed to react on him like a draught of cold air and set him coughing." 12

—*stirred:* "Mr Featherstone rubbed the knob of his stick and made a brief convulsive show of laughter, which had much the same genuineness as an old whist-player's chuckle over a bad hand." 12

—*abrupt:* " '**Mrs Waule**, you had better go.'

"Even those neighbours who had called Peter Featherstone an old fox, had never accused him of being insincerely polite, and his sister was quite used to the peculiar absence of ceremony with which he marked his sense of blood-relationship." 12

—*quizzical:* "He continued to look at **Fred** with the same twinkle and with one of his habitual grimaces, alternately screwing and widening his mouth; and when he spoke, it was in a low tone, which might be taken for that of an informer ready to be bought off, rather than for the tone of an offended senior. He was not a man to feel any strong moral indignation even on account of trespasses against himself. It was natural that others should want to get an advantage over him, but then, he was a little too cunning for them." 12

Peter Featherstone, Mary Garth, Mrs Waule, and Rosamond

—hating his relations: "For the old man's dislike of his own family seemed to get stronger as he got less able to amuse himself by saying biting things to them. Too languid to sting, he had the more venom refluent in his blood." 32

—spending on his funeral: "He loved money, but he also loved to spend it in gratifying his peculiar tastes, and perhaps he loved it best of all as a means of making others feel his power more or less uncomfortably." 34

—using his imagination: " . . . in writing the programme for his burial he certainly did not make clear to himself that his pleasure in the little drama of which it formed a part was confined to anticipation. In chuckling over the vexations he could inflict by the rigid clutch of his dead hand, he inevitably mingled his consciousness with that livid stagnant presence, and so far as he was preoccupied with a future life, it was with one of gratification inside his coffin. Thus old Featherstone was imaginative, after his fashion." 34

Will Ladislaw. " . . . when he lifted his hat, Dorothea could see a pair of grey eyes rather near together, a delicate irregular nose with a little ripple in it, and hair falling backward; but there was a mouth and chin of a more prominent, threatening aspect than beloved to the type of the grandmother's miniature. Young Ladislaw did not feel it necessary to smile, as if he were charmed with this introduction to his future second cousin and her relatives; but wore rather a pouting air of discontent." 9

—enraptured: "But what a voice! It was like the voice of a soul that had once lived in an Æolian harp." 9

—amused: "Mr Will Ladislaw's sense of the ludicrous lit up his features very agreeably: it was the pure enjoyment of comicality; and had no mixture of sneering and self-exaltation." 9

—cousin's report: " 'But so far is he from having any desire for a more accurate knowledge of the earth's surface, that he said he should prefer not to know the sources of the Nile, and that there should be some unknown regions preserved as hunting-grounds for the poetic imagination . . . .

" 'It is, I fear, nothing more than a part of his general inaccuracy and indisposition to thoroughness of all kinds, which would be a bad augury for him in any profession, civil or sacred, even were he so far submissive to ordinary rule as to choose one.' " 9

—dilettante: "Genius, he held, is necessarily intolerant of fetters: on the one hand it must have the utmost play for its spontaneity; on the other, it may confidently await those messages from the universe which summon it to its peculiar work, only placing itself in an attitude of receptivity towards all sublime chances." 10

—experimenter: "The attitudes of receptivity are various, and Will had sincerely tried many of them. He was not excessively fond of wine, but he had several times taken too much, simply as an experiment in that form of ecstasy; he had fasted till he was faint, and then supped on lobster; he had made himself ill with doses of opium. Nothing greatly original had resulted from these measures . . . . The superadded circumstance which would evolve the genius had not yet come; the universe had not yet beckoned." 10

—hair: "[It] was not immoderately long, but abundant and curly . . . . " 19

—as a painter: " 'And what is a portrait of a woman? Your painting and Plastik are poor stuff after all. They perturb and dull conceptions instead of raising them. Language is a finer medium.'

" 'Yes, for those who can't paint,' said **Naumann**. "there you have perfect right. I did not recommend you to paint, my friend.'

"The amiable artist carried his sting, but Ladislaw did not choose to appear stung." 19

—touched: "Why was he making any fuss about **Mrs Casaubon**? And yet he felt as if something had happened to him with regard to her." 19

—shy: "She met Ladislaw with that exquisite smile of goodwill which is unmixed with vanity, and held out her hand to him. He was the elder by several years, but at that moment he looked much the younger, for his transparent complexion flushed suddenly and he spoke with a shyness extremely unlike the ready indifference of his manner with his male companion . . . . " 21

—controlling feelings: " . . . the idea of this dried-up pedant, this elaborator of small explanations about as important as the surplus stock of false antiquities kept in a vendor's back chamber, having first got this adorable young creature to marry him, and then passing his honeymoon away from her, groping after his mouldy futilities (Will was given to hyperbole)—this sudden picture stirred him with a sort of comic disgust: he was divided between the impulse to laugh aloud and the equally unseasonable impulse to burst into scornful invective. For an instant he felt that the struggle was causing a queer contortion of his mobile features, but with a good effort he resolved it into nothing more offensive than a merry smile." 21

—smile: "Will Ladislaw's smile was delightful, unless you were angry with him beforehand: it was a gush of inward light illuminating the transparent skin as well as the eyes, and playing about every curve and line as if some **Ariel** were touching them with a new charm, and banishing for ever the traces of moodiness." 21

—smitten: "She was not coldly clever and indirectly satirical, but adorably simple and full of feeling. She was an angel beguiled. It would be a unique delight to wait and watch for the melodious fragments in which her heart and soul came forth so directly and ingenuously. The Æolian harp again came into his mind." 21

—contrast of light: "The first impression on seeing Will was one of sunny brightness, which added to the uncertainty of his changing expression. Surely, his very features changed their form; his jaw looked sometimes large and sometimes small; and the little ripple in his nose was a preparation for metamorphosis. When he turned his head quickly his hair seemed to shake out light, and some persons thought they saw decided genius in this coruscation. **Mr Casaubon**, on the contrary, stood rayless." 21

—conversationalist: " . . . it seemed to **Dorothea** that Will had a happier way of drawing her husband into conversation and of deferentially listening to him than she had ever observed in any one before . . . . Will talked a good deal himself, but what he said was thrown in with such rapidity, and with such an unimportant air of saying something by the way, that it seemed a gay little chime after the great bell." 22

—in love: " . . . Will did not know what to say, since it would not be useful for him to embrace her slippers, and tell her that he would die for her . . . . " 22

—*cousinly comment:* " 'I trust I may be excused for desiring an interval of complete freedom from such distractions as have been hitherto inevitable, and especially from guests whose desultory vivacity makes their presence a fatigue.' " 29

—*devoted:* "It was a question whether gratitude which refers to what is done for one's self ought not to give way to indignation at what is done against another . . . . 'It is the most horrible of virgin-sacrifices,' said Will; and he painted to himself what were **Dorothea**'s inward sorrows as if he had been writing a choric wail. But he would never lose sight of her: he would watch over her—if he gave up everything else in life he would watch over her, and she should know that she had one slave in the world." 37

—*in bliss:* " 'I remember them [previous conversations] all,' said Will, with the unspeakable content in his soul of feeling that he was in the presence of a creature worthy to be perfectly loved. I think his own feelings at that moment were perfect, for we mortals have our divine moments, when love is satisfied in the completeness of the beloved object." 37

—*gratitude:* "In his inmost soul Will was conscious of wishing to tell **Dorothea** what was rather new even in his own construction of things—namely, that **Mr Casaubon** had never done more than pay a debt towards him. Will was much too good a fellow to be easy under the sense of being ungrateful. And when gratitude has become a matter of reasoning there are many ways of escaping from its bonds." 37

—*contented:* "There was a gentleness in his tone which came from the unutterable contentment of perceiving—what **Dorothea** was hardly conscious of—that she was travelling into the remoteness of pure pity and loyalty towards her husband. Will was ready to adore her pity and loyalty, if she would associate himself with her in manifesting them." 37

—*electrified:* "When **Mrs Casaubon** was announced he started up as from an electric shock, and felt a tingling at his finger-ends. Any one observing him would have seen a change in his complexion, in the adjustment of his facial muscles, in the vividness of his glance, which might have made them imagine that every molecule in his body had passed the message of a magic touch. And so it had . . . . Will, too, was made of very impressible stuff. The bow of a violin drawn near him cleverly, would at one stroke change the aspect of the world for him, and his point of view shifted as easily as his mood. Dorothea's entrance was the freshness of morning." 39

—*surprised with **Rosamond**:* "Will Ladislaw, meanwhile, was mortified, and knew the reason of it clearly enough. His chances of meeting **Dorothea** were rare; and here for the first time there had come a chance which had set him at a disadvantage. It was not only, as it had been hitherto, that she was not supremely occupied with him, but that she had seen him under circumstances in which he might appear not to be supremely occupied with her. He felt thrust to a new distance from her . . . . " 43

—*sensitive:* "And Will was of a temperament to feel keenly the presence of subtleties: a man of clumsier perceptions would not have felt, as he did, that for the first time some sense of unfitness in perfect freedom with him had sprung up in **Dorothea**'s mind, and that their silence, as he conducted her to the carriage, had had a chill in it." 43

—*vocation:* " . . . he was beginning thoroughly to like the work . . . and he studied the political situation with as ardent an interest as he had ever given to poetic metres or mediaevalism. It is undeniable that but for the desire to be where **Dorothea** was . . . he would probably have been rambling in Italy sketching plans for several dramas, trying prose and finding it too jejune, trying verse and finding it too artificial, beginning to copy 'bits' from old pictures, leaving off because they were 'no good,' and observing that, after all, self-culture was the principal point; while in politics he would have been sympathising warmly with liberty and progress in general . . . .

"Ladislaw had now accepted his bit of work, though it was not that indeterminate loftiest thing which he had once dreamed of as alone worthy of continuous effort. His nature warmed easily in the presence of subjects which were visibly mixed with life and action, and the easily-stirred rebellion in him helped the glow of public spirit." 46

—a gypsy: "As Lydgate had said of him, he was a sort of gypsy, rather enjoying the sense of belonging to no class; he had a feeling of romance in his position, and a pleasant consciousness of creating a little surprise wherever he went . . . his irritation had gone out towards **Mr Casaubon**, who had declared beforehand that Will would lose caste. 'I never had any caste,' he would have said . . . and the quick blood would have come and gone like breath in his transparent skin." 46

—and children: "He had a fondness, half artistic, half affectionate, for little children—the smaller they were on tolerably active legs, and the funnier their clothing, the better Will liked to surprise and please them." 46

—predilection for lying down: "Another [oddity] was, that in houses where he got friendly, he was given to stretch himself at full length on the rug while he talked, and was apt to be discovered in this attitude by occasional callers for whom such an irregularity was likely to confirm the notions of his dangerously mixed blood and general laxity." 46

—and a friend: "The two men were not at all alike, but they agreed none the worse. **Lydgate** was abrupt but not irritable, taking little notice of megrims in healthy people, and Ladislaw did not usually throw away his susceptibilities on those who took no notice of them." 46

—and a friend's wife: "With **Rosamond**, on the other hand, he pouted and was wayward—nay, often uncomplimentary, much to her inward surprise; nevertheless he was gradually becoming necessary to her entertainment by his companionship in her music, his varied talk, and his freedom from [**Lydgate**'s] grave preoccupation which . . . confirmed her dislike of the medical profession." 46

—happy fly in amber: "He would not go out of her reach. He saw no creature among her friends to whom he could believe that she spoke with the same simple confidence as to him. She had once said that she would like him to stay; and stay he would, whatever fire-breathing dragons might hiss around her." 47

—sanguine: "Will easily felt happy when nothing crossed his humour, and by this time the thought of vexing **Mr Casaubon** had become rather amusing to him, making his face break into its merry smile, pleasant to see as the breaking of sunshine on the water . . . . " 47

—singing: "Sometimes, when he took off his hat, shaking his head backward, and showing his delicate throat as he sang, he looked like an incarnation of the spring whose spirit filled the air—a bright creature, abundant in uncertain promises." 47

—*invidious comparison:* "Why should he be compared with an Italian carrying white mice? That word quoted from **Mrs Cadwallader** seemed like a mocking travesty wrought in the dark by an impish finger . . . .

"An Italian with white mice!—on the contrary [thought **Dorothea**], he was a creature who entered into every one's feelings, and could take the pressure of their thought instead of urging his own with iron resistance." 50

—*time for decision:* " . . . if he could only be sure that she cared for him more than for others; if he could only make her aware that he stood aloof until he could tell his love without lowering himself—then he could go away easily, and begin a career which at five-and-twenty seemed probable enough in the inward order of things, where talent brings fame, and fame everything else which is delightful." 51

—*tongue-tied:* "It had seemed to him as if they were like two creatures slowly turning to marble in each other's presence, while their hearts were conscious and their eyes were yearning. But there was no help for it. It should never be true of him that in this meeting to which he had come with bitter resolution he had ended by a confession which might be interpreted into asking for her fortune. Moreover, it was actually true that he was fearful of the effect which such confessions might have on **Dorothea** herself." 54

—*told of the codicil:* " 'Great God! What do you mean?' said Will, flushing over face and ears, his features seeming to change as if he had had a violent shake. 'Don't joke; tell me what you mean.'

" 'You don't really know?' said **Rosamond**, no longer playful, and desiring nothing better than to tell in order that she might evoke effects . . . .

" 'Pray don't say any more about it,' said Will, in a hoarse under-tone extremely unlike his usual light voice. 'It is a foul insult to her and to me.' Then he sat down absently, looking before him, but seeing nothing." 59

—*ready for a fight:* "Like most people who assert their freedom with regard to conventional distinction, he was prepared to be sudden and quick at quarrel with any one who might hint that he had personal reasons for that assertion—that there was anything in his blood, his bearing, or his character to which he gave the mask of an opinion. When he was under an irritating impression of this kind he would go about for days with a defiant look, the colour changing in his transparent skin as if he were on the *qui vive,* watching for something which he had to dart upon." 60

—*accosted:* " 'Excuse me, Mr Ladislaw—was your mother's name **Sarah Dunkirk**?'

"Will, starting to his feet, moved backward a step, frowning, and saying with some fierceness, 'Yes sir, it was. And what is that to you?' . . .

"**Raffles** on his side had not the same eagerness for a collision which was implied in Ladislaw's threatening air. The slim young fellow with his girl's complexion looked like a tiger-cat ready to spring on him." 60

—*a munificent offer:* " 'My unblemished honour is important to me. It is important to me to have no stain on my birth and connections. And now I find there is a stain which I can't help. My mother felt it, and tried to keep as clear of it as she could, and so will I . . . . What I have to thank you for is that you kept the money till now, when I can refuse it. It ought to lie with a man's self that he is a gentleman. Good-night, sir' . . . .

"No third person listening could have thoroughly understood the impetuosity of Will's repulse or the bitterness of his words. No one but himself then knew how everything connected with the sentiment of his own dignity had an immediate bearing for him on his relation to **Dorothea** and to **Mr Casaubon**'s treatment of him. And in the rush of impulses by which he flung back that offer of **Bulstrode**'s, there was mingled the sense that it would have been impossible for him ever to tell Dorothea that he had accepted it." 61

—slip of the tongue: " 'I have never done you an injustice. Please remember me,' said **Dorothea**, repressing a rising sob.

" 'Why should you say that?' said Will, with irritation. 'As if I were not in danger of forgetting everything else.' " 62

—beside himself: " 'Don't touch me!' he said, with an utterance like the cut of a lash, darting from [**Rosamond**] and changing from pink to white and back again, as if his whole frame were tingling with the pain of the sting . . . .

"It would have been safer for Will in the first instance to have taken up his hat and gone away; but he had felt no impulse to do this; on the contrary, he had a horrible inclination to stay and shatter Rosamond with his anger. It seemed as impossible to bear the fatality she had drawn down on him without venting his fury as it would be to a panther to bear the javelin-wound without springing and biting." 78

—agony and lack of tact: " 'I had no hope before—not much—of anything better to come. But I had one certainty—that she believed in me. Whatever people had said or done about me, she believed in me—that's gone! . . .

" 'Explain! Tell a man to explain how he dropped into hell! Explain my preference! I never had a *preference* for her, and more than I have a preference for breathing. No other woman exists by the side of her. I would rather touch her hand if it were dead, than I would touch any other woman's living.' " 78

—entanglement? "And what seemed a foreboding was pressing upon him as with slow pincers—that his life might come to be enslaved by this helpless woman who had thrown herself upon him in the dreary sadness of her heart. But he was in gloomy rebellion against the fact that his quick apprehensiveness foreshadowed to him, and when his eyes fell on Rosamond's blighted face it seemed to him that he was the more pitiable of the two . . . .

"It seemed to him this evening as if the cruelty of his outburst to Rosamond had made an obligation for him, and he dreaded the obligation: he dreaded **Lydgate**'s unsuspecting goodwill: he dreaded his own distaste for his spoiled life, which would leave him in motiveless levity." [*word?*] 79

—sensitive empathy: "Will was very open and careless about his personal affairs, but it was among the more exquisite touches in nature's modelling of him that he had a delicate generosity which warned him into reticence here. He shrank from saying that he had rejected **Bulstrode**'s money, in the moment when he was learning that it was **Lydgate**'s misfortune to have accepted it." 79

—susceptibility: "For a creature of Will's susceptible temperament—without any neutral region of indifference in his nature, ready to turn everything that befell him into the collisions of a passionate drama—the revelation that **Rosamond** had made her happiness in any way dependent on him was a difficulty which his outburst of rage towards her had immeasurably increased for him." 82

Featherstone Relations

Martha (*née* **Featherstone**) **Cranch**, "living with some wheeziness in the Chalky Flats, could not undertake the journey; but her son, as being poor **Peter**'s own nephew, could represent her advantageously . . . . [She] said that nobody need be surprised if he left the best part of his money to those who least expected it." 32

—*speaking softly:* "Poor Mrs Cranch was bulky, and breathing asthmatically, had the additional motive for making her remarks unexceptionable and giving them a general bearing, that even her whispers were loud and liable to sudden bursts like those of a deranged barrel-organ." 35

Tom Cranch, "who, having come all the way from the Chalky Flats to represent his mother and watch his uncle **Jonah**, also felt it his duty to stay and to sit chiefly in the kitchen to give his uncle company. Young Cranch was not exactly the balancing point between the wit and the idiot—verging slightly towards the latter type, and squinting so as to leave everything in doubt about his sentiments except that they were not of a forcible character." 32

Jonah Featherstone. "To the poorer and least favoured it seemed likely that since Peter had done nothing for them in his life, he would remember them at the last. Jonah argued that men liked to make a surprise of their wills. . . . " 32

—*sticking it out:* "Brother Jonah, for example (there are such unpleasant people in most families; perhaps even in the highest aristocracy . . .) having come down in the world, was mainly supported by a calling which he was modest enough not to boast of, though it was much better than swindling either on exchange or turf, but which did not require his presence at Brassing so long as he had a good corner to sit in and a supply of food. He chose the kitchen-corner, partly because he liked it best, and partly because he did not want to sit with **Solomon**, concerning whom he had a strong brotherly opinion. Seated in a famous arm-chair and in his best suit, constantly within sight of good cheer, he had a comfortable consciousness of being on the premises . . . and he informed **Mary Garth** that he should not go out of reach of his brother **Peter** while that poor fellow was above ground." 32

—*jocular:* "The troublesome ones in a family are usually either the wits or the idiots. Jonah was the wit among the Featherstones and joked with the maid-servants when they came about the hearth, but seemed to consider **Miss Garth** a suspicious character, and followed her with cold eyes." 32

Solomon Featherstone. "Brother Solomon and Sister **Jane** were rich, and the family candour and total abstinence from false politeness with which they were always received seemed to them no argument that their brother in the solemn act of making his will would overlook the superior claims of wealth." 32

—*characteristics:* "He was a large-cheeked man, nearly seventy, with small furtive eyes, and was not only of much blander temper but thought himself much deeper than his brother **Peter**; indeed not likely to be deceived in any of his fellow-men, inasmuch as they could not well be more greedy and deceitful than he suspected them of being. Even the invisible powers, he thought, were likely to be soothed by a bland parenthesis here and there—coming from a man of property, who might have been as impious as others." 32

—*his views:* " 'I shouldn't be sorry to hear he'd remembered *you,* **Mr Trumbull**,' said Solomon. 'I never was against the deserving. It's the undeserving I'm against.' " 32

Joshua Rigg. " ' . . . there is a new face come out from behind that broad man queerer than any of them: a little round head with bulging eyes—a sort of frog-face—do look. He must be of another blood, I think.' " 34

—*surprise:* " . . . a strange mourner who had plashed among them as if from the moon . . . a man perhaps about two or three and thirty, whose prominent eyes, thin-lipped, downward-curved mouth, and hair sleekly brushed away from a forehead that sank suddenly above the ridge of the eyebrows, certainly gave his face a batrachian unchangeableness of expression. Here, clearly was a new legatee . . . . " 35

—*the legatee:* "[He] showed a notable change of manner . . . putting business questions with much coolness. He had a high chirping voice and a vile accent." 35

—*son of his mother:* "The result is sometimes a frog-faced male, desirable, surely to no order of intelligent beings. Especially when he is suddenly brought into evidence to frustrate other people's expectations—the very lowest aspect in which a social superfluity can present himself." 41 *See* Mrs Rigg MF

Rigg Featherstone [his name changed to inherit]—*characteristics:* "[His] low characteristics were all of the sober, water-drinking kind. From the earliest to the latest hour of the day he was always as sleek, neat, and cool as the frog he resembled, and old **Peter** had secretly chuckled over an offshoot almost more calculating, and far more imperturbable, than himself. I will add that his finger-nails were scrupulously attended to, and that he meant to marry a well-educated young lady (as yet unspecified) whose person was good, and whose connections, in a solid middle-class way, were undeniable. Thus his nails and modesty were comparable to those of most gentlemen; though his ambition had been educated only by the opportunities of a clerk and accountant in the smaller commercial houses of a seaport." 41

—*ambition:* "The cool and judicious Joshua Rigg had not allowed his parent to perceive that Stone Court was anything less than the chief good in his estimation, and he had certainly wished to call it his own. But as **Warren Hastings** [H] looked at gold and thought of buying Daylesford, so Joshua Rigg looked at Stone Court and thought of buying gold. He had a very distinct and intense vision of his chief good, the vigorous greed which he had inherited having taken a special form by dint of circumstance: and his chief good was to be a money-changer . . . . The one joy after which his soul thirsted was to have a money-changer's shop on a much-frequented quay, to have locks all round him of which he held the keys, and to look sublimely cool as he handled the breeding coins of all nations, while helpless Cupidity looked at him enviously from the other side of an iron lattice. The strength of that passion had been a power enabling him to master all the knowledge necessary to gratify it." 53

Borthrop Trumbull, "a distinguished bachelor and auctioneer of those parts, much concerned in the sale of land and cattle: a public character, indeed, whose name was seen on widely-distributed placards, and who might reasonably be sorry for those who did not know of him. He was second cousin to Peter Featherstone, and had been treated by him with more amenity than any other relative, being useful in matters of business, and in that programme of his funeral which the old man had himself dictated, he had been named a Bearer.

"There was no odious cupidity in Mr Borthrop Trumbull—nothing more than a sincere sense of his own merit, which, he was aware, in case of rivalry might tell against competitors; so that if **Peter Featherstone**, who so far as he, Trumbull, was concerned, had behaved like as good a soul as ever breathed, should have done anything handsome by him, all he could say was, that he had never fished and fawned, but had advised him to the best of his experience, which now extended over twenty years from the time of his apprenticeship at fifteen, and was likely to yield a knowledge of no surreptitious kind. His admiration was far from being confined to himself, but was accustomed professionally as well as privately to delight in estimating things at a high rate.

"He was an amateur of superior phrases, and never used poor language without immediately correcting himself—which was fortunate, as he was rather loud, and given to predominate, standing or walking about frequently, pulling down his waistcoat with the air of a man who is very much of his own opinion, trimming himself rapidly with his forefinger, and marking each new series in these movements by a busy play with his large seals. There was occasionally a little fierceness in his demeanour, but it was directed chiefly against false opinion, of which there is so much to correct in the world that a man of some reading and experience necessarily has his patience tried." ¶32

—professional: "On the whole, in an auctioneering way, he was an honourable man, not ashamed of his business, and feeling that 'the celebrated **Peel**, now **Sir Robert**,' if introduced to him, would not fail to recognise his importance." 32

—grandiloquent: " 'Oh yes, anybody may ask,' said Mr Trumbull, with loud and good-humoured though cutting sarcasm. 'Anybody may interrogate. Any one may give their remarks an interrogative turn,' he continued, his sonorousness rising with his style." 32

" 'It commences well.' (Things never began with Mr Borthrop Trumbull: they always commenced, both in private life and on his handbills.)" 32

—insider status: "Mr Borthrop Trumbull really knew nothing about old Featherstone's will; but he could hardly have been brought to declare any ignorance unless he had been arrested for misprision of treason." 32

"[He] was handling his watch-seals and trimming his outlines with a determination not to show anything so compromising to a man of ability as wonder or surprise." 35

—demeanour: "He pushed aside his plate, poured out his glass of ale and drew his chair a little forward, profiting by the occasion to look at the inner side of his legs, which he stroked approvingly—Mr Trumbull having all those less frivolous airs and gestures which distinguish the predominant races of the north." 32

—pneumonia: "Mr Trumbull was a robust man, a good subject for trying the expectant theory upon—watching the course of an interesting disease when left as much as possible to itself, so that the stages might be noted for future guidance; and from the air with which he described his sensations **Lydgate** surmised that he would like to be taken into his medical man's confidence, and be represented as a partner in his own cure . . . .

" 'Never fear, sir; you are not speaking to one who is altogether ignorant of the *vis medicatrix*,' said he, with his usual superiority of expression, made rather pathetic by difficulty of breathing. And he went without shrinking through his abstinence from drugs, much sustained by application of the thermometer which implied the importance of his temperature . . . .

"The auctioneer was not an ungenerous man, and liked to give others their due, feeling that he could afford it. He had caught the words 'expectant method,' and rang chimes on this and other learned phrases to accompany the assurance that Lydgate 'knew a thing or two more than the rest of the doctors—was far better versed in the secrets of his profession than the majority of his compeers.' " 45

—in his element: "And surely among all men whose vocation requires them to exhibit their powers of speech, the happiest is a prosperous provincial auctioneer keenly alive to his own jokes and sensible of his encyclopaedic knowledge . . . [he] had a kindly liquid in his veins; he was an admirer by nature, and would have liked to have the universe under his hammer, feeling that it would go at a higher figure for his recommendation." 60

Mrs Jane (*née* **Featherstone**) **Waule**. " 'That gig seems to me more funereal than a hearse. But then Mrs Waule always has black crape on . . . .

" 'They are as rich as Jews, those Waules and Featherstones; I mean, for people like them, who don't want to spend anything. And yet they hang about my uncle like vultures, and are afraid of a farthing going away from their side of the family. But I believe he hates them all [said **Fred**].'

"The Mrs Waule who was so far from being admirable in the eyes of these distant connections, had happened to say this very morning (not at all with a defiant air, but in a low, muffled, neutral tone, as of a voice heard through cotton wool) that she did not wish 'to enjoy their good opinion.' " 12

—face: "[The fire] made no difference to the chill-looking purplish tint of Mrs Waule's face, which was as neutral as her voice; having mere chinks for eyes, and lips that hardly moved in speaking." 12

—inured: "Indeed, she herself was accustomed to think that entire freedom from the necessity of behaving agreeably was included in the Almighty's intentions about families." 12

—sacred belief: "Notwithstanding her jealousy of the **Vincys** and **Mary Garth**, there remained as the nethermost sediment in her mental shallows a persuasion that her brother **Peter Featherstone** could never leave his chief property away from his blood relations . . . . " 12

—sticking to it: " . . . the lady who had been Jane Featherstone for twenty-five years before she was Mrs Waule found it good to be there every day for hours. Without other calculable occupation than that of observing the cunning **Mary Garth** (who was so deep that she could be found out in nothing) and giving occasional dry wrinkly indications of crying—as if capable of torrents in a wetter season—at the thought that they were not allowed to go into Mr Featherstone's room." 32

—emotional: " 'But you can't take your own time to die in, Brother,' began Mrs Waule, with her usual woolly tone. 'And when you lie speechless you may be tired of having strangers about you, and you may think of me and my children'——but here her voice broke under the touching thought which she was attributing to her speechless brother; the mention of ourselves being naturally affecting." 32

John Waule, " 'only three-and-twenty, though steady beyond anything.' " 12

Miscellaneous. " . . . some nephews, nieces, and cousins, arguing with still greater subtility as to what might be done by a man able to 'will away' his property and give himself large treats of oddity, felt in a handsome sort of way that there was a family interest to be attended to, and thought of Stone Court as a place which it would be nothing but right for them to visit . . . . In fact there was a general sense running in the Featherstone blood that everybody must watch everybody else, and that it would be well for everybody else to reflect that the Almighty was watching him." 32

—cousins: "The two cousins were elderly men from Brassing, one of them conscious of claims on the score of inconvenient expense sustained by him in presents of oysters and other eatables to his rich cousin Peter: the other entirely saturnine, leaning his hands and chin on a stick, and conscious of claims based on no narrow performance but on merit generally: both blameless citizens of Brassing, who wished that **Jonah Featherstone** did not live there." 35

—second cousin: "[He] was a Middlemarch mercer of polite manners and superfluous aspirates." 35

Others

Bambridge, horse-dealer. "Mr Bambridge had more open manners [than **Horrock**], and appeared to give forth his ideas without economy. He was loud, robust, and was sometimes spoken of as being 'given to indulgence'—chiefly in swearing, drinking, and beating his wife. Some people who had lost by him called him a vicious man; but he regarded horse-dealing as the finest of the arts, and might have argued plausibly that it had nothing to do with morality. He was undeniably a prosperous man, bore his drinking better than others bore their moderation, and, on the whole, flourished like the green bay-tree . . . the minute retentiveness of his memory was chiefly shown about the horses he had himself bought and sold; the number of miles they would trot you in no time without turning a hair being, after the lapse of years, still a subject of passionate asseveration, in which he would assist the imagination of his hearers by solemnly swearing that they never saw anything like it. In short, Mr Bambridge was a man of pleasure and a gay companion." 23

—salesmanship: " . . . Mr Bambridge was finding it worth his while to say many impressive things about the fine studs he had been seeing and the purchases he had made on a journey in the north from which he had just returned. Gentlemen present were assured that when they could show him anything to cut out a blood mare, a bay, rising four, which was to be seen at Doncaster if they chose to go and look at it, Mr Bambridge would gratify them by being shot from here to Hereford.' " 71

Bowyer. " 'I suppose it is the fashion to sing comic songs in a rhythmic way, leaving you to fancy the tune—very much as if it were tapped on a drum?'

" 'Ah, you have heard Mr Bowyer,' said **Rosamond**, with one of her rare smiles." 16

" 'What will you when you are forty? Like Mr Bowyer, I suppose—just an idle, living in **Mrs Beck**'s front parlour—fat and shabby, hoping somebody will invite you to dinner—spending your morning in learning a comic song. . . .' " 25

—able at harassment: " 'It was Bowyer who did it,' said **Mr Standish**, evasively. 'I know it as well as if he had been advertised. He's uncommonly good at ventriloquism, and he did it uncommonly well, by God! **Hawley** has been having him to dinner lately: there's a fund of talent in Bowyer.' " 51

Lady Chettam, "who attributed her own remarkable health to home-made bitters united with constant medical attendance, entered with much exercise of the imagination into **Mrs Renfrew**'s account of symptoms, and into the amazing futility in her case of all strengthening medicines.

" 'Where can all strength of those medicines go, my dear?' said the mild but stately dowager . . . . ' " 10

—tact: " 'Who, my dear?' said Lady Chettam, a charming woman, not so quick as to nullify the pleasure of explanation." 10

Mr Chichely, "a middle-aged bachelor and coursing celebrity, who had a complexion something like an Easter egg, a few hairs carefully arranged, and a carriage implying the consciousness of a distinguished appearance." 10

—on women: " 'Ay, to be sure, there should be a little devil in a woman,' said Mr Chichely, whose study of the fair sex seemed to have been detrimental to his theology. 'And I like them blond, with a certain gait, and a swan neck.' " 10

—on reform: " 'Hang your reforms!' said Mr Chichely. 'There's no greater humbug in the world. You never hear of a reform, but it means some trick to put in new men' . . . .

"**Lydgate** had really lost sight of the fact that Mr Chichely was his Majesty's coroner . . . . " 16

Dagley. " 'Think of . . . those poor Dagleys, in their tumble-down farm-house, where they live in the back kitchen and leave the other rooms to the rats!' " 39

—in residence: "Mr Dagley himself made a figure in the landscape, carrying a pitchfork and wearing his milking-hat—a very old beaver flattened in front. His coat and breeches were the best he had, and he would not have been wearing them on this week-day occasion if he had not been to market and returned later than usual, having given himself the rare treat of dining at the public table of the Blue Bull." 39

—having 'dined': "It was a maxim about Middlemarch, and regarded as self-evident, that good meat should have good drink, which last Dagley interpreted as plenty of table ale well followed up by rum-and-water. These liquors have so far truth in them that they were not false enough to make poor Dagley seem merry: they only made his discontent less tongue-tied than usual. He had also taken too much in the shape of muddy political talk, a stimulant dangerously disturbing to his farming conservatism, which consisted in holding that whatever is, is bad, and any change is likely to be worse. He was flushed, and his eyes had a decidedly quarrelsome stare as he stood still grasping his pitchfork . . . . " 39

—saying his peace: " 'I'm no more drunk nor you are, nor so much . . . . I can carry my liquor, an' I know what I mean. An' I mean as the King 'ull put a stop to't, for them say it as knows it, as there's to be a Rinform, and them landlords as never done the right thing by their tenants 'ull be treated i' that way as they'll hev to scuttle off.' " 39

Mrs Dagley. "Overworked Mrs Dagley—a thin, worn woman, from whose life pleasure had so entirely vanished that she had not even any Sunday clothes which could give her satisfaction in preparing for church—had already had a misunderstanding with her husband since he had come home, and was in low spirits, expecting the worst." 39

Mrs Dollop, "the landlady of the Tankard in Slaughter Lane . . . became more and more convinced by her own asseveration, that Doctor **Lydgate** meant to let the people die in the Hospital, if not to poison them, for the sake of cutting them up without saying by your leave or with your leave . . . . " 45

"[She] had often to resist the shallow pragmatism of customers disposed to think that their reports from the outer world were of equal force with what had 'come up' in her mind." 71

Dunkirk, "the richest man in the congregation. Soon [**Bulstrode**] became an intimate there, honoured for his piety by the wife, marked out for his ability by the husband, whose wealth was due to a flourishing city and west-end trade. . . . The business was a pawnbroker's, of the most magnificent sort both in extent and profits; and on a short acquaintance with it Bulstrode became aware that one source of magnificent profit was the easy reception of any goods offered, without strict inquiry as to where they came from." 61

Mrs Dunkirk, "a simple pious woman, left with all the wealth in and out of the magnificent trade, of which she never knew the precise nature, had come to believe in **Bulstrode** . . . . It was natural that after a time marriage should have been thought of between them. But Mrs Dunkirk had qualms and yearnings about her daughter, who had long been regarded as lost both to God and her parents. It was known that the daughter had married, but she was utterly gone out of sight. The mother, having lost her son, imagined a grandson, and wished in a double sense to reclaim her daughter. If she were found, there would be a channel for property . . . . Efforts to find her must be made before Mrs Dunkirk would marry again. Bulstrode concurred, but after advertisement as well as other modes of inquiry had been tried, the mother believed that her daughter was not to be found, and consented to marry without reservation of property.

"The daughter had been found, but only one man besides Bulstrode knew it, and he [**Raffles**] was paid for keeping silence and carrying himself away." 61

Mrs Farebrother, "the Vicar's white-haired mother, befrilled and kerchiefed with dainty cleanliness, upright, quick-eyed, and still under seventy. . . . The old lady was evidently accustomed to tell her company what they ought to think, and to regard no subject as quite safe without her steering. She was afforded leisure for this function by having all her little wants attended to by **Miss Winifred**." 17

Mr Gambit, "a practitioner just a little lower in status than **Wrench** or **Toller**, and especially esteemed as an accoucheur, of whose ability **Mr Mawmsey** had the poorest opinion on all other points, but in doctoring, he was wont to say in an undertone, he placed Gambit above any of them." 45

"He was a stout husky man with a ring on his fourth finger . . . .

"He had not indeed great resources of education, and had had to work his own way against a good deal of professional contempt, but he made none the worse accoucheur for calling the breathing apparatus 'longs.' " 45

Christy Garth "was getting cheap learning and cheap fare in Scotland, having to his father's disappointment taken to books instead of that sacred calling 'business.' " 40

—*vocation:* "[He] held it the most desirable thing in the world to be a tutor, to study all literatures and be a regenerate **Porson**, and . . . was an incorporate criticism on poor **Fred**, a sort of object-lesson given to him by the educational mother. Christy himself, a square-browed, broad-shouldered masculine edition of his mother not much higher than Fred's shoulder—which made it the harder that he should be held superior—was always as simple as possible, and thought no more of Fred's disinclination to scholarship than of a giraffe's, wishing that he himself were more of the same height." 57

—*progress:* " 'He has paid his expenses for the last year by giving lessons, carrying on hard study at the same time. He hopes soon to get a private tutorship and go abroad.' " 57

Letty Garth, "with an air of superiority . . . . " 24

" 'How rude you look, pushing and frowning, as if you wanted to conquer with your elbows! **Cincinnatus**, I am sure, would have been sorry to see his daughter behave so.' (**Mrs Garth** delivered this awful sentence with much majesty of enunciation, and Letty felt that between repressed volubility and general disesteem, that of the Romans inclusive, life was already a painful affair.)" 24

—*pleased:* "But she was made exultant by having her chin pinched and her cheek kissed by **Mr Farebrother**—an incident which she narrated to her mother and father." 40

—*rapt:* "Letty herself, showing as to her mouth and pinafore some slight signs that she had been assisting at the gathering of the cherries which stood in a coral-heap on the tea-table, was now seated on the grass, listening open-eyed to the reading [of *Ivanhoe*]." 57

—*fighting back:* " 'Yes, I can. Mother, please say that I am to go,' urged Letty, whose life was much checkered by resistance to her depreciation as a girl." 57

Hackbutt, "a rich tanner of fluent speech, whose glittering spectacles and erect hair were turned with some severity towards innocent **Mr Powderell**." 18

—*knowledgeable:* "Mr Hackbutt, whose fluent speech was at that time floating more widely than usual, and leaving much uncertainty as to its ultimate channel, was heard to say in Mr **Hawley**'s office that the article in question 'emanated' from **Brooke** of Tipton, and that Brooke had secretly bought the "Pioneer" some months ago." 37

—*on the nondispensing of drugs:* " ' . . . nothing is more offensive than this ostentation of reform, where there is no real amelioration.' " 45

Mrs Hackbutt. " . . . there was a sudden strong desire within her for the excitement of an interview in which she was quite determined not to make the slightest allusion to what was in her mind.

"Hence **Mrs Bulstrode** was shown into the drawing-room, and Mrs Hackbutt went to her, with more tightness of lip and rubbing of her hands than was usually observable in her, these being precautions adopted against freedom of speech. She was resolved not to ask how **Mr Bulstrode** was." 74

Frank Hawley, "lawyer and town-clerk, who rarely presented himself at the board, but now looked in hurriedly, whip in hand . . . . '**Farebrother** has been doing the work . . . without pay, and if pay is to be given, it should be given to him. I call it a confounded job to take the thing away from Farebrother.' " 18

" 'It seems to me that you have been crammed with one side of the question, **Mr Brooke**,' said Mr Frank Hawley, who was afraid of nobody, and was a Tory suspicious of electioneering intentions." 18

—*Tory views:* " '[**Brooke**] has got the freak of being a popular man now, after dangling about like a stray tortoise. So much the worse for him. I've had my eye on him for some time. He shall be prettily jumped upon. He's a damned bad landlord . . . . As to his paper, I only hope he may do the writing himself. It would be worth our paying for.' " 37

—*speaking out:* "[He] started up, and said in his firm resonant voice, 'Mr Chairman, I request that before any one delivers his opinion on this point I may be permitted to speak on a question of public feeling, which not only by myself, but by many gentlemen present, is regarded as preliminary.'

"Mr Hawley's mode of speech, even when public decorum repressed his 'awful language,' was formidable in its curtness and self-possession." 71

Horrock, the 'vet.' "In Mr Horrock there was certainly an apparent unfathomableness which offered play to the imagination. Costume, at a glance, gave him a thrilling association with horses (enough to specify the hat-brim which took the slightest upward angle just to escape the suspicion of bending downwards), and nature had given him a face which by dint of Mongolian eyes, and a nose, mouth, and chin seeming to follow his hat-brim in a moderate inclination upwards, gave the effect of a subdued unchangeable sceptical smile, of all expressions the most tyrannous over a susceptible mind, and, when accompanied by adequate silence, likely to create the reputation of an invincible understanding, an infinite fund of humour—too dry to flow, and probably in a state of immovable crust—and a critical judgment which, if you could ever be fortunate enough to know it, would be *the* thing and no other. It was a physiognomy seen in all vocations, but perhaps it has never been more powerful over the youth of England than in a judge of horses." 23

—*inscrutable:* "Mr Horrock looked before him with as complete a neutrality as if he had been a portrait by a great master." 23

Julia Ladislaw. " 'It is a peculiar face,' said **Dorothea**, looking closely. 'Those deep grey eyes rather near together—and the delicate irregular nose with a sort of ripple in it—and all the powdered curls hanging backward. Altogether it seems to me peculiar rather than pretty. There is not even a family likeness between her and your mother [**Mrs Casaubon**].' " 9

—*her portrait:* "**Dorothea** could fancy that it was alive now—the delicate woman's face which yet had a headstrong look, a peculiarity difficult to interpret . . . . Here was a woman who had known some difficulty about marriage. Nay, the colours deepened, the lips and chin seemed to get larger, the hair and eyes seemed to be sending out light, the face was masculine [**Will**'s?] and beamed on her with that full gaze which tells her on whom it falls that she is too interesting for the slightest movement of her eyelid to pass unnoticed and uninterpreted. The vivid presentation came like a pleasant glow to Dorothea: she felt herself smiling . . . . " 28

—*her husband:* " ' . . . there was nothing to be said against her husband except that he was a Polish refugee who gave lessons for his bread . . . .

" ' . . . my grandfather was a patriot—a bright fellow—could speak many languages—musical—got his bread by teaching all sorts of things. They both died rather early.' " 37

Madame Laure. "[She] paused a little and then said, slowly, *'I meant to do it.'*

"**Lydgate**, strong man as he was, turned pale and trembled: moments seemed to pass before he rose and stood at a distance from her.

" 'There was a secret, then,' he said at last, even vehemently. 'He was brutal to you: you hated him.'

" 'No! he wearied me; he was too fond: he would live in Paris, and not in my country; that was not agreeable to me.'

" 'Great God!' said Lydgate, in a groan of horror. 'And you planned to murder him?'

" 'I did not plan: it came to me in the play—*I meant to do it.*' " 15 *See Topicon* LM:Love—*infatuation*

Captain Lydgate, "the baronet's third son, who, I am sorry to say was detested by our **Tertius** of that name as a vapid fop 'parting his hair from brow to nape in a despicable fashion' (not followed by Tertius himself), and showing an ignorant security that he knew the proper thing to say on every topic . . . to **Rosamond** this visit was a source of unprecedented but gracefully-concealed exultation. She was so intensely conscious of having a cousin who was a baronet's son staying in the house that she imagined the knowledge of what was implied by his presence to be diffused through all other minds; and when she introduced Captain Lydgate to her guests, she had a placid sense that his rank penetrated them as if it had been an odour." 58

—*characteristics:* " . . . his low brow, his aquiline nose bent on one side, and his rather heavy utterance, might have been disadvantageous in any young gentleman who had not a military bearing and mustache to give him what is doted on by some flower-like blond heads as 'style.' He had, moreover, that sort of high-breeding which consists in being free from the petty solicitudes of middle-class gentility, and he was a great critic of feminine charms." 58

Sir Godwin Lydgate, uncle. "Don't set your wife to write to me when you have anything to ask. It is a roundabout wheedling sort of thing which I should not have credited you with. I never choose to write to a woman on matters of business. As to my supplying you with a thousand pounds, or only half that sum, I can do nothing of the sort. My own family drains me to the last penny." 65

Mr Mawmsey "was not only an overseer (it was about a question of outdoor pay that he was having an interview with **Lydgate**), he was also asthmatic and had an increasing family: thus, from a medical point of view, as well as from his own, he was an important man; indeed, an exceptional grocer, whose hair was arranged in a flame-like pyramid, and whose retail deference was of the cordial, encouraging kind—jocosely complimentary, and with a certain considerate abstinence from letting out the full force of his mind." 45

Dr Minchin "was usually said to have more 'penetration' [than **Dr Sprague**]." 16

—*and religion:* "On this ground it was (professionally speaking) fortunate for Dr Minchin that his religious sympathies were of a general kind, and such as gave a distant medical sanction to all serious sentiment, whether of Church or Dissent, rather than any adhesion to particular tenets . . . [he] was quite sure that man was not a mere machine or a fortuitous conjunction of atoms . . . [he] liked to keep the mental windows open and objected to fixed limits . . . . He objected to the rather free style of anecdote in which Dr Sprague indulged, preferring well-sanctioned quotations, and liking refinement of all kinds: it was generally known that he had some kinship to a bishop, and sometimes spent his holidays at 'the palace.' " 18

—characteristics: "Dr Minchin was soft-handed, pale-complexioned, and of rounded outline, not to be distinguished from a mild clergyman in appearance . . . . " 18

Henrietta Noble, "[**Mrs Farebrother**'s] sister, a tiny old lady of meeker aspect, with frills and kerchief decidedly more worn and mended . . . . " 17

—her besetting vice: "Meanwhile tiny Miss Noble carried on her arm a small basket, into which she diverted a bit of sugar, which she had first dropped in her saucer as if by mistake; looking round furtively afterwards, and reverting to her tea-cup with a small innocent noise as of a tiny timid quadruped. Pray think no ill of Miss Noble. That basket held small savings from her more portable food, destined for the children of her poor friends among whom she trotted on fine mornings, fostering and petting all needy creatures being so spontaneous a delight to her, that she regarded it much as if it had been a pleasant vice that she was addicted to. Perhaps she was conscious of being tempted to steal from those who had much that she might give to those who had nothing, and carried in her conscience the guilt of that repressed desire." 17

—a report: " '. . . a wonderfully quaint picture of self-forgetful goodness, and **Ladislaw** gallants her about sometimes. I met them one day in a back street: you know Ladislaw's look—a sort of **Daphnis** in coat and waistcoat, and this little old maid reaching up to his arm—they looked like a couple dropped out of a romantic comedy.' " 50

—happy: "[She was] making tender little beaver-like noises . . . . " 52

—denominated: " ' . . . Henrietta Noble never was a whist-player.' (**Mrs Farebrother** always called her tiny old sister by that magnificent name.)" 52

—calamity: " 'I have lost my tortoise-shell lozenge-box. I fear the kitten has rolled it away,' said the tiny old lady, involuntarily continuing her beaver-like notes . . . .

" '**Mr Ladislaw** gave it me,' said Miss Noble. 'A German box—very pretty, but if it falls it always spins away as far as it can.' " 80

—affair of the heart: " 'If Henrietta Noble forms an attachment to any one, Mrs Casaubon,' said [**Farebrother**'s] mother, emphatically—'she is like a dog—she would take their shoes for a pillow and sleep the better.'

" '**Mr Ladislaw**'s shoes, I would,' said Henrietta Noble." 80

Plymdale. " 'I think it would be as well for gentlemen not to give their remarks a personal bearing . . . . I shall vote for the appointment of **Mr Tyke**, but I should not have known, if **Mr Hackbutt** hadn't hinted it, that I was a Servile Crawler.' " 18

Mrs Selina (31) **Plymdale** "thought that **Rosamond** had been educated to a ridiculous pitch, for what was the use of accomplishments which would be all laid aside as soon as she was married?" 16 *See* **Mrs Harriet Bulstrode**—*confidante* CHM

—characteristics: " . . . a round-eyed sharp little woman, like a tamed falcon." 31

—judging kindly: "[Her] maternal view was, that **Rosamond** might possibly now have retrospective glimpses of her own folly; and feeling the advantages to be at present all on the side of her son, was too kind a woman not to behave graciously . . . .

" . . . her native sharpness softened by a fervid sense that she was taking a correct view." 64

" 'I think we must not set down people's bad actions to their religion,' said falcon-faced Mrs Plymdale . . . . " 74

Ned Plymdale, "(one of the good matches in Middlemarch, though not one of its leading minds) . . . . " 27

"How different [**Lydgate**] was from young Plymdale or **Mr Caius Larcher**. These young men had not a notion of French, and could speak on no subject with striking knowledge, except perhaps the dyeing and carrying trades, which of course they were ashamed to mention; they were Middlemarch gentry, elated with their silver-headed whips and satin stocks, but embarrassed in their manners and timidly jocose . . . . " 27

—characteristics: "He had also reasons, deep rather than ostensible, for being satisfied with his own appearance. To superficial observers his chin had too vanishing an aspect, looking as if it were being gradually reabsorbed. And it did indeed cause him some difficulty about the fit of his satin stocks, for which chins were at that time useful." 27

—a rival: " . . . as [**Lydgate**] took his seat with easy confidence on the other side of her, young Plymdale's jaw fell like a barometer towards the cheerless side of change." 27

Powderell, "a retired ironmonger of some standing—his interjection being something between a laugh and a Parliamentary disapproval. 'We must let you have your say. But what we have to consider is not anybody's income— it's the souls of the poor sick people'—here Mr Powderell's voice and face had a sincere pathos in them." 18

—kindly: "Even good Mr Powderell, who in his constant charity of interpretation was inclined to esteem **Lydgate** the more for what seemed a conscientious pursuit of a better plan, had his mind disturbed with doubts during his wife's attack of erisipelas . . . . " 45

—at an auction: " 'I'll bid a pound!' said Mr Powderell, in a tone of resolved emotion, as of a man ready to put himself in the breach. Whether from awe or pity, nobody raised the price on him." 60

John Raffles. "He was a man obviously on the way towards sixty, very florid and hairy, with much grey in his bushy whiskers and thick curly hair, a stoutish body which showed to disadvantage the somewhat worn joinings of his clothes, and the air of a swaggerer, who would aim at being noticeable even at a show of fireworks, regarding his own remarks on any other person's performance as likely to be more interesting than the performance itself . . . .

"Such were the appearance and mental flavour of Mr Raffles, both of which seemed to have a stale odour of travellers' rooms in the commercial hotels of that period." 41

—departing: "Raffles, walking with the uneasy gait of a town loiterer obliged to do a bit of country journeying on foot, looked as incongruous amid this moist rural quiet and industry as if he had been a baboon escaped from a menagerie." 41

—poise: "Mr Raffles on most occasions kept up the sense of having been educated at an academy, and being able, if he chose, to pass well everywhere; indeed, there was not one of his fellow-men whom he did not feel himself in a position to ridicule and torment, confident of the entertainment which he thus gave to all the rest of the company." 41

Mr Raffles' demise is imminently expected

—*morning after:* "The difference between his morning and evening self was not so great as his companion had imagined that it might be; the delight in tormenting was perhaps even the stronger because his spirits were rather less highly pitched. Certainly his manners seemed more disagreeable by the morning light." 53

—*cunning:* "Mr Raffles ended with a jocose snuffle: no man felt his intellect more superior to religious cant. And if the cunning which calculates on the meanest feelings in men could be called intellect, he had his share, for under the blurting rallying tone with which he spoke to **Bulstrode**, there was an evident selection of statements, as if they had been so many moves at chess." 53

—*gregarious:* " . . . few men were more impatient of private occupation or more in need of making themselves continually heard than Mr Raffles." 53

—*at an auction:* "His large whiskers, imposing swagger, and swing of the leg, made him a striking figure; but his suit of black, rather shabby at the edges, caused the prejudicial inference that he was not able to afford himself as much indulgence as he liked." 60

—*greatly changed:* "But for his pallor and feebleness, **Bulstrode** would have called the change in him entirely mental. Instead of his loud tormenting mood, he showed an intense, vague terror, and seemed to deprecate Bulstrode's anger, because the money was all gone—he had been robbed—it had half of it been taken from him. He had only come here because he was ill and somebody was hunting him—somebody was after him: he had told nobody anything, he had kept his mouth shut . . . the fact being that the links of consciousness were interrupted in him, and that his minute terror-stricken narrative to **Caleb Garth** had been delivered under a set of visionary impulses which had dropped back into darkness." 69

—*dying:* "At a glance he knew that Raffles was not in the sleep which brings revival, but in the sleep which streams deeper and deeper into the gulf of death." 70

—*observed:* " . . . a change in the stertorous breathing was marked enough to draw [**Bulstrode**'s] attention wholly to the bed, and forced him to think of the departing life, which had once been subservient to his own—which he had once been glad to find base enough for him to act on as he would. It was his gladness then which impelled him now to be glad that the life was at an end." 70

—*posthumous report:* " . . . he takes a stiff glass. Damme if I think he meant to turn king's evidence, but he's that sort of bragging fellow, the bragging runs over hedge and ditch with him, till he'd brag of a spavin as if it 'ud fetch money. A man should know when to pull up.' " 71

Dr Sprague, "who was considered the physician of most 'weight' . . . divested his large heavy face of all expression, and looked at his wineglass while **Lydgate** was speaking. Whatever was not problematical and suspected about this young man—for example, a certain showiness as to foreign ideas, and a disposition to unsettle what had been settled and forgotten by his elders—was positively unwelcome to a physician whose standing had been fixed thirty years before by a treatise on Meningitis, of which at least one copy marked 'own' was bound in calf." 16

—*the chaplaincy:* "Dr Sprague, the rugged and weighty, was, as every one had foreseen, an adherent of **Mr Farebrother**. The Doctor was more than suspected of having no religion, but somehow Middlemarch tolerated this deficiency in him . . . his neighbours call[ed] him hard-headed and dry-witted; conditions of texture which were also held favourable to the storing of judgments connected with drugs." 18

—*a presence:* "[He] was superfluously tall; his trousers got creased at the knees, and showed an excess of boot at a time when straps seemed necessary to any dignity of bearing; you heard him go in and out, and up and down, as if he had come to see about the roofing." 18

—*standing with colleagues:* "In short, he had weight, and might be expected to grapple with a disease and throw it; while **Dr Minchin** might be better able to detect it lurking and to circumvent it. They enjoyed about equally the mysterious privilege of medical reputation, and concealed with much etiquette their contempt for each other's skill. Regarding themselves as Middlemarch institutions, they were ready to combine against all innovators, and against non-professionals given to interference." 18

Mr Standish. " 'A fine woman, Miss Brooke! An exceptionally fine woman, by God!' said Mr Standish, the old lawyer, who had been so long concerned with the landed gentry that he had become landed himself, and used that oath in a deep-mouthed manner as a sort of armorial bearings, stamping the speech of a man who held a good position." 10

—*at a will-reading:* "Mr Standish was not a man who varied his manners: he behaved with the same deep-voiced, offhand-civility to everybody, as if he saw no difference in them, and talked chiefly of the hay crop . . . . " 35

Tantripp. " 'When Tantripp was brushing my hair the other day [said **Celia**], she said that **Sir James**'s man knew from **Mrs Cadwallader**'s maid that Sir James was to marry the eldest **Miss Brooke**.' " 4

" . . . a solid-figured woman who had been with the sisters at Lausanne." 48

—*moved:* " 'God bless you, madam!' said Tantripp, with an irrepressible movement of love towards the beautiful, gentle creature for whom she felt unable to do anything more, now that she had finished tying the bonnet." 48

—*alarmed:* " 'Why, madam, you've never been in bed this blessed night,' burst out Tantripp, looking first at the bed and then at **Dorothea**'s face, which in spite of bathing had the pale cheeks and pink eyelids of a *mater dolorosa*. 'You'll kill yourself, you will. Anybody might think now you had a right to give yourself a little comfort.' " 80

—*on widow's weeds:* " ' . . . if anybody was to marry me flattering himself I should wear those higeous weepers two years for him, he'd be deceived by his own vanity, that's all.' " 80

Mr Thesiger, "a moderate evangelical, wished for the appointment of his friend **Mr Tyke**, a zealous able man . . . . Mr Thesiger's manners had so much quiet propriety that objectors could only simmer in silence." 18

Mr Toller. "The long-established practitioners, Mr Wrench and Mr Toller . . . agreed that Lydgate was a jackanapes, just made to serve Bulstrode's purpose." 18

"Mr Toller shared the highest practice in the town and belonged to an old Middlemarch family: there were Tollers in the law and everything else above the line of retail trade. Unlike our irascible friend **Wrench**, he had the easiest way in the world of taking things which might be supposed to annoy him, being a well-bred, quietly facetious man, who kept a good house, was very fond of a little sporting when he could get it, very friendly with **Mr Hawley**, and hostile to **Mr Bulstrode**. It may seem odd that with such pleasant habits he should have been given to the heroic treatment, bleeding and blistering and starving his patients, with a dispassionate disregard to his personal example; but the incongruity favoured the opinion of his ability among his patients, who commonly observed that Mr Toller had lazy manners, but his treatment was as active as you could desire:—no man, said they, carried more seriousness into his profession: he was a little slow in coming, but when he came, he *did* something. He was a great favourite in his own circle, and whatever he implied to any one's disadvantage told doubly from his careless ironical tone." 45

Rev. Walter Tyke, "[whose] sermons were all doctrine . . . . " 16

" . . . a man entirely given to his clerical office, who was simply curate at a chapel of ease in St Peter's parish, and had time for extra duty. Nobody had anything to say against Mr Tyke, except that they could not bear him, and suspected him of cant." 18

—*apostolic:* " 'Practically [said **Lydgate**] I find that what is called being apostolic now, is an impatience of everything in which the parson doesn't cut the principal figure. I see something of that in Mr Tyke at the Hospital: a good deal of his doctrine is a sort of pinching hard to make people uncomfortably aware of him.' " 50

Mr Wrench, "medical attendant to the **Vincy** family, [who] very early had grounds for thinking lightly of **Lydgate**'s professional discretion . . . . " 11

—*characteristics:* "Mr Wrench was a small, neat, bilious man, with a well-dressed wig: he had a laborious practice, an irascible temper, a lymphatic wife and seven children; and he was already rather late before setting out on a four-miles drive to meet **Dr Minchin** on the other side of Tipton . . . . Great statesmen err, and why not small medical men?" 26

—*techy:* "Country practitioners used to be an irritable species, susceptible on the point of honour; and Mr Wrench was one of the most irritable among them." 26

—*in close circumstances:* "[**Lydgate**] could not imagine himself . . . in such a home as Wrench had—the doors all open, the oil-cloth worn, the children in soiled pinafores, and lunch lingering in the form of bones, black-handled knives and willow-pattern. But Wrench had a wretched lymphatic wife who made a mummy of herself indoors in a large shawl, and he must have altogether begun with an ill-chosen domestic apparatus." 36

—*irritated:* "Mr Wrench, generally abstemious, often drank wine rather freely at a party, getting the more irritable in consequence.

" ' . . . I say the most ungentlemanly trick a man can be guilty of is to come among the members of his profession with innovations which are a libel on their time-honoured proceedings. That is my opinion, and I am ready to maintain it against any one who contradicts me.' Mr Wrench's voice had become exceedingly sharp." 45

Minor Figures

Mrs Abel "thought, like the servants at The Shrubs, that the strange man belonged to the unpleasant 'kin' who are among the troubles of the rich . . . [she] agreed with her husband that there was 'no knowing,' a proposition which had a great deal of mental food for her, so that she shook her head over it without further speculation." 69

Bagster, " 'one of those candidates who come from heaven knows where, but dead against Ministers, and an experienced Parliamentary man.' " 38

Master Bunney, "who was putting in some garden seeds, and [**Dorothea**] discoursed wisely with that rural sage about the crops that would make the most return on a patch of ground, and the result of sixty years' experience as to soils—namely, that if your soil was pretty mellow it would do, but if there came wet, wet, wet to make it all of a mummy, why then——." 80

Byles, " 'the butcher as his bill has been running on for the best o' joints since last Michaelmas was a twelvemonth . . . . ' " 71

Baby **Arthur** (54) **Chettam**. " . . . his upper lip; see how he is drawing it down, as if he meant to make a face. Isn't it wonderful! He may have his little thoughts.' " 50

" . . . that unconscious centre and poise of the world, who had the most remarkable fists all complete even to the nails, and hair enough, really, when you took his cap off, to make—you didn't know what—in short, he was **Bouddha** in a Western form." 50

children. "[**Ladislaw**] had somehow picked up a troop of droll children, little hatless boys, with their galligaskins much worn and scant shirting to hang out, little girls who tossed their hair out of their eyes to look at him, and guardian brothers at the mature age of seven. This troop he had led out on gypsy excursions to Haskell Wood at nutting-time, and since the cold weather had set in he had taken them on a clear day to gather sticks for a bonfire in the hollow of a hillside, where he drew out a small feast of gingerbread for them, and improvised a Punch-and-Judy drama with some private home-made puppets." 46

Clintup. "He was a diffident though distinguished nurseryman and feared that the audience might regard his bid [for a sharp-edged fender] as a foolish one." 60

Timothy Cooper "was a wiry old labourer, of a type lingering in those times—who had his savings in a stocking-foot, lived in a lone cottage, and was not to be wrought on by any oratory, having as little of the feudal spirit, and believing as little, as if he had not been totally unacquainted with the Age of Reason and the Rights of Man." 56

Crabbe, "the glazier, who gathered much news and groped among it dimly." 71

Crowse, " 'with his empty face and neat umbrella, and mincing little speeches. What right have such men to represent Christianity [said **Mary**]—as if it were an institution for getting up idiots genteelly . . . . ' " 52

Dibbitts, apothecary, " 'will get rid of his stale drugs, then. I'm fond of little Dibbitts [said **Toller**]—I'm glad he's in luck.' " 45

Dill. " 'He'll be drove away, whether or no,' said Mr Dill, the barber, who had just dropped in. 'I shaved **Fletcher**, **Hawley**'s clerk, this morning . . . and he says they're all of one mind to get rid o' **Bulstrode**.' " 71

"Mr Dill affected to laugh in a complimentary way at **Mrs Dollop**, as a woman who was more than a match for the lawyers, being disposed to submit to much twitting from a landlady who had a long score against him." 71

Dover, the silversmith, "was willing to reduce [the debt] by taking back a portion of the plate and any other article which was as good as new. 'Any other article' was a phrase delicately implying jewellery . . . . " 58

Kit Downes. " 'Think of Kit Downes, uncle, who lives with his wife and seven children in a house with one sitting-room and one bed-room hardly larger than this table!' " 39

Miss Winifred Farebrother, "the Vicar's elder sister, well-looking like himself, but nipped and subdued as single women are apt to be who spend their lives in uninterrupted subjection to their elders." 17

farmer. "A young farmer, acquainted with Mr Bambridge, came into the Red Lion, and entered into conversation about parting with a hunter, which he introduced at once as **Diamond**, implying that it was a public character." 23

Mrs Fitchett, the lodge-keeper's wife. "The phaeton was driven onwards . . . leaving Mrs Fitchett laughing and shaking her head slowly, with an interjectional 'Sure*ly*, sure*ly*— from which it might be inferred that she would have found the country-side somewhat duller if the Rector's lady had been less free-spoken and less of a skinflint." 6

Flavell, " 'the Methodist preacher, was brought up for knocking down a hare that came across his path when he and his wife were walking out together. He was pretty quick, and knocked it on the neck . . . .

" 'Well, now, Flavell in his shabby black gaiters, pleading that he thought the Lord had sent him and his wife a good dinner, and he had a right to knock it down, though not a mighty hunter before the Lord, as **Nimrod** was—I assure you it was rather comic . . . . ' " 39

Fletcher, law clerk. " ' . . . what's more against one's stomach than a man coming and making himself bad company with his religion, and giving out as the Ten Commandments are not enough for him, and all the while he's worse than half the men at the tread-mill? Fletcher said so himself.' " 71

Fly. "She took his fore-paws in one hand, and lifted up the forefinger of the other, while the dog wrinkled his brows and looked embarrassed. 'Fly, Fly, I am ashamed of you,' **Mary** was saying in a grave contralto. 'This is not becoming in a sensible dog; anybody would think you were a silly young gentleman.' " 52

Hiram Ford, a waggoner, "who had a dim notion of London as a centre of hostility to the country." 56

" 'We war on'y for a bit o' foon,' said Hiram, who was beginning to see consequences. 'That war all we war arter.' " 56

Alfred Garth. " 'But I have saved my little purse for Alfred's premium: I have ninety-two pounds. He can go to **Mr Hanmer**'s now; he is just at the right age.' " 24

Ben Garth, "an energetic young male with a heavy brow . . . . " 24

"[He] had fetched his own old bow and arrows, and was making himself dreadfully disagreeable, **Letty** thought, by begging all present to observe his random shots, which no one wished to do except **Brownie**, the active-minded but probably shallow mongrel . . . . " 56

Jim Garth. " ' . . . it will be five years before Jim is ready to take to business.' " 40

Mrs Goby, "as respectable a woman as any in Parley Street, who had money in trust before her marriage . . . . " 45

Griffin. " 'Griffin and his wife told me only today, that **Mr Tyke** said they should have no more coals if they came to hear you preach.' " 17

Fanny Hackbutt " 'comes at half-past eleven. I am not getting a great income now,' said **Mrs Garth**, smiling." 24

Hanmer, an engineer prepared to teach Alfred Garth. 24

Hawley, "just come from his law studies in town . . . . Young Hawley, an accomplished billiard-player, brought a cool fresh hand to the cue." 66

Hicks. " 'I found poor Hicks's judgment unfailing; I never knew him wrong. He was coarse and butcher-like, but hé knew my constitution. It was a loss to me his going off so suddenly [said **Lady Chettam**].' " 10

Hopkins, "the meek-mannered draper opposite, was the first to act on this inward vision [of gossip], being the more ambitious of a little masculine talk because his customers were chiefly women." 71

House-surgeon. "[**Dr Minchin**] had been inwardly annoyed, however, when he had asked at the Infirmary about the woman [**Nancy Nash**] he had recommended two days before, to hear from the house-surgeon, a youngster who was not sorry to vex Minchin with impunity, exactly what had occurred. . . . " 45

" 'We have a capital house-surgeon and dispenser, a clear-headed, neat-handed fellow [said **Lydgate**]." 45

Job " 'has only to speak about very plain things.' " 24

Jonas, a dyer. " 'Ah, there's better folks spend their money worse [than **Bulstrode**],' said a firm-voiced dyer, whose crimson hands looked out of keeping with his good-natured face." 71

Keck, " 'who manages the 'Trumpet.' I saw him the other day with **Hawley** [said **Chettam**]. His writing is sound enough, I believe, but he's such a low fellow, that I wished he had been on the wrong side.' " 38

—a rival: " . . . asserting that **Ladislaw**, if the truth were known, was not only a Polish emissary [spy] but crack-brained, which accounted for the preternatural quickness and glibness of his speech when he got on to a platform . . . . It was disgusting to Keck to see a strip of a fellow, with light curls round his head, get up and speechify by the hour against institutions 'which had existed when he was in his cradle.' " 46

Ladislaw, father. " 'And I never knew much of my father, beyond what my mother told me; but he inherited the musical talents. I remember his slow walk and his long thin hands, and one day remains with me when he was lying ill, and I was very hungry, and had only a little bit of bread.' " 37

" 'It was at Boulogne I saw your father [said **Raffles**]—a most uncommon likeness you are of him, by Jove! mouth—nose—eyes—hair turned off your brow just like his—a little in the foreign style.' " 60

Sarah (53) *née* **Dunkirk** (60) **Ladislaw**, **Will**'s mother. " . . . she died by an accident—a fall—four years ago. It is curious that my mother, too, ran away from her family, but not for the sake of her husband. She never would tell me anything about her family, except that she forsook them to get her own living —went on the stage, in fact. She was a dark-eyed creature, with crisp ringlets, and never seemed to be getting old. You see I come of rebellious blood on both sides.' " 37

Caius Larcher: *see* **Ned Plymdale** O

Edwin (60) **Larcher**, "the eminent carrier . . . . 'In my opinion **Farebrother** is too lax for a clergyman.' " 18

—*affluent:* "[His] great success in the carrying business . . . warranted his purchase of a mansion near Riverston already furnished in high style by an illustrious Spa physician—furnished indeed with such large framefuls of expensive flesh-painting in the dining-room, that **Mrs Larcher** was nervous until reassured by finding the subjects to be Scriptural." 60

Limp, "a meditative shoemaker, with weak eyes and a piping voice." 71

" . . . after taking a draught, [he] placed his flat hands together and pressed them hard between his knees, looking down at them with blear-eyed contemplation, as if the scorching power of **Mrs Dollop**'s speech had quite dried up and nullified his wits until they could be brought round again by further moisture." 71

Liret. "**Dorothea** had never been tired of listening to old Monsieur Liret when **Celia**'s feet were as cold as possible, and when it had really become dreadful to see the skin of his bald head moving about." 5

Charles (65) **Lydgate**, uncle, "who was a doctor of divinity (also a pleasing though sober kind of rank, when sustained by blood)." 36

Martha, "a little confused on the score of her kitchen apron, but collected enough to be sure that 'mum' was not the right title for this queenly young widow with a carriage and pair." 77

Mrs Mawmsey, "a woman accustomed to be made much of as a fertile mother—generally under attendance more or less frequent from **Mr Gambit**, and occasionally having attacks which required **Dr Minchin**." 45

Miss Morgan "was already far on in morning lessons with the younger [**Vincy**] girls in the school-room." 11

"Everything looked blooming and joyous except Miss Morgan, who was brown, dull, and resigned, and . . . just the sort of person for a governess." 16

Music master. "**Rosamond** played admirably. Her master at **Mrs Lemon**'s school . . . was one of those excellent musicians here and there to be found in our provinces, worthy to compare with many a noted Kapellmeister in a country which offers more plentiful conditions of musical celebrity." 16

Nancy Nash, charwoman, "became a subject of compassionate conversation in the neighbouring shops of Churchyard Lane as being afflicted with a tumour at first declared to be as large and hard as a duck's egg, but later in the day to be about the size of 'your fist.' " 45

" . . . much prejudice against **Lydgate**'s method as to drugs was overcome by the proof of his marvellous skill in the speedy restoration of Nancy Nash after she had been rolling and rolling in agonies from the presence of a tumour both hard and obstinate, but nevertheless compelled to yield." 45

Adolf Naumann, "a dark-eyed animated German . . . . " 19

" 'See now! My existence pre-supposes the existence of the whole universe—does it *not*? and my function is to paint . . . . ' " 19

Mr Peacock, whose practice [**Lydgate**] had paid something to enter on . . . had many patients among [the **Vincy**s'] connections and acquaintances." 11

Pegwell. " '[The roan, said **Bambridge**] belonged to Pegwell, the corn-factor; he used to drive him in his gig seven years ago, and he wanted me to take him, but I said, "Thank you, Peg. I don't deal in wind-instruments." ' " 23

Samuel Powderell. " . . . brother Samuel's cheek had the same purple round as ever . . . . " 47

Pratt, the butler, "a red-cheeked man given to lively converse with **Tantripp**, and often agreeing with her that it must be dull for Madam." 37

" 'I wish every book in that library was built into a caticom for your master,' said **Tantripp** to Pratt . . . .

"Pratt laughed. He liked his master very well, but he liked Tantripp better." 48

—knowing: "Of course, as a servant who was to be told nothing, he knew the fact of which **Ladislaw** was still ignorant, and had drawn his inferences; indeed, had not differed from his betrothed **Tantripp**, when she said, '*Your* master was as jealous as a fiend—and no reason.' " 54

Pritchard. " 'Have you got nothing else for my breakfast, Pritchard?' said **Fred**, to the servant who brought in coffee and buttered toast . . . . " 11

Mrs Renfrew, "the colonel's widow, was not only unexceptionable in point of breeding, but also interesting on the ground of her complaint, which puzzled the doctors, and seemed clearly a case wherein the fulness of professional knowledge might need the supplement of quackery." 10

Mrs Rigg, "in whose sex frog-features, accompanied with fresh-coloured cheeks and a well-rounded figure, are compatible with much charm for a certain order of admirers." 41

Dr Spanning. " 'He spoke very handsomely of my late tractate on the Egyptian Mysteries—using, in fact, terms which it would not become me to repeat.' " 37

Spilkins, "a young **Slender** of the neighbourhood, who was reckless with his pocket-money and felt his want of memory for riddles." 60

Mrs Strype. "[**Bulstrode**] would defend Mrs Strype the washerwoman against **Stubb**'s unjust exaction on the score of her drying-ground, and he would himself scrutinise a calumny against Mrs Strype." 16

Mrs Taft, "who was always counting stitches and gathered her information in misleading fragments caught between the rows of her knitting, had got it into her head that **Mr Lydgate** was a natural son of **Bulstrode**'s, a fact which seemed to justify her suspicions of evangelical laymen." 26

Tegg. "[**Bulstrode**] would take a great deal of pains about apprenticing Tegg the shoemaker's son, and he would watch over Tegg's churchgoing . . . . " 16

Saint Theresa of Avila. "Who . . . has not smiled with some gentleness at the thought of the little girl walking forth one morning hand-in-hand with her still smaller brother, to go and seek martyrdom in the country of the Moors? Out they toddled from rugged Avila, wide-eyed and helpless-looking as two fawns, but with human hearts, already beating to a national idea, until domestic reality met them in the shape of uncles, and turned them back from their great resolve." P

Harry Toller. " '**Lydgate** has been living at a great rate for a young beginner,' said Mr Harry Toller, the brewer. 'I suppose his relations in the North back him up.' " 63

Sophy Toller. " 'She is such a very nice girl—no airs, no pretensions, though on a level with the first . . . . I mean that Sophy is equal to the best in the town, and she is contented with that.' " 64

Trawley. " ' . . . what has become of Trawley? I have quite lost sight of him. He was hot on the French social systems, and talked of going to the Backwoods to found a sort of Pythagorean community. Is he gone?'

" 'Not at all. He is practicing at a German bath, and has married a rich patient.' " 17

Lord Triton " 'is precisely the man: full of plans for making the people happy in a soft-headed sort of way. That would just suit **Mrs Casaubon**.' " 54

Mrs Truberry, "who had scented peerages in the air from the very first introduction of the Reform question, and would sign her soul away to take precedence of her younger sister, who had married a baronet." 84

Mr Tucker "was the middle-aged curate, one of the 'inferior clergy,' who are usually not wanting in sons . . . [and] was just as old and musty-looking as she would have expected **Mr Casaubon**'s curate to be; doubtless an excellent man who would go to heaven (for **Celia** wished not to be unprincipled), but the corners of his mouth were so unpleasant. Celia thought with some dismalness of the time she should have to spend as bridesmaid at Lowick, where the curate had probably no pretty little children whom she could like, irrespective of principle." 9

Vesalius [H]. " ' . . . the only way he could get to know anatomy . . . was by going to snatch bodies at night, from graveyards and places of execution. . . .

" 'Oh, he had a good deal of fighting to the last. And they did exasperate him enough at one time to make him burn a good deal of his work. Then he got shipwrecked just as he was coming from Jerusalem to take a great chair at Padua. He died rather miserably.' " 45

Mrs Vigo "had been reader and secretary to royal personages, and in point of knowledge and sentiments even **Dorothea** could have nothing to object to her." 54

Bob Vincy. " 'You are always finding fault with Bob because he is not Fred.'

" 'Oh, no, mamma, only because he is Bob.' " 11

Louisa Vincy, "Mrs Vincy's darling, now ran to her with wide-eyed serious excitement, saying, 'O mamma, mamma. The little man [Rumpelstiltskin] stamped so hard on the floor he couldn't get his leg out again!' " 63

Vincy boy. "**Mary** secretly rejoiced that the youngest of the three was very much what her father must have been when he wore a round jacket, and showed a marvellous nicety of aim in playing at marbles, or in throwing stones to bring down the mellow pears." 87

Wakley [H]. " 'I disapprove of Wakley,' interposed **Dr Sprague**, 'no man more: he is an ill-intentioned fellow, who would sacrifice the respectability of the profession, which everybody knows depends on the London Colleges, for the sake of getting some notoriety for himself. There are men who don't mind about being kicked blue if they can only get talked about.' " 16

Also mentioned

Abel, hand at Stone Court	69
Archdeacon visited by Mr Casaubon	37
Bailiff at Stone Court, under Bulstrode	53
Baldwin, the tax-gatherer, part of the gossip about Bulstrode	71
Mrs Ballard, schoolmistress, whose pupils walk two by two	40
Trapping Bass, a poacher	84
Mrs Beck, lodging-house keeper to Mr Bowyer	25
Captain Beevor, who dragged his wife around by her hair	55
Mrs Beevor, who married Captain Beevor soon after widowhood	55
Justice Blakesley, the local magistrate	56
Bott, a tenant with good clay on his land for bricks	40
Mrs Bretton, the late; whose large house in Lowick Gate would suit Rosamond	36
Briggs, groom at Freshitt	84
Ellen Bulstrode, a daughter treated by Lydgate	26, 74
Kate Bulstrode, another daughter a little young for marriage	31, 74
Bunch, to be hanged as a sheep-stealer	4
Cadwallader, youngest daughter, age 5	8
Callum, clerk to Caleb Garth	56
Carp, who did not write enthusiastically of Casaubon's preliminary work	29
Mrs Carter, cook at Tipton Grange	6
Cheshire, remembered by Mrs Taft for radical cures with irons	45
Clemmens, a Brassing solicitor who drew Featherstone's last will	35
Clergyman at the Lowick church; new in the desk	47
Clerk at the bank, who revealed the source of Lydgate's funds	71
Coleman, whose house required the visit of a doctor	81
Courier at Rome—experienced	20
Crichley, a portraitist	84
Mrs Croly, celebrated beauty who made a conquest of Sir Godwin Lydgate in 1790	64
Curate at Tipton vicarage, with ill-shod but merry children	3
Jacob Dagley, a tenant's son who has killed a leveret	39
De Bracy—family name of Mrs Cadwallader	6
Archie Duncan, who told Sarah Dunkirk about her family's questionable business	60
Dunkirk son, who died	61
Faulkner, who had bought a horse from Bambridge in '19	71
Female friend of Mrs Mawmsey	45
Rev. Freke—"the brick-and-mortar incumbent"	8
Fulke, in the Colonial Office; known to Chettam	49
Garratt, lady's maid at Freshitt	50
Giles, an unsuccessful candidate for Parliament from Middlemarch	38
Grainger, a patient who lost much weight before dying	10
Grampus, a colonial governor mentioned by Chettam	49
Lord Grinsell, step-father of Mrs Beevor	55
Gripp & Co., Middlemarch publishers, who brought out Mary Garth's book on Plutarch	87
Clara Harfager, with a portion: her friends don't know what to do with her	62
Arabella Hawley, who went into a consumption	36
Housekeeper at Stone Court, under Bulstrode	53
John, groom to Sir James Chettam	3
Johnson, Brooke's gamekeeper: thought preacher Flavell a hypocrite for killing a hare	39
Jonas, a servant to Mr Casaubon	5
Joseph, auctioneer's assistant	60
Mrs Kell, housekeeper at the Grange	62
Kibble, Brassing purveyor of silverware	36
Leonard Lamb, B. A., of Finsbury; taught John Raffles (who called him Ba-Lamb)	41
Mrs Larcher, whose children got the measles and were treated by Mr Wrench	26, 60
Mrs Lemon, keeper of an elegant school for young ladies	11
Lovegood, steward to Sir James Chettam	3, 34
Mainwaring, Fred's more fortunate schoolmate	12

Manservant to Sir James Chettam: meets Lydgate on the road	29
Lord Medlicote, who gave land and timber for the Middlemarch hospital	13, 23
Lord Megatherium, a connection of Mrs Cadwallader's	6
Mrs Mengan, sister to Captain Lydgate; daughter of the baronet	58
nurse of the Chettam baby; oracular	50
Oliver, the local M.P. who is a Peelite	38
Organist at St Peter's, who teaches Rosamond	16
Philomicron ("lover of small things"); a writer of letters to the editor	17
Pike, a scholar whose ridicule Mr Casaubon feared	29
Pinkerton, incumbent Member of Parliament for Middlemarch	6, 51
Miss Pippin, putatively in love with Pumpkin	3
Lord Plessy, who lay in bed and played dominoes	38
Mme Poinçon, a schoolmistress in Lausanne	1
Political personage from Brassing, speaking fully for the reforming interests	51
Protheroe, a surgeon to visit the Hospital from Brassing for exceptional operations	45
Pumpkin, putatively in love with Miss Pippin	3
Robisson, a former employer of Mrs Abel to whom she provided alcohol	70
Sadler, a mercer with good damask	36
Schoolmaster and schoolmistress, discussing a new bell with Dorothea	80
Sheriff of the county	34
Spicer, shoemaker and parish-clerk in Middlemarch	70
Spicer, his brother; the bell-hanger in Lowick Gate	70
Mrs Sprague, discussing Mrs Bulstrode's calamity; elderly and old-fashioned	74
Staymaker and his wife, friends of Nancy Nash in her illness	45
Steward to Lord Medlicote, looking for a hunter	23
Stubb, who had an exaction against Mrs Strype's drying-ground	16
Lord Tapir, a connection of Mrs Cadwallader's	6
Tench, a scholar whose ridicule Mr Casaubon feared	29
Mrs Teveroy, Lord Grinsell's second wife	55
Tom, assistant to Caleb Garth, a boy of seventeen	56
the **Torbits**, who were in debt	64
Truberry, who had gone over to the Reform side at his wife's instigation	84
Vincy uncle, a clergyman now deceased	11
Vyan, Fred's more fortunate schoolmate	12
Mrs Walsingham, of Melspring, mother of the present Mrs Truberry	84
Waule, the late; "a warm man was Waule."	12
Rebecca, **Joanna**, and **Elizabeth Waule**, daughters of Jane	12
Webbe, medical man from Crabsley; to visit the Hospital twice a week	45
Miss Willoughby, a high-born schoolfellow of Rosamond's	36
Mrs Wimple, a patient of Dr Minchin's	18
Wright, groom to Mr Brooke	6
Yoddrell, with a farm near Frick	56

Gwendolen Harleth
[compare the portrait on page 534]

Published in eight parts by John Blackwood February-September 1876 **DD**

Daniel Deronda

Book I: The Spoiled Child

Daniel Deronda observes a beautiful woman playing at roulette at a continental gambling resort. She feels his glance and begins to lose. Later **Gwendolen Harleth** learns who he is but does not meet him. A letter calls her home. 1 Her mother tells her their livelihood is gone in a financial crash. Gwendolen raises money on a necklace, but while she considers remaining a day to play, a packet is brought to her: it is the necklace with a note from a "Stranger." She feels humiliated. She decides to go home at once. 2

Flashback: Gwendolen arrives at her mother's new home, Offendene. **Mrs Davilow** and four Davilow daughters explore. **Isabel**, the youngest, opens a panel and reveals a dead face. Gwendolen shudders and demands it be shut up, locked, and the key delivered to her. Her uncle, **Rev. Henry Gascoigne**, his wife, Mrs Davilow's sister, and their daughter **Anna** arrive to welcome them. Mr Gascoigne tells them of society in the neighbourhood and agrees to inquire about mount for Gwendolen. 3 Gwendolen's dominance and egoism are described. 4 She is invited to the **Arrowpoints**' and meets their daughter **Catherine** and **Julius Klesmer**, a formidable visiting musician. She patronizes the ridiculous Mrs Arrowpoint, who perceives it. She sings and has a success, though Klesmer is not impressed. His words wound; she is mortified. 5

Rex Gascoigne returns and participates with Gwendolen in charades and costumed *tableaux*. He falls heavily in love. During a presentation, Gwendolen is terrified when the panel hiding the dead face flies open. Isabel had unlocked it to satisfy her curiosity. She confesses. Gwendolen is subject to bouts of dread for no apparent reason. She cannot spend the night alone. 6 Anna fears for Rex and warns him, fruitlessly. A hunt: Gwendolen rides fearlessly and does well; left behind, Rex is thrown and hurt slightly. He tells his father of his love, and Mr Gascoigne reconnoiters. He determines that Gwendolen is not in love. But Rex makes his try; she reacts with violent aversion, and he is bitterly hurt. 7 Rex goes to bed; then gets up with plans to go to Canada. Anna wants to go with him; they speak to their father and he gently dissuades them. 8

Mallinger Grandcourt moves in at Diplow Hall, the house of his uncle, **Sir Hugo Mallinger**. There is excitement at the arrival of a very eligible bachelor. Gwendolen will be seen by him at a forthcoming Archery Meeting. 9 The Meeting occurs and Gwendolen has an immense success. As she receives a gold star for her feats Mr Grandcourt is brought to meet her. 10

Book II: Meeting Streams

Grandcourt impresses: calm, relaxed, cold, impeccable in speech. Gwendolen is repulsed by his hanger-on **Lush**. She is surprised by, later almost afraid of Grandcourt. They dance, and they walk. 11 Grandcourt at home with Lush shows cruelty to his dog. He disdains the idea of marrying heiress **Miss Arrowpoint**; he prefers Gwendolen. Lush expostulates and is ignored. 12 He pays great attentions to Gwendolen, but she turns them aside, and he is irritated. She decides to accept him but has fears. Her mother questions: she will not commit. Her uncle sternly brings her to the point: she will do it. Lush imports a woman and two children and has a plan to prevent the marriage. 13

As the archery begins, Gwendolen gets a note urging a rendezvous for news of Grandcourt. She goes. **Lydia Glasher** tells her she left her husband nine years before for Grandcourt. She has her two children with her. Gwendolen promises not to marry Grandcourt and to keep it all a secret. She leaves to join the **Langens** at Dover and travel with them. 14

Mallinger reaches Leubronn after Gwendolen has left. He encounters his uncle Sir Hugo Mallinger and Deronda. Sir Hugo praises Gwendolen. Daniel denies interest. 15 His boyhood with his uncle, and his discovery that there is a mystery: who were his parents? He grows, sings beautifully, looks wonderful; at Eton he is reserved. Sir Hugo marries. Daniel's development in character and beauty of personality are detailed. He goes on to Cambridge, where he meets **Hans Meyrick** and helps him to a scholarship, at cost to himself. Hans wins, Daniel loses. He wanted to leave anyway. Hans secretly writes Sir Hugo telling all. So Sir Hugo is tolerant and blesses Daniel's plans to travel. 16

Rowing on the Thames at dusk, Deronda sees a sad-looking young girl on the bank. On his return to the spot, he realizes she is planning to drown herself. He intervenes and persuades her to come with him. He will take her to the Meyricks. 17 We see diminutive **Mrs Meyrick** and her diminutive daughters **Kate**, **Amy** and **Mab**, at home, reading aloud and dreaming of good deeds. They welcome **Mirah Lapidoth** with sympathy and delight. 18

Book III: Maidens Choosing

Daniel is bemused, excited and apprehensive after his adventure. He worries at what his efforts to find Mirah's family may reveal. 19 Mirah tells Mrs Meyrick the story of her abduction by her father and her later life: her stay in America, training, exploitation, her fears of entrapment and flight to England; her failure to find traces of her mother and the despair which led her to the river. Daniel is entranced by her, but he leaves with the Mallingers for two months abroad: he will see Gwendolen gambling at Leubronn. 20

Gwendolen returns to Offendene and commiserates with her mother, who is sick at heart. They canvass options and consider their situation. Gwendolen rallies her mother courageously and says she has a plan. She writes a note to Klesmer, asking him to call. 21 Klesmer and Catherine discover they love each other. Catherine goes to tell her parents, who are beside themselves. She is firm: she will marry Klesmer even if she is disinherited, which is their threat. 22 Gwendolen consults Klesmer on her prospects for a career on the stage. He is kind but candid. She feels burning hurt but holds her head up. She will take a job as governess. 23 She suggests selling her jewels but notices the necklace Deronda returned to her and superstitiously saves it out of the collection. 24

Back from Leubronn, Grandcourt plans to pursue Gwendolen, despite Lush's remonstrance. Lush tells him of the scene with Lydia Glasher, but Grandcourt persists in sending Gwendolen a note. 25 Gwendolen and the Rector speak: her prospective employer will come to meet her. She despairs. Her mother brings a note from Grandcourt: new thoughts start up. 26 She waits for him, sure she will reject him: disgust and indignation at his past are still strong. He arrives and presses her, promising relief to her mother. His manner and words are perfection. It is "Yes." He kisses her hand; she asks that Lush be dismissed and he agrees at once. She tells her mother: no little cottage, no life for her as a governess. 27

Book IV: Gwendolen Gets Her Choice

The Gascoignes are apprised. Gwendolen's conscience makes her sleepless. Grandcourt sends a large diamond and a cheque. They ride, and she is exhilarated. He gives Lush his *congé* with £300 a year to stay within call. Mrs Davilow is anxious: how does Gwendolen really feel? Grandcourt is intrigued. Lush writes Sir Hugo, who hopes to buy Diplow outright. He asks Deronda to be his emissary. 28 At his home, Grandcourt languidly pays homage. Deronda observes, and Gwendolen needs him desperately. Grandcourt leaves to see his mistress. 29 At Gadsmere we learn Lydia's story: an abusive marriage, a first-born dead; her flight to glamour and wealth. Grandcourt tells her he will marry; she is devastated. He asks for the diamonds he will give his bride; she refuses to give them up unless directly to her at the last minute. He thinks her mad but has to give in. She gets him to light a cigar. They part in mutual fear. 30

Gwendolen is a beautiful bride. Grandcourt is surprisingly in love. But at their new home there is the packet of diamonds, with a vitriolic note from Lydia. Grandcourt finds his love in terrified, morbid hysterics. 31 Mirah, happy with the Meyricks, makes it clear that she is a Jewess. A portrait of Deronda at twenty-five: at a loss to find a mission in life. Travelling with his uncle, Deronda enters a synagogue for the first time. A patriarch sees him and asks him who his mother was. He retreats coldly. Back in London, he visits the Meyricks and hears Mirah sing. He knows Hans will return soon, and he fears his reaction to Mirah. He will continue his search for Mirah's family. 32

Roaming through the Jewish quarter, Deronda sees an archetypal Jew and buys a book from him. Then he finds **Ezra Cohen**, pawn-broker, and his family including his mother (sensitive to a question about a daughter) and precocious **Jacob Alexander**. They are charmed by him. He will return to pledge a diamond ring. He is unhappy at the thought that these are Mirah's family. 33 He returns and joins the Sabbath dinner. The Jewish archetype joins the group. He is **Mordecai**, obviously very ill. He prays, then leaves. Ezra Cohen offers Deronda £40 for his ring, and the transaction is made. 34

Book V: Mordecai

Their honeymoon over, the Grandcourts come to the Mallingers' to meet their world. Deronda is there: she is cold and brittle at first, then suddenly reveals deep sadness in a glance at him. She is wretched: she has fatally misunderstood her power in marriage to the suppressive, sadistic Grandcourt. She reverences Deronda, who feels for her. 35 Hanger-on **Vandernoodt** fills Deronda in on the Glasher family. As he takes it in, he understands her much better. He counsels her compassionately. She drinks it in. 36 Hans has returned, and Deronda is disconcerted to learn he is in love with Mirah and has painted her. They argue over this. He calls to see Mirah, who has been amused by Hans. They discuss her singing for Klesmer. Deronda loves. 37

Mordecai yearns for a young ideal who will sit at his feet and absorb his thought and his dreams. He frightens little Jacob. He knows he is dying, and his agitation builds. 38 Klesmer calls and hears Mirah sing. He likes it and invites her to sing at his home. He will offer advice and teachers. The Meyricks and Mirah are ecstatic. Hans advises a new dress. 39 Deronda rows on the river and sees Mordecai above him at Blackfriars. They go together to the book shop and confer. Mordecai asks about his forebears, and Deronda tells what he knows. Mordecai is surer than ever; Deronda is impressed. They part after Mordecai declines to discuss the Cohens and a mysterious daughter. 40

Book VI: Revelations

Deronda reflects on his time with Mordecai. He speculates on the validity of his enthusiasm and his own possible role. 41 He goes with Mordecai to a club, the "Philosophers," and hears the talk. Inspired by his presence, Mordecai rapturizes on the Jews and their future national home. The others are unconvinced but awed by his fervour. 42 Moved by his experience, Mordecai reminisces: he reveals himself as the Ezra who was Mirah's brother. He tells of her abduction, his mother's despair. Deronda fears to reveal what he knows: Mordecai is frail and faint. 43 Meanwhile, Gwendolen copes, visiting her mother and uncle to say a trip to London is in prospect. 44 She hears Mirah sing at the Mallingers' and pleads with Deronda not to give up on her. 45

Deronda, by appointment, comes to Mordecai and tells him Mirah is safe and near. With Mrs Meyrick's help he finds and furnishes lodgings. 46 With Mordecai in his new home, Mirah comes. They reunite in love. 47 Stung by Grandcourt's suggestion that Deronda dallies with Mirah, Gwendolen goes to invite her to sing. She hears Deronda and quickly learns that he is revered as a benefactor, nothing more. At home, Grandcourt orders her never to go there again. He tells her Lush will come to tell her about his will. Lush gives her an abstract which shows that absent a son born to her Lydia's son will inherit. She expresses her satisfaction and has dinner with Grandcourt in perfect calm. She thinks of leaving him but decides to keep it all to herself. Riding, she sees Lydia, showing herself vindictively. She is amazed that Grandcourt cuts her dead and thinks of his death as the way out. At a party she publicly asks Deronda to visit the next afternoon. He comes; shyness overwhelms her. She stutters out a plea to be shown how to be better. Sorrow for her ties his tongue. In walks Grandcourt, pleased not to have been fooled. Deronda leaves. Grandcourt tells her they will yacht in the Mediterranean. 48 Sir Hugo sends for Deronda. He gives him a letter from his mother. Deronda asks if his father is living: "no." Sir Hugo asks forgiveness for pain; Deronda shakes his hand. 49

Book VII: The Mother and the Son

Sir Hugo gives Deronda a letter from his mother, the **Princess Leonora Halm-Eberstein**. She summons him to Genoa to meet with her and receive property she has withheld. He goes, and he waits nearly three weeks: she comes at last. 50 They meet. She is pleased with his looks. She tells him she had been a great singer and had not wanted a son. His father was a Jew; she is a Jew. Deronda exults at the news; she is startled: he carries her father's Jewish spirit in him. He deeply sympathizes with her, and she is touched although resentful that **Joseph Kalonymos** has forced her to break the wall between Deronda and his Jewishness. They part for a time. 51 Deronda has a long letter from Hans, with comments on Mirah and the support the Klesmers are giving her. His "hope" for Mirah no longer irritates Deronda. Hans reports that Gwendolen and Grandcourt are yachting in the Mediterranean. Mirah and Mrs Meyrick talk: Mirah has seen her father. She fears his shrinking before Mordecai. Mrs Meyrick gets her to promise that if he appears, they will be told. She is sensitive about Gwendolen and Deronda's possible interest in her. 52

A second audience: Deronda is clear on his mission; his mother guesses that he loves a Jewess. He is silent. She probes, and he describes Mirah but says he has no assurance of her love. He half-accuses, half-forgives her; she does not accept blame and says farewell. He leaves an older man. 53 Grandcourt exults in yachting despotism; Gwendolen's hatred grows and terrifies her. A storm damages the yacht; they must put in at Genoa for a week. They encounter Deronda, to general amazement; Grandcourt insists on going out sailing in a small craft he would handle himself. Gwendolen resists but has to give in. 54 Deronda has finished his business but waits still at Genoa, thinking of offering moral support to Gwendolen. He sees her brought in by sailors, soaking wet and distracted. Grandcourt has drowned. Deronda wires Sir Hugo and the Rector, asking that Mrs Davilow come at once. 55

Deronda sees Gwendolen, who tells him of her hatred and wish to kill; the knife she had secreted in her room; her seeing Deronda and drawing back from murderous thoughts. She tells of Grandcourt, knocked into the water, coming up and calling for the rope: and she held her hand and wished him dead. A second time, and she held the rope and did not throw it. Then she leaped in after him, terrified of herself. But he was drowned. Deronda in his mind discounts her guilt but is glad of her remorse and foresees that Good will triumph in her. 56 He comes and tells her she bears no guilt: cramp prevented Grandcourt from reaching the boat. She begs that he not forsake her; he goes; she weeps. 57

Book VIII: Fruit and Seed

A domestic scene at the Davilows' is interrupted by a telegram to say that Grandcourt is drowned. Mrs Davilow will leave at once. Rex, present when the news comes, is much torn up: his love is as strong and hopeless as ever. His father prepares to leave for Genoa. 58 Sir Hugo arrives at Genoa. Deronda meets him. They discuss Gwendolen and Grandcourt's surprising will with its meagre £2,000 a year for her, then Deronda's mother and his new situation. Sir Hugo warns him strongly against "eccentricity." 59 In Mainz, Deronda meets Kalonymos and assures him of his gratitude. Kalonymos is delighted to see his resemblance to **Daniel Charisi**, his grandfather, and to learn he takes his Jewishness seriously. He delivers the Charisi chest to Deronda, whose statement of intent and commitment seems to clarify both for him. 60

Hans rushes the news of Grandcourt's death to the Meyricks'. His blithe prediction of romance for Deronda infuriates Mirah, who blows him up. He walks her home penitently, but fearing she is headed for hurt. Mirah is beside herself, wracked by jealousy and self-contempt; Mordecai raptly awaits Deronda's return. He lectures profoundly; she has her own view. 61 Leaving a house where she has sung, Mirah senses her father following her. He accosts her and spins a fantasy of devotion deserted. She invites him to come in and see his son; he begs off and cadges her purse. She tells Mordecai, weeping. 62 Deronda arrives, and there is a climactic scene with Mordecai, witnessed by Mirah. Deronda announces that he is a Jew. He is committed to help his people. Mordecai is ecstatic. Mirah is partly reassured as to Gwendolen. 63

Gwendolen is anxious to leave Genoa. Her mother knows a little now, as Sir Hugo has told the Rector the purport of Grandcourt's will. Both are incensed at Gwendolen's shabby treatment. Sir Hugo confirms his friendship. When her mother asks, Gwendolen confirms that she knows all and approves. Sir Hugo offers his London house for the time. 64 Gwendolen asks him to get a message to Deronda: she asks him what she should accept under the will. He advises her to take all: anything else would create pain for her mother, wonder and inquiry among the public. He takes a gentle leave. 65 Having gambled all Mirah's money away, Lapidoth goes again to the well. Mordecai castigates him but allows him to stay. Mirah is gentle but offers no caress. He broods. 66

Deronda visits Hans to tell his news. Hans has already heard it, has been on an opium binge and is out of sorts. He tells Deronda Mirah is his: she is jealous of Gwendolen. 67 Deronda eagerly goes to her. She is out; he reads with Mordecai, having taken off his heavy ring in the heat. Lapidoth enters and sees it at once. In a moment he has fled with it and sought a ship. Mirah's agony at this is mitigated by Deronda's profession of love and proposal of marriage. The lovers are in bliss. 68 Deronda has tried twice to tell Gwendolen of his new situation but her own emotional state has prevented. Now he comes a third time and gets it out: he is a Jew; he will leave England for years; he will devote himself to establishing a national centre for Jews. She is stricken and can barely speak. He goes, sorrowing for her. 69 Joyous marriage in the Jewish rite for Deronda and Mirah; loving, uniting death for Mordecai. 70

The mutual proposals and acceptances of Klesmer and Miss Arrowpoint are in the *Topicon* at LM:Love—*mutual discovery;* and the scene in the library with her parents shortly after is at A:Parents—*thunderstruck.*

Contents

Title Role

Daniel Deronda, at Leubronn: "There was a calm intensity of life and richness of tint in his face that on a sudden gaze from him was rather startling, and often made him seem to have spoken, so that servants and officials asked him automatically, 'What did you say, sir?' when he had been quite silent." 15

—face: "But in the nephew Daniel Deronda the family faces of various types, seen on the walls of the gallery, found no reflex. Still he was handsomer than any of them, and when he was thirteen might have served as model for any painter who wanted to image the most memorable of boys: you could hardly have seen his face thoroughly meeting yours without believing that human creatures had done nobly in times past, and might do more nobly in time to come." 16

—feminine quality: "He had not lived with other boys, and his mind showed the same blending of child's ignorance with surprising knowledge which is oftener seen in bright girls." 16

—disturbing new idea: "Daniel felt the presence of a new guest who seemed to come with an enigmatic veiled face, and to carry dimly-conjectured, dreaded revelations. The ardour which he had given to the imaginary world in his books suddenly rushed towards his own history and spent its pictorial energy there, explaining what he knew, representing the unknown. The uncle whom he loved very dearly took the aspect of a father who held secrets about him—who had done him a wrong—yes, a wrong: and what had become of his mother, from whom he must have been taken away?—Secrets about which he, Daniel, could never inquire; for to speak or be spoken to about these new thoughts seemed like falling flakes of fire to his imagination.

"Those who have known an impassioned childhood will understand this dread of utterance about any shame connected with their parents. The impetuous advent of new images took possession of him with the force of fact for the first time told, and left him no immediate power for the reflection that he might be trembling at a fiction of his own. The terrible sense of collision between a strong rush of feeling and the dread of its betrayal, found relief at length in big slow tears, which fell without restraint . . . . " ¶16

—sensitive: " . . . there was hardly a delicacy of feeling this lad was not capable of." 16

—singer: "Daniel had not only one of those thrilling boy voices which seem to bring an idyllic heaven and earth before our eyes, but a fine musical

instinct, and had early made out accompaniments for himself on the piano, while he sang from memory." 16

—*admired:* "The boy came forward with unusual reluctance. He wore an embroidered holland blouse which set off the rich colouring of his head and throat, and the resistant gravity about his mouth and eyes as he was being smiled upon, made their beauty the more impressive. Every one was admiring him." 16

—*predilections:* "But Daniel's tastes were altogether in keeping with his nurture: his disposition was one in which everyday scenes and habits beget not *ennui* or rebellion, but delight, affection, aptitudes; and now the lad had been stung to the quick by the idea that his uncle—perhaps his father—thought of a career for him which was totally unlike his own, and which he knew very well was not thought of among possible destinations for the sons of English gentlemen . . . now, in spite of his musical gift, he set himself bitterly against the notion of being dressed up to sing before all those fine people who would not care about him except as a wonderful toy." 16

—*at school:* "Every one, his tutor included, set him down as a reserved boy, though he was so good-humoured and unassuming, as well as quick both at study and sport, that nobody called his reserve disagreeable. Certainly his face had a great deal to do with that favourable interpretation; but in his instance the beauty of the closed lips told no falsehood." 16

—*innate kindness:* "But hatred of innocent human obstacles was a form of moral stupidity not in Deronda's grain; even the indignation which had long mingled itself with his affection for **Sir Hugo** took the quality of pain rather than of temper; and as his mind ripened to the idea of tolerance towards error, he habitually linked the idea with his own silent grievances." 16

—*character:* "Deronda's early-wakened susceptibility, charged at first with ready indignation and resistant pride, had raised in him a premature reflection on certain questions of life; it had given a bias to his conscience, a sympathy with certain ills, and a tension of resolve in certain directions, which marked him off from other youths much more than any talents he possessed." 16

—*goal:* "There had sprung up in him a meditative yearning after wide knowledge which is likely always to abate ardour in the fight for prize acquirement in narrow tracks. Happily he was modest, and took any secondrateness in himself simply as a fact, not as a marvel necessarily to be accounted for by a superiority." 16

—*rare quality:* "Daniel had the stamp of rarity in a subdued fervour of sympathy, an activity of imagination on behalf of others, which did not show itself effusively, but was continually seen in acts of considerateness that struck his companions as moral eccentricity." 16

"He had his flashes of fierceness, and could hit out upon occasion, but the occasions were not always what might have been expected. For in what related to himself his resentful impulses had been early checked by a mastering affectionateness. Love has a habit of saying 'Never mind' to angry self, who, sitting down for the nonce in the lower place, by-and-by gets used to it." 16

—*ambition*: "Certainly Deronda's ambition, even in his spring-time, lay exceptionally aloof from conspicuous, vulgar triumph, and from other ugly forms of boyish energy; perhaps because he was early impassioned by ideas, and burned his fire on those heights. One may spend a good deal of energy in disliking and resisting what others pursue, and a boy who is fond of somebody else's pencil-case may not be more energetic than another who is fond of giving his own pencil-case away." 16

—*ethic:* "Still, it was not Deronda's disposition to escape from ugly scenes: he was more inclined to sit through them and take care of the fellow least able to take care of himself. It had helped to make him popular that he was sometimes a little compromised by this apparent comradeship. For a meditative interest in learning how human miseries are wrought—as precocious in him as another sort of genius in the poet who writes a Queen Mab at nineteen—was so infused with kindliness that it easily passed for comradeship." 16

—*studies:* "Every one interested in him agreed that he might have taken a high place if his motives had been of a more pushing sort, and if he had not, instead of regarding studies as instruments of success, hampered himself with the notion that they were to feed motive and opinion—a notion which set him criticising methods and arguing against his freight and harness when he should have been using all his might to pull . . . .

"He found the inward bent towards comprehension and thoroughness diverging more and more from the track marked out by the standards of examination: he felt a heightening discontent with the wearing futility and enfeebling strain of a demand for excessive retention and dexterity without any insight into the principles which form the vital connections of knowledge. . . .

"He longed now to have the sort of apprenticeship to life which would not shape him too definitely, and rob him of the choice that might come from a free growth." 16

—*school friendship:* "Deronda was content, and gave **Meyrick** all the interest he claimed, getting at last a brotherly anxiety about him, looking after him in his erratic moments, and contriving by adroitly delicate devices not only to make up for his friend's lack of pence, but to save him from threatening chances. Such friendship easily becomes tender: the one spreads strong sheltering wings that delight in spreading, the other gets the warm protection which is also a delight. Meyrick was going in for a classical scholarship, and his success, in various ways momentous, was the more probable from the steadying influence of Deronda's friendship." 16

—*on the river:* "Rowing in his dark-blue shirt and skull-cap, his curls closely clipped, his mouth beset with abundant soft waves of beard, he bore only disguised traces of the seraphic boy 'trailing clouds of glory.' " 17

—*a grown man now:* "Still, even one who had never seen him since his boyhood might have looked at him with slow recognition, due perhaps to the peculiarity of the gaze which **Gwendolen** chose to call 'dreadful,' though it had really a very mild sort of scrutiny. The voice, sometimes audible in subdued snatches of song, had turned out merely a high barytone; indeed, only to look at his lithe powerful frame and the firm gravity of his face would have been enough for an experienced guess that he had no rare and ravishing tenor such as nature reluctantly makes at some sacrifice. Look at his hands: they are not small and dimpled with tapering fingers that seem to have only a deprecating touch: they are long, flexible firmly-grasping hands, such as **Titian** has painted in a picture where he wanted to show the combination of refinement with force. And there is something of a likeness, too, between the faces belonging to the hands—in both the uniform pale-brown skin, the perpendicular brow, the calmly penetrating eyes.

Daniel sees a girl on the banks of the Thames

"Not seraphic any longer: thoroughly terrestrial and manly; but still of a kind to raise belief in a human dignity which can afford to acknowledge poor relations." ¶17

—riverbank vision: "It was clear to him as an onyx cameo: the brown-black drapery, the white face with small, small features and dark, long-lashed eyes. His mind glanced over the girl-tragedies that are going on in the world, hidden, unheeded, as if they were but tragedies of the copse or hedge-row, where the helpless drag wounded wings forsakenly, and streak the shadowed moss with the red moment-hand of their own death." 17

—stimulus: " . . . the new image of helpless sorrow easily blent itself with what seemed to him the strong array of reasons why he should shrink from getting into that routine of the world which makes men apologise for all its wrong-doing, and take opinions as mere professional equipment—why he should not draw strongly at any thread in the hopelessly-entangled scheme of things." 17

—moved: " 'Great God!' the words escaped Deronda in a tone so low and solemn that they seemed like a prayer become unconsciously vocal. The agitating impression this forsaken girl was making on him stirred a fibre that lay close to his deepest interest in the fates of women—'perhaps my mother was like this one.' The old thought had come now with a new impetus of mingled feeling, and urged that exclamation in which both East and West have for ages concentrated their awe in the presence of inexorable calamity." 17

—fervour: "To say that Deronda was romantic would be to misrepresent him; but under his calm and somewhat self-repressed exterior there was a fervour which made him easily find poetry and romance among the events of everyday life." 19

—apprehension: "Deronda's thinking went on in rapid images of what might be: he saw himself guided by some official scout into a dingy street; he entered through a dim doorway, and saw a hawk-eyed woman, rough-headed, and unwashed, cheapening a hungry girl's last bit of finery; or in some quarter only the more hideous for being smarter, he found himself under the breath of a young Jew talkative and familiar, willing to show his acquaintance with gentleman's tastes, and not fastidious in any transactions with which they would favour him—and so on through the brief chapter of his experience in this kind. Excuse him: his mind was not apt to run spontaneously into insulting ideas, or to practise a form of wit which identifies **Moses** with the advertisement sheet; but he was just now governed by dread, and if **Mirah**'s parents had been Christian, the chief difference would have been that his forebodings would have been fed with wider knowledge. It was the habit of his mind to connect dread with unknown parentage, and in this case as well as his own there was enough to make the connection reasonable." 19

—stoic: "No reasoning as to the foundations of custom could do away with the early-rooted feeling that his birth had been attended with injury for which his father was to blame; and seeing that but for this injury **Grandcourt**'s prospect might have been his, he was proudly resolute not to behave in any way that might be interpreted into irritation on that score." 25

—balance: " . . . the mental balance in Deronda, who was moved by an affectionateness such as we are apt to call feminine, disposing him to yield in ordinary details, while he had a certain inflexibility of judgment, and independence of opinion, held to be rightfully masculine." 28

—*susceptibility:* "[**Gwendolen**'s past] implied a nature liable to difficulty and struggle—elements of life which had a predominant attraction for his sympathy, due perhaps to his early pain in dwelling on the conjectured story of his own existence. Persons attracted him, as **Hans Meyrick** had done, in proportion to the possibility of his defending them, rescuing them, telling upon their lives with some sort of redeeming influence; and he had to resist an inclination, easily accounted for, to withdraw coldly from the fortunate." 28

—*the feminine:* " . . . there was something beyond his habitual compassionate fervour—something due to the fascination of her womanhood. He was very open to that sort of charm, and mingled it with the consciously Utopian pictures of his own future; yet any one able to trace the folds of his character might have conceived that he would be more likely than many less passionate men to love a woman without telling her of it. Sprinkle food before a delicate-eared bird: there is nothing he would more willingly take, yet he keeps aloof, because of his sensibility to checks which to you are imperceptible." 28

—*disturbing:* "His face had that disturbing kind of form and expression which threatens to affect opinion—as if one's standard were somehow wrong. (Who has not seen men with faces of this corrective power till they frustrated it by speech or action?) His voice, heard now for the first time, was to **Grandcourt**'s toneless drawl, which had been in her ears every day, as the deep notes of a violoncello to the broken discourse of poultry and other lazy gentry in the afternoon sunshine. Grandcourt, she inwardly conjectured, was perhaps right in saying that Deronda thought too much of himself—a favourite way of explaining a superiority that humiliates." 29

—*his glance:* " . . . with his usual directness of gaze—a large-eyed gravity, innocent of any intention. His eyes had a peculiarity which has drawn many men into trouble; they were of a dark yet mild intensity, which seemed to express a special interest in every one on whom he fixed them, and might easily help to bring on him those claims which ardently sympathetic people are often creating in the minds of those who need help. In mendicant fashion, we make the goodness of others a reason for exorbitant demands on them." 29

—*for the underdog:* "We fall on the leaning side; and Deronda suspected himself of loving too well the losing causes of the world. Martyrdom changes sides, and he was in danger of changing with it, having a strong repugnance to taking up that clue of success which the order of the world often forces upon us and makes it treason against the common weal to reject. And yet his fear of falling into an unreasoning narrow hatred made a check for him: he apologised for the heirs of privilege; he shrank with dislike from the loser's bitterness and the denunciatory tone of the unaccepted innovator." 32

—*too much sympathy:* "A too reflective and diffusive sympathy was in danger of paralysing in him that indignation against wrong and that selectness of fellowship which are the conditions of moral force; and in the last few years of confirmed manhood he had become so keenly aware of this that what he most longed for was rather some external event, or some inward light, that would urge him into a definite line of action, and compress his wandering energy. He was ceasing to care for knowledge—he had no ambition for practice —unless they could both be gathered up into one current with his emotions, and he dreaded, as if it were a dwelling-place of lost souls, that dead anatomy of culture which turns the universe into a mere ceaseless answer to queries, and knows, not everything, but everything else about everything—as if one should be ignorant of nothing concerning the scent of violets except the scent itself for which one had no nostril. But how and whence was the needed event to come?—the influence that would justify partiality, and make him what he longed to be yet was unable to make himself—an organic part of social life, instead of roaming in it like a yearning disembodied spirit, stirred with a vague social passion, but without fixed local habitation to render fellowship real?" 32

—a sadness seen: " 'I can't do anything to help her—nobody can, if she has found out her mistake already. And it seems to me that she has a dreary lack of the ideas that might help her. Strange and piteous to think what a centre of wretchedness a delicate piece of human flesh like that might be, wrapped round with fine raiment, her ears pierced for gems, her head held loftily, her mouth all smiling pretence, the poor soul within her sitting in sick distaste of all things! But what do I know of her? There may be a demon in her to match the worst husband, for what I can tell. She was clearly an ill-educated, worldly girl: perhaps she is a coquette.' " 35

—on old things: " 'To delight in doing things because our fathers did them is good if it shuts out nothing better; it enlarges the range of affection—and affection is the broadest basis of good in life.' " 35

—new insight: "Gwendolen knowing of that woman and her children, marrying **Grandcourt**, and showing herself contented, would have been among the most repulsive of beings to him; but Gwendolen tasting the bitterness of remorse for having contributed to their injury was brought very near to his fellow-feeling." 36

—irritated: "He was conscious of that peculiar irritation which will sometimes befall the man whom others are inclined to trust as a mentor—the irritation of perceiving that he is supposed to be entirely off the same plane of desire and temptation as those who confess to him.' " 37

—his birth: "Many of us complain that half our birthright is sharp duty. Deronda was more inclined to complain that he was robbed of this half; yet he accused himself, as he would have accused another, of being weakly self-conscious and wanting in resolve . . . . To Daniel the words Father and Mother had the altar-fire in them: and the thought of all closest relations of our nature held still something of the mystic power which had made his neck and ears burn in boyhood." 37

—opaque: "Sometimes he had longed for the sort of friend to whom he might possibly unfold his experience . . . for he had found it impossible to reciprocate confidences with one who looked up to him. But he had no expectation of meeting the friend he imagined. Deronda's was not one of those quiveringly-poised natures that lend themselves to second-sight." 37

—tolerant: "His nature was too large, too ready to conceive regions beyond his own experience, to rest at once in the easy explanation, 'madness,' whenever a consciousness showed some fulness and conviction where his own was blank." 40

—fateful meeting: " . . . opposite to [**Mordecai**] was a face not more distinctively oriental than many a type seen among what we call the Latin races: rich in youthful health, and with a forcible masculine gravity in its repose, that gave the value of judgment to the reverence with which he met the gaze of this mysterious son of poverty who claimed him as a long-expected friend. The more exquisite quality of Deronda's nature—that keenly perceptive sympathetic emotiveness which ran along with his speculative tendency—was never more thoroughly tested. He felt nothing that could be called belief in

the validity of Mordecai's impressions concerning him or in the probability of any greatly effective issue: what he felt was a profound sensibility to a cry from the depths of another soul; and accompanying that, the summons to be receptive instead of superciliously prejudging. Receptiveness is a rare and massive power, like fortitude; and this state of mind now gave Deronda's face its utmost expression of calm benignant force—an expression which nourished Moredecai's confidence and made an open way before him." 40

—facing it: "This strong man whose gaze was sustainedly calm and his finger-nails pink with health, who was exercised in all questioning and accused of excessive mental independence, still felt a subduing influence over him in the tenacious certitude of the fragile creature before him, whose pallid yellow nostril was tense with effort as his breath laboured under the burthen of eager speech. The influence seemed to strengthen the bond of sympathetic obligation. In Deronda at this moment the desire to escape what might turn into a trying embarrassment was no more likely to determine action than the solicitations of indolence are likely to determine it in one with whom industry is a daily law." 40

—conscience: "And Deronda's conscience included sensibilities beyond the common, enlarged by his early habit of thinking himself imaginatively into the experience of others." 41

—speculation: "Nay, it was conceivable that as **Mordecai** needed and believed that he had found an active replenishment of himself, so Deronda might receive from Mordecai's mind the complete ideal shape of that personal duty and citizenship which lay in his own thought like sculptured fragments certifying some beauty yearned after but not traceable by divination." 41

—a romantic: "Feelings had lately been at work within him which had very much modified the reluctance he would formerly have had to think of himself as probably a Jew. And, if you like, he was romantic. That young energy and spirit of adventure which have helped to create the world-wide legends of youthful heroes going to seek the hidden tokens of their birth and its inheritance of tasks, gave him a certain quivering interest in the bare possibility that he was entering on a like track—all the more because the track was one of thought as well as action." 41

—caution: "His own experience of the small room that ardour can make for itself in ordinary minds had had the effect of increasing his reserve; and while tolerance was the easiest attitude to him, there was another bent in him also capable of becoming a weakness—the dislike to appear exceptional or to risk an ineffective insistence on his own opinion." 43

—attraction: "Moreover, he liked being near her—how could it be otherwise? She was something more than a problem: she was a lovely woman, for the turn of whose mind and fate he had a care which, however futile it might be, kept soliciting him as a responsibility, perhaps all the more that, when he dared to think of his own future, he saw it lying far away from this splendid sad-hearted creature, who, because he had once been impelled to arrest her attention momentarily, as he might have seized her arm with warning to hinder her from stepping where there was danger, had turned to him with a beseeching persistent need." 48

—yearning: "He had not the Jewish consciousness, but he had a yearning grown the stronger for the denial which had been his grievance, after the obligation of avowed filial and social ties." 43

The Princess Halm-Eberstein greets her repudiated son

—facing an agony: "The feeling Deronda endured in these moments he afterwards called horrible. Words seemed to have no more rescue in them than if he had been beholding a vessel in peril of wreck—the poor ship with its many-lived anguish beaten by the inescapable storm.

"How could he grasp the long-growing process of this young creature's wretchedness?—how arrest and change it with a sentence? He was afraid of his own voice . . . . He felt himself holding a crowd of words imprisoned within his lips, as if the letting them escape would be a violation of awe before the mysteries of our human lot." ¶48

—vulnerability: " . . . he had never throughout his relations with **Gwendolen** been free from the nervous consciousness that there was something to guard against not only on her account but on his own—some precipitancy in the manifestation of impulsive feeling—some ruinous inroad of what is but momentary on the permanent chosen treasure of the heart—some spoiling of her trust, which wrought upon him now as if it had been the retreating cry of a creature snatched and carried out of his reach by swift horsemen or swifter waves, while his own strength was only a stronger sense of weakness." 50

—hearing a repudiation: "[The Princess] seemed to fling out the last words against some possible reproach in the mind of her son, who had to stand and hear them—clutching his coat-collar as if he were keeping himself above water by it, and feeling his blood in the sort of commotion that might have been excited if he had seen her going through some strange rite of a religion which gave a sacredness to crime." 51

—a mission: " 'The effect of my education can never be done away with. The Christian sympathies in which my mind was reared can never die out of me,' said Deronda, with increasing tenacity of tone. 'But I consider it my duty—it is the impulse of my feeling—to identify myself, as far as possible, with my hereditary people, and if I can see any work to be done for them that I can give my soul and hand to I shall choose to do it.' " 53

—declaration: " 'Your will was strong, but my grandfather's trust which you accepted and did not fulfil—what you call his yoke—is the expression of something stronger, with deeper, farther-spreading roots, knit into the foundations of sacredness for all men. You renounced me—you still banish me—as a son'—there was an involuntary movement of indignation in Deronda's voice—'But that stronger Something has determined that I shall be all the more the grandson whom also you willed to annihilate.' " 53

—leaving her: "He felt an older man. All his boyish yearnings and anxieties about his mother had vanished. He had gone through a tragic experience which must for ever solemnise his life and deepen the significance of the acts by which he bound himself to others." 53

—new knowledge: "He beheld the world changed for him by the certitude of ties that altered the poise of hopes and fears, and gave him a new sense of fellowship, as if under cover of the night he had joined the wrong band of wanderers, and found with the rise of morning that the tents of his kindred were grouped far off." 55

—the new crisis: "Against his better will, he shrank from the task that was laid on him: he wished, and yet rebuked the wish as cowardly, that she could bury her secrets in her own bosom. He was not a priest. He dreaded the weight of this woman's soul flung upon his own with imploring dependency." 56

—hearing it all: "He was completely unmanned . . . it seemed that the lot of this young creature, whose swift travel from her bright rash girlhood into this agony of remorse he had had to behold in helplessness, pierced him the deeper because it came close upon another sad revelation of spiritual conflict: he was in one of those moments when the very anguish of passionate pity makes us ready to choose that we will know pleasure no more, and live only for the stricken and afflicted." 56

—conclusion: " . . . **Gwendolen**'s confession . . . convinced him the more that there had been throughout a counterbalancing struggle of her better will. It seemed almost certain that her murderous thought had had no outward effect—that, quite apart from it, the death was inevitable. Still, a question as to the outward effectiveness of a criminal desire dominant enough to impel even a momentary act, cannot alter our judgment of the desire . . . . He held it likely that Gwendolen's remorse aggravated her inward guilt, and that she gave the character of decisive action to what had been an inappreciably instantaneous glance of desire." 56

"But her remorse was the precious sign of a recoverable nature; it was the culmination of that self-disapproval which had been the awakening of a new life within her; it marked her off from the criminals whose only regret is failure in securing their evil wish. Deronda could not utter one word to diminish that sacred aversion to her worst self—that thorn-pressure which must come with the crowning of the sorrowful Better, suffering because of the Worse." 56

—forgiving: "When he saw **Sir Hugo**'s familiar figure descending from the railway carriage, the life-long affection, which had been well accustomed to make excuses, flowed in and submerged all newer knowledge that might have seemed fresh ground for blame." 59

—with his grandfather's friend: "The moment wrought strongly on Deronda's imaginative susceptibility: in the presence of one linked still in zealous friendship with the grandfather whose hope had yearned towards him when he was unborn, and who though dead was yet to speak with him . . . he seemed in himself to be touching the electric chain of his own ancestry; and he bore the scrutinising look of **Kalonymos** with a delighted awe, something like what one feels in the solemn commemoration of acts done long ago but still telling markedly on the life of to-day." 60

—clarity: " 'I shall call myself a Jew,' said Deronda, deliberately, becoming slightly paler under the piercing eyes of his questioner. 'But I will not say that I shall profess to believe exactly as my fathers have believed. Our fathers themselves changed the horizon of their belief and learned of other races. But I think I can maintain my grandfather's notion of separateness with communication. I hold that my first duty is to my own people, and if there is anything to be done towards restoring or perfecting their common life, I shall make that my vocation.'

"It happened to Deronda at that moment, as it has often happened to others, that the need for speech made an epoch in resolve. His respect for the questioner would not let him decline to answer, and by the necessity to answer he found out the truth for himself." 60

—transformation: "He came back with something like a discovered charter warranting the inherited right that his ambition had begun to yearn for: he came back with what was better than freedom—with a duteous bond which his experience had been preparing him to accept gladly, even if it had

been attended with no promise of satisfying a secret passionate longing never yet allowed to grow into a hope." 63

—confessed to himself: "But now he dared avow to himself the hidden selection of his love. Since the hour when he left the house at Chelsea in full-hearted silence under the effect of **Mirah**'s farewell look and words—their exquisite appealingness stirring in him that deeply-laid care for womanhood which had begun when his own lip was like a girl's—her hold on his feeling had helped him to be blameless in word and deed under the difficult circumstances we know of." 63

—unleashed: "His mother had compelled him to a decisive acknowledgment of his love, as **Joseph Kalonymos** had compelled him to a definite expression of his resolve. This new state of decision wrought on Deronda with a force which surprised even himself. There was a release of all the energy which had long been spent in self-checking and suppression because of doubtful conditions . . . his judgment no longer wandering in the mazes of impartial sympathy, but choosing, with that noble partiality which is man's best strength, the closer fellowship that makes sympathy practical—exchanging that bird's-eye reasonableness which soars to avoid preference and loses all sense of quality, for the generous reasonableness of drawing shoulder to shoulder with men of like inheritance." 63

—a greeting: " 'We have the same people. Our souls have the same vocation. We shall not be separated by life or by death.' " 63

—his ambition: " 'Since I began to read and know, I have always longed for some ideal task, in which I might feel myself the heart and brain of a multitude—some social captainship, which would come to me as a duty, and not be striven for as a personal prize. You [**Mordecai**] have raised the image of such a task for me—to bind our race together in spite of heresy. You have said to me—"Our religion united us before it divided us—it made us a people before it made Rabbanites and Karaites." I mean to try what can be done with that union—I mean to work in your spirit. Failure will not be ignoble, but it would be ignoble for me not to try.' " 63

—an apprehension: "**Mirah**, he knew, felt herself bound to him by deep obligation, which to her sensibilities might give every wish of his the aspect of a claim; and an inability to fulfil it would cause her a pain continually revived by their inevitable communion in care for **Ezra**. Here were fears not of pride only, but of extreme tenderness. Altogether, to have the character of a benefactor seemed to Deronda's anxiety an insurmountable obstacle to confessing himself a lover, unless in some inconceivable way it could be revealed to him that Mirah's heart had accepted him beforehand." 63

—kind advice: " 'What makes life dreary is the want of motive; but once beginning to act with the penitential, loving purpose you have in your mind, there will be unexpected satisfactions—there will be newly-opening needs—continually coming to carry you on from day to day. You will find your life growing like a plant . . . .

" 'This sorrow, which has cut down to the root, has come to you while you are so young—try to think of it, not as a spoiling of your life, but as a preparation for it . . . . You can, you will, be among the best of women, such as make others glad that they were born.' " 65

Daniel and Mirah

—*her father a thief:* " '**Mirah**, let me think that he is my father as well as yours—that we can have no sorrow, no disgrace, no joy apart. I will rather take your grief to be mine than I would take the brightest joy of another woman. Say you will not reject me—say you will take me to share all things with you. Say you will promise to be my wife—say it now. I have been in doubt so long—I have had to hide my love so long. Say that now and always I may prove to you that I love you with complete love.' " 68

—*definitive statement:* " 'The idea that I am possessed with [he said to **Gwendolen**] is that of restoring a political existence to my people, making them a nation again, giving them a national centre, such as the English have, though they too are scattered over the face of the globe. That is a task which presents itself to me as a duty. I am resolved to begin it, however feebly. I am resolved to devote my life to it. At the least, I may awaken a movement in other minds, such as has been awakened in my own.' " 69

Gwendolen

Gwendolen Harleth. "She was bending and speaking English to a middle-aged lady seated at play beside her; but the next instant she returned to her play, and showed the full height of a graceful figure, with a face which might possibly be looked at without admiration, but could hardly be passed with indifference." 1

—*observed:* "The darting sense that he was measuring her and looking down on her as an inferior, that he was of different quality from the human dross around her, that he felt himself in a region outside and above her, and was examining her as a specimen of a lower order, roused a tingling resentment which stretched the moment with conflict. It did not bring the blood to her cheeks, but sent it away from her lips." 1

—*that evening:* "The Nereid in sea-green robes and silver ornaments, with a pale sea-green feather fastened in silver falling backward over her green hat and light-brown hair, was Gwendolen Harleth. She was under the wing or rather soared by the shoulder of the lady who had sat by her at the roulette-table . . . . " 1

—*admired:* " ' . . . I think her complexion one of her chief charms. It is a warm paleness: it looks thoroughly healthy. And that delicate nose with its gradual little upward curve is distracting. And then her mouth—there never was a prettier mouth, the lips curl backward so finely, eh, **Mackworth**?' " 1

—*entitlement undermined:* "The first effect of this letter on Gwendolen was half stupefying. The implicit confidence that her destiny must be one of luxurious ease, where any trouble that occurred would be well clad and provided for, had been stronger in her own mind than in her mamma's, being fed there by her youthful blood and that sense of superior claims which made a large part of her consciousness. It was almost as difficult for her to believe suddenly that her position had become one of poverty and humiliating dependence, as it would have been to get into the strong current of her blooming life the chill sense that her death would really come . . . . Her impulse was to survey and resist the situation rather than to wail over it." 2

—*gambler:* "Gwendolen's imagination dwelt on this course [of playing to win needed funds] and created agreeable consequences, but not with unbroken confidence and rising certainty as it would have done if she had been touched with the gambler's mania. She had gone to the roulette-table not because of passion, but in search of it . . . . " 2

Daniel watches Gwendolen at the gaming table

—*self-belief:* "She had a *naïve* delight in her fortunate self, which any but the harshest saintliness will have some indulgence for in a girl who had every day seen a pleasant reflection of that self in her friends' flattery as well as in the looking-glass. And even in this beginning of troubles, while for lack of anything else to do she sat gazing at her image in the growing light, her face gathered a complacency gradual as the cheerfulness of the morning. Her beautiful lips curled into a more and more decided smile, till at last she took off her hat, leaned forward and kissed the cold glass which had looked so warm. How could she believe in sorrow? If it attacked her, she felt the force to crush it, to defy it, or run away from it, as she had done already. Anything seemed more possible than that she could go on bearing miseries, great or small." 2

—*resentful:* "Gwendolen reddened with the vexation of wounded pride. . . . He knew very well that he was entangling her in helpless humiliation: it was another way of smiling at her ironically, and taking the air of a supercilious mentor. Gwendolen felt the bitter tears of mortification rising and rolling down her cheeks. No one had ever before dared to treat her with irony and contempt." 2

—*forebears:* "She had no notion how her maternal grandfather [**Armyn**] got the fortune inherited by his two daughters, but he had been a West Indian— which seemed to exclude further question; and she knew her father's family was so high as to take no notice of her mamma, who nevertheless preserved with much pride the miniature of a **Lady Molly** in that connection." 3

—*spoiled:* "Having always been the pet and pride of the household, waited on by mother, sisters, governess, and maids, as if she had been a princess in exile, she naturally found it difficult to think her own pleasure less important than others made it, and when it was positively thwarted felt an astonished resentment apt, in her cruder days, to vent itself in one of those passionate acts which look like a contradiction of habitual tendencies." 3

—*an incident:* "Though never even as a child thoughtlessly cruel, nay, delighting to rescue drowning insects and watch their recovery, there was a disagreeable silent remembrance of her having strangled her sister's canary-bird in a final fit of exasperation at its shrill singing which had again and again jarringly interrupted her own. She had taken pains to buy a white mouse for her sister in retribution, and though inwardly excusing herself on the ground of a peculiar sensitiveness which was a mark of her general superiority, the thought of that infelonious [*sic*] murder had always made her wince." 3

—*self-protective:* "Gwendolen's nature was not remorseless, but she liked to make her penances easy, and now that she was twenty and more, some of her native force had turned into a self-control by which she guarded herself from penitential humiliation. There was more show of fire and will in her than ever, but there was more calculation underneath it." 3

—*goal:* " . . . this delicate-limbed sylph of twenty meant to lead. For such passions dwell in feminine breasts also. In Gwendolen's, however, they dwelt among strictly feminine furniture, and had no disturbing reference to the advancement of learning or the balance of the constitution; her knowledge being such as with no sort of standing-room or length of lever could have been expected to move the world. She meant to do what was pleasant to herself in a striking manner; or rather, whatever she could do so as to strike others with admiration and get in that reflected way a more ardent sense of living, seemed pleasant to her fancy." 4

—will: "Other people allowed themselves to be made slaves of, and to have their lives blown hither and thither like empty ships in which no will was present: it was not to be so with her, she would no longer be sacrificed to creatures worth less than herself, but would make the very best of the chances that life offered her, and conquer circumstance by her exceptional cleverness." 4

—confidence: ". . . Gwendolen's confidence lay chiefly in herself. She felt well equipped for the mastery of life. With regard to much in her lot hitherto, she held herself rather hardly dealt with, but as to her 'education' she would have admitted that it had left her under no disadvantages. In the schoolroom her quick mind had taken readily that strong starch of unexplained rules and disconnected facts which saves ignorance from any painful sense of limpness, and what remained of all things knowable, she was conscious of being sufficiently acquainted with through novels, plays, and poems. About her French and music, the two justifying accomplishments of a young lady, she felt no ground for uneasiness; and when to all these qualifications, negative and positive, we add the spontaneous sense of capability some happy persons are born with, so that any subject they turn attention to impresses them with their own power of forming a correct judgment on it, who can wonder if Gwendolen felt ready to manage her own destiny?" 4

—center of all: "If when they were under the stress of travelling, she did not appear at the breakfast-table till every one else had finished, the only question was, how Gwendolen's coffee and toast should still be of the hottest and crispest; and when she appeared with her freshly-brushed light-brown hair streaming backward and awaiting her mama's hand to coil it up, her long brown eyes glancing bright as a wave-washed onyx from under their long lashes, it was always she herself who had to be tolerant . . . . " 4

—charm: "Always she was the princess in exile, who in time of famine was to have her breakfast-roll made of the finest-bolted flour from the seven thin ears of wheat, and in a general decampment was to have her silver fork kept out of the baggage. How was this to be accounted for? The answer may seem to lie quite on the surface—in her beauty, a certain unusualness about her, a decision of will which made itself felt in her graceful movements and clear unhesitating tones, so that if she came into the room on a rainy day when everybody else was flaccid and the use of things in general was not apparent to them, there seemed to be a sudden, sufficient reason for keeping up the forms of life; and even the waiters at hotels showed the more alacrity in doing away with crumbs and creases and dregs with struggling flies in them. This potent charm, added to the fact that she was the eldest daughter . . . may seem so full a reason for Gwendolen's domestic empire, that to look for any other would be to ask the reason of daylight when the sun is shining." 4
For that other possible reason, see II:317

—demanding egoism: " . . . I am forced to doubt whether even without her potent charm and peculiar filial position Gwendolen might not still have played the queen in exile, if only she had kept her inborn energy of egoistic desire, and her power of inspiring fear as to what she might say or do. However, she had the charm, and those who feared her were also fond of her; the fear and the fondness being perhaps both heightened by what may be called the iridescence of her character—the play of various, nay, contrary tendencies

. . . a moment is room wide enough for the loyal and mean desire, for the outlash of a murderous thought and the sharp backward stroke of repentance." 4

—*in song:* "Gwendolen was not nervous: what she undertook to do she did without trembling, and singing was an enjoyment to her. Her voice was a moderately powerful soprano (some one had told her it was like **Jenny Lind**'s), her ear good, and she was able to keep in tune, so that her singing gave pleasure to ordinary hearers, and she had been used to unmingled applause. She had the rare advantage of looking almost prettier when she was singing than at other times . . . . " 5

—*excited:* "Gwendolen, in spite of her wounded egoism, had fulness of nature enough to feel the power of [**Klesmer**'s] playing, and it gradually turned her inward sob of mortification into an excitement which lifted her for the moment into a desperate indifference about her own doings, or at least a determination to get a superiority over them by laughing at them as if they belonged to somebody else. Her eyes had become brighter, her cheeks slightly flushed, and her tongue ready for any mischievous remarks." 5

—*grace and mediocrity:* "Perhaps it would have been rash to say then that she was at all exceptional inwardly, or that the unusual in her was more than her rare grace of movement and bearing, and a certain daring which gave piquancy to a very common egoistic ambition, such as exists under many clumsy exteriors and is taken no notice of. For I suppose that the set of the head does not really determine the hunger of the inner self for supremacy: it only makes a difference sometimes as to the way in which the supremacy is held attainable, and a little also to the degree in which it can be attained; especially when the hungry one is a girl, whose passion for doing what is remarkable has an ideal limit in consistency with the highest breeding and perfect freedom from the sordid need of income." 6

—*limits:* "She rejoiced to feel herself exceptional; but her horizon was that of the genteel romance where the heroine's soul poured out in her journal is full of vague power, originality, and general rebellion, while her life moves strictly in the sphere of fashion; and if she wanders into a swamp, the pathos lies partly, so to speak, in her having on her satin shoes. Here is a restraint which nature and society have provided on the pursuit of striking adventure; so that a soul burning with a sense of what the universe is not, and ready to take all existence as fuel, is nevertheless held captive by the ordinary wire-work of social forms and does nothing particular." 6

—*terrified:* " . . . a piercing cry from Gwendolen, who stood without change of attitude, but with a change of expression that was terrifying in its terror. She looked like a statue into which a soul of Fear had entered: her pallid lips were parted; her eyes, usually narrowed under their long lashes, were dilated and fixed . . . the touch of her mother's arm had the effect of an electric charge; Gwendolen fell on her knees and put her hands before her face. She was still trembling, but mute, and it seemed that she had self-consciousness enough to aim at controlling her signs of terror, for she presently allowed herself to be raised from her kneeling posture and led away. . . . " 6

—*spurious compliment:* "She liked to accept as a belief what was really no more than delicate feigning. [**Klesmer**] divined that the betrayal into a passion of fear had been mortifying to her, and wished her to understand that he took it for good acting. Gwendolen cherished the idea that now he was struck with her talent as well as her beauty, and her uneasiness about his opinion was half turned to complacency." 6

—*wonderment:* "She wondered at herself in these occasional experiences, which seemed like a brief remembered madness, an unexplained exception from her normal life; and in this instance she felt a peculiar vexation that her helpless fear had shown itself, not, as usual, in solitude, but in well-lit company." 6

—*religion:* "She had no permanent consciousness of other fetters, or of more spiritual restraints, having always disliked whatever was presented to her under the name of religion, in the same way that some people dislike arithmetic and accounts: it had raised no other emotion in her, no alarm, no longing: so that the question whether she believed it had not occurred to her, any more than it had occurred to her to inquire into the conditions of colonial property and banking, on which, as she had had many opportunities of knowing, the family fortune was dependent." 6

—*irrationality:* "What she unwillingly recognised, and would have been glad for others to be unaware of, was that liability of hers to fits of spiritual dread, though this fountain of awe within her had not found its way into connection with the religion taught her or with any human relations. She was ashamed and frightened, as at what might happen again, in remembering her tremor on suddenly feeling herself alone, when, for example, she was walking without companionship and there came some rapid change in the light. Solitude in any wide scene impressed her with an undefined feeling of immeasurable existence aloof from her, in the midst of which she was helplessly incapable of asserting herself." 6

—*vulnerability:* "The little astronomy taught her at school used sometimes to set her imagination at work in a way that made her tremble: but always when some one joined her she recovered her indifference to the vastness in which she seemed an exile; she found again her usual world in which her will was of some avail, and the religious nomenclature belonging to this world was no more identified for her with those uneasy impressions of awe than her uncle's surplices seen out of use at the Rectory. With human ears and eyes about her, she had always hitherto recovered her confidence, and felt the possibility of winning empire." 6

—*repulsion:* "Besides, she objected, with a sort of physical repulsion, to being directly made love to. With all her imaginative delight in being adored, there was a certain fierceness of maidenhood in her." 7

—*hearing of an accident:* "Gwendolen rather valued herself on her superior freedom in laughing where others might only see matter for seriousness. Indeed, the laughter became her person so well that her opinion of its gracefulness was often shared by others; and it even entered into her uncle's course of thought at this moment, that it was no wonder a boy should be fascinated by this young witch—who, however, was more mischievous than could be desired." 7

—*side remark:* " 'Mamma, I wonder how girls manage to fall in love. It is easy to make them do it in books. But men are too ridiculous.' " 7

—*an aunt's view:* " 'There are things in Gwendolen I cannot reconcile myself to. My **Anna** is worth two of her, with all her beauty and talent. It looks so very ill in her that she will not help in the schools with Anna—not even in the Sunday-school. What you or I advise is of no consequence to her: and poor **Fanny** is completely under her thumb.' " 7

—*out of sorts:* "But the wisdom of ages has hinted that there is a side of the bed which has a malign influence if you happen to get out on it; and this accident befalls some charming persons rather frequently. Perhaps it had befallen Gwendolen this morning. The hastening of her toilet, the way in which **Bugle** used the brush, the quality of the shilling serial mistakenly written for her amusement, the probabilities of the coming day, and, in short, social institutions generally, were all objectionable to her. It was not that she was out of temper, but that the world was not equal to the demands of her fine organism." 7

"The perception that poor **Rex** wanted to be tender made her curl up and harden like a sea-anemone at the touch of a finger." 7

—wooed: " 'Pray don't make love to me! I hate it.' She looked at him fiercely.

"**Rex** turned pale and was silent, but could not take his eyes off her, and the impetus was not yet exhausted that made hers dart death at him. Gwendolen herself could not have foreseen that she should feel in this way. It was all a sudden, new experience to her . . . the life of passion had begun negatively in her. She felt passionately averse to this volunteered love." 7

—shift: "She could not help seeing his wretchedness and feeling a little regret for the old Rex who had not offended her. Decisively, but with some return of kindliness, she said—

" 'About making love? Yes. But I don't dislike you for anything else.'

"There was just a perceptible pause before he said a low 'good-bye' . . . .

"**Mrs Davilow** . . . presently came into the drawing-room, where she found Gwendolen seated on the low couch, her face buried, and her hair falling over her figure like a garment. She was sobbing bitterly. 'My child, my child, what is it?' cried the mother . . . she pressed her cheek against Gwendolen's head, and then tried to draw it upward. Gwendolen gave way, and letting her head rest against her mother, cried out sobbingly, 'Oh mamma, what can become of my life? there is nothing worth living for!'

" 'Why , dear?' said Mrs Davilow . . . .

" 'I shall never love anybody. I can't love people. I hate them.'

" 'The time will come, dear, the time will come.'

" Gwendolen was more and more convulsed with sobbing; but putting her arms round her mother's neck with an almost painful clinging, she cried brokenly, 'I can't bear any one to be very near me but you.'

"Then the mother began to sob, for this spoiled child had never shown such dependence on her before: and so they clung to each other." 7

—resentful: " 'Mamma, I see now why girls are glad to be married—to escape being expected to please everybody but themselves.' " 9

—at archery: "Perhaps she had never looked so well. Her face was beaming with young pleasure in which there were no malign rays of discontent; for being satisfied with her own chances, she felt kindly towards everybody and was satisfied with the universe." 10

—conversation breaks: "(Pause, wherein Gwendolen recalled what she had heard about **Grandcourt**'s position, and decided that he was the most aristocratic-looking man she had ever seen.) . . . .

" (Pause, during which Gwendolen thought that a man of extremely calm, cold manners might be less disagreeable as a husband than other men, and not likely to interfere with his wife's preferences.) . . . .

"(Pause, during which it occurred to Gwendolen that a man of cold and distinguished manners might possibly be a dull companion; but on the other hand she thought that most persons were dull, that she had not observed husbands to be companions—and that after all she was not going to accept **Grandcourt**.) . . . .

"(Pause, wherein Gwendolen was thinking that men had been known to choose some one else than the woman they most admired, and recalled several experiences of that kind in novels.)" 11

—pique: "And this **Mr Grandcourt**, who seemed to feel his own importance more than he did hers—a sort of unreasonableness few of us can tolerate —must not take for granted that he was of great moment to her, or that because others speculated on him as a desirable match she held herself altogether at his beck." 11

—frisson: "But for some mysterious reason—it was a mystery of which she had a faint wondering consciousness—she dared not be satirical: she had begun to feel a wand over her that made her afraid of offending **Grandcourt**." 11

—reflexively rude: "But she, poor child, had had no design in this action, and was simply following her antipathy and inclination, confiding in them as she did in the more reflective judgments into which they entered as sap into leafage." 11

—ignorant: "Gwendolen had no sense that these men were dark enigmas to her, or that she needed any help in drawing conclusions about them—**Mr Grandcourt** at least. The chief question was, how far his character and ways might answer her wishes; and unless she were satisfied about that, she had said to herself that she would not accept his offer." 11

—hard to get: "Whether **Grandcourt** had been offended or not there was no judging: his manners were unchanged, but Gwendolen's acuteness had not gone deeper than to discern that his manners were no clue for her, and because these were unchanged she was not the less afraid of him." 13

—apprehensive, but: "This subjection to a possible self, a self not to be absolutely predicted about, caused her some astonishment and terror: her favourite key of life—doing as she liked—seemed to fail her, and she could not foresee what at a given moment she might like to do. The prospect of marrying **Grandcourt** really seemed more attractive to her than she had believed beforehand that any marriage could be: the dignities, the luxuries, the power of doing a great deal of what she liked to do, which had now come close to her, and within her choice to secure or to lose, took hold of her nature as if it had been the strong odour of what she had only imagined and longed for before." 13

"Gwendolen wished to mount the chariot and drive the plunging horses herself, with a spouse by her side who would fold his arms and give her his countenance without looking ridiculous." 13

—a big mistake: "Certainly, with all her perspicacity, and all the reading which seemed to her mamma dangerously instructive, her judgment was consciously a little at fault before **Grandcourt**. He was adorably quiet and free from absurdities—he would be a husband to suit with the best appearance a woman could make. But what else was he? He had been everywhere, and seen everything. *That* was desirable, and especially gratifying as a preamble to his supreme preference for Gwendolen Harleth. He did not appear to enjoy anything much. That was not necessary: and the less he had of particular tastes or desires, the more freedom his wife was likely to have in following

hers. Gwendolen conceived that after marriage she would most probably be able to manage him thoroughly." 13

—*decision:* "And on the whole she wished to marry him; he suited her purpose; her prevailing, deliberate intention was, to accept him." 13

" . . . she wished to accept him if she could. At this moment she would willingly have had weights hung on her own caprice." 13

—*teasing:* " '[He] has all the qualities that would make a husband tolerable—battlement, veranda, stables &c., no grins and no glass in his eye.' " 13

—*hearing her uncle:* "Gwendolen became pallid as she listened to [his] admonitory speech. The ideas it raised had the force of sensations. Her resistant courage would not help her here, because her uncle was not urging her against her own resolve; he was pressing upon her the motives of dread which she already felt; he was making her more conscious of the risks that lay within herself." *See* **Rev. Henry Gascoigne** OP—*authoritative.*

—*recovered:* "Gwendolen looked lovely and vigorous as a tall, newly-opened lily the next morning: there was a reaction of young energy in her, and yesterday's self-distrust seemed no more than the transient shiver on the surface of a full stream." 14

—*her predecessor:* "Gwendolen, watching **Mrs Glasher**'s face while she spoke, felt a sort of terror: it was as if some ghastly vision had come to her in a dream and said, 'I am a woman's life.' " 14

—*disillusion:* "Gwendolen had certainly hardened in the last twenty-four hours: her mother's trouble evidently counted for little in her present state of mind, which did not essentially differ from the mood that makes men take to worse conduct when their belief in persons or things is upset. Gwendolen's uncontrolled reading, though consisting chiefly in what are called pictures of life, had somehow not prepared her for this encounter with reality." 14

—*rallying:* " 'Never mind. I don't mind. I will do something. I will be something. Things will come right. It seemed worse because I was away. Come now! you must be glad because I am here.'

"Gwendolen felt every word of that speech. A rush of companionate tenderness stirred all her capability of generous resolution; and the self-confident projects which had vaguely glanced before her during her journey sprang instantaneously into new definiteness. Suddenly she seemed to perceive how she could be 'something.' It was one of her best moments, and the fond mother, forgetting everything below that tide-mark, looked at her with a sort of adoration." 21

—*sign of development:* " . . . perhaps she had never before in her life felt so inwardly dependent, so consciously in need of another person's opinion. There was a new fluttering of spirit within her, a new element of deliberation in her self-estimate which had hitherto been a blissful gift of intuition." 23

—*pain coming:* "The belief that to present herself in public on the stage must produce an effect such as she had been used to feel certain of in private life, was like a bit of her flesh—it was not to be peeled off readily, but must come with blood and pain." 23

—*the truth hurts:* "Gwendolen had never in her life felt so miserable. No sob came, no passion of tears, to relieve her. Her eyes were burning; and the noonday only brought into more dreary clearness the absence of interest from her life. All memories, all objects, the pieces of music displayed, the open piano—the very reflection of herself in the glass—seemed no better than the packed-up shows of a departing fair. For the first time since her consciousness began, she was having a vision of herself on the common level, and had lost the innate sense that there were reasons why she should not be slighted, elbowed, jostled—treated like a passenger with a third-class ticket, in spite of private objections on her own part." 23

—*her speech:* " . . . it was never her aspiration to express herself virtuously so much as cleverly—a point to be remembered in extenuation of her words, which were usually worse than she was." 24

—amour propre: "Gwendolen's daring was not in the least that of the adventuress; the demand to be held a lady was in her very marrow; and when she had dreamed that she might be the heroine of the gaming-table, it was with the understanding that no one should treat her with the less consideration, or presume to look at her with irony as **Deronda** had done." 24

—*lost:* "And poor Gwendolen had never dissociated happiness from personal pre-eminence and *éclat.* That where these threatened to forsake her, she should take life to be hardly worth the having, cannot make her so unlike the rest of us . . . . Surely a young creature is pitiable who has the labyrinth of life before her and no clue—to whom distrust in herself and her good fortune has come as a sudden shock, like a rent across the path that she was treading carelessly.

"In spite of her healthy frame, her irreconcilable repugnance affected her even physically: she felt a sort of numbness and could set about nothing; the least urgency, even that she should take her meals, was an irritation to her; the speech of others on any subject seemed unreasonable, because it did not include her feeling and was an ignorant claim on her. It was not in her nature to busy herself with the fancies of suicide to which disappointed young people are prone: what occupied and exasperated her was the sense that there was nothing for her but to live in a way she hated." 24

—*talisman:* "But the movement of mind which led her to keep the necklace . . . came from that streak of superstition in her which attached itself both to her confidence and her terror—a superstition which lingers in an intense personality even in spite of theory and science; any dread or hope for self being stronger than all reasons for or against it. Why she should suddenly determine not to part with the necklace was not much clearer to her than why she should sometimes have been frightened to find herself in the fields alone; she had a confused state of emotion about **Deronda**—was it wounded pride and resentment, or a certain awe and exceptional trust? It was something vague and yet mastering, which impelled her to this action about the necklace." 24

—*humbled:* "To be a queen disthroned is not so hard as some other down-stepping: imagine one who had been made to believe in his own divinity finding all homage withdrawn, and himself unable to perform a miracle that would recall the homage and restore his own confidence. Something akin to this illusion and this helplessness had befallen the poor spoiled child, with the lovely lips and eyes and the majestic figure—which seemed now to have no magic in them." 26

—*her ethic:* "The impulse [to flee] had come—not only from her maidenly pride and jealousy, not only from the shock of another woman's calamity thrust close on her vision, but—from her dread of wrong-doing, which was vague, it is true, and aloof from the daily details of her life, but not the less strong. Whatever was accepted as consistent with being a lady she had no scruple about; but from the dim region of what was called disgraceful, wrong, guilty, she shrank with mingled pride and terror . . . . " 27

—ignorance: "Gwendolen had about as accurate a conception of marriage —that is to say, of the mutual influences, demands, duties of man and woman in the state of matrimony—as she had of magnetic currents and the law of storms." 27

—love? "True, the question of love on her own part had occupied her scarcely at all in relation to **Grandcourt**. The desirability of marriage for her had always seemed due to other feelings than love; and to be enamoured was the part of the man, on whom the advances depended." 27

—his past: "What others might think, could not do away with a feeling which in the first instance would hardly be too strongly described as indignation and loathing that she should have been expected to unite herself with an outworn life, full of backward secrets which must have been more keenly felt than associations with *her* . . . . Gwendolen had found no objection to **Grandcourt**'s way of being enamoured before she had had that glimpse of his past, which she resented as if it had been a deliberate offence against her His advances to her were deliberate, and she felt a retrospective disgust for them. Perhaps other men's lives were of the same kind—full of secrets which made the ignorant suppositions of the woman they wanted to marry a farce at which they were laughing in their sleeves." 27

—temptation: "And she—ah, piteous equality in the need to dominate!—she was overcome like the thirsty one who is drawn towards the seeming water in the desert, overcome by the suffused sense that here in this man's homage to her lay the rescue from helpless subjection to an oppressive lot. . . .

" 'You will tell me now, I hope, that **Mrs Davilow**'s loss of fortune will not trouble you further. You will trust me to prevent it from weighing upon her. You will give me the claim to provide against that.'

"The little pauses and refined drawlings with which this speech was uttered, gave time for Gwendolen to go through the dream of a life. As the words penetrated her, they had the effect of a draught of wine, which suddenly makes all things easier, desirable things not so wrong, and people in general less disagreeable. She had a momentary phantasmal love for this man who chose his words so well, and who was a mere incarnation of delicate homage. Repugnance, dread, scruples—these were dim remembered pains, while she was already tasting relief under the immediate pain of hopelessness. She imagined herself already springing to her mother, and being playful again." 27

—the moment: "She seemed to herself to be, after all, only drifted towards the tremendous decision:—but drifting depends on something besides the currents, when the sails have been set beforehand." 27

—conscience: "But her resolution was dogged by the shadow of that previous resolve which had at first come as the undoubting movement of her whole being . . . she was appalled by the idea that she was going to do what she had once started away from with repugnance. It was new to her that a question of right or wrong in her conduct should rouse her terror; she had known no compunction that atoning caresses and presents could not lay to rest. But here had come a moment when something like a new consciousness was awaked." 28

—ill omen: "She seemed on the edge of adopting deliberately, as a notion for all the rest of her life, what she had rashly said in her bitterness . . . that

it did not signify what she did; she had only to amuse herself as best she could. That lawlessness, that casting away of all care for justification, suddenly frightened her: it came to her with the shadowy array of possible calamity behind it—calamity which had ceased to be a mere name for her; and all the infiltrated influences of disregarded religious teaching, as well as the deeper impressions of something awful and inexorable enveloping her, seemed to concentrate themselves in the vague conception of avenging power." 28

—*blameless:* "This maiden had been accustomed to think herself blameless; other persons only were faulty." 28

—*naïve:* "Poor Gwendolen had no awe of unmanageable forces in the state of matrimony, but regarded it as altogether a matter of management, in which she would know how to act." 28

—*startled:* "One day, indeed, he had kissed not her cheek but her neck a little below her ear; and Gwendolen, taken by surprise, had started up with a marked agitation which made him rise too and say, 'I beg your pardon—did I annoy you?' 'Oh, it was nothing,' said Gwendolen, rather afraid of herself, 'only I cannot bear—to be kissed under my ear.' She sat down again with a little playful laugh, but all the while she felt her heart beating with a vague fear: she was no longer at liberty to flout him as she had flouted poor **Rex**." 29

—*caring:* "Why did she care so much about the opinion of this man who was 'nothing of any consequence'? She had no time to find the reason—she was too much engaged in caring." 29

—*changed:* " . . . there had been changes going on within her since that time at Leubronn: the struggle of mind attending a conscious error had wakened something like a new soul, which had better, but also worse, possibilities than her former poise of crude self-confidence: among the forces she had come to dread was something within her that troubled satisfaction." 29

—*apprehension:* " . . . Gwendolen, young, headlong, eager for pleasure, fed with the flattery which makes a lovely girl believe in her divine right to rule—how quickly might life turn from expectancy to a bitter sense of the irremediable!" 35

Gwendolen Grandcourt

—*first seen after her honeymoon:* "The white silk and diamonds—it may seem strange, but she did wear the diamonds on her neck, in her ears, in her hair—might have something to do with the new imposingness of her beauty, which flashed on [**Deronda**] as more unquestionable if not more thoroughly satisfactory than when he had first seen her at the gaming-table . . . as he saw her receiving greetings with what seemed a proud cold quietude and a superficial smile, there seemed to be at work within her the same demonic force that had possessed her when she took him in her resolute glance and turned away a loser from the gaming-table." 35

—*and first glance:* " . . . before he could speak, she had turned on him no smile, but such an appealing look of sadness, so utterly different from the chill effort of her recognition at table, that his speech was checked." 35

—*volatile:* " . . . in [her] nature there was a combination of proud reserve with rashness, of perilously-poised terror with defiance, which might alternately flatter and disappoint control. Few words could less represent her than 'coquette.' She had a native love of homage, and belief in her own power, but no cold artifice for the sake of enslaving." 35

Gwendolen Grandcourt
[compare the portrait on page 502]

—a change: "And the poor thing's belief in her power, with her other dreams before marriage, had often to be thrust aside now like the toys of a sick child, which it looks at with dull eyes, and has no heart to play with, however it may try." 35

—and ***Deronda****:* "There was not the faintest touch of coquetry in the attitude of her mind towards him: he was unique to her among men, because he had impressed her as being not her admirer but her superior: in some mysterious way he was becoming a part of her conscience, as one woman whose nature is an object of reverential belief may become a new conscience to a man." 35

—frustrated: "She felt sick with irritation—so fast do young creatures like her absorb misery through invisible suckers of their own fancies—and her face had gathered that peculiar expression which comes with a mortification to which tears are forbidden." 35

—paralyzed: "Any endurance seemed easier than the mortal humiliation of confessing that she knew all before she married him, and in marrying him had broken her word. For the reasons by which she had justified herself when the marriage tempted her . . . were now as futile as the burnt-out lights which set off a child's pageant. Her sense of being blameworthy was exaggerated by a dread both definite and vague. The definite dread was lest the veil of secrecy should fall between her and **Grandcourt**, and give him the right to taunt her. With the reading of that letter had begun her husband's empire of fear." 35

—trapped by pride: "Gwendolen, indeed, with all that gnawing trouble in her consciousness, had hardly for a moment dropped the sense that it was her part to bear herself with dignity, and appear what is called happy. In disclosure of disappointment or sorrow she saw nothing but a humiliation which would have been vinegar to her wounds." 35

—husbandly will: " . . . **Grandcourt** had become a blank uncertainty to her in everything but this, that he would do just what he willed, and that she had neither devices at her command to determine his will, nor any rational means of escaping it." 35

—the diamonds: " 'Oh, please not. I don't think diamonds suit me.'

" 'What you think has nothing to do with it,' said **Grandcourt**. His *sotto voce* imperiousness seeming to have an evening quietude and finish, like his toiler. 'I wish you to wear the diamonds.'

" 'Pray excuse me, I like these emeralds,' said Gwendolen, frightened in spite of her preparation. That white hand of his which was touching his whisker was capable, she fancied, of clinging round her neck and threatening to throttle her; for her fear of him, mingling with the vague foreboding of some retributive calamity which hung about her life, had reached a superstitious point.

" 'Oblige me by telling me your reason for not wearing the diamonds when I desire it,' said Grandcourt. His eyes were still fixed upon her, and she felt her own eyes narrowing under them as if to shut out an entering pain.

"Of what use was the rebellion within her? She could say nothing that would not hurt her worse than submission." 35

—a new consciousness: "It had been Gwendolen's habit to think of the persons around her as stale books, too familiar to be interesting. **Deronda** had lit up her attention with a sense of novelty not by words only, but by

imagined facts: his influence had entered into the current of that self-suspicion and self-blame which awakens a new consciousness." 35

—cynosure: "It was remarked that she carried herself with a wonderful air, considering that she had been nobody in particular, and without a farthing to her fortune. If she had been a duke's daughter, or one of the royal princesses, she could not have taken the honours of the evening more as a matter of course. Poor Gwendolen! It would by-and-by become a sort of skill in which she was automatically practised, to bear this last great gambling loss with an air of perfect self-possession." 36

—submitting: " 'You will not go on being selfish and ignorant.'

"She did not turn away her glance or let her eyelids fall, but a change came over her face—that subtle change in nerve and muscle which will sometimes give a childlike expression even to the elderly: it is the subsidence of self-assertion." 36

—the husband: "Why could she not rebel, and defy him? She longed to do it. But she might as well have tried to defy the texture of her nerves and the palpitation of her heart. Her husband had a ghostly army at his back, that could close round her wherever she might turn." 36

—straight talk: " 'It is the curse of your life—forgive me—of so many lives, that all passion is spent in that narrow round, for want of ideas and sympathies to make a larger home for it. Is there any single occupation of mind that you care about with passionate delight or even independent interest? . . . The refuge you are needing from personal trouble is the higher, the religious life, which holds an enthusiasm for something more than our own appetites and vanities. The few may find themselves in it simply by an elevation of feeling; but for us who have to struggle for our wisdom, the higher life must be a region in which the affections are clad with knowledge.'

"The half-indignant remonstrance that vibrated in Deronda's voice came, as often happens, from the habit of inward argument with himself rather than from severity towards Gwendolen; but it had a more beneficent effect on her than any soothings . . . . For the moment she felt like a shaken child—shaken out of its wailings into awe . . . . " 36

—conflict transmuted: " 'But if feelings rose—there are some feelings—hatred and anger—how can I be good when they keep rising? And if there came a moment when I felt stifled and could bear it no longer—' she broke off, and with agitated lips looked at **Deronda**, but the expression on his face pierced her with an entirely new feeling. He was under the baffling difficulty of discerning, that what he had been urging on her was thrown into the pallid distance of mere thought before the outburst of her habitual emotion. It was as if he saw her drowning while his limbs were bound. The pained compassion which was spread over his features as he watched her, affected her with a compunction unlike any she had felt before . . . . " 36

—improbability: " . . . it was as far from Gwendolen's conception that **Deronda**'s life could be determined by the historical destiny of the Jews, as that he could rise into the air on a brazen horse, and so vanish from her horizon in the form of a twinkling star." 44

—in a trap: " . . . now that she was a wife, the sense that **Grandcourt** was gone to Gadsmere was like a red heat near a burn. She had brought on herself this indignity in her own eyes—this humiliation of being doomed to a terrified silence lest her husband should discover with what sort of consciousness she had married him; and as she had said to **Deronda**, she 'must

go on.' After the intensest moments of secret hatred towards this husband who from the very first had cowed her, there always came back the spiritual pressure which made submission inevitable. There was no effort at freedom that would not bring fresh and worse humiliation." 44

—alert: "With her long sight and self-command she had the rare power of quickly distinguishing persons and objects on entering a full room . . . . " 45

—declaration: " 'If you despair of me, I shall despair. Your saying that I should not go on being selfish and ignorant has been some strength to me. If you say you wish you had not meddled—that means, you despair of me and forsake me. And then you will decide for me that I shall not be good. It is you who will decide, because you might have made me different by keeping as near to me as you could, and believing in me.' " 45

—decision: " 'If I am to have misery anyhow,' was the bitter refrain of her rebellious dreams, 'I had better have the misery that I can keep to myself.' Moreover, her capability of rectitude told her again and again that she had no right to complain of her contract, or to withdraw from it." 48

—consolations of religion: "Church was not markedly distinguished in her mind from the other forms of self-presentation, for marriage had included no instruction that enabled her to connect liturgy and sermon with any larger order of the world than that of unexplained and perhaps inexplicable social fashions. While a laudable zeal was labouring to carry the light of spiritual law up the alleys where law is chiefly known as the policeman, the brilliant Mrs Grandcourt, condescending a little to a fashionable Rector and conscious of a feminine advantage over a learned Dean, was, so far as pastoral care and religious fellowship were concerned, in as complete a solitude as a man in a lighthouse." 48

—dark thoughts: "The thought of his dying would not subsist: it turned into as with a dream-change into the terror that she should die with his throttling fingers on her neck avenging the thought. Fantasies moved within her like ghosts, making no break in her more acknowledged consciousness and finding no obstruction in it: dark rays doing their work invisibly in the broad light." 48

—acknowledgment: "With all her early indulgence in the disposition to dominate, she was not one of the narrow-brained women who through life regard all their own selfish demands as rights, and every claim upon themselves as an injury. She had a root of conscience in her, and the process of purgatory had begun for her on the green earth: she knew that she had been wrong." 54

—bondage: " . . . the husband to whom she had sold her truthfulness and sense of justice, so that he held them throttled into silence, collared and dragged behind him to witness what he would, without remonstrance." 54

—quarrelling? " . . . even if she had shrunk from quarrelling on other grounds, quarreling with **Grandcourt** was impossible: she might as well have made angry remarks to a dangerous serpent ornamentally coiled in her cabin without invitation. And what sort of dispute could a woman of any pride and dignity begin on a yacht?" 54

—self-dread: "Side by side with the dread of her husband had grown the self-dread which urged her to flee from the pursuing images wrought by her pent-up impulse. The vision of her past wrong-doing, and what it had brought on her, came with a pale ghastly illumination over every imagined

deed that was a rash effort at freedom, such as she had made in her marriage." 54

—touchstone: "Moreover, she had learned to see all her acts through the impression they would make on **Deronda**: whatever relief might come to her, she could not sever it from the judgment of her that would be created in his mind. Not one word of flattery, of indulgence, of dependence on her favour, could be fastened on by her in all their intercourse, to weaken his restraining power over her (in this way Deronda's effort over himself was repaid); and amid the dreary uncertainties of her spoiled life the possible remedies that lay in his mind, nay, the remedy that lay in her feeling for him, made her only hope. He seemed to her a terrible-browed angel from whom she could not think of concealing any deed so as to win an ignorant regard from him: it belonged to the nature of their relation that she should be truthful, for his power over her had begun in the raising of a self-discontent which could be satisfied only by genuine change." 54

—fear as a safeguard: "And so it was. In Gwendolen's consciousness, Temptation and Dread met and stared like two pale phantoms, each seeing itself in the other—each obstructed by its own image; and all the while her fuller self beheld the apparitions and sobbed for deliverance from them." 54

—hatred beaten off: "It was sometimes after a white-lipped, fierce-eyed temptation with murdering fingers had made its demon-visit that these best moments of inward crying and clinging for rescue would come to her, and she would lie with wide-open eyes in which the rising tears seemed a blessing, and the thought, 'I will not mind if I can keep from getting wicked,' seemed an answer to the indefinite prayer." 54

—developed: "Mrs Grandcourt was handsomer than Gwendolen Harleth: her grace and expression were informed by a greater variety of inward experience, giving new play to her features, new attitudes in movement and repose; her whole person and air had the nameless something which often makes a woman more interesting after marriage than before, less confident that all things are according to her opinion, and yet with less of deer-like shyness—more fully a human being." 54

—incubus: "He continued standing with his air of indifference, till she felt her habitual stifling consciousness of having an immovable obstruction in her life, like the nightmare of beholding a single form that serves to arrest all passage though the wide country lies open." 54

"The walls had begun to be an imprisonment, and while there was breath in this man he would have the mastery over her. His words had the power of thumbscrews and the cold touch of the rack. To resist was to act like a stupid animal unable to measure results." 54

—hatred: "She was afraid of her own hatred, which under the cold iron touch that had compelled her to-day had gathered a fierce intensity. As she sat guiding the tiller under her husband's eyes, doing just what he told her, the strife within her seemed like her own effort to escape from herself. She clung to the thought of **Deronda**: she persuaded herself that he would not go away while she was there—he knew that she needed help. The sense that he was there would save her from acting out the evil within. And yet quick, quick, came images, plans of evil that would come again and seize her in the night, like furies preparing the deed that they would straightway avenge." 54

—brought to land: " . . . pale as one of the sheeted dead, shivering, with wet hair streaming, a wild amazed consciousness in her eyes, as if she had

waked up in a world where some judgment was impending, and the beings she saw around were coming to seize her . . . Gwendolen gave scared glances, and seemed to shrink in terror as she was carefully, tenderly helped . . . her wet clothes clinging about her limbs, and adding to the impediment of her weakness. Suddenly her wandering eyes fell on **Deronda**, standing before her, and immediately, as if she had been expecting him and looking for him, she tried to stretch out her arms, which were held back by her supporters, saying, in a muffled voice—

" 'It is come, it is come! He is dead!' " 55

—afterward: "But her long hair was gathered up and coiled carefully, and, through all, the blue stars in her ears had kept their place: as she started impulsively to her full height, sheathed in her white shawl, her face and neck not less white, except for a purple line under her eyes, her lips a little apart with the peculiar expression of one accused and helpless, she looked like the unhappy ghost of that Gwendolen Harleth whom Deronda had seen turning with firm lips and proud self-possession from her losses at the gaming-table." 56

—her hand held: "That grasp was an entirely new experience to Gwendolen: she had never before had from any man a sign of tenderness which her own being had needed, and she interpreted its powerful effect on her into a promise of inexhaustible patience and constancy." 56

—confession: " 'All sorts of contrivances in my mind—but all so difficult. And I fought against them—I was terrified at them—I saw his dead face . . . ever so long ago I saw it; and I wished him to be dead. And yet it terrified me. I was like two creatures. I could not speak—I wanted to kill—it was as strong as thirst—and then directly—I felt beforehand I had done something dreadful, unalterable—that would make me like an evil spirit. And it came—it came.' " 56

" 'That all made it so hard when I was forced to go in the boat. Because when I saw you it was an unexpected joy, and I thought I could tell you everything—about the locked-up drawer and what I had not told you before. And if I had told you, and knew it was in your mind, it would have less power over me. I hoped and trusted in that. For after all my struggles and my crying, the hatred and rage, the temptation that frightened me, the longing, the thirst for what I dreaded, always came back. And that disappointment—when I was quite shut out from speaking to you, and I was driven to go in the boat—brought all the evil back, as if I had been locked in a prison with it and no escape. Oh, it seems so long ago now since I stepped into that boat! I could have given up everything in that moment, to have the forked lightning for a weapon to strike him dead.' " 56

—the facts: " 'I don't know how it was—he was turning the sail—there was a gust—he was struck—I know nothing—I only know that I saw my wish outside me . . . .

" 'I saw him sink, and my heart gave a leap as if it were going out of me. I think I did not move. I kept my hands tight. It was long enough for me to be glad, and yet to think it was no use—he would come up again. And he *was* come—farther off—the boat had moved. It was all like lightning. "The rope!" he called out in a voice—not his own—I hear it now—and I stooped for the rope—I felt I must—I felt sure he could swim, and he would come back whether or not, and I dreaded him. That was in my mind—he would come back.

Paralysis

" 'But he was gone down again, and I had the rope in my hand—no, there he was again—his face above the water—and he cried again—and I held my hand, and my heart said, "Die!"—and he sank, and I felt "It is done—I am wicked, I am lost!"—and I had the rope in my hand—I don't know what I thought—I was leaping away from myself—I would have saved him then. I was leaping from my crime, and there it was—close to me as I fell—there was the dead face—dead, dead. It can never be altered. That was what happened. That was what I did. You know it all. It can never be altered.' " 56

—*a parting:* "He rose as he spoke, and she gave him her hand submissively. But when he had left her she sank on her knees, in hysterical crying. The distance between them was too great. She was a banished soul—beholding a possible life which she had sinned herself way from." 57

—*her need:* "But the force, the tenacity of her nature had thrown itself into that dependence, and she would no more let go her hold on **Deronda**'s help, or deny herself the interview her soul needed, because of witnesses, than if she had been in prison in danger of being condemned to death." 64

—*infusion of hope:* "[**Deronda**'s] words were like the touch of a miraculous hand to Gwendolen. Mingled emotions streamed through her frame with a strength that seemed the beginning of a new existence, having some new powers or other which stirred in her vaguely . . . . But the new existence seemed inseparable from Deronda: the hope seemed to make his presence permanent." 65

—*a certain love:* "Mighty Love had laid his hand upon her; but what had he demanded of her? Acceptance of rebuke—the hard task of self-change—confession—endurance. If she cried towards him, what then? She cried as the child cries whose little feet have fallen backward—cried to be taken by the hand, lest she should lose herself." 65

—*memory loss:* "In fact, poor Gwendolen's memory had been stunned, and all outside the lava-lit track of her troubled conscience, and her effort to get deliverance from it, lay for her in dim forgetfulness." 65

—*recuperating:* "She was experiencing some of that peaceful melancholy which comes from the renunciation of demands for self, and from taking the ordinary good of existence, and especially kindness, even from a dog, as a gift above expectation." 69

—*her best hope:* "Her supreme need of [**Deronda**] blinding her to the separateness of his life, the whole scene of which she filled with his relation to her . . . . Had he not first risen on her vision as a corrective presence which she had recognised in the beginning with resentment, and at last with entire love and trust? She could not spontaneously think of an end to that reliance, which had become to her imagination like the firmness of the earth, the only condition of her walking." 69

—*setback*: " . . . he found her in a state of deep depression, overmastered by those distasteful miserable memories which forced themselves on her as something more real and ample than any new material out of which she could mould her future. She cried hysterically, and said that he would always despise her. He could only seek words of soothing and encouragement; and when she gradually revived under them, with that pathetic look of renewed childlike interest which we see in eyes where the lashes are still beaded with tears, it was impossible to lay another burthen on her." 69

—*an earthquake:* " . . . she was for the first time feeling the pressure of a vast mysterious movement, for the first time being dislodged from her supremacy in her own world, and getting a sense that her horizon was but a dipping onward of an existence with which her own was revolving. All the troubles of her wifehood and widowhood had still left her with the implicit impression which had accompanied her from childhood, that whatever surrounded her was somehow specially for her . . . . but here had come a shock which went deeper than personal jealousy—something spiritual and vaguely tremendous that thrust her away, and yet quelled all anger into self-humiliation." 69

—*and then:* " 'I am going to marry.'

"At first there was no change in Gwendolen's attitude: she only began to tremble visibly; then she looked before her with dilated eyes, as at something lying in front of her, till she stretched her arms out straight, and cried with a smothered voice—

" 'I said I should be forsaken. I have been a cruel woman. And I am forsaken.' " 69

—*her last words:* "I only thought of myself, and I made you grieve. It hurts me now to think of your grief. You must not grieve any more for me. It is better—it shall be better with me because I have known you." 70

Other Principals

Rev. Henry Gascoigne. "He had some agreeable virtues, some striking advantages, and the failings that were imputed to him all leaned toward the side of success.

"One of his advantages was a fine person, which perhaps was even more impressive at fifty-seven than it had been earlier in life. There were no distinctively clerical lines in the face, no official reserve or ostentatious benignity of expression, no tricks of starchiness or of affected ease: in his Inverness cape he could not have been identified except as a gentleman with handsome dark features, a nose which began with an intention to be aquiline but suddenly became straight, and iron-grey hair. Perhaps he owed this freedom from the sort of professional make-up which penetrates skin tones and gestures and defies all drapery, to the fact that he had once been **Captain Gaskin**, having taken orders and a diphthong but shortly before his engagement to **Miss Arkyn**.

"If anyone had objected that his preparation for the clerical function was inadequate, his friends might have asked who made a better figure in it, who preached better or had more authority in his parish? He had a native gift for administration, being tolerant both of opinions and conduct, because he felt himself able to overrule them, and was free from the irritations of conscious feebleness. He smiled pleasantly at the foible of a taste which he did not share—at floriculture or antiquarianism for example, which were much in vogue among his fellow-clergyman in the diocese; for himself, he preferred following the history of a campaign, or divining from his knowledge of **Nesselrode**'s motives what would have been his conduct if our cabinet had taken a different course.

"Mr Gascoigne's tone of thinking after some long-quieted fluctuations had become ecclesiastical rather than theological; not the modern Anglican, but what he would have called sound English, free from nonsense such as became a man who looked at a national religion by daylight, and saw it in its relations to other things.

"No clerical magistrate had greater weight at sessions, or less of mischievous impracticableness in relation to worldly affairs. Indeed, the worst imputation thrown out against him was worldliness: it could not be proved that he forsook the less fortunate, but it was not to be denied that the friendships he cultivated were of a kind likely to be useful to the father of six sons and two daughters; and bitter observers . . . remarked that the colour of his opinions had changed in consistency with this principle of action. But cheerful, successful worldliness has a false air of being more selfish than the acrid, unsuccessful kind, whose secret history is summed up in the terrible words, 'Sold but not paid for.' " ¶3

—fatherly: " . . . he was interrupted by seeing poor **Rex** come in with a face which was not the less handsome and ingratiating for being pale and a little distressed. He was secretly the favourite son, and a young portrait of the father; who, however, never treated him with any partiality—rather, with an extra rigour." 7

—a son's love: "Mr Gascoigne was inwardly going through some self-rebuke for not being more wary, and was now really sorry for the lad; but every consideration was subordinate to that of using the wisest tactics in the case. He had quickly made up his mind, and could answer the more quietly—

" 'My dear boy, you are too young to be taking momentous, decisive steps of that sort. This is a fancy which you have got into your head during an idle week or two: you must set to work at something and dismiss it. There is every reason against it. An engagement at your age would be totally rash and unjustifiable; and moreover, alliances between first cousins are undesirable. Make up your mind to a brief disappointment. Life is full of them. We have all got to be broken in; and this is a mild beginning for you.' " 7

—with his family: "It was a noticeable group that these three creatures made, each of them with a face of the same structural type—the straight brow, the nose suddenly straightened from an intention of being aquiline, the short upper lip, the short but strong and well-hung chin: there was even the same tone of complexion and set of the eye. The grey-haired father was at once massive and keen-looking; there was a perpendicular line in his brow which when he spoke with any force of interest deepened, and the habit of ruling gave him an air of reserved authoritativeness. **Rex** would have seemed a vision of the father's youth, if it had been possible to imagine Mr Gascoigne without distinct plans and without command, smitten with a heart sorrow, and having no more notion of concealment than a sick animal; and **Anna** was tiny copy of Rex, with hair drawn back and knotted, her face following his in its changes of expression, as if they had one soul between them." 8

—query: " 'You think, I suppose, that you have had a shock which has changed all your inclinations, stupefied your brains, unfitted you for anything but manual labour, and given you a dislike to society? Is that what you believe?' " 8

—rumour: "He held it futile, even if it had been becoming, to show any curiosity as to the past of a young man whose birth, wealth, and consequent leisure made many habits venial which under other circumstances would have been inexcusable." 9

—background: "To the Rector, whose father (nobody would have suspected it, and nobody was told) had risen to be a provincial corn-dealer, aris-

tocratic heirship resembled regal heirship in excepting its possessor from the ordinary standard of moral judgments." 13

—clear-headed: "But the Rector's was a firm mind, grasping its first judgments tenaciously and acting on them promptly, whence counter-judgments were no more for him than shadows fleeting across the solid ground to which he adjusted himself." 13

—matrimonial prospect: "**Grandcourt**, the almost certain baronet, the probable peer, was to be ranged with public personages, and was a match to be accepted on broad general grounds national and ecclesiastical. Such public personages, it is true, are often in the nature of giants which an ancient community may have felt pride and safety in possessing, though, regarded privately, these born eminences must often have been inconvenient and even noisome." 13

—authoritative: "The Rector's mode of speech always conveyed a thrill of authority, as of a word of command: it seemed to take for granted that there could be no wavering in the audience, and that every one was going to be rationally obedient . . . .

" . . . you hold your fortune in your own hands—a fortune such as rarely happens to a girl in your circumstances—a fortune in fact which almost takes the question out of the range of mere personal feeling, and makes your acceptance of it a duty . . . . And I must point out to you that in case Mr Grandcourt were repelled without your having refused him—without your having intended ultimately to refuse him, your situation would be a humiliating and painful one. I, for my part, should regard you with severe disapprobation, as the victim of nothing else than your own coquetry and folly.' " 13

—benign: "He wished his niece parks, carriages, a title—everything that would make this world a pleasant abode; but he wished her not to be cynical—to be, on the contrary, religiously dutiful, and have warm domestic affections." 13

—adversity: "Mr Gascoigne's worth of character, a little obscured by worldly opportunities—as the poetic beauty of women is obscured by the demands of fashionable dressing—showed itself to great advantage under this sudden reduction of fortune. Prompt and methodical, he had set himself not only to put down his carriage, but to reconsider his worn suits of clothes, to leave off meat for breakfast, to do without periodicals, to get **Edwy** from school and arrange hours of study for all the boys under himself, and to order the whole establishment on the sparest footing possible. For all healthy people economy has its pleasures, and the Rector's spirit had spread through the household." 24

—missed: " . . . his cheerful, complacent activity and spirit of kind management, even when mistaken, [was] more of a comfort than the neutral loftiness which was every day chilling [**Gwendolen**]." 44

—optimist: "Mr Gascoigne had come to the conclusion that **Grandcourt** was a proud man, but his own self-love, calmed through life by the consciousness of his general value and personal advantages, was not irritable enough to prevent him from hoping the best about his niece's husband because her uncle was kept rather haughtily at a distance." 44

—peace: " . . . the Rector maintained his cheerful confidence in the goodwill of patrons and his resolution to deserve it by diligence in the fulfilment of his duties, whether patrons were likely to hear of it or not; doing nothing solely with an eye to promotion except, perhaps, the writing of two ecclesias-

tical articles, which, having no signature, were attributed to some one else, except by the patrons who had a special copy sent them, and these certainly knew the author but did not read the articles. The Rector, however, chewed no poisonous cud of suspicion on this point: he made marginal notes on his own copies to render them a more interesting loan, and was gratified that the Archdeacon and other authorities had nothing to say against the general tenor of his argument.

"Peaceful authorship!—living in the air of the fields and downs, and not in the thrice-breathed breath of criticism—bringing no Dantesque leanness; rather, assisting nutrition by complacency, and perhaps giving a more suffusive sense of achievement than the production of a whole *Divina Commedia.*" ¶58

Henleigh Mallinger Grandcourt. "He was slightly taller than [**Gwendolen**], and their eyes seemed to be on a level; there was not the faintest smile on his face as he looked at her, not a trace of self-consciousness or anxiety in his bearing; when he raised his hat he showed an extensive baldness surrounded with a mere fringe of reddish-blond hair, but he also showed a perfect hand; the line of feature from brow to chin undisguised by beard was decidedly handsome, with only moderate departures from the perpendicular, and the slight whisker too was perpendicular. It was not possible for a human aspect to be freer from grimace or solicitous wrigglings; also it was perhaps not possible for a breathing man wide awake to look less animated . . . Grandcourt's bearing had no rigidity, it inclined rather to the flaccid. His complexion had a faded fairness resembling that of an actress when bare of the artificial white and red; his long narrow grey eyes expressed nothing but indifference." 11

—*summed up:* " 'He is not ridiculous.' " 11

—*speech:* "He spoke with a fine accent, but with a certain broken drawl, as of a distinguished personage with a distinguished cold on his chest." 11

—*mannerism:* " . . . Grandcourt, who listened with an impassive face and narrow eyes, his left fore-finger in his waistcoat-pocket, and his right slightly touching his thin whisker." 11

—*mode of speaking:* "Grandcourt, like many others, had two remarkably different voices. Hitherto we have heard him speaking in a superficial interrupted drawl suggestive chiefly of languor and *ennui.* But this last brief speech was uttered in subdued, inward, yet distinct tones, which **Lush** had long been used to recognise as the expression of a peremptory will." 12

"Grandcourt's speeches this morning were, as usual, all of that brief sort which never fails to make a conversational figure when the speaker is held important in his circle. Stopping so soon, they give signs of a suppressed and formidable ability to say more, and have also the meritorious quality of allowing lengthiness to others." 13

—*reptilian:* "That absence of demonstrativeness which she was glad of, acted as a charm in more senses than one, and was slightly benumbing. Grandcourt after all was formidable—a handsome lizard of a hitherto unknown species, not of the lively, darting kind. But **Gwendolen** knew hardly anything about lizards, and ignorance gives one a large range of probabilities. This splendid specimen was probably gentle, suitable as a boudoir pet: what may not a lizard be, if you know nothing to the contrary? Her acquaintance with Grandcourt was such that no accomplishment suddenly revealed in him would have surprised her. And he was so little suggestive of drama, that it hardly occurred to her to think with any detail how his life of thirty-six years had been passed: in general, she imagined him always cold and dignified, not likely ever to have committed himself. He had hunted the tiger—had he ever been in love or made love?" 13

—rumour discounted: "But if Grandcourt had really made any deeper or more unfortunate experiments in folly than were common in young men of high prospects, he was of an age to have finished them. All accounts can be suitably wound up when a man has not ruined himself [thought the Rector], and the expense may be taken as an insurance against future error. This was the view of practical wisdom; with reference to higher views, repentance had a supreme moral and religious value. There was every reason to believe that a woman of well-regulated mind would be happy with Grandcourt." 13

—languid: " 'Starting away,' however, was not the right expression for the languor of intention that came over Grandcourt, like a fit of diseased numbness, when an end seemed within easy reach: to desist then, when all expectation was to the contrary, became another gratification of mere will, sublimely independent of definite motive." 14

—passions: "Grandcourt's passions were of the intermittent, flickering kind: never flaming out strongly." 15 *See Topicon* S:Emotions—*passion missing*

—complexion: " . . . he lingered over his toilet, and certainly came down with a faded aspect of perfect distinction which made fresh complexions, and hands with the blood in them, seem signs of raw vulgarity . . . . " 25

—skittish: " . . . on the other hand, the certainty of acceptance was just 'the sort of thing' to make him lapse hither and thither with no more apparent will than a moth." 25

—unpredictable: "**Lush** had had his patron under close observation for many years, and knew him perhaps better than he knew any other subject; but to know Grandcourt was to doubt what he would do in any particular case . . . . But Lush had some general certainties about Grandcourt, and one was, that of all inward movements those of generosity were the least likely to occur in him." 25

—intrigued: "And he also considered himself to be wooing: he was not a man to suppose that his presence carried no consequences; and he was exactly the man to feel the utmost piquancy in a girl whom he had not found quite calculable." 27

—aroused: "At that moment his strongest wish was to be completely master of this creature—this piquant combination of maidenliness and mischief: that she knew things which had made her start away from him, spurred him to triumph over that repugnance; and he was believing that he should triumph." 27

"The evident hesitation of this destitute girl to take his splendid offer stung him into a keenness of interest such as he had not known for years." 27

—vignette: "The chair of red-brown velvet brocade was a becoming background for his pale-tinted well-cut features and exquisite long hands: omitting the cigar, you might have imagined him a portrait by **Moroni**, who would have rendered wonderfully the impenetrable gaze and air of distinction, and a portrait by that great master would have been quite as lively a companion as Grandcourt was disposed to be." 28

—*his* fiancée: " . . . he believed that this girl was rather exceptional in the fact that, in spite of his assiduous attention to her, she was not in love with him; and it seemed to him very likely that if it had not been for the sudden poverty which had come over her family, she would have not have accepted him . . . . On the whole, Grandcourt got more pleasure out of this notion than he could have done out of winning a girl of whom he was sure that she had a strong inclination for him personally. And yet this pleasure in mastering reluctance flourished along with the habitual persuasion that no woman whom he favoured could be quite indifferent to his personal influence; and it seemed to him not unlikely that by-and-by **Gwendolen** might be more enamoured of him than he of her. In any case she would have to submit; and he enjoyed thinking of her as his future wife, whose pride and spirit were suited to command every one but himself. He had no taste for a woman who was all tenderness to him, full of petitioning solicitude and willing obedience. He meant to be master of a woman who would have liked to master him, and who perhaps would have been capable of mastering another man." 28

—*mastery:* "Grandcourt himself was not jealous of anything unless it threatened his mastery—which he did not think himself likely to lose." 28

—*courtship converse:* "His answers to her lively questions about what he had seen and done in his life, bore drawling very well. From the first she had noticed that he knew what to say; and she was constantly feeling not only that he had nothing of the fool in his composition, but that by some subtle means he communicated to her the impression that all the folly lay with other people, who did what he did not care to do . . . . Then Grandcourt's behaviour as a lover had hardly at all passed the limit of an amorous homage which was inobtrusive as a wafted odour of roses, and spent all its effect in a gratified vanity." 29

—*old adherence:* "No one talked of **Mrs Glasher** now, any more than they talked of the victim in a trial for manslaughter ten years before: she was a lost vessel after whom nobody would send out an expedition of search; but Grandcourt was seen in harbour with his colours flying, registered as seaworthy as ever.

"Yet in fact Grandcourt had never disentangled himself from Mrs Glasher. His passion for her had been the strongest and most lasting he had ever known; and though it was now as dead as the music of a cracked flute, it had left a certain dull disposedness, which on the death of her husband three years before had prompted in him a vacillating notion of marrying her, in accordance with the understanding often expressed between them during the days of his first ardour." 30

—*incapability:* "He could not shake her nor touch her hostilely; and if he could, the process would not bring the diamonds. He shrank from the only sort of threat that would frighten her—if she believed it. And in general, there was nothing he hated more than to be forced into anything like violence even in words: his will must impose itself without trouble." 30 *This key element in his nature Gwendolen never understands, to her great cost.*

—*defied:* "He was in a state of disgust and embitterment quite new in the history of their relation to each other. It was undeniable that this woman whose life he had allowed to send such deep suckers into his had a terrible power of annoyance in her; and the rash hurry of his proceedings had left her opportunities open. His pride saw very ugly possibilities threatening it . . . . " 30

—*extreme statement:* " 'You have made me feel uncommonly ill with your folly,' said Grandcourt, apparently choosing this statement as the strongest possible use of language." 30

—*very annoyed:* "The effect that clung and gnawed within Grandcourt was a sense of imperfect mastery." 30

—*impression made:* "[**Deronda**'s] notion of Grandcourt as a 'remnant' was founded on no particular knowledge, but simply on the impression which ordinary polite intercourse had given him that Grandcourt had worn out all his natural healthy interest in things." 35

—*returned from the honeymoon:* "The bridegroom had neither more nor less easy perfection of costume, neither more nor less well-cut impassibility of face, than before his marriage. It was to be supposed of him that he would put up with nothing less than the best in outward equipment, wife included; and the bride was what he might have been expected to choose." 35

—*observant:* "Grandcourt had a delusive mood of observing whatever had an interest for him, which could be surpassed by no sleepy-eyed animal on the watch for prey . . . . If Grandcourt cared to keep any one under his power he saw them out of the corners of his long narrow eyes, and if they went behind him, he had a constructive process by which he knew what they were doing there. He knew perfectly well where his wife was, and how she was behaving." 35

—*unmasked:* "[**Gwendolen**] had found a will like that of a crab or a boa-constrictor which goes on pinching or crushing without alarm at thunder. Not that Grandcourt was without calculation of the intangible effects which were the chief means of mastery; indeed he had a surprising acuteness in detecting that situation of feeling in Gwendolen which made her proud and rebellious spirit dumb and helpless before him." 35

—*domestic bliss:* "Why should a gentleman whose other relations in life are carried on without the luxury of sympathetic feeling, be supposed to require that kind of condiment in domestic life? What he chiefly felt was that a change had come over the conditions of his mastery, which, far from shaking it, might establish it the more thoroughly. And it was established." 35

—*his politics:* " . . . he embraced all Germans, all commercial men, and all voters liable to use the wrong kind of soap, under the general epithet of 'brutes,' but he took no action on these much agitated questions beyond looking from under his eyelids at any man who mentioned them, and retaining a silence which served to shake the opinions of timid thinkers." 48

—*his taste:* "His taste was fastidious, and **Gwendolen** satisfied it: he would not have liked a wife who had not received some elevation of rank from him; nor one who did not command admiration by her mien and beauty; nor one whose nails were not of the right shape; nor one the lobe of whose ear was at all too large and red; nor one who, even if her nails and ears were right, was at the same time a ninny, unable to make spirited answers." 48

—*his preference:* "These requirements may not seem too exacting to refined contemporaries whose own ability to fall in love has been held in suspense for lack of indispensable details; but fewer perhaps may follow him in his contentment that his wife should be in a temper which would dispose her to fly out if she dared, and that she should have been urged into marrying him by other feelings than passionate attachment. Still, for those who prefer command to love, one does not see why the habit of mind should change precisely at the point of matrimony." 48

—*not jealous:* " . . . having taken on himself the part of husband, he was not going in any way to be fooled, or allow himself to be seen in a light that could be regarded as pitiable. This was his state of mind—not jealousy; still, his behaviour in some respects was as like jealousy as yellow is to yellow, which colour we know may be the effect of very different causes." 48

—*suppressive:* " the continual liability to Grandcourt's presence and surveillance seemed to flatten every effort to the level of the boredom which his manner expressed: this negative mind was as diffusive as fog, clinging to all objects, and spoiling all contact." 48

—*power:* "He knew the force of his own words. If this white-handed man with the perpendicular profile had been sent to govern a difficult colony, he might have won reputation among his contemporaries. He had certainly ability, would have understood that it was safer to exterminate than to cajole superseded proprietors, and would not have flinched from making things safe in that way." 48

—*fastidious:* "Like all proud, closely-wrapped natures, he shrank from explicitness and detail, even on trivialities, if they were personal: a valet must maintain a strict reserve with him on the subject of shoes and stockings. And clashing was intolerable to him: his habitual want was to put collision out of the question by the quiet massive pressure of his rule." 48

—*blind spot:* "Grandcourt's view of things was considerably fenced in by his general sense, that what suited him, others must put up with. There is no escaping the fact that want of sympathy condemns us to a corresponding stupidity. *Mephistopheles* thrown upon real life, and obliged to manage his own plot, would inevitably make blunders." 48

—*obtuse:* "He conceived that she did not love him: but was that necessary? She was under his power, and he was not accustomed to soothe himself, as some cheerfully-disposed persons are, with the conviction that he was very generally and justly beloved. But what lay quite away from his conception was, that she could have any special repulsion for him personally. How could she? He himself knew what personal repulsion was—nobody better: his mind was much furnished with a sense of what brutes his fellow-creatures were, both masculine and feminine; what odious familiarities they had, what smirks, what modes of flourishing their handkerchiefs, what costume, what lavender water, what bulging eyes, and what foolish notions of making themselves agreeable by remarks which were not wanted. In this critical view of mankind there was an affinity between him and **Gwendolen** before their marriage, and we know that she had been attractingly wrought upon by the refined negations he presented to her. Hence he understood her repulsion for **Lush**. But how was he to understand or conceive her present repulsion for Henleigh Grandcourt?

"Some men bring themselves to believe, and not merely maintain, the non-existence of an external world; a few others believe themselves objects of repulsion to a woman without being told so in plain language. But Grandcourt did not belong to this eccentric body of thinkers. He had all his life had reason to take a flattering view of his own attractiveness, and to place himself in fine antithesis to the men who, he saw at once, must be revolting to a woman of taste. He had no idea of a moral repulsion, and could not have believed, if he had been told it, that there may be a resentment and disgust which will gradually make beauty more detestable than ugliness, through exasperation at that outward virtue in which hateful things can flaunt themselves or find a supercilious advantage." 54

—*keen pleasure:* "Grandcourt had an intense satisfaction in leading his wife captive after this fashion: it gave their life on a small scale a royal representation and publicity in which everything familiar was got rid of, and everybody must do what was expected of them whatever might be their private protest—the protest (kept strictly private) adding to the piquancy of despotism." 54

—*complacent:* "But his soul was garrisoned against presentiments and fears: he had the courage and confidence that belong to domination, and he was at that moment feeling perfectly satisfied that he held his wife with his bit and bridle. By the time they had been married a year she would cease to be restive." 54

—*courage:* " . . . he had set his mind on this boating, and carried out his purpose as something that people might not expect him to do, with the gratified impulse of a strong will which had nothing better to exert itself upon. He had remarkable physical courage, and was proud of it—or rather he had a great contempt for the coarser, bulkier men who generally had less." 54

Ezra (Mordecai) Lapidoth. "A man in threadbare clothing, whose age was difficult to guess—from the dead yellowish flatness of the flesh, something like an old ivory carving—was seated on a stool against some bookshelves that projected beyond the short counter, doing nothing more remarkable than reading the yesterday's *Times,* but when he let the paper rest on his lap and looked at the incoming customer, the thought glanced through Deronda that precisely such a physiognomy as that might possibly have been seen in a prophet of the Exile, or in some New Hebrew poet of the mediaeval time. It was a finely typical Jewish face, wrought into intensity of expression apparently by a strenuous eager experience in which all the satisfaction had been indirect and far off, and perhaps by some bodily suffering also, which involved that absence of ease in the present.

"The features were clear-cut, not large; the brow not high but broad, and fully defined by the crisp black hair. It might never have been a particularly handsome face, but it must always have been forcible; and now with its dark, far-off gaze, and yellow pallor in relief on the gloom of the backward shop, one might have imagined one's self coming upon it in some past prison of the Inquisition, which a mob had suddenly burst open, while the look fixed on an incidental customer seemed eager and questioning enough to have been turned on one who might have been a messenger either of delivery or of death." ¶33

—*dressed for the Sabbath:* "Mordecai had no handsome Sabbath garment, but instead of the threadbare rusty black coat of the morning he wore one of light drab, which looked as if it had once been a handsome loose paletot now shrunk with washing, and this change of clothing gave a still stronger accentuation to his dark-haired, eager face, which might have belonged to the prophet **Ezekiel** . . . . " 34

—*at prayer:* "[He] delivered himself alone at some length, in a solemn chanting tone, with his chain slightly uplifted and his thin hands clasped easily before him. Not only in his accent and tone, but in his freedom from the self-consciousness which has reference to others' approbation, there could hardly have been a stronger contrast to the Jew at the other end of the table. It was an unaccountable conjunction—the presence among these common, prosperous, shopkeeping types, of a man who, in an emaciated threadbare condition, imposed a certain awe on **Deronda**, and an embarrassment at not meeting his expectations." 34

—*yearning:* "For many winters, while he had been conscious of an ebbing physical life, and a widening spiritual loneliness, all his passionate desire had concentred itself in the yearning for some young ear into which he could pour his mind as a testament, some soul kindred enough to accept the spiritual product of his own brief, painful life, as a mission to be executed." 38

"His inward need for the conception of this expanded, prolonged self was reflected as an outward necessity. The thoughts of his heart (that ancient phrase best shadows the truth) seemed to him too precious, too closely inwoven with the growth of things not to have a further destiny. And as the more beautiful, the stronger, the more executive self took shape in his mind, he loved it beforehand with an affection half identifying, half contemplative and grateful." 38

—*fateful meeting:* "Imagine—we all of us can—the pathetic stamp of consumption with its brilliancy of glance to which the sharply-defined structure of features reminding one of a forsaken temple, give already a far-off look as of one getting unwillingly out of reach; and imagine it on a Jewish face naturally accentuated for the expression of an eager mind—the face of a man little above thirty, but with that age upon it which belongs to time lengthened by suffering, the hair and beard still black throwing out the yellow pallor of the skin, the difficult breathing giving more decided marking to the mobile nostril, the wasted yellow hands conspicuous on the folded arms: then give to the yearning consumptive glance something of the slowly dying mother's look when her one loved son visits her bedside, and the flickering power of gladness leaps out as she says, 'My boy!'—for the sense of spiritual perpetuation in another resembles that maternal transference of self." 40

—*confident forecast:* " 'The world grows, and its frame is knit together by the growing soul; dim, dim at first, then clearer and more clear, the consciousness discerns remote stirrings. As thoughts move within us darkly, and shake us before they are fully discerned—so events—so benign they are knit with us in the growth of the world. You have risen within me like a thought not fully spelled: my soul is shaken before the words are all there. The rest will come—it will come.' " 40

" 'Your doubts lie as light as dust on my belief.' " 40

—*reliable?* "This Mordecai happened to have a more pathetic aspect, a more passionate, penetrative speech than a social reformer with coloured views of the new moral world in parallelograms, or than an enthusiast in sewage; still he came under the same class. It would be only right and kind to indulge him a little, to comfort him with such help as was practicable; but what likelihood was there that his notions had the sort of value he ascribed to them? In such cases a man of the world knows what to think beforehand." 41

—*moved:* " ' . . . the spirit of my youth has been stirred within me, and this body is not strong enough to bear the beating of its wings. I am as a man bound and imprisoned through long years: behold him brought to speech of his fellow and his limbs set free: he weeps, he totters, the joy within him threatens to break and overthrow the tabernacle of flesh.' " 42

—*after his oration:* "Before [**Deronda**] stood, as a living, suffering reality, what hitherto he had only seen as an effort of imagination, which, in its comparative faintness, yet carried a suspicion of being exaggerated: a man steeped in poverty and obscurity, weakened by disease, consciously within the shadow of advancing death, but living an intense life in an invisible past and future, careless of his personal lot, except for its possibly making some obstruction to a conceived good which he would never share except as a brief inward vision—a day afar off, whose sun would never warm him, but into which he threw his soul's desire, with a passion often wanting to the personal motive of healthy youth. It was something more than a grandiose transfiguration of the parental love that toils, renounces, endures, resists the suicidal promptings of despair—all because of the little ones, whose future becomes present to the yearning gaze of anxiety." 42 *See Topicon* FM:Jews—*for his nation*

—transformed: "The quiet tenacity of his ordinary self differed as much from his present exaltation of mood as a man in private talk, giving reasons for a revolution of which no sign is discernible, differs from one who feels himself an agent in a revolution begun." 42

—greatness: "Yes, greatness: that was the word which **Deronda** now deliberately chose to signify the impression that Mordecai made on him . . . this man, however erratic some of his interpretations might be—this consumptive Jewish workman in threadbare clothing, lodged by charity, delivering himself to hearers who took his thoughts without attaching more consequences to them than the Flemings to the ethereal chimes ringing above their market-places—had the chief elements of greatness: a mind consciously, energetically moving with the larger arch of human destinies, but not the less full of conscience and tender heart for the footsteps that tread near and need a leaning-place; capable of conceiving and choosing a life's task with far-off issues, yet capable of the unapplauded heroism which turns off the road of achievement at the call of the nearer duty whose effect lies within the beatings of the hearts that are close to us, as the hunger of the unfledged bird to the breast of its parent." 43

—enthusiast: " 'Mordecai is an enthusiast [said **Deronda**]. I should like to keep that word for the highest order of minds—those who care supremely for grand and general benefits to mankind.' " 46

—wonderful news: " 'What was prayed for has come to pass: **Mirah** has been delivered from evil.'

"Mordecai's grasp relaxed a little, but he was panting with a sort of tearless sob.

" '**Deronda** went on: 'Your sister is worthy of the mother you honoured.'

"He waited there, and Mordecai, throwing himself backward in his chair, again closed his eyes, uttering to himself almost inaudibly for some minutes in Hebrew, and then subsiding into a happy-looking silence. Deronda, watching the expression in his uplifted face, could have imagined that he was speaking with some beloved object: there was a new suffused sweetness, something like that on the faces of the beautiful dead. For the first time Deronda thought he discerned a family resemblance to Mirah." 46

—his faith: " 'Seest thou, **Mirah**,' he said once, after a long silence, 'the *Shemah,* wherein we briefly confess the divine Unity, is the chief devotional exercise of the Hebrew; and this made our religion the fundamental religion for the whole world; for the divine Unity embraced as its consequence the ultimate unity of mankind. See, then—the nation which has been scoffed at for its separateness, has given a binding theory to the human race. Now, in complete unity a part possesses the whole as the whole possesses every part: and in this way human life is tending toward the image of the Supreme Unity: for as our life becomes more spiritual by capacity of thought, and joy therein, possession tends to become more universal, being independent of gross mate-

rial contact; so that in a brief day the soul of a man may know in fuller volume the good which has been and is, nay, is to come, than all he could possess in a whole life where he had to follow the creeping paths of the senses. In this moment, my sister, I hold the joy of another's future within me: a future which these eyes will not see, and which my spirit may not then recognise as mine. I recognise it now, and love it so, that I can lay down this poor life upon its altar and say: "Burn, burn indiscernibly into that which shall be, which is my love and not me." ' " 61

—his father: " 'Seest thou,' he presently added, 'our lot is the lot of Israel. The grief and the glory are mingled as the smoke and the flame. It is because we children have inherited the good that we feel the evil. These things are wedded for us, as our father was wedded to our mother.' " 62

—dying: "He chose to be dressed and sit up in his easy-chair as usual. **Deronda** and **Mirah** on each side of him, and for some hours he was unusually silent, not even making the effort to speak, but looking at them occasionally with eyes full of some restful meaning, as if to assure them that while this remnant of breathing-time was difficult, he felt an ocean of peace beneath him.

"It was not till late in the afternoon, when the light was falling, that he took a hand of each in his and said, looking at Deronda, 'Death is coming to me as the divine kiss which is both parting and reunion—which takes me from your bodily eyes and gives me full presence in your soul. Where thou goest, Daniel, I shall go. Is it not begun? Have I not breathed my soul into you? We shall live together.' " 70

Mirah Lapidoth. "**Deronda** . . . saw at a few yards' distance from him a figure which might have been an impersonation of the misery he was unconsciously giving voice to: a girl hardly more than eighteen, of low slim figure, with most delicate little face, her dark curls pushed behind her ears under a large black hat, a long woollen cloak over her shoulders. Her hands were hanging down clasped before her, and her eyes were fixed on the river with a look of immovable, statue-like despair." 17

—glance: "Her look was something like that of a fawn or other gentle animal before it turns to run away: no blush, no special alarm, but only some timidity which yet could not hinder her from a long look before she turned. . . . He had no right to linger and watch her: poorly-dressed, melancholy women are common sights; it was only the delicate beauty, the picturesque lines and colour of the image that were exceptional, and these conditions made it the more markedly impossible that he should obtrude his interest upon her . . . . He fell again and again to speculating on the probable romance that lay behind that loneliness and look of desolation; then to smile at his own share in the prejudice that interesting faces must have interesting adventures; then to justify himself for feeling that sorrow was the more tragic when it befell delicate, childlike beauty." 17

—approached: "Her little woman's figure as she laid her delicate chilled hands together one over the other against her waist, and went a step backward while she leaned her head forward as if not to lose her sight of his face, was unspeakably touching." 17

—reflecting: " 'I thought it was not wicked. Death and life are one before the Eternal. I know our fathers slew their children and then slew themselves, to keep their souls pure. I meant it so. But now I am commanded to live. I cannot see how I shall live.' " 17

—*distrait:* "Sorrowful isolation had benumbed her sense of reality, and the power of distinguishing outward and inward was continually slipping away from her. Her look was full of wondering timidity, such as the forsaken one in the desert might have lifted to the angelic vision before she knew whether his message were in anger or in pity." 17

—*introduced:* "For an instant she looked up at **Deronda**, as if she were referring all this mercy to him, and then again turning to **Mrs Meyrick**, said with more collectedness in her sweet tones than he had heard before—

" 'I am a stranger. I am a Jewess. You might have thought I was wicked.' " 18

—*qualities:* "Her voice, her accent, her looks—all the sweet purity that clothed her as with a consecrating garment made [**Deronda**] shrink the more from giving her, either ideally or practically, an association with what was hateful or contaminating." 19

—*recovering:* " . . . when she came down in **Mab**'s black dress, her dark hair curling in fresh fibrils as it gradually dried from its plenteous bath, she looked like one who was beginning to take comfort after the long sorrow and watching which had paled her cheek and made deep blue semicircles under her eyes." 20

—*Jewish consciousness:* " ' . . . it comforted me to believe that my suffering was part of the affliction of my people, my part in the long song of mourning that has been going on through ages and ages. For if many of our race were wicked and made merry in their wickedness—what was that but part of the affliction borne by the just among them, who were despised for the sins of their brethren?' " 20

—*her wanderings:* " 'My thoughts were stronger than I was: they rushed in and forced me to see all my life from the beginning; ever since I was carried away from my mother I had felt myself a lost child taken up and used by strangers, who did not care what my life was to me, but only what I could do for them. It seemed all a weary wandering and heart-loneliness—as if I had been forced to go to merry-makings without the expectation of joy. And now it was worse. I was lost again, and I dreaded lest any stranger should notice me and speak to me. I had a terror of the world . . . . And I began to think that my despair was the voice of God telling me to die.' " 20

—*demeanour:* "Her theatrical training had left no recognizable trace; probably her manners had not much changed since she played the forsaken child at nine years of age; and she had grown up in her simplicity and truthfulness like a little flower-seed that absorbs the chance confusion of its surroundings into its own definite mould of beauty. **Deronda** felt that he was making acquaintance with something quite new to him in the form of womanhood. For Mirah was not childlike from ignorance: her experience of evil and trouble was deeper and stranger than his own. He felt inclined to watch her and listen to her as if she had come from a far-off shore inhabited by a race different from our own." 20

—*a report:* " '**Mab** says our life has become like a fairy tale, and all she is afraid of is that Mirah will turn into a nightingale again and fly away from us. Her voice is just perfect: not loud and strong, but searching and melting, like the thoughts of what has been. That is the way old people like me feel a beautiful voice.' " 32

—*her religion:* " 'Oh yes. I like what I have always seen there [at the Synagogue], because it brings back to me the same feelings—the feelings I would not part with for anything else in the world.'

"After this, any criticism, whether of doctrine or of practice, would have seemed to these generous little people [the **Meyricks**] an inhospitable cruelty. Mirah's religion was of one fibre with her affections, and had never presented itself to her as a set of propositions." 32

—*after his absence:* "The dainty neatness of her hair and dress, the glow of tranquil happiness in a face where a painter need have changed nothing if he had wanted to put it in front of the host singing 'peace on earth and goodwill to men,' made a contrast to his first vision of her that was delightful to **Deronda**'s eyes." 32

—*unself-conscious:* "The circumstances of her life had made her think of everything she did as work demanded from her, in which affectation had nothing to do; and she had begun her work before self-consciousness was born." 32

—*about to sing:* "Imagine her—it is always good to imagine a human creature in whom bodily loveliness seems as properly one with the entire being as the bodily loveliness of those wondrous transparent orbs of life that we find in the sea—imagine her with her dark hair brushed from her temples, but yet showing certain tiny rings there which had cunningly found their own way back, the mass of it hanging behind just to the nape of the little neck in curly fibres, such as renew themselves at their own will after being bathed into straightness like that of water-grasses. Then see the perfect cameo her profile makes, cut in a duskish shell where by some happy fortune there pierced a gem-like darkness for the eye and eyebrow; the delicate nostrils defined enough to be ready for sensitive movements, the finished ear, the firm curves of the chin and neck entering into the expression of a refinement which was not feebleness." 32

—*her people:* " 'I will never separate myself from my mother's people. I was forced to fly from my father; but if he came back in age and weakness and want, and needed me, should I say, "This is not my father"? If he had shame, I must share it. It was he who was given to me for my father, and not another. And so it is with my people. I will always be a Jewess. I will love Christians when they are good, like you. But I will always cling to my people. I will always worship with them.' " 32

—*acclimated:* " . . . Mirah appeared to enjoy speaking of what she felt very much as a little girl fresh from school pours forth spontaneously all the long-repressed chat for which she has found willing ears. For the first time in her life Mirah was among those whom she entirely trusted, and her original visionary impression that **Deronda** was a divinely-sent messenger hung about his image still, stirring always anew the disposition to reliance and openness." 37

—*appraised:* " . . . **Lady Pentreath**, who had said in her violoncello voice—

" 'Well, your Jewess is pretty—there's no denying that. But where is her Jewish impudence? She looks as demure as a nun. I suppose she learned that on the stage.' " 45

—*a great apprehension:* " ' . . . when the thought haunts me how it would be if my father were to come and show himself before us both, what seems as if it would scorch me most is seeing my father shrinking before **Ezra**' . . . .

She was silent a moment or two, and then said, in a new tone of yearning compassion, 'And we are his children—and he was once young like us—and my mother loved him. Oh! I cannot help seeing it all close, and it hurts me like a cruelty.' " 52

—*new feeling:* "Of one element in her changed mood she could have given no definite account: it was something as dim as the sense of approaching weather-change, and had extremely slight external promptings, such as we are often ashamed to find all we can allege in support of the busy constructions that go on within us, not only without effort but even against it, under the influence of any blind emotional stirring. Perhaps the first leaven of uneasiness was laid by **Gwendolen**'s behaviour on that visit which was entirely superfluous as a means of engaging Mirah to sing, and could have no other motive than the excited and strange questioning about **Deronda**. Mirah had instinctively kept the visit a secret, but the active remembrance of it had raised a new susceptibility in her, and made her alive as she had never been before to the relations Deronda must have with that society which she herself was getting frequent glimpses of without belonging to it." 52

—*experience:* "Her peculiar life and education had produced in her an extraordinary mixture of unworldliness, with knowledge of the world's evil, and even this knowledge was a strange blending of direct observation with the effects of reading and theatrical study." 52

—*dislike:* " . . . **Gwendolen**, who was increasingly repugnant to her—increasingly, even after she had ceased to see her; for liking and disliking can grow in meditation as fast as in the more immediate kind of presence." 52

—*oblivious:* "But her uneasiness had not reached that point of self-recognition in which she would have been ashamed of it as an indirect, presumptuous claim on **Deronda**'s feeling. That she or any one else should think of him as her possible lover was a conception which had never entered her mind . . . . " 52

—*disquiet:* "Airy possibilities to which she could give no outline, but to which one name and one figure [**Gwendolen**] gave the wandering persistency of a blot in her vision. Here lay the vaguer source of the hidden sadness rendered noticeable to **Hans** by some diminution of that sweet ease, that ready joyousness of response in her speech and smile, which had come with the new sense of freedom and safety; and had made her presence like the freshly-opened daisies and clear bird-notes after the rain." 52

—*resolute calm:* "The force of her nature had long found its chief action in resolute endurance, and to-day the violence of feeling which had caused the first jet of anger had quickly transformed itself into a steady facing of trouble, the well-known companion of her young years. But while she moved about and spoke as usual, a close observer might have discerned a difference between this apparent calm, which was the effect of restraining energy, and the sweet genuine calm of the months when she first felt a return of her infantine happiness." 61

—*jealousy and love:* "But what difference could this pain of hers make to any one else? It must remain as exclusively her own, and hidden, as her early yearning and devotion towards her lost mother. But unlike that devotion, it was something that she felt to be a misfortune of her nature—a discovery that what should have been pure gratitude and reverence had sunk into selfish pain, that the feeling she had hitherto delighted to pour out in words was degraded into something she was ashamed to betray—an absurd longing that she who had received all and given nothing should be of importance where she was of no importance—an angry feeling towards another woman who possessed the good she wanted.

"But what notion, what vain reliance could it be that had lain darkly within her and was now burning itself into sight as disappointment and jealousy? It was as if her soul had been steeped in poisonous passion by forgotten dreams of deep sleep, and now flamed out in this unaccountable misery. For with her waking reason she had never entertained what seemed the wildly unfitting thought that **Deronda** could love her." ¶61

—passion: "But her feeling was no longer vague: the cause of her pain—the image of **Mrs Grandcourt** by **Deronda**'s side drawing him farther and farther into the distance, was as definite as pincers on her flesh. In the *Psyche*-mould of Mirah's frame there rested a fervid quality of emotion sometimes rashly supposed to require the bulk of a **Cleopatra**; her impressions had the thoroughness and tenacity that give to the first selection of passionate feeling the character of a life-long faithfulness." 61

—accosted: "The presence of this unreverend father now, more than ever, affected Mirah with the mingled anguish of shame and grief, repulsion and pity—more than ever, now that her own world was changed into one where there was no comradeship to fence him from scorn and contempt." 62

—filial reverence: "Her heart had begun to beat faster with the prospect of what was coming in the presence of **Ezra**; and already in this attitude of giving leave to the father whom she had been used to obey—in this sight of him standing below her, with a perceptible shrinking from the admission which he had been indirectly asking for, she had a pang of the peculiar, sympathetic humiliation and shame—the stabbed heart of reverence—which belongs to a nature intensely filial." 62

—an opening: " . . . **Deronda**'s suddenly revealed sense of nearness to them: there seemed to be a breaking of day around her which might show her other facts unlike her forebodings in the darkness." 63

—canker: "Deronda was not to blame, but he had an importance for Mrs Grandcourt which must give her some hold on him. And the thought of any close confidence between them stirred the little biting snake that had long lain curled and harmless in Mirah's gentle bosom." 63

—bride-to-be: "But now she was glowing like a dark-tipped yet delicate ivory-tinted flower in the warm sunlight of content, thinking of any possible grief as part of that life with **Deronda** which she could call by no other name than good. And he watched the sober gladness which gave new beauty to her movements and her habitual attitudes of repose, with a delight which made him say to himself that it was enough of personal joy for him to save her from pain . . . . Mirah was ready to believe that he had been a rescuing angel to many besides herself. The only wonder was, that she among them all was to have the bliss of being continually by his side." 70

Sir Hugo Mallinger "was an easy-tempered man, tolerant both of differences and defects; but a point of view different from his own concerning the settlement of the family estates fretted him rather more than if it had concerned Church discipline or the ballot, and faults were the less venial for belonging to a person whose existence was inconvenient to him." 15

—annoyance: "In no case could **Grandcourt** have been a nephew after his own heart; but as the presumptive heir to the Mallinger estates he was the sign and embodiment of a chief grievance in the baronet's life—the want

of a son to inherit the lands, in no portion of which had he himself more than a life-interest. For in an ill-advised settlement which his father, **Sir Francis**, had chosen to make by will, even Diplow with its modicum of land had been left under the same conditions as the ancient and wide inheritance of the two Toppings— Diplow, where Sir Hugo had lived and hunted through many a season in his younger years, and where his wife and daughters ought to have been able to retire after his death." 15

—nephew: ". . . nothing had since occurred to make them hate each other more than was compatible with perfect politeness, or with any accommodation that could be strictly mutual." 15

—contented: " 'You remember **Napoleon**'s *mot—je suis un ancêtre,'* said Sir Hugo, who habitually undervalued birth, as men after dining well often agree that the good of life is distributed with wonderful equality." 15

—painted: "In Sir Hugo's youthful portrait with rolled collar and high cravat, **Sir Thomas Lawrence** had done justice to the agreeable alacrity of expression and sanguine temperament still to be seen in the original, but had done something more than justice in slightly lengthening the nose, which was in reality shorter than might have been expected in a Mallinger." 16

—fine parent: " . . . 'Nunc,' as Sir Hugo had taught him to say; for the baronet was the reverse of a strait-laced man, and left his dignity to take care of itself. Him **Daniel** loved in that deep-rooted filial way which makes children always the happier for being in the same room with father or mother, though their occupations may be quite apart. Sir Hugo's watch-chain and seals, his handwriting, his mode of smoking and of talking to his dogs and horses, had all a rightness and charm about them to the boy which went along with the happiness of morning and breakfast time." 16

—author: " . . . the books he had written were all seen under the same consecration of loving belief which differenced what was his from what was not his, in spite of general resemblance. Those writings were various, from volumes of travel in the brilliant style, to articles on things in general, and pamphlets on political crises; but to Daniel they were alike in having an unquestionable rightness by which other people's information could be tested." 16

—blind spot: "The mistakes in his behaviour to **Deronda** were due to that dulness towards what may be going on in other minds, especially the minds of children, which is among the commonest deficiencies even in good-natured men like him; when life has been generally easy to themselves, and their energies have been quietly spent in feeling gratified.

"No one was better aware than he that Daniel was generally suspected to be his own son. But he was pleased with that suspicion; and his imagination had never once been troubled with the way in which the boy himself might be affected, either then or in the future, by the enigmatic aspect of his circumstances. He was as fond of him as could be, and meant the best by him. And considering the lightness with which the preparation of young lives seems to lie on respectable consciences, Sir Hugo Mallinger can hardly be held open to exceptional reproach.

"He had been a bachelor till he was five-and-forty, had always been regarded as a fascinating man of elegant tastes; what could be more natural, even according to the index of language, than that he should have a beautiful boy like the little Deronda to take care of?" ¶16

—disposition: "Hardly any man could be more good-natured than Sir Hugo, indeed in his kindliness, especially to women, he did actions which others would have called romantic; but he never took a romantic view of them, and in general smiled at the introduction of motives on a grand scale, or of reasons that lay very far off." 32

—a farewell: " 'God bless you, Dan! . . . . Whatever else changes for you, it can't change my being the oldest friend you have known, and the one who has all along felt the most for you. I couldn't have loved you better if you'd been my own . . . . However—things must be as they may.' It was a defensive measure of the baronet's to mingle purposeless remarks with the expression of serious feeling." 50

—letting down easily: "[His] manner of implying that one's gifts are not of the highest order [reports **Hans**] is so exceedingly good-natured and comfortable that I begin to feel it an advantage not to be among those poor fellows at the tip-top." 52

—apprehensive: " 'I have long expected something remarkable from you **Dan**; but, for God's sake, don't go into any eccentricities! I can tolerate any man's difference of opinion, but let him tell it me without getting himself up as a lunatic. At this stage of the world, if a man wants to be taken seriously he must keep clear of melodrama. Don't misunderstand me. I am not suspecting you of setting up any lunacy on your own account. I only think you might easily be led arm in arm with a lunatic, especially if he wanted defending. You have a passion for people who are pelted, Dan. I'm sorry for them too; but so far as company goes, it's a bad ground of selection. . . .

" 'I hope you are not going to set a dead Jew above a living Christian.' " 59

—on testamentary disposition: " 'And it's a chilling thought that you go out of this life only for the benefit of a cousin. A man gets a little pleasure in making his will, if it's for the good of his own curly heads; but it's a nuisance when you're giving and bequeathing to a used-up fellow like yourself, and one you don't care two straws for. It's the next worse thing to having only a life interest in your estates.' " 64

—paradox: "It was among the usual paradoxes of feeling that Sir Hugo, who had given his fatherly cautions to **Deronda** against too much tenderness in his relations with the bride, should now feel rather irritated against him by the suspicion that he had not fallen in love as he ought to have done." 64

—public figure: "For Sir Hugo was a man who liked to show himself and be affable, a Liberal of good lineage, who confided entirely in Reform as not likely to make any serious difference in English habits of feeling, one of which undoubtedly is the liking to behold society well fenced and adorned with hereditary rank." 69

Supporting Roles

Miss Catherine Arrowpoint, "unfortunately also dressed in white, immediately resembled a *carte-de-visite* in which one would fancy the skirt alone to have been charged for. Since Miss Arrowpoint was generally liked for the amiable unpretending way in which she wore her fortunes, and made a softening screen for the oddities of her mother, there seemed to be some unfitness in **Gwendolen**'s looking so much more like a person of social importance." 5

—*kind:* "The trying little scene at the piano had awakened a kindly solicitude towards [**Gwendolen**] in the gentle mind of Miss Arrowpoint, who managed all the invitations and visits . . . . " 5

—*provoking:* " . . . Miss Arrowpoint each time they met raised an unwonted feeling of jealousy in [**Gwendolen**]; not in the least because she was an heiress, but because it was really provoking that a girl whose appearance you could not characterise except by saying that her figure was slight and of middle stature, her features small, her eyes tolerable, and her complexion sallow, had nevertheless a certain mental superiority which could not be explained away—an exasperating thoroughness in her musical accomplishment, a fastidious discrimination in her general tastes, which made it impossible to force her admiration and kept you in awe of her standard. This insignificant-looking young lady of four-and-twenty, whom any one's eyes would have passed over negligently if she had not been Miss Arrowpoint, might be suspected of a secret opinion that Miss Harleth's acquirements were rather of a common order; and such an opinion was not made agreeable to think of by being always veiled under a perfect kindness of manner." 6

—*sympathetic:* "The exception to this willing aloofness [of the women from **Gwendolen**] was Miss Arrowpoint, who often managed unostentatiously to be by her side, and talked to her with quiet friendliness.

" 'She knows, as I do, that our friends are ready to quarrel over a husband for us,' thought Gwendolen, 'and she is determined not to enter into the quarrel.'

" 'I think Miss Arrowpoint has the best manners I ever saw,' said **Mrs Davilow** . . . .

" 'I wish I were like her,' said Gwendolen." 11

—*appraised:* " . . . the daughter's looks and manners require no allowances, any more than if she hadn't a sixpence. She is not beautiful; but equal to carrying any rank.' " 12

—*a problem:* "[She had] a clear head and a strong will. The **Arrowpoints** had already felt some anxiety owing to these endowments of their Catherine. She would not accept the view of her social duty which required her to marry a needy nobleman or a commoner on the ladder towards nobility; and they were not without uneasiness concerning her persistence in declining suitable offers." 22

—*a trend:* "Catherine Arrowpoint had no corresponding restlessness to class with [**Klesmer**'s]: notwithstanding her native kindliness she was perhaps too coolly firm and self-sustained. But she was one of those satisfactory creatures whose intercourse has the charm of discovery; whose integrity of faculty and expression begets a wish to know what they will say on all subjects or how they will perform whatever they undertake; so that they end by raising not only a continual expectation but a continual sense of fulfilment—

the systole and diastole of blissful companionship. In such cases the outward presentment easily becomes what the image is to the worshipper. It was not long before the two became aware that each was interesting to the other; but the 'how far' remained a matter of doubt." 22

Fanny Davilow. " . . . Mrs Davilow's motherly tenderness clung chiefly to her eldest girl, who had been born in her happier time." 3

"Mrs Davilow's worn beauty seemed the more pathetic for the look of entire appeal which she cast at **Gwendolen** . . . . " 3

—*stimulated:* "[**Mrs Gascoigne**] had said interjectionally to her sister, 'It would be a mercy, Fanny, if that girl were well married!' to which Mrs Davilow, discerning some criticism of her darling in the fervour of that wish, had not chosen to make any audible reply, though she had said inwardly, 'You will not get her to marry for your pleasure'; the mild mother becoming rather saucy when she identified herself with her daughter." 9

—*cautious:* "Since that scene after poor **Rex**'s farewell visit, the mother had felt a new sense of peril in touching the mystery of her child's feeling, and in rashly determining what was her welfare: only she could think of welfare in another shape than marriage." 9

—*loved:* "A figure appearing under the portico brought a rush of new and less selfish feeling in **Gwendolen**, and when springing from the carriage she saw the dear beautiful face with fresh lines of sadness in it, she threw her arms round her mother's neck, and for the moment felt all sorrows only in relation to her mother's feeling about them." 21

—*poor guide:* "And the trials of matrimony were the last theme into which Mrs Davilow could choose to enter fully with this daughter." 27

—*time has passed:* "Mrs Davilow's delicate face showed only a slight deepening of its mild melancholy, her hair only a few more silver lines, in consequence of the last year's trials . . . . " 58

Anna Gascoigne. " 'You have outgrown Anna, my dear,' putting his arm tenderly round his daughter, whose shy face was a tiny copy of his own, and drawing her forward. 'She is not so old as you by a year, but her growing days are certainly over.' " 3

" 'I am not at all clever, and I never know what to say. It seems so useless to say what everybody knows, and I can think of nothing else, except what papa says.' " 3

—*ill at ease:* " . . . any one looking at [**Gwendolen**] for the first time might have supposed that long galleries and lackeys had always been a matter of course in her life; while her cousin Anna, who was really more familiar with these things, felt almost as much embarrassed as a rabbit suddenly deposited in that well-lit space." 5

—*performing:* "Anna had caused a pleasant surprise; nothing could be neater than the way in which she played her little parts; one would even have suspected her of hiding much sly observation under her simplicity." 6

—*apprehensive:* "Anna admired her cousin—would have said with simple sincerity, '**Gwendolen** is always very good to me,' and held it in the order of things for herself to be entirely subject to this cousin; but she looked at her with mingled fear and distrust, with a puzzled contemplation as of some wondrous and beautiful animal whose nature was a mystery, and who, for anything Anna knew, might have an appetite for devouring all the small creatures that were her own particular pets." 7

—*sisterly:* " 'Oh **Rex**, I cannot bear it. You will make yourself very unhappy.' Here Anna burst into tears.

" 'Nannie, Nannie, what on earth is the matter with you?' said Rex. A little impatient at being kept in this way, hat on and whip in hand.

" 'She will not care for you one bit—I know she never will!' said the poor child in a sobbing whisper. She had lost all control of herself.

"Rex reddened and hurried away from her out of the hall door, leaving her to the miserable consciousness of having made herself disagreeable in vain." 7

—*a regret:* " 'I should have done with going out, and gloves, and crinoline, and having to talk when I am taken to dinner—and all that.' " 8

—*sister's pain:* " . . . and Anna, to whom the thought of [**Rex**] was part of the air she breathed, was ill at ease with the lively cousin who had ruined his happiness. She tried dutifully to repress any sign of her changed feeling; but who in pain can imitate the glance and hand-touch of pleasure?" 9

—*visitor:* "Anna Gascoigne felt herself much at home with the **Meyrick** girls, who knew what it was to have a brother, and to be generally regarded as of minor importance in the world." 52

Rex Gascoigne. "He was a fine open-hearted youth, with a handsome face strongly resembling his father's and **Anna**'s, but softer in expression than the one, and larger in scale than the other: a bright, healthy, loving nature, enjoying ordinary, innocent things so much that vice had no temptation for him, and what he knew of it lay too entirely in the outer courts and little-visited chambers of his mind for him to think of it with great repulsion. Vicious habits were with him 'what some fellows did—stupid stuff' which he liked to keep aloof from. He returned Anna's affection as fully as could be expected of a brother whose pleasures apart from her were more than the sum total of hers; and he had never known a stronger love." 6

—*in love:* " . . . he was too completely absorbed in a first passion to have observation for any person or thing. He did not observe **Gwendolen**; he only felt what she said or did, and the back of his head seemed to be a good organ of information as to whether she was in the room or not. Before the end of the first fortnight he was so deeply in love that it was impossible for him to think of his life except as bound up with Gwendolen's. He could see no obstacles, poor boy; his own love seemed a guarantee of hers, since it was one with the unperturbed delight in her image, so that he could no more dream of her giving him pain than an Egyptian could dream of snow. She sang and played to him whenever he liked, was always glad of his companionship in riding, though his borrowed steeds were often comic, was ready to join in any fun of his, and showed a right appreciation of **Anna**. No mark of sympathy seemed absent. That because Gwendolen was the most perfect creature in the world she was to make a grand match, had not occurred to him. He had no conceit—at least, not more than goes to make up the necessary gum and consistence of a substantial personality: it was only that in the young bliss of loving he took Gwendolen's perfection as part of that good which had seemed one with life to him, being the outcome of a happy, well-embodied nature." 6

—*thrilled:* " . . . her figure, her long white throat, and the curves of her cheek and chin were always set off to perfection by the compact simplicity of her riding dress. He could not conceive a more perfect girl; and to a youthful lover like Rex it seems that the fundamental identity of the good, the true, and the beautiful, is already extant and manifest in the object of his love.

Most observers would have held it more than equally accountable that a girl should have like impressions about Rex, for in his handsome face there was nothing corresponding to the undefinable stinging quality—as it were a trace of demon ancestry—which made some beholder hesitate in their admiration of **Gwendolen**." 7

—handicapped hunting: "If [**Gwendolen**] had thought of him, it would have struck her as a droll picture that he should be gradually falling behind, and looking round in search of gates: a fine lithe youth, whose heart must be panting with all the spirit of a beagle, stuck as if under a wizard's spell on a stiff clerical hackney, would have made her laugh with a sense of fun much too strong for her to reflect on his mortification." 7

—wooing rejected: " 'Be as cross with me as you like—only don't treat me with indifference,' said Rex, imploringly. 'All the happiness of my life depends on your loving me—if only a little—better than any one else.'

"He tried to take her hand, but she hastily eluded his grasp . . . .

"To Rex at twenty the joy of life seemed at an end more absolutely than it can do to a man at forty." 7

—reaction: " . . . the chief thought of his mother and **Anna** was how to tend this patient who did not want to be well, and from being the brightest, most grateful spirit in the household, was metamorphosed into an irresponsive, dull-eyed creature who met all affectionate attempts with a murmur of 'Let me alone.' " 8

—new report: "Rex Gascoigne—you remember a head you admired among my sketches, a fellow with a good upper lip, reading law—has got some rooms in town now not far off us, and has had a neat sister (upper lip also good) staying with him the last fortnight." 52

—aftermath: " . . . **Mr Gascoigne** was inclined to regard the little affair which had caused him so much anxiety the year before as an evaporation of superfluous moisture, a kind of finish to the baking process which the human dough demands." 58

—father's pride: " . . . Rex was that romance of later life which a man sometimes finds in a son whom he recognises as superior to himself, picturing a future eminence for him according to a variety of famous examples." 58

—his rival's death: "In Rex's nature the shame was immediate, and overspread like an ugly light all the hurrying images of what might come, which thrust themselves in with the idea that **Gwendolen** was again free—overspread them, perhaps, the more persistently because every phantasm of a hope was quickly nullified by a more substantial obstacle . . . .

"These thoughts, which he wanted to master and suspend, were like a tumultuary ringing of opposing chimes that he could not escape from by running. During the last year he had brought himself into a state of calm resolve, and now it seemed that three words had been enough to undo all that difficult work, and cast him back into the wretched fluctuations of a longing which he recognised as simply perturbing and hopeless. And at this moment the activity of such longing had an untimeliness that made it repulsive to his better self. Excuse poor Rex: it was not much more than eighteen months since he had been laid low by an archer who sometimes touches his arrow with a subtle, lingering poison." 58

—his burden: "This sort of passion had nested in the sweet-natured, strong Rex, and he had made up his mind to its companionship, as if it had

been an object supremely dear, stricken dumb and helpless, and turning all the future of tenderness into a shadow of the past. But he had also made up his mind that his life was not to be pauperised because he had had to renounce one sort of joy; rather, he had begun life again with a new counting-up of the treasures that remained to him, and he had even felt a release of power such as may come from ceasing to be afraid of your own neck." 58

Lydia Glasher. "An impressive woman, whom many would turn to look at again in passing; her figure was slim and sufficiently tall, her face rather emaciated, so that its sculpturesque beauty was the more pronounced, her crisp hair perfectly black, and her large anxious eyes also what we call black. Her dress was soberly correct, her age perhaps physically more advanced than the number of years would imply, but hardly less than seven-and-thirty. An uneasy-looking woman: her glance seemed to presuppose that people and things were going to be unfavourable to her, while she was nevertheless ready to meet them with resolution." 13

—encounter: "[**Gwendolen**] could take in the whole figure of this stranger and perceive that she was unmistakeably a lady, and one who must once have been exceedingly handsome." 14

—the message: " 'You are very attractive, **Miss Harleth**. But when he first knew me, I too was young. Since then my life has been broken up and embittered. It is not fair that he should be happy and I miserable, and my boy thrust out of sight for another.'

"These words were uttered with a biting accent, but with a determined abstinence from anything violent in tone or manner." 14

—history: "It was full ten years since the elopement of an Irish officer's beautiful wife with young **Grandcourt**, and a consequent duel where the bullets wounded the air only, had made some little noise. Most of those who remembered the affair now wondered what had become of that Mrs Glasher whose beauty and brilliancy had made her rather conspicuous to them in foreign places, where she was known to be living with young Grandcourt." 30

"At first she was comparatively careless about the possibility of marriage. It was enough that she had escaped from a disagreeable husband and found a sort of bliss with a lover who had completely fascinated her . . . . She was an impassioned, vivacious woman, fond of adoration, exasperated by five years of marital rudeness; and the sense of release was so strong upon her that it stilled anxiety for more than she actually enjoyed." 30

—first child: " . . . the one spot which spoiled her vision of her new pleasant world, was the sense that she had left her three-year-old boy, who died two years afterwards, and whose first tones saying 'mamma' retained a difference from those of the children that came after." 30

—expectant: "Her head, which, spite of emaciation, had an ineffaceable beauty in the fine profile, crisp curves of hair, and clearly-marked eyebrows, rose impressively above her bronze-coloured silk and velvet, and the gold necklace which Grandcourt had first clasped round her neck years ago." 30

—contrast: "Imagine the difference in rate of emotion between this woman whom the years had worn to a more conscious dependence and sharper eagerness, and this man whom they were dulling into a more and more neutral obstinacy." 30

—speech: "She had a quick, incisive way of speaking that seemed to go with her features, as the tone and *timbre* of a violin go with its form." 30

—the news has come: "She knew her helplessness, and shrank from testing it by any appeal—shrank from crying in a dead ear and clinging to dead knees, only to see the immovable face and feel the rigid limbs. She did not weep nor speak: she was too hard pressed by the sudden certainty which had as much of chill sickness in it as of thought and emotion." 30

—hatred: "This woman with the intense eager look had had the iron of the mother's anguish in her soul, and it had made her sometimes capable of a repression harder than shrieking and struggle. But underneath the silence there was an outlash of hatred and vindictiveness: she wished that the marriage might make two others wretched, besides herself." 30

—making a stand: "She was suffering the horrible conflict of self-reproach and tenacity. She saw . . . herself left behind in lonely uncertainty . . . all the wretchedness of a creature who had defeated her own motives. And yet she could not bear to give up a purpose which was a sweet morsel to her vindictiveness . . . .

" 'Yes, I am foolish . . . . If you will indulge me in this one folly, I will be very meek—I will never trouble you.' She burst into hysterical crying, and said again almost with a scream—'I will be very meek after that.'

"There was a strange mixture of acting and reality in this passion. She kept hold of her purpose as a child might tighten its hand over a small stolen thing, crying and denying all the while." 30

—wasted malice: "Lydia, feeding on the probabilities in her favour, devoured her helpless wrath along with that pleasanter nourishment; but she could not let her discretion go entirely without the reward of making a *Medusa*-apparition before **Gwendolen**, vindictiveness and jealousy finding relief in an outlet of venom, though it were as futile as that of a viper already flung to the other side of the hedge." 48

Princess Leonora Halm-Eberstein*—the letter:*

"To my son, **Daniel Deronda**

"My good friend and yours, **Sir Hugo Mallinger**, will have told you that I wish to see you. My health is shaken, and I desire there should be no time lost before I deliver to you what I have long withheld. Let nothing hinder you from being at the *Albergo dell' Italia* in Genoa by the fourteenth of this month. . . .Wait for me—the Princess Halm-Eberstein. Bring with you the diamond ring that Sir Hugo gave you. I shall like to see it again—your unknown mother,

"Leonora Halm-Eberstein" 50

—first view: "She was covered, except as to her face and part of her arms, with black lace hanging loosely from the summit of her whitening hair to the long train stretching from her tall figure. Her arms, naked from the elbow, except for some rich bracelets, were folded before her, and the fine poise of her head made it look handsomer than it really was . . . his chief consciousness was that her eyes were piercing and her face so mobile that the next moment she might look like a different person. For even while she was examining him there was a play of the brow and nostril which made a tacit language . . . . Suddenly, she let fall his hand, and placed both hers on his shoulders, while her face gave out a flash of admiration in which every worn line disappeared and seemed to leave a restored youth." 51 *See* page 517

"She was a remarkable-looking being. What was it that gave her son a painful sense of aloofness?—Her worn beauty had a strangeness in it as if she were not quite a human mother, but a *Melusina*, who had ties with some world which is independent of ours." 51

—career: " 'I was a great singer, and I acted as well as I sang. All the rest were poor beside me. Men followed me from one country to another. I was living a myriad lives in one. I did not want a child.' " 51

—double consciousness: "The varied transitions of tone . . . were as perfect as the most accomplished actress could have made them. The speech was in fact a piece of what may be called sincere acting: this woman's nature was one in which all feeling—and all the more when it was tragic as well as real—immediately became matter of conscious representation: experience immediately passed into drama, and she acted her own emotions. In a minor degree this is nothing uncommon, but in the Princess the acting had a rare perfection of physiognomy, voice, and gesture. It would not be true to say that she felt less because of this double consciousness: she felt—that is, her mind went through—all the more, but with a difference: each nucleus of pain or pleasure had a deep atmosphere of the excitement or spiritual intoxication which at once exalts and deadens." 51

—her father's suppression: " 'I was to be what he called "the Jewish woman" under pain of his curse. I was to feel everything I did not feel, and believe everything I did not believe. I was to feel awe for the bit of parchment in the *mezuza* over the door; to dread lest a bit of butter should touch a bit of meat; to think it beautiful that men should bind the *tephillin* on them, and women not—to adore the wisdom of such laws, however silly they might seem to me. I was to love the long prayers in the ugly synagogue, and the howling, and the gabbling, and the dreadful fasts, and the tiresome feasts, and my father's endless discoursing about Our People, which was a thunder without meaning in my ears. I was to care for ever about what Israel had been, and I did not care at all. I cared for the wide world, and all that I could represent in it. I hated living under the shadow of my father's strictness. Teaching, teaching for everlasting—"this you must be," "that you must not be"—pressed on me like a frame that got tighter and tighter as I grew. I wanted to live a large life, with freedom to do what every one else did, and be carried along in a great current, not obliged to care.' " 51

—cowed: " 'I had an awe of my father—always I had had an awe of him: it was impossible to help it. I hated to feel awed—I wished I could have defied him openly; but I never could. It was what I could not imagine: I could not act it to myself that I should begin to defy my father openly and succeed. And I never would risk failure.' " 51

—separateness: " 'I rid myself of the Jewish tatters and gibberish that make people nudge each other at sight of us, as if we were tattooed under our clothes, though our faces are as whole as theirs. I delivered you from the pelting contempt that pursues Jewish separateness. I am not ashamed that I did it. It was the better for you.' " 51

—touched: "His single impulse was to kneel by her and take her hand gently between his palms, while he said in that exquisite voice of soothing which expresses oneness with the sufferer—

" 'Mother, take comfort!'

"She did not seem inclined to repulse him now, but looked down at him and let him take both her hands to fold between his. Gradually tears gathered, but she pressed her handkerchief against her eyes and then leaned her cheek against his brow, as if she wished that they should not look at each other." 51

—second marriage: " 'I made believe that I preferred being the wife of a Russian noble to being the greatest lyric actress of Europe; I made believe—I acted that part. It was because I felt my greatness sinking away from me, as I feel my life sinking now. I would not wait till men said, "She had better go." ' " 51

—a second audience: " . . . she presently entered, dressed in a loose wrap of some soft silk, in colour a dusky orange, her head again with black lace floating about it, her arms showing themselves bare from under her wide sleeves. Her face seemed even more impressive in the sombre light, the eyes larger, the lines more vigorous. You might have imagined her a sorceress who would stretch forth her wonderful hand and arm to mix youth-potions for others, but scorned to mix them for herself, having had enough of youth." 53

—her portrait: " 'Had I not a rightful claim to be something more than a mere daughter and mother? The voice and the genius matched the face. Whatever else was wrong, acknowledge that I had a right to be an artist, though my father's will was against it. My nature gave me a charter.' " 53

—as to love: " 'I am not a loving woman. That is the truth. It is a talent to love—I lacked it. Others have loved me—and I have acted their love. I know very well what love makes of men and women—it is subjection. It takes another for a larger self, enclosing this one'—she pointed to her own bosom. 'I was never willingly subject to any man. Men have been subject to me.' " 53

—summary: " 'What then? It is all over. Another life! Men talk of "another life," as if it only began on the other side of the grave. I have long entered on another life.' With the last words she raised her arms till they were bare to the elbow, her brow was contracted in one deep fold, her eyes were closed, her voice was smothered: in her dusky flame-coloured garment, she looked like a dreamed visitant from some region of departed mortals." 53

Joseph Kalonymos. "[**Deronda**] happened to take his seat in a line with an elderly man from whom he was distant enough to glance at him more than once as rather a noticeable figure—his ample white beard and felt hat framing a profile of that fine contour which may as easily be Italian as Hebrew." 32

" 'He was my father's friend. He knew of your birth: he knew of my husband's death, and once, twenty years ago, after he had been away in the Levant, he came to see me and inquire about you. I told him that you were dead: I meant you to be dead to all the world of my childhood. If I had said you were living, he would have interfered with my plans: he would have taken on him to represent my father, and have tried to make me recall what I had done. What could I do but say you were dead? The act was done.' " 51

—the clue: " 'But Joseph Kalonymos had heard my father speak of the **Deronda** branch, and the name confirmed his suspicion. He began to suspect what had been done. It was as if everything had been whispered to him in the air. He found out where I was. He took a journey into Russia to see me; he found me weak and shattered. He had come back again, with his white hair, and with rage in his soul against me. He said I was going down to the grave clad in falsehood and robbery—falsehood to my father and robbery of my own child.

Daniel Deronda meets Joseph Kalonymos

" 'He accused me of having kept the knowledge of your birth from you, and having brought you up as if you had been the son of an English gentleman . . . . This man's words were like lion's teeth upon me.' " 51

—*at his bank*: " . . . seated at a table arranging open letters, was the white-bearded man whom he had seen the year before in the synagogue at Frankfort. He wore his hat—it seemed to be the same old felt hat as before—and near him was a packed portmanteau with a wrap and overcoat upon it. On seeing **Deronda** enter he rose, but not did not advance or put out his hand. Looking at him with small penetrating eyes which glittered like black gems in the midst of his yellowish face and white hair, he said in German—

" 'Good! It is now you who seek me, young man.' " 60

—*hair:* "Then deliberately laying aside his hat and showing a head thickly covered with white hair, he stroked and clutched his beard while he looked examiningly at the young face before him." 60

—*traveller:* " ' . . . I am beyond my threescore years and ten, and I am a wanderer, carrying my shroud with me.' " 60

—*satisfied:* " 'Our youth fell on evil days; but this we have won: we increase our wealth in safety, and the learning of all Germany is fed and fattened by Jewish brains—though they keep not always their Jewish hearts.' " 60

—*self-described:* " 'And since I was a ripe man, I have been what I am now, for all but age—loving to wander, loving transactions, loving to behold all things, and caring nothing about hardship. **Charisi** thought continually of our people's future: he went with all his soul into that part of our religion: I, not. So we have freedom, I am content. Our people wandered before they were driven. Young man, when I am in the East, I lie much on deck and watch the greater stars. The sight of them satisfies me. I know them as they rise, and hunger not to know more.' " 60

—*envoi:* "With that they parted; and almost as soon as **Deronda** was in London, the aged man was again on shipboard, greeting the friendly stars without any eager curiosity." 60

Julius Klesmer, "being a felicitous combination of the German, the Sclave [Slav], and the Semite, with grand features, brown hair floating in artistic fashion, and brown eyes in spectacles. His English had little foreignness except its fluency; and his alarming cleverness was made less formidable just then by a certain softening air of silliness which will sometimes befall even Genius in the desire of being agreeable to Beauty." 5

—*disappointed:* " 'No, truly, but that makes nothing,' said Herr Klesmer, suddenly speaking in an odious German fashion with staccato endings, quite unobservable in him before, and apparently depending on a change of mood, as Irishmen resume their strongest brogue when they are fervid or quarrelsome. 'That makes nothing. It is always acceptable to see you sing.' " 5

—*candor:* " 'Yes, it is true; you have not been well taught,' said Herr Klesmer, quietly. Woman was dear to him, but music was dearer. 'Still, you are not quite without gifts. You sing in tune, and you have a pretty fair organ. But you produce your notes badly; and that music which you sing is beneath you. [The **Bellini** aria] is a form of melody which expresses a puerile state of culture—a dandling, canting, see-saw kind of stuff—the passion and thought of people without any breadth of horizon. There is a sort of self-satisfied folly about every phrase of such melody; no cries of deep, mysterious passion—no conflict—no sense of the universal. It makes men small as they listen to it.' " 5

—*performing:* " . . . he certainly fetched as much variety and depth of passion out of the piano as that moderately responsive instrument lends itself to, having an imperious magic in his fingers that seemed to send a nerve-thrill through ivory key and wooden hammer, and compel the strings to make a quivering lingering speech for him." 5

—*incongruous:* "Fancy an assemblage where the men had all that ordinary stamp of the well-bred Englishman, watching the entrance of Herr Klesmer— his main of hair floating backward in massive inconsistency with the chimney-pot hat, which had the look of having been put on for a joke above his pronounced but well-modelled features and powerful clear-shaven mouth and chin; his tall thin figure clad in a way which, not being strictly English, was all the worse for its apparent emphasis of intention. Draped in a loose garment with a Florentine *berretta* on his head, he would have been fit to stand by the side of **Leonardo da Vinci**; but how when he presented himself in trousers which were not what English feeling demanded about the knees?—and when the fire that showed itself in his glances and the movements of his head, as he looked round him with curiosity, was turned into comedy by a hat which ruled that mankind should have well-cropped hair and a staid demeanour, such, for example, as **Mr Arrowpoint**'s, whose nullity of face and perfect tailoring might pass everywhere without ridicule? One sees why it is often better for greatness to be dead, and to have got rid of the outward man." 10

—*eligible:* "Klesmer was eminently a man of honour, but marriages rarely begin with formal proposals; and moreover, **Catherine**'s limit of the conceivable did not exactly correspond with her mother's." 22

—*fascinating:* "Klesmer was as versatile and fascinating as a young *Ulysses* on a sufficient acquaintance—one whom nature seemed to have first made generously and then to have added music as a dominant power using all the abundant rest, and, as in **Mendelssohn**, finding expression for itself not only in the highest finish of execution, but in that fervour of creative work and theoretic belief which pierces the whole future of a life with the light of congruous, devoted purpose. His foibles of arrogance and vanity did not exceed such as may be found in the best English families . . . . " 22

—*after dinner:* " . . . Klesmer's eloquence, gesticulatory and other, went on for a little while like stray fireworks accidentally ignited, and then sank into immovable silence. **Mr Bult** was not surprised that Klesmer's opinions should be flighty, but was astonished at his command of English idiom and his ability to put a point in a way that would have told at a constituents' dinner—to be accounted for probably by his being a Pole, or a Czech, or something of that fermenting sort, in a state of political refugeeism which had obliged him to make a profession of his music . . . . " 22

—*irked:* " 'I was sure he had too much talent to be a mere musician.'

" 'Ah, sir, you are under some mistake there,' said Klesmer, firing up. 'No man has too much talent to be a musician. Most men have too little. A creative artist is no more a mere musician than a great statesman is a mere politician. We are not ingenious puppets, sir, who live in a box and look out on the world only when it is gaping for amusement. We help to rule the nations and make the age as much as any other public men.

Julius Klesmer comes to listen to Mirah (Mrs Meyrick lets him in)

" 'We count ourselves on level benches with legislators. And a man who speaks effectively through music is compelled to something more difficult than parliamentary eloquence.' " 22

—*turned out:* "Klesmer made his most deferential bow in the wide doorway of the ante-chamber—showing also the deference of the finest grey kerseymere trousers and perfect gloves (the 'masters of those who know' are happily altogether human)." 23

—*stung:* "He had wished as delicately as possible to rouse in **Gwendolen** a sense of her unfitness for a perilous, difficult course; but it was his wont to be angry with the pretensions of incompetence, and he was in danger of getting chafed." 23

—*compassionate:* "Our speech even when we are most single-minded can never take its line absolutely from one impulse; but Klesmer's was as far as possible directed by compassion for poor **Gwendolen**'s ignorant eagerness to enter on a course of which he saw all the miserable details with a definiteness which he could not if he would have conveyed to her mind." 23

—*candor:* " 'You have asked my judgment on your chances of winning. I don't pretend to speak absolutely; but measuring probabilities, my judgment is—you will hardly achieve more than mediocrity.' " 23

—*come to call:* " . . . there was seen bowing towards **Mrs Meyrick** a figure . . . tall and physically impressive even in his kid and kerseymere, with massive face, flamboyant hair, and gold spectacles . . . . " 39

—*outsize:* "Klesmer's personality, especially his way of glancing round him, immediately suggested vast areas and a multitudinous audience, and probably they made the usual scenery of his consciousness . . . . Klesmer was vain, but not more so than many contemporaries of heavy aspect, whose vanity leaps out and startles one like a spear out of a walking-stick; as to his carriage and gestures, these were as natural to him as the length of his fingers; and the rankest affectation he could have shown would have been to look diffident and demure. While his grandiose air was making Mab feel herself a ridiculous toy to match the cottage piano, he was taking in the details around him with a keen and thoroughly kind sensibility . . . he had had large acquaintance with the variety and romance which belong to small incomes." 39

—*verdict:* " . . . with a sudden unknitting of his brow and with beaming eyes, he put out his hand and said abruptly, 'Let us shake hands: you are a musician.' " 39

—*ceremonious:* "Thereupon Klesmer bowed round to the three sisters more grandly than they had ever been bowed to before. Altogether it was an amusing picture—the little room with so much of its diagonal taken up in Klesmer's magnificent bend to the small feminine figures like images a little less than life-size, the grave **Holbein** faces on the walls, as many as were not otherwise occupied, looking hard at this stranger who by his face seemed a dignified contemporary of their own, but whose garments seemed a deplorable mockery of the human form." 39

Lapidoth. "Once a handsome face, with bright colour, it was now sallow and deep-lined, and had that peculiar impress of impudent suavity which comes from courting favour while accepting disrespect. He was lightly made and active, with something of youth about him which made the signs of age seem a disguise; and in reality he was hardly fifty-seven. His dress was shabby, as when she had seen him before." 62

—*contrast:* "The figure of **Mirah**, with her beauty set off by the quiet, careful dress of an English lady, made a strange pendant to this shabby, foreign-looking, eager, and gesticulating man, who withal had an ineffaceable jauntiness of air, perhaps due to the bushy curls of his grizzled hair, the smallness of his hands and feet, and his light walk." 62

—*an inscription:* "The father read it, and had a quick vision of his marriage day, and the bright, unblamed young fellow he was in that time; teaching many things, but expecting by-and-by to get money more easily by writing; and very fond of his beautiful bride **Sara**—crying when she expected him to cry, and reflecting every phase of her feeling with mimetic susceptibility. Lapidoth had travelled a long way from that young self, and thought of all that this inscription signified with an unemotional memory, which was like the ocular perception of a touch to one who has lost the sense of touch, or like morsels on an untasting palate, having shape and grain, but no flavour." 62

—*gambler:* "[He was] ruled by the possibility of staking something in play or betting which presented itself with the handling of any sum beyond the price of staying actual hunger, and left no care for alternative prospects or resolutions. Until he had lost everything he never considered whether he would apply to **Mirah** again or whether he would brave his son's presence." 66

—*self-delusive:* "Lapidoth counted on the fascination of his cleverness—an old habit of mind which early experience had sanctioned; and it is not only women who are unaware of their diminished charm, or imagine that they can feign not to be worn out." 66

—*callous:* "This haggard son, speaking as from a sepulchre, had the incongruity which selfish levity learns to see in suffering and death, until the unrelenting pincers of disease clutch its own flesh. Whatever preaching he might deliver must be taken for a matter of course, as a man finding shelter from hail in an open cathedral might take a little religious howling that happened to be going on there.

"Lapidoth was not born with this sort of callousness: he had achieved it." 66

—*castigated:* "As **Ezra** ended, Lapidoth threw himself into a chair and cried like a woman, burying his face against the table—and yet, strangely, while this hysterical crying was an inevitable reaction in him under the stress of his son's words, it was also a conscious resource in a difficulty; just as in early life, when he was a bright-faced curly young man, he had been used to avail himself of this subtly-poised physical susceptibility to turn the edge of resentment or disapprobation." 66

—*ingratiating:* "He was behaving with much amiability, and trying in all ways at his command to get himself into easy domestication with his children—entering into **Mirah**'s music, showing himself docile about smoking, which **Mrs Adam** could not tolerate in her parlour, and walking out in the square with his German pipe and the tobacco with which Mirah supplied him." 67

—*watching for a chance:* "The imperious gambling desire within him, which carried on its activity through every other occupation, and made a continuous web of imagination that held all else in its meshes, would hardly have been under the control of a protracted purpose, if he had been able to lay his hand on any sum worth capturing . . . Lapidoth felt himself under an irritating completeness of supply in kind as in a lunatic asylum where everything was made safe against him." 68

—theft: " . . . the imaginary action of taking the ring which kept repeating itself like an inward tune, sank into a rejected idea. He satisfied his urgent longing by resolving to go below . . . by no distinct change of resolution, rather by a dominance of desire, like the thirst of the drunkard—it so happened that in passing the table his fingers fell noiselessly on the ring, and he found himself in the passage with the ring in his hand. It followed that he put on his hat and quitted the house. . . . and before he was out of the square his sense of haste had concentrated itself on selling the ring and getting on shipboard." 68

Thomas Cranmer Lush, "a middle-aged man with dark full face and fat hands, who seemed to be on the easiest terms with both [**Klesmer** and **Grandcourt**], and presently led the way in joining the Arrowpoints, whose acquaintance had already been made by both him and Grandcourt. Who this stranger was [**Gwendolen**] did not care much to know . . . . " 11 (28)

—dislikable: "[**Gwendolen**] was subject to physical antipathies, and Mr Lush's prominent eyes, fat though not clumsy figure, and strong black grey-besprinkled hair of frizzy thickness, which, with the rest of his prosperous person, was enviable to many, created one of the strongest of her antipathies." 11

—sinecure: "Lush, being a man of some ability, had not known **Grandcourt** for fifteen years without learning what sort of measures were useless with him, though what sort might be useful remained often dubious. In the beginning of his career he held a fellowship, and was near taking orders for the sake of a college living, but not being fond of that prospect accepted instead the office of travelling companion to a marquess, and afterwards to young Grandcourt, who had lost his father early, and who found Lush so convenient that he had allowed him to become prime minister in all his more personal affairs. The habit of fifteen years had made Grandcourt more and more in need of Lush's handiness, and Lush more and more in need of the lazy luxury to which his transactions on behalf of Grandcourt made no interruption worth reckoning." 12

—kickable: "I cannot say that the same lengthened habit had intensified **Grandcourt**'s want of respect for his companion since that want had been absolute from the beginning, but it had confirmed his sense that he might kick Lush if he chose—only he never did choose to kick any animal, because the act of kicking is a compromising attitude . . . . " 12

—softened: "But what son of a vicar who has stinted his wife and daughters of calico in order to send his male offspring to Oxford, can keep an independent spirit when he is bent on dining with high discrimination, riding good horses, living generally in the most luxuriant honey-blossomed clover—and all without working?" 12

—complacent: "Since in his own opinion he had never done a bad action, it did not seem necessary to consider whether he should be likely to commit one if his love of ease required it. Lush's love of ease was well satisfied at present, and if his puddings were rolled towards him in the dust, he took the inside bits and found them relishing." 12

—annoyed: "This morning, for example, though he had encountered more annoyance than usual, he went to his private sitting-room and played a good hour on the violoncello." 12

—policy: "It was Lush's policy and inclination to gratify everybody when he had no reason to the contrary; and the baronet always treated him well, as

one of those easy-handled personages who, frequenting the society of gentlemen, without being exactly gentlemen themselves, can be the more serviceable, like the second-best articles of our wardrobe, which we use with a comfortable freedom from anxiety." 25

—sensitive: "He wished for himself what he felt to be good, and was not conscious of wishing harm to any one else; unless perhaps it were just now a little harm to the inconvenient and impertinent **Gwendolen**. But the easiest-humoured amateur of luxury and music, the toad-eater the least liable to nausea, must be expected to have his susceptibilities. And Mr Lush was accustomed to be treated by the world in general as an apt, agreeable fellow: he had not made up his mind to be insulted by more than one person." 25

—dismissal: " 'I do *not* like Mr Lush's company.'

" 'You shall not have it. I'll get rid of him.'

" 'You are not fond of him yourself?'

" 'Not in the least. I let him hang on me because he has always been a poor devil,' said **Grandcourt**, in an *adagio* of utter indifference. 'They got him to travel with me when I was a lad. He was always that coarse-haired kind of brute—a sort of cross between a hog and a dilettante.' " 27

—change coming: "He might easily cause **Grandcourt** a great deal of annoyance, but it would be to his own injury, and to create annoyance was not a motive with him . . . . It was nothing new that Grandcourt should show a perverse wilfulness, yet in his freak about this girl he struck Lush rather newly as something like a man who was *fey*—led on by an ominous fatality; and that one born to his fortune should make a worse business of his life than was necessary, seemed really pitiable." 28

—equable: "He had only the small movements of gratified self-loving resentment in discerning that this marriage fulfilled his own foresight in not being as satisfactory as the supercilious young lady had expected it to be, and as **Grandcourt** wished to feign that it was. He had no persistent spite much stronger than what gives the seasoning of ordinary scandal to those who repeat it and exaggerate it by their conjectures. With no active compassion or goodwill, he had just as little active malevolence, being chiefly occupied in liking his particular pleasures, and not disliking anything but what hindered those pleasures—everything else ranking with the last murder and the last *opera buffa*, under the head of things to talk about." 48

Hans Meyrick, "a youth who had come as an exhibitioner from Christ's Hospital, and had eccentricities enough for a **Charles Lamb**." 16

—characteristics: "Only to look at his pinched features and blond hair hanging over his collar reminded one of pale quaint heads by early German painters; and when this faint colouring was lit up by a joke, there came sudden creases about the mouth and eyes which might have been moulded by the soul of an aged humorist. . . . Hans Meyrick—he had been daringly christened after **Holbein**—felt himself the pillar, or rather the knotted and twisted trunk, round which these feeble climbing plants [his mother and three sisters] must cling. There was no want of ability or of honest well-meaning affection to make the prop trustworthy: the ease and quickness with which he studied might serve him to win prizes at Cambridge . . . . The only danger was, that the incalculable tendencies in him might be fatally timed, and that his good intentions might be frustrated by some act which was not due to habit but to capricious, scattered impulses. He could not be said to have any

one bad habit; yet at longer or shorter intervals he had fits of impish recklessness, and did things that would have made the worst habits." 16

—*accident-prone:* "Hans was made for mishaps: his very limbs seemed more breakable than other people's—his eyes more of a resort for uninvited flies and other irritating guests." 32

—*back from Rome:* " . . . the blond Hans in his weird youth as the presiding genius of the littered place—his hair longer than of old, his face more whimsically creased, and his high voice as usual getting higher under the excitement of rapid talk." 37

—*autobiographical:* " 'Since I got into the scrape of being born, everything I have liked best has been a scrape either for myself or somebody else. Everything I have taken to heartily has somehow turned into a scrape. My painting is the last scrape; and I shall be all my life getting out of it. You think now I shall get into a scrape at home. No; I am regenerate. You think I must be over head and ears in love with **Mirah**. Quite right; so I am. But you think I shall scream and plunge and spoil everything. There you are mistaken—excusably, but tremendously mistaken. I have undergone baptism by immersion. Awe takes care of me.' " 37

—*light-hearted:* " 'I don't found my romantic hopes on a woman's sentiments,' said Hans, perversely inclined to be the merrier when he was addressed with gravity. 'I go to science and philosophy for my romance. Nature designed **Mirah** to fall in love with me. The amalgamation of races demands it—the mitigation of human ugliness demands it—the affinity of contrasts assures it. I am the utmost contrast to Mirah—a bleached Christian, who can't sing two notes in tune. Who has a chance against me?' " 37

—*reappraised:* ". . . what Hans called his hope now seemed to **Deronda**, not a mischievous unreasonableness which roused his indignation, but an unusually persistent bird-dance of an extravagant fancy; and he would have felt quite able to pity any consequent suffering of his friend's, if he had believed in the suffering as probable. But some of [his] busy thought . . . was given to the argument that Hans Meyrick's nature was not one in which love could strike the deep roots that turn disappointment into sorrow: it was too restless, too readily excitable by novelty, too ready to turn itself into imaginative material, and wear its grief as a fantastic costume." 52

—*observer:* " . . . many fragments of observation and gradually gathered knowledge . . . convinced him not only that **Mrs Grandcourt** had a passion for **Deronda**, but also, notwithstanding his friend's austere self-repression, that Deronda's susceptibility about her was the sign of concealed love. Some men, having such a conviction, would have avoided allusions that could have roused that susceptibility; but Hans's talk naturally fluttered towards mischief, and he was given to a form of experiment on live animals which consisted in irritating his friends playfully. His experiments had ended in satisfying him that what he thought likely was true." 61

—*silenced:* " . . . he longed that his speechless companionship should be eloquent in a tender, penitent sympathy which is an admissible form of wooing a bruised heart." 61

—*confession:* " 'I've been smoking opium. I always meant to do it some time or other, to try how much bliss could be got by it; and having found myself just now rather out of other bliss, I thought it judicious to seize the opportunity. But I pledge you my word I shall never tap a cask of that bliss again. It disagrees with my constitution.' " 67

—*cat out of the bag:* " 'Our friendship—my friendship—can't bear the strain of behaving to you like an ungrateful dastard and grudging you your happiness. For you *are* the happiest dog in the world. If **Mirah** loves anybody better than her brother, *you are the man.'* " 67

—*calmer, but:* "Hans appeared to have recovered his vivacity, but **Deronda** detected some feigning in it, as we detect the artificiality of a lady's bloom from its being a little too high-toned and steadily persistent (a 'Fluctuating Rouge' not have yet appeared among the advertisements). Also, with all his grateful friendship and admiration for Deronda, Hans could not help a certain irritation against him such as extremely incautious, open natures are apt to feel when the breaking of a friend's reserve discloses a state of things not merely unsuspected but the reverse of what had been hoped and ingeniously conjectured." 69

Mrs Meyrick "had three girls to educate and maintain on a meagre annuity." 16

—*and family:* " . . . they were fastidious in some points, and could not believe that the manners of ladies in the fashionable world were so full of coarse selfishness, petty quarrelling, and slang as they are represented to be in what are called literary photographs. The Meyricks had their little oddities, streaks of eccentricity from the mother's blood as well as the father's, their minds being like mediaeval houses with unexpected recesses and openings from this into that, flights of steps and sudden outlooks.

"But mother and daughters were all united by a triple bond—family love; admiration for the finest work, the best action; and habitual industry." 18

"They were all alike small, and so in due proportion with their miniature rooms." 18

—*characteristics:* "Mrs Meyrick was reading aloud from a French book: she was a lively little woman, half French, half Scotch, with a pretty articulateness of speech that seemed to make daylight in her hearer's understanding. Though she was not yet fifty, her rippling hair, covered by a quakerish net cap, was chiefly grey, but her eyebrows were brown as the bright eyes below them; her black dress, almost like a priest's cassock with its row of buttons, suited a neat figure hardly five feet high." 18

—*newspaper:* "She was a great reader of news, from the widest-reaching politics to the list of marriages; the latter, she said, giving her the pleasant sense of finishing the fashionable novels without having read them, and seeing the heroes and heroines happy without knowing what poor creatures they were." 61

Others

Mr Arrowpoint, "a host and a perfect gentleman, of whom no one had anything to say but that he had married **Miss Cuttler**, and imported the best cigars . . . . " 5 *See Topicon* A:Parents—*thunderstruck*

Mrs Arrowpoint. *See Topicon* A:Parents—*thunderstruck*

—*offended:* " . . . though not a splenetic or vindictive woman, [she] had her susceptibilities . . . . It was occasionally recalled that she had been the heiress of a fortune gained by some moist or dry business in the city, in order fully to account for her having a squat figure, a harsh parrot-like voice, and a systematically high head-dress; and since these points made her externally rather ridiculous, it appeared to many only natural that she should have what are called literary tendencies . . . .

"**Gwendolen**, who had a keen sense of absurdity in others . . . it followed in her mind, unreflectingly, that because Mrs Arrowpoint was ridiculous she was also likely to be wanting in penetration . . . . " 5

Lord Brackenshaw, "a middle-aged peer of aristocratic seediness in stained pink, with easy-going manners which would have made the threatened Deluge seem of no consequence." 7

—*at his meet:* " 'For my part, I am not magnanimous; I should like to win. But, confound it! I never have the chance now. I'm getting old and idle. The young ones beat me. As old **Nestor** says—the gods don't give us everything at one time. I was a young fellow once, and now I am getting an old and wise one. Old, at any rate; which is a gift that comes to everybody if they live long enough, so it raises no jealousy.' " 10

—*at his meal:* "And every year the amiable Lord Brackenshaw, who was something of a *gourmet,* mentioned **Byron**'s opinion that a woman should never be seen eating—introducing it with a confidential—'The fact is'—as if he were for the first time admitting his concurrence in that sentiment of the refined poet." 11

Bult, "an esteemed party man who, rather neutral in private life, had strong opinions concerning the districts of the Niger, was much at home also in the Brazils, spoke with decision of affairs in the South Seas, was studious of his Parliamentary and itinerant speeches, and had the general solidity and suffusive pinkness of a healthy Briton on the central table-land of life. **Catherine**, aware of a tacit understanding that he was an undeniable husband for an heiress, had nothing to say against him but that he was thoroughly tiresome to her. Mr Bult was amiably confident, and had no idea that his insensibility to counterpoint could ever be reckoned against him. **Klesmer** he hardly regarded in the light of a serious human being who ought to have a vote; and he did not mind Miss Arrowpoint's addiction to music any more than her probable expenses in antique lace." 22

Daniel Charisi, physician; adamant Jew and father of **Leonora**. *See* **Princess Leonora Halm-Eberstein** SR

—*daughter's view:* " 'I tell you, he never thought of his daughter except as an instrument. Because I had wants outside his purpose, I was to be put in a frame and tortured . . . . I have after all been the instrument my father wanted. —"I desire a grandson who shall have a true Jewish heart. Every Jew should rear his family as if he hoped that a Deliverer might spring from it." ' " 53

—*his way:* " 'He said, "Let us bind ourselves with duty, as if we were sons of the same mother." That was his bent from first to last—as he said, to fortify his soul with bonds. It was a saying of his, "Let us bind love with duty; for duty is the love of law; and law is the nature of the Eternal." ' " 60

—*his will:* " 'He had an iron will in his face: it braced up everybody about him. When he was quite young he had already got one deep upright line in his brow . . . . Daniel Charisi used to say, "Better a wrong will than a wavering; better a steadfast enemy than an uncertain friend; better a false belief than no belief at all." What he despised most was indifference.' " 60

—*his priority:* " 'What he used to insist on was that the strength and wealth of mankind depended on the balance of separateness and communication, and he was bitterly against our people losing themselves among the Gentiles; "It's no better," said he, "than the many sorts of grain going back from their variety into sameness." He mingled all sorts of learning; and in that he was like our Arabic writers in the golden time. We studied together, but he went beyond me. Though we were bosom friends, and he poured himself out to me, we were as different as the inside and the outside of the bowl. I stood up for no notions of my own. I took Charisi's sayings as I took the shape of the trees: they were there, not to be disputed about. It came to the same thing in both of us: we were both faithful Jews, thankful not to be Gentiles.' " 60

Mrs Charisi. " 'My mother was English—a Jewess of Portuguese descent. My father married her in England.' " 51

Addy Cohen, "The young woman answering to 'Addy'—a sort of paraquet [parrakeet] in a bright blue dress, with coral necklace and earrings, her hair set up in a huge bush—looked as complacently lively and unrefined as her husband . . . . " 33

—*dressed for the Sabbath:* "Young Mrs Cohen was clad in red and black, with a string of large artificial pearls wound round and round her neck: the baby lay asleep in the cradle under a scarlet counterpane . . . . " 34

Adelaide Rebekah Cohen. " 'And will you give me a kiss this evening?' said **Deronda**, with a hand on each of her little brown shoulders.

"Adelaide Rebekah (her miniature crinoline and monumental features corresponded with the combination of her names) immediately put up her lips to pay the kiss in advance . . . . " 33

—*dressed for the Sabbath,* "in braided amber . . . . " 34

—*at table:* "[She] stood on the chair with her whole length exhibited in her amber-coloured garment, her little Jewish nose lengthened by compression of the lip in the effort to make a suitable appearance." 34

Eugenie Esther Cohen. "[Her mother carried] a black-eyed little one, its head already well covered with black curls, and deposited it on the counter, from which station it looked round with even more than the usual intelligence of babies." 33

Ezra Cohen, "whose flourishing face glistening on the way to fatness was hanging over the counter in negotiation with some one . . . . " 33

—*pawn-broker proud:* "If an amiable self-satisfaction is the mark of earthly bliss, **Solomon** in all his glory was a pitiable mortal compared with Mr Cohen—clearly one of those persons who, being in excellent spirits about themselves, are willing to cheer strangers by letting them know it . . . . **Deronda**, not in a cheerful mood, was rashly pronouncing this Ezra Cohen to be the most unpoetic Jew he had ever met with in books or life: his phraseology was as little as possible like that of the Old Testament; and no shadow of a Suffering Race distinguished his vulgarity of soul from that of a prosperous pink-and-white huckster of the purest English lineage." 33

—no martyr: "Ezra Cohen was not clad in the sublime pathos of the martyr, and his taste for money-getting seemed to be favoured with that success which has been the most exasperating difference in the greed of Jews during all the ages of their dispersion. This Jeshurun of a pawnbroker was not a symbol of the great Jewish tragedy; and yet was there not something typical in the fact that a life like **Mordecai**'s—a frail incorporation of the national consciousness, breathing with difficult breath—was nested in the self-gratulating ignorant prosperity of the Cohens?" 42

Jacob Alexander Cohen, "a robust boy of six and a younger girl, both with black eyes and black-ringed hair—looking more Semitic than their parents as the puppy lions show the spots of far-off progenitors . . . the boy had run forward into the shop with an energetic stamp, and setting himself about four feet from Deronda, with his hands in the pockets of his miniature knicker-bockers, looked at him with a precocious air of survey." 33.

—project: " 'Have you got a knife?' says Jacob, coming closer. His small voice was hoarse in its glibness, as if it belonged to an aged commercial soul, fatigued with bargaining through many generations." 33

—listening: " . . . here the marvellous Jacob, whose *physique* supported a precocity that would have shattered a Gentile of his years . . . . " 33

—dressed for the Sabbath, "in black velveteen with scarlet stockings." 34

—friend: "During that time little Jacob had advanced into knickerbockers, and into that quickness of apprehension which has been already made manifest in relation to hardware and exchange. He had also advanced in attachment to **Mordecai**, regarding him as an inferior, but liking him none the worse, and taking his helpful cleverness as he might have taken the services of an enslaved Djinn." 38

—frightened: " . . . the sunken dark eyes and hoarse accents close to him, the thin grappling fingers, shook Jacob's little frame into awe, and while **Mordecai** was speaking he stood trembling with a sense that the house was tumbling in and they were not going to have dinner any more. But when the terrible speech had ended and the pinch was relaxed, the shock resolved itself into tears; Jacob lifted up his small patriarchal countenance and wept aloud . . . Jacob, feeling the danger wellnigh over, howled at ease, beginning to imitate his own performance and improve upon it—a sort of transition from impulse into art often observable." 38

—under instruction: "It is worth while [reports **Hans**] to catch our prophet's expression when he has that remarkable type of young Israel on his knee, and pours forth some Semitic inspiration with a sublime look of melancholy patience and devoutness. Sometimes it occurs to Jacob that Hebrew will be more edifying to him if he stops his ears with his palms, and imitates the venerable sounds as heard through that muffling medium. When **Mordecai** gently draws down the little fists and holds them fast, Jacob's features all take on an extraordinary activity, very much as if he were walking through a menagerie and trying to imitate every animal in turn, succeeding best with the owl and the peccary." 52

—age: " . . . his age usually strikes one as being like the Israeltish garments in the desert, perhaps near forty, yet with an air of recent production.

. . . Judging from this modern Jacob at the age of six, my astonishment is that his race has not bought us all up long ago, and pocketed our feebler generations in the form of stock and scrip, as so much slave property." 52

Mrs Cohen. "[He] was not soothed when he saw a vigorous woman beyond fifty enter and approach to serve him. Not that there was anything very repulsive about her: the worst that could be said was that she had that look of having made her toilet with little water, and by twilight, which is common to unyouthful people of her class, and of having presumably slept in her large earrings, if not in her rings and necklace." 33

—a question: " 'And you have no daughter?'

"There was an instantaneous change in the mother's face. Her lips closed more firmly, she looked down, swept her hands outward on the counter, and finally turned her back on **Deronda** . . . . . " 33

—dressed for the Sabbath: "The grandmother was arrayed in yellowish brown with a large gold chain in lieu of the necklace, and by this light her yellow face with its darkly-marked eyebrows and framing roll of grey hair looked as handsome as was necessary for picturesque effect." 34

Davilow sisters. "Of the girls, from **Alice** in her sixteenth year to **Isabel** in her tenth, hardly anything could be said on a first view, but that they were girlish, and that their black dresses were getting shabby." 3

—**Alice**. " 'And I have [given Alice lessons] because you asked me. But I don't see why I should, else. It bores me to death; she is so slow. She has no ear for music, or language, or anything else. It would be much better for her to be ignorant, mamma: it is her *rôle,* she would do it well.'

" 'That is a hard thing to say of your poor sister, **Gwendolen**, who is so good to you, and waits on you hand and foot.' " 3

—**Isabel**, "a plain and altogether inconvenient child with an alarming memory . . . . " 3

—greeted: "Then, of course, notice had to be taken of the four other girls whom **Gwendolen** had always felt to be superfluous: all of a girlish average that made four units utterly unimportant, and yet from her earliest days an obtrusive influential fact in her life. She was conscious of having been much kinder to them than could have been expected. And it was evident to her that her uncle and aunt also felt it a pity there were so many girls:—what rational persons could feel otherwise, except poor mamma, who never would see how **Alice** set up her shoulders and lifted her eyebrows till she had no forehead left, how **Bertha** and **Fanny** whispered and tittered together about everything, or how **Isabel** was always listening and staring and forgetting where she was, and treading on the toes of her suffering elders?" 3

—newly poor: "Behind, of course, were the sad faces of the four superfluous girls, each, poor thing—like those other many thousand sisters of us all—having her peculiar world which was of no importance to any one else, but all of them feeling **Gwendolen**'s presence to be somehow a relenting of misfortune: where Gwendolen was, something interesting would happen; even her hurried submission to their kisses, and 'Now go away, girls,' carried the sort of comfort which all weakness finds in decision and authoritativeness." 21

—present: " . . . the four girls, **Alice** with the high shoulders, **Bertha** and **Fanny** the whisperers, and **Isabel** the listener, were all present on this family occasion . . . . " 28

—time has passed: " . . . the four girls had bloomed out a little from being less in the shade . . . . " 58

Captain Davilow. "This [having an establishment], rather mysteriously to **Gwendolen**, appeared suddenly possible on the death of her step-father Captain Davilow, who had for the last nine years joined his family only in a brief and fitful manner, enough to reconcile them to his long absences, but she cared much more for the fact than for the explanation. All her prospects had become more agreeable in consequence." 3

—family memories: "**Gwendolen**, immediately thinking of the unlovable step-father whom she had been acquainted with the greater part of her life while her frocks were short, said—

" 'Why did you marry again, mamma? It would have been nicer if you had not.'

"**Mrs Davilow** coloured deeply, a slight convulsive movement passed over her face, and straightway shutting up the memorials she said, with a violence quite unusual in her—

" 'You have no feeling, child!'

"Gwendolen, who was fond of her mamma, felt hurt and ashamed, and had never since dared to ask a question about her father." 3

—mystery: " 'I have made up my mind [said **Gwendolyn**] not to let other people interfere with me as they have done.' " 3

—bad choice: " . . . **Mrs Davilow**, conscious that she had always been seen under a cloud as poor dear **Fanny**, who had made a sad blunder with her second marriage . . . . " 3

—offense (abuse?): "[**Gwendolen**] was the eldest daughter, towards whom her mamma had always been in an apologetic state of mind for the evils brought on her by a step-father . . . . " 4

—thief: " 'All my best ornaments were taken from me long ago.'

"**Mrs Davilow** coloured. She usually avoided any reference to such facts about **Gwendolen**'s step-father as that he had carried off his wife's jewellery and disposed of it." 24

Mrs Nancy Gascoigne bore a family likeness to her sister [Mrs Davilow]. But she was darker and slighter, her face was unworn by grief, her movements were less languid, her expression more alert and critical as that of a rector's wife bound to exert a beneficent authority. Their closest resemblance lay in a non-resistant disposition, inclined to imitation and obedience; but this, owing to the difference in their circumstances, had led them to very different issues.

"The younger sister had been indiscreet, or at least unfortunate in her marriages; the elder believed herself the most enviable of wives, and her pliancy had ended in her sometimes taking shapes of surprising definiteness. Many of her opinions, such as those on church government and the character of **Archbishop Laud**, seemed too decided under every alteration to have been arrived at otherwise than by a wifely receptiveness." ¶3

Glasher children. "The children were lovely—a dark-haired girl of six or more, a fairer boy of five." 13

"The handsome little fellow was puffing out his cheeks in trying to blow a tiny trumpet which remained dumb. His hat hung backward by a string, and his brown curls caught the sun-rays. He was a cherub." 14

" . . . the children of Gadsmere—**Mrs Glasher**'s four beautiful children, who had dwelt there for about three years." 30

—at home: "The children were all there. The three girls, seated round their mother near the window, were miniature portraits of her—dark-eyed, delicate-featured brunettes with a rich bloom on their cheeks, their little nostrils and eyebrows singularly finished as if they were tiny women, the eldest being barely nine. The boy [**Henleigh**] was seated on the carpet at some distance, bending his blond head over the animals from a Noah's ark, admonishing them separately in a voice of threatening command, and occasionally licking the spotted ones to see if the colours would hold. **Josephine**, the eldest, was having her French lesson; and the others, with their dolls on their laps, sat demurely enough for images of the Madonna." 30

"He acquitted himself with all the advantage of a man whose grace of bearing has long been moulded on an experience of boredom—nursed the little **Antonia**, who sat with her hands crossed and eyes upturned to his bald head, which struck her as worthy of observation . . . . It was only the two eldest girls who had known him as a continual presence . . . . " 30

Sara Lapidoth. " 'Oh, I believe the mother's good,' said Mrs Meyrick, with rapid decisiveness, 'or was good . . . . A good woman, you may depend: you may know it by the scoundrel the father is. Where did the child get her goodness from? Wheaten flour has to be accounted for.' " 20

—remembered: " 'I think my life began with waking up and loving my mother's face: it was so near to me, and her arms were round me, and she sang to me. One hymn she sang so often, so often: and then she taught me to sing it with her: it was the first I ever sang. They were always Hebrew hymns she sang; and because I never knew the meaning of the words they seemed full of nothing but our love and happiness.' " 20

Lady Louisa Mallinger, the former **Miss Raymond**, "after having had three daughters in quick succession, had remained for eight years till now that she was over forty without producing so much as another girl . . . . " 15

—a little slow: "Lady Mallinger felt apologetically about herself as a woman who had produced nothing but daughters in a case where sons were required, and hence regarded the apparent contradictions of the world as probably due to the weakness of her own understanding." 20

—at breakfast: "[She] had not been listening, her mind having been taken up with her first sips of coffee, the objectionable cuff of her sleeve, and the necessity of carrying **Theresa** to the dentist—innocent and partly laudable preoccupations, as the gentle lady's usually were. Should her appearance be inquired after, let it be said that she had reddish blond hair (the hair of the period), a small Roman nose, rather prominent blue eyes and delicate eyelids, with a figure which her thinner friends called fat, her hands showing curves and dimples like a magnified baby's." 28

—entertaining: "Lady Mallinger, with fair matronly roundness and mildly prominent blue eyes, moved about in her black velvet, carrying a tiny white dog on her arm as a sort of finish to her costume . . . . " 35

Meyrick sisters. "The candles were on a table apart for **Kate**, who was drawing illustrations for a publisher; the lamp was not only for the reader but for **Amy** and **Mab**, who were embroidering satin cushions for 'the great world.' " 18

—the group: "The daughters were to match the mother, except that **Mab** had **Hans**'s light hair and complexion, with a bossy irregular brow and other

quaintnesses that reminded one of him. Everything about them was compact, from the firm coils of their hair, fastened back *à la Chinoise,* to their grey skirts in puritan nonconformity with the fashion, which at that time would have demanded that four feminine circumferences should fill all the free space in the front parlour. All four, if they had been wax-work, might have been packed easily in a fashionable lady's travelling trunk. Their faces seemed full of speech, as if their minds had been shelled, after the manner of horse-chestnuts, and become brightly visible." 18

—a welcome: " 'We will take care of you—we will comfort you—we will love you,' cried **Mab**, no longer able to restrain herself, and taking [**Mirah**'s] small right hand caressingly between both her own." 18

—worship: " '**Kate** burns a pastille before his portrait every day,' said **Mab**. 'And I carry his signature in a little black-silk bag round my neck to keep off the cramp. And **Amy** says the multiplication-table in his name. We must all do something extra in honour of him, now he has brought you to us.' " 20

—bursting out: " 'But everything in the world must come to an end some time. We must bear to think of that,' said **Mab**, unable to hold her peace on this point. She had already suffered from a bondage of tongue which threatened to become severe if **Mirah** were to be too much indulged in this inconvenient susceptibility to innocent remarks.

"**Deronda** smiled at the irregular, blond face, brought into strange contrast by the side of Mirah's . . . . " 32

—spotted: "But imagine **Mab**'s feeling when, suddenly fixing his eyes on her, he said decisively, 'That young lady is musical, I see!' She was a mere blush and sense of scorching.

" 'Yes,' said **Mirah** on her behalf. 'And she has a touch.'

" 'Oh, please, Mirah—a scramble, not a touch,' said Mab, in anguish, with a horrible fear of what the next thing might be: this dreadfully divining personage —evidently **Satan** in grey trousers—might order her to sit down to the piano, and her heart was like molten wax in the midst of her. But this was cheap payment for her amazed joy when Klesmer said benignantly, turning to **Mrs Meyrick**, 'Will she like to accompany Miss Lapidoth and hear the music on Wednesday?' " 39

Mr Middleton, "the actual curate, was said to be quite an acquisition: it was only a pity he was so soon to leave." 3

—discussed: " '[**Rex**]is cleverer than Mr Middleton, and everybody but you calls Mr Middleton clever' [said **Anna**].

" 'So he may be in a dark-lantern sort of way. But he *is* a stick. If he had to say, "Perdition catch my soul, but I do love her," he would say it in just the same tone as, "Here endeth the second lesson." ' " 6

" 'For no one ever thought of laughing at Mr Middleton before you. Every one said he was nice-looking, and his manners perfect. I am sure I have always been frightened at him because of his learning and his square-cut coat, and his being a nephew of the bishops and all that.' " 6

—touched: "**Miss Gwendolen**, quite aware that she was adored by this unexceptionable young clergyman with pale whiskers and square-cut collar, felt nothing more on the subject than that she had no objection to be adored: she turned her eyes on him with calm mercilessness . . . . " 6

Leonora Morteira. " 'My mother died [said the **Princess**] when I was eight years old, and then my father allowed me to be continually with my aunt Leonora and be taught under her eyes, as if he had not minded the danger of her encouraging my wish to be a singer, as she had been.' " 51

Lady Pentreath. " 'It's a sort of troubadour story,' said Lady Pentreath, an easy, deep-voiced old lady; 'I'm glad to find a little romance left among us. I think our young people now are getting too worldly wise.' " 35

—dancing: " 'Mr **Deronda**, you are the youngest man; I mean to dance with you. Nobody is old enough to make a good pair with me. I must have a contrast.' And the contrast certainly set off the old lady to the utmost. She was one of those women who are never handsome till they are old, and she had the wisdom to embrace the beauty of age as early as possible. What might have seemed harshness in her features when she was young, had turned now into a satisfactory strength of form and expression which defied wrinkles, and was set off by a crown of white hair; her well-built figure was well covered with black drapery, her ears and neck comfortably caressed with lace, showing none of those withered spaces which one would think it a pitiable condition of poverty to expose. She glided along gracefully enough, her dark eyes still with a mischievous smile in them as she observed the company. Her partner's young richness of tint against the flattened hues and rougher forms of her aged head had an effect something like that of a fine flower against a lichenous branch." 36

The "Philosophers" 42

" 'They are few—like the cedars of Lebanon—poor men given to thought.'

Buchan, "the saddler, was Scotch."

" 'Ay,' said Buchan, in a rapid thin Scotch tone which was like the letting in of a little cool air on the conversation . . . 'with all deference, I would beg t'observe that we have got to examine the nature of changes before we have a warrant to call them progress . . . . ' "

Croop, "the dark-eyed shoemaker, was probably more Celtic than he knew."

Gideon, "the optical instrument maker, was a Jew of the red-haired, generous-featured type easily passing for Englishmen of unusually cordial manners . . . . "

" 'I'm a rational Jew myself. I stand by my people as a sort of family relations, and I am for keeping up our worship in a rational way . . . . But I am for getting rid of all our superstitions and exclusiveness. There's no reason now why we shouldn't melt gradually into the populations we live among . . . . And I'm for the old maxim, "A man's country is where he's well off." ' "

—Jews and Palestine: " 'As to the connection of our race with Palestine, it has been perverted by superstition till it's as demoralizing as the old poor-law. The raff and scum go there to be maintained like able-bodied paupers, and to be taken special care of by the angel **Gabriel** when they die. It's no use fighting against facts We must look where they point; that's what I call rationality. The most learned and liberal men among us who are attached to our religion are for clearing our liturgy of all such notions as a literal fulfilment of the prophecies about restoration, and so on. Prune it of a few useless rites and literal interpretations of that sort, and our religion is the simplest of all religions, and makes no barrier, but a union, between us and the rest of the world.' "

Goodwin, "wood-inlayer . . . well-built, open-faced, pleasant-voiced . . . . "

Lilly, "the pale, neat-faced copying clerk, whose light-brown hair was set up in a small parallelogram above his well-filled forehead, and whose shirt, taken with an otherwise seedy costume, had a freshness that might be called insular, and perhaps even something narrower."

—the Jews: " 'Well, whatever the Jews contributed at one time, they are a stand-still people,' said Lilly. 'They are the type of obstinate adherence to the superannuated. They may show good abilities when they take up liberal ideas, but as a race they have no development in them.' "

Marrables, "the florid laboratory assistant . . . . "

Miller, "a man in a pepper-and-salt dress, with blond hair, short nose, broad forehead and general breadth, who, holding his pipe slightly uplifted in the left hand, and beating his knee with the right, was just finishing a quotation from **Shelley** . . . an exceptional second-hand bookseller who knew the insides of books, had at least grandparents who called themselves German, and possibly far-away ancestors who denied themselves to be Jews . . . . "

Pash, "the watchmaker, was a small, dark, vivacious, triple-baked Jew."

—nationality: " ' . . . with us in Europe the sentiment of nationality is destined to die out. It will last a little longer in the quarters where oppression lasts, but nowhere else. The whole current of progress is setting against it.' "

Minor Figures

Mrs Adam. "When Mrs Adam opened the door to let in the father, she could not help casting a look at the group, and after glancing from the younger man to the elder, said to herself as she closed the door, 'Father, sure enough.' " 66

Ephraim Alcharisi (formerly **Charisi**). " 'Your father was different. Unlike me—all lovingness and affection. I knew I could rule him; and I made him secretly promise me, before I married him, that he would put no hindrance in the way of my being an artist. My father was on his deathbed when we were married: from the first he had fixed his mind on my marrying my cousin Ephraim.' " 51

" ' . . . he made it the labour of his life to devote himself to me: wound up his money-changing and banking, and lived to wait upon me—he went against his conscience for me. As I loved the life of my art, so he loved me.' " 51

Madame Alcharisi. " 'I was the Alcharisi you have heard of [said the **Princess**]: the name had magic wherever it was carried. Men courted me. **Sir Hugo Mallinger** was one who wished to marry me. He was madly in love with me.' " 51

Amaryllis. "And in spite of [the Rector's] practical ability, some of his experience had petrified into maxims and quotations. Amaryllis fleeing desired that her hiding-place should be known; and that love will find out the way 'over the mountain and over the wave' may be said without hyerbole in this age of steam. **Gwendolen**, he conceived, was an Amaryllis of excellent sense but coquettish daring; the question was whether she had dared too much." 15

Astorga. " 'I shall introduce you to Astorga: he is the foster-father of good singing and will give you advice.' " 39

Banks, "the bailiff, with whom [**Daniel**] had ridden about the farms on his pony . . . there came back the recollection of a day some years before when he was drinking **Mrs Banks**'s whey, and Banks said to his wife with a wink and a cunning laugh, 'He features the mother, eh?' " 16

Boatman. "[**Deronda**] stayed behind to hear from the remaining boatman that her husband had gone down irrecoverably, and that his boat was left floating empty. He and his comrade had heard a cry, had come up in time to see the lady jump in after her husband, and had got her out fast enough to save her from much damage." 55

Boy. " . . . a melancholy little boy, with his knees and calves simply in their natural clothing of epidermis, but for the rest of his person in a fancy dress. He alone had his face turned towards the doorway, and fixing on it the blank gaze of a bedizened child stationed as a masquerading advertisement on the platform of an itinerant show, stood close behind a **lady** deeply engaged at the roulette-table." 1

Lady Brackenshaw, "a gracious personage who, adorned with two fair little girls and a boy of stout make, sat as lady paramount." 10

Brecon. " '. . . for God's sake don't come out as a superior expensive kind of idiot, like young Brecon, who got a Double First, and has been learning to knit braces ever since.' " 16

Brewitt, " 'the blacksmith, said to me the other day that his 'prentice had no mind to his trade, "and yet, sir," said Brewitt, "what would a young fellow have if he doesn't like the blacksmithing?" ' " 58

Bugle, lady's maid at Offendene.

Rev. Clintock. " 'Who is that with **Gascoigne**?' said the archdeacon, neglecting a discussion of military manœvres on which, as a clergyman, he was naturally appealed to." 5

Clintock the younger, "a hopeful young scholar, who had already suggested some 'not less elegant than ingenious' emendations of Greek texts—said . . . 'By George! who is that girl with the awfully well-set head and jolly figure?' " 5

Count. " 'I now began to feel a horrible dread of this man [said **Mirah**], for he worried me with his attentions, his eyes were always on me: I felt sure that whatever else there might be in his mind towards me, below it all there was scorn for the Jewess and the actress . . . . The Count was neither very young nor very old: his hair and eyes were pale; he was tall and walked heavily, and his face was heavy and grave except when he looked at me. He smiled at me, and his smile went through me with horror; I could not tell why he was so much worse to me than other men.' " 20

Countess and her **gambling neighbour**. "The white bejewelled fingers of an English countess were very near touching a bony, yellow, crab-like hand stretching a bared wrist to clutch a heap of coin—a hand easy to sort with the square, gaunt face, deep-set eyes, grizzled eyebrows, and ill-combed scanty hair which seemed a slight metamorphosis of the vulture. And where else would her ladyship have graciously consented to sit by that dry-lipped feminine figure prematurely old, withered after short bloom like her artificial flowers, holding a shabby velvet reticule before her, and occasionally putting in her mouth the point with which she pricked her card?" 1

Croupier. " 'Faites votre jeu,* mesdames et messieurs,' said the automatic voice of destiny from between the moustache and imperial of the croupier . . . . 'Le jeu de va plus,' said destiny . . . . " 1 [*For one of GE's linguistic accomplishments, this elementary mistake is bewildering: *Faîtes vos jeux* would be the expression when addressing a crowd of players.]

Joel Dagge, "a blacksmith's son who also followed the hounds under disadvantages, namely, on foot . . . on this occasion showed himself that most useful of personages, whose knowledge is of a kind suited to the immediate occasion: he not only knew perfectly well what was the matter with the horse, how far they were both from the nearest public-house and from Pennicote Rectory, and could certify to **Rex** that his shoulder was only a bit out of joint, but also offered experienced surgical aid." 7

"Joel being clearly a low character, it is happily not necessary to say more of him to the refined reader, than that he helped Rex to get home with as little delay as possible." 7

Dowager. " 'For my part I think [**Gwendolyn**] odious,' said a dowager. 'It is wonderful what unpleasant girls get into vogue. Who are these **Langens**? Does anybody know them?' " 1

Dymock. " 'Its only fault is a dark curate with broad shoulder and broad trousers who ought to have gone into the heavy drapery line.' " 69

Juliet Fenn. "It was impossible to be jealous of Juliet Fenn, a girl as middling as mid-day market in everything but her archery and her plainness, in which last she was noticeably like her father: underhung and with receding brow resembling that of the more intelligent fishes." 11

" . . . a young lady whose profile had been so unfavourably decided by circumstances over which she had no control, that **Gwendolen** some months ago had felt it impossible to jealous of her." 35

Fetch, "the beautiful liver-coloured water-spaniel, which sat with its fore-paws firmly planted and its expressive brown face turned upward, watching **Grandcourt** with unshaken constancy . . . . I fear that Fetch was jealous, and wounded that her master gave her no word or look; at last it seemed that she could bear this neglect no longer, and she gently put her large silky paw on her master's leg . . . poor thing, whimpered interruptedly, as if trying to repress that sign of discontent, and at last rested her head beside the appealing paw, looking up with piteous beseeching . . . . But when the amusing anguish burst forth in a howling bark, Grandcourt pushed Fetch down without speaking . . . . Fetch, having begun to wail, found, like others of her sex, that it was not easy to leave off; indeed, the second howl was a louder one, and the third was like unto it." 12

Fraser. "The tutor, an able young Scotchman who acted as **Sir Hugo Mallinger**'s secretary, roused rather unwillingly from his political economy, answered with the clear-cut emphatic chant which makes a truth doubly telling in Scotch utterance—

" 'Their own children were called nephews . . . for the propriety of the thing; because, as you know very well, priests don't marry, and the children were illegitimate.' " 16

Mrs Gadsby. " . . . no lady of good position followed the Wessex hunt: no one but Mrs Gadsby, the yeomanry captain's wife, who had been a kitchen-maid and still spoke like one." 7

Gambler, "a man with the air of an emaciated beau or worn-out libertine, who looked at life through one eye-glass, and held out his hand tremulously when he asked for change. It could surely be no severity of system, but rather some dream of white crows, or the induction that the eighth of the month was lucky, which inspired the fierce yet tottering impulsiveness of his play." 1

Warham Gascoigne, "who was studying for India with a Wanchester 'coach,' having no time to spare, and being generally dismal under a cram of everything except the answers needed at the forthcoming Examination . . . ." 6

"The Rector cherished a fatherly delight, which he allowed to escape him only in moderation. Warham, who had gone to India, he had easily borne parting with . . . . " 58

Colonel Glasher, an Irish officer. "At that early time **Grandcourt** would willingly have paid for the freedom to be won by a divorce; but the husband would not oblige him, not wanting to be married again himself, and not wishing to have his domestic habits printed in evidence." 30

The **Gogoffs**. " 'Why did you ask the Gogoffs? When you write invitations in my name, be good enough to give me a list, instead of bringing down a giantess on me without my knowledge. She spoils the look of the room.' " 12

Hafiz. "The only large thing of its kind in the [**Meyricks**'] room was Hafiz, the Persian cat, comfortably poised on the brown leather back of a chair, and opening his large eyes now and then to see that the lower animals were not in any mischief." 18

" . . . Hafiz, seated a little aloft with large eyes on the alert, regarding the whole scene as an apparatus for supplying his allowance of milk." 52

Lady Flora Hollis "proposed after luncheon, when some of the guests had dispersed, and the sun was sloping towards four o'clock, that the remaining party should make a little exploration." 13

—*curious:* "Lady Flora Hollis, a lively middle-aged woman, well endowed with curiosity, felt a sudden interest in making a round of calls with **Mrs Torrington** . . . . " 15

Italian. "Standing close to [the **Tradesman**'s] chair was a handsome Italian, calm, statuesque, reaching across him to place the first pile of napoleons from a new bagful just brought him by an **envoy** with a scrolled mustache. The pile was in half a minute pushed over to an old bewigged **woman** with eye-glasses pinching her nose. There was a slight gleam, a faint mumbling smile about the lips of the old woman; but the statuesque Italian remained impassive, and—probably secure in an infallible system which placed his foot on the neck of chance—immediately prepared a new pile." 1

Baron Langen, "a gentleman with a white mustache and clipped hair: solid-browed, stiff, and German." 1

" 'A very good furniture picture.' " 1

Baroness Langen. " 'Your baroness is always at the roulette-table,' said **Mackworth**. 'I fancy she has taught the girl to gamble.'

"'Oh, the old woman plays a very sober game; drops a ten-franc piece here and there. The girl is more headlong.' " 1

Mr Lassman. "But it is hard to resign one's self to Mr Lassman's wicked recklessness, which they say was the cause of the failure." 2

" 'You said in your letter it was Mr Lassmann's [*sic*] fault we had lost our money. Has he run away with it all?

" 'No, dear, you don't understand. There were great speculations: he meant to gain. It was all about mines and things of that sort. He risked too much.' " 21

Miss Lawe. " . . . it was rather exasperating to see how **Gwendolen** eclipsed others: how even the handsome Miss Lawe, explained to be the daughter of **Lady Lawe**, looked suddenly broad, heavy, and inanimate . . . . " 5

Joseph Leo. " 'My master at Vienna said, "Don't strain it further: it will never do for the public:—it is gold, but a thread of gold dust." ' " 20

" 'This is Joseph Leo's music,'

" 'Yes, he was my last master—at Vienna: so fierce and so good,' said **Mirah**, with a melancholy smile. 'He prophesied that my voice would not do for the stage. And he was right.' " 39

Franz Liszt [H]. "**Klesmer** was not yet a Liszt, understood to be adored by ladies of all European countries with the exception of Lapland . . . . " 22

Hugues le Malingre, "who came in with the Conqueror—and also apparently with a sickly complexion which had been happily corrected in his descendants." 16

Henleigh Mallinger, "younger brother . . . had married **Miss Grandcourt**, and taken her name along with her estates, thus making a junction between two equally old families . . . . " 16

Miss Merry. " '**Jocosa** (this was her name for Miss Merry), let down my hair.' " 3

" 'With the girls so troublesome, and Jocosa so dreadfully wooden and ugly, and everything make-shift about us . . . . ' " 3

" '**Gwendolen** will not rest without having the world at her feet,' said Miss Merry, the meek governess . . . . " 4

"Good Miss Merry, whose air of meek depression, hitherto held unaccountable in a governess affectionately attached to the family, was now at the general level of circumstances, did not expect any greeting, but busied herself with the trunks and the **coachman**'s pay . . . . " 21

—time has passed: " . . . the good Jocosa preserved her serviceable neutrality towards the pleasures and glories of the world as things made for those who were not 'in a situation.' " 58

Bishop Mompert. " 'The bishop's views are of a more decidedly Low Church colour than my own . . . but though privately strict, he is not by any means narrow in public matters.' " 24

Mrs Mompert. " 'Don't be alarmed, my dear. She would like to have a more precise idea of you than my report can give . . . she herself exercises a close supervision over her daughters' education, and that makes her less anxious as to age. She is a woman of taste and also of strict principle, and objects to have a French person in the house.' " 24

" 'It is a good thing that you have an engagement of marriage to offer as an excuse, else she might feel offended. She is rather a high woman.'

" 'I am rid of that horror,' thought **Gwendolen**, to whom the name of Mompert had become a sort of Mumbo-jumbo." 28

Primrose, "his father's grey nag, a good horse enough in his way, but of sober years and ecclesiastical habits . . . . " 7

Railway official "also seemed without resources, and his innocent demeanour in observing **Gwendolen** and her trunks was rendered intolerable by the cast in his eye; especially since, being a new man, he did not know her, and must conclude that she was not very high in the world." 21

Ram. "He was an elderly son of **Abraham**, whose childhood had fallen on the evil times at the beginning of this century, and who remained amid this smart and instructed generation as a preserved specimen, soaked through and through with the effect of the poverty and contempt which were the common heritage of most English Jews seventy years ago. He had none of the oily cheerfulness observable in **Mr Cohen**'s aspect: his very features—broad and chubby—showed that tendency to look mongrel without due cause which, in a miscellaneous London neighbourhood, may perhaps be compared with the marvels of imitation in insects, and may have been nature's imperfect effort on behalf of the purer Caucasian to shield him from the shame and spitting to which purer features would have been exposed in the times of zeal.

"Mr Ram dealt ably in books in the same way that he would have dealt in tins of meat and other commodities—without knowledge or responsibility as to the proportion of rottenness or nourishment they might contain. But he believed in **Mordecai**'s learning as something marvellous, and was not sorry that his conversation should be sought by a bookish gentleman, whose visits had twice ended in a purchase. He greeted **Deronda** with a crabbed goodwill, and putting on large silver spectacles, appeared at once to abstract himself in the daily accounts." ¶40

Robinson, "the attorney . . . would have been naturally piqued if he had been asked to meet a set of people who passed for his equals." 69

Lord Slogan, "an unexceptionable Irish peer, whose estate wanted nothing but drainage and population . . . . " 9

Mrs Startin, housekeeper at Offendene. " 'But as to fires, I've had 'em in all the rooms for the last week, and everything is well aired. I could wish some of the furniture paid better for all the cleaning it's had, but I *think* you'll see the brasses have been done justice to.' " 3

Tradesman. "There too, very near the fair **countess**, was a respectable London tradesman, blond and soft-handed, his sleek hair scrupulously parted behind and before, conscious of circulars addressed to the nobility and gentry, whose distinguished patronage enabled him to take his holidays fashionably, and to a certain extent in their distinguished company. Not his the gambler's passion that nullifies appetite, but a well-fed leisure, which in the intervals of winning money in business and spending it showily, sees no better resource than winning money in play and spending it yet more showily—reflecting always that Providence had never manifested any disapprobation of his amusement, and dispassionate enough to leave off if the sweetness of winning much and seeing others lose had turned to the sourness of losing much and seeing others win." 1

Tradesman. ". . . . a deaf and grisly tradesman was casting a flinty look at certain cards, apparently combining advantages of business with religion. . . . " 32

Vandernoodt. " 'Do you think her pretty, Mr Vandernoodt?'

" 'Very. A man might risk hanging for her—I mean a fool might.' " 1

" . . . a man of the best Dutch blood imported at the revolution: for the rest, one of those commodious persons in society who are nothing particular themselves, but are understood to be acquainted with the best in every department; close-clipped, pale-eyes, *nonchalant,* as good a foil as could well be found to the intense colouring and vivid gravity of **Deronda** . . . . Mr Vandernoodt was an industrious gleaner of personal details, and could probably tell everything about a great philosopher or physicist except his theories or discoveries . . . . " 35

—conversation: "Mr Vandernoodt, who had the mania of always describing one thing while you were looking at another, was quite intolerable with his insistence on **Lord Blough**'s kitchen, which he had seen in the north." 35

Vendor. "[Advantages] shoutingly proposed to him in Jew-dialect by a dingy man in a tall coat hanging from neck to heel, a bag in hand, and a broad low hat surmounting his chosen nose . . . . " 32

Mrs Vulcany "once remarked that **Miss Harleth** was too fond of the gentlemen; but we know that she was not in the least fond of them—she was only fond of their homage—and women did not give her homage." 11

Wiener. "**Gwendolen**'s dominant regret was that after all she had only nine louis to add to the four in her purse: these Jew dealers were so unscrupulous in taking advantage of Christians unfortunate at play!" 2

Youth. "Turning into an old book-shop to ask the exact time of service at the synagogue, [**Deronda**] was affectionately directed by a precocious Jewish youth, who entered cordially into his wanting not the fine new building of the Reformed but the old Rabbinical school of the orthodox, and cheated him like a pure Teuton, only with more amenity, in his charge for a book quite out of request as one 'nicht so leicht zu bekommen.' " 32

Also mentioned

Adonis in a George the Fourth wig, at the gambling resort	1
Madame Alcharisi, the singer who became a Princess	36
Angus, captain of Grandcourt's yacht	54
Archdeacon, intimate at Quetcham Hall	3
Armyn, Gwendolen's maternal grandfather; a West Indian planter	3
Admiral Arrowpoint, one of Nelson's men; a doctor's son	35
Austrian baron with a long moustache and short affection	59
Mrs Banks, wife of Sir Hugo's bailiff	16
Bazley, agent for Lord Brackenshaw and not at all an ill-natured man	21
blacksmith in Diplow, optimistic at a new development	9
Blenny, who once lived at Offendene	15
Lord Blough, whose kitchen Vandernoodt had seen in the north	35
Ladies Beatrice and **Maria Brackenshaw**, not yet old enough to hunt	7
Cambridge Don, to be interested in Daniel	16
Christian servant, opening the door at Ezra Cohen's on the sabbath	34
clerk at the bank in Mainz	60
coachman who drives Gwendolen from the station	21
Cohen daughter/sister, who will never be restored to her family as Mirah has been	46
companion, a much worse-looking man than Mirah's father, seen in the street	52
courier who accompanies Sir Hugo to Genoa	59
Lady Cragstone, a gambler	28
Crane, out-of-doors servant at Offendene	35
crew on the Grandcourt yacht: picturesque	54
The **Cushats**, invited to visit Grandcourt	12
Miss Cuttler, dry or moist goods heiress who married Mr Arrowpoint	5
Sally Dagge, who has twice dislocated her shoulder	7
Fenn, who bequeathed his unfortunate looks to his daughter; M.P. for West Orchards	11

The **Fitzadams**, of the Worcestershire branch	35
Fletcher, lessee of collieries at Gadsmere	30
Mrs French, housekeeper to Sir Hugo	16
functionary at a gambling resort: an envoy with a scrolled mustache	1
Edwy Gascoigne, a daughter	3
Lotta Gascoigne, who went black-berrying with her sister Anna	3, 52
Gaskin, a provincial corn-dealer and father of the Rector	13
Gawcome, lessee of collieries at Gadsmere	30
Gibbs, valet on the yacht in the Mediterranean	54
Glasher son, abandoned by his mother at three; dead at five	30
governess to the Davilow daughters	3
Lord Grampian, with whom Bishop Mompert is close	24
Grapnell & Co., who failed for a million	2
Miss Graves, a governess or teacher Gwendolen does not wish to emulate	21
groom for Lord Brackenshaw, with whom Mr Gascoigne consults	3
groom at Offendene	7
Prince Halm-Eberstein, and five children; the family of Deronda's mother	51
Harleth, the late; father of Gwendolen and of high family	3
Lady Molly Harleth, whose miniature Mrs Davilow kept	3
Haynes, who wanted to rent Offendene	2
Hollis, invited to visit Grandcourt	12
Hutchins manservant to Grandcourt	25
Italian lady, who lived with Mirah and her father in New York	20
Jarrett, the village carpenter who helped prepare the stage at Offendene	6
Jeffries, groom and driver at Offendene, departed	21
Jenning, who wrote a poem in four cantos on croquet	5
Jewish vendor, dingy in a tall coat; in Frankfort	32
Jodson, who died, leaving a house available for Mrs Davilow	44, 58
Kalonymos sons, living in ease and luxury in Mainz	60
labourer, elderly, preparing a barouche at the railway station	21
lady, deeply engaged at the roulette table	1
Lady Lawe, mother of a handsome girl	5
Leek, a farmer near Offendene	21
Leonora, aunt of Daniel Deronda's mother; a singer and teacher	51
Mackworth, part of the gambling scene at Leubronn	1
foreign maid warranted against seasickness	54
old maidservant, to the Meyricks in Chelsea	39
Sir Francis Mallinger, who made an ill-advised estate settlement	15
Lady Amabel Mallinger, who had singing lessons with Mirah	69
Lady Theresa Mallinger, a daughter in need of the dentist	28
Two other **Mallinger** daughters	35
Marshall, a jeweller at Wanchester	21
master for theater and singing, who taught Mirah in New York	20
Madame Meunier, a schoolmistress Gwendolen has known	21
Meyrick, father of Hans: an engraver of some distinction, now dead eleven years	16
Nash, the bone-setter, who has reset dislocated shoulders	7
Lady Clementina (**Pentreath**?), with nine daughters, to be taught singing	36
Lord Pentreath, invited to meet the Grandcourts with his wife	35
Phoebe, the Meyricks' maid	18
Puller, a scholar contemporary of Daniel's	16
the **Quallons**, neighbours of Offendene	3
Quicksett, a scholar contemporary of Daniel's	16
Raymond, brother to Lady Mallinger, and Mrs Raymond; and various little Raymonds	35
Edgar Raymond, age four	35
rower, who helped bring Gwendolen to land; wet through; ran off	55
sailors, helping Gwendolen; rough, bronzed men	55
Sarah, servant to the Cohens, who sometimes minds the shop	46
Scrogg, a county historian	64
servant in chasseur's livery, representing the Princess Halm-Eberstein	50
servants in the Princess's anteroom, observing Daniel with surprise	51
servants at Gadsmere, to the Glashers	30
Mr Sinker, eminent counsel	35
Lord Stannery, a relative of Grandcourt's, whose peerage he might inherit	28
Stillfox, tutor to Rex Gascoigne	7

Canon Stopley, who had wanted to attend the Archery Meeting	10
Captain and Mrs Torrington, invited to visit Grandcourt	12
sister of Mrs Torrington, visiting Grandcourt	29
Turvey, valet to Sir Hugo	16
valet to Lord Brackenshaw, handing out the bows at an archery picnic	14
valet to Henleigh Grandcourt; an old servant who was in Genoa with him	25, 56
old woman, winning for the moment at roulette	1

Epilogue

The following is from the final chapter of GE's last fictional work, Impressions of Theophrastus Such (1879). *This chapter 18, "The Modern Hep! Hep! Hep!" is exhaustively extracted in the Topicon at FM:Jews. The title is an anti-Semitic cry which may have originated during the Crusades as an acronym for* Hierosolyma est perdita—*"Jerusalem is Lost." The term was applied to an outbreak of anti-Jewish riots which occurred in Germany in 1819.*

"If we are to consider the future of the Jews at all, it seems reasonable to take as a preliminary question: Are they destined to complete fusion with the peoples among whom they are dispersed, losing every remnant of a distinctive consciousness as Jews; or, are there in the breadth and intensity with which the feeling of separateness, or what we may call the organised memory of a national consciousness, actually exists in the world—wide Jewish communities—the seven millions scattered from east to west—and again, are there in the political relations of the world, the conditions present or approaching for the restoration of a Jewish state planted on the old ground as a centre of national feeling, a source of dignifying protection, a special channel for special energies which may contribute some added form of national genius, and an added voice in the councils of the world? . . .

"Why are we so eager for the dignity of certain populations of whom perhaps we have never seen a single specimen, and of whose history, legend, or literature we have been contentedly ignorant for ages, while we sneer at the notion of a renovated national dignity for the Jews, whose ways of thinking and whose very verbal forms are on our lips in every prayer which we end with an Amen?

"Some of us consider this question dismissed when they have said that the wealthiest Jews have no desire to forsake their European palaces, and go to live in Jerusalem. But in a return from exile, in the restoration of a people, the question is not whether certain rich men will choose to remain behind, but whether there will be found worthy men who will choose to lead the return. Plenty of prosperous Jews remained in Babylon when Ezra marshalled his band of forty thousand and began a new glorious epoch in the history of his race, making the preparation for that epoch in the history of the world which has been held glorious enough to be dated from for evermore.

"The hinge of possibility is simply the existence of an adequate community of feeling as well as widespread need in the Jewish race, and the hope that among its finer specimens there may arise some men of instruction and ardent public spirit, some new Ezras, some modern Maccabees, who will know how to use all favouring outward conditions, how to triumph by heroic example, over the indifference of their fellows and the scorn of their foes, and will steadfastly set their faces towards making their people once more one among the nations . . . .

"Pagans in successive ages said, 'These people are unlike us, and refuse to be made like us: let us punish them.' The Jews were steadfast in their separateness, and through that separateness Christianity was born . . . . There is still a great function for the steadfastness of the Jew: not that he should shut out the utmost illumination which knowledge can throw on his national history, but that he should cherish the store of inheritance which that history has left him.

"Every Jew should be conscious that he is one of a multitude possessing common objects of piety in the immortal achievements and immortal sorrows of ancestors who have transmitted to them a physical and mental type strong enough, eminent enough in faculties, pregnant enough with peculiar promise, to constitute a new beneficent individuality among the nations, and, by confuting the traditions of scorn, nobly avenge the wrongs done to their Fathers.

"There is a sense in which the worthy child of a nation that has brought forth illustrious prophets, high and unique among the poets of the world, is bound by their vision.

"Is bound?

"Yes, for the effective bond of human action is feeling, and the worthy child of a people owning the triple name of Hebrew, Israelite, and Jew, feels his kinship with the glories and the sorrows, the degradation and the possible renovation of his national family." ¶TS 18

William Blackwood & Sons **TS**
1879

Impressions of Theophrastus Such

"That a gratified sense of superiority is at the root of barbarous laughter may be at least half the truth. But there is a loving laughter in which the only recognised superiority is that of the ideal self, the God within, holding the mirror and the scourge for our own pettiness as well as our neighbours." 1

Commentators have taken differing views on the name of the Narrator. The historical Theophrastus, disciple and successor to Aristotle, had one name. But the Narrator GE gives us is an Englishman. Englishmen have patronymics. So, although the erudite explain the title of the work as an abbreviation importing the idea of a series of essays on characters ("Such a person as . . . "), we consider that GE has given him a full name—inspired perhaps by that idea, but a full name nonetheless.

Figures are presented in the order of their appearance in their respective chapters, regardless of relative importance.

Précis

The Narrator presents himself as a lonely but amiable, altruistic bachelor, principally concerned that he not be perceived as cruelly or unfairly judging his contemporaries in the sketches to follow. He breathlessly insists on his fallibility and egoism: he cannot perceive his own flaws. He relies ultimately on God's forgiveness of his pettiness and asks the reader's indulgence of his determination to write. 1 His first excursion is into the past. He fondly and with seeming objectivity describes his country parson father and the latter's career. He reminisces nostalgically on the sylvan scenes of his childhood. The descriptions and comments at times compellingly evoke GE herself. 2

Proteus Merman writes for periodicals and indulges in inconclusive research which scatters his energies. He marries prematurely. He has a startling insight which impeaches the theories and work of the great **Grampus**

and he writes this up and sends it to him. It obtains circulation and notoriety, and scientific colleagues circle the wagons and attack Merman, more libellously than accurately. He is deeply wounded and fights back. He neglects his regular work but produces an eloquent 60 pages which he considers a full refutation and proof of his theory. He gets it printed, but it is greeted with either sarcasm or neglect. His reputation as sober thinker, safe writer, and sound lawyer is injured; his wife **Julia** struggles to make ends meet. Now a poor man, he gets little help because he seems unsafe. He takes a job well beneath him. His basic idea is quietly adopted and validated by his rivals. 3

The late, highly respectable and unobtrusive **Lentulus** is described (in the voice of a respectful and seemingly *naïve* Theophrastus) as a mysterious savant who holds the key to true poetry and right philosophy, though he does not reveal them. By the end of the essay, the narrator has shown his penetration: Lentulus was hopelessly conceited, but so ignorant and inept in propounding his ideas that he never encountered probing discourse or contradiction. His silence kept his complacency and absurdity hidden from the light of day. 4 **Hinze** is a gentleman of obsequious manners and oily deference. He is incapable of sincerity but always punctiliously correct. He goads the narrator to rage and embarrasses his interlocutors by his worshipfulness. His is the funniest character and the most memorable Impression in the book. 5

The narrator reviews manifestations of **Touchwood**'s bad temper. He is adamant that "temper" is no excuse: such behaviour cannot be atoned for. 6 Retired cotton manufacturer **Spike** is of good appearance, vapid conversation, and abysmal ignorance. He typifies the working of Adam Smith's "invisible hand." 7 The narrator's friend **Mordax** is a man of parts but highly resistant to new information or ideas not first conceived by himself. The narrator's own valet, **Pummel**, is similarly reluctant ever to admit that he is hearing something new. 8 The young **Mixtus** was absorbed in religious and philanthropical activity, but since his marriage to **Scintilla**, his ardour in these directions has been submerged by her indifference and that of her friends. He has become rich and his ideas are disregarded. He no longer knows who he is. 9

Ideas may be better heard if presented in French, and here the idea is that the ridiculous must be pointed out where it exists and not imagined where it does not. Beware of burlesquing the affecting, the truly pathetic, the grand. Caricature as a technique is abused. Society's moral fabric is endangered. [*Did GE get up on the wrong side of the bed one morning and go to a particularly ribald, irreverent Pantomime? Her humourless, frantic, apocalyptic prose is way over the top, and there is no Impression of any Character in the chapter.*] 10 The question is plagiarism. **Euphorion** treats it lightly, and it is held very difficult to prove. We hear the fable of an animals' conclave to determine the source of the honeycomb. 11 **Ganymede** was the youngest child and a beautiful boy and man. A proficient writer, he has grown accustomed to amazing others by his youthfulness. He is fat now, but he does not realize he makes a different impression than formerly. Ingrained self-image prevails. 12

Commentary on the hypocrisies of self-deception and the castigation of others for one's own sins. Abuses of the imagination—undisciplined and untruthful—are ascribed to the flighty **Callista**. The narrator brilliantly discourses on the high, transcending literary and artistic imagination—more in GE's voice than that of her English bachelor alter ego—in passages which should be far better known than they are. 13 Monopolizers of conversation are recognised as bores; why not over-productive writers? **Pepin** is a case in point: he got into print prematurely and has been trapped in a mode of spurious authority ever since, with no serious, veracious work produced. He protects himself with a bitter arrogance but is privately an amiable fellow. 14

Vorticella, the wife of an important townsman, sees her book on the Channel Islands favorably reviewed by local and distant organs. She shows her files to the young Narrator and when she returns interrogates him. She suffers from the disease of magnified self-importance consequent on having had a book published. 15 The Narrator strenuously attacks a perceived tendency to divide public dishonesty and rottenness from private tenderness and affections and forgive the former if the latter are present. "Morals" and "Morality" are not limited to the personal: they must apply to public welfare. This essay is pure polemic, without humour, without "Impression." 16

The Narrator and **Trost** debate technology and the likelihood of man's retaining control of the machines he invents. With scientific sophistication, the Narrator cogently projects a Darwinian struggle which will be won by the perfected inanimate. Trost is out-talked. There is no human foible, no humour, no "Impression." 17 The last segment of the work is an eloquent essay attacking anti-Semitism. It has no business in TS and nothing to do with its point. 18

Contents

The Narrator

Theophrastus Such. "I am a bachelor, without domestic distractions of any sort, and have all my life been an attentive companion to myself, flattering my nature agreeably on plausible occasions, reviling it rather bitterly when it mortified me, and in general remembering its doings and sufferings with a tenacity which is too apt to raise surprise if not disgust at the careless inaccuracy of my acquaintances, who impute to me opinions I never held, express their desire to convert me to my favourite ideas, forget whether I have ever been to the East, and are capable of being three several times astonished at my never having told them before of my accident in the Alps, causing me the nervous shock which has ever since notably diminished my digestive powers." 1

—absurd: " . . . I must still come under the common fatality of mankind and share the liability to be absurd without knowing that I am absurd. It is in the nature of foolish reasoning to seem good to the foolish reasoner. . . . While there are secrets in me unguessed by others, these others have certain items of knowledge about the extent of my powers and the figure I make with them, which in turn are secrets unguessed by me." 1

—introductory: "Thus if I laugh at you, O fellow-men! if I trace with curious interest your labyrinthine self-delusions, note the inconsistencies in your zealous adhesions, and smile at your helpless endeavours in a rashly chosen part, it is not that I feel myself aloof from you: the more intimately I seem to discern your weaknesses, the stronger to me is the proof that I share them. How otherwise could I get the discernment?—for even what we are averse to, what we vow not to entertain, must have shaped or shadowed itself within us as a possibility before we can think of exorcising it." 1

—dependent: "I really do not want to learn from my enemies: I prefer having none to learn from. Instead of being glad when men use me despitefully, I wish they would behave better and find a more amiable occupation for their intervals of business. In brief, after a close intimacy with myself for a longer period than I choose to mention, I find within me a permanent longing for approbation, sympathy, and love." 1

—his love: "Yet I am a bachelor, and the person I love best has never loved me, or known that I loved her." 1

—alone: "Though continually in society, and carrying about the joys and sorrows of my neighbours, I feel myself, so far as my personal lot is concerned, uncared for and alone." 1

—author: " . . . as to intellectual contribution, my only published work was a failure, so that I am spoken of to inquiring beholders as 'the author of a book you have probably not seen.' (The work was a humorous romance, unique in its kind, and I am told is much tasted in a Cherokee translation, where the jokes are rendered with all the serious eloquence characteristic of the Red races.)" 1

—characteristics: "Then, in some quarters my awkward feet are against me, the length of my upper lip, and an inveterate way I have of walking with my head foremost and my chin projecting. One can become only too well aware of such things by looking in the glass, or in that other mirror held up to nature in the frank opinions of street-boys . . . . " 1

—fortune: "It is to be borne in mind that I am not rich, have neither stud nor cellar, and no very high connections such as give to a look of imbecility a certain prestige of inheritance through a title line . . . . " 1

—change of heart: "Clearly enough, if anything hindered my thought from rising to the force of passionately interested contemplation, or my poor pent-up pond of sensitiveness from widening into a beneficent river of sympathy, it was my own dulness, and though I could not make myself the reverse of shallow all [at] once, I had at least learned where I had better turn my attention . . . . I have not attained any lofty peak of magnanimity, nor would I trust beforehand in my capability of meeting a severe demand for moral heroism. But that I have at least succeeded in establishing a habit of mind which keeps watch against my self-partiality and promotes a fair consideration of what touches the feelings or the fortunes of my neighbours, seems to be proved by the ready confidence with which men and women appeal to my interest in their experience." 1

—willing ear: "My acquaintances tell me unreservedly of their triumphs and their piques; explain their purposes at length, and reassure me with cheerfulness as to their chances of success; insist on their theories and accept me as a dummy with whom they rehearse their side of future discussions; unwind their coiled-up griefs in relation to their husbands, or recite to me examples of feminine incomprehensibleness as typified in their wives; mention frequently the fair applause which their merits have wrung from some persons, and the attacks to which certain oblique motives have stimulated others." 1

—humility: " . . . I occasionally, in the glow of sympathy which embraced me and my confiding friend on the subject of his satisfaction or resentment, was urged to hint at a corresponding experience in my own case; but the signs of a rapidly lowering pulse and spreading nervous depression in my previously vivacious interlocutor, warned me . . . I took it as an established inference that these fitful signs of a lingering belief in my own importance were generally felt to be abnormal . . . I am really at the point of finding that this world would be worth living in without any lot of one's own. Is it not possible for me to enjoy the scenery of the earth without saying to myself, I have a cabbage-garden in it?" 1

—authorship: "My conversational reticences about myself turn into garrulousness on paper—as the sea-lion plunges and swims the more energetically because his limbs are of a sort to make him shambling on land. The act of writing, in spite of past experience, brings with it the vague, delightful illusion of an audience nearer to my idiom than the Cherokees, and more numerous than the visionary One for whom many authors have declared themselves willing to go through the pleasing punishment of publication." 1

"Thus I make myself a charter to write, and keep the pleasing, inspiring illusion of being listened to, though I may sometimes write about myself. What I have already said on this too familiar theme has been meant only as a preface, to show that in noting the weaknesses of my acquaintances I am conscious of my fellowship with them." 1

—dreams of difference: "I have often had the fool's hectic of wishing about the unalterable, but with me that useless exercise has turned chiefly on the conception of a different self, and not, as it usually does in literature, on the advantage of having been born in a different age, and more especially in one where life is imagined to have been altogether majestic and graceful. With my present abilities, external proportions, and generally small provision

for ecstatic enjoyment, where is the ground for confidence that I should have had a preferable career in such an epoch of society? An age in which every department has its awkward-squad seems in my mind's eye to suit me better." 2

—*contemporary:* "I gather, too, from the undeniable testimony of [**Aristotle**'s] disciple **Theophrastus**, that there were bores, ill-bred persons, and detractors even in Athens, of species remarkably corresponding to the English, and not yet made endurable by being classic; and altogether, with my present fastidious nostril, I feel that I am the better off for possessing Athenian life solely as an inodorous fragment of antiquity." 2

—*objective:* " . . . I might have been one of those benignant lovely souls who, without astonishing the public and posterity, make a happy difference in the lives close around them, and in this way lift the average of earthly joy." 2

—*remembering the present:* "All reverence and gratitude for the worthy Dead on whose labours we have entered, all care for the future generations whose lot we are preparing; but some affection and fairness for those who are doing the actual work of the world, some attempt to regard them with the same freedom from ill-temper, whether on private or public grounds, as we may hope will be felt by those who will call us ancient!" 2

"I at least am a modern with some interest in advocating tolerance, and notwithstanding an inborn beguilement which carries my affection and regret continually into an imagined past, I am aware that I must lose all sense of moral proportion unless I keep alive a stronger attachment to what is near, and a power of admiring what I best know and understand." 2

—*scenes of childhood:* " . . . there is a pair of eyes . . . that once perhaps learned to read their native England through the same alphabet as mine—not within the boundaries of an ancestral park, never even being driven through the county town five miles off, but—among the midland villages and markets, along by the tree-studded hedgerows, and where the heavy barges seem in the distance to float mysteriously among the rushes and the feathered grass . . . my eyes at least have kept their early affectionate joy in our native landscape, which is one deep root of our national life and language." 2

—*benignant:* "I would at all times rather be reduced to a cheaper estimate of a particular person, if by that means I can get a more cheerful view of my fellow-men generally . . . . It would have been a grief to discover that [**Lentulus**] was bitter or malicious, but by finding him to be neither a mighty poet, nor a revolutionary poetical critic, nor an epoch-making philosopher, my admiration for the poets and thinkers whom he rated so low would recover all its buoyancy . . . . " 4

—*curious:* "Hence I deliberately attempted to draw out **Lentulus** in private dialogue, for it is the reverse of injury to a man to offer him that hearing which he seems to have found nowhere else. And for whatever purposes silence may be equal to gold, it cannot be safely taken as an indication of specific ideas." 4

—*humour misapplied:* "The art of spoiling is within reach of the dullest faculty: the coarsest clown with a hammer in his hand might chip the nose off every statue and bust in the Vatican, and stand grinning at the effect of his work. Because wit is an exquisite product of high powers, we are not therefore forced to admit the sadly confused inference of the monotonous jester that he is establishing his superiority over every less facetious person, and over every topic on which he is ignorant or insensible, by being uneasy until he has distorted it in the small cracked mirror which he carries about with him as a joking apparatus." 10

—*corrosion of values:* "This is what I call debasing the moral currency: lowering the value of every inspiring fact and tradition so that it will command less and less of the spiritual products, the generous motives which sustain the charm and elevation of our social existence—that something besides bread by which man saves his soul alive [*see* Exhibit XI]. The bread-winner of the family may demand more and more coppery shillings, or assignats, or greenbacks for his day's work, and so get the needful quantum of food; but let that moral currency be emptied of its value—let a greedy buffoonery debase all historic beauty, majesty, and pathos, and the more you heap up the desecrated symbols the greater will be the lack of the ennobling emotions which subdue the tyranny of suffering, and make ambition one with social virtue [*see* Exhibit XI]." 10

—*viewing with alarm:* "This is the impoverishment that threatens our posterity:—a new famine, a meagre fiend with lewd grin and clumsy hoof, is breathing a moral mildew over the harvest of our human sentiments. These are the most delicate elements of our too easily perishable civilisation." 10

—*against plagiarism:* "I protest against the use of these majestic conceptions [as to a universal property in ideas] to do the dirty work of unscrupulosity and justify the non-payment of conscious debts which cannot be defined or enforced by the law . . . . Surely the acknowledgement of a mental debt which will not be immediately detected, and may never be asserted, is a case to which the traditional susceptibility to 'debts of honour' would be suitably transferred." 11

—*others' property:* "But it is fair to maintain that the neighbour who borrows your property, loses it for a while, and when it turns up again forgets your connection with it and counts it his own, shows himself so much the feebler in grasp and rectitude of mind. Some absent persons cannot remember the state of wear in their own hats and umbrellas, and have no mental check to tell them that they have carried home a fellow-visitor's more recent purchase: they may be excellent householders, far removed from the suspicion of low devices, but one wishes them a more correct perception, and a more wary sense that a neighbour's umbrella may be newer than their own." 11

—*aging:* " 'Well,' said I, 'youth seems the only drawback that is sure to diminish. You and I have seven years less of it than when we last met.'

" 'Ah?' returned **Ganymede**, as lightly as possible, at the same time casting an observant glance over me, as if he were marking the effect of seven years on a person who had probably begun life with an old look, and even as an infant had given his countenance to that significant doctrine, the transmigration of ancient souls into modern bodies." 12

—*self-image:* "It is true that he no longer hears expressions of surprise at his youthfulness . . . but this sort of external evidence has become an unnecessary crutch to his habitual inward persuasion. His manners, his costume, his suppositions of the impression he makes on others, have all their former correspondence with the dramatic part of the young genius. As to the incongruity of his contour and other little accidents of *physique,* he is probably no more aware that they will affect others as incongruities than *Armida* is conscious how much her rouge provokes our notice of her wrinkles . . . .

"But let us be just enough to admit that there may be old-young coxcombs as well as old-young coquettes." 12

—*correspondence:* "It is my way when I observe any instance of folly, any queer habit, any absurd illusion, straightway to look for something of the same type in myself, feeling sure that amid all differences there will be a certain correspondence; just as there is more or less correspondence in the natural history even of continents widely apart, and of islands in opposite zones." 13

—*analysis:* " . . . I pursue this plan . . . of using my observation as a clue or lantern by which I detect small herbage or lurking life; or I take my neighbour in his least becoming tricks or efforts as an opportunity for luminous deduction concerning the figure the human genus makes in the specimen which I myself furnish." 13

—*judging others:* "To judge of others by oneself is in its most innocent meaning the briefest expression for our only method of knowing mankind; yet, we perceive, it has come to mean in many cases either the vulgar mistake which reduces every man's value to the very low figure at which the valuer himself happens to stand; or else, the amiable illusion of the higher nature misled by a too generous construction of the lower." 13

—*encountering a talker:* "There is a monotony and narrowness already to spare in my own identity; what comes to me from without should be larger and more impartial than the judgment of any single interpreter. On this ground even a modest person, without power or will to shine in the conversation, may easily find the predominating talker a nuisance, while those who are full of matter on special topics are continually detecting miserably thin places in the web of that information which he will not desist from imparting. Nobody that I know of ever proposed a testimonial to a man for thus volunteering the whole expense of the conversation.

"Why is there a different standard of judgment with regard to a writer who plays much the same part in literature as the excessive talker plays in what is traditionally called conversation?" 14

—*published comment:* "Clearly there is a sort of writing which helps to keep the writer in a ridiculously contented ignorance; raising in him continually the sense of having delivered himself effectively, so that the acquirement of more thorough knowledge seems as superfluous as the purchase of costume for a past occasion. He has invested his vanity (perhaps his hope of income) in his own shallownesses and mistakes, and must desire their prosperity. Like the professional prophet, he learns to be glad of the harm that keeps up his credit, and to be sorry for the good that contradicts him. It is hard enough for any of us, amid the changing winds of fortune and the hurly-burly of events, to keep quite clear of a gladness which is another's calamity; but one may choose not to enter on a course which will turn such gladness into a fixed habit of mind, committing ourselves to be continually pleased that others should appear to be wrong in order that we may have the air of being right." 14

—*on writing a book:* "I would by no means make it a reproach to [**Vorticella**] that she wrote no more than one book; on the contrary, her stopping there seems to me a laudable example. What one would have wished, after experience, was that she had refrained from producing even that single volume, and thus from giving her self-importance a troublesome kind of double incorporation which became oppressive to her acquaintances . . . . " 15

—*lie required:* "Here was a judgment on me. Orientally speaking, I had lifted up my foot on the steep descent of falsity and was compelled to set it down on a lower level." 15

—*question of morality:* " 'Surely your pity is misapplied,' said I, rather dubiously, for I like the comfort of trusting that a correct moral judgment is the strong point in woman (seeing that she has a majority of about a million in our islands) . . . . 'I should have thought you would rather be sorry for **Mantrap**'s victims—the widows, spinsters, and hard-working fathers whom his unscrupulous haste to make himself rich has cheated of all their savings. . . . ' " 16

—*treachery and rapacity:* "And since we are sometimes told of such maleficent kings that they were religious, we arrive at the curious result that the most serious wide-reaching duties of man lie quite outside both Morality and Religion—the one of these consisting in not keeping mistresses (and perhaps not drinking too much), and the other in certain ritual and spiritual transactions with God which can be carried on equally well side by side with the basest conduct towards men." 16

—*general welfare:* "Thoroughness of workmanship, care in the execution of every task undertaken, as if it were the acceptance of a trust which it would be a breach of faith not to discharge well, is a form of duty so momentous that if it were to die out from the feeling and practice of a people, all reforms of institutions would be helpless to create national prosperity and national happiness." 16

—*metaphor:* " 'Precisely,' said I, with a meekness which I felt was praiseworthy; it is the feebleness of my capacity, bringing me nearer than you to the human average, that perhaps enables me to imagine certain results better than you can. Doubtless the very fishes of our rivers, gullible as they look, and slow as they are to be rightly convinced in another order of facts, form fewer false expectations about each other than we should form about them if we were in a position of somewhat fuller intercourse with their species; for even as it is we have continually to be surprised that they do not rise to our carefully selected bait. Take me then as a sort of reflective and experienced carp; but do not estimate the justice of my ideas by my facial expression.' " 17

—*Jewish nationhood:* " . . . when the dread and hatred of foreign sway had condensed itself into dread and hatred of the Romans, many Conservatives became Zealots, whose chief mark was that they advocated resistance to the death against the submergence of their nationality. Much might be said on this point towards distinguishing the desperate struggle against a conquest which is regarded as degradation and corruption, from rash, hopeless insurrection against an established native government; and for my part (if that were of any consequence) I share the spirit of the Zealots. I take the spectacle of the Jewish people defying the Roman edict, and preferring death by starvation or the sword to the introduction of **Caligula**'s deified statue into the temple, as a sublime type of steadfastness." 18

The *Topicon* extracts much of the Narrator's discourse. Characteristic items are under A:Ancestor, A:Parents, FM:Behaviour, FM:Jews, GB:Regions, GP:History, H:Cause and Effect, H:Nobility, H:Social class, LC:Authorship, LC:Conversation, LM:Man, LM:Marriage, LM:Woman, M:Imagination, M:Mind, S:Egoism (several entries), S:Ideal and Idealism, S:Laughter, SR:Memories, and TP:Clergy

TS 1

I Looking Inward

Lippus ("bleary-eyed"). " . . . though I can hardly be so blundering as Lippus and the rest of those mistaken candidates for favour whom I have seen ruining their chance by a too elaborate personal canvass . . . . "

Jean-Jacques Rousseau [H]. "But the incompleteness which comes of self-ignorance may be compensated by self-betrayal. A man who is affected to tears in dwelling on the generosity of his own sentiments makes me aware of several things not included under those terms. Who has sinned more against those duteous reticences than Jean Jacques? Yet half our impressions of his character come not from what he means to convey, but from what he unconsciously enables us to discern." *See Topicon* LC:Authorship—*autobiography*

Minutius Felix. " 'Your own fault, my dear fellow!' said [he] one day that I had incautiously mentioned this uninteresting fact [of **Such**'s aloneness]." *See* Exhibit X

Artisan. "Once, when zeal lifted me on my legs, I distinctly heard an enlightened artisan remark, 'Here's a rum cut!'—and doubtless he reasoned the same way as . . . . "

Glycera. " . . . the elegant Glycera, when she politely puts on an air of listening to me, but elevates her eyebrows and chills her glance in sign of predetermined neutrality: both have their reasons for judging the quality of my speech beforehand."

Friend. "I leave my manuscripts to a judgment outside my imagination, but I will not ask to hear it, or request my friend to pronounce, before I have been buried decently, what he really thinks of my parts, and to state candidly whether my papers would be most usefully applied in lighting the cheerful domestic fire. It is too probable that he will be exasperated at the trouble I have given him of reading them; but the consequent clearness and vivacity with which he could demonstrate to me that the fault of my manuscripts, as of my own published work, is simply flatness, and not that surpassing subtilty which is the preferable ground of popular neglect—this verdict, however instructively expressed, is a portion of earthly discipline of which I will not beseech my friend to be the instrument."

TS 2

II Looking Backward

Father. " . . . I am contented that my father was a country parson, born much about the same time as **Scott** and **Wordsworth** . . . I am rather fond of the mental furniture I got by having a father who was well acquainted with all ranks of his neighbours, and am thankful that he was not one of those aristocratic clergymen who could not have sat down to a meal with any family in the parish except my lord's—still more that he was not an earl or a marquis."

—tithe: "They grumbled at their obligations towards him; but what then? It was natural to grumble at any demand for payment, tithe included, but also natural for a rector to desire his tithe and look well after the levying. A Christian pastor who did not mind about his money was not an ideal prevalent among the rural minds of flat central England, and might have seemed to introduce a dangerous laxity of supposition about Christian laymen who happened to be creditors. My father was none the less beloved because he

was understood to be of a saving disposition, and how could he save without getting his tithe?"

—*popular:* "The sight of him was not unwelcome at any door, and he was remarkable among the clergy of his district for having no lasting feud with rich or poor in his parish. I profited by his popularity, and for months after my mother's death, when I was a little fellow of nine, I was taken care of first at one homestead and then at another; a variety which I enjoyed much more than my stay at the Hall, where there was a tutor."

—*conservative:* "To my father's mind the noisy teachers of revolutionary doctrine were, to speak mildly, a variable mixture of the fool and the scoundrel; the welfare of the nation lay in a strong Government which could maintain order; and I was accustomed to hear him utter the word 'Government' in a tone that charged it with awe, and made it part of my effective religion, in contrast with the word 'rebel,' which seemed to carry the stamp of evil in its syllables, and, lit by the fact that *Satan* was the first rebel, made an argument dispensing with more detailed inquiry."

TS 3

III How We Encourage Research

Proteus Merman. "Twenty years ago Merman was a young man of promise, a conveyancer with a practice which had certainly budded . . . . Meanwhile he occupied himself in miscellaneous periodical writing and in a multifarious study of moral and physical science. What chiefly attracted him in all subjects were the vexed questions which have the advantage of not admitting the decisive proof or disproof that renders many ingenious arguments superannuated."

—*the opposite sex:* "[His] flexibility was naturally much helped by his amiable feeling towards woman, whose nervous system, he was convinced, would not bear the continuous strain of difficult topics . . . . Indeed his tastes were domestic enough to beguile him into marriage when his resources were still very moderate and partly uncertain."

—*creation:* "In the first development and writing out of his scheme, Merman had a more intense kind of intellectual pleasure than he had ever known before. His face became more radiant, his general view of human prospects more cheerful . . . . The possession of an original theory which has not yet been assailed must certainly sweeten the temper of a man who is not beforehand ill-natured. And Merman was the reverse of ill-natured."

—*fighting on:* "That his counter-theory was fundamentally the right one he had a genuine conviction, whatever collateral mistakes he might have committed; and his bread would not cease to be bitter to him until he had convinced his contemporaries that **Grampus** had used his minute learning as a dust-cloud to hide sophistical evasions . . . and that the best preparation in this matter was a wide survey of history and a diversified observation of men."

—*frustration:* "Unable to get his answers printed, he had recourse to that more primitive mode of publication, oral transmission or button-holding, now generally regarded as a troublesome survival, and the once pleasant, flexible Merman was on the way to be shunned as a bore. His interest in new acquaintances turned chiefly on the possibility that they would care about the Magicodumbras and Zuzumotzis; that they would listen to his complaints and exposures of unfairness, and not only accept copies of what he had written on the subject, but send him appreciative letters in acknowledgment."

—*poisoned:* "This was the sad truth. Merman felt himself ill-used by the world, and thought very much worse of the world in consequence. The gall of his adversaries' ink had been sucked into his system and ran in his blood. He was still in the prime of life, but his mind was aged by that eager monotonous construction which comes of feverish excitement on a single topic and uses up the intellectual strength."

Grampus [Greenland whale]. " . . . after spending some hours over the epoch-making work of Grampus, a new idea seized him . . . .

" 'That fellow Grampus, whose book is cried up as a revelation, is all wrong about the Magicodumbras and the Zuzumotzis, and I have got hold of the right line.' "

—*rebuttal:* "This article in which **Merman** was pilloried and as good as mutilated—for he was shown to have neither ear nor nose for the subtleties of philological and archæological study—was much read and more talked of, not because of any interest in the system of Grampus . . . but because the sharp epigrams with which the victim was lacerated, and the soaring fountains of acrid mud which were shot upward and poured over the fresh wounds, were found amusing in recital."

Julia Merman. "**Merman** started up in bed. The night was cold, and the sudden withdrawal of warmth made his wife first dream of a snowball, and then cry—

" 'What is the matter, Proteus?' "

—*humbled:* " 'Oh no, **Proteus**, dear. I do believe what you say is right. That is my only guide. I am sure I never have any opinions in any other way: I mean about subjects . . . . I know I said once that I did not want you to sing "Oh ruddier than the cherry," because it was not in your voice. But I cannot remember ever differing from you about *subjects*. I never in my life thought any one cleverer than you.' "

—*gallant:* "The brave and affectionate woman whose small outline, so unimpressive against an illuminated background, held within it a good share of feminine heroism, did her best to keep up the charm of home and soothe her husband's excitement; parting with the best jewel among her wedding presents in order to pay rent, without ever hinting to her husband that this sad result had come of his undertaking to convince people who only laughed at him."

—*resignation:* "She was a resigned little creature, and reflected that some husbands took to drinking and others to forgery: hers had only taken to the Magicodumbras and Zuzumotzis, and was not unkind . . . . "

Lord Narwhal [sea unicorn]. " . . . Grampus knew nothing of the book until his friend Lord Narwhal sent him an American newspaper . . . . "

Professor Sperm N. Whale. " . . . a spirited article by the well-known Professor . . . which was rather equivocal in its bearing . . . . "

Butzkopf [Grampus in German] and **Dugong** [sea cow], "both men whose signatures were familiar to the Teutonic world . . . asking their Master whether he meant to take up the combat, because, in the contrary case, both were ready."

—*second round:* "Butzkopf made [**Merman**'s rebuttal] the subject of an elaborate *Einleitung* to his important work, *Die Bedeutung des Ægyptischen*

Labyrinthes; and Dugong, in a remarkable address which he delivered to a learned society in Central Europe, introduced Merman's theory with so much power of sarcasm that it became a theme of more or less derisive allusion to men of many tongues."

M. Cachalot [sperm whale] "had not read either **Grampus** or **Merman**, but he heard of their dispute in time to insert a paragraph upon it . . . . "

M. Porpesse, "also, availing himself of **M. Cachalot**'s knowledge, reproduced it in an article with certain additions . . . . "

Ziphius [bottle-nosed dolphin] et al. "[**Merman**] had even found cases in which Ziphius, **Microps**, **Scrag Whale** the explorer, and other Cetaceans of unanswerable authority, were decidedly at issue with **Grampus**. Especially a passage cited by this last from that greatest of fossils **Megalosaurus** was demonstrated by Merman to be capable of three different interpretations, all preferable to that chosen by Grampus . . . . "

Loligo [cuttlefish] et al. "The fluent Loligo, the formidable **Shark**, and a younger member of his remarkable family known as **S. Catulus** [shark pup] made a special reputation by their numerous articles, eloquent, lively, or abusive, all on the same theme, under titles ingeniously varied, alliterative, sonorous, or boldly fanciful . . . . They tossed him on short sentences; they swathed him in paragraphs of winding imagery; they found him at once a mere plagiarist and a theorizer of unexampled perversity, ridiculously wrong about *potzis* and ignorant of Pali . . . . "

TS 4

IV A Man Surprised at His Originality

Lentulus. "The majority of his acquaintances, I imagine, have always thought of him as a man justly unpretending and as nobody's rival; but some of them have perhaps been struck with surprise at his reserve in praising the works of his contemporaries, and have now and then felt themselves in need of a key to his remarks on men of celebrity in various departments."

—unexceptionable: "He was a man of fair position, deriving his income from a business in which he did nothing, at leisure to frequent clubs and at ease in giving dinners; well-looking, polite, and generally acceptable in society as a part of what we may call its bread-crumb—the neutral basis needful for the plums and spice."

—grudging: "Why, then, did he speak of the modern **Maro** [**Virgil**] or the modern **Flaccus** [**Horace**] with a peculiarity in his tone of assent to other people's praise which might almost have led you to suppose that the eminent poet had borrowed money of him and showed an indisposition to repay? He had no criticism to offer, no sign of objection more specific than a slight cough, a scarcely perceptible pause before assenting, and an air of self-control in his utterance—as if certain considerations had determined him not to inform against the so-called poet, who to his knowledge was a mere versifier."

—as to philosophy: "But time wearing on, I perceived that the attitude of Lentulus towards the philosophers was essentially the same as his attitude towards the poets; nay, there was something so much more decided in his mode of closing his mouth after brief speech on the former, there was such an air of rapt consciousness in his private hints as to his conviction that all

thinking hitherto had been an elaborate mistake, and as to his own power of conceiving a sound basis for a lasting superstructure . . . . "

—obscurity: "I only meditated approvingly on the way in which a man of exceptional faculties, and even carrying within him some of that fierce refiner's fire which is to purge away the dross of human error, may move about in society totally unrecognised, regarded as a person whose opinion is superfluous, and only rising into a power in emergencies of threatened blackballing."

—ignorance: "We need not go far to learn that a prophet is not made by erudition. Lentulus at least had not the bias of a school; and if it turned out that he was in agreement with any celebrated thinker, ancient or modern, the agreement would have the value of an undesigned coincidence not due to forgotten reading."

—appearance: "No man's appearance could be graver or more gentlemanlike than that of Lentulus as we walked along the Mall . . . . His wristbands and black gloves, his hat and nicely clipped hair, his laudable moderation in beard, and his evident discrimination in choosing his tailor, all seemed to excuse the prevalent estimate of him as a man untainted with heterodoxy, and likely to be so unencumbered with opinions that he would always be useful as an assenting and admiring listener."

—conceited: "This Lentulus certainly was [a good fellow], in the sense of being free from envy, hatred, and malice; and such freedom was all the more remarkable an indication of native benignity, because of his gaseous, illimitably expansive conceit. Yes, conceit; for that his enormous and contentedly ignorant confidence in his own rambling thoughts was usually clad in a decent silence, is no reason why it should be less strictly called by the name directly implying a complacent self-estimate unwarranted by performance. Nay, the total privacy in which he enjoyed his consciousness of inspiration was the very condition of its undisturbed placid nourishment and gigantic growth."

—silence a benefit: "But Lentulus was at once so unreceptive, and so little gifted with the power of displaying his miscellaneous deficiency of information, that there was really nothing to hinder his astonishment at the spontaneous crop of ideas which his mind secretly yielded . . . . He might have been mischievous but for the lack of words: instead of being astonished at his inspirations in private, he might have clad his addled originalities, disjointed commonplaces, blind denials, and balloon-like conclusions, in that mighty sort of language which would have made a new Koran for a knot of followers."

—caveat from ***Theophrastus:*** "I mean no disrespect to the ancient Koran, but one would not desire the roc to lay more eggs and give us a whole wing-flapping brood to soar and make twilight."

TS 5

V A Too Deferential Man

Hinze. " . . . there are studious, deliberate forms of insincerity which it is fair to be impatient with: Hinze's, for example . . . his family is Alsatian, but he has been settled in England for more than one generation. He is the superlatively deferential man, and walks about with murmured wonder at the wisdom and discernment of everybody who talks to him. He cultivates the low-toned *tête à tête,* keeping his hat carefully in his hand and often stroking it, while he smiles with downcast eyes, as if to relieve his feelings under the pressure of the remarkable conversation which it is his honour to enjoy at the present moment."

—disconcerting: "**Felicia** was evidently embarrassed by his reverent wonder, and, in dread lest she should seem to be playing the oracle, became somewhat confused . . . . But this made no difference to Hinze's rapt attention and subdued eagerness of inquiry. He continued to put large questions, bending his head slightly that his eyes might be a little lifted in awaiting her reply . . . .

"Here was an occasion for Hinze to smile down on his hat and stroke it. . . . Hinze appeared so impressed with the plenitude of [Felicia's] revelations that he recapitulated them, weaving them together with threads of compliment— 'As you very justly observed'; and—'It is most true, as you say,' and— 'It were well if others noted what you have remarked.' "

—"ass": "Some listeners incautious in their epithets would have called Hinze an 'ass.' For my part I would never insult that intelligent and unpretending animal who no doubt brays with perfect simplicity and substantial meaning to those acquainted with his idiom, and if he feigns more submission than he feels, has weighty reasons for doing so—I would never, I say, insult that historic and ill-appreciated animal, the ass, by giving his name to a man whose continuous pretence is so shallow in its motive, so unexcused by any sharp appetite as this of Hinze's."

—others' opinions: "In general, Hinze delights in the citation of opinions, and would hardly remark that the sun shone without an air of respectful appeal or fervid adhesion. The 'Iliad,' one sees, would impress him little if it were not for what **Mr Fugleman** has lately said about it; and if you mention an image or sentiment in **Chaucer** he seems not to heed the bearing of your reference, but immediately tells you that **Mr Hautboy**, too, regards Chaucer as a poet of the first order, and he is delighted to find that two such judges as you and Hautboy are at one."

—status: "He is very well off in the world, and cherishes no unsatisfied ambition that could feed design and direct flattery . . . he has had the education and other advantages of a gentleman without being conscious of marked result, such as a decided preference for any particular ideas or functions."

—mind: "His mind is furnished as hotels are, with everything for occasional and transient use."

—judgment: "His nature is not tuned to the pitch of a genuine direct admiration, only to an attitudinising deference which does not fatigue itself with the formation of real judgments. All human achievement must be wrought down to this spoon-meat—this mixture of other persons' washy opinions and his own flux of reverence for what is third-hand, before Hinze can find a relish for it."

—*correctness:* "He has no more leading characteristic than the desire to stand well with those who are justly distinguished; he has no base admirations, and you may know by his entire presentation of himself, from the management of his hat to the angle at which he keeps his right foot, that he aspires to correctness."

—*summarized:* "Hinze has not the stuff in him to be at once agreeably conversational and sincere, and he has got himself up to be at all events agreeably conversational. Notwithstanding this deliberateness of intention in his talk he is unconscious of falsity, for he has not enough of deep and lasting impression to find a contrast or diversity between his words and his thoughts. He is not fairly to be called a hypocrite, but I have already confessed to the more exasperation at his make-believe reverence, because it has no deep hunger to excuse it."

Felicia, "who is certainly a clever woman, and, without any unusual desire to show her cleverness, occasionally says something of her own or makes an allusion which is not quite common."

—*good citizen:* "Felicia's acquaintances know her as the suitable wife of a distinguished man, a sensible, vivacious, kindly-disposed woman, helping her husband with graceful apologies written and spoken, and making her receptions agreeable to all comers. But you have imagined that **Hinze** had been prepared by general report to regard this introduction to her as an opportunity comparable to an audience of the Delphic Sibyl."

—*conversation:* "When she had delivered herself on the changes in Italian travel, on the difficulty of reading **Ariosto** in these busy times, on the want of equilibrium in French political affairs, and on the pre-eminence of German music, he would know what to think."

Tulpian "is appealed to on innumerable subjects, and if he is unwilling to express himself on any one of them, says so with instructive copiousness: he is much listened to, and his utterances are registered and reported with more or less exactitude. But I think he has no other listener who comports himself as Hinze does—who, figuratively speaking, carries about a small spoon ready to pick up any dusty crumbs of opinion that the eloquent man may have let drop."

—*quirks:* "Tulpian, with reverence, be it said, has some rather absurd notions, such as a mind of large discourse often finds room for: they slip about among his higher conceptions and multitudinous acquirements like disreputable characters at a national celebration in some vast cathedral, where to the ardent soul all is glorified by rainbow light and grand associations: any vulgar detective knows them for what they are."

TS 6

VI Only Temper

Touchwood. "He is by turns insolent, quarrelsome, repulsively haughty to innocent people who approach him with respect, neglectful of his friends, angry in face of legitimate demands, procrastinating in the fulfilment of such demands, prompted to rude words and harsh looks by a moody disgust with his fellow-men in general—and yet, as everybody will assure you, the soul of honour, a steadfast friend, a defender of the oppressed, an affectionate-hearted creature."

—antagonistic: "Touchwood's bad temper is of the contradicting pugnacious sort. He is the honourable gentleman in opposition, whatever proposal or proposition may be broached . . . . An invitation or any sign of expectation throws him into an attitude of refusal. Ask his concurrence in a benevolent measure: he will not decline to give it, because he has a real sympathy with good aims; but he complies resentfully, though where he is let alone he will do much more than any one would have thought of asking for. No man would shrink with greater sensitiveness from the imputation of not paying his debts, yet when a bill is sent in with any promptitude he is inclined to make the tradesman wait for the money he is in such a hurry to get."

—reversal: "If Touchwood's behaviour affects you very closely you had better break your leg in the course of the day: his bad temper will then vanish at once; he will take a painful journey on your behalf; he will sit up with you night after night; he will do all the work of your department so as to save you from any loss in consequence of your accident; he will be even uniformly tender to you till you are well on your legs again, when he will some fine morning insult you without provocation, and make you wish that his generous goodness to you had not closed your lips against retort."

—amends: " . . . Touchwood's atoning friendliness has a ring of artificiality. Because he formerly disguised his good feeling towards you he now expresses more than he quite feels. It is in vain. Having made you extremely uncomfortable last week he has absolutely diminished his power of making you happy to-day: he struggles against this result by excessive effort, but he has taught you to observe his fitfulness rather than to be warmed by his episodic show of regard."

TS 7

VII A Political Molecule

Spike, "an elector who voted on the side of Progress though he was not inwardly attached to it under that name."

—characteristics: "He was a political molecule of the most gentlemanlike appearance, not less than six feet high, and showing the utmost nicety in the care of his person and equipment. His umbrella was especially remarkable for its neatness, though perhaps he swung it unduly in walking. His complexion was fresh, his eyes small, bright, and twinkling. He was seen to great advantage in a hat and greatcoat—garments frequently fatal to the impressiveness of shorter figures; but when he was uncovered in the drawing-room, it was impossible not to observe that his head shelved off too rapidly from the eyebrows towards the crown, and that his length of limb seemed to have used up his mind so as to cause an air of abstraction from conversational topics. He appeared, indeed, to be preoccupied with a sense of his exquisite cleanli-

ness, clapped his hands together and rubbed them frequently, straightened his back, and even opened his mouth and closed it again with a slight snap, apparently for no other purpose than the confirmation to himself of his own powers in that line."

—conversationalist: "Sometimes Spike's mind, emerging from its preoccupation, burst forth in a remark delivered with smiling zest; as, that he did like to see gravel walks well rolled, or that a lady should always wear the best jewellery, or that a bride was a most interesting object; but finding these ideas received rather coldly, he would relapse into abstraction, draw up his back, wrinkle his brows longitudinally, and seem to regard society, even including gravel walks, jewellery, and brides, as essentially a poor affair."

—intellectual interests: " . . . though he seemed rather surprised at the consideration that **Alfred the Great** was a Catholic, or that apart from the Ten Commandments any conception of moral conduct had occurred to mankind, he was not stimulated to further inquiries on these remote matters. Yet he aspired to what he regarded as intellectual society, willingly entertained beneficed clergymen, and bought the books he heard spoken of, arranging them carefully on the shelves of what he called his library, and occasionally sitting alone in the same room with them."

—political might-have-been: " . . . he understood his own trading affairs, and in this way became a genuine, constant political element. If he had been born a little later he could have been accepted as an eligible member of Parliament, and if he had belonged to a high family he might have done for a member of the Government. Perhaps his indifference to 'views' would have passed for administrative judiciousness, and he would have been so generally silent that he must often have been silent in he right place."

Mrs Spike, "influential as a woman who belonged to a family with a title in it, and who had condescended in marrying him . . . had to blush a little at what was called her husband's 'radicalism'—an epithet which was a very unfair impeachment of Spike, who never went to the root of anything."

TS 8

VIII The Watch-Dog of Knowledge

Mordax "is an admirable man, ardent in intellectual work, public-spirited, affectionate, and able to find the right words in conveying ingenious ideas or elevated feeling. Pity that to all these graces he cannot add what would give them the utmost finish—the occasional admission that he has been in the wrong, the occasional frank welcome of a new idea as something not before present to his mind! But no: Mordax's self-respect seems to be of that fiery quality which demands that none but the monarchs of thought shall have an advantage over him, and in the presence of contradiction or the threat of having his notions corrected, he becomes astonishingly unscrupulous and cruel for so kindly and conscientious a man."

Acer. " 'You are fond of attributing those fine qualities to Mordax . . . but I have not much belief in virtues that are always requiring to be asserted in spite of appearances against them. True fairness and goodwill show themselves precisely where his are conspicuously absent.' "

Laniger, "who has a temper but no talent for repartee, having been run down in a fierce way by **Mordax**, is inwardly persuaded that the highly-lauded man is a wolf at heart: he is much tried by perceiving that his own friends seem to think no worse of the reckless assailant than they did before. . . . "

Corvus, "who has lately been flattered by some kindness from Mordax, is unmindful enough of Laniger's feeling to dwell on this instance of good-nature with admiring gratitude."

Judas [H]. "The deed of Judas has been attributed to far-reaching views, and the wish to hasten his Master's declaration of himself as the Messiah. Perhaps—I will not maintain the contrary—Judas represented his motive in this way, and felt justified in his traitorous kiss; but my belief that he deserved, metaphorically speaking, to be where **Dante** saw him, at the bottom of the Malebolge, would not be the less strong because he was not convinced that his action was detestable."

Pummel. "I have a sort of valet and factotum, an excellent, respectable servant, whose spelling is so unvitiated by non-phonetic superfluities that he writes *night* as *nit*. One day, looking over his accounts, I said to him jocosely, 'You are in the latest fashion with your spelling, Pummel: most people spell 'night' with a *gh* between the *i* and the *t*, but the greatest scholars now spell it as you do.' 'So I suppose, sir,' says Pummel; 'I've see it with a *gh*, but I've noways give into that myself.' "

—*unastonished:* "You would never catch Pummel in an interjection of surprise. I have sometimes laid traps for his astonishment, but he has escaped them all, either by a respectful neutrality, as of one who would not appear to notice that his master had been taking too much wine, or else by that strong persuasion of his all-knowingness which makes it simply impossible for him to feel himself newly informed. If I tell him that the world is spinning round and along like a top, and that he is spinning with it, he says, 'Yes, I've heard a deal of that in my time, sir,' and lifts the horizontal lines of his brow a little higher, balancing his head from side to side as if it were too painfully full . . . . His utmost concession is, that what you state is what he would have supplied if you had given him *carte blanche* instead of your needless instruction, and in this sense his favourite answer is, 'I should say.' "

—*superior:* "But while he is never surprised himself, he is constantly imagining situations of surprise for others. His own consciousness is that of one so thoroughly soaked in knowledge that further absorption is impossible, but his neighbours appear to him to be in the state of thirsty sponges which it is a charity to besprinkle . . . . He is fond of discoursing to the lad who acts as **shoe-black** and general subaltern, and I have overheard him saying to that small upstart, with some severity, 'Now don't you pretend to know, because the more you pretend the more I see your ignorance'—a lucidity on his part which has confirmed my impression that the thoroughly self-satisfied person is the only one fully to appreciate the charm of humility in others."

TS 9

IX A Half-Breed

Mixtus. "To most observers he appears to be simply one of the fortunate and also sharp commercial men who began with meaning to be rich and have become what they meant to be: a man never taken to be well-born, but surprisingly better informed than the well-born usually are, and distingushed among ordinary commercial magnates by a personal kindness which prompts him not only to help the suffering in a material way through his wealth, but also by direct ministration of his own; yet with all this, diffusing, as it were, the odour of a man delightedly conscious of his wealth is an equivalent for the other social distinctions of rank and intellect which he can thus admire without envying."

—*in youth:* " . . . his chosen associates were men and women whose only distinction was a religious, a philanthropic, or an intellectual enthusiasm, when the lady on whose words his attention most hung was a writer of minor religious literature . . . . At that time Mixtus thought himself a young man of socially reforming ideas, of religious principles and religious yearnings . . . . His opinions were of a strongly democratic stamp, except that even then, belonging to the class of employers, he was opposed to all demands in the employed that would restrict the expansiveness of trade."

—*his present acquaintance:* "This society regards him as a clever fellow in his particular branch, seeing that he has become a considerable capitalist, and as a man desirable to have on the list of one's acquaintance. But from every other point of view Mixtus finds himself personally submerged: what he happens to think is not felt by his esteemed guests to be of any consequence, and what he used to think with the ardour of conviction he now hardly ever expresses. He is transplanted, and the sap within him has long been diverted into other than the old lines of vigorous growth."

—*and now:* "He has not lost the kindness that used to make him a benefactor and succourer of the needy, and he is still liberal in helping forward the clever and industrious; but in his active superintendence of commercial undertakings he has contracted more and more of the bitterness which capitalists and employers often feel to be a reasonable mood towards obstructive proletaries. Hence many who have occasionally met him when trade questions were being discussed, conclude him to be indistinguishable from the ordinary run of moneyed and money-getting men. Indeed, hardly any of his acquaintances know what Mixtus really is, considered as a whole—nor does Mixtus himself know it."

Apollos, "an eloquent congregational preacher, who had studied in Germany and had liberal advanced views then far beyond the ordinary teaching of his sect."

Scintilla. "Why, he married Scintilla, who fascinated him as she had fascinated others, by her prettiness, her liveliness, and her music."

—*milieu:* " . . . though without fortune, [she] associated with families of Greek merchants living in a style of splendour, and with artists patronised by such wealthy entertainers."

—*particular:* "Now this lively lady knew nothing of Non-conformists, except that they were unfashionable: she did not distinguish one conventicle from another . . . . In general, people who appeared seriously to believe in any sort of doctrine, whether religious, social, or philosophical, seemed rather absurd to Scintilla. Ten to one these theoretic people pronounced oddly, had some reason or other for saying that the most agreeable things were wrong, wore objectionable clothes, and wanted you to subscribe to something. They were probably ignorant of art and music, did not understand *badinage,* and, in fact, could talk of nothing amusing."

—*not particular:* "If Scintilla had no liking for the best sort of nonconformity, she was without any troublesome bias towards Episcopacy, Anglicanism, and early sacraments, and was quite contented not to go to church."

—*wifely:* "**Mixtus**, she felt, was an excellent creature, quite likable, who was getting rich; and Scintilla meant to have all the advantages of a rich man's wife. She was not in the least a wicked woman; she was simply a pretty animal of the ape kind, with an aptitude for certain accomplishments which education had made the most of."

TS 10

X Debasing the Moral Currency

Clarissa Such. "We soak our children in habits of contempt and exultant gibing, and yet are confident that—as Clarissa one day said to me—'We can always teach them to be reverent in the right place, you know.' And doubtless if she were to take her boys to see a burlesque **Socrates**, with swollen legs, dying in the utterance of cockney puns, and were to hang up a sketch of this comic scene among their bedroom prints, she would think this preparation not at all to the prejudice of their emotions on hearing their tutor read that narrative of the *Apology* which has been consecrated by the reverent gratitude of ages."

TS 11

XI The Wasp Credited with the Honeycomb

Euphorion. "No man, I imagine, would object more strongly than Euphorion to communistic principles in relation to material property, but with regard to property in ideas he entertains such principles willingly, and is disposed to treat the distinction between Mine and Thine in original authorship as egoistic, narrowing, and low."

—*intellectual creations:* " . . . it is his habit to talk with a Gallic largeness and refer to the universe: he expatiates on the diffusive nature of intellectual products, free and all-embracing as the liberal air; on the infinitesimal smallness of individual origination compared with the massive inheritance of thought on which every new generation enters; on that growing preparation for every epoch through which certain ideas or modes of view are said to be in the air, and, still more metaphorically speaking, to be inevitably absorbed, so that every one may be excused for not knowing how he got them."

—*pretension:* "But Euphorion would be very sorry to have it supposed that he is unacquainted with the history of ideas, and sometimes carries even into minutiæ the evidence of his exact registration of names in connection with quotable phrases or suggestions: I can therefore only explain the apparent infirmity of his memory in cases of larger 'conveyance' by supposing that he is accustomed by the very association of largeness to range them at once under those grand laws of the universe in the light of which Mine and Thine disappear and are resolved into Everybody's or Nobody's, and one man's particular obligations to another melt untraceably into the obligations of the earth to the solar system in general."

Aquila "is too agreeable and amusing for any one who is not himself bent on display to be angry at his conversational rapine—his habit of darting down on every morsel of booty that other birds may hold in their beaks, with an innocent air, as if it were all intended for his use, and honestly counted on by him as a tribute in kind. Hardly any man, I imagine, can have had less trouble in gathering a showy stock of information than Aquila. On close inquiry you would probably find that he had not read one epoch-making book of modern times, for he has a career which obliges him to much correspondence and other official work, and he is too fond of being in company to spend his leisure moments in study; but to his quick eye, ear, and tongue, a few predatory excursions in conversation where there are instructed persons, gradually furnish surprisingly clever modes of statement and allusion on the dominant topic."

Sir Hong Kong Bantam [named in 9]. " . . . the insignificant Bantam, hitherto silent, seemed to spoil the flow of ideas by stating that the product could not be taken as less than a hundred and seventeen, **Aquila** would glide on in the most graceful manner . . . causing Bantam to be regarded by all present as one of those slow persons who take irony for ignorance, and who would warn the weasel to keep awake. How should a small-eyed, feebly crowing mortal like him be quicker in arithmetic than the keen-faced forcible Aquila, in whom universal knowledge is easily credible?"

Hoopoe et al. "Hardly any kind of false reasoning is more ludicrous than this on the probabilities of origination. It would be amusing to catechise the guessers as to their exact reasons for thinking their guess 'likely': why Hoopoe of John's has fixed on **Toucan** of Magdalen; why **Shrike** attributes its peculiar style to **Buzzard**, who has not hitherto been known as a writer; why the fair **Columba** thinks it must belong to the reverend **Merula**; and why they are all alike disturbed in their previous judgment of its value by finding that it really came from **Skunk**, whom they had either not thought of at all, or thought of as belonging to a species excluded by the nature of the case."

Skunk. "Clearly they were all wrong in their notion of the specific conditions, which lay unexpectedly in the small Skunk, and in him alone—in spite of his education nobody knows where, in spite of somebody's knowing his uncles and cousins, and in spite of nobody's knowing that he was cleverer than they thought him."

TS 12

XII 'So Young!'

Ganymede "was once a girlishly handsome precocious youth . . . many circumstances have conspired to keep up in Ganymede the illusion that he is surprisingly young. He was the last born of his family, and from his earliest memory was accustomed to be commended as such to the care of his elder brothers and sisters: he heard his mother speak of him as her youngest darling with a loving pathos in her tone, which naturally suffused his own view of himself, and gave him the habitual consciousness of being at once very young and very interesting . . . his deficiencies and excesses were alike to be accounted for by the flattering fact of his youth, and his youth was the golden background which set off his many-hued endowments."

—to his credit: "If we imagine with due charity the effect on Ganymede, we shall think it greatly to his credit that he continued to feel the necessity of

being something more than young, and did not sink by rapid degrees into a parallel of that melancholy object, a superannuated youthful phenomenon. Happily he had enough of valid, active faculty to save him from that tragic fate."

—*appearance in youth:* "I saw something of him through . . . the time of rich chesnut [*sic*] locks, parted not by a visible white line, but by a shadowed furrow from which they fell in massive ripples to right and left. In these slim days he looked the younger for being rather below the middle size, and though at last one perceived him contracting an indefinable air of self-consciousness, a slight exaggeration of the facial movements, the attitudes, the little tricks, and the romance in shirt-collars, which must be expected from one who, in spite of his knowledge, was so exceedingly young, it was impossible to say that he was making any great mistake about himself."

—*self-conscious:* "He was only undergoing one form of a common moral disease: being strongly mirrored for himself in the remark of others, he was getting to see his real characteristics as a dramatic part, a type to which his doings were always in correspondence."

—*after an absence:* "He had lost his slimness, and that curved solidity which might have adorned a taller man was a rather sarcastic threat to his short figure . . . a stranger would now have been apt to remark that Ganymede was unusually plump for a distinguished writer, rather than unusually young."

Wife. "He had married . . . and as if to keep up his surprising youthfulness in all relations, he had taken a wife considerably older than himself."

TS 13

XIII How We Come to Give Ourselves False Testimonials, And Believe in Them

Heloisa et al. " . . . it does seem surprising that Heloisa should be disgusted at **Laura**'s attempts to disguise her age, attempts which she recognises so thoroughly because they enter into her own practice; that **Semper**, who often responds at public dinners and proposes resolutions on platforms, though he has a trying gestation of every speech and a bad time for himself and others at every delivery, should yet remark pitilessly on the folly of precisely the same course of action in **Ubique**; that **Aliquis**, who lets no attack on himself pass unnoticed, and for every handful of gravel against his windows sends a stone in reply, should deplore the ill-advised retorts of **Quispiam**, who does not perceive that to show oneself angry with an adversary is to gratify him."

Pilulus. " 'A person with your tendency of constitution should take as little sugar as possible,' said Pilulus to **Bovis** somewhere in the darker decades of this century. 'It has made a great difference to **Avis** since he took my advice in that matter: he used to consume half a pound a-day.' "

Bovis "had never said inwardly that he would take a large allowance of sugar, and he had the tradition about himself that he was a man of the most moderate habits; hence, with this conviction, he was naturally disgusted at the saccharine excesses of **Avis**."

Mrs Bovis. " 'Twenty-six large lumps every day of your life, **Mr Bovis**,' says his wife . . . .

" 'You drop them into your tea, coffee, and whisky yourself, my dear, and I count them.' "

Callista "is always ready to testify of herself that she is an imaginative person, and sometimes adds in illustration, that if she had taken a walk and seen an old heap of stones on her way, the account she would give on returning would include many pleasing particulars of her own invention, transforming the simple heap into an interesting castellated ruin."

—casual: "And, in fact, I find on listening to Callista's conversation, that she has a very lax conception even of common objects, and an equally lax memory of events. It seems of no consequence to her whether she shall say that a stone is overgrown with moss or with lichen, that a building is of sandstone or of granite, that **Meliboeus** once forgot to put on his cravat or that he always appears without it; that everybody says so, or that one stock-broker's wife said so yesterday; that **Philemon** praised **Euphemia** up to the skies, or that he denied knowing any particular evil of her . . . . Her supposed imaginativeness is simply a very usual lack of discriminating perception, accompanied with a less usual activity of misrepresentation, which, if it had been a little more intense, or had been stimulated by circumstance, might have made her a profuse writer unchecked by the troublesome need of veracity."

TS 14

XIV The Too Ready Writer

Adrastus, "whose professional engagements might seem more than enough for the nervous energy of one man, and who yet finds time to print essays on the chief current subjects, from the tri-lingual inscriptions, or the idea of the infinite among the prehistoric Lapps, to the Colorado beetle and the grape disease in the south of France, is generally praised if not admired for the breadth of his mental range and his gigantic powers of work."

Theron, "who has some original ideas on a subject to which he has given years of research and meditation, has been waiting anxiously from month to month to see whether his condensed exposition will find a place in the next advertised programme, but sees it, on the contrary, regularly excluded, and twice the space he asked for filled with the copious brew of **Adrastus**, whose name carries custom like a celebrated trade-mark."

Pepin. "In the vivacious Pepin I have often seen the image of my early youth . . . he is industrious while I was idle . . . Pepin, while feeling himself powerful with the stars in their courses, really raises some dust here below."

—in a hurry: "He is no longer in his springtide, but having been always busy he has been obliged to use his first impressions as if they were deliberate opinions, and to range himself on the corresponding side in ignorance of much that he commits himself to; so that he retains some characteristics of a comparatively tender age, and among them a certain surprise that there have not been more persons equal to himself. Perhaps it is unfortunate for him that he early gained a hearing, or at least a place in print, and was thus encouraged in acquiring a fixed habit of writing, to the exclusion of any other breadwinning pursuit."

—critic: " . . . he finds himself under an obligation to be skilled in various methods of seeming to know; and having habitually expressed himself before he was convinced, his interest in all subjects is chiefly to ascertain that he has not made a mistake, and to feel his infallibility confirmed. That impulse

to decide . . . has hardened into 'style,' and into a pattern of peremptory sentences; the sense of ability in the presence of other men's failures is turning into the official arrogance of one who habitually issues directions which he has never himself been called on to execute . . . . "

—*misleading impression:* "Is this fellow-citizen of ours, considered simply in the light of a baptised Christian and tax-paying Englishman, really as madly conceited, as empty of reverential feeling, as unveracious and careless of justice, as full of catch-penny devices and stagey attitudinising as on examination his writing shows itself to be? By no means. He has arrived at his present pass in 'the literary calling' through the self-imposed obligation to give himself a manner which would convey the impression of superior knowledge and ability. He is much worthier and more admirable than his written productions . . . . "

Bombus. "[**Pepin**] is on the way to become like the loud-buzzing, bouncing Bombus who combines conceited illusions enough to supply several patients in a lunatic asylum with the freedom to show himself at large in various forms of print."

TS 15

XV Diseases of Small Authorship

Vorticella, "who flourished in my youth not only as a portly lady walking in silk attire, but also as the authoress of a book entitled 'The Channel Islands, with Notes and an Appendix.' "

—*intimidating:* " . . . Vorticella's personality had an effect on me something like that of a powerful mesmeriser when he directs all his ten fingers towards your eyes, as unpleasantly visible ducts for the invisible stream. I felt a great power of contempt in her, if I did not come up to her expectations."

—*the disease:* "Poor Vorticella might not have been more wearisome on a visit than the majority of her neighbours, but for this disease of magnified self-importance belonging to small authorship. I understand that the chronic complaint of 'The Channel Islands' never left her. As the years went on and the publication tended to vanish in the distance for her neighbours' memory, she was still bent on dragging it to the foreground, and her chief interest in new acquaintances was the possibility of lending them her book, entering into all details concerning it, and requesting them to read her album of 'critical opinions.' "

Volvox. " 'The fact is that no critic in this town is fit to meddle with such subjects, unless it be Volvox, and he, with all his command of language, is very superficial. It is Volvox who writes in the "Monitor." I hope you noticed how he contradicts himself?' "

Vibrio, " 'who writes the playful notice in the "Medley Pie," has a clever hit at **Volvox** in that passage about the steeplechase of imagination, where the loser wants to make it appear that the winner was only run away with. . . . Vibrio is a poor little tippling creature, but, as **Mr Carlyle** would say, he has an eye, and he is always lively.' "

Gregarina, "whose distinction was that she had had cholera, and who did not feel herself in her true position with strangers until they knew it."

Male author. "I have known a man with a single pamphlet containing an assurance that somebody else was wrong, together with a few approved quotations, produce a more powerful effect of shuddering at his approach than ever **Vorticella** did with her varied octavo volume, including notes and appendix."

Monas, "who had also written his one book . . . and not only carried it in his portmanteau when he went on visits, but took the earliest opportunity of depositing it in the drawing-room, and afterwards would enter to look for it, as if under pressure of a need for reference, begging the lady of the house to tell him whether she had seen 'a small volume bound in red.' One hostess at last ordered it to be carried into his bedroom to save his time; but it presently reappeared in his hands, and was again left with inserted slips of paper on the drawing-room table."

TS 16

XVI Moral Swindlers

Melissa. "Talking to Melissa in a time of commercial trouble, I found her disposed to speak pathetically of the disgrace which had fallen on **Sir Gavial Mantrap** . . . ."

—*questioned:* " 'Oh, all that about the Companies, I know was most unfortunate . . . . But **Sir Gavial** made a good use of his money, and he is a thoroughly *moral* man . . . .

" 'Sir Gavial is an excellent family man—quite blameless there, and so charitable round his place at Tiptop . . . . I think a man's morals should make a difference to us . . . I *am* sorry for Sir Gavial Mantrap.' "

Sir Gavial Mantrap, disgraced "because of his conduct in relation to the Eocene Mines, and to other companies ingeniously devised by him for the punishment of ignorance in people of small means: a disgrace by which the poor titled gentleman was actually reduced to live in comparative obscurity on his wife's settlement of one or two hundred thousand in the consols."

—*aftermath:* " ' . . . he is eating well, lying softly, and after impudently justifying himself before the public, is perhaps joining in the General Confession with a sense that he is an acceptable object in the sight of God, though decent men refuse to meet him.' "

Barabbas, " 'whose life, my husband tells me, is most objectionable, with actresses and that sort of thing. I think a man's morals should make a difference to us. I'm not sorry for Mr Barabbas . . . . "

TS 17

XVII Shadows of the Coming Race

Trost. "My friend Trost, who is no optimist as to the state of the universe hitherto . . . is confident that at some future period within the duration of the solar system, ours will be the best of all possible worlds—a hope which I always honour as a sign of beneficent qualities . . . . "

—*reassurance:* " 'But' says Trost, treating me with cautious mildness . . . 'you forget that these wonder-workers are the slaves of our race, need our tendance and regulation, obey the mandates of our consciousness, and are only deaf and dumb bringers of reports which we decipher and make use of. They are simply extensions of the human organism, so to speak, limbs immeasurably more powerful, ever more subtle finger-tips, ever more mastery over the invisibly great and the invisibly small. Each new machine needs a new appliance of human skill to construct it, new devices to feed it with material, and often keener-edged faculties to note its registrations or performances. How then can machines supersede us?—they depend upon us. When we cease, they cease.' "

TS 18

XVIII The Modern Hep! Hep! Hep!

Editor's note: There is not a single character, not a single coined name, not a single "Impression" anywhere in this essay, which appears to have been tacked onto TS so that GE would see it in print before she died. In effect, she buried it with hardly a trace. It is extensively abstracted in the *Topicon,* however, particularly at FM:Jews, and a portion of it is an Epilogue to the chapter on *Daniel Deronda* at page 594.

Also mentioned

(Historical figures excluded)

Aliquis, who lets no attack on himself pass unnoticed	13
Avis, who took too much sugar before Pilulus spoke to him	13
Buzzard, who might have written something	11
Catulus, a younger scientist who attacks Merman	3
Columba, who attributed a writing to the reverend Merula	11
Crespi, an artist	9
Euphemia, praised by Philemon	13
Fugleman, who pontificates on the *Iliad*	5
Hautboy, who is pleased to consider Chaucer a great poet	5
Jacobson, believed to be Jewish and thought unpleasant	18
Johns, preaching with a solemn twang at a Baptist chapel in the lowest suburbs	9
Laura, like **Heloisa**, making a practice of disguising her advancing age with makeup	13
Megalosaurus, that greatest of fossils	3
Melibœus, of sartorial uncertainty	13
Rev. Merula, to whom a writing was attributed by Columba	11
Microps, scientific researcher	3
Philemon, with ambivalent and contradictory reports of Euphemia	13
Quispiam, whose ill-advised retorts to criticism are themselves criticised by Aliquis	13
Rosemary, creator of a sculpture called "Babes in the Wood"	5
Scrag Whale, explorer	3
Semper, a poor but frequent public speaker	13
Shark, a younger scientist who attacks Merman	3
shoe-black, a small subaltern in the Narrator's household	8
Shrike, who made an erroneous attribution	11
Toucan, of Magdalen, who might have written something	11
Dr Tuffle, who wrote in the "Regulator"	4
Ubique, criticised by Semper for inept public speaking	13

The Lifted Veil

The narrator **Latimer** tells us he foresees his death and describes it. He has parapsychological gifts, including "prevision." A younger brother, he tells of his rigid father, who tried to impose on him a career unsuited to his talents and predilections. Forced to study science, he read Shakespeare on the sly. He went to Geneva to study at age sixteen and made a friend, **Charles Meunier**. He becomes ill and in convalescence tended by his father (who has come from London to be with him, a fact Latimer never notices) has a clairvoyant vision of Prague. Intrigued, he tries to induce a vision of Venice but fails. Waiting for his father, who has planned an excursion for him, he has a vision of his father and two ladies: **Mrs Filmore**, a neighbour at home, and her husband's orphaned niece, **Bertha Grant**. They vanish, but moments later Latimer sees them, hears his father speak the exact words of the vision, and faints.

When he wakes, his father explains about Bertha. Latimer finds he is intermittently, involuntarily telepathic. Others' thoughts, banal and annoying, obtrude on his consciousness. He hates his brother **Alfred**, partly because he seems destined for Bertha. Latimer is fascinated by her because he cannot read her mind. Infatuated, he gives her a ring for her birthday, but does not see it on her finger. He asks about it: she shows she wears it on a chain in her bosom. He is undone. In Vienna, he envisions her as his wife. He hates Alfred, wishing him dead. He faints. On to Prague: will it be as he saw it? Yes. 1

At home: Bertha and Alfred are engaged. He goes out riding. Latimer calls on Bertha, and they walk and talk. He bursts out his love; she turns it aside. At home he learns Alfred has been thrown and killed. After 18 months, Latimer and Bertha marry. He is ecstatic for a time, but her manner grows cold and withdrawn. His father dies. He can read her mind now, and he is repulsed. It is silent war for seven years. Then a maid leaves and Bertha hires **Mrs Archer**, who gains mysterious influence with her. Latimer gradually is losing his telepathic capabilities, and Bertha seems more cheerful.

A letter from Meunier: he will visit. Bertha and Archer fall out; Archer becomes ill; Bertha nurses her attentively. Meunier says she will die. He wants to try the results of a transfusion after death. Bertha watches and will not leave until death occurs. The transfusion brings Mrs Archer back just as Bertha reenters to face her accusation of trying to poison Latimer. Latimer and Bertha separate. She lives on half their wealth, pitied and admired; he wanders before coming home to die. 2

The Protagonist

Latimer. "I have lately been subject to attacks of *angina pectoris,* and in the ordinary course of things, my physician tells me, I may fairly hope that my life will not be protracted many months." 1

—*death foreseen:* "Just as I am watching a tongue of blue flame rising in the fire, and my lamp is burning low, the horrible contraction will begin at my chest. I shall only have time to reach the bell, and pull it violently, before the sense of suffocation will come . . . . The sense of suffocation increases: my lamp goes out with a horrible stench: I make a great effort, and snatch at the bell again. I long for life, and there is no help. I thirsted for the unknown: the thirst is gone. O God, let me stay with the known, and be weary of it: I am content. Agony of pain and suffocation—and all the while the earth, the fields, the pebbly brook at the bottom of the rookery, the fresh scent after the rain, the light of the morning through my chamber-window, the warmth of the hearth after the frosty air—will darkness close over them for ever?" 1

—*death:* "Darkness—darkness—no pain—nothing but darkness: but I am passing on and on through the darkness: my thought stays in the darkness, but always with a sense of moving onward." 1

—*childhood remembered:* "My childhood perhaps seems happier to me than it really was, by contrast with all the after-years. For then the curtain of the future was as impenetrable to me as to other children: I had all their delight in the present hour, their sweet indefinite hopes for the morrow; and I had a tender mother: even now, after the dreary lapse of long years, a slight trace of sensation accompanies the remembrance of her caress as she held me on her knee—her arms round my little body, her cheek pressed on mine." 1

—*disconcerted by visions:* "Already I had begun to taste something of the horror that belongs to the lot of a human being whose nature is not adjusted to simple human conditions" 1

—*new sensibility:* "This was the obtrusion on my mind of the mental process going forward in first one person, and then another, with whom I happened to be in contact: the vagrant, frivolous ideas and emotions of some uninteresting acquaintance—**Mrs Filmore**, for example—would force themselves on my consciousness like an importunate, ill-played musical instrument, or the loud activity of an imprisoned insect." 1

"But this superadded consciousness, wearying and annoying enough when it urged on me the trivial experience of indifferent people, became an intense pain and grief when it seemed to be opening to me the souls of those who were in a close relation to me—when the rational talk, the graceful attentions, the wittily-turned phrases, and the kindly deeds, which used to make the web of their characters, were seen as if thrust asunder by a microscopic vision, that showed all the intermediate frivolities, all the suppressed egoism, all the struggling chaos of puerilities, meanness, vague capricious memories, and indolent make-shift thoughts, from which human words and deeds emerge like leaflets covering a fermenting heap." 1

—tongue-tied: " . . . my constitutional timidity and distrust had continued to benumb me, and the words in which I had sometimes premeditated a confession of my love, had died away unuttered. The same conflict had gone on within me as before—the longing for an assurance of love from **Bertha**'s lips, the dread lest a word of contempt and denial should fall upon me like a corrosive acid. What was the conviction of a distant necessity to me? I trembled under a present glance, I hungered after a present joy, I was clogged and chilled by a present fear." 2

—overwhelmed: "The girl whose light fingers grasped me, whose elfish charming face looked into mine—who, I thought, was betraying an interest in my feelings that she would not have directly avowed—this warm-breathing presence again possessed my senses and imagination like a returning syren [*sic*] melody which had been overpowered for an instant by the roar of threatening waves. It was a moment as delicious to me as the waking up to a consciousness of youth after a dream of middle age." 2

—new feeling: "As I saw into the desolation of my father's heart, I felt a movement of deep pity towards him, which was the beginning of a new affection—an affection that grew and strengthened in spite of the strange bitterness with which he regarded me in the first month or two after my brother's death. If it had not been for the softening influence of my compassion for him—the first deep compassion I had ever felt—I should have been stung by the perception that my father transferred the inheritance of an eldest son to me with a mortified sense that fate had compelled him to the unwelcome course of caring for me as an important being . . . . There is hardly any neglected child for whom death has made vacant a more favoured place, who will not understand what I mean." 2

"My softened feeling towards my father made this the happiest time I had known since childhood—these last months in which I retained the delicious illusion of loving Bertha, of longing and doubting and hoping that she might love me." 2

—reversal: "Our positions were reversed. Before marriage she had completely mastered my imagination, for she was a secret to me; and I created the unknown thought before which I trembled as if it were hers. But now that her soul was laid open to me, now that I was compelled to share the privacy of her motives, to follow all the petty devices that preceded her words and acts, she found herself powerless with me, except to produce in me the chill shudder of repulsion—powerless, because I could be acted on by no lever within her reach. I was dead to worldly ambitions, to social vanities, to all the incentives within the compass of her narrow imagination, and I lived under influences utterly invisible to her." 2

—suicide? "For a long while she lived in the hope that my evident wretchedness would drive me to the commission of suicide; but suicide was not in my nature. I was too completely swayed by the sense that I was in the grasp of unknown forces, to believe in my power of self-release. Towards my own

destiny I had become entirely passive; for my one ardent desire had spent itself, and impulse no longer predominated over knowledge." 2

—*pity:* "There was still pity in my soul for every living thing, and **Bertha** was living—was surrounded with possibilities of misery." 2

The Other Principal

Bertha Grant *in a vision:* " . . . the lady on the left of my father was not more than twenty, a tall, slim, willowy figure, with luxuriant blond hair, arranged in cunning braids and folds that looked almost too massive for the slight figure and the small-featured, thin-lipped face they crowned. But the face had not a girlish expression: the features were sharp, the pale grey eyes at once acute, restless, and sarcastic. They were fixed on me in half-smiling curiosity, and I felt a painful sensation as if a sharp wind were cutting me. The pale-green dress, and the green leaves that seemed to form a border about her pale-blond hair, made me think of a Water-Nixie . . . and this pale, fatal-eyed woman, with the green weeds, looked like a birth from some cold sedgy stream, the daughter of an aged river." 1

—*intriguing:* " . . .she made the only exception, among all the human beings about me, to my unhappy gift of insight. About Bertha I was always in a state of uncertainty . . . no womanly character could seem to have less affinity for that of a shrinking, romantic, passionate youth than Bertha's. She was keen, sarcastic, unimaginative, prematurely cynical, remaining critical and unmoved in the most impressive scenes, inclined to dissect all my favourite poems, and especially contemptuous towards the German lyrics which were my pet literature at that time." 1

—*coquette:* " . . . I conclude that her vanity and love of power were intensely gratified by the belief that I had fainted on first seeing her purely from the strong impression her person had produced on me . . . without a grain of romance in her, Bertha had that spirit of intrigue which gave piquancy to the idea that the brother of the man she meant to marry was dying with love and jealousy for her sake . . . I believe she must inwardly have delighted in the tremors into which she threw me by the coaxing way in which she patted my curls, while she laughed at my quotations. Such caresses were always given in the presence of our friends; for when we were alone together, she affected a much greater distance towards me, and now and then took the opportunity, by words or slight actions, to stimulate my foolish timid hope that she really preferred me." 1

—*foreseen:* " 'Madman, idiot! why don't you kill yourself, then?' It was a moment of hell. I saw into her pitiless soul—saw its barren worldliness, its scorching hate . . . . I shuddered—I despised this woman with the barren soul and mean thoughts; but I felt helpless before her, as if she clutched my bleeding heart, and would clutch it till the last drop of life-blood ebbed away. She was my wife, and we hated each other." 1

"Behind the slim girl Bertha, whose words and looks I watched for, whose touch was bliss, there stood continually that Bertha with the fuller form, the harder eyes, the more rigid mouth—with the barren selfish soul laid bare; no longer a fascinating secret, but a measured fact, urging itself perpetually on my unwilling sight." 1

—*on marriage:* " 'What! your wisdom thinks I must love the man I'm going to marry? The most unpleasant thing in the world. I should quarrel with him; I should be jealous of him; our *ménage* would be conducted in a very ill-bred manner. A little quiet contempt contributes greatly to the elegance of life.' " 2

—deceptive: "And she made me believe that she loved me. Without ever quitting her tone of *badinage* and playful superiority, she intoxicated me with the sense that I was necessary to her, that she was never at ease unless I was near her, submitting to her playful tyranny . . . . Out of the subtlest web of scarcely perceptible signs, she set me weaving the fancy that she had always unconsciously loved me better than **Alfred**, but that, with the ignorant fluttered sensibility of a young girl, she had been imposed on by the charm that lay for her in the distinction of being admired and chosen by a man who made so brilliant a figure in the world as my brother. What was it to me that I had the light of my wretched prevision on the fact that now it was I who possessed at least all but the personal part of my brother's advantages?" 2

—marriage: " . . . Bertha in her white silk and pale-green leaves, and the pale hues of her hair and face, looked like the spirit of the morning." 2

—a change: "But I was conscious of a growing difference in her manner towards me; sometimes strong enough to be called haughty coldness, cutting and chilling me as the hail had done that came across the sunshine on our marriage morning; sometimes only perceptible in the dexterous avoidance of a *tête-tête* walk or dinner to which I had been looking forward. I had been deeply pained by this—had even felt a sort of crushing of the heart, from the sense that my brief day of happiness was near its setting; but still I remained dependent on Bertha, eager for the last rays of a bliss that would soon be gone for ever, hoping and watching for some after-glow more beautiful from the impending night." 2

—moment of truth: "The terrible moment of complete illumination had come to me, and I saw that the darkness had hidden no landscape from me, but only a blank prosaic wall: from that evening forth, through the sickening years which followed, I saw all round the narrow room of this woman's soul—saw petty artifice and mere negation where I had delighted to believe in coy sensibilities and in wit at war with feeling—saw the light floating vanities of the girl defining themselves into the systematic coquetry, the scheming selfishness, of the woman—saw repulsion and antipathy harden into cruel hatred, giving pain only for the sake of wreaking itself." 2

—growing fear: "But she had begun to suspect, by some involuntary betrayals of mine, that there was an abnormal power of penetration in me—that fitfully, at least, I was strangely cognisant of her thoughts and intentions, and she began to be haunted by a terror of me, which alternated every now and then with defiance." 2

—charmed: "Bertha was much struck by the unexpected fascinations of a visitor [**Meunier**] whom she had expected to find presentable only on the score of his celebrity, and put forth all her coquetries and accomplishments. Apparently she succeeded in attracting his admiration, for his manner towards her was attentive and flattering." 2

—at the deathbed: "She wore a rich *peignoir,* and her blond hair was half-covered by a lace cap: in her attire she was, as always, an elegant woman, fit to figure in a picture of modern aristocratic life: but I asked myself how that face of hers could ever have seemed to me the face of a woman born of woman, with memories of childhood, capable of pain, needing to be fondled? The features at that moment seemed so preternaturally sharp, the eyes were so hard and eager—she looked like a cruel immortal, finding her spiritual

feast in the agonies of a dying race. For across those hard features there came something like a flash when the last hour had been breathed out, and we all felt that the dark veil had completely fallen. What secret was there between Bertha and this woman?" 2

Supporting Roles

Father. "He was a firm, unbending, intensely orderly man, in root and stem a banker, but with a flourishing graft of the active landholder, aspiring to county influence: one of those people who are always like themselves from day to day, who are uninfluenced by the weather, and neither know melancholy nor high spirits." 1

—*Greek and Latin:* "My father was not a man to underrate the bearing of Latin satirists or Greek dramatists on the attainment of an aristocratic position. But, intrinsically, he had slight esteem for 'those dead but sceptred spirits,' having qualified himself for forming an independent opinion by reading **Potter**'s 'Æschylus,' and dipping into **Francis**' 'Horace.' " 1

—*a perception:* "I knew my father's thought about me: 'That lad will never be good for anything in life: he may waste his years in an insignificant way on the income that falls to him: I shall not trouble myself about a career for him.' " 2

—*his favourite, dead:* "My father had been one of the most successful men in the money-getting world: he had had no sentimental sufferings, no illness. The heaviest trouble that had befallen him was the death of his first wife. But he married my mother soon after; and I remember he seemed exactly the same, to my keen childish observation, the week after her death as before. But now, at last, a sorrow had come—the sorrow of old age, which suffers the more from the crushing of its pride and its hopes, in proportion as the pride and hope are narrow and prosaic." 2

Charles Meunier, "a youth whose intellectual tendencies were the very reverse of my own . . . . He was an orphan, who lived on a miserable pittance while he pursued the medical studies for which he had a special genius . . . . Charles was poor and ugly, derided by Genevese *gamins,* and not acceptable in drawing-rooms. I saw that he was isolated, as I was, though from a different cause, and, stimulated by a sympathetic resentment, I made timid advances towards him . . . there sprang up as much comradeship between us as our different habits would allow . . . . " 1

—*heard from:* "Meunier had now a European reputation, but his letter to me expressed that keen remembrance of an early regard, an early debt of sympathy, which is inseparable from nobility of character: and I too felt as if his presence would be to me like a transient resurrection into a happier pre-existence." 2

—*blossomed:* "Meunier was now a brilliant figure in society, to whom elegant women pretended to listen, and whose acquaintance was boasted of by noblemen ambitious of brains. He repressed with the utmost delicacy all betrayal of the shock which I am sure he must have received from our meeting, or of a desire to penetrate into my condition and circumstances, and sought by the utmost exertion of his charming social powers to make our reunion agreeable."

—*concentrating:* "For the next twenty minutes I forgot everything but Meunier and the experiment in which he was so absorbed, that I think his senses would have been closed against all sounds or sights which had no relation to it." 2

Alfred. " . . . already a tall youth at Eton. My brother was to be [my **father**'s] representative and successor; he must go to Eton and Oxford, for the sake of making connections, of course . . . . " 1

"At Basle we were joined by my brother Alfred, now a handsome self-confident man of six-and-twenty—a thorough contrast to my fragile, nervous, ineffectual self . . . . Alfred, from whom I had been almost constantly separated, and who, in his present stage of character and appearance, came before me as a perfect stranger, was bent on being extremely friendly and brother-like to me. He had the superficial kindness of a good-humoured, self-satisfied nature, that fears no rivalry, and has encountered no contrarieties. . . . There must always have been an antipathy between our natures.

"As it was, he became in a few weeks an object of intense hatred to me; and when he entered the room, still more when he spoke, it was as if a sensation of grating metal had set my teeth on edge. My diseased consciousness was more intensely and continually occupied with these thoughts and emotions . . . . I was perpetually exasperated with the petty prompting of his conceit and his love of patronage, with his self-complacent belief in **Bertha Grant**'s passion for him, with his half-pitying contempt for me—seen not in the ordinary indications of intonation and phrase and slight action, which an acute and suspicious mind is on the watch for, but in all their naked skinless complication." ¶1

—about to ride: " . . . my brother himself appeared at the door, florid, broad-chested, and self-complacent, feeling what a good-natured fellow he was not to behave insolently to us all on the strength of his great advantages." 2

—self-sufficient: "But then, again, my exasperating insight into Alfred's self-complacent soul, his freedom from all the doubts and fears, the unsatisfied yearnings, the exquisite tortures of sensitiveness, that had made the web of my life, seemed to absolve me from all bonds towards him. This man needed no pity, no love; those fine influences would have been as little felt by him as the delicate white mist is felt by the rock it caresses." 2

Others

Archer. "She was a tall, wiry, dark-eyed woman, this Mrs Archer, with a face handsome enough to give her coarse hard nature the odious finish of bold, self-confident coquetry . . . . I seldom saw her, but I perceived that she rapidly became a favourite with her mistress . . . . " 2

—upset: " . . . there had been some quarrel between **Bertha** and this maid . . . . I had overheard Archer speaking in a tone of bitter insolence, which I should have thought an adequate reason for immediate dismissal. No dismissal followed; on the contrary Bertha seemed to be silently putting up with personal inconveniences from the exhibitions of this woman's temper." 2

—agitation: " ' . . . there seems a strange prompting in her to say something which pain and failing strength forbid her to utter; and there is a look of hideous meaning in her eyes, which she turns continually toward her mistress. In this disease the mind often remains singularly clear to the last.' " 2

—*in extremis:* "The face was pinched and ghastly, a cold perspiration was on the forehead, and the eyelids were lowered so as almost to conceal the large dark eyes." 2

—*resurrection:* "The dead woman's eyes were wide open, and met [**Bertha**'s] in full recognition—the recognition of hate. With a sudden strong effort, the hand that Bertha had thought for ever still was pointed towards her, and the haggard face moved. The gasping eager voice said—

" 'You mean to poison your husband . . . the poison is in the black cabinet . . . I got it for you . . . you laughed at me, and told lies about me behind my back, to make me disgusting . . . because you were jealous . . . are you sorry . . . now?"

"The lips continued to murmur, but the sounds were no longer distinct. Soon there was no sound . . . . " 2

Letherall "was a large man in spectacles, who one day took my small head between his large hands, and pressed it here and there in an exploratory, suspicious manner—then placed each of his great thumbs on my temples, and pushed me a little way from him, and stared at me with glittering spectacles. The contemplation appeared to displease him, for he frowned sternly, and said to my father, drawing his thumbs across my eyebrows—

" 'The deficiency is there, sir—there and here,' he added, touching the upper sides of my head, 'here is the excess. That must be brought out, sir, and this must be laid to sleep.' " 1

Minor Figures

Mrs Filmore. "She was a commonplace middle-aged woman, in silk and cashmere . . . . " 1

Fletcher " 'is going to be married, and she wants me to ask you to let her husband have the public-house and farm at Molton. I wish him to have it. You must give the promise now, because [she] is going to-morrow morning. . . . ' " 2

Housekeeper "will have rushed out of the house in a fury, two hours before, hoping that **Perry** will believe she has gone to drown herself." 1

Perry "is alarmed at last and is gone out after her." 1

Scullery-maid "is asleep on a bench: she never answers the bell; it does not wake her." 1

Also mentioned

attendants at Archer's bedside: one at first, then replaced by two	2
doctor to the family; away at the time of Archer's illness	2
Filmore husband, a nonentity	1
groom, who accompanied Latimer on his little white pony	1
Pierre, manservant attending Latimer in Geneva	1
Schmidt, German courier in Geneva, whose mind intrudes on Latimer	1

Brother Jacob

David Faux, a butler's nephew, decides to be a confectioner. He feels constrained by the social consequences of the choice and decides to seek his fortune in the new world, taking his mother's store of guineas with him. He has abstracted them and is about to bury them when his idiot brother **Jacob** appears with his pitchfork. He distracts Jacob with lozenges he was bringing to **Sally Lunn**. He tells him that, planted, the guineas will produce lozenges. He had planned to leave openly, allowing his mother to discover her loss in his presence, but now he has to leave at once, and so he does at crack of dawn. But he finds Jacob digging up the box of guineas. He has to walk on with Jacob beside him, carrying his bundle at the end of the pitchfork. Jacob has found candy in his tailcoat and keeps a hold of the tail. At last, after plying him with beer, David gets free of a sleeping idiot and catches the coach to Liverpool. 1

Six years pass. A new confectioner's shop opens in Grimworth. Faux has become **Edward Freely**, and his shop windows impress. Leading housewives begin to patronize. He gains standing. Casting his eye about, he decides a suitable mate would be **Penelope Palfrey**, daughter of a distinguished family. He maneuvers invitations and becomes a presence at the house, to the disgust of suitor **John Towers**. The campaign includes the portrait of an **Admiral Freely**, with one arm and one eye, and pleas to be taught **Mrs Palfrey**'s recipe for brawn. He inveigles **Mr Palfrey** into his sanctum and talks about expecta-tions from a fond uncle in Jamaica. The engagement is announced. Faux/ Freely spots an advertisement: his father is dead; he is wanted. 2

He has worked for six years as a cook in Jamaica and saved. Now, he sees a chance for a legacy, and he goes, meets his elder brother **Jonathan**, and collects. His mother and father had been scrupulous as to his rights despite his theft. The Palfreys come to call—and so does the idiot Jacob, ecstatic to see David and eating a pie. Jacob has learned where David is from talk at home. David tries pretense, but Jacob is too much for him. He insists on sitting with them, so the Palfreys leave. David does not sleep. The townspeople gather to watch, and interest is general. Jonathan Faux comes for Jacob, and the jig is up. Palfrey leaves in disgust: the engagement is off. Jacob refuses to leave: the sweets are too good. Grocer **Prettyman** takes

Jonathan to lunch and learns all. The details, including the theft, permeate the town. David is ostracized. He abandons the shop and disappears. Penny marries Towers. *Nemesis* is triumphant. 3

Contents

Principals

David Faux, the youngest of seven sons, "carried home the pleasing illusion that a confectioner must be at once the happiest and the foremost of men, since the things he made were not only the most beautiful to behold, but the very best eating . . . so that when his father declared he must be put to a trade, David chose his line without a moment's hesitation; and, with a rashness inspired by a sweet tooth, wedded himself irrevocably to confectionery." 1

—imaginative: "He was a young man of much mental activity, and, above all, gifted with a spirit of contrivance; but then, his faculties would not tell with great effect in any other medium than that of candied sugars, conserves, and pastry . . . . David could invent delightful things in the way of drop-cakes, and he had the widest views of the sugar department, but in other directions he certainly felt hampered by the want of knowledge and practical skill, and the world is so inconveniently constituted, that the vague consciousness of being a fine fellow is no guarantee of success in any line of business." 1

—grandiose: "His soul swelled with an impatient sense that he ought to become something very remarkable—that it was quite out of the question for him to put up with a narrow lot as other men did: he scorned the idea that he could accept an average . . . . No position could be suited to Mr David Faux that was not in the highest degree easy to the flesh and flattering to the spirit." 1

—literary? " . . . his ideas might not have been below a certain mark of the literary calling; but his spelling and diction were too unconventional." 1

—characteristics: " . . . a young gentleman of pasty visage, lipless mouth, and stumpy hair . . . . " 1

—unwary: "This ingenious young man, Mr David Faux, thought he had achieved a triumph of cunning when he had associated himself in his brother's rudimentary mind with the flavour of yellow lozenges. But he had yet to learn that it is a dreadful thing to make an idiot fond of you, when you yourself are not of an affectionate disposition: especially an idiot with a pitchfork—obviously a difficult friend to shake off by rough usage." 1

—no more crime: "Besides, he would have been greatly hurt not to be thought well of in the world: he always meant to make a figure, and be thought worthy of the best seats and the best morsels." 1

—provoked: "But David was by no means impetuous; he was a young man greatly given to calculate consequences, a habit which has been held to be the foundation of virtue. But somehow it had not precisely that effect in David: he calculated whether an action would harm himself, or whether it

would only harm other people. In the former case he was very timid about satisfying his immediate desires, but in the latter he would risk the result with much courage." 1

—returned with new name: "**Mr Edward Freely** was a man whose impulses were kept in due subordination: he held that the desire for sweets and pastry must only be satisfied in a direct ratio with the power of paying for them." 2

—good times: "Only it happened at Grimworth, which, to be sure, was a low place, that the maids and matrons could do nothing with their hands at all better than cooking; nor even those who had always made heavy cakes and leathery pastry. And so it came to pass, that the progress of civilisation at Grimworth was not otherwise apparent than in the impoverishment of men, the gossiping idleness of women, and the heightening prosperity of Mr Edward Freely." 2

—gaining respect: "Mr Freely was becoming a person of influence in the parish; he was found useful as an overseer of the poor, having great firmness in enduring other people's pain, which firmness, he said, was due to his great benevolence; he always did what was good for people in the end." 2

—at the club: " . . . he was sometimes a little free in his conversation, more than hinting at a life of Sultanic self-indulgence which he had passed in the West Indies, shaking his head now and then and smiling rather bitterly, as men are wont to do when they intimate that they have become a little too wise to be instructed about a world which has long been flat and stale to them." 2

—beau: "It may seem incredible that a confectioner should have ideas and conversation so much resembling those to be met with in a higher walk of life, but it must be remembered that he had not merely travelled, he had also bow-legs and a sallow, small-featured visage, so that nature herself had stamped him for a fastidious connoisseur of the fair sex." 2

—smitten: "He thought [**Penny**'s] prettiness comparable to the loveliest things in confectionery; he judged her to be of submissive temper—likely to wait upon him as well as if she had been a negress, and to be silently terrified when his liver made him irritable; and he considered the **Palfrey** family quite the best in the parish . . . . On the whole, he thought her worthy to become Mrs Edward Freely, and all the more so, because it would probably require some ingenuity to win her." 2

Jacob Faux, "a very healthy and well-developed idiot, who consumed a dumpling about eight inches in diameter every day . . . . " 1

" . . . **David**, being a timid young man, had a considerable dread and hatred of Jacob, as of a large personage who went about habitually with a pitchfork in his hand." 1

—unexpected: " . . . the sound of a large body rustling towards him with something like a bellow was such a surprise to **David** . . . in the same moment he looked up and saw his dear brother Jacob close upon him, holding the pitchfork so that the bright smooth prongs were a yard in advance of his own body, and about a foot off David's . . . he kept his ground and smiled at Jacob, who nodded his head up and down, and said, 'Hoich, Zavy!' in a painfully equivocal manner." 1

—some faculty: "David, you understand, was not an intense idiot, but within a certain limited range knew how to choose the good and reject the evil: he took one lozenge, by way of test, and sucked it as if he had been a

philosopher; then, in as great an ecstasy at its new and complex savour as **Caliban** at the taste of **Trinculo**'s wine, chuckled and stroked this beneficent brother, and held out his hand for more; for, except in fits of anger, Jacob was not ferocious or needlessly predatory." 1

—dangerous: "Jacob was quiet as long as he was treated indulgently; but on the slightest show of anger, he became unmanageable, and was liable to fits of fury which would have made him formidable even without his pitchfork. There was no mastery to be obtained over him except by kindness or guile." 1

—where he likes it: "It soon appeared that Jacob could not be made to quit his dear brother **David** except by force. He understood, with a clearness equal to that of the most intelligent mind, that **Jonathan** would take him back to skimmed milk, apple-dumpling, broad-beans and pork. And he had found a paradise in his brother's shop. It was a difficult matter to use force with Jacob, for he wore heavy nailed boots, and if his pitchfork had been mastered, he would have resorted without hesitation to kicks. Nothing short of using guile to bind him hand and foot would have made all parties safe." 3

Supporting Roles

Miss Penelope Palfrey. "For it was no less a person than Miss Penelope Palfrey, second daughter of the **Mr Palfrey** who farmed his own land, that had attracted **Mr Freely**'s peculiar regard, and conquered his fastidiousness, and no wonder, for the Ideal, as exhibited in the finest waxwork, was perhaps never so closely approached by the Real as in the person of the pretty Penelope. Her yellowish flaxen hair did not curl naturally, I admit, but its bright crisp ringlets were such smooth, perfect miniature tubes, that you would have longed to pass your little finger through them, and feel their soft elasticity. She wore them in a crop, for in those days, when society was in a healthier state, young ladies wore crops long after they were twenty, and Penelope was not yet nineteen.

"Like the waxen ideal, she had round blue eyes, and round nostrils in her little nose, and teeth such as the ideal would be seen to have, if it ever showed them. Altogether, she was a small, round thing, as neat as a pink and white double daisy, and as guileless; for I hope it does not argue guile in a pretty damsel of nineteen, to think that she should like to have a beau and be 'engaged,' when her elder sister had already been in that position a year and a half." ¶2

—dreams: "And all the while Penny was imagining the circumstances under which **Mr Freely** would make her an offer: perhaps down by the row of damson-trees, when they were in the garden before tea; perhaps by letter. . . . But, however he might make the offer, she would not accept it without her father's consent: she would always be true to Mr Freely, but she would not disobey her father. For Penny was a good girl, though some of her female friends were afterwards of opinion that it spoke ill for her not to have felt an instinctive repugnance to Mr Freely." 2

Mrs Palfrey, "like other geniuses, wrought by instinct rather than by rule, and possessed no receipts;—indeed, despised all people who used them, observing that people who pickled by book, must pickle by weights and measures, and such nonsense; as for herself, her weights and measures were the tip of her finger and the tip of her tongue, and if you went nearer, why of course for dry goods like flour and spice, you went by handfuls and pinches, and for wet, there was a middle-sized jug . . . . Knowledge of this kind is like

Titian's colouring: difficult to communicate; and as Mrs Palfrey, once remarkably handsome, had now become rather stout and asthmatical, and scarcely ever left home, her oral teaching could hardly be given anywhere except at Long Meadows. Even a matron is not insusceptible to flattery, and the prospect of a visitor whose great object would be to listen to her conversation, was not without its charms to Mrs Palfrey." 2

Steene, "since his marriage . . . openly preferred discussing the nature of spavin with a coarse neighbour, and was angry if the pudding turned out watery—indeed, was simply a top-booted 'vet,' who came in hungry at dinner-time; and not in the least like a nobleman turned Corsair out of pure scorn for his race, or like a renegade with a turban and crescent, unless it were in the irritability of his temper. And scorn is such a very different thing in top-boots!" 2

—host: "This brutal man had invited a supper-party for Christmas eve, when he would expect to see mince-pies on the table . . . . He would storm at her, she was certain; and before all the company; and then she should never help crying . . . . " 2

Mrs Steene. "It was young Mrs Steene, the veterinary surgeon's wife, who first gave way to temptation. I fear she had been rather over-educated for her station in life, for she knew by heart many passages in 'Lalla Rookh,' the 'Corsair,' and the 'Siege of Corinth,' which had given her a distaste for domestic occupations . . . . " 2

—contretemps: "Mrs Steene had prepared her mince-meat, and had devoted much butter, fine flour, and labour, to the making of a batch of pies in the morning; but they proved to be so very heavy when they came out of the oven, that she could only think with trembling of the moment when her husband should catch sight of them . . . . " 2

—expedient: "Suddenly the thought darted through her mind that this once she might send for a dish of mince-pies from Freely's: she knew he had some . . . indeed, making mince-pies at all was a great expense, when they were not sure to turn out well: it would be much better to buy them ready-made. You paid a little more for them, but there was no risk of waste." 2

Others

Mrs Chaloner, "had given a general order for the veal sweet-breads and the mutton kidneys . . . . " 2

—leadership: "Mrs Chaloner, the rector's wife, was among the earliest customers at the shop, thinking it only right to encourage a new parishioner who had made a decorous appearance at church . . . . Mrs Chaloner ordered wine-biscuits and olives, and gave **Mr Freely** to understand that she should find his shop a great convenience." 2

Jonathan Faux "had told his son very frankly, that he must not look to being set-up in business by *him:* with seven sons . . . it was pretty well if they got a hundred apiece at his death." 1

Miss Fullilove, "the timber-merchant's daughter, was quite sure that if she were **Miss Penny Palfrey**, she would be cautious; it was not a good sign when men looked so much above themselves for a wife." 2

Mrs Gate, "at the large carding-mill, who, having high connections frequently visiting her, might be expected to have a large consumption of ratafias and macaroons." 2

Mrs Mole. "The third step [for **Mrs Steene**] was to harden herself by telling the fact of the bought mince-pies to her intimate friend Mrs Mole, who had already guessed it, and who subsequently encouraged herself in buying a mould of jelly, instead of exerting her own skill, by the reflection that 'other people' did the same sort of thing." 2

Letitia Palfrey, "who had a prouder style of beauty [than **Penny**'s], and a more worldly ambition, was engaged to a wool-factor, who came all the way from Cattelton to see her; and everybody knows that a wool-factor takes a very high rank, sometimes driving a double-bodied gig. Letty's notions got higher every day . . . . " 2

Mr Palfrey. "We know how easily the great Leviathan may be led, when once there is a hook in his nose or a bridle in his jaws. Mr Palfrey was a large man, but, like Leviathan's, his bulk went against him when once he had taken a turning. He was not a mercurial man, who easily changed his point of view. Enough. Before two months were over, he had given his consent to **Mr Freely**'s marriage with his daughter **Penny**, and having hit on a formula by which he could justify it, fenced off all doubts and objections, his own included. The formula was this: 'I'm not a man to put my head up an entry before I know where it leads.' " 2

Mr Prettyman. " 'He's an amusing fellow,' said Mr Prettyman, the highly respectable grocer . . . 'and I've no objection to his making one at the Oyster Club; but he's a bit too fond of riding the high horse. He's uncommonly knowing, I'll allow; but now came he to go to the Indies? . . . When folks go so far off, it's because they've got little credit nearer home . . . . However, he's got some good rum; but I don't want to be hand and glove with him, for all that.' " 2

Mr Rodd, "the Baptist minister, had requested that, so far as was compatible with the fair accommodation of other customers, the sheep's trotters might be reserved for him." 2

John Towers, "whose cheeks were of the finest pink, set off by a fringe of dark whisker, was quite eclipsed by the presence of the sallow **Mr Freely**." 2

"To be sure, there was young Towers always coming to the house; but **Penny** felt convinced he only came to see her brother, for he never had anything to say to her, and never offered her his arm, and was as awkward and silent as possible." 2

Uncle, "the butler at the great house close by Brigford, had made a pet of [**David**] in his early boyhood, and it was on a visit to this uncle that the confectioners' shops in that brilliant town had, on a single day, fired his tender imagination." 1

Minor Figures

Zephaniah Crypt, testator. " . . . the trustees of [his] Charity, under the stimulus of a late visitation by commissioners, were beginning to apply long-accumulating funds to the rebuilding of the Yellow Coat School . . . . " 2

Jonathan Faux. " 'My mother may do as she likes about having you to see her, but, for my part, I don't want to catch sight of you on the premises again. When folks have taken a new name, they'd better keep to their new 'quinetance.' " 3

Sally Lunn, "[who] had been an early flame of [**David**'s] . . . . " 1

Mining-agent, "who was a great *bon vivant,* even [and the **doctor** and the **curate**] began to rely on **Freely** for the greater part of their dinner, when they wished to give an entertainment of some brilliancy." 2

Squire Palfrey "had been respected by the last Grimworth generation as a man who could afford to drink too much in his own house." 2

Mrs Tibbits. "[**David**] was sure there was nothing average about him; even such a person as Mrs Tibbits, the washerwoman, perceived it, and probably had a preference for his linen." 1

Also mentioned

Mrs Cleve, whose trustee let a shop in Grimworth to a stranger	2
cow-boy, who is employed by Mr Faux	1
curate, who turned to a special commercial organ when entertaining	2
doctor, whose cook was not satisfactory	2
errand-boy, sent by the confectioner	2
Mrs Faux, a forgiving mother	1,2
Miss Fothergill, who became Mrs Prettyman	2
—her sister, who had married a London mercer	2
Freely, sallow swain	2
Fullilove, timber-merchant in Grimworth	2
Luff, a Grimworth draper	2
Lunn, father of Sally	1
Moffat, auctioneer, who died without leaving anyone in the business	2
Palfreys, the; who farmed their own land in Grimworth	2
Palfrey brother, friends with Towers	2
Palfrey sister, engaged for a year and a half	2
Strutt, attorney for Jonathan Faux's estate	2
wife of the local doctor, who patronized the new confectionery	2

Jubal in his Prime

THE POETRY

The Poetry: Introductory

The more notable poetry of George Eliot, leaving aside *The Spanish Gypsy,* was published at GE's behest by Blackwood: in 1874 (*The Legend of Jubal and Other Poems*) and then expanded in 1878 (*The Legend of Jubal and Other Poems, Old and New*). Where no other date of composition can be determined, we have used the publication date.

The contents and sequence of the two collections were as follows:

1874	1878
The Legend of Jubal	The Legend of Jubal
Agatha	Agatha
Armgart	Armgart
How Lisa Loved the King	How Lisa Loved the King
A Minor Prophet	A Minor Prophet
Brother and Sister	Brother and Sister
Stradivarius	Stradivarius
Two Lovers	A College Breakfast-Party
Arion	Two Lovers
"O May I Join the Choir Invisible"	Self and Life
	"Sweet Evenings Come and Go, Love"
	The Death of Moses
	Arion
	"O May I Join the Choir Invisible"

After a group of shorter poems datable to the early years, and the epic *Spanish Gypsy,* we have presented below the poems in the order of the 1878 edition, followed by Eliot's shorter poetry from the middle and later years in the order given by van den Broek's CSP (see below).

Margaret Reynolds has written a fine brief article on Eliot's poetry for the *Oxford Reader's Companion to George Eliot,* to which the reader can turn for valuable context and cogent specific commentary. She confirms our perception that the epigraphs Eliot inserted in her last three novels are, when not taken from other authors, her original poetry, and we have provided those original epigraphs at the end of this section. The very recent appearance of Antonie van den Broek's wonderful *The Complete Shorter Poetry of George Eliot* (2005; *see* Supplementary Comment to the Bibliography, page xxx) gives us great confidence that this presentation is complete.

Contents

Early Poems

Farewell

Knowing that shortly I must put off this tabernacle (2 Peter 1:14)

As o'er the fields by evening's light I stray,
I hear a still, small whisper—"Come away"!
Thou must to this bright, lovely world soon say
Farewell!

The mandate I'd obey, my lamp prepare,
Gird up my garments, give my soul to pray'r,
And say to earth and all that breathe earth's air
Farewell!

Thou sun, to whose parental beam I owe
All that has gladden'd me while here below—
Moon, stars, and covenant confirming bow,
Farewell!

Ye verdant meads, fair blossoms, stately trees,
Sweet song of birds, and soothing hum of bees—
Refreshing odours, wafted on the breeze,
Farewell!

Ye patient servants of creation's lord
Whose mighty strength is govern'd by his word,
Who raiment, food and help in toil afford,
Farewell!

Ye feebler, freer tribes, that people air,
Fairy like insects, making buds your lair,
Ye that in water shine, and frolic there,
Farewell!

Books that have been to me as chest of gold,
Which, miser like, I secretly have told,
And for them love, health, friendship, peace have sold,
Farewell!

Blest volume! whose clear truth-writ page, once known,
Fades not before heaven's sunshine or hell's moan
To thee I say not, of earth's gifts alone,
Farewell!

Dear kindred, whom the lord to me has given,
Must the dear tie that binds us, now be riven?
No! say I *only* till we meet in heaven,
Farewell!

There shall my newborn senses find new joy,
New sounds, new sights my eyes and ears employ,
Nor fear that word that here brings sad alloy,
Farewell!

July 1839

Sonnet

Oft, when a child, while wand'ring far alone,
That none might rouse me from my waking dream,
And visions with which fancy still would teem
Scare by a disenchanting earthly tone;
If, haply, conscious of the present scene,
I've marked before me some untraversed spot
The setting sunbeams had forsaken not,
Whose turf appeared more velvet-like and green
Than that I walked and fitter for repose:
But ever, at the wished-for place arrived,
I've found it of those seeming charms deprived
Which from the mellowing power of distance rose:
To my poor thought, an apt though simple trope
Of life's dull path and earth's deceitful hope.

September 1839

Question and Answer

"Where blooms, O my Father, a thornless rose?"
"That can I not tell thee, my child;
Not one on the bosom of earth e'er grows,
But wounds whom its charms have beguiled."

"Would I'd a rose on my bosom to lie!
But I shrink from the piercing thorn;
I long, but dare not its point defy,
I long, and I gaze forlorn."

"Not so, O my child, round the stem again
Thy resolute fingers entwine—
Forego not the joy for its sister pain,
Let the rose, the sweet rose, be thine!"

September 1840

(untitled)

Mind the rich store of nature's gifts to man
Each has his loves, close wedded to his soul
By fine associations' golden links.
As the Great Spirit bids creation teem
With conscious being and intelligence,
So man His miniature resemblance gives
To matter's every form a speaking soul,
An emanation from his spirit's fount,
The impress true of its peculiar seal.
Here finds he thy best image, sympathy!

February 1842

(untitled)

As tu vu la lune se lever
Dans un ciel d'azur sans voile?
Mille gouttes de rosée réflechissent
Sa lumière, comme autant d'étoiles.

Un violet du printemps cueilles
Et le caches bien dans ton sein,
De la délicieuse odeur
Tu et tes vêtements seront pleins.

Ainsi lorsqu'une belle âme se montre
Elle revêtit tant de ses charmes:—
Ainsi son souvenir gardons
Quoique, hélas! il tire nos larmes.

August 20, 1849

William Blackwood & Sons **SG**
1868

The Spanish Gypsy

As if a strong, delightful water that we knew only as a river appeared in the character of a fountain; as if one whom we had wondered at as a good walker or inexhaustible pedestrian, began to dance; as if ***Mr Bright****, in the middle of a public meeting, were to oblige the company with a song—no, no, not like that exactly, but like something quite new—is the appearance of George Eliot in the character of a poet. "The Spanish Gypsy," a poem in five books, originally written, as a prefatory note informs us, in the winter of 1864-65, and, after a visit to Spain in 1867, re-written and amplified, is before us. It is a great volume of three hundred and fifty octavo pages; and the first thing which strikes the reader is, that it is a good deal longer than he expected it would be. This is bad, to begin with. What right has anybody to make a poem longer than one expected? The next thing that strikes one is—at all events, the next thing that struck me was, as I very hastily turned over this book—that the fine* largo *of the author's manner, continued through so many pages, was a very little burdensome in its effect . . . .*

"There is only one living mind which could have given us poetico-psychological studies of human character like these. There is no comparison in range of faculty between such a mind and ***John Clare****'s. Is it not strange, and almost pathetic, that an uncultivated peasant could sing, and touch us with music, as no speech could; and yet that a highly cultivated mind like George Eliot's should almost overwhelm our judgment by the richness and volume of what it pours forth in the name of song; and yet that we are compelled to say the bird-note is missing?"*

—Matthew Browne (*Contemporary Review,* VIII, 1868)

Editor's Note: We make no pretense to expertise in poetry, though we love it and read it often. We think *The Spanish Gypsy* a powerful, touching work of art. Technically, it is extraordinary: it is nearly impossible to find a clumsy phrase, an inapposite word, a discord in tone. The scansion is about perfect. The characters are plausible, the three principals memorable, the Gypsy chief Zarca epically heroic. The arc of the story line is compelling. We suspect the indifferent attention to the work since its initial good publishing success grows from a simple, damning fact: it is not a novel.

Book I

We are in Andalusia, in southern Spain, in the town of Bedmár, formerly Moorish and still a single mile north of Moorish territory. It is the end of the fifteenth century. The Inquisition has just been introduced; the Jews will shortly be expelled from the country. Five men sit in a tavern, three talking: **Lorenzo**, the host; **Blasco**, a silversmith; and **Juan**, lutenist and minstrel. (Two silent figures are **Roldan**, jaded street entertainer, and his lame son **Pablo**.) They speculate on **Duke Silva**'s military plans, watch him riding past. They discuss the severe Prior, the Duke's uncle. **Captain Lopez** enters and reports in disgust there will be no sally against the Moorish forces. The Duke instead will marry immediately. The lady is **Fedalma**, raised by the late Duchess, and an "infidel." Juan is deeply, hopelessly in love with her. Lopez's remarks anger him, but he turns to song. This upsets Roldan, whose son sings for pence, while Juan sings for nothing. Juan apologizes and will sing no more. Roldan and Pablo leave for the plaza with their monkey, the gloomy **Annibal**. There is talk of banishing the Gypsies and the Jews, which Blasco opposes for practical reasons. Lopez will escort a group of Gypsies from one prison to another. Their chief is described by Juan as a paragon. All leave for the plaza. i

The Plaça Santiago: Roldan exhibits Annibal's tricks, then does his magic and tumbling. Pablo begins to play the viol. The acts end; all wait for a dance to commence; Fedalma appears and dances. The crowd is rapt and thrilled, but a file of Gypsy prisoners interrupts. Lopez is stringent in command. The prisoners are chained in couples except for one man, who faces Fedalma. Their eyes meet; she is awed and uneasy. The gloomy bell tolls evening. The prisoners pass; the crowd looks for her; she is gone. ii

In the castle, Silva has doffed his mail and carefully arrayed himself to call on Fedalma. His nature is not of a piece—part masterly, part introspective: a nature "quiveringly poised in reach of storms." **Fr Isidor**, the Prior, comes and questions him on the decision not to sally against the Moors. He attacks his plan to marry, calling Fedalma infidel, a "lewd Herodias." Silva is furious. The Prior tells him Fedalma is at that moment dancing before the populace. Silva, aghast, rushes to find her. As he is giving orders for a search, she walks in. She says she danced because the impulse was strong to give herself and the people pleasure. He cannot but forgive. He says they must be married secretly at once: she needs protection. They look at family jewels. The prisoners pass in the street. Silva goes. She studies the jewels and is struck by a gold necklace. She wonders if she has known it before. Juan enters. He takes charge of the casket and goes. Fedalma keeps the necklace. She will ask for the Gypsy leader **Zarca**'s release after she is wed. iii

In a street by the castle, Juan and an admirer, **Pepíta**, talk. She pouts because he does not love her. He sings to her but will not allow for love: he is a poet. She is sad and leaves; he sings about her. iv

The Prior in his office considers a scurrilous letter accusing Fedalma. It may be false; he does not care: he will submit her to the Inquisition. He is disappointed in his nephew Silva. He was the elder brother but chose the Church. He scorns rules for man in general; perjury can serve the holy truth. He prays, and vows that tomorrow Fedalma will be taken and locked away. v

In Fedalma's chamber, she meditates in the night. A newly dead bird falls in the room, a message on it for her: her father is coming. He appears:

he is the leader she saw in the street. He describes the gown and clasps she had worn when Spaniards snatched her. She acknowledges him. He calls her to her destiny. She accepts it, tells him she will marry the Duke and win the Gypsies, the *Zíncala,* freedom. He scoffs. The Duke would risk rebellion if he helped them. She knows the secret of the gate. She must aid, and go with them. She refuses. He tells her she cannot change who she is. She will be queen in their new land, promised to them in Africa. Trapped, she gives in. She writes Silva a letter and leaves her betrothal ring. She goes with Zarca. vi

Book II

Silva leads his troop back to Bedmár, eager to see Fedalma. The priest who will marry them is with him. **Don Alvar** intercepts him with Fedalma's letter and tells of the Prior's attempt to seize her. Silva is devastated and grieving in her boudoir when he hears Pablo singing. He summons the boy and his father and orders Roldan to find the gypsy camp, promising gold for his retirement on his return. The boy and Annibal will stay in the astrologer's tower. i

We are high up in the tower of Abderahman. **Salomo Sephardo**, Jew and confidant to Silva, hears Silva's request that Pablo and Annibal be sheltered for a time. He tells Sephardo of his intent to seek Fedalma, asking for astrological guidance. They discuss Jewish persecution and the study of the stars. ii

In a castle hall, attendants and soldiers are gathered. **Don Amador** is reading aloud over much noise. The boy **Arias** is singing. Don Amador loses patience and issues threats. There is a disagreement, and Arias tries to settle it with a badly phrased question to the Duke, who slaps him and stalks out. iii

In the Plaça Santiago, Lorenzo and Blasco talk. There are rumors of trouble: the Inquisition? Silva has given his authority to **Don Diego**. A **market-woman** passes an apple with a message in it to Lorenzo. It is a letter from Zarca to the Moorish king **El Zagal** reporting plans to invest Bedmár. Lorenzo says he will take the apple to the astrologer's tower. iv

Book III (in one scene)

We are in a Moorish valley, where the *Zincala* camp. Juan has been sleeping, and girls have stolen his buttons and other ornaments. He strums his lute; the girls want to dance; he will not play until his property is restored. Eventually it is. He plays and sings; the boys sneak in and steal the buttons and other items and run off. **Hinda**, the girls' ringleader, is distraught.

Fedalma appears, in Moorish dress. She is sick at heart. She asks Juan if he has news of Bedmár. He offers to go: she declines this. Juan leaves her, and moments later Zarca arrives. He hints at plans involving Silva. The Moorish captain El Zagal has made him his representative in Africa. He questions Fedalma on her resolve and fidelity. He goes to duty, and she ponders her fate.

Amazingly, Silva appears. They cling to each other. He is alone. Zarca enters and thrusts his sword between them. Zarca threatens vengeance for Spanish persecution. Silva pleads his love. Zarca proclaims Gypsy solid strength. They debate fiercely, Fedalma makes her choice: fidelity and her people. Zarca offers safe conduct to Silva, but he chooses to stay with

Fedalma and the *Zíncala*. Fedalma is horrified: he would be under oath to obey her father and be subservient to Gypsy rule. She begs him to go. No: he will take the oath; the Gypsies gather as witnesses to hear him do it.

Book IV

The scene is still the valley. Silva watches for Juan. He feels torn by old faith and loyalties. His superficial view of religion haunts him now. But his choice is love, not honor. He has chosen no absolution. In a long soliloquy he defies God and infamy for his love: "I have the right to choose my good or ill, A right to damn myself!" Speaking their (Romany?) speech, the soldiers discuss him and their lack of trust in him. They sing their curse and chant of solidarity until they hear echoing song on the desert: all are moving out, toward Almería. i

The hall in the castle at Bedmár. The Moors and Gypsies have won a great battle and taken the town, killing many. Three corpses lie under mantles. Zarca has been sleeping: now he wakes. He looks at the dead with regret, noting that blows at guilt hurt innocence in the shock. He thinks sadly of the pain to his daughter. Sephardo enters. He identifies the dead: the Duke's friend **Alvar**; the singer **Arias**; and another. Zarca orders decent burial. He recalls Fedalma's plea, "When you see fair hair be pitiful." Sephardo goes. ii

Once again, the Plaça Santiago. There is a stake with fagots, and a gibbet. The townspeople surround drawn-up Moorish soldiers. Zarca enters. He tells them that the Prior, whose death at the stake he had forestalled, will be dealt with now, but not with Christian cruelty. Fr Isidor will not be burned alive but hanged—a speedy death. **Nadar** reports: Silva is mad with rage and grief and has disappeared. He warns Zarca to be careful. Silva appears, beside himself. He accuses Zarca of treachery to him by not telling his plans to take Bedmár and kill his friends. Zarca reminds him of his gypsy oath. Silva asks if any still might be spared. He sees his uncle brought in to die and screams for his life. Fr Isidor anathematizes him as apostate traitor. Silva begs for death. The soldiers quickly take the Prior to the gibbet. Silva renounces his oath, tears off his Gypsy badge. He looks up to see the Prior hanged and, unhinged, takes out a dagger and stabs Zarca. Falling, Zarca calls for Fedalma. She comes and sees all in an instant. Zarca entrusts her with the future of her people. She calls on them to acknowledge her: they all assent. Zarca orders Silva's release. Fedalma will not look at him. He leaves. Zarca dies and is carried off in state. iii

Book V (in one scene)

We are in the port of Almería. The boats are being loaded with Gypsies and their possessions. Moors watch and speculate on the hells of others. Nadar supervises. Fedalma is there, thinking ahead and knowing failure will come: Zarca's absence leaves the Gypsies ready to scatter. Already **Hassan** has contracted to fight with the Moors, taking many with him. Fedalma thinks of the joy she renounced. Juan points out Silva, in pilgrim's dress. She goes to bid farewell. He is going to Rome for absolution. Fedalma: "Our marriage rite is our resolve that we will each be true to high allegiance, higher than our love." They gaze and gaze at each other, and then they part. He watches her ship: straining, he "knew not if he gazed on aught but blackness overhung by stars."

Fedalma receives a Visitor

Contents

Principals

Fedalma. "Sudden, with gliding motion like a flame/That through dim vapor makes a path of glory,/A figure lithe, all white and saffron-robed,/Flashed right across the circle, and now stood/With ripened arms uplift and regal head,/Like some tall flower whose dark and intense heart/Lies half within a tulip-tinted cup." I ii

—*dancing:* "Even the chance-strayed delicate tendrils black,/That backward 'scape from out her wreathing hair—/Even the pliant folds that cling transverse/When with obliquely soaring bend altern/She seems a goddess quitting earth again—/Gather expression—a soft undertone/And resonance exquisite from the grand chord/Of her harmoniously bodied soul." I ii

—*proud of it:* "Yes, it was true. I was not wrong to dance . . . . A brightness soft/as of the angels moving down to see/Illumined the broad space. The joy, the life/Around, within me, were one heaven: I longed/To blend them visibly: I longed to dance/Before the people—be as mounting flame/To all that burned within them! Nay, I danced;/There was no longing: I but did the deed/Being moved to do it Oh! I seemed new-waked/To life in unison with a multitude—/Feeling my soul upborne by all their souls,/ Floating within their gladness! Soon I lost/All sense of separateness: Fedalma died/As a star dies, and melts into the light./ I was not, but joy was, and love and triumph." I iii

—*called:* "To be the angel of a homeless tribe:/To help me bless a race taught by no prophet/And make their name, now but a badge of scorn,/A glorious banner floating in their midst,/Stirring the air they breathe with impulses/Of generous pride, exalting fellowship/Until it soars to magnanimity." I vi

—*her choice:* "But her choice was made./Slowly, while yet her father spoke, she moved/From where oblique with deprecating arms/She stood between the two who swayed her heart:/Slowly she moved to choose sublimer pain;/ Yearning, yet shrinking; wrought upon by awe,/Her own brief life seeming a little isle/Remote through visions of a wider world/With fates close-crowded; firm to slay her joy/That cut her heart with smiles beneath the knife,/Like a sweet babe foredoomed by prophecy./ She stood apart, yet near her father: stood/Hand clutching hand, her limbs all tense with will/That strove 'gainst anguish, eyes that seemed a soul/Yearning in death towards him she loved and left." III

—*a future leaderless:* "In a little while, the tribe/That was to be the ensign of the race,/And draw it into conscious union,/Itself would break in small and scattered bands/That, living on scant prey, would still disperse/And propagate forgetfulness. Brief years,/And that great purpose fed with vital fire/That might have glowed for half a century,/Subduing, quickening, shaping, like a sun—/Would be a faint tradition, flickering low/In dying memories, fringing with dim light/The nearer dark." V

—*on her father's death:* "We/With our poor petty lives have strangled one/That ages watch for vainly . . . . My father held within his mighty frame/A people's life: great futures died with him/Never to rise, until the time shall ripe/Some other hero with the will to save/The outcast Zíncali." V

Duke Silva. "To keep the Christian frontier—such high trust/Is young Duke Silva's; and the time is great." I i

—*status*: "Born de la Cerda, Calatravan knight,/Count of Segura, fourth Duke of Bedmár/Offshoot from that high stock of old Castile/Whose topmost branch is proud **Medina Celi**—/Such titles with their blazonry are his/Who keeps this fortress, its sworn governor,/Lord of the valley, master of the town,/ Commanding whom he will . . . . " I i

—*caparisoned:* "Night-black the charger, black the rider's plume,/But all between is bright with morning hues—/Seems ivory and gold and deep blue gems,/And starry flashing steel and pale vermilion,/All set in jasper: on his surcoat white/Glitter the sword-belt and the jewelled hilt,/Red on the back and breast the holy cross,/And 'twixt the helmet and the soft-spun white/Thick tawny wavelets like the lion's mane/Turn backward from his brow, pale, wide, erect,/Shadowing blue eyes—blue as the rain-washed sky/That braced the early stem of Gothic kings/He claims for ancestry. A goodly knight,/A noble caballero, broad of chest/And long of limb." I i

—*ambivalence:* "Silva was both the lion and the man;/First hesitating shrank, then fiercely sprang,/Or having sprung, turned pallid at his deed/And loosed the prize, paying his blood for nought./A nature half-transformed, with qualities/That oft betrayed each other, elements/Not blent but struggling, breeding strange effects,/Passing the reckoning of his friends or foes./ Haughty and generous, grave and passionate;/With tidal moments of devoutest awe,/Sinking anon to farthest ebb of doubt;/ Deliberating ever, till the sting/Of a recurrent ardor made him rush/Right against reasons that himself had drilled/And marshalled painfully. A spirit framed/ Too proudly special for obedience,/Too subtly pondering for mastery:/born of a goddess with a mortal sire,/ Heir of flesh-fettered, weak divinity,/Doom-gifted with long resonant consciousness/And perilous heightening of the sentient soul." I iii

—*aghast:* "O god, it's true then! —true that you,/A maiden nurtured as rare flowers are,/The very air of heaven sifted fine/Lest any mote should mar your purity,/Have flung yourself out on the dusty way/For common eyes to see your beauty soiled!/You own it true—you danced upon the Plaça?" I iii

—*mollified:* "You shrink no more/from gazing men, than from the gazing flowers/That, dreaming sunshine, open as you pass." I iii

—*tormented in his choice:* "Now the former life/Of close-linked fellowship, the life that made/His full-formed self, as the impregnate sap/Of years successive frames the full-branched tree—/Was present in one whole; and that great trust/His deed had broken turned reproach on him/From faces of all witnesses who heard/His uttered pledges; saw him hold high place/Centring reliance; use rich privilege/That bound him like a victim-nourished god/By tacit covenant to shield and bless;/assume the Cross and take his knightly oath/Mature, deliberate: faces human all,/And some divine as well as human:

Silva has lost his head, Zarca his life

"His/who hung supreme, the suffering Man divine/Above the altar; Hers, the Mother pure/Whose glance informed his masculine tenderness/With deepest reverence; the Archangel armed/Trampling man's enemy: all heroid forms/That fill the world of faith with voices, hearts,/And high companionship, to Silva now/Made but one inward and insistent world/With faces of his peers, with court and hall/And deference, and reverent vassalage,And filial pieties—one current strong,/The warmly mingled life-blood of his mind,/Sustaining him even when he idly played/With rules, belief, charges, and ceremonies/As arbitrary fooling Such revenge/Is wrought by the long travail of mankind/On him who scorns it, and would shape his life/Without obedience." ¶IV i

—*beside himself:* "Sweeping like some pale herald from the dead,/Whose shadow-nurtured eyes, dazed by full light,/See nought without, but give reverted sense/to the soul's imagery, Silva came,/The wondering people parting wide to get/Continuous sight of him as he passed on—/This high hidalgo, who through blooming years/Had shone on men with lunetary calm. . . . Bareheaded now, carrying an unsheathed sword,/And on his breast, where late he bore the cross,/Wearing the Gypsy badge; his form aslant,/ Driven, it seemed, by some invisible chase,/Right to the front of **Zarca**." IV iii

Zarca. "JUAN: We have a Gypsy in Bedmár whose frame/Nature compacted with such fine selection,/'Twould yield a dozen types: all Spanish knights,/From him who slew **Rolando** at the pass/Up to the mighty **Cid**; all deities,/Thronging in Olympus in fine attitudes;/Or all hell's heroes whom the poet saw/Tremble like lions, writhe like demigods." I i

—*stripped:* "JUAN: He wore fine mail, a rich-wrought sword and belt,/And on his surcoat black a broidered torch,/A pine-branch flaming, grasped by two dark hands./ But when they stripped him of his ornaments/It was the baubles lost their grace, not he./ His eyes, his mouth, his nostril, all inspired/With scorn that mastered utterance of scorn,/With power to check all rage until it turned/ To ordered force, unleashed on chosen prey—/It seemed the soul within him made his limbs/And made them grand. The baubles were well gone./ He stood the more a king, when bared to man." I i

—*appraised:* JUAN: Oh, he is dangerous!/Granáda with this Zarca for a king/Might still maim Christendom. He is of those/Who steal the keys from snoring Destiny/And make the prophets lie. A Gypsy, too,/Suckled by hunted beasts, whose mother-milk/Has filled his veins with hate." I iii

—*mission:* "So abject are the men whose blood we share:/Untutored, unbefriended, unendowed;/No favorites of heaven or of men./Therefore I cling to them! Therefore no lure shall draw me to disown them, or forsake/The meagre wandering herd that lows for help/And needs me for its guide . . . ." I vi

—*exhortation:* "Nay, never falter: no great deed is done/By falterers who ask for certainty./No good is certain, but the steadfast mind,/The undivided will to seek the good:/'Tis that compels the elements, and wrings/A human music from the indifferent air./ The greatest gift the hero leaves his race/Is to have been a hero. Say we fail!—/We feed the high tradition of the world,/And leave our spirit in our children's breasts." I vi

—*his men and duty:* "Ay metal fine/In my brave Gypsies. Not the lithest Moor/Has lither limbs for scaling, keener eye/To mark the meaning of the furthest speck/That tells of change; and they are disciplined/By faith in me, to such obedience/As needs no spy. My scalers and my scouts/Are to the

Moorish force they're leagued withal/As bow-string to the bow; while I their chief/ Command the enterprise and guide the will/Of Moorish captains, as the pilot guides/With eye-instructed hand the passive helm." III

—bringing justice: "Punishing cruel wrong by cruelty/We copy Christian crime. Vengeance is just:/Justly we rid the earth of human fiends/Who carry hell for pattern in their souls./But in high vengeance there is noble scorn:/It tortures not the torturer, nor gives/Iniquitous payment for iniquity./The great avenging angel does not crawl/To kill the serpent with a mimic fang;/He stands erect, with sword of keenest edge/That slays like lightning." IV ii

Supporting Roles

Fr Isidor, the Prior. JUAN: "As a black eagle with gold beak and claws/Is like a raven. Even in his cowl,/Covered from head to foot, the Prior is known/ From all the black herd round. When he uncovers/And stands white-frocked, with ivory face, his eyes/Black-gleaming, black his coronal of hair/Like shredded jasper, he seems less a man/With struggling aims, than pure incarnate Will,/Fit to subdue rebellious nations, nay,/That human flesh he breathes in, charged with passion/Which quivers in his nostril and his lip,/But disciplined by long in-dwelling will/To silent labor in the yoke of law." I i

LORENZO: "My mind is this: the Father is so holy/'Twere sin to wish his soul detained from bliss./ Easy translation to the realms above,/The shortest journey to the seventh heaven,/Is what I'd never grudge him." I i

—excoriation: "Miserable man!/Your strength will turn to anguish, like the strength/of fallen angels. Can you change your blood?/You are a Christian, with the Christian awe/In every vein. A Spanish noble, born/To serve your people and your people's faith./ Strong, are you? Turn your back upon the Cross—/Its shadow is before you. Leave your place: /Quit the great ranks of knighthood: you will walk/For ever with a tortured double self,/A self that will be hungry while you feast,/Will blush with shame while you are glorified,/Will feel the ache and chill of desolation,/Even in the very bosom of your love./ Make yourself with woman, fit for what?/To make the sport of Moorish palaces,/A lewd **Herodias** . . . ." I iii

—his target: "Suspicion is a heaven-sent lamp, and I—/I, watchman of the Holy Office, bear/That lamp in trust. I will keep faithful watch./The Holy Inquisition's discipline/Is mercy, saving her, if penitent—/God grant it!—else—root up the poison-plant,/Though 'twere a lily with a golden heart!/ This spotless maiden with her pagan soul/Is the arch-enemy's trap: he turns his back/On all the prostitutes, and watches her/To see her poison men with false belief/In rebel virtues. She has poisoned Silva . . . . " I v

—his precepts: "The fence of rules is for the purblind crowd;/They walk by averaged precepts: sovereign men,/Seeing by God's light, see the general/By seeing all the special—own no rule/But their full vision of the moment's worth./ 'Tis so God governs, using wicked men—/Nay, scheming fiends, to work his purposes./ Evil that good may come? Measure the good/Before you say what's evil. Perjury?/ I scorn the perjurer, but I will use him/To serve the holy truth. There is no lie/Save in his soul, and let his soul be judged./I know the truth, and act upon the truth." I v

—to the scaffold: "The Father came bareheaded, frocked, a rope/Around his neck,—but clad with majesty,/The strength of resolute undivided souls/ Who, owning law, obey it. In his hand/He bore a crucifix, and praying, gazed/

Solely on that white image . . . Isidor/Lifted his eyes to look around him—calm,/Prepared to speak last words of willingness/To meet his death—last words of faith unchanged,/That, working for Christ's kingdom, he had wrought/Righteously." IV iii

—seeing the apostate: "Back from me, traitorous and accursed man!/ Defile not me, who grasp the holiest,/With touch or breath! Thou foulest murderer!/ Fouler than **Cain** who struck his brother down/In jealous rage, thou for thy base delight/Hast oped the gate for wolves to come and tear/ Uncounted brethren, weak and strong alike,/The helpless priest, the warrior all unarmed/ Against a faithless leader: on thy head/Will rest the sacrilege, on thy soul the blood./These blind barbarians, misbelievers, Moors,/Are but as **Pilate** and his soldiery;/Thou, **Judas**, weighted with that heaviest crime/ Which deepens hell! . . . O most wretched man!/Whose memory shall be of broken oaths—/Broken for lust—I turn away mine eyes /For ever from you." IV iii

Juan, "the spare man with the lute,/Who makes you dizzy with his rapid tongue,/Whirring athwart your mind with comment swift/On speech you would have finished by and by,/Shooting your bird for you while you are loading,/ Cheapening your wisdom as a pattern known,/Woven by any shuttle on demand./ Can never sit quite still, too: sees a wasp/And kills it with a movement like a flash;/Whistles low notes or seems to thrum his lute/As a mere hyphen 'twixt two syllables/Of any steadier man; walks up and down/And snuffs the orange flowers and shoots a pea/To hit a streak of light let through the awning./Has a queer face: eyes large as plums, a nose/Small, round, uneven, like a bit of wax/Melted and cooled by chance.

"Thin-fingered, lithe,/And as a squirrel noiseless, startling men/Only by quickness. In his speech and look/A touch of graceful wildness, as of things/Not trained or tamed for uses of the world;/Most like the Fauns that roamed in days of old . . . . For Juan was a minstrel still, in times/When minstrelsy was held a thing outworn . . . . So Juan was a troubadour revived,/Freshening life's dusty road with babbling rills/Of wit and song, living 'mid harnessed men/With limbs ungalled by armor, ready so/To soothe them weary, and to cheer them sad./ Guest at the board, companion in the camp,/A crystal mirror to the life around,/ Flashing the comment keen of simple fact/Defined in words; lending brief lyric voice/To grief and sadness; hardly taking note/Of difference betwixt his own and others';/But rather singing as a listener/To the deep moans, the cries, the wild strong joys/Of universal Nature, old yet young.

"Such Juan, the third talker, shimmering bright/As butterfly or bird with quickest life." ¶I i

—talker: "ZARCA: I fitted all my memories with the chat/Of one named Juan—one whose rapid talk/Showers like the blossoms from a light-twigged shrub,/If you but cough beside it." I vi

—friend: "Juan who went and came/To soothe two hearts, and claimed nought for his own?/Friend more divine than all divinities,/Quenching his human thirst in others' joy." IV i

Pablo. "[She] left this boy, lame from his birth,/And sad and obstinate, though when he will/He sings God-taught such marrow-thrilling strains/As seem the very voice of dying Spring,/ A flute-like wail that mourns the blossoms gone,/And sinks, and is not, like their fragrant breath,/With fine transition on the trembling air./ He sits as if imprisoned by some fear,/Motionless, with wide eyes that seem not made/For hungry glancing of a twelve-year'd boy/To mark the living thing that he could tease,/But for the gaze of some primeval sadness/Dark twin with light in the creative ray./ This little PABLO has his spangles took/And large rosettes to hide his poor left foot/Rounded like any hoof (his mother thought/God willed it so to punish all her sins)." I i

—*singing:* " 'Twas Pablo, like the wounded spirit of song/Pouring melodious pain to cheat the hour/For idle soldiers in the castle court . . . **Silva** then/ Bethought him whence the voice came, framed perforce/Some outward image of a life not his/That made a sorrowful centre to the world:/A boy lame, melancholy-eyed, who bore/A viol—yes, that very child he saw/This morning eating roots by the gateway . . . . " II i

Salomo Sephardo—in **Abderahman**'s tower. "In carved dark-oaken chair, unpillowed, sleeps/Right in the rays of Jupiter a small man,/In skull-cap bordered close with crisp gray curls,/And loose black gown showing a neck and breast/ Protected by a dim-green amulet;/Pale-faced with finest nostril wont to breathe/Ethereal passion in a world of thought;/Eyebrows jet-black and firm, yet delicate;/Beard scant and grizzled; mouth shut firm, with curves/So subtly turned to meanings exquisite,/You seem to read them as you read a word/Full-vowelled, long-descended, pregnant—rich/With legacies from long, laborious lives." II ii

—*warning:* "But note this—I am a Jew;/And while the Christian persecutes my race,/I'll turn at need even the Christian's trust/Into a weapon and a shield for Jews." II ii

Others

Don Alvar. "It was his friend Don Alvar whom he saw/Reining his horse up, face to face with him,/Sad as the twilight, all his clothes ill-girt—/As if he had been roused to see one die,/And brought the news to him whom death had robbed." II i

—*dead:* "But this young Alvar/Was doubly noble, as a gem that holds/Rare virtues in its lustre; and his death/Will pierce **Don Silva** with a poisoned dart." IV ii

Don Amador. "To what good end is it that I . . . am reading aloud in a clerkly manner from a book which hath been culled from the flowers of all books, to instruct you in the knowledge befitting those who would be knights and worthy hidalgos? I had as lief be reading in a belfry . . . .Wherefore am I master of the Duke's retinue, if my voice is to run along like a gutter in a storm?" II iii

Annibal. "I said the souls were five—besides the dog./ But there was still a sixth, with wrinkled face,/Grave and disgusted with all merriment/Not less than **Roldan**. It is ANNIBAL,/The experienced monkey who performs the tricks,/Jumps through the hoops, and carries round the hat./ Once full of sallies and impromptu feats,/Now cautious not to light on aught that's new/Lest he be whipped to do it o'er again/From A to Z, and make the gentry laugh:/A misanthropic monkey, gray and grim,/Bearing a lot that has no remedy/For want of concert in the monkey tribe." I i

—*visitor:* "The cautious monkey, in a Moorish dress,/A tunic white, turban and scimitar,/Wears these stage garments, nay, his very flesh,/With silent protest; keeps a neutral air/As aiming at a metaphysic state/'Twixt 'is' and 'is not;' lets his chain be loosed/By sage **Sephardo**'s hands, sits still at first,/Then trembles out of his neutrality,/Looks up and leaps into Sephardo's lap,/And chatters forth his agitated soul,/Turning to peep at **Pablo** on the floor." II ii

Arias, "a stripling of fifteen, sings by snatches in a boyish treble, as he walks up and down, and tosses back the nuts which another youth flings towards him." II iii

—impudent: "Nay, **Don Amador**; **King Alfonso**, they say, was a heretic . . . noble birth gives us more leave to do ill if we like . . . .

"Why nobles are only punished now and then, in a grand way, and have their heads cut off, like the **Grand Constable**. I shouldn't mind that." II iii

—dead: "This fair and curly youth was Arias,/A son of the Pachecos. . . . " IV ii

Blasco. "His right-hand guest is solemn as the dog,/Square-faced and massive: BLASCO is his name,/A prosperous silversmith from Aragon;/In speech not silvery, rather tuned as notes/From a deep vessel made of plenteous iron,/Or some great bell of slow but certain swing/That, if you only wait, will tell the hour/As well as flippant clocks that strike in haste/And set off chiming a superfluous tune . . . . " I i

Hinda, "Prettiest and boldest, tucks her kirtle up/As wallet for the stolen buttons—then/Bends with her knife to cut from off the hat/The aigrette and long feather . . . Hinda swift as thought leaps back,/But carries off the spoil triumphantly,/And leads the chorus of a happy laugh/Running with all the naked-footed imps/Till with safe survey all can face about/And watch for signs of stimulating chase,/While Hinda ties long grass around her brow/to stick the feather in with majesty." III

—loyal: "She'd sooner be a rat and hang on thorns/To parch until the wind had scattered her,/Than be an outcast, spit at by her tribe." III

—on the quay: "Below [Fedalma] sat/Slim mischievous Hinda, happy, red-bedecked/With rows of berries, grinning, nodding oft,/And shaking high her small dark arm and hand . . . . " V

Iñez, "the old trusted nurse . . . . " I iii

FEDALMA: "Nay, my lord,/You must not blame her, dear old nurse. She cried. Why, you would have consented too, at last." I iii

—her mistress gone: "Motionless all—save where old Iñez lay/Sunk on the floor holding her rosary,/Making its shadow tremble with her fear./ And **Silva** passed her by because she grieved . . . . " II i

Lopez. "Entered with resonant step, another guest—/A soldier: all his keenness in his sword,/His eloquence in scars upon his cheek,/His virtue in much slaying of the Moor:/With brow well-creased in horizontal folds/To save the space, as having nought to do:/Lips prone to whistle whisperingly—no tune,/But trotting rhythm: meditative eyes,/Most often fixed upon his legs and spurs:/Styled Captain Lopez."

Lorenzo. "MINE HOST is one: he with the well-arched nose,/Soft-eyed, fat-handed, loving men for nought/But his own humor, patting old and young/Upon the back, and mentioning the cost/With confidential blandness, as a tax/That he collected much against his will/From Spaniards who were all his bosom friends:/Warranted Christian—else how keep an inn,/Which calling asks true faith? Though like his wine/Of cheaper sort, a trifle over-new . . . . Our host . . . was born ten years too soon,/Had heard his mother call him **Ephraim**,/Knew holy things from common, thought it sin/To feast on days when Israel's children mourned/So had to be converted with his sire,/To doff the awe he learned as Ephraim,/And suit his manners to a Christian name." I i

Pepíta. "[To **Juan**] I think you like me not. I wish you did./ Sometimes you sing to me and make me dance,/Another time you take no heed of me,/Not though I kiss my hand to you and smile./But **Andrès** would be glad if I kissed him." I iv

Roldan. The silent ROLDAN has his brightness too,/But only in his spangles and rosettes./ His parti-colored vest and crimson hose/Are dulled with old Valencian dust, his eyes/With straining fifty years at gilded balls/To catch them dancing, or with brazen looks/At men and women as he made his jests/Some thousand times and watched to count the pence/His wife was gathering. His olive face/Has an old writing in it, characters/Stamped deep by grins that had no merriment . . . . Roldan would gladly never laugh again;/Pensioned, he would be grave as any ox,/And having beans and crumbs and oil secured/Would borrow no man's jokes for evermore./ 'Tis harder now because his wife is gone,/Who had quick feet, and danced to ravishment/Of every ring jewelled with Spanish eyes,/But died . . . . " I i

El Zagal. " . . . that fierce lion/Grisly El Zagal, who has made his lair/In Guadix' fort, and rushing thence with strength/Half his own fierceness, half the untainted heart/Of mountain bands that fight for holiday,/Wastes the fair lands that lie by Alcalá,/Wreathing his horse's neck with Christian heads." I i

Minor Figures

Alda. "Thin Alda's face, sad as a wasted passion,/Leaned o'er the nodding baby's . . . . " I i

Arbués, the grand Inquisitor in Aragon. BLASCO: "He had a shell/like any lobster: a good iron suit/From top to toe beneath the innocent serge./ That made the tell-tale sound. But then came shrieks./ The chanting stopped and turned to rushing feet,/And in the midst lay Master Arbués,/Felled like an ox. 'Twas wicked butchery." I i

Boabdil, "the waverer, who usurps/A throne he trembles in, and fawning licks/The feet of conquerors . . . . " I i

Don Diego, "the fiery Don." I i

Enriquez. "Serves the infidels right! They have sold Christians enough to people half the towns in Paradise." II iii

Fabian. "Oh, the very tail of our chance has vanished. The royal army is breaking up—going home for the winter." II iii

Hita "is decked/With an embroidered scarf across her rags . . . . " III

Hurtado. "Yes, yes, through the pass of By-and-by, you go to the valley of Never. We might have done a great feat . . . . " II iii

Ismaël. HINDA: "It could be no one else/But Ismaël. He catches all the birds,/Knows where the speckled fish are, scales the rocks/And sings and dances with me when I like./How should I marry and not marry him?" III

—*on the quay:* " . . . the black-maned Ismaël,/Who held aloft his spoil, and clad in skins/Seemed the Boy-prophet of the wilderness/Escaped from tasks prophetic." V

José. "Nonsense, **Arias**! /Nobles have their heads cut off because their crimes are noble. /If they did what was unknightly, they would come to shame." II iii

Lambra. "[You were] the child,/Sole offspring of my flesh, that Lambra bore/One hour before the Christian, hunting us,/Hurried her on to death." I vi

Father of **Lorenzo**. "His father was a convert, chose the chrism/As men choose physic, kept his chimney warm/With smokiest wood upon a Saturday,/Counted his gains and grudges on a chaplet,/And crossed himself asleep for fear of spies;/Trusting the God of Israel would see/'Twas Christian tyranny that made him base." I i

Lola. "Fat Lola leaned upon the balcony/With arms that might have pillowed **Hercules** . . . . " I i

Fr Marcos "says [**Fedalma**] will not confess/And love not holy water; says her blood/Is infidel; says the Duke's wedding her/Is union of light with darkness." I i

Market-woman. "Good, good, sir! Taste and try. See, here is one/Weighs a man's head. The best are bound with tow . . . . '/Tis called the Miracle. You open it, /And find it full of speech." II iv

Nadar. "Ay, but this sleek hound [**Silva**],/Who slipped his collar off to join the wolves,/Has still a heart for none but kennelled brutes./He rages at the taking of the town,/Says all his friends are butchered . . . I would sooner be/A murdered Gypsy's dog, and howl for him,/Than be this Spaniard." IV iii

Pepe. " 'twixt the rails/The little Pepe showed his two black beads,/His flat-ringed hair and small Semitic nose,/Complete and tiny as a new-born minnow . . . . " I i

Pepita, "blondest maid/In all Bedmár—Pepita, fair yet flecked,/Saucy of lip and nose, of hair as red/As breasts of robins stepping on the snow—/Who stands in front with little tapping feet,/And baby-dimpled hands that hide enclosed/Those sleeping crickets, the dark castanets." I ii

Priest. "His glance/Took in with much content the priest who rode/Firm in his saddle, stalwart and broad-backed,/Crisp-curled, and comfortably secular,/Right in the front of him." II i

Ramon. JUAN: "You hear the trumpet? There's old Roman's blast./ No bray but his can shake the air so well./He takes his trumpeting as solemnly/As angel charged to wake the dead; thinks war/Was made for trumpeters, and their great art/Made solely for themselves who understand it./ His features all have shaped themselves to blowing,/And when his trumpet's bagged or left at home/He seems a chattel in a broker's booth,/A spoutless watering-can, a promise to pay/No sum particular." I i

Tralla, "with thorns for pins, sticks two rosettes/Upon her threadbare woollen . . . . " III

Wife. " . . . holding in her arms/The baby senior, stood **Lorenzo**'s wife/All negligent, her kerchief discomposed/By little clutches, woman's coquetry/Quite turned to mother's cares and sweet content." I i

Zind. "Marauding Spaniards . . . doubtless snatched you up,/When Zind, your nurse, as she confessed, was urged/By burning thirst to wander towards the stream/And leave you on the sand some paces off/Playing with pebbles, while she dog-like lapped." I vi

The Departure for Africa

Also mentioned

Abderahman, for whom the astrological tower in Silva's castle is named	II ii
Don Alonzo, lord of Aguilar, for whom Blasco made a silver dish	I i
Andrès, who apparently loves Pepíta	I iv
Attila [H], great leader of the depredations of the Huns	I i
Blas, who is quoted commenting on rumors and on catching a fish	I i II ii
Marquis of Cadiz, mentioned in passing	II iii
Catalan, old, blind and wandering: taught Pablo music	I ii
Duchess Diana, the late mother of the Duke, who raised Fedalma	I i
Fray Domingo, who might have to take over the reading	II iii
King Ferdinand of Aragon: a fine presence and proper limbs	I i
Grand Constable, who had his head cut off	II iii
Hassan, a gypsy left in charge in the field by Zarca	III
Saint James [H]	I i
Ponce de Leon [H], seen in camp	I I
Medina Celi, supreme in Castile	I i
Nouna, attending Fedalma in the gypsy camp	III
Perez, manservant to Silva	I iii
Quintin, commenting on rumors	I i
Salomo, allegedly in dangerous discourse with Fedalma	I v
Sebastian, quoted commenting on rumors	I I

Lyrics and Songs

Should I long that dark were fair?
Say, O song!
Lacks my love aught, that I should long?

Dark the night, with breath all flow'rs,
And tender broken voice that fills
With ravishment the listening hours:
Whisperings, wooings,
Liquid ripples and soft ring-dove cooings
In low-toned rhythm that love's aching stills.
Dark the night,
Yet is she bright,
For in her dark she brings the mystic star,
Trembling yet strong, as is the voice of love,
From some unknown afar.
O radiant Dark! O darkly-fostered ray!
Thou hast a joy too deep for shallow Day. I i

Maiden, crowned with glossy blackness,
Lithe as panther forest-roaming,
Long-armed naiad, when she dances,
On a stream of ether floating—
Bright, O bright Fedalma!

Form all curves like softness drifted,
Wave-kissed marble roundly dimpling,
Far-off music slowly wingéd
Gently rising, gently sinking—
Bright, O bright Fedalma!

Pure as rain-tear on a rose-leaf,
Cloud high-born in noonday spotless,
Sudden perfect as the dew-bead,

Gem of earth and sky begotten—
Bright, O bright Fedalma!

Beauty has no mortal father,
Holy light her form engendered
Out of tremor, yearning, gladness,
Presage sweet and joy remembered—
Child of Light, Fedalma! I i

Spring comes hither,
Buds the rose;
Roses wither,
Sweet spring goes.
Ojalà, would she carry me!

Summer soars—
Wide-winged day
White light pours,
Flies away.
Ojalà, would he carry me!

Soft winds blow,
Westward born,
Onward go
Toward the morn.
Ojalà, would they carry me!

Sweet birds sing
O'er the graves
Then take wing
O'er the waves
Ojalà, would they carry me! I ii

Warm whispering through the slender olive leaves
Some to me a gentle sound,
Whispering of a secret found
In the clear sunshine 'mid the golden sheaves:
Said it was sleeping for me in the morn,
Called it gladness, called it joy,
Draw me on—"Come hither, boy"—
To where the blue wings rested on the corn.
I thought the gentle sound had whispered true—
Thought the little heaven mine,
Leaned to clutch the thing divine,
And saw the blue wings melt within the blue. I ii

It was in the prime
Of the sweet Spring-time.
In the linnet's throat
Trembled the love-note,
And the love-stirred air
Thrilled the blossoms there.
Little shadows danced
Each a tiny elf,
Happy in large light
And the thinnest self.

It was but a minute
        In a far-off Spring,
        But each gentle thing,
Sweetly-wooing linnet,
Soft-thrilled hawthorn tree,
        Happy shadowy elf
        With the thinnest self,
Life still on in me
O the sweet, sweet prime
Of the past Spring-time!   I ii

Day is dying! Float, O song,
        Down the westward river,
Requiem chanting to the Day—
        Day, the mighty Giver.

Pierced by shafts of Time he bleeds,
        Melted rubies sending
Through the river and the sky,
        Earth and heaven blending;

All the long-drawn earthy banks
        Up to cloud-land lifting:
Slow between them drifts the swan,
        'Twixt two heavens drifting.

Wings half open, like a flow'r
        Inly deeper flushing,
Neck and breast as virgin's pure—
        Virgin proudly blushing.

Day is dying! Float, O swan,
        Down the ruby river;
Follow, song, in requiem
        To the mighty Giver.   I ii

Memory
Tell to me
What is fair,
Past compare
        In the land of Tubal?

Is it Spring's
Lovely things,
Blossoms white,
Rosy dight?
        Then it is Pepíta

Summer's crest
Red-gold tressed,
        Corn-flowers peeping under?—
Idle noons,
Lingering moons,

Sudden cloud,
Lightning's shroud,
Sudden rain,
Quick again
        Smiles where late was thunder?—
Are all these
Made to please?
        So too is Pepíta.
Autumn's prime,
Apple-time,
Smooth cheek round,
Heart all sound?—Is it this
You would kiss?
        Then it is Pepíta.

You can bring
No sweet thing,
But my mind
Still shall find
        It is my Pepíta.

Memory
Sings to me
It is she—
She is fair
Past compare
        In the land of Tubal. I iv

Came a pretty maid
        By that moon's pure light,
Loved me well, she said,
        Eyes with tears all bright,
            A pretty maid!

But too late she strayed,
        Moonlight pure was there;
She was nought but shade
        Hiding the more fair,
            The heavenly maid! I iv

The world is great: the birds all fly from me,
The stars are golden fruit upon a tree
All out of reach: my little sister went,
            And I am lonely.

The world is great: I tried to mount the hill
Above the pines, where the light lies so still,
But it rose higher: little Lisa went,
            And I am lonely.

The world is great: the wind comes rushing by,
I wonder where it comes from; sea-birds cry
And hurt my heart: my little sister went,
And I am lonely.

The world is great: the people laugh and talk,
And make loud holiday: how fast they walk!
I'm lame, they push me: little Lisa went,
And I am lonely. II I

O bird that used to press
Thy head against my cheek
With touch that seemed to speak
And ask a tender "yes"—
Ay de mi, my bird!

O tender downy breast
And warmly beating heart,
That beating seemed a part
Of me who gave it rest—
Ay de mis, my bird! II i

There was a holy hermit
Who counted all things loss
For Christ his Master's glory:
He made an ivory cross,

And as he knelt before it
And wept his murdered Lord,
The ivory turned to iron,
The cross became a sword.

The tears that fell upon it,
They turned to red, red rust,
The tears that fell from off it
Made writing in the dust.
The holy hermit, gazing,
Saw words upon the ground:
"The words be red for ever
With the blood of false Mahound." II iii

At the battle of Clavijo
In the days of King Ramiro,
Help us Allah! cried the Moslem,
Cried the Spaniard, Heaven's chosen,
God and Santiago!

Straight out-flushing like the rainbow,
See him come, celestial Baron,
Mounted knight, with red-crossed banner,
Plunging earthward to the battle,
Glorious Santiago!

As the flame before the swift wind,
See, he fires us, we burn with him!
Flash our swords, dash Pagans backward—
Victory he! pale fear is Allah!
                        God with Santiago! II iii

All things journey: sun and moon,
Morning, noon, and afternoon,
                Night and all her stars:
'Twixt the east and western bars
                Round they journey,
                        Come and go!
                We go with them!
For to roam and ever roam
Is the Zíncali's loved home.

Earth is good, the hillside breaks
By the ashen roots and makes
                Hungry nostrils glad:
Then we run till we are mad,
                Like the horses,
                        And we cry,
                None shall catch us!
Swift winds wing us—we are free—
Drink the air—we Zíncali!

Falls the snow: the pine-branch split,
Call the fire out, see it flit,
                Through the dry leaves run,
Spread and glow, and make a sun
                In the dark tent:
                        O warm dark!
                Warm as conies!
Strong fire loves us, we are warm!
Who the Zíncali shall harm?

Onward journey: fires are spent;
Sunward, sunward! lift the tent,
                Run before the rain,
Through the pass, along the plain.
                Hurry, hurry,
                        Lift us, wind!
                Like the horses.
For to roam and ever roam
Is the Zíncali's loved home.   III

Push off the boat,
                Quit, quit the shore,
                        The stars will guide us back:—
O gathering cloud,
                O wide, wide sea,
                        O waves that keep no track!

On through the pines!
            The pillared woods,
                  Where silence breathes sweet breath:—
O labyrinth,
            O sunless gloom,
                  The other side of death! IV i

Brother, hear and take the curse
      Curse of soul's and body's throes,
      If you hate not all our foes,
      Cling not fast to all our woes,
            Turn false Zíncala!
      May you be accurst
      By hunger and by thirst
            By spikéd pangs,
            Starvation's fangs
            Clutching you alone
When none but peering vultures hear your moan.
      Curst by burning hands,
            Curst by aching brow,
            When on sea-wide sands
                  Fever lays you low;
            By the maddened brain
      When the running water glistens,
      And the deaf ear listens, listens,
            Prisoned fire within the vein,
            On the tongue and on the lip
                  Not a sip
            Even from the earth or skies;
            Hot the desert lies
      Pressed into your anguish,
      Narrowing earth and narrowing sky
            Into lonely misery.

            Lonely may you languish
      Through the day and through the night,
      Hate the darkness, hate the light,
            Pray and find no ear,
            Feel no brother near,
            Till on death you cry,
            Death who passes by,
            And anew you groan,
Scaring the vultures all to leave you living lone:
            Curst be soul's and body's throes
            If you love the dark men's foes,
      Cling not fast to all the dark men's woes,
                  Turn false Zíncala!

            Swear to hate the cruel cross,
                  The silver cross!
            Glittering, laughing at the blood
                  Shed below it in a flood

When it glitters over Moorish porches;
        Laughing at the scent of flesh
When it glitters where the faggot scorches,
        Burning life's mysterious mesh:
                Blood of wandering Israël
                Blood of wandering Ismaël
        Blood, the drink of Christian scorn,
        Blood of wanderers, sons of morn
                Where the life of men began:
                        Swear to hate the cross!—

Sign of all the wanderers' foes,
Sign of all the wanderers' woes—
                Else its curse light on you!
Else the curse upon you light
Of its sharp red-sworded might.
May it lie a blood-red blight
On all things within your sight:
On the white base of the morn,
On the meadows and the corn,
On the sun and on the moon,
On the clearness of the noon,
On the darkness of the night.

May it fill your aching sight—
Red-cross sword and sword blood-red—
Till it press upon your head,
Till it lie within your brain,
Piercing sharp, a cross of pain,
Till it lie upon your heart,
                Burning hot, a cross of fire,
Till from sense in every part

Pains have clustered like a stinging swarm
                        In the cross's form,
And you see naught but the cross of blood,
And you feel nought but the cross of fire:
Curst by all the cross's throes
If you hate not all our foes,
Cling not fast to all our woes,
                Turn false Zíncala!   III

The 1878 Edition

Macmillan's and *Atlantic Monthly;* May 1870 **LJ**
Completed January 13, 1869

The Legend of Jubal

" . . . he was the father of all such as handle the harp and organ."
—*Genesis* 4:21

Cain has killed and been banished and marked. He has found his way to an eastward land where for a time all is peace, plenty, and idleness. He and his family labor "gently." One day, **Lamech** in play with his children throws a stone which kills his boy. Cain, seeing this, realizes that God has followed him. Content is gone: work becomes the norm. All things in nature are seen anew as precious, because death will come and end their enjoyment. Lamech's sons vow that through industry and effort they will leave something behind when they in turn die. They are **Jabal**, the tranquil herder of flocks; **Tubal-Cain**, the restless fabricator of metals; and **Jubal**, unsure of his calling. No women are given names in the poem, but Jabal has a **sister** who helps him in the milking.

Tubal-Cain's products include materials for weapons and torture, but also for agriculture and social good. Jubal watches and reflects. He wanders, listening to birds and human speech. Realizing his calling is as a musician, he makes a lyre. There is a sylvan scene of play, presided over by the **mother** (presumably Cain's wife). Jubal begins to play and "Joy took the air and took each breathing soul." The youths and maidens dance. Tubal-Cain watches in wonder at this "power in metal shape which made strange bliss." Jubal is acclaimed, but a problem develops: he has many imitators. He becomes weary of "hearing himself." He decides to travel and seek new music. He finds the land of the race of **Seth**, **Adam**'s last-born.

Here he abides a long, long time, making music heartening to the people. He climbs peak after peak but hears no celestial music. At last, for the first time he sees the overwhelming ocean: he sits down, discouraged, and drops his lyre. The world is too much for him. He has lost his voice. He decides to go home. He is confident of recognition and welcome, and after much travail he finds his old haunts. But he is shocked by change: paths are now paven roads; small towns are cities. He sinks down to rest—and suddenly hears music. A great crowd with lyres and cymbals, flutes and psalteries, are coming, and they sing his name! It is a memorial celebration. He is thrilled. He rushes among them and tells them who he is. But they do not believe him. They scorn and pummel him for his sacrilege. He flees and falls to earth, to die.

And a vision—his angel—comes. The angel reminds him of his great gift of music and the great choice he made: to cling to it and give it to the world. It tells him he is forever blessed, that he will forever shine in men's souls—a god. Jubal finds himself translated: his grave is the All-creating Presence.

Title Role

Jubal "But Jubal had a frame
Fashioned to finer senses, which became
A yearning for some hidden soul of things,
Some outward touch complete on inner springs
That vaguely moving bred a lonely pain,
A want that did but stronger grow with gain
Of all good else, as spirits might be sad
For lack of speech to tell us they are glad." 148-55

—wandering: "Then with such blissful trouble and glad care
For growth within unborn as mothers bear,
To the far woods he wandered, listening,
And heard the birds their little stories sing
In notes whose rise and fall seemed melted speech—
Melted with tears, smiles, glances—that can reach
More quickly through our frame's deep-winding night,
And without thought raise thought's best fruit,
delight." 268-75

—idea: "It was his thought he saw; the presence fair
Of unachieved achievement, the high task,
The struggling unborn spirit that doth ask
With irresistible cry for blood and breath,
Till feeding its great life we sink in death." 302-306

—challenged: "Jubal must dare as great beginners dare,
Strike form's first way in matter rude and bare,
And, yearning vaguely toward the plenteous quire
Of the world's harvest, make one poor small lyre.
He made it, and from out its measured frame
Drew the harmonic soul, whose answers came
With guidance sweet and lessons of delight
Teaching to ear and hand the blissful Right . . . . " 340-47

—mission: "Then Jubal poured his triumph in a song—
The rapturous word that rapturous notes prolong
As radiance streams from smallest things that burn,
Or thought of loving into love doth turn.
And still his lyre gave companionship
In sense-taught concert as of lip with lip.
Alone amid the hills at first he tried
His wingèd song; then with adoring pride

And bridegroom's joy at leading forth his bride,
He said, 'This wonder which my soul hath found,
This heart of music in the might of sound,
Shall forthwith be the share of all our race
And like the morning gladden common space:
The song shall spread and swell as rivers do,
And I will teach our youth with skill to woo
This living lyre, to know its secret will,
Its fine division of the good and ill.
So shall men call me sire of harmony,
And where great Song is, there my life shall be.' " 350-68

—fulfilment: "Then from the east, with glory on his head
Such as low-slanting beams on cornwaves spread,
Came Jubal with his lyre: there 'mid the throng,
Where the blank space was, poured a solemn song,
Touching his lyre to full harmonic throb
And measured pulse, with cadences that sob,
Exult and cry, and search the inmost deep
Where the dark sources of new passion sleep.
Joy took the air, and took each breathing soul,
Embracing them in one trancèd whole . . . . " 410-20

—acclaim: "All clung with praise to Jubal: some besought
That he would teach them his new skill; some caught,
Swiftly as smiles are caught in looks that meet,
The tone's melodic change and rhythmic beat . . . .
And thus did Jubal to his race reveal
Music their larger soul, where woe and weal
Filling the resonant chords, the song, the dance,
Moved with a wider-wingèd utterance." 462-65, 468-71

—hemmed in: " 'Hearing myself,' he said, 'hems in my life,
And I will get me to some far-off land,
Where higher mountains under heaven stand
And touch the blue at rising of the stars,
Whose song they hear where no rough mingling mars
The great clear voices." 475-80

—new land: "He lingered wandering for many an age,
And, sowing music, made high heritage
For generations far beyond the Flood—
For the poor late-begotten human brood
Born to life's weary brevity and perilous good." 505-509

—aged: "And now to ignorant eyes
No sign remained of Jubal, **Lamech**'s son,
That mortal frame wherein was first begun
The immortal life of song. His withered brow
Pressed over eyes that held no lightning now,
His locks streamed whiteness on the hurrying air,
The unresting soul had worn itself quite bare
Of beauteous token, as the outworn might

Jubal knows the end has come

Of oaks slow dying, gaunt in summer's light.
His full deep voice toward thinnest treble ran:
He was the rune-writ story of a man." 558-68

—rejected: "But ere the laughter died from out the rear,
Anger in front saw profanation near;
Jubal was but a name in each man's faith
For glorious power untouched by that slow death
Which creeps with creeping time; this too, the spot,
And this the day, it must be crime to blot,
Even with scoffing at a madman's lie:
Jubal was not a name to wed with mockery.

Two rushed upon him: two, the most devout
In honor of great Jubal, thrust him out,
And beat him with their flutes." 690-99

" . . . he sought the screen
Of thorny thickets, and there fell unseen.
The immortal name of Jubal filled the sky,
While Jubal lonely laid him down to die." 703-706

—a vision: "The face bent over him like silver night
In long-remembered summers; that calm light
Of days which shine in firmaments of thought,
That past unchangeable, from change still wrought.
And gentlest tones were with the vision blent:
He knew not if that gaze the music sent,
Or music that calm gaze: to hear, to see,
Was but one undivided ecstasy:
The raptured senses melted into one,
And parting life a moment's freedom won
From in and outer, as a little child
Sits on a bank and sees blue heavens mild
Down in the water, and forgets its limbs,
And knoweth nought save the blue heaven that
swims." 720-33

" 'Jubal,' the face said, 'I am thy loved Past,
The soul that makes thee one from first to last.
I am the angel of thy life and death,
Thy outbreathed being drawing its last breath.
Am I not thine alone, a dear dead bride
Who blest thy lot above all men's beside?" 734-9

"And on the mountains in thy wandering
Thy feet were beautiful as blossomed spring,
That turns the leafless wood to love's glad home,
For with thy coming Melody was come.
This was thy lot, to feel, create, bestow,
And that immeasurable life to know
From which the fleshly self falls shrivelled, dead,
A seed primeval that has forests bred." 766-73

"It is the glory of the heritage
Thy life has left, that makes thy outcast age:
Thy limbs shall lie dark, tombless on this sod,
Because thou shinest in man's soul, a god,
Who found and gave new passion and new joy
That nought but Earth's destruction can destroy." 774-80

—translation: "The words seemed melting into symphony,
The wings upbore him, and the gazing song
Was floating him the heavenly space along,
Where mighty harmonies all gently fell
Through veiling vastness, like the far-off bell,
Till, ever onward through the choral blue,
He heard more faintly and more faintly knew
Quitting mortality, a quenched sun-wave
The All-creating Presence for his grave." 783-91

His Brothers

Jabal "Jabal, the eldest, bore upon his face
The look of that calm river-god, the Nile,
Mildly secure in ower that needs not guile . . . .
Now Jabal learned to tame the lowing kine,
And from their udders drew the snow-white wine
That stirs the innocent joy, and makes the stream
Of elemental life with fulness teem . . . ." 132-5, 156-9

—his role: "This was the work of Jabal: he began
The pastoral life, and, sire of joys to be,
Spread the sweet ties that bind the family
O'er dear dumb souls that thrilled at man's caress,
And shared his pains with patient helpfulness." 185-9

Tubal-Cain " . . . was restless as the fire
That aglows and spreads and leaps from high to higher
Where'er is aught to seize or to subdue;
Strong as a storm he lifted or o'er threw,
His urgent limbs like rounded granite grew . . . .
But strength that still on movement must be fed,
Inspiring thought of change, devices bred,
And urged his mind through earth and air to rove
For force that he could conquer if he strove,
For lurking forms that might new tasks fulfil
And yield unwilling to his stronger will." 135-9, 142-7

—his work: "But Tubal-Cain had caught and yoked the fire,
Yoked it with stones that bent the flaming spire
And made it roar in prisoned servitude
Within the furnace, till with force subdued
It changed all forms he willed to work upon,
Till hard from soft, and soft from hard, he won." 190-95

"Each day he wrought, and better than he planned,
Shape breeding shape beneath his restless hand.
(The soul without still helps the soul within,
And its deft magic ends what we begin.)" 204-7

—results: "Each day saw the birth
Of various forms which, flung upon the earth,
Seemed harnless toys to cheat the exacting hour,
But were as seeds instinct with hidden power.
The axe, the club, the spikèd wheel, the chain,
Held silently the shrieks and moans of pain;
And near them latent lay in share and spade,
In the strong bar, the saw, and deep-curved blade,
Glad voices of the hearth and harvest-home,
The social good, and all earth's joy to come." 214-23

"Thus to mixed ends wrought Tubal; and they say,
Some things he made have lasted to this day;
As, thirty silver pieces that were found
By **Noah**'s children buried in the ground.
He made them from mere hunger of device,
Those small white discs; but they became the price
The traitor **Judas** sold his Master for;
And men still handling them in peace and war
Catch foul disease, that comes as appetite,
And lurks and clings as withering, damning blight." 224-33

"But Tubal-Cain wot not of treachery,
Nor greedy lust, nor any ill to be,
Save the one ill of sinking into nought,
Banished from action and act-shaping thought.
He was the sire of swift-transforming skill,
Which arms for conquest man's ambitious will;
And round him gladly, as his hammer rung,
Gathered the elders and the growing young:
These handled vaguely and those plied the tools,
Till, happy chance begetting conscious rules,
The home of Cain with industry was rife,
And glimpses of a strong persistent life,
Panting through generations as one breath,
And fillng with its soul the blank of death." 234-47

The Patriarch

Cain "When Cain was driven from Jehovah's land
He wandered eastward, seeking some far strand
Ruled by kind gods who asked no offerings
Save pure field-fruits, as aromatic things,
To feed the subtler sense of frames divine
That lived on fragrance for their food and wine:
Wild joyous gods, who winked at faults and folly,
And could be pitiful and melancholy.

He never had a doubt that such gods were;
He looked within, and saw them mirrored there." 1-10

—the mark: " . . . and that red brand,
The scorching impress of Jehovah's hand,
Was still clear-edged to his unwearied eye,
Its secret firm in time-fraught memory.
He said, 'My happy offspring shall not know
That the red life from out a man may flow
When smitted by his brother.' True, his race
Bore each one stamped upon his new-born face
A copy of the brand no wit less clear;
But every mother held that little copy dear." 30-40

—seeing death: "He will not wake;
This is the endless sleep, and we must make
A bed deep down for him beneath the sod;
For know, my sons, there is a mighty God
Angry with all man's race, but most with me . . . .
This is Jehovah's will, and he is strong;
I thought the way I travelled was too long
For Him to follow me: my thought was vain!
He walks unseen, but leaves a track of pain,
Pale Death His footprint is, and He will come again!" 66-81

The Family

Lamech "Till, hurling stones in mere athletic joy,
Strong Lamech struck and killed his fairest boy,
And tried to wake him with the tenderest cries.
And fetched and held before the glazèd eyes
The things they best had loved to look upon;
But never glance or smile or sigh he won." 58-63

Mother "Here the broad-bosomed mother of the strong
Looked, like **Demeter**, placid o'er the throng
Of young lithe forms . . . . " 383-5

Sister "Near [**Jabal**] his sister, deft, as women are,
Plied her quick skill in sequence to his thought
Till the hid treasures of the milk she caught
Revealed like pollen 'mid the petals white,
The golden pollen, virgin to the light." 173-7

Also mentioned

Demeter, goddess of the fields and harvest 384
Judas, who betrayed the Master for thirty pieces of silver 230
Noah, patriarch of the great Flood 227
Seth, the last-born son of Adam 498

Agatha

In the black forest mountains, fifteen miles from Freiburg, lies the tiny watering-place of St Märgen where there is a small peasant's cottage. Here live **Agatha** and her frail, blind cousins **Kate** and **Nell**. A visitor, the **Countess Linda**, calls, and Agatha tells of her life. She had been an orphan who cared for an old couple who, when they died, left her their cottage and all in it. She tells of her work for neighbors and how she has been cared for. She likes her plain clothes. The Countess says farewell. The young folk sometimes play gentle jokes on the three old women. The populace enjoys a song, written by poet **Hans**, the tailor (*see* Lyrics and Songs).

"Come with me to the mountain, not where rocks
Bear harsh above the troops of hurrying pines,
But where the earth spreads soft and rounded breasts
To feed her children; where the generous hills
Lift a green isle betwixt the sky and plain
To keep some Old World things aloof from change." 1-6

Title Role

Agatha "Old Agatha, whose cousins **Kate** and **Nell**
Are housed by her in Love and Duty's name,
They being feeble, with small withered wits,
And she believing that the higher gift
Was given to be shared. So Agatha
Shares her one room, all neat on afternoons,
As if some memory were sacred there
And everything within the four low walls
An honored relic." 79-87

"Agatha
Sat at her knitting, aged, upright, slim,
And spoke her welcome with mild dignity.
She kept the company of kings and queens
And mitred saints who sat below the feet

Of Francis with the ragged frock and wounds;
And Rank for her meant Duty, various,
Yet equal in its worth, done worthily." 133-40

—*occupations:* "O that is easy earning
We help the neighbors, and our bit and sup
Is never failing: they have work for us
In house and field, all sorts of odds and ends,
Patching and mending, turning o'er the hay,
Holding sick children—there is always work;
And they are very good—the neighbors are:
Weigh not our bits of work with weight and scale,
But glad themselves with giving us good shares
Of meat and drink . . . . " 167-77

—*special duty:* " . . . and in the big farm-house
When cloth comes home from weaving, the good wife
Cuts me a piece—this very gown—and says:
'Here, Agatha, you old maid, you have time
To pray for **Hans** who is gone soldiering:
The saints might help him, and they have much to do,
'Twere well they were besought to think of him.'
She spoke half jesting, but I pray, I pray
For poor young Hans." 177-84

—*narrator's report:* "I stayed among those hills; and oft heart more
Of Agatha. I liked to hear her name,
As that of one half grandame and half saint,
Uttered with reverent playfulness. The lads
And younger men all called her mother, aunt,
Or granny, with their pet diminutives,
And bade their lasses and their brides behave
Right well to one who surely made a link
'Twixt faulty folk and God by loving both . . . . " 284-92

Sancta Maria "Holy little Mary, dear
As all the sweet home things she smiles upon,
The children and the cows, the apple-trees,
The cart, the plough, all named with that caress
Which feigns them little, easy to be held,
Familiar to the eyes and hand and heart.
What though a Queen? She puts her crown away
And with her little Boy wears common clothes,
Caring for common wants, remembering
That day when good **Saint Joseph** left his work
To marry her with humble trust sublime." 23-33

Countess Linda "One long summer's day
An angel entered at the rose-hung gate,
With skirts pale blue, a brow to quench the pearl,
Hair soft and blonde as infants', plenteous
As hers who made the wavy lengths once speak

The grateful worship of a rescued soul . . . .
The angel was a lady, noble, young,
Taught in all seemliness that fits a court,
All lore that shapes the mind to delicate use,
Yet quiet, lowly, as a meek white dove
That with its presence teaches gentleness.
Men called her Countess Linda . . . her years were few
Her outward beauties all in budding time,
Her virtues the aroma of the plant
That dwells in all its being, root, stem, leaf,
And waits not ripeness." 87-92, 96-101, 103-107

"Fair Countess Linda sat upon the bench,
Close fronting the old knitter, and they talked
With sweet antiphony of young and old." 143-5

Also mentioned

Saint Ann, the virgin's mother	254-5
Saint Elizabeth, "the lowly queen"	121
Saint Francis, of Assisi	138
Angel Gabriel	358
Hans, who has gone for a soldier	180
Poet **Hans**, the tailor, who made songs for the people	306
Saint Joseph, consort of Mary	32
Kate, cousin to Agatha	79
Michael, an inn-keeper	148
Nell, cousin to Agatha	79
Toni, waggoner whose load crushed and killed him	330-31
Saint Ursula	120

A Song

Midnight by the chapel bell!
Homeward, homeward all, farewell!
I with you, and you with me,
Miles are short with company.
Heart of Mary, bless the way,
Keep us all by night and day!

Moon and stars at feast with night
Now have drunk their fill of light.
Home they hurry, making time
Trot apace, like merry rhyme.
Heart of Mary, mystic rose,
Send us all a sweet repose!

Swiftly through the wood down hill,
Run till you can hear the mill.
Toni's ghost is wandering now,
Shaped just like a snow-white cow.
Heart of Mary, morning star,
Ward off danger, near or far!

Toni's wagon with its load
Fell and crushed him in the road
'Twixt these pine-trees. Never fear!
Give a neighbor's ghost good cheer.
Holy Babe, our God and Brother,
Bind us fast to one another!

Hark! the mill is at its work,
Now we pass beyond the murk
To the hollow, where the moon
Makes her silvery afternoon.
Good Saint Joseph, faithful spouse,
Help us all to keep our vows!

Here the three old maidens dwell,
Agatha and Kate and Nell;
See, the moon shines on the thatch,
We will go and shake the hatch.
Heart of Mary, cup of joy,
Give us mirth without alloy!

Hush, 'tis here, no noise, sing low,
Rap with gentle knuckles—so!
Like the little tapping birds,
On the door; then sing good words.
Meek Saint Anna, old and fair,
Hallow all the snow-white hair!

Little maidens old, sweet dreams!
Sleep one sleep till morning beams.
Mothers ye, who help us all,
Quick at hand, if ill befall.
Holy Gabriel, lily-laden
Bless the aged mother-maiden!

Forward, mount the broad hillside
Swift as soldiers when they ride.
See the two towers how they peep,
Round-capped giants, o'er the steep.
Heart of Mary, by thy sorrow,
Keep us upright through the morrow!

Now they rise quite suddenly
Like a man from bended knee
Now Saint Märgen is in sight,
Here the roads branch off—good night!
Heart of Mary, by thy grace,
Give us with the saints a place!

Armgart

The first scene in this verse-drama opens with **Walpurga**, a maiden lady slightly lame, and **Graf Dornberg**, talking about the great opera singer **Armgart**, cousin to Walpurga and the beloved of the Graf, who at that moment is singing the lead in Gluck's *Orfeo ed Euridice.* Her friend and manager **Leo** is with her. Armgart's talent and personality are evidently extraordinary. She and Leo now appear: the performance has been a sensation. She wears a star royalty has sent her. Leo criticizes a trill she interpolated, and they argue. They discuss music, art, and Armgart. A supper is laid, but the Graf goes and will come next day. I

The Graf and Armgart talk about music, her career, the perils of success. He reminds her he has waited: now he proposes marriage. She declines: "The man who marries me must wed my Art—Honor and cherish it, not tolerate." He sadly acknowledges that they must part. II

A year has passed. Armgart has had throat trouble. **Doctor Grahn** says she is fine now. Walpurga worries. Armgart has burst out of the house on learning that a *Fidelio* was to be performed: she intended to sing the part—she and no one else. The Doctor is reassuring and leaves, to return later. III

In two hours, Armgart and Leo enter. Armgart is speechless. The Doctor enters, and Armgart comes to life, accusing him of murdering her voice. He says she is overwrought and asks Leo for his view. Leo shrugs and walks out. The Doctor is calm, but in leaving asks for a word with Walpurga. IV

Armgart asks Walpurga to go for a walk. She refuses and rebukes the singer. She says the Graf is back. There is a knock—it is a letter from him. He extends his sympathy but cannot come: he is off on a long mission to the Caucasus. Armgart is glad, and bitter, full of self-pity. She wants to go out, but the door is locked: **Gretchen** has gone shopping. Walpurga has had enough: she excoriates Armgart for unfeeling lording it over everyone. Armgart is touched. Leo comes, and Walpurga leaves them alone. As though noticing him for the first time, Armgart asks about his music: is it played? will it last? No to both. He advises her to keep to the stage as an actress. She says no: she would be mediocre. She asks for advice: she will take humble work, teaching singing in another town. He agrees. She will go to Freiburg, Walpurga's beloved old home. Armgart will bury her dead joy. V

Title Role

Armgart WALPURGA: "She was stiller than is her wont
But once, at some such trivial word of mine,
As that the highest prize might yet be won
By her who took the second—she was roused.
'For me,' she said, 'I triumph or I fail.
I never strove for any second prize.'
GRAF: Poor human-hearted singing bird! She bears
Cæsar's ambition in her delicate breast,
And nought to still it with but quivering song!" I

—her power: GRAF: "Is it most her voice
Subdues us? or her instinct exquisite,
Informing each old strain with some new grace
Which takes our sense like any natural good?
Or most her spiritual energy
That sweeps us in the current of her song?" I

—her triumph "Tell them, **Leo**, tell them
How I outsang your hope and made you cry
Because **Gluck** could not hear me. That was folly!
He sang, not listened: every linkèd note
Was his immortal pulse that stirred in mine,
And all my gladness is but part of him." I

—praised: "I am not glad with that mean vanity
Which knows no good beyond its appetite
Full feasting upon praise! I am only glad,
Being praised for what I know is worth the praise;
Glad of the proof that I myself have part
In what I worship! . . .
Think you I felt myself a *prima donna?*
No, but a happy spiritual star
Such as old **Dante** saw, wrought in a rose
Of light in Paradise, whose only self
Was consciousness of glory wide-diffused,
Music, life, power—I moving in the midst
With a sublime necessity of good." I

—hubris? "If the world brings me gifts
Gold, incense, myrrh—'twill be the needful sign
That I have stirred it as the high year stirs
Before I sink to winter." I

—goal: "I sing for love of song and that renown
Which is the spreading act, the world-wide share,
Of good that I was born with." II

Dante

—a woman: "Yes, I know
The oft-taught Gospel: 'Woman, thy desire
Shall be that all superlatives on earth
Belong to men, save the one highest kind—
To be a mother. Thou shalt not desire
To do aught best save pure subservience:
Nature has willed it so!' O blessed Nature!
Let her be arbitress; she gave me voice
Such as she only gives a woman child,
Best of its kind, gave me ambition too,
That sense transcendent which can taste the joy
Of swaying multitudes, of being adored
For such achievement, needed excellence,
As man's best art must wait for, or be dumb.
Men did not say, when I had sung last night,
' 'Twas good, nay, wonderful, considering
She is a woman' . . . ." II

—advice "You are bitter, Graf.
Forgive me; seek the woman you deserve,
All grace, all good, who has not yet found
A meaning in her life, nor any end
Beyond fulfilling yours. The type abounds." II

—assurance: "Oh, I can live unmated, but not live
Without the bliss of singing to the world,
And feeling all my world respond to me." II

—distraught: " . . . you have murdered it!
Murdered my voice—poisoned the soul in me,
And kept me living.
You never told me that your cruel cures
Were clogging films—a mouldy dead'ning blight—
A lava-mud to crust and bury me,
Yet hold me living in a deep, deep tomb,
Crying unheard for ever! Oh, your cures
Are devil's triumphs: you can rob, maim, slay,
And keep a hell on the other side your cure
Where you can see your victim quivering
Between the teeth of torture . . . O misery, misery!
You might have killed me, might have let me sleep
After my happy day and wake—not here,
Where all is faded, flat—a feast broke off—
Banners all meaningless—exulting words
Dull, dull—a drum that lingers in the air
Beating to melody which no man hears." IV

"You never told me, never gave me choice
To die a singer, lightning-struck, unmaimed,
Or live what you would make me with your cures—
A self accursed with consciousness of change . . .
. . . Oh, I had meaning once,
Like day and sweetest air. What am I now?

The millionth woman in superfluous herds.
Why should I be, do, think? 'Tis thistle-seed,
That grows and grows to feed the rubbish-heap." IV

—self-pity: "Prisoned now,
Prisoned in all the petty mimicries
Called woman's knowledge, that will fit the world
As doll-clothes fit a man. I can do nought
Better than what a million women do—
Must drudge among the crowd and feel my life
Beating with passion through an insect's horn
That moves a millet-seed laboriously.
If I *would* do it!" V

—stricken by remorse: "Yet you speak truth;
I wearied you [**Walpurga**], it seems; took all your help
As cushioned nobles use a weary serf,
Not looking at his face." V

Graf Dornberg "We should but lose
Were **Armgart** borne too commonly and long
Out of the self that charms us. Could I choose,
She were less apt to soar beyond the reach
Of woman's foibles, innocent vanities,
Fondness for trifles like that pretty star
Twinkling beside her cloud of ebon hair." I

—warning: "You said you dared not think what life had been
Without the stamp of eminence; have you thought
How you will bear the poise of eminence
With dread of sliding? Paint the future out
As an unchecked and glorious career,
'Twill grow more strenuous by the very love
You bear to excellence, the very fate
Of human powers, which tread at every step
On possible verges." II

—the question: "I came not to seek
Any renunciation save the wife's,
Which turns away from other possible love
Future and worthier, to take his love
Who asks the name of husband." II

Doctor Grahn "She can take no harm.
'Twas time for her to sing; her throat is well.
It was a fierce attack, and dangerous;
I had to use strong remedies . . . . " III

—attacked: "A sudden check has shaken you, poor child!
All things seem livid, tottering to your sense,
From inward tumult. Stricken by a threat
You see your terrors only." IV

Leo

—scolding: "Will you ask the house
To teach you singing? Quit your *Orpheus* then,
And sing in farces grown to operas,
Where all the prurience of the full-fed mob
Is linked with melodic impudence:
Jerk forth burlesque bravuras, square your arms
Akimbo with a tavern wench's grace,
And set the splendid compass of your voice
To lyric jibs. Go to! I thought you meant
To be an artist—lift your audience
To see your vision, not trick forth a show
To please the grossest taste of grossest numbers." I

—praise indeed: "**Armgart** stood
As if she had been new-created there
And found her voice which found a melody.
The minx! **Gluck** had not written, nor I taught:
Orpheus was Armgart, Armgart Orpheus." I

—his music: ARMGART: "They hardly ever play your music?
LEO: No!
Schubert too wrote for silence: half his work
Lay like a frozen Rhine till summers came
That warmed the grass above him. Even so!
His music lives now with a mighty youth." V

Walpurga, "who advances with a slight lameness of gait . . . . " I

—cousinly affection: "Nay, I fear
My love is little more than what I felt
For happy stories when I was a child.
[**Armgart**] fills my life that would be empty else,
And lifts my nought to value by her side." I

—frank: "I say, then, you are simply fevered, mad:
You cry aloud at horrors that would vanish
If you would change the light, throw into shade
The loss you aggrandize, and let day fall
On good remaining, nay on good refused
Which may be gained now." V

—the worm turns: "Ay, such a mask
As the few born like you to easy joy,
Cradled in privilege, take for natural
On all the lowly faces that must look
Upward to you! what revelation now
Shows you the mask or gives presentiment
Of sadness hidden? You who every day
These five years saw me limp to wait on you
And thought the order perfect which gave me,

The girl without pretension to be aught,
A splendid cousin for my happiness:
To watch the night through when her brain was fired
With too much gladness—listen, always listen
To what *she* felt, who having power had right
To feel exorbitantly, and submerge
The souls around her with the poured-out flood
Of what must be ere she were satisfied!
That was feigned patience, was it? Why not love,
Love nurtured even with that strength of self
Which found no room save in another's life? V

"Where is the rebel's right for you alone?
Noble rebellion lifts a common load;
But what is he who flings his own load off
And leaves his fellows toiling? Rebel's right?
Say rather, the deserter's." V

—slaves and Jews: "We touch afar.
For did not swarthy slaves of yesterday
Leap in their bondage at the Hebrews' flight,
Which touched them through the three-
millennial dark?" V

Also mentioned

Julius Cæsar [H], of high ambition I
Gretchen, the maid who has the key V
Paulina, who is singing *Fidelio* V
Schroder-Devrient [H], great singer of the day I
Franz Schubert [H], whose music was largely unheard in his time V

How Lisa Loved the King

We are in late 13th century Palermo, capital of Sicily. It is high festival: the French have just been evicted, and **King Pedro III of Aragon** is the much-admired monarch. He rides in procession before the people. **Lisa**, daughter of **Bernardo**, a Florentine merchant now in business here, sees the king and is overwhelmed with ecstatic love. Her admirer **Perdicone** is utterly forgotten. She can think of nothing else: if the King only knew of her devotion she would die in peace and happiness. She takes to her bed and is pining away. Her parents watch in dismay: if they lose her, they will have no purpose in life.

At her bedside one day, they see a small revival. She asks them to fetch the singer **Minuccio**. He could be her messenger to the King. He sings for her, and she feels better. She says she would die happy if she knew the King was aware of her feelings. Minuccio promises and goes to his friend the poet **Mico**. He asks him to write a *canzòn* "divinely sad, sinlessly passionate and meekly mad," and Mico agrees. It is done in two days, and Minuccio goes to the court. At the right moment, he sings.

All are transfixed. The King asks Minuccio to explain, and in his ear alone Minuccio tells Lisa's tale. Pedro vows to visit her that very evening. Minuccio rushes to Lisa and gives all the details. She revives and dresses herself and her hair. The King, feigning an accidental encounter, calls on Bernardo and asks him about his daughter. He learns of depression, recent revival. He goes to her room. A gentle remonstrance is blissful to her, and she promises to be well.

The King tells **Queen Costanza** the story. She suggests they both pay a call. Lisa and family receive them. King Pedro tells her he will henceforth be her cavalier and will carry her colors. But he also tells her to listen to the man who loves and would wed her. He offers her a kiss, and her reply confirms her love and service, but asks the Queen's permission as to the kiss. The Queen likes this. There quickly follows betrothal with Perdicone, to whom the King gives large and fruitful lands. The populace like the outcome much. The envoi reminds us the story is from Boccaccio's *Decameron*.

Principals

Lisa. "Who was it felt the deep mysterious glow,/The impregnation with supernal fire/Of young ideal love—transformed desire,/Whose passion is but worship of that Best/Taught by the many-mingled creed of each young breast?/ 'Twas gentle Lisa, of no noble line . . . . " 47-51

—*attractions:* "She had a pensive beauty, yet not sad;/Rather, like minor cadences that glad/The hearts of little birds amid spring boughs;/ And oft the trumpet or the joust would rouse/Pulses that gave her cheek a finer glow,/ Parting her lips that seemed a mimic bow/By chiselling Love for play in coral wrought,/Then quickened by him with the passionate thought,/The soul that trembled in the lustrous night/Of slow long eyes. Her body was so slight,/ It seemed she could have floated in the sky,/And with the angelic choir made symphony;/ But in her cheek's rich tinge, and in the dark/Of darkest hair and eyes, she bore a mark/Of kinship to her generous mother earth . . . . " 77-91

—*seeing the King:* " . . . great Love his essence had endued/With **Pedro**'s form, and entering subdued/The soul of Lisa, fervid and intense,/Proud in its choice of proud obedience/To hardship glorified by perfect reverence.

"Sweet Lisa homeward carried that dire guest,/And in her chamber through the hours of rest/The darkness was alight for her with sheen/Of arms, and plumèd helm, and bright between/Their commoner gloss, like the pure living spring/ 'Twixt porphyry lips, or living bird's bright wing/ 'Twixt golden wires, the glances of the king/Flashed on her soul, and waked vibrations there/Of known delights love-mixed to new and rare:/ The impalpable dream was turned to breathing flesh . . . . " 126-40

—*longing:* "She watched all day that she might see him pass/With knights and ladies; but she said, 'Alas!'/ Though he should see me, it were all as one/He saw a pigeon sitting on the stone/Of wall or balcony: some colored spot/His eye just sees, his mind regardeth not . . . . I shall die,/And he will never know who Lisa was . . . . " 159-64, 166-7

—*a visitor:* "Her cheek already showed a slow faint blush,/But soon the voice, in pure full liquid rush,/Made all the passion, that till now she felt,/ Seem but cool waters that in warmer melt/Finished the song, she prayed to be alone/ With kind **Minuccio**; for her faith had grown/To trust him as if missioned like a priest/With some high grace, that when his singing ceased/ Still made him wiser, more magnanimous/Than common men who had no genius." 263-72

—*another visitor:* "[His] words, that touch upon her hand from him/ Whom her soul worshipped, as far seraphim/Worship the distant glory, brought some shame/Quivering upon her cheek, yet thrilled her frame/With such deep joy she seemed in paradise,/In wondering gladness, and in dumb surprise/That bliss could be so blissful . . . . " 476-82

—*in bliss:* "She thought no maid betrothed could be more blest;/For treasure must be valued by the test/Of highest excellence and rarity,/And her dear joy was best as best could be;/There seemed no other crown to her delight/Now the high loved one saw her love aright." 507-12

—*avowal:* " 'Monsignor, I know well that were it known/To all the world how high my love had flown,/There would be few who would not deem me mad,/Or say my mind the falsest image had/Of my condition and your lofty place./But heaven has seen that for no moment's space/Have I forgotten you to be the king,/Or me myself to be a lowly thing—/A little lark, enamoured of the sky,/That soared to sing, to break its breast, and die . . . I loved you, love you, and shall always love./But that doth mean, my will is ever yours,/Not only when your will my good insures,/But if it wrought me what the world calls harm —/Fire, wounds, would wear from your dear will a charm/That you will be my knight is full content,/And for that kiss—I pray, first for the queen's consent.' " 625-34, 640-6

King Pedro of Aragon. " 'Twas told that Pedro, King of Aragon,/Was welcomed master of all Sicily,/A royal knight, supreme as kings should be/In strength and gentleness that make high chivalry." 16-19

—*cynosure:* "His the best jennet, and he sat it best;/His weapon, whether tilting or in rest,/Was worthiest watching, and his face once seen/Gave to the promise of his royal mien/Such rich fulfilment as the opened eyes/Of a loved sleeper, or the long-watched rise/Of vernal day, whose joy o'er stream and meadow flies." 36-42

—*moved by music:* "But most such sweet compulsion took the mood/Of Pedro (tired of doing what he would)./ Whether the words which that strange meaning bore/Were but the poet's feigning or aught more,/Was bounden question, since their aim must be/At some imagined or true royalty." 373-8

—*moved by the tale:* "The king had features pliant to confess/The presence of a manly tenderness—/son, father, brother, lover, blent in one,/In fine harmonic exaltation—/The spirit of religious chivalry. He listened, and **Minuccio** could see/The tender, generous admiration spread/O'er all his face, and glorify his head/With royalty that would have kept its rank/Though his brocaded robes to tatters shrank." 389-98

—*instant decision:* " 'So sweet a maid,/In nature's own insignia arrayed,/ Though she were come of unmixed trading blood/That sold and bartered ever since the Flood,/Would have the self-contained and single worth/Of radiant jewels born in darksome earth. **Raona** were a shame to Sicily,/Letting such love and tears unhonored be:/Hasten, **Minuccio**, tell her that the king/To-day will surely visit her when vespers ring.' " 399-408

—*remonstrance:* " 'Lady, what is this? /You, whose sweet youth should others' solace be,/Pierce all our hearts, languishing piteously. /We pray you, for the love of us, be cheered,/Nor be too reckless of that life, endeared/To us who know your passing worthiness,/And count your blooming life as part of our life's bliss.' " 469-75

Supporting Roles

Costanza (Constance), the Queen: " . . . a fair deep-breasted queen/A-horseback, with blonde hair and tunic green/Gold-bordered . . . . " 170-3

—*hearing the story:* "The queen had that chief grace/Of womanhood, a heart that can embrace/All goodness in another woman's form;/And that same day, ere the sun lay too warm/On southern terraces, a messenger/Informed **Bernardo** that the royal pair would straightway visit him and celebrate/Their gladness at his daughter's happier state,/Which they were fain to see." 565-73

Minuccio, "entreated, gladly came./ (He was a singer of most gentle fame—/A noble, kindly spirit, not elate/That he was famous, but that song was great—/Would sing as finely to this suffering child/As at the court where princes on him smiled.) / Gently he entered and sat down by her,/Asking what sort of strain she would prefer—/The voice alone, or voice with viol wed;/ Then, when she chose the last, he preluded/With magic hand, that summoned from the strings/Aërial spirits, rare yet vibrant wings/That fanned the pulses of his listener/And waked each sleeping sense with blissful stir." 249-262

—in performance: "He waited till the air had ceased to move/To ringing silver, till Falernian wine/Made quickened sense with quietude combine,/And then with passionate descant made each ear incline." 323-6

"The strain was new. It seemed a pleading cry,/And yet a rounded perfect melody,/Making grief beauteous as the tear-filled eyes/Of little child at little miseries./ Trembling at first, then swelling as it rose,/Like rising light that broad and broader grows,/It filled the hall, and so possessed the air/That not one breathing soul was present there,/Though dullest, slowest, but was quivering/In music's grasp, and forced to hear her sing." 363-372

Others

Bernardo, "a rich Florentine,/Who from his merchant-city hither came/ To trade in drugs; yet kept an honest fame,/And had the virtue not to try and sell/Drugs that had none. He loved his riches well,/But loved them chiefly for his **Lisa**'s sake,/Whom with a father's care he sought to make/The bride of some true honorable man . . . . " 53-60

Mico, "a poet-friend, a Siennese." 301

—the commission: " ' . . . write me a canzòn divinely sad,/Sinlessly passionate and meekly mad/With young despair, speaking a maiden's heart/Of fifteen summers, who would fain depart /From ripening life's new-urgent mystery—/Love-choice of one too high her love to be—/But cannot yield her breath till she has poured/Her strength away in this hot-bleeding word/Telling the secret of her soul to her soul's lord.' " 305-13

Perdicone, "Whose birth was higher than his fortunes were . . . . " 62

—struck: " 'Twas Perdicone's friends made overtures/To good **Bernardo**: so one dame assures/Her neighbor dame who notices the youth/Fixing his eyes on **Lisa** . . . . " 71-4

—success: " . . . There was betrothal made that very morn/Twixt Perdicone, youthful, brave, well-born,/And **Lisa**, whom he loved . . . . " 651-3

Mico's Song

Love, thou didst see me, light as morning's breath,
Roaming a garden in a joyous error,
Laughing at chases vain, a happy child,
Till of thy countenance the alluring terror
In majesty from out the blossoms smiled,
From out their life seeming a beauteous death.

O Love, who so didst choose me for thine own,
Taking this little isle to thy great sway,
See now, it is the honor of thy throne
That what thou gavest perish not away,
Nor leave some sweet remembrance to atone
By life that will be for this brief life gone:
Hear, ere the shroud o'er these frail limbs be thrown—

Since every king is vassal unto thee,
My heart's lord needs must listen loyally—
O tell him I am waiting for my Death!

Tell him, for that he hath such royal power
'Twere hard for him to think how small a thing,
How slight a sign, would make a wealthy dower
For one like me, the bride of that pale king
Whose bed is mine at some swift-nearing hour.
Go to my lord, and to his memory bring
That happy birthday of my sorrowing
When his large glance made meaner gazers glad,
Entering the bannered lists: 'twas then I had
The wound that laid me in the arms of Death.

Tell him, O Love, I am a lowly maid,
No more than any little knot of thyme
That he with careless foot may often tread;
Yet lowest fragrance oft will mount sublime
And cleave to things most high and hallowèd,
As doth the fragrance of my life's springtime,
My lowly love, that soaring seeks to climb
Within his thought, and make a gentle bliss,
More blissful than if mine, in being his:
So shall I live in him and rest in Death. 327-62

A Minor Prophet

This 325-line work begins as an intermittently witty lampoon of the pious adherence of one **Elias Baptist Butterworth** to the principles and practices of vegetarianism, with obeisances to phrenology and transcendantalism. It is largely unmentioned in biographies (Margaret Reynolds thinks it "very funny"). We found it in the 1894 twelve-volume set, *George Eliot's Works,* published by Thomas Y. Crowell & Co., New York—the source of most of the illustrations reproduced in this work—which gives it a date (confirmed by van den Broek).

The narrator, **Colin Clout** (a name borrowed from Spenser), is appalled at the utopian predictions Elias makes of a perfect, uniform world. Colin, who seems to speak with the author's voice, likes untidiness, difference, the ungainly, the ugly, the pathetic. The poem rises from parody to purpose—it becomes, indeed, a paean of faith in human dignity and progress, part of which is extracted in the *Topicon* under M:Belief. *Here, we believe, is the most eloquent statement of personal faith GE made in a published work.*

Elias Baptist Butterworth. "I have a friend, a vegetarian seer,
By name Elias Baptist Butterworth,
A harmless, bland, disinterested man,
Whose ancestors in **Cromwell**'s day believed
The Second Advent certain in five years,
But when **King Charles the Second** came instead,
Revised their date and sought another world:
I mean—not heaven but—America . . . they did insist
Somewhat too wearisomely on the joys
Of their Millennium, when coats and hats
Would all be of one pattern, books and songs
All fit for Sundays, and the casual talk
As good as sermons preached extempore." 1-8

—*phrenological:* "And in Elias the ancestral zeal
Breathes strong as ever, only modified
By Transatlantic air and modern thought.
You could not pass him in the street and fail
To note his shoulder's long declivity,

Beard to the waist, swan-neck, and large pale eyes;
Or, when he lifts his hat, to mark his hair
Brushed back to show his great capacity—
A full grain's length at the angle of the brow
Proving him witty, while the shallower men
Only seem witty in their repartees.
Not that he's vain, but that his doctrine needs
The testimony of his frontal lobe." 21-33

—*transcendental:* "On all points he adopts the latest views;
Takes for the key of universal Mind
The 'levitation' of stout gentlemen;
Believes the Rappings are not spirits' work,
But the Thought-atmosphere's, a steam of brains
In correlated force of raps, as proved
By motion, heat, and science generally . . . . " 34-40

"*So* the Thought-atmosphere is everywhere:
High truths that glimmered under other names
To ancient sages, whence good scholarship
Applied to Eleusinian mysteries—
The Vedas—Tripitaka—Vendidad—
Might furnish weaker proof for weaker minds
That thought was rapping in the hoary past,
And might have edified the Greeks by raps
At the greater Dionysia, if their ears
Had not been filled with Sophoclean verse." 43-52

—*futuristic:* "And when all Earth is vegetarian—
When, lacking butchers, quadrupeds die out,
And less Thought-atmosphere is reabsorbed
By nerves of insects parasitical,
Those higher truths, seized now by higher minds
But not expressed (the insects hindering)
Will either flash out into eloquence,
Or better still, be comprehensible
By rappings simply, without need of roots." 53-61

"Earth will hold
No stupid brutes, no cheerful queernesses,
No naïve cunning, grave absurdity.
Wart-pigs with tender and parental grunts,
Wombats much flattened as to their contour,
Perhaps from too much crushing in the ark,
But taking meekly that fatality;
The serious cranes, unstung by ridicule;
Long-headed, short-legged, solemn-looking curs,
(Wise, silent critics of a flippant age);
The silly straddling foals, the weak-brained geese
Hissing fallaciously at sound of wheels—
All these rude products will have disappeared
Along with every faulty human type.
By dint of diet vegetarian
All will be harmony of hue and line,
Bodies and minds all perfect, limbs well-turned,
And talk quite free from aught erroneous." 116-33

Colin Clout. "I am Colin Clout.
A clinging flavor penetrates my life—
My onion is imperfectness: I cleave
To nature's blunders, evanescent types
Which sages banish from Utopia.
'Not worship beauty?' say you. Patience, friend!
I worship in the temple with the rest;
But by my hearth I keep a sacred nook
For gnomes and dwarfs, duck-footed waddling elves
Who stitched and hammered for the weary man
In days of old. And in that piety
I clothe ungainly forms inherited
From toiling generations, daily bent
At desk, or plough, or loom, or in the mine,
In pioneering labors for the world." 172-86

—his faith: "I too rest in faith
That man's perfection is the crowning flower,
Toward which the urgent sap in life's great tree
Is pressing—seen in puny blossoms now,
But in the world's great morrows to expand
With broadest petal and with deepest glow." 217-22

* * *

"Presentiment of better things on earth
Sweeps in with every force that stirs our souls
To admiration, self-renouncing love,
Or thoughts, like light, that bind the world in one:
Sweeps like the sense of vastness, when at night
We hear the roll and dash of waves that break
Nearer and nearer with the rushing tide,
Which rises to the level of the cliff
Because the wide Atlantic rolls behind
Throbbing respondent to the far-off orbs." 316-325

Written July 1869; published in the 1874 collection **BS**

Brother and Sister

I.

I cannot choose but think upon the time
When our two lives grew like two buds that kiss
At lightest thrill from the bee's swinging chime,
Because the one so near the other is.

He was the elder and a little man
Of forty inches, bound to show no dread,
And I the girl that puppy-like now ran,
Now lagged behind my brother's larger tread.

I held him wise, and when he talked to me
Of snakes and birds, and which God loved the best,
I thought his knowledge marked the boundary
Where men grew blind, though angels knew the rest.
    If he said 'Hush!' I tried to hold my breath
    Wherever he said 'Come!' I stepped in faith.

II.

Long years have left their writing on my brow,
But yet the freshness and the dew-fed beam
Of those young mornings are about me now,
When we two wandered toward the far-off stream

With rod and line. Our basket held a store
Baked for us only, and I thought with joy
That I should have my share, though he had more,
Because he was the elder and a boy.

The firmaments of daisies since to me
Have had those mornings in their opening eyes,
The bunchèd cowslip's pale transparency
Carries that sunshine of sweet memories,
    And wild-rose branches take their finest scent
    From those blest hours of infantine content.

III.

Our mother bade us keep the trodden ways,
Stroked down my tippet, set my brother's frill,
Then with the benediction of her gaze
Clung to us lessening, and pursued us still

Across the homestead to the rookery elms,
Whose tall old trunks had each a grassy mound,
So rich for us, we counted them as realms
With varied products: here were earth-nuts found,

And here the Lady-fingers in deep shade;
Here sloping toward the Moat the rushes grew,
The large to slit for pith, the small to braid:
While over all the dark rooks cawing flew,

    And made a happy strange solemnity,
    A deep-toned chant from life unknown to me.

IV.

Our meadow-path had memorable spots:
One where it bridged a tiny rivulet,
Deep hid by tangled blue Forget-me-nots;
And all along the waving grasses met

My little palm, or nodded to my cheek,
When flowers with upturned faces gazing drew
My wonder downward, seeming all to speak
With eyes of souls that dumbly heard and knew.

Then came the copse, where wild things rushed unseen,
And black-scathed grass betrayed the past abode
Of mystic gypsies, who still lurked between
Me and each hidden distance of the road.

    A gypsy once had startled me at play,
    Blotting with her dark smile my sunny day.

V.

Thus rambling we were schooled in deepest love,
And learned the meanings that give words a soul,
The fear, the love, the primal passionate store,
Whose shaping impulses make manhood whole.

Those hours were seed to all my after good;
My infant gladness, through eye, ear, and touch,
Took easily as warmth a various food
To nourish the sweet skill of loving much.

For who in age shall roam the earth and find
Reasons for loving that will strike out love
With sudden rod from the hard year-pressed mind?
Were reasons sown as thick as stars above,

    'Tis love must see them, as the eye sees light:
    Day is but Number to the darkened sight.

Going fishing

VI.

Our brown canal was endless to my thought;
And on its banks I sat in dreamy peace,
Unknowing how the good I loved was wrought,
Untroubled by the fear that it would cease.

Slowly the barges floated into view
Rounding a grassy hill to me sublime
With some Unknown beyond it, whither flew
The parting cuckoo toward a fresh spring time.

The wide-arched bridge, the scented elder-flowers,
The wondrous watery rings that died too soon,
The echoes of the quarry, the still hours
With white robe sweeping-on the shadeless noon,
Were but my growing self, are part of me,
My present Past, my root of piety.

VII.

Those long days measured by my little feet
Had chronicles which yield me many a text;
Where irony still finds an image meet
Of full-grown judgments in this world perplext

One day my brother left me in high charge,
To mind the rod, while he went seeking bait,
And bade me, when I saw a nearing barge,
Snatch out the line, lest he should come too late.

Proud of the task, I watched with all my might
For one whole minute, till my eyes grew wide,
Till sky and earth took on a strange new light
And seemed a dream-world floating on some tide—
A fair pavilioned boat for me alone
Bearing me onwards through the vast unknown.

VIII.

But sudden came the barge's pitch-black prow,
Nearer and angrier came my brother's cry,
And all my soul was quivering fear, when lo!
Upon the imperilled line, suspended high,

A silver perch! My guilt that won the prey,
Now turned to merit, had a guerdon rich
Of hugs and praises, and made merry play,
Until my triumph reached its highest pitch

When all at home were told the wondrous feat,
And how the little sister had fished well.
In secret, though my fortune tasted sweet,
I wondered why this happiness befell.
'The little lass had luck,' the gardener said:
And so I learned, luck was with glory wed.

IX.

We had the self-same world enlarged for each
By loving difference of girl and boy:
The fruit that hung on high beyond my reach
He plucked for me, and oft he must employ

A measuring glance to guide my tiny shoe
Where lay firm stepping-stones, or call to mind
'This thing I like my sister may not do
For she is little, and I must be kind.'

Thus boyish Will the nobler mastery learned
Where inward vision over impulse reigns,
Widening its life with separate life discerned,
A Like unlike, a Self that self restrains.
His years with others must the sweeter be
For those brief days he spent in loving me.

X.

His sorrow was my sorrow, and his joy
Sent little leaps and laughs through all my frame;
My doll seemed lifeless and no girlish toy
Had any reason when my brother came.

I knelt with him at marbles, marked his fling
Cut the ringed stem and made the apple drop,
Or watched him winding close the spiral string
That looped the orbits of the humming top.

Grasped by such fellowship my vagrant thought
Ceased with dream-fruit dream-wishes to fulfil;
My aëry-picturing fantasy was taught
Subjection to the harder, truer skill
That seeks with deeds to grave a thought-tracked line,
And by 'What is,' 'What will be' to define.

XI.

School parted us; we never found again
That childish world where our two spirits mingled
Like scents from varying roses that remain
One sweetness, nor can evermore be singled.

Yet the twin habit of that early time
Lingered for long about the heart and tongue:
We had been natives of one happy clime,
And its dear accents to our utterance clung.

Till the dire years whose awful name is Change
Had grasped our souls still yearning in divorce,
And pitiless shaped them in two forms that range
Two elements which sever their life's course.
But were another childhood-world my share,
I would be born a little sister there.

Stradivarius

This 143-line poem is published in the Crowell edition of *George Eliot's Works*, with, unusually for Crowell, no date given. Haight seems to intimate that it was written in 1869, the year GE's journal mentions the violin-maker as a possible subject. Van den Broek's headnote takes us no further. As noted above, the poem was included in her poetry collection, *The Legend of Jubal and Other Poems,* published in 1874.

The ant and the grasshopper: **Antonio Stradivari** makes violins with persistency, accuracy and, above all, diligence. His friend **Naldo** doesn't see the point of such labor and lectures him on the fine spontaneity true Art requires. Stradivari eloquently articulates his mission, his satisfaction in it, and the necessity of his approaching it with total integrity. Naldo asks for a loan, saying that a great idea requires hatching, and the bird must be fed meanwhile. Stradivari tells him the hatching secret is Work and suggests he get on with it.

Antonio Stradivari "... him
Who a good century and half ago
Put his true work in that brown instrument
And by the nice adjustment of its frame
Gave it responsive life, continuous
With the master's finger-tips and perfected
Like them by delicate rectitude of use." 5-11

—proper credit: "Another soul was living in the air
And swaying it to true deliverance
Of high invention and responsive skill:—
That plain white-aproned man who stood at work
Patient and accurate full fourscore years,
Cherished his sight and touch by temperance
And since keen sense is love of perfectness
Made perfect violins, the needed paths
For inspiration and high mastery." 17-25

—viewpoint:

" 'Who draws a line and satisfies his soul,
Making it crooked where it should be straight?
An idiot with an oyster-shell may draw
His lines along the sand, all wavering,
Fixing no point or pathway to a point;
An idiot one remove may choose his line,
Straggle and be content; but God be praised,
Antonio Stradivari has an eye
That winces at false work and loves the true,
With hand and arm that play upon the tool
As willingly as any singing bird
Sets him to sing his morning roundelay,
Because he likes to sing and likes the song.' " 70-83

—the player:

" 'Twere purgatory here to make them ill;
And for my fame—when any master holds
Twixt chin and hand a violin of mine,
He will be glad that Stradivari lived,
Made violins, and made them of the best.' " 87-91

—God's part:

"I give them instruments to play upon,
God choosing me to help Him.'
" 'What! were God at fault for violins, thou absent?'
" 'Yes;
He were at fault for Stradivari's work.' " 94-7

" 'My work is mine,
And, heresy or not, if my hand slacked
I should rob God—since He is fullest good—
Leaving a blank instead of violins.
I say, not God Himself can make man's best
Without best men to help Him.' " 102-7

—dismissal:

" 'If thou wilt call thy pictures eggs
I call the hatching, Work. 'Tis God gives skill,
But not without men's hands: He could not make
Antonio Stradivari's violins
Without Antonio. Get thee to thy easel.' " 139-43

Giuseppe

" 'Why, many hold Giuseppe's violins
As good as thine.'
" 'May be: they are different.
His quality declines: he spoils his hand
With over-drinking.' " 98-101

Joseph Joachim [H] "Who holds the strain afresh incorporate
By inward hearing and notation strict
Of nerve and muscle . . . . " 13-16

Naldo

" . . . a painter of eclectic school,
Taking his dicers, candlelight and grins
From **Caravaggio**, and in holier groups
Combining Flemish flesh with martyrdom—
Knowing all tricks of style at thirty-one,
And weary of them . . .
Naldo would tease him oft to tell his aims."
44-49, 52

" 'Tis a petty kind of fame
At best, that comes of making violins;
And saves no masses, either. Thou wilt go
To purgatory none the less.' " 83-86

Written in early 1874, published July 1878 **CB**
Macmillan's Magazine

A College Breakfast-Party

Over nine hundred lines are devoted to a conversation among some familiarly named personages, of whom **Hamlet** is doubtless the best known. His host is the faithful **Horatio**; and the other guests are sentence-spinner **Osric**; ardent, rash and radical **Laertes**; discursive **Rosencranz**; grave **Guildenstern**; and a polished **Priest**. Be it understood that these are Englishmen, the venue being "our English Wittenberg."

Ashton describes the work as "a versified symposium of views about faith, science, God, love, and duty . . . . Questions about 'the social Ought' and its difficult relation to the 'individual claim' are raised, though in the—for George Eliot—straitjacket form of blank verse such questions have an unfortunate sonority and pomposity which was absent from their successful embodiment in the life of *Middlemarch*." (p.333)

The discussion ends; the participants say good-bye, and Hamlet wanders along the river. He takes a nap and dreams. The narrator speculates that visions may have warned him that talking too quickly leaves the soul empty.

Hamlet "Blond, metaphysical, and sensuous,
Questioning all things and yet half convinced
Credulity were better; held inert
'Twixt fascinations all opposites,
And half suspecting that the mightiest soul
(Perhaps his own?) was union of existences,
Having no choice but choice of everything:
As, drinking deep to-day for love of wine,
To-morrow half a Brahmin, scorning life
As mere illusion, yearning for that True
Which has no qualities; another day
Finding the fount of grace in sacraments,
And purest reflex of the light divine
In gem-bossed pyx and broidered chasuble,
Resolved to wear no stockings and to fast
With arms extended, waiting ecstasy;

But getting cramps instead, and needing change,
A would-be pagan next . . . . " 4-21

—first question:
" 'I crave direction, Father, how to know
The sign of that imperative whose right
To sway my act in face of thronging doubts
Were an oracular gem in price beyond
Urim and Thummin [*sic*] lost to Israel.
That bias of the soul, that conquering die
Loaded with golden emphasis of Will—
How find it where resolve, once made, becomes
The rash exclusion of an opposite
Which draws the stronger as I turn aloof.' " 140-9

Guildenstern
" 'Ay,' said Guildenstern,
With friendly nod, 'the Father, I can see,
Has caught you up in his air-chariot.
His thought takes rainbow-bridges, out of reach
By solid obstacles, evaporates
The coarse and common into subtilties,
Insists that what is real in the Church
Is something out of evidence, and begs
(Just in parenthesis) you'll never mind
What stares you in the face and bruises you.' " 239-48

Horatio
" . . . a friend
With few opinions, but of faithful heart,
Quick to detect the fibrous spreading roots
Of character that feed men's theories,
Yet cloaking weaknesses with charity
And ready in all service save rebuke." 23-8

Laertes
" 'I protest,'
Burst in Laertes, 'against arguments
That start with calling me a butterfly,
A bubble, spark, or other metaphor
Which carries your conclusions as a phrase
In quibbling law will carry property . . . .
For those who know it, pain is solely pain:
Not any letters of the alphabet
Wrought syllogistically pattern-wise,
Nor any cluster of fine images,
Nor any missing of their figured dance
By blundering molecules.' " 72-7, 91-6

—on gratitude:
" 'I am no optimist whose faith must hang
On hard pretence that pain is beautiful
And agony explained for men at ease
By virtue's exercise in pitying it.
But this I hold: that he who takes one gift
Made for him by the hopeful work of man,
Who tastes sweet bread, walks where he will unarmed,
His shield and warrant the invisible law,

Who owns a hearth and household charities,
Who clothes his body and his sentient soul
With skill and thoughts of men, and yet denies
A human good worth toiling for, is cursed
With worse negation than the poet feigned
In **Mephistopheles**. The Devil spins
His wire-drawn argument against all good
With sense of brimstone as his private lot
And never drew a solace from the Earth.' " 566-582

—old nations: "Old nations breed old children, wizened babes
Whose youth is languid and incredulous,
Weary of life without the will to die;
Their passions visionary appetites
Of bloodless spectres wailing that the world
For lack of substance slips from out their grasp;
Their thoughts the withered husks of all things dead,
Holding no force of germs instinct with life,
Which never hesitates but moves and grows." 668-77

Osric " . . . spinner of fine sentences,
A delicate insect creeping over life
Feeding on molecules of floral breath,
And weaving gossamer to trap the sun . . . . " 31-4

—expostulation: " 'Truce, I beg!'
Said Osric with nice accent. 'I abhor
That battling of the ghosts, that strife of terms
For utmost lack of color, form, and breath,
That tasteless squabbling called Philosophy:
As if a blue-winged butterfly afloat
For just three days above the Italian fields,
Instead of sipping at the heart of flowers,
Poising in sunshine, fluttering towards its bride,
Should fast and speculate, considering
What were if it were not? or what now is
Instead of that which seems to be itself?
Its deepest wisdom surely were to be
A sipping, marrying, blue-winged butterfly;
Since utmost speculation on itself
Were but a three days' living of worse sort—
A bruising struggle all within the bounds
Of butterfly existence.' " 56-72

—art and world: "Hatred, war, vice, crime, sin, those human storms,
Cyclones, floods, what you will—outbursts of force—
Feed art with contrast, give the grander touch
To the master's pencil and the poet's song,
Serve as Vesuvian fires or navies tossed
On yawning waters, which when viewed afar
Deepen the claim sublime of those choice souls
Who keep the heights of poesy and turn
A fleckless mirror to the various world,

Giving its many-named and fitful flux
An imaged, harmless, spiritual life,
With pure selection, native to art's frame,
Of beauty only, save its minor scale
Of ill and pain to give the ideal joy
A keener edge." 752-66

Priest " 'Would add that sacramental grace is grace
Which to be known must first be felt, with all
The strengthening influxes that come by prayer.' " 102-5

—the Soul: " 'The Church demands no more, has standing room
And basis for her doctrine: this (no more)—
That the strong bias which we name the Soul,
Though fed and clad by dissoluble waves,
Has antecedent quality, and rules
By veto or consent the strife of thought,
Making arbitrament that we call faith.' " 132-8

—the Presence: " 'Take your wit,
Your highest passion, widest-reaching thought:
Show their conditions if you will or can,
But though you saw the final atom-dance
Making each molecule that stands for sign
Of love being present, where is still your love?
How measure that, how certify its weight?
And so I say, the body of the Church
Carries a Presence, promises and gifts
Never disproved—whose argument is found
In lasting failure of the search elsewhere
For what it holds to satisfy man's need.' " 188-99

Rosencranz "None said, 'Let Darkness be,' but Darkness was;
And in it waited with Teutonic ease,
An argumentative Leviathan,
Blowing cascades from out his element,
The thunderous Rosencranz . . . . " 51-5

—human good: " 'Your human good, which you would make supreme,
How do you know it? Has it shown its face
In adamantine type, with features clear,
As this republic, or that monarchy?
As federal grouping, or municipal?
Equality, or finely shaded lines
Of social difference? ecstatic whirl
And draught intense of passionate joy and pain,
Or sober self-control that starves its youth
And lives to wonder what the world calls joy?
Is it in sympathy that shares men's pangs
Or in cool brains that can explain them well?
Is it in labor or in laziness?
In training for the tug of rivalry
To be admired, or in the admiring soul?

In risk or certitude? In battling rage
And hardy challenges of Protean luck,
Or in a sleek and rural apathy
Full fed with sameness? Pray define
your Good . . . .' " 360-78

—irked: "But Rosencranz,
Deaf as the angry turkey-cock whose ears
Are plugged by swollen tissues when he scolds
At men's pretensions . . . . " 409-12

* * *

"Each now said 'Good-bye.'
Such breakfast, such beginning of the day
Is more than half the whole. The sun was hot
On southward branches of the meadow elms,
The shadows slowly farther crept and veered
Like changing memories, and **Hamlet** strolled
Alone and dubious on the empurpled path
Between the waving grasses of new June
Close by the stream where well-compacted boats
Were moored or moving with a lazy creak
To the soft dip of oars. All sounds were light
As tiny silver bells upon the robes
Of hovering silence. Birds made twitterings
That seemed but Silence self o'erfull of love.
'Twas invitation all to sweet repose;
And Hamlet, drowsy with the mingled draughts
Of cider and conflicting sentiments,
Chose a green couch . . . .
And then he dreamed a dream so luminous
He woke (he says) convinced; but what it taught
Withholds as yet. Perhaps those graver shades
Admonished him that visions told in haste
Part with their virtues to the squandering lips
And leave the soul in wider emptiness." 875-92, 903-8

Also mentioned

Saint Anselm [H], philosopher, monk; Archbishop of Canterbury 899
Auguste Comte [H], philosopher, founder of Positivism 899
Charles Darwin [H], paleobiologist, author of *The Origin of Species* 899
Democritus [H], ancient Greek philosopher 898
Epicurus [H], ancient philosopher 174
Pythagoras [H], Greek philosopher and mathematician 898
Arthur Schopenhauer [H], German philosopher 899
Socrates [H], philosopher immortalized by Plato 532
Voltimand, with whom the Priest had an appointment 205
Zeno [H]—"the Stoic" 174

Two Lovers

Two lovers by a moss-grown spring:
        They leaned soft cheeks together there,
        Mingles the dark and sunny hair,
And heard the wooing thrushes sing.
            O budding time!
            O love's blest prime!

Two wedded from the portal stept:
        The bells made happy carollings,
        The air was soft as fanning wings,
White petals on the pathway slept.
            O pure-eyed bride!
            O tender pride!

Two faces o'er a cradle bent:
        Two hands above the head were locked;
        These pressed each other while they rocked,
Those watched a life that love had sent.
            O solemn hour!
            O hidden power!

Two parents by the evening fire:
        The red light fell about their knees
        On heads that rose by slow degrees
Like buds upon the lily spire.
            O patient life!
            O tender strife!

The two still sat together there,
        The red light shone about their knees;
        But all the heads by slow degrees
Had gone and left that lonely pair.
            O voyage fast!
            O vanished past!

The red light shone upon the floor
        And made the space between them wide;
        They drew their chairs up side by side,
Their pale cheeks joined, and said, "Once more!"
            O memories!
                    O past that is!

Two Lovers by a Moss-grown Spring

First published in the 1878 collection **SL**

Self and Life

SELF

Changeful comrade, Life of mine,
    Before we two must part,
I will tell thee, thou shalt say,
    What thou hast been and art.
Ere I lose my hold of thee
Justify thyself to me.

LIFE

I was thy warmth upon thy mother's knee
    When light and love within her eyes were one;
We laughed together by the laurel-tree,
    Culling warm daisies 'neath the sloping sun;
        We heard the chickens' lazy croon,
            Where the trellised woodbines grew,
        And all the summer afternoon
            Mystic gladness o'er thee threw.
                Was it person? Was it thing?
                Was it touch or whispering?
                It was bliss and it was I:
                Bliss was what thou knew'st me by.

SELF

Soon I knew thee more by Fear
    And sense of what was not,
Haunting all I held most dear
    I had a double lot:
Ardor, cheated with alloy,
Wept the more for dreams of joy.

LIFE

Remember how thy ardor's magic sense
  Made poor things rich to thee and small things great;
How hearth and garden, field and bushy fence,
  Were thy own eager love incorporate;
    And how the solemn, splendid Past
      O'er thy early widened earth
    Made grandeur, as on sunset cast
      Dark elms near take mighty girth.
        Hands and feet were tiny still
        When we knew the historic thrill,
        Breathed deep breath in heroes dead,
        Tasted the immortals' bread.

SELF

Seeing what I might have been
  Reproved the thing I was,
Smoke on heaven's clearest sheen,
  The speck within the rose.
By revered ones' frailties stung
Reverence was with anguish wrung.

LIFE

But all thy anguish and thy discontent
  Was growth of mine, the elemental strife
Towards feeling manifold with vision blent
  To wider thought: I was no vulgar life
    That, like the water-mirrored ape,
      Not discerns the thing it sees,
    Nor knows its own in others' shape,
      Railing, scorning, at its ease.
        Half man's truth must hidden lie
        If unlit by Sorrow's eye.
        I by Sorrow wrought in thee
        Willing pain of ministry.

SELF

Slowly was the lesson taught
  Through passion, error, care;
Insight was with loathing fraught
  And effort with despair.
Written on the wall I saw
'Bow!' I knew, not loved, the law.

LIFE

But then I brought a love that wrote within
  The law of gratitude, and made thy heart
Beat to the heavenly tune of seraphin

Whose only joy in having is, to impart:
Till then, poor Self—despise thy ire,
Wrestling 'gainst my mingled share,
Thy faults, hard falls, and vain desire
Still to be what others were—
Filled, o'erflowed with tenderness
Seeming more as thou wert less,
Knew me through that anguish past
As a fellowship more vast.

SELF

Yes, I embrace thee, changeful Life!
Far-sent, unchosen mate!
Self and thou, no more at strife,
Shall wed in hallowed state.
Willing spousals now shall prove
Life is justified by love.

"Sweet Evenings Come and Go, Love"

"La noche buena se viene,
La noche buena se va,
Y nosotros nos iremos
Y no volveremos mas."
—Old *Villancico.*

Sweet evenings come and go, love,
They came and went of yore:
This evening of our life, love,
Shall go and come no more.

When we shall have passed away, love,
All things will keep their name;
But yet no life on earth, love,
With ours will be the same.

The daisies will be there, love,
The stars in heaven will shine:
I shall not feel thy wish, love,
Nor thou my hand in thine.

A better time will come, love,
And better souls be born:
I would not be the best, love,
To leave thee now forlorn.

First published in the 1878 collection **DM**

The Death of Moses

Moses “Moses, who spake with God as with his friend,
And ruled his people with the twofold power
Of wisdom that can dare and still be meek,
Was writing his last word, the sacred name
Unutterable of that Eternal Will
Which was and is and evermore shall be.
Yet was his task not finished, for the flock
Needed its shepherd and the life-taught sage
Leaves no successor; but to chosen men,
The rescuers and guides of Israel,
A death was given called the Death of Grace,
Which freed them from the burden of the flesh
But left them rules of the multitude
And loved companions of the lonely. This
Was God’s last gift to Moses, this the hour
When soul must part from self and be but soul.” 1-16

—resisting: “But Moses cried,
Firm as a seer who waits the trusted sign:
‘Reap thou the fruitless plant and common herb—
Not him who from the womb was sanctified
To teach the law of purity and love.’
And **Zamaël** baffled from his errand fled.” 54-59

—the summons: “But Moses, pausing, in the air serene
Heard now that mystic whisper, far yet near,
The all-penetrating Voice, that said to him,
‘Moses, the hour is come and thou must die.’
‘Lord, I obey; but thou rememberest
How thou, Ineffable, didst take me once
Within thy orb of light untouched by death.’
Then the voice answered, ‘Be no more afraid:
With me shall be thy death and burial.
So Moses waited, ready now to die.” 60-9

—the struggle: " 'O spirit! child of mine!
A hundred years and twenty thou hast dwelt
Within this tabernacle wrought of clay.
This is the end: come forth and flee to heaven.'

But the grieved soul with plaintive pleading cried,
'I love this body with a clinging love:
The courage fails me, Lord to part from it.'

'O child, come forth! For thou shalt dwell with me
About the immortal throne where seraphs joy
In growing vision and in growing love.'

Yet hesitating, fluttering, like the bird
With young wing weak and dubious, the soul
Stayed." 79-91

—the victory: "But behold! Upon the death-dewed lips
A kiss descended, pure, unspeakable—
The bodiless Love without embracing Love
That lingered in the body, drew it forth
With heavenly strength and carried it to heaven." 91-5

Gabriel "God spake to Gabriel, the messenger
Of mildest death that draws the parting life
Gently, as when a little rosy child
Lifts up its lips from off the bowl of milk
And so draws forth a curl that dipped its gold
In the soft white—thus Gabriel draws the soul.
'Go bring the soul of **Moses** unto me!'
And the awe-stricken angel answered, 'Lord,
How shall I dare to take his life who lives
Sole of his kind, not to be likened once
In all the generations of the earth?' " 17-27

Michaël "Then God called Michaël, him of pensive brow,
Snow-vest and flaming sword, who knows and acts:
'Go bring the spirit of **Moses** unto me!'
But Michaël with such grief as angels feel,
Loving the mortals whom they succor, pled:
'Almighty, spare me; it was I who taught
Thy servant Moses; he is part of me
As I of thy deep secets, knowing them.' " 28-35

Zamaël "Then God called Zamaël, the terrible.
The angel of fierce death, of agony
That comes in battle and in pestilence
Remorseless, sudden or with lingering throes.
And Zamaël, his raiment and broad wings
Blood-tinctured, the dark lustre of his eyes
Shrouding the red, fell like the gathering night
Before the prophet. But that radiance
Won from the heavenly presence in the mount
Gleamed on the prophet's brow and dazzling pierced

Its conscious opposite: the angel turned
His murky gaze aloof and inly said:
'An angel this, deathless to angel's stroke.' " 36-48

" 'Who is now left upon the earth
Like him to teach the right and smite the wrong?' " 103-4

" 'No prophet like him lives or shall arise
In Israel or the world for evermore.' " 107-8

" 'His burial is hid with God.
We stood far off and saw the angels lift
His corpse aloft until they seemed a star
That burnt itself away within the sky.' " 111-14

* * *

"Then through the gloom without them and within
The spirit's shaping light, mysterious speech,
Invisible Will wrought clear in sculptured sound,
The thought-begotten daughter of the voice,
Thrilled on their listening sense: 'He has no tomb
He dwells not with you dead, but lives as Law.' " 117-22

Arion

Arion, whose melodic soul
Taught the dithyramb to roll
  Like forest fires, and sing
  Olympian suffering,

Had carried his diviner lore
From Corinth to the sister shore
  Where Greece could largelier be,
  Branching o'er Italy.

Then weighted with his glorious name
And bags of gold, aboard he came
  'Mid harsh seafaring men
  To Corinth bound again.

The sailors eyed the bags and thought:
"The gold is good, the man is nought—
  And who shall track the wave
  That opens for his grave?"

With brawny arms and cruel eyes
They press around him where he lies
  In sleep beside his lyre,
  Hearing the Muses quire.

He waked and saw this wolf-faced Death
Breaking the dream that filled his breath
  With inspiration strong
  Of yet unchanted song.

"Take, take my gold and let me live!"
He prayed, as kings do when they give
  Their all with royal will,
  Holding born kingship still.

To rob the living they refuse,
One death or other he must choose,
  Either the watery pall
  Or wounds and burial.

"My solemn robe then let me don,
Give me high space to stand upon,
  That dying I may pour
  A song unsung before."

It pleased them well to grant this prayer,
To hear for nought how it might fare
  With men who paid their gold
  For what a poet sold.

In flowing stole, his eyes aglow
With inward fire, he neared the prow
  And took his god-like stand,
  The cithara in hand.

The wolfish men all shrank aloof.
And feared this singer might be proof
  Against their murderous power,
  After his lyric hour.

But he, in liberty of song,
Fearless of death or other wrong,
  With full spondaic toll
  Poured forth his mighty soul:

Poured forth the strain his dream had taught,
A nome with lofty passion fraught
  Such as makes battles won
  On fields of Marathon.

The last long vowels trembled then
As awe within those wolfish men:
  They said, with mutual stare,
  Some god was present there.

But lo! Arion leaped on high
Ready, his descant done, to die;
Not asking, "Is it well?"
  Like a pierced eagle fell.

According to Greek legend, Arion was rescued by a dolphin. He reached Corinth ahead of the sailors and confronted them. They were all executed on the spot.

Written in August 1867; first published in the 1874 collection **OM**

O May I Join the Choir Invisible

O may I join the choir invisible
Of those immortal dead who live again
In minds made better by their presence: live
In pulses stirred to generosity.
In deeds of daring rectitude, in scorn
For miserable aims that end with self,
In thoughts sublime that pierce the night like stars,
And with their mild persistence urge men's search
To vaster issues.
So to live is heaven:
To make undying music in the world,
Breathing as beauteous order that controls
With growing sway the growing life of man.
So we inherit that sweet purity
For which we struggled, failed, and agonized
With widening retrospect that bred despair.
Rebellious flesh that would not be subdued,
A vicious parent shaming still its child
Poor anxious penitence, is quick dissolved;
Its discords, quenched by meeting harmonies,
Die in the large and charitable air.
And all our rare, better, truer self,
That sobbed religiously in yearning song,
That watched to ease the burden of the world,
Laboriously tracing what must be,
And what may yet be better—saw within
A worthier image for the sanctuary,
And shaped it forth before the multitude
Divinely human, raising worship so
To higher reverence more mixed with love—
That better self shall live till human Time
Shall fold its eyelids, and the human sky
Be gathered like a scroll within the tomb
Unread for ever.

This is life to come,
Which martyred men have made more glorious
For us who strive to follow. May I reach
That purest heaven, be to other souls
The cup of strength in some great agony,
Enkindle generous ardor, feed pure love,
Beget the smiles that have no cruelty—
Be the sweet presence of a good diffused,
And in diffusion ever more intense.
So shall I join the choir invisible
Whose music is the gladness of the world.

Five years before she completed her creation of Dorothea Brooke, GE here enunciates the consolatory principles of that lady's life, summarized in the famous envoi *at the end of* Middlemarch:

"Her finely-touched spirit had still its fine issues, though they were not widely visible. Her full nature . . . spent itself in channels which had no great name on the earth. But the effect of her being on those around her was incalculably diffusive: for the growing good of the world is partly dependent on unhistoric acts; and that things are not so ill with you and me as they might have been, is half owing to the number who lived faithfully a hidden life, and rest in unvisited tombs."

Shorter Poems
From the Middle and Later Years

In a London Drawingroom

The sky is cloudy, yellowed by the smoke.
For view there are the houses opposite
Cutting the sky with one long line of wall
Like solid fog: far as the eye can stretch
Monotony of surface and of form
Without a break to hang a guess upon.
No bird can make a shadow as it flies,
For all is shadow, as in ways o'erhung
By thickest canvass, where the golden rays
Are clothed in hemp. No figure lingering
Pauses to feed the hunger of the eye
Or rest a little on the lap of life.
All hurry on and look upon the ground,
Or glance unmarking at the passers by
The wheels are hurrying too, cabs, carriages
All closed, in multiplied identity.
The world seems one huge prison-house and court
Where men are punished at the slightest cost,
With lowest rate of colour, warmth and joy.

December 1865

Arms! To Arms!

(*from Depping's Spanish ballads*)

With two thousand Moorish horsemen
    Reduan lays waste the plain,
Seizes all the herds and pushes
    Past the frontier of Jasa;
Spies the turrets of the city—
    Arrow-swift he leaves them far,

Scours the fruitful lands dividing
All the towered holds of war.
And Baeza's bells high swinging
Arms! to Arms! in haste are ringing.

On he marches in such silence,
Seems as it had been agreed
'Twixt the mutely hanging trumpet
And the hushed, unneighing steed.
But at last the watchman posted
Darkly like the stars at noon
Send their threatening signals onward:
Torch to torch is answering soon
And Baeza's bells high swinging
Arms! to Arms! in haste are ringing.

Night is in their van to shroud them
With her banners floating black,
But behind them are the bonfires
They have left upon their track:
Flames that wave instead of harvests,
Coiling around the cottage wall,
Fiery serpents that illumine
Ruin's wicked festival.
And Baeza's bells high swinging
Arms! to Arms! in haste are ringing.

Towards the front of sudden danger
All the brave prepare to go:
Cavaliers take polished lances,
Men afoot the trusty bow,
Proud Jaen sends forth her nobles,
Hurrying townsmen spread alarm,
Humming, swarming, sharp'ning weapons,
Angry wasps at threat of harm.
And Baeza's bells high swinging
Arms! to Arms! in haste are ringing.

Now the gates of morn are open
And the Christians ope their gates;
Meet the Moor at half a league thence,
Clashing weapons, clashing hates.
With the din the air is maddened,
Echoes hurry in dismay,
Fifes are shrieking, drums are roaring
Men are shouting, horses neigh.
And Baeza's bells high swinging
Arms! to Arms! in haste are ringing.

1866

Ex Oriente Lux

When first the earth broke from her parent ring
Trembling an instant ere her separate life
Had found the unfailing pulse of night and day,
Her inner half that met the effusive Sun
Had earlier largesse of his rays and thrilled
To the celestial music of the dawn
While yet the western half was cold and sad,
Shivering beneath the whisper of the stars.
So Asia was the earliest home of light:
The little seeds first germinated there,
Birds first made bridals, and the year first knew
Autumnal ripeness. Ever wandering sound
That dumbly throbbed within the homeless vast
Took sweet imprisonment in song and speech—
Like light more beauteous for shattering,
Parted melodious in the trembling throat
Of the first matin bird; made utterance.
From the full-rounded lips of that young race
Who moved by the omnipresent Energy
Dividing towards sublimer union,
Clove sense and image subtilly in twain,
Then wedded them, till heavenly Thought was born.

1866

In the South

O gentle brightness of late autumn morns!
The dear Earth like a patient matron left
By all she loved and reared, still smiles and loves.
The fields low-shorn gleam with a paler gold,
The olives stretch their shadows; on the vines
Forgotten bunches breathe out mellowness,
And little apples poised upon their stems
Laugh sparkling high above the mounting sun.
Each delicate blade and bossy arching leaf
Is silvered with the dew; the plough o'erturns
The redolent earth, and with slow-broadening belt
Of furrowed brownness, makes mute prophecy.
The far off rocks take breathing colours, bathed
In the aërial ocean of clear blue;
The palm soars in the silence, and the towers
And scattered villages seem still to sleep
In happy morning dreams.

1867

Will Ladislaw's Song

O me, O me, what frugal cheer
  My love doth feed upon!
A touch, a ray, that is not here,
  A shadow that is gone.

A dream of breath that might be near,
  An inly-echoed tone,
The thought that one may think me dear,
  The place where one was known,

The tremor of a banished fear,
  An ill that was not done—
O me, O me, what frugal cheer
  My love doth feed upon!

MM V 47 (June 1872)

Erinna

Eliot begins by quoting scholarship (not legible): "Erinna died in early youth when chained by her mother to the spinning-wheel. She had as yet known the charm of existence in imagination alone. Her poem called 'The Spindle' . . . containing only 300 hexameter verses, in which she probably expressed the restless and aspiring thoughts which crowded on her youthful mind as she pursued her monotonous work, has been deemed by many of the ancients of such high poetic merit as to entitle it to a place beside the epics of Homer. Four lines are extant. The dialect is the mixture of Doric and Æolic spoken at Rhodes where Erinna was born; the date about B.C. 612."

  'Twas in the isle that Helios saw
Uprising from the sea a flower-tressed bride
  To meet his kisses—Rhodes, the filial pride
  Of god-taught craftsmen who gave Art its law:
  She held the spindle as she sat,
  Erinna with the thick-coiled mat
  Of raven hair and deepest agate eyes,
  Gazing with a sad surprise
  At surging visions of her destiny
  To spin the byssus drearily
  In insect labour, while the throng
Of Gods and men wrought deeds that poets wrought in song.

  Visions of ocean-wreathed Earth
Shone through with light of epic rhapsody
  Where Zeus looked with Olympus and the sea
  Smiled back with Aphrodite's birth;
  Where heroes sailed on daring quests
  In ships that knew and loved their guests;
  Where the deep-bosomed matron and sweet maid
  Died for others unafraid;
  Where Pindus echoed to the Ionian shore
  Songs fed with action and the love
  Of primal work, where Themis saw
Brute Fear beneath her rod ennobled into awe.

Hark, the passion in her eyes
Changes to melodic cries
Lone she pours her lonely pain.
Song unheard is not in vain:
The god within us plies
His shaping power and moulds in speech
Harmonious a statue of our sorrow,
Till suffering turn beholding and we borrow,
Gazing on Self apart, the wider reach
Of solemn souls that contemplate
And slay with full-beamed thought the darling Dragon Hate.

"Great Cybele, whose ear doth love
The piercing flute, why is my maiden wail
Like hers, the loved twice lost, whose dear hands pale
Yearning, severed seemed to move
Thin phantoms on the night-black air?
But thou art deaf to human care:
Thy breasts impartial cherish with their food
Strength alike of ill and good.
The dragon and the hero, friend and foe,
Who makes the city's weal, and who its woe,
All draw their strength from thee; and what I draw
Is rage divine in limbs fast bound by narrow law.

"But Pallas, thou dost choose and bless
The nobler cause, thy maiden height
And terrible beauty marshalling the fight
Inspire weak limbs with stedfastness.
Thy virgin breast uplifts
The direful aegis, but thy hand
Wielded its weapon with benign command
In Rivalry of highest gifts
With strong Poseidon whose earth-shaking roll
Matched not the delicate tremors of thy spear
Piercing Athenian land and drawing thence
With conquering beneficence
Thy subtly chosen dole
The sacred olive fraught with light and plenteous cheer,
What, though thou pliest the distaff and the loom?
Counsel is thine, to sway the doubtful doom
Of cities with a leaguer at their gate;
Thine the device that snares the hulk elate
Of purblind force and saves the hero or the State."

1873-6

I grant you ample leave

"I grant you ample leave
To use the hoary formula 'I am'
Naming the emptiness where thought is not;
But fill the void with definition. 'I'
Will be no more a datum than the words
You link false inference with, the 'Since' and 'so'
That, true or not, make up the atom-whirl.
Resolve your 'Ego', it is all one web
With vibrant ether clotted into worlds:
Your subject, self, or self-assertive 'I'
Turns nought but object, melts to molecules,
Is tripped from naked Being with the rest
Of those rag-garments named the Universe.
Or if, in strife to keep your 'Ego' strong
You make it weaver of the etherial light,
Space, motion, solids and the dream of Time—
Why, still 'tis Being looking from the dark,
The core, the centre of your consciousness,
That notes your bubble-world: sense, pleasure, pain,
What are they but a shifting otherness,
Phantasmal flux of moments?"

1874?

Mordecai's Hebrew Verses

"Away from me the garment of forgetfulness,
Withering the heart;
The oil and wine from presses of the Goyim,
Poisoned with scorn.
Solitude is on the sides of Mount Nebo,
In its heart a tomb:
There the buried ark and golden cherubim
Make hidden light:
There the solemn faces gaze unchanged,
The wings are spread unbroken:
Shut beneath in silent awful speech
The Law lies graven.

"Solitude and darkness are my covering,
And my heart a tomb;
Smite and shatter it, O Gabriel!
Shatter it as the clay of the founder
Around the golden image."

DD V 38 (December 1875)

'Mid my gold-brown curls

'Mid my gold-brown curls
   There twined a silver hair:
I plucked it idly out
And scarcely knew 'twas there.
Coiled in my velvet sleeve it lay
And like a serpent hissed:
"Me thou canst pluck and fling away,
   One hair is lightly missed;
But how on that near day
When all the wintry army muster in array?"

1873-6

Fragments from a Note-book

I would not have your beauties in exchange
For the sweet thoughts your beauty breeds in me.

(*suggested by Sappho,* Fr. 17)

For shaken creeds are as the tottering poles,
The Earth reels madly to the maddened sense
And men, because they numbered falsely, hold
   All number false.

Mercy haunts lazar-houses, sighs and weeps
O'er famished clowns, but opes its nostrils wide
To scent the blood of nobles.

The ocean-meadow where the dark flocks play
Of wandering clouds whose shepherd is the day.

Master in loving! till we met
I lacked the pattern thy sweet love hath set:
I hear Death's footstep—must we then forget?—
      Stay, stay—not yet!

Epigraphs

GE began consistently using epigraphs she composed herself while writing *Felix Holt* (1866; she called them "mottoes"). She used them extensively in *Middlemarch* and *Daniel Deronda.* Occasionally she would quote others. Punctuations vary from edition to edition. When in doubt, it's van den Broek. We disregard the occasional unsigned prose epigraph.

Felix Holt (1866)

He left me when the down upon his lip
Lay like the shadow of a hovering kiss.
"Beautiful mother, do not grieve," he said;
"I will be great, and build our fortunes high,
And you shall wear the longest train at court,
And look so queenly, all the lords shall say,
'She is a royal changeling: there's some crown
Lacks the right head, since hers wears nought but braids.' "
O, he is coming now—but I am grey:
And he—— FH 1

A jolly parson of the good old stock,
By birth a gentleman, yet homely too,
Suiting his phrase to Hodge and Margery
Whom he once christened, and has married since.
A little lax in doctrine and in life,
Not thinking God was captious in such things
As what a man might drink on holidays,
But holding true religion was to do
As you'd be done by—which could never mean
That he should preach three sermons in a week.
FH 2

'Twas town, yet country too; you felt the warmth
Of clustering houses in the wintry time;
Supped with a friend, and went by lantern home.
Yet from your chamber window you could hear
The tiny bleat of new-yeaned lambs, or see
The children bend beside the hedgerow banks
To pluck the primroses. FH 3

1st Citizen. Sir, there's a hurry in the veins of youth
That makes a vice of virtue by excess.
2d Citizen. What if the coolness of our tardier veins
Be loss of virtue?
1st Citizen. All things cool with time—
The sun itself, they say, till heat shall find
A general level, nowhere in excess.
2d Citizen. 'Tis a poor climax, to my weaker thought,
That future middlingness. FH 5

Though she be dead, yet let me think she lives,
And feed my mind, that dies for want of her. FH 6 *postscr*

M. It was but yesterday you spoke him well—
You've changed your mind so soon?
N. Not I—'tis he
That, changing to my thought, has changed my mind.
No man puts rotten apples in his pouch
Because their upper side looked fair to him.
Constancy in mistake is constant folly. FH 7

Truth is the precious harvest of the earth.
But once, when harvest waved upon a land,
The noisome cankerworm and caterpillar,
Locusts, and all the swarming foul-born broods,
Fastened upon it with swift, greedy jaws,
And turned the harvest into pestilence.
Until men said, What profits it to sow? FH 11

This man's metallic; at a sudden blow
His soul rings hard. I cannot lay my palm,
Trembling with life, upon that jointed brass.
I shudder at the cold unanswering touch;
But if it press me in response, I'm bruised. FH 14

And doubt shall be as lead upon the feet
Of thy most anxious will. FH 15

It is a good and soothfast saw;
Half-roasted never will be raw;
No dough is dried once more to meal,
No crock new-shapen by the wheel;
You can't turn curds to milk again,
Nor Now, by wishing, back to Then;
And having tasted stolen honey,
You can't buy innocence for money. FH 17

Consistency?—I never changed my mind,
Which is, and always was, to live at ease. FH 19

Her gentle looks shot arrows, piercing him
As gods are pierced, with poison of sweet pity. FH 22

Your fellow-man?—Divide the epithet:
Say rather, you're the fellow, he the man. FH 25

The fields are hoary with December's frost.
I too am hoary with the chills of age.
But through the fields and through the untrodden woods
Is rest and stillness—only in my heart
The pall of winter shrouds a throbbing life. FH 34

M. Check to your queen!
N. Nay, your own king is bare,
And moving so, you give yourself checkmate. FH 35

See now the virtue living in a word!
Hobson will think of swearing it was noon
When he saw Dobson at the May-day fair,
To prove poor Dobson did not rob the mail.
'Tis neighbourly to save a neighbour's neck:
What harm in lying when you mean no harm?
But say 'tis perjury, then Hobson quakes—
He'll none of perjury!
Thus words embalm
The conscience of mankind; and Roman laws
Bring still a conscience to poor Hobson's aid. FH 36

The down we rest on in our aêry dreams
Has not been plucked from birds that live and smart:
'Tis but warm snow, that melts not. FH 38

He rates me as the merchant does the wares
He will not purchase—"quality not high!—
'Twill lose its colour opened to the sun,
Has no aroma, and, in fine, is naught—
I barter not for such commodities—
There is no ratio betwixt sand and gems."
'Tis wicked judgment! For the soul can grow,
As embryos, that live and move but blindly,
Burst from the dark, emerge regenerate,
And lead a life of vision and of choice. FH 41

I am sick at heart. The eye of day,
The insistent summer noon, seems pitiless,
Shining in all the barren crevices
Of weary life, leaving no shade, no dark,
Where I may dream that hidden waters lie. FH 44

We may not make this world a paradise
By walking it together with clasped hands
And eyes that meeting feed a double strength.
We must be only joined by pains divine,
Of spirits blent in mutual memories. FH 45

Why, there are maidens of heroic touch,
And yet they seem like things of gossamer
You'd pinch the life out of, as out of moths.
O, it is not loud tones and mouthingness,
T'is not the arms akimbo and large strides,
That make a woman's force. The tiniest birds,
With softest downy breasts, have passions in them
And are brave with love. FH 46

The devil tempts us not—'tis we tempt him,
Beckoning his skill with opportunity. FH 47

Nay, falter not—'tis an assured good
To seek the noblest—'tis your only good
Now you have seen it; for that higher vision
Poisons all meaner choice for evermore. FH 49

The maiden said, I wis the londe
Is very fair to see,
But my true-love that is in bonde
Is fairer still to me. FH 51

Our finest hope is finest memory:
And those who love in age think youth is happy,
Because it has a life to fill with love. FH *Epilogue*

Middlemarch (1871-2)

1st Gent. Our deeds are fetters that we forge ourselves.
2d Gent. Ay, truly: but I think it is the world
That brings the iron." MM 4

"My lady's tongue is like the meadow blades,
That cut you stroking them with idle hand.
Nice cutting is her function: she divides
With spiritual edge the millet-seed,
And makes intangible savings." MM 6

"Oh, rescue her! I am her brother now,
And you her father. Every gentle maid
Should have a guardian in each gentleman." MM 8

1st Gent. An ancient land in ancient oracles
Is called "law-thirsty:" all the struggle there
Was after order and a perfect rule.
Pray, where lie such lands now?
2d Gent. Why, where they lay of old—in human
souls. MM 9

1st Gent. How class your man?—as better than the most,
Or, seeming better, worse beneath that cloak?
As saint or knave, pilgrim or hypocrite?
2d Gent. Nay, tell me how you class your wealth of books,
The drifted relics of all time. As well
Sort them at once by size and livery:
Vellum, tall copies, and the common calf
Will hardly cover more diversity
Than all your labels cunningly devised
To class your unread authors. MM 13

Follows here the strict receipt
For that sauce to dainty meat,
Named Idleness, which many eat
By preference, and call it sweet:
First watch for morsels, like a hound,
Mix well with buffets, stir them round
With good thick oil of flatteries,
And froth with mean self-lauding lies.
Serve warm: the vessels you must choose
To keep it in are dead men's shoes. MM 14

"Black eyes you have left, you say,
Blue eyes fail to draw you;
Yet you seem more rapt to-day,
Than of old we saw you.

Oh, I track the fairest fair
Through new haunts of pleasure;
Footprints here and echoes there
Guide me to my treasure:

Lo! she turns—immortal youth
Wrought to mortal stature,
Fresh as starlight's aged truth—
Many namèd Nature!" MM 15

The clerkly person smiled and said,
Promise was a pretty maid,
But being poor she died unwed. MM 17

"Oh, sir, the loftiest hopes on earth
Draw lots with meaner hopes: heroic breasts,
Breathing bad air, run risk of pestilence;
Or, lacking lime-juice when they cross the Line,
May languish with the scurvy." MM 18

A child forsaken, waking suddenly,
Whose gaze afeard on all things round doth rove,
And seeth only that it cannot see
The meeting eyes of love. MM 20

"Your horses of the Sun," he said,
"And first-rate whip Apollo!
Whate'er they be, I'll eat my head,
But I will beat them hollow." MM 23

"Let the high Muse chant loves Olympian:
We are but mortals, and must sing of man." MM 27

1st Gent. All times are good to seek your wedded home
Bringing a mutual delight.
2d Gent. Why, true.
The calendar hath not an evil day
For souls made one by love, and even death
Were sweetness, if it came like rolling waves
While they two clasped each other, and foresaw
No life apart. MM 28

How will you know the pitch of that great bell
Too large for you to stir? Let but a flute
Play 'neath the fine-mixed metal: listen close
Till the right note flows forth, a silvery rill:
Then shall the huge bell tremble—then the mass
With myriad waves concurrent shall respond
In low soft unison. MM 31

"*1st Gent.* Such men as this are feathers, chips, and straws,
Carry no weight, no force.
2d Gent. But levity
Is causal too, and makes the sum of weight.
For power finds its place in lack of power;
Advance is cession, and the driven ship
May run aground because the helmsman's thought
Lacked force to balance opposites." MM 34

Wise in his daily work was he [Caleb Garth]
To fruits of diligence.
And not to faiths or polity,
He plied his utmost sense.
These perfect in their little parts,
Whose work is all their prize—
Without them how could laws, or arts,
Or towered cities rise? MM 40

I would not creep along the coast, but steer
Out to mid-sea, by guidance of the stars. MM 44

Was never true love loved in vain,
For truest love is highest gain.
No art can make it: it must spring
Where elements are fostering.
So in heaven's spot and hour
Springs the little native flower,
Downward root and upward eye,
Shapen by the earth and sky. MM 47

Surely the golden hours are turning grey
And dance no more, and vainly strive to run:
I see their white locks streaming in the wind—
Each face is haggard as it looks at me,
Slow turning in the constant clasping round
Storm-driven. MM 48

A task too strong for wizard spells
        This squire had brought about;
'Tis easy dropping stones in wells,
        But who shall get them out? MM 49

Party is Nature too, and you shall see
By force of Logic how they both agree:
The Many in the One, the One in Many:
All is not Some, nor Some the same as Any:
Genus holds species, both are good or small;
One genus highest, one not high at all;
Each species has its differentia too,
This is not That, and He was never You,
Though this and that are AYES, and you and he
Are like one to one, or three to three. MM 51

Hath she her faults? I would you had them too.
They are the fruity must of soundest wine;
Or say, they are regenerating fire
Such as hath turned the dense black element
Into a crystal pathway for the sun. MM 55

They numbered scarce eight summers when a name
        Rose on their souls and stirred such motions there
As thrill the buds and shape their hidden frame
        At penetration of the quickening air:
His name who told of loyal Evan Dhu,
        Of quaint Bradwardine, and Vich Ian Vor,
Making the little world their childhood knew
        Large with a land of mountain, lake, and scaur,
And larger yet with wonder, love, belief
        Toward Walter Scott, who living far away
Sent them this wealth of joy and noble grief.
        The book and they must part, but day by day,
                To lines that thwart like portly spiders ran,
                They wrote the tale, from Tully Veolan.
MM 57

They said of old the Soul had human shape,
But smaller, subtler than the fleshly self,
So wandered forth for airing when it pleased.
And see! beside her cherub-face there floats
A pale-lipped form aerial whispering
Its promptings in that little shell her ear. MM 59

1st Gent. Where lies the power, there let the blame lie too.
2d Gent. Nay, power is relative; you cannot fright
The coming pest with border fortresses,
Or catch your carp with subtle argument.
All force is twin in one: cause is not cause
Unless effect be there; and action's self
Must needs contain a passive. So command
Exists but with obedience. MM 64

Now is there civil war within the soul;
Resolve is thrust from off the sacred throne
By clamorous Needs, and Pride the grand-vizier
Makes humble compact, plays the supple part
Of envoy and deft-tongued apologist
For hungry rebels. MM 67

Our deeds still travel with us from afar,
And what we have been makes us what we are. MM 70

Full souls are double mirrors, making still
An endless vista of fair things before,
Repeating things behind. MM 72

Pity the laden one; this wandering woe
May visit you and me. MM 73

Would it were yesterday and I i' the grave,
With her sweet faith above for monument. MM 78

—internal lyrics from Middlemarch:

Why should our pride make such a stir to be
And be forgot? What good is like to this,
To do worthy the writing, and to write
Worthy the reading and the world's delight? MM 43

And see Will Ladislaw's song, page 727

Daniel Deronda (1876)

Let thy chief terror be of thine own soul:
There, 'mid the throng of hurrying desires
That trample on the dead to seize their spoil,
Lurks vengeance, footless, irresistible
As exhalations laden with slow death,
And o'er the fairest troop of captured joys
Breathes pallid pestilence. DD Bk 1

This man contrives a secret 'twixt us two,
That he may quell me with his meeting eyes
Like one who quells a lioness at bay. DD 2

What name doth Joy most borrow
When life is fair?
"To-morrow"
What name doth best fit Sorrow
In young despair?
"To-morrow" DD 8

I'll tell thee, Berthold, what men's hopes are like:
A silly child that, quivering with joy,
Would cast its little mimic fishing-line
Baited with loadstone for a bowl of toys
In the salt ocean. DD 9

1st Gent: What woman should be? Sir, consult the taste
Of marriageable men. This planet's store
In iron, cotton, wool, or chemicals—
All matter rendered to our plastic skill,
Is wrought in shapes responsive to demand:
The market's pulse makes index high or low,
By rule sublime. Our daughters must be wives,
And to be wives must be what men will choose:
Men's taste is women's test. You mark the phrase?
'Tis good, I think?—the sense well winged and poised
With t's and s's.
2d Gent. Nay, but turn it round
Give us the test of taste. A fine *menu*—
Is it to-day what Roman epicures
Insisted that a gentleman must eat
To earn the dignity of dining well? DD 10

I will not clothe myself in wreck—wear gems
Sawed from cramped finger-bones of women drowned;
Feel chilly vaporous hands of ireful ghosts
Clutching my necklace; trick my maiden breast
With orphans' heritage. Let your dead love
Marry its dead. DD 14

Life is a various mother: now she dons
Her plumes and brilliants, climbs the marble stairs
With head aloft, nor ever turns her eyes
On lackeys who attend her; now she dwells
Grim-clad up darksome alleys, breathes hot gin,
And screams in pauper riot.
But to these
She came a frugal matron, neat and deft,
With cheerful morning thoughts and quick device
To find the much in little. DD 18

We please our fancy with ideal webs
Of innovation, but our life meanwhile
Is in the loom, where busy passion plies
The shuttle to and fro, and gives our deeds
The accustomed pattern. DD 22

He brings white asses laden with the freight
Of Tyrian vessels, purple, gold, and balm,
To bribe my will: I'll bid them chase him forth,
Nor let him breathe the taint of his surmise
On my secure resolve.
Ay, 'tis secure;
And therefore let him come to spread his freight.
For firmness hath its appetite and craves
The stronger lure, more strongly to resist;
Would know the touch of gold to fling it off;
Scent wine to feel its lip the soberer;
Behold soft byssus, ivory, and plumes
To say, "They're fair, but I will none of them,"
And flout Enticement in the very face.
DD 26

Desire has trimmed the sails, and Circumstance
Brings but the breeze to fill them. DD 27

No penitence and no confessional:
No priest ordains it, yet they're forced to sit
Amid deep ashes of their vanished years. DD 30

Aspern. Pardon, my lord—I speak for Sigismund.
Fronsberg. For him? Oh, ay—for him I always hold
A pardon safe in bank, sure he will draw
Sooner or later on me. What his need?
Mad project broken? fine mechanic wings
That would not fly? durance, assault on watch,
Bill for Epernay, not a crust to eat?
Aspern. Oh, none of these, my lord; he has escaped
From Circe's herd, and seeks to win the love
Of your fair ward Cecilia: but would win
First your consent. You frown.
Fronsberg. Distinguish words
I said I held a pardon, not consent. DD 37

Fairy folk a-listening
Hear the seed sprout in the spring,
And for music to their dance
Hear the hedgerows wake from trance,
Sap that trembles into buds
Sending little rhythmic floods
Of fairy sound in fairy ears.
Thus all beauty that appears
Has birth as sound to finer sense
And light-clad intelligence. DD 44

Behold my lady's carriage stop the way,
With powdered lacquey and with champing bay;
She sweeps the matting, treads the crimson stair,

Her arduous function solely "to be there."
Like Sirius rising o'er the silent sea,
She hides her heart in lustre loftily. DD 45

Ever in his soul
That larger justice which makes gratitude
Triumphed above resentment. 'Tis the mark
Of regal natures, with the wider life,
And fuller capability of joy:—
Not wits exultant in the strongest lens
To show you goodness vanished into pulp
Never worth "thank you"—they're the devil's friars,
Viewed to be poor as he in love and trust,
Yet must go begging of a world that keeps
Some human property. DD 49

She held the spindle as she sat.
Erinna with the thick-coiled mat
Of raven hair and deepest agate eyes,
Gazing with a sad surprise
At surging visions of her destiny—to spin the byssus drearily
In insect-labour, while the throng
Of gods and men wrought deeds that poets wrought in song. DD 50

GE used the last eight lines of the first stanza of Erinna as the epigraph for DD 51. See page 727

Deeds are the pulse of Time, his beating life,
And righteous or unrighteous, being done,
Must throb in after-throbs till Time itself
Be laid in stillness, and the universe
Quiver and breathe upon no mirror more. DD 57

The godhead in us wrings our noble deeds
From our reluctant selves. DD 67

The Lifted Veil (Cabinet Edition, 1878)

Give me no light, great Heaven, but such as turns
To energy of human fellowship;
No powers beyond the growing heritage
That makes completer manhood.

Indexes of Characters and Persons given entries in this volume

Characters with Surnames

All those given entries in this volume are shown below. For others, refer to any particular work for citations in the "Also mentioned" sections. Illustration pages are in italics.

Characters without Surnames

Generic Characters

Historical, Biblical, and Literary Figures

About the Editor

Until 1988, GEORGE NEWLIN had spent his professional career combining activities in law and finance with volunteer service in the arts and serious avocational musical performance. At that time, he withdrew from most of his activities in venture capital and assets management and began developing his concept for a new kind of analytical literary anthology, beginning with the works of Charles Dickens. His *Everyone in Dickens* was published in three volumes in 1995, and a topical concordance, *Every Thing in Dickens,* appeared the following year. Subsequent works on Dickens concentrated on assembling historical documents and other materials to provide a context for the study of *A Tale of Two Cities* (1998) and *Great Expectations* (2000). His monumental four-volume work *Everyone and Everything in Trollope* was published by M.E. Sharpe in 2004. Having completed his volumes on George Eliot, he has begun work on a four-volume anthology of the prose and poetry of Thomas Hardy. Mr Newlin has phased out of most of his not-for-profit work in the arts but continues to give piano concerts. His specialty is the Beethoven piano concertos.

Printed in the United States
by Baker & Taylor Publisher Services